Consumer Behavior in Action

Consumer Behavior in Action

Real-Life Applications for Marketing Managers

Geoffrey P. Lantos

Routledge
Taylor & Francis Group

LONDON AND NEW YORK

To Joshua, Kristina, Jessica, Kayla, and Holly—
my favorite consumers.

First published 2011 by M.E. Sharpe

Published 2015 by Routledge
2 Park Square, Milton Park, Abingdon, Oxon OX14 4RN
711 Third Avenue, New York, NY 10017, USA

Routledge is an imprint of the Taylor & Francis Group, an informa business

Notices
No responsibility is assumed by the publisher for any injury and/or damage to
persons or property as a matter of products liability, negligence or otherwise,
or from any use of operation of any methods, products, instructions or ideas
contained in the material herein.

Practitioners and researchers must always rely on their own experience and
knowledge in evaluating and using any information, methods, compounds, or
experiments described herein. In using such information or methods they should
be mindful of their own safety and the safety of others, including parties for
whom they have a professional responsibility.

Product or corporate names may be trademarks or registered trademarks, and
are used only for identification and explanation without intent to infringe.

Library of Congress Cataloging-in-Publication Data

Lantos, Geoffrey Paul, 1952–
  Consumer behavior in action : real-life applications for marketing managers /
by Geoffrey P. Lantos.
      p. cm.
  Includes bibliographical references and index.
  ISBN 978-0-7656-2090-3 (pbk. : alk. paper)
  1. Consumer behavior. I. Title.

HF5415.32.L37 2010
658.8′342—dc22   2009048086

ISBN 13: 9780765620903 (pbk)

CONTENTS

THE STUDY OF CONSUMER BEHAVIOR

Consumer behavior (CB) investigates the thought processes and actions of *consumers*—ultimate end users (rather than business buyers or organizational consumers). Consumers choose how to allocate their available resources of money, time, and energy to select, purchase, consume (use), and dispose of *products*—goods, services, ideas, or anything else that satisfies customers' personal needs or desires or that solves personal marketplace problems.

This field of study is inherently interesting. You are all consumers and have personally experienced most phenomena taught in this textbook. However, you have done so without realizing the conceptual underpinnings of your marketplace behaviors and their consequent marketing strategy implications, which you will experience in this book.

The Most Important and Exciting Area in Marketing

Understanding CB is job number one for any consumer marketer. Proper product design and development, pricing, placement in distribution channels, and promotion (marketing communication) are all founded upon the marketer's knowledge of consumers. CB is one of the most exciting areas of marketing. Every day, all around you, marketers use various messages and media to inform, persuade, and influence your purchasing decisions. Marketers' efforts compete with other stimuli for your attention—and for your hard-earned money!

Studying CB is useful for a number of reasons: It allows businesspeople to make better marketing management decisions; helps government lawmakers to make more informed public policy decisions about their consumer constituents' welfare; and benefits consumers (that means everyone!) who wish to learn how to become better buyers (we hope you do!). It can also deepen your understanding of both society and human behavior in general. You will find yourself thinking about this course as you read print ads and view TV commercials, go shopping, try new products, surf the Web, and otherwise get involved in the marketplace.

A Multifaceted Field of Study

Learning about CB will help you to understand yourself better since this field borrows from most of the social (behavioral) sciences, which study human society, individual relationships, and individuals' thinking and behavior. Social science disciplines of relevance to CB include cultural anthropology, sociology, psychology, communication theory, economics, and management science. CB blends these disciplines with marketing management theory, practice, and research to understand people's consumption behavior in society.

THE PURPOSE OF THIS BOOK

A Theoretical Book

CB is a *theoretical* field. As such it presents and discusses abstract concepts to help *describe, explain, predict,* and, some critics contend, *control* marketplace behavior. Most CB textbooks do a fine job of presenting conceptual material and illustrating it with examples.

To make this material more interesting, this book provides background discussions for each exercise in a down-to-earth, highly engaging, conversational writing style. Each background section uses an abundant blend of contemporary examples that you will recognize and relate to and classic examples that are interesting and contain pertinent lessons. Each exercise includes learning objectives, background, review questions, and in-class and written applications questions. Each chapter concludes with a list of key concepts, a summary that captures key facts presented in the chapter, and a list of references for further independent study and use in written applications exercises.

AN APPLIED BOOK

Like almost all business and marketing courses, CB is also an *applied* field. As such, CB uses social science theories to solve marketing management, public policy, and consumer problems. As has been observed, there is nothing as practical as a good theory, and good theory leads to good practice. Executive recruiting firm Spencer Stuart conducted a survey of chief executive officers, chief marketing officers, and other senior executives that revealed communication and innovation as two of the key skills in which many senior marketers are deficient. To address this, we especially emphasize applications of CB theory for managers in the areas of advertising and new product development. This book also shows you how to become a more informed, shrewder consumer.

ADS AND SCENARIOS: HEALTHY EXERCISE

Ideas learned without application will not stick. We learn best by rolling up our sleeves and immersing ourselves in the material. Confucius was right—people learn best by doing.

Using the applied experiential exercises in this book can help you become an active participant in learning, thereby gaining better mastery of the theoretical material. Hence, this book is titled "Consumer Behavior in *Action*." Each exercise uses several *active learning strategies*. These techniques are designated to help you, alone or in groups, to actively use your knowledge.

Action learning is a connection of theory and practice that puts concepts in concrete form and provides a context for understanding abstract matter. The Association to Advance Collegiate Schools of Business (AACSB) looks for evidence of active learning when accrediting business schools, where students are involved with either real or practice-field examples that illustrate the ideas they are studying. The exercises in this book provide both types of exercises.

Today's best professors are not merely teachers, but designers of learning *experiences*. The experiences this book provides will allow you to learn by doing on your own, driven at your own pace and guided by your own interests. Raised in the visual and very interactive environments of video games, the Internet, and mobile communication devices, young adults are accustomed to this way of learning and the joys of interactive experience. You expect learning to be about doing, and with this book it is!

To some degree, every CB textbook leads students to think about their own marketplace behavior, utilize the World Wide Web, conduct consumer research, or make classroom presentations. No textbook that we are aware of does *all* of these things. But this book does—and more!

LEARNING OBJECTIVES

The exercises herein contain assignments with a high degree of real-world content. They may relate to your personal experiences, making them more interesting and relevant while increasing your involvement in the learning process.

Specifically, the exercises have been designed to achieve the following general learning objectives:

- To allow you to experience deriving CB theories, concepts, and principles and then applying them to specific real-world situations. This sharpens understanding and aids retention of these ideas.
- To demonstrate the practicality of the material, both professionally (for marketing decision makers and public policy influencers) and personally (for consumers).
- To solidify and test your understanding of the material and to challenge you to think about it in a useful and involving way.
- To serve as catalysts for in-class participation, exchange of information, and oral presentations (in teams or individually).
- To provide out-of-class involvement in applied activities and writing assignments.
- To stimulate creative thinking.
- To make learning fun, enjoyable, entertaining, relevant, and personally and professionally useful.

THE BOOK'S STRUCTURE AND FLOW

This book is organized to answer three fundamental questions: *Who* buys? *How* do they go about buying? And *why* do they buy?

The *who* question is answered in terms of the marketer's *market segmentation* strategy, covered in the second chapter of Part I and emphasized in depth throughout the textbook. The *how* issue is dealt with in Part II on the *consumer decision-making process*. Finally, the *why* issue is explored in Part III on *external sociocultural influences* and in Part IV on *individual psychological influences*.

THE LOGIC OF THE BOOK'S ORGANIZATION

The four parts can be covered in any sequence. However, it makes sense to cover most, if not all, of the material in Part I first. This section gives an overview of CB and covers foundational material on market segmentation that is further developed in Parts III and IV.

Within each part, the order of chapters can be switched to suit the instructor's personal preference. However, the authors' experience is that the material in this book's later chapters flows best from the earlier parts. That is, the discussion of *psychology* builds on that of *sociology,* and, further, the CB applications of both of these social sciences are better understood in light of knowledge about the *consumer decision process*.

Likewise, information in later chapters builds most logically upon material in earlier chapters within any given part of the book. For example, the more microlevel sociological material is best grasped after you are familiar with the more macrolevel sociological matter. Also, the psychology chapters are logically arranged to coincide with stages in the consumer decision-making process, which are covered earlier in the book.

Furthermore, later exercises at times refer back to similar and related concepts in earlier exercises so you can see how the material ties together. In fact, this book is more integrative than other CB books. It continually shows how various seemingly disparate concepts tie together.

OVERVIEW OF THE FOUR PARTS

Part I reviews the fundamentals of marketing most relevant to CB, notably *market segmentation*. This part also provides some general overview material on CB that paints the "big picture."

Before looking at the various influences on consumer decision making (CDM), we first describe the *CDM process* in general (Part II, Chapter 3) as well as each of the *specific stages* in that process (Part II, Chapter 4).

The rest of the book investigates sociocultural and psychological influences on CB. It proceeds from a macro/societal standpoint to a micro/individual/psychological perspective. Thus, Part III investigates *societal influences* on CB, beginning with the most macro influences—society and culture—and ending with micro interpersonal influences.

Part IV deals with micropsychological influences, arranged in the order in which they sequentially influence CDM. We begin with personality and lifestyle, arguably the most fundamental influences on CB. These are closely tied to many of the sociocultural factors and are the most observable of the psychological factors.

Then we investigate motivation, which is related most closely to the initial phase in the CDM process: problem recognition. We also investigate personality and motivation since these two psychological variables, and most of the societal influences, interact to determine lifestyle.

The next concept is perception—the gateway to the learning process. Perception is associated with the search-for-information phase (second stage) of the CDM process.

Finally, we investigate attitudes, which are formed during the alternative evaluation stage (third phase) and are based on learned information. Attitudes lead to a buying decision (fourth stage), and they might be modified during the postpurchase evaluation stage (final phase).

EMPHASIS ON MARKETING RESEARCH, ADVERTISING, AND NEW PRODUCT DEVELOPMENT

All textbooks vary somewhat in breadth and depth of coverage. Our selected topics are the most mainstream subjects covered by most textbooks. These topics lend themselves to interactive applications. This book places extra emphasis on marketing research, advertising, and new product development. The author is convinced that it is important to understand how consumer research can be used to learn about the nuances of a marketer's particular customers. Advertising and new product development, like marketing research, are the key areas in which marketers can invest for a brand's future. New products fuel corporate growth, and advertising builds brand equity, which is necessary to sustain a brand for the long haul.

NOTES ON THE EXERCISES

Each exercise begins with learning objectives: what you should know and be able to do as a result of reading the background to the exercise and working through the application questions. Every exercise has enough background to provide you with adequate "ammunition" to complete application questions for that exercise.

We have tried to cut through the complexity found in some textbooks, making the material as lucid as possible. To do so, in some cases we have provided conceptualizations that are unique to this book. For instance, in Exercise 6.1 on subcultural segmentation, six general themes related to subcultures are identified and applied to the major bases for subcultural segmentation. In Exercise 9.2, changes in family composition are identified and associated with both a traditional and modern family life cycle formulation. In Exercise 10.1, we discuss the relationship between the degree of innovativeness in Booz Allen Hamilton's new product classification system and that in Robertson's scheme for classifying innovations based on behavioral change.

MULTIPLE SYNONYMOUS TERMS—SAYING THE SAME THING DIFFERENT WAYS

Unlike most textbooks, which favor one term over another, this book includes multiple terms for key concepts. This is important for your future work as a marketer since, unfortunately, the language of textbooks and professionals varies, with different companies and industries using dissimilar terms and phrases for essentially the same idea. Knowing these various terminologies will be of genuine benefit when you find yourself laboring in the marketing vineyards. Alternatively, your professor might tell you to just use the term that he or she prefers.

For example, the term *associative learning* is sometimes called *incidental learning*. Hence, it is introduced as associative (incidental) learning. Likewise, attitude-based choices are variously referred to as affective choices and hedonic choices. Therefore, these terms are introduced as attitude-based (affective, hedonic) choices. Attitude strength also is known as attitude importance and attitude intensity, and so it appears as attitude strength (importance, intensity). Occasionally, common abbreviations follow a term, such as *attitude toward the ad* (A_{ad}), where A_{ad} is a common abbreviation for *attitude toward the ad*.

Note that all key concepts for a chapter are in **boldfaced** type the first time they are used in the chapter. Glossary terms are also **bolded**.

TEN TYPES OF APPLICATIONS ASSIGNMENTS

The fifty-five exercises contain ten types of applications assignments that can be done during class discussions and formal oral presentations as well as outside the classroom as written assignments. These applications exercises are designed to achieve the book's objectives.

The Applications Exercises Matrix on pages xiv through xvi indicates which types of applications are found in each exercise (e.g., "A" stands for "Analysis of advertisements"). If you are looking for a certain type of application, you will find this grid useful.

Here are the ten types of applications assignments:

1. **Analysis of Advertisements (A).** Many exercises ask you to think about how various print and/or Internet ads apply behavioral concepts, how effectively they do so, and how, if at all, the ads can improve their usage of these concepts. While some of the print ads are classics, most are contemporary.
2. **Scenarios (S).** Various exercises present a series of short scenarios to be analyzed in light of concepts learned. These test your understanding of the material and its application. You will find these scenarios to be engaging and a good platform for critical thinking.
3. **Introspective Exercises (I).** Some exercises ask you to recall, think about, and analyze, examples of your own CB related to a particular topic or concept. This demonstrates the relevance of the material to you personally and in

some cases can assist you in becoming a savvier consumer. Many of these introspective exercises work especially well as show-and-tell oral presentations.

4. **Interactive Web Exercises (W).** Several exercises require you to visit corporate or other Web sites in order to simulate decision making (DM) or otherwise learn about CB in an interactive environment. Through these exercises you will also learn about effective Internet advertising, sources of consumer information, and how to become a more astute *Netizen*—citizen of the Internet. You can "compare notes" with your classmates on their Web experiences during class discussions.

5. **Fieldwork Exercises (F).** Certain exercises ask you to implement an experimental or survey-based field research procedure. This allows you to develop an understanding of how various principles were derived as well as gain a feel for conducting consumer research on a small scale. Fieldwork exercises are also useful in generating classroom discussion on your experiences.

6. **Quantitative Exercises (Q).** A few exercises require you to do mathematical calculations to arrive at decisions. This reminds you that "number crunching" is not just for accountants and the folks in finance. Effective marketers can analyze numerical data such as marketing research statistics and decision models so as to develop sound marketing strategies.

7. **Creative Exercises (C).** Some exercises ask you to creatively apply your CB knowledge to designing ads or other marketing strategies and tactics. The marketing field is most closely associated with *creativity*—the ability to generate novel and useful ideas for solving marketing problems.

8. **Debatable Issues (D).** Several exercises pose controversial issues for analysis in order to heat up class discussion.

9. **Ethical Analysis (E).** Several exercises ask you to analyze the morality of certain marketing practices, requiring you to use moral reasoning and apply ethical theory as presented in Exercise 1.

10. **Marketplace Analysis (M).** A few exercises request you to think about what is going on in the marketplace with regard to course concepts, based on your own knowledge and experiences.

IN-CLASS OR OUT-OF-CLASS ASSIGNMENTS

The applications sections at the end of each exercise contain both in-class and out-of-class assignments, with suggestions for in-class discussions as well as out-of-class written assignments. Your instructor will select which questions to assign for in-class discussion, written assignments, and in-class presentations, either individually or in teams.

Each exercise begins with a background on the subject matter of the exercise to provide you with the knowledge you need to complete the applications. For a more detailed background (especially useful for written exercises or those to be presented orally) you might wish to do additional reading in other CB textbooks or articles and books found in the chapter's reference list.

1. IN-CLASS APPLICATIONS

Each exercise can easily be integrated into your instructor's lesson plan using the section entitled In-Class Applications. These discussions give you the opportunity to compare your personal experiences and ideas with those of your classmates. Your instructor can choose whether to have you discuss each exercise as an entire class or in small discussion groups where you can pool and integrate your answers before presenting them to the whole class for their reactions.

2. WRITTEN APPLICATIONS

Each exercise also contains a section entitled Written Applications. These are questions that can be answered in three to five pages, excluding attached ads or other exhibits. You will answer some or all of the questions in the Written Applications section of your assigned exercise—whatever it takes to have a quality paper of about three to five pages.

In the applications that ask you to analyze advertisements, you are instructed not only to discuss the ads in the application but also to find and discuss additional ads illustrating the concept of interest. The ads you find and analyze will generally either be print ads from magazines and newspapers or online ads.

3. ORAL PRESENTATIONS

The introspective, Internet, and fieldwork exercises can all make for brief, interesting, and informative student oral class presentations. These presentations can be done individually and/or in small groups. The latter approach can help develop the teamwork and interpersonal skills you will need as a marketer.

The purposes of these presentations are:

- To enhance your oral communication and professional presentation skills.
- To develop your ability to work cooperatively with other persons (teamwork and interpersonal skills).
- To provide a change of pace and an additional learning vehicle for the class sessions.

For team presentations, each team's members are jointly responsible for presenting answers to the In-Class Applications questions for the exercise assigned to them. Your team should present your own answers and involve your classmates in the exercise. You can gain student involvement by requesting your classmates to also answer some of the questions in the exercise, encouraging your peers to ask your team members questions and/or to react to your team's comments, thereby engaging in a dialogue with them.

Unless your instructor tells you otherwise, you are free to format your presentation any way you see fit—as individual talks by each team member, as a panel discussion among team members, as a lecture/discussion between teammates and class members, as a role-playing exercise, and so on. You may also use more than one of these pedagogies during your presentation—only your imagination and creativity limit you! You are encouraged to use audiovisual materials such as PowerPoint slides, online video clips, Web site visitations, charts, handouts, and so on.

Each team presentation should take approximately twelve to fifteen minutes (with a lot of involvement from your class members, it might take longer). You may choose to answer some or all of the questions in the In-Class Applications exercise section of your assigned exercise, and you may decide to add one or more questions of your own—whatever it takes to have a quality presentation lasting about twelve to fifteen minutes.

Important Note. In preparation for the presentation, all students in the class should review the Background section to the exercise that a team will be presenting on a given date as well as any additional information on the topic in your textbook.

Important Note for Instructors Only. (No peeking by students!) An instructor's manual with very extensive answers to the applications questions is available online for adopting instructors. It also contains additional examples for each exercise that illustrate the various concepts presented in the exercises.

APPLICATIONS EXERCISES MATRIX

The following template shows you which exercises in the book contain which types of applications exercises as described in the Preface. The applications are of the following types:

- Analysis of advertisements (symbolized by A)
- Scenarios (S)
- Introspective exercises (I)
- Interactive Web exercises (W)
- Fieldwork exercises (F)
- Quantitative exercises (Q)
- Creative exercises (C)
- Debatable issues (D)
- Ethical analysis (E)
- Marketplace analysis (M)

The matrix checks off which types of applications each exercise contains.

PREFACE EXHIBIT

Exercise		A	S	I	W	F	Q	C	D	E	M
1.1	Types of Needs and Wants	✓								✓	
1.2	Marketing Management Philosophies		✓					✓	✓		
1.3	The Multiple Influences on Consumer Behavior	✓		✓							
1.4	Traditional Theories of Consumer Behavior	✓	✓	✓							
2.1	Segmentation Strategies	✓								✓	
2.2	Brand Positioning	✓						✓			
2.3	Benefit Segmentation	✓						✓		✓	✓
3.1	The Economics Perspective on Consumer Decision Making		✓	✓	✓						✓
3.2	Your College Choice Decision		✓	✓		✓		✓			
3.3	Consumer Decision Making in an On-line Environment			✓	✓				✓		
3.4	Involvement, Perceived Risk, and Risk Reduction Strategies	✓		✓		✓					✓
3.5	Levels of Decision Making (Learning Stages)	✓		✓		✓					
3.6	Types of Consumer Purchasing Decisions	✓	✓	✓					✓	✓	
4.1	Problem Recognition	✓		✓	✓	✓		✓	✓		✓
4.2	Information Search			✓							
4.3	Alternative Evaluation: The Process and Evaluative Criteria	✓		✓		✓					✓
4.4	Alternative Evaluation: Decision Models	✓	✓	✓			✓				
4.5	Alternative Evaluation Using Shopping Bots			✓	✓						
4.6	Decisions: Outlet and Brand Choices			✓		✓		✓			
4.7	Postpurchase Outcomes	✓	✓	✓		✓		✓			✓
5.1	Overview of Components of Culture	✓	✓	✓	✓	✓		✓			
5.2	Cultural Artifacts: Creating a Time Capsule			✓	✓	✓		✓			✓
5.3	American Cultural Values	✓		✓	✓				✓		✓
5.4	Violating Cultural Norms		✓	✓	✓	✓					✓
6.1	Subcultural Segmentation	✓						✓	✓	✓	
6.2	Subcultures and You	✓		✓				✓			
7.1	Social Class Segmentation	✓						✓	✓		
7.2	Social Class and You	✓		✓		✓		✓			
7.3	Social Stratification Using a Multiple-Item Index		✓	✓			✓				
8.1	Types of Reference Groups	✓	✓	✓							✓
8.2	Types of Reference Group Influence	✓	✓	✓				✓	✓	✓	
8.3	Social Power	✓		✓				✓			
9.1	Family Decision-Making Roles	✓		✓						✓	✓
9.2	Family Life Cycle Stages	✓									

(continued)

PREFACE EXHIBIT *(continued)*

Exercise		A	S	I	W	F	Q	C	D	E	M
9.3	Family Influences and You	✓		✓				✓			
10.1	Categories of Innovations and Product Characteristics That Influence Adoption and Diffusion	✓	✓	✓		✓		✓			✓
10.2	Word-of-Mouth Communication and Opinion Leaders	✓		✓	✓	✓		✓		✓	
11.1	Freudian Personality Theory	✓		✓	✓	✓		✓			
11.2	Building a Brand Image	✓		✓	✓	✓		✓			✓
11.3	Measuring Personality and Brand Image	✓		✓	✓	✓	✓	✓			✓
11.4	Psychographics: VALS2 and Claritas PRIZM Lifestyle Segmentation			✓	✓	✓		✓			✓
12.1	Rational and Emotional Motives	✓	✓		✓				✓	✓	
12.2	Motivational Conflict	✓	✓	✓							✓
12.3	Maslow's Hierarchy of Needs	✓						✓			✓
13.1	Marketing to Selective and Subjective Perception	✓	✓	✓	✓	✓					
13.2	The Absolute Threshold Level and Subliminal Messages	✓		✓	✓					✓	✓
13.3	Weber's Law: The Just Noticeable Difference			✓	✓	✓				✓	✓
13.4	Surrogate Indicators	✓		✓		✓				✓	✓
13.5	Gestalt Psychology's Principles of Perceptual Organization	✓	✓		✓						
14.1	Memory, Retention, and Retrieval	✓	✓	✓	✓	✓					✓
14.2	Elements of the Learning Process	✓	✓	✓				✓		✓	✓
14.3	Theories of Learning	✓	✓	✓	✓			✓		✓	
15.1	The Tricomponent (ABC) Attitude Model and the Elaboration Likelihood Model	✓	✓			✓					
15.2	The Cognitive Decision-Making Perspective	✓	✓	✓			✓				
15.3	The Affective Experiential Perspective and the Conative Behavioral Influence Perspective	✓	✓					✓			

ACKNOWLEDGMENTS

This book was made possible with the support of the Stonehill College Undergraduate Research Experience (SURE) program during two summers, as well as a Stonehill College faculty research grant during those summers and two sabbatical semesters. Nan Mulford, Bonnie Troupe, and Kathy Conroy, coordinators of the SURE program and of Stonehill's Office of Academic Development, lent their support and gave their ever-friendly and helpful advice and encouragement along the way.

I gratefully acknowledge my two student assistants who served as Stonehill SURE Scholars. Rosemary Leal Borden (1997) and Jacqueline M. Lombard (2002) were equal partners with me in planning and gathering preliminary information for the applications exercises. As the SURE Research Associates on the project, Rosemary and Jackie were key contributors to the birth and initial development of this book. Their insights into student concerns, diligence in conducting magazine and Web searches for ads, and meticulous proofreading of copy were instrumental in making a better book. Their creativity in dreaming up scenarios, thoughtful analyses concerning answers to the assignments questions for the Instructor's Manual, as well as their unflagging loyalty to the project and strong, independent work ethic all contributed tremendously to the quality of this book.

Also worthy of great thanks are the developmental edition publishers, Bruce and Lorelei Bendinger, as well as their dedicated staff of assistants at The Copy Workshop, Patrick Aylward and Eugenia Velazquez. Lorelei had faith in and patience with this project when larger publishers did not. Bruce and Lorelei both offered encouragement and excellent creative suggestions at each stage of preparing the manuscript for prepublication. Bruce provided many of the titles for the scenarios. Patrick's eagle-eyed copyediting and technical assistance was invaluable.

I would like to thank my co-laborers at M.E. Sharpe. Harry Briggs, executive editor, was encouraging and enthusiastic about this project from day one. Throughout the book's intermediate and final development, he provided encouragement and thoughtful advice. Elizabeth Granda, associate editor, and Stacey Victor, production editor slogged along with me as the book moved from manuscript to published book.

I am also very indebted to Dr. Gail Tom, professor of Marketing at California State University in Sacramento, California. The inspiration for this project came from her book *Applications of Consumer Behavior: Readings and Exercises,* published in 1984 by Prentice-Hall, Inc. Many of the exercises in this book have their genesis in her book, which I had used for teaching Consumer Behavior (CB) until I began creating an early version of this textbook. Dr. Tom cheerfully and generously gave me permission to piggyback off of her trailblazing efforts.

I wish to thank Professor Ted Jula of Stonehill College for his expertise in providing accurate information for Exercises 3.3 and 4.5 on e-commerce. Professor Nadia Abgrab of Salve Regina College contributed her expertise and suggestions for Exercise 4.6 concerning retail influences.

Thanks go to a number of Stonehill students who lent assistance. Neil Sullivan, an accounting major, and Courtney George, a marketing major, both from the class of 2003, as well as Matthew Renzullo, a multidisciplinary studies major (2004), gave the manuscript a meticulous reading, offering suggestions for adding and deleting material and examples, as well as structural and mechanical changes. The result is an easier-to-read and more interesting book. And, thanks to Meghan Willis (2006), a finance major, to Mahrukh Mahmood (2006), an international studies and foreign languages major, and to Mallory Cole (2007), a communications and political science double major, for their uncanny ability to translate my atrocious handwriting and to type in my edits. Meghan's prior experience in the publishing field and with PageMaker software proved invaluable. Mallory, an aspiring editor, also helped with editing. Mallory O'Neill, a 2009 marketing major, assisted with answers to review questions and compiled the extra examples and conceptual material in the Instructor's Manual. Brianna Kastukarch (2007), a communications and sociology major, Jessica Peragine (2007), a communications major, Amanda Rubin (2007), a marketing major, Jenna Walsh (2008), a marketing major, and political science major Matt Durand (2010), all helped with edits and updates on the semifinal draft. Marketing major Courtney Osier (2011) created the PowerPoint slides for the instructor's Web site, along with her brother, finance major Douglas Osier, Jr. (2011), and marketing major Heather Tellier (2011) wrote the test bank. Finally, Carolyn McGuinness, Stonehill College Business Administration Department administrative assistant, helped with finalizing the glossary.

I also gratefully acknowledge the useful feedback and ideas from CB classes from 2002 through 2009 for their informal and formal feedback. Thanks also to Kristen Eastey (2002), a marketing major, and to Nicole Duff (2006), a history major and education minor who tabulated and analyzed the student surveys.

And, I would be remiss not to thank an additional twenty-eight years worth of CB students for their thoughts, examples, and suggestions on how to more effectively teach this material. This book and its Instructor's Manual are very much a product of their input.

I am indebted to my mother, Janice, who instilled in me the love for advertising and marketing, and my father, Peter, a business executive who inspired me to study business. I also thank my children, Joshua, Kristina, Jessica, and Kayla for the interesting examples of CB their lives have provided. Their imprint is found within these pages.

Most of all, I wish to acknowledge and thank my Lord and Savior, Jesus Christ, for inspiring me and leading me through this undertaking, bringing me together with my student assistants to work on this project, and for the talents and abilities with which He has gifted me. He is the author of all knowledge. All we have and accomplish is by His grace and mercy.

Geoffrey P. Lantos
Professor of Business Administration
Marketing Major Program Director
Stonehill College, North Easton, Massachusetts

INTRODUCTION TO CONSUMER BEHAVIOR AND MARKETING MANAGEMENT

CCONSUMER BEHAVIOR OVERVIEW

Chapter 1 provides a bird's-eye view of the field of consumer behavior (CB). Exercise 1.1 reviews the fundamental types of consumer needs and wants that marketers strive to satisfy in accordance with the marketing concept. Exercise 1.2 discusses different marketing management philosophies that vary in the degree to which the marketer satisfies consumer wants and needs. Exercise 1.3 takes a sweeping look at the numerous influences on CB. Exercise 1.4 reviews some of the traditional theories of human motivation underlying CB.

MARKET SEGMENTATION

Chapter 2 summarizes some of the basics of market segmentation, a concept that is fundamental to understanding CB and marketing management. Exercise 2.1 provides a hands-on approach to mastering market segmentation strategies, which are used to select target markets. Exercise 2.2 discusses brand positioning, a means of differentiating the marketer's brand from competitors for the targeted market. Exercise 2.3 covers benefit segmentation, a technique that both segments a market and positions a product within that market.

HOW THE EXERCISES WORK

As noted in the Preface, there are ten types of applications in this book. Each exercise begins with Objectives. Then, the Background section provides essential information to enable you to do the applications assignments.

LEARNING BY DOING

Throughout this book, we want you to learn by doing, not just by remembering the theories. Each exercise is designed to help you become familiar with a basic principle of CB, not just in theory but also in practice.

Throughout, you will see that we believe that the best way to learn about CB is by putting it into action. The study of CB is dynamic: You are always rolling up your sleeves and trying to figure out the ever-changing marketplace. Every marketing problem is a new challenge as well as an opportunity, and every marketing solution creates new problems.

So let's learn. And let's put that learning to work!

CONSUMER BEHAVIOR OVERVIEW

This first chapter covers some basics and sets the scene for the study of **consumer behavior (CB)**. Exercise 1.1 begins by discussing the different types of wants and needs that marketers identify and satisfy via their **products**, which are tangible goods, intangible services, ideas, or anything else that can satisfy customers' needs or desires. There are two types of needs: utilitarian needs (also known as functional or instrumental needs) and hedonic needs (experiential needs). Each type is satisfied by a distinct marketing strategy.

ORGANIZATION OF CHAPTER ONE

Exercise 1.2 introduces various philosophies of marketing management. Some marketing philosophies focus on customer needs and wants while others focus on the interests of the organization or society. The marketing management philosophy determines the nature of the consumer marketing strategy.

Exercise 1.3 previews the rest of the textbook by observing the multiple influences on CB, each of which is later discussed in more detail. These include:

1. Elements of the decision-making process
2. Sociocultural influences
3. Individual psychological influences

Exercise 1.4 investigates some traditional theories of CB. These are most likely to be held by marketing executives who borrow ideas from fields of social (behavioral) science, such as economics, psychology, and sociology.

EXERCISE 1.1. TYPES OF NEEDS AND WANTS

OBJECTIVES

1. To show that CB is usually a form of problem solving.
2. To demonstrate that sometimes CB involves not problem solving but rather creating desired feelings and experiences.
3. To illustrate the two basic types of needs and wants that products satisfy—utilitarian needs and hedonic needs—and how marketers appeal to each in their marketing communications.
4. To help you recognize how ads appeal to these two categories of needs and wants.

BACKGROUND

MARKETING AND TWO KINDS OF CUSTOMERS

Marketing is the business function that identifies and anticipates customers' needs and wants, creates products to satisfy those needs and wants, and then delivers the products through various techniques of pricing, distribution, and promotion. The essence of marketing is the satisfaction of human needs and wants through the exchange of values between a buyer (customer) and a seller (marketer).

Marketing's task is to serve customers **efficiently** (getting more accomplished while using fewer resources) and **effectively** (so as to produce the best effects for both buyer and seller) as a means to the organization's end of earning money for its owners. Marketing is like playing tennis—those who do not serve well lose!

The served customers are of two general types and are from two different markets: (1) business markets, and (2) consumer markets. **Business (business-to-business, B2C, organizational) customers** are those who buy on behalf of a business organization. Business buyers acquire goods and services that enter into the production of other goods and services that facilitate an organization's operation or that can be resold.

The second type of customer market is **consumers**—people who purchase or use products to satisfy their own or other people's personal needs and wants or to solve their marketplace problems. Whereas consumers buy for someone's ultimate consumption, business buyers purchase in an organizational context. Consumer customers reside in the living room or den, not in the boardroom or office.

Organizational buyers are human beings too. They are subject to emotions; need for status and risk aversion; and other personal factors discussed throughout this book. So, much of what you will learn about CB applies in a business-buying context as well.

CB AS PROBLEM SOLVING AND SATISFACTION OF NEEDS AND WANTS

Traditionally, CB is viewed as a problem-solving process. Products are purchased and consumed as solutions to consumer problems caused by unsatisfied needs and wants. Google, eBay, and Swiffer all filled unmet desires for unlimited information, infinite product choice, and really fast housecleaning, respectively.

What the customer considers of value and buys is not merely a product, it is a **utility**—the product satisfies needs or provides solutions to problems. The most basic issue of marketing is how best to satisfy customers' needs and wants. **Needs** are states of felt deprivation of essential physiological requirements for optimal life conditions. Being mandatory, needs are satisfied by necessities (e.g., clothing, shelter, and rest). **Wants** are the forms that human needs take as determined by society and individual preferences. They are requirements for non-necessities (luxuries), that is, products that are desirable but not mandatory (e.g., a steak to satisfy the hunger need or a frosty glass of lemonade for the thirst need). Plasma TVs, sports cars, yachts, and backyard Jacuzzis can all satisfy wants. However, where to draw the line between wants and needs is not always clear since what constitutes a luxury changes in a dynamic environment. Technology becomes increasingly indispensible—today, most people cannot survive without cell phones and high-speed Internet access, and young people need their iPhones, too. However, during the Great Recession of 2008–2009, people considered appliances such as dishwashers or clothes dryers as more discretionary.

TWO PERSPECTIVES: INFORMATION PROCESSING VERSUS EXPERIENTIAL

Paradigms are models, perspectives, or worldviews providing fundamental assumptions regarding what we are studying and how to study it. One problem-solving perspective of CB is the **information-processing paradigm**. This view of CB is largely objective and rational, oriented toward problem solving by acquiring and analyzing information to determine the best solution to the problem. This is largely the viewpoint of Part II on consumer decision making and of Part IV, which concerns consumer psychology, especially how consumers process information and learn.

But what a brutally dull world this would be if we just bought things to satisfy pedestrian needs and wants. Fortunately, we also have desires and even whims. Consequently, the **experiential paradigm** of CB recognizes that often consumers try not to solve practical problems but rather to pursue the more subjective, emotional, and symbolic aspects of consumption. In this experiential paradigm, the emphasis is on the experiential aspects of consumption, where feelings of enjoyment or pleasure are key outcomes.

UTILITARIAN AND HEDONIC NEEDS

Each of these paradigms relates primarily to one of two categories of needs and wants: utilitarian and hedonic. Exhibit 1.1 summarizes the discussion that follows.

EXHIBIT 1.1   Utilitarian and Hedonic Needs

Utilitarian/Functional/ Instrumental Needs	Hedonic/Experiental/ Transformational Needs
• Utilitarian—satisfies useful needs. Examples: save time or money, improve your health. • Functional—performs a practical function. Examples: keeps your engine running smoothly, keeps accurate time. • Instrumental—product is instrumental to providing a material benefit. Examples: disinfects germ-laden areas, relieves pain fast.	• Hedonic—provides pleasure. Examples: the taste of food, the smooth texture of silk. • Experiential—provides experiences and indulgences. Examples: experience driving excitement, experience thrills and chills. • Transformational—transforms the experience of buying and using the product. Examples: the status of a luxury automobile, the coolness of the latest fashion.
Cognitive/rational decision making. Objective product criteria: instrinsic to the product and easily verified.	Experiential/emotional decision making. Subjective product criteria: extrinsic to the product and subject to individual taste.

UTILITARIAN NEEDS

Utilitarian (functional, instrumental) needs include practical, rational, objective, concrete, economic, and cognitive needs. The product performs a useful (utilitarian) function (functional), solves a specific consumption-related problem, or is instrumental in providing a material benefit. Cases in point: Detergent gets clothes clean, acne medicine shrivels pimples, and motor oil keeps a car's engine running smoothly. Utilitarian consumers engage in reasoned problem solving to satisfy their desires. The paradigm is one of cognitive (thinking) information processing by buyers to figure out how to best satisfy their needs and wants.

The product attributes that consumers seek are objective performance criteria (easily verified) that are intrinsic to the product. Example: Functional soft drinks laced with nutritional supplements, such as Diet Coke Plus, a no-calorie soda fortified with vitamins and minerals.

HEDONIC NEEDS

People buy experiences in addition to solutions to problems. **Hedonic (experiential, transformational) needs** include emotional, social, nonrational, subjective, abstract, symbolic, sensory, self-expressive, and aesthetic needs. The product creates feelings or experiences, providing an opportunity for indulgence ("That looks like it would be fun to try!") rather than solving a pragmatic problem ("That plaster compound will help me fix the hole in the wall").

Hedonic products are purchased for such "useless" things as pure enjoyment (e.g., recreation), fun (entertainment), fantasy (perfume), sensory pleasure (Diet Coke "Just for the taste of it!"), emotional arousal (roller coasters), aesthetic appreciation (art, music), or personal expression (ringtones). Starbucks sells not just a cup of joe but rather a coffee-drinking experience in stores featuring comfy furniture, funky décor, and way-cool music. You do not drink a 7-Eleven Slurpee for nutrition—you indulge in one for fun, "brain freeze," and a colored tongue.

Experiential marketing—providing customers with experiences, not just products—is often the name of the marketing game. Recognizing this, with its RAZR, Motorola transformed itself from a tech-driven cell phone seller to a provider of music, video, and Internet access wherever people roam.

Hedonic needs for self-expression are called **symbolic (value-expressive, expressive) needs**, reflecting a buyer's *self-concept*. Here, the consumer asks, "Who am I?" "Who do others think I am?" or "Who do I want others to think I am?" For instance, driving a flashy sports car says something about the driver's personality.

Many of these hedonic needs are social in nature. The product attributes sought are subjective performance criteria, evaluated differently by each individual and influenced by personal tastes and preferences. Subjective attributes contrast with objective intrinsic attributes, such as size and weight. Rather, they are extrinsic to the product and more integral to the consumer's self-concept.

Hedonic needs provide emotional involvement. The paradigm for experiential needs is one of emotional experiencing. Consumers experience not just thoughts but also feelings.

Of course, a given product can satisfy both utilitarian as well as hedonic needs. While a car may be purchased to satisfy basic transportation needs, it can also fulfill needs for self-expression (sports cars) and sociability ("family" cars). Most foods are bought for both sustenance and pleasure. A watch might be purchased either to tell time (Timex) or as an upscale badge of sophistication (Rolex).

MARKETING IMPLICATION

The bottom-line mandate for marketers is to view themselves not as product purveyors but rather as satisfiers of consumer needs and wants and solvers of customer problems! The focus in product development will not be on adding gee-whiz bells and whistles to products that do not appeal to customers (e.g., car dashboards with more knobs and buttons than an airplane cockpit). Rather, emphasis should be on developing goods and services that meet unsatisfied needs better than competitive products. Also, promotion will focus less on the product and more on the consumer needs and wants that the product satisfies (e.g., a beautiful lawn, not fertilizer).

ETHICAL SATISFACTION OF NEEDS AND WANTS

Sometimes this book will engage in an ethical analysis of marketing strategies to satisfy needs and wants. In the wake of numerous openly exposed scandals in the business and marketing worlds, modern marketers are concerned not just with *doing well* through effective and efficient marketing strategy; they are also focused on *doing good* through ethical marketing tactics.

Ethics is the study of morality, a set of principles or rules of right and wrong designed to guide our thinking and behavior. **Moral** means right, good, and proper decisions, behaviors, policies, and institutions. This contrasts with **immoral**—wrong, bad, and improper decisions, behaviors, policies, and institutions. **Ethical issues** are problems, situations, or opportunities that require a person or organization to choose among several courses of action (including no action) that must be evaluated as right or wrong. Ethical issues arise whenever there is serious potential harm or benefit to any individual or group ("stakeholders") from a particular decision or behavior. The choices are differentially consistent or inconsistent with **moral standards**—rules or guidelines by which we should live. Moral standards are accepted principles of right and wrong for guiding individual or group behavior. Examples include fairness, honesty, dependability, and courage, among many commonly recognized values.

Moral reasoning (ethical reasoning) is the rational reasoning process whereby people determine if human decisions, behaviors, institutions, or policies are in accordance with or in violation of moral standards, thereby analyzing ethical issues. Moral reasoning is done by a conscientious **moral agent**—an individual or institution that engages in moral decision making and has responsibility to make an ethical decision. In a marketing (or any other) situation, that person could be you!

REVIEW QUESTIONS

1. How does a consumer customer differ from a business (organizational) customer? Why does this distinction matter?

2. What is meant by the statement: "CB is a problem-solving process"? What is the marketing implication?

3. How do needs differ from wants? Cite examples of products that satisfy primarily needs and others that fulfill mainly wants.

4. What is the distinction between the information-processing perspective and the experiential perspective for studying CB?

5. What is meant by utilitarian (functional, instrumental) needs? What kinds of products satisfy these needs?

6. What is meant by hedonic (experiential, transformational) needs? What kinds of products satisfy these desires?

7. Why is the distinction between utilitarian and hedonic needs important to product development? To advertising?

IN-CLASS APPLICATIONS

Discuss the following:

1. Analyze each of the advertisements in Exhibits 1.2 through 1.6. Explain which general category (or categories) of consumer needs and wants—utilitarian and hedonic—the ad suggests the product satisfies. Describe the specific buyer needs and wants that the ad suggests the product satisfies.

2. For each ad, could the featured product be effectively advertised as satisfying the other general category of needs and wants (if these are not already appealed to in the ad)? Describe the specific needs in this category that the product could satisfy.

3. For each ad, could the featured product be effectively advertised by appealing to other specific needs in the category analyzed in Question 1? To which such needs could it appeal?

4. Do you find any potential ethical issues in any of these ads?

WRITTEN APPLICATIONS

1. Answer Questions 1 through 3 in the In-Class Applications above for these four ads.

2. Find four additional ads and repeat the analysis in Questions 1 through 3 in the In-Class Applications. (Note: Ads found can be in magazines or newspapers, direct mail pieces, or downloaded Web sites.)

EXERCISE 1.2. MARKETING MANAGEMENT PHILOSOPHIES

OBJECTIVES

1. To illustrate that not all firms are oriented to satisfying the needs and wants of their consumers. There are different marketing management philosophies that can guide marketing efforts.

2. To review and illustrate the different marketing management philosophies that focus on various aspects of the marketplace—the firm's production and distribution, its products, its customers' needs and wants, and societal welfare—and to demonstrate that each philosophy can be successful in different market situations.

3. To help you appreciate the managerial and ethical superiority of the more sophisticated marketing concept and societal marketing concept in most marketing environments, and to understand that these concepts cannot be implemented without a sound understanding of CB based on consumer research.

4. To enable you to recognize marketers' use of each of these philosophies and the conditions under which each philosophy will be successful.

5. To help you form ethical convictions on the controversial issues of consumer sovereignty and corporate social responsibility.

EXHIBIT 1.2   Bayer Ad

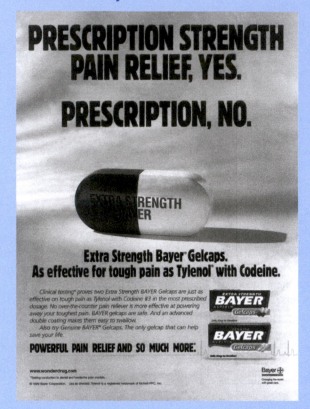

EXHIBIT 1.3   Crystal Light Ad

EXHIBIT 1.4   Ban Roll-On Ad

EXHIBIT 1.5   De Beers Ad

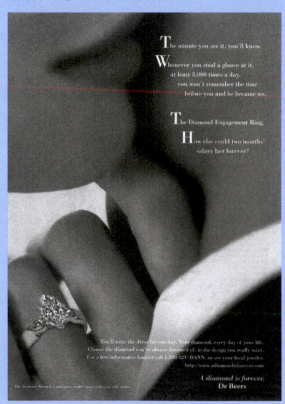

EXHIBIT 1.6   Pepperidge Farm Ad

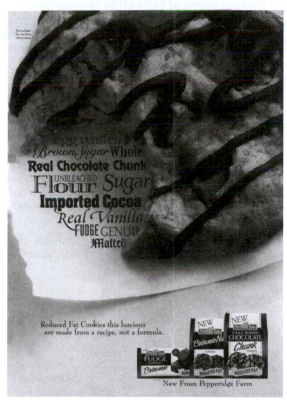

BACKGROUND

The underlying premise of Exercise 1.1 was that to most effectively market their wares, marketers must understand the nature of the needs and wants they are attempting to satisfy and then gratify them via their marketing program, with all focus on the customer. However, some firms place more emphasis on their organization's interests rather than their customers. Nonetheless, in recent years some enlightened marketers have begun balancing the needs of both their business and customers against those of society's well-being. All of these approaches reflect a different marketing management philosophy.

Deciding how to weigh the sometimes conflicting interests of the organization, its customers, and society gives rise to five major alternative **philosophies of marketing management**—how companies plan, implement, and control their marketing programs with their target markets in order to achieve their organizational and marketing objectives.

These five philosophies of marketing management are a reflection of an organization's level of marketing sophistication, and they parallel the evolution of marketing in the United States through various historical eras.

Due to their market situations or lack of marketing savvy, many organizations may still be in one of the earlier stages. While market situations might justify the use of less sophisticated marketing management philosophies, lack of marketing acumen certainly does not.

We shall review each marketing philosophy and show the kinds of marketing environments in which each can be successful. Exhibit 1.7 summarizes key points for each philosophy.

THE PRODUCTION CONCEPT

The earliest and least sophisticated marketing management philosophy and stage of marketing evolution is the **production concept (production orientation)**—the organizational philosophy that says consumers are primarily interested in products that are readily *affordable* and easily *available*. The production concept suggests that marketing managers should direct their efforts toward improving production efficiency via cost-cutting

---

EXHIBIT 1.7   Overview of Philosophies of Marketing Management

Philosophy	What is it?	When was it popular?	Marketplace conditions	Shortcomings
Production Concept	Make products affordable and available	Industrial Revolution (late 1800s–early 1900s)	• Unaffordable prices • Uncompetitive markets • Seller's markets	• Assumes all buyers want is affordability and availability • Vulnerable to competition offering better products and promotions
Product Concept	Make quality products and/or unique products	Early 1900s	• Poor product quality • Consumers seeking innovation and differentiation	• Focus on the firm, not its customers • Neglects consumer • Relies on word of mouth
Selling Concept	Aggressive promotion of branded products	1930s and 1940s	• Unsought goods • Overcapacity	• Views consumer as easily persuaded and manipulated, not sovereign • Overemphasizes branding • Focuses on short-term transactions, not customer relationships
Marketing Concept	Identify and satisfy unsatisfied consumer needs and wants better than competitors using consumer research	After 1950–Today	• Competitive marketplace	• Satisfaction of consumer desires might not be in individual's or society's best interest
Societal Marketing Concept	Balance consumer desires and company requirements with societal welfare	Since the late 1960s	• Consumers' needs and wants conflict with their best long-run interests and/or with societal welfare	• Open to discussion

methods in the factory that lower per-unit costs so as to lower the product's price, enhancing distribution efficiency by shaving distribution costs, and improving supply chain management by making the right goods available to the right people at the right time and place. Two marketing mix elements are critical: price and place (distribution). The focus is operational excellence—creating a lean and efficient value-delivery system.

All the marketer needs to know about CB is who buys the product, what price they are willing to pay, and where they prefer to purchase it. Otherwise, it is pretty much a "take-it-or-leave-it" approach to the buyer. There is a lack of concern for considerations that are weighed to various degrees in the more sophisticated marketing philosophies: the quality and uniqueness of the firm's products, their marketing communication process, the customer's needs and wants, and the society's well-being.

The production concept was born in the late 1870s during the Industrial Revolution—the era of assembly line mass production of standardized products using interchangeable parts, a period now known in marketing circles as the *production era*. The classic example is Henry Ford's Model T of the early twentieth century. Ford's objective was to make an affordable car for the masses, not just the elite. To achieve this, Ford used assembly line mass production, cranking out one standardized model, the Model T, in basic black.

Today, this philosophy can still be successful, primarily in four market situations:

1. Where a product's price is too high to be affordable by most people or is in a very price-sensitive market. Texas Instruments came to dominate the market for handheld calculators by lowering its

costs and hence its price. Dell expanded the market for home computers by efficiently making and selling computers online. Southwest Airlines appealed to cost-conscious travelers.

2. Where there is a concern for convenient availability. Witness Wal-Mart: The focus is on (a) low prices, achieved by large-scale purchasing from suppliers and a very efficient distribution system to squeeze out costs, and (b) conveniently available distribution. Stores are located off of highway exit ramps and in densely populated areas, with virtually everything available under one roof.

3. In a relatively uncompetitive market where the producer need not fret about other firms developing better products or selling them more aggressively. For instance, before the 1990s deregulation, public utilities had monopolies in their local markets, enabling them to concentrate on low-cost, efficient production rather than on marketing.

4. In a **seller's market**—a marketplace condition where product demand exceeds product supply. There is lack of availability due to reasons such as shortages of product components, patent protection, a monopoly on resources, or a complex technology that competitive firms have difficulty mastering. The result is an ability for the seller to not worry about not fully satisfying buyers.

However, in the long run, competitors will enter the market, develop better products, and aggressively promote them, making production orientation a recipe for disaster.

THE PRODUCT CONCEPT

Although the Model T made personal transportation affordable to the masses, the car was nonetheless a mess, the butt of jokes. At any given moment it might stall or a wheel could fall off. Benefits to owning a Model T did not include reliability and safety. Ford failed to follow the next, slightly more sophisticated marketing approach: the **product concept (product orientation)**. This marketing management philosophy alleges that consumers are interested in products that offer the most quality and performance and/or have unique features.

This orientation is epitomized by the old adages "A quality product sells itself" and "If you build a better mousetrap, the world will beat a path to your door." Consequently, in addition to concentrating on affordability (price) and availability (place), managers should also emphasize product development and improvement, inventing the greatest thing since sliced bread and then finding ways to make it competitively superior.

The product concept assumes that consumers seek out reasonably priced, easily available, but also well-made and innovative products. Henry Ford said: "There is one rule for industrialists and that is: Make the best quality of goods possible at the lowest cost possible." Some packaged goods companies practiced this philosophy in the early twentieth century's more competitive *product era.* For example, Milton Hershey believed that affordable, well-distributed, quality chocolates would fly off the store shelves. Until the early 2000s, Microsoft also had an "if-we-build-it-they-will-come" attitude. Growing rivals such as Firefox, Google, and open-source software suppliers forced Microsoft to modify their philosophy.

Unfortunately, like the production concept, the product concept suffers a lack of concern for selling the product and genuinely meeting customer needs and desires. Currently, this marketing philosophy typifies many entrepreneurs and technology-driven, engineering-centered companies that believe affordable, available, high-quality innovative products are all that is necessary for a sale. Likewise, clothing designers typically work in ivory tower studios without consulting customers.

Today, the product concept can succeed in market situations where buyers believe product quality is lacking; consumers are seeking something innovative or different; and/or there is perceived brand superiority (in the buyers' eyes), such as with popular artists or extremely well-liked brands.

However, there are three potentially fatal flaws with the product concept. First, it is focused inward on the firm and its technologies and products, rather than outward toward its customers' needs and problems. The trouble is that buyers might prefer a better solution to their mouse problem but not necessarily a better mousetrap. Perhaps a house cat will suffice! In fact, product concept practitioners use the "dead mouse" principle where they appear, catlike, on consumers' front porches each morning with a freshly killed, unwanted rodent. That is, there might be no market for the product! Many modern high-tech gizmos suffer *feature creep*—the addition of unnecessary bells and whistles simply because they are technologically possible and the designers think they are cool, not because consumers want the resulting complex, overengineered products. PC software has become "bloatware"—memory-hogging programs that munch disk space and pile on features that folks neither want or use, and often do not even know exist.

Excessive product focus can cause **marketing myopia**. This narrow-sightedness or tunnel vision leads managers to define a company as a product producer or expert in a particular technology. Thus viewed, Dupont is a chemical processor, and 3M is in coating and bonding technology. Marketing myopia can eventually make a company's products obsolete as new products and technologies displace its offerings. Instead, a firm should view itself as a satisfier of consumer needs and wants and solver of customer problems. For example, Hollywood in the 1950s said they were in the movie business, not the entertainment business. Consequently, they failed to immediately enter the new television business. Today, in the wake of electronic media such as DVD and downloads at Web sites like Movielink.com, the smartest people in Hollywood realize that they are in the information and entertainment content business.

Second, the product concept causes firms to forget the fact that they are not selling products but rather bundles of **benefits**—satisfactions of needs and wants. For example, health and beauty aids manufacturers do not really sell cosmetics but rather the satisfaction of beauty, charm, sex appeal, and even hope. According to Visa's research, what their credit card means to their customers is universal acceptance, a safe transaction, and a convenient form of payment.

And finally, the product concept assumes that people will automatically find out from others about the better mousetrap. However, word of mouth is notoriously slow, is subject to communication omissions and distortions, and the message might never reach the ears of most target market members. In a highly competitive, crowded, noisy marketplace, a marketer must work hard to be heard, using some form of **marketing communication**—persuasive communication directed to people in the marketplace to encourage them to accept the marketer's product.

THE SELLING CONCEPT

The need for marketing communication suggests a third, more sophisticated philosophy: the **selling concept (selling orientation)**. If people do not need or want a better mousetrap, they can be persuaded that they do via marketing communications. So to move the merchandise, a firm must undertake a large-scale promotional effort using a **promotional mix**—the specific combination of marketing communication techniques used in a marketing communication strategy. This includes aggressive, catchy use of one or more of the following promotional tools:

1. **Advertising**: any paid form of nonpersonal promotion by an identified sponsor making predominant use of the mass communication media.
2. **Personal selling** (direct selling): personal persuasive communication in a conversation between an organizational representative and one or more prospective customers, designed to influence the latter's purchase decision (i.e., for the ultimate purpose of making a sale).
3. **Sales promotion (promotions, promotional marketing)**: short-term incentives to encourage sale of a product. These entail indirect price cuts, such as coupons, rebates, and two-for-the-price-of-ones, and extra tangible value added to the product, such as sweepstakes, contests, and premiums.
4. **Public relations (PR)**: the communications function that builds good relations and a good reputation with the organization's various publics by obtaining favorable publicity, building up a good "corporate image," and handling or heading off unfavorable rumors, stories, and events. The target audience is broader than the product's or firm's target market: it is the organization's **publics (stakeholders, constituencies)**. These include all individuals and groups that have an interest in the firm, can affect it by their behavior, and are affected by how it conducts business: customers, stockholders, employees, suppliers and distributors, creditors, local communities, government regulatory agencies, and others. Marketers are sometimes responsible for a particular type of PR, **publicity**—nonpaid or nonpersonal newsworthy media exposure concerning a firm and its products.

Practitioners of the selling concept do not take customers' desires as a given. Rather, they believe that consumer wants can be persuasively molded to fit the product. This philosophy came into vogue during the Great Depression of the 1930s and lasted until about 1950—the sales era. During this epoch the U.S.

economy shifted from being a seller's market to a **buyer's market**—a marketplace condition where supply outpaces demand. Due to increased competition for limited demand, marketers began using marketing communication to persuade consumers to buy their **brand**—a name, term, symbol, design, or a combination that identifies the goods or services of one seller or a group of sellers and distinguishes them from those of competitors. Brands signaled quality, giving consumers confidence that their hard-earned dollars were being wisely spent. Brand names also added to the product's psychological value (vs. purely functional value), offering enhanced benefits such as social confidence (Sure deodorant) and brand image.

Some marketers still believe that a "hard sell" is necessary to move merchandise, particularly in two marketing circumstances: (1) Where the marketer sells **unsought goods**—products for which consumers have a dormant or **latent need**, a need that must be awakened and kindled by promotion. Examples include life insurance, cemetery plots, estate planning, and tires. (Are yours in good shape?) The marketer's job is to create a felt need and convince prospects of the product's benefits. (2) Where there is overcapacity or it is critical to work down excessive inventory.

There are three problems inherent to the selling concept:

1. It has a distorted view of human nature, seeing consumers as easily persuaded or even manipulated into buying unnecessary merchandise. However, all the best research suggests that usually consumers are **sovereign**, or in control of their decision making, personally responsible, and not controlled by outside forces. Although consumers can be influenced, they cannot be controlled.
2. Clever, heavily promoted brands do not guarantee success. "Buy Samson deodorant—it's strong!" probably will not make the cash register ring.
3. The selling concept is shortsighted, fixating on the immediate **transaction**—a single exchange agreement or one-shot sale. Instead, marketers should try to establish a long-term relationship with customers by continually fulfilling their unsatisfied desires via **relationship marketing (retention marketing)**. This type of marketing develops long-term, value-laden relationships between brands and customers by continually fulfilling buyers' unsatisfied desires. However, the selling concept maximizes short-term sales at the expense of the long-run profits that can be earned by bringing customers back for more.

THE MARKETING CONCEPT

The flaws in the selling concept led to the **marketing concept (marketing orientation)**—a marketing management philosophy that suggests that the ticket to business success is to identify what consumers want and need, and then to gear the entire marketing program to satisfying those needs and desires more effectively and efficiently than the competition. This yields a **competitive advantage**—an advantage over competitors gained by offering consumers greater value than rivals do. The overarching focus is on consumers' needs and wants rather than the firm, its products, or its promotional prowess. Consumers rule! This is known as being customer-focused, customer-oriented, or customer-centric. The marketing concept has three pillars: **market orientation, long-run profit orientation**, and **cross-functional integration**.

First, *market orientation* refers to the firm's understanding of customers and competitors, the two main parties (in addition to the seller) in the *market*, a place where buyers and sellers gather to trade. Two information-gathering activities used here are **marketing intelligence** and **marketing research**. **Marketing intelligence** is the acquisition of knowledge about everyday marketplace events through the use of ongoing procedures. Information is gathered by reading trade publications, talking to industry professionals, attending trade shows, and scouring the Internet (read, walk, talk, and surf, respectively). *Marketing research* is the formal, systematic, objective collection of information to solve a specific marketing problem using scientific, empirical techniques such as surveys, focus groups, and experiments. This includes **consumer research**, which studies consumers to gain information about them that is of use to marketers.

Second, *consumer research* is used to (a) understand who the customer is (the target market) and define the customer's demographic, lifestyle, and marketplace behavioral characteristics; (b) gain a better knowledge of how the consumer buys (i.e., the consumer's decision-making process); and (c) acquire insight into why customers buy, including the influence of the sociocultural environment and the effect of the individual's psychological makeup.

Long-run profit orientation is the recognition that the firm lives to serve and satisfy its customers in order to earn *profits*, the excess of revenues over outlays in a given period of time. Profits are the businessperson's compensation for hard work and risk-taking activity. Profitability over the long haul is preferred over short-term sales volume or market share because the latter can always be bought via heavy advertising, price-cutting, and sales promotions, but these activities can be profitless, especially if current sales rob future sales as customers stockpile.

Third, in *cross-functional integration* the best-in-class organizations instill a marketplace focus in all of their employees as well as in outside partners such as component parts suppliers, distributors, and advertising agencies. Thus viewed, marketing is not just a business function but also a philosophy of business, being everyone's business! In market-focused firms, all employees and partners must understand how their jobs contribute to customer satisfaction and add customer value. Examples include the accountant who bills the customer in a manner that ensures understanding, the engineer who designs a user-friendly high-tech product, and the financial manager who helps set a reasonable and affordable price and attractive interest rates on installment payments for high-ticket items.

The marketing concept says that there are four stages in the marketing process: (1) identify unsatisfied or undersatisfied consumer needs and wants in one or more market segments using marketing intelligence and marketing research; (2) develop a superior product for meeting those needs and desires, focusing not so much on **features**—physical product attributes (characteristics)—but more on benefits—psychological satisfaction of needs and wants that users derive from the product's features; (3) market the product in a customer-pleasing manner (attractive price, convenient distribution, and informative and entertaining promotion); and (4) follow up after the sale to ensure that superior customer contentment was achieved, either personally with each customer or through large-scale customer satisfaction surveys.

The marketing concept fixes the flaws in the selling concept, suggesting that the consumer truly is *sovereign*—king or queen of the marketplace kingdom. In today's competitive market, with innovations resulting largely from marketing research that illuminates how a firm and its rivals are faring vis-à-vis the consumer, most companies enjoy long-term success only by practicing the marketing concept.

THE SOCIETAL MARKETING CONCEPT

Whereas the marketing concept matches the firm's capabilities with the customer's needs, the **societal marketing concept** balances consumer interests and company requirements with *societal well-being*, or society's collective needs. This marketing philosophy mandates marketers to serve and satisfy customers more efficiently and effectively than competitors in a way that maintains or even enhances the individual's and society's welfare, while maintaining the firm's profits.

This enlightened concept recognizes that while the marketing concept results in a satisfied customer and a profitable firm, it might encourage actions that conflict with consumers' and society's best long-term interests. Consider that Kraft Foods now has a heightened sensitivity to the increasing number of overweight and obese Americans and stopped airing a TV commercial depicting a group of teens sitting around, lethargically sprawled out in a living room stuffing themselves with Double Stuf Oreos. Kraft's ads now portray products in the context of a nutritious snack or meal, such as Mini Oreos with milk. Kraft's product development team is reducing calories per serving in existing and new products and seeking ways to lower fat content and add vitamins and minerals.

The societal marketing concept was founded during the late 1960s and early 1970s, based on the idea of **corporate social responsibility (CSR)**, in which business assumes the obligation to optimize the positive effects and minimize the negative effects of its actions on society. American business organizations are inherently social institutions as well as economic enterprises. Firms should therefore weigh the social consequences of their activities and carefully balance them with their responsibilities to various *stakeholders*, considering both short-term and long-term effects on these stakeholder groups.

The social responsibilities of business include obedience of federal, state, and local laws; environmental protection; production of safe products; provisions for worker health and safety; nondiscrimination in hiring, firing, and promotion; recognition of employee rights in the workplace; and corporate philanthropy, which includes contributing to society with cash or products, community involvement by supporting employees in such endeavors as mentoring students or volunteering for a community cause, and undertaking green initiatives such as including environmental concerns in production processes.

All but the last of these special responsibilities are ethical responsibilities to do no harm. Corporate philanthropy, while widely adopted, remains controversial since critics contend it lies outside the firm's mandate to maximize shareholder value. However, this might not be the case, since many customers prefer to buy from socially responsible organizations and many employees and business partners favor associating with such firms.

The societal marketing concept recognizes three situations in which the marketing concept falls short and satisfying customers might not be desirable: (1) Sometimes, people have needs and wants that are inappropriate because satisfying them so would go against society's best interests. Many controversial "sin" products, such as cigarettes, alcoholic beverages, CDs with lyrics promoting violence, and gambling casinos would be examples. Coca-Cola, PepsiCo, and Cadbury Schweppes all have policies banning advertising for their nutritionally challenged beverages featuring or aimed at kids who are younger than twelve years old. Kellogg's does, too; plus it has pledged to crank out more nutritious products. (2) Some people have needs and wants that are not in their own best self-interest. For years McDonald's cooked their French fries in beef tallow, which was high in fat content and cholesterol, but they no longer do so; nonetheless, they have retained their French fries' taste. (3) Some people have needs of which they are unaware, such as to get into better physical shape, get more sleep, or satisfy spiritual needs. Here, the marketer's job is to market a product that satisfies these latent needs and educate consumers on the products' importance for their lives.

At times government mandates or encourages CSR activities. Here, marketers have no choice—the law requires social responsibility. Seat belts and air bags are no longer optional for car manufacturers to install, and autos must meet federal emissions standards. And with a bit of prodding from federal regulators, U.S. automakers are finally rolling out hybrids and researching electric cars.

REVIEW QUESTIONS

1. Describe each of the five marketing management philosophies, when each was popular, the marketplace conditions in which each is best practiced, and the potential shortcomings of each philosophy.
2. What is meant by a seller's market and a buyer's market? Which marketing management philosophy will be most effective in each of these two marketplace conditions and why?
3. What are the three characteristics of the marketing concept?
4. Discuss the two information-gathering tools that are available for marketers practicing a marketing orientation.
5. What is corporate social responsibility? What are some commonly recognized corporate social responsibilities? How does CSR relate to the societal marketing concept?

IN-CLASS APPLICATIONS

1. Marketers would have us believe that consumers are sovereign—king or queen, totally in control of their decisions and not subject to undue influence by the marketer. Renowned philosopher John Stuart Mill observed, "Over himself, over his own body and soul, the individual is sovereign." However, Abraham Lincoln believed, "You can't fool all of the people all of the time," suggesting that perhaps you can fool some of the people some of the time. P.T. Barnum opined, "There is a sucker born every minute." And some wag proclaimed that "a fool and his money are soon parted."

   So, do you believe that the consumer is sovereign? Don't marketers have power over consumers? Are there some types of market situations or consumer groups where this might be the case?
2. The ideas of corporate social responsibility and the societal marketing concept sound noble, but are they practical? Will companies voluntarily practice them? If so, why, and if not, why not?

   Furthermore, is it in society's best interest for marketers to define what is "socially responsible"? What are some arguments against corporate social responsibility and the societal marketing concept? Consider: What are a corporation's primary responsibilities?
3. Identify which marketing management philosophy is best illustrated in each of the following scenarios. In each case, explain whether or not the marketing environment described suggests that the use of that marketing management philosophy is justifiable and should be successful.

→ *Scenario A. The Talking Refrigerator.* Buster studied mechanical engineering in college and graduate school. Since then he has been a weekend tinkerer, designing and developing some pretty interesting products.

Buster's latest and greatest invention is something he calls the talking refrigerator. As a shopper loads it with food, she talks into the refrigerator's "ear" (a microphone), listing each item she is depositing in the refrigerator. She can also record nonrefrigerated foods stored in the pantry. The computer inside the refrigerator remembers this information. Likewise, when food is taken out of the refrigerator or pantry to be eaten, the appliance is told this in order to catalogue it.

The purpose of all this? When it is mealtime, the consumer tells the refrigerator which meal it is (including snacks), how many people will be eating, and how hungry they are. The computer then suggests what food is in stock and how much should be prepared to eat.

→ *Scenario B. The Gadonia Airport.* The city of Gadonia recently opened a new commuter airport. The location was chosen to be in close proximity to other venues of public transportation like the bus station and taxi service. Runways were designed to maximize daily traffic in and out of the airport.

Computerization of virtually all operating functions was projected to lower operating costs by 15 percent below the average for all of the nation's commuter airports. This has allowed for a slight reduction in most airfares, making the airport a more attractive alternative to other business and pleasure travel modes.

→ *Scenario C. The Blasphemers Rock!* The Blasphemers is a new modern rock group that has just broken upon the scene. Lead singer Frank McMeel explains their inspiration process: "Our stuff is real crude, dude. We kinda sit around the studio shootin' the breeze, drinkin' some 'adult beverages' until we get inspired to produce something really evil that'll really offend parents of the teens and kids who buy our music."

"Some fans love this, but sometimes at concerts we can tell that we really gross out the others. We've even seen some of them walk out in the middle of a concert. I don't know if we lose CD sales, but we don't care. We're in it for fun and to change the world!"

→ *Scenario D. Florida Swampland Development.* The Florida Swampland Development Company sells vacation property to upper-income people with cash to burn. Prospective customers are flown for free to the vacation property, where the sales force strongly attempts to push the property using a team-selling approach. Prospects are walked through sample developed properties, shown videos of satisfied customers enjoying their vacation places, and are wined and dined until they break open their wallets.

→ *Scenario E. Elect a Radical.* Anne Nethers, a member of the Radically Independent Party, is running for town Selectperson in South Aridtown. Anne faces stiff opposition from two better-known candidates with better-articulated positions on the issues. She feels that the most important thing she can do to win the election is to get her face in front of the public. Anne's strategy is to increase her name recognition through advertising locally on the radio, encouraging people to put up signs on their front lawns, and making personal appearances at town hall meetings, where she plans to sway people to her somewhat muddled viewpoints on the issues.

→ *Scenario F. Phil Anthropic Publications.* Phil Anthropic had been in the business of producing soft-core pornography magazines, videos, and Web sites. Following a religious conversion, he repented and totally changed the nature of his business. Now, all of his media channels speak out on the evils of excessive media sex and violence. He encourages people to boycott advertisers in such media and relies on donations from believers in his cause. Phil no longer makes big bucks, but he feels fulfilled in his work.

→ *Scenario G. Register at Wotzamatta U.* The State University, Wotzamatta U, has finally gone online with its registration process. Whereas students used to travel to the registrar's office prior to the semester's commencement to register for courses, now they can register on the registrar's home page any time before the semester starts.

Cost savings have been tremendous. In fact, the registrar's office was even able to lay off two employees due to the time savings. Also, as an unanticipated byproduct, students are grumbling a lot less about the time and hassle of the registration process.

→ *Scenario H. California's Cars.* At the dawn of the twenty-first century, in order to cut down on air pollution, the California state government required the automobile industry to produce a certain quota of electric cars for sale in the state as a precondition to their selling any other cars in California. Unfortunately, car manufacturers experienced trouble selling the electric cars because consumers found several problems with them.

First, electric automobile engines aren't powerful enough to move full-size cars at any reasonable speed. Therefore, the vehicles had to be built flimsily, making them potential death traps in accidents. Second, the narrow range of an electric car's battery means that one cannot drive long distances without stopping every few hours to recharge it. Third, they have a top speed lower than the speed limit on major highways, so they will cause people to take longer to get where they want to go.

WRITTEN APPLICATIONS

1. Answer In-Class Applications Questions 1 and 2. Anticipate objections to your viewpoints, and defend yourself against these objections.

2. Using information from the business press or your imagination, develop a real or fictitious scenario illustrating each of the five marketing management philosophies. In each case, explain whether or not the marketing environment suggests that the use of that marketing management philosophy is justifiable and should be successful.

EXERCISE 1.3. THE MULTIPLE INFLUENCES ON CONSUMER BEHAVIOR

OBJECTIVES

1. To give a broad overview of the many influences on consumer decision making, each of which will be covered in greater depth during this course.
2. To encourage you to remember that the purchase of a given product is influenced by a convergence of many different interacting factors, all worthy of marketers' consideration.
3. To help you recognize the multiple influences being appealed to in a single advertisement.
4. To enable you to think about the multiple influences at work in your own consumer decision making.

BACKGROUND

There are many things that make consumers tick. To confirm this, just look at the list of topics in this book's Table of Contents. Although you will study one factor at a time in this course, in practice the variables exert simultaneous influence and they interact with one another. This book divides these influences into three general categories: (1) decision making, (2) sociocultural, and (3) psychological.

When studying these influences, CB theorists have borrowed from theories of many academic and applied disciplines, including marketing management, cultural anthropology, sociology, psychology, economics, and mass and interpersonal communication. While it is true that studying CB is not rocket science, you should recognize that buyer behavior is quite complex, not to mention ever-changing.

Some of the major categories of influence and specific influences on CB within each category are summarized in Exhibit 1.8. The following is a brief overview of these factors.

1. **Decision process influences**: These factors affect the stages in the purchase decision process.
   - *Level of involvement:* The degree of importance and relevance of the purchase to the consumer in purchase and usage situations, ranging from high to low.
   - *Level of decision making:* The consumer's amount of prior consumer information on and experience with buying the product. This covers everything from extensive problem solving due to little or no prior experience, to routine purchasing and extensive experience, with limited decision making in between. Routine purchases include brand loyalty—(regularly re-buying the same brand due to preference and inertia—repurchasing the same brand out of mere habit).

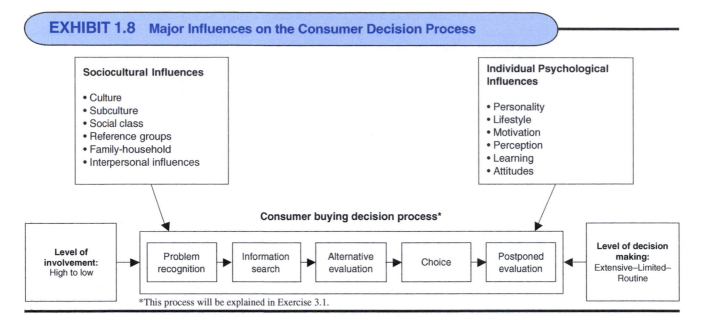

EXHIBIT 1.8   Major Influences on the Consumer Decision Process

- *Situational factors:* A purchase decision is affected by the shopping environment (e.g., product display, in-store advertising), and the usage environment (e.g., individual versus social consumption, purchase for self versus a gift for someone else).
2. **Sociocultural influences:** Societal and social influences range from the broad culture down to interpersonal relations. Most of the following sociocultural factors can serve either separately or together as a basis for market segmentation and target marketing.
   - *Culture:* A society's socially acquired thought and behavior patterns, such as values, behavioral standards, language, traditions, and symbols. International marketers segment the marketplace based on cultural differences.
   - *Subculture:* Subgroups within society that share some unique thought and behavior patterns. These include ethnic, religious, and generational groups, plus geographic regions.
   - *Social class:* A status hierarchy whereby groups and individuals are classified based on prestige derived from socioeconomic factors such as occupation, income, and education. This hierarchy is broadly construed as the upper class, middle class, and lower class.
   - *Reference groups:* Social groups that influence a person's thoughts or actions, such as clubs, organizations, and religious congregations, as well as individual friends and colleagues.
   - *Family/household:* Influences from members of one's family or household, such as continuing to purchase the branded products one's parents always used.
   - *Interpersonal influences:* Opinion leaders and others to whom consumers turn for word-of-mouth information and advice, especially for more complex, risky, and socially visible products. New products are often targeted initially toward opinion leaders, and marketers look for creative ways to stimulate word-of-mouth communication.
3. **Individual psychological influences:** The consumer's mental processes and behavior during decision making. Each of these can also serve as a foundation for targeted marketing.
   - *Personality:* A buyer's unique, characteristic behavior and thought patterns. Examples of personality traits are extroverted, self-confident, sociable, and risk-loving. (Segmentation example: Pepsi-Cola—"For those who think young"—targets the young at heart.)
   - *Lifestyle:* How consumers live and spend time and money. Example lifestyle groups include couch potatoes, sports fanatics, bookworms, and computer nerds. (Segmentation example: Tom's of Maine health-care products target health-conscious, active people.)
   - *Motivation:* Reasons why consumers buy. Motivation entails needs and wants, goals, and desires that move people toward or away from products. These include rational, instrumental, economic motives (e.g., survival, safety, achievement) and emotional, hedonic motives (e.g., love, status, fun).

Marketers must stimulate and appeal to motives that are appropriate to the product. (Segmentation example: benefit segmentation).

- *Perception:* A process whereby consumers select, organize, and interpret sensory information (sights, sounds, odors, etc.) to form a meaningful picture of their world. Since people selectively and subjectively perceive their worlds, their perceptions often deviate from reality. Marketers create perceptions, appeal to existing perceptions, and correct misperceptions. (Segmentation example: Appealing to gender by creating brands positioned for males versus females [e.g., Marlboro versus Virginia Slims cigarettes].)
- *Learning:* Changes in a consumer's thinking and behavior arising from experience. Consumer learning can range from the simple, such as recalling brand names and slogans, to the complex, such as discovering the best way to purchase a house. Most marketing communications try to teach consumers something about the brand. (Segmentation example: Targeting consumers unaware of a brand with highly informative ads versus reaching consumers having much brand experience with "reminder" ads.)
- *Attitudes:* A consumer's consistently favorable or unfavorable evaluations, feelings, and tendencies toward an object or idea, such as a product, brand, store, or salesperson. Most promotional activity tries to form, change, or maintain brand attitudes. (Segmentation example: Attitudinal segmentation, such as politicians who use a different appeal for their supporters than for their detractors.)

Here is an example of how many of the above factors are influential when purchasing even a simple tube of toothpaste:

- *Level of involvement:* Toothpaste is a low-involvement purchase, not a significant part of people's everyday lives. It is therefore a challenge for a toothpaste marketer to interest consumers in the brand.
- *Level of decision making:* Most consumers would consider toothpaste to be a routine purchase; many are brand loyal. Hence, little thought goes into the decision. This is a challenge for marketers of new brands and of unpopular brands.
- *Culture:* In American society it is a cultural truism that "cleanliness is next to godliness," and brushing one's teeth after every meal is a cultural ritual. Toothpaste marketers can appeal to these cultural beliefs.
- *Reference groups:* People often buy brands that promise to give a whiter smile or fresher breath, and some brands are even available in pretty packages to match bathroom decor.
- *Family:* According to one survey, 62 percent of college students still buy the same brand of toothpaste they used while living at home. Consequently, marketers often depict toothpaste as an all-family product (in the stereotypical ad, the entire family gathers in the bathroom to brush happily).
- *Situational factors:* The number of shelf facings (the more the better) and in-store location of a brand (end-of-aisle is prime real estate) might influence the buying decision.
- *Motivation:* Marketers educate people to buy toothpaste for reasons such as preventing bad breath, providing a sexy smile, and alleviating worries about such nasties as cavities, tartar, and gingivitis.
- *Perception:* Consumers might buy toothpaste with blue speckles because they wrongly believe that the toothpaste will be more effective.

REVIEW QUESTIONS

1. What are the three general categories of multiple influences on CB that are discussed in this book? Briefly explain the nature of each category.
2. What are the two major influences on the consumer decision process? Briefly describe each.
3. Cite the major sociocultural influences on CB and how marketers can use each of them.
4. List the major individual psychological influences on CB and how marketers can use each of them.

IN-CLASS APPLICATIONS

1. Find as many multiple influences on CB as you can in Exhibits 1.9 through 1.12, and describe how each might affect consumers.

2. For each product featured in Exhibits 1.9 through 1.12, which of the various multiple influences do you think is the most important in the decision process and why? Why would this be important for the marketer to know in each case?

EXHIBIT 1.9   Dole Pineapple Fun Shapes Ad

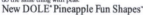

EXHIBIT 1.10   Avery Dennison Ad

EXHIBIT 1.11   Grey Poupon Ad

EXHIBIT 1.12   Purina One Ad

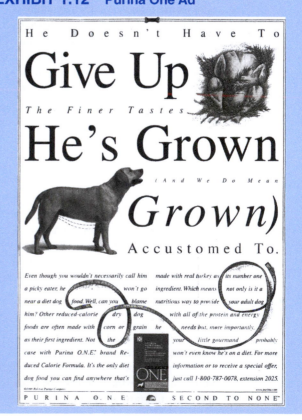

3. Think of a purchase you recently made that was influenced by many of the factors discussed in Exercise 1.3. Describe how your buying behavior was affected by these influences. Were one or two of these factors most dominant? Did any of the influences either reinforce each other or conflict with one another?

WRITTEN APPLICATIONS

1. Answer Questions 1 and 2 in the In-Class Applications for three of the ads in Exhibits 1.9 through 1.12. Could any of these ads be altered so as to appeal to any of the other buying influence factors outlined in this exercise? If so, explain how.

2. Find three additional ads and repeat the analysis you did in the previous question.

3. Answer In-Class Application Question 3. Then, interview a classmate or someone else to see how their purchase of this or a similar product was affected by the multiple influences.

EXERCISE 1.4. TRADITIONAL THEORIES OF CONSUMER BEHAVIOR

OBJECTIVES

1. To summarize some of the classic social (behavioral) science theories of human (and, hence, consumer) behavior that have been adapted by marketers to understand CB.
2. To introduce several of the major theories discussed later in this course.
3. To demonstrate that each theory is only a partial explanation for human behavior and to illustrate how each theory best explains for certain products, consumers, and purchase/usage situations.
4. To give you practice in recognizing the application of these theories to various consumer scenarios and advertisements.
5. To help you clarify your own philosophy of life that motivates your behavior, including your CB.

BACKGROUND

THE NATURE OF SOCIAL SCIENCE THEORIES

During the 1960s, marketing professors developed expertise in the **social (behavioral) sciences**—scientific disciplines in which the actions and reactions of humans and animals are studied through observational and experimental methods. Much of their research was based on **theories**—propositions about various aspects of the world founded on observation that allow marketers to *describe*, *explain*, *predict*, and perhaps *control* certain phenomena. These theories were largely borrowed from social sciences such as cultural anthropology, sociology, psychology, economics, political science, and history.

The social science theory that marketers believe in is a major factor influencing their consumer marketing decisions. For example, if a marketer subscribes to economic theory, believing consumers respond primarily to economic stimuli, that seller will attempt to influence the consumer chiefly with financial incentives such as better quality or more quantity for the consumer's money and sales promotions. However, if the marketer believes social influence theory is influential, then marketing efforts will be dominated by appeals to social status and peer pressure.

THE APPLICATION OF SOCIAL SCIENCE THEORIES TO MARKETING

Professor Philip Kotler, in a classic marketing article, summarized five different behavioral models from the social science literature that can help marketing strategists to understand buyers' *sociocultural influences* and *psychological processes*. Kotler noted that each model represented a radically different conceptualization of human behavior.

What follows are descriptions of four theories described by Kotler that were borrowed from economics, psychology, and sociology., Each theory outlined in Exhibit 1.13 is only a partial answer to the burning questions, "What drives human nature?" and "What makes the consumer tick?" However, each theory is

EXHIBIT 1.13	Four Traditional Theories of Consumer Behavior			
	Type of Theory	Discipline	Founder	Key Marketing Implications
1.	Utilitarian Economic Consumer	Microeconomics	Alfred Marshall	Offer consumers a value proposition.
2.	Classical Conditioned Consumer	Psychology	Ivan Pavlov	Use concept of drive, cues, association, and reinforcement to condition.
3.	Irrational, Hedonic, Psychoanalytic Consumer	Psychology	Sigmund Freud	Use motivation research, symbolism, irrational and subconscious appeals, and subliminal advertising.
4.	Social-Psychological Consumer	Sociology	Thorstein Veblen	Emphasize social appeals such as conspicuous consumption and social status.

useful in gaining insight into CB for certain types of *products*, *consumers*, and *situations*, the three variables upon which the answer to the "Why do they buy?" question regarding CB often depends. Each theory offers several implications for marketing practice.

MARSHALL'S ECONOMIC MODEL: THE UTILITARIAN, ECONOMIC CONSUMER (EARLY 1900S)

THE THEORY

Early twentieth century economist Alfred Marshall formulated the first CB theory, and it concerned economics' rational choice. **Economics** is the social science concerned with the allocation of scarce resources to produce products that satisfy consumers' unlimited needs and wants. Marketing, as the management discipline focusing on the exchange of values between a buyer and seller (marketer) to satisfy buyers' needs and wants, has its roots in economics.

Marshall's neoclassical economic theory of the consumer was designed to describe, explain, and predict which bundles of goods consumers would buy at various quantities and prices. **Pragmatic (instrumental, utilitarian)** consumers carefully allocate their scarce household resources among various purchase alternatives to maximize their expected utility—the satisfactions of needs, solutions of problems, pleasure, or happiness that the product provides. **Rationality** means buyers make choices that produce the very best (optimal) results for themselves, maximizing utility within the constraints imposed by their financial budgets.

Thus viewed, purchase decisions are based on rational, purposeful, thoughtful, self-interested economic calculations. Consumers wisely spend their incomes to get the most utility for each dollar spent: the most "bang for the buck." They are assumed to have "perfect marketplace information," being aware of the prices, features and benefits, and availability of all marketplace options, as well as knowing their own preferences.

THE MARKETING IMPLICATIONS

The assumptions of rationality—that buyers always carefully act in their own best interest and that they possess perfect information—are not always realistic. In fact, buyers often make *satisfactory* (pretty good) rather than *optimal* (the very best for the money) decisions, a process called **satisficing**. This is so because their information search is both *selective*, meaning it is not always worth expending the time and effort necessary to get perfect information in order to obtain the very best deal, and *subjective*, or biased and distorted.

Nonetheless, Marshall's model of CB is at least a rough approximation of some types of marketplace behaviors. Notably, a buzzword in marketing communications these days is **value**—customers obtain the optimum combination of quantity and quality for their dollars. The **value proposition** is an offer by a marketer that entails maximizing the ratio: (quantity + quality) ÷ price. Alternatively, value maximization means maximizing the difference between the customer's benefits and costs. For example, Target has an "expect more, pay less" strategy featuring designer products with prices set for low-to-middle income pocketbooks. During the 2008 recession, DiGiorno pizza's advertising calculated that under "DiGiornonomics," a delivery pizza cost more than twice as much as a DiGiorno pizza baked at home. Subway's five-dollar footlong subs propelled the chain to success during the late 2000s Great Recession.

Marshall's model suggests marketers can:

1. Give consumers more product quantity or additional products for their money than competitors. Value-added sales promotions such as bonus packs and premiums do this.
2. Offer better product **quality**—enhanced or additional features, or a product that performs better or lasts longer—for the same price as competitors. Better quality can even be offered for a higher price if consumers believe it is worth paying more to get more. Starbucks gives superior coffee in a pleasant atmosphere, Volvo provides extra safety in cars, and the United Parcel Service (UPS) gives more reliability in delivery services.
3. Promote the wonderful "value" offered to consumers, as seen in value-price brands, such as fast-food "value meals" and brands found in bargain basements.
4. Charge a lower price. Many sales promotions offer indirect price cuts through techniques such as price-off deals, rebates, and coupons.

PAVLOV'S LEARNING MODEL: THE CONDITIONED CONSUMER (1930S)

THE THEORY

Although derived from the 1870s experiments of physiologist Ivan Pavlov, this theory was not adapted in marketing circles until the 1930s, when several large ad agencies hired behaviorists-practitioners of Pavlov's theory of **conditioning**, a passively learned, low-involvement associative process of automatic responses or habits produced primarily by repetition plus reinforcement (reward) of the responses. The Pavlovian model suggests that much of our behavior is automatic, unthinking, knee-jerk reactions to environmental stimuli—a model of man as machine, a passive automaton. It is an example of a model of human **psychology**, the social science that studies human thought and behavior.

Pavlov's learning model incorporates the following five concepts:

1. **Drives**: internal tension states activated by unsatisfied needs and wants. Drives include primary biological drives (needs), such as hunger, thirst, and sex, and secondary learned drives (wants), such as affiliation, self-esteem, power, and achievement.
2. **Cues (stimuli)**: environmental stimuli received through the five senses (sights, sounds, smells, flavors, and tactile stimuli).
3. **Association**: a linkage between two or more cues.
4. **Responses**: a person's reactions to the cue(s) in an effort to reduce the drive. These include both observable behavior, such as talking and waving, and unobservable reactions, such as thinking or learning.
5. **Reinforcement**: a reward resulting from a response to a stimulus that leads to a reduction in a drive's strength. Water is rewarding because it quenches thirst and participating in a team sport satisfies both affiliation and achievement drives. Reinforcement increases the probability that the behavior to obtain the reward will be repeated.

The Pavlovian learning paradigm, summarized in Exhibit 1.14, is known as **classical conditioning**. In Pavlov's experiments, hungry dogs (drive) were exposed to meat paste (unconditioned or natural stimulus) associated with the ringing of a bell (conditioned or unnatural stimulus). The dogs naturally salivated upon exposure to the meat paste (unconditioned response). After repetitive pairings of the ringing bell followed by the reinforcement of being fed some meat paste, they drooled at the sound of the bell—a conditioned response.

In a marketing context, consumers who are hungry (drive) might be alert for restaurant signs. Upon spotting the Golden Arches (cue) they might go into McDonald's and order some burgers and fries (response), which they sit down and enjoy eating (reinforcement).

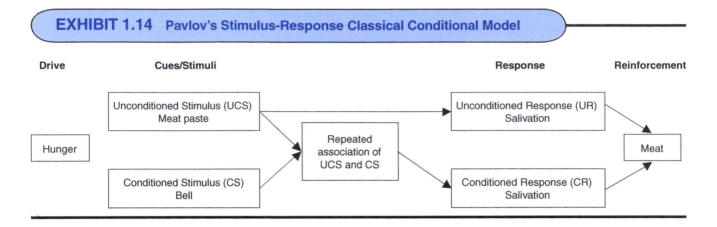

EXHIBIT 1.14   **Pavlov's Stimulus-Response Classical Conditional Model**

THE MARKETING IMPLICATIONS

Marketers can link their brands to a particular need or drive through repeated association. Such linkage, referred to as **need association**, can be especially effective if marketing communications are timed (via time of day, week, month, or year) to appeal to drives when they peak, since the stronger the drive the more quickly and completely the conditioning will be completed. Consequently, Campbell's advertises heavily during winter snowstorms, and a lot of toy advertising occurs just before Christmas.

Directional advertising, which consumers use to locate a product they wish to buy, capitalizes on need association. This involves media such as the Yellow Pages, movie listings, classified ads, point-of-purchase displays, smart banner ads (keyword-activated banner ads that pop up when users input keywords in a search engine), and highway billboards telling what attractions can be found at the next exit. Also, promotion should appeal to the strongest product-related drives, such as hunger for candy bars ("Snickers satisfies"), fear for seat belts ("Buckle up for safety"), and sex for fragrances, marketed as aromatic aphrodisiacs.

Through **mood association** advertisers can attach a certain mood or feeling to their brands. Repeated association with stimuli evokes a conditioned or unconditioned response such as relaxation, recreation, and companionship. For instance, a well-liked song (unconditioned stimulus) can create feelings of happiness and pleasure (unconditioned response). Or a popular sportscaster's voice might incite feelings of excitement related to sports events, which then rubs off on the advertised brand.

Mood association explains the popularity of event marketing sponsorship: When marketers connect their brands with the intense emotional experiences of attending sports events, rock concerts, and Spring Break vacation spots—bang!—the thrills come back the way the bell worked with Pavlov's dogs.

In **cue association**, marketers repeatedly expose consumers to unique marketing cues, such as logos, jingles, slogans, or familiar environmental cues with their attendant feelings, such as the bells and buzzers of video arcades. In their ads, advertisers should use repetition of the brand name, slogan, and other cues to be remembered. This is especially true for relatively unimportant low-involvement products whose advertising does not actively engage consumers. Important: It is not just what you say but how often you say it.

Marketers can make it easy for consumers to respond, either to make an inquiry for more information or to purchase the brand. Ways to break down purchase barriers include reasonably low prices, widespread distribution, and friendly salespeople. Response devices used by direct marketers include toll-free numbers, e-mail addresses, and easy-to-navigate Web sites.

Marketers should provide postpurchase reinforcement in the form of quality products that satisfy consumer expectations, advertising that reassures buyers they made a good choice, and courteous, efficient postpurchase customer service.

Marketers can build brand habits (automatic responses) through means such as offering quality products, employing helpful salespeople, and using **loyalty marketing (continuity programs, frequent buyer programs, frequency marketing)** that encourage repeat patronage by offering reinforcement through ongoing, long-term incentives and rewards such as frequent buyer programs and brand clubs.

A major drawback to the Pavlovian model is that it challenges the notion of consumer sovereignty, hich says that consumers can ultimately decide for themselves and cannot be manipulated by playing on their drives, creating moods, and otherwise controlling them.

FREUD'S PSYCHOANALYTICAL MODEL: THE EMOTIONAL/HEDONIC CONSUMER (1950S)

THE THEORY

Sigmund Freud (1856–1939) discussed repressed (hidden), subconscious, instinctual, and symbolic motivations. This was popularized in marketing circles during the 1950s when ad agencies and marketing researchers focused on tapping into such motives using motivational research techniques.

Freud's basic ideas were as follows:

- While there are conscious, mostly utilitarian, needs that the consumer is both able and willing to discuss, there are also **subconscious motives**. These are mostly social and psychological needs of a hedonic nature that consumers are either *unable* or *unwilling* to discuss, either because the needs are latent or because talking about and/or gratifying hedonic needs is socially unacceptable. However, many of these latent or deep-seated needs can be uncovered via probing conversation conducted by a trained psychoanalyst.
- Many motives are *instinctual*, or innate and universal in a species. Needs such as sex and security are not reasoned, and such instinctual needs are too antisocial to be verbally expressed. They, too, can only be discovered through deep probing.
- Many subconscious motivations are of a symbolic nature. **Symbols** are objects, characters, or other concrete representations of ideas, concepts, or other abstractions. The instinctual need for oral gratification might be manifested in symbolic behavior such as cigarette smoking, just as lollipop sucking could be a symbolic substitute for a mother figure, and a cigar might be a phallic symbol. It follows that suggestive symbols can be used to excite subconscious motives. So, a cigar might arouse a woman's sex drive or a man's need for dominance.

THE MARKETING IMPLICATIONS

There might be flaws in **survey research**, which asks direct (undisguised), straightforward questions in a highly structured (versus flexible) format (i.e., the same questions are asked of all respondents in a predetermined sequence). Survey queries often result in two problems: unwillingness and inability to answer questions because the needs are *latent*—deep-seated, hidden below the surface.

To overcome the problem of consumers' unwillingness or inability to answer questions, Viennese psychologist Ernest Dichter (1907–1991) built on Freudian psychoanalysis and pioneered **motivation (motivational) research** in the 1940s and 1950s. Dichter's methods involved consumer research using probing and indirect questions to drill down deep into consumers' subconscious minds to discover the motives or "real reasons" people buy what they are unable or unwilling to discuss. Such methodologies are popular in **exploratory research**. This preliminary research is conducted in a marketing research project to (a) clarify the nature of a research problem or issue (e.g. "Are sales down because of a poor advertising message, a too-high price, or shoddy product quality?"); (b) develop and screen alternative solutions to the problem (e.g., various advertising slogans); and (c) generate testable hypotheses (e.g., "Consumers will prefer the funny slogan to the serious slogan").

Exploratory research uses **qualitative research**, in which detailed descriptions or narratives of events are collected. This is in contrast to **quantitative research**, which is the systematic scientific investigation of quantitative properties of various phenomena and their relationships (i.e., collecting data that take numerical form). Qualitative research does not provide conclusive evidence on which of the alternative solutions to choose, but rather yields directional guidance through background learning. Motivational exploratory research is designed to gain deep insights into consumer thinking and behavior, which provides useful information into subsequent **conclusive research**—research providing information used to reach conclusions or make decisions on alternative courses of action regarding advertising, product development, sales approaches, and so on.

Semiotics (semiotic studies, semiology) is the study of symbols and signs—something that has meaning, such as words, images, body language, and so on. For example, in an Apple Computer commercial, a hip-looking dude wipes the nose of a sickly looking businessman who symbolizes Windows PCs and smugly asserts Apple's immunity to computer viruses.

On a deeper level, marketers can use suggestive symbols to excite consumers' subconscious motives. Brand images are often built around these symbolic connotations. The Prudential Insurance rock symbolizes security and stability, easing the anxious consumer.

Marketers can appeal to the subconscious and to **emotions**—feelings that are not physically controllable. Examples of Freudian appeals commonly used in advertising include:

- *Sex appeals:* Marketers seduce customers into buying through this approach. For instance, they can suggest that if a man purchases a certain brand of cologne, members of the opposite sex will swarm around him so much he will have to beat them off with a stick.
- *Fear appeals:* Through these, marketers scare buyers into purchasing. A classic 1930s example was Lifebuoy deodorant soap's suggestion that if you do not wash with it you will offend people with your "B.O." (body odor)
- *Fantasy and wish fulfillment appeals:* Marketers lure customers into buying with promises of unrealized pleasures and forbidden fruits, appealing to their fantasies. Many diversionary activities help people take a break from reality. They escape into a good book, an enjoyable movie, or a fun TV show, or they go on a dream vacation.

VEBLEN'S SOCIAL-PSYCHOLOGICAL MODEL: THE SOCIAL CONSUMER (1950s)

THE THEORY

Thorstein Veblen (1857–1929) was one of the founding fathers of modern **sociology**, the social science that investigates social behavior and human groups within society. In 1899 Veblen penned the influential tome *The Theory of the Leisure Class,* in which he further developed Aristotle's notion that man is primarily a social animal heavily influenced by people and social groups.

In this book, Veblen famously coined the term "**conspicuous consumption**," consumption of consumer goods and leisure activities and display of social status to impress those around us. This motivation is relevant for *conspicuous* (readily observable to others) products such as cars, houses, and clothing, all of which serve the *display* function. Even everyday items such as pens can suggest status: For a mere $95 to $450 you can buy a Cross Verve "writing instrument" (it's not just a "pen"!), with a platinum or gold finish. Would pure functionality motivate someone to buy a $24,000 diamond-studded gold mobile phone from Sony Ericsson? You've heard of bling or ice—slang for the flashy, bejeweled accessories that scream out "Look how rich I am!" Would you purchase a $14,800 crocodile bag from Gucci? Too expensive? Is $200 to $400 asking too much for a Coach bag? How about shiny, big chrome rims for the wheels on your car—only $8,000 a set!

According to Veblen, most people try to emulate the purchases of the wealthy, attempting to keep up with the proverbial Joneses, copying the lifestyles of the rich and famous. So-called *aspirational brands* appeal to this desire to "wanna be" like those Joneses. This explains the success of Trump Ice—the diamond of bottled water—as the Donald Trump name has become an aspiration for success in fields such as real estate, golf courses, and gambling casinos. Prestige fragrances (perfumes and colognes) with names of celebrities are another example.

In the wake of the Great Recession of the late 2000s, some observers believe that "inconspicuous consumption" is in: It is fashionable to be frugal and chic to be cheap. People are no longer spendthrifts but rather are into thrift and savvy shopping. It is now prestigious to tout the good deals one finds. That is, the Marshallian consumer prevails over the Veblenian consumer, but that person brags about it. Also, we have moved from having to being, from boasting about our merchandise to bragging about our activities and experiences, such as travel to exotic locales and esoteric hobbies.

THE MARKETING IMPLICATIONS

Marketers must be acutely aware of social influences on individual tastes and preferences. The following approaches work best for products that are visible and socially consumed.

1. Groups and social classes that influence purchases must be identified and associated with the brand through ads featuring similar people, celebrity endorsers, product placement in high-end venues, and so on.
2. Marketers might consider using upscale, uptown imagery (high class) and social status ("snob") appeals for products purchased as badges of rank or distinction. This makes the wares more desirable by associating them with a high social class.
3. Marketers can employ social appeals, including gaining social approval, engaging in socially correct behavior, and appealing to peer pressure, envy, and hopping on the bandwagon ("Join the crowd"), as well as recalling and reliving social experiences through product consumption.

REVIEW QUESTIONS

1. Describe each of the four traditional social science theories of CB—Marshall's utilitarian economic consumer, Pavlov's classically conditioned buyer, Freud's emotional and hedonic consumer, and Veblen's social-psychological consumer. Then, name several significant marketing implications of each model.
2. Cite the types of products, consumers, and usage situations each model seems to best explain.
3. What is the relationship between economics and the value proposition? What are some ways marketers can offer their customers a better value?
4. Describe the nature of conditioning and the major elements of the classical conditioning process.
5. Explain the differences between motivational research and survey research. When is each appropriate?
6. How do marketers use semiotics?
7. Explain conspicuous consumption and the types of products and consumers for which it might be important.

IN-CLASS APPLICATIONS

1. Identify and explain which theory or theories of CB are being portrayed in the following scenarios. Briefly explain.
   → *Scenario A. Barbie's New Car.* In the past month, Barbie's automobile died, so now Barbie needs another car. She always desired a brand new Jaguar, which she believes to be "eye-catching" and "rich-looking." The Jaguar is a symbol of the freedom, wildness, and attention that she, too, always wanted.

   However, because she has just graduated from college and is beginning to embark on a new career, Barbie can't afford a Jaguar. Instead, she decides to purchase a Chevrolet. Hey, the Chevy gets her to her destinations and it still lets her live out her fantasies!
   → *Scenario B. Paul Plans to Buy a Laptop.* Recently, Paul began looking to magazines, electronic stores, online recommendations, and friends to gather information on various models and features of laptop computers. He wishes to purchase the "right" laptop: one that would allow him to do his schoolwork, play various computer games, and go online to download music and videos, all within a reasonable budget.

   Although Paul realizes that top-of-the-line laptops are fairly expensive for students, he has decided to spend between $1,500 and $2,000 on the computer, printer, fax machine, and scanner. This is a reasonable price range that allows him to satisfactorily obtain a computer suitable to his needs.
   → *Scenario C. Wash Pam's Hair.* Pam is a regular user of Suave shampoo. However, recently she decided to purchase a new type of hair cleanser, Herbal Essence Rose shampoo and conditioner. She justifies the purchase by claiming the product is "all natural" and healthy for her hair. Further, it's a good deal at a bargain price.

   However, Pam's friends believe that there is another underlying reason that she doesn't wish to share with them: to show off her gorgeous, silky, shiny hair. In fact, since the shampoo purchase, she has gone on a spending spree, purchasing all kinds of frivolous items, a whole new wardrobe, and a brand new car. It appears that another side of Pam has been unleashed.
   → *Scenario D. Anne Satisfies Her Thirst.* Anne suddenly became thirsty while walking from her college dorm room to class on a hot summer's day. On the way, she remembered seeing an advertisement

for a new vitamin-enriched bottled water called Heaven-Up. In this ad, the satisfied expression on the model's face indicates that her thirst is quenched as a swarm of men hover around her.

Anne decided to purchase Heaven-Up since it is the "in drink" among the college community. Boy was she surprised. Not only did she lose her thirst, but she was also quite lively at her 2:30 P.M. class!

→ *Scenario E. Bill's First Impressions.* Bill grew up watching the "Happy the Clown" TV show every weekday. Each morning Happy would tell the kiddies in the audience to start their day with a big bowl of Banana Wackies cereal as he sang the Banana Wackies jingle. Bill would nag his mother on every shopping trip to buy Banana Wackies, and she usually complied. Then, he'd often eat a bowl while watching "Happy the Clown."

Bill can't quite explain it, but to this day he still enjoys Banana Wackies cereal, not to mention clowns!

→ *Scenario F. Lou Loves Lollipops.* Lou loves lollipops, sucking on them morning, afternoon, and night. When a marketing researcher once asked him what his favorite snack is and why he likes it, Lou couldn't explain why he craves lollipops so much.

Later, someone later told him that it had to do with an oral fixation from his early childhood—that lollipops represent the sexual satisfaction Lou felt drinking from his mother's breast. Lou thinks that might be a bit far-fetched, but he nevertheless loves his lollipops.

→ *Scenario G. Mel O'Dee's Makeup.* Mel O'Dee is young but not in love—yet! She spends a lot of money on perfume, hair styling products, makeup, jewelry, and so on, hoping that these will attract the man of her dreams. As she applies these items each day she envisions that man. Maybe . . . just maybe . . . today she will meet him and he'll sweep her off her feet and into his muscular arms.

2. Each of the theories of CB discussed in this exercise relates to a worldview, life view, or philosophy of life—a set of fundamental beliefs about the nature of the world, what is important in life, and what gives us a sense of purpose, direction, and goals to guide our actions. A philosophy of life serves as a motivating force in peoples' lives. This worldview underlies one's values, thinking processes, and decision making.

For example, Marshall's economic man seems rather materialistic, seeking fortune and wealth. He is selfish, out to maximize his own gain, very cold and calculating, albeit rational, logical, and efficient. Similarly, can you describe the philosophies of life that seem to be subscribed to by the Pavlov, Freud, and Veblen models? Describe the person who believes in each of these worldviews.

What other philosophies of life are there? What is important to people who subscribe to each of these philosophies?

What is your philosophy of life? Is one worldview better than the others? Why or why not?

Written Applications

1. Identify which theory or theories of CB are being portrayed in each of the ads in Exhibits 1.15 through 1.18.

2. For the product in each ad, could another theory of CB not directly evident in the ad also be effectively used to promote the product? Explain how this could be done and whether that would be a better answer to the question "What makes the consumer tick?" for buyers of this product.

3. Find four more ads, each of which illustrates a different theory of CB (i.e., find one ad for each of the four theories discussed in this Exercise). Then, answer Questions 1 and 2 for each of these four ads.

4. Which theory do you think best describes your own general human behavior (excluding your CB)? Explain. For instance, if you are a creature of habit, Pavlov's theory would explain your actions. If you are always trying to impress your friends, Veblen's theory would apply.

Which theory do you think best describes your own CB? Explain. Is there a difference between the theory driving your general behavior and that motivating your CB? If so, explain why you think this is so. If not, is this lack of a difference to be expected?

Does this mean that certain advertising and personal selling appeals are more likely to cause you to buy a certain product or brand? Can you cite an example or two?

EXHIBIT 1.15   Ritz Crackers Ad

EXHIBIT 1.16   American Express Ad

EXHIBIT 1.17   Nivea Ad

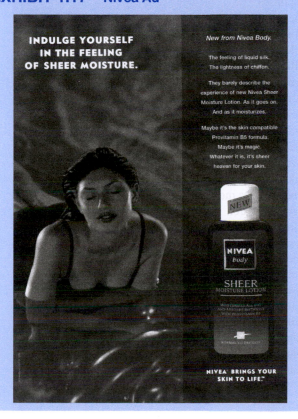

EXHIBIT 1.18   Movado Ad

KEY CONCEPTS

advertising
association
benefits
brand
business (organizational) customers
buyer's market
classical conditioning
competitive advantage
conclusive research
conditioning
conspicuous consumption
consumer behavior
consumer research
consumer sovereignty
consumers
corporate social responsibility (CSR)
cross-functional integration
cue association
cues (stimuli)
decision heuristics
decision process influences (decision-making influences)
drives
economics
emotions
ethical issues
ethics
experiential marketing
experiential paradigm
exploratory research
features
hedonic (experiential, transformational) needs
immoral
individual psychological influences
information-processing paradigm
latent need
long-run profit orientation
loyalty marketing (continuity programs, frequent buyer programs, frequency marketing)
market orientation
marketing
marketing communication
marketing concept (marketing orientation)
marketing intelligence
marketing management philosophies
marketing myopia
marketing research
Marshall's utilitarian economic consumer

mood association
moral
moral agent
moral standards
motivation (motivational) research
need association
needs
paradigms
personal selling (direct selling)
philosophies of marketing management
pragmatic (instrumental, utilitarian) consumers
product
product concept (product orientation)
product quality
production concept (production orientation)
promotional mix
psychology
public relations ("PR")
publicity
publics (stakeholders, constituencies)
qualitative research
reinforcement
relationship marketing
responses
sales promotion (promotions, promotional marketing)
satisficing
seller's market
selling concept (selling orientation)
semiotics
social (behavioral) sciences
societal marketing concept
sociocultural influences
sociology
sovereign
stakeholders
subconscious motives
survey research
symbolic (value-expressive, expressive) needs
symbols
theories
transaction
unsought goods
utilitarian (functional, instrumental) needs
utility
value
value proposition
wants

SUMMARY

Definitions and synonymous terms for all key terms in chapter summaries can be found in both the Glossary and within the chapter. This chapter provided an overview of disciplines of consumer behavior (CB), which views customers as problem solvers. However, a more recent view is that sometimes buyers create sought-after feelings and experiences.

Exercise 1.1 described two basic categories of consumer needs. The problem-solving information processing paradigm focuses primarily on utilitarian needs, while the experiential perspective concerns itself mainly with hedonic needs. This suggests that during development of a product and its promotional message, marketers should concentrate on attributes that will satisfy the appropriate types of needs and wants. The preferred marketing research approach to investigate consumer needs and wants and the favored marketing communication method to appeal to them varies according to whether the needs and wants satisfied by the product are utilitarian or hedonic.

Ethics concerns what is moral versus what is immoral. Ethical decision makers face ethical issues.

Different marketing management philosophies regarding the importance of and means to satisfy consumer needs and wants were outlined in Exercise 1.2. In order of increasing sophistication and historical sequence of development, these philosophies of marketing are: the production concept, the product concept, the selling concept, the marketing concept (which considers consumers as being sovereign), and the societal marketing concept (which emphasizes that satisfaction of consumer desires must fulfill the firm's mandate to practice corporate social responsibility [CSR]).

Exercise 1.3 provided an overview of the course, stressing that even the simplest purchases are subject to the following multiple and sometimes interacting influences:

- Decision process influences—factors such as the level of involvement, level of decision making, and situational variables
- Sociocultural influences—societal and social influences ranging from the broad culture down to interpersonal relations
- Individual psychological influences—the consumer's mental and physical activities during decision making, such as motivation, perception, and learning

Finally, Exercise 1.4 completed the introduction to CB by reviewing some traditional CB theories based on the social sciences of economics, psychology, and sociology. Four theories of human and consumer behavior were summarized:

- Marshall's utilitarian economic consumer seeks to get the most utility for his or her money, suggesting that marketers offer consumers a value proposition.
- Pavlov's classical conditioned consumer, a stimulus-response model of human psychology, learns through a passive, low-involvement process of responding automatically to frequently repeated cues and rewards. This suggests that sellers can appeal to driven consumers with cues presented repetitively in order to evoke buying responses that are then reinforced.
- Psychologist Sigmund Freud's emotional, hedonic, psychoanalytical consumer is driven by subconscious motives, unreasoned instincts, symbolic motives, and the need for pleasure, suggesting marketers use motivation research to discover such motives that consumers are ordinarily unable or unwilling to discuss and then appeal to them in marketing communications.
- Sociologist Thorstein Veblen's social-psychological consumer is concerned with conspicuous consumption.

Chapter 2 will delve into the marketer's most fundamental strategic decision: market segmentation, or how to divide the marketplace into groups of customers sharing common needs and wants.

REFERENCES

Alreck, Pamela L., and Settle, Robert B. (1999). "Strategies for Building Consumer Brand Preference." *Journal of Product and Brand Management,* 8, 2, 130–144.

Anderson, Paul F. (1986). "On Method in Consumer Research: A Critical Relativist Perspective." *Journal of Consumer Research,* 13, 2, 155–173.

Bendinger, Bruce. (2002). *The Copy Workshop Workbook, Really New Edition.* Chicago, IL: The Copy Workshop.

Bhat, Subodh, and Reddt, Srinivas K. (1998). "Symbolic and Functional Positioning of Brands." *Journal of Consumer Research,* 15, 1, 32–43.

Danziger, Pamela N. (2004). *Why People Buy Things They Don't Need.* Chicago, IL: Dearborn Trade Publishing.

Dunfee, Thomas W., Smith, N. Craig, and Ross, William T., Jr. (1999). "Social Contracts and Marketing Ethics." *Journal of Marketing,* 63, 3, 14–32.

Eisenberg, Lee. (2009). *Shoptimism: Why the American Consumer Will Keep on Buying No Matter What.* New York: Free Press.

Ferrell, O.C., Fraedrich, John, and Ferrell, Linda. (2008). *Business Ethics: Ethical Decision Making and Cases.* Boston: Houghton Mifflin Company.

Friedman, Milton. (1970). "The Social Responsibility of Business Is to Increase Profits." *New York Times Magazine,* 33 (13 September), 122–126.

Hirschman, Elizabeth C., and Holbrook, Morris B. (1982). "Hedonic Consumption: Emerging Concepts, Methods, and Propositions." *Journal of Marketing,* 46, 3, 92–101.

Holbrook, Morris B., and Hirschman, Elizabeth C. (1982). "The Experiential Aspects of Consumption: Consumer Fantasies, Feelings, and Fun." *Journal of Consumer Research,* 9, 2, 132–140.

Hunt, Shelby. (1984). "Marketing and Machiavellianism." *Journal of Marketing,* 48, 3, 30–42.

Johar, J. S., and Sirgy, M. Joseph. (1991). "Value-Expressive versus Utilitarian Advertising Appeals: When and Why to Use Which Appeal." *Journal of Advertising,* 20, 3, 23–34.

John, Joby. (2003). *Fundamentals of Customer-Focused Management.* Westport, CT: Praeger.

Kotler, Philip. (1965). "Behavioral Models for Analyzing Buyers." *Journal of Marketing,* 29, 4, 37–45.

Lantos, Geoffrey P., and Cooke, Simon. (2003). "Corporate Socialism Unethically Masquerades as 'CSR': The Difference Between Being Ethical, Altruistic, and Strategic in Business." *Strategic Direction,* 19, 6, 31–35.

Levitt, Ted. (1960). "Marketing Myopia." *Harvard Business Review,* 38, 4, 45–56.

Mowen, John C. (1988). "Beyond Consumer Decision Making." *Journal of Consumer Marketing,* 5, 1, 15–25.

Mrudula, E. (ed.) (2005). *Corporate Philanthropy, a Win-Win Model.* Hyderabad, India: The ICFAI University Press.

Packard, Vance. (1957). *The Hidden Persuaders.* New York: David McKay.

Pollay, Richard W. (1986). "The Distorted Mirror: Reflections on the Unintended Consequences of Advertising." *Journal of Marketing,* 50 (April), 18–36.

Richard, Michael D., Womack, James A., and Allaway, Arthur W. (1993). "Marketing Myopia: An Integrated View." *Journal of Product and Brand Management,* 2, 3, 49–54.

Rundle-Thiele, Sharyn, Ball, Kim, and Gillespie, Meghan. (2008). "Raising the Bar: From Corporate Social Responsibility to Corporate Social Performance." *Journal of Consumer Marketing,* 25, 4, 245–253.

Shavitt, Sharon. (1992). "Evidence for Predicting the Effectiveness of Value-Expressive versus Utilitarian Appeals: A Reply to Johar and Sirgy." *Journal of Advertising,* 21, 2, 47–52.

Shukla, Paurav. (2008). "Conspicuous Consumption among Middle Age Consumers: Psychological and Brand Antecedents." *Journal of Product and Brand Management,* 17, 1, 25–36.

Smith, N. Craig, and Quelch, John A. (1993). *Ethics in Marketing.* Homewood, IL: Richard D. Irwin.

Veblen, Thorstein. (1953). *The Theory of the Leisure Class* (1899; reprint). New York: New American Library.

This chapter further illustrates material that is foundational to the study of consumer behavior (CB). Marketing strategy begins with getting the basics correct: segmentation, targeting, and positioning.

Chapter 1 discussed types of consumer needs and wants, management philosophies marketers use to either neglect or concentrate on satisfying needs and wants, and different social science theories concerning what motives underlie those needs and wants.

Market segmentation is a managerial process that identifies groups of consumers who share similar or common needs and wants or problems to be solved as well as underlying motivations for marketplace behavior. Before marketing activity begins, marketers must identify, describe, and understand a group of current and prospective customers with common needs and wants, known as a **target market**. For instance, Target stores do not mass market, they target market, pursuing working mothers between the ages of twenty-five and fifty-four.

A proper understanding of the target market drives all elements of the **marketing mix**—the controllable marketing decision variables known as the *four P's*: product, price, place, and promotion. The firm uses these to meet the needs of its target market.

Many of the topics in this textbook constitute a basis or foundation for **segmenting** or dividing the market and then defining a target market. Such market segmentation foundations include *sociocultural variables* such as international cultures, domestic subcultures, social classes, membership groups, family situations, and opinion leaders. They also encompass *psychological variables*, including motivation, personality types, psychographics, stages in the learning process, and attitudes toward the brand.

ORGANIZATION OF CHAPTER TWO

Exercise 2.1 reviews three broad bases for segmenting markets (i.e., demographics, psychographics, and behavioristic [behavioral]) and the three broad market segmentation strategies: (undifferentiated [mass] marketing, differentiated marketing [multiple segmentation], and concentrated [niche] marketing).

Exercise 2.2 discusses the important strategic decision of positioning. or psychologically differentiating a product for a target market.

Finally, given that consumers ultimately purchase products for their **benefits** (satisfactions of needs and wants), **benefit segmentation** is investigated in Exercise 2.3. Benefit segmentation is based on the idea that target market members share common needs and wants.

EXERCISE 2.1. SEGMENTATION STRATEGIES

OBJECTIVES

1. To point out the importance of identifying, describing, understanding, and appealing to a desirable customer group, known as a target market, and to enumerate the prerequisites for effective market segmentation.
2. To describe and give specific examples of the bases (variables) that can be used as foundations for segmenting the marketplace: demographics, psychographics, and buyer behavior (behavioristic or behavioral segmentation).

3. To explain and contrast three broad target market strategies for deciding the extent to which the consumer marketplace should be segmented: undifferentiated (mass) marketing, differentiated marketing (multiple segmentation), and concentrated (niche) marketing, including the advantages and disadvantages of each approach.
4. To help you understand the kinds of situations in which each of the three segmentation strategies is appropriate.
5. To enable you to recognize and evaluate advertisers' use of market segmentation variables and target market strategies and their linkage to an advertisement's creative strategy.

BACKGROUND

PRODUCT DIFFERENTIATION AND MARKET SEGMENTATION AS COMPETITIVE ADVANTAGES

The era of "one size fits all" in the marketplace is, for the most part, long gone. Fact is, one size fits none! So, most marketers practice **product differentiation**. Items in a product line differ from each other and/ or from rivals' offerings in one of three ways.

1. They are better than competitive brands, *physically* or *tangibly*, by "building a better mousetrap" (product concept). Erectile dysfunction drug Levitra is better than Viagra because it works in sixteen minutes. Another competitor, Cialis, can last as long as thirty-six hours. HP computers were the first to allow users to watch movies without waiting for Windows to launch and offered the first touchscreen, all-in-one desktop, resulting in the advertising tagline, "The computer is personal again."
2. They are superior to rivals *psychologically* or *intangibly*. Marketers promote the trustworthiness of their brand names ("Trust Tylenol"), craft *brand images* (Mr. Clean is tough, yet friendly), and position their brands as being different (see Exercise 2.2). Unless there are patentable physical distinctions, psychological differences are usually more difficult for rivals to imitate since they entail feelings and imagery.
3. They offer a variety of products. Companies provide multiple product line items that differ from one another, including multiple sizes, quality levels, styles, feature combinations, options, flavors, and scents. While Henry Ford standardized automobile production, General Motors founder William Durant offered buyers a vast array of brands, models, and colors. Charmin is packed in red for those who want more strength and blue for those seeking more softness. Today's consumers can choose from miles of aisles of cars, clothing, and electronic equipment. The album-oriented rock genre that dominated FM radio in the 1970s and 1980s has been splintered into so many formats that three of them begin with the letter "A" (active, alternative, and adult rock).

Product differentiation can offer one or more of three competitive edges: (1) satisfying customers better than the competitors do, (2) offering the same customers more variety, and (3) satisfying various groups of people with different needs. Exhibit 2.1 summarizes product differentiation strategies. Regarding factor (3), sellers may also pursue one or more differentiated markets through market segmentation. The basic idea underlying market segmentation is that consumer preferences for products and the way they are marketed are not uniform or homogenous, but are instead heterogeneous. Women want one thing, men want another. Kids like some flavors, adults prefer others.

PREREQUISITES FOR EFFECTIVE SEGMENTATION

For market segmentation to succeed, seven marketplace requirements must be met.

1. *Differentiability:* Heterogeneity between groups and homogeneity within groups regarding product requirements: Customer needs must be different enough among consumers to merit distinct marketing programs (heterogeneity). At the same time, some consumers share similar desires (homogeneity) so that they can be clustered together into a market segment and appealed to with the same marketing program.

EXHIBIT 2.1   Product Differentiation

```
                        ┌──────────────────────────┐
                        │  Strategies to create product │
                        │  distinctions in buyers' eyes │
                        └──────────────────────────┘
        ┌─────────────────────┼─────────────────────┐
┌───────────────────┐ ┌───────────────────┐ ┌───────────────────┐
│ Physical/Tangible     │ │ Psychological/Intangible │ │ Product Variety       │
│ Differences:          │ │ Differences: Trusted brand│ │ Marketing:            │
│ Quality of performance,│ │ name, brand image     │ │ Quality levels, sizes,│
│ features, options     │ │                       │ │ styles, flavors, scents│
└───────────────────┘ └───────────────────┘ └───────────────────┘
        └─────────────────────┼───────────┐   ┌───────┘
                    ┌───────────────────┐ ┌───────────────────┐
                    │ Better customer       │ │ More variety,         │
                    │ satisfaction          │ │ less boredom          │
                    └───────────────────┘ └───────────────────┘
```

2. *Identifiability and divisibility:* Members of differentiated segments must be clearly identifiable along one or more bases (variables) for segmentation in order to create market profiles, such as descriptions of the segments. The data for carving the market into segments of similar customers must either be readily available from research suppliers or easily acquired through primary consumer research.

3. *Measurability:* There need to be ways to measure the important parameters of each identified market regarding relative attractiveness to the marketer. Segments should be compared along criteria such as size, growth rate, purchasing power, presence and nature of competition, and forecasted sales potential.

4. *Substantiality (profitability, attractiveness):* Based on the measurements, one or more of the market groups must be found to be attractive—large and lucrative enough to generate profits that justify serving it through a unique marketing program.

5. *Accessibility (reachability):* At least one of the substantial segments must be effectively and efficiently reachable through distribution and promotional strategies. For instance, the organization should be able to gain distribution in the stores in which targeted customers shop, and the marketer should be able to afford advertising in the media they use.

6. *Actionability:* It must be possible to design and implement a separate marketing mix for each substantial and accessible targeted group. Actionability might be limited by legal requirements such as restrictions on advertising to children, social expectations such as community standards for good taste, and cost requirements such as payments for securing prime retail shelf space or the high cost of advertising media.

7. *Responsiveness:* Each actionable market segment should favorably respond to the marketing program designed for it. For example, business-class fliers are less price-sensitive and more willing to pay higher airfares to get perks like more legroom and wider seats than are leisure fliers.

THE MARKET SEGMENTATION PROCESS

The process of dividing and serving (divide and conquer!) the market consists of three sequential stages, summarized in Exhibit 2.2.

STEP 1. MARKET SEGMENTATION

Market segmentation involves subdividing the marketplace into distinct and meaningful subsets of customers. Each group merits a separate marketing program to satisfy targeted consumers' particular needs and desires as suggested by the marketing concept.

> **EXHIBIT 2.2** **The Market Segmentation Process**

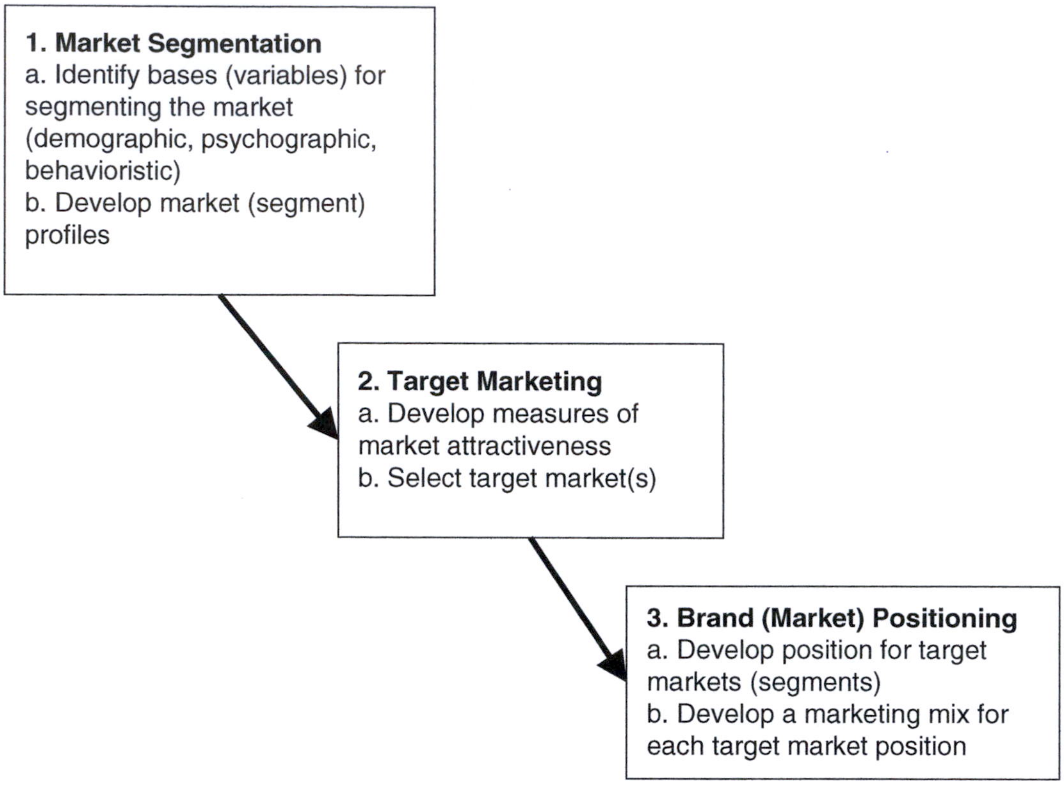

1. Market Segmentation
a. Identify bases (variables) for segmenting the market (demographic, psychographic, behavioristic)
b. Develop market (segment) profiles

2. Target Marketing
a. Develop measures of market attractiveness
b. Select target market(s)

3. Brand (Market) Positioning
a. Develop position for target markets (segments)
b. Develop a marketing mix for each target market position

Step 1A. Identify Bases (Variables) for Segmentation. Segmentation begins by identifying the fundamental bases (variables) for dividing the market: demographics, psychographics, and behavior. The chosen variables should serve as predictors of CB. Exhibit 2.3 summarizes the discussion that follows.

(**Demographics** are states of being that describe consumers' observable characteristics. Demographics include variables such as geographic factors (region, urban/suburban/rural, city size, county size, state size, population, climate, and terrain), age, sex, income, occupation, ethnicity, race, religion, social class, marital status, household size, family life cycle stage, and other human descriptors (see Part III, External Sociocultural Influences on Consumer Behavior). **Demographic segmentation** uses demographic variables to describe a consumer's observable characteristics.

Demographic variables are simple and inexpensive to obtain via **secondary data,** which is information gathered by someone else for another purpose. Such data is available from government sources (e.g., the U.S. Census Bureau at www.census.gov and FedStats at www.fedstats.gov/programs/index.html) and nongovernmental sources (e.g., *Sales and Marketing Management Survey of Buying Power* and *Editor and Publisher Market Guide*). Alternatively, the data can be procured via **primary research** (self-generated data, mostly from simple survey questions such as, "What is your age?").

Unfortunately, demographics merely describe consumers. They do not explain buyer behavior. The underlying reason a consumer makes a purchase is not simply because she is thirty-seven, for example (although turning twenty-one is often a cause for celebration).

Age and sex remain the most popular segmentation factors. Individuals relate to people of their own age and sex who are pictured in advertisements, who serve as salespeople, and who approach them as survey fieldworkers. Regarding sex, Beef jerky is stereotypically for guys: rough, rugged, and stinky. It is distributed in "guy" venues such as convenience stores and do-it-yourself depots. Women are the primary

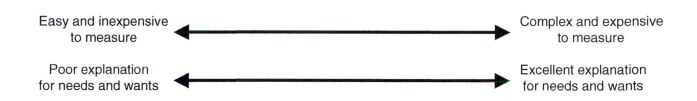

EXHIBIT 2.3   Consumer Marketing Segmentation Bases

Demographic Variables— States of Being	Psychographic Variables— States of Mind and Action	Behavioristic Variables— States of Action
Geography, age, sex, income, occupation, ethnicity, race, religion, social class, marital status, household size, family life cycle, etc.	Personality, lifestyle, motivation, attitudes, interests, opinions	End use, usage rate, usage experience, purchase/usage occasion, loyalty status, marketing factor sensitivity, innovativeness, opinion leadership, buyer readiness state, benefits sought, etc.

Easy and inexpensive to measure ◄──────────────────────► Complex and expensive to measure

Poor explanation for needs and wants ◄──────────────────────► Excellent explanation for needs and wants

(core) customers for no-cal sodas, but Coke Zero targets men from college age up with black packaging, a more sugary-tasting sweetener, and irreverent marketing that appeals to men who have become calorie-conscious with age.

Psychographics adds *states of mind* and consequent *states of action* to states of being. Psychographics include internal and external personal factors such as personality and lifestyle, motivation, and activities, interests, and opinions (AIOs).

Psychographic information is not as readily available as demographic data via secondary data sources. It is also more difficult to accurately obtain through primary research. Consequently, it is usually acquired from specialized research firms. This is worth the cost because psychographics helps explain CB better than demographics do. People buy things because of what they think, and how they feel and behave rather than because they are in a particular income bracket or age group. After a psychographic segment is found, marketers usually search for common demographic descriptors of segment members so they can more easily be identified and reached via appropriate media.

For instance, people who live in so-called red states are often NASCAR-loving, gun-toting, God-fearing Republicans from the rural, suburban, and small-town heartland that stretches from the Deep South through the Great Plains and into the mountain states. Blue state residents, by contrast, are highly secular, latte-sipping, diversity-embracing Democrats concentrated in the urban areas on the two coasts and around the Great Lakes.

Behavioristic (behavioral, usage) segmentation encompasses *states of action* within the marketplace. For instance, Nintendo Wii targets not only the core videogaming market of teen boys and young men but also "dabblers," "lapsed gamers," and "nongamers," including girls, women, and seniors. Behavioral bases include the following.

- *End use (function).* Many items have multiple uses. Clorox liquid bleach can serve as an insecticide, a wound cleaner, a cure for rashes, and a household cleaner. Women often have swimsuits for leisure swimming versus more revealing ones for sunbathing.
- *Usage rate (usage status).* Typical categories are heavy users, medium users, light users, lapsed users (previous product or brand users who are now nonusers), nonusers, first-time users, and potential users. Often, **Pareto's Law (the heavy-half theory)** is operational—half of a brand's customers account for

a disproportionately larger amount of a brand's overall sales volume. For instance, often 80 percent of sales result from 20 percent of customers. Business travelers who fly frequently are known as road warriors.

- *Usage experience.* A high-tech-gadget user could be a neophyte versus an "old pro."
- *Purchase (usage) occasion.* Some products can be used for various activities or events. Each usage constitutes a basis for segmentation. Folgers coffee can be "the best part of waking up" or served to guests. Nuts are eaten for individual snacking and at parties.
- *Loyalty status/commitment level.* A buyer could be a first timer or a regular user. The latter may be brand loyal, a brand switcher purchasing whatever is on sale or choosing brands offering promotional incentives, or a variety seeker switching among varieties of a given brand or between different brands for a change of pace.
- *Marketing factor sensitivity.* Price sensitivity, deal proneness, and advertising responsiveness all describe people who are highly receptive to certain marketing mix variables.
- *Buyer readiness state.* This is a measure of learning: degree of awareness, interest, or information; attitude toward a product or brand; and any prior purchase and usage experience.
- *Benefits sought.* Benefits are the satisfaction of buyers' needs and wants. For example, the "dashboard diner" market entails people who like to eat in their cars because it is quick and easy, and who therefore patronize quick-serve restaurant drive-thrus.

As is true of psychographic groups, behavioristic groups are usually also described demographically so they can be readily identified and reached.

Technology has led to the increasing popularity of behavioral segmentation. **Behavioral targeting (marketing, tracking)** involves matching ads to interests indicated by recency and frequency of CBs, collected unobtrusively via Internet *cookies,* which are small text files that Web servers and ad networks place on users' hard drives. Behavioral targeting uses collaborative filtering technology that recognizes when Web site visitors are seeking a particular product or service and then serves an ad relevant to their search at a later date on another Web page. For example, a Web surfer could be looking at real estate listings on a daily newspaper site on Monday, and then on Thursday, while reading the sports section, that person would be served an ad from a real estate agent. Netflix scans users' rental histories and their film ratings to suggest movies they would likely enjoy. Another use of high-tech behavioral segmentation is shopper loyalty cards. Consumers give retailers some of their personal information to get the cards, which offer discounts and other rewards when presented at checkout.

Step 1B. Develop Market Profiles. A **market segment profile** is a description of the group of people emerging from the market segmentation process known as a *market segment*, using the selected segmentation variable(s). Two or more variables may be combined. Example: Men between the ages of thirty-five and forty-four living in New England who have a family consisting of a wife and one or more children (all demographics), enjoy taking family vacations (psychographics), and are frequent business travelers (behavioristic). Adding more variables narrows the market to a more finely tuned group.

STEP 2. TARGET MARKETING

Target marketing (market targeting) is the act of evaluating, selecting, and serving the market segment(s) that the organization can accommodate most effectively and efficiently.

Step 2A. Develop Measures of Market Attractiveness. Evaluation involves developing measures of **market attractiveness**, a gauge of the potential profitability of each market segment. Issues to consider include whether the organization has the resources to serve each segment; each segment's size, growth rate, and buying power; costs of serving each segment; and size and nature of competitors serving the same segment and consumer loyalty to those rivals.

Step 2B. Select Target Markets. Next, the firm selects and focuses on one or more segments to pursue, known as *target markets*, each described by a *market segment profile* statement. For instance, Ferrari, a customer-made Italian sports car, chases males forty-five to fifty, 65 percent of whom are repeat buyers and 60 percent of whom own a private jet.

STEP 3. BRAND (MARKET) POSITIONING

The final step in the process of choosing and serving markets is **brand (market) positioning**.

Step 3A. Develop Positioning for Target Markets. **Positioning** entails physically and/or psychologically differentiating the firm's offering for each target market from those of competitors pursuing the same or similar segments. Whereas target marketing considers the customers, positioning also considers competitors. A **positioning statement** is a summary of the product's positioning discussing its key points of distinction appealing to the targeted segment.

Step 3B. Develop a Marketing Mix for Each Target Market. Positioning is done via formulation of a unique, competitive marketing mix for each target segment. For instance, a product can take a high-quality, high-price, snob-appeal position, being sold in upscale stores by sophisticated salespeople.

THREE TARGET MARKET STRATEGIES

During the market segmentation and target marketing stages of the segmentation process, two important decisions must be made. First is the degree to which the market will be segmented, that is, the number of variables used (e.g., age versus both age and sex) and number of levels of each variable (e.g. four versus eight age groups). The more variables and the more levels of each variable used, the more precisely segments can be described, although this costs more time, money, and effort. The second important decision is how many segments to select as target markets (one or more than one) and the nature of these segments (broad vs. narrow).

Accordingly, there are three general **target market (market coverage) strategies**, which are plans for targeting a firm's marketing efforts to members of the marketplace: (1) undifferentiated (mass) marketing, (2) differentiated marketing (multiple segmentation), and (3) concentrated (niche) marketing. These market coverage strategies are outlined in Exhibit 2.4.

UNDIFFERENTIATED MARKETING

Undifferentiated marketing (mass marketing, market aggregation) involves no market segmentation. The marketer pursues the entire market or largest segment of it with one product and one marketing program. There is neither product differentiation nor market differentiation (segmentation). Mass distribution and mass promotion are the name of the marketing game.

Once popular, this "one-size-fits-all" approach, which seldom fits anyone, is rarely used today except in several fairly uncommon situations:

- In less competitive markets where precise customer satisfaction is not necessary.
- In small markets where segmentation would result in groups too small to profitably serve.
- For commodities, such as milk, sugar, salt, fruits and vegetables, and number 2 pencils, which virtually everybody consumes for similar reasons.
- For "All-American" brands satisfying universal needs, such as Hershey, "The great American chocolate bar," and *USA Today,* "The nation's newspaper."

Undifferentiated marketing has the advantage of being *economical* in that no costs are incurred in researching different groups and designing and administering separate marketing programs to each. However, it can be *ineffective*: In trying to appeal to everyone, a marketer ends up appealing to no one. To quote the wise sages, "You can't be all things to all people."

Undifferentiated marketing can also be *inefficient*, involving wasted effort and high expense in trying to reach everyone, including those not interested in the product. And customer satisfaction is low because

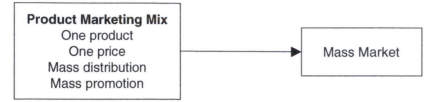

EXHIBIT 2.4   Three Market Coverage Strategies

1. Undifferentiated (Mass) Marketing

Product Marketing Mix
One product
One price
Mass distribution
Mass promotion

→ Mass Market

2. Differentiated Marketing (Multiple Segmentation)

Product Marketing Mix 1 → Market Segment (Target Market) 1

Product Marketing Mix 2 → Market Segment (Target Market) 2

Product Marketing Mix 3* → Market Segment (Target Market) 3

3. Concentrated (Niche) Marketing

Product Marketing Mix → Market Segment (Target Market)

*Either one product or differentiated products can be offered along with unique marketing programs for each segment.

diverse and unique needs and wants are not being fulfilled. Consequently, even traditional mass marketers now segment the market. McDonald's has two key customer groups: (1) the primary (core) target market (the most important target market focus) of young families with kids, and (2) the secondary target market (of lesser importance and focus) of young adults who eat on the run.

DIFFERENTIATED MARKETING

Differentiated marketing (multisegment [multimarket] marketing, segmented marketing, multiple segmentation) entails dividing the total market into two or more market segments and pursuing at least two of them with two or more marketing strategies (one strategy per segment). There are two approaches: (1) the same product can be offered to each target market but with a separate marketing program, and (2) differentiated products and unique marketing programs can be aimed at each segment.

Multiple segmentation is more *effective* than mass marketing because it results in better customer satisfaction, leading to higher sales and customer loyalty. However, differentiated marketing is more costly since multiple markets must be researched and two or more marketing programs are formulated and implemented. However, this strategy can be more *efficient* on a per-person-reached basis than undifferentiated marketing because the wasted expense of trying to reach nearly everyone is spared.

CONCENTRATED MARKETING

Concentrated (niche) marketing is increasingly popular. It divides the market into groups and then focuses exclusively on one and only one often narrowly defined, small, underserved segment with one product and one marketing mix. Especially where the segment is very specialized and neglected by other marketers, a concentrated strategy results in higher levels of customer satisfaction and less competition. Thus, the "size-friendly" Freedom Paradise Resort in Mexico accommodates overweight guests with facilities for plus-sized vacationers with larger and sturdier chairs, wider doorways, and plus-size gift shirts in the gift shop.

Niching can also result in lower costs due to specialization and limiting the reach of the marketing program, making it especially attractive to smaller firms with limited resources as well as smaller divisions of larger firms. Further, the marketer might be seen as a specialist who knows the target customer group so well that it satisfies their desires better than other companies selling to that niche. Today's puny niche markets might eventually become tomorrow's mainstream giants, as has occurred with many ethnic foods.

However, it's not always true that in niches there are riches. Concentrated marketing can also be a risky strategy since the marketer is putting all eggs in one basket. If the market dries up, the seller is out of business. Also, the size of the organization's business is limited by the size of the single segment. And, if the segment grows, this might attract larger competitors. Also the marketer might acquire a focused image or reputation that limits entry into other potentially lucrative market segments.

Technology encourages and enables niche marketing. In his book *The Long Tail: Why the Future of Business Is Selling Less of More,* Chris Anderson proposes the **long-tail theory**. As the Internet makes it easy and cheap to offer a vast array of content, consumers turn away from mass market hit products they sort of want, such as best-selling books, chart-topping songs, and blockbuster movies. Instead, they turn toward niche products they really desire, such as obscure books, songs, and movies. So, we find Amazon .com offering "earth's biggest selection"; eBay, on which you can find anything to suit your personal tastes; and online music store Rhapsody selling songs not available in retail stores. Anderson believes that the future of demand stimulation lies not at the head of the curve where the mass market exists, but rather down the "long tail" of niches. Technology empowers niche-pursuing marketers with detailed consumer data, which enables them to microtarget messages.

THE ULTIMATE MARKET SEGMENTATION: INDIVIDUALIZED MARKETING

During the 1990s a new trend took hold: **individualized (one-to-one, segment-of-one, markets of one) marketing**. Here, marketers push segmentation to the max, serving each individual consumer with a tailor-made marketing program. Of course, for many personal services, such as fitness trainers, financial advisers, and lawyers, one-to-one marketing has always been the modus operandi. With individualized marketing we have come full circle since days long gone, when the local merchant knew you by name and your personal preferences.

Today, via what sounds oxymoronic, **mass customization**—mass production of goods with differing individual specifications through the use of components that may be assembled in a number of different configurations—many producers can now achieve flexible, low-cost manufacturing without lengthy production runs of one product. Aided by Internet technology, for example, customer relationship management (CRM) software by providers such as Salesforce.com and NetSuite, Inc. allows individual dialogue with and tracking of transaction data and online behavior of each customer; it is feasible and economical for each buyer to be given exactly what his or her heart desires, mimicking job-shop production. For example, CVS's ExtraCare loyalty program enables highly targeted marketing efforts, with promotional offers at the register, coupons, e-mail, and direct mail. Individualized marketing is a form of **direct marketing**, marketing by the manufacturer directly to the end user or buyer without use of any intermediaries. Sellers interact directly with buyers, using media such as mail, phone, e-mail, and Web sites to obtain a direct *response*, usually a sale or inquiry for more information.

Personalized computers, customized CDs, and jeans designed just for buyers are all familiar products of mass customization. Such mass customization entails **co-creation**, in which customers participate in creating their products. On the LEGO Factory Web site, children can create and design the sets of their dreams. Apple's customers can download music inexpensively from their online music store to create a custom jukebox on an iPod. Many professors now order course material specifically for their courses that is packaged as customized, bound books.

REVIEW QUESTIONS

1. What is the underlying rationale for market segmentation?
2. How does market segmentation differ from product differentiation?

3. What are the prerequisites for effective market segmentation?
4. Outline the three-stage market segmentation process, including the two substeps in each major stage.
5. Describe and give specific examples of each of the three major categories of market segmentation bases.
6. Describe the three general target market strategies, explaining the strengths and limitations of each.

IN-CLASS APPLICATIONS

1. Which general bases and specific variables for defining market segments, if any, do each of the ads in Exhibits 2.5 through 2.8 seem to be using? Describe the resulting target market profile.

Are there any other variables that the ad's product could effectively use for segmentation? If so, explain which bases could be used and why, and describe the resulting market segment profiles.

How, if at all, would use of these additional variables change the ad's creative strategy, that is, the message (what is said about the brand, such as the selling theme or slogan) and the creative execution of the message (how the message is said or presented).

2. Which target market strategy—undifferentiated, differentiated, or concentrated—is being used by the brands shown in each of the ads in Exhibits 2.5 through 2.8? Why do you suppose each chose that strategy? Would you recommend an alternative? If so, what and why?

3. One controversial marketing strategy is price discrimination in which different prices are set for different market segments. Prices are not based on differential costs of serving those segments, but are founded on varying levels of demand among segments. Examples: senior citizens are granted discounts, ladies get admitted to some nightclubs free on "ladies' nights," and students who can afford full freight help subsidize the tuition of those who cannot. Price discrimination is legal. But is it ethical?

WRITTEN APPLICATIONS

1. Answer In-Class Applications Questions 1 and 2 for each of the ads (Exhibits 2.5–2.8). Be as creative as you can be in suggesting modified creative strategies.

2. After analyzing these ads, find three more ads that each use a different target marketing strategy. Repeat the same analysis as in the previous question for each of these ads.

EXERCISE 2.2. BRAND POSITIONING

OBJECTIVES

1. To show the importance and purpose of both positioning and subsequent repositioning in developing marketing strategy for a branded product.
2. To describe the criteria used in physical and psychological brand positioning.
3. To help you understand how advertising can be used to position or reposition a brand.
4. To give you practice in creatively psychologically positioning a brand in different ways.

BACKGROUND

POSITIONING DEFINED

Brand (market) positioning entails designing a *physical* product and its *psychological* image. Positioning allows targeted consumers to understand and appreciate what the marketing entity stands for or means in relation to its competitors, helping the marketer to differentiate his or her offering from competitors within the market segment.

EXHIBIT 2.5   Wal-Mart Ad

EXHIBIT 2.6   Prudential Ad

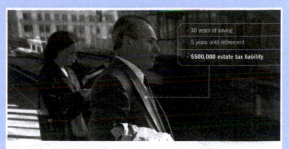

EXHIBIT 2.7   Tylenol Ad

EXHIBIT 2.8   Bulova Ad

Although positioning is the third stage in the process of market segmentation (see Exercise 2.1), it is also the first step in the development of a marketing strategy for each targeted segment, setting the foundation for the marketing mix decisions (See the third box in Exhibit 2.2).

PHYSICAL POSITIONING AND PSYCHOLOGICAL POSITIONING

Physical positioning (physical product differentiation) entails distinguishing the marketer's product from the rivals via tangible product attributes—physical product characteristics, such as styling, color, and odor—or by making it of better quality or higher performance. Physically, Lexus positions itself as a luxury car providing perfection in all of the details, while Volvo is solidly positioned on safety. Shell gasoline contains Platformate, Johnson's baby shampoo has a "no tears" formula, and Charmin Ultra Strong bathroom tissue is five times stronger when wet.

However, many brands of products in commodity categories are virtually physically indistinguishable. Examples: nasal spray, deodorant, margarine, detergent, and alkaline batteries. Also, attributes are too often easy to copy. To set their brand apart from the crowd, marketers of such parity or easily imitated products practice **psychological positioning (psychological product differentiation)**, creating "induced" brand differences in buyers' minds via advertising and promotion. Whereas the brand's physical position is tangible and concrete, its psychological position is abstract and intangible, creating a subjective consumer meaning concerning what the brand is like and what it represents.

A given physical product can have multiple subjective consumer meanings, depending on how the marketer brands, packages and labels, prices, places, and promotes it. For example, for many years Pepsi-Cola has been more than just carbonated cola—it is a young person's drink, "The Choice for a New Generation."

Although critics abhor the idea of "creating differences where there are no real differences," the result of psychological positioning for some buyers is **psychological value added (intangible value, perceptual value)**. Customers of psychologically positioned brands get extra utility and are therefore willing to pay more for it. Hence, a woman might feel more glamorous because she uses Elizabeth Taylor's perfume as opposed to a brand endorsed by everyday Jills.

THE DIMENSIONS OF PSYCHOLOGICAL POSITIONING

Psychological brand positioning involves locating the brand in the buyer's mind relative to three interrelated dimensions: uses, target markets, and competition.

1. *Uses (applications, functions).* These are a brand's "reasons for being." A soda pop could be used as a thirst quencher as well as a facilitator of social relationships. Raisins can serve as a snack or a baking ingredient.
2. *Target market users or user imagery.* A brand can be positioned as appropriate for a specific user group. Lucky Brand Jeans and Juicy Couture charm bracelets are for the fashionistas.
3. *The competition or competitive set.* This is a group of various alternative products and brands that consumers consider as substitutes for their brand. Emphasis is on the brand's superiority to all the others via head-to-head comparisons on one or more brand attributes. Gillette positions MACH 3 as "the best a man can get." Bratz dolls are anti-Barbie: ultra fashionable with bare midriffs, bee-stung lips, trendy duds, and funky names.

Comparison (comparative) advertising claims that the brand is superior to one or more explicitly named brands on one or more attributes (e.g., "People like Kraft Cheese Nips better than Cheez-It crackers"). It is usually employed by follower brands trying to surpass the market leader. Schick slices Gillette razors, Coors and Miller ask beer drinkers to can Budweiser, Pizza Hut delivers a slice to Domino's, Reebok boots Nike, and Apple takes a bite out of Windows-based PCs. In effect, challengers say, "Hey, they might be number one, but we're just as good as they are!"

A popular type of competitive differentiation is **value positioning**—differentiating a brand by suggesting it gives consumers more for their money. Value positionings include less for a much lower price (no-frills cell phones), the same for a lower price (Wal-Mart), and more for the same price (Lexus).

Competitive positioning can also entail **product class (category) positioning**—defining the boundaries of the product class, done either broadly or narrowly, suggesting other competitive products. Diet Pepsi can be positioned narrowly against other diet colas, or increasingly more broadly against all diet sodas, all other colas, all low-calorie beverages, or even all beverages. Stovetop stuffing competes against "belly stuffer" side dishes such as potatoes, rice, and noodles.

In short, psychological positioning is done for brands in a product class where the product has many alternative uses, potential target markets, and possible competitors, including within other product categories. Once the use has been established, the target market and competition more or less become evident.

Consider Red Bull, positioned by product category as an energy drink. The physical position is distinct: Red Bull contains caffeine, vitamins, carbohydrates, and amino acids. The psychological position is an energy booster (use) for twenty-somethings (users) to be consumed after work before hitting the dance clubs (usage situation).

PSYCHOLOGICAL POSITIONING THROUGH ADVERTISING

An **advertising appeal (selling premise, unique selling proposition)** is a basic advertising message that summarizes the brand's positioning in a statement explaining how a brand in a particular product category has a specific use that satisfies a target market's needs better than do competitor products and brands.

An example is Carnation Instant Breakfast. The physical position is a flavored sugary powder fortified with protein, vitamins, and minerals. When added to milk it dissolves to make the milk more palatable and nutritious.

However, more significant for the marketing of this brand than this physical position is its psychological position, based on the product's promoted use, target market, and competition.

1. *Use.* Instant Breakfast's name, packaging, and advertising all suggest that it be used as a meal replacement at breakfast time.
2. *Competition.* Drinking Instant Breakfast is a substitute for more traditional quick breakfasts such as cereal, oatmeal, toast and jam, and toaster pastries. To a lesser extent, Instant Breakfast provides an alternative to larger, more traditional breakfasts, such as bacon and eggs, waffles, and pancakes, plus the accompanying beverage.
3. *Target market.* Instant Breakfast's targeted customers are busy people, especially working adults and on-the-run students with limited discretionary time to spend in the morning preparing and consuming breakfast. The selling premise is that Instant Breakfast is easier to prepare while being just as delicious and nutritious as traditional breakfasts.

However, Instant Breakfast could have been given many different positions by varying the definitions of the brand's use, targeted customers who want that use, and competitive products and brands that fulfill the desired use for those customers. It could, for instance, be branded, packaged, and promoted as Gulpees, a delicious snack beverage when added to milk (use) for children (users) who love to drink soda, Kool-Aid, and other yummy beverages (competitive products and brands) between meals.

REPOSITIONING IN A DYNAMIC MARKETPLACE

A marketplace with changing conditions sometimes mandates creating a new brand position, a process known as **repositioning (relaunching, restaging, remarketing)**—staking out a new and different brand position due to marketplace dynamics. Such brand reinvention becomes necessary due to four changes, three of which are related to one of the four bases for psychological positioning: uses, target markets, and competitors. The fourth marketplace dynamic is technology.

New uses come from changes in society, such as evolving values, behavioral standards, and customs. With an antismoking mood and new laws prohibiting public smoking, Wrigley's spearmint gum repositioned from providing chewing enjoyment to being a smoking alternative. The Subway sandwich company repositioned its menu as a healthy choice by featuring low-fat sandwiches in ads starring Jared S. Fogle, who lost 235 pounds in a one-year "Subway diet."

Changes in the demographic composition of the population or changing needs within target groups result in new desirable target market(s). Johnson & Johnson repositioned their baby powder and shampoo as appropriate for adults during the 1970s birth dearth. Kellogg's Frosted Flakes is now marketed to adults and children since Kellogg's discovered that parents were secretly digging into the sugar-laden cereal.

In a shifting competitive landscape, new foes enter the marketplace and old ones grow, decline, or exit. Years ago, Mountain Dew repositioned from a frumpy hillbilly image to an edgy, youthful personality as rival sodas pursued teenagers. Faced with no-frills airlines, American Airlines, long the preferred carrier of discriminating corporate travelers, repositioned itself as the top provider of value travel, offering more legroom and service for the same price as the low-fare carriers.

Changes in the technological environment led to changed physical as well as psychological positioning. As microwave ovens became common, Cheez Whiz repositioned itself from a cheese spread to a fast, convenient, microwaveable cheese sauce. Microsoft modified their organizational position from providing only software for the personal computer to software for the Internet and wireless mobile devices such as cell phones and PDAs.

A possible problem in repositioning for well-established brands is a loss in brand equity—the value consumers assign to a brand above and beyond its functional characteristics, including brand name awareness, perceived brand quality, brand associations, brand image, and brand loyalty. Due to loss of goodwill in the current target market from brand repositioning, a marketer could lose a loyal consumer franchise while never convincing new target customers that the brand now stands for something different that they desire. If Jaguar (sporty, stylish, historic, and British) were to try to reposition themselves as more like Lexus (conservative, expensive, modern, luxurious, and slightly Japanese), this might alienate current customers while possibly failing to attract many new ones. Case in point: Volkswagen attempted to move up-market with the luxury Touareg sports utility vehicle and Phaeton sedan models. However, that confused car buyers, who associate VW with zippy, affordable cars.

There are, nonetheless, many interesting examples of brands that made a successful 180-degree turn-around in the marketplace via repositioning. For example, you might not know the following surprising origins for some of today's household name products.

- Welch's grape juice was first positioned as a wine substitute before being repositioned as a regular fruit drink.
- Coca-Cola was originally advertised as a brain tonic and later as a high-class fountain drink. Today, we know Coca-Cola as the leading all-American soft drink.
- Early on, Canada Dry was used as a mixer for alcoholic drinks. It was also positioned by consumers themselves as a medicine when feeling sick. Presently, Canada Dry is positioned as a club soda and a mainstream soft drink.
- We now know Vaseline petroleum jelly as a multiuse product. However, can you picture this product being used as a machine lubricant? That was its original use.
- Post-it Notes were previously marketed as an adhesive used on fabrics to cut out patterns for making clothing. The manufacturers believed it would be a success because it was less messy and a lot easier than using chalk on fabric. But it was a flop. Post-it Notes are now used by virtually everyone who wants to leave someone else, or themselves, a note.
- Whereas Old Spice was once known as a cheap cologne for older men, the brand's recent irreverent repositioning advertising —spoofs of classic Old Spice ads featuring a sailor—along with new products such as deodorant and body washes, have brought it favor with younger guys.

REVIEW QUESTIONS

1. Define and explain the nature of both physical positioning and psychological positioning.
2. What is the purpose of brand positioning and why is it important in today's marketplace?
3. Outline and describe the dimensions of psychological positioning, giving an example of each.
4. What is repositioning? What marketplace dynamics sometimes necessitate the repositioning of a brand?

IN-CLASS APPLICATIONS

1. Develop at least three psychological positionings for the nutritional drink Instant Breakfast, along with the advertising appeal (selling premise) behind each. Which one of these do you think would be most successful in the marketplace? Why?

2. Each of the following pairs of ads in Exhibits 2.9 through 2.17 illustrates two psychological positionings (one old, one new) for a branded product (four ads in the case of Listerine). Describe the original and the more recent positionings in terms of use, target market, and competition. Then, explain the advertising appeal based on the brand's position.

What changing marketplace conditions do you think mandated the new position in each case? In your opinion, how effective was each repositioning? Can you dream up another position for each of these products?

WRITTEN APPLICATIONS

1. Answer Question 2 in the In-Class Applications for two of the products featured in the Exhibits 2.9 through 2.17. In addition, locate another ad for one of these products (possibly online) and describe its positioning.

2. Find ads for two other products that have a clear psychological position. Describe the positioning strategy used by each using the criteria discussed in this exercise. Then, develop two alternative positionings for each brand. Would either of these positions work well, given current marketplace conditions?

EXERCISE 2.3. BENEFIT SEGMENTATION

OBJECTIVES

1. To demonstrate the importance and usefulness of benefit segmentation as the ultimate application of market segmentation to satisfy consumer needs and wants.
2. To explain and illustrate the relationship between psychological positioning and benefit segmentation.
3. To help you decide on the ethics of creating psychological brand distinctions where physical brand differences do not exist.
4. To recognize the application of benefit positioning in conjunction with positioning by use, target market, and competition.

BACKGROUND

FEATURES AND BENEFITS

Consumer product developers focus on features and benefits. **Benefits** are the satisfactions of buyers' needs and wants as delivered by the product's **features**—physical attributes that provide benefits. Lightweight luggage (feature) is portable (benefit). A fluorescent (feature) clock glows in the dark (function or use), and so is easy to read (benefit).

Marketers do not view consumers as being interested in products and their features per se but in the benefits that those products and features deliver. This is because benefits are the consumer needs satisfied by the brand's features. For example, you purchase a snow blower for the satisfaction of quickly clearing the snow without breaking your back. Consumers seek clean, clear skin, not a bar of soap.

Features are objective product information that consumers translate into subjective *benefits*—what the features mean to them or do for them. "The sweater is $95 and 100 percent cashmere" means "The sweater is expensive and soft." Each product feature must yield one or more consumer benefits so that buyers want that attribute. Marketing communications should focus primarily on the product's benefits since these are the reasons consumers buy a product.

EXHIBIT 2.9   Kleenex Ad, 1920s

EXHIBIT 2.10   Kleenex Ad: Timely Tips by Little Lulu

EXHIBIT 2.11   Listerine Ad, 1950s: For Dandruff Treatment

EXHIBIT 2.12   Listerine Ad, 1950s: For Cough or Sore Throat

EXHIBIT 2.13   Listerine Ad, 1950s: For Fresh Breath

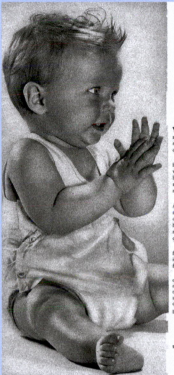

EXHIBIT 2.14   Marlboro Ad, 1970

EXHIBIT 2.15   Marlboro Ad, 1984

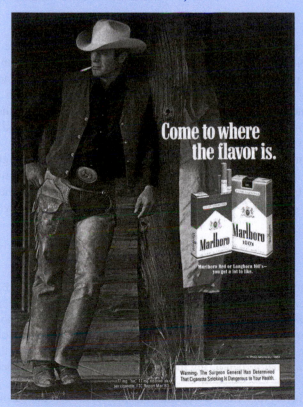

EXHIBIT 2.16   Miller Ad, 1950

EXHIBIT 2.17   Miller Ad, 1981

MARKET SEGMENTATION AND BENEFITS

Recall that the purpose of market segmentation is to discover groups of consumers who share similar needs and desires, that is, they seek similar product benefits. Since many products deliver multiple benefits simultaneously, each of which is most important to a particular segment of customers, dividing the marketplace according to benefits sought is good marketing practice. In buying detergent, one group of customers is interested in tough, powerful cleaning, while another customer cluster prefers color protection. Still other groups favor whitening, brightening, odor removal, stain fighting, fabric protection, or safeness for tender skin. Each customer group is a potential benefit segment.

Consequently, many brands focus on promoting one particular benefit. Thus, Tide is the tough, powerful cleaner, while Cheer offers color protection, Gain has an odor-removing formula, and Oxydol whitens clothes. The benefit of light beer for men is that it does not fill them up fast, so they can drink more, while for women light beer's benefit is that it contains fewer calories, so they will not gain weight as easily.

THE NATURE OF BENEFIT SEGMENTATION

Benefit segmentation, then, involves dividing the market based on benefits desired from a product because various groups of consumers seek different features and benefits for the same product. Segmenting by benefits is one technique of *behavioristic segmentation*. Theoretically, benefit segmentation is the most effective way to segment a market since it is based on the notion that a market segment consists of people who want the same satisfactions from a product. For example, some people prefer a low price, yielding the benefit of saving money. Others seek high product quality, delivering more enjoyment, better performance, or a longer-lasting product.

All other market segmentation variables are merely imperfect surrogates (substitutes) for the real reasons (benefits) consumers purchase. For example, the variable old age suggests the consumer has many medical needs, although this is not always the case. High income implies a desire for luxury goods, although a high-income consumer may nonetheless be quite frugal.

However, benefits sought are the consumer needs satisfied by the brand's features. So, theoretically, benefits desired by consumers should determine their purchase and usage behavior much more accurately than demographic or psychographic variables. This is because benefits are the causal factors of CB rather than merely descriptive consumer characteristics that tend to correlate with or are associated with CB.

As a type of psychological positioning, benefit segmentation helps marketers define and differentiate their brands from competitors. If most other mint candy brands talk up the "fresh breath" benefit ("breath mints") and, instead, you promote the cool sweet taste benefit ("candy mints"), you will be perceived as unique and will face less immediate competition than if you were to position your product as another "breath mint."

Benefit segmentation was first popularized in the late 1960s in a classic article that divided the toothpaste market into four benefit segments. The *sensory* segment consisted of people wanting flavor and a pleasing product appearance. Demographically, these were children who used spearmint-flavored toothpaste brands such as Colgate and Stripe. *Sociables* comprised teens and young people who tended to be smokers. They sought bright teeth and were heavy users of Ultrabrite, Macleans, and Plus White. *Worriers* focused on the benefit of decay prevention. They were primarily large families who heavily used Crest. People wanting low prices made up the *independent* segment. They tended to be men who purchased whatever brand happened to be on sale.

Toothpaste marketers still practice benefit segmentation. Some brands focus on therapeutic benefits (Crest fights cavities and Colgate Luminous strengthens enamel), while others emphasize cosmetic benefits (Close-Up gives you pearly whites and fresh breath). Some brands even tout multiple benefits, although this has the danger of muddying the brand's position. For example, Aquafresh has three stripes, each delivering a different benefit: white fights cavities, blue provides great taste, and red delivers fresh breath. Crest Pro-Health promises to address all five major health care problems identified by dentists—cavities, gingivitis, plaque, tooth sensitivity, and tartar buildup—plus, it fights stains and freshens breath! The trend is toward brands promoting multiple benefits.

BENEFIT SEGMENTATION AS ANOTHER POSITIONING DIMENSION

In addition to use, target market, and competition, benefits are another dimension on which to psychologically position a brand. Benefit segmentation can be combined with these other positioning dimensions.

REVIEW QUESTIONS

1. Explain the relationship between features and benefits. How do features and benefits tie in to market segmentation?
2. Why can benefit segmentation be considered the most direct and useful means of market segmentation?
3. How can benefit segmentation be practiced as a form of psychological positioning?

IN-CLASS APPLICATIONS

1. There are many other toothpaste brands you have probably seen advertised in the marketplace: Colgate, Aim, Aquafresh, Listerine, Mentadent, Arm & Hammer, Sensodyne, and Rembrandt, among others. Some come in various formulations such as tartar control, baking soda, gum care, and special sparkles and flavors for kids.

What benefits do each of these brands' features yield? Describe demographically and/or psychographically the target market that is most interested in each of these benefits.

2. Is it ethical to position a brand as unique by promoting a specific benefit when many other brands in the category also deliver that benefit? Think, for example, about laundry detergents: Tide claims tough,

powerful cleaning; Cheer promises color protection; and Gain provides sunshine scent and removes odors. Yet, every brand of detergent can more or less do all of these things.

3. For each of the Web site ads in Exhibits 2.18 through 2.20, describe the toothpaste's prominent feature(s), the benefits delivered by the features, and the target market that seeks those benefits.

Do you believe the benefit segmentation evidenced in each ad is effective? Why or why not? If not, how could it be improved or changed? How do these ads differ from those you've seen in traditional print media (magazines and newspapers)? Why do you think this difference exists?

4. For the three magazine ads that follow the Web toothpaste ads (Exhibits 2.21–2.23), describe the brand's positioning (psychological and /or physical), using the four positioning criteria discussed in both this exercise and in Exercise 2.2.

WRITTEN APPLICATIONS

1. Answer In-Class Application Questions 3 and 4. Then, choose one of the brands in one of the ads from Exhibits 2.18 through 2.20 and create a print (magazine or newspaper) ad for it, using positioning consistent with the online ad. Describe how your print ad differs from the Web ad and why.

2. Find three more ads for three different brands within a product category of your choosing, each of which uses a different method of benefit segmentation. Repeat the analysis for Questions 3 and 4 above for this set of ads.

KEY CONCEPTS

advertising appeal (selling premise, unique
   selling proposition)
behavioral targeting (marketing, tracking)
behavioristic (behavioral, usage)
   segmentation
benefit segmentation
benefits
brand concepts
brand image
brand (market) positioning
co-creation
comparison (comparative) advertising
concentrated (niche) marketing
demographic segmentation
demographics
differentiated marketing (multiple
   segmentation, multimarket strategy)
direct marketing
features
individualized (one-to-one, segment-of-one,
   markets-of-one) marketing
long-tail theory
market attractiveness
market segment profile

market segmentation
marketing mix
mass customization
Pareto's Law (the heavy-half theory)
physical positioning (physical product
   differentiation)
positioning
positioning statement
primary reserach
product class (category) positioning
product differentiation
psychographics
psychological positioning (psychological
   product differentiation)
psychological value added
repositioning
secondary data
segmenting
target market
target market (market coverage) strategies
target marketing (market targeting)
undifferentiated marketing (mass marketing,
   market aggregation)
value positioning

EXHIBIT 2.18   Tom's of Maine Ad

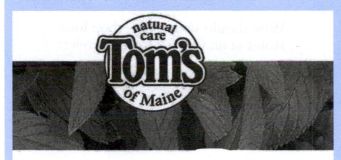

What's New · Natural Fluoride-Free Toothpaste for Children

Flavor ▼
Silly Strawberry

Size ▼
4 OZ.

Quantity ▼

add to basket

Not all items are available in all sizes.

reviews | ingredients

EXHIBIT 2.19   Dr. Wolfe's Aloe-Dent Ad

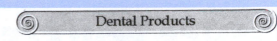

Dental Products & Oral Hygiene

Mouth Rinse

Dentistry;Breath fresheners and natural Whole Leaf Aloe Veraconcentrate are now formulated together with Subtle Energy Solutions %liquid minerals technology. This potent formula effectively eliminates mouth odors and stimulates the healing ofirritated tissues in the mouth, promoting healthy teeth and gums. TheAloe-Dent mouth rinse contains No fluoride, No sugar andNo alcohol. The result is an outstanding mouth rinse that leaves yourmouth feeling and smelling minty fresh.

Dr. Bill Wolfe's Tooth Gel ...ALOE-DENT

Scientific laboratory studies have demonstrated the bacteriocidal, virucidal and anti-inflammatory effects of the gel fromthe Whole Leaf Aloe Vera Plant. Now the soothing effects of Aloe Gel are formulated with the Subtle Energy Solutions liquid minerals technology. This potent formula helps to facilitate the removal of dental plaque and tartar (the cause of dental disease) and to stimulate the healing of inflamed tissues andsensitive teeth, promoting healthy teeth and gums. The Subtle EnergySolutions Tooth Gel contains contains No fluoride, No sugar and NoSodium Lauryl Sulfate. The result is a unique tooth gel for moderndental health.

EXHIBIT 2.20   Close-Up Ad

Product Details

FRESHENING Red Gel
- Zesty cinnamon mouthwash built right in for long-lasting, fresh breath protection
- Cavity-fighting formula
- Great-tasting way to clean, freshen, whiten and protect teeth

WHITENING Cinnamon Sparkle Gel
- Micro-crystals safely clean away surface stains to make teeth even whiter and brighter
- Zesty cinnamon mouthwash with a gentle whitening formula for fresher breath and a sparkling smile
- Whitens teeth, fights cavities, gives you a cleaner mouth and fresher breath

NEW WHITENING Mint Sparkle Gel
- Contains tingly, tasty mint mouthwash for long-lasting fresh breath
- Gently cleans, freshens, whitens and protects teeth
- Micro-crystals safely clean away surface stains to make teeth even whiter and brighter

"Gel-A-Friend"

EXHIBIT 2.21   Lincoln Ad

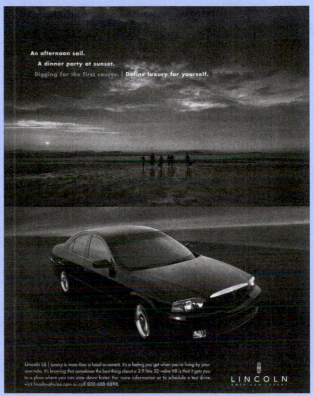

EXHIBIT 2.22　**Healthy Choice Ad**

EXHIBIT 2.23　**Alpha Omega Fine Watches Ad**

SUMMARY

All key concepts and their synonyms are defined within the chapter and in the Glossary.

This chapter explored a foundational CB topic: market segmentation, which seeks to target groups of customers known as target markets.

One way to do battle in a competitive marketplace is via product differentiation through (1) being physically or tangibly better than competitors, (2) being superior to rivals psychologically or intangibly, and (3) using product variety. When this is done in conjunction with pursuing one or more particular target markets, market segmentation is being practiced.

Exercise 2.1 reviewed the three-step market segmentation process:

1. *Market segmentation:* There are three variables (bases) for marketplace division: demographics (states of being), psychographics (states of mind and consequent states of action), and behavioristic (behavioral) segmentation (states of action). From the target market's description along these dimensions, market segment profiles are developed.
2. *Target marketing:* Measures of market attractiveness are developed, and then target markets are identified.
3. *Market positioning:* This involves designing a physical marketing entity and its brand image. It also entails developing a marketing mix for each target market position.

There are seven prerequisites for effective segmentation: differentiability, identifiability and divisibility, measurability, substantiality (profitability, attractiveness), accessibility (reachability), actionability, and responsiveness.

There are three broad target market strategies, each with strengths and limitations: undifferentiated marketing, differentiated marketing, and concentrated marketing. The long-tail theory says the Internet makes it easy and cheap to offer a vast amount of content, so consumers turn from mass market hit products they sort of want toward niche products they really desire. Individualized marketing, a form of direct marketing, often entails mass customization. Through co-creation, customers participate in creating their products.

Exercise 2.2 further investigated brand positioning (physical positioning and psychological positioning, which creates added psychological value). Psychological positioning can be achieved via alternative uses, possible target markets or user imagery, and competitors. One tool here is comparison advertising. Competitive positioning includes product class positioning. An advertising appeal summarizes the positioning in a brief statement typically mentioning the product category, the brand's use, the target market's needs, and competitor products and brands.

In an ever-changing marketplace, repositioning may become necessary due to shifts in societal values and norms (mandating new uses), demographics (suggesting new target markets), competitors (leading to new competitive positioning), and technology (resulting in new physical and psychological positioning). However, caution must be taken not to destroy existing brand equity.

Exercise 2.3 explored benefit segmentation, based on the distinction between benefits and features. Benefit segmentation involves dividing the marketplace into groups of consumers, each of which is especially concerned with receiving a particular product benefit. This is a very powerful segmentation technique because benefits are the consumer needs and wants delivered by the product.

Benefit segmentation is another dimension of psychological positioning and, as such, can readily be combined with use, target market, and competition positioning dimensions so as to create a meaningful psychological uniqueness for the marketer's brand.

REFERENCES

Anderson, Chris. (2006). *The Long Tail: Why the Future of Business Is Selling Less of More.* New York: Hyperion.

Dalgic, Tevfik. (2006). *Handbook of Niche Marketing: Principles and Practice.* New York: Best Business Books.

Dibb, Sally, and Simkin, Lyndon. (2008). *Market Segmentation Success—Making It Happen!* New York: Haworth Press.

Dickson, Peter R., and Ginter, James L. (1987). "Market Segmentation, Product Differentiation, and Marketing Strategy." *Journal of Marketing,* 51, 2, 11–27.

Engel, James F., Fiorillo, Henry F., and Cayley, Murray A., eds. (1972). *Market Segmentation: Concepts and Applications.* New York: Holt, Rinehart, and Winston.

Frank, Ronald E., Massey, William F., and Wind, Yoram. (1972). *Market Segmentation.* Englewood Cliffs, NJ: Prentice Hall.

Green, Paul E., Krieger, Abba M., and Schaffer, Catherine M. (1985). "Quick and Simple Benefit Segmentation." *Journal of Advertising Research,* 25, 3, 9–15.

Haley, Russell I. (1968). "Benefit Segmentation: A Decision-Oriented Research Tool." *Journal of Marketing,* 32, 3, 30–35.

———. (1984). "Benefit Segmentation—20 Years Later." *Journal of Consumer Marketing,* 1, 4, 5–14.

Pine, Joseph B. II, and Gilmore, James H. (2000). *Markets of One—Creating Customer-Unique Value through Mass Customization.* Boston: Harvard Business School Press.

Ries, Al, and Trout, Jack. (1981). *Positioning: The Battle for Your Mind.* New York: McGraw-Hill.

Schmidt, Bernard H. (1999). *Experiential Marketing.* New York: The Free Press.

Smith, Wendell R. (1956). "Product Differentiation and Market Segmentation as Alternative Marketing Strategies." *Journal of Marketing,* 21, 3, 3–8.

Wansink, Brian, and Park, Sea Bum. (2000). "Methods and Measures That Profile Heavy Users." *Journal of Advertising Research,* 40, 4, 61–72.

Weinstein, Art. (1994). *Market Segmentation: Using Demographics, Psychographics, and Other Niche Marketing Techniques to Predict Model Customer Behavior.* Chicago: Probus Publishing.

Wells, William D. (1975). "Psychographics: A Critical Review." *Journal of Marketing Research,* 12, 2, 196–213.

PART

II

THE CONSUMER DECISION-MAKING PROCESS

The study of consumer behavior (CB) is about market choice behavior. Consumers decide between two or more competing alternatives, which can be brands (Brand X or Brand Z?), products (e.g., potatoes, stuffing, or rice?), stores (e.g., Kmart or Wal-Mart?), payment methods (cash, check, credit, or debit?), and even whether to make a purchase ("Just looking").

Consequently, we view CB as a process occurring over time. We are concerned not just with the purchase decision itself but also with how a decision is reached, that is, prepurchase behavior. Also, we wish to understand the outcomes of the decision, that is, postpurchase behavior, such as product usage, satisfaction, doubts about the wisdom of the decision, and product disposition.

Part II focuses on the decision process, which is (more or less) rational. Thoughtful, reasoned action is taken to satisfy an individual's needs and wants and solve his or her problems. Even emotional decisions can be viewed within the context of this step-by-step process. The two broad influences on consumer decision making are sociocultural and psychological, which will be discussed in Parts III and IV.

OVERVIEW OF CONSUMER DECISION MAKING

Chapter 3 provides an overview of the consumer decision process and its five stages. Exercise 3.1 covers the earliest model of consumer decision making, formulated by microeconomists. The model is found to have several deficiencies that are overcome by behavioral models of consumers.

Exercises 3.2 and 3.3 outline the five-stage consumer decision process and look at a variety of decision-making scenarios, including the process you went through to select your college or university, and information sought and decisions made on the World Wide Web. Exercises 3.4 and 3.5 look at two important factors that determine whether the consumer will use the entire five-stage consumer decision process: the consumer's level of involvement and degree of decision making. Finally, Exercise 3.6 illustrates some common consumer purchasing decisions based on possible combinations of degree of involvement and level of decision making.

57

STAGES IN CONSUMER DECISION MAKING

The five stages of consumer decision making are investigated in Chapter 4: (1) problem recognition (Exercise 4.1); (2) information search (Exercise 4.2); (3) alternative evaluation (Exercises 4.3, 4.4, and 4.5); (4) purchase decision (choice; Exercise 4.6); and (5) postpurchase behavior (Exercise 4.7). The marketer's goal is to understand each stage and favorably influence consumers in that stage through marketing activities.

You will be engaged in every stage.

Traditionally, consumer researchers have viewed consumers as engaged in a conscious, logical decision-making process with five steps: (1) problem recognition, (2) information search, (3) alternative evaluation, (4) purchase, and (5) postpurchase outcomes. This chapter takes a broad view of this decision process as well as short-cut variations on it that occur either when consumers are less involved in decision making (DM) and/or have much prior information on and experience with DM for a particular product.

ORGANIZATION OF CHAPTER THREE

Exercise 3.1 presents the traditional microeconomics perspective of consumer DM and its limitations. Exercise 3.2 reviews the five-stage consumer decision process model used for important decisions and information-intensive purchases, such as choosing a college. This process can occur in an online environment, as you will experience in Exercise 3.3.

Exercise 3.4 explores how DM varies depending on the buyer's level of involvement—how important the product and its purchase are to the buyer. Exercise 3.5 shows how the consumer's level of DM—his degree of prior information and experience—can also affect the extent to which he will proceed through the carefully reasoned, five-stage decision process. Exercise 3.6 combines different levels of involvement and DM to illustrate six general types of purchasing situations.

EXERCISE 3.1. THE ECONOMICS PERSPECTIVE ON CONSUMER DECISION MAKING

OBJECTIVES

1. To familiarize you with the earliest theory of consumer choice, which is based on microeconomics.
2. To help you understand the limitations of most assumptions underlying the rational economic consumer perspective and to illustrate how modern marketers view consumers.
3. To enable you to see the limitations of the economics perspective by demonstrating that some consumer behavior (CB) is irrational.

BACKGROUND

THE FIELD OF ECONOMICS

An **economy** is the institutional structure through which individuals in a society coordinate their diverse wants and desires. An **economic system** is the means by which the economy is organized, setting the parameters for business decisions and consumer DM.

Economics is the social science concerned with the allocation of scarce resources (land, labor, and capital) to produce products satisfying consumers' unlimited needs and wants, given the society's institutional structures. Economics answers three fundamental societal questions: (1) What commodities will be produced and in what quantities? (2) How will they be made (by whom, with what resources and technology)? (3) To whom will they be distributed?

There are two major branches of economics: microeconomics and macroeconomics. The study of **microeconomics** has two perspectives:

1. Individual business decisions, known as the neoclassical (microeconomic) theory of the firm. Business organizations face the profit-maximization problem, deciding which price and output alternatives maximize the firm's earnings.
2. Individual consumer choices, called the neoclassical theory of consumption, which concerns consumer DM. This analyzes the consumer satisfaction (utility) maximization problem regarding quantities of assorted products (goods and services) to purchase at particular prices.

A key assumption underlying microeconomics is **rationality**. Rational decisions are made that produce the best possible or most preferred (optimal) results for the decision maker, given the decider's resource constraints and knowledge of the environment. The individual firm rationally maximizes profit through price and output decisions, and the individual consumer rationally maximizes satisfaction through purchase decisions.

Macroeconomics deals primarily with aggregates such as the total amount of products produced by society and the absolute levels of prices. It addresses issues such as level of growth of measures of national output, such as Gross National Product and Gross Domestic Product, interest rates, unemployment, inflation, the availability of credit, and business cycles. In this exercise we will only discuss microeconomics, even though macroeconomic variables do influence consumer DM, especially for durable goods purchases. However, a consumer's personal situation (job security, income level, amount of savings, etc.) can have a greater effect on spending than the health of the national economy.

THREE ECONOMIC SYSTEMS

The three systems for organizing economic activity are the command system, the market economy, and the mixed economy.

In the **command system (socialism, collectivism, statism, centrally planned economies, command economies)**, a government body arranges economic activities. Typically, there is a central government agency making economic decisions on peoples' occupations, what goods they need at what prices, along with collective or governmental ownership and administration of the means of production and distribution of goods.

In a **market economy (laissez faire, capitalist, free enterprise system)**, the means of production and distribution are privately or corporately owned, and development is proportionate to the accumulation and reinvestment of profits gained in a free market. The government leaves its citizens alone regarding all economic activities, except for regulating illegal activities. The market economy has two major characteristics: a free market and privately owned means of production and distribution.

- A **free market** is characterized by open competition. The goods produced, their prices, and the wages of workers employed to produce the goods are not controlled by the government. Instead, they are allowed to fluctuate according to the forces of supply and demand. Consequently, there are no import or export controls, wage or price controls, government price supports, or other government interventions in the marketplace. Buyers and sellers freely and mutually agree on the terms of exchange. This avoids the surpluses or shortages that inevitably occur when a government authority tampers with the forces of supply and demand. Examples of government intervention are surplus crops rotting due to high prices caused by price supports and the long gas lines caused by the 1970s energy crisis, in which gasoline price controls resulted in artificially low gas prices. A free market also maximizes producer and consumer freedom.
- The means of production and distribution are privately or corporately owned (versus government owned). Consequently, there is freedom of privately owned businesses to operate competitively for profit with minimal government regulation (only enough necessary to protect consumer interests and to ensure fair competition among producers). Workers can move freely between jobs, and everyone is able to enter the market to buy or sell. Competition helps ensure lower prices, product safety, quality, variety, and innovation.

A **mixed economy** is a blend of command and market economies, of socialism and capitalism. Economic decisions are primarily made freely as in a market economy, but there is more government intervention, motivated by a desire to help the economy (although poor government decisions can harm the economy) such as through wage and price controls and import tariffs and quotas. Most modern economies in democratic nations are of the mixed variety.

MARKETING AND ECONOMICS

Focused on the production and distribution of products, economics is the father social science to **marketing**—the management discipline concerned with the exchange between a buyer (consumer or business customer) and seller (marketer) that allocates scarce resources in order to meet the customer's product-related needs and the seller's profit-related needs. Economists formulated the first theory of CB. The current behavioral views of buyer DM are a result of the inadequacies of many of the assumptions underlying this early view of consumer DM. The modern perspective on CB comes from other behavioral science disciplines, notably cultural anthropology, sociology, and psychology (see Parts III and IV of this book).

THE MICROECONOMIC THEORY OF THE UTILITARIAN, ECONOMIC CONSUMER

The **neoclassical microeconomic model of consumer DM** is based on economist Alfred Marshall's theory of consumption, which says that consumer decisions are based on buyers' careful allocation of their scarce financial resources among various purchase alternatives so as to purchase a bundle of goods and services that maximize their *utility* (satisfaction). The utilitarian approach suggests that buyers make careful, rational cost-benefit calculations using perfect information to determine the *optimal* combination of goods they can obtain, subject to their resource constraints.

KEY ASSUMPTIONS UNDERLYING MARSHALL'S THEORY OF THE UTILITARIAN CONSUMER

1. Consumers are **rational**. This assumes that consumers make **optimal decisions**. These choices produce the very best results for consumers, given their resource (money, time, and energy) constraints. Buyers make purchase decisions based on purposeful, thoughtful, self-interested economic calculations whereby each person wisely spends his or her limited income to get the most satisfaction for each dollar spent.

   The golden rule of utility optimization is to maximize the buyer's expected utility per dollar spent. This yields the greatest benefit-cost ratio for customers. They always get the most for their money, which maximizes **value**—the optimum quantity plus quality per dollar spent. When it becomes more (less) costly to buy or do something, people will do it less (more).
2. Consumers have perfect information that is costless to acquire. They are aware of all marketplace alternatives and their prices and are cognizant of the utility yielded by each item.
3. Consumers are **self-interested**. They are motivated by maximization of their own utility (as long as it does not come at others' expense—that would be selfish).
4. Consumers are **sovereign**. They are in control of their DM, personally responsible, and not subject to manipulation by outside forces. Needs and wants come only from within the buyer rather than from environmental forces such as other people, mass media, or marketing communications. Tastes and preferences, therefore, cannot be molded or manipulated by producers. It follows that advertising, personal selling, and other persuasive marketing efforts are wasted.

A CONSUMER BEHAVIORIST EVALUATION OF THE MICROECONOMIC THEORY OF THE UTILITARIAN, ECONOMIC CONSUMER

Modern economists and marketers argue that the assumption that people make only reasoned, self-interested choices is flawed. The overriding problem is that the microeconomic theory of the individual consumer is **normative (prescriptive, evaluative)**—it explains the way the rational consumer should behave, based on *deductive (inferential) reasoning*. This contrasts with the behavioral approach that is **positive (descriptive)**, or founded on *inductive investigation* (empirical—deriving general principles or laws from specific facts or observations), which is applied in consumer research. The fact is that consumers are not mechanical, calculating robots, surgically comparing all alternatives for the very best deal. Let us therefore revisit the four neoclassical microeconomic assumptions: (1) consumers are rational; (2) consumers have perfect and costless information; and (3) consumers are self-interested, and (4) consumers are sovereign.

Consumers are rational. The unreality of rationality is explained by the concept of **bounded rationality**. People are only as rational as their limited resources, knowledge, and time will permit. There are inherent limits on rational thought and DM. In a complex and uncertain world, humans make decisions under the constraints of limited cognitive (knowledge) and time (as well as financial) resources. Also, they often gain emotional utility that is hard to quantify. For instance, a $2.50 aspirin makes us feel better than a 10-cent one.

There is a burgeoning new field known as **behavioral economics**—economic psychology that investigates behavioral influences on economic decisions. Behavioral economics adds to neoclassical economic theory the common-sense notion that people are often short-sighted, emotional, impulsive, and far from coldly irrational, even acting against their own best interests. Examples pointed out in best-selling books such as *Freakonomics* and *Predictably Irrational: The Hidden Forces That Shape Our Decisions* include procrastination, addiction, and spitefulness. However, this is nothing new: John Maynard Keynes coined the term "animal spirits" for such behaviors in his now canonical *General Theory of Employment, Interest, and Money.*

Hence, rather than being optimizers (satisfaction maximizers), consumers often **satisfice**, or settle for a satisfactory (rather than the optimal) brand as a satisfier of their wants and needs. Patronizing convenience stores for food and personal care items even though product prices are higher than at supermarkets and drug stores, or standing in line every day for four-dollar coffee seems hardly economical or reasonable. Yet, even these patronages can be viewed as perfectly rational when the **opportunity cost**—the next best use of the consumer's time after the current activity—is taken into account.

Hence, by extending the concept of cost to include nonmonetary costs and benefits, we can see that almost every purchase maximizes the ratio of satisfaction to cost to some degree. Cost includes not just a product's price but also time, effort, and other scarce resources, plus opportunity costs. Benefits can be emotional and hedonic, not just utilitarian.

Consider this. Most consumers would rather buy twelve light bulbs for one dollar each over the course of a year than pay eight dollars for a single light bulb that lasts an entire year. At the time of purchase, the single eight-dollar light bulb seems expensive, while the one -dollar bulbs appear to be a good deal. However, a consumer would save four dollars by buying the expensive, longer-lived bulb. and would forego the hassle of repeatedly going to the store, using gasoline to get there, and expending energy to replace the old bulb. An explanation lies in the *time value of money*: The consumer might have a high *discount rate*—a dollar today might be worth much more to somebody than a dollar tomorrow. Therefore, that person will be reluctant to spend a lot of money immediately and will instead favor expending more funds later on.

Now, ponder the following statements about various common patterns of seemingly irrational CB to decide just how rational or irrational each type of behavior really is.

- *"Impulse purchasing*—buying without deliberate, careful planning—is unwise and irrational." This is often true, as consumers are sometimes concerned with instant gratification rather than their long-term best interests (e.g., cupcakes taste good but are not good for you). However, impulse buying can be rational. A spontaneous gift for a sick friend might be totally justifiable. Or one could experience "love at first sight" with a dress or suit jacket seen in a department store and buy it on impulse to achieve emotional satisfaction.

  In his best-selling book *Blink: The Power of Thinking Without Thinking,* Malcolm Gladwell argues that much thinking happens in a blink of an eye with a decisive glance. When you meet someone for the first time or read the first few sentences of a book you're thinking of buying, your mind takes about two seconds to jump to a series of conclusions, which are often quite accurate. What goes on in that first two seconds could be viewed as perfectly rational: It is still thinking, but it is more rapid fire than the deliberate, conscious DM that we usually associate with rational thinking. However, Gladwell warns readers about leaping to conclusions, as marketers can manipulate our first impressions.

- *"Brand loyalty*—purchasing the same brand regularly due to a strong preference for it without considering buying competitive brands—is foolish due to possibly overlooking new and better alternatives."

However, brand loyalty can be justified if the shopper feels that the expected benefits of seeking out a better brand aren't worth expending the necessary time and effort (resource constraints).

- *"Brand switching*—changing brands from purchase to purchase—is nonoptimal if the shopper has a preferred brand that satisfies her needs." However, a buyer could become bored with a particular brand and so engages in variety seeking—the buyer searches for something new within a product category, such as different flavors of food or scents of cologne, even though she is satisfied with the most recently purchased brand. Furthermore, the consumer might wish to determine via personal experience whether a new brand yields even more utility per dollar than his or her favorite brand.
- "It is not rational to buy a product based on **emotion**—feelings that are not physically controllable, such as fear, anger, excitement, and vanity." However, satisfying such emotional motives still yields satisfaction, so rationality should be broadly interpreted to include such emotional motives as beauty and prestige. After all, consumers can satisfy hedonic needs as well as practical utilitarian needs by consuming goods and services.

In each of these four generalized examples of CB, what looks to be irrational behavior actually turns out to be, on closer inspection, rational indeed!

Consumers have perfect and costless information. To make a rational decision, a consumer requires complete product information on price, competitive strengths and weaknesses, product availability, and so on. But this is often lacking, as is often the case with technical, complex products. Buyers are at a disadvantage relative to sellers who, as product experts, can take advantage of customers' ignorance (a condition known as *information asymmetry*). Even for something as simple as concentrated detergent, many consumers have trouble understanding that, while the price per ounce is higher (because there is less water), the cost per wash is actually lower.

Further, information acquisition can be costly in terms of time, money, and effort. Consequently, an information search is usually highly selective. It is not always worth spending the resources needed to gather perfect information to be able to obtain the very best deal.

In short, although people do not always know for certain whether a particular product will, per dollar spent, maximize their utility, they usually know whether that product satisfies their needs and desires at a reasonable price. And the imperfection of consumer information provides marketers with an opportunity to supply customers with favorable product data so as to influence their purchase decisions.

Consumers are self-interested. It is probably safe to say that most of the time, most people act in their own best self-interest. However, there is sometimes **altruism**—the compassionate caring for one's fellow humans that leads to deemphasizing self-interest and focusing instead on maximizing others' welfare, usually at the expense of one's own concerns. Altruism practices self-sacrifice for general causes such as the public good or the environment and helping others, and it includes philanthropic giving and volunteerism. Altruistic behavior is bound by what is perceived as right, proper, moral, or appropriate.

For instance, *empathy*—feeling compassion for others—is an emotion that can lead to selfless behavior. Ask any parent: They sacrifice time, money, and energy for their kids. Is this rational? What about purchasing environmentally friendly products or fair trade goods (agricultural products and handicrafts produced in developing countries that promote sustainability) even though they cost more? Being patriotic and "buying American" even though foreign brands might offer a better value? Being concerned for corporate social responsibility actions such as not testing on animals, not using sweatshop labor, or contributing from corporate coffers to the "cause of the week"?

Nonetheless, altruistic acts would seem to be self-interested since "random acts of kindness" usually lead to that warm glow and sense of moral satisfaction that comes from helping. Furthermore, because we tend to "reap what we sow," other self-interested benefits accrue from altruistic behavior. For instance, the sacrificing parent may reasonably expect to be cared for in old age by the grown children who have come to appreciate those earlier sacrifices.

Consumers are sovereign. Due to lack of perfect (or even good) buyer information, the assumption of consumer sovereignty is sometimes flawed. Consumers also do not always "call the shots" where there is little competition (hence little variety, lower quality, and higher prices), when the consumer segments are vulnerable to manipulation (e.g., children, mentally challenged, and very sick people), and where unscrupulous marketers practice deception. At the very least, consumers can be influenced by marketing efforts.

REVIEW QUESTIONS

1. Explain the difference between microeconomics and macroeconomics.
2. Describe the three economic systems. Which one characterizes U.S. economic policy?
3. Summarize the key assumptions underlying the microeconomic theory of the utilitarian consumer. Which of these assumptions do consumer behaviorists accept and why? Which assumptions do they reject and why?
4. What is rational behavior? Cite four generalized examples of apparently irrational CBs that, on closer consideration, actually can be considered as rational behaviors.
5. What are the primary modern marketing implications stemming from the microeconomics perspective described in this exercise?

IN-CLASS APPLICATIONS

1. Can you determine any rational basis for each of the following apparently irrational CBs?
   a. Many consumers are unwilling to pay a little more money initially for appliances, furniture, and other durable goods that can save them a great deal of money in the long run by being higher quality, working better, or lasting longer. Instead, they purchase the "cheap junk" to save a few bucks today. For instance, they might prefer an item that is half the price even though it will only last one-fourth as long.
   b. Most consumers leave a tip for a server in a restaurant, even if that establishment is so far away from home that they never expect to return. The size of the tip usually depends on the quality of service. People are even more likely to leave a tip (and a more generous tip) in a restaurant to which they expect they'll return.
   c. Many workers have their employer withhold more money than necessary from their paychecks for tax purposes because they love to get a big tax refund check at the end of the year. They view this behavior as rational because it forces them to save money rather than frivolously spending it. They can later use their government-issued refund check for important big-ticket purchases such as a family vacation or a new car.
   d. American consumers love to gamble with their money, from buying lottery tickets and going to the racetrack to playing the slot machines in a casino. Most of the time they lose, and the expected value of gambling in commercial establishments is negative since the establishment must earn a profit. However, there's always the slim chance of making lots of easy money.
   e. Some people purchase flight insurance before embarking on an airline flight, even though the probability of dying or being injured in an airline crash is extremely remote—much lower than that of perishing or being harmed in an automobile accident.
   f. Sometimes consumers take advantage of a two-for-one sale on infrequently bought packaged goods such as a bottle of spice, even if they really only need one item for the foreseeable future.
   g. Many people buy Girl Scout cookies from daughters of friends. Although they are quite tasty, the cookies cost much more than cookies of equal quality in a supermarket.
   h. Individuals generally prefer to "blow" a bonus on some big, frivolous purchase but would shudder at the thought of paying for it with their regular salary or by withdrawing money from their savings account.
2. Describe the decision(s) that the consumer(s) in each of the following scenarios should make if they are acting in a purely rational manner:
   → *Scenario A*. One year ago Chris paid $45 for a ticket to a basketball game to be played later this week. Yesterday, his friend Hugh paid $45 cash for a ticket to the same game. And a sick buddy who couldn't attend gave their mutual friend, Leo, a free ticket today. All three men have looked forward to attending the Big Game.

   On game day, however, there is a blinding snowstorm, making driving quite hazardous. Who should be most willing and who should be least willing to brave the storm and attend the game: Chris, who purchased his ticket long ago; Hugh, who just recently shelled out $45; or Leo, who got a free ticket?

→ *Scenario B.* Kitty accidentally booked a $300 ski trip and a $150 snowboarding trip for the same weekend. Both packages include food, lodging, and weekend lift passes, and they are both nonrefundable. Because they were both sale priced, neither package is transferable to others. Which weekend getaway package should Kitty use?

→ *Scenario C.* Lois, in an effort to become more physically active during the winter months, recently bought a pair of bowling shoes and a pair of in-line skates. She planned to go bowling and frequent the local roller skating rink during the wintertime. However, after trying each of these sports, she discovered that she really didn't care for either one very much.

    Lois's friend took her ice-skating, and Lois loved it. Now, she's considering giving up bowling and Rollerblading and instead buying a new pair of ice skates. But since they are now used, she knows she could only get pennies on the dollar for her bowling shoes and in-line skates. What should she do?

→ *Scenario D.* Rosie is such a ditz. She misplaced her $300 Gucci handbag and the used Coach handbag that she bought at the local thrift outlet for $5. She loved them both equally, despite the cost differential. Fortunately, neither bag contained money, credit cards, or anything of significant value when she lost it. Should Rosie be more concerned about one loss over the other?

→ *Scenario E.* Ray was dining out at a restaurant with some close friends. Although the original agreement was that they'd ask for separate checks and each pay for their own meal, he got the sudden urge to pick up the tab for everyone. His own bill would have been $22, but he ended up blowing $125. Was Ray a wise consumer?

→ *Scenario F.* Gail paid a $50 annual fee to become a member of a wholesale club, thinking she could save money (more than $50) by shopping there over the next year. However, she later found she could get better deals on virtually everything at a Discounter Dick's, which doesn't charge a membership fee.

    Gail wonders whether she should continue to patronize the wholesale club in order to make her $50 investment worthwhile. After all, she does save some money there compared to all other stores in the area except for Discounter Dick's.

3. How "perfect" is your information? It's time to play *The Price Is Right*. All books and notes on the floor, and no running to the supermarket to get the answers! Your instructor will ask you to write on an index card or slip of paper or to use the classroom response system ("clickers") to guess what you should pay at a supermarket when buying:
   a. A dozen grade A large eggs
   b. A gallon of whole milk
       The professor will then collect your answers and plot a frequency distribution of responses on the board. Did everyone agree? What lessons do we learn from this?

WRITTEN APPLICATIONS

1. Thinking about the nature of and relationship between economic systems and marketing, describe some economic situations or conditions under which marketing activities would either be nonexistent or of minimal importance, and, hence, an understanding of consumers would be unnecessary. Are any of these likely future scenarios?

2. Describe a situation in which either your own CB or that of another consumer you know followed that of the rational microeconomic model. Describe another situation where your or another person's CB seemed irrational according to this model. Why do you suppose the behavior was rational in the first situation but irrational in the second?

EXERCISE 3.2. YOUR COLLEGE CHOICE DECISION

OBJECTIVES

1. To familiarize you with the stages in the consumer decision-making process (CDM) and the marketing management implications of each stage.

2. To make this five-stage decision process meaningful to you personally by having you recall and describe how you arrived at the decision to attend your college or university.
3. To recognize how marketers try to influence each stage of consumer DM by describing how colleges' marketing activities tried to influence you at every stage of your college choice decision process.
4. To help you use this decision-making model in future important decisions.
5. To enable you to recognize and differentiate the different stages in the consumer decision-making process.
6. To have you learn to creatively develop marketing strategies to influence consumers at each stage of the consumer decision-making process.

BACKGROUND

Decisions, decisions, decisions! Today's consumers face more choices than ever before. One university study found that people make anywhere from three hundred to seventeen hundred decisions each day, ranging from when to get up and what to wear to deciding what to eat and in which activities to get involved.

In the marketplace, we are bombarded with choices. It is not just a matter of choosing Coke or Pepsi. Each cola comes in numerous varieties, such as sugar-free; caffeine-free; cherry, vanilla, or lemon flavors; and with different packaging, such as bottles, cans, jugs, or even industrial-size drums (kidding). Starbucks has more than nineteen thousand ways it can serve a cup of coffee, with five kinds of milk to stir into it. You can order the tall, grande, or venti; add foam or no foam; get it extra hot; and you have a choice among three brands of artificial sweeteners!

However, some people complain about *brand proliferation* (excessive choices among brands, often with minimal distinctions between them), which increases decision difficulty. In his book *The Paradox of Choice: Why More Is Less,* Professor Barry Schwartz argued that too many choices—in everything from retail shopping and picking a mortgage to selecting a 401(k) retirement plan—causes stress, paralysis, and frustration with choosing. Faced with overload, he says people typically react in one of three ways: (1) they freeze and make no choice; (2) they make a poor decision; or (3) they make the right choice but then second guess it.

TYPES OF DECISIONS

A **consumer decision** entails selecting an alternative from among two or more choices. The **consumer decision-making process** entails the steps consumers go through to make decisions between marketplace alternatives. Alternatives include product choice (e.g., fly a plane or take the train; buy boxers or briefs); brand choice (McDonald's or Burger King); store choice (Target or Kohl's); brand item options (colors, styles, scents, flavors, etc.); paying with cash, credit, or debit; using paper bags or plastic, and even whether or not to make a purchase at all. Focus in this exercise is primarily on brand choice decisions, since this is the most common type of choice.

DECISION MAKING: A FIVE-STAGE PROCESS

There are five sequential stages in the consumer decision-making process, which are overviewed in Exhibit 3.1. At the end of each of the first three stages in the flow chart, there is a "hold" box, indicating that the consumer can either temporarily or permanently stop the process for reasons such as lack of time or money, a belief that there are no good alternatives to choose from, or perceived difficulty of learning to use a product.

The marketer's general task is to lead consumers through the five stages. We will describe consumer activities at each step of the decision continuum and the marketer's specific corresponding tasks at each stage.

STAGE 1. PROBLEM RECOGNITION

Problem recognition (need recognition, need arousal) is the consequence of an unsatisfied felt need or want or an unsolved problem. It occurs when the consumer experiences a discrepancy between her *desired (ideal) state of affairs* and her *actual (current) state of affairs.*

EXHIBIT 3.1   The Consumer Decision-Making Process

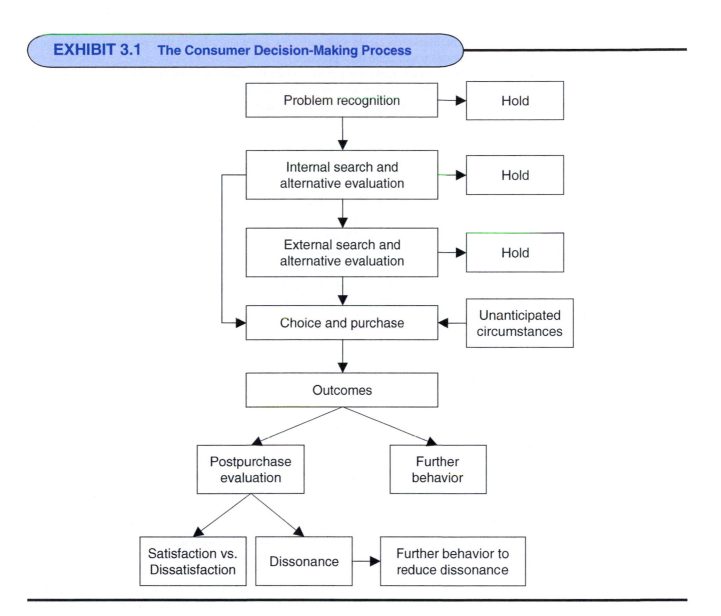

For sellers, consumer problems offer marketing opportunities:

- Develop a product that does a better job than competitive brands in satisfying consumers' needs and wants or solving their problems.
- Use **problem-solution (problem-resolution) advertising**—an advertising formula that raises a problem and dramatically shows how the product solves it ("Fight pimples fast!"). Also, employ consultative personal selling strategies that describe the consumer problem and then explain how the marketer's product effectively solves that problem.
- Increase consumer dissatisfaction with currently used products or brands (perhaps employing comparison advertising, which names competitors). Then show how your brand offers a better solution.
- Make consumers aware of **latent (subconscious, covert) problems (needs)**—those issues consumers are unaware of, hidden below the surface of consciousness. Examples include being underinsured or not getting a fully balanced diet.

Despite what marketing's critics say, it is doubtful that marketers can actually create desires and problems. This is because needs originate either from within the consumer's psychological makeup or from the sociocultural environment. Marketers create want satisfiers, not wants, that is, they promote satisfaction of people's already existing desires through their products.

It is actually latent desires that marketers tap into when they appear to be "creating" needs. So, Tide detergent for sensitive skin might make people who have had allergic reactions to detergent realize, "Aha, I must have sensitive skin. I should buy Tide for sensitive skin."

Stage 2. Information Search

In order to satisfy his need or solve his problem, in the **information search** stage, the consumer seeks marketplace **information**—data that reduces uncertainty or changes the buyer's beliefs. The search for information begins with an **internal search**—a consumer scans his or her memory to try to recall a satisfactory solution to the problem. Memory can be based on either prior personal experience or exposure to marketplace information. If an internal search reveals a viable purchase option, the buyer purchases it.

The marketing implications of internal search are:

- Make certain that marketing communications are memorable and persuasive so that the brand immediately pops into buyers' minds as their problems' solution.
- Ensure that experiences people have with the brand are positive so they share their experience with others encountering similar problems.

If the customer's internal search fails to yield an acceptable option, that person undertakes an **external (environmental) search**, or a motivated and conscious decision to seek information to solve the problem. Here, consumers make two decisions regarding their search process:

1. *Degree of search:* how much time and effort to put into searching. Generally, an information search is selective: It makes sense to continue searching only if the additional expected benefits (e.g., cost savings, obtaining higher quality products) exceed the extra anticipated costs (i.e., monetary expenses, like gasoline for car travel costs, and nonmonetary costs, such as lost time and the headaches of fighting traffic). The implication is that marketers must not drown customers in data and should make the shopping process as painless as possible.
2. *Direction of search:* which sources of information to use. Consumers employ not only marketer-controlled or commercial sources (e.g., salespeople, advertising, and packaging) but also nonmarketer-controlled or noncommercial sources (e.g., word-of-mouth recommendations from others, editorial and news material, and consumer-oriented Web sites). And shoppers use both public or nonpersonal sources (e.g., in-store displays, sales promotions, and neutral [unbiased] sources such as *Consumer Digest*) and private or personal sources (e.g., telemarketing, colleagues, and professional advice).

The marketer's job is to

- use those controllable marketing sources that research suggests consumers are most likely to turn to for the product category, and
- try, if possible, to influence the nonmarketing sources (e.g., suggesting personal referrals).

Stage 3. Alternative Evaluation

The **alternative evaluation** stage occurs simultaneously with external search. Here, the consumer decides which *evaluative criteria* (e.g., price, quality, style, etc.) will be used to compare alternatives as well as the *relative importance (weights)* of those criteria. She then compares the brands or the criteria to determine her most preferred one.

The consumer considers brands in her **evoked (consideration, choice, decision) set**, the group of brands evaluated. This assessment results in formation of **beliefs**, perceptions about the performance of each brand on each criterion (e.g., Continental Airlines offers friendly service, a little more legroom, and has good on-time performance).

If beliefs about a brand's performance are all generally positive (especially on the most important attributes), the consumer develops a positive **brand attitude**, an overall evaluation of the brand on purchase criteria. A **buying (purchase) intention** is then formed toward the consumer's *preferred brand*—the alternative for which the consumer has the most positive attitude.

The marketer's task throughout alternative evaluation is twofold:

- During product development, focus on achieving excellent performance on the criteria that are most important to the target market.
- Promote the brand's outstanding performance on those criteria while downplaying criteria on which the brand performs poorly (e.g., a brand of light beer would not tout "watery" and "tasteless").

STAGE 4. PURCHASE DECISION

One's choice from among the considered alternatives occurs during the **purchase decision** stage. Here, a shopper might select a less attractive alternative to his most-favored brand due to *unanticipated circumstances,* such as a deal on one of the less-favored brands or a change in personal circumstances such as loss of a job that precludes buying an expensive item.

The implications for marketers trying to affect the purchase decision are:

- A major influence for retail-distributed goods is in-store merchandising (e.g., displays, ample shelf space, in-store advertising, and sales assistance). Catchy or informative packaging can also sway the customer's choice.
- For Internet-distributed products, ease of purchase is critical. Too many consumers give up halfway through the purchase process online because it is too confusing!

STAGE 5. POST-PURCHASE BEHAVIOR

Today's relationship-oriented marketers focus on the final **postpurchase behavior (postpurchase outcomes)** stage. Concerns include:

- Following up after the sale to ensure that customer satisfaction has been achieved, that is, consumer expectations are met and desires are fulfilled, and postpurchase dissonance (doubt) has been addressed. Today's marketers are constantly engaged in activities to reduce dissatisfaction and/or dissonance, such as customer satisfaction surveys, offering after-sale service and support, cheerfully handling complaints, and reinforcing the purchase decision via reassuring advertising and follow-up sales calls.
- Taking advantage of opportunities to sell more merchandise to current customers, for example, cross-selling related merchandise such as software to use with hardware and upgrading consumers to higher-end merchandise on future purchases.
- Making service offers, such as extended warranties and extended service contracts, which allow buyers to increase the amount of time after a purchase during which the manufacturer will fix the product at no additional charge.
- Offering generous trade-ins or buy-back arrangements.

REVIEW QUESTIONS

1. Outline and briefly describe the five-stage consumer decision-making process.
2. Discuss the major marketing implications of each stage of the buyer decision process.

IN-CLASS APPLICATIONS

Your decision to attend your college was probably a high-involvement, extended decision-making situation that involved the carefully reasoned five-stage decision process. Think back to that decision process in answering the following questions.

1. Describe the five-stage decision process you used in choosing your current college. Focus on the following stages and issues in each stage.
   a. Problem recognition: What happened to trigger the process?
   b. Information search: Were you able to rely on an internal search? How extensive was your external information search? What sources of information did you employ during this external search? Did you learn more from personal or impersonal sources? Marketer- or nonmarketer-controlled sources? Why did you use those information sources? Which sources were most influential?
   c. Alternative evaluation: How many institutions were in your evoked set? What criteria did you use for comparing them? Which criteria were most important to you? Which of your beliefs do you think most influenced your decision?
   d. Choice: What was your first choice? Where did the college you now attend rank within your evoked set? Did any unanticipated circumstances affect your ultimate decision?
   e. Postpurchase behavior: Are you satisfied with your choice? Why or why not? What things (if any) do students complain about at your university? Have you experienced any dissonance regarding your decision? If so, explain the nature of your doubts. What other important postpurchase outcomes have occurred?
2. What, if anything, would you do differently if you were to go through this college-choice process again (say, if you transferred to another school or decided to go on to graduate school)?
3. Consider either your own decision process or the college decision-making process for what you consider to be the "typical" high school student (if it differs from your own behavior). How could knowledge of this decision process be used by a college marketing manager (e.g., the admissions director) for favorably influencing each stage of the college choice process?
4. There will be life after college. Before you know it, you will be a college graduate. Important DM will continue. You'll be grappling with big issues: Where to live, what to do for a career, where to work, whom to marry, whether and how many children to have, and, more immediately, where to find a happy hour with free chicken wings.

   Trace through the DM process you envision yourself using for an important decision you'll make after college. Does thinking about this choice in advance better prepare you to eventually make it?
5. Explain which stage of the CDM process each of the following consumers is in. Then identify a strategy that a marketing manager could use to help the consumer in that stage act favorably toward the marketer's brand.
   → *Scenario A. Penny Abhors a Vacuum.* Penny is very disappointed with her recent purchase of a new Ablaze vacuum cleaner. In the Blossom Brothers department store, she looked at different models and brands. However, the salesperson convinced her that the Ablaze was the best vacuum cleaner for her money even though she thought that it was actually the wrong choice because it was too big and powerful.

      Regardless, she decided to buy that brand because she trusted the salesperson. When she first tried it at home, the machine took in virtually everything in sight—almost including her cat. This was just one of the many things with which she was not satisfied. What finally did it was when smoke started to come from the vacuum cleaner and it almost caught on fire.

      One thing is for sure, Penny will never buy another Ablaze vacuum cleaner again, nor will she patronize the retail store from which she purchased it, except to complain to that salesperson.
   → *Scenario B. Eve Is Up and At 'Em.* Eve has so much on her mind, so much to do, and so little time in which to do it. Recently, she has been forgetting to attend some very important meetings with her work colleagues and has been having a difficult time keeping dinner dates with her friends.

      Eve currently has a daily planner on her office desk. However, she is frequently away from her office desk and is often on the run. For this reason, it seems more practical to find a mobile device that alerts her to what her daily activities are. Hopefully, she can find time in her busy schedule to accomplish this task.
   → *Scenario C. Chris's Car CD.* Chris finally decided there were three features that he absolutely had to have in a new car stereo. The CD player had to be capable of track searching, multiple disc loading, and Bluetoooth interface.

Chris inspected each of the brands in Ernie's Electronics Emporium very carefully, looking for the strengths one car stereo had over the others on his evaluative criteria. Consequently, he narrowed down his selection to three brands. He planned to check for these three brands at two other retail stores down the street from Ernie's to see if he could find a better deal on any of them.

Chris has his work cut out for him, doesn't he?

→ *Scenario D. Dan Digs Digital.* Dan has just learned that his grown daughter, Sally Mae, is taking digital photographs of his grandchildren and posting them on the Internet under their family home page. She has talked to Dan about buying his first ever computer and hooking up to the Internet, so he can download pictures of the grandkids. Dan is wondering how to get started in shopping around for a home computer so he can take up this hobby.

→ *Scenario E. The One-Man Search Engine.* Al is shopping for a Joe Satriani CD online. He visits Amazon. com, types Joe's name into the search engine, and inspects the list of albums, prices, dates, and list of tracks from each album. He also samples several tunes from a few albums. Pleased with these guitar riffs, he proceeds to the Music Boulevard Web site to see if he can get better prices, sample more music from Satriani's various albums, and find one of the albums that was out of stock at CDNow.

→ *Scenario F. Carrie Goes to Pot.* Carrie was interested in purchasing a hot pot to reheat her coffee at work. She looked at retail flyers for several discount and department stores but found nothing. She visited several home appliance shops with no luck. Finally, she checked several shopping Web sites but couldn't locate the product.

Consequently, she sent e-mail requests to these Web sites asking for information on availability and prices of hot pots. She is still waiting to hear from the customer service reps.

→ *Scenario G. Crock Shock.* Meg bought a Crock-Pot yesterday. Today, she made beef stew in it, but the stew came out soggy. "This Crock-Pot is a crock of @%&*!" she cursed.

WRITTEN APPLICATIONS

1. Answer Questions 2 and 4 in the In-Class Applications. For the second question, get some insight by discussing the issue with fellow students and/or college graduates. For the third question, get ideas by talking to one or more people who have already gone through that decision process.

2. Take a small-scale survey of about a half dozen randomly selected students on your campus (not your friends), asking them to describe the college decision process they went through. Describe and summarize your findings.

What are the marketing implications for the admissions recruiters at your school? Discuss your findings and suggestions with admissions personnel at your college. How did they react and what ideas did they have?

EXERCISE 3.3. CONSUMER DECISION MAKING IN AN ONLINE ENVIRONMENT

OBJECTIVES

1. To familiarize you with the Internet as a source of information useful in the CD process.
2. To make you aware of both the advantages and limitations of shopping on the Web.
3. To give you skills for using online shopping (electronic shopping or e-shopping) technology.
4. To enable you to experience how the theory of the CDM process applies to electronic shopping.
5. To have you discover how marketers can influence consumer DM in an online environment.

BACKGROUND

The **Internet** has come of age. In the twenty-first century, the ability to obtain information, either as a consumer or as a manager, and to communicate with others electronically is necessary regardless of your major or profession. The Internet is now a major and growing channel of distribution and communication for business and consumer products alike, especially since more and more people are accessing it mobilely through Internet-enabled smartphones.

Overview of the Internet

The **Internet** is a worldwide means of exchanging information and communication via a computer network consisting of smaller, interconnected networks. The Internet links both public and private computer systems to allow users to access information and documents from distant sources.

The **World Wide Web (WWW),** the most popular component of the Internet and its main commercial constituent, supports a graphical interface retrieval system that organizes information into thousands of interconnected pages or documents called **Web (home, start, welcome) pages**. These introductory pages or opening screens of a Web site make navigation simple and exciting. Each home page is like a book cover or gateway, acting as the starting point to additional information and entertainment.

For marketers, the WWW is a medium of both advertising and both **e-commerce**, the direct sale of goods and services on the Internet, and **m-commerce**, mobile e-commerce conducted from smartphones. Facilitating this are **hyperlinks (links)**. These connect Web sites electronically and allow consumers to travel through cyberspace in a nonsequential manner. Also helpful for people to easily find information on the Internet are **search engines**, which are computer programs that make finding information simple. Users can type in a name, word, or phrase and the search engine will scour the Net to locate relevant information and Web site addresses.

The World Wide Web as Shopping Medium

Of all the options available to Internet advertisers, the WWW holds the greatest potential because of its ability to combine several of the unique qualities of the other media (i.e., print, sound, and motion) into one, while allowing for two-way communication between advertiser and customer. It enables detailed and full-color graphics, audio transmission, delivery of in-depth messages, demonstration, twenty-four-hour availability, and two-way information exchanges between the advertiser and the customer. A Web site can provide corporate and product information as well as allow the consumer to make a purchase.

Online Shopping: A Major Shift in Consumer Behavior

Since the late 1990s, a relatively rapid change has occurred in CB: almost everyone shops online. The WWW has changed how consumers learn about products and stores, get coupons and discounts, read product reviews, and buy things. It allows easier comparison shopping, greater contact among consumers (e.g., recommendations), and easier feedback from consumer to marketer.

In almost every durable goods product category, before they buy, people go online, whether it is for a car, pharmaceutical product, or apparel. In 2008, 74 percent of people in North America were Internet users, and more than 49 percent used search engines on a typical day. Sixty-two percent of Internet users use general search engines and 26 percent use shopping-specific search engines (shopping bots) when researching products online. Although more than one-third of all U.S. households shopped online in 2006, Internet shopping represented only 5 percent of American retail sales. There is much growth potential as Web sites improve and consumers become more comfortable with online shopping. All major retailers now have Web sites, and many make a significant percent of their sales online. More shopping Web sites are adding search capabilities to enable searching by particular product characteristics and help customers find specific items in local stores; they also feature customer and product ratings and reviews, as well as videos featuring the likes of author interviews on bookstore sites and models in clothing.

The most recent shift in online CB concerns mobile shopping. This has led to the practice of **mobile marketing (mobile commerce, m-commerce)**, which entails marketing and advertising over wireless networks so consumers can use their Internet-enabled smartphones, e-readers, portable entertainment players, and other wireless devices to get product/price and store information, find store locations, obtain coupons, and make purchases.

Mobile shopping sites are offered by retailers (e.g., Amazon, eBay, Toys R Us, Walgreens, Wal-Mart, Best Buy) and others (e.g., Google). Some consumers now use their smartphones to locate stores, gather product and price information, and buy. Mobile shopping sites usually have fewer features than regular Web sites but are sized for small screens and are more easily navigated. Some permit checkout on the mobile site while others direct users back to the regular site in order to complete the transaction.

Another new development is the availability of mobile device applications, or apps, which make mobile shopping easier. Branded apps are mostly free, although some charge a nominal fee. They include games, information (e.g., a documentary), and utility (e.g., Sherwin-Williams' paint-color selection; Kraft's 99-cent iFood Assistant with 7,000 recipes, a dish of the day, and a grocery store locater; Nationwide insurance's app that lets customers file claims from the accident scene, including sending photos; Barnes & Noble's app letting shoppers snap pictures of any book on its shelves and then open a trove of details about the book).

CONSUMER ADVANTAGES OF ONLINE SHOPPING

The case for electronic shopping is compelling:

- Consumers can save time through quick access to information about a company or store and its products. A Web site must have useful **navigational tools**. These devices help consumers efficiently navigate (find their way) through a Web site. These guides include hyperlinks, home and section icons ("click here" blocks), a site-specific search engine, a site map that is accessible from every page, a navigation bar, and even gift finders specific to gender or age.
- E-shopping can save money for several reasons. *Shopping bots* ("shopbots"), such as mySimon, search the Web for a product and show you all the places it is sold and the lowest price. Shopping online also saves money on gas and car maintenance. And low distribution costs allow e-tailers to keep prices low. Many Web sites list promotion or coupon codes to enter prior to checkout, and several sites (e.g., couponcabin.com, BradsDeals.com) help consumers get any existing discounts. Purchases made outside of the Web site's home state are not taxed. There is, however, usually the added cost of shipping.
- Internet shopping provides greater availability of information, thereby facilitating comparison shopping. A given site can offer a wealth of information on a company, product specifications, costs, purchase information, and so on. Links will direct users to even more information if they wish. Third-party sites such as Edmunds.com or Cars.com offer information on warranty, trade-in value, incentives, and so on. Real-time information is available as sites can be constantly updated.
- Communication is often two-way via e-mail so you can have questions answered and better communicate your exact needs. More than any other medium, the Internet allows consumers to directly interact with an advertiser, increasing customer involvement and satisfaction, and building a relationship between the advertiser and the customer.
- E-shopping is convenient—you can do it 24/7, without leaving the comfort of your home or office, even in your jammies.
- The selection is much better. Web sites such as Amazon.com can offer millions of items out of their virtual inventories. Customization by merchants like Dell means you can have the product designed to your specifications.
- Buyers sometimes feel like they are in better control of buying in the absence of salesperson or shopping pal pressure. Also, there are fewer marketing distractions, such as the store's snack rack, that induce an unwanted impulse purchase.
- Unlike marketing communications from many other sources, Internet information is not intrusive or interruptive (forced on consumers). Instead, buyers seek out Web advertising and are therefore highly engaged with it and view it as credible.
- Consumers have a greater sense of confidentiality when buying sensitive products such as condoms since there is no personal contact (although sites often track your purchase behavior).

- Objective user reviews are often available. At Amazon.com you can get customers' product reviews. Reviews of local business are available at sites such as Google Maps, Yahoo! Local, and Yelp.com.

CONSUMER DISADVANTAGES OF ONLINE SHOPPING

There are a number of limitations with buying online.

- Customers are unable to physically inspect the merchandise—purchases are made sight unseen. You can buy farmhouse cheese on the Internet, but you cannot taste it first. You can purchase a used car on eBay, which is approximately like selecting your spouse through voice mail.
- Buyers must wait for product delivery rather than being able to immediately take the merchandise home, although often you can order merchandise online and pick it up the same day at the local store.
- Customer service (responding to customer e-mail inquiries, inventory look-up, product return policies, etc.) still often leaves something to be desired.
- Consumer privacy can be threatened by unwanted spam (unsolicited e-mail), pop-up ads, and the like. Private information might be shared with other firms because Web site privacy policies often do not guarantee that a shopper's personal data will not be shared with other online marketers without permission.
- Consumer security is sometimes sketchy. Customer information might leak to hackers and other undesirables. Identity theft results when hackers can steal credit card numbers, login usernames and passwords, and other personally identifiable information.
- It can be expensive to order and then return goods. Because consumers are buying without actually seeing the items, and since exact colors might not reproduce on computer or smartphone monitors, consumers often end up returning merchandise and getting stuck with large return shipping charges.
- Internet shopping might not satisfy **nonbuying (nonfunctional) shopping motives**, needs unrelated to acquisition of one or more products that are more psychosocial in nature. These nonbuying needs include recreation (getting out of the house and diversion from the daily routine), physical activity, sensory stimulation (e.g., smelling perfume, handling merchandise, and enjoying background music), social experiences and community (not just virtual community), and status and authority over retail clerks.

In other words, a great deal of shopping behavior satisfies hedonic needs rather than utilitarian needs. Brick-and-mortar stores such as Niketown provide an entire shopping experience. In the late 1990s, some Net enthusiasts predicted the demise in physical retailing due to the rise in Internet shopping. However, the existence of nonbuying motives, along with the other limitations of buying online, suggests otherwise.

VARIATIONS IN CONSUMER INTERNET SHOPPING

CB regarding use of the Internet varies. Some consumers either lack access or resist using this new channel of distribution, primarily due to privacy and security concerns. Other shoppers choose to browse the Web so as to gather information and then toddle on down to the store to negotiate a purchase face-to-face with the retailer, such as when purchasing cars.

A smaller number of shoppers visit retail stores first and then buy from an e-tailer. Still others do all the shopping online: gathering information, negotiating, purchasing, and either arranging for delivery or picking up merchandise in the store.

Most consumers begin searching by using broad generic terms such as "gifts" or a product category name. Closer to time of purchase, they narrow down their search to specifics regarding product attributes they are seeking and the brand name.

INSTRUCTIONS FOR LOGGING ON AND USING THE INTERNET FOR SHOPPING

We know that you are already very familiar with surfing the WWW. Here, we will concentrate on using the Web for consumer shopping. The procedure is as follows:

Since most people start shopping online by using a search engine, on your favorite Web browser (Internet

Explorer, Firefox, MSN Explorer, etc.), select a search engine by pointing your browser to it (e.g., www.google.com, www.Yahoo.com, www.MSN.com, www.Bing.com), typing in a keyword or phrase in the search engine's search box, or clicking on the "Search Web" button. Most portals (search engines serving as entry/starting points for Internet exploration) also have a shopping link to get you started. You should use more than one search engine because you will get different results with different search engines.

In the space for search, key in the type of product or service you are interested in (be specific), and click on the Search button or Enter key. On the screen, you will see the number of references found. If there are no matches, try typing another word or product name in the search box.

You can greatly increase your chances of success by understanding the search features offered by each site (e.g., surrounding a phrase with quotation marks might limit the search only to those documents in which those words appear in sequence).

Once you get the listing of references, all you have to do is to click on the links—words, terms, and phrases in blue—and you will be "surfing." Everything is menu-driven, so you really need not be a computer jock!

A few suggestions on how to narrow your search:

- You can try shopping for your item store by store. Or, you can go to the shopping section of a portal and search from there. If you are short on time, try any of the "metasearch" sites that use many search engines at once, such as MetaCrawler, Monstercrawler, Mamma, or Dogpile.

- Almost all search engines have an "advanced search" or "options" area; taking a few minutes to read the instructions on more specific searches can save you time in the long run. These allow you to limit searches to parameters such as a date frame or publication source, or to use Boolean search language, i.e., logical terms, such as AND, OR, and NOT, helping you to define a search more precisely.

- If there is a certain sequence of words you want to search, put the phrase in quotation marks.

- If broad categories yield too many results (such as "car classifieds"), be more specific to find what you want ("Corvette classifieds").

- If your keywords do not yield the results you are after, try synonyms. You can find these in a thesaurus in your word processor.

- In most search engines, you can put a plus sign (+) in front of a word that must be included in all results. An example is city guides+Seattle. Similarly, put a minus sign (–) in front of a word that should not appear in the results (python–Monty).

- Another alternative is to click on the "shop" icon on your Web browser. You can then either do a search as above or click on one of the product category links.

- Still another possibility is to try one of the more popular shopping sites. The largest players in online retailing are Amazon.com and eBay.com. Other general e-tailers include Buy.com, Barnesandnoble.com, BestBuy.com, and Overstock.com. All major retailers now have Web sites, usually found by typing www.storename.com (replace "storename" with the retailer's name). Other top product research Web sites are Google, Yahoo!, ConsumerReports.com, WalMart.com, MSN, and Ask.com.

- Also increasingly popular are recommendations or warnings by other consumers, found on **customer review sites**. Business-listing sites by Google (maps.google.com is the most desired home for local businesses), Yahoo! and others such as Yelp, Citysearch, and AOL Local let consumers rave about their favorite businesses or complain about poor service, allowing shoppers to get credible personal opinions about local businesses and services. The reviews can dramatically raise a Web site's visibility in search engines, with reviews and star ratings often cited in search results. For example, a search for "Los Angeles chiropractor" returns not only links to Web sites but also a ten-item list of local chiropractors with their addresses, reviews, star ratings, and a local map at the top of the page. Beware, though: Unfortunately, some unethical marketers write fake reviews or aggressively seek favorable reviews by offering incentives such as iPods and gift certificates.

- Yet another option is to try some of the following generic placeholders: marketplace.com, PlanetRetail.com, or www.ismall.com.

- Still another possibility is to use a shopping bot, which can be useful for comparison shopping feature-by-feature and dollar-by-dollar. Bots do not sell anything; they search for and compare products for you (See Exercise 4.5). For example, Travelocity.com, Priceline.com, and Expedia.com can find the best prices for your traveling needs, while Brandwise.com and AJMadison.com do so for your home appliances desires. To locate virtually anything, try sites such as Bargainfinder, Become, Shopzilla, and Yahoo! Shopping. Other popular bots include bottomdollar.com, CompareNet.com, PriceSCAN.com, PriceGrabber.com, and MyBasics.com.

REVIEW QUESTIONS

1. What is the Internet and how has it changed consumer shopping behavior?
2. What is mobile commerce and how does it differ from traditional electronic commerce?
3. Explain the major advantages and disadvantages of Internet shopping for consumers.
4. Describe some basic strategies for shopping online.
5. In what sense does the existence of nonbuying (nonfunctional) motives for shopping argue against the replacement of traditional bricks-and-mortar retailing with e-tailing?

IN-CLASS APPLICATIONS

1. Discuss your experiences with shopping on the Internet. How long have you been shopping online? How often do you shop online? What motivates you to shop online? How do you find e-shopping compares with shopping in brick-and-mortar stores? Which sites have you shopped on and why did you shop there? What kinds of products have you purchased? Were you a satisfied customer? Have you ever had a bad experience with online shopping? Are there certain kinds of products you prefer to buy online and others you favor buying off line? Why?

If you've never bought anything online, explain why not. Do you expect to do so in the future? Why or why not? Do you know anyone who has never bought anything online? Why haven't they done so?

2. Could any nonbuying motives apply to Internet shopping? How could marketers tap into these nonfunctional motives?

3. Take a stand on each of the following controversial issues:
   a. State governments should raise revenues by taxing sales on Internet transactions. (Currently, Internet sales aren't taxed, unlike retail sales in most states.)
   b. States should not regulate or ban Internet sales by marketers of products such as cars, contact lenses, mortgages, and wine. (Some states say that buying such products without personal contact between buyers and sellers could harm buyers, such as sales of wines to minors and badly fitting contact lenses.)

4. Discuss your experiences as you complete the shopping assignment in the following written application by answering the seven questions in the written application.

WRITTEN APPLICATIONS

Your instructor will assign each student a product or service to "buy," according to the following list arranged by the first letter of students' last names. Or, if you or your instructor prefer, you may "purchase" a product of your own choosing.

You will be required to gather information about your product or service via the Internet, although you need not actually purchase it. You may use any of the sites listed below as well as those discussed in the background section of this exercise and others you are aware of or encounter during your shopping "trip."

Letters A through D—Entertainment: Amazon.com, CDNow.com, Barnesandnoble.com, Reel.com, Buy.com, BestBuy.com

Letters E through G—Apparel and Jewelry: Nordstrom.com, LLBean.com, Gap.com, Levis.com, Bluefly.com, BrooksBrothers.com, JCrew.com

Letters H through J—Gifts and Flowers: RedEnvelope.com, Wine.com, Sparks.com, 1800flowers.com, Hallmark.com, WalMart.com

Letters K through M—Cosmetics: Clinique.com, BobbiBrown.com, Avon.com, Macys.com, CosmeticsCounter.com, SmashBox.com

Letters N through Q—Health and Beauty Aids: drugstore.com, productscan.com, RegoTrading.com

Letters R through T—House and Garden: Garden.com, Furniture.com, Target.com, CrateandBarrel.com, MarthaStewart.com

Letters U through Z—Computer hardware or software: CompUSA.com, Newegg.com, Buy.com, Gateway.com, Dell.com, CompUSA.com, AppleComputer.com, CDW.com

Other suggested categories: Some other suggested product classes to explore include: hobby, craft, and novelty items; toys; hotels and travel (e.g., for spring break!); health care products and services; jewelry and watches; office and school supplies; pet supplies; and automotive. Visit the "shopping" section of your browser or search engine to get a list of category links on which you can click.

Browse at several locations to gather information about your product, and then discuss the following seven issues. You may attach portions of printouts as exhibits to facilitate your discussion.

1. List the names of five or more brands (or of service providers) in your product category that you would consider buying or using.
2. Briefly describe the search procedure you used to gather data on these brands. Did you use search engines, shopping bots, or a combination of these?
3. Describe each brand or service package in terms of main features or attributes, including price, and the benefits those features provide.
4. Compare/rate the five brands or service packages on your important criteria and indicate your final choice. Describe the process you use to arrive at this decision.
5. Discuss in detail the following issues related to your experience with Web sites you visited. You might want to compare some of the different sites you explored on these issues.
   a. Sources, amount, and type of information available. Was the site more "hard sell" (informative and designed to make an immediate sale) or primarily "soft sell" (entertaining, indirectly promoting the product via informational or lifestyle presentations)?
   b. Ease of accessing and digesting information (compare to other information sources consumers typically use for this product or service category). Were navigational tools easy to use? Was the site visually appealing?
   c. Quality, relevance, and credibility of information in making purchase decisions. Does it appear to be unbiased? Are there interactive elements whereby you can contact the company or e-tailer with questions, suggestions, comments, and complaints?
   d. Ease of making a purchase (if you actually buy something).
6. Summarize your experience while surfing the Internet as a consumer. Have you shopped on the Internet before? Do you plan on doing so in the future? Why or why not? Have you ever shopped from a mobile device? How, if at all, did this experience compare with shopping from a computer?
7. Which stages in the CD process would be similar or the same when shopping online as opposed to shopping off line and which would be different? How would they differ? Are some stages easier to get through online or off line? Explain.

EXERCISE 3.4. INVOLVEMENT, PERCEIVED RISK, AND RISK REDUCTION STRATEGIES

OBJECTIVES

1. To give you insight into the nature and critical importance of the concept of involvement in influencing the extent and nature of the CDM process.
2. To show you that there are several facets to involvement, and to demonstrate their distinctions: cognitive involvement versus affective involvement, and product involvement versus purchase involvement.
3. To explain the three mediating factors of CB that determine the degree of involvement: (1) the product, (2) the consumer, and (3) the purchase or consumption situation.
4. To give you practice in discerning the extent of involvement as it differs (a) among products, (b) among consumers, and (c) in various situations.
5. To explain the connection between involvement and perceived risk.

6. To demonstrate the different types of perceived risk inherent in searching for, buying, and consuming a product, and to enable you to recognize these risks from advertisements.
7. To explain risk-reduction strategies (RRSs), which consumers use to reduce perceived risk, and corresponding risk relievers, or actions marketers take to reduce perceived risk.
8. To give you practice in identifying RRSs and risk relievers suggested by ads.
9. To help you understand RRSs you use as a consumer and the corresponding risk relievers marketers offer you.
10. To give you practice in conducting survey research and to thereby learn about levels of the various types of involvement, perceived risks, and RRSs.

BACKGROUND

VARIATIONS IN THE CONSUMER DECISION PROCESS

Calculated consumer DM is the exception rather than the rule. For example, you might habitually buy your favorite brand without even considering competing alternatives. There are two general individual difference variables that affect whether or not the consumer goes through a carefully reasoned decision process: (1) the level of DM (consumer's learning stage) and (2) the level of involvement.

The **level of decision making (DM) (consumer's learning stage)** is the degree of prior information and experience the consumer has with the product category and its alternatives. If he or she has extensive knowledge of the product and brands, then he or she need not conduct a careful search and alternative evaluation. Level of DM is examined in Exercise 3.5. In this exercise we investigate the other determinant of whether or not a consumer proceeds fully through the five-stage decision-making model: the level of involvement.

THE NATURE OF CONSUMER INVOLVEMENT

INVOLVEMENT DEFINED

Involvement is the extent to which the purchase decision has perceived personal importance and relevance for the buyer. Specifically, involvement is the degree of interest in and concern by the consumer in a particular situation for the object of involvement: a product, purchase of a particular product or the marketing communication for that product.

If the consumer is involved with a purchase decision, problem recognition is important and he or she is motivated to extensively search for information to help select the product. The one exception is if the level of DM is low, i.e., the consumer is knowledgeable and experienced and therefore does not need to extensively search (See Exercise 3.5). If involvement is low, information search and alternative evaluation will be limited, regardless of the level of DM.

Exhibit 3.2 summarizes the major variables related to involvement discussed in this exercise.

SEMANTIC DIFFERENTIAL SCALES TO MEASURE INVOLVEMENT

Involvement is sometimes measured on **semantic differential scales**—measures consisting of a series of seven-point rating scales using bipolar (opposite) adjectives to anchor the beginning and end of each scale item. Consumers could rate a product category or brand as very important (7) to very unimportant (1), very interesting to very uninteresting, very relevant to very irrelevant, exciting to unexciting, meaningful to meaningless, appealing to unappealing, fascinating to ordinary, priceless to worthless, necessary to unnecessary, and involving to uninvolving.

TYPES OF CONSUMER INVOLVEMENT

INVOLVEMENT CLASSIFIED BY NEED SATISFIED: COGNITIVE INVOLVEMENT AND AFFECTIVE INVOLVEMENT

Corresponding to utilitarian (functional, instrumental) needs is **cognitive involvement**, or thoughtful involvement. Related to hedonic (experiential, transformational) needs is **affective involvement**, or emotional

EXHIBIT 3.2   **A Model of Consumer Involvement**

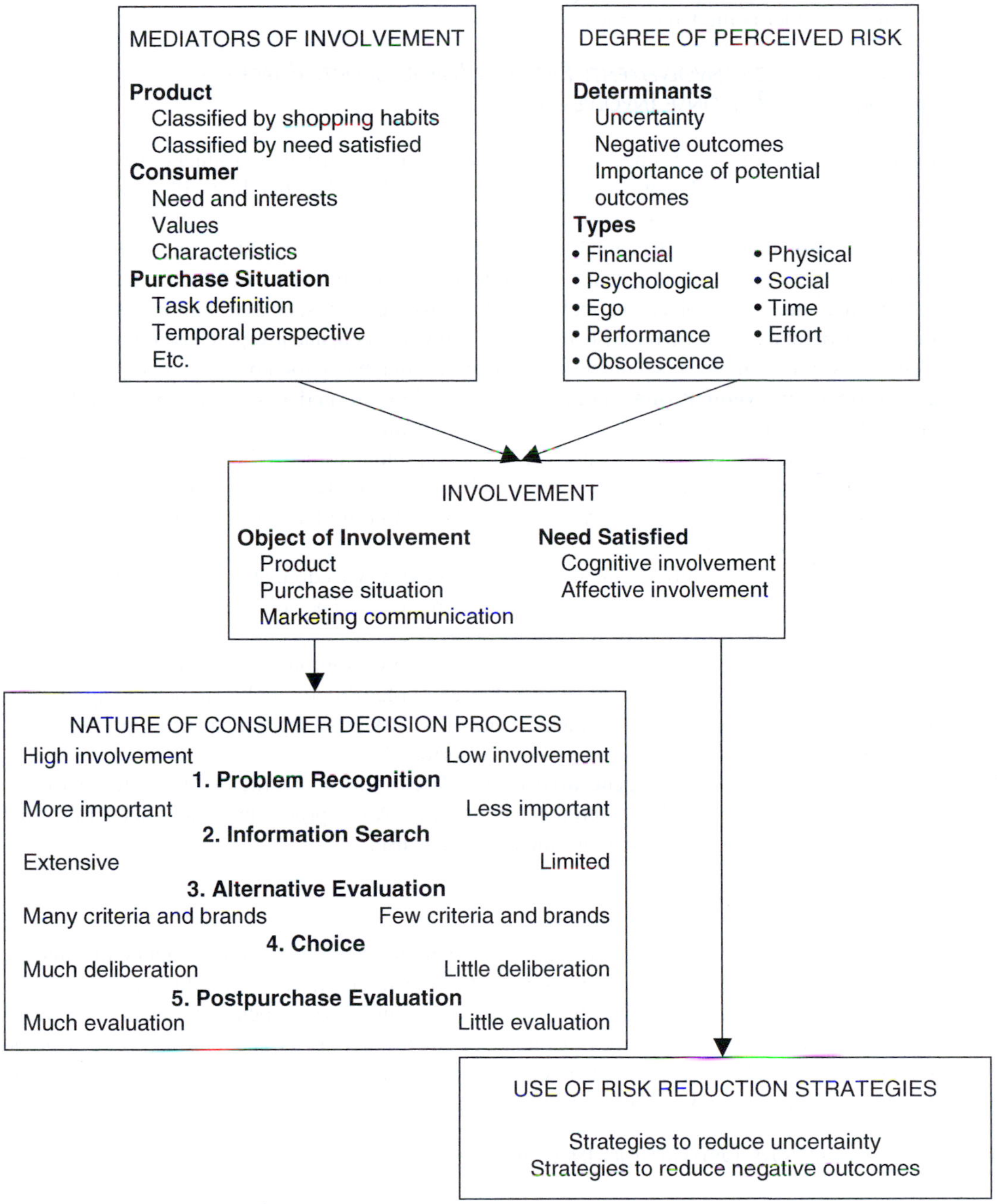

MEDIATORS OF INVOLVEMENT

Product
    Classified by shopping habits
    Classified by need satisfied
Consumer
    Need and interests
    Values
    Characteristics
Purchase Situation
    Task definition
    Temporal perspective
    Etc.

DEGREE OF PERCEIVED RISK

Determinants
    Uncertainty
    Negative outcomes
    Importance of potential
    outcomes
Types
- Financial   • Physical
- Psychological   • Social
- Ego   • Time
- Performance   • Effort
- Obsolescence

INVOLVEMENT

Object of Involvement   **Need Satisfied**
    Product   Cognitive involvement
    Purchase situation   Affective involvement
    Marketing communication

NATURE OF CONSUMER DECISION PROCESS

High involvement	Low involvement
1. Problem Recognition	
More important	Less important
2. Information Search	
Extensive	Limited
3. Alternative Evaluation	
Many criteria and brands	Few criteria and brands
4. Choice	
Much deliberation	Little deliberation
5. Postpurchase Evaluation	
Much evaluation	Little evaluation

USE OF RISK REDUCTION STRATEGIES

Strategies to reduce uncertainty
Strategies to reduce negative outcomes

involvement. If there is a high level of cognitive involvement, consumers wish to make a rational, informed decision and put lots of thought into it. With a high level of affective involvement, consumers can be passionate about or experience intense feelings for the product. High affective involvement is found in **value-expressive products**—products that provide social or aesthetic utility or have symbolic meaning regarding the user's self-image, suggesting to others something about who we are, such as macho, intellectual, or thoroughly modern. Value-expressive products are high in **ego involvement**, which is the importance of a product to a consumer's **self-image (self-concept)**, or who the individual believes he or she resembles and how others view this individual. Thus, wearing "cool" clothing or driving a "hot" car would positively reflect a consumer's self-concept.

A consumer can experience high or low cognitive and affective involvement simultaneously, and one can be high while the other is moderate or low.

Involvement Classified by the Object of Involvement: Product Involvement, Purchase Situation Involvement, and Message Response Involvement

Product involvement is a consumer's inherent degree of interest in a particular product or brand, and it is an enduring involvement. People do not take pictures of their first Big Mac, but they will photograph their first car and they will wear their favorite sports team's jersey.

Purchase situation involvement (decision involvement) is a consumer's extent of concern for and interest in the purchase process for a particular item, that is, it is situational, short-term involvement. It is possible to have high purchase situation involvement but low product involvement, such as a skinny person buying a book on weight control for an obese friend. Also, high product involvement and low purchase involvement can occur simultaneously, for example, when purchasing a new shirt in a hurry for a big party one hour away.

Message-response involvement (marketing communication, advertising involvement) is the consumer's degree of interest in paying attention to and learning from (message-related involvement) and/or being entertained by (executional involvement) marketing communications. Where product involvement and/or purchase involvement is high, we would expect advertising involvement to be high, as well. However, if an ad is particularly entertaining or relevant, there could be high advertising involvement while product and purchase involvement are low.

Marketers try to raise message involvement, if possible. One way to do that is to send consumers via traditional offline ads to a Web site to interact with or even create ads. The ads' message involvement can be measured by **engagement**, the amounts of time and effort consumers spend on an ad.

A **sticky Web site** is an engaging site that is able to attract repeat visitors and have them stay for extended time periods by being interesting and/or entertaining. For example, Proctor and Gamble's beinggirl.com teen advice site promotes the Always and Tampax brands. Its "ask Iris" section answers questions like, "Will a shark attack me if I swim in the ocean during my period?"

Another technique is to solicit **user-generated (created) content**, encouraging Web site visitors to create and pass along their own ads. However, this can backfire. A site promoting Chevrolet's Tahoe led to user-created ads passed around the Web that ridiculed its gas use.

High-Involvement versus Low-Involvement Media

Advertising media can also vary in level of consumer involvement. Print media (newspapers, magazines, direct mail, and catalogs) and electronic interactive media (the Internet, interactive kiosks, and mobile media such as cell phones and digital music players) tend to be of high involvement for consumers actively seeking information or entertainment. On the other hand, broadcast media (TV and radio) and out-of-home media (billboards, bus advertising, etc.) are inclined to be of low involvement, as audience members passively receive information and only half pay attention to the ads, if at all.

Three Mediating ("It Depends") Factors Determining Involvement

What is it that determines whether or not the purchase of a product by a consumer in a particular situation is involving? It depends on the product, the consumer, and the purchase and consumption situations. These are the three general **mediating (contingency) variables** ("it depends" factors) of CB. The answer to specific questions regarding CB is often that "it depends" on one or more of these variables.

Mediating Factor 1: The Product

Product involvement is the consumer's cognitive and emotional states reflecting the degree that person feels a product category is interesting, relevant, and possibly even exciting. For example, fashionistas find clothing and fashion more interesting and exciting than do others.

Note that *involvement* is not the same as *importance*. For instance, most people would agree that having good tires is important, but most individuals are not very interested in or excited about buying new tires.

Although degree of involvement for any given product varies among consumers, some products tend to be inherently more high involvement: jewelry, furniture, clothing, MP3 players, and dinner at a restaurant. On the other hand, sponge mops, paper towels, bathroom deodorizers, and shoe polish are usually low involvement.

We now look at several ways to classify products that correlate with product involvement.

Products Classified by Shopping Habits. Generally, high-involvement goods tend to be either **shopping goods**, products for which consumers carefully and comparatively evaluate alternatives during the shopping process, or **specialty goods**, items for which consumers have very strong brand preferences. Both such products are usually high priced and infrequently bought, such as appliances, jewelry, and cars. Most low-involvement items are **convenience goods**, products purchased frequently and with minimal shopping effort, such as packaged foods and personal care items. However, there are always exceptions to these general rules. For example, if a consumer's favorite food is peanut butter and this person strongly favors Jif, for that buyer this would be a high-involvement specialty good.

Search, Experience, and Credence Goods. There are three types of products, depending on if and how consumers obtain useful information on them: search goods, experience goods, and credence goods. **Search goods** are composed of **search attributes**, objective, tangible product attributes on which consumers can obtain useful, objective **brand-attribute information** or facts about various brands' performance on important attributes through prepurchase search and alternative evaluation. Examples of search attributes include price, color, size, shape, miles per gallon, and energy efficiency ratings. Many such features are utilitarian in nature and can be quantitatively measured. Gathering information before buying is the easiest, least expensive, and often the least risky way to learn about such products. Search goods are generally high involvement, infrequently purchased utilitarian durables such as computers, cars, and appliances. Consequently, the prepurchase search will be fairly extensive. Hence, marketers should provide consumers of search goods with the desired information and make sure that it is truthful since consumers are able to check other information sources for confirmation (not to mention that to do otherwise would be unethical).

Experience goods are composed of **experience attributes**, which are mostly intangible and subjectively evaluated. For example, defining tasty food is very subjective: One person's perfect squid sushi is another's garden hose on rice. Therefore, the extent of prepurchase search for experience goods will be minimal. They are called experience attributes because the best way to learn about how a brand performs on these attributes is by personal experience, either through prepurchase sampling and demonstration or through postpurchase consumption and evaluation. These are the easiest, cheapest, and least risky ways to learn about experience goods, as opposed to prepurchase search for search goods.

The ability of a deodorant to stop wetness is best assessed for yourself, as is whether a toilet tissue is really "the softest ever." Experience goods tend to be moderate or low involvement, frequently purchased, hedonic nondurables. Most are rich in sensory experiences such as taste (food, beverages), smell (perfume, scented candles), touch (hand lotions, fabrics), aural experiences (CDs, stereos sets), and visual experiences (movies, TV shows).

Information from prepurchase sources, such as advertising, ratings services, and even friends, is of little value since "there's no accounting for taste." After all, how often have you been disappointed by a friend's suggestion to eat at a particular restaurant or by a movie or book critic's recommendation?

Marketers of experience goods should provide consumers with personal experiences prior to purchase, such as free samples and trial offers or test runs of durable goods such as appliances and consumer electronics. iTunes lets you sample musical artists before you make their songs a permanent part of your play list. Likewise, Amazon.com permits you to read an excerpt from a book before you order it.

Credence goods are products high in **credence attributes**. These features are hidden or unknown and not easily discernible. Consumers are unable to evaluate brand performance on these criteria either before or after purchase and consumption, because they either lack the knowledge to do so or cannot justify the cost of doing so. For example, whether vitamin-enriched or fiber-fortified foods are really helping us stay healthy is difficult to know. It is hard to compare the effectiveness of various brands of motor oil or to determine the efficacy of some prescription medications that do not immediately alleviate obvious symptoms. Sometimes credence goods can be evaluated, but only after extensive usage or when the product ultimately fails to perform well or at all. Examples include auto reliability, mutual fund performance, and the cholesterol-inhibiting ability of a drug.

Credence products tend to be items that are complex in nature or require special expertise to evaluate, such as fine wine; professional services such as knee surgery, a brake job, or legal advice; and products with less discernable results, such as engine coolant. Due to this uncertainty, credence goods are generally high in perceived risk and, consequently, tend to be fairly high in involvement.

Consumers might try to get prepurchase information on credence goods but typically lack confidence in the data. Instead, buyers often resort to simple *decision heuristics*, rules of thumb, such as purchasing well-known brand names, buying brands endorsed by experts, or relying on trusted friends' recommendations. Therefore, marketers encourage consumers to use quick and easy means of assessing the quality of credence goods, such as company or brand name, the number of years they have been in business, and other surrogate (substitute) indicators of quality.

MEDIATING FACTOR 2: THE CONSUMER

Whether a given product is of enduring involvement depends on the consumer's needs and wants, values, family situation, professional or work life, hobbies and interests, religious faith, and other personal characteristics. We have wine connoisseurs, health nuts, beach bums, clotheshorses, cigar aficionados, and auto enthusiasts, among other types of product fetishists.

Highly involved consumers usually make good target customers who are more likely to be frequent buyers, buy in high volume, purchase higher-end versions, encourage others to buy, and so on.

MEDIATING FACTOR 3: THE PURCHASE SITUATION

The third "it depends" factor affecting involvement is the **purchase situation**, which consists of factors peculiar to a particular time, place, or location that affect the buyer's decision. This relates to short-term and situational purchase involvement. Situational influences include:

- The *physical surroundings*. For example, buying in an upscale versus downscale store or purchasing online versus at a store (i.e., buying by browser versus being a store browser).
- The *social situation*. For instance, shopping with family or cruising with friends in the mall.
- The *purchase occasion*. For example, taking the family out to dinner.
- The *task definition*. This is the purpose for buying and consuming, such as procuring paper and notebooks to use at school. Generally, there are three purchase purposes: for one's personal use, for household use, or for someone else, such as a gift or buying with the expectation of reimbursement from the one for whom one is purchasing. Buying on behalf of a loved one or friend usually raises the level of involvement.
- The *temporal perspective*. For example, time available for shopping or being rushed versus taking a leisurely shopping excursion.
- The *degree of personal responsibility* associated with the decision. For instance, being the "gopher" versus making the choice yourself.
- *Antecedent states*. These are momentary moods, such as anger or anxiety, and temporary conditions, such as sickness or being flush with cash.

PERCEIVED RISK AND INVOLVEMENT

PERCEIVED RISK DEFINED AND CONCEPTUALIZED

Another factor determining the degree of involvement is the level of risk perceived by the consumer in purchasing the product in a particular situation. This **perceived risk** is the extent of uncertainty the consumer believes (perceives) exists about possible negative consequences associated with the purchase and use of a product.

You pay your money, you take your chances. The gown might create a sensation—or not. The caviar might be delectable—or inedible. The new car might be a delight to drive—or the source of constant headaches.

You should understand several things about perceived risk:

- The risk is perceived. It is what the consumer believes to be true and so it could differ from objective reality. Hence, marketers must understand risk from the consumer's viewpoint, not simply from a detached, objective perspective.
- Risk is a function of (1) uncertainty or lack of advance knowledge, (2) possible negative outcomes or the probability of losses, and (3) the importance to the consumer of the losses arising from those undesirable consequences.
- People are risk averse. They are more afraid of a loss than they are concerned with a gain of equal magnitude. Losses loom larger than gains, for instance, a dollar won is valued less than a dollar lost. Strictly speaking, this is irrational behavior.
- Involvement and perceived risk are positively correlated. The more involved the consumer is, the greater the number of perceived risks associated with the purchase.
- Perceived risk is undesirable from both the consumer's and the marketer's perspective. Since they do not like perceived risk, consumers to seek to minimize it. Marketers should assist them in reducing this risk by providing risk relievers, or marketing strategies to lessen perceived risk. This is very important: If risk is great enough, customers will either refrain from buying or else select a competitive brand perceived as a "safer" choice.

CONSUMER RISK REDUCTION STRATEGIES

For the marketer to know which risk relievers to offer consumers, the basic consumer **risk-reduction strategies (RRSs)** must be understood. These are the actions consumers take to handle and lessen perceived risk. These strategies include:

- Purchasing the least expensive alternative, thereby minimizing possible financial loss.
- Buying the most expensive alternative. Although this sounds contradictory to the previous strategy, a high price usually indicates high quality.
- Purchasing a brand with a positive brand image or from a store with a favorable store image.
- Buying a smaller product size or version to minimize negative consequences.
- Seeking information via prepurchase search and alternative evaluation.
- Relying on the advice of others who are considered more trustworthy than marketers.
- Seeking one or more sources of reassurance, either from marketers (e.g., money-back guarantees, trial periods) or from others ("I love your new house").
- Becoming or remaining brand loyal to increase certainty.
- Buying heavily advertised brands, which are presumed to be of higher quality.

TYPES OF PERCEIVED RISKS AND MARKETERS' CORRESPONDING RISK RELIEVERS

The type of risk reliever a marketer should use to reduce perceived risk depends on the type of risk the consumer faces:

Financial (economic, monetary) risk is the likely loss of money associated with purchasing and using a product. It includes not only the product's up-front sticker price (invoice cost or transaction price) but also costs of acquisition, ownership and maintenance, and disposal. An important financial risk reliever in the marketer's arsenal is offering a better value through a lower purchase price, giving better quality or performance for the money. There are also *price protection plans*, guarantees that a marketer's price is the lowest. If a consumer finds a lower price elsewhere, the marketer will match it, either before or after the purchase. In a variation, when consumers buy nonrefundable airline tickets and the fares drop before departure, most airlines refund the difference via a travel voucher for a future flight, minus the airlines ticket change fee, typically $50 to $100.

During the Great Recession of 2008–2009, financial risk relievers gained new importance as marketers unveiled a slew of guarantees, rebates, and freebies for those dissatisfied or who became unemployed; a practice called *altruism marketing*. General Motors offered a money-back guarantee to dissatisfied customers, JetBlue waived flight-cancelation fees (up to $100 per ticket) for customers who lost their jobs, and under the Hyundai Assurance Plus plan, Hyundai made up to three car payments for their customers who lost their jobs during the first year of ownership and let them return the product without incurring a penalty or damaging their credit record if they failed to find work.

Social risk is a possible loss of face, prestige, and approval of significant others, such as friends and family, due to not buying and using a product or as a consequence of purchasing and using a socially unacceptable product. Social risk relievers include making products appear to be popular or affiliated with a desirable social group, advertising that emphasizes the social approval brand users receive, using consumer testimonials, and employing bandwagon appeals ("We're #1! or "Everyone's buying it").

Ego risk entails potential loss of prestige, status, and respect due to purchasing and using a product. Ego risk is based on ego involvement and **self-ego**, one's sense of self-worth. We have a need to defend, enhance, and express our self-concept and self-ego. Socially visible products help us to do this, as they are often symbols of who we are and what we have accomplished. Examples: a hair-coloring product might leave a consumer's hair with a strange-looking hue, frumpy clothing can lower one's self-esteem, and driving a junk-box car can be an embarrassment. The key ego risk reliever is a favorable brand personality that target market members can identify with or aspire to.

Performance (functional) risk involves the possibility that the product will not perform as expected, that is, it will not satisfy the functional needs it is meant to fulfill. There are several performance risk relievers: building and testing the product for quality; creating realistic (not exaggerated) expectations to avoid consumer disappointment with product performance; letting prospects try the product via samples, trial periods, demonstrations, and the like; providing installation, setup, and training in the case of technology products; and offering guarantees and warranties, including **extended warranties**. The latter are service contracts covering repairs, maintenance, or replacement for a specific time beyond the product's normal warranty period on product performance. Sears' Kidvantage program pledges to replace any clothing that wears out before a child outgrows it.

Physical (safety) risk is possible harm that can come from the product malfunctioning, thereby posing a physical hazard to the health and safety of users, others in close proximity to the users, and possibly even the ecological environment. Useful physical risk relievers include performance risk relievers discussed previously, building safeguards into the product to make it "idiot proof," including instructional materials and warning labels to promote safe use, having the product certified for safety by an independent testing organization, and providing after-sale assistance to ensure safe use of the product.

Psychological risk entails uneasiness, mental anguish, and fear that the product will not provide emotional or intellectual satisfaction. Consumers wonder whether they will feel good, comfortable, or at ease with the product. For example, vacationers question whether they will enjoy a new vacation spot, while others experience angst over figuring out what to order in an ethnic restaurant. Psychological risk relievers include enlisting testimonials from satisfied users; letting consumers actually or vicariously (e.g., via a DVD or downloaded simulation) gain prepurchase product experience through trial periods, samples, and so on; developing and promoting well-known brand names (e.g., Kindercare Day Care Centers); providing advertising, salespeople, and customer service lines that reassure and reinforce the customer; and making the decision reversible through guarantees, warranties, and money-back offers.

Time risk is the perceived excessive time devoted to any stage in the consumer decision process, such as prepurchase search or learning how to operate a purchased item. The overriding time risk reliever is for the marketer to provide concise, easily understood prepurchase information; alleviate time-consuming postpurchase problems by providing simple assembly and operating instructions and offering toll-free service lines; and provide time guarantees (e.g., Trans World Airlines [TWA] gave away one thousand bonus miles to passengers on any domestic flights that arrived more than fifteen minutes late or were canceled).

Effort risk is the amount of exertion that the consumer fears having to put into buying and using the product. It tends to be closely correlated to time risk. For example, there is the "learning curve" required when learning to use a technically complex product. Marketers should consider these effort risk relievers: simplicity in product design; easily understood, "user friendly" operating instructions; a helpful and courteous customer service staff to assist perplexed customers; and developing devices that are laborsaving, such as an electric can opener or a garage door opener.

Obsolescence risk is the risk that the purchased product will quickly become outdated, usually being superseded by a new, advanced version. Hi-tech products (can you say "HD DVD video player?") and fashion and fad items (which lack a successor) are prone to this risk. Obsolescence risk relievers include offering free or low-cost upgrades, making later versions of hardware compatible with the earlier versions of the hardware, leasing the product for a limited time, and only making infrequent but major product changes rather than frequent but minor product alterations.

REVIEW QUESTIONS

1. What is involvement? How can a consumer's involvement be measured?
2. Explain the difference between:
   a. Cognitive involvement and affective involvement. What type of consumer needs do each of these kinds of involvement relate to?
   b. Product involvement, purchase situation involvement, and message-response involvement.
3. Describe the influences of each of the three mediating factors on involvement.
4. Explain the nature of search, experience, and credence products and how each affects the nature of product involvement and search activity.
5. What is perceived risk? What three factors determine perceived risk?
6. Explain the difference and relationship between consumer RRSs and risk relievers.
7. Describe each of the nine types of perceived risk, the types of consumers and products likely to be affiliated with each risk, and effective RRSs for each.

IN-CLASS APPLICATIONS

1. Select one or more products for which you can discuss involvement with your classmates. Candidates include stereo equipment, cross-country skis, dog food, aspirin, perfume, Mother's Day or Father's Day greeting cards, frozen vegetables, mountain bicycles, and sunscreen. You may select one or more other products if you wish.

Discuss whether you have a high, moderate, or low level of involvement for each product and why.

Is involvement influenced by the nature of the consumer (e.g., sex, age, hobbies, personal characteristics), product (e.g., convenience, shopping, or specialty good; search, experience, or credence good; level of overall perceived risk or types of perceived risks), and situation (e.g., shopping situation)?

Describe the nature and level of cognitive involvement and affective involvement for each product.

2. The background discussion noted that "it is possible to have high purchase situation involvement but low product involvement," as well as to have "high product involvement but low purchase involvement." Cite general as well as specific examples of where both of these situations could prevail.

3. Think about a high-involvement purchase you recently made that was laden with perceived risks. Describe the types of risks, the RRSs you used, and the risk relievers that the marketer employed or could have employed.

4. Analyze the ads in Exhibits 3.3 to 3.7 in order to discuss the following:
   a. Whether there is any evidence of an appeal to cognitive involvement, affective involvement, or ego involvement. Do you think each ad succeeds in creating a high degree of message-response involvement? How does each ad attempt to do this?
   b. Describe the types of perceived risk that could arise in the purchase and use of each product.
   c. Does each ad offer the consumer one or more risk relievers? If it does not, are there any risk relievers that the ad could discuss?

WRITTEN APPLICATIONS

1. Conduct a survey of at least ten students on your campus (or any ten people, if you prefer) for three of the products in Question 1. Answer the questions by developing a brief questionnaire to learn about the degree and nature of your respondents' involvement with the product. (Hint: Try using semantic differential scales.) Also, find out about perceived risks experienced by your respondents and any risk-reduction strategies they use.

2. Answer Questions 3 and 4 in the In-Class Applications for three of the ads.

3. Find three more ads, each for a moderate- to high-involvement product, and repeat the analysis in Questions 3 and 4 in the In-Class Applications.

EXHIBIT 3.3   Colgate Ad

EXHIBIT 3.4   Tropicana Ad

EXHIBIT 3.5   Jergens Ad

EXHIBIT 3.6   Take Control Ad

EXHIBIT 3.7   Roche Pharmaceuticals Ad

EXERCISE 3.5. LEVELS OF DECISION MAKING (LEARNING STAGES)

OBJECTIVES

1. To help you to understand the nature and importance of the concept of levels of decision making (DM) and how this variable influences the extent and nature of the consumer decision-making process.
2. To enable you to distinguish between product involvement and levels of DM.
3. To have you recognize the different levels of DM and how prior information and experience shape the decision-making process.
4. To give you practice developing appropriate marketing strategies for consumers in each level of DM.
5. To provide you with experience with consumers' learning stages by conducting survey research.

BACKGROUND

THE CONCEPT OF CONSUMER DECISION-MAKING LEVELS

The second general individual difference variable affecting the nature and extent of the consumer decision-making (CDM) process is the consumer's **level of decision making (consumer's learning stage, decision process continuum, consumer problem-solving approach)**, the degree of prior information and experi-

EXHIBIT 3.8 Levels of Decision Making Continuum			
Characteristics	Extended Decision Making (EDM)	Limited Decision Making (LDM)	Routine Decision Making (RDM)
Prior information and experience	Low	Moderate	High
Product class knowledge	Low	Moderate to high	High
Brand knowledge	Low	Moderate to low	High
Thought, time, and effort devoted to search	High	Moderate	Low
Degree of purchase involvement	High	Moderate	Low
Common product-market scenarios	New products, infrequently bought products, first-time purchases	Growth stage of PLC, new and improved brands enter, infrequently purchased products, repeated problem solving	Convenience goods in mature categories
Consumer strategies	Learn about product class	Seek brand-attribute information, use decision heuristics	Simplify decision making by establishing routines, brand loyalty, and inertia
Recommended marketing strategies	Build primary demand, help frame decision making, give personal assistance	Build selective demand, physical and psychological brand differentiation	Reminder advertising, sales promotions, new channels, marketing innovations

ence the consumer has with the product category and some of its brands. There are three learning stages that represent the amounts of previous learning and product experience. Consequently, each stage entails a different degree of time and effort for DM, which has important implications for marketing strategies.

THREE CONSUMER LEARNING STAGES

We will now investigate the three levels of DM in the order in which consumers typically progress through them as they learn about a product class and its brands. Exhibit 3.8 summarizes the three stages.

EXTENDED DECISION MAKING

The first consumer-learning stage is variously known as **extended decision making (EDM), extended problem solving, extensive DM, extensive problem solving, complex DM, midrange problem solving,** or **considered purchases**. EDM is a learning stage where the consumer has little or no prior knowledge of and experience with the product class or alternative brands within that product category.

General EDM scenarios include the following: purchase of new products about which buyers lack experience; very infrequently purchased items where consumers' prior information and experience is either largely forgotten or irrelevant due to changing market conditions caused by factors such as emerging technology and the entrance of new brands; and a person's first-time purchases in categories that are life-stage or age driven, such as one's first car or a tuxedo rental.

The primary goal of consumers practicing EDM is to gather information on the product category and learn what it is, how it functions, what its advantages are over predecessor products (e.g., the merits of an MP3 player over a DVD player), what the important purchase criteria are (e.g., storage capacity in an MP3 player); and how alternatives perform on the criteria. There is high purchase involvement so consumers will move thoughtfully, carefully, and completely through the entire five-stage consumer DM process.

Marketers targeting EDM consumers should employ one or more of the following strategies:

- Encourage category learning through marketing communications that build **primary (generic) demand**, or understanding of and a felt need for the product category. The early automobile was hawked as a "horseless carriage," superior to the horse and carriage (faster, more horsepower, and no horse poop to clean up!). **Primary (generic) demand advertising** builds primary demand. This type of advertising is heavy with information and often refers to another more detailed information source, such as a Web site or toll-free number.
- Build **secondary (selective, brand) demand**, a favorable attitude toward the marketer's brand. This uses **secondary (selective, brand) demand advertising,** which is promotion that emphasizes brand superiority.
- Help the consumer frame (structure) DM to favor the seller. Marketers can stress the importance of buying criteria upon which their brands perform strongly and can direct consumers to third-party information sources that give their brands a favorable rating.
- Enlist a sales force to assist customers and use customer service reps to help with postpurchase issues.

LIMITED DECISION MAKING

The second level of DM is **limited decision making (LDM; limited problem solving)**. The consumer has some familiarity and perhaps experience with the product class and one or more of its brands and so engages in a somewhat restricted information search, primarily on performance of some brands on the buying criteria.

LDM conditions include the growth stage of the product life cycle. Consumers have some product experience during this stage, in which the following are common scenarios: New brands enter the market; pioneer brands are improved, often adding variations such as new styles, options, varieties, and so on; and infrequently bought items are subject to changing marketplace circumstances, such as new technology.

LDM also characterizes two general shopping situations: **repeated problem solving**; a buying situation in which a consumer considers buying a different brand than they have in the past, which can result in brand switching, and **variety (novelty) seeking**, searching for something new out of boredom or dissatisfaction.

The primary goal of consumers practicing LDM is to acquire brand-attribute information to make a brand choice decision. Moderate purchase involvement prevails during LDM. Consumers seek information more selectively than in EDM, often bypassing data on the product category that they already possess. Compared with EDM, fewer information sources are consulted, evaluation of brands is limited to one or a few vital criteria, the number of brands evaluated is restricted, and the consumer is not motivated to visit as many retail outlets or Web sites. Although buyers still proceed through the entire decision-making process, there is generally less time and effort expended during each stage.

Tasks of the marketers targeting LDM consumers include:

- Using promotional efforts to increase selective demand. Salespeople tout the virtues of their wares and advertisers employ comparison advertising.
- Developing product improvements, line extensions (varieties and versions of current products, such as new flavors and scents), sales promotions, price reductions, and other means of brand differentiation to entice consumers to switch brands.

ROUTINE DECISION MAKING

The third consumer learning stage is **routine decision making (RDM; routine problem solving, nominal DM, habitual DM, routinized response behavior, routine buying behavior, programmed decisions)**. In RDM, the consumer has extensive information on and experience with the product class and one, or (usually) many, brands. He or she usually buys the same brand repeatedly.

There are two general RDM situations:

- **Brand (customer) loyalty:** repeat buying of a particular brand due to a strong preference and emotional attachment. Brand-loyal customers exhibit high product involvement but low purchase involvement. In the United States, brands commanding high customer loyalty include Hershey's, Sony, Kraft, Crayola, Kellogg's, Nintendo's Wii, Rolls Royce, and Johnson & Johnson.

- **Inertia (repeat purchases, habitual buying)**: regularly purchasing the same brand out of habit, convenience, or indifference. In physics, "inertia" is the tendency of a body to maintain its resting state or uniform motion unless acted on by an outside force. Inert consumers don't switch brands unless enticed to do so by rival brands. Such customers consider competing brands to be fairly similar, find their usual brand satisfactory, and have no strong brand commitment. They feel low involvement for both the product and the purchase situation.

Inertia can also occur for high-tech products as a result of **switching costs**, the psychological, physical, and economic costs that buyers face in switching between technologies or products. Examples include buying, installing, and learning new home financial planning or tax preparation software and learning how to operate a new brand of digital camera.

Brand loyalty and inertia are common because people are creatures of habit who establish routines to simplify their lives. RDM buyers wish to minimize time and effort in shopping. Accordingly, in RDM there is a high probability of only visiting one store or Web site. RDM is most likely to occur for frequently bought products in mature categories. There is a low level of purchase involvement.

Marketers facing RDM customers should realize the importance of maintenance marketing activities, that is, customer retention and relationship marketing efforts. These activities include:

- Developing simple reminder and reinforcement advertising to keep the marketer's name top-of-mind and let the consumer know the brand is still a major player.
- Using occasional promotional deals to reward and retain current customers.
- Making continuous product improvements and offering more product variety.
- Gaining new channels of distribution to make purchasing more convenient.

REVIEW QUESTIONS

1. What is the level of DM? How do the extent and nature of DM vary in each of the stages of the level of DM?
2. How does the level of DM differ from the level of product involvement?
3. Describe the nature of the decision-making process of each of the three levels of DM—EDM, LDM, and RDM—as well as typical product-market scenarios for each. Also, discuss appropriate marketing strategies in each of these stages.

IN-CLASS APPLICATIONS

1. Consumers who view a product as high involvement, all else equal, go through the complete five-stage decision-making process. Consumers undergoing extensive problem solving also go through the entire consumer decision process, everything else constant. Likewise, consumers for whom a product is low involvement tend to truncate the decision process, as do consumers in the routine decision-making stage.

So, aren't the levels of DM continuum and involvement continuum really the same idea? After all, at one end of each spectrum consumers make thorough decisions and at the other end they do not. Correct?

2. Which learning stage would you be in if you were shopping for each of the following products: a house to live in on your own (or with a friend or two) after college graduation (assume this is financially feasible!), a portable MP3 player, and a pick-me up candy bar? (After today's class, you might feel you need and earned it!)

For each of these products, explain how your previous information and experience would put you in that learning stage and what the nature of your decision process would be. How could knowledge of the level of DM you are in help the marketer who wishes to target marketing communications toward you?

3. Explain which learning stage the typical consumer would be in for the products in Exhibits 3.9 to 3.12. What does this suggest for the nature of each advertiser's marketing communications?

Is each ad "on track" in terms of content and style for consumers in this learning stage? Can you suggest improvements in any of the ads to better appeal to consumers at that learning stage?

EXHIBIT 3.9   Prevnar Ad

EXHIBIT 3.10   Maxwell House Ad

EXHIBIT 3.11   Dove Ad

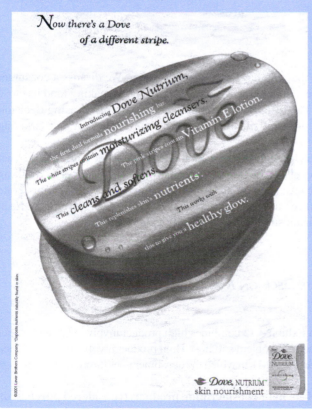

EXHIBIT 3.12   StarBand. Ad

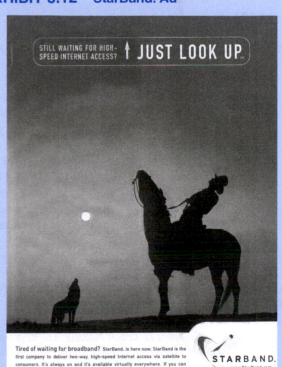

WRITTEN APPLICATIONS

1. Answer Question 2 in the In-Class Applications, replacing "you" in Question 2 with "college students in general." Do this by taking a survey of at least ten students at your university (or ten other individuals from a similar age group), replacing "you" in the question with "people of age __." Describe the typical consumer's learning stage for each product as well as any exceptions, i.e., any respondents whose learning stages are different from most. What factors account for any such differences?

2. Answer Question 3 in the In-Class Applications for the ads. Be sure to explain who you believe is the "typical consumer" for each ad, and check your assumptions by discussing the ad with one or more of these people where feasible.

3. Find three other ads, each targeting people at a particular stage in the levels of DM (each ad's product should correspond to a different stage). Repeat the analysis in Question 3 in the In-Class Applications for each ad.

EXERCISE 3.6. TYPES OF CONSUMER PURCHASING SITUATIONS

OBJECTIVES

1. To help you recognize the most common types of consumer buying situations by linking the concepts of product involvement and the consumer's level of decision making (DM).
2. To give you insight into the most effective marketing strategies for customers in each purchasing situation.
3. To familiarize you with the nature of brand loyalty and how it is measured.
4. To give you practice in recognizing different purchase decision situations in ads and scenarios.

BACKGROUND

OVERVIEW OF CONSUMER PURCHASE DECISION SITUATIONS

This exercise pulls together all of the material that you have read in this chapter. We discuss a consumer decision-making paradigm that combines product involvement and level of decision making (and its close correlate, the level of purchase involvement). The result is six common **consumer purchasing decision (decision making) situations**. Each purchase decision situation calls for a particular type of marketing program.

Exhibit 3.13 presents a paradigm of consumer decision-making situations based on the degree of product involvement and the consumer's level of DM (level of purchase involvement). There are four cells resulting from dichotomizing each dimension into two levels: high versus low product involvement; high/moderate information search (high purchase involvement) versus low search/habit (low purchase involvement). Each cell contains one or two types of purchase decision situations, for a total of six types.

SIX TYPES OF CONSUMER PURCHASE DECISION SITUATIONS

CELL 1: HIGH PRODUCT INVOLVEMENT, HIGH-TO-MODERATE DECISION MAKING/ PURCHASE INVOLVEMENT

Complex Decision Making. The upper-left cell in Exhibit 3.13 combines high product involvement with either extended DM (complex DM) or limited DM (repeated problem solving). High product involvement combined with extended DM yields **complex decision making (CDM),** in which the consumer goes through the five-stage consumer decision process.

Products typically bought under complex DM are **high-consideration products (considered purchases),**

EXHIBIT 3.13   Types of Consumer Purchasing Decision Situations

	High involvement	Low involvement	
High to moderate information search (EDM, LDM) and purchase involvement	Complex decision making (CDM) Repeated problem solving (RPS) (LDM)	Variety seeking (LDM) Impulse purchasing (LDM)	Little to moderate prior information and experience
Low search habit (RDM) and low purchase involvement	Brand loyalty	Inertia	Much prior information and experience

Level of Decision Making

Degree of Product Involvement

such as houses, cars, major appliances, consumer electronics, personal computers, and Internet services. Most are shopping goods and search goods.

Repeated Problem Solving (RPS). **Repeated problem solving (RPS)** entails high product involvement and limited DM. Buyers have some prior category knowledge and, perhaps, experience. They do a somewhat limited search for a different brand than previously bought for reasons such as dissatisfaction with earlier brands, discontinuation of brands, the entry of new brands, changes in marketing mixes of existing brands, or retail unavailability of favored brands.

In RPS, as in CDM, the entire five-stage decision procedure is carefully undertaken. However, in RPS (as in limited DM in general), the process is somewhat abbreviated, with fewer information sources, attributes, and alternatives typically being evaluated.

The marketer targeting CDM and RPS consumers should try to move them through each stage of the decision process, satisfying their extensive information needs and rationally convincing them of the superiority of the brand.

CELL 2: LOW PRODUCT INVOLVEMENT, HIGH-TO-MODERATE DECISION MAKING/ PURCHASE INVOLVEMENT

The cell in the top right corner of Exhibit 3.13 illustrates two situations where there is low product involvement but nonetheless high-to-moderate DM (purchase involvement). Some search and evaluation occurs despite low product involvement, suggesting limited DM.

This can occur in many situations, such as buying a gift, shopping with someone else and trying to impress them as a careful shopper, attempting to save money on an expensive albeit boring product like a vacuum cleaner, and teaching a child how to be a prudent shopper.

Besides these specific cases, there are two more general purchasing situations that fit cell 2: variety seeking and impulse buying.

Variety Seeking. **Variety (novelty)** seeking entails searching for something different from the previous purchase within the product category, such as new flavors of food, scents of cologne, or brands, even though the consumer has been satisfied with past varieties and brands bought.

Even if product involvement is low, consumers who are content with their most recent purchase are nonetheless more likely to seek variety and consequently become either variety seekers (who stick with their preferred brand but try out different versions of it) or brand switchers. Variety seeking is most likely to occur for frequently purchased hedonic products and occasional products—here today, gone tomorrow—such as fast-food feeders' rotating "limited time" sandwich specials that generate extra visits, promotional talking points, and brand buzz.

The marketing implication is to add variety to the product line through seasonal products or **product line extensions**. Seasonal items are only available at certain times of the year, such as seasonal brews (Oktoberfest beer). Product line extensions are additions to product lines sporting the existing brand name, such as new styles, colors, flavors, scents, ingredients, additives, performance levels, and so on.

Impulse Buying. Cell 2 also includes the **impulse (unplanned) purchase**, a spontaneous buying situation where neither problem recognition nor a buying intention in a particular product category existed prior to entering a store or visiting a Web site. The purchased brand differs from what the consumer originally planned (possibly including no planned purchase at all).

The impulse buy is a spur-of-the-moment act, usually triggered by some in-store (or Web site) stimulus, such as a product display, point-of-sale promotion, or a pop-up or search ad on the Internet. For instance, those wallet-friendly one-dollar DVDs dispensed by Redbox vending machines near checkout lines in supermarkets and Walmart trigger numerous impulse buys. Impulse purchasing is spontaneous (versus thoughtful), urgent (even compulsive), often emotional, and frequently made seeking instant gratification, with the consumer at times feeling out of control. Impulse purchases are most likely frequently purchased hedonic products.

Here, marketers should use in-store and on-location impulse triggers, notably point-of-purchase displays. Also, shelf placement is critical: The more shelf space a brand occupies, the more likely it is to be bought, and "eye level is buy level." In-store samples (e.g., perfume) can also induce an impulse purchase, as can see-through blister packaging for products such as digital mobile devices. This is known in some circles as the **behavioral influence perspective,** which uses environmental stimuli such as merchandising and packaging to modify CB. Impulse purchases can also be increased by building a *sticky Web site*, one that is able to attract repeat visitors and have them stay for extended time periods by providing useful information and entertainment.

CELL 3: HIGH PRODUCT INVOLVEMENT, LOW DECISION MAKING/PURCHASE INVOLVEMENT

Brand Loyalty Conceptualized. In the third cell of Exhibit 3.13 (bottom left corner), we find high product involvement combined with habitual purchase behavior, that is, low purchase involvement. The major reason is brand (customer) loyalty. This could be indicated by **behavioral brand loyalty**—repeat purchasing of a brand. For high-involvement, expensive, infrequently purchased durables, repeat purchase or customer retention is a valid measure of loyalty. For instance, the automobile industry averages loyalty rates of about 50 percent: One of two buyers repurchases the same brand of car. However, the word *loyalty* suggests more than just behavior: There is also **attitudinal (emotional) brand loyalty**, an emotional attachment and brand preference. Brand loyalty is preferential habitual buying: The consumer feels an emotional attachment to the brand, almost as if wedded to it ("It's my Tide." "That's my Luvs." You are tied to Tide, love Luvs, and are close to Close-Up). Mac users are not called the "Mac faithful" for nothing.

Consequently, **brand (customer) loyalty** is preferential attitudinal and behavioral responses toward one or more brands in a product category expressed by a decision-making unit (an individual or household) over time. It involves repeat purchase behavior due to a positive attitude toward or preference for the brand. In addition, **multibrand loyalty (brand cluster loyalty)** occurs when a consumer is loyal to more than one brand in a category. Usually this is for reasons of variety seeking while remaining "true blue" to the preferred brand.

It is also possible for consumers to be **company loyal**, having favorable attitudinal and behavioral responses toward a firm and its various offerings. Nike has a loyal following and so has branched out from running shoes to all sorts of sports apparel. Similarly, customers can be **store loyal**, having favorable attitudinal and behavioral responses toward a retailer and its various offerings. Retail gift cards have become a lure for attracting and retaining new customers.

Reasons for Brand Loyalty. People become brand loyal for several reasons:

- The favored brand better satisfies consumers' needs and wants than competitive options do.
- Reduction of perceived risk. High-involvement products usually have important perceived risks. Sticking with a favorite brand enhances certainty, thereby reducing perceived risk.
- To simplify DM. Brand loyalty is the path of least resistance. This is a weaker reason, however, since inertia (cell 4 discussed below) also makes buying easier.
- Maintenance of self-image. Brand image can reinforce the consumer's self-concept ("I'm a Ford Mustang kind of guy").

Measuring Brand Loyalty. Brand loyalty can be measured using behavioral research such as scanner data. This information, which is captured at the point of sale, can measure a decision-making unit's (not just an individual's but also a household's) proportion of purchases within a category devoted to particular brands (e.g., 60 percent of the time brand Q is bought and 40 percent of the time the infamous brand X is purchased). This provides a measure known as the brand's **share of category requirements**.

Brand loyalty can also be assessed for frequently bought items by brand-choice sequences. For example, Miss Frump buys brand F this week, brand F next week, followed in subsequent weeks by brands Z, F, Z, Y, and F. For infrequently bought products such as cars, one subsequent repeat purchase might indicate loyalty.

Another behavioral measurement of customer loyalty is the length of time a customer has been buying a brand. A shopper who has been purchasing a brand regularly for ten years would be considered more loyal than one who has been doing so for four years.

However, relying on behavioral data alone is inadequate because it might only measure **spurious loyalty,** behavior that resembles brand loyalty but is not genuine loyalty caused by both true brand preference and regular buying. Rather, it is merely **repeat purchase behavior (behavioral brand loyalty)**, buying a brand repeatedly due to factors such as indifference, convenience, low price, or unavailability of the preferred brand (versus brand preference). Consequently, in addition to behavioral data, marketers should also collect attitudinal or preference data such as measures of customer satisfaction, intent to repurchase, and **brand advocacy**, a measure of attitudinal loyalty that entails planning to recommend or recommending the brand to others. Brand advocacy can be measured simply by asking customers how likely they are to recommend a specific brand to a friend. Such customers can be leveraged to drive word-of-mouth campaigns (see Exercise 10.2).

A relatively recent measurement of brand advocacy (and, hence, customer loyalty) is the **net promoter score**, a measure of the relative number of advocates for the brand versus complainers against it. The idea is that the most loyal customers are willing to put their own reputations on the line when serving as brand advocates. The score is derived from one simple ten-point scale survey question: "How likely is it that you would recommend (Company X) to a friend or colleague?" Answers yield the percentage of brand promoters (scoring 9 or 10), indifferent customers (7 or 8), and detractors (0 to 6) who are chronic complainers about the firm. The net detractor score is derived by subtracting the detractor percentage from the promoter percentage. The average company scores between 5 and 10 percent, meaning promoters barely outnumber detractors.

Additionally, marketers can use **brand tradeoff analysis**, a measure of customer loyalty based on how large a price differential between the customer's favored brand and second-preferred brand offered at a lower price would induce that person to switch to the second-preferred brand. This is a measure of **cross elasticity of demand**, or how a change in the price of one alternative results in a change of sales in another (either a substitute, as here, or a complement).

The Importance of Brand-Loyal Customers. The ultimate marketing goal is to gain brand-loyal customers, that is, to create a **consumer brand franchise**. These valuable customers have the following characteristics:

- They are less price sensitive, willing to pay a premium price to obtain their preferred option. There is no need to bribe them with price deals (the exploitation potential argument).
- They are more likely to search elsewhere if their favored brand is out of stock ("Accept no substitute!"). Therefore, marketers do not need to incur the heavy expense associated with achieving intensive distribution, i.e., if the product does not have to be widely available (operating efficiency argument).
- They exhibit **competitive insulation**. This is the ability of a brand to resist the conquest marketing efforts of rivals who are attempting to win the brand's customers' favor through price promotions and persuasive promotion (competitive insulation argument). (Giving in to these flirtatious temptations is adultery!)
- They require less advertising and promotion to ensure their repeat patronage (operating efficiency argument).
- They are more inclined to be brand advocates (brand evangelists), spreading the brand gospel to others, thereby reducing promotional costs associated with attracting new customers (goodwill argument).
- They tend to buy more often, in greater quantities, and remain customers longer.
- They are more likely to buy licensed products. These goods carry a manufacturer's brand name or logo but are produced by other firms that pay the manufacturer royalties on sales.
- They are more prone to procure product line extensions and brand franchise extensions, items in other product categories featuring the same brand name (e.g., Compaq Internet appliances, Neutrogena shampoo; brand extensions argument).
- They generate lower transactions costs associated with activities such as handling returns, reworking defective items, and managing complaints (customer efficiency argument).
- They are more motivated and willing to provide feedback to marketers.
- They might invest in a company's stock.

Strategies for Gaining Brand-Loyal Customers. Since nurturing brand-loyal customers is lucrative, astute marketers strive to develop a loyal base. The following are strategies for building a consumer brand franchise.

- Design a superior product and promote it as such.
- Use the risk relievers discussed in Exercise 3.5 to reduce perceived risk.
- Develop a strong brand image with which people either identify or to which they aspire.
- Use **loyalty marketing (continuity programs, frequent buyer programs, frequency marketing)**, which encourages repeat patronage by offering incentives and rewards such as accumulating points redeemable for prizes, instant discounts, and special privileges. Sales promotion programs like these build long-term customer relationships rather than merely encouraging short-term brand switching.
- Offer club marketing programs. Membership in some sort of semi-exclusive "club" is extended to regular customers (e.g., Burger King Kids' Club, Harley Davidson's Harleys Owners Group [HOG]), giving customers a sense of ownership.
- Use **affinity marketing**—affiliating with a special interest group to which customers are already loyal (e.g., credit cards co-branded with the name of a university).
- Create **switching costs**. These are psychological, physical, and economic expenses consumers will incur if they switch to a rival brand. Such costs include an investment in learning about the new brands (e.g., mastering a new computer operating system or how to quickly navigate through a store), developing a relationship with a different salesperson, or foregoing "preferred customer" benefits such as discounts and reward programs.
- Encourage children and teens to buy the product: "Get 'em while they're young and influential." (Candy cigarettes, anyone?) Companies that target college students are reaching them when they're making many purchasing decisions for the first time, choosing everything from soap to banking services. The result can be lifelong customers.
- Offer **bundled pricing (price packaging)**, a group of related products sold in a package where the total price of the component products is less than if each product were sold separately. For example, telephone, cable, and wireless companies vie for customer loyalty by offering packages that can include local telephone, long distance phone calls, cable TV, Internet access, cellular service, paging, and satellite service. This offers savings as well as the convenience of a single bill.

CELL 4: LOW PRODUCT INVOLVEMENT, LOW DECISION MAKING/PURCHASE INVOLVEMENT

The final cell in the bottom right corner of Exhibit 3.13 shows **inertia (repeat purchase, habitual buying)**, regularly purchasing the same brand (low decision making/purchase involvement) out of habit, convenience, or indifference (low product involvement). Like brand loyalty, this is **habitual buying**, regularly purchasing with little thought one or more brands in a given category. While brand loyalty occurs for more involving products, inertia occurs for low-involvement items. The reason for repeat patronage for a brand-loyal customer is commitment. In the case of inertia, habitual buying is the result of passive indifference or acceptance. The inert customer's goal is to simplify life: It just is not worth the time and effort to search for possible better alternatives. Convenience goods with minimal brand differences are typically bought through inertia.

One marketing implication of inertia is to make competitors' customers an "offer they can't refuse" so they switch to the seller's brand. Coupons, sweepstakes and contests, rebates, and other promotional offers can zap easily swayed customers out of their lazy, inert states. Also, repetitive consumer exposure to advertising cues such as slogans, jingles, and trade characters help keep the inert brand top-of-mind to ensure continued habitual purchase. Widespread distribution is also important because if the brand is unavailable the consumer will readily switch to another brand. A competitive price will also keep customers coming back for more.

REVIEW QUESTIONS

1. Name and describe each of the six types of consumer purchasing decision situations in terms of level of involvement and level of decision making as well as the consumer decision process. Suggest example products or buying scenarios for each.
2. Cite major marketing strategy implications for each of the six decision situations.
3. What is brand loyalty, what causes customers to become brand loyal, what are the different ways loyalty can be measured, why is it important for marketers to capture loyal customers, how can marketers do so, and how does brand loyalty differ from repeat purchase behavior?

IN-CLASS APPLICATIONS

1. Think of an example of a product and brand you have bought in each of the six purchasing decision situations: Did your level of product involvement and level of decision making match the paradigm in Exhibit 3.13 in each case? Was it the type of product you would ordinarily expect to be purchased in this buying situation? Why do you think you bought the product in this fashion (e.g., why did you buy impulsively)?

   Explain the marketing strategies that were used by competing brands to try to influence you in each case as well as how successful they were. Did the marketing strategies make sense in light of the purchasing situation in each case?

   What could a marketer of a competitive brand do to change the nature of the buying situation to work in his favor in each situation? For instance, how might a marketer move you from being brand loyal or from inertia with a competitive brand toward brand loyalty to at least trying the marketer's brand?
2. The concept of variety seeking suggests that a marketer should crank out more product variations. Yet some people complain about unnecessary product proliferation. They feel there is too much variety, which results in consumer confusion and superfluous and superficial differentiation. Do you agree? Is this situation good or bad for consumers?
3. The behavioral influence perspective used to trigger impulse purchases seems to try to manipulate consumers. Is this unethical? Does it invalidate consumer sovereignty?
4. Are each of the following consumers brand loyal? Explain how brand loyalty can be measured.
   → *Scenario A. Bobbi on the Bubble.* Bobbi buys Bubbles soap 70 percent of the time, Soapee soap 20 percent of the time, and the other 10 percent of her soap purchases go to Latherup soap.
   → *Scenario B. Check Out Meg's Chocolate Choices.* Meg procures Candee bar chocolate today, Yumee Nums wafer bar tomorrow, Candee bar for each of the next two days, then Twinkles chocolate drops.

She finishes the week with a Candee bar. She repeats the pattern over the next two weeks, except she skips one day for Lent (Meg has low willpower).

→ *Scenario C. Jack's Snacks.* Jack has purchased Snackie Crackie cereal the last dozen times he's ventured to the Super Duper Shop and Drop store. He's been willing to pay the 15- to 25-cent premium they charge over his next favorite brand, Banana Wackies. Today, Banana Wackies offered a one-dollar-off coupon to Jack, and he took the bait.

→ *Scenario D. Mac Names That Tuna.* Mac says he is very satisfied overall with his recent purchase of Teennee Tinee tuna fish. He rates it a 6 or 7 using a 7-point scale (7 = very satisfied) on each of 8 attributes.

5. Which of the six purchasing situations applies to each of the products advertised in Exhibits 3.14 to 3.18? Does each ad effectively appeal to consumers in that type of purchasing situation? Explain. What other marketing strategies could be used to appeal to consumers in this buying situation?

WRITTEN APPLICATIONS

1. Answer In-Class Applications Question 1. Then, for each of the six products you discussed, ask someone else how they went about making a purchase decision for that product. Classify each of their purchase processes into one of the six purchasing decision situations. For people who were in a decision-making situation different from yours, explain what factors account for the difference.

2. Answer In-Class Applications Question 5.

3. Find an advertisement for a product that is typically bought in each of the six purchase situations in Exhibit 3.13. Does each ad effectively appeal to consumers in that type of purchasing situation? Explain.

What other marketing strategies could be used to appeal to consumers in this buying situation?

EXHIBIT 3.14   Hilton Ad

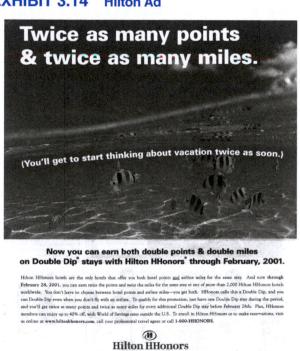

EXHIBIT 3.15   Pepto-Bismol Ad

EXHIBIT 3.16   Adobe Ad

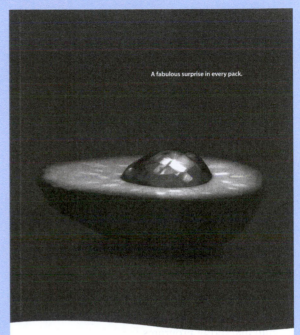

EXHIBIT 3.17   Quaker Oatmeal Ad

EXHIBIT 3.18   Purina Ad

KEY CONCEPTS

affective involvement

affinity marketing

alternative evaluation

altruism

attitudinal (emotional) brand loyalty

behavioral brand loyalty (purchase brand loyalty)

behavioral economics

behavioral influence perspective

beliefs

bounded rationality

brand advocacy

brand attitude

brand (customer) loyalty

brand franchise extensions (brand expansions)

brand tradeoff analysis

brand-attribute information

bundled pricing (price packaging)

buying (purchase) intention

club marketing programs

cognitive involvement

command system (socialism, collectivism, statism, centrally planned economies, command economies)

company loyal

competitive insulation

complex decision making (CDM)

consumer brand franchise

consumer decision

consumer decision-making process

consumer purchasing decision situations (decision making)

convenience goods

credence attributes

credence goods

cross elasticity of demand

customer review sites

e-commerce

economic system

economics

economy

effort risk

ego involvement

ego risk

emotion

engagement

evoked (consideration, choice, decision) set

experience attributes

experience goods

extended decision making (EDM) (extended problem solving, extensive DM, extensive problem solving, complex DM, midrange problem solving, considered purchases)

extended warranties

external (environmental) search

financial (economic, monetary) risk

free market

habitual buying

high-consideration products (considered purchases)

hyperlinks (links)

impulse (unplanned) purchase

inertia (repeat purchases, habitual buying)

information

information search

internal search

Internet

involvement

latent (subconscious, covert) problems (needs)

level of decision making (consumer's learning stage)

limited decision making (LDM; limited problem solving)

loyalty marketing (continuity programs, frequent buyer programs, frequency marketing)

macroeconomics

market economy (laissez faire, capitalist, or free enterprise system)

marketing

m-commerce

mediating (contingency) variables

message-response involvement (advertising involvement)

microeconomics

mixed economy

mobile marketing (mobile commerce, m-commerce)

multibrand loyalty (brand cluster loyalty)

navigational tools

neoclassical microeconomic model of consumer decision making

net promoter score

nonbuying (nonfunctional) shopping motives

normative (prescriptive, evaluative)

obsolescence risk

opportunity cost

optimal decisions

perceived risk

performance (functional) risk

physical (safety) risk

positive (descriptive)

(continued)

KEY CONCEPTS *(continued)*

postpurchase behavior (postpurchase outcomes)

primary (generic) demand

primary (generic) demand advertising

problem recognition (need recognition, need arousal)

problem-solution (problem-resolution) advertising

product involvement

product line extensions

psychological risk

purchase decision

purchase situation

purchase situation involvement (decision involvement)

rational

rationality

repeat purchase behavior (behavioral brand loyalty)

repeated problem solving

risk averse

risk-reduction strategies (RRSs)

risk relievers

routine decision making (RDM; routine problem solving, nominal DM, habitual DM, routinized response behavior, routine buying behavior, programmed decisions)

satisfice

search attributes

search engines

search goods

secondary (selective, brand) demand

secondary (selective, brand) demand advertising

self-ego

self-image (self-concept)

self-interested

semantic differential scales

share of category requirements

shopping goods

social risk

sovereign

specialty goods

spurious loyalty

sticky Web site

store loyal

switching costs

time risk

user-generated (created) content value

value

value proposition

value-expressive products

variety (novelty) seeking

Web (home, start, welcome) pages

World Wide Web

SUMMARY

This chapter introduced the consumer decision-making process, which might be truncated where there is either a low degree of involvement and/or a low level of decision making. Exercise 3.1 examined consumer decision making (DM) from the economics perspective. The difference between microeconomics and macroeconomics was discussed. Economics provides the foundation for marketing. Three systems for organizing economic activity are (1) the command system, (2) the market economy, and (3) a mixed economy.

The microeconomic model of CDM analyzes consumer demand to determine what goods people buy, in what quantities, and at what prices. Consumers purchase to maximize their utility within the constraints of a financial budget, so they must be pragmatic or utilitarian. Microeconomics also assumes that people make optimal decisions. However, the microeconomic theory of the individual consumer is normative, not positive, with the following highly questionable assumptions:

- Rationality. Bounded rationality suggests there are inherent limits on rational thought and DM. Rather than behaving optimally, consumers satisfice, as in the cases of impulse purchasing, brand loyalty, brand switching, and emotional purchasing.
- Self-interest. One exception for self-interest is altruism.
- Perfect and costless information.
- Sovereign consumers. However, buyers can be influenced by marketing efforts.

The economic model suggests the importance of offering consumers a value proposition.

Exercise 3.2 overviewed the consumer decision process and consumer decisions. The stages and marketing implications of each stage are as follows:

1. Problem recognition. Develop a product superior to competitors' for solving consumers' problems, and use problem-solution advertising. Making consumers aware of latent problems is not the same as creating desires.
2. Information search. Search for information includes (a) internal search, suggesting marketers use memorable promotional efforts and ascertain that consumers' brand experiences are positive, and (b) external search, implying marketers know their customers' search habits and provide them with the correct amount and type of information, determine preferred sources of information, and promote the product through the appropriate channels.
3. Alternative evaluation. Consumers decide the relative importance of evaluative criteria used to compare alternatives, evaluating brands in their evoked sets. This leads to formulation of beliefs, resulting in brand attitudes and buying intentions. Marketers should focus on developing products that yield excellent performance on the most important criteria and promoting the brand's excellent performance on those criteria.
4. Choice. As a result of unanticipated circumstances, the brand gaining the most positive attitude and purchase intention is not always bought. Marketers should use in-store merchandising and catchy packaging, and own or be linked to Web sites where purchasing is easy.
5. Postpurchase behavior. These outcomes should be monitored in terms of customer satisfaction, postpurchase dissonance, and other postpurchase behaviors on which to capitalize.

In Exercise 3.3 CDM on the Internet using navigational tools was described and experienced firsthand. There are several advantages as well as limitations to shopping online. One issue is lack of fulfillment of nonbuying (nonfunctional) shopping motives.

Exercise 3.4 introduced involvement, which is measured using semantic differential scales. Unless the level of decision making (DM) is low, consumers who are highly involved with a product and/or with its purchase are motivated to search out and process marketplace information.

Types of involvement classified by the type of need satisfied by the product are cognitive involvement and affective involvement. A high level of cognitive involvement means consumers make a rational, informed choice and search a lot. A high level of affective involvement means consumers can have intense feelings for value-expressive products, which entail ego involvement and self-concept.

Types of involvement classified by the object of involvement are product involvement, purchase situation involvement, and message-response (advertising) involvement. Where product involvement and/or purchase involvement is high, so is message involvement. Advertising involvement is measured by engagement, something marketers try to raise using techniques such as directing consumers to a Web site to interact with or even create ads as well as user-generated (created) content. Advertising media differ in the extent to which they involve consumers.

There are three general mediating factors that determine the degree of involvement:

1. The product. Classified by consumer shopping habits, these include shopping goods, specialty goods (both tend to be high involvement), and convenience goods (usually low involvement). A product can also be categorized as search goods (generally high involvement), experience goods (usually moderate or low involvement), and credence goods (typically fairly high involvement).
2. The consumer. Personal characteristics such as values and interests influence a person's product involvement.
3. The purchase situation. Purchase involvement is short term and situational. Buyers might be involved with the purchase of a product but not the product itself.

Involvement is also a function of perceived risk, which is a determined by uncertainty about possible negative consequences and the importance to the consumer of undesirable outcomes. Perceived risk is caused by risk averseness. Marketers' risk relievers include providing product information to reduce uncertainty and offering guarantees and warranties to lessen negative consequences. The appropriate risk reliever depends on a number of consumer risk reduction strategies (RRSs), which can reduce either potential negative consequences or uncertainty.

Types of perceived risk, each of which is more likely for certain kinds of consumers and products, are financial risk, social risk, ego risk (based on ego involvement), performance risk, physical risk, psychological risk, time risk, effort risk, and obsolescence risk.

Exercise 3.5 investigated the level of DM, which is based on someone's extent of prior information and experience about both the product category and its brands. Customers at a high (low) level of DM give extensive (little) thought, search, and time to the purchase decision. Consumers at a high (low) level of DM exhibit high (low) purchase involvement. While the level of DM correlates with purchase involvement, it does not always vary directly with product involvement. There can be high (low) product involvement and low (high) DM.

Consumers in extended decision making (EDM) have little or no prior knowledge of and experience with the product class and its brands. These consumers perform extensive searches. A marketer targeting such customers should build primary (generic) demand while also encouraging secondary (selective, brand) demand, assist consumers in framing DM so as to favor the seller, and use salespeople and customer service personnel to aid customers.

Consumers in limited decision making (LDM) have familiarity and perhaps experience with the product class and one or more of its brands. However, they require additional brand-attribute information, such as in repeated problem solving, usually either leading to brand switching or variety seeking. Such consumers seek brand-attribute information, but sometimes they use decision heuristics. Marketers pursuing these shoppers should build secondary demand and focus on physical and psychological brand differentiation.

Customers in routine decision making (RDM) try to simplify the buying process by routinely purchasing one or a limited repertoire of brands, as in the programmed decision scenarios of brand loyalty and inertia. Marketers targeting these buyers should run reminder and reinforcement advertisements, offer sales promotions, seek out new distribution channels, and provide other marketing innovations to keep customers in RDM returning to the brand.

Exercise 3.6 combined the dimension of the level of product involvement (high versus low) with the level of DM (purchase involvement; high versus low) to yield a four-cell matrix containing six general types of consumer purchasing decision situations (see Exhibit 3.13). Each has particular strategy implications. The high product involvement–high level of DM cell includes complex decision making (CDM) for high-consideration products and repeated problem solving (RPS).

The low product involvement–high DM cell includes: first, variety seeking for frequently purchased hedonic products and temporary occasional products, the need for which can be satisfied through product line extensions, and second, impulse purchasing, suggesting marketers use the behavioral influence perspective.

The high product involvement–DM cell includes brand loyalty (attitudinal and behavioral) and sometimes multibrand loyalty. Some types of products are more likely to capture brand loyalty than others, and people become brand loyal for several reasons. Brand loyalty can be measured using behavioral research such as scanner data. These data can capture the brand's share of category requirements, brand-choice sequences, and length of time a consumer has been buying a brand. However, behavioral data might merely indicate spurious loyalty or repeat purchase behavior. In order to capture the attitudinal component, researchers should also collect attitudinal or preference data such as measures of customer satisfaction, intent to repurchase, brand advocacy as measured by the net promoter score, and brand trade-off analysis to determine cross-elasticity of demand.

There are several reasons why a consumer brand franchise is valuable, including competitive insulation. Strategies to gain brand-loyal customers include using loyalty marketing, club marketing programs, and affinity marketing; creating switching costs; and offering bundled pricing, among others.

The final DM cell is high product involvement—low DM cell: inertia.

REFERENCES

Ainscough, Thomas L., and Luckett, Michael G. (1996). "The Internet for the Rest of Us: Marketing on the World Wide Web." *Journal of Consumer Marketing,* 13, 2, 36–47.

Andrews, J. Craig, and Durvasula, Srinivas. (1990). "A Framework for Conceptualizing and Measuring the Involvement Construct in Advertising Research." *Journal of Advertising,* 19, 4, 27–40.

Ariely, Dan. (2008). *Predictably Irrational: The Hidden Forces That Shape Our Decisions.* New York: Harper Collins.

Arnold, Mark J., and Reynolds, Kristy E. (2003). "Hedonic Shopping Motivations." *Journal of Retailing,* 79, 77–95.

Back, Ki-Joom. (2003). "A Brand Loyalty Model Involving Cognitive, Affective, and Conative Brand Loyalty and Customer Satisfaction." *Journal of Hospitality and Tourism Research,* 27, 4, 419–443.

Bauer, Raymond A. (1960). "Consumer Behavior as Risk Taking." In R.S. Hancock, ed., *Proceedings of the American Marketing Association.* Chicago: American Marketing Association, 389–398.

Baumol, William J., and Blinder, Alan S. (1998). *Macroeconomics: Principles and Policy,* 7th ed. Fort Worth, TX: Dryden Press.

Becker, Gary S. (1962). "Irrational Behavior and Economic Theory." *Journal of Political Economy,* 70, 1, 1–13.

———. (1965). "A Theory of the Allocation of Time." *Economic Journal,* 40, 299 (September), 493–450.

Belch, Michael A., and Willis, Laura A. (2002). "Family Decision at the Turn of the Century: Has the Changing Structure of Households Impacted the Family Decision-Making Process?" *Journal of Consumer Behaviour,* 2, 2, 111–124.

Belk, Russell W. (1975). "Situational Variables and Consumer Behavior." *Journal of Consumer Research,* 2, 3, 157–164.

Bettman, James R. (1973). "Perceived Risk and Its Components." *Journal of Marketing Research,* 10, 2, 184–190.

Brafman, Ori, and Brafman, Rom. (2008). *Sway: The Irresistible Pull of Irrational Behavior.* New York: Doubleday.

Breitenbach, Craig S., and Van Doren, Doris C. (1998). "Value-Added Marketing in the Digital Domain: Enhancing the Utility of the Internet." *Journal of Consumer Marketing,* 15, 5, 558–575.

Buchanin, Mark. (2007). *The Social Atom.* London: Bloomsbury Publishing.

Copeland, Melvin T. (1923). "Relation of Consumers' Buying Habits to Marketing Methods." *Harvard Business Review,* 1 (April), 282–289.

Cox, Donald F., ed. (1967). *Risk Taking and Information Handling in Consumer Behavior.* Boston: Division of Research, Graduate School of Business Administration, Harvard University.

Crawford, Merle, and Di Benedetto, Anthony. (2008). *New Products Management,* 9th ed. Boston: McGraw-Hill.

Curtin, Richard T. (1982). "Indicators of Consumer Behavior: The University of Michigan Surveys of Consumers." *Public Opinion Quarterly,* 46, 340–352.

Duffy, Dennis L. (2003). "Internal and External Factors Which Affect Consumer Loyalty." *Journal of Consumer Marketing,* 20, 5, 480–485.

———. (2005). "The Evolution of Customer Loyalty Strategy." *Journal of Consumer Marketing,* 22, 5, 284–286.

Feather, Frank. (2000). *FutureConsumer.com: The Webolution of Shopping to 2010.* Toronto: Warwick Publishing.

Gigerenzer, Gerd, and Selten, Reinhard. (2001). *Bounded Rationality.* Cambridge: MIT Press.

Gladwell, Malcolm. (2005). *Blink: The Power of Thinking Without Thinking.* New York: Back Bay Books.

Harford, Tim. (2008). *The Logic of Life.* New York: Random House.

Hausman, Angela. (2000). "A Multi-level Investigation of Consumer Motivations in Impulse Buying Behavior." *Journal of Consumer Marketing,* 17, 5, 403–429.

Heyne, Paul A. (1997). *The Economic Way of Thinking,* 8th ed. New York: Macmillan.

Hirschman, Elizabeth C., and Wallendorf, Melanie. (1980). "Some Implications of Variety Seeking for Advertising and Advertisers." *Journal of Advertising,* 9, 2, 17–19.

Jacoby, Jacob, and Chestnut, Robert. (1978). *Brand Loyalty: Measurement and Management.* New York: Wiley.

Jacoby, Jacob, and Kyner, David B. (1973). "Brand Loyalty vs. Repeat Purchasing Behavior." *Journal of Marketing Research,* 10, 1, 1–9.

Jaillet, Helene F. (2003). "Web Metrics: Measuring Patterns in Online Shopping." *Journal of Consumer Behaviour,* 2, 4, 369–381.

Joines, Jessica L., Scherer, Clifford W., and Scheufele, Dietram A. (2003). "Exploring Motivations for Consumer Web Use and Their Implications for e-Commerce." *Journal of Consumer Marketing,* 20, 2, 90–108.

Katona, George. (1974). "Psychology and Consumer Economics." *Journal of Consumer Research,* 1, 1, 1–8.

Levitt, Steven, and Dubner, Stephen. (2005). *Freakonomics: A Rogue Economist Explores the Hidden Side of Everything.* New York: HarperCollins.

Mowen, John C. (1988). "Beyond Consumer Decision Making." *Journal of Consumer Marketing,* 5, 1, 15–25.

Nelson, Philip. (1970). "Information and Consumer Behavior." *Journal of Political Economy,* 78, 2, 311–329.

———. (1974). "Advertising as Information." *Journal of Political Economy,* 82, 4, 729–754.

Nicosia, Francesco. (1966). *Consumer Decision Processes.* New York: Prentice-Hall.

Olshavsky, Richard W., and Granbois, Donald H. (1979). "Consumer Decision Making—Fact or Fiction?" *Journal of Consumer Research,* 6, 2, 93–100.

Parsons, Andrew. (2002). "Brand Choice in Gift Giving: Recipient Influence." *Journal of Product and Brand Management,* 11, 4, 237–248.

Paul, Pallab. (1996). "Marketing on the Internet." *Journal of Consumer Marketing,* 13, 4, 27–39.

Quester, Pascale, and Lim, Ai Lin. (2003). "Product Involvement/Brand Loyalty: Is There a Link?" *Journal of Product and Brand Management,* 12, 1, 22–38.

Reichheld, Frederick. (2003) "The One Number You Need to Grow." *Harvard Business Review,* 81, 12, 1–9.

Rook, Dennis W. (1987). "The Buying Impulse." *Journal of Consumer Research,* 14, 2, 174–188.

Roselius, Ted. (1971). "Consumer Rankings of Risk Reduction Strategies." *Journal of Marketing,* 35, 1, 56–61.

Rowley, Jennifer, and Dawes, Jillian. (2006). "Disloyalty: A Closer Look at Nonloyals." *Journal of Consumer Marketing,* 17, 6, 538–549.

Rubinstein, Ariel. (1998). *Modeling Bounded Rationality.* Cambridge, MA: MIT Press.

Schwartz, Barry. (2004). *The Paradox of Choice: Why More Is Less,* New York: Ecco.

Sen, Amartya. (1987) "Rational Behavior." In J. Eatwell, M. Millgate, and P. Newman (eds.), *The New Palgrave Dictionary of Economics.* London and Basingstoke: Macmillan.

Sheth, Jagdish, and Venkatesan, N. (1968). "Risk Reduction Processes in Repetitive Consumer Behavior." *Journal of Marketing Research,* 5, 3, 307–310.

Silvera, David H., Lavack, Anne M., and Kropp, Fredric. (2008). "Impulse Buying: The Role of Affect, Social Influence, and Subjective Well-Being." *Journal of Consumer Marketing,* 25, 1, 23–33.

Simon, Herbert A. (1957). "A Behavioral Model of Rational Choice." *Quarterly Journal of Economics,* 69, 2, 99–118.

———. (1982). *Models of Bounded Rationality* (3 vols.). Cambridge, MA: MIT Press.

———. (1983). *Reason in Human Affairs.* Stanford: Stanford University Press.

Slama, Mark E., and Tashchian, Armen. (1985). "Selected Socioeconomic and Demographic Characteristics Associated with Purchasing Involvement." *Journal of Marketing,* 49, 1, 72–82.

Strahilevitz, Michal, and Myers, John G. (1998). "Donations to Charity as Purchase Incentives: How Well They Work May Depend on What You Are Trying to Sell." *Journal of Consumer Research,* 24, 4, 434–446.

Tauber, Edward. (1972). "Why Do People Shop?" *Journal of Marketing,* 36, 1, 46–59.

Van Raaij, Fred. (1981). "Economic Psychology." *Journal of Economic Psychology,* 1, 1–24.

Wood, Stacy L., and Moreau, Page C. (2006). "From Fear to Loathing? How Emotion Influences the Evaluation and Early Use of Innovations." *Journal of Marketing,* 70, 3, 44–57.

Zaichkowsky, Judith Lynne. (1985). "Measuring the Involvement Construct in Marketing." *Journal of Consumer Research,* 12, 3, 341–352.

ORGANIZATION OF CHAPTER FOUR

This chapter investigates in more detail each of the five phases of the consumer decision process used by highly involved, relatively uninformed, inexperienced consumers. It focuses on how marketers can influence consumer decisions at each stage. Exercise 4.1 begins with the first stage, problem recognition, to learn about its determinants. The next phase, information search, is then investigated in Exercise 4.2, focusing on the degree to which consumers search and the sources of information they seek.

Then, alternative evaluation is analyzed in Exercises 4.3, 4.4, and 4.5 to see the various types of evaluative criteria and decision rules consumers use to consider and compare alternatives. In Exercise 4.6 the decision-making stage is covered to learn of the influences on consumer choices, both in a traditional retail setting as well as in a virtual retail environment. In Exercise 4.7 the important postpurchase outcomes phase is reviewed, including concepts of relationship marketing, customer satisfaction, and dissonance.

EXERCISE 4.1. PROBLEM RECOGNITION

OBJECTIVES

1. To understand the nature of the problem recognition stage and factors triggering it.
2. To learn how marketers can successfully use new product development and advertising to move consumers through this stage.
3. To gain experience developing product ideas and advertisements by using problem analysis.
4. To identify appeals to problem recognition in ads and Web sites.
5. To form an opinion on the controversial issue of whether marketers create consumer problems and cause people to buy things they do not need.

BACKGROUND

CONSUMER BEHAVIOR AS PROBLEM SOLVING

Marketers usually view consumers as conscious problem solvers seeking to satisfy their needs and wants. **Problem solving** is the process whereby consumers take thoughtful, reasoned action to find a solution to satisfy their needs, where the solution is purchase of a product. As a wise marketing sage once observed, "Consumers don't purchase products—they buy solutions to their problems." Accordingly, a man buys charm and sophistication, not cologne; a woman purchases hope, not perfume.

THE FIRST PHASE—PROBLEM RECOGNITION

The first stage of consumer decision making (CDM) is appropriately called **problem recognition (need arousal, need state)**, which is the result of a consumer's unsolved problem or a felt (unsatisfied) need or

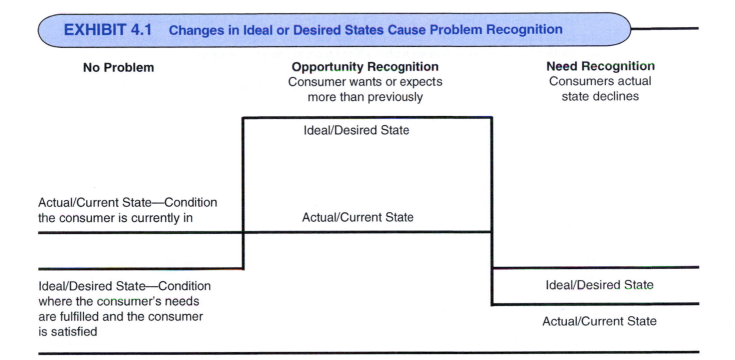

EXHIBIT 4.1   Changes in Ideal or Desired States Cause Problem Recognition

want. It involves a significant gap between a consumer's actual (current) state of affairs and the buyer's desired (ideal) state of affairs caused by an unsolved problem or an unsatisfied need or want. In the ideal state the consumer's needs are fulfilled and satisfaction is achieved. The consumer's goal: to close the gulf between the desired and actual states.

How Problem Recognition Arises

The gap between the actual and ideal circumstances can arise in two ways, as illustrated in Exhibit 4.1, via opportunity recognition or need recognition.

In **opportunity recognition**, the consumer's ideal state increases and that person wants and expects more than previously. Reasons why consumers "raise the bar" on their desires and expectations include:

- *Life circumstances change.* When you graduate college you will need to upgrade from sweatshirts, jeans, and baseball caps to a professional wardrobe and to trade in that seedy backpack for an elegant leather briefcase.
- *Individual development leads to changing needs.* A child eventually outgrows picture books and wants chapter books instead.
- *New products become available.* Once you watch high-definition TV, the old analog TV with the digital converter box will no longer do.
- *The purchase of one item creates the need for a related product.* When you purchase a DVD player, you need some DVDs to play in it.
- *What is "in" or "cool" changes.* New fashion items (e.g., clothing styles), trendy items (the hot "flavor of the month"), and even fad items (e.g., Emo music, Mentos and Coke).
- *New information reveals* the extent to which the actual conditions deviate from the desired circumstances, such as when a medical report in *The Journal of the American Medical Association* tells us that aspirin can help to prevent heart attack.
- *External stimuli.* Examples: the wonderful aroma wafting out of a bakery or pizzeria triggers a desire for their delicacies; a record store blasting the latest Breaking Benjamin CD makes one want to run in and buy it.

The discrepancy between the actual and desired states is also widened via **need recognition**, where the actual state declines. (Note that this particular use of the term *need recognition* is one type of problem recognition but is not synonymous with it.) Need recognition has several causes:

- Assortment depletion or wear and tear. Examples: running out of tissues, eggs, or milk; an old suit becomes threadbare.
- Becoming dissatisfied with one's current brand.
- A change in one's financial status. Examples: suffering a pay cut, inheriting a fortune from crazy Uncle Ernie.
- Boredom induces variety seeking.

MARKETING OPPORTUNITIES DURING THE PROBLEM RECOGNITION STAGE

NEW PRODUCT DEVELOPMENT

The first opportunity is to develop and launch new products that trigger problem recognition. The most successful new products are based on knowledge of unsatisfied needs and wants.

Problem-Based Ideation. The most fruitful way to develop new products is to use **problem-based ideation (problem-solution route, problem find–problem solve approach)**. The procedure involves discovering unsatisfied needs and wants and developing new products to satisfy them. Marketing research methodologies can be used to isolate problems. Techniques include customer satisfaction surveys, focus groups, in-depth interviews, user observation, complaint e-mails, and online community chatter.

Marketers then conceive, develop, test, and launch new products that better solve the problems or satisfy the desires than anything else currently offered in the marketplace. Product conception can involve individual creativity or using group ideation meetings, such as brainstorming sessions. Clorox found that consumers feared the harshness of bleach, wished to use it in spot applications, and were concerned that excess bleach could affect colors of other items in the wash. The user solution: Apply the bleach only where needed, have full control of the dosage, and have it in a convenient form that avoids skin contact. The marketer's creative product solution: the Clorox Bleach Pen.

Problem Analysis. One well-known approach to finding and solving problems is **problem analysis (problem detection, needs analysis)**. The procedure involves the following steps: (1) Determine an activity or product where consumers are believed to have unsatisfied needs or unsolved problems. (2) Use surveys or focus groups with target market consumers to gather a list of those needs and problems. (3) Employ creative thinking to generate product ideas to solve one or more of the problems on the list.

There are two types of problem analysis: activity analysis and product analysis. **Activity (process) analysis** focuses on a particular activity or process, such as washing the car, entertaining guests, or getting some exercise. Consumer research is used to ascertain what problems consumers experience while performing the activity, how severe or important each problem is, and the frequency of each problem's occurrence. Customers can also be asked to propose new product ideas that are solutions to the problems.

Product analysis uncovers problems that consumers associate with using a particular product, employing the same procedure as activity analysis. For example, consumer complaints about spaghetti being a messy food to eat may have led to the development of SpaghettiOs or even the electric fork!

OTHER MARKETING STRATEGY IMPLICATIONS OF PROBLEM RECOGNITION

Here are some other strategies enterprising marketers can use to capitalize on this stage:

- Launch complementary items for new products (software, supplies, maintenance products).
- Emphasize to customers the importance of staying on top of cutting-edge developments, such as recent fashions, trends, and fads related to products you produce.

- Make your new products socially visible to create opportunity recognition when people see others using the "latest and greatest." This can be done via loaning or giving products to popular people, holding special events built around the product, seeking customer referrals, or using social media such as Facebook pages, YouTube channels, or Twitter tweeters.
- Use **problem-solution (problem-resolution) advertising**, which raises a problem and dramatically demonstrates how the product solves it. For example, ads for Sherwin-Williams paint for kids' rooms addressed the problem of children getting their grimy paws all over the walls and offered a more stain-resistant paint. A variation of problem-solution advertising promotes a brand on the basis of problem prevention for so-called unsought goods, such as insurance, tires, or baby monitors.
- Employ primary (generic) demand advertising (e.g., "Pork—The other white meat").
- Utilize secondary (selective) demand advertising (e.g., "Brand Alpha beat Brand Beta two-to-one in taste tests").
- Use **consultative personal selling**. In this persuasive sales approach, salespeople are not merely order takers but rather probe deeply to find out what problems customers want to solve and then offer appropriate solutions.
- Pursue market segments with changing needs. Children and teens, college graduates, newlyweds, new parents, and newly retired people are all individuals whose new life circumstances cause problem recognition, be it for a companion of the opposite sex, a uniform for a new job, supplies for a newborn, or furniture for a down-sized home.
- Use **behavioral influence techniques**. Retail environmental stimuli and ecological design, such as merchandising and packaging, can induce need recognition and modify buying behavior. Supermarkets place the most frequently purchased products (e.g., milk, bread, and eggs) at the back of the store so customers must walk past hundreds of other tempting items on the way in and out. They position impulse items (candy, potato chips, etc.) where they are most likely to be seen by consumers: near checkout counters, at the ends of aisles, and at eye level on the shelves. Bars serve free salty snacks to stimulate thirst. To arouse hunger, fast-food restaurant signs liberally use the color orange, which has strong appetite appeal.

CAN PROBLEM RECOGNITION BE CREATED?

A controversial suggestion is to create "false" problems or unsatisfied needs and "wicked" wants through advertising and promotion, which can then be satisfied by the promoter's product. But is "creation of desires" really possible? Do ads and salespeople create problems such as "waxy yellow buildup," "houseitosis" (smelly house), and "dog breath"? Do ads manufacture a problem by saying something like, "The dirt you can't see"? Who knew they needed furniture perfume until Febreze debuted or oversized fleece blankets with sleeves until cheesy TV commercials flogged Snuggies? Do marketers sometimes offer solutions for invented problems? Are they selling us a bill of goods we do not want or need? If so, then we must deny the concept of consumer sovereignty and admit that we are all dupes at the hands of marketers.

However, the marketing concept suggests that needs and wants preexist products. Needs are not for products—products are for needs! Marketers do not create *wants*—they create *want satisfiers*! In each of the preceding examples, the wants must have existed before the product, perhaps below the surface of consciousness—*latent (subconscious, covert)* needs. For instance, the Snuggie solves the problem of the blanket slipping from your shoulders on cold winter nights.

Demand cannot be created. It can only be discovered via consumer research and then satisfied via marketing activities. The best evidence we have of this is the astronomical failure rate of new products, which ranges anywhere from 35 percent to 90 percent depending on the product market. If there was a formula for creating desires, surely all marketers would use it and thus never fail!

Consequently, the strategy recommendation is not to "create" needs but rather to make people aware of **latent (covert) problems** they had not given much thought to or were unaware of. Much public service advertising awakens problem recognition (e.g., "Friends don't let friends drive drunk"). The Oral B Indicator toothbrush, which changes color when it is worn out, heightened consumer awareness of the need to dispose of and replace old toothbrushes.

Consumer Activities Immediately Following Problem Recognition

Once people have recognized the problem, they can put the decision process on hold. The choice procedure is halted, either permanently or temporarily, due to (1) resource constraints on further action, such as limited time, money, energy, or mental capacity; (2) a decision to wait to buy for reasons such as a price drop or an improved version of the product coming out; or (3) the perception that the discrepancy between the actual and desired states is too small, making action unnecessary. For example, while an old article of clothing might appear somewhat worn out, it might be so comfortable that the owner does not much care about this problem.

The possible marketing opportunities in the problem recognition stage are to (1) help consumers alleviate constraints, such as through financing, saving consumers time by offering delivery, and making learning about the product easy through simple sales and promotional presentations; (2) convince customers that they should not postpone purchasing (e.g., advertising saying "Offer available while supplies last," or salespeople who use the *standing-room-only technique*—a suggestion that the product might be gone if prospects delay buying); or (3) point out the critical importance of the problem.

More commonly, the consumer decides against putting the decision process on hold and proceeds to the second stage, information search.

Review Questions

1. Define problem recognition, and identify and describe the two major causes of this stage.
2. Cite the major marketing opportunities suggested by the problem recognition stage.
3. Describe problem-based ideation.
4. What is problem analysis and what is its relationship to problem-based ideation? Outline the procedure used during problem analysis.
5. Why shouldn't marketers try to manufacture consumer problems for their products to solve?
6. Cite and describe the two possible outcomes in the decision process following problem recognition. What are the marketing implications of the hold outcome?

In-Class Applications

1. What unsolved consumer problems do college students typically have? What needs and wants of yours aren't fulfilled? Which of the various sources of opportunity recognition and need recognition are the source of your problems? Do you believe that there is a segment of consumers (other than college students) who share any of your problems? If so, describe this group.

   Does this suggest an idea for a new product or else an improved version of an existing product? If so, describe your new product concept in terms of three elements that often make up product concept statements (used to get consumer reactions to the idea): (1) the product form (i.e., physical attributes, what the product is); (2) its functions or uses and applications the product could serve (what the product does); and (3) delivered benefits (the product's satisfaction of consumer needs and wants). An example is a toothpaste (form) that whitens teeth (function) to make you attractive to the opposite sex (benefit).

2. Do you really agree with the marketers' argument that they can't create consumer problems but only solve existing problems? Or do you believe that marketers can manipulate consumer demand?

   Consider the following: (1) Oxygenated bottled water sales grew in the early 2000s, allegedly providing athletes with the oxygen needed for training and endurance. Yet experts have debated whether this drink really improves athletic performance. Did these marketers create a "false" need or "wicked" want? (2) A firm recently launched a diet pill for dogs that curbs a dog's appetite. But if dogs don't feed themselves, are weight-loss pills for canines really necessary? Why is this issue of creating false needs important for marketers? For legislators and government regulators?

3. How, if at all, could each of the following recently launched products satisfy needs or wants or solve problems:
   a. Giant Cheetos: These are like regular Cheetos, only they are the size of ping pong balls.
   b. Bubble Calendar: A four-foot tall wall calendar with Bubble-Wrap-like bubbles to pop for each day of the year.
   c. Oreo Fun Stix: Straw-shaped Oreos that can be used to drink milk.

4. Problem recognition can occur either through need recognition or opportunity recognition. Before class, visit each of the following Web sites and determine whether consumers would visit each site because of need recognition and/or opportunity recognition: eBay.com, jaguar.com, and netgrocer .com.

5. How does each of the advertisements in Exhibits 4.2 through 4.5 seem to be creating a marketing opportunity out of problem recognition? Specifically, how does each ad tap into need recognition, problem recognition, or latent needs? How does each ad use problem-solution advertising, advertising that creates awareness of needs, or some other technique to capitalize on the problem recognition stage?

WRITTEN APPLICATIONS

1. You are to develop a product concept using product analysis based on one of the research approaches previously discussed (customer satisfaction survey, focus group, in-depth interview, user observation, or online community chatter). Your problem analysis should either use product analysis or activity analysis to uncover consumer problems.

A survey sample should be limited to about ten target market members. A focus group should involve about six targeted consumers. In-depth interviews can be conducted with two or three people. Several users can be observed using a product in a natural setting. You can ask them questions if you wish. Another alternative is to explore any online communities or social networking sites that might be relevant for unearthing problems.

From your results, use creative thinking, either alone or with others, to develop a product concept, including product form, function(s), and benefit(s). If you want to get creative and add ideas for branding, packaging, logos, and the like, you have our blessing.

Finally, create one or more ads for at least one of these products, using one or more of the advertising formats related to problem recognition: ads tapping into the "latest and greatest" developments (trends, fashions, or fads), problem-solution advertising, primary demand advertising, or secondary demand advertising.

2. Answer Question 5 in the In-Class Applications above.

3. Find and discuss four more ads that tap into problem recognition differently than those in Exhibits 4.2 through 4.5.

EXERCISE 4.2. INFORMATION SEARCH

OBJECTIVES

1. To demonstrate the importance of internal information search and how marketers can influence consumers in this stage.
2. To give you practice in making effective marketing decisions regarding two important factors related to the external information search stage: (a) how much information to give consumers and (b) which sources of information to use in conveying this data to them, recognizing the strengths and limitations of each information source.
3. To reflect on your own internal search and external search activities and how marketing efforts influence them.

BACKGROUND

If a consumer decides to act on the recognized problem, he or she proceeds to the information search stage. **Information** is data that reduces uncertainty, thereby lowering perceived risk. Information can change an individual's beliefs regarding the desirability of a particular brand. **Information search** is the second stage of the consumer decision process, during which the consumer seeks marketplace information.

EXHIBIT 4.2   American Plastics Council Ad

EXHIBIT 4.3   Fidelity Investments Ad

EXHIBIT 4.4   Castrol GTX Ad

EXHIBIT 4.5   Remington Ad

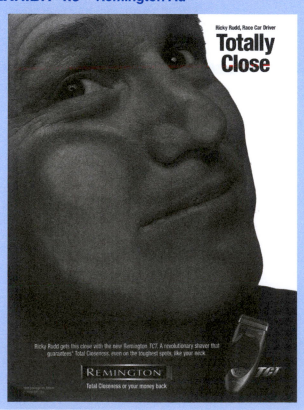

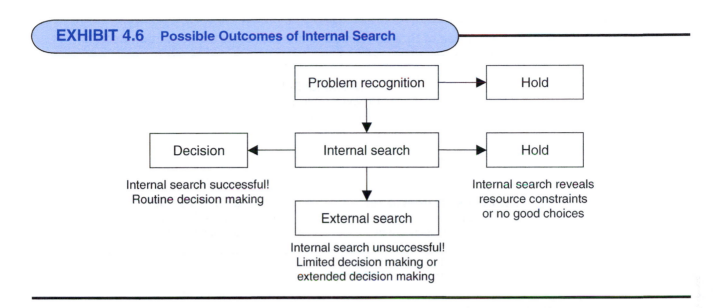

EXHIBIT 4.6   Possible Outcomes of Internal Search

Problem recognition → Hold

Decision ← Internal search → Hold

Internal search successful!
Routine decision making

Internal search reveals
resource constraints
or no good choices

Internal search ↓ External search

Internal search unsuccessful!
Limited decision making or
extended decision making

INTERNAL SEARCH

Internal search occurs following problem recognition and prior to external search. Here, consumers try to recall whether they have enough information to make an intelligent purchase decision, based on prior learning or personal product experience. Internal search occurs before external search since it consumes less time and money.

Exhibit 4.6 shows the three possible outcomes of internal search. This search will usually lead immediately to a purchase decision if the buyer is in routine DM. Here, the solution readily pops into the consumer's mind, who will likely buy the preferred option.

Alternatively, prior learning or personal experiences might inform a consumer that there are no alternatives worthy of consideration or that there are too many resource constraints—limited time, money, energy, or mental capacity for solving the problem. So, that person will put the decision process on either temporary or permanent hold.

Consumers start first with internal search, which is often the only kind of information search. Exhibit 4.7 provides an overview of types of brands residing in buyers' memories during internal search. At this time, consumers think about their **awareness set (retrieval set)**. This is the group of brands the buyer is aware of in the product category during internal search. These brands are retrieved from the **universal set**, which is composed of all brands in the product class.

An important subset of this awareness set is composed of brands considered as possible solutions to the problem, referred to as the **evoked (consideration, choice, decision) set**. This consists of brands that the shopper will consider, compare, and evaluate—alternatives that are "on the short list." This suggests that it is important for a brand to be regarded favorably. The positive memories can be built via unique promotional efforts (e.g., Verizon's Test Man), sales promotions (e.g., special events), and other creative marketing communications. If the memories are experience-based, marketers must ascertain that they are founded on a satisfactory product encounter stemming from high product quality and excellent need satisfaction.

Other brand groups in the awareness set are the **inert set**, brands in the awareness set toward which the buyer is indifferent, and the **inept set**, alternatives in the awareness set the consumer views as unacceptable. There is hope for a brand in the typical consumer's inert set. If the marketer is able to provide this shopper with convincing, favorable information or with a satisfactory free trial experience, then the brand could move into the buyer's consideration set. However, it is probably a lost marketing cause to attempt to move an inept brand into the consideration set through persuasion or trial because the consumer will be very skeptical and disinterested. To avoid this, an inept brand's marketer needs to discover sources of dissatisfaction and negative attitudes and then take corrective action to improve the product.

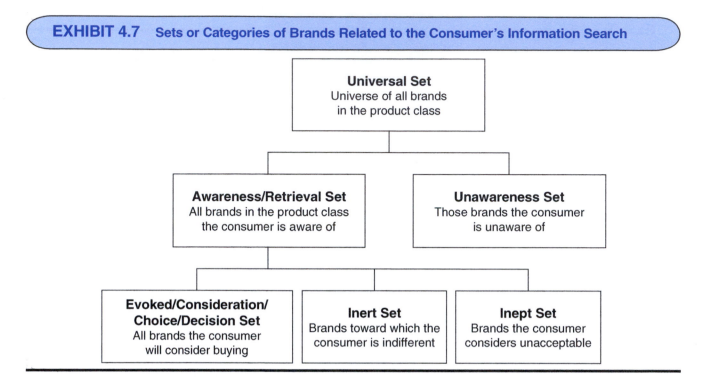

EXHIBIT 4.7   Sets or Categories of Brands Related to the Consumer's Information Search

OVERVIEW OF EXTERNAL SEARCH

If internal search reveals too much uncertainty to make a reasoned decision, the consumer enters **the external (environmental) search** stage, seeking information from the marketing environment. External searches are performed prior to purchase (**prepurchase search**). This is a goal-oriented search that follows problem recognition and is driven by a desire to acquire a want-satisfying or problem-solving product. This contrasts with **postpurchase search**, which is an external search that sometimes occur after purchase and use of the product for reasons such as reducing doubt and alleviating dissatisfaction.

There are two issues marketers need to consider during the information search stage: (1) the **degree of search**, how much consumers will search during an external search; and (2) the **direction of search**, which information sources they will use and the relative importance of each information source.

THE DEGREE OF SEARCH

Several variables determine the degree of external search:

1. Number of sources consulted (e.g., the number of stores or Web sites visited, the quantity of ads read)
2. Amount of information sought from each source
3. Total time spent searching
4. Number of alternatives evaluated (i.e., evoked set size)
5. Number of criteria used to appraise the options

The degree of prepurchase search is influenced by the extent of consumer involvement and the consumer's learning stage. A consumer will search more in high-involvement situations, where the benefits of search (e.g., perceived risk reduction) are relatively high. The less prior information and experience a consumer possesses (i.e., a higher level of DM), the more search is required. In extended DM situations, the benefits of search will be greatest since there is little existing consumer knowledge. The overriding

EXHIBIT 4.8   **Consumer Information Sources**

	Personal Sources	Nonpersonal Sources
Marketer-controlled/ Commercial Sources	Salespeople Trade shows Telemarketers Consumer hotlines	Media advertising Sales promotions Point-of-purchase Packaging
Nonmarketer-controlled/ Noncommercial Sources	Word of mouth Professional advice Personal experience	Publicity Neutral/independent sources

caution for marketers is that consumers do not necessarily prefer more information to less! Consequently, marketers should be selective in providing information.

THE DIRECTION OF SEARCH

The second major external search issue is the **direction of search** activity, that is, which information sources consumers use and the relative importance of each source. Exhibit 4.8 provides a taxonomy of consumer information sources. It employs two useful ways to classify them: personal versus impersonal and marketer versus nonmarketer (commercial versus noncommercial).

Personal sources are individuals with whom the consumer has direct, one-on-one contact, such as friends, family, colleagues, neighbors, and professionals, whereas nonpersonal sources are those that do not involve other people. The latter include mass media **advertising**, or any paid form of nonpersonal promotion by an identified sponsor making predominant use of the mass communication media; publicity, which is nonpaid, nonpersonal, newsworthy media exposure concerning a firm and its products; and neutral sources (usually unbiased) such as professional reviewers's new car reviews in the *New York Times* or *USA Today*, user reviews found on Web sites such as Amazon.com, government Web sites, and consumer review and information sites such as Yelp and Citysearch for reviews of restaurants and destinations, iLike for music recommendations, and Zillow for real estate information.

Marketer-controlled (commercial, advocate) sources originate with and are directed by the marketer, whereas non-marketer-controlled (noncommercial) sources stem from and are controlled by communicators other than marketers, such as friends, professionals, product users, and the media. The latter include neutral (independent) sources. Third-party information is provided to the general public in news editorials; consumer ratings publications such as *Consumer Reports;* product-focused magazines such as *Car and Driver;* shopping magazines such as *Lucky* and *Domino;* government and scientific reports on subjects such as health and diet (e.g., U.S. Surgeon General's reports); satisfaction ratings by organizations such as J.D. Power and Associates; and personal blogs. Many noncommercial sources are now available on line, such as Zagat's restaurant ratings and reviews and TripAdvisor reviews of hotels, restaurants, and attractions.

A lot of marketing activity is designed to stimulate nonmarketing information. One strategy entails targeting *opinion leaders*. These influential individuals are seen by their peers as product experts who provide reliable information (see Exercise 10.2). Other ways marketers stimulate noncommercial information transmission include targeting professional advisors, such as financial planners, auto mechanics, and home decorators; currying favorable media publicity; and setting up chat rooms on their Web sites.

MARKETING ADVANTAGES AND DISADVANTAGES OF CONSUMER INFORMATION SOURCES

In choosing an information source, marketers must know which sources consumers generally prefer for the their products. Additionally, sellers must consider that each of these general categories of information has communication advantages and disadvantages in terms of effectiveness (high communication that yields desired effects) and *efficiency* (low cost, both in total and per person reached).

Nonpersonal and Personal Sources. Usually, consumers use nonpersonal mass media sources to gain awareness of and information on a new or unfamiliar product. As buyers move closer to the decision to actually try and perhaps adopt a product, they lean more heavily on personal sources of information, such as friends and salespeople. Personal sources are also preferred where buyers lack competence to intelligently judge a product, such as high-tech items and professional services.

Marketing advantages for personal sources include high credibility and information that can be tailored to the recipient's information needs. Disadvantages include limited market reach and the higher cost (per person reached). Nonpersonal sources have the strengths of broad reach and efficiency (low per-person cost), countered by the weakness of providing nontailored information. This can result in a mass appeal that is less interesting and sought after, as well as being more annoying and intrusive.

Marketer-Controlled and Non-Marketer-Controlled Sources. Marketer-controlled sources allow control over what is said, as well as how, where, when, and how often it is said. However these commercial sources are less credible because they are biased, and total promotional expenses can be high (although, except for sales calls, they are usually low-cost on a per-person reached basis).

Non-marketer-controlled sources provide more credibility due to their perceived neutrality. They are also "free" to the marketer (although there can be costs involved in pursuing and influencing them). Noncommercial sources, unfortunately, offer no control over what is said and how it is said, and they lack direction over where, when, and how often the message is transmitted.

TWO OTHER TYPES OF INFORMATION SEARCH

Besides prepurchase search, two other types of external search can occur outside of the consumer DM process: ongoing search and accidental search. **Ongoing (exploratory) search** is regular search undertaken to gather a bank of information for potential future use or to experience fun or pleasure. Hobbyists, such as car buffs, often gather information of interest just to stay on the cutting edge. And some people enjoy recreational shopping.

Together, prepurchase and ongoing search constitute **deliberate search**, active information acquisition in either the form of prepurchase or ongoing search activity. **Accidental (incidental) search**, on the other hand, is passive information acquisition via involuntary exposure. This yields data that is not necessarily of interest to the consumer. Such search occurs through passive viewing of broadcast commercials and outdoor billboards, unsolicited word-of-mouth communication, and seeing banner, pop-up, or e-mail ads online.

REVIEW QUESTIONS

1. What is internal search? Describe each of the "sets" formed during information search and the marketing implication for each. What are the other marketing implications of the internal search phase?
2. What is external search and what are the two major issues for marketers to confront during external search?
3. What factors influence the degree of prepurchase search and what is its major marketing implication?
4. Describe the classification scheme for consumer information sources (found in Exhibit 4.8). Cite the major advantages and disadvantages of each of the four general types of sources shown in Exhibit 4.8 (e.g., marketer-controlled, personal sources).

IN-CLASS APPLICATIONS

1. Consider your personal experiences with purchasing a high-involvement product versus a low-involvement item. Describe the nature of and differences between the internal search process for each product. In each case, what was the outcome of your internal search?

2. Answer Question 1, comparing an extended decision making (EDM) buying situation with a limited decision making (LDM) and then a routine decision making (RDM) situation that you have encountered.

3. Answer the first two questions in the context of external search (instead of internal search) that you undertook. How influential were marketer-controlled information sources on your purchase decision in each case?

4. Think of a time when you used ongoing (exploratory) search and another occasion when you used accidental (incidental) search. What types of information sources did you use in each case? How, if at all, did the information sources in each situation contribute to an eventual purchase decision? Would you choose to use these sources again?

WRITTEN APPLICATIONS

1. Answer Questions 1 through 4 in the In-Class Applications. Then, ask someone else these same questions (this could be another student in your class familiar with the material). Summarize that person's responses and compare them with your answers. What differences do you notice between the two sets of responses, and what factors might account for those differences?

2. Think of a product you'd like to purchase in the not-too-distant future, or else recall a product you recently purchased. Describe how you would engage or have engaged in an external search for that product. Be sure to discuss (a) the degree of search and (b) the general and specific types of sources you would or did seek. Explain reasons for all choices you made or will make.

Then, take the role of a marketer of that product. Discuss which commercial sources of information you would use in communicating with your customers, why you selected them, and which, if any, noncommercial sources you might attempt to influence and how you would try to sway them.

EXERCISE 4.3. ALTERNATIVE EVALUATION: THE PROCESS AND EVALUATIVE CRITERIA

OBJECTIVES

1. To provide an overview of the alternative evaluation process and the nature of consumer research used to understand this process.
2. To familiarize you with the different types of evaluative criteria.
3. To give you insight into your own alternative evaluation process.
4. To enable you to analyze the use of evaluative criteria and means–end chain analysis in advertising.
5. To give you experience using consumer research to discover the alternative evaluation process that consumers use for a particular product.
6. To give you practice using knowledge of the nature of evaluative criteria for product design, analytical attribute analysis, and advertising copywriting.

BACKGROUND

OVERVIEW OF THE ALTERNATIVE EVALUATION PROCESS

The third stage in the consumer decision-making process—**prepurchase alternative evaluation**—is comparing evaluative criteria (attributes) of various alternatives identified during information search in order to choose among them. If this information is favorable enough, consumers then form a **buying intention**, a plan to select an alternative. Exhibit 4.9 provides an overview of the alternative evaluation process.

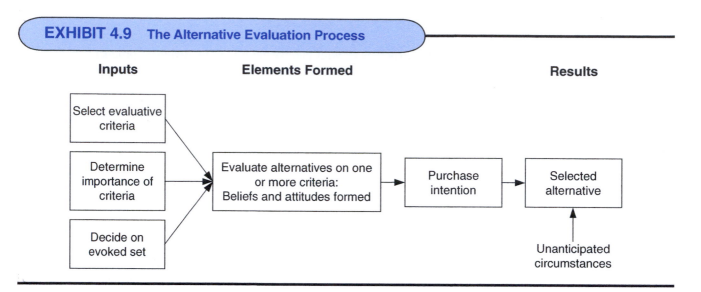

EXHIBIT 4.9   The Alternative Evaluation Process

INPUTS TO ALTERNATIVE EVALUATION

In order for a customer to evaluate alternatives, three inputs are required, as shown in Exhibit 4.9. First, buyers decide on **evaluative (choice, decision, buying, purchase) criteria** (sometimes just referred to as **criteria**), those attributes or characteristics of alternatives used by consumers to consider, compare, evaluate, and select one or more alternatives. These criteria include the product's physical features, such as price, quality, and style, and consumer benefits (satisfactions provided by the features), such as saving money and having comfort. Second, customers determine the **importance weights (weights)**, the relative importance of these criteria. Finally, buyers decide on the members of their evoked set.

MENTAL BUILDING BLOCKS FORMED DURING ALTERNATIVE EVALUATION

The first mental building block formed during alternative evaluation is **beliefs**, the consumer's perception of how each alternative performs on the critical criteria. These beliefs give rise to an **attitude**, a favorable or unfavorable evaluation of an alternative based on the customer's beliefs. If beliefs about a brand are generally positive, then the attitude will be positive. Third, a **buying intention (purchase intention, intention to buy, behavioral intention, purchase plan, propensity to buy)** is a plan to buy the most favorable option—the one for which the consumer feels *brand preference*.

THE NATURE OF ALTERNATIVE EVALUATION

In most cases, consumers make **attribute-based choices**, decisions made by comparing brand performance on the evaluative criteria, as outlined in Exhibit 4.9. However, there are two other types of alternative evaluation decision models: attitude-based choices and decision heuristics.

Consumers sometimes make decisions that are not based not on specific brand-attribute comparisons. **Attitude-based (affective, hedonic) choices** are the result of general attitudes toward, summary impressions of, or feelings and emotions associated with the product. Example: "I like Campbell's soups—they bring back happy childhood memories."

Shortcut **decision heuristics** are quick rules of thumb usually confined to one easily used criterion. A consumer's rule might be "Buy the brand mom always bought" or "Buy whatever is on sale."

RESULTS OF ALTERNATIVE EVALUATION

Barring any unanticipated circumstances, such as a retail stockout on the preferred brand or peer pressure to buy a less-preferred brand, consumers will select their favored alternative. Alternatively, the decision process might be put on hold, either temporarily or permanently, due to resource constraints and/or perceived lack of alternatives worth pursuing.

THE NATURE OF EVALUATIVE CRITERIA

Evaluative criteria are a subset of **product criteria**, attributes in a product, regardless of whether or not they matter to buyers. That is, product criteria may or may not be *evaluative criteria* used to select among options. Product criteria for a restaurant include the nature and color of the furniture, but it is doubtful that these are evaluative criteria used to select a restaurant.

Evaluative criteria answer the question, "What features and benefits do buyers look for when they purchase this product?" **Salient attributes** come readily to buyer's minds and are on the tip of their tongues if asked. Hence, although research respondents will mention them when asked what criteria they use in judging brands in a product class, salient attributes are not necessarily evaluative criteria. A criterion could be salient, for example, due to frequent exposure to an advertisement that mentions it (the toothpaste is "minty fresh!"; the cola is "refreshing"; the beer is "drinkable"), a recent article read (a story on soaring crime rates could prime the "safety" attribute in selecting a neighborhood in which to dwell), or a recent personal experience such as a problem incurred. A follow-up probe to determine why a respondent mentioned a characteristic might reveal whether it is cited because it is salient or truly important to the respondent.

Important attributes are criteria that are significant to the consumer. Bought brands should rate highly on them. Clearly, the marketer must perform well on these important characteristics. It is possible, however, that even though an attribute is important, it is not used to compare brands because the consumer believes that all brands perform more or less equally on that criterion. For example, a pitch that "Soapee soap will get your hands and face really clean" won't make the cash registers ring. There has to be something more: Perhaps one brand fights bacteria, another smells particularly nice, and a third comes in a unique shape.

Consumers evaluate brands on **determinant attributes**. These criteria are important and are used to distinguish brands, because not all alternatives are equal. A toaster oven's ability to brown bread evenly is important but not determinant. Think about what makes you buy one brand rather than another in a given category product. This is its determinant attribute.

THE GENERAL TYPES OF CHOICE CRITERIA: FEATURES AND BENEFITS

Product features (physical attributes, product specifications [specs]) constitute the *tangible product* or the objective, physical properties of a product such as its size, shape, styling, color, and other aspects of product design. A shampoo's features include its ingredients, pH balance, alkaline contents, and degree of concentration. Product development activities are concerned with forming features, each delivering one or more product benefits. There are also *intangible* or abstract features, such as endorsement by a product-testing agency, years of experience in the field, and reputation for excellence.

Product **benefits** are subjective satisfactions, consumption goals, or desired consequences consumers get from the features, such as ease of use and comfort. **Functional benefits** relate to *utilitarian (functional) needs* and concern the product's end uses or applications, the activity yielding desired benefits. Functional benefits answer the questions, "What is the product used for?" and "What are its practical applications?" Shampoo can be used to clean hair and make it glisten.

The other two types of benefits relate to *hedonic (experiential) needs*. **Experiential (hedonic) benefits** answer the questions, "How does it feel to use the product?" and "What kind of experiences does the product provide?" A shampoo brand's experiential benefits could include leaving hair feeling soft, having a clean scent, and looking bright and shiny.

Symbolic benefits relate to *brand imagery* and symbolic needs for self-expression to reflect one's *self-concept*. Symbolic benefits answer the question, "What types of people use the brand?" A shampoo brand's promoted symbolic benefits might include leaving hair looking young, giving hair a sexy appearance, and being associated with glamorous, sophisticated, upscale women.

As Exhibit 4.10 shows, features generally give rise to *functional benefits*, which in turn might lead to either *experiential benefits* and/or *symbolic benefits*. For example, Certs mints have a drop of Retsyn

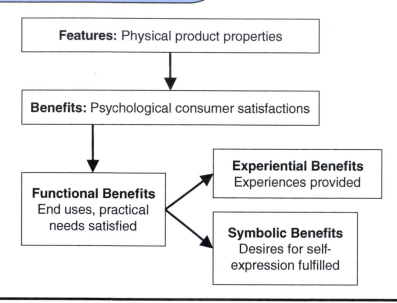

EXHIBIT 4.10   Types of Choice Criteria

Features: Physical product properties

Benefits: Psychological consumer satisfactions

Functional Benefits End uses, practical needs satisfied

Experiential Benefits Experiences provided

Symbolic Benefits Desires for self-expression fulfilled

(feature), which provides fresh breath (function), making your mouth feel fresh (experiential benefit), and giving you sex appeal (symbolic benefit).

MEANS-END CHAIN ANALYSIS LINKS FEATURES AND BENEFITS TO PERSONAL VALUES

Means-end chain analysis is based on the idea that product features are the means for obtaining the ends, which are product benefits and personal values. Exhibit 4.11 shows the relationship between the elements of the means-end chain. The consumer's ultimate ends are to fulfill **personal values**—beliefs about what constitutes an ideal state of being and doing. Personal values answer the question, "Why are the product's benefits important to the buyer?"

There are two types of consumer values. **Terminal values** are personal desirable end *states of being* (existence), or how people would like to eventually experience their lives; examples include achievement at work, financial security, and self-respect. **Instrumental values** are ideal *states of doing* or modes of conduct required to achieve the terminal states of being. These include hard work, frugality, helpfulness, honesty, and obedience.

Evaluative criteria are a means to the end of fulfilling these instrumental values. So, having hands that look and feel clean (benefit) might be critical since people value beauty. Possessing younger-looking hands (benefit) is significant because we treasure youth (personal value).

As another example of a means-end chain analysis, flavored potato chips might have the feature of sour cream and onion flavor, which yields the hedonic benefits of tasting good and having guests enjoy themselves more, and the symbolic benefit of party givers feeling they are good hosts. The terminal value in this case would be social recognition and friendship.

CONSUMER RESEARCH TO OBTAIN INFORMATION ON THE ALTERNATIVE EVALUATION PROCESS

Before designing a product and crafting its promotion, the marketer must determine which evaluative criteria consumers use in evaluating the product, the relative importance of each criterion in the decision process, the brands in consumers' evoked sets, and consumers' beliefs about how evoked set alternatives perform on the criteria. Research inputs are required on each of these.

EXHIBIT 4.11   Means-Ends Chain Analysis

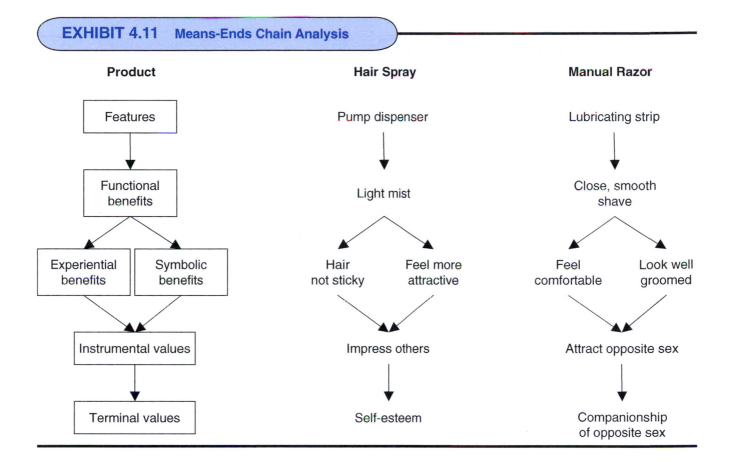

INPUT 1: EVALUATIVE CRITERIA USED

To discover what the important and determinant criteria are, researchers usually employ a large-scale survey or small-scale focus groups. Respondents are asked to recall which criteria they used to evaluate a given product. Researchers request the following types of information: "How do you compare different brands of antihistamines?" "What do you look for in deciding which cold or allergy medicine you'll buy?" "How do you go about choosing among brands of antihistamines?"

These researchers must be alert for **response bias**, a survey respondent's conscious or unconscious misrepresentation of the truth. Response bias can be deliberate or nondeliberate falsification.

Deliberate falsification is an unwillingness to tell the truth (e.g., someone who will not admit drinking to excess). Deliberate falsification concerning attributes used in choosing is most likely to occur due to **social desirability bias**, a respondent's desire to appear proper, seem rational, gain prestige, or avoid embarrassment. Consumers tend to overstate the importance of rational utilitarian criteria such as price and quality, while they underplay the significance of emotional hedonic attributes, such as image and pleasure. Hence, when asked why she chooses to fly first class instead of coach, a businesswoman might explain that it provides an environment in which she can get her work done rather than that she favors the free drinks and prestige.

Nondeliberate falsification is the unconscious misrepresentation or inability to tell the truth due to factors such as faulty memory, fatigue, and unfamiliarity. It may be a result of ambiguous characteristic (i.e., they have multiple meanings or are too abstract). The attribute "convenient" applied to a store could have a place dimension (close to home), a time dimension (open 24/7, speedy service), or a use dimension (friendly salespeople who are easy to deal with). "Locally grown" has no standardized meaning. About half of all consumers consider it to be within 100 miles of where an item is purchased. Others consider it to be within their state or region (e.g., New England).

EXHIBIT 4.12   Rating Scales for Measuring Relative Importance of Criteria

Basic Rating Scale

Very
important   1 2 3 4 5 6 7   Very
                                    unimportant

Evaluative Scale

Very
favorable   3 2 1 0 -1 -2 -3   Very
                                       unfavorable

Rank Order Importance Scale

Please mark the following soft drink attributes in order of importance to you by placing a 1 next to the most important attribute, a 2 next to the the second most important attribute, and so on until you have ranked all six.

____ Sweetness   ____ Price
____ Carbonation   ____ Calories
____ Taste   ____ Caffeine/Caffeine free

INPUT 2: RELATIVE IMPORTANCE OF CRITERIA

Once a list of important and determinant attributes has been developed, the marketer must discover each characteristic's importance weight. This type of research uses surveys employing **rating scales** that ask interviewees to estimate the magnitude of "something" on a continuum, as illustrated in Exhibit 4.12. In this case, the "something" is an attribute's importance, estimated by the respondent indicating how important that attribute is by checking off or circling a point on a five- or seven-point scale from "very important" to "very unimportant."

However, a characteristic might be rated very important because the consumer considers the presence of that attribute to be undesirable, such as sourness in a beverage. To overcome this difficulty, the analyst can instead use an **evaluative scale**, which tells not only the *magnitude* but also the *direction* of the importance rating. The evaluative scale shows "very favorable" or "very good" at one end and "very unfavorable" or "very poor" at the other. The ratings on the positive end of the scale range from 1 to 3, while those on the negative side go from –1 to –3. Thus, having a particular characteristic, such as smooth texture in a beverage, might be rated by a respondent as +2, while another criterion, such as a fruity taste, might be rated as –3. The assumption is that the further from the midpoint of the scale (0) a consumer rates an attribute, the more strongly he or she feels about that criterion and the more important it is.

Alternatively, respondents can be given a **rank-order importance scale** in which they rank a list of product criteria in order of personal importance. In a snack chip, flavor could be ranked first in importance, saltiness second, and crunchiness third. Another possibility is to use a **constant sum scale**, in which respondents are asked to divide a constant quantitative sum or amount among evaluative criteria to indicate their relative importance, such as dividing twenty points among five characteristics according to their relative importance.

INPUT 3: ALTERNATIVES IN THE EVOKED SET

Next, researchers need to know which brands are members of the consumer's evoked set. Usually, a straightforward survey is used. Respondents are asked about brands they consider in choosing within a product category. One of three methods is employed: In *aided recall,* consumers make a selection from a given list of brands. In *unaided recall,* they try to remember brands off the top of their head. In *recognition,* respondents view pictures of brand identity elements, such as logotypes, packages, brand names, trade characters, and advertisements, and then state which of the pictured brands they typically consider.

INPUT 4: BELIEFS ABOUT ALTERNATIVES' PERFORMANCE ON THE CRITERIA

Finally, researchers ask about consumers' *beliefs* about how every brand performs on each attribute. This is measured by **brand ratings**, again using rating scales. Typically, for each alternative in a buyer's evoked set, a listing of product criteria and brands is presented. Respondents then rate each brand's performance on each attribute, from very satisfactory to very unsatisfactory, usually using either a five- or seven-point rating scale.

APPLICATIONS OF KNOWLEDGE OF THE ALTERNATIVE EVALUATION PROCESS

NEW PRODUCT DEVELOPMENT APPLICATIONS

One approach for developing new products is **analytical attribute analysis**, in which marketers examine product characteristics to generate new product ideas and design new or improved products. The underlying idea is that a future product change must come from altering one or more of a product's criteria, such as making a battery last longer or improving the creaminess of a pudding.

One approach is to enhance one or more criteria ("longer lasting"). Another technique is to add one or more criteria to an existing product, such as Kleenex with lotion. The addition of berries as a perceived healthful ingredient has sold lots of cereal (e.g., Berry Burst Cheerios and Special K Red Berries) and alcoholic beverages (Skyy Berry vodka and Bacardi Razz rum with natural raspberry).

Analytical attribute analysis begins with consumer research. Its goal is to understand the consumer benefits that are not being adequately delivered in the marketplace. As the problem recognition stage suggests, there is a **gap** between consumer ideal and actual states of affairs, and so this research is sometimes called **gap analysis**.

After identifying these benefits, marketers write a **product concept statement.** This verbal description of a new product idea describes its *form* (physical attributes), product *functions* (functional benefits), and delivered *benefits* (both hedonic and symbolic).

Next, marketers work with the technical groups—the research and development, engineering, and product design departments—to create a product with features that will deliver the desired benefits. The following are some idea generation techniques used to develop better products with analytical attribute analysis.

Dimensional Analysis. **Dimensional analysis (attribute listing)** begins with an exhaustive listing of all of the physical features (dimensions) of a product that developers think need improvement or modification. For each characteristic, the analyst asks either consumers or managers; "How can we change or improve this attribute to better deliver benefits?"

Possibilities include the following:

- Changing the nature of dimensions (e.g., concentrated detergent, mini versions of cookies).
- Improving characteristics (e.g., resealable packaging, more chocolate flavor in a candy bar).
- Adding attributes (e.g., Chips Ahoy! cookies with peanut butter chips and candy pieces, Edy's ice cream with bits of Girl Scout cookies).
- Borrowing a dimension from another product category (e.g., Bounty quilted napkins applied the strength and durability of their paper towels to napkins).

Attribute Extension. **Attribute extension (parameter analysis)** starts with a characteristic that has recently changed in the marketplace and then extends that change to see what (if any) benefits will accrue to consumers. For instance, low-fat foods and low-calorie sodas inevitably led to no-fat and zero-calorie versions. Spectator sport events have been lasting longer, so a twenty-four-hour marathon sport would satisfy the insatiable sports fan.

ADVERTISING AND PROMOTION APPLICATIONS

During or immediately following product development, the promotions experts should develop marketing communications to describe the benefits that the product will deliver and the personal values it will fulfill. Knowing about determinant purchase criteria, their relative importance, and the various evoked-set brands' performances on these attributes enables marketers to most effectively promote those products by focusing on the brand's superior performance on those criteria. However, keep in mind the maxim, "emphasize benefits, not features." Consumers do not buy products—they purchase bundles of benefits.

Especially for new products and inexperienced buyers, marketers can influence consumer evaluations by framing the alternatives. **Framing** is the way in which a decision problem is presented to the decision maker, such as suggesting that certain criteria (those the brand best performs on) are most important. Accordingly, Volvo might emphasize its superior comfort and safety while suggesting that these are the key criteria in buying a car.

REVIEW QUESTIONS

1. Describe the alternative evaluation process, including inputs into it, the process of formation of beliefs and attitudes, and the outcomes of the process.
2. Explain the difference between each of the following:
   a. Salient, important, and determinant attributes
   b. Attitude-based and attribute-based choices
   c. Features and benefits, and the three types of benefits: functional, experiential, and hedonic
3. Describe the logic behind and the process of means-end chain analysis.
4. Describe (a) the nature of research done, (b) possible problems of response bias, and (c) remedies for the various types of response bias that can occur when collecting data for each of the following four elements of the alternative evaluation process:
   a. Evaluative criteria used
   b. Relative importance of the criteria
   c. Alternatives in the evoked set
   d. Consumers' beliefs about alternatives' performance on the criteria
5. Explain how knowledge of the alternative evaluation process could be used to improve:
   a. Product development efforts
   b. Promotional efforts

IN-CLASS APPLICATIONS

1. Describe the alternative evaluation process you recently used in buying a product. What were your evaluative criteria and the relative importance of those criteria? Which and how many brands were in your evoked set?

   What were your beliefs about those brands' performances on the criteria? Did the brand that you intended to buy perform best on those criteria overall?
2. Think about athletic shoes. As a class, brainstorm a list of attributes that are
   a. salient but not necessarily determinant,
   b. important but not necessarily determinant, and
   c. determinant.
3. For each of the ads in Exhibits 4.13 through 4.16, which of the general types of evaluative criteria (features, functional benefits, experiential benefits, and symbolic benefits) are being emphasized? Which specific criteria (e.g., contains lemon scent, delicious, sophisticated, etc.) are being used within each of these general categories? Do you think each of these criteria is important to consumers? Is each determinant? What other criteria, if any, could each of the ads have emphasized? Would this have been more effective?

   Also, find at least one means-end chain consisting of the sequence "feature-function-benefit-personal values" in each ad (you might need to infer the personal value).

EXHIBIT 4.13   Neutrogena Ad

EXHIBIT 4.14   Braun Ad

EXHIBIT 4.15   Rembrandt Ad

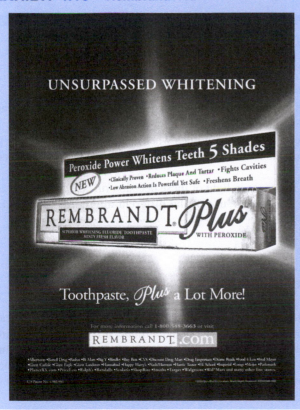

EXHIBIT 4.16   Fresh Step Ad

WRITTEN APPLICATIONS

1. Answer Question 3 in the In-Class Applications.
2. Find three more ads, each of which emphasizes one or more evaluative criteria as the ad's major appeal or emphasis. Repeat the analysis in Question 3 in the In-Class Applications for each of the ads you find.
3. Select a product category commonly used by college students (e.g., cell phones, laptop computers, knapsacks).
   a. Design a small-scale survey using ten members of the target market to discover the following:
      i.   Which criteria consumers use. Point out any sources of response bias you suspect might have occurred in your survey. If you wish, you may try building a means-end chain with one or several of your respondents.
      ii. The relative importance of those criteria. This will require a second round of questioning (using different respondents if you wish) after you've determined the criteria they use. Which type of rating scale did you use and why?
      iii. Alternatives in the evoked set. How did you ascertain these? How large was the typical evoked set?
      iv. Beliefs about performance of alternatives in the evoked set on the criteria. Do you suspect any types of response bias here?
   b. Develop a new product concept using an analytical attribute analysis technique. The product idea can range from a radically new-to-the-world product (e.g., nonmelting ice cubes) to an incremental innovation (e.g., sugar-free spicy cola Jell-O). You can try dimensional analysis based on your attribute list or attribute extension using one of the characteristics.
   c. Design a print ad for your new product idea that promotes the product on its various evaluative criteria. Discuss the general and specific types of criteria it uses and why this ad will help persuade people to buy this product.

EXERCISE 4.4. ALTERNATIVE EVALUATION: DECISION MODELS

OBJECTIVES

1. To help you understand and recognize the different decision models consumers use to evaluate alternatives, as well as the situations in which they are most likely to use each.
2. To give you insight into how you have applied decision rules when shopping.
3. To learn how knowledge of the decision models can give insight into new product development and promotion strategies.
4. To enable you to evaluate advertising messages in light of these decision rules.
5. To be able to quantitatively analyze consumers' use of the different alternative evaluation rules.

BACKGROUND

DECISION MAKING DURING THE ALTERNATIVE EVALUATION PROCESS

This exercise continues the discussion of the alternative evaluation process begun in Exercise 4.3. Recall that consumers form brand beliefs that they combine to develop a brand attitude, arrived at by applying **decision models (decision rules, alternative evaluation rules, decision strategies, information-processing strategies, choice rules)**. These decision rules are shoppers' procedures used to evaluate the performance of evoked set alternatives on their choice criteria. This exercise describes how consumers employ these decision rules to form attitudes and buying intentions toward the brands.

| EXHIBIT 4.17 | Brand Evaluation Data for the Camera Market: Multiattribute Attitude Model |

Criterion	Importance*	Alpha**	Beta	Gamma	Delta	Epsilon
Image quality	4	10	8	6	4	1
Ease of use	3	8	9	8	3	5
Camera size	2	6	8	10	7	8
Price	1	4	3	5	8	7

*Importance of each criterion is scored on a scale where 1 = least important and 4 = most important.
**Brand ratings are scored on a scale where 1 = very poor performance and 10 = excellent performance.

DECISION RULES AND THE BRAND-ATTRIBUTE MATRIX

In this exercise, you will see how an understanding of decision rules typically used by consumers for a particular product class has ramifications for new product development and advertising and promotion. The focus is on **information integration theory**, the cognitive algebra consumers apply in using their brand-attribute knowledge to make marketplace decisions.

It will help the following discussion to have a working example, say, the purchase of a digital camera. Exhibit 4.17 presents a **brand-attribute matrix (decision matrix)**. This chart shows brand ratings on determinant attributes for a product, in this case a camera. Exhibit 4.17 could represent marketplace data collected from a sample survey of camera buyers, or it could be brand-attribute information for an individual consumer.

The first column in this exhibit shows that when buying a camera, consumers consider a brand's performance on four very general determinant evaluative criteria: image quality, ease of use, camera size, and price. The second column reveals the importance weight for each criterion, which could be on either a rating scale of 1 (very unimportant) to 4 (very important) or a ranking scale, where "4" is the most important attribute and "1" is the least important attribute.

The next five columns list the five brands under consideration: Alpha, Beta, Gamma, Delta, and Epsilon. Listed in the column under each brand are consumer beliefs or ratings of that alternative's performance on each of the four criteria. These beliefs are scored on a scale of 1 (very poor) to 10 (excellent).

The brand selected by the consumer depends on which of the four decision rules is used.

The detailed discussion that follows is summarized in Exhibit 4.23, p. 135. You might wish to periodically refer to this exhibit to review and compare the various decision rules. Generally, most decision models fall under one of two categories: compensatory decision rules and noncompensatory decision rules.

COMPENSATORY DECISION MODELS

Compensatory decision rules (linear compensatory models) use all of the brand-attribute information in Exhibit 4.17 to compute one of two types of attribute scores: (1) a weighted score in the weighted linear compensatory model or (2) a summated score in the unweighted model. A brand's score can be thought of as a representation of the consumer's brand attitude, abbreviated "A_B," for "attitude toward the brand." All else equal, the consumer will choose the brand in a product category with the highest total brand score, determined by adding the performance ratings on all of the determinant characteristics (with or without using importance weights).

This decision rule is called a compensatory decision strategy because a high rating on one attribute compensates for a lower score on another criterion. Hence, trade-offs are made among the brand's performances on the various criteria. Accordingly, a car that is a gas guzzler might still be acceptable because it yields high performance. Compensatory decision rules are utility-maximizing decision strategies to select the optimal brand that use all available brand-attribute information and maximize overall performance.

WEIGHTED LINEAR COMPENSATORY DECISION MODELS

The **weighted linear compensatory rule (weighted additive rule)** is a weighted (consumers consider each attribute's relative importance) linear compensatory decision model. This traditional **multiattribute attitude model** is represented by the formula:

$$A_{jk} = \sum w_{ik} b_{ijk} \ ,$$

where i = attribute i
    j = brand j
    k = consumer k (Her name must be "Kay!")
    A_{jk} = consumer k's attitude score for brand j (A_B)
    w_{ik} = the importance weight assigned to attribute i by consumer k
    b_{ijk} = consumer k's belief about the performance of brand j on attribute i
    n = number of attributes on which the product category's brands are evaluated

The consumer's overall attitude toward any given brand is a weighted sum of beliefs about the brand's performance on each of the attributes. The higher the sum, the more positive is the attitude. This particular multiattribute model is sometimes called the **infinite ideal point attitude model (vector attribute model)**, since theoretically consumers prefer an unlimited or "infinite" amount of each criterion. In a TV set, people want better picture quality, more durability, a longer guarantee, and greater convenience.

The marketing implications are focus on excellent performance in the most important characteristics during product development and promotion of performance in marketing communications.

Looking at Exhibit 4.17, we can quantitatively measure brand preferences for A_B as follows:

Alpha (α) = $(4 \times 10) + (3 \times 8) + (2 \times 6) + (1 \times 4) = 80$
Beta (β) = $(4 \times 8) + (3 \times 9) + (2 \times 8) + (1 \times 3) = 78$
Gamma (γ) = $(4 \times 6) + (3 \times 8) + (2 \times 10) + (1 \times 5) = 73$
Delta (δ) = $(4 \times 4) + (3 \times 3) + (2 \times 7) + (1 \times 8) = 47$
Epsilon (ε) = $(4 \times 1) + (3 \times 5) + (2 \times 8) + (1 \times 7) = 42$

So, the Alpha brand is preferred since it has the highest score (80), followed by Beta (78), then Gamma (73), next Delta (47), with Epsilon being the least preferred (42). The consumer will form a buying intention for Alpha and, barring any unanticipated situational constraints such as unavailability or a special one-day price break on a competitive brand, Alpha will be bought.

UNWEIGHTED LINEAR COMPENSATORY DECISION MODELS

A second type of linear compensatory model is one in which the attributes are not weighted, that is, all criteria are equal in importance. The formula for determining the consumer's attitude using such an **unweighted linear compensatory decision model (unweighted rule, simple additive rule, equal weight rule)** is:

$$A_{jk} = \sum b_{ijk}$$

We simply total the consumer's brand ratings (beliefs) for a particular brand. In the camera example, the brand ratings would be: Alpha = 10 + 8 + 6 + 4 = 28; Beta = 8 + 9 + 8 + 3 = 28; Gamma = 6 + 8 + 10 + 5 = 29; Delta = 4 + 3 + 7 + 8 = 22; Epsilon = 1 + 5 + 8 + 7 = 21. So, neglecting weights, Gamma becomes the preferred brand (29), nosing out Alpha and Beta (both 28). This simple additive rule tends to be used where the consumer has limited time, energy, or motivation to carefully consider weights.

EXHIBIT 4.18   Brand Evaluation Data for the Soda Pop Market: Finite Ideal Point Model

Criterion	Ideal Amount	Zeta	Eta	Theta	Kappa	Lambda
Carbonation	4	10	8	6	4	1
Sweetness	8	8	7	8	3	5
Calories	2	6	8	10	7	8
Caffeine	5	4	3	5	8	7

FINITE IDEAL POINT MODELS

In contrast to infinite ideal point decision rules, there are products for which a moderate amount of an attribute is preferred. This is known as the **finite ideal point (attribute adequacy, additive difference) attitude model**.

For example, in a soda pop, too much carbonation would become undesirable as bubbles burst out of the consumer's nose and too much sweetness might taste nasty. The finite ideal point rule is the model of moderation, especially used for experience goods where people do not want too much of a good thing. Accordingly, light beer has a moderate amount of calories and alcohol. Each attribute has an ideal level, such as, "4" on a scale of 1 to 10.

To illustrate, Exhibit 4.18 shows the same numerical data as Exhibit 4.17, except that the example is an experience good, soda pop, where moderation on attributes is desired. We also use different brand names just to keep it almost interesting. The figure indicates the ideal amount of each characteristic. Also, we assume all criteria are equal in importance (although attribute weightings could be added). The exhibit shows that, on a scale of 1 to 10, consumers want a moderate amount of carbonation (4), a fairly high level of sweetness (8), few calories (2), and a moderate amount of caffeine (5).

Examining the data in Exhibit 4.18, we can calculate attitude scores for each of the soda brands by summing up absolute values of the differences between a brand's ideal and actual levels on each attribute, indicated by $\left| I_{jk} - b_{ijk} \right|$:

Zeta (ζ) = |4 − 10| + |8 − 8| + |2 − 6| + |5 − 4| = 6 + 0 + 4 + 1 = 11
Eta (η) = |4 − 8| + |8 − 7| + |2 − 8| + |5 − 3| = 4 + 1 + 6 + 2 = 13
Theta (θ) = |4 − 6| + |8 − 8| + |2 − 10| + |5 − 5| = 2 + 0 + 8 + 0 = 10
Kappa (κ) = |4 − 4| + |8 − 3| + |2 − 7| + |5 − 8| = 0 + 5 + 5 + 3 = 13
Lambda (λ) = |4 − 1| + |8 − 5| + |2 − 8| + |5 − 7| = 3 + 3 + 6 + 2 = 14

Theta, with the lowest score (10), is the preferred brand. In fact, it meets the ideal level on two attributes.

The clear marketing implication is to develop a product with the target market's ideal level of each characteristic and then promote the brand as being the "perfect fit" for the consumer.

OBSERVATIONS ON COMPENSATORY DECISION MODELS

Compensatory decision rules entail a **brand-based evaluation strategy (choice by processing brands [CPB], processing by brands [PBB], brand-choice sequence)**, evaluating one brand at a time across all attributes (instead of comparing all brands across one criterion at a time). For example, first the consumer evaluates the Alpha brand on all attributes to arrive at an overall evaluation, and then does likewise for the Beta brand, followed successively by an assessment of all brands in her evoked set. Then she selects her overall preferred brand.

Although compensatory rules tend to be rather complex and time-consuming, they do capture all available information and, as a result, the consumer ends up selecting the optimal brand (barring unanticipated circumstances).

Due to their complexity and time-consuming nature, we expect compensatory models to be used where one or more of the following conditions exist:

- There is a high involvement decision and/or extended DM. Consequently, consumers are willing to spend the time, effort, and energy to select, as Hallmark says, "the very best."
- There is adequate time to fully deliberate before deciding.
- Buyers have the expertise needed to conduct an exhaustive search.
- There are just a few alternatives and/or determinant attributes, so each alternative can be carefully considered on all criteria without information overload (strain on the brain!).

Compensatory rules can be used as the second stage in a **phased decision strategy (multistage choice process)**—a two-step decision process. The first stage entails quickly paring down a large number of alternatives to a more manageable number, using one of the quicker and easier noncompensatory rules that follow. The second phase uses a compensatory rule to more fully evaluate the remaining alternatives.

NONCOMPENSATORY DECISION MODELS

Noncompensatory decision rules do not permit high performance on one attribute to compensate for a low rating on another criterion—no trade-offs are allowed. Only the most important brand-attribute information is considered. For example, a consumer might wish to search for the least expensive brand, regardless of its performance on other criteria.

Noncompensatory rules are simpler than compensatory strategies in that no mathematical attitude scores need be implicitly computed. However, these choice strategies do not take into account all available data and so only yield a satisfactory decision (satisficing).

Nonetheless, these easy methods simplify DM for the customer, saving time, energy, and effort. Therefore, such alternative evaluation rules tend to be used when one or (usually) several of the following conditions exist:

- There is a low involvement decision and/or limited DM.
- The consumer experiences time pressure.
- Nonexpert buyers do not have the ability to carefully consider all options on all criteria.
- There are too many alternatives and/or attributes to carefully consider.

Often, noncompensatory strategies are used as the first phase in a phased decision strategy to quickly weed out some options so that the remaining alternatives can be more carefully assessed via a compensatory rule.

There are four types of noncompensatory strategies. The first two rules we will examine use choice by processing brands. The third and fourth, however, employ **choice by processing attributes (CPA; processing by attributes [PBA], dimensional processing, attribute search sequence)**, in which all brands are compared, one criterion at a time. Also, the first two noncompensatory strategies weight all characteristics equally, whereas the third and fourth rules rank the criteria.

CONJUNCTIVE DECISION RULE

The **conjunctive decision rule** considers all (or any, or the first) brands that surpass a cutoff, a minimum acceptable level (MAL) or minimum standard of performance on each and every determinant criterion. An alternative is either considered further for a final choice (phased decision strategy) or is chosen if it exceeds the consumer's minimum performance standards for each evaluative criterion. For example, in selecting a house using a phased decision conjunctive strategy, a buyer might require that it be no more than thirty minutes from work, have at least three bedrooms, cost less than $275,000, be no older than twenty-five years, and be situated on at least two acres. These stipulations preclude the need to carefully examine most homes on the market. In low-involvement purchases, the consumer can use a conjunctive rule to quickly choose the first brand encountered that meets all MALs rather than weeding out many possibilities as with the phased strategy.

Exhibit 4.19 revisits our camera example from Exhibit 4.17. Now, instead of importance levels for each

---

EXHIBIT 4.19   **Brand Evaluation Data for the Camera Market: Conjunctive Model**

Criterion	Minimum Standard	Alpha	Beta	Gamma	Delta	Epsilon
Image quality	4	10	8	6	4	1
Ease of use	5	8	9	8	3	5
Camera size	7	6	8	10	7	8
Price	2	4	3	5	8	7

EXHIBIT 4.20   **Brand Evaluation Data for the Camera Market: Disjunctive Model**

Criterion	Minimum Standard	Alpha	Beta	Gamma	Delta	Epsilon
Image quality	7	10	8	6	4	1
Ease of use	8	8	7	8	3	5
Camera size	Not critical	6	8	10	7	8
Price	Not critical	4	3	5	8	7

---

criterion, all attributes are equally important and the consumer establishes a cutoff level of performance on each attribute.

The MAL for image quality in the Exhibit 4.19 example is 4, eliminating Epsilon since it only rates a 1 on this attribute. For ease of use a brand must score at least a 5, which weeds out Delta. Camera size must rate at least a 7, so Alpha is out of the running. The remaining brand, Beta, surpasses the price standard of 2, and so it is selected.

If Beta had also rated lower than 2 on price, no brand would have met all the cutoffs. Then what? There are several possibilities. No brand would have been purchased, the decision would have been postponed, the consumer would have relaxed her cutoffs, or another decision rule would have been used instead of the conjunctive rule.

Notice how the conjunctive rule leads to a different decision than both the weighted and unweighted compensatory decision strategies. Note also that even though Alpha outperforms Beta on two of the criteria, it is not selected because it fails to meet just one cutoff (camera size). So, when a consumer uses the conjunctive rule, a superior brand can be eliminated simply because it falls below the cutoff on just one criterion!

DISJUNCTIVE DECISION RULE

As with the conjunctive model, in the **disjunctive decision rule** cutoffs are established, but now there are MALs for only two or three key criteria, often at a very high performance level. The consumer considers all brands (or any, or the first) that meet or exceed the key cutoff(s), regardless of performance on the other less important criteria.

For example, a boxy gas guzzler might be an acceptable car if it has excellent power and that is the key criterion. In an emergency purchase (say, a new radiator for a car badly leaking radiator fluid), availability is key, price, quality, and other criteria be darned.

Exhibit 4.20 illustrates the disjunctive model, using data identical to that in Exhibit 17.3 (conjunctive model). However, only two attributes are critical: image quality and ease of use. Note that the minimum standards on these key criteria are now both set at a very high level.

The minimum standard of 7 on image quality rules out all but the Alpha and Beta brands. The cutoff of 8 on ease of use then eliminates the Beta brand. Therefore, Alpha is selected, even though it ranks two scale points below Beta on camera size.

If Beta had also performed below this cutoff, thereby eliminating the only remaining brand, several things could happen: No brand would be purchased, the decision would be delayed, one or more MALs would be lowered, or another decision rule would be selected.

PRODUCT DEVELOPMENT AND PROMOTIONAL IMPLICATIONS OF CONJUNCTIVE AND DISJUNCTIVE RULES

The conjunctive and disjunctive rules have two things in common. First, they both use CPB in which one brand at a time is evaluated across all its attributes. Second, they both establish minimum standards on all or critical determinant characteristics that the chosen brand must meet or exceed.

The implication for product development in categories where brands are selected using the conjunctive rules is to make sure that the brand performs at least at the cutoff levels on the several or many criteria. However, it needn't perform above the cutoff levels to be selected. Where the disjunctive rule is used, the emphasis is on meeting very high performance standards on the one or few critical criteria.

The marketing communication ramification for these two decision rules is to promote the brand as meeting or surpassing the MAL on the determinant attributes. For instance, ads for Static Guard focus solely on the ability to eliminate static cling.

LEXICOGRAPHIC AND ELIMINATION-BY-ASPECTS DECISION MODELS

The next two noncompensatory decision strategies—lexicographic and elimination by aspects—share two characteristics. First, both use CPA—they compare brands across criteria, i.e. one attribute at a time. Second, they do so by rank ordering characteristics and then comparing brands across one attribute at a time, beginning with the most important criterion and proceeding through the less critical criteria, if necessary.

For product development, the use of these two consumer decision rules suggests that marketers should focus on the most important criteria. An implication for promotion is that comparative advertising should compare brands attribute by attribute on the most important characteristics.

Lexicographic Decision Model. Using the **lexicographic decision rule,** the consumer first ranks the evaluative criteria in order of perceived importance. He then compares alternatives on the most important attribute and selects the one scoring highest, regardless of how it performs on the other criteria. You could call this the "instant winner model."

However, if two or more brands tie their ratings on that most critical criterion, the buyer then compares those tied brands on the second-most important characteristic, selecting the alternative that performs best on that dimension. However, if there is again a tie, he proceeds to the third-highest-weighted attribute, comparing the remaining tied alternatives. If there continue to be ties, the consumer proceeds through the remaining criteria in order of importance, until one of the remaining brands outperforms the others.

For example, the consumer might begin a search for hotels by looking for the lowest-priced option. If three out of the many hotels in the marketplace were all equally inexpensive, she would then inspect those three on her next-most important criterion, say, prestige of the hotel's name. If two of these three brands were equally prestigious, she would size these two up on her third-most-significant attribute, (e.g., service level). If one of the brands rated better than the other on the service criterion, she would choose it. Even if there were other, less important determinant criteria, these attributes would not be necessary to evaluate the brands.

To illustrate the lexicographic rule, Exhibit 4.21 uses the soda pop market data of Exhibit 4.18, except that instead of the ideal amount of each criterion, we now note its importance, rated on a scale of one to ten. Since sweetness is the most important of these four attributes, the consumer begins by comparing all brands on sweetness. Alternatives Zeta and Theta are tied for top performance on sweetness, so the other brands are eliminated. Next, the customer compares just these two tied brands on the second most significant criterion, calories. Here, Theta is the better performer, and so it is chosen.

If consumers use a lexicographic rule, product development should concentrate primarily on excellence of the most important criterion. If competitors are able to match a brand on that criterion, the brand must

EXHIBIT 4.21	Brand Evaluation Data for the Soda Pop Market: Lexicographic Model					
Criterion	Importance	Zeta	Eta	Theta	Kappa	Lambda
Carbonation	3	10	8	6	4	1
Sweetness	7	8	7	8	3	5
Calories	5	6	8	10	7	8
Caffeine	2	4	3	5	8	7

also focus on great performance on the second-most important criterion, and on down through the other important attributes.

Where the lexicographic rule governs, promotional messages should hammer home the alternative's superior performance on the most important attribute. Often, this focused promotion is done in conjunction with targeting a benefit segment. Marketers promote the most important benefit, pursuing benefit segments such as quality-oriented consumers, status-oriented buyers, or deal-prone customers.

Alternatively, if the brand performs best on a particular characteristic, the marketer can try to frame (structure) consumers' decisions by persuading them that it is the most important criterion, and then promote the brand's superiority on that characteristic (e.g., "Purchase the most prestigious brand" or "Shop at the least expensive store").

Elimination-by-Aspects Rule (Sequential Elimination Model). The **elimination-by-aspects rule (sequential elimination model)**, like the lexicographic rule, begins by ranking the criteria in order of perceived importance. However, the next step involves determining a cutoff for each criterion (as is done in the conjunctive and disjunctive models). Then, as with the lexicographic rule, the customer compares brands on the most important criterion first. However, instead of trying to pick an instant winner on this most critical criterion, she instead weeds out those alternatives that meet or exceed the cutoff. You could call this the "weeding out model."

The remaining brands are then compared on the next-most-important criterion to eliminate those that do not at least meet the consumer's cutoff on that characteristic. The process continues successively through the less important criteria, excluding brands from further consideration as they fail to meet each criterion's cutoff, until only one alternative remains and is chosen. Since the elimination-by-aspects rule tends to take into account more criteria than the lexicographic rule, it is more likely to result in a purchase that is close to optimal.

A consumer choosing a shirt using the elimination-by-aspects rule might begin by eliminating all foreign brands, then exclude those remaining brands that are not a solid color, next preclude remaining options that cost more than $50, and finally reject remaining shirts that aren't 100 percent cotton, leaving only one brand to purchase.

To illustrate the elimination-by-aspects model, Exhibit 4.22 reproduces the data from Exhibit 4.21 for the lexicographic model, except it adds minimum standards for each criterion in the third column. The consumer will begin brand evaluation with the most critical criterion, sweetness. Brands Kappa and Lambda are eliminated since they fall below the cutoff of 6. The buyer then evaluates the remaining three alternatives, Zeta, Eta, and Theta, on the next-most-important criterion, calories, with Zeta falling short of the acceptable standard. Remaining contenders, Eta and Theta are sized up on the third-most-important characteristic, carbonation. Theta falls flat, so Eta is anointed as the chosen brand. Note that Eta is selected even though it is not the best performer on the most important criterion, sweetness.

Because users of the lexicographic rule focus on one or a select few characteristics, product developers and advertisers need to concentrate just on beating rivals on those key criteria. However, with the sequential elimination model, hurdles must generally be surpassed on many of the determinant attributes. Comparative advertising can suggest how the brand is superior on the criteria, starting with the most important characteristic and successively eliminating competitors for their inferior performances on the various attributes.

| EXHIBIT 4.22 | Brand Evaluation Data for the Soda Pop Market: Elimination-by-Aspects Model |

Criterion	Importance	Cutoff	Zeta	Eta	Theta	Kappa	Lambda
Carbonation	3	7	10	8	6	4	1
Sweetness	7	6	8	7	8	3	5
Calories	5	7	6	8	10	7	8
Caffeine	2	5	4	3	5	8	7

DECISION HEURISTICS (CHOICE HEURISTICS)

A third general category of decision rules is known as **decision heuristics (choice heuristics, heuristics)**, mental rules of thumb that generally focus on a single criterion to simplify consumer DM, speed up the process, and help consumers cope with information overload. Examples are "Buy the least expensive brand." "Purchase the brand with the best-known name." "Buy the same brand you purchased last time." "Choose the brand rated highest by *Consumer Reports*." An example of a brand-specific decision rule is "Select Iota, the brand our family always used."

Decision heuristics, which can clearly lead to nonoptimal (non-utility-maximizing) choices, are most likely to be used where buyers:

- have insufficient product category information,
- lack ability to intelligently select, and
- don't have the motivation or involvement to make a careful decision.

For shoppers using decision heuristics, product development and promotion should focus on the key criterion and either reinforce currently used heuristics or create new decision rules that can work in the marketer's favor, such as buying by price.

AFFECT REFERRAL (AFFECTIVE CHOICE) RULE

Affect referral (affective choice, hedonic choice) does not ground decisions in specific brand-attribute comparisons but rather in global attitudes, holistic impressions, or emotions associated with a brand. Affect referral can also be thought of as the "How will it make me feel?" decision heuristic. For instance, young consumers buy mobile electronic devices not just because they are useful, but also because they are perceived as cool.

This decision rule prevails under one or more of the following conditions:

- The product primarily gives hedonic benefits (e.g., colorful scented candles).
- The buyer has much previous information and experience with the category, resulting in emotional ties.
- There is primarily affective involvement, rather than cognitive involvement.

The suggestion for product development on goods where affect referral prevails is to design products that will give the user positive emotional experiences, which can often be achieved through sensory marketing, or appealing to the senses (e.g., the smell of a cologne or the bright colors of a package).

The promotional implication is to create messages provoking an overall good feeling about the brand. This can be done through the use of humor (Bud Light), cute characters (Pillsbury Doughboy), and appeals to nostalgia (the movie *Toy Story* appealed to baby-boomer parents, who bought their youngsters some of the toys featured in the film that they were nostalgic about, such as Mr. Potato Head and Slinky) or through scenarios that show the pleasures experienced while using the product (e.g., the thrill of driving a sports

---

EXHIBIT 4.23   The Alternative Evaluation Decision Models

1. **Compensatory decision rules (linear compensatory models)**—Buyers use all available brand-attribute information: They select the brand that provides the highest total attitude score when performance ratings for all determinant attributes are added, with or without importance weights, as follows:
   a. **Weighted linear compensatory rules (weighted additive rules)**—Importance weights for the criteria are used. This traditional **multiattribute attitude model** is represented by the formula $A_{jk} = \sum w_{ij} b_{ijk}$. It is an **infinite ideal point model.**
   b. **Unweighted linear compensatory rules (simple additive rules)**—Importance weights aren't included—all attributes are assumed to be equally important.
       The above can be either be **infinite ideal point models**—consumers prefer an unlimited amount of each criterion—or **finite ideal point models**—consumers desire a moderate amount of each characteristic.
       Compensatory models use a **brand-based evaluation strategy (choice by processing brands)**—one brand at a time is evaluated across all attributes.
2. **Noncompensatory decision rules**—Consumers do not permit high performance on one attribute to compensate for a low rating on another criterion. Only the most important, not all, brand-attribute information is considered. Therefore, these models don't yield a "best" decision; they will only lead to a satisfactory decision—**satisficing.**
   The first two noncompensatory rules use **choice by processing brands (brand-based evaluation strategy)**—evaluating one brand at a time across all attributes:
   a. **Conjunctive decision rule**—Buyers consider all (or any, or the first) brands that surpass a cutoff or minimum acceptable level (MAL) of performance on each determinant criterion.
   b. **Disjunctive decision rule**—Buyers establish cutoffs for a limited number of key criteria, often at a very high performance level. They consider all (or any, or the first) brands that meet or exceed each of these cutoffs.

   The next two noncompensatory rules use **choice by processing attributes**—comparing all brands across one criterion at a time:
   c. **Lexicographic decision rule**—Buyers rank the criteria in order of importance and select the brand scoring highest on the most important criterion. If two or more brands tie, they continue through the remaining attributes in order of importance, stopping when one of the remaining brands outperforms the others and selecting it.
   d. **Elimination by aspects rule (sequential elimination rule)**—Consumers rank the criteria in order of importance and then eliminate all brands that don't meet or exceed a cutoff on the most important criterion. They next go to the second-most important criterion and weed out remaining brands that don't meet or exceed a cutoff on it, continuing until only one of the remaining brands outperforms the others.
3. **Decision (choice) heuristics**—Buyers employ shortcut rules of thumb that generally focus on a *single criterion* to simplify their decision making.
4. **Affect referral rule (affective choice rule)**—Unlike the other three categories of decision strategies, affect referral decision rules are not *attribute-based choices* but rather are *attitude-based decisions*—due to global attitudes, holistic impressions, or emotions associated with a product or brand.

---

car). In effect, a consumer's attitude toward the ad (A_{ad}) helps determine her attitude toward the brand (A_b)—good feelings from the ads rub off on the brand.

    An overview of the decision strategies is found in Exhibit 4.23.

REVIEW QUESTIONS

1. Describe each of the four major categories of consumer decision models—compensatory, noncompensatory, decision heuristics, and affect referral—in terms of
   a. nature and amount of information used,
   b. procedure for using information, and
   c. marketing strategy implications.
2. Compare the two compensatory decision rules—weighted compensatory rules and unweighted compensatory rules—in terms of
   a. use of importance values, and
   b. assumption of finite vs. infinite ideal point models.
3. Compare the four noncompensatory rules—conjunctive, disjunctive, lexicographic, and elimination by aspects—in terms of
   a. use of choice by processing brands vs. choice by processing attributes,
   b. use of importance values (weighting, ranking, or neither),
   c. use of cutoffs (minimum standards), and
   d. marketing strategy implications.

4. Compare decision heuristics and the affect referral rule in terms of
    a. use or nonuse of criteria and number of criteria used, and
    b. attitude-based vs. attribute-based choices.

IN-CLASS APPLICATIONS

1. Are the compensatory decision rules descriptive of how consumers actually behave? Do you know anyone who sits down and computes an attitude score for each brand in his or her evoked set? If not, then of what use are these models to the marketing manager?

2. Describe purchases you have made using the following strategies:
    a. Compensatory decision rule. Which specific type of decision rule did you use: weighted linear compensatory, infinite ideal point, simple additive, or finite ideal point? Did this choice of strategy seem to yield you the optimal alternative as theory suggests?
    b. Noncompensatory decision rule. Which specific type of decision rule did you use: conjunctive, disjunctive, lexicographic, or elimination by aspects? Was this a good choice of decision rules for this product?
    c. Decision heuristics. What was the specific rule of thumb you used? Was it a good idea to use this choice heuristic?
    d. Affective choice rule. Do you think this was a wise way to select this product?

3. Which type of decision rule is the consumer employing in each of the following scenarios? Does that decision strategy appear to be an appropriate one for the type of product being purchased? If not, what would be a better choice of rule to use and why?
    → *Scenario A. Ted's Dream Car Comes True.* Ted, a true perfectionist, did not want to settle for anything less than the best. The need for a new car hit him very suddenly due to his new profession as a songwriter and producer who commutes into the city every weekday. Consequently, he needed an automobile that is very economical on gas (25 miles per gallon in the city minimum) and appears sporty, consistent with his image as a young man on the move. Also, Ted felt that this new vehicle should have a rear defroster and a good CD player.

    For a long time, Ted could not find a vehicle that met all of his needs, even though he visited several dealerships and dozens of Web sites. However, one day by pure chance (or, was it fate?) he came across the car of his dreams sitting alone in the lot of a car dealer on the outskirts of town—it was everything he desired!

    → *Scenario B. Rick's College Choice Strategy.* Rick, a junior in high school, tackled the task of finding a college or university that offered a good theater program. He wrote a list of features he deemed to be important in colleges. Examples were whether the school offered an excellent theater program, whether it was a two- or four-year institution, if it was a single-sex or coed college, inclusion of certain school/community organizations, and level of tuition.

    However, Rick found that some of the features were more important than others. He viewed the strength of a college's theater program to be most critical, followed closely by being coed (Rick wanted to have some fun at school, too!) and having a Christian fellowship group. After much thought, he had a good plan for evaluating the colleges on his list and decided to estimate how well each college performed on the features.

    Rick did not want to exclude a college from his evoked set just because it was lacking on one attribute. Rather, he wanted to be very careful to get the best of everything, if possible.

    → *Scenario C. Rose Phone Home.* Rose wished to purchase a new cordless telephone. However, she wanted the phone to have memory capability of up to 100 phone numbers (hey—she's a popular gal!). This was a MUST, she told a sales associate at the Local Yokal electronic store. However, the sales rep still showed her a phone with less memory than what she wanted, the 80RET by TenorPacific. Rose immediately disconnected this phone from her list of possibilities. After much shopping around, she finally purchased her phone at Phone Central, the model 100MEM with 200-name storage by ToneUSA.

    → *Scenario D. Bea's Perfume Is Nothing to Sniff At.* Bea wrote out a list of product characteristics she desires in a woman's perfume, determining that her desired fragrance must be affordable (no more than $60 for 5 fluid ounces) and have a prestigious brand name. Most important, Bea wanted her perfume to have a passionate, mysterious scent. She didn't know quite how she would evaluate cologne on that criterion, but she had a feeling that the fragrance would hit her square in the face when she encountered it.

While in a Julio's department store, Bea began critiquing perfumes that were less than $12 per ounce based on whether she felt their scents were simultaneously mysterious and passionate. All of the colognes that did not have these qualities were not considered further. Finally, Bea found the fragrance she deemed to be the most desirable of them all, Smoking Mystique.

→ *Scenario E. Auntie Is the Burger Queen.* Aunt Droid wanted good quality hamburger meat to serve her dinner guests one evening, so she went to the Park and Splurge store. Most important to her was less than 8 percent fat (Auntie is trying to shed a few pounds!). Second most important was a price less than $3.29 per pound. When she got to the store she found only one packet of hamburger that was 93 percent lean. Even though it was $3.39 a pound, she bought it.

→ *Scenario F. Polly Wants a Potato Chip.* Polly is choosing among potato chip brands. She considers fat content to be most important, followed by resealable package, and then price. She immediately eliminates all but two brands, Brand X and Brand Y, because they are too high in fat content. She notes that Brand X lacks a resealable container, so she selects Brand Y.

4. The following is a brand-attribute matrix for Hank's decision on what brand of digital video recorder to buy.

Criterion	Importance	Minimum Standard	Ideal	Ajax	Apex	Acme
Maximum recording capacity	5	30 hours (3 rating)	5	2	4	5
Monthly service fees	3	Less than $10/month (3 rating)	5	3	5	3
Number of advanced capabilities	2	Three or more (4 rating)	5	4	3	4
On-screen program guide quality	3	Rating of 3	5	4	3	2

Attribute importance ratings as well as brand ratings for the Ajax, Apex, and Acme brands are on a 1 (low) to 5 (high) scale. Minimum standards are set for each attribute's rating.
Determine which brand Hank will select using each of the following decision rules.
a. Weighted linear compensatory infinite ideal point model
b. Weighted linear compensatory finite ideal point model
c. Simple additive model
d. Conjunctive decision model
e. Disjunctive decision model (assume no minimum standards for number of advanced capabilities and on-screen program guide quality)
f. Lexicographic decision model
g. Elimination-by-aspects model

5. Analyze each of the ads in Exhibits 4.24 through 4.28 to determine which decision model it assumes consumers use when choosing among brands in the advertised product category. In your judgment, is each ad effectively helping to frame (structure) the decision for the consumer?

Cite another decision model each ad could have appealed to, discuss whether or not this would be more effective for assisting the consumer in selecting this product, and describe how the ad would need to be altered to be consistent with this decision rule.

WRITTEN APPLICATIONS

1. Answer Question 2 in the In-Class Applications. Then, ask someone you know the same questions (of course, this will require that you be able to explain each decision rule if your respondent isn't a CB classmate). Report the results.
2. Answer Question 3 from the In-Class Applications.

EXHIBIT 4.24   Renova Ad

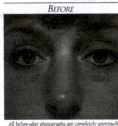
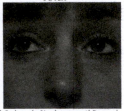

EXHIBIT 4.25   Flonase Ad

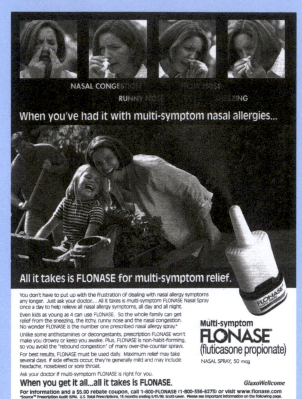

EXHIBIT 4.26   Mazda Ad

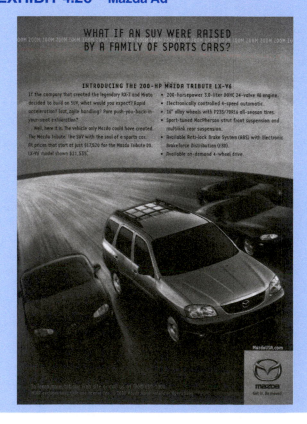

EXHIBIT 4.27   Dentyne Ad

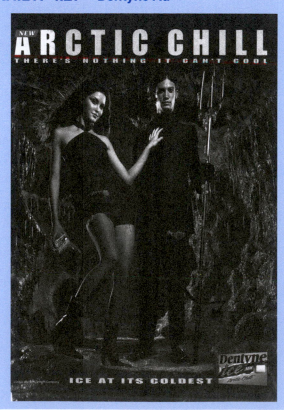

EXHIBIT 4.28   Allergan Refresh Tears Ad

3. Find two more ads, where each seems to suggest that the consumer uses a particular compensatory decision rule (each ad should suggest a different compensatory rule). Also find two ads that indicate that the customer employs a different noncompensatory rule. Repeat the analysis in all of the questions found in Question 5 in the In-Class Applications above for each ad that you find.

EXERCISE 4.5. ALTERNATIVE EVALUATION USING SHOPPING BOTS

OBJECTIVES

1. To apply the theoretical material on the alternative evaluation process from Exercises 4.3 and 4.4 to evaluating brands in an online environment.
2. To become familiar with the two types of shopping bots.
3. To get firsthand experience in using shopping bots to make purchase decisions.
4. To understand the strengths and limitations of shopping bots.

BACKGROUND

THE NATURE OF SHOPPING BOTS

A very efficient way to facilitate the alternative evaluation process is to comparison shop on line using **shopping bots (shopbots, buyer agents, virtual sales assistants, shopping search engines, comparison shopping sites, robot search engines)**. These specially designed Internet search engines are used to locate and compare brand alternatives, telling users price information about brands and/or providing product recommendations. These comparison shopping sites troll the Internet in search of information using specified evaluative criteria that are either user-stated or search-engine specified. The purpose is to systematically find brand-attribute information. Bots act like **meta-engines (metasearch tools)**, which are search engines that hunt multiple search engines simultaneously for words and phrases, combine results, remove duplicate entries, and present a single listing.

A shopbot employs a robot ("bot") or intelligent agent to roam the Internet in search of information. Most shopping bots claim to eliminate the searching necessary to identify the right product at the best price. They take a consumer's query, visit e-tailers that might have the sought product, bring the user the results, and present the findings in a consolidated, compact format showing brand performance on attributes.

Once a search has been performed, the user needs to assign relevance rankings to the items retrieved. The intelligent agent uses this information in the next iteration to modify its search operation. Bots do not sell anything—they search for and compare products for you. However, many also provide access to an order form.

Beware: Bots are not always concerned with the consumer's best interest since most are for-profit ventures, collaborating with various manufacturers and Internet marketers. Shopping bots earn money by directing consumers to Internet merchants, charging either listing fees or click-through fees. However, some e-tailers use their own shopping bots, using collaborative filtering technologies to recommend products to shoppers based on tracking their purchasing patterns.

Two Types of Shopping Bots

The two types of shopping bots are comprehensive and product specific. **Comprehensive shopbots** provide comprehensive coverage in many product categories. Examples of comprehensive robot search engines include ShopWiki, mySimon, Netmarket, Smarter, Shopzilla, PriceGrabber, Shopping.com, AlltheWeb, Epinions, PlanetRetail, CheapUncle, DealNews, ZDNet, ThisNext, and ConsumerSearch. Some sites offer consumer (user) product reviews, such as Epinions.com. Usually, there is a five-star rating, the number of reviews that rating is based on, and the actual written reviews. Other sites, such as CheapUncle and NexTag, present professional (expert) product reviews. ConsumerSearch.com contains both user and expert reviews, and it examines the reviews for credibility and consolidates the analyses. ThisNext is a cross between a social networking and Web shopping site, dubbed "shopcasting." Some general search engines, such as Yahoo! and Ask, offer comparison shopping sites. Other popular comprehensive shopbots include PriceSCAN, DealTime, BottomDollarFood, and CompareNet. You can type "comparison shopping sites" or a similar phrase into any search engine to discover even more shopping bots.

The second type of shopping bots focuses on a specific product range. For example, Travelocity, Expedia, Orbitz, CheapTickets, and Lowestfare can find the best deals in travel. Bookfinder locates books, Realtor gives real estate listings, and CDPricecompare gives the lowest prices on books, music, movies, and more. In the field of computers, Pricewatch compares computers and components ranging from motherboards to notebook batteries and StreetPrices evaluates computers and peripherals as well as other electronic devices such as camcorders and CD players.

Strengths and Limitations of Shopping Bots

Consumer benefits for using shopbots include convenience, saving time and money, acquiring broad information, and free and easy comparison shopping. The best bots provide simple navigation, well-organized results, sorting by total cost (including shipping, handling, taxes, and restocking fees), and prices from a large number of retailers.

Bots are less useful if you're looking for experience goods requiring prepurchase experience via examination and testing, such as clothing and jewelry. Such items are more taste-driven and are difficult to objectively compare as shopping bots do. Unfortunately, some retailers are anxious about consumers being overly concerned with price and have designed their sites to either refuse the robot admission to the site or confuse the robot.

Keep the following caveats in mind when evaluating shopping bots. Bots do not guarantee the best price for the best product or service; bots do not evaluate and compare all retailers. Some favor retailers who have paid a high price to be listed, and others are biased due to partnerships with retailers and manufacturers.

SHOPPING BOT TIPS

- Search via shopping bots using specific terms if you know what you are looking for (e.g., brand name, color, model).
- Get information from at least three different bots.
- Factor in additional costs along with product prices (e.g., shipping and handling costs, taxes, and restocking fees).
- Carefully read purchase security policies.
- Print copies of completed order forms and keep confirmation/account numbers for your records.
- Verify that a product is in stock before you purchase it.

If this exercise leaves you curious for even more information about shopping bots, you can find it at BotSpot.com.

REVIEW QUESTIONS

1. What are shopping bots? How do they work?
2. What are the major types of shopbots? Give some examples of each.
3. Describe the strengths and limitations of shopbots.

IN-CLASS APPLICATIONS

1. Discuss your experiences, if any, in using shopping bots prior to beginning this exercise. What advantages did you find as compared to "old-fashioned" information search? Disadvantages?

2. Describe your experiences by completing the shopping exercise below.

WRITTEN APPLICATIONS

1. Visit three different shopping bots in search of brand-attribute information in a product category of your choosing. Your instructor might specify which bots to use and which category to search. Or, you can try shopbots mentioned in the background section of this exercise (several of which will perhaps be defunct by the time you do this exercise).

    Another possibility is to type search terms such as "shopping bots," "shopbots," and "shopping search engine" into several different search engines (such as Google, Yahoo!, Alta Vista, Dogpile, HotBot, Lycos, Bing, and others found by clicking on the "Search" button in your browser). This will help you learn about current and relevant search sites.

    Write a summary report of your shopping experience on each shopping bot. You may attach portions of printouts as exhibits to facilitate your discussion. In comparing the shopping bots, consider the following issues.

    a. *Evaluative criteria used.* Did the shopping bot specify these for you or could you choose your own? If the bot chose attributes for you, were they the same as your own determinant criteria? If not, did this severely limit their usefulness? Was the bot restricted in the types of evaluative criteria used (i.e., did it use both features and one or more of the three types of benefits discussed in Exercise 4.3)?

    b. *Importance of the criteria.* Were you able to make this decision or did the bot either weight the attributes for you or assume they were all equal in importance? Did the bot's weighting scheme help or hinder your evaluation of brands?

    c. *Members of the evoked set.* Did the bot determine these for you or were you allowed to input your own brands? Did the bot's evoked set in any way constrain your alternative evaluation process?

    d. What types of brand-evaluation (ratings) information did the bot use? Was it quantitative (e.g., rating scales, price points), qualitative (descriptive information), or both? Was all of the bot's information objective (easily verifiable search attributes such as price, size, and weight) or was some of it subjective (experience attributes such as "enjoyable," "fun," "tastes good," etc.)?

    e. Which type of decision rule did the shopping bot seem to use? Does this make sense for the product category you were searching? Did use of this decision rule restrict the bot's usefulness for you? Which decision model, if any, might be more appropriate for this product?

    f. Summarize your experience using shopping bots. How did it compare to using corporate Web sites to gather brand-attribute information?

    g. Evaluate the privacy policies of the three shopbots that you used. Are they easy to find? Are they clear? Do they seem to protect the consumer's right to privacy?

EXERCISE 4.6. DECISIONS: OUTLET AND BRAND CHOICES

OBJECTIVES

1. To understand and critically analyze the evaluative criteria that influence selection of outlets (retail stores and Web sites).
2. To explain how the macroenvironment, microenvironment, and personal purchase situational factors can all influence brand choice decisions when shopping.
3. To understand and critically analyze the factors in the purchase environment that affect brand choices, as well as their implications for both retailers and manufacturers.
4. To gain additional understanding into your own shopping behavior.
5. To acquire experience in evaluating a retailer's performance on evaluative criteria and purchase environment factors.

BACKGROUND

OVERVIEW OF THE CHOICE PROCESS

This exercise describes the path to purchase known as "the last mile," that is, the **choice (shopping) process**, or all activities between formation of a purchase intention and buying the product in retail outlets. **Retail outlets** are commercial markets for goods or services that shoppers visit to purchase merchandise, that is, retail stores (physical entities) and Web sites (virtual entities).

Although some people would rather grout the bathroom tile than set foot in a mall, for others shopping is the other great American pastime (baseball being the first one). There are a lot more people going to malls on Sundays than to football games. For retailers and the manufacturers whose brands they carry, the in-store experience provides the moment of truth—a brand choice (purchase decision).

Retail marketing comes in three forms: (1) manufacturers branding and selling their products at retail, (2) retailers branding and promoting their own products at retail, and (3) retailers branding and promoting their own stores and chains.

Recall that the alternative evaluation process culminates in a preferred alternative—the brand toward which the consumer has the most favorable attitude. This positive attitude results in a favorable buying intention. Usually, a most favorable brand attitude and buying intention leads to the purchase of the preferred alternative. However, there might be nonfulfillment of purchase intentions for several reasons:

1. Sometimes a decision is made to purchase the product, but the brand-choice decision is deferred until the consumer has selected a place to shop and is inside a store or on a Web site. Therefore, we shall first examine the evaluative criteria used in the store choice decision.
2. There might be unanticipated circumstances that intervene between the intention to buy and the actual purchase decision. The result is that instead of both the planned product and brand being

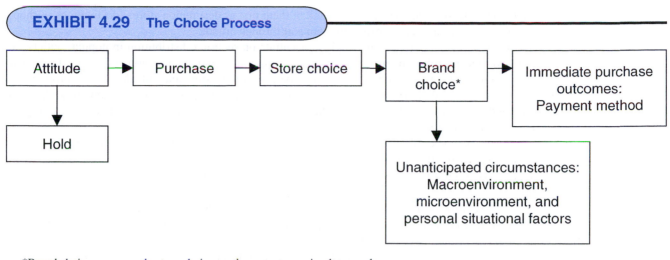

EXHIBIT 4.29   The Choice Process

Attitude → Purchase → Store choice → Brand choice* → Immediate purchase outcomes: Payment method

Attitude → Hold

Brand choice* → Unanticipated circumstances: Macroenvironment, microenvironment, and personal situational factors

*Brand choice can precede store choice, or they can occur simultaneously.

bought, there might be either (a) no purchase or (b) a brand substitution—the intended product is bought but the planned brand is not. This discussion includes the unanticipated circumstances that can affect brand choice decisions.

Finally, we briefly describe the immediate purchase outcomes: purchase and consumption of the product. Exhibit 4.29 summarizes all of these factors.

STORE CHOICE

There are two levels of store choice decision—type of outlet (e.g., discount vs. department store) and brand of outlet (e.g., Target vs. Costco).

TYPE OF OUTLET CHOICE

First, the shopper must determine where to buy the desired product. In addition to brick-and-motar retail stores there are also nonstore retailers—distribution channels other than retail outlets, including catalogers, mail order marketers, television shopping, direct sales, part-plan marketers (home parties, such as Mary Kay, Tupperware), and e-tailers.

For example, suppose you want to rent a video—where do you go? A few years ago, a video rental shop was an obvious choice, but you could also patronize a grocery store, a convenience store, and, in some cases, other secondary outlets such as gas stations and dry cleaners. Or you could even rent within the comfort of your home via video-on-demand from your local cable, satellite, or phone company. The latter option along with online services such as Netflix and Blockbuster Online, which deliver ordered videos under subscription plans through mail or via digital downloads, have largely replaced retail rentals.

STORE BRAND CHOICE: STORE SELECTION CRITERIA

Once an outlet type has been determined, the buyer's second choice decision concerns the brand of store. Usually, store selection entails routine DM—consumers have strong store preferences or might even be store loyal. In fact, there is a trend toward dominance of store choice decisions over brand-choice decisions. This is due in part to declining brand loyalty, with brand decisions increasingly being made by retailers. As a consequence, consumers do not say, "I want a Sony," or "I'd like a Panasonic," but rather, "I've got to go to Best Buy to check out what they've got in digital TVs." Major merchants, such as CarMax, AutoNation

USA, and Home Depot, want customers to think of them first as destination stores (destinations to shop). Once people arrive, a salesperson will help them sort through brands.

Consequently, manufacturers increasingly concentrate on securing distribution in popular outlets and obtaining favorable **merchandising**—the advertising, promotion, and organization of the sale of a particular brand within a store. Merchandising generally involves both in-store and outside-of-store promotional activities, including special pricing, assortment, coupon dispensers, posters, point-of-purchase displays, adequate shelf space allotments, favorable shelf positioning, in-store audio, and signage. This helps to facilitate shoppers' in-store brand decisions.

Store choices are analogous to brand choices: Consumers evaluate store alternatives on their evaluative criteria using a decision rule. The major distinction between a store choice and a brand choice is in the types of evaluative criteria used. The following are the most important store selection criteria.

Store Image. Analogous to brand image, **store image** is the buyer's overall perception or impression of the store's personality and of the type of person who shops there. Store image is a function of both the physical and psychological characteristics the marketer uses to position the store. A shop can be highbrow or lowbrow, classy or classless, a place to be seen shopping or a place you would be embarrassed to be seen patronizing. A store can have an image of carrying fine merchandise or of selling cheap junk.

Store Brands. **Store brands (private labels, dealer brands, in-house labels, own labels)** are brands that are owned, sponsored, and controlled by the retailer. Examples include Sam's Choice soda at Wal-Mart and Arizona jeans from JCPenney. Retailers use such brands as lower-price alternatives to manufacturers' brands as well as to help build store loyalty, and earn higher profit margins.

Retail Advertising. Retail advertising comes in two basic types. **Price-and-item advertising** usually has the message, "Here are the brands we are currently featuring at these spectacular prices." Other essential information can be included, such as hours of operation and location. **Image advertising** is retail advertising that helps to craft a store image via the people, places, and situations it includes.

Physical Store Attributes. A store's tangible characteristics can also be used to create a retail image. For example, if a store appears clean and modern, customers assume the merchandise is fashionable and up-to-date. Physical store characteristics include exterior architecture—storefront, signs, entrances, display windows, store visibility in the surrounding area, parking availability, and traffic congestion—and interior characteristics—lighting, music, temperature, restroom facilities, flooring, aisle width, overall cleanliness, colors, scents, wall textures, décor, store layout (floor space allotted for merchandise and traffic), department locations, product groupings, noise level, and in-store advertising and merchandising.

Price. Although price has historically been used by merchants to draw in customers, price promotions are now being deemphasized in the wake of findings that they tend to cannibalize sales from the future or shift sales among brands within the store rather than from store to store. Instead, "everyday low price" strategies, popularized by Wal-Mart, became prevalent in the 1980s and 1990s and are now rampant in the fast-food industry with 99-cent menus.

Some retailers still attract patrons through price discounts known as **loss leaders**, reduced prices on high-margin items to attract customers who are expected to buy other merchandise at full price while in the store. Fast-food feeders offer enticing discounts on sandwiches to lure consumers. Once customers are inside, cashier suggestions and in-store displays push add-ons, such as drinks, sides, and other high-margin items.

Customer Services. Customer services can increase customer satisfaction (credit, alterations, installation, and shopper information); increase convenience (telephone ordering, catalogs, home delivery, easy "no-questions-asked" merchandise return, and package carry out); and provide special benefits (gift wrapping, gift registries, product repair, and complaint offices).

Generally, stores position themselves as being either price-oriented, with minimal service levels (e.g., most supermarkets and mass merchandisers employing order-taking clerks), or customer service-oriented, with higher prices (e.g., department stores and specialty stores with knowledgeable "customer service consultants").

Outlet Location. Consumers prefer to shop at locations that are conveniently located close to home. If stores are viewed as roughly equal on the other criteria or if there is no strong store preference, distance and driving time can be the make-or-break factor. Therefore, Wal-Mart locates near highway ramps and Radio Shack outlets are situated so that 94 percent of the population lives within five miles of one.

Hours of Operation. Today's busy shoppers demand more than the traditional "banker's hours" of 9:00 A.M. to 4:00 P.M. Evenings, weekends, and "round-the-clock" hours are expected.

Nature and Quality of Assortment. This attribute becomes significant especially when a consumer has not yet made a brand choice and wants to evaluate and select from among many brands. Two important merchandise mix considerations are width and depth:

1. **Width** refers to the number of different products a retailer carries. A store can offer either a wide assortment (many products, permitting one-stop shopping, something time-pressured consumers increasingly seek) or a narrow selection (few products, allowing for specialization).
2. **Depth** refers to variety within a merchant's product category or department, which can be either shallow (little variety) or deep (much variety). Whereas mass merchandisers tend to offer wide but somewhat shallow assortments, specialty stores such as The Limited and "category killers" like Toys 'R Us offer narrow but very deep assortments.

Store Personnel. The nature and appearance of store employees, including salespeople, stock clerks, cashiers, and customer service reps, are important. Employees should be knowledgeable, friendly, cheerful, enthusiastic, helpful (but not overbearing), and professional in appearance.

Store Patrons. Customers prefer to shop at stores that attract members of their social milieu (social class and social groups). Teenagers do not want to be seen in an "old fogy's" store, nor do elitists wish to darken the door of a dollar store.

Consumer Logistics. **Consumer logistics** is the speed and ease with which patrons are able to move into and through a store, including parking, entering, browsing, checkout, and exit. Customer logistics is affected by physical factors such as store location, store layout, aisle width, crowding, and length of checkout lines (shoppers' number one complaint).

UNANTICIPATED FACTORS AFFECTING PRODUCT AND BRAND CHOICE

The shopping process concludes with a decision on whether or not to buy. If a purchase is to be made, decisions about when to purchase and what product type and brand to buy follow. Sometimes these final choices deviate from the buyer's original intentions.

CHOICE ON WHETHER OR NOT TO BUY

One possibility here is a no-purchase decision, where the buyer decision process is temporarily or permanently shelved for reasons such as lack of desirable alternatives; constrained consumer resources; and changing macroenvironmental, microenvironmental, and personal circumstances. **Shopper marketing** is the orchestration of in-store marketing activities and the retail environment to turn browsers into buyers at the point of sale. The idea is that the retail store itself is an important marketing medium. Shopper marketing includes the traditional 4 Ps of product (packaging, graphics, etc.), price (e.g., discounts, coupons), place (shelving, product positioning, etc.), and promotion (e.g., in-store TV, shopping basket ads).

DECISION ON WHEN TO BUY

Timing of the purchase can be influenced by macroenvironmental factors such as the season of the year, microenvironmental factors such as product publicity, personal situational factors such as receiving a bonus at work, and purchase environment conditions such as a sales promotion.

DECISIONS ON WHAT PRODUCT AND BRAND TO BUY: THREE CATEGORIES OF UNANTICIPATED FACTORS

We shall now discuss the three categories of unanticipated circumstances affecting product and brand choice (Exhibit 4.29).

THE MACROENVIRONMENT

Macroenvironmental events occur in society at large. Societal changes that could take the consumer by surprise and an example of each are listed below:

- The sociocultural environment: Faced with increased social and workplace pressure to quit smoking, a consumer suddenly decides to abandon this habit.
- The technological environment: The product to be purchased becomes technologically obsolete.
- The economy: A recession causes customers to postpone buying major-ticket items such as large appliances.
- The natural environment: In the face of rising energy costs a consumer postpones or abandons purchasing an energy-gulping appliance or car.
- Politics and the law: New export controls make a product unavailable.

THE MICROENVIRONMENT

The manufacturer's or retailer's **microenvironment (operating environment)** entails factors close to the company affecting its ability to effectively serve its customers, thereby causing buyers to either fulfill or not fulfill their original purchase intentions.

The following are changes in the microenvironment and an example of each:

- Competitors: A rival comes out with an improved or lower-cost product.
- Channels of distribution: Online sellers offer an easier, cheaper way for the consumer to purchase the product.
- Suppliers: A supply shortage means the product must bear a higher price to cover the increased input costs.
- Other publics or stakeholders: A magazine prints an unfavorable review of a product.

PERSONAL SITUATIONAL FACTORS

Personal purchase situational factors consist of variables peculiar to a particular time, place, or location that affect the buyer's decision. For example, the time since her last meal could significantly affect a consumer's purchase decision between a one-pint versus a half-gallon carton of ice cream. Situational factors are largely beyond a marketer's influence. However, in some cases a retailer can partially control them through manipulating elements of the shopping environment, such as serving food samples.

THE PURCHASE ENVIRONMENT: IN-STORE VARIABLES INFLUENCING BRAND CHOICE DECISIONS

In-store variables can be a potent influence on consumer DM. Consider the following factors.

PACKAGING: THE MANUFACTURER'S CONTROLLABLE IN-STORE INFLUENCE

An important function of a product's **packaging**—the product's container or wrapper, plus inserts and labeling—is to promote that product. The package as "the silent salesman" provides the last opportunity to deliver a selling message before the customer makes a purchase. A well-designed package "grabs" the shopper's attention through bright colors, bold typeface, and distinctive graphics, and it can reinforce the brand image. For example, if a new hair conditioner is positioned as "bright" and "uniquely you," a yellow box with a mirrored surface on top can reinforce this.

ATMOSPHERICS

Atmospherics is the conscious design of physical retail or service environment space (servicescape) and its various dimensions, making the store an attractive place to shop and helping to positively shape the shopping experience. Store dimensions such as lighting, layout, décor, fixtures, furnishings, colors, aromas, music and other sounds, temperature, merchandise layout, and salespeople's dress, attitudes, and behaviors are all designed to affect buyers' feelings and actions. For instance, bright lighting can create excitement, while subdued lighting can induce a mellow mood. Atmospherics influence consumer judgments of the store's quality and image, amount of time spent in the store, and nature and volume of merchandise purchased. For example, bargain basements deliberately use narrow aisles, harsh lighting, and overloaded counters to create a bargain image. Starbuck's Wi-Fi connections, comfy couches, and hip music make patrons want to linger over another cup of java. Atmospherics can also differentiate a store. Consequently, most large retailers now have "signature scents" exclusive to their stores. At a Sony Style outlet, the subtle scent of vanilla and mandarin orange relaxes shoppers and makes buying consumer electronics less intimidating, especially for women.

To create an atmosphere online, Internet retailers such as Amazon and eBay also use graphics, colors, layout, content, and **interactivity**—opportunities for e-shoppers to interact with a firm's personnel through e-mail, chat rooms, and blogs. Other online atmospheric tools include animation, music and sounds, and other navigational tools.

IN-STORE MEDIA

Point-of-purchase (POP) displays (point-of-sale displays), which are especially effective in self-service outlets, include banners, shelf signs, kiosks, ads on shopping carts, in-store broadcasts, and other ads found in retail outlets, including racks, shelves, or bins that hold the product. In conjunction with the package, they can clinch the sale. Displays not only grab attention but also jumpstart sales because there is a consumer belief that "if an item is displayed, it must be on sale." Buyers beware: This might not be the case.

Other forms of in-store media include on-shelf advertisements, product demonstrators and sample dispatchers, coupon-dispensing machines, shopping cart ads, in-store radio ads, commercials on video monitors in checkout lines, and video kiosks.

SALESPEOPLE

In outlets other than self-service stores, where package influence prevails, salespeople have perhaps the greatest purchase-environment influence on shopper decisions. Naturally, consumers prefer sales personnel who are credible—knowledgeable and trustworthy individuals who consider the buyer's best interests (rather than just their own commissions). Salespeople should also be likeable and attractive. Ideally, sales representatives are demographically and psychographically similar to store customers, for people feel more comfortable with "their own kind" and are more likely to trust their opinions.

SALES PROMOTIONS

Sales promotions (promotions, promotional marketing) are short-term incentives to encourage immediate sale of a product. They can take the form of either price promotions, that is, indirect price reductions (e.g., on-shelf coupons, instant rebates), or tangible value added to the product (e.g., gift-with-purchase, "buy one get one free"). In-store samples, such as food morsels handed out by demonstrators, can induce an impulse purchase. Tried-and true promotions such as loyalty programs (e.g., spend $100 and you get a coupon good for $5 off your next purchase) and gift cards are meant to keep customers returning for more (gift card redeemers often purchase additional merchandise, too). E-tailers also use promotions such as samples, electronic coupons, and sweepstakes and contests to encourage people to visit or return to a Web site.

IN-STORE PRODUCT PLACEMENT

In-store product placement concerns in-store positioning, shelf space, and shelf positioning. **In-store positioning** refers to the placement of the product in the store. For instance, Ocean Spray craisins (dried cranberries) could be located in the produce aisle, positioned as a fruit; the snack section, positioned as a snack; the baked goods aisle, marketed as an ingredient; or the dried fruit section, positioned as a fruit snack. The amount of **shelf space** is the number of *shelf facings*, that is, rows displaying a product. Up to a point, the more shelf space a brand occupies, the more units will be sold: "Stack it high, and watch it fly!" **Shelf positioning (shelving)** concerns the shelf location of a brand. New items are most likely to be stocked at eye level since it is the best place to trigger an impulse purchase ("Eye level is buy level"). Shoulder-to-waist level is second best.

IMMEDIATE PURCHASE DECISION OUTCOMES

PAYMENT METHOD

Once product and brand choices have been made, one last decision follows: method of payment for the selected alternative. ("Will that be cash, charge, or debit? Visa, MasterCard, or Discover card?") In our cashless society, more and more consumers are paying with personal checks, traveler's checks, money orders, charge checks (checks issued by a credit or charge card company as a cash advance), bank cards, and debit cards.

CONSUMPTION

The final outcome of the purchase is consumption or usage. Consumption can occur immediately. However, usage is generally postponed until some time after the purchase. A product might be consumed by someone other than the buyer, such as a family member, houseguest, or gift recipient.

REVIEW QUESTIONS

1. Outline and explain the important evaluative criteria that influence outlet selection.
2. What are the three major categories of unanticipated circumstances affecting product and brand choice? Cite several examples from each category.
3. What are the primary factors in the purchase environment affecting buyer decisions and how does each influence those decisions? How can manufacturers and retailers make decisions to influence purchases by considering these factors?

IN-CLASS APPLICATIONS

1. Which store criteria are important to you in selecting the following:
   a. Music store
   b. Clothing outlet
   c. Restaurant
   d. Place to buy sporting goods
   e. Professional service provider (hair stylist, tax accountant, doctor, etc.)
   What is the relative importance of the criteria for each of these products? Which decision rule (from Exercise 4.4) best describes how you go about choosing an alternative for each?

2. Think of a recent purchase you made for which the brand bought differed from the brand you originally intended to buy. Which unanticipated factor(s) accounted for the difference? Are there any lessons to be learned by either a manufacturer or a retailer?

WRITTEN APPLICATIONS

1. Trace through the store and brand choice process, as outlined in Exhibit 4.29, that you recently experienced for a fairly high-involvement, routine decision when shopping in a bricks-and-mortar retail environment. Describe as many factors as you can recall that intervened between your initial brand attitudes and your actual brand purchase. Your discussion should include your store choice decision, including the evaluative criteria and decision rule you used in selecting a store. Explain any unanticipated macroenvironment, microenvironment, and personal situational factors that helped influence your brand choice decision. Finally, discuss the influence and effectiveness of the elements in the retail purchase environment in your brand selection decision-making process.

What implications of this process are there for the retailer and manufacturer involved? In particular, what are they doing especially well, what do they need to do to improve their marketing programs, and what new things could they be doing to better take advantage of the consumer choice process discussed in this exercise?

2. Visit a small independent retailer, such as a grocer, bookstore, record store, or clothing store. Determine how the merchant meets direct competition from large retail chains, supermarkets, discount stores, department stores, superstores, or other types of retail outlets.

You can use a personal interview, observation, and/or discussions with customers as well as your own informed analysis. Or perform your analysis for a full-price department store competing with a discounter such as Kmart, or vice versa.

Include in your discussion an evaluation of the merchant's performance on store choice criteria and the purchase environment, with special emphasis on strategies and tactics used to influence product and brand choices, increase sales, or sway the timing of sales. Include any recommendations on how you think the retailer could improve in any of these areas.

EXERCISE 4.7. POSTPURCHASE OUTCOMES

OBJECTIVES

1. To recognize how marketers must understand, appeal to, and take advantage of postpurchase outcomes, such as postpurchase evaluation (resulting in satisfaction/dissatisfaction and possible dissonance).
2. To get practice in seeking marketing opportunities from postpurchase behavior.

BACKGROUND

BUILDING CUSTOMER RELATIONSHIPS

The product has been purchased and consumed. Marketing mission accomplished? Nope! A common fallacy is that the marketer's job ends with the sale. However, modern marketers realize that you can't just "love 'em and leave 'em."

The old school of marketing centered on the **transaction**, a single exchange between a buyer and seller or one-time sale—it was a "one night stand." Such **transactional marketing** emphasizes making the immediate sale and new customer acquisition via **conquest (acquisition) marketing**, in which competitors' customers are targeted, and new product users who have never purchased items in the product category are enticed.

In contrast, today's marketers strive to build *long-term relationships* with their existing customers, realizing that effective marketing continues even *after* the sale. **Relationship (retention) marketing** involves all organizational activities that develop long-term, value-laden relationships between brands and customers through marketers' efforts to continually fulfill buyers' unsatisfied desires. Such relationships are built from having both **brand insight**—a marketer's deep understanding of the brand—and **consumer insight**—a marketer's deep customer knowledge stemming from consumer research. The focus is on satisfying and retaining existing customers. Retention marketing is more important to large, established firms with a large market share to defend. Smaller companies are hungrier and use *offensive* marketing tactics, such as comparison advertising, to pursue rivals' customers.

Relationship marketing activities are designed to develop trust and commitment. Consumers must have confidence in the honesty and integrity of the marketer and in the quality and reliability of the seller's goods. They must also care about maintaining a valued relationship. Dell lost customers' trust and commitment when customer service slipped but is now regaining it after redoubling service efforts.

Why the focus on current customers? Although precise statistics are elusive, it is said that it costs five times as much (some say six to ten times) to capture a new customer as it does to hang onto an existing one. Even farmers know that it is easier and cheaper to harvest fields they've already planted than to cultivate fields.

Today's marketers want customers for life, and they even calculate the **lifetime value of a customer (LVC; lifetime customer value [LCV], lifetime value [LTV])**. This estimation projects a customer's financial worth over the entire history of that customer's relationship with a company. It is calculated by subtracting the acquisition costs and ongoing costs of serving a customer from the customer's continuing revenue stream.

Building an enduring relationship with a consumer can be expensive. For example, a major pizza chain might value a young adult's future business at $8,000 in future revenue. LVC is calculated by subtracting initial costs to attract a customer with advertising and promotional offers ($100) and future costs of selling to and servicing the buyer ($4,900). They should therefore be willing to spend up to $3,000 ($8,000 minus $5,000) to acquire that customer.

Consumers are rightly viewed as the most valuable assets on the balance sheet (although accountants never place them there). Therefore, they should be maintained with at least as much care as a firm's best plant and equipment.

The firm adds value at each consumer *touchpoint* or interaction by continually staying in touch with buyers, providing individualized attention to them, offering any needed after-sale service, providing valued information, and distributing extra incentives through loyalty marketing activities.

These relationship marketing activities usually rely on collection or maintenance of a **customer database**. This lists each customer along with contact information (including address, phone number, and e-mail address), demographic and psychographic characteristics, and purchase transaction history. Such a database is the foundation for **customer relationship management (CRM)**—activities to encourage repeat patronage offer reinforcement through incentives and rewards, including the capture, storage, and analysis of customer information that will help optimize those rewards. CRM programs require **longitudinal research**, or consumer research on attitudes and behaviors of individual customers gathered over time. For example, all the transactional information on Dick Tater over the last year might be used to gauge the strength of his relationship with a particular firm.

Overview of Postpurchase Outcomes

There are several **postpurchase outcomes (postacquisition behaviors)**. Marketers are especially interested in these aspects of CB that follow the purchase and acquisition of a product (Exhibit 4.30).

Customer Satisfaction/Dissatisfaction

Satisfaction Defined and Conceptualized

Consumer satisfaction/dissatisfaction (CS/D) is critical because the generic goal of marketing activity is customer satisfaction. Satisfaction is a function of a consumer's desires and expectations. A product's performance should at least meet, and preferably exceed, consumers' desires (what they need or want to get)

EXHIBIT 4.30   **Postpurchase Outcomes**

```
                              ┌─────────────┐
                              │  Purchase   │
                              └──────┬──────┘
                                     │
                                     ▼
                         ┌────────────────────┐
                         │ Consumption/usage* │
                         └─────────┬──────────┘
                   ┌───────────────┴───────────────┐
                   ▼                                ▼
      ┌───────────────────────────┐   ┌──────────────────────────┐
      │ Postpurchase evaluation   │   │ Postpurchase behavior    │
      │ outcomes                  │   │                          │
      └────────┬─────────┬────────┘   └─────┬──────────┬─────────┘
               │         │                  │          │         │
               ▼         ▼                  ▼          ▼         ▼
      ┌──────────┐ ┌──────────┐ ┌──────────┐ ┌──────┐ ┌─────────┐
      │Satisfac- │ │Postpur-  │ │ Repeat   │ │Brand │ │ Other   │
      │tion/     │ │chase     │ │purchase  │ │switch│ │behavior │
      │dissatis- │ │disson-   │ │          │ │ing   │ │         │
      │faction   │ │ance      │ │          │ │      │ │         │
      └────┬─────┘ └────┬─────┘ └────┬─────┘ └──────┘ └─────────┘
           │            │            ▲  │
           ▼            └────────────┘  ▼
  ┌─────────────────┐        ┌──────────────┐
  │  Complaining    │        │ Brand loyalty│
  │  behavior       │        │              │
  └─────────────────┘        └──────────────┘
```

*As is traditionally done, we assume purchase leads to usage. However, items sometimes go unused in certain product categories (e.g., health and fitness equipment, small kitchen appliances, health foods and supplements, club memberships). Reasons include items being bought just because they were on sale, maintenance hassles, and difficulties learning to use or problems with using the product.

and *expectations* (what they expect to get). **Consumer satisfaction/dissatisfaction (CS/D)** is a postpurchase state in which a customer's desires and expectations are fulfilled (met or exceeded), or not.

The first requirements to be met are **desires**, the needs and wants to be fulfilled or problems to be solved. Consumers want products to deliver a certain level of benefit. You want the beverage to satisfy your thirst and the air freshener to leave the room smelling pleasant.

A second factor contributing to satisfaction is **expectations**, prepurchase beliefs about the level of product performance on all of the important criteria. You expect the cell phone to not drop calls and the refrigerator to keep food cool and fresh. If the consumer's expectations and desires have been achieved or surpassed, then he or she is satisfied. If expectations or desires are not met, the customer is dissatisfied.

SATISFACTION AND PERFORMANCE

Product performance is the degree to which the product fulfills consumer desires and expectations. It has two dimensions: instrumental performance and symbolic performance. **Instrumental performance** entails outcomes of product purchase and usage related to *utilitarian (instrumental)* needs. Failure to deliver the desired and expected instrumental performance is believed to result in dissatisfaction as consumers' minimal requirements are not met. **Dissatisfiers**, such as long wait times and dirty tables in a restaurant, are related to dissatisfaction with instrumental performance.

However, achieving the wanted and anticipated performance levels on instrumental attributes is not enough to deliver satisfaction. Satisfaction frequently requires meeting or exceeding desired and expected levels of **symbolic performance**, outcomes of product purchase and usage related to *hedonic needs*, such as enjoyment, fun, and entertainment. These are known as **satisfiers**. In a restaurant these would include order takers who greet patrons courteously and managers who are visible and ready to assist customers.

When the consumer compares actual (or, more accurately, perceived) product performance against desires and expectations, three outcomes are possible:

1. **Satisfaction**—positive confirmation of expectations and desires: The buyer receives what was expected.
2. **Delight**—positive disconfirmation of expectations and desires: A pleasant surprise ensues. The consumer gets more than expected and is therefore thrilled.
3. **Dissatisfaction**—negative disconfirmation of expectations and desires: An unpleasant surprise occurs because the customer received less than what was expected and desired.

WHY CUSTOMER SATISFACTION IS SO IMPORTANT

Although 100 percent customer satisfaction is like a unicorn or mermaid—something marketers can all imagine but none will ever see—marketers must strive for this ideal. Customer satisfaction is important to avoid **market damage**—harm done by dissatisfied customers. The following types of market damage can arise.

Exit or defection. Dissatisfied customers vote with their feet and either exit the market altogether or else defect to another brand. The firm thereby forfeits their lifetime consumer value and must incur extra marketing costs to acquire new customers. Marketers monitor **churn rate**, which is the number or percentage of customers who defect in a given period of time.

Complaining. Dissatisfied customers often engage in **consumer-complaining behavior (CCB)**, courses of action a consumer may take if he or she is dissatisfied, which can ruin a marketer's business. According to one commonly used classification scheme for CCB, consumers can take several courses of action: voice responses, private responses, and public (third-party) responses.

Voice responses. These are complaints made directly to the firm. This can actually be a very useful feedback source a company can use to improve the value it delivers to customers. Consequently, smart firms monitor and act upon consumer complaints. However, if a marketer receives few or even no complaints, it does not mean that everything is hunky dory. The fact is that, for reasons we will discuss, very few consumers bother to complain. Consequently, marketers need to be proactive in learning about customer gripes by seeking them out.

Private responses are negative word-of-mouth communications. For example, think about your conversations with fellow students regarding "good" versus "bad" professors on your campus. Which type do you enjoy discussing more?

Although many complaints never reach the marketer (or the professor!), they do spread to potential customers (or other students). According to one estimate, there are nine such complaints to friends, relatives, colleagues, and neighbors per dissatisfied customer, more than twice the number of compliments passed on by contented customers.

The Internet provides much grist for the negative word-of-mouth mill via online forums, chat rooms, bulletin boards, e-mail messages, blogs, YouTube videos, and hate Web sites such as "I hate McDonald's," "Toys R Us Sucks," and the "U-Hell" Web site about U-Haul rentals. One bad customer experience can be revisited in perpetuity in the digital space. Instead of nine complaints, there are likely to be 90, 900, or even 900,000!

Public, or *third-party, responses.* These can include seeking legal redress, such as in local small claims court, and negative publicity. The latter response might be in the form of a letter or e-mail written to the editor of a publication or a complaint report filed with an organization such as a municipality, a consumer protection agency, a consumer group such as Consumers Union or the U.S. Public Interest Research Group, a local media outlet, or the Better Business Bureau. Another third-party response is to organize or participate in a product **boycott**, in which dissatisfied customers organize to encourage people to abstain from purchasing the product. Such actions can lead to highly visible negative publicity for the firm.

No action. Dissatisfied customers can also choose to not take action. A great many people decide to suffer in silence. However, on ethical grounds, a marketer should not want to cause misery.

MARKETING IMPLICATIONS OF THE SATISFACTION STAGE

Expectations Management. It is important to create realistic consumer expectations. If a marketer raises the expectations bar so high that she cannot fulfill it, she will have dissatisfied customers. Yet, many marketers over-promise in their "brag-and-boast" advertising (e.g., "Best in town," "Unsurpassed," and "Second to none"). The old maxims that "honesty pays," you should "walk the talk," "under-promise and over-deliver" are certainly true in marketing communication. Southwest Airlines typically leads the airline industry in terms of customer satisfaction scores, and they promise little more than peanuts.

Product Quality. **Product quality** entails giving buyers something for their money that meets their desires and fulfills their expectations. That is, a quality product satisfies its customers. Thus viewed, quality is a subjective assessment of the product ("Quality is in the eye of the beholder"). This is *perceived quality*.

But since competitive brands might also meet or exceed consumer expectations, it is also useful to think of quality as actual competitive superiority or excellence on important evaluative criteria. This is *actual quality*—quality that can be objectively assessed, such as by J.D. Power and Associates' Initial Quality Study. This annual study reports problems with new vehicles that owners experienced during the first ninety days of ownership.

Guarantees and Warranties. Money-back guarantees and product warranties are written promises about a product's integrity. A **guarantee** relates to the *customer*—it ensures customer satisfaction; otherwise, money will be refunded ("satisfaction guaranteed"). Wal-Mart accepts returned goods without argument and with a smile.

A **warranty** relates to the *product*. It constitutes a written promise about a product's integrity that outlines the manufacturer's responsibility for repairing or replacing defective parts, spelling out the terms of resti-tution, or exactly what parts of the product are covered and the payout, plus the time period for coverage. Tupperware replaces broken parts decades after purchase, and Zippo lighters offers a lifetime warranty on all of its products, with no disclaimers whatsoever. Both guarantees and warranties assure buyers that they will be compensated if a product doesn't meet reasonable expectations.

The Importance of Restitution. The **recovery process (customer winback)** for counteracting bad customer experiences develops reasonable strategies for rectifying complaints—turning dissatisfaction into action! Customer winback typically entails making **restitution (redress)**, providing compensation for things gone wrong. Restitution can be in the form of discounts, coupons, free gifts, even apologies—whatever the consumer considers to be just compensation for time, money, and aggravation.

Making amends is essential since customers recovered are significantly more loyal than customers who have never experienced a problem! The **recovery paradox** says that effective recovery can make customers more satisfied and less likely to provide negative word of mouth than if the product had been perfect the first time. In fact, it costs less to win back past customers than to acquire new ones.

Consequently, more and more hotels, airlines, car rental companies, and other service providers are embracing **service recovery**—responding when service goes wrong to turn potentially negative situations into positive ones. In so doing, most service organizations empower customer service personnel to im-mediately solve a problem and offer disgruntled customers restitution. Service recovery works best when a front-line employee apologizes, fixes a problem, and offers something of value to compensate for the customer's anguish and lost time. It is a good idea to also enlist customers' opinions of what went wrong and how the firm could fix it, as occurred when JetBlue Airways phoned passengers who had waited hours for a flight that was then abruptly canceled.

Customer Service and Support. Perhaps no other issue matters as much to the typical enterprise as customer service. It can help cement a customer relationship if done correctly, but failure to pick up the phone or show up at the appointed time can kill whatever relationship already existed. After-sale ("after-market") customer service and support (product support services) can enhance customer satisfaction and add value to the total product. Customer service and support are called *enhancers* since they can enhance customer satisfaction and can delight (not just satisfy) the customer. While providing value-added *enhancers* can increase customer satisfaction, not offering them has little effect on dissatisfaction since enhancers are not expected. Such extra value added over and above the buyer's expectations can be tangible, such as manufacturers sewing extra buttons inside pants or a Web site offering coupons and games. However, extra value is usually intangible, such as easy credit, free training, and around-the-clock customer service.

Consumer Research Can Monitor Customer Satisfaction. Tracking customer satisfaction and complaints is vital. Silence is not necessarily golden in light of estimates that up to 80 or 90 percent of disgruntled customers do not bother to complain. Such apathy is often due to inertia (buyers believe it is not worth the bother), a belief that the company is incapable of handling their problem, or a lack of knowledge on how or where to contact the company.

There are three techniques for tracking consumer satisfaction and complaining behavior:

1. Customer satisfaction (CS) research. This typically uses written surveys asking customers to evaluate the product. Many service establishments, such as restaurants and hotels, and some retailers ask customers to fill out surveys and mail them back postage paid. The surveys query buyers regarding their overall evaluation of goods or service quality as well as their degree of CS/D with each attribute. Typically these are five-point Likert scales anchored "very satisfied" to "very dissatisfied." Additionally, the customer might be asked to offer suggestions for improvement and/or to discuss problems and matters for corrective action.

2. Making it easy for customers to complain. This is often the responsibility of a customer service department or department of customer satisfaction. Channels for complaining include follow-up (inquiry) phone calls to customers, toll-free customer service lines, e-mail where customers can contact the firm and lodge compliments or complaints, and allowing customer reviews on the marketer's Web site. Although it is scary to permit customers to post what they wish about your brand on your site, both the positive and negative feedback let you know where you are excelling and where you need to improve.

3. Monitor social media such as Twitter chatter and Facebook conversations.

POSTPURCHASE DISSONANCE

DISSONANCE DEFINED AND CONCEPTUALIZED

Postpurchase dissonance (buyer's remorse, regret) is a consumer's postchoice doubt or anxiety over whether he selected the best alternative. Dissonance is caused by awareness that one or more of the unselected alternatives might be superior to what the buyer purchased because they offer better performance on some attributes. Buyers second-guess themselves with questions such as, "Should I have purchased a front-wheel drive rather than a rear-wheel drive car?" and "Should I have bought the name brand (Tylenol) rather than a private label (Rite Aid)?"

Buyer's remorse is an example of what psychologists call **cognitive dissonance**. This psychological discomfort results when two **cognitions**, bits of knowledge and/or perceptions, are inconsistent or do not fit together.

For example, the knowledge that "I bought Brand F" and "Brand A is superior to Brand F on many dimensions" creates dissonance. Knowing that chocolate causes cavities and is fattening creates uncomfortable tensions or discomfort if you have just scarfed down a three-ounce Snickers bar. This causes a person to reappraise one of the conflicting cognitions in order to reduce the cognitive dissonance and instead achieve **consonance**, psychological balance or consistency among cognitions, including knowledge of one's actions. In order to restore consonance, a cigarette smoker who is confronted with evidence on the risks of smoking can either quit smoking or can deny or discount the risks of smoking.

The most common way to achieve consonance is to seek additional information that confirms the wisdom of selecting the chosen brand. As a result, postpurchase search follows the brand choice decision.

Dissonance is not the same as dissatisfaction. Dissatisfaction is the belief that a product does not meet desires and/or expectations. You can be reasonably satisfied with your decision yet still experience doubt that it was the best possible choice. Although dissonance is usually transitory, it can degenerate into dissatisfaction if a marketer does not take the steps to deal with it.

Postpurchase dissonance is most likely to arise under the following conditions:

- High involvement with the product and/or purchase situation. Buyers will not experience much dissonance over buying a box of toothpicks for $1.29 only to discover they could have shopped the Pick N Save store and gotten them for $1.09. They do experience dissonance, however, if they buy an expensive software program requiring customer support and then learn that the manufacturer is going out of business.
- High perceived risk.
- A difficult choice with no clear winner. The more choices there are, the more the alternatives seem similar, and the more the unchosen alternatives contain desirable attributes, the higher the dissonance.
- The decision is made of the consumer's free will—there is **volitional control**. If there was no uncontrollable influence, such as peer pressure or a governmental mandate, the responsibility for the decision rests solely with the buyer, who then frets about whether she did the best thing. But if a parochial school student must purchase a school uniform she does not like, she will not second-guess her purchase since it was not her free choice.
- The choice is irrevocable—there is no turning back and the buyer must remain committed. This means the customer cannot return the product or get her money back.
- The buyer is prone to high anxiety. Such people tend to experience more dissonance because they worry more.

CONSUMER STRATEGIES TO REDUCE DISSONANCE

Since dissonance is uncomfortable, consumers are motivated to take action to reduce doubt. Consumer dissonance-reduction strategies include:

- Conducting a postpurchase information search to confirm the wisdom of the purchase decision. This includes seeking positive information about the chosen brand and negative data on the rejected alternatives.
- Seeking approval and reassurance from friends and experts that the decision was wise.
- Increasing the perceived attractiveness of the purchased brand, such as by weighting more heavily the attributes on which the chosen alternative performs best or by perceiving that it performs better on certain criteria than it really does.
- Decreasing the perceived attractiveness of rejected alternatives.
- Decreasing the importance of the purchase decision ("I won't use it much") or the importance of the negative information. ("So what if I overpaid?")
- Concluding that all alternatives are virtually identical and so it does not really matter which one was selected.
- Making the purchase revocable by returning the product, selling it, or giving it away to someone else.
- Ignoring any dissonant information or else subjectively interpreting it to be favorable.
- Lowering one's level of expectations ("Oh well, there were no good options anyway").

MARKETING STRATEGIES TO REDUCE CONSUMER DISSONANCE

Through awareness of these consumer strategies for dissonance alleviation, a marketer can try to reduce consumer dissonance by either improving one or more marketing mix elements or helping consumers with their dissonance-reduction strategies as follows.

- Monitoring the extent and causes of dissonance using marketing research tracking methods, such as written surveys and inbound and outbound phone calls, as well as monitoring customer e-mails, chat rooms, blogs, wikis, and other electronic forums.
- Using marketing communications to reduce dissonance among postpurchase information seekers to bolster their choice. Such promotional material can include:
  a. Running reinforcement advertising. These reassuring ads, aimed at recent purchasers, stress the product's quality, value, and superiority to the competition. ("Aren't you glad you use Dial? Don't

you wish everybody did?") They can also include positive consumer comments from feedback sources such as consumer review sites and social media conversations.

b. Offering other nonpersonal marketing communications. These include instructional materials, buyers' "club" newsletters, and package inserts emphasizing product superiority.

c. Using personalized marketing communications. One-on-one promotion assures the buyer that she made a smart choice. This can include congratulatory or thank-you letters or e-mail messages; follow-up phone calls to ensure the product is working well; salesperson follow-up visits; consumer training; and other in-person contacts emphasizing what a good value the consumer got, how to properly use the product, and how to get the most out of it. For instance, some bicycle stores invite customers to bring their new bikes back after thirty days for a free tune-up, where salespeople follow up to make sure customers are pleased with their purchase and make any necessary adjustments.

d. Setting up forums for the exchange of nonmarketer sources of communication. Such forums can include customer clubs and Web site chat rooms where customers can discuss product experiences. (Caution: Chat rooms can also turn into gripe or hate rooms!)

e. Providing generous warranties, guarantees, price-protection plans, easy return or exchange policies, and other means of reducing irrevocability.

f. Using ongoing customer relationship marketing strategies as discussed earlier.

g. Trying to cause or increase dissonance among competitive brand users in order to encourage them to revoke their decision or else buy the marketer's brand the next time. Techniques include using comparison advertising, offering a better deal to consumers if they return the competitors' product, and paying them to switch. Care must be taken, however, not to unethically disparage the competitor's brand, thereby turning your brand into a bully.

MISCELLANEOUS POSTPURCHASE BEHAVIOR OUTCOMES

Following consumption, there are further behavioral patterns of interest to marketers that often create additional marketing opportunities.

- Repeat purchase behavior. This is not necessarily brand loyalty caused by brand preference but might instead be merely rebuying the same brand due to factors such as convenience, low price, unavailability of the preferred brand, perceived lack of better alternatives, or inertia.

- The need for consumer financing. This sometimes arises for big-ticket purchases. Retailers and manufacturers both use "easy credit" as an opportunity to increase sales, although this has curtailed since the financial crisis of 2008 and 2009.

- A need for complementary products. **Complementary products** are consumed in conjunction with the purchased item. Hence, manufacturers increasingly **cross-promote (cross-sell)**. They—sell (promote) product sets (related items) in their product lines simultaneously. Examples: washers and dryers, skate guards and ice skates. A home purchase stimulates sales of carpeting, furniture, and home-remodeling goods and services. E-mail makes one-to-one cross-selling easy to do, since buyers' past purchases can be tracked. Amazon.com monitors from which product categories a consumer frequently buys, as well as specific choices, and then sends that person e-mail messages promoting related merchandise. Such products are often **tie-in (captive) products**, related items, such as software, that must be used in conjunction with the main product, such as hardware.

  Such complementary items often use **captive-product pricing,** a pricing strategy whereby they break even in selling the main product (e.g., video game consoles sold at cost) or even take a loss (e.g., free cell phones or cable TV boxes), but they make a large profit margin on the captive product (e.g., video games, cell phone service) since the consumer feels required to purchase it.

- The desire for upgrades. Trading up to higher quality levels may eventually arise. Upgrades can include adding features or quality to the purchased product. You no sooner buy a laptop computer than you find you need more memory, a more powerful chip for speed, and a webcam.

- The need for consumer education. This can be necessary for technically complex products, which require consumer instruction on proper assembly, usage, and ultimate disposal. Such information can be provided through media such as package enclosures, CDs, and product Web sites. This education can be monetized. Apple collects $99 a year for each of two personalized customer service and education offerings.

- A need for maintenance and after-market products. Many big-ticket purchases such as cars and computers need to be regularly serviced to stay in tip-top shape. **After-market products** are goods and services, usually parts and accessories, associated with the upkeep or repair of a previously purchased product (e.g., automobile batteries, tires, and tune-ups).
- Word-of-mouth referrals. Consumers can be given incentives to recommend a product to others. Enticements include discounts on future purchases, free goods and services, and other merchandise.
- Product nonuse. How often do fruits and vegetables rot in refrigerators or packages of chips sit on shelves growing stale after their expiration dates? Probably too often. Marketers of such neglected perishable goods can use prominent expiration dates, reminding customers to consume the item and suggesting new uses for the product to speed consumption.
- Product returns. Rented products need to be returned by consumers. Sometimes follow-up is necessary as a reminder. Although late returns can lead to penalties, marketers should weight the added revenue against possible lost consumer goodwill, as Blockbuster Video discovered when such fees enraged some of their customers.
- Product disposal (disposition, divestment). Options here include throwing it away, recycling it, trading it in, selling (remarketing) it to another consumer or to a middleman, giving it away, or loaning or renting it. Some manufacturers set up a **reverse supply chain**, a series of activities required to retrieve a used product from a customer and either dispose of or reuse it. Socially responsible marketers encourage recycling by offering special incentives, using educational efforts, and by manufacturing containers that are easily recycled or reused. Both trading in and reselling present marketing opportunities such as offering trade-ins and buyback arrangements and selling refurbished used products.
- Regifting. **Regifting** entails recycling of consumers' new or (gasp!) used presents, passing them off as new gifts. There are the "gifts that keep on giving," such as the fruitcake that gets passed, like a family heirloom, from one sibling to the next, or the dreaded frog candlestick holders. (Surely, 'tis better to regift than to receive.)
- Product recalls. While marketers hope recalls never happen, for safety-related problems they often do. If marketers discover such a difficulty, they are morally obligated to issue a recall, since failing to do so could contribute to consumer harm.

REVIEW QUESTIONS

1. What is relationship marketing and why is it so important?
2. Outline the major categories of postpurchase outcomes, and summarize why each is important to marketers.
3. Explain how consumer satisfaction/dissatisfaction (CS/D) arises, the origins of the desires and expectations that determine CS/D, and why CS/D is important to marketers. Then, describe marketing strategies that can enhance customer satisfaction.
4. What is postpurchase dissonance and how does it differ from dissatisfaction? In which types of purchase situations is dissonance most likely to occur? Describe consumer strategies that reduce dissonance and marketer strategies that help alleviate dissonance.
5. Discuss some of the marketing opportunities that might arise from the miscellaneous postpurchase behavior outcomes described in the exercise.

IN-CLASS APPLICATIONS

1. Each of the following scenarios contains several postpurchase outcomes that marketers ignore at their peril. Find as many postpurchase evaluation outcomes and postpurchase behavior outcomes as you can in each situation. What types of marketing opportunities and/or threats are presented in each scenario to marketers of the purchased brand and their competitors?
   → *Scenario A. Emerrex Impresses Al.* Al received an article in the mail about how the Emerrex 500Z widescreen television was on the *Electronics Monthly* top-ten list of quality televisions. The article

helped reassure him that the Emerrex 500Z he recently picked up at an electronics store did, indeed, live up to its promises.

He was also pleased that Emerrex let him spread out his payments over twenty-four months at only 1.9 percent interest. Al also loves that they offered him a built-in personal video recorder for less than a compatible one sold separately would have cost.

Al invited a bunch of his friends over to watch the Super Bowl on his Emerrex. Several of them told him how impressed they were with the TV (even though the game turned out to be boring). He then showed his closeups of buddies the article Emerrex had mailed him.

→ *Scenario B. HotTop Ain't So Hot.* Mark had a not-so-good experience with his new HotTop digital stove. Every time he tried to cook something, the food would still be ice cold to lukewarm, at best.

As a consequence, Mark tried to get a refund from the manufacturer, but to no avail. He now warns his friends, family members, work colleagues, people he sits next to on the commuter rail—almost anybody and everybody!—about this terrible product.

→ *Scenario C. Mercantile Means Business!* About a year ago, Candy bought a home CD recorder (burner) from the Mercantile Corp. The warranty registration form asked what Candy felt were a lot of personal questions about other electronic products she owns or is interested in acquiring. It also requested information about her hobbies and interests. But she mailed Mercantile the postcard to secure the full twelve-month warranty.

Since then, Candy has received a mailing every week informing her of other Mercantile electronics products or asking her to upgrade to newer models of the CD recorder she purchased. She also got a survey with a postage-paid reply envelope asking her to rate her new recorder on more than twenty features (several of which she didn't even know the product had!).

Candy just doesn't know whether it is worth taking up Mercantile on their latest offer—an extended three-year full warranty for only $99.95. If this is what having a "customer relationship" is all about, Candy wants none of it!

→ *Scenario D. The Dovers Get Duped.* Ben and Eileen Dover interviewed three different builders about the sunroom they dreamed of adding to their house. They settled on Pete Sakes, who finished the job in record time. Although Pete kept assuring them that he used only the finest materials and offered better workmanship than his competitors, the Dovers were dismayed when Pete finished the job and the bill was almost 10 percent over budget.

Also, the floorboards squeaked and the screen door rattled, making the Dovers wonder in jest whether the place might not be haunted. And, when the paint started to peel just three months later, they sensed that something was amiss. Ben and his bride were especially distraught when an acquaintance told them that he had a sunroom built a few months earlier for about $1,000 less than the Dovers had paid and was fully delighted with the room.

When they called Mr. Sakes to discuss these issues, the Dovers were surprised and angry to find his line had been disconnected. Further investigation revealed he had skipped town for unknown reasons.

→ *Scenario E. Chet's Sportzkatz Adventures.* Chet spent months scouring Web sites and reading car magazines before he settled on buying the Sportzkatz 911Z roadster. The price matched or beat all of the other two-seat sports cars he had test-driven. Further, the Scratch 'n Dent dealership from which he bought the 911Z was most accommodating: They offered a free 500-mile checkup, called Chet two weeks after the purchase to see whether he had any questions or issues, and even sent a service rep to his home one cold winter morning when his engine wouldn't turn over properly. Also, they gave him a password to the Sportzkatz.com chat room, where he had fun trading stories with other 911Z owners.

However, Chet soon read in both *Consumer Reports* and *Car and Driver* that two other models he had seriously considered both received better overall customer satisfaction ratings and that some 911Zs experienced repeated problems with the ignition.

2. As a class, brainstorm as many possible postpurchase outcomes as you can think of that might occur after a young couple purchases their first life insurance policy. What are the marketing implications of each of these outcomes?

3. Identify the postacquisition behaviors suggested in each of the ads in Exhibits 4.31 through 4.33. Is each ad effectively taking advantage of each of these behaviors? What other recommendations can you offer each advertiser for effective postpurchase behavior management? (These suggestions need not be confined to advertising.)

EXHIBIT 4.31   Neutrogena Ad

EXHIBIT 4.32   Andersen Windows Ad

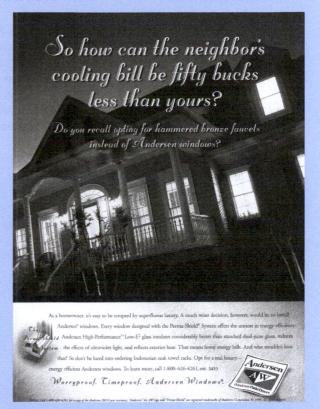

EXHIBIT 4.33   Viagra Ad

WRITTEN APPLICATIONS

1. Answer Question 3 in the In-Class Applications. Then, find three more ads that suggest several post-purchase outcomes. Repeat the analysis used in Question 3.

2. Describe a purchase with which you were very satisfied or dissatisfied. What did the marketer do very well or very poorly to contribute to your postpurchase attitude? What suggestions can you offer this marketer to ensure customer satisfaction in the future?

3. Describe a purchase for which you suffered dissonance. What did the marketer do (or not do) to contribute to your trepidation? What suggestions can you offer this marketer to reduce dissonance in future efforts?

KEY CONCEPTS

accidental (incidental) search
activity (process) analysis
advertising
affect referral (affective choice, hedonic choice)
after-market products
analytical attribute analysis
atmospherics
attitude
attitude-based (affective, hedonic) choices
attribute extension (parameter analysis)
attribute-based choices
awareness set (retrieval set)
behavioral influence techniques
beliefs
benefits
boycott
brand franchise
brand insight
brand ratings
brand-attribute matrix (decision matrix)
brand-based evaluation strategy (choice by processing brands [CPB], processing by brands [PBB], brand-choice sequence)
buying intention (purchase intention, intention to buy, behavioral intention, purchase plan, propensity to buy)
captive-product pricing
choice by processing attributes (CPA) (processing by attributes [PBA], dimensional processing, attribute search sequence)
choice (shopping) process
churn rate
cognitions
cognitive dissonance
compensatory decision rules (linear compensatory models)
complementary products
comprehensive shopbots
conjunctive decision rule
conquest (acquisition) marketing
consonance

constant sum scale
consultative personal selling
consumer insight
consumer logistics
consumer satisfaction/dissatisfaction (CS/D)
consumer-complaining behavior (CCB)
cross-promote (cross-sell)
customer database
customer relationship management (CRM)
decision models (decision rules, alternative evaluation rules, decision strategies, information-processing strategies, choice rules)
decision heuristics (choice heuristics, heuristics)
degree of search
deliberate search
delight
depth
desires
determinant attributes
dimensional analysis (attribute listing)
direction of search
disjunctive decision rule
dissatisfaction
dissatisfiers
elimination-by-aspects rule (sequential elimination model)
evaluative (choice, decision, buying, purchase) criteria (or, criteria)
evaluative scale
evoked (consideration, choice, decision) set
expectations
experiential (hedonic) benefits
external (environmental) search
finite ideal point (attribute adequacy, additive difference) attitude model
framing
functional benefits
gap
gap analysis

(continued)

KEY CONCEPTS *(continued)*

guarantee
image advertising
importance weights (weights)
important attributes
inept set
inert set
infinite ideal point attitude model (vector attribute model)
information
information integration theory
information search
in-store positioning
instrumental performance
instrumental values
interactivity
internal search
latent (covert) problems
lexicographic decision rule
lifetime value of a customer (LVC; lifetime customer value [LCV], lifetime value [LTV])
longitudinal research
loss leaders
macroenvironmental events
market damage
marketer-controlled (commercial, advocate) sources
means-end chain analysis
merchandising
meta-engine (metasearch tool)
microenvironment (operating environment)
multiattribute attitude model
need recognition
neutral (independent) sources
noncompensatory decision rules
non-marketer-controlled (noncommercial) sources
nonpersonal sources
ongoing (exploratory) search
opportunity recognition
packaging
personal sources
personal values
phased decision strategy (multistage choice process)
point-of-purchase (POP) displays (point-of-sale displays)
postpurchase dissonance (buyer's remorse, regret)
postpurchase outcomes (postacquisition behaviors)
postpurchase search
prepurchase alternative evaluation
prepurchase search
price-and-item advertising
problem analysis (problem detection, needs analysis)
problem recognition (need arousal, need state)

problem solving
problem-based ideation (problem-solution route, problem find–problem solve approach)
problem-solution (problem-resolution) advertising
product analysis
product concept statement
product criteria
product features (physical attributes, product specifications [specs])
product performance
product quality
publicity
rank-order importance scale
rating scales
recovery paradox
recovery process (customer winback)
regifting
relationship (retention) marketing
response bias
restitution (redress)
retail outlets
reverse supply chain
sales promotions (promotions, promotional marketing)
salient attributes
satisfiers
service recovery
shelf positioning (shelving)
shelf space
shopper marketing
shopping bots (shopbots, buyer agents, virtual sales assistants, shopping search engines, comparison shopping sites, robot search engines)
social desirability bias
store brands (private labels, dealer brands, in-house labels, own labels)
store image
symbolic benefits
symbolic performance
terminal values
tie-in (captive) products
transaction
transactional marketing
universal set
unweighted linear compensatory decision model (unweighted rule, simple additive rule, equal weight rule)
volitional control
warranty
weighted linear compensatory rule (weighted additive rule)
width
word-of-mouth (WOM) communication

SUMMARY

This chapter explored each of the five stages in the consumer decision-making process. Exercise 4.1 focused on problem recognition, which arises via opportunity recognition or need recognition. Marketers can develop new products using problem-based ideation such as problem analysis to identify problems (either activity analysis or product analysis).

Other marketing implications of the problem recognition stage include using problem-solution advertising, employing primary demand advertising, utilizing secondary demand advertising, deploying consultative salespeople, using behavioral influence techniques, and stimulating latent needs.

Following problem recognition, the buyer might put the procedure on hold for particular reasons, yielding various marketing opportunities. Otherwise, the consumer proceeds to prepurchase information search, gathering information (Exercise 4.2). This search commences with an internal search of the awareness set, evoked set, inert set, and inept set.

Internal search leads to a purchase decision in routine DM. Here, marketers should ascertain that consumers remember the brand favorably, putting it in their evoked sets.

If the internal search fails to yield sufficient information, the consumer enters the external search stage—prepurchase search. Additionally, buyers can engage in ongoing search and accidental search.

Degree of prepurchase search is influenced by the extent of consumer involvement and the consumer's learning stage. Regarding the direction of prepurchase search, information sources consumers use can be classified as personal or nonpersonal and marketer controlled (commercial) or non-marketer controlled (noncommercial). Exhibit 15.3 summarizes each of these information sources, such as neutral sources.

Prepurchase information search occurs concurrently with prepurchase alternative evaluation (Exercise 4.3). The inputs to alternative evaluation are the evaluative criteria, their relative importance, and the evoked set. Here, consumers rate the options on criteria to form beliefs and attitudes, thereby forming a buying intention, although they might also put the process on hold.

Marketers distinguish among salient attributes, important attributes, and determinant attributes. Consumers usually make attribute-based choices, although they might also make attitude-based choices or use decision heuristics.

Marketers need to distinguish between a product's features and benefits, which include functional, experiential, and symbolic benefits. Generally, features give rise to functional benefits, leading to experiential and/or symbolic benefits. From these linkages follows the idea of the means-end chain analysis. The ends are consumers' personal values, including terminal values and instrumental values.

Consumer researchers must discover what evaluative criteria consumers use, the relative importance of the criteria, alternatives in the evoked set, and consumers' beliefs about alternatives' performance on the criteria. Either a large-scale survey or small-scale focus groups ask respondents about evaluative criteria, although a potential problem is response bias, such as social desirability bias.

To discover attributes' importance weights, research uses survey instruments with rating scales such as evaluative scales, rank-order importance scales, and constant sum scales.

Knowledge of the alternative evaluation process for a product can be employed during new product development by using analytical attribute analysis such as via gap analysis. Marketers then write a product concept statement. Analytical attribute methodologies include dimensional analysis and attribute extension.

Knowing about determinant purchase criteria, their relative importance, and the performance of brands in the evoked set on these attributes enables effective product promotion by focusing on the brand's superior performance on those criteria, through tools such as comparative advertising and framing.

Exercise 4.4 described how brand-attribute matrix data is combined to form brand attitudes using one or more decision models. There are four general decision strategies according to information integration theory:

1. Compensatory decision rules use all available brand-attribute information and, hence, are utility-maximizing decision strategies. They include weighted linear compensatory rules and unweighted

linear compensatory decision models. The traditional multiattribute attitude model, represented by the formula

$$A_{jk} = \sum w_{ik} b_{ijk},$$

is an infinite ideal point model that suggests marketers should focus on excellent performance of the most important characteristics during product development and promote this performance in marketing communications. Unweighted linear compensatory decision models assume all attributes are equally important to buyers, and they can either be infinite ideal point models or finite ideal point models. Compensatory decision models assume a brand-based evaluation strategy. Because they are complex and time-consuming, these models are used only for certain buying conditions, notably high-involvement decisions and/or extended decision-making situations, as well as in the second stage of a phased decision strategy.

2. Noncompensatory decision rules use only the most important brand-attribute information to yield a satisfactory decision. However, they are simpler to use than compensatory strategies and are likely to be employed under opposite conditions. Such models are often used in the first stage of a phased decision strategy. There are four types of noncompensatory strategies: conjunctive decision rules, disjunctive decision rules, lexicographic decision rules, and elimination-by-aspects rules. The first two rules use choice by processing brands and the last two use choice by processing attributes. Each is used under particular buying conditions and has marketing implications.

3. Decision heuristics are used when buyers have insufficient information, lack ability to intelligently select, and do not have the motivation or involvement to make a careful decision. Implications for product development and promotion include the need to focus on the key criterion and to reinforce existing heuristics or create new decision rules.

4. Affect referral rules are attitude-based decisions. They are used where the product gives hedonic benefits, buyers have much previous information and experience, and there is primarily affective involvement. The suggestion for product development is to design products that will give the user positive emotional experiences. The promotional implication is to create an overall good feeling about the brand.

Exercise 4.5 involved the alternative evaluation process in an online environment using shopping bots, which act like meta-engines. Bots can be comprehensive or focused on a specific product range. There are a number of consumer benefits for browsing using shopbots, but they also have particular limitations.

Exercise 4.6 described the choice process in retail outlets. Manufacturers concentrate on securing distribution in popular outlets and obtaining merchandising. Two levels of store-choice decision are type of outlet and brand of outlet. Regarding outlet type, shoppers select between retail stores and nonstore retailers. Store choices are analogous to brand choices, but in selecting at which store to shop, consumers use different evaluative criteria, including store image, store brands, retail advertising (price-and-item advertising and image advertising), price (including loss leaders), nature and quality of assortment (including width and depth), and consumer logistics.

The shopping process concludes with a decision on whether or not to buy. The purchase choice is followed by decisions about when to purchase and what type product and brand to purchase. Final selections sometimes deviate from the buyer's original intentions due to unanticipated circumstances.

There are also four categories of unanticipated circumstances that affect product and brand choice: macroenvironmental events, the microenvironment, personal situational factors, and the purchase environment. The latter includes retail stores, service establishments, and various nonstore direct marketing environments. Influential factors include atmospherics (online, these include interactivity and navigational tools), point-of-purchase displays, in-store media, and in-store positioning decisions such as shelf positioning. The last important decision is method of payment, which can be by check, cash, credit cards, charge cards, and debit cards.

The postpurchase outcomes stage was covered in Exercise 4.7 and is summarized in Exhibit 4.30. Today, instead of transactional marketing emphasizing conquest marketing, marketers strive to build long-term customer relationships via relationship marketing in order to capture the lifetime value of the customer.

Such relationships are founded upon brand insight and customer insight. A customer database is used in customer relationship management to build customer trust and commitment, leading to a consumer brand franchise achieved through tools such as customer loyalty programs and longitudinal research.

One critical postpurchase evaluation outcome is consumer satisfaction/dissatisfaction. If both desires and expectations are met or exceeded by perceived product performance, the customer is satisfied. Product performance includes both instrumental and symbolic performance. When the consumer compares actual (or perceived) product performance against her desires and expectations, the result can be either satisfaction, delight, or dissatisfaction. The origin of desires is needs and wants. Consumer satisfaction is important to firms in order to avoid market damage, including consumer-complaining behavior and boycotts, among other undesirable circumstances.

Marketing implications of the nature of satisfaction include the following:

- Expectations management is important; realistic expectations should be created.
- Product quality is critical.
- Money-back guarantees or product warranties can ensure customer satisfaction.
- Restitution is important for the recovery process of dissatisfied customers. Service providers should offer service recovery.
- After-sale customer service and product support services are important.
- Competitors' dissatisfied customers can be pursued.
- Customer satisfaction and complaints can be monitored by conducting customer satisfaction research and providing channels for customers to complain.

A second important postpurchase evaluation outcome is postpurchase dissonance, cognitive dissonance caused by inconsistent cognitions. Instead of dissonance, people seek consonance via additional information that confirms the wisdom of their selection.

Postpurchase dissonance is not dissatisfaction. Dissonance arises under particular marketplace circumstances. Consumers use a number of strategies to reduce dissonance. Armed with knowledge of dissonance, marketers can implement one or more strategies to reduce consumer dissonance.

Postpurchase behaviors that create marketing opportunities include the desire for complementary products that can be cross-promoted or sold as tie-in products, the need for aftermarket products, regifting, and product disposal, including establishment of a reverse supply chain.

REFERENCES

Anderson, Eugene W., Fornell, Claes, and Lehmann, Donald R. (1994). "Customer Satisfaction, Market Share, and Profitability: Findings from Sweden." *Journal of Marketing,* 58, 3, 53–66.

Beales, Howard, Mazis, Michael B., Salop, Steven C., and Staelin, Richard. (1981). "Consumer Search and Public Policy." *Journal of Consumer Research,* 8, 1, 11–22.

Beatty, Sharon W., and Smith, Scott M. (1987). "External Search Effort: An Investigation Across Several Product Categories." *Journal of Consumer Research,* 14, 1, 83–95.

Belk, Russell W. (1975). "Situational Variables and Consumer Behavior." *Journal of Consumer Research,* 2, 3, 157–164.

Block, Peter H., Sherrell, Daniel L., and Ridgway, Nancy M. (1986). "Consumer Search: An Extended Framework." *Journal of Consumer Research,* 13, 1, 127–131.

Bruner, Gordon C., III, and Pomazal, Richard J. (1988). "Problem Recognition: The Crucial First Stage in the Consumer Decision Process." *Journal of Consumer Marketing,* 5, 1, 53–63.

Burton, Scott, and Babin, Laurie A. (1989). "Decision-Framing Helps Make the Sale." *Journal of Consumer Marketing,* 6, 2, 15–24.

Büschken, Joachim. (2004). *Higher Profits Through Customer Lock-in.* Mason, OH: South-Western.

Calder, Bobby J. (1981). "Cognitive Consistency and Consumer Behavior." In Harold H. Kassarjian and Thomas S. Robertson (eds.), *Perspectives in Consumer Behavior,* 3d ed. Glenview, IL: Scott, Foresman, and Company.

Churchill, Gilbert A., Jr., and Surprenant, Carol F. (1983). "An Investigation into the Determinants of Customer Satisfaction." *Journal of Marketing Research,* 19, 4, 491–504.

Cobb, Cathy J., and Hoyer, Wayne D. (1986). "Planned Versus Impulse Purchase Behavior." *Journal of Retailing,* 62 (Winter), 384–409.

Corbae, Gerald, Jensen, Jacob B., and Schneider, Dirk. (2003). *Marketing 2.0—Strategies for Closer Customer Relationships.* Heidelberg, Germany: Springer-Verlag.

Cummings, William H., and Venkatesan, M. (1976). "Cognitive Dissonance and Consumer Behavior: A Review of the Evidence." *Journal of Marketing Research,* 13, 3, 303–308.

Curry, David J., and Wortzell, Lawrence H. (1988). "Prices and Price/Quality Relationships: A Longitudinal Analysis." *Journal of Marketing,* 52, 1, 36–51.

Diener, Betty J., and Greyser, Stephen A. (1978). "Consumer Views of Redress Needs." *Journal of Consumer Marketing,* 42, 4, 21–27.

Duke, Charles R., and Mount, Andrew S. (1996). "Rediscovering Importance-Performance Analysis of Products." *Journal of Product and Brand Management,* 5, 2, 43–54.

Festinger, Leon. (1957). *A Theory of Cognitive Dissonance.* Stanford, CA: Stanford University Press.

Fisher, James E., Garrett, Dennis E., Arnold, Mark J., and Ferris, Mark E. (1999). "Dissatisfied Consumers Who Complain to the Better Business Bureau." *Journal of Consumer Marketing,* 16, 6, 576–589.

Gabarino, Ellen, and Johnson, Mark S. (1999). "The Different Roles of Satisfaction, Trust, and Commitment in Customer Relationships." *Journal of Marketing,* 63, 2, 70–87.

Gilly, Mary C., and Gelb, Betsy D. (1982). "Post-Purchase Consumer Processes and the Complaining Consumer." *Journal of Consumer Research,* 9, 3, 323–328.

Goldman, Arieh, and Johansson, J. K. (1978). "Determinants of Search for Lower Prices: An Empirical Assessment of the Economics of Information Theory." *Journal of Consumer Research,* 5, 3, 176–186.

Griffin, Jill. (2002). *Customer Loyalty: How to Earn It, How to Keep It.* San Francisco: Jossey-Bass.

Griffin, Jill, and Lowenstein, Michael W. (2001). *Customer WinBack: How to Recapture Lost Customers—And Keep Them Loyal.* San Francisco: Jossey-Bass.

Gutman, Jonathan. (1997). "Means-Ends Chains as Goals Hierarchies." *Psychology & Marketing,* 14, 6, 545–560.

———. (1982). "A Means-End Chain Model Based on Consumer Categorization Processes." *Journal of Marketing,* 46, 2, 60–72.

Harris, Godfrey. (2000). *Don't Take Our Word for It: Everything You Need to Know About Making Word-of-Mouth Advertising Work for You.* Gloucestershire, UK: Cowcombe House.

Hennig-Thurau, Thorsten, and Hansen, Ursula, eds. (2000). *Relationship Marketing: Gaining Competitive Advantage Through Customer Satisfaction and Customer Retention.* Berlin: Springer-Verlag.

Hocutt, Mary Ann, Bowers, Michael R., and Donavan, Todd D. (2006). "The Art of Service Recovery: Fact or Fiction?" *Journal of Service Marketing,* 20, 3, 199–207.

Horn, Sam. (2006). *POP! Stand Out in Any Crowd.* New York: Perigee Books.

Hoyer, Wayne D. (1984). "An Examination of Consumer Decision Making for a Common Repeat Purchase Product." *Journal of Consumer Research,* 11, 3, 822–829.

Hunt, Shelby. (1970). "Post-Transactional Communication and Dissonance Reduction." *Journal of Marketing,* 34, 1, 46–51.

Jacoby, Jacob, and Chestnut, Robert W. (1978). *Brand Loyalty: Measurement and Management.* New York: Wiley & Sons.

Jacoby, Jacob, Berning, Carol K., and Dietvorst, Thomas F. (1977). "What About Disposition?" *Journal of Marketing,* 41, 2, 22–28.

Jacoby, Jacob, Szybillo, George J., and Busato-Schach, Jacqueline. (1977). "Information Acquisition Behavior in Brand Choice Situations." *Journal of Consumer Research,* 5, 4, 209–216.

Kau, Ah-Keng, and Loh, Elizabeth Wan-Yiun. (2006). "The Effects of Service Recovery on Consumer Satisfaction: A Comparison Between Complainants and Non-complainants." *Journal of Service Marketing,* 20, 2, 101–111.

Kaufman-Scarborough, Carol, and Linquist, Jay D. (2002). "E-Shopping in a Multiple Channel Environment." *Journal of Consumer Marketing,* 19, 4, 333–350.

Kotler, Philip. (1973–1974). "Atmospherics as a Marketing Tool." *Journal of Retailing,* 49 (Winter), 40–64.

Kracklauer, Alexander H., and D. Quinn Mills, eds. (2004). *Collaborative Customer Relationship Management: Taking CRM to the Next Level.* Berlin: Springer-Verlag.

Laroche, Michel, Kim, Chankon, and Matsui, Takayoshi. (2003). "Which Decision Heuristics Are Used in Consideration Set Formation?" *Journal of Consumer Marketing,* 20, 3, 192–209.

Maddox, R. Neil. (1981). "Two-Factor Theory and Consumer Satisfaction: Replication and Extension." *Journal of Consumer Research,* 8, 1, 97–102.

Magnini, Vincent P., Ford, John B., Markowski, Edward P., and Honeycutt, Earl D., Jr. (2007). "The Service Recovery Paradox: Justifiable Theory or Smoldering Myth?" *Journal of Service Marketing,* 21, 2, 213–225.

Mantel, Susan Powell, and Kardes, Frank R. (1999). "The Role of Direction of Comparison, Attribute-Based Processing, and Attitude-Based Processing in Consumer Preference." *Journal of Consumer Research,* 25, 4, 335–351.

Mitchell, Jack. (2003). *Hug Your Customers: The Proven Way to Personalize Sales and Achieve Astounding Results.* New York: Hyperion Books.

Newell, Frederick. (2000). *Loyalty.com: Customer Relationship Management in the New Era of Internet Marketing.* New York: McGraw-Hill.

Newman, Joseph W. (1977). "Consumer External Search: Amount and Determinants." In A.G. Woodside, J.N. Sheth, and P.D. Bennett (eds.), *Consumer and Industrial Buying Behavior.* New York: North-Holland, 79–94.

Nyer, Prashanth U. (2000). "An Investigation into Whether Complaining Can Cause Increased Consumer Satisfaction." *Journal of Consumer Marketing,* 17, 1, 9–19.

Pham, Michel Tuan. (1998). "Representativeness, Relevance, and the Use of Feelings in Decision Making." *Journal of Consumer Research,* 25, 2, 144–159.

Richens, Marsha S. (1983). "Negative Word-of-Mouth by Dissatisfied Consumers: A Pilot Study." *Journal of Advertising,* 47, 1, 68–78.

Rowley, Jennifer. (2000). "Product Search in E-Shopping: A Review and Research Propositions." *Journal of Consumer Marketing,* 17, 1, 20–35.

Saucier, Rick. (2001). *Influencing Sales Through Store Design.* Lewiston, NY: The Edwin Mellen Press.

Scammon, Debra L. (1977). "'Information Load' and Consumers." *Journal of Consumer Research,* 4, 3, 148–155.

Sheth, Jagdish, and Parvatiyar, Atul, eds. (2000). *Handbook of Relationship Marketing.* Thousand Oaks, CA: Sage Publications.

Spreng, Richard A., Mackenzie, Scott B., and Olshavsky, Richard W. (1996). "A Reexamination of the Determinants of Consumer Satisfaction." *Journal of Marketing,* 60, 3, 15–32.

Stauss, Bernd, and Seidel, Wolfgang. (2005). *Complaint Management: The Heart of CRM.* Mason, OH: South-Western.

Stigler, George J. (1961). "The Economics of Information." *Journal of Political Economy,* 69, 3, 213–255.

Thomassen, Lars, Lincoln, Keith, and Aconis, Anthony. (2006). *Retailization: Brand Survival in the Age of Retailer Power.* London, UK: Kogan Page Limited.

Trocchia, Philip J., and Swindler, Jamda. (2002). "An Investigation of Product Purchase and Subsequent Non-consumption." *Journal of Consumer Marketing,* 19, 3, 188–204.

Tsiros, Michael, and Mittal, Vikas. (2000). "Regret: A Model of Its Antecedents and Consequences in Consumer Decision Making." *Journal of Consumer Research,* 26, 4, 401–417.

Underhill, Paco. (1999). *Why We Buy: The Science of Shopping.* New York: Simon & Schuster.

Urbany, Joel E. (1986). "An Experimental Examination of the Economics of Information." *Journal of Consumer Research,* 13, 2, 257–271.

Zimmer, Mary R., and Golden, Linda L. (1988). "Impressions of Retail Stores: A Content Analysis of Consumer Images." *Journal of Retailing,* 64 (Fall), 265–293.

PART

III

EXTERNAL SOCIOCULTURAL
INFLUENCES ON CONSUMER
BEHAVIOR

THE NATURE OF SOCIOCULTURAL INFLUENCES

Sociocultural (sociological) forces consist of influences from the cultural and social environment. These range from the overall society and its culture to significant others such as family, friends, and colleagues. This societal environment has a significant impact on consumer lifestyles and how they evaluate, buy, and use products.

Part III discusses all major societal spheres of influence. It commences with the broad macro impact of **society**, a large cluster of people sharing a common culture, i.e., an aggregate of people within a nation or group of nations who usually share a common language and heritage. We then proceed through **social categories**, aggregate groups within a society share common demographic, socioeconomic, psychological, and/or behavioral status, such as ethnic subcultures and social classes. The text then moves to the narrow, more immediate micro social groups and interpersonal influences characterized by close interactions and interpersonal communication.

The pages ahead apply concepts from various social science disciplines: **cultural anthropology**, the scientific study of the development of human cultures; **demography**, the science of describing a society's broad vital population characteristics; **sociology**, the scientific investigation of the formation and function of social forces and institutions that affect contemporary society (such as families, religious institutions, and workplaces) as well as peoples' personal lives (such as cliques and juvenile gangs); and **social psychology**, the scientific inquiry into social behavior within social groups and among individuals, which includes the influence of group members on one another and the impact of the group on individual decisions, such as conforming to the group's ideology.

These behavioral sciences are not just academic disciplines. Nearly every major advertising agency and many large consumer marketers hire professional consultants from these fields, either on staff or on retainer, to provide consumer insight.

Chapters 5, 6, and 7 investigate broad, impersonal sociocultural factors. Chapter 5 discusses the effects of cultural influences on buyer behavior. Cultural influences encompass common patterns of thinking and a person's behavior within society. Specific aspects of society and their importance to consumer marketers are investigated. These include tangible and intangible components, values, and behavioral norms. Chapter 6 presents subcultural influences. Each general social category has its own cultural characteristics (e.g., ethnic, religious, geographic, and generational groups).

167

Chapter 7 concerns social class influences, which rank members of society according to status, power, and wealth.

Chapters 8, 9, and 10 cover personal influences on consumers. Chapter 8 investigates reference groups, formal and informal social groups that heavily affect consumers. The most significant of all reference groups is the family—people dwelling together who are related by blood, marriage, or adoption. Family influences are covered in Chapter 9. Chapter 10 focuses on interpersonal influences, especially how people, including opinion leaders, affect others' acceptance of new products.

SOCIOCULTURAL SEGMENTATION

Each of these levels of sociocultural influence forms a base for market segmentation. Culture is useful for international or cross-cultural market segmentation (e.g., Western versus Eastern culture or secular versus religious society). As American culture becomes more culturally diverse, we are seeing increasing emphasis on *subcultural* segmentation, such as pursuing the burgeoning Hispanic or evangelical Christian markets; social classes are alive and well in the United States, even though we like to think that all people are created equal. Social groups and opinion leaders can also be targeted as highly influential markets.

All of these sociocultural influences are useful for segmentation because they combine to affect a consumer's lifestyle—how a person spends his or her time and hard-earned money. Since all of the sociocultural factors are gradually evolving, consumer lifestyles are ever-changing as well.

A major trend in this evolution is diversity: The United States is increasingly pluralistic, with markets becoming more fractionalized and splintered. Minority groups are becoming a larger percentage of the population, there is a widening gap between rich and poor, and we are witnessing further diversification of the family structure. This trend has created numerous lifestyle groups for marketers to target, abolishing the façade of a single American lifestyle.

The broadest and most pervasive of all sociocultural factors shaping consumer decision making is **culture**, the symbols, values, and beliefs, that is, the total way of life, shared by members of a society. A **society** is an aggregate group of people within a nation or group of nations who usually share a common language and heritage, that is, a large cluster of people sharing a common culture. Culture is investigated by **cultural anthropologists**, social scientists who systematically investigate the various factors that make up society.

Anthropologists learn about cultures using **ethnography**, the study of living cultures through fieldwork and firsthand accounts. Ethnography helps anthropologists understand society from its citizens' point of view. Ethnographers spend considerable periods of time with local people, making detailed observations and interviewing them regarding their practices (interviews occur either during or following the observed behavior).

For applied business research, ethnography entails entering customers' natural environments (home, work, retail stores, etc.) to better gain a realistic perspective of their attitudes, behaviors, and product needs. This "day-in-the-life" or "fly-on-the-wall" research has, since its inception in the 1960s, proven particularly useful for new product developers wishing to uncover and identify emerging and unmet consumer needs, especially desires that customers are unwilling or unable to articulate. After spending anywhere from a few hours or days to several months studying a culture, ethnographers identify what is missing in people's lives—the perfect cell phone, home appliance, or piece of furniture—and then work with engineers and designers to help generate ideas for products to fill those needs.

Ethnographic research offers a much deeper and richer level of insight than other qualitative research techniques such as focus groups and in-depth interviews. However, it can be quite expensive and time-consuming. Consequently, many firms use consultants rather than hiring their own anthropologists. Xerox, one of the first firms to use applied ethnography, hired an anthropologist to conduct workplace ethnographic research. The anthropologist presented her findings in a film showing office workers struggling to make copies on a Xerox machine. This led Xerox engineers to create the familiar green button that lets us walk up to the machine and easily make a copy. Similarly, anthropologists from the design firm IDEO helped Procter & Gamble develop the idea for P&G's Magic Reach tool after watching people struggle to clean their bathrooms. The device's long handle and swivel get into those hard-to-reach places.

IMPORTANT CHARACTERISTICS OF CULTURE

There are several important cultural traits we can glean from our definition:

1. As the total way of life of society, culture is pervasive or comprehensive. Omnipresent in our lives, it surrounds us and affects everything we own, think, feel, and do: the food we eat, the clothes we wear, the language we speak, and the activities we undertake. And yet, although culture is so vital to our functioning, like air, we are hardly aware of it because we are immersed in it.
2. Culture is learned or acquired, it is not biologically inherited. All that is not of the natural world, but rather is of human origin, makes up culture. For example, in American culture, people learn that "cleanliness is next to godliness." Consequently, Americans' mornings are spent washing up and grooming before taking on the day. In contrast, some Europeans bathe less frequently and do not use deodorant. Food preferences are also learned—would you eat cod semen at a Japanese banquet or pigeon's head at a Chinese meal? In Japan you can dine on squid, ox tongue, eel, cactus, and chicken wing ice cream—items not likely to be added to Lunchables packages any time soon.

3. Cultural learning is transmitted by members of society through socializing (societal) institutions (socialization agents), social groups and organizations that teach people how to function in society. These include (a) the family or home, where most values, attitudes, and behaviors originate; (b) educational institutions; (c) religious organizations, where moral values are learned; (d) local communities; (e) workplaces; and (f) the media (newspapers, magazines, radio, television, movies, video games, the Internet, and mobile media such as cell phones and iPods). Media content includes consumer advertising, which is an important part of our "pop" (popular) culture.

4. Culture evolves from generation to generation, with most change being evolutionary, not revolutionary. The image of cigarette smokers has fallen from the days of Humphrey Bogart and Lauren Bacall, when smoking was stylish and sophisticated as epitomized by the smoking jacket. Now, smokers are tossed out of offices and bars and must huddle in doorways on cold days, taking drags and tossing their butts into the streets. On the other hand, although tattoos were once relegated to male sailors and circus sideshow freaks, men and women of all social classes now sport them. Your father came from an era when men only wore two pieces of jewelry: a watch and a wedding band—necklaces and earrings were never seen on men.

CULTURAL CHANGE

Three general categories of societal change that are of particular relevance to marketers are social trends, fashions, and fads. **Social trends** are long-term, broad directions of change in a society. Typically, a series of related events over time provide evidence of a trend. For instance, increased sales of organic and natural foods might suggest consumer interest in healthy food choices. The rise of the iPod and TiVo could indicate a trend toward media personalization.

According to *American Demographics* magazine, major trends that have endured since the 1980s include the growing power of women due to their entry into the workforce, the increasingly diverse marketplace, an explosion of entrepreneurship, focus on health and alternative medicine, and rising demand for adult education. Other examples of trends include computer literacy, health and wellness, casual lifestyles, abstinence (from alcohol, tobacco, and even casual sex), tolerance of diverse behaviors and lifestyles, and cocooning—spending lots of time around hearth and home rather than going "out on the town."

Companies that miss a trend neglect an important market opportunity and often end up playing catch-up. The U.S. auto industry spent decades paying the cost of ignoring early signs that consumers wanted cars to be smaller, higher in quality, and more fuel efficient.

Fashions are styles that are adopted by a group of consumers for some time, ranging from several years to more than a decade. They tend to be shorter-lived than trends but endure longer than fads. Seismic fashion shifts occur about twice a decade. The bell-bottoms of the 1970s gave way to tight-fitting jeans in the 1980s, pleated khakis in the 1990s, and low-rise capris in the 2000s.

Styles often come from revival and recycling rather than innovation. Skinny jeans, Bermuda shorts, and platform shoes are all retreads that are barely tweaked for today's younger generation. Boomers wore crinkly peasant skirts, corset belts, and chunky turquoise jewelry when they were young. The current young generation—not yet born when these styles were au courant—has adopted them, oblivious to their history. Hip-huggers are popular again—only they are now called "low-rise jeans." Bell-bottoms, capris, bootcut jeans for girls, miniskirts, polo shirts, and madras patchwork prints also recently returned from the 1960s and 1970s. Like trends, fashions often provide a significant, albeit brief market opportunity.

Fads are short-lived fashions that are taken up with great enthusiasm for a brief, period of time, usually by relatively few people. Sales take off like a rocket but soon drop like a bomb. Think Davy Crockett coonskin caps and Hula-hoops (1950s); pet rocks (mid-1970s); disco (late 1970s); Rubik's Cubes and Cabbage Patch Kids (early 1980s); baby-on-board signs (late 1980s); slap bracelets (early 1990s); pogs (mid-1990s); Furbies and Beanie Babies (late 1990s); bobbleheads, thongs, and U.S. flags on cars (early 2000s); Harry Potter, big sunglasses, Texas hold 'em poker, and flare jeans (mid-2000s); and Crocs, emo music, skinny jeans, and Sudoku puzzles (late 2000s). Short-lived alternatives to beer have included wine coolers (1980s); dry beer (early 1990s); and flavored malt drinks (early 2000s). A fad's main appeal is simply that it is hot—the latest and greatest. Fads present brief marketing opportunities—catch the wave or miss out.

The difficulty is in distinguishing fads from fashions. Low-carbohydrate products burned bright in the early 2000s for about two years, then quickly all but burned out, with remaining marketers ending up serving niches. The same thing happened a few years later with organic foods. Reality TV shows became all the rage in the early 2000s, but after about five years their popularity began to slide, as was previously true for Westerns, spy shows, and hospital dramas.

It is much easier to distinguish trends from fads:

- Trends are broader in scope and popularity, and consequently can be expressed in different ways. Health foods endure while fad foods such as oat bran, fish oil, and wrap sandwiches come and go.
- A given trend is usually supported by other trends and demographic and societal changes. Hence, it satisfies multiple needs, thereby fitting most people's lifestyles. The back-to-nature and outdoors movement fits in with the popularity of walking, hiking, bicycling, camping, mountain climbing, fishing, racquetball, and so on—a range of activities from tame to adventurous, individual to group, and competitive to collaborative. It also meshes with lifestyle integration of fitness and weight control, the environmental movement, and desired escape from structured time schedules. Physical fitness is a trend with various faddish manifestations that come and go (pumping iron, in-line skating, and skateboarding).
- Trends grow and decline much more slowly than fads, which pop up overnight like mushrooms and dandelions and have a life span about as long as such vegetation. While there has been an overall trend toward eating healthier, fad diets such as the Zone and South Beach diets don't have staying power.
- Trends provide long-term benefits, whereas fads appeal to uniqueness, being up on the latest and greatest, or hopping on the bandwagon. Cell phones, e-mail, instant messaging, and social networking are here to stay since they meet important needs for staying in touch with friends, family, and the office. But the 1970s citizens band radio fad was merely about chatting in the car or truck for the fun of it.
- Trends are flexible and modifiable for individual needs. Health and wellness can be achieved through diet, exercise, smoking cessation, and stress-reduction techniques, whereas a grapefruit diet and yoga are limited in application and appeal.

ORGANIZATION OF CHAPTER 5

The four exercises in this chapter explore various cultural constituents. Exercise 5.1 looks at the assorted symbolic, knowledge-based, attitudinal, and behavioral components of culture and relates them to consumer behavior (CB) and societal change.

Exercise 5.2 examines the material components of culture, focusing on the United States and marketing's role in our materialistic, acquisitive culture. Exercise 5.3 investigates values, the most important knowledge-based element of culture. And Exercise 5.4 examines norms, the most significant of all behavioral cultural constituents.

EXERCISE 5.1. OVERVIEW OF COMPONENTS OF CULTURE

OBJECTIVES

1. To enable you to recognize and categorize the different elements that constitute culture.
2. To help you understand how marketers infuse their marketing communications with cultural components to appeal to members of society and allow you to experience how they appeal to consumers.
3. To have you witness how advertising reflects changes in cultural components over time and differences in these elements across cultures.

BACKGROUND

This exercise broadly categorizes various **cultural components (cultural cues)**, the basic elements constituting a society's culture. These components are illustrated with marketing examples and advertisements

> **EXHIBIT 5.1   Components of Culture (Cultural Cues)**
>
> **Symbols**: Tangibles, words, images, pictures, colors, shapes, numbers, animals, music, product semiotics, trade characters. advertising icons.
>
> **Material components/cultural artifacts:** Visible, tangible items, including commercial products.
>
> **Cognitive components/abstract elements:**
>   **Cultural knowledge:**
>   Cultural values/social values/core values
>   Cultural beliefs: Cultural truisms/folk wisdom, superstitions, common knowledge, myths, legends
>   Language
>   Religion
>   Politics
>   Cultural attitudes
>   **Cultural behavior and activities:**
>   Cultural norms:
>   Customs
>   Conventions
>   Etiquette
>   Rituals
>   Mores: Legal codes, moral (ethical) norms
>   Cultural activities

that incorporate them. The four broad categories of cultural cues are summarized in Exhibit 5.1: symbols, material artifacts, cognitive components (knowledge and attitudes), and behaviors.

Symbols: Making the Intangible Tangible

Symbols are objects, characters, and other concrete, tangible representations of abstract, intangible ideas. Cultural communication uses symbols to convey information quickly and easily, something advertisers strive to do. Symbols come in several forms:

- Tangible items are physical representations of cultural ideas. The terrorists who attacked the World Trade Center and Pentagon on 9/11 chose those buildings because they symbolized U.S. financial and military power.
- Words are used to verbally communicate cultural ideas. Marketers are interested in the meanings and images conveyed by the words they select to communicate with customers.
- Pictorial images, colors, shapes, numbers, animals, and music can all be symbolic, and their meanings can differ across cultures. While the number 7 is lucky in the United States and Morocco, it is unlucky in Ghana and Kenya. A dove represents serenity and peace in the United States but death in some Asian cultures.

Marketers have been embarrassed by cross-cultural symbolic gaffes. Merrill Lynch used a bull to represent strength, but some foreign customers viewed it instead as a source of meat. An advertiser in England and Ireland displayed the "V" peace sign, which in those nations is equivalent to an American giving someone the finger. Samsonite offered suitcases in purple and black in the Mexican market where, unfortunately, these colors are associated with death and mourning.

As is true of all aspects of culture, symbols change over time. The letter "X" used to stand for pornography ("X-rated"), but it now means extreme, edgy, and youthful (as in Generation X, ESPN's X Games, and Nissan Xterra).

Semiotics (semiotic studies, semiology) is the study of signs (i.e., something that has meaning, such as words, images, body language, etc.) and symbols. **Product semiotics** investigates unique symbolic qualities of products and brands. Porcelain china and paper plates both hold food, but one is more appropriate for serving guests a fine meal and the other is better for burgers at a picnic. The cigar has always been looked upon as a symbol of success, achievement, and celebration. The Harley-Davidson motorcycle represents rugged individualism, freedom, and rebellion.

Many brands use **trade characters (advertising icons, product mascots)**, people or animals that symbolize a brand. Betty Crocker stands for the motherly care the company puts into preparing their baked products. The Energizer Bunny represents longevity, perseverance, and determination. Ronald McDonald personifies fun and family values.

CULTURAL ARTIFACTS: THE MATERIAL COMPONENTS OF CULTURE

Cultural artifacts (material components) are physical aspects of society. They include tangible items such as homes, cars, books, appliances, tools—in fact, all commercial products.

Certain cultures are associated with specific products. The United States is the land of hamburgers, hot dogs, blue jeans, and Coca-Cola. The Netherlands is associated with tulips, wooden clogs, and Gouda cheese. Britain is known for tea, rain boots (Mackintosh), and Shetland sweaters.

Some products are associated with specific eras. The 1900–1909 period ushered in the Ford car, Crayola crayons, and the Teddy Bear; 1910–1919 gave birth to the telephone, crossword puzzles, and construction toys such as Erector sets and Tinkertoys; the 1940s launched Tide detergent and Timex watches; the 1950s introduced TV dinners and muscle cars with huge tailfins; the 1960s birthed Handi-Wrap plastic wrap and Ziploc bags; and the 1970s introduced VCRs, disco music, and the smiley face, whose 1990s descendant was the happy face emoticon typed on computer keyboards ☺.

Some of these products have not changed at all (crossword puzzles and the Teddy Bear). Others evolved slowly (new colors of Crayola crayons and new formulas of Tide detergent), while others have changed radically (you would not still drive an early Ford auto for everyday transportation) and some no longer exist (button shoes and girdles).

COGNITIVE COMPONENTS: THE WAY WE THINK

The **cognitive components** of society's "collective consciousness" are thoughts, values, ideas, and other intangibles that influence and help define a society. Cultural knowledge and cultural attitudes are two categories of cognitive components.

CULTURAL KNOWLEDGE

Cultural knowledge is a general awareness shared by a society's citizens. It includes cultural values, cultural beliefs, language, and summary constructs such as religion and politics. **Cultural values (core values, social values)** are abstract ideals about general goals and desirable means for achieving those goals that are widely shared in a society. They are a culture's beliefs about what is and is not desirable regarding goals or ends (terminal values) and the means to achieve those goals (instrumental values). Examples of American cultural values focused on goals are accomplishment, activity, comfort, efficiency and practicality, and social recognition. Cultural values focusing on means for attaining goals include ambition, cheerfulness, cleanliness, courage, and self-control.

Marketing efforts should appeal to society's dominant core values whenever possible. G.I. Joe, an American cultural icon, represents the American values of heroism, patriotism, and courage.

Some ideals are **ethical values**, standards for acting morally and doing the right and proper thing. Ethical values are either good and helpful (e.g., freedom, equality, and nondiscrimination) or bad and harmful (e.g., deception, violation of rights, and injustice).

One of the most important ingredients in ethical decision making is the central role of ethical values. It is especially important to be aware of these values when traveling abroad since standards of right and wrong may be different, such as the acceptability of bribery and of treating women as second-class citizens. Although *culture relativists* say, "When in Rome, do as the Romans do," *cultural absolutists* say that moral truths exist regardless of society—certain actions are just plain right or wrong, that is, a society may be endorsing unethical values, as when the United States permitted slavery.

Cultural beliefs, a second general type of cultural knowledge, are a society's ideas about reality that may or may not be true. The following are common cultural beliefs:

- **Cultural truisms (folk wisdom)**. These pithy sayings express commonly held beliefs such as "Time is money" and "You can't teach an old dog new tricks." As is true of all cultural elements, cultural beliefs change over time. During the 1920s, many people believed that education was wasted on a girl and a woman's place was in the home. Many cultural truisms are not universally accepted. Some say, "Absence makes the heart grow fonder," while others insist "Out of sight, out of mind." Many believe that "Knowledge is power," but others insist "Ignorance is bliss" and "What you don't know won't hurt you."

  A provocative example of a marketing cultural belief is that green M&Ms are an aphrodisiac. This is an example of an **urban legend**—a cultural belief passed along from person to person that is not true. The M&Ms legend reportedly started circulating among randy college guys during the 1970s. After decades of skirting the legend, M&M/Mars finally cashed in with TV commercials and print ads featuring the seductive female M&M character, Green, sporting bedroom eyes and luscious lips.

- **Superstitions** are ideas that result from ignorance, fear of the unknown, or trust in magic or chance. Examples include the beliefs that astrology can help foretell the future, one should play his or her "lucky number" in a lottery, and 13 is an unlucky number. Marketers were in seventh heaven about a calendar quirk on July 7, 2007, and its link to the lucky number 777. Hotels, casinos, and retailers held 7-centric promotions and events, such as Wal-Mart's "Lucky in Love Wedding Search," in which seven couples won a July 7 wedding ceremony and reception.

- **Common knowledge** is a set of educated beliefs shared by most members of society, such as computer literacy and common courtesy.

- **Myths** are stories containing symbolic elements expressing a society's key values, ideals, emotions, and dreams. These often feature a clash between good and evil and serve as a moral guide. Superman, Dr. Jekyll and Mr. Hyde, E.T., and Santa Claus, whose modern image was developed in the 1930s through a series of Coca-Cola ads, are all mythical.

- **Legends** are stories about revered people who are a combination of myth and history. Legendary figures include Elvis Presley, Babe Ruth, Davy Crockett, Paul Bunyan, Princess Diana, John Lennon, and Michael Jordan.

  Language, a third type of cultural knowledge, permits effective communication within a society. Marketers must be careful with literal translations from one language to another, as idioms and figures of speech do not smoothly translate. You might run into difficulty if you tell a Frenchman he is "out to lunch" and he orders pate or, explain to a Spanish woman that you are "tackling some problems" and she assumes you fight bulls.

A fourth kind of cultural knowledge suggests that certain topics shouldn't be discussed among polite company—religion and politics. Consequently, marketers should exercise caution when incorporating religion and politics into their marketing communications so as not to offend people. **Religion** is a belief in and reverence for a supernatural power(s) recognized as the creator(s) and governor(s) of the universe. Religious beliefs influence what people regard as truth on big-picture issues such as the nature of reality, the meaning of life, the existence and nature of the afterlife, and the makeup of morality. Religious beliefs affecting CB include "It is wrong to eat meat," "Don't smoke tobacco," and "Don't go shopping on Sunday."

Politics concerns the activities and affairs of government and politicians. Marketers are ever vigilant to monitor and lobby for or against laws passed by legislatures and interpreted by the judiciary on issues such as product safety, fair pricing and distribution, and deceptive advertising. But many marketers are loath to get involved. When asked to endorse an opponent of conservative Jesse Helms in a North Carolina U.S. Senate race, Michael Jordan observed, "Republicans buy shoes, too."

CULTURAL ATTITUDES

Cultural attitudes are very general positive or negative evaluations in society regarding issues and practices, such as the proper roles of men and women in society, whether smoking in public is acceptable, and whether ironing clothes is necessary. For instance, Europeans are less inhibited about their bodies than Americans are, so there is little social stigma in men unzipping and peeing in public if nature calls. This illustrates that cultural attitudes give rise to cultural behavior.

Cross-cultural attitudes are reflected in advertising. Slapstick violence in humorous advertising is accepted in the United States but not in Europe. However, the U.S. ad market is more squeamish about sexual images and nudity compared with Europe and many other parts of the world.

BEHAVIORAL COMPONENTS: THE WAY WE ACT

Cultures vary with regard to how people behave in certain situations. The two categories of behavioral components are cultural norms and cultural activities.

CULTURAL NORMS

Cultural norms are informal societal rules or standards for appropriate or inappropriate behavior. Such behavioral standards determine what is "normal," i.e., the way things ought to be. Cultural norms permeating society include customs, conventions, etiquette, and rituals.

Customs are norms handed down over generations that define culturally acceptable behaviors in specific situations, often special occasions. For example, it is customary to hold ceremonies for such milestone events as weddings and graduations, and it is expected that ham will be served at Easter dinner and turkey at Thanksgiving dinner.

Conventions are norms regarding the conduct of everyday life. They concern the proper way to do things such as entertain guests, landscape a yard, and dress for work. Conventions, like most aspects of culture, evolve slowly. Recall that during the 1990s, dress in the American workplace became more casual, with employees switching from gray flannel suits to gray flannel shirts. Children once carried books to school either in their arms or in a briefcase, but they now lug them in backpacks. During the 1970s, a 10 percent tip in a restaurant was fine; in the 1990s it had risen to 15 percent; and now it is approaching 20 percent. However, in most countries tips are still only 10 percent and in some countries there is no tipping at all or it only exists in certain cities.

Conventions related to CB can change. During the energy shortage of 2001, some hotels began charging "energy fees" in addition to their posted and advertised rates, thereby breaking the convention that customers should not have to pay such surprising add-on charges.

Etiquette (decorum) is the set of rules that govern socially acceptable behavior. If you violate rules of etiquette, you are rightly considered ill-mannered, or even uncivilized, but not immoral.

Standards of etiquette vary among cultures. For example, territoriality is a person's defense of their territory, or personal space. In the United States, people stay about three to four feet away from others, whereas in some European countries people stand almost nose to nose.

A **ritual (ritual behavior)** is a series of expressive, symbolic behaviors that occur in a fixed sequence and are frequently repeated over time. Rituals can be mundane, everyday, and private activities. They include grooming rituals such as shampooing and shaving daily or brushing one's teeth after every meal. Rituals can also be important and public, such as **rites of passage**. These ceremonies recognize people's change in social status, life situation, or other significant events. Examples include birthday parties, retirement dinners, graduation ceremonies, and bar mitzvahs.

Rituals frequently are associated with **ritual artifacts**, items used in conjunction with rituals, such as a retirement gold watch, a communion cup, or a white wedding gown. Associated with Christmas are Christmas trees, mistletoe, wreaths, and colored lights. Birthdays bring to mind candles, cake, and wrapping paper. Gift giving is a public ritual that involves purchasing, exchanging, and evaluating gifts at these rites of passage.

Social and entertainment events are often ritualistic and goods-laden, such as dinner and the theater, baseball games and hot dogs, and Super Bowl viewing parties. Holidays are also often rich in ritual, presenting marketers opportunities to sell ritual artifacts. Thanksgiving, Christmas, Easter, and the Fourth of July all include ritualistic consumption such as feasting and gift giving.

MORES

Mores are norms with a strong moral overtone. They usually prohibit forbidden behavior, such as incest, cannibalism, and the exhibition of skin by women in fundamentalist Muslim countries. Violating a more constitutes a moral breach and usually results in some sort of social sanction, such as peer disapproval, ostracism, or even imprisonment. The two important types of mores are legal codes and moral norms.

Legal codes are a code of laws adopted by a town, state, or nation enforcing mores via government sanctions for wrongdoing. There are laws that marketers are obliged to obey concerning matters such as selling cigarettes and alcohol to minors, gambling, consumer protection, price discrimination, and truth in advertising.

Moral norms (ethical norms) are standards of behavior that require, prohibit, or allow certain specific actions to avoid causing harm to others (e.g., prohibitions against stealing, lying, and injuring) or to help people (e.g., encouragement of donating money and time to charities). For example, most people in the United States feel it is wrong for youngsters to consume alcoholic beverages.

CULTURAL ACTIVITIES

Cultural activities involve how people in a society spend time and money. We can be occupied with leisure or work, be alone or with others, or pursue sports or the arts.

Acceptable activities change over time. For example, ballroom dancing was thought to spark sexual passions in the early 1900s, as was jitterbug dancing during the 1940s and the Twist in the 1960s. In the early 2000s "freak dancing" or "dirty dancing," in which boys thrust their pelvises into girls' behinds, caused consternation among parents, and songs such as Sisqo's "Thong Song" and "Bootylicious" by Destiny's Child encouraged this practice. What do you suppose dancing will be like in the 2020s?

REVIEW QUESTIONS

1. Describe the four major categories of cultural cues and examples of specific types of elements included in each category. Explain the marketing relevance of each of these categories.
2. What are the major types of symbols? Which ones are marketers most likely to use?
3. How do cognitive components of culture differ from material artifacts? What are the major types of cognitive components marketers can tap into?
4. Cite examples of cultural behavior and activities and how they present marketing opportunities.

IN-CLASS APPLICATIONS

1. Identify and explain which cultural components are found in the following scenarios. Classify each broadly (i.e., symbols, material artifacts, cognitive components, cultural attitudes, and cultural behavior) and narrowly (e.g., words, superstitions, and customs).
   → *Scenario A. Bob Courts Candy.* Bob has an important first date tomorrow with the captain of the cheerleading team, Candy. He wants to do it right, so he purchases a pair of Calvin Klein slacks and a bottle of CK cologne.
   → *Scenario B. Dick Does Digital.* Dick is shopping for a digital TV. He wishes to be on the leading edge with his home entertainment center. Dick knows it will be expensive, but wants to impress his friends with his technological savvy as well as entertain them in style.
   → *Scenario C. Lynn Goes Online for Goodies.* Lynn has been invited to her friend's home for dinner. She offers to bring a dessert. Pressed for time because she has a demanding full-time job, she orders a dessert and bottle of wine from the Peapod online home shopping service. They promise to deliver to her door within three hours.
   → *Scenario D. Professor Looks Very Professionally Professorial.* Arthur Vary is trying to cultivate an intellectual image for himself as a newly minted assistant professor of marketing, so he decided to buy a pair of eyeglasses even though his vision is 20/20. Professor Vary also took up pipe smoking to look contemplative, although he knows it is unhealthy. Further, Arthur invested in a classical music collection to craft the academic image and lined his office bookshelf with all of the complimentary review copies of textbooks received from publishers to make it appear that he is well read. Professor Vary also invested in a cap and gown for the many academic convocations and graduations he knows he will be attending during his career.
   → *Scenario E. Herr Krauss Goes Native.* Heimlich Krauss, a German citizen, recently moved to New York City to head up the marketing function within a U.S. subsidiary of his corporation. He wanted

to adjust to the United States as quickly as possible. In order to do so, Mr. Krauss took to drinking Coca-Cola, bought a Chevrolet, frequented McDonald's, and shopped at Sears. He also bought a German-English dictionary and some English language CDs to improve his command of the language. Heimlich then began regularly attending New York Yankees games, where he patriotically stood for the national anthem, splurged on hot dogs and Budweiser beer, took a seventh-inning stretch, and rooted for the Bronx Bombers.

2. Identify an example of each of the four broad categories of cultural characteristics that has influenced your CB or the behavior of college students in general. Note any significant differences between American and international students in the class.

3. One way to generate new product ideas is to use trend extrapolation, which means to identify a broad current change in society (demographically, technologically, socially, politically, etc.) and assume it will continue into the future. Analysts then ask what new needs or wants this trend creates and what new products could be developed to satisfy the emerging needs and wants.

    What new product ideas are suggested by each of the following cultural trends?

    a. Sit-down meals are giving way to grazing as time-strapped consumers eat on the run throughout the day.
    b. People are down-aging, acting younger and younger (e.g., 80-year-old marathon runners).
    c. Weddings are becoming more formal, individualistic, and expensive.
    d. People want to simplify their lives—"less is more."

4. Identify as many cultural cues as you can in each of the ads from U.S. media in Exhibits 5.2 through 5.6. Which of these elements might not work well in some other foreign cultures? Why not?

WRITTEN APPLICATIONS

1. Answer Question 3 in the In-Class Applications. For one of your new product ideas, suggest several other cultural trends with which it would be consistent. Then, check your assumption by surveying about six target market members (be sure to clearly describe that market) to see whether they find it an attractive new product idea and why or why not. Do any of them mention any of the trends?

2. Answer Question 4 in the In-Class Applications. Identify and describe specific societies in which one or more of these ads might not be acceptable.

3. Visit one or more of the following Web sites, which contain archives of advertisements:
    * Adflip.com: The world's largest archive of classic print ads.
    * Ad*Access at http://library.duke.edu/digitalcollections/adaccess/: Over 7,000 advertisements printed in U.S. and Canadian newspapers and magazines between 1911 and 1955.
    * adclassix.com/rareads.htm: A specialist in original vintage ads.
    * AdForum.com (AdForum allows you to search by country as well as by time period): http://adland.tv/: Carries 40,000 TV and radio spots in Quicktime format. The site is strong in both U.S. and international ads.

On these sites, find two ads from different time periods (e.g., the 1940s and the 1980s) and two ads from different countries (e.g., the United States and France). Discuss differences reflected in cultural characteristics found in each ad.

EXERCISE 5.2. CULTURAL ARTIFACTS: CREATING A TIME CAPSULE

OBJECTIVES

1. To help you understand the contribution of cultural artifacts to society.
2. To have you describe cultural artifacts from various eras, working from your memory and conducting online research.
3. To give you insight into the role of marketing activities in contributing to a society's cultural artifacts.

EXHIBIT 5.2 Lorrilard Tobacco Company Ad

EXHIBIT 5.3 Purina One Ad

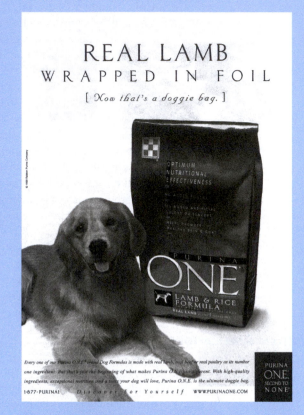

EXHIBIT 5.4 Hefty Ad

EXHIBIT 5.5 Bounty Ad

EXHIBIT 5.6   Egg Beaters Ad

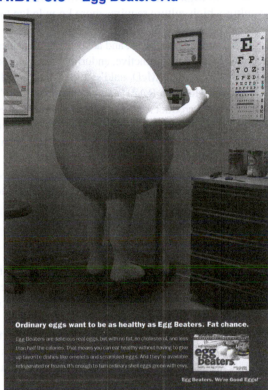

Ordinary eggs want to be as healthy as Egg Beaters. Fat chance.

Egg Beaters are delicious real eggs, but with no fat, no cholesterol, and less than half the calories. That means you can eat healthy without having to give up favorite dishes like omelets and scrambled eggs. And they're available refrigerated or frozen. It's enough to turn ordinary shell eggs green with envy.

Egg Beaters. We're Good Eggs!

BACKGROUND

THE NATURE OF CULTURAL ARTIFACTS

Recall that one of the four broad categories of cultural components is cultural artifacts. These come in two general categories: (1) **privately owned consumer goods** are owned by individuals and households, and include houses, appliances, video games, and packaged foods, and (2) **public goods** are owned and maintained by a governmental entity and are available for everyone's use. Examples include infrastructure such as highways, bridges, airports, and parking garages, as well as government buildings, museums, and parks.

After a culture has dissipated, cultural artifacts are sometimes left behind, which cultural anthropologists study via observational research as **physical trace evidence**. We have all heard tales of archaeological digs that uncover relics such as remnants of broken pottery, chipped portions of artwork, and parts of tools.

Artifacts come and go. In American culture, cuff links and three-piece suits are now virtually a thing of the past, tie clasps are becoming extinct, and even briefcases are being replaced by tote bags, athletic bags, and knapsacks.

MARKETING ARTIFACTS AND POP CULTURE

Products, brands, advertisements, retail outlets, and service establishments all contribute to our culture. Some marketing artifacts form parts of the **popular ("pop," mass) culture**—the culture of mainstream appeal, such as movies, TV shows, popular books, music, fashion, sports, toys and games (including video games), and magazines. Popular culture is not rooted in cultural tradition. It is mass produced and standardized, shaped more by marketing surveys than by the spontaneous expression of a people's experience. A visible aspect of pop culture is consumer advertising, with images, slogans, and icons that become ingrained in the people's consciousness.

Pop culture contrasts with **high culture**, elite activities such as museum-caliber art, opera, and ballet. Compared with pop culture, high culture requires more knowledge to understand, is less accessible, and is more exclusive in content, style, and appeal.

Product elements, such as brands, packages, and advertising characters sometimes become so highly recognized that they become **product icons**, distinctive, enduring brand symbols that hold significant nostalgic value or deep meaning for consumers, such as McDonald's golden arches and the Nike checkmark. In fact, products such as the Apple iPod and the Motorola RAZR cell phone are "so cool" that they take on iconic status.

Trade characters are a type of product icon. Many fictitious creatures and characters, such as the Pillsbury Doughboy, the Michelin Man, and the Jolly Green Giant, have become well known in popular culture. Many are more recognizable than business tycoons, artists, and even U.S. presidents!

New up-and-comers are always being invented, such as the Aflac Duck and the Geico Gecko. There is almost universal recognition of more-established advertising icons, such as the Keebler elves, Mr. Clean, and the Campbell's soup kids. All are friendly, familiar parts of the cultural landscape, and even little children can readily recognize them.

TIME CAPSULES: PRESERVING CULTURAL ARTIFACTS

Time capsule is a tool for preserving contemporary cultural artifacts to help future generations to learn more about an earlier epoch. Product relics from bygone eras include caster oil, girdles, button shoes, Nehru jackets, women's and men's garter belts, bomb shelters, white cotton gloves, chastity belts, and pillbox hats. (OK twenty-somethings, look them up!)

A time capsule from the 1990s might contain videotapes of the movies *Wayne's World* and *Titanic,* a Nintendo Game Boy, a Zap-It super saturator water gun, records by kid rappers Kris Kross, 90210 dolls, a Giga Pet, a Baby-sitters Club book, a David Letterman Top-10 list, a Beanie Baby, a sport utility vehicle, and a pair of Nike Air Jordans.

It is interesting to note that, to celebrate the launch of the new millennium, Kellogg's Frosted Flakes held a promotion featuring product icon Tony the Tiger on the back panel of the cereal box inviting kids to create a time capsule for this momentous event. Hey, if the kiddies can do it, so can you! So get busy preparing the application below.

REVIEW QUESTIONS

1. Cite and describe two major categories of material artifacts. Into which category would most consumer goods fall?
2. What types of cultural artifacts do marketers contribute to the popular culture?
3. What is a time capsule and how does it relate to the concept of physical trace evidence?

IN-CLASS APPLICATIONS

1. What objects would you put into a time capsule to represent the first decade of the twenty-first century for someone living in the future? It could be for a child, a future archaeologist, or even an alien being curiously unearthing your time capsule 100, 1,000, or even 1,000,000 years from now.

Think primarily in terms of privately owned items (most of which will be consumer goods), but also include some public goods that represent the culture at large. For example, for the year 1946, the first year of the post–World War II era, popular music included "Day by Day" by Frank Sinatra, "Prisoner of Love" by Perry Como, and "Ole Buttermilk Sky" by Hoagy Carmichael; the latest literature consisted of *Animal Farm* by George Orwell, *The Iceman Cometh* by Eugene O'Neill, and *All the King's Men* by Robert Penn Warren; while top movies were *It's a Wonderful Life,* starring James Stewart, and *The Best Years of Our Lives,* featuring Fredric March and Myrna Loy. Representations of public goods could include original manuscripts, photographs, and other memorabilia from President Harry Truman's career, such as slips of paper featuring his famous phrases "The buck stops here" and "If you can't stand the heat, get out of the kitchen." You can also try to tangibly illustrate some of the other cultural characteristics from Exercise 5.1: symbols, cognitive components, and cultural behavior.

What do these objects tell us about the nature of our culture? Which marketing artifacts are especially positive contributions with beneficial effects on society and which are particularly negative contributors with harmful influences on the decade's culture?

Your professor might opt to have class members bring in cultural artifacts to represent the current year. These could then be buried by class members in a box somewhere on campus (or else just kept in a box in your professor's office) to be opened in a year or more by a later class, which, in turn, could create its own time capsule.

2. Select another decade that you are somewhat familiar with (or would like to learn about), and answer Question 1 for that decade.

3. Try your hand at forecasting new artifacts (e.g., new products) or modifications of existing artifacts for the next ten years. How will these affect other cultural components?

WRITTEN APPLICATIONS

1. From the In-Class Applications, answer Questions 1 and 2 for the decades of the 1980s and 1990s, and Question 3. You might want to do some research on the Internet by visiting several search engines and typing in "time capsule," "history of time capsules," "fads and fashions," and similar phrases.

EXERCISE 5.3. AMERICAN CULTURAL VALUES

OBJECTIVES

1. To help you understand the nature of cultural values by examining several popular classification schemes.
2. To have you observe and understand how advertisers incorporate cultural values into their advertising appeals and relate them to product features.
3. To give you experience in witnessing how American cultural values have both survived and evolved over time and how American values differ from those in other societies, as revealed through examining advertising from different decades and cultures.
4. To have you compare your own personal values with those of American society and to reflect on how any differences between these two values sets influence your receptivity to advertisements featuring mainstream American cultural values.
5. To provoke thought and discussion on the nature of the intertwining cause-and-effect relationship between advertising and cultural values by analyzing ads to determine whether advertising shapes or reflects society's values.

BACKGROUND

CULTURAL VALUES AND PERSONAL VALUES

Societal values are significant because their very general nature causes them to influence all other cultural constituents (cultural beliefs, attitudes, norms, and activities). In Exercise 5.1 we defined cultural values (core values, social values) as abstract ideals about general goals and desirable means for achieving those goals that are widely shared in a society. Core values are general, abstract ideals, positive or negative, not tied to any specific object or situation.

Universal cultural values are cherished across many different cultures, from New York to New Delhi. This is because values correspond to underlying common human psychological needs. Most American ideals are universal cultural values, such as freedom, liberty, and being healthy, successful, and active.

Where cultures differ, however, is the relative importance they attach to such values. For instance, personal success is regarded more highly in individualistic cultures such as most Western societies. Some cultures clash over values. Islamic terrorists wage war against Western cultural values of individual freedom, women's rights, democracy, and free enterprise. This relative weight of various values within a culture forms a culture's **value system**. In the United States, honesty is valued over thrift and career success is treasured more than politeness. Americans place a very high value on private property, especially as embodied in the home.

There are also **personal values (self-oriented values)**, ideals most important to an individual that shape how the person thinks and behaves in almost every situation. Personal values usually mirror cultural, sub-cultural, and social group values but are held at an individual level rather than at a societal level. Personal values sometimes deviate from social values.

VALUES AND EVALUATIVE CRITERIA

Cultural values, in turn, determine which **product-specific values** or evaluative criteria buyers use for selecting among brands in a product category. For example, someone who values good physical health might look for food attributes such as vitamin-enriched and low in fat, cholesterol, and carbohydrates.

Recall from Exercise 4.3 the idea of a **means-end chain analysis**—product attributes are the *means* for obtaining the *ends*, which are the consumer benefits the product attributes provide. However, the ultimate ends are not simply benefits. Rather, the consumer's ultimate goal is to fulfill *personal values*.

For example, a mother might purchase a high-priced snack food that provides health benefits because she values her family's health. A businessperson might buy a new version of a personal digital assistant advertised to contain the latest technological feature because she values being up to date.

Do not confuse *societal values* or *personal values* with *evaluative criteria*, which are specific product dimensions such as price, size, and quality level. Values are general beliefs related to many products. For example, safety and quality are two general values that people seek in many goods, whereas safety and quality could also be specific features of products that people valuing safety and quality look for.

CLASSIFYING CULTURAL VALUES

We now review several of the more common classification schemes for values. You will notice that there is a lot of overlap among them.

HOFSTEDE'S CULTURAL DIMENSIONS

Cross-cultural (transnational) differences in values were proposed in 1980 by Dutch psychologist Geert Hofstede, who found in his survey research four general value dimensions, to which a fifth value has since been added: **individualism versus collectivism, uncertainty avoidance, masculinity versus femininity, power distance, and time orientation**.

Individualism versus Collectivism. This describes the extent to which a culture focuses on individuals and their welfare rather than groups and their well-being. In **collectivist cultures**, people subordinate their personal goals to those of the group to which they owe allegiance, such as relatives, friends, and organizations. Decisions are made on the basis of group harmony and consensus. In **individualistic cultures**, people are more concerned with personal goals, individual experiences, variety, pleasure, and freedom than with group welfare. The United States is a very individualistic country. Individualism is expressed through behaviors such as body piercing, burning custom CDs, and buying customized cell phone ring tones, vanity license plates, and vanity Web site domain names (e.g., GeoffreyLantos.com).

Uncertainty Avoidance. This dimension is a measure of the degree to which a culture prefers structured situations to unstructured situations and is willing to tolerate ambiguity and unusual behavior. Societies high in uncertainty avoidance prefer formal rules, absolute truth, the advice of experts, and straightforward product information. Cultures low in uncertainty avoidance are more open to change and new experiences. They tolerate less information content in advertising. The United States is relatively low in uncertainty avoidance. It is a nation of risk takers who are open to change. American society is postmodernist—questioning absolute truth and tolerating personal differences.

Masculinity versus Femininity. This concerns the extent to which sex roles are clearly defined in a culture. In **masculine cultures**, there are clear distinctions between masculine values such as assertiveness, success, competition, and materialism, and feminine values such as warm personal relationships, nurturance, equality, and preserving the environment. In **feminine cultures**, there are no rigid gender roles and both sexes are concerned with quality of life, caring for others, and modesty. The United States scores moderately on the index of masculinity.

Power Distance. This refers to the degree to which members of a society are considered equal in terms of status, authority, and wealth and there is acceptance of social inequality and hierarchical relationships, such as superiors versus subordinates.

Some cultures, as in Japan, emphasize strict vertical relationships and base decisions on levels of authority, such as authoritative spokespersons in advertising. Other societies, as in the United States, foster a high degree of equality and informality, with decisions founded on facts and reasoning among peers and colleagues.

Time Orientation. This refers to the extent to which members of society are oriented to the past, present, or future. The United States is oriented to the future and the present, believing that "Time waits for no man," "Time is money," and we must "do it yesterday," indicating that "there's no time like the present."

Time orientation is also concerned with whether a society is **polychromic**, or oriented toward multitasking (e.g., talking on a cell phone while walking, studying while watching television), or **monochromic**, focusing on doing one thing at a time. The United States is increasingly polychromic.

GLOBAL VALUES

Perhaps the most inclusive scheme of values is shown in Exhibit 5.7, which sets out **global values**, which are abstract and apply across many specific situations. Global values contrast with **domain-specific values**, ideals that hold only for a particular set of activities, such as family, the workplace (corporate values), or religion.

The greatest means of distinguishing between cultural values within societies is Hofstede's individualism-collectiveism dimension. Global values can be lumped into three broad groups: *individualism, collectiveism,* and *mixed.* They can be further organized into seven broad categories: maturity, security, self-direction, prosocial behavior (serving others), restrictive conformity (conforming to others' expectations), achievement, and enjoyment of life.

Other global values that are often said to characterize the American way of life include:

- *Activity.* Americans believe that keeping busy is healthy and natural, and they have a strong work ethic. The United States tends to equate idleness with evil, reflected in the folk wisdom "The devil finds work for idle hands."
- *Efficiency and practicality.* Efficiency means valuing anything that saves time and money. Practicality esteems laborsaving products to accomplish utilitarian tasks and solve problems.
- *Progress.* This entails "getting ahead" and doing better, often by using technology.
- *Humanitarianism.* This entails helping those who are less fortunate and rooting for the "underdog," as well as defending individual rights and being generous toward charitable causes.
- *Respect for societal institutions.* Americans traditionally placed their faith in institutions such as family, schools, houses of worship, business, and government. However, this faith has recently waned in light of various ethics scandals and financial mismanagement among institutional leaders.
- *Mastery of the environment.* This is the extent to which society lives in harmony with nature as opposed to attempting to dominate, exploit, and overcome it. In recent years, Americans have renewed their respect for the natural environment, exercising concern for pollution, overcrowded landfills, recycling, and their ecological footprint.

DOMAIN-SPECIFIC AMERICAN VALUES

In addition to these global values there are domain-specific values relevant to a particular area of activity. These are influenced by cultural values. Examples include materialism, which is relevant to marketplace behavior, and health, which is pertinent to family and self. Values relevant to the marketplace are called

EXHIBIT 5.7 Core Global American Values

MIXED	
Maturity * Mature love * True friendship * Wisdom * A world of beauty + Courageous	**Security** * National security * Freedom * Inner harmony * Family security * A world at peace

INDIVIDUAL	**COLLECTIVE**
Self-Direction * Sense of accomplishment * Self respect + Imaginative + Independent + Broadminded + Intellectual + Logical	**Prosocial** * Equality * Salvation + Forgiving + Helpful + Belief in God + Honest + Loving

Achievement	**Enjoyment**	**Restrictive Conformity**
* Social recognition * An exciting life + Ambitious + Capable	* Comfortable life * Pleasure * Happiness + Cheerful	+ Obedient + Polite + Self-controlled + Clean + Responsible

Key:
* = Terminal values
+ = Instrumental values

consumption-specific values and are evaluative criteria. For retail stores, these could include a broad assortment and courteous salespeople, whereas for products they include durability and stylishness.

Domain-specific values that are important to Americans include:

- *Materialism.* Americans place high value on acquiring money and material goods—the so-called "good life." People often judge others superficially by the quantity and quality of their possessions. Many ads reinforce this mindset by implying that "you are what you own," often conveyed through a brand image.
- *The home.* Almost two-thirds of all Americans own a home. Home ownership and making the home attractive are highly esteemed. Many products, from home entertainment centers and home furnishings to lawn care products and landscaping services, are pitched as turning a house into a "home."
- *A balance of work and leisure.* Work is valued both as an end itself (the Protestant work ethic) and as a means to an end (to finance leisure and pleasure). Working too much is viewed as workaholism, while not working enough is considered slothful. "In all things moderation."
- *Family and children.* Americans cherish providing for and spending quality time with the family— so-called "family values." Many ads feature family activities.
- *Health and fitness.* Americans have become more health conscious over the past several decades, eating better, getting more exercise, avoiding unhealthy products such as cigarettes, fatty foods, and

consuming too much alcohol. There is a recent concern about obesity, especially in children, with advertisers of children's "junk foods" under attack. Hershey's even put an antioxidant seal on its dark chocolate to indicate that the treats contain nutrients to protect cells from damage due to oxidation.

- *Hedonism.* Pleasure is sought through the purchase of many hedonic products.
- *Youthfulness.* The United States is a culture obsessed with looking and acting young, of being "young at heart." Consequently, Americans are afloat in products such as Botox (cosmetic injections for the wrinkle-phobic), hair coloring to keep the gray away, and diet products to feel and appear young.
- *Technology.* Americans have a fascination with technological advances that help them realize the good value of progress. Hence, high-tech products such as mobile wireless devices and high-definition TVs are pitched as the latest and greatest leading-edge marvels.

ROKEACH'S TERMINAL AND INSTRUMENTAL VALUES

Psychologist Milton Rokeach defines **terminal values** as ends (shown with an asterisk in Exhibit 5.7) or ideal end *states of being* (existence). The latter describes how people would like to eventually experience their lives. Such values include achieving mature love, true friendship, and wisdom. According to Rokeach, terminal values should be the ultimate motivators of CB.

Instrumental values are ideal *states of doing*. They are the means (indicated with a plus sign in Exhibit 5.7) or modes of conduct required to achieve terminal values. Examples include being courageous, imaginative, and independent. Americans believe deeply in education, innovation, risk taking, and plain hard work as the means to a better life.

In light of *personal values*, people who highly regard the set of values at one end of Exhibit 5.7 tend to deem the ideals on the chart's opposite side (top versus bottom, and left versus right) less important. Hence, someone who places high worth on maturity and security (top of the figure) would value less enjoyment (bottom), while a person who esteems self-direction and achievement (left) would not value prosocial behavior and restrictive conformity (right). Due to people's personal values, universal agreement does not exist on these values within the culture at large.

FOCUS-OF-ORIENTATION VALUES

Another common value-classification scheme places values into one of three broad categories depending on the **focus of orientation**: personal, social, and material values.

We have already discussed personal values (self-oriented values), which reflect the objectives and approaches to life that individual members of the culture find desirable. American and other Western cultures are more oriented toward personal values such as activity, hard work, materialism, postponed gratification, abstinence, and religion, whereas some other cultures are more inclined toward personal values such as passivity, leisure, nonmaterialism, immediate gratification, sensual gratification, and secularity.

Social Values (Other-Oriented Values). This set of values reflects a culture's view of what constitutes appropriate relationships between individuals and groups. U.S. and other Western societies are more geared toward casual relationships, competitiveness, individualism, youth orientation, performance, immediate family, masculinity, and diversity. Other cultures cherish formality, cooperation, collectivism, seniority, position, extended family, femininity, and uniformity.

Material Values (Environment-Oriented Values). This group of values prioritizes society's relationships with the various aspects of the broad environment: ecological (physical or natural environment), economic, and technical. The United States is concerned with order and cleanliness, optimism and problem solving, progress and change, and risk taking. Other societies value disorder, fatalism, tradition, security, and stability.

EVOLVING CULTURAL VALUES

Many traditional Western values are slowly changing. Some people speak of "traditional values" versus "new values." Exhibit 5.8 gives some examples of these changes. During the cultural revolution of the 1960s on

> **EXHIBIT 5.8** **Changing Values in Western Civilization**

From	To
Traditional family life	Alternative families
Patriotism	Globalism and multiculturalism
Respect for institutions	Self-reliance
Mastery of environment	Harmony with nature and environmental stewardship
Hard work	Leisure
Abstinence	Sensuality
Master nature	Admire nature
Postponed gratification	Immediate gratification
Devotion to God	Humanism ("Man is the measure of all things") and secularism
Rugged individualism	Collectivism
Individual rights	Group rights (e.g., women's and minority rights)
Equality of opportunity	Equality of outcome

both sides of the Atlantic Ocean, old-fashioned values such as individual responsibility and self-sacrifice declined in favor of individual freedom and self-indulgence. However, in the aftermath of the tragic events of 9/11, many observers believe the pendulum is swinging back in the direction of the values in the left-hand column of Exhibit 5.8. Some of the fundamental human values that many Americans seem to be returning to include family, patriotism, community, work-life balance, integrity, compassion, and authenticity.

REVIEW QUESTIONS

1. Describe each of the following schemes for classifying cultural values: Hofstede's cultural dimensions, core global American values, Rokeach's terminal and instrumental values, and focus-of-orientation values.
2. Explain the relationship between cultural values and personal values and between global values and domain-specific values.
3. What is the nature of the relationship between values and evaluative criteria?

IN-CLASS APPLICATIONS

1. Which set of values in Exhibit 5.8 do you personally tend to subscribe to: those in the left-hand column or those in the right-hand column? Why do you prefer this particular set of personal values? Do your personal values ever clash with those of other important people in your life? How do you handle any consequent conflict? Toward which of these two value sets do you believe the United States (or Western civilization in general) is heading? Can you cite any evidence?
2. For each of the advertisements in Exhibits 5.9–5.15, find as many American cultural values as you can that are implicitly appealed to in that ad. Briefly discuss each of the values. Is each a terminal value or instrumental value? A global value or a domain-specific value? Also, give your opinion on whether each ad effectively uses these values.

   Which product attributes (physical features or consumer benefits) are, or else could be, linked to the various values in each ad? How would you do so?
3. The ads in Exhibits 5.9 through 5.15 came from a special millennium advertising section in the January 2000 issue of *Good Housekeeping* magazine. This issue celebrated one hundred years of the Good Housekeeping Institute, which evaluates advertised products for quality and awards its Good House-

keeping Seal of Approval. Each ad was designed to be a "salute to our shared history," celebrating the partnership between the advertisers and the magazine regarding innovation in some of the most successful and well-known brands in the world. However, each ad also illustrates American cultural values, both those prevalent when the product the ad featured was launched and those values now dominant.

Your assignment is as follows:

    a. Discuss the American cultural values that are common to most or all of the ads. Are they effectively employed in each ad?

    b. Describe any values unique to each ad. Are these values appropriately associated with the product?

    c. For each ad, explain how values seem to have either endured or evolved from when the product was launched until the dawn of the new millennium.

4. In 1917 British novelist Norman Douglas remarked, "You can tell the ideals of a nation by its advertisements." Do you agree? Do you believe that advertising helps shape a nation's values or does it merely reflect and appeal to already existing values? Is it a mirror or mindbender? A barometer or an arbiter? Does art imitate life or does life imitate art? Explain. What is the implication of your answer for advertising practitioners?

WRITTEN APPLICATIONS

1. Answer Questions 2 and 3 in the In-Class Applications for two of the ads in Exhibits 5.9 through 5.15. Also, discuss what other values could be associated with each of the four ads you discuss and how these values could be incorporated into advertising.

2. Repeat Question 2 in the In-Class Applications for three more ads that you find.

3. Answer Question 4 in the In-Class Applications.

4. Which of your own personal values differ from those of your society? Does this influence your own receptivity to any of the ads you have observed in Section A?

5. Visit one or more of the following Web sites from Exercise 5.1 (Written Applications Question #3) to view ads from different time periods or cultures: Adflip.com, Ad*Access at http://library.duke.edu/digitalcollections/adaccess/, adclassix.com/rareads.htm, and AdForum.com.

(AdForum is probably your best bet as it allows you to search by country as well as by time period.) Describe how these ads vary over three different decades (pick any three you like) or three different cultures (your choices) by selecting at least three ads from each time period or culture.

EXERCISE 5.4. VIOLATING CULTURAL NORMS

OBJECTIVES

1. To help you understand the nature and different types of cultural norms.
2. To help you gain an appreciation for marketers' sensitivity to cultural norms, which they must avoid violating.
3. To enable you to think about and experience firsthand the consequences of violating cultural norms.

BACKGROUND

THE NATURE OF CULTURAL NORMS

Recall that cultural norms determine socially acceptable boundaries for behavior, either in general or in specific situations. These norms are transmitted by example, by word of mouth, and through religious teachings. Some examples your parents probably taught you include do not "buck" the line, never stare at people, and knock on a closed door before entering. At college, you should not rummage through your roommate's personal stuff looking for something or take someone else's seat in a class where students have their "own" seats (officially assigned or not).

EXHIBIT 5.9   La-Z-Boy Ad

EXHIBIT 5.10   Jell-O Ad

EXHIBIT 5.11   AARP Ad

A Health Insurance Program That Should Interest All Practical, Serious Individuals (You Know, Like Yourself).

If you've spent any time comparing health insurance alternatives, you know some programs offer more choices in coverage than others. AARP Health Care Options offers AARP Members a variety of competitively priced plans. The result is that, with AARP Health Care Options, you can expect to find the coverage that's best for you and your budget, now and as your needs change.

Should you have any questions call AARP Health Care Options to talk with a customer service professional. They'll answer your health insurance questions and help you understand your options.

And once you're part of the Program, the same kind of thoughtful help will always be just a phone call away. The goal is simply for you to get the most out of your health insurance. After all, you've earned it.

AARP HEALTH CARE OPTIONS
Insured by
UNITED HEALTHCARE INSURANCE COMPANY
METROPOLITAN LIFE INSURANCE COMPANY

1-800-245-1212, Ext. 820

for a free, no-obligation information kit, including benefits, costs, limitations, exclusions and eligibility requirements

Weekdays 7 a.m. to 11 p.m., Saturdays 9 a.m. to 5 p.m., ET   www.aarphealthcare.com

EXHIBIT 5.12   Maytag Ad

Commemorative Advertising Section

Good Housekeeping INSTITUTE CENTENNIAL

Maytag has learned a thing or two about the way Americans live in the more than 100 years it has been making appliances. Today, Maytag focuses on combining consumer-driven insights with innovation to design a full line of appliances known for superior quality and reliability—products that make life a lot easier.

Those insights have inspired product innovations at Maytag like the Gemini range, the award-winning Neptune washer and dryer, and the Atlantis washer.

Their latest introduction, the Maytag Gemini range, is a totally new kind of kitchen appliance, featuring two ovens in the space of a conventional range. It allows you to prepare two separate dishes at different temperatures at the same time—bringing the family together for a complete hot meal.

Another example of innovation built on insight is the Maytag Neptune high-efficiency washer and dryer, a revolutionary laundry duo unlike any other on the market today. Along with a breakthrough front-loading design, the Maytag Neptune washer and dryer provide outstanding stain removal, remarkable clothing care, large-tub capacity, easy access and substantial water and energy savings.

If you prefer a top-loading washer, Maytag's newest laundry product, the Atlantis, gets clothes clean and keeps whites white—all in an ergonomically designed package that makes loading and unloading easy. It also features a 30-day detergent dispenser that eliminates the need to measure and pour with every wash load—a truly great idea.

This is just the beginning of Maytag's commitment to innovation built on insight. Watch for more exciting new products planned for 2000 and beyond.

MAYTAG.COM
Bringing innovation home.

EXHIBIT 5.13 Jolly Time Pop Corn Ad

Commemorative Advertising Section

Grandpa Smith, Founder

A perfect treat for young and old.

JOLLY TIME POP CORN

A 1932 Jolly Time advertisement in Good Housekeeping magazine

Pop corn has to be the world's most fun food. That's why 85 years ago great-grandpa Cloid Smith thought, "Pop corn should be on every store shelf in America." So he did it.

Soon, families across America were munching and crunching and enjoying this former country-store secret. And just as soon, there were lots of other pop corn products on the market—some good, some not so good.

But the Smith family remained committed to bringing value, performance, taste—and fun—to every family in America. Jolly Time was the first pop corn to pop consistently, the first pop corn with a package to match the excitement contained inside, and the first pop corn to stay fresh on the store shelf. Perhaps that's why Jolly Time has held the Good Housekeeping Seal longer than any food product (since 1925!).

Now, the third and fourth generation Smiths are wowing American families with exciting new products—like Blast O Butter Microwave Pop Corn, the ultimate

theatre-style butter microwave pop corn. And Jolly Time's newest product, Jolly Time White & Buttery Microwave Pop Corn...there's nothing like it. From double butter to low fat, Jolly Time has a product for every taste.

Most of all, the Smith family is committed to fun, as evidenced by 85 years devoted to making sure that your family has a blast eating America's favorite treat... Jolly Time Pop Corn.

Jolly Time's newest product, white pop corn flavored with real butter

The Funn family characters are the newest addition to the Jolly Time family, created to remind you that Jolly Time Pop Corn is all about fun!

Jolly Time Pop Corn

Pop in on us at www.jollytime.com

EXHIBIT 5.14 Sun-Maid

Commemorative Advertising Section

Five Foods That Cut Living Costs made with SUN-MAID Raisins

California Sun-Maid Raisins

California Associated Raisin Co.

Raisins are an ancient food, for which we can probably thank those forward-thinking Egyptians once again. They discovered the process of sun-drying fruit, concentrating flavors and nutrients. Today, California's vineyards supply most of the world's raisins, and the Sun-Maid® brand is the pride of more than 1,200 California raisin growers.

A key element of the Sun-Maid philosophy is its commitment to the family farm, where its grapes are grown, and where painstaking efforts are employed year-round to turn those grapes into the succulent morsels of fruit we love.

Sun-Maid joined the roster of products that were tested and approved by Good Housekeeping in 1918. An indispensable ingredient in mincemeat pie, oatmeal cookies and apple strudel—and a convenient and healthy snack—Sun-Maid Raisins have been the world's favorite for some 80 years, and a household name in 50 countries around the world.

Sun-Maid Growers over the years have expanded their product offerings to include raisin bread and a line of nutritious, all-natural dried fruit snacks. And as we become ever more health and fitness-conscious, Sun-Maid products will surely be kitchen staples far into the new millennium.

SUN·MAID®

EXHIBIT 5.15 Pond's Ad

Commemorative Advertising Section

A Beauty Hint

Since its early breakthroughs in the 1840s, Pond's® has consistently made its mark in the beauty industry through countless innovations. The Pond's Institute draws on more than four decades of research and experience to create revolutionary advances in skin care—year after year. To meet the changing needs of women, all new Pond's products are the result of an ongoing dialogue between the Pond's Institute and the consumer.

It's a customer-first philosophy that has resulted in such products as Age Defying Complex, which has been proven to dramatically reduce the signs of aging, Pond's Cleansing and Make-Up Remover Towelettes, which clean gently down to the pores, removing even waterproof make-up...and the Clear Solutions line, which helps control oil without drying or tightening the skin.

Amid all the buzz about great "new" beauty products with natural, herbal bases, Pond's can honestly stake a longstanding claim to that territory. Because Pond's has been harnessing nature's gifts in its products since its founding in the 1840s. The original Pond's Extract was created using the secrets of an Oneida Indian healer.

A version of cold cream has existed since the days of Cleopatra, but it was specially mixed by pharmacists and available only to wealthy women. In 1907, Pond's invented the first shelf-stable cream, thus making available to all women a cold cream that deep-cleans and moisturizes the skin in one step.

Since 1846, Pond's mission has remained constant—to make every woman look and feel beautiful.

Pond's Cold Cream Introduced in 1907

Pond's Age Defying Complex 1994

Pond's Cleansing and Make-Up Remover Towelettes 1998

Pond's Clear Solutions 1999

POND'S.

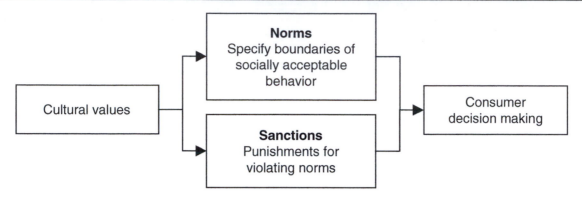

EXHIBIT 5.16   The Relationship of Norms to Values, Sanctions, and Consumer Behavior

Source: Adapted from Hawkins, and Mothersbaugh, *Consumer Behavior,* 11th ed. (Boston: Irwin McGraw Hill, 2010), p. 43.

Cultural norms change over time. For example, today more and more people are neglecting to respond to party and wedding invitations with an RSVP. Fist bumping (two people tapping fists lightly) is replacing the handshake, a gesture that goes back to medieval times when opponents clasped each other's weapons arms to indicate that they were friendly and unarmed. Unlike half a decade ago, today foul language is spoken by children and sometimes to teachers and other adults, whom they sometimes address by first name.

Norms also vary by place. Most college students are reasonably well-mannered around their professors or in class but tend to cut loose in the dorms and even more so at weekend campus parties.

And norms certainly vary across cultures: Saudi Arabian women must be fully covered (except for their eyes) at all times; greetings in Asian countries include bowing instead of shaking hands; blinking one's eyes is considered impolite in Taiwan; folding one's arms over the chest is deemed disrespectful in Fiji; putting your hands in your pockets is viewed as rude in Malaysia; and in Portugal one must always kiss both cheeks in greeting as a sign of respect and admiration. In Italy, gum chewing is considered rude; talking to a stranger of the opposite sex is considered a come-on in Egypt; and in Brazil, eating a sandwich with a knife and fork is good manners.

Norms express *cultural values*, which, unlike many norms, are not tied to any specific object or situation. Hence, values determine which behaviors are desirable. People are expected to "conform to the norm." Without norms, social chaos, or at least confusion, would result. Consequently, **social sanctions**—penalties for violating norms—are usually administered, ranging from frowns, teasing, and ridicule to ostracism and imprisonment.

Exhibit 5.16 summarizes this relationship between values, norms, sanctions, and CB.

THE TYPES OF CULTURAL NORMS

A given cultural norm can take the form of one or more of any of the following categories:

- *Customs (traditions).* These norms are handed down from generation to generation and are specific to certain situations. Example: Marriages arranged by parents in Middle Eastern cultures.
- *Conventions.* Norms regarding proper conduct in everyday life or routine behavior. Example: You should greet someone by shaking hands.
- *Etiquette (decorum).* The set of rules that govern socially acceptable behavior. Example: Always say "please" and "thank you."
- *Rituals.* A series of symbolic behaviors that occur in a fixed sequence and are frequently repeated. Example: At your college graduation you will wear a cap and gown, process in and out, and stand and sit at the proper times (and probably party hardy afterwards!).

- *Mores (ethical norms).* Norms with a strong moral overtone, usually avoiding a taboo or forbidden behavior. These standards of conduct require, prohibit, or allow certain specific actions to avoid harming others. Example: It is wrong to tell a lie.
- *Legal codes.* Norms that, like mores, are usually based on moral values, but these codes are enforced legally with government sanctions when violated. Example: When you move to a new community, a neighbor might warn you, "You should not drive over 20 miles per hour in any residential zone in this town."

MARKETING SENSITIVITY TO NORMS

Marketers need to be culturally sensitive so they do not violate norms in their marketing practices. Tobacco advertisers have been raked across the coals for allegedly targeting teens with their advertising and merchandising. Parents might not appreciate a food marketer who encourages children to play with their food. Trying to market birthday pies instead of birthday cakes would probably flop because it violates a custom.

Marketers must remain abreast of norms, which, as a cultural component, often slowly evolve. For instance, some auto dealerships featuring "no bicker stickers" are now discouraging bargaining over car prices, which is how cars historically have been bought. It is no longer socially acceptable for food companies to target kids with junky foods. Instead, all major food manufacturers are reexamining their product lines, trimming fat, sugar, calories, and carbs. Gambling was once considered by most Americans to be morally wrong and many forms constituted criminal activities, but now gambling is generally considered to be acceptable if it is organized as a state lottery for a good cause, is heavily marketed, or is euphemistically called "gaming."

REVIEW QUESTIONS

1. What are cultural norms? Cite some examples.
2. Cite and describe the different types (categories) of cultural norms.
3. How do sanctions reinforce cultural norms?
4. Why is it important for marketers to be sensitive to cultural norms, both in the domestic market and when marketing internationally?

IN-CLASS APPLICATIONS

1. Because cultural norms are informal, people tend to be unaware of them and take them for granted. Only when these norms are broken do they realize that what is considered normal in some cultures is regarded as abnormal in others. Still other norms are universally held in virtually all cultures and are never to be violated. Breaking these norms causes others discomfort.

   Consider each of the following deviations from cultural norms. How would you categorize each broken norm (custom, convention, etiquette, ritual, more, or legal code)? Which norms are universal and which are culturally bound to Western society and/or the United States?

   Describe how you think people would react if you were to break the following norms:

   a. Ride an elevator, but upon entrance do not turn around. Face your fellow passengers.
   b. Take a seat next to someone in the library or cafeteria, even though there are empty chairs all around the table and other empty tables.
   c. Stand about four inches away from someone you are having a conversation with (a friend or a stranger). Maintain this distance throughout the conversation.
   d. Ask someone for his or her seat while riding on mass transit.
   e. Serve dinner guests dessert before the main course, followed by leftovers.
   f. Offer to pay cash for dinner at the end of a meal at a friend's home.
   g. Wear pajamas to class (not just a sweatshirt or T-shirt with sweatpants or shorts).
   h. Tell someone not to have a nice day.
   i. Smoke a cigarette in church.
   j. Open some of your friend's presents at her party without being asked to do so.

    k. Bring your CD or DVD player or iPod to another class (not CB!) and blare one of your favorite songs during class.

    l. Pick your nose in a job interview (only if you do not really wish to land the job!) or while having a meeting with your faculty advisor (only if you do not wish to get a letter of recommendation!).

    m. Rummage through the refrigerator of an acquaintance (not a good friend).

    n. When inviting guests over to your house, don't offer them a seat. Rather, demand that they sit on the floor, and then you take a seat.

    o. Sit down and hang out in a college faculty lounge. Try to strike up a conversation with faculty you might not even know.

    p. Ask an acquaintance (not a good friend) an intimate question such as "What areas of your life are you struggling with?" or "How is your marriage working out for you?"

    q. Buy and present as a gift to your pastor, priest, or other spiritual leader a risqué T-shirt (e.g., "FBI—Female Body Inspector").

2. Can you think of any other examples where you, another person, or even a marketer has broken a cultural norm? What was the outcome in each case?

3. Visit ExecutivePlanet.com's home page. You will find business culture guides for various countries. Click on the link for a country that interests you, and then click on some of its links. Discuss any implications you can think of from what you learn here that an American marketer should be aware of regarding marketing communications (including personal selling).

WRITTEN APPLICATIONS:

1. Repeat Question 1 in the In-Class Applications, only this time you must actually break three of the above norms. Only do this if your instructor asks you to and you are brave enough. Otherwise, "Don't try these at home, kids!" Instead, just speculate on what would happen if you violated each norm. You can test these unusual behaviors for fun on your (soon to be former?) friends, family (hopefully they won't disown you), and/or peers (who will no longer admit that you are one of them).

2. Answer Question 2 above by thinking about your own experience and interviewing three people. Try to find at least one marketing example that seems to be violating a cultural norm.

3. Answer Question 3.

KEY CONCEPTS

cognitive components	customs
collectivist cultures	demography
common knowledge	domain-specific values
consumption-specific values	ethical values
conventions	ethnography
cultural activities	etiquette (decorum)
cultural anthropologists	fads
cultural anthropology	fashions
cultural artifacts (material components)	feminine cultures
cultural attitudes	focus of orientation
cultural beliefs	global values
cultural components (cultural cues)	high culture
cultural knowledge	individualism versus collectivism
cultural norms	individualistic cultures
cultural truisms (folk wisdom)	instrumental values
cultural values (core values, social values)	legal codes
culture	legends

(continued)

KEY CONCEPTS *(continued)*

masculine cultures
masculinity versus femininity
material values (environment-oriented values)
means-end chain analysis
monochromic
moral norms (ethical norms)
mores
myths
personal values (self-oriented values)
physical trace evidence
politics
polychromic
popular ("pop," mass) culture
power distance
privately owned consumer goods
product icons
product semiotics
product-specific values
public goods
religion
rites of passage
ritual artifacts

ritual (ritual behavior)
rituals
semiotics (semiotic studies, semiology)
social categories
social psychology
social sanctions
social trends
social values (other-oriented values)
socializing (societal) institutions (socialization agents)
society
sociocultural (sociological) forces
sociology
superstitions
symbols
terminal values
time capsule
time orientation
trade characters (advertising icons, product mascots)
uncertainty avoidance
universal cultural values
urban legend
value system

SUMMARY

Chapter 5 began our look at external sociocultural influences on CB, which allow apply social science disciplines including cultural anthropology, demography, sociology, and social psychology. This chapter covered culture, studied by cultural anthropologists using ethnography. Culture is pervasive (comprehensive); learned (acquired); transmitted by socializing institutions; and evolves slowly. Three types of societal change are relevant to marketers: social trends, fashions, and fads. There are a number of ways to distinguish trends from fads.

Exercise 5.1 overviewed pervasive cultural components summarized in Exhibit 5.1: Symbols, studied through semiotics and product semiotics and represented in marketing by trade characters, among others; material components; cognitive components, including cultural knowledge (cultural values, including ethical values, cultural beliefs [cultural truisms, superstitions, common knowledge, myths and legends, and language], religion and politics; and cultural attitudes); cultural behavior and activities (cultural norms [customs, conventions, etiquette, rituals [rites of passage and ritual artifacts], mores [legal codes and moral norms], and cultural activities). Marketers need to be culturally sensitive so they do not violate any of these cultural cues in their marketing practices.

Exercise 5.2 dealt in more depth with cultural artifacts, which include privately owned consumer goods and public goods. Material artifacts are sometimes left behind after a culture has dissolved. Cultural anthropologists study these artifacts to gain a better understanding of the society.

Tangible parts of any modern culture include marketing elements, which form parts of popular culture. Consumer advertising's elements become well-known parts of the pop culture. One way to communicate pop culture to future generations is via the time capsule. Product semiotics studies product elements such as brands, packages, and advertising characters, which sometimes become so highly recognized that they become icons.

Exercise 5.3 concerned cultural values, most of which are universal. Cultures differ in their value systems. Cultural and personal values determine which product-specific values people use when deciding, relating to means-end chain analysis.

There are a number of systems for classifying cultural values. Cross-cultural (transnational) differences in values are most associated with Hofstede's general value dimensions along which cultures can vary: individualism versus collectivism, uncertainty avoidance, masculinity versus femininity, power distance, and time orientation, including polychromic and monochromic cultures.

A comprehensive scheme of values is found in global values (Exhibit 5.7). There are a number of global American values. Global values contrast with domain-specific values. The Rokeach value classification system differentiates terminal values from instrumental values. The focus of orientation values classification includes personal, social, and material values. Many traditional Western values are slowly evolving (see Exhibit 5.8).

Exercise 5.4 delved further into the fourth category of cultural cues—cultural norms—which change over time and place. Norms express cultural values and failure to adhere to them often results in social sanctions.

REFERENCES

Berger, Arthur Asia. (1984). *Signs in Contemporary Culture: An Introduction to Semiotics.* New York: Longman.

Demirjian, Turan Senduger, and Tian, Robert. (2007). *Perspectives in Consumer Behavior: An Anthropological Approach.* Fort Worth, TX: Fellows Press of America.

de Mooij, Marieke. (2004). *Consumer Behavior and Culture: Consequences for Global Marketing and Advertising.* Thousand Oaks, CA: Sage Publications.

Hawkins, Del I., and Mothersbaugh, David L. (2004). *Consumer Behavior: Building Marketing Strategy,* 9th ed. Boston: McGraw-Hill Irwin.

Hofstede, Geert. (1980). *Culture's Consequences.* Beverly Hills, CA: Sage Publications.

Holbrook, Morris. (1987). "Mirror, Mirror, on the Wall, What's Unfair in the Reflections on Advertising." *Journal of Marketing,* 51, 3, 95–103.

Hoyer, Wayne D., and MacInnis, Deborah J. (2007). *Consumer Behavior,* 4th ed. Boston: Houghton Mifflin.

Kramer, Thomas, and Block, Lauren. (2007). "Conscious and Nonconscious Components of Superstitious Beliefs in Judgment and Decision Making." *Journal of Consumer Research,* 34, 4, 783–793.

Laermer, Richard. (2008). *2011—Trendspotting for the Next Decade.* New York: McGraw-Hill.

Lantos, Geoffrey P. (1987). "Advertising: Looking Glass or Molder of the Masses?" *Journal of Public Policy and Marketing,* 6, 104–128.

Letscher, Martin G. (1994). "How to Tell Fads from Trends." *American Demographics,* December, 38–41.

McCracken, Grant. (1986). "Culture and Consumption: A Theoretical Account of the Structure and Meaning of Consumer Goods." *Journal of Consumer Research,* 13, 1, 71–84.

Mick, David. (1986). "Consumer Research and Semiotics: Exploring the Mythology of Signs, Symbols, and Significance." *Journal of Consumer Research,* 13, 2, 196–213.

Milner, Laura M., Fodness, Dale, and Speece, Mark. (1993). "Hofsted's Research on Cross-Cultural Work-Related Values: Implications for Consumer Behavior." In W. Fred Van Raaij and Gary J. Bamossy (eds.), *European Advances in Consumer Research.* Amsterdam: Association for Consumer Research, 70–76.

Pollay, Richard W. (1986). "The Distorted Mirror: Reflections on the Unintended Consequences of Advertising." *Journal of Marketing,* 50, 2, 18–36.

Rokeach, Milton. (1973). *The Nature of Human Values.* New York: The Free Press.

———. (1979). *Understanding Human Values.* New York: The Free Press.

Rook, Dennis W. (1985). "The Ritual Dimensions of Consumer Behavior." *Journal of Consumer Research,* 12, 3, 251–264.

Samuel, Lawrence R. (2002). *Brought to You By—Postwar Television Advertising and the American Dream.* Austin, TX: University of Texas Press.

Schwartz, Shalom H., and Bilsky, Wolfgang. (1987). "Toward a Universal Psychological Structure of Human Values." *Journal of Personality and Social Psychology,* 53, 3, 550–562.

Sproles, George P. (1981). "Analyzing Fashion Life Cycles—Principles and Perspectives." *Journal of Marketing,* 45, 4, 116–124.

Sunderand, Patricia L., and Denny, Rita M. (2007). *Doing Anthropology in Consumer Research.* Walnut Creek, CA: Left Coast Press.

Vinson, Donald E., Scott, Jerome E., and Lamont, Lawrence R. (1977). "The Role of Personal Values in Marketing and Consumer Behavior." *Journal of Marketing,* 41, 2, 44–50.

Zakia, Richard D., and Nadin, Mihai. (1987). "Semiotics, Advertising and Marketing." *Journal of Consumer Marketing,* 4, 2, 5–12.

SUBCULTURAL INFLUENCES

In this chapter and Chapter 7 we investigate subcultures and social classes. These **social categories,** aggregate groups within a culture, have a particular level of social status demographically, socioeconomically, psychologically, and/or behaviorally.

The two exercises in this chapter further investigate U.S. culture by breaking it down into **subcultures (microcultures)**, which are cultural subgroups within the **macroculture**, the mainstream culture at large. Members of a subculture share unique cultural characteristics while retaining many of the significant cultural components of the society at large. Examples include Hispanics, Jews, Midwesterners, and Generation Y. **Subcultural influences** include the values, norms, symbols, and other unique cultural components of these subcultures.

Segmentation of consumer markets on the basis of subculture is becoming more common. Many U.S. residents are associated with one or more subculture, and the influence of these lifestyle groups is powerful.

ORGANIZATION OF CHAPTER SIX

Exercise 6.1 investigates subcultural segmentation and its major bases: ethnicity, religion, geographic region, and age cohorts. You will witness specific examples of subcultural segments that can provide great niche marketing opportunities.

Most of us are members of several subcultures, all of which can strongly influence our CB. Exercise 6.2 provides an opportunity to consider your own subcultural identities, how they influence your marketplace behavior, and how they affect efforts of marketers to appeal to you effectively.

EXERCISE 6.1. SUBCULTURAL SEGMENTATION

OBJECTIVES

1. To familiarize you with the different bases for subcultural segmentation—ethnicity, religion, geography, and age—and to enable you to describe the major segments using each.
2. To make you aware of six major considerations for subcultural marketing.
3. To enable you to analyze how advertisers become more effective by using their understanding of subcultural markets.
4. To have you take a stand on the controversial issue of targeting minorities with potentially dangerous products.
5. To have you use your own understanding of subcultural segments to design ads that appeal to members of those segments.

BACKGROUND

Chapter 5 was concerned with the white mainstream culture in the United States. However, there is a major trend toward cultural pluralism in that diversity of racial, ethnic, or religious backgrounds is increasingly accepted. Each of the following subcultural groups is also a lifestyle group with unique cultural characteristics. It is important for marketers to understand the unique thinking and behavior patterns of diverse consumer groups.

BASES FOR FORMING SUBCULTURES

The major subcultural segmentation variables are (1) ethnic background (race, nationality, and language); (2) religion; (3) geographic region; and (4) generation or age cohort. In addition, there are many other subcultures frequently targeted by marketers but not reviewed here, including the college market; the gay, lesbian, bisexual, and transgender (GLBT) market; the deaf community; political preference groups; Goth and punk youth; and the physically disabled market.

A few marketers have even formulated or else targeted their own type of microculture. **Consumption subcultures** are groups whose members share an avocational interest and hence a commitment to a particular product category, brand, or consumption activity. Examples include Trekkies or Trekkers (the Star Trek subculture), Harley-Davidson riders, hot-rodders, scrapbookers, karate kids, and skydivers. Pursuing like-minded consumers who spontaneously connect around a product or service is called **tribal marketing**. For example, magazines such as *Cooking Light* and *Bon Appétit* have sponsored culinary fairs and supper club events.

MAJOR SUBCULTURAL SEGMENTATION CONSIDERATIONS

There are six important considerations for subcultural marketers. Later, we will revisit each one for each of the four major variables for subcultural segmentation.

SUBCULTURES SERVE AS A BASIS FOR MARKET SEGMENTATION

Subcultures provide an important foundation for market segmentation in a pluralistic society. While marketers usually describe them with identifiable demographic descriptors, they also understand the lifestyle implications of these variables.

Many subcultures can be further divided into **sub-subcultures**, which are subcultures within subcultures. Therefore, many subcultures can be subsegmented into smaller, more homogenous groups, each with its own distinctive language, symbols, customs, and other cultural characteristics. For example, the Hispanic (Spanish-language-speaking) subculture can be further segmented by country of origin, such as Mexico, Puerto Rico, or Cuba. Chinese Americans constitute the largest group of Asian Americans. The so-called disabled market consists of three submarkets: adults with disabilities, parents of disabled children, and caretakers such as siblings and grandparents.

Consumers can also be cross-classified by two subcultural segmentation variables, such as baby boomer blacks. Subcultural cross-classification often occurs when geography is used in conjunction with one of the other three subcultural segmentation variables. This is common practice because subcultural segments often cluster geographically. For instance, gays and lesbians congregate in large cities such as San Francisco or New York as well as in Provincetown, Massachusetts. Numerous Mormons live in Utah, many senior citizens reside in Florida, a disproportionate number of Jews dwell in New York City, and lots of Asian Americans inhabit the West Coast.

MARKETERS SHOULD APPEAL TO SUBCULTURAL CHARACTERISTICS

Marketers must understand and appeal to the norms, values, and other cultural components of a subculture in order to effectively communicate with and appeal to its members. For example, each ethnic, religious, geographic, and age subculture has its own kind of music that can be included in commercials, such as salsa, polka, gospel, bluegrass, and big band.

However, as Exhibit 6.1 shows, while a person might simultaneously be in one or more microcultures, he or she is still a member of the core culture. Hence, the individual will exhibit mass market cultural characteristics that do not conflict with those of his or her subculture as well as unique traits of the subculture(s).

To respect the subculture, marketers must avoid violating or offending members' sensitivities along their

EXHIBIT 6.1   Subcultures Demonstrate Unique Consumer Behavior

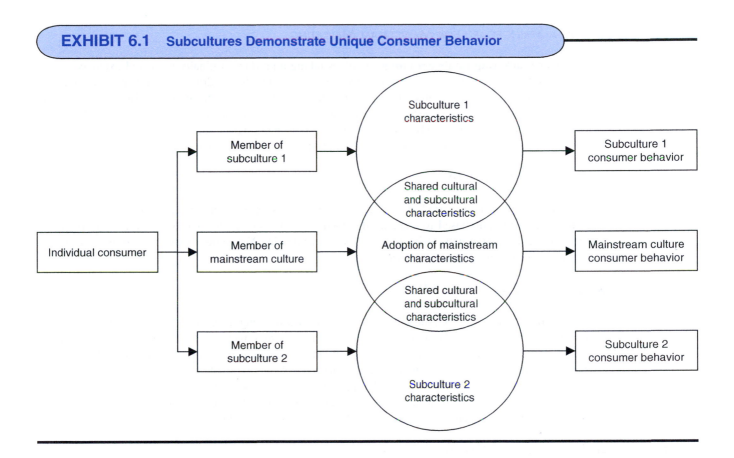

subcultural characteristics. Unfortunately, advertisers have butchered foreign languages with mistranslations in ethnic markets. This happened when an airline ran an ad that promoted leather seats. The translation was interpreted by Hispanics as either "sit naked" or "fly naked." One of the biggest blunders is to mistranslate advertising copy. The Perdue chicken slogan, "It takes a tough man to make a tender chicken," was wrongly translated into Spanish as, "It takes a sexually excited man to make a chick affectionate." Another was the Coors beer slogan, "Turn it Loose," which in Spanish became, "Suffer from Diarrhea."

Such mistakes usually occur because companies simply use an in-house translator who speaks the language but is not fluent. A more accurate method is the use of **backtranslation**, or having someone fluent in both languages, translate English to the foreign language and then having a second person conversant in both languages translate it back again to English.

Another problem is that the creative idioms so often used in ads do not translate word-for-word into another culture. You cannot talk about "knocking one out of the ballpark" to someone in Albania. Marketers must be familiar with the subculture's special jargon. A Kraft ad in black magazines featured the headline "You go, Mom!" a play on the black female exclamation, "You go, girl!"

Negative stereotypes of subcultures must be avoided. It is not smart to portray Generation Xers as angst-ridden slackers, devout Christians as dogmatic and bigoted, or all African Americans as musical or athletic. A marketer's best bet is to employ the services of marketing research firms and advertising agencies that specialize in a subcultural market, such as youth researchers and ethnic (multicultural) advertising agencies.

MARKETING TO SUBCULTURES

Generally, subcultures are on the rise, with most growing in absolute size and many expanding relatively as a percentage of the population. Many members of particular subcultures are also achieving upward social mobility—higher incomes, education, and occupational status. They are also gaining political clout, recognition, and visibility.

SUBCULTURES SERVE AS A SPRINGBOARD FOR MAINSTREAM MARKETING

Crossover marketing (mainstreaming) involves taking a product originally marketed exclusively to a particular subculture and broadening its appeal to the macroculture. Sports drinks such as Gatorade originated among the consumption subculture of serious athletes and branched out from there. Ethnic foods, such as Mexican burritos, tacos, and even guacamole sauce, are now universally consumed. The U.S. Hispanic-owned food company Goya Foods first targeted the Caribbean immigrant sub-subculture, then branched out to Latin American and Mexican foods. Today, its products are found in mainstream U.S. supermarkets.

SUBCULTURES DEMONSTRATE UNIQUE CBs

Subcultures exhibit unique product and brand preferences, shopping patterns, and media habits. In fact, products are often purchased to make a "statement" about a subculture with which a person identifies. Texans wear ten-gallon hats, string ties, and boots, while Gen Yers enjoy body art, extreme sports, and hopping into a mosh pit at a rock concert.

SUBCULTURES ARE EXPOSED TO SPECIALIZED MEDIA

Specialized media exist to reach subcultural groups through advertising. There are alternative rock radio stations for Gen Yers, *We* magazine for Americans with disabilities, *Latina* magazine for Hispanics, and the Web site Africana.com for African Americans. The social networking site Disaboom.com targets people with disabilities through social networking features like those found on Facebook plus information such as career advice, disability rights, and disability scholarships. Such media appeal to subcultural members who appreciate that marketers are singling out their subculture for attention. Ads run in these formats can be modified to better appeal to subcultural members. These media outlets are cost effective for reaching subcultural niches.

THE FOUR MOST POPULAR SUBCULTURAL BASES

We will now explore the four most common subcultural bases for subcultural segmentation, relating each type of subculture to the six major subcultural considerations outlined earlier.

ETHNIC SUBCULTURES

Marketers used to exclusively target the Anglo mainstream culture in the United States (90 percent of the U.S. population in 1950), defined by the U.S. Census Bureau as "non-Hispanic whites." Today, marketers use **multicultural (ethnic, minority) marketing**, which targets groups whose members share subcultural components based on a common race, nationality, or language.

Simply stated, ethnicity is founded on passport or pigment. Definitions of ethnic minorities can be based on one or more of the following: (1) racial groups (white or Caucasian, black or African American, yellow or Asian American, and red or American Indian); (2) nationality groups founded on country of origin (e.g., Asian Americans can come from Korea, Thailand, Japan, China, etc.); and (3) language groups sharing a common mother tongue. For instance, **Hispanics (Latinos)** share the Spanish language in either their primary language or the language of an ancestor, but Hispanics can be of various races and nationalities. Although racial and nationality groups are recorded separately by the U.S. Census Bureau, they clearly overlap, and so marketers can use them together to define ethnicity. The top three ethnic groups—African Americans, Hispanic Americans, and Asian Americans—now represent just under one-third (32 percent) of the U.S. population.

The following are the six major ethnic segmentation considerations.

Ethnic Groups Serve as a Basis for Market Segmentation. Clearly, the trend is toward multicultural marketing, both in the United States and in some countries abroad, such as the United Kingdom and Australia. Each of the major ethnic groups can be divided into ethnic sub-subcultures using segmentation variables such as country of origin; language preference (that of the homeland versus the **host culture**—the culture immigrants have adopted); **assimilation**, the process whereby ethnic group members learn and adapt to the values, language, and other cultural characteristics of the host culture, thereby replacing their native subcultural traits; **acculturation**, learning to function within the dominant culture while retaining one's original culture; and **subcultural identification**, the degree to which ethnic group members retain their cultural identity, primarily through socializing institutions such as schools, churches, and neighborhoods. Some ethnic peoples who have lived in the United States their entire lives develop a need to reconnect with their country and culture of origin, a phenomenon marketers call **retro-acculturation**.

Ethnic subcultures tend to cluster geographically, notably in areas of the adopted nation closest to their country of origin (e.g., Asians on the West Coast). Geographic grouping is evident in ethnic neighborhoods within major cities, such as Chinatown, Little Poland, and Little Haiti.

Increasingly, minority individuals, like Tiger Woods, are claiming multiple ethnic identities. Consequently, Mattel launched Barbie's friend Kayla, its first-ever multiethnic doll, designed to be interpreted as Asian, Hispanic, or any combination of various ethnic groups.

Marketers Should Appeal to Ethnic Group Characteristics. The United States has long been referred to as a "cultural melting pot," but this label is outdated. The United States is now viewed as an "ethnic mosaic," a "salad bowl," or an "American rainbow," suggesting acculturation, or assimilation. Members of many subcultural groups bond with each other to maintain their ethnic identities and preserve their cultural traditions and values.

Ethnic consumers, especially those with high subcultural identification, are more responsive to marketing techniques that appeal to their cultural characteristics. For instance, a growing number of retailers are promoting the Hispanic tradition of celebrating Three Kings Day every January 6 as a way to extend the holiday buying season.

It can be hazardous to rely on simple ethnic stereotypes. Too many marketers still spring for cheap laughs, portraying black women as mean, Hispanic men as loose, and Asians as martial artists. Not all blacks bounce basketballs while listening to hip-hop music. Asian Americans do not all live in Chinatown or work in nail salons. In fact, Asian Americans as a group rank highest for median household income, level of education, and business ownership.

Ethnic Subcultures Are Rising. Ethnic groups are increasing in sheer numbers, in purchasing power, and as influencers of urban trends. Growth in numbers is being fueled largely by high immigration and high *fertility rates*, which refers to the average number of babies born to childbearing women during their reproductive years (generally more than two children per family for ethnic groups). Because immigrants tend to be younger and generally have more children, they are becoming a larger part of the nation's younger population. The old are mostly white, and the young are increasingly ethnically diverse. Marketers recognize the shift. Beer ads, for example, are targeted at younger, ethnic people.

The year 2050 is forecast to be the tipping point after which non-Hispanic whites will no longer comprise the majority of the U.S. population. Most ethnic groups are also achieving upward social mobility and more political power and status within the mainstream culture.

Ethnic Groups Serve as a Springboard for Mainstream Marketing. Crossover marketing of minority market products abounds, with notable examples including ethnic foods, music, fashion, and movies. In the case of ethnic minorities, mainstreaming is known as **de-ethnicitization**. Hot sauces and zesty cuisine, including Cajun, Caribbean, and Asian, are going mainstream, driven by burgeoning ethnic groups. Tabasco sauce is hotter than ever! In the early 1990s, sales of salsa, originally a Hispanic and Southern food, surpassed ketchup sales for the first time ever in the United States. Once tucked away in the supermarket's ethnic aisle, tortillas are now familiar to most Americans, and are often called "wraps" to seem more ethnically neutral.

Urban marketing refers to marketing efforts that reflect the trends and attitudes originating in cities, driven by young African American and Hispanic consumers' choices in entertainment and fashion. Coca-Cola, Pepsi-Cola, Dr. Pepper, Reebok, and other advertisers have moved urban music stars, such as Jay-Z and LL Cool J, from targeted ethnic ads to mainstream ads because today's youth are increasingly color-blind and culture blind. Young Americans are especially prone to adopt characteristics of other cultures, a process known as **intraculteralism**. This differs from **multiculturalism**, in which distinct ethnicities are celebrated, and, in the case of *multicultural marketing*, are specifically targeted.

Ethnic Groups Demonstrate Unique CBs. Minority consumers exhibit behavioral patterns at variance from mainstream consumers. Each group has specific product preferences, especially regarding food, clothing, music, and hair and skin care products. For instance, African American consumers seem to enjoy shopping more than the other groups and are more fashion conscious. However, some behavioral distinctions between ethnic and mainstream consumers disappear after controlling for differences in income, education, concentration in central cities, and other socioeconomic indicators. In other words, these demographic factors are better viewed as correlates of certain ethnic CBs than membership in an ethnic group. For example, CB researchers have reported that blacks and Hispanics are more brand loyal than Anglo consumers. However, many ethnic consumers live in areas with restricted retail outlet choices. It is actually geography more than ethnicity that determines brand-switching behavior.

Ethnic Groups Are Exposed to Specialized Media. Specialty media exist for marketers to reach all ethnic groups and, increasingly, many ethnic subgroups. Some of these are ethnic language media. Typically, minority consumers are heavier users of ethnic national TV networks such as BET, Univision, and Telemundo, and local radio stations. Neighborhood media, such as outdoor and transit, also reach geographically concentrated ethnic consumers, who are generally lighter users of print media.

RELIGIOUS SUBCULTURES

Interest in religion, from evangelical Christianity to New Age mysticism, has increased in recent years. This trend is evidenced by best-selling books about religion such as Tim LaHaye and Jerry Jenkins's *Left Behind* series, Pastor Rick Warren's *The Purpose-Driven Life,* Dan Brown's *The Da Vinci Code,* Rhonda Byrne's *The Secret,* and renewed interest in C.S. Lewis's *The Chronicles of Narnia.* Other evidence in popular media includes TV shows such as *Touched by an Angel* and *Joan of Arcadia,* athletes openly praying before a game, Madonna's lovefest with kabbalah, and the public's fascination with paranormal activity and the occult, as evidenced by Harry Potter's escapades.

Religion provides people with important cultural characteristics, notably moral values, beliefs about "big-picture" issues such as sex, family life, and even the meaning of life, and norms, including activities, customs, rituals, and mores.

Religion as a Basis for Market Segmentation. In the United States, the principal organized religious faiths include Protestantism, Catholicism, Judaism, and Islam (the Muslim faith). A number of other religions and religious cults exist with smaller numbers of believers, such as Buddhism and Jehovah's Witnesses.

However, there has been a decline in participation in organized religion. This is primarily because Americans are becoming more pluralistic and individualistic in their religious beliefs. Consequently, most religions contain sub-subcultures, which are by and large defined by conservatism, the extent to which the teachings of the faith are taken literally and seen as the only truth.

Protestantism includes many different denominations, such as Baptist, Methodist, and Lutheran. Each Protestant denomination has branches, such as southern and conservative Baptists. Catholics consist of traditionalists, charismatics, and liberals. Members of the Jewish faith are either Orthodox (ultra-conservative), Conservative, or Reformed.

Each religious subculture and sub-subculture has a demographic profile. For example, within Protestantism, the socioeconomic status of Episcopalians is high, while Methodists are average, and Baptists skew low. One-third of all Baptists are black and one-half of all blacks are Baptist. Catholics are heavily Hispanic, with two-thirds of all Hispanics practicing Catholicism. Each religious subgroup also has subcultural characteristics, such as Orthodox Jews adhering to strict Old Testament dietary regulations and many devout Catholics still abstaining from eating meat on Friday.

Religious groups sometimes cluster geographically. Baptists and Evangelicals congregate in the South's Bible Belt; a disproportionate number of Catholics are found in the Northeast, as well as in areas of high Hispanic concentration; and Jews are most likely to live in New England, especially in urban areas.

Marketers Should Appeal to Religious Groups' Characteristics. Religious values and norms are an important consideration when communicating with religious subcultures, and there are significant distinctions between religious groups. Catholics tend to be more traditional, with a focus on family ties. Protestants still believe in the Protestant work ethic as well as individual responsibility and self-control. Jews stress individual responsibility, education, and achievement. Muslims cling to family norms and hold conservative beliefs regarding drug and alcohol use and sexual permissiveness.

Unfortunately, religious stereotypes persist: Jews are typecast as wealthy, stingy, and shrewd, and Evangelicals are perceived as backwoods buffoons who are self-righteous and hypocritical.

Some Religious Subcultures Are Rising. While the influence of organized religion has waned, religious subcultures remain strong. Growth rates vary widely between the various groups. The Catholic Church attributes most of its growth since the 1970s to the blossoming Hispanic population. Evangelical Christians are a rapidly growing and increasingly influential subculture. The group is characterized by a strong belief in and literal interpretation of the Bible. Muslims, while currently a minority, are the world's fastest-growing religious group.

Religious Subcultures Serve as a Springboard for Mainstream Marketing. Bagels and matzo balls were originally associated with the Jewish subculture but are now mass-marketed. Today, even pagans wear Christian crosses as necklaces. Children's videos featuring Christian fare such as *McGee and Me* and *VeggieTales* are mass marketed. Christian-themed movies include the *Left Behind* series and *The Passion of the Christ*. Also popular are Christian rock artists such as DC Talk, Jars of Clay, Switchfoot, Third Day, and Skillet, and rap/metalists P.O.D.

Religious Subcultures Demonstrate Unique CBs. CB can be influenced strongly by religious convictions. Examples include purchasing products that are associated with the celebration of religious rituals (confirmations and baptisms) and holidays (Christmas as the primary buying season). Religions also have unique symbols and artifacts, such as crosses, doves, fish, and communion cups for Christians, and rainbows, crystals, and unicorns for New Agers.

Religious beliefs and customs dictate the use or nonuse of certain products. Dietary laws for observant Jews mean that pork and shellfish are forbidden. Many Jewish cuisines and cleaning products must be kosher, with "U" and "P" marks on food packaging to indicate that the food meets Jewish dietary laws. However, some kosher products are going mainstream as non-Jews look for these marks as indicators that the food or cleaning product is pure and wholesome. Mormons would make a very poor target for tobacco products, liquor, and items containing caffeine, the consumption of which is forbidden. Because Catholics believe in sex for procreation rather than recreation, practicing Catholics are not a good market for birth control products.

Religious Subcultures Are Exposed to Specialized Media. All major religious groups have specialty media targeting them, notably magazines and radio stations. We see conservative Christians reading *Christianity Today* magazine, watching Christian TV shows such as Pat Robertson's *The 700 Club* and the Trinity Broadcasting Network, listening to former host James Dobson's radio show *Focus on the Family*, and even tuning in to Christian cable channels such as Z Music Television, which plays contemporary Christian music.

REGIONAL SUBCULTURES

Different geographic areas display unique subcultures. Many Americans have a strong sense of regional identification (e.g., New England "Yankees," Southern belles, and Heartlanders). Different geographic areas have their own cultural characteristics, such as language, style of dress, popular foods, and preferred pastimes. Such distinctions are determined by regional characteristics that include ethnic and religious mixes of citizens, climate, and natural resources. Such distinctions suggest that what works in Austin might flop in Boston or what plays in Peoria might not be tops in Texas. Consequently, the trend is toward regional marketing campaigns with decentralized strategic planning and decision making.

Geographic Subcultures as a Basis for Market Segmentation. A common geographic breakout for the United States includes New England, the Northeast or Mid-Atlantic region, the Southeast or South Atlantic, the Midwest, Mountain states, the Southwest, Plains states, the Pacific Northwest, and the Great Plains.

Such areas differ demographically: The Northeast is older, largely white, with fewer children; the West is younger and more diverse.

Demographically, regions often overlap with other subcultures. Recall that ethnic groups, religions, and age groups collect geographically. Hispanics dominate large portions of counties in a span of states stretching from California to Texas, African Americans are strongly represented in the South as well as selected urban areas in the Northeast and Midwest, the Asian presence is relatively large and highly concentrated in a few scattered Western counties, and American Indians are concentrated in select pockets of Oklahoma as well as the Southeast, Upper Midwest, and the West. Similarly, many evangelicals populate the Bible Belt and Mormons abound in Utah. Many seniors inhabit Florida and Cape Cod, and many college students can be located in and around Boston and other big cities.

Geographic behavioral differences can also be identified. Southerners, unused to the hurry and crowding of Northeastern cities, tend to consider Northeasterners rude and unfriendly. Northeasterners, unaccustomed to the South's relaxed speech and courtesy, sometimes believe Southerners are slow and stupid.

By targeting regional sub-subcultures, many marketers and retailers practice **micromarketing**, a market segmentation practice varying marketing efforts down to the zip code and neighborhood levels. Kmart stocks each of its stores with fashion, food, and everyday items preferred in each location's community.

Marketers Should Appeal to Regional Characteristics. Values, norms, language, and other cultural indicators vary widely across the nation. Southern culture revolves around the home, family, and church, while southwestern society is more geared toward casual outdoor entertaining, comfortable clothes, and active sports. There are even regional sports cultures, with marketers using local sports heroes in their geographically targeted advertising. Language varies across the country. A submarine sandwich is variously known as a hero, a hoagie, a grinder, a poor boy, a Dagwood, a Giddy Burger, or a Torpedo. Do you prefer tube steaks, wieners, franks, frankfurters, or would you just settle for a hot dog? Radio commercials for Newbury Comics, a New England music store, tap into the local vernacular by promising its patrons a "wicked good time."

Despite the differences, marketers must be wary of negative stereotypes. Most Southerners are not shiftless, redneck Bible thumpers; many New Englanders are not prim, proper, and thrifty; and there are West Coast dwellers who actually are neither beach bums nor surfer dudes.

Some Regional Subcultures Are Rising. The growth trend in the population, jobs, and even political power is moving away from the "frostbelt" and toward the "sunbelt." The balance of population is shifting rapidly from the North and East to the South and West, notably the Mountain states and the Pacific Northwest. The three megastates of California, Texas, and Florida are still growing, albeit at a slower pace than previously. Recently, high growth has been experienced by Arizona, North Carolina, Nevada, and Colorado.

Geographic Subcultures Serve as a Springboard for Mainstream Marketing. Trends in fashions, music, and hot products often originate on the West and East coasts, and then migrate into the Heartland, as happened with Seattle "grunge" music and fashion of the early 1990s. Country music spread from its Southern roots in the 1970s. NASCAR, now the number-two spectator sport (behind the NFL), has rural roots in the Southeast during the outlaw culture of the Prohibition era, when rum-running moonshiners raced one another, using the same hot rods they also employed to evade federal agents.

Regional Subcultures Demonstrate Unique CBs. Product preferences differ from coast to coast. For example, styles of dress vary, with the Southwest being the most casual (to go with their outdoorsy lifestyle) and New England being most conservative.

Regional cuisines vary. Pennsylvania is known for Philly cheese steak, soft pretzels and mustard, shoofly pie, and Pennsylvania Dutch cookery. Louisiana is famous for Cajun cooking and Creole recipes. Southerners love their hominy grits, hush puppies, moon pies, shrimp Creole, collard greens, black-eyed peas, and sweet potato pie. If you shop at a Wal-Mart in Louisiana, you can pick up a bag of fishy-flavored Zapp's Cajun Crawtator potato chips!

Sales figures on certain products skew high in some areas and low in others. Detroit is big on Rollerblades, bowling balls, and popcorn, while Bostonians go for pasta, fish, sailing, and Porsches. People in Concord, New Hampshire, are nuts—they eat a lot of peanuts, mixed nuts, and cashews.

Regionalized Media. Regional media include city, state, and regional magazines; regional newspapers such as the *New York Times* and the *Los Angeles Times;* regional cable news networks such as Northwest Cable News and New England Cable News; and regional editions of most national publications, which feature local as well as national news and advertising. Also, general media preferences vary by locale, with Sunbelt dwellers exposed to less TV and newspapers and more to radio and outdoor media such as billboards.

GENERATIONAL SUBCULTURES (AGE COHORTS): TALKIN' 'BOUT MY GENERATION

A **generation (generational cohort, birth cohort, age subculture)** is a group of people born in the same era (typically seventeen to twenty-three years in duration) who have experienced a common social, political, historical, technological, and economic environment as well as a similar significant, defining, or formative life events. Some of the latter are **light-bulb memories**—vivid recollections of significant historical events, such as the space shuttle Challenger explosion of 1986, the 9/11 attacks on the United States, and the Virginia Tech massacre of 2007. Consequently, the members of a generational cohort have much in common regarding values, norms, behaviors, and other cultural characteristics.

Marketers should distinguish three age-related phenomena to help them understand any given age group:

1. **Age effects (life cycle effects).** Differences due to age include (a) physical distinctions, such as older people having difficulty seeing and hearing, and (b) psychological differences, such as younger people craving edgy fun and excitement. People in a given age bracket (e.g., teenagers, who are thirteen to nineteen years of age) are known as an **age cohort**, not to be confused with a generational cohort.
2. **Life-stage effects.** Distinctions arising from moving through important personal life events, such as getting a driver's license, going through parenthood, and confronting retirement.
3. **Cohort effects.** Differences due to one's birth year and when one grew up. Early generational experiences shared among cohorts form values and life skills. This explains why in the 1960s, Benny Goodman music was nostalgic for middle-aged adults, whereas in the 1980s and 1990s Beatles and Rolling Stones tunes became sentimental for this same age group. So, it is fallacious to believe that a twenty-year-old living in the dawn of the twenty-first century will think, talk, and act like one living in 1900, 1950, or even 1990.

The following are our six subcultural considerations applied to age cohorts.

1. *Generational Cohorts as a Basis for Market Segmentation.* **Generational marketing** is a segmentation scheme that divides the marketplace on the basis of generational cohorts. The five generations that have attracted marketing attention are as follows:
   ➤ *Pre-Depression Generation (born before 1930).* The **pre-Depression (GI) generation** grew up in tough times, during the Great Depression and World War II. Many were deprived of material goods and a solid education. They went on to mature during the prosperous 1950s. This group makes up the older end of today's **mature market (seniors)**, variously defined as people over 50, 55, or 60.
   ➤ *Depression Generation (b. 1930–1946).* The **Depression generation** is sometimes labeled the **silent generation, postwar cohort,** or **bridge generation.** Living as youngsters during the Depression or World War II, they came of age during the 1950s or early 1960s, a period of economic growth and relative social tranquility.
   ➤ *Baby Boom Generation (b. 1946–1964).* The **baby boom generation (baby boomers, boomers)** makes up more than 40 percent of the U.S. population. Born during the prosperous years following World War II, they were the offspring of GIs returning from the war to establish families. Boomers came of age amidst mass affluence and social and political upheaval in the 1960s, and stagflation (high inflation and unemployment) in the 1970s. Many were participants in the sexual and drug revolutions of the 1960s, and consequently are sometimes called the "Woodstock" generation

(named after the 1969 music festival in Woodstock, New York). They ushered in a radically new set of values concerning gender equality, sexual orientation, premarital sex, and the environment. Demographically, they have high levels of education and income. Many are parents or grandparents in dual-income households.

➤ *Generation X (b. 1965–1978).* **Generation Xers (Gen X)** were born during what is known as the **baby bust** (because of its small size relative to the baby boom). They are sometimes called **busters, Xers, postboomers, the shadow generation, the MTV generation, thirteeners** (the thirteenth generation produced in America since its founding), and **the Nike generation** (after the company's "live-for-the moment" philosophy). The baby bust was the first era during which a large segment of society grew up in either dual-income or single-parent households. Gen Xers came of age during the prosperous 1980s and early 1990s.

Many spent their early years in day care centers and experienced the divorce of their parents while growing up. This led to their acceptance of extended or "alternative" families, which can include stepparents, half-siblings, close friends, and "relationship partners" such as in common-law marriages and same-sex couples. Generation X is slowly replacing the aging boomers in the workplace, and they have the lowest level of loyalty to institutions such as companies, government, and church. It has been suggested that they be renamed "Generation E" because they are entrepreneurial, educated, and e-mail savvy.

➤ *Generation Y (b. 1978–2000).* Members of the **Generation Y (Gen Y)** cohort arrived during the so-called **baby boomlet** or the **echo baby boom** (born to parents of the baby boom generation). They are also known as the **Internet generation**, the **Net generation**, or **N-generation** (because many came of age during the birth and early development of the Internet); **millennials** or the **millennium generation** (they were young in the year 2000); and **Generation Next**. They are more diverse racially and ethnically as well as in terms of socioeconomic status than Generation Xers.

This cohort grew up during a booming economy, widespread computer literacy, a technology boom, and unprecedented diversity in the population regarding ethnicity, beliefs, values, and other cultural characteristics. Since they matured in prosperous times and in smaller families with fewer children, they were pampered and are consequently materialistic and self-absorbed. Interestingly, they are also caring, tolerant, and well traveled. They were raised in an era of many social concerns: divorce was common, AIDS was a global epidemic, and international terrorism grew.

Most Gen Yers were raised in dual-income or single-parent households, spent time in day care, and were latchkey kids (they were home alone after school). Consequently, they were responsible for helping out with family shopping during their teen years, resulting in a sophisticated, marketing-savvy generation that is highly skeptical of advertisers and politicians who are not authentic. They will not buy from manufacturers or retailers with dubious environmental or humanitarian records. Having grown up with technology, they use it constantly—for work, leisure, and maintaining relationships. Work-life balance is important to this generation. They are hardworking, entrepreneurial, and candid.

2. *Marketers Should Appeal to Generational Characteristics.* In order to appeal to someone, you must understand them. **Cohort analysis** is a research method used to describe an aggregate of people (usually a birth cohort or marriage cohort) in terms of present as well as future values, attitudes, and lifestyles. These cultural characteristics are formed during an age cohort's "coming of age"—their teen years and early adulthood. Age cohort differences in such characteristics give rise to generation gaps (perhaps they should be called "cohort chasms"!). To appeal to any given age group and avoid these gaps, marketers must strive to understand the target cohort.

People often strive to achieve as adults what they were deprived of as children. For instance, the pre-Depression generation, having grown up in hard economic times, is concerned with material security. Because many members of Generation X matured in unstable homes, they care about establishing secure families.

Marketers must be wary of stereotyping all members of a generation. Those in the older generations despise being portrayed as old, crotchety, senile, frail geezers, especially since many are quite active. Likewise, most Gen Xers resent being pegged as apathetic slackers since many have achieved career success through hard work.

3. *Some Age Cohorts Are Rising.* Generations vary in terms of economic, buying, and political power. Members of the Depression generation hold many positions of power at the top rungs of the corporate

and government ladders. The majority of people from the pre-Depression and Depression generations are financially secure. But the baby boomers make up the largest segment of the population and continue to gain in positions of power within business and the government.

4. *Age Subcultures Serve as a Springboard for Mainstream Marketing.* Crossover marketing, which reaches across generations, can occur due to *upward diffusion.* (This also occurs across ethnic groups, crossing over from marketing a given product to a minority to the majority.) Many styles of music, fashion, and video games originate at the lower rungs of the socioeconomic ladder, in this case the younger cohorts, and then trickle upward. Extreme sports such as skateboarding, in-line skating, and motocross or BMX biking originated with the youth of Generations X and Y and became more universally popular. The adoption of "retro" styles by younger generations also illustrates generational crossover.

5. *Generations Demonstrate Unique CBs.* Product preferences vary by generation. For example, musical tastes reflect genres listened to during the teen years through early adulthood. The pre-Depression generation favors big band jazz and the Depression generation likes swing music. TV commercials aimed at baby boomers are replete with oldies and classic rock, while those targeted toward Generations X and Y contain alternative rock and rap.

6. *Specialized Media for Age Cohorts.* Each generation has media targeted directly toward it. For the pre-Depression and Depression generations, there is *AARP: The Magazine* and *50 Plus* magazine. Baby boomers are tuned into VH1, oldies radio stations, and National Public Radio. Baby busters read magazines such as *Spin* and watch Fox network TV shows such as *The Simpsons* and *Family Guy.* Magazines such as *Maxim, Spin,* and *Details,* have been developed for Generation Y. Web sites featuring music and online games are popular with both Generations X and Y. These online and wireless-centric consumers live in a different world from those who were raised on print media. Tech-savvy cohorts can be difficult to reach due to the Internet's fragmentation.

REVIEW QUESTIONS

1. Explain the relationship between social categories, subcultures, and social classes.
2. What are the four primary bases for subcultural marketing? Cite and describe major groups within each of these segmentation schemes. What other bases are also sometimes used for subcultural marketing?
3. Cite six important subcultural considerations discussed in the exercise and an example of each for all four primary bases of subcultural segmentation.
4. Cite and explain the three important bases for ethnic segmentation.
5. What is the relationship between micromarketing and geodemographic segmentation?
6. What are the three age-related phenomena marketers need to distinguish when practicing generational marketing?

IN-CLASS APPLICATIONS

Note: When you find advertisements and create your own ads for the following questions, in addition to using ethnic, religious, geographic, and generational subcultures, you are welcome to explore other subcultural groups, such as college students, the physically handicapped, liberal Democrats, surfer dudes, and so on.

1. Describe the subcultural target market for each of the ads in Exhibits 6.2 through 6.7, being as specific and descriptive as possible. Do any ads target either a sub-subculture or two or more subcultures simultaneously? How does each ad try to appeal to subcultural characteristics? Can any of the ads' appeals be improved in any way?

Are you able to find any examples of crossover marketing or appeals to unique patterns of CB in any of these ads? What kind of medium do you suppose each ad was found in?

2. It is controversial to target certain "vulnerable" groups with "socially irresponsible" products, such as those that are frivolous, i.e., don't satisfy a "genuine" need or else create a "false" problem (e.g., a back scratcher shaped like a paw); those marketed with false claims (weight loss remedies that can help you lose five pounds a day while eating all you want); unhealthy goods (chewing tobacco); potentially dangerous items (handguns and fireworks); or products considered immoral (condoms).

EXHIBIT 6.2   **Betty Crocker Ad**

EXHIBIT 6.3   *Yankee* **Magazine Ad**

EXHIBIT 6.4   **Rosary Ad**

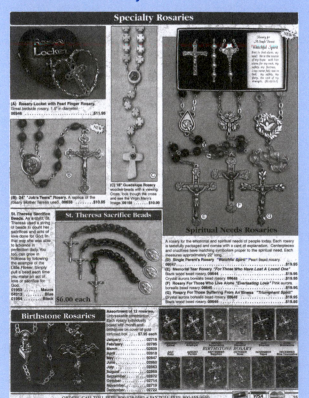

EXHIBIT 6.5   **American Family Association Ad**

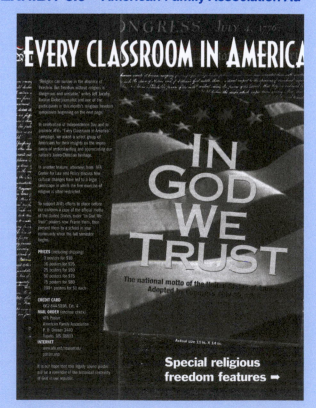

EXHIBIT 6.6   AARP Ad

EXHIBIT 6.7   Levi's Ad

Groups cited as being particularly susceptible to marketing efforts for such products include children, the very elderly, recent immigrants, those of low education, the mentally handicapped, shopaholics, and the recently bereaved. Such people are presumably easily deceived or manipulated, or otherwise more vulnerable to unscrupulous business practices, not fitting the model of the "sovereign" consumer or of the "reasonable person." Therefore, these categories of consumers require extra government protection.

For example, children are considered a vulnerable group. Some believe it is unethical to target this group with advertisements for unhealthy fare such as double cheeseburgers with bacon, large fries, and 64-ounce super-caffeinated cola. The mass marketing of these products may have contributed to childhood obesity. Fast-food restaurants have been unsuccessfully sued for hawking such unhealthy fare.

Another category sometimes added to the list of "vulnerable" groups is ethnic minorities. Several marketers of "sin" products, such as cigarettes, malt liquor and hard alcohol, and gambling, have come under fire for specifically targeting groups in ethnic neighborhoods, using local media such as flyers and in-store signage.

For example, a billboard for a brand of malt liquor in a black neighborhood in East St. Louis exclaimed, "It'll do the trick." Another said "The power of (brand name)—it works every time," suggesting the product can be used by men to get women drunk. One tobacco company was criticized for selling single cigarettes to African Americans who couldn't afford to buy a whole pack. Critics also point out the large number of liquor stores in Hispanic neighborhoods.

Given that they market such potentially detrimental products to mainstream markets, do you think it is wrong for purveyors of "sin" products to target minorities, especially those of lower income and educational levels living in inner cities? Why or why not? If you believe that such minority marketing is legitimate, should there be stipulations on how the marketing is done? If so, describe.

How do you think marketers justify marketing potentially harmful goods to ethnic minorities?

Do you agree with the marketers or the critics? How do you feel about mainstream marketers such as Chevrolet sponsoring religious concerts or otherwise affiliating themselves with religious groups or events? Should there be separation of church and marketing? Why or why not?

WRITTEN APPLICATIONS

1. Answer Question 1 in the In-Class Applications for four of the ads. If you are a member of any of these subcultures, does the ad appeal to you personally? Why or why not? If you are not a member of any of these subcultures, interview someone who is and get that person's perspective on the advertising's appeal (or lack thereof).

2. Find two additional ads for which you can answer Question 1 in the In-Class Applications. These advertisements can come from either specialized subcultural media or mainstream media that are either targeting one or more particular subcultures or attempting to popularize a subcultural product via crossover marketing.

3. Create an ad for any advertising medium that will appeal to one (or more) subcultures. Answer Question 1 in the In-Class Applications for that ad.

4. Answer Question 2 in the In-Class Applications. In addition to offering your own opinion, solicit the opinion of a member of one of the disadvantaged groups.

EXERCISE 6.2. SUBCULTURES AND YOU

OBJECTIVES

1. To help you understand how your own values, norms, attitudes, and other cultural characteristics are influenced by the subculture(s) to which you belong.
2. To have you recognize how advertisers try to influence you by appealing to your subcultural heritage.
3. To have you use your understanding of your own subculture(s) to design an ad that would appeal to members of your subculture.

BACKGROUND

The Background section for Exercise 6.1 provides all the information you will need for this exercise. This exercise is presented only as a written application, not as an in-class application. Although students could discuss their written reports in class, many might find much of it too personal. Therefore, instructor discretion is advised on using this as an in-class application.

WRITTEN APPLICATIONS

1. In order of personal importance, list all of the subcultures of which you are a member. You should be able to come up with at least two from the four major bases for subcultural segmentation. You might also be able to add other subcultures using other bases, such as college students, political preference groups, and consumption subcultures.

For each subculture, briefly explain why being a member of that subculture is or is not important to you. Would this affect your susceptibility to marketing efforts targeting your subcultural group?

2. For each subculture to which you belong, describe the cultural characteristics that you personally share with typical members of the subculture (if any), as well as cultural characteristics on which you deviate from typical subcultural group members (if any). Might these deviations matter to a marketer?

3. Describe some ways in which your CB has been influenced by your subcultural characteristics.

4. Find at least two print advertisements, each targeted toward at least one of your subcultural groups. (If you belong to more than two subcultures, you may limit the number of ads to two.) How does each ad try to appeal to group members' subcultural characteristics?

Why does each ad appeal or not appeal to you personally? (Answer in light of your self-assessment of your standing on the subcultural characteristics as described in Questions 1 and 2.) Could the appeal of each ad be improved in any way? Can you find any examples of crossover marketing or appeals to unique patterns of CB in any of the ads? In what type of media did each ad appear? Was each media vehicle an appropriate choice for each advertiser?

5. Create an ad for a product that interests you by appealing to one or more of the subcultures to which you belong. Then, answer Question 4 for your ad (except for the last question regarding media in which the ads appeared). Explain in which media vehicles (media by brand name, e.g., *The Jewish Advocate* newspaper or *Sunset* magazine, a West Coast publication) you would run your ad and why.

KEY CONCEPTS

acculturation	generational marketing
age cohort	Hispanics (Latinos)
age effects (life-cycle effects)	host culture
assimilation	intraculturalism
baby boom generation (baby boomers, boomers)	life-stage effects
backtranslation	light-bulb memories
cohort analysis	macroculture
cohort effects	mature market (seniors)
consumption subcultures	micromarketing
crossover marketing (mainstreaming)	multicultural marketing (ethnic marketing, minority
de-ethnicitization	marketing)
Depression generation (silent generation, postwar	multiculturalism
cohort, bridge generation)	pre-Depression (GI) generation
generation (generational cohort, birth cohort, age	retro-acculturation
subculture)	social categories
Generation X (Gen X, baby bust, busters, Xers,	sub-subcultures
postboomers, shadow generation, MTV generation,	subcultural identification
thirteeners, the Nike generation)	subcultural influences
Generation Y (Gen Y, baby boomlet, echo baby boom,	subcultures (microcultures)
Internet generation, Net generation, N-generation,	tribal marketing
millennials, millennium generation, Generation Next)	urban marketing

SUMMARY

Chapter 6 investigated one type of social category. This chapter concerned subcultures within the macroculture and their subcultural influences. The major subcultural segmentation variables are: ethnic background (race, nationality, and language); religion; geographic region; and generational cohort. Also of interest to some marketers are consumption subcultures.

Exercise 6.1 identified six important subcultural segmentation considerations along which we discussed each of the four major variables used for subcultural segmentation as follows:

1. Subcultures provide a foundation for market segmentation based on identifiable descriptors and the lifestyle implications of the resulting groups. Many subcultures can be further divided into sub-subcultures. Consumers can be cross-classified by two subcultural segmentation variables, notably when geography is used in conjunction with one of the other three subcultural segmentation variables, since subcultural segments often cluster geographically.

2. Marketers should appeal to subcultural characteristics while avoiding offending subculture members' sensitivities, such as portraying them with negative stereotypes.

3. Most subcultures are rising, growing in absolute and relative size. Members of these groups are achieving upward social mobility and enhanced political clout.

4. Subcultures sometimes serve as springboards for mainstreaming, including de-ethnicitization of ethnic products.
5. Subcultures exhibit unique CBs such as product and brand preferences, shopping patterns, and media habits.
6. These specialized media habits suggest the existence of specialized subcultural media.

Exercise 6.1 investigated each of the four major variables for subcultural segmentation along these six themes. Regarding ethnicity, more marketers are pursuing multicultural marketing. Ethnic minorities can be defined on one or more of three bases: (a) racial groups, (b) nationality groups, and (c) language groups. The three major ethnic subgroups are African Americans (blacks), Hispanics, and Asian Americans.

The major ethnic segmentation considerations are as follows:

1. The trend is toward ethnic segmentation, both in the United States and in some countries abroad. Important bases for ethnic sub-subcultures are country of origin, degree of acculturation or assimilation to the host culture, and subcultural identification.
2. Ethnic groups respond to messages emphasizing their cultural characteristics. Avoid relying on simple ethnic stereotypes. Backtranslation avoids language blunders.
3. Ethnic subcultures exhibit high growth rates due to both high fertility rates and high immigration rates. Most ethnic groups are achieving upward social mobility as well as more political power and status.
4. Crossover marketing of ethnic products occurs with urban marketing. Young Americans are especially prone to intraculteralism, which differs from multiculturalism.
5. Unique behavioral patterns are exhibited by minority consumers, such as higher brand loyalty, although some differences between ethnic and mainstream consumers disappear after controlling for income, education, and other socioeconomic indicators.
6. Specialty media exist for all ethnic groups and, increasingly, for many ethnic subgroups. Minority consumers heavily use broadcast media and local radio but lightly use print media.

Regarding religious subcultures, people derive important values and beliefs from their religion that, in turn, shape their cultural characteristics. In the United States, the principal organized religious faiths include Protestantism, Catholicism, Judaism, and Islam.

The major religion segmentation themes are as follows:

1. Most religions have sub-subcultures, usually defined by conservatism. Each subculture and sub-subculture has its own demographic profile and subcultural characteristics, and some geographic regions have a heavy concentration of particular religions.
2. Values and norms are heavily influenced by religion. Unfortunately, stereotypes persist.
3. While organized religious influence has waned somewhat, religious subcultures remain strong. The United States is increasingly pluralistic and individualistic in its religious beliefs. Evangelical Christians and Muslims are rapidly expanding in numbers and influence.
4. Examples of religious crossover marketing exist, especially in various media.
5. Religious beliefs and customs sometimes influence consumption and shopping patterns, dictating some products' use (Kosher foods) or nonuse (alcohol and tobacco).
6. All major religious groups have their own media, notably magazines and radio stations.

Regional subcultures are determined by geographic characteristics such as ethnic and religious mixes of citizens, climate, and natural resources. The trend is toward regional marketing.

The major regional segmentation themes are as follows:

1. Regions differ demographically, often overlapping with other subcultures. Targeting regional sub-subcultures, many marketers and retailers practice micromarketing.
2. Cultural indicators such as language and mannerisms vary widely across the United States.
3. The growth trend in the population, jobs, and political power is shifting rapidly from the North and the East to the South and West.

4. Geographic crossovers are common, with trends often originating on the West and East coasts, and then migrating into the "Heartland."
5. Product preferences in styles of dress, food, and sporting goods differ from coast to coast.
6. Regional media can be used to target specific areas.

A fourth basis for subcultural segmentation is the consumer's age. Members of any one generation share light-bulb memories. Marketers should distinguish three age-related phenomena: (1) age effects, (2) life stage effects, and (3) cohort effects. Generational marketing divides the marketplace on the basis of age cohorts.

There are five generations that have attracted the most marketing attention: the pre-Depression generation—the older end of today's mature market (seniors); the Depression generation; the baby boom generation; Generation X, and Generation Y. The major generational segmentation themes are:

1. Diversity within each generation is based on ethnicity, geography, social class, and behavior.
2. Cohort analysis can be used to understand a cohort's values, attitudes, and lifestyles. Exercise 6.1 examined some of the key cultural characteristics for each of the five age cohorts.
3. The various cohorts vary regarding economic, buying, and political power.
4. Crossover marketing opportunities across generations arise due to the upward diffusion that occurs for minorities. Some fashions originate at the lower rungs of the ladder of social esteem (minority groups and younger age cohorts) and trickle upward within society.
5. Nonetheless, each generation retains its own unique product and media preferences, including specialty media for each generation.

Exercise 6.2 enabled you to apply your knowledge of subcultures from Exercise 6.1 to understanding your own personal subcultures and how these influence your CBs.

REFERENCES

The Barna Group. (2005). "Annual Barna Group Survey Describes Changes in America's Religious Beliefs and Practices." http://www.barna.org/barna-update/article/5-barna-update/181-annual-barna-group-survey-describes-changes-in-americas-religious-beliefs-and-practices (accessed June 16, 2006).

Brown, Mary, and Orsborn, Carol. (2006). *BOOM: Marketing to the Ultimate Power Consumer—The Baby-Boomer Woman.* New York: AMACOM, 2006.

Cimino, Richard, and Lattin, Don. (1999). "Choosing My Religion." *American Demographics,* April, 60–65.

Faura, Juan. (2005). *Hispanic Marketing Grows Up: Exploring Perceptions and Facing Realities.* Ithaca, NY: Paramount Market Publishing.

Gibson, Campbell. (1993). "The Four Baby Booms." *American Demographics,* November, 36–40.

Green, Brent. (2005). *Marketing to Leading-Edge Baby Boomers: Perceptions, Principles, Practices, Predictions,* 2nd ed. Ithaca, NY: Paramount Market Publishing.

Gronbach, Kenneth W. (2008). *The Age Curve: How to Profit from the Coming Demographic Storm.* New York: AMACOM.

Halter, Marilyn. (2000). *Shopping for Identity.* New York: Schocken Books.

Hapoienu, S. L. (1990). "The Rise of Micromarketing." *Journal of Business Strategy,* 1, 37, 37–42.

Harris, Leslie M., ed. (2003). *After Fifty: How the Baby Boom Will Redefine the Mature Market.* Ithaca, NY: Paramount Market Publishing.

Howe, Neil, and Strauss, William. (2000). *Millennials Rising: The Next Great Generation.* New York: Vintage Books.

Katsanis, Lea Prevel. (1994). "The Ideology of Political Correctness and Its Effect on Brand Strategy." *Journal of Product and Brand Management,* 3, 2, 5–14.

Kaufman-Scarborough, Carol. (2000). "Asian-American Consumers as a Unique Market Segment: Fact or Fallacy?" *Journal of Consumer Research,* 17, 2, 249–162.

Korgaonkar, Pradeep K., Karson, Eric J., and Lund, Daulatram. (2000). "Hispanics and Direct Marketing Advertising." *Journal of Consumer Research,* 17, 2, 137–157.

Korzenny, Felipe, and Korzenny, Betty Ann. (2005). *Hispanic Marketing: A Cultural Perspective.* Burlington, MA: Elsevier/Butterworth-Heinemann.

Kosmin, Barry A., and Keysar, Ariela B. (2006). *Religion in a Free Market.* Ithaca, NY: Paramount Market Publishing.

McDaniel, Stephen W., and Burnett, John J. (1991). "Targeting the Evangelical Segment." *Journal of Advertising Research,* 31, 4, 26–33.

Michman, Ronald D. (2003). *Lifestyle Marketing: Reaching the New American Consumer.* Westport, CT: Praeger Publishers.

Miller, Pepper, and Kemp, Herb. (2005). *What's Black About It? Insights to Increase Your Share of a Changing African-American Market.* Ithaca, NY: Paramount Market Publishing.

Morgan, Carol M., and Levy, Doran J. (2002). *Marketing to the Mindset of Boomers and Their Elders.* St. Paul, MN: Attitude Base, The Brewer House.

Moschis, George P., Lee, Euehun, Mathur, Anil, and Strautman, Jennifer. (2000). *The Maturing Marketplace: Buying Habits of Baby Boomers and Their Parents.* Westport, CT: Quorum Books.

Moschis, George P., and Mathur, Anil. (2007). *Baby Boomers and Their Parents: Surprising Findings about Their Lifestyles, Mindsets, and Well-Being.* Ithaca, NY: Paramount Market Publishing.

Mueller, Barbara. (2008). *Communicating with the Multicultural Consumer: Theoretical and Practical Perspectives.* New York: Peter Lang.

Muley, Miriam. (2009). *The 85% Niche: The Power of Women of All Colors—Latina, Black, and Asian.* Ithaca, NY: Paramount Market Publishing.

Napoli, Julie, and Ewing, Michael T. (2001). "The Net Generation." *Journal of International Consumer Marketing,* 13, 1, 21–34.

Nyren, Chuck. (2005). *Advertising to Baby Boomers.* Ithaca, NY: Paramount Market Publishing.

Paul, Pamela. (2001). "Echo Boomerang." *American Demographics,* June, 45–49.

———. (2001). "Getting Inside Generation Y." *American Demographics,* September, 43–49.

Roberts, James A., and Manolis, Chris. (2000). "Baby Boomers and Busters: An Exploratory Investigation of Attitudes Toward Marketing, Advertising, and Consumerism." *Journal of Consumer Marketing,* 17, 6, 481–499.

Rossman, Marlene L. (1994). *Multicultural Marketing.* New York: American Management Association, 153–157.

Schouten, John W., and McAlexander, James H. (1995). "Subcultures of Consumption." *Journal of Consumer Research,* 22, 1, 43–61.

Smith, N. Craig, and Cooper-Martin, Elizabeth. (1997). "Ethics and Target Marketing: The Role of Product Harm and Consumer Vulnerability." *Journal of Marketing,* 61, 3, 1–20.

Strauss, William, and Howe, Neil. (2006). *Millennials and the Pop Culture: Strategies for a New Generation of Consumers in Music, Movies, TV, Internet and Video Games.* Great Falls, VA: Life Course Associates.

Stroud, Dick. (2007). *The Fifty-Plus Market.* London: Kogan Page.

Sturdivant, Frederick D. (1973). "Subculture Theory: Poverty, Minorities, and Marketing." In Scott Ward and Thomas S. Robertson (eds.), *Consumer Behavior: Theoretical Sources.* Englewood Cliffs, NJ: Prentice-Hall, 469–520.

Tharp, Marye C. (2001). *Marketing and Consumer Identity in Multicultural America.* Thousand Oaks, CA: Sage Publications.

Valdés, M. Isabel. (2000). *Marketing to American Latinos (Part 1): A Guide to the In-Culture Approach.* Ithaca, NY: Paramount Market Publishing.

———. (2002). *Marketing to American Latinos (Part 2): A Guide to the In-Culture Approach.* Ithaca, NY: Paramount Market Publishing.

Wolburg, Joyce M. (2005). "Drawing the Line Between Targeting and Patronizing: How 'Vulnerable' Are the Vulnerable?" *Journal of Consumer Marketing,* 22, 5, 287–288.

Yarrow, Kit, and O'Donnell, Jayne. (2009). *Gen Buy: How Tweens, Teens, and Twenty-Somethings Are Revolutionizing Retail.* San Francisco, CA: Jossey-Bass.

Zill, Nicholas, and Robinson, John. (1997). "The Generation X Difference." *American Demographics,* April, 24–33.

Zogby, John. (2008). *The Way We'll Be: The Zogby Report on the Transformation of the American Dream.* New York: Random House.

CHAPTER 7

SOCIAL CLASS INFLUENCES

In this chapter we investigate another type of social category, social class. Western cultures use class systems to rank groups or individuals hierarchically within society or a social group with respect to social status and place them into groups called **strata** (singular is stratum). This ranking system is referred to as **social stratification**.

Socioeconomic status (SES; social status) is an individual's or group's position within a hierarchical social structure. SES is the relative ranking of members of each social class stratum (group) based on factors such as wealth, power, and prestige. Cultural anthropologists and sociologists describe two basic systems whereby society can be stratified: the **caste system** and the **class system** stratify preindustrial and very traditional societies.

The caste system is found in India, with priests and scholars at the top rung of the social ladder and outcasts or untouchables at the bottom. Ancient Roman society used a caste system, with the patricians, or aristocrats, up top and the plebeians, or commoners, down below. In medieval Europe, the lords of the manor lorded it over the serfs.

In a caste system, social prestige is not acquired. One's social rank is *ascribed*, based on uncontrollable characteristics given at birth, such as the social status of one's parents, race, and gender. Status is *formally defined* and clearly identified with markers such as clothing, jewelry, makeup, and other personal accessories. Members of each stratum have a strong identity, and a rigid hierarchy exists among caste members. **Social mobility** does not exist. One cannot climb up or down the social ladder, and social intercourse between members of different castes is forbidden.

A class system stratifies members of most modern societies. **Social class** is a means for ranking groups of people hierarchically in either an industrial or postindustrial society based on social status. Members of a given class share approximately the same amount of social status, while people in other classes have either more or less status. One's position in society is achieved via contributions to society through performance in various societal roles, such as work and accomplishments in the community, church, and family. Class is informally defined. There are no clear labels or obvious indicators of status or strong class identity. Status is subjectively assigned using criteria that are sometimes vague and open to dispute. This results in a lack of consensus on what social class any given person belongs to and disagreement on the number and nature of social classes within a society. Social mobility and interaction between members of different social classes is common. Social mobility, the ability to move up (upward mobility) and down (downward mobility) through the social hierarchy, is of importance to marketers who suggest upward mobility via purchase of their brand.

Although we might not feel comfortable with it, social class distinctions are a fact of life, like the difference between urban and rural or north and south. You might feel that the existence of social classes is unfair in a society where we value egalitarianism and a nation founded on the cultural beliefs that "all men are created equal." Social classes exist because, while all people are equal in human worth, they are not equivalent in human abilities and efforts. Since talents and levels of industry differ, some people achieve more than others in their societal roles.

In general, a class society is divided into upper, middle, and lower classes. Accordingly, products are said to be *upscale*, *midscale* (broadscale), and *downscale*. Exhibit 7.1 shows the diamond-shaped three-class model of social class found in the United States and many other Western societies. Note that there is a broad middle class and smaller upper and lower classes.

Exhibit 7.1 also demonstrates that marketers can simultaneously slice the consumer market in several ways, such as by social class and ethnic group. Social classes are indicated as horizontal strata and ethnic groups as

213

EXHIBIT 7.1   The Relationship between Social Class and Ethnic Subculture

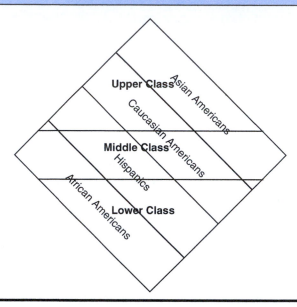

diagonal slices through those strata. For instance, Asian Americans tend to be of higher socioeconomic status than Caucasian Americans, although they cut through all three social classes. As one moves up the social class diamond, subcultural influences tend to dissipate as assimilation occurs. Lower-class members of any given ethnic group are more prone to retain the jargon, foods, clothing, and other cultural characteristics associated with their ethnic group. Consequently, some marketers segment the marketplace based on subculture and then target a particular social class within a subculture, such as upper-class African Americans.

The potential for social class as a market segmentation variable was first noted in the 1940s when W. Lloyd Warner discovered that each of the social class groups he identified displayed unique purchase motivations and shopping behaviors. He realized that class groupings are more than just an economic phenomenon—they also have psychosocial and lifestyle connotations.

Social class and consumption are inexorably intertwined. Chess, wine, and brie are considered as more upscale than checkers, beer, and Velveeta. Members of the upper class are more apt to drive a Volvo than a Chevy and to wear Tommy Hilfiger rather than Lee jeans.

ORGANIZATION OF CHAPTER SEVEN

In Exercise 7.1, we observe how marketers use a popular scheme—the Coleman-Rainwater social standing hierarchy—for structuring social classes to segment their markets and then effectively marketing toward their targeted social class. Exercise 7.2 will give you a chance to consider your own social class standing, how it influences your marketplace behavior, and how your social status affects efforts of marketers to appeal to you. Finally, Exercise 7.3 will help you see and calculate how consumer researchers assign consumers to a social class.

EXERCISE 7.1. SOCIAL CLASS SEGMENTATION

OBJECTIVES

1. To familiarize you with the Coleman-Rainwater social standing hierarchy.
2. To give you insight into and the ability to recognize how marketers use social class positioning in their advertising.

3. To help you understand how marketers can simultaneously target members of adjacent social classes by using either an upward pull strategy or by appealing to the overprivileged or underprivileged within an adjacent social class.
4. To enable you to use knowledge of the social class hierarchy to design ads that appeal to members of various social classes.

BACKGROUND

SOCIAL CLASS AND SEGMENTATION

Social classes form a useful basis for segmenting consumer markets because occupants of a given social class often share common demographics, ways of thinking (values, beliefs, and attitudes), lifestyles (ways of spending time and money), and behaviors, including CB.

At one end of the social ladder we find Jacques Perrier, who drinks the finest bourbon and champagne. He is a lucrative target for super-premium prestige vodka brands such as Grey Goose, Belvedere, and Chopin, which are priced at $25 to $200 per bottle, and he patronizes hotels like the Ritz-Carlton and Four Seasons. At the other end of the social class spectrum resides Joe Six-Pack, who might knock back cheap Thunderbird or Boone's Farm wine or popular-priced, bottom-shelf beer such as Keystone, Busch, Natural, and Miller High Life. Joe stays at Motel 6 or Super 8 motels when splurging on holiday.

The trend is toward **two-tier marketing**, in which marketing efforts are either up-market (e.g., distributing products through exclusively positioned top-tier retailers such as Neiman Marcus, Nordstrom, Bloomingdale's, Lord & Taylor, and Saks Fifth Avenue) or down-market (e.g., selling through lower-end value-priced mass merchants or off-price chains such as Wal-Mart and Kmart, or via warehouse clubs such as Costco and BJ's), not toward the middle market. The thinking is that we are experiencing an "hour-glass economy" in which the middle group is disappearing and people are either trading up or down. Hence, mid-tier department stores (JCPenney, Macy's, and Sears) and mid-tier specialty stores (Abercrombie & Fitch and Gap) are losing ground to upscale specialty stores among affluent shoppers and to discounters among less privileged consumers and bargain hunters. Even traditional supermarkets are experiencing competition from discount supercenters such as Wal-Mart on the lower end and specialty food stores such as Trader Joe's and Whole Foods at the upper end.

Likewise, successful products aim either uptown or downtown. Kraft macaroni and cheese is a highly successful brand, but it is in danger of being caught in the middle and squeezed by rivals at both the upper end of the market (Annie's Deluxe macaroni and cheese) and low end (Wal-Mart's store brand). Levi Strauss, which sold through midscale retailers, once avoided discounters. However, they were squeezed from the middle by high-fashion denim brands such as newcomers Diesel and Lucky. Consequently, Levi's launched a signature line for discounters and the premium Red Tag brand for upscale venues. Conagra chases both higher-income and budget-conscious customers, offering rival brands: Marie Callender's and Chef Boyardee; Healthy Choice and Banquet; Orville Redenbacher and Act II. Budweiser is squeezed by superpremium brews such as Amstel Light and Carlsburg at one end and discount beers that Joe Six-Pack drinks at the other end.

Knowledge of a target market's social class enables a marketer to formulate a product position and brand image consistent with the actual or desired lifestyle of target market members. Based on a brand's positioning and image, all elements of the marketing mix are chosen: the product's quality level and add-on features (higher quality and extras for higher-class customers); high versus low price points; choice of up-market versus down-market retailers to sell through; and creation of appropriate marketing communications that appeal to differences among social classes in lifestyles, languages, and cultural characteristics.

Exhibit 7.2 shows the relationship between culture, subculture, and social class. It demonstrates that an individual can simultaneously exhibit CBs of the core culture as well as of subculture(s) and social class, which may overlap. Exhibit 7.2 also illustrates that consumers who are overprivileged and/or aspiring members of a social class will exhibit CBs of the next-highest social class as well as some aspects of buyer behavior found in their own social class.

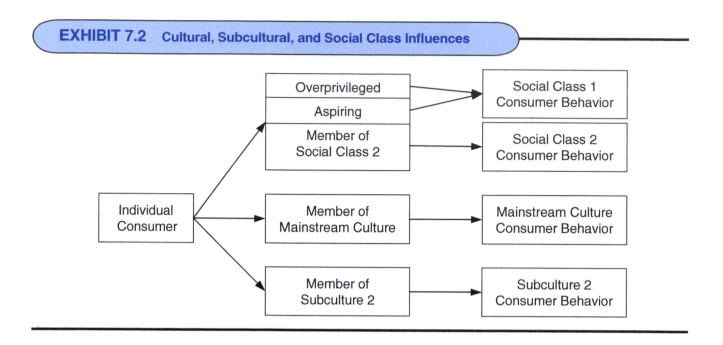

EXHIBIT 7.2   Cultural, Subcultural, and Social Class Influences

TARGETING OF MULTIPLE SOCIAL CLASSES

There are two complicating factors causing some marketers to target two or more adjacent social classes simultaneously with one marketing program: (1) upward social mobility and (2) relative occupational class income. The latter gives rise to the overprivileged and underprivileged segments in each social class (see Exhibit 7.2). Due to these factors, marketers sometimes position their marketing programs toward more than just one social class.

UPWARD SOCIAL MOBILITY

Many consumers wish to achieve **upward social mobility** and take action to achieve a higher social status. This is usually done through educational or occupational achievement. Such consumers have a **subjective social class**—a class with which they identify and perhaps to which they aspire but to which they do not belong. Consequently, using an **upward pull strategy**, a marketer positions a brand as an **aspirational brand**. These brands are believed to assist the customer in achieving the trappings of the next rung on the social ladder. To help climb the societal steps, these consumers **trade up**, or splurge on luxury goods that they find emotionally satisfying and that are symbolic of upward social mobility, such as big flat-screen TVs and expensive golf clubs.

The upward pull strategy involves marketing communications using values, lifestyles, and other characteristics of the social class that target market members wish to attain. Simultaneously, the marketer reaches current members of the upper social class as a second target market. Therefore, an ad pursuing aspiring lower-middle-class customers can position itself as an upper-middle-class (one rung above lower middle class) brand through its language, characters, setting, and other imagery.

Many luxury car brands (Mercedes, Jaguar, Lexus) offer entry-level models for social climbers, who they hope will later trade up to their higher-end models. While the wealthy consumer is still a core customer, high-end retailers are paying close attention to aspiring middle-class shoppers and have been adding more high-style merchandise at not-quite-so-high prices.

RELATIVE OCCUPATIONAL CLASS INCOME: THE OVERPRIVILEGED AND UNDERPRIVILEGED

Within a given social class there are a wide range of incomes. **Relative occupational class income (ROCI)** is the relationship of a family's total income to the median income of other families in the same social class. The three ROCI categories are: (1) the **overprivileged** families, who have an income higher than the average in their class; (2) the **underprivileged**, who are below their social class average income; and (3) **class average** households, which have typical income levels for their class.

The **relative income hypothesis** says that although the overprivileged and underprivileged generally share the same patterns of thinking and behavior as other members of their social class, their purchasing patterns often differ due to their higher or lower incomes. Specifically, the overprivileged tend to buy like those in the class above them and the underprivileged mimic the purchasing habits of those in the social category below them (due to budget constraints). Consequently, a marketer targeting the lower-upper class can simultaneously appeal to the overprivileged members of the upper-middle class, which is one rung lower on the social ladder.

SOCIAL CLASS CATEGORIES

THE WARNER INDEX OF STATUS CHARACTERISTICS HIERARCHY

There is little agreement among sociologists as to how many distinct social classes are necessary to fully describe the American class structure. Although most societies can be characterized as having three broad classes—upper, middle, and lower—the number of social strata defined in the various classification schemes ranges from two to as many as nine. There are more than a dozen distinctive classification systems.

An early and still popular classification system is W. Lloyd Warner's six-category scheme: upper-upper class, lower-upper class, upper-middle class, lower-middle class, upper-lower class, and lower-lower class. We will examine this scheme further in Exercise 7.3.

THE COLEMAN-RAINWATER SOCIAL STANDING HIERARCHY

The **Coleman-Rainwater social standing (social class) hierarchy** contains three general groupings with seven social classes as follows: **upper Americans** (upper-upper, lower-upper, and upper-middle), **middle Americans** (middle class and working class), and **lower Americans** (upper-lower and lower-lower). Unlike Warner's ISC, Coleman-Rainwater's classification system distinguishes between the middle class (white-collar workers) and the working class (blue-collar workers). In fact, Coleman-Rainwater's "middle Americans" are approximately equivalent to Warner's "lower-middle" class. Coleman-Rainwater's other class labels are identical to those found in Warner's six-class system, although Coleman-Rainwater adds a working class.

Since this is a very popular scheme, we will use it as the basis for defining and understanding the different social classes in the United States today. The following section features a capsule description of each of Coleman and Rainwater's social classes, which is useful for marketers to segment their markets and then effectively position and market their products.

1. UPPER AMERICANS (14 PERCENT): AMERICA'S "QUALITY MARKET"

Upper-upper (0.3 percent): The "capital S" society world of inherited wealth, these individuals enjoy the following: aristocratic names and socially prominent blue blood families; "prep school" followed by Ivy League colleges and master's degrees; beautiful homes in the best "gold coast" areas; luxury cars and extensive travel. This group includes prominent physicians and lawyers as well as owners of major business establishments, but working is optional. They form the nucleus of the best country clubs and sponsor major charitable events. Members provide leadership and funds for community and civic activities and often serve on boards of directors for major corporations or as trustees for nonprofit organizations. They dress conservatively, avoid ostentatious purchases (since they are accustomed to wealth), emphasize self-expression, buy quality merchandise, and reflect an ideal of "spending with good taste." This is not a major market segment because of its small size. Examples include the Rockefeller and Kennedy families.

Lower-upper (1.2 percent): The **nouveau riche**, which literally means "new money" or "new wealth." This group is the newer social elite of first-generation earned wealth. They might be extremely wealthy, but since the money is still relatively new they have not yet been fully accepted by the community's upper crust. Members include current professional and corporate leaders as well as entertainment and sports celebrities. Most have earned master's degrees. They live in the better suburban neighborhoods and high-rise apartment buildings and are influentials in society—business leaders and the professional elite. These self-made people are active in community affairs and public issues.

The lower-upper class can be further segmented into two subgroups: (a) those who slowly acquired their wealth through professional accomplishments and tend to maintain upper-middle-class lifestyles and (b) those who rapidly gained wealth, such as entrepreneurs, sports stars, and entertainers. The first subgroup is secure in their luxury lifestyle and turned off by ostentation. Members of the second subgroup are frequently unable to join the same exclusive clubs or command the respect of the upper uppers. High achievers, they flaunt their wealth through conspicuous consumption and spend money lavishly (and often tastelessly) to display their newfound riches. Examples include Bill Gates, Ted Turner, and Donald Trump.

Upper-middle (12.5 percent): This is the intellectual elite. They are successful professionals, independent businesspeople, and corporate managers. Their income is derived from profits and fees. Members' educational levels range from bachelor's degrees to professional and graduate degrees. This group lives in above-average residential areas, emphasizes education for their children, and lacks the wealth and status of the upper class. Their social position has been achieved mainly through their occupational achievements. Lifestyle centers on active involvement in private clubs and in arts and charities in local communities. Women in this group are more likely to be employed, active, and self-expressive than women in the other groups.

More important than status are housing quality and location, as well as product quality, appearance, and value. This group is a prime market for "the finer things in life": luxury goods and high-priced homes to serve as symbols of their achievements.

2. MIDDLE AMERICANS (70 PERCENT)

Middle class (32 percent): This group includes average-income white-collar workers, owners of small businesses, and highly paid, socially ambitious blue-collar workers, who receive income from weekly, biweekly, or monthly salaries. Most have college degrees or completed some college courses. They do not reach high levels in their organizations, live in modest suburban homes in average residential neighborhoods, and tend to be involved in church-sponsored activities. Respectability is important. They care what the neighbors think and try to do the "proper" things. This group consists of two segments: traditionalists who value home ownership, high moral standards, and family; and nontraditionalists who reflect the values of the upper-middle class because they are upwardly mobile. Nontraditionalist women are more likely to work and are less oriented toward meal preparation and child rearing. Nontraditionalists are also more likely to make purchases based on status considerations. Both groups generally avoid upscale furnishings and enjoy do-it-yourself projects. With limited incomes, they balance their desire for current consumption with wants for future security.

Working class (38 percent): This group includes average-pay blue-collar workers. They hold positions in factories, construction companies, service industries (police, bartenders, deliverymen), and sales. Members generally have completed high school and are paid hourly wages. Jobs tend to be monotonous, although affluence is possible if the individual is a member of a union. Work is seen as a means to "buy" enjoyment. This group tends to stay close to their parents and relatives and live in older parts of town in modest homes or apartments often located in marginal urban neighborhoods, decaying suburbs, or rural areas. They have traditional values; husbands are generally the breadwinners and only about one-third of the women are employed. Most seek security for and protection of their possessions rather than advancement.

This group has money for consumer products and, along with the middle class, represents the mass market for many consumer goods. Their uncreative jobs lead to a pattern of impulse purchasing in an attempt to escape from the dull routine—buy for today rather than plan for tomorrow. Consequently, effective advertising appeals to fantasy and escape. Working-class people take pride in their work and view themselves as the often unappreciated backbone of the nation. Husbands typically have a "macho" self-image and are big sports fans. They prefer new-model cars and appliances. Members take their recreation seriously and are good targets for pickup trucks, campers, hunting equipment, powerboats, and beer.

3. Lower Americans (16 percent)

Upper-lower (9 percent): These are the working poor. They work in unskilled minimum-wage jobs and their living standard is just above poverty. They may not have completed high school and live in marginal housing that is often located in depressed and decaying neighborhoods. Crime, drugs, and gangs cause them to be concerned about their family's safety and their children's future. Lack of education and opportunities makes it difficult to move up the social hierarchy; consequently, they are frustrated and angry about not being able to share in the "American Dream" of upward social mobility.

Members of this group live from paycheck to paycheck and rarely plan for the future. Most and sometimes all of their income goes to rent, heat, food, and medicine. Their behavior is often considered "crude" and "trashy" by members of higher social strata.

Lower-lower (7 percent): This is the bottom rung on the social ladder or our nation's poor. These individuals subsist on government welfare. They are usually unemployed for long periods of time or else have the "dirtiest" jobs, such as dishwasher or garbageman. Most have only grade school educations and some are illiterate. Many of the children in this group are illegitimate. Some of the people at this level have criminal records. Apathy, fatalism, and impulsive consumption are characteristic of their day-to-day existence. The challenge to marketers is to meet the needs of this group while still earning a profit.

REVIEW QUESTIONS

1. Explain the relationship between social stratification and social class.
2. Compare the two major systems for stratifying a society in terms of four important criteria.
3. Why is social class a useful variable for market segmentation?
4. Describe how the concepts of upward social mobility and relative occupational class income can each result in targeting two adjacent social classes simultaneously with one marketing program.
5. Describe the Coleman-Rainwater Social Standing Hierarchy and its use by marketers.

IN-CLASS APPLICATIONS

1. Using the Coleman-Rainwater Social Class Hierarchy, identify what you believe is the social class target market(s) for each of the ads in Exhibits 7.3 through 7.7. Explain why you believe the social class you have identified is the target market.

Do any of these ads seem to be using either an upward pull strategy or an appeal to either the overprivileged or underprivileged within a given social class? If so, describe that appeal. Would it be possible to promote each product to one or more other social classes in addition to or instead of the one targeted in the ad? If so, how would this change the nature of the advertising?

2. Some people say the United States is becoming a mass-market society, and so targeting consumers by social class will become less important in the future. Others believe that differences between social classes are actually growing more pronounced, perhaps with the middle class shrinking (the so-called hourglass economy—"the rich get richer and the poor get poorer"), and consequently social class segmentation will become even more critical. Which view do you believe is correct? Can you cite any evidence to support your position?

WRITTEN APPLICATIONS

1. Answer Question 1 in the In-Class Applications for four of the ads. For products you believe could be targeted to social classes other than the currently targeted market, design a new ad for that market. Discuss your ad's use of social class appeal.

2. Find three additional ads, each of which seems to be targeted toward a different social class. Answer Question 1 in the In-Class Applications for each of these ads.

3. Answer Question 2 in the In-Class Applications.

EXHIBIT 7.3   Tide Ad

EXHIBIT 7.4   *The National Enquirer* and *Star* Subscription Ad

EXHIBIT 7.5   Cascade Ad

EXHIBIT 7.6   Iberia Airlines Ad

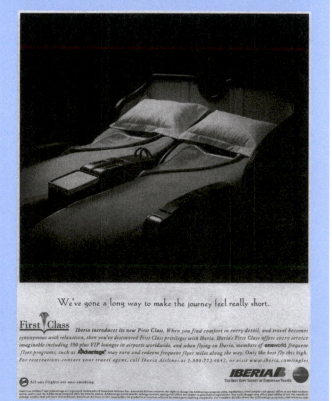

EXHIBIT 7.7   State Farm Insurance Ad

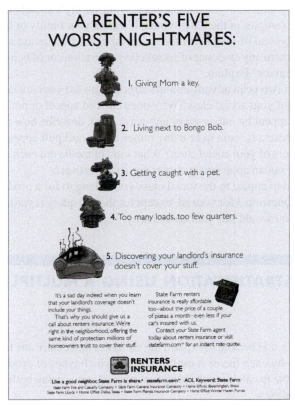

EXERCISE 7.2. SOCIAL CLASS AND YOU

OBJECTIVES

1. To determine which social class in the Coleman-Rainwater Social Class Hierarchy you belong to and to be able to cite evidence for this.
2. To gain insight into how your social class has influenced your CB.
3. To understand how advertisers try to influence you by appealing to your social class characteristics and aspirations.
4. To use your knowledge of your social class to design an ad that would appeal to members of your social class.

BACKGROUND

See the Background section for Exercise 7.1, which provides all the information you will need for this exercise, which is presented only as a written application, not as an in-class application. Although students could discuss their written reports in class, many might find much of it too personal. Therefore, instructor discretion is advised on using this as an in-class application.

WRITTEN APPLICATIONS

1. Which social class described in the Coleman-Rainwater Social Class Hierarchy do you believe best describes you and your family or household? Explain.

Show the descriptions of these social classes to one or more family/household members. Report on whether or not they agree with your assessment and briefly summarize any discussion you have with them about this and anything new you learned about your family's social class and/or CB.

2. Cite some examples of the CB of yourself and/or your family or household members that seem either very typical or atypical of members of your social class. If there are any deviations, why do you suppose that this is so? Is there any evidence of social class aspirations or of being overprivileged or underprivileged in any of this behavior? Explain.

3. Find at least two print advertisements targeted toward your social class. How does each ad try to appeal to members of your social class? Why does each ad appeal or not appeal to you personally? Can each ad's social class appeal be improved in any way? If so, describe how and why.

Do either of these ads seem to be using either an upward pull appeal or an appeal to the over- or underprivileged members of your social class? What kind of media did each ad appear in? Was the media vehicle in which each ad ran an appropriate choice for its advertiser?

4. Create an ad to appeal to the social class you belong to for a product that interests you. Then, answer the questions in Question 3 for your ad, except for the last query regarding media. Instead, explain in which media vehicles you would run your ad and why.

EXERCISE 7.3. SOCIAL STRATIFICATION USING A MULTIPLE-ITEM INDEX

OBJECTIVES

1. To know and be able to explain the variables that contribute to determining an individual's social class, why each factor is useful, and for which types of products each is most valuable.
2. To be able to calculate an individual's social status using both Warner's and Hollingshead's multi-item indexes.
3. To know the advantages of and to figure out the limitations and potential pitfalls in using a multi-item index to measure social class.

BACKGROUND

In this exercise you will find out more about the marketing research variables and research methodologies used to determine the social class of an individual or group of people for purposes of target marketing. You shall see from your experience in using such methods that, while they have the appearance of objectivity because they are quantitative, there are still serious shortcomings that make them more subjective than marketing researchers would wish.

OBJECTIVE MARKETING APPROACHES TO MEASURING SOCIAL CLASS

Marketers determine peoples' social class using the **objective method**, in which researchers collect data on various **socioeconomic status (SES) variables (stratification variables)**. These factors include occupation, education, and amount of income. These are **proxy factors (surrogate variables)** because either separately or combined together they serve as substitute (surrogate) indicators of social status, a complex concept that cannot be fully captured even by combinations of such variables. An objective variable can be used alone as a *single-item index* or in conjunction with several other socioeconomic variables in a *multi-item index*. However, neither alone nor together are they the same thing as socioeconomic status—they are merely measures that approximate status. In all cases, the researcher gathers **primary data**, original data collected for the first time, to learn about peoples' social status. This is usually done using sample surveys, where people fill out a questionnaire asking them to rate themselves on various socioeconomic variables. The researcher then translates this information to a social class standing, as you will do in the Applications section of this exercise. Observational methods are also used for gathering primary data. This might entail driving through a neighborhood or going into homes to check out social class indicators such as living room furniture and other expensive or expressive possessions.

Marketers also use secondary data obtained from research services that supply geodemographic data combining geographic, demographic, and lifestyle statistics to describe micro-regions.

SINGLE-ITEM INDEXES

When you first meet someone, you ask questions such as "What do you do for a living?" "Where do you live?" and "Where did you go to college?" (However, it would violate a cultural norm to ask them about their income!) What you are really doing is gathering information one variable (question) at a time, which will help you, subconsciously perhaps, determine that person's social class. This allows you to see how much they have in common with you.

Single-item indexes estimate social class using a single proxy indicator. However, since social class is a multidimensional concept that comprises multiple components such as education, occupation, source and amount of income, wealth, and location of residence, single-item indexes are usually of limited accuracy in predicting a person's social class.

Single-item indexes are quick and easy to use, and allow one to correlate CB with an important predictor variable. For example, for predicting who attends the theater or art museums or subscribes to intellectual magazines, the single variable "education" might suffice.

KEY SINGLE-ITEM INDEX VARIABLES USED TO DETERMINE SOCIAL CLASS

The following are variables commonly used in single-item indexes. The first three variables—occupation, education, and income—are the most closely associated with social status. They tend to be highly correlated with one another.

Occupation. Occupation is usually the best single indicator of a person's social class because it so highly correlates with most of the other dimensions, notably education and income. Hence, occupation is the most widely used single-item index in consumer research on social class.

Generally, higher-status occupations are defined in terms of ownership and control of the means of production as well as influence over the labor power of others. Various surveys have shown remarkable stability in the prestige ratings people assign to various occupations, both over time and across nations. Rated high are professional and business positions such as physician, scientist, and lawyer. Occupations requiring skilled labor, such as building contractor, medical lab technician, and electrician are ranked in the middle. Unskilled jobs, such as gas station attendant and taxi driver are found near the bottom rung of the social status ladder.

Occupation can be used to locate target customers for self-expressive lifestyle products such as dressy attire, vacations, and hobbies (e.g., playing the piano or collecting artwork). Employment also correlates highly with the purchase of work-related tools of the trade such as pickup trucks, home office products, professional memberships publications, and occupational uniforms.

Education. Schooling is important because it is the major means for achieving upward social mobility. Where and what you learn help determine where and what you earn. Education level is useful for predicting sales of cultural events such as season ballet tickets and classical music performances. It also correlates strongly with the purchase of intellectually-oriented goods such as magazine subscriptions, book club memberships, and educational toys.

Income. Income can be measured at either the personal or household level. It helps determine social status as well as purchasing power. However, income generally does not predict consumption to the same degree as occupation and education. Income level provides the means to live high but is not the main reason for lifestyle product purchases.

Two components of income are:

- *Source of income:* This includes interest on inherited wealth or investments, salary, wages, or government transfer payments.
- *Amount of income:* The dollar amount earned per time period, such as an hourly wage or annual salary plus bonus and stock dividends. Under $25,000 per year puts a household at the bottom rung of the ladder, $50,000 to $100,000 in the middle, and over $200,000 up top.

Many marketers target the upper classes for the same reason Willie Sutton robbed banks—that is where they believe the money (income) is! However, they mistakenly consider income as synonymous with social class. These two variables are not always highly correlated. While incomes do rise moving up through the classes, huge overlaps remain between the incomes of different classes. For example, a school teacher earning $40,000 a year would be middle class, while a brick layer making $70,000 would remain working class despite the earnings differential. Many low-status jobs pay a high income, especially if unionized. Conversely, some high-status occupations offer relatively low incomes. (If you want to earn oodles of money, do not become a college professor!)

The concept of relative occupational class income (Exercise 7.1) supports this lack of equivalence between income and social class. There is a wide range of income within a given social class, which results in the over- and underprivileged within each class. For example, overprivileged middle-class consumers are more likely than their lower-income cohorts to own campers, tractor lawnmowers, and backyard swimming pools.

Income as a single-item predictor variable is best used to forecast sales of expensive, nonnecessity, nonstatus items. Examples are ownership of a washer and drier versus going to the Laundromat, or subscribing to premium cable or satellite TV. Income in conjunction with one or more other socioeconomic variables is required to accurately predict purchases of expensive and expressive items, such as jewelry (Tiffany versus costume jewelry) and make of automobile (Mercedes versus Hyundai).

OTHER SINGLE-ITEM INDEX VARIABLES DETERMINING SOCIAL CLASS

Although occupation, education, and income, either individually or collectively, are the factors most often used to determine social standing, the following socioeconomic variables can also be fruitful for insights into CB.

Amount and Source of Wealth. Do not confuse wealth with income. **Income** is a flow of money—literally, the amount of money regularly coming into a household. **Wealth** entails accumulated economic assets minus liabilities (debts). It is a stock reflecting a lifetime's accumulation of income, investments, and inheritances. Wealth includes liquid assets, such as cash, checking and savings accounts, and mutual funds, as well as nonliquid assets, such as homes and cars. Liabilities include mortgages and unpaid credit card balances. Measurement of wealth includes both the amount and the source of wealth, which can range from inheritance ("old money") down to charity and transfer payments.

Consumer buying power (state-of-wallet) is how much a person can purchase, and it is determined by three variables: (1) wealth, (2) income, and (3) access to credit, enabling borrowing against future earnings or wealth. The credit crisis that began in 2008 greatly hurt marketers of big-ticket items that target consumers of all social classes who had become addicted to easy credit and using their home equity as a piggy bank against which to borrow. For example, tighter credit means fewer car loans and, therefore, fewer car sales. It also means that homeowners do not have easy access to money from refinancing or home equity loans, which impacts sales of durable goods.

Social Interactions/Affiliations. People prefer to associate with "their own kind." As a result, most personal social intercourse occurs with members of one's own social class, although some exchange happens with those of adjacent classes. Interpersonal interactions consist of both individual and social group affiliations, including professional associations, religious institutions, and social organizations. It makes a difference if someone hangs with the gang at the pool hall or at the country club swimming pool.

Material Possessions. Material goods are symbols of success in most societies. They help define social status, notably when these products are **status symbols**. These items are visible, physical representations of membership in, or aspiration to, a particular social class or status group and serve as "badges" of achievement and distinction.

The item that is the greatest indicator of social status in the United States is the home; including its *location* (the "right" or "wrong" side of the tracks, skid row versus the North Shore, gated community versus trailer park) and *house type* (size, style, and condition). Big-ticket items in the home, from furniture to appliances, also count. The acid test of social status is the living room, including furniture and accessories (flooring, drapes, fireplace, etc.) and condition (cleanliness, organization, and general ambience). Other status markers include fine china, sterling silverware, and priceless antiques.

Leisure Activities. The uptown crowd prefers more aristocratic pursuits, such as frequenting the opera; boating (from sailing to yachting); horseback riding; individualistic sports such as tennis, golf, downhill skiing, and scuba diving; and vacations in exotic locales such as the Bahamas or Dubai. The downtown gang prefers attending the roller derby, building models, frequenting taverns, engaging in team sports such as bowling, and vacationing at the homes of friends and relatives.

A major leisure activity for most Americans is enjoying the media. The upper classes watch PBS, listen to NPR, and are heavy consumers of highbrow print media such as *Architectural Digest* and *Washingtonian* magazines. The lower classes enjoy daytime quiz shows, soap operas, talk shows, and "reality" programs. They reader gossip magazines such as *The National Enquirer* and *Soap Opera Digest.*

MULTI-ITEM INDEXES

Generally, an **index measure (composite measure, composite variable, multi-item variable)** is a research measurement combining two or more variables to measure a single concept. Index measures allow for a richer description and usually have better explanatory power than using each of the single variables in isolation. **Multi-item (composite variable) social class index measures** recognize that social class is a multidimensional construct, an amalgamation of several socioeconomic and demographic variables. Such indexes acknowledge that social class is a multidimensional construct affected by all of the factors just examined.

Multi-item measures usually have better explanatory power than single-item indexes. Typically index measures are computed as *weighted averages*—some variables are counted more heavily in calculating the index number because they have greater explanatory power. Two important multi-item indexes to measure social class are the Index of Status Characteristics (ISC) and the Index of Social Position (ISP).

WARNER'S INDEX OF STATUS CHARACTERISTICS (ISC)

Warner's Index of Status Characteristics (ISC), developed by W. Lloyd Warner and his associates in the late 1940s, uses four socioeconomic factors, weighting each one as follows (weights or relative importance values are in parentheses): occupation (4), source of income (3), house type (3), and dwelling area (2).

To compute an individual's ISC score, each weight is multiplied by a person's rating or score on the corresponding variable. The individual's standing on each variable is assigned using a seven-point rating scale ranging from 1 (very high status) to 7 (very low status). (Note: Lower scores indicate higher SES in both of the multi-item indexes discussed in this exercise.)

Exhibit 7.8 summarizes the ranges of scores and weights for Warner's system. The equation to calculate social status is:

$$ISC\ score = (occupation\ rating\ score \times 4) + (source\ of\ income\ score \times 3) +$$
$$(house\ type\ score \times 3) + (dwelling\ area\ score \times 2)$$

Example: Mike R. and Tellie Phone. Suppose we have a small neighborhood convenience store owner, Mike R. Phone, who operates a profitable business and lives with his wife, Tellie, in a modest, three-bedroom house in a typical residential neighborhood. Mike and Tellie feel that they have done well for themselves, considering they left school after eighth grade. Mike's ISC score could be calculated using the following ratings:

Occupation = 5
Source of income = 3
House type = 4
Dwelling area = 4

Using the equation to calculate an ISC score:

$$Mike\ R.\ Phone's\ ISC\ score = (5 \times 4) + (3 \times 3) + (4 \times 3) + (4 \times 2) = 49$$

EXHIBIT 7.8   Weights and Scores for Warner's Index of Status Characteristics (ISC)

Scale item	Description	Score
Occupation Scale (Weight of 4)	Professionals and large business proprietors	1
	Semiprofessionals and officials of large businesses	2
	Clerks and kindred workers	3
	Skilled workers	4
	Proprietors of small businesses	5
	Semiskilled workers	6
	Unskilled workers	7
Source of Income Scale (Weight of 3)	Inherited wealth	1
	Earned wealth	2
	Profits and fees	3
	Salary	4
	Wages	5
	Private relief	6
	Public relief and nonrespectable income	7
House Type Scale (Weight of 3)	Excellent houses	1
	Very good houses	2
	Good houses	3
	Average houses	4
	Fair houses	5
	Poor houses	6
	Very poor houses	7
Dwelling Area Scale (Weight of 2)	Very high: Gold Coast, North Shore, etc.	1
	High: the better suburbs and apartment house areas, houses with spacious yards	2
	Above average: areas all residential, space around houses, apartment areas in good condition	3
	Average: residential neighborhoods, no deterioration in the area	4
	Below average: area not quite holding its own, beginning to deteriorate, business entering	5
	Low: considerably deteriorated, run-down, and semi-slum	6
	Very low: slum	7

The last step is to convert this ISC score to a social status level by using the scale provided in Exhibit 7.9. This figure divides individuals into one of six social status groups and shows the percent of the population Warner found in each of these six social classes. The Phone family's score of 49 translates to the lower-middle class.

Hollingshead Index of Social Position (ISP)

The **Hollingshead Index of Social Position (ISP)** is a two-item index that was created by August Hollingshead in the 1950s. It uses two variables: occupation (weighted 7) and education (weighted 4). Exhibit 7.10 summarizes the weighting and scoring system for the ISP.

The equation for figuring someone's SES employing the Hollingshead ISP is:

$$ISP\ score = (occupation\ score \times 7) + (education\ score \times 4)$$

For example, we can calculate the Hollingshead ISP score for Mike and Tellie Phone as follows:

$$ISP\ score = (3 \times 7) + (6 \times 4) = 45$$

Exhibit 7.11 shows the five social class categories for Hollingshead ISP scores. The Phone family's ISP score of 45 puts them solidly in the middle class.

EXHIBIT 7.9 Social Class Categories for Warner ISC Scores

ISC Score	Social Class Equivalent	Population Breakdown
12–17	Upper-upper class	1.4%
18–24	Lower-upper class	1.6%
25–37	Upper-middle class	10.2%
38–50	Lower-middle class	28.8%
51–62	Upper-lower class	33.0%
63–84	Lower-lower class	25.0%

EXHIBIT 7.10 Weights and Scores for Hollingshead's Index of Social Position (ISP)

Scale item	Description	Score
Occupation Scale (Weight of 7)	Higher executives of large concerns, proprietors, and major professionals	1
	Business managers, proprietors of medium-sized businesses, and lesser professionals	2
	Administrative personnel, owners of small businesses, and minor professionals	3
	Clerical and sales workers, technicians, and owners of little businesses	4
	Skilled manual employees	5
	Machine operators and semiskilled employees	6
	Unskilled employees	7
Education Scale (Weight of 4)	Professional (M.A., M.S., M.E., M.D., Ph.D., LL.B., and the like)	1
	Four-year college graduate	2
	One to three years college (also business schools)	3
	High school graduate	4
	Ten to 11 years of school (part high school)	5
	Seven to nine years of school	6
	Less than seven years of school	7

EXHIBIT 7.11 Social Class Categories for Hollingshead ISP Scores

ISP Score	Social Class Equivalent
11–17	Upper class
18–31	Upper-middle class
32–47	Middle class
48–63	Lower-middle class
64–77	Lower class

OTHER POPULAR MULTI-ITEM INDEXES

Although you will not work with them in this exercise, there are several other multi-item indexes used to determine people's social class. The **Census Bureau's Index of Socioeconomic Status** is a three-factor social status index using occupation, income, and education. It produces four social class categories: upper (15.1 percent of the population), upper-middle (34.5 percent), middle (34.1 percent), and lower-middle (16.3 percent). Another multi-item index, the **Computerized Status Index (CSI),** combines education, occupation, area of residence, and income.

By now you might be wondering: "Which index should be used?" As with single-item indexes, the answer depends on which variables would best seem to logically explain purchase and use of a marketer's product. For example, an intellectually oriented product, such as a visit to an art museum, might require the Hollingshead ISP rather than the Warner's ISC since the former includes education but the latter excludes this variable.

Review Questions

1. Outline the major consumer research techniques used to measure social status.
2. What are the three most commonly used single-item index variables for assessing people's social class? In what circumstances is each most useful and for what types of products is each best employed?
3. Describe the nature and use of multi-item indexes in general and, in particular, of Warner's and Hollingshead's social class indexes.
4. What are the major limitations in using a multi-item index for measuring social class?

In-Class Applications

1. Evaluate the social class of your family or household using the Warner ISC and Hollingshead ISP. Also, assess your family's social status on each of the single-item index variables that do not appear in these two multi-item indexes.

    Has this information changed your perception of your social class from what you believed it was using the Coleman-Rainwater classification scheme in Exercise 7.2? If so, does it now better agree with what other family members told you about your family's social class in Exercise 7.2? Does it better predict your CB than the Coleman-Rainwater classification system? Explain.
2. Answer questions (a) through (e) below based on the information provided for each of the individuals in the scenarios that follow. Then answer summary question (f).
    a. Compute each person's social class using both Warner's ISC and Hollingshead's ISP. Be sure to show all calculations.
    b. Discuss any differences you made in the assignment of individuals to social classes with the Warner and Hollingshead indexes. What are the implications of any discrepancies for marketing decision making?
    c. Compare your classifications of each individual using both indexes with those of your classmates. What are the marketing implications of these discrepancies?
    d. Cite as many socioeconomic variables as you can that could be used to determine each individual's social status but that are not used in either of these two indexes. Describe each person's social status on each of these variables. How does this additional information alter your perception of each person's social class, if any, from that found using the multi-item indexes?
    e. What is your overall conclusion regarding each person's social class?

       Describe a marketing program that could be created for one of these individuals by knowing the likely CB of a typical member of his or her social class.
       → *Scenario A. Take a Look at Nan.* Nan is an optometrist employed by Good Vision Eye Care. Her annual salary is $120,000. Nan lives in a swank top-floor penthouse suite she purchased on Manhattan's Upper East Side. This location is what PRIZM (a marketing research firm) calls an "Urban Gold Coast" neighborhood—one with high median household incomes, populated by individuals aged eighteen to twenty-four and sixty-five or older, and dotted with urban upscale high-rises.

       Nan's penthouse has three bedrooms, a living room, kitchen, two baths, a wet bar, and a safe where she stores the $1.5 million dollars she has earned from working the past twenty years and the $2.5 million she inherited from her now dearly departed, wealthy Uncle Tom. Nan is a member of both the Manhattan Conservative Baptist Church and the Upper East Side Optical Society. She has been living in New York City since she graduated three years ago from the Jefferson Davis School of Optometry in Richmond, Virginia. She enjoys shooting pool (and the breeze!) at the Urban Gold Coast Bar & Grill and betting at the New Yack dog track.
       → *Scenario B. Manuel Laber—Hard at Work.* Manuel Laber works on an automotive assembly line installing spark plugs, earning $7.50 per hour. He lives in a poor black ghetto in downtown Detroit, where he shares a bathroom and kitchen with three other people in the rundown, one-room apartment he rents. Last year, Manuel earned a master's degree in business administration from the University of Michigan, but he subsequently decided that the management profession was not for him.

Mr. Laber is a member of the Ann Arbor Kiwanis Club and of the Pitch N' Putt Country Club, where he tees off every Saturday morning, weather permitting. He takes pride in pulling into these organizations' parking lots in his spiffy new BMW.

→ *Scenario C. A Not-So-Beautiful Mind.* From his ratty appearance, you would not have a clue that Sonny Dillon is a professor at Wotza Matta U, an Ivy League university. After all, he looks like a bum—not unclean, just a mess, all slovenly, wrinkled, and unkempt. However, he has a brilliant mind, is a real firecracker in the classroom, writes research reports for the top-tier academic journals, and is active as president of the All-Star Academic Society, so the school lets him stay.

With his handsome endowed chair's salary you would expect him to live in a really nice house, but Sonny chooses to live in a flophouse hotel room and grabs his meals from the local greasy spoon where he hangs out with his buddies. The students think he is crazy to live there—you would not want to drive your car through the neighborhood, even with all the car windows rolled up!

They say Professor Dillon does not have two pennies to rub together because he gives away most of his salary to his needy neighbors and financially struggling students. Although students consider him cool, they also think he's a little off!

f. Based on your experiences in quantifying individuals' social classes using the Warner and Hollingshead multi-item indexes, cite the various problems you find with using so-called objective measures of a person's social class. Can you think of solutions for any of these problems?

WRITTEN APPLICATION

1. Complete the In-Class Applications questions for Exercise 7.3, excluding Question 2c.

KEY CONCEPTS

aspirational brand
caste system
Census Bureau's Index of Socioeconomic Status
class average
class system
Coleman-Rainwater social standing (social class)
    hierarchy
Computerized Status Index (CSI)
consumer buying power (state-of-wallet)
Hollingshead Index of Social Position (ISP)
income
index measure (composite measure, composite variable,
    multi-item variable)
lower Americans
lower-lower
lower-upper
middle Americans
middle class
multi-item (composite variable) social class indexes
nouveau riche
objective method
overprivileged
primary data
proxy factors (surrogate variables)

relative income hypothesis
relative occupational class income (ROCI)
single-item indexes
social class (societal rank)
social mobility
social stratification
socioeconomic status (SES; social status)
socioeconomic status (SES) variables (stratification
    variables)
status symbols
stratum (pl. strata)
subjective social class
trade up
two-tier marketing
underprivileged
upper Americans
upper-lower
upper-middle
upper-upper
upward pull strategy
upward social mobility
Warner's Index of Status Characteristics (ISC)
wealth
working class

SUMMARY

The social class system is founded on the concept of social stratification based on socioeconomic status. A society can be stratified via the caste system, where social prestige is ascribed, formally defined, objectively assigned, and closed to social mobility, or the class system, where social status is achieved, informally defined, subjectively assigned, and open to social mobility.

In order to stratify people in a class system we use social class. Exercise 7.1 described the use of social class as a market segmentation variable. Social class provides a useful basis for segmentation because members of a given social class often share common demographics, ways of thinking, lifestyles, and behaviors. Some consumers display their social status via conspicuous consumption.

There is a trend toward two-tier marketing. Knowledge of a targeted social class enables marketers to formulate a product position and brand image consistent with the actual or desired lifestyle of target market members. All elements of the marketing mix are chosen based on this knowledge.

There are two complicating factors that cause marketers to target at least two social classes simultaneously with one marketing program: upward social mobility and relative occupational class income.

Many consumers have a subjective social class. To climb the social ladder, many buyers trade up. Using an upward pull strategy, a marketer positions a brand as an aspirational brand. Hence, marketers do not always target their marketing programs toward their customers' current social class but rather toward their social class aspirations.

Relative occupational class income results in further segmentation of a class into the overprivileged, the underprivileged, and class average families. The relative income hypothesis says that the overprivileged and underprivileged have purchasing patterns that often differ from others in their social class due to their dissimilar relative income: the overprivileged buy like those in the class above them and the underprivileged like those in the social category below them.

Most class societies can be characterized as having three broad classes—upper, middle, and lower—and these people are said to be upscale, midscale, and downscale, respectively. However, classification schemes do differ. A commonly used system is the Coleman-Rainwater Social Standing Hierarchy, which describes three general groupings encompassing seven social classes: (1) upper Americans (upper-upper, lower-upper, including the nouveau riche, and upper-middle), (2) middle Americans (middle class, including traditionalists and nontraditionalists, and working class), and (3) lower Americans (upper-lower and lower-lower).

Exercise 7.2 encouraged you to apply your knowledge of social classes from Exercise 7.1 to understand your own personal social class situation and how this influences your CB.

In Exercise 7.3, the research variables and methodologies for investigating peoples' social class were investigated. Marketers use objective methods employing socioeconomic status (SES) variables such as occupation, education, and amount of income. These are proxy factors serving as substitute indicators for the very complex concept of social status. An objective variable can be used alone as a single-item index or in conjunction with several other socioeconomic variables as a multi-item index.

Primary data collection methods, including sample surveys and observational techniques, can be used to learn about peoples' social status. Also useful is secondary data, such as that provided by research services supplying geodemographic data.

Single-item indexes are usually less accurate in predicting social class than are multi-item indexes, but they are quicker and easier to use, allowing correlation of CB with an important predictor variable. The most often used single-item index variables are all achieved, not ascribed. Especially used here are occupation, education, and income, all highly interrelated.

Occupation is generally viewed as the best single proxy indicator of a person's social class because it so highly correlates with most of the social class dimensions. Occupation can be used to locate target customers for self-expressive lifestyle products and for occupation-related goods. Education is important because it is the major means for achieving upward social mobility and is useful for predicting sales of taste-oriented activities and of intellectually oriented goods.

Income (personal or household) entails both source of income and amount of income. Income is not the same as social class because, while incomes do rise moving up through the classes, there remain huge overlaps between the incomes of different classes. Supporting this lack of equivalence between income and social class is the concept of relative occupational class income. Income alone is best used to forecast sales of expensive, nonnecessity, nonstatus items. Income in conjunction with one or more other socioeconomic variables is required to best predict purchases of expensive and expressive items. Other socioeconomic variables useful for insights into social class and CB include wealth, consumer buying power, personal and social group affiliations, material possessions (especially those used as status symbols), and leisure activities.

Multi-item social class indexes use index measures, which combine two or more variables to measure a single concept, allowing for a richer description and having better explanatory power than each of the single variables of which it is comprised taken alone. Usually index measures are computed as weighted averages.

Two multi-item indexes to measure social class are Warner's Index of Status Characteristics (ISC) and the Hollingshead Index of Social Position (ISP). To compute an individual's ISC score, each weight is multiplied by a person's rating on the corresponding variable using the formula: ISC score = (occupation rating score × 4) + (source of income score × 3) + (house type score × 3) + (dwelling area score × 2). The individual's standing on each variable is assigned using a seven-point rating scale, from 1 (very high status) to 7 (very low status). Exhibit 7.8 summarizes the ranges of scores and weights. The resulting score is then converted to a social class standing by using the categories provided in Exhibit 7.9.

The Hollingshead ISP is a two-item index. Exhibit 7.10 summarizes the weighting and scoring system for the ISP. Exhibit 7.11 provides the social class categories for the calculated ISP scores using the formula: ISP score = (occupation score × 7) + (education score × 4).

There are several other multi-item indexes used to determine people's social class. The Census Bureau's Index of Socioeconomic Status is a three-factor social status index that is based on occupation, income, and education. The Computerized Status Index combines education, occupation, area of residence, and income.

To choose the most appropriate multi-item index, one must consider which variables best explain purchase and use of a marketer's product. By working through the applications in Exercise 7.3, you figured out the shortcomings of using these "objective," multi-item indexes.

REFERENCES

Coleman, Richard P. (1983). "The Continuing Significance of Social Class to Marketing." *Journal of Consumer Research,* 10, 3, 265–280.

Coleman, Richard P., and Rainwater, Lee. (1978). *Standing in America: New Dimensions of Class.* New York: Basic Books.

Hauser, Robert M., and Featherman, David L. (1977). *The Process of Stratification.* New York: The Academic Press.

Henry, Paul. (2002). "Systematic Variation in Purchase Orientations." *Journal of Consumer Marketing,* 19, 5, 424–438.

Hollingshead, August B., and Redlich, Fredrick C. (1958). *Social Class and Mental Illness: A Community Study.* New York: Wiley.

Lenski, Gerhard E. (1954). "Status Crystallization: A Non-Vertical Dimension of Social Status." *American Sociological Review,* 19 (August), 405–412.

Martinueau, Pierre. (1958). "Social Classes and Spending Behavior." *Journal of Marketing,* 23, 4, 121–129.

Munson, J. Michael, and Spivet, Austin W. (1981). "Product and Brand-User Stereotypes among Social Classes." *Journal of Advertising Research,* 21, 4, 37–46.

Myers, James H., and Mount, John F. (1973). "More on Social Class vs. Income as Correlates of Buyer Behavior." *Journal of Marketing,* 37, 2, 71–73.

Peters, William H. (1970). "Relative Occupational Class Income: A Significant Variable in the Marketing of Automobiles," *Journal of Marketing,* 34, 2, 74–77.

Schaninger, Charles M. (1981). "Social Class versus Income Revisited: An Empirical Investigation." *Journal of Marketing Research,* 18, 2, 192–208.

Silverstein, Michael J., and Fiske, Neil. (2003). *Trading Up: The New American Luxury.* New York: Penguin Books.

Sivadas, Eugene, Mathew, George, and Curry, David J. (1997). "A Preliminary Examination of the Continuing Significance of Social Class to Marketing: A Geodemographic Replication." *Journal of Consumer Marketing,* 14, 6, 463–479.

Warner, W. Lloyd, Meeker, Marchia, and Eells, Kenneth. (1949). *Social Class in America: A Manual of Procedure for the Measurement of Social Status.* Chicago: Scientific Research Associates.

REFERENCE GROUPS AND SOCIAL INFLUENCES

Personal social influences are important because people are social creatures and are made for relationships with one another. From the earliest chapters of Genesis we read that it is not good for people to be lone rangers; we need community. Poet John Donne said, "No man is an island, entire of itself; every man is a piece of the continent, a part of the main." As social animals, individuals inevitably and naturally collect into social groups, such as in bars, golf clubs, civic clubs, and faith communities, much as primitive people congregated into tribes. Because people feel most comfortable with others who are similar to themselves, "like" tends to group with "like" (i.e., "birds of a feather flock together").

SOCIAL GROUPS, SOCIAL AGGREGATES, AND SOCIAL CATEGORIES

This chapter concerns the influence on buying behavior of the **social group**—a set of individuals who regularly interact to satisfy common needs or accomplish individual or mutual goals, and who share views regarding norms, values, or beliefs. This definition highlights three characteristics of a social group: regular interaction, common goals, and shared ideology.

1. Regular ongoing interaction and interdependence. Group members influence each other's thinking and behavior. There is a sense of community; a feeling of group membership or of belonging within the group, ideally a feeling of "sharing and caring." Group members have certain implicitly or explicitly defined relationships. Their behaviors are interdependent and they have mutually interlocking roles.
2. Common individual or mutual goals or needs and wants. Social group objectives include survival, accomplishing work, providing solace and comfort for one another, entertaining and relaxing with members, sharing information, and establishing friendships.
3. A shared ideology of values, beliefs, attitudes, and norms. Group members are "of one mind" in ways that are important to the group and its individual participants. This social tie that binds helps maintain the group's **cohesiveness,** or the degree to which social group participants are bonded through a shared ideology. Where necessary, the shared belief system also ensures **conformity,** a change in a group member's beliefs, attitudes, or actions as a reaction to real or perceived group pressure. Young people are especially likely to conform.

Using these three criteria, one can conclude that a bunch of people milling around at a sporting event or in a shopping mall would not constitute a social group. They will never be together again as a group, do not share mutual goals, and have no common ideology (other than, perhaps, liking the place where they are congregating). Such a crowd is a **social aggregate**, a bunch of people who have nothing in common except temporarily occupying the same time and place.

Also, do not confuse a social group with a **social category**, in which aggregates of persons share common status demographically, socioeconomically, psychologically, and/or behaviorally (i.e., such as subcultures and social classes). Mothers, Roman Catholics, working class people, and sports car owners are all social categories, but they fail to meet our three criteria for being social groups.

The manner in which social groups function and how their members influence one another is studied by **sociologists**—social scientists who investigate sociology—and **social psychologists**—social scientists who study social psychology.

REFERENCE GROUPS AND REFERENCE PEOPLE

Of all the various types of social groups, marketers are most interested in the **reference group**, a social group used as a reference point or frame of reference for shaping an individual's thinking (especially goals and ideology) and behavior. Similarly significant is the **reference person (reference other, reference figure, or significant other)**. A reference person is an influential individual used as a reference point or frame of reference for shaping someone's thinking and behavior.

A reference person usually symbolizes or represents a reference group and embodies key attributes of the group, serving as a model member of that group. He or she is respected and admired, and projects an image that people can either *identify* with or *emulate* (aspire to be like).

Reference people used by advertisers include:

- *Celebrities:* well-known individuals, such as sports icons, TV and film stars, authors, and political and religious leaders. Many consumers emulate such persons because they admire them.
- The *common man or typical consumer:* everyday, ordinary consumers whom target market members can identify with and trust. People most readily relate to those in their own social category, classified by the key demographic variables of age and sex (e.g., young men).
- *Experts:* people "in the know" by virtue of education, training, or experience. They are therefore considered credible as long as they are also seen as trustworthy. Examples include professional service providers, chefs (for food items), and company executives or employees.

ORGANIZATION OF CHAPTER 8

The three exercises in this chapter focus on the CB influence of reference groups and reference persons. Exercise 8.1 describes the various types of reference groups to which marketers can appeal. You will examine the social groups you belong to or aspire to join and how they influence your CB. Exercise 8.2 explores the various types of reference group influence that marketers use, while Exercise 8.3 demonstrates how marketers tap into various types of social power to influence CB.

EXERCISE 8.1. TYPES OF REFERENCE GROUPS

OBJECTIVES

1. To provide insight into how and when social groups affect buyer behavior.
2. To identify the different types of reference groups and their influence on CB.
3. To demonstrate how marketers can tap into the various types of reference groups in order to affect marketplace behavior.
4. To investigate on your own reference groups and their influence on your CB.

BACKGROUND

Most of us are members of multiple social groups. As a college student, you might belong to a family, friendship cliques, a dorm or group of apartment mates, a sports team, student organizations, and a religious congregation. As you read about the different types of social groups in this exercise, keep in mind your own groups and their influence on you and your CB.

There are three ways reference groups can influence your CB. First, they can affect what you buy. For instance, families sway what children eat for breakfast and watch on television. Friends recommend what movies to see and the brands of DVD players their peers should buy. Second, many products are purchased to achieve a sense of belonging or to make a statement about who we are, both as individuals and as members of social groups. Starbucks is less about coffee and more about a community—a cool place to hang out, sip joe, and socialize. You might buy a Putztown University sweatshirt to exhibit your PU affiliation or a T-shirt to signify your loyalty to your fraternity, Tappa Kegga Beer. Third, group members sometimes make joint decisions. Coworkers decide what radio station to play at work, friends determine where to go on spring break together, or a romantic couple chooses which restaurant to patronize on their next date.

CHARACTERISTICS OF PRODUCTS AFFECTED BY REFERENCE GROUPS

The following are characteristics of products most likely to be influenced by reference groups. In almost all cases, there is a high level of product involvement.

- Socially visible or conspicuous products that are publicly consumed are high in perceived social risk. These products are often bought to make statements about who we are or to which groups we belong. Examples include clothing, sporty cars, cosmetics, and furniture. Reference groups especially influence *brand choices* for conspicuous items (as opposed to *product choices*). This is due to the importance of brand image—a mental impression reflecting the brand's personality. A classy woman will want a handbag made by the likes of Louis Vuitton, Prada, or Gucci.
- Luxuries or nonnecessities are expensive products that are not affordable for many people and therefore connote status. Uniqueness of ownership occurs for items such as expensive consumer electronic devices, pricey jewelry, and recreational vehicles.
- For private luxuries, social group influence is strongest for deciding whether or not to acquire the *product,* rather than choosing a particular *brand.* Product ownership connotes exclusivity but the brand for private luxuries remains hidden from public view. However, reference groups do influence brand choices for public luxuries, or nonnecessities consumed in public. For example, some brands, such as Coach handbags, Calloway golf clubs, and Mercedes-Benz cars, ooze luxury. On the other hand, private necessities such as soap powder and paper goods lack conspicuous brands. Consequently, reference group influence is minimal for these products.
- There are some products about which buyers lack confidence in their ability to make an informed decision, such as insurance, health care, and other professional services. Consequently, people look to reference groups or reference persons for buying assistance.
- Products that are relevant to the group are influenced by reference groups. For a church, the choice of a version of the Bible would be high in group influence but selection of an alcoholic beverage would be irrelevant.

Exhibit 8.1 summarizes the influence of reference groups for products and brands based on distinguishing necessities from luxuries and private consumer goods from public consumer goods.

TYPES OF SOCIAL GROUPS

In order to better understand how marketers capitalize on social group influence, it is helpful to be familiar with the different types of social groups identified by sociologists. These groups are classified by membership, type of contact, formality of structure, and nature of attraction.

1. GROUPS CLASSIFIED BY MEMBERSHIP

Membership Groups. **Membership groups** are social groups to which an individual belongs, that is, he or she has achieved formal or informal acceptance by the group. Advertisers can demonstrate their product being consumed by such groups and display how their wares can help one to fit in. Marketers also create membership "clubs" based on their brand as a type of relationship marketing, such as Burger King's Kids' Club and hotel "clubs," which allow access to specific floors that feature perks such as restricted key-card access. Some membership groups are composed of people with an interest in a product, such as the Conservative Book Club. **Brand communities** are groups of consumers who feel a common bond or shared purpose associated

EXHIBIT 8.1   Reference Group Influence on Publicly and Privately Consumed Luxuries and Necessities

Where the product is consumed

	In private	In public	
Necessity	**Private Necessities** Examples: Mattress, canned peaches, refrigerator, toilet paper, deodorant, hot water heater	**Public Necessities** Examples: Wristwatch, car, cell phone, shoes, shirts, blouses	**Low**
Luxury	**Private Luxuries** Examples: Hot tub, Blu-Ray player, wine cellar, designer clothes, original artwork	**Public Luxuries** Examples: Digital camera, jewelry, private jet, designer handbag, yacht	**High**
	Low	High	

Type of product (left axis)

Reference group influence on product choice (right axis)

Reference group influence on brand choice

with a consumer product. Harley-Davidson established the million-member Harley Owners Group (HOG) in response to Harley-Davidson owners' desire to share their passion and show their pride through group events, such as attending HOG rallies and wearing branded Harley motorcycle clothing.

Nonmembership Groups. **Nonmembership groups** are social groups to which a person does not belong but might qualify to join. A subtype of the nonmembership group category is the **aspiration group**, which possesses a positive attraction that causes people to want to join, such as business administration students longing to join the ranks of successful business entrepreneurs.

An **anticipatory aspiration group** is an aspiration group that a person hopes and *expects* to join, such as college students becoming college alumni or entry-level business neophytes eventually turning into senior executives. Marketers appeal to consumers' hopes and dreams to join such groups by associating usage of their product with climbing to the top, often using an upward social mobility message, such as "dressing for success" in the business world.

Symbolic reference groups are nonmembership groups that an individual admires but does not expect to qualify to join. A sports fan might purchase a sports jersey with a team logo to symbolize her identification with the group. Celebrity-studded advertising plays on some peoples' unrealistic dreams to be like their superstar heroes. Other ads playing off symbolic reference groups use idealized "everyday" people and situations, for example, impossibly handsome guys and gorgeous gals into whom we can presumably be magically transformed if we buy and use the promoted brand.

2. GROUPS CLASSIFIED BY TYPE OF CONTACT

Contact type refers to the level of interpersonal contact between group members. Generally, as group size increases interpersonal contact decreases.

Primary Groups. **Primary groups** are contact groups characterized by *small size*, which allows for frequent interpersonal contact on a one-on-one basis, as occurs within families and among good friends; and a *highly shared ideology*, with members valuing each other's ideals, opinions, and beliefs, as often occurs within families and among roommates. Primary groups are quite influential on CB.

Secondary Groups. Traits of **secondary groups** are *large size.* Face-to-face interaction is more sporadic and less comprehensive, which leads to the formation of smaller primary groups—such as Sunday school groups within very large church congregations or work teams within a big corporation—and a *less strongly shared ideology.* Secondary groups are less influential on members' thoughts and actions than primary groups and are therefore less useful to marketers (e.g., a labor union trying to influence members' political ideologies).

Virtual Groups. **Virtual groups (virtual communities, online communities, cybercommunities, social media)** are interactive media outlets containing *user-generated content,* in which consumers can comment on or contribute to the medium's content or one another's comments, thereby building community. These Internet forum slack face-to-face relationships; rather, there is indirect but usually frequent interaction via techniques such as blogging and chatting. Content can be submitted and updated quickly, and content providers can receive consumer feedback in real time. For instance, in iVillage's chat rooms, users have formed groups on everything from fertility and parenting to fitness and nutrition.

Social networking sites, such as Facebook and MySpace, are online communities in which consumers can comment on or contribute to the medium's content and interact. Users create their own pages, where they post information on their interests, favorite games, movies, and even brands, as well as search for others with similar interests.

Social networking sites help members accomplish personal and career goals. These sites are broader in scope than earlier online networks, such as AOL chat rooms and Yahoo! member groups. Major sites bring chat, home pages, photos, and file sharing under one virtual roof with an easy interface. In these general interest community centers, primarily young people post personal information, make "friends" online, and blog about breakups or Friday night plans or comment on current events.

There are also many age-targeted sites. These include sites for wee ones, such as Webkinz.com (a place to interact with other kids online); tweens (ages eight to twelve), such as ClubPenguin (a place for kids to explore, play games, and learn basic computer skills safely) and tweenland (youngsters can create personal pages with videos, photos, and blogs, most with strict parental controls); and oldsters, such as Winster.com (a game-oriented site for female baby boomers) and Eons.com (described as MySpace for boomers).

Other sites are targeted toward specific groups such as college students (Bebo); ethnic groups (Black-Planet, MiGente, and Asian Avenue, aimed at blacks, Hispanics, and Asians, respectively); social activists (Care2, TakingITGlobal); businesspeople (LinkedIn, Ryze); mothers (Clubmom, Newbaby.com); lefties (both left-handed people and political leftists); and product hobbyists from gardening to golf (auto enthusiasts use CarDomain and carspace.com, and photo sharers go to Flickr).

Marketers generate buzz by posting status updates announcing sales promotions, special events, and the like, and creating fun brand profiles (profile pages) on mass social networking sites like MySpace and Facebook. Brand communities are of two types: commercially sponsored brand communities and consumer-driven brand communities. **Commercially sponsored brand communities** are set up by companies as "relationship-building" Web sites. Here, people can leave postings about themselves and the brands, become a brand fan, get information, play games, get tools, read blogs, receive special insider offers, and so on. Visitors can leave e-mail addresses, which firms then use for communications. Members post questions for each other and leave advice. At mycoke.com you can "Meet friends, make music, and perform" with the help of music- and video-sharing software. Here, visitors can write about their favorite bands, mix and share music, upload short videos, and rack up points for free Coke products. Sheraton.com invites travelers to share trip photos, commentary, and videos. Kellogg's and Jenny Craig both host online support groups for women trying to lose weight.

The brand profile pages on such sites, where people can be made aware via offline ads, allow marketers to promote their brand with photos, customer reviews, and so on; make sales; provide information; and offer branded applications such as ringtones that users can add to their own pages. For example, American Eagle Outfitter's MySpace page is mostly an ad for the youth-oriented clothing chain, but it also features discussion forums that cover topics from fashion to store employment.

By monitoring the conversations in branded virtual communities, marketers garner special insights into consumer needs and desires. Procter & Gamble's beinggirl.com is a teen community site where teen girls can get product advice from experts in women's health, users' opinions, participate in polls, and otherwise stay "plugged in." P&G thereby gathers data and tests new products.

However, building interactive relationships with consumers on such sites requires marketers to yield control and take risks. Consequently, marketers must closely monitor the sites for lewd images and profanity. Nonetheless, leaving critical posts up lends credibility. A well-known case involved Chevrolet's make-your-own-ad site for its Tahoe SUV. Several visitors created ads criticizing its fuel use, circulating them on the Internet. Chevrolet did not censor these sentiments.

Companies are also establishing wikis, Web sites that allows visitors to make changes, contributions, or corrections. Examples include eBay, which allows users to write answers to frequently asked questions, and T-Mobile's Sidekick wiki, a forum for users to tell others how to get more out of their T-Mobile phones.

In addition to company-sponsored brand communities, there are also **consumer-driven brand communities,** social networking sites about brands created by consumers such as NissanClub, created by a Nissan loyalist for the brand's buffs to post pictures, find parts, and chat about upcoming designs. For any type of virtual group, the Internet allows for a less inhibited information flow since there is no face-to-face contact and because people feel more comfortable writing certain things than saying them. Although negative and even ugly comments are at times posted, marketers must accept this as part of the Web culture.

Indirect Reference Groups. **Indirect reference groups** are reference groups or persons with whom a person lacks face-to-face contact. Nonetheless, the individual can observe and thus be influenced by these reference people. Usually, they are celebrities, politicians, or other public personalities. Indirect reference groups can also include people "on the street," such as well-dressed individuals at a public outing.

3. GROUPS CLASSIFIED BY FORMALITY OF STRUCTURE

This dimension concerns whether the organization's structure is explicitly spelled out (formal groups) or only implicitly known (informal groups).

Formal Groups. **Formal groups** have a formal, explicit organization, usually defined in writing, and possibly including a charter, regular meeting times, and officers or positions. Specific roles exist for the various positions, such as leading meetings and collecting dues. Organizational goals are explicitly stated. There is also generally a list of members and membership requirements. Examples include business work groups, community service organizations' volunteer teams, alumni associations, business clubs, and tenant organizations. Some products advertise their use by such groups, such as Lotus Notes assisting employee work groups. Some formal groups brand themselves, as in college-branded T-shirts, coffee mugs, and affinity (branded) credit cards.

Informal Groups. **Informal groups** have implicit rather than explicit positions, roles, and goals. They are usually either socially based or founded on common interests. Examples include family, friendship cliques, and shopping, sports, and donation groups. Often advertisements portray such groups using the advertised product, such as good friends socializing with a soft drink.

4. GROUPS CLASSIFIED BY ATTRACTION OR INFLUENCE

This dimension refers to the desirability that membership or association within a particular group has for an individual. The possibilities are contactual, disclaimant, and dissociative groups.

Contactual Groups. **Contactual groups** are membership groups that people are proud of, such as sports teams, health clubs, or college chapters of the American Marketing Association. Marketers emphasize the social acceptance of their products by such groups and how their wares can help one better accommodate oneself to the group, such as owning the "right" tennis racket for a tennis club. Merchandise exhibiting an organization's logo appeals to contactual groups.

Disclaimant Groups. **Disclaimant groups** are negative membership groups whose ideology the individual rejects. A drug user could decide to abandon his drug-using pals. Insensitive parents might force their unwilling youngster to join the Future Violinists of America.

Demarketing (unselling, conversional marketing) involves "unselling" products or behaviors associated with a membership group whom the marketer wishes to turn into a disclaimant group. In effect, the message is, "Leave the group!" One common approach to creating negative demand is to reposition socially undesirable or unhealthy behaviors that teenagers' and young adults' peers might regard as "cool" as actually being "uncool" things they should disclaim, such as smoking, drinking, drug use, and "casual sex." By using this approach, the Partnership for a Drug-Free America has claimed some success in de-glamorizing drugs.

Dissociative Groups. **Dissociative groups (avoidance groups)** are negative nonmembership groups whose values the individual rejects and with which the person wishes to avoid association. Marketers affiliated with the negative group, product, or behavior can try to make it acceptable or even glamorous. For example, in the 1960s, when motorcycles had a negative "Hell's Angels" persona, Honda successfully changed their product's image by declaring, "You meet the nicest people on a Honda." An opposite strategy is to try to maintain or increase the negative image of harmful behaviors, as was done by the public service campaigns "Don't drink and drive" and "Give a hoot, don't pollute."

REVIEW QUESTIONS

1. What are the three key characteristics of a social group? How do social groups differ from social aggregates and social categories?
2. What are reference groups and reference persons? What types of reference persons do marketers use?
3. Describe three general situations where reference groups influence CB.
4. For what types of products is reference group influence most potent?
5. Describe the four classification criteria for social groups, the types of groups classified along these criteria, and which of these groups are most useful for marketers and how marketers use them.

IN-CLASS APPLICATIONS

1. a. To which social groups do you feel the greatest sense of loyalty? Why are you loyal to them?
   b. Describe each group you listed in 1a with respect to the three defining characteristics of social groups: interaction, common needs and goals, and shared ideology.
   c. Classify each of your social groups according to the four classification criteria: your membership in each, the type of contact you have, the formality of the group's structure, and the nature of your attraction to the group.
   d. Describe which of these groups has had an influence on your purchase behavior and the nature of this influence. Also, describe any instances where you recall marketers trying to use reference group influence using social groups similar to your own groups. How effective do you believe the marketer's influence attempt was in each instance?
2. In each of the following scenarios:
   a. Explain whether the group described is a social group, social aggregate, or social category. If it is a social group, explain how it fulfills the three defining characteristics of a social group. If it isn't a social group, explain how it fails to fulfill one or more of these criteria.
   b. For those groups that are social groups, explain whether each is a primary group or secondary group, as well as a formal group or an informal group.
   c. For those groups that are social groups, describe a reference person who could be effectively used by advertisers to appeal to members of the group.
      → *Scenario A. Fields of Soccer Dads.* Stu, Graham, and Phil are three "soccer dads" who coach their children's soccer teams. They see one another every Saturday during the fall soccer season at the Mudville soccer fields. After most games, they get together to trade stories about how the kids on their teams are performing.
      → *Scenario B. Moms at the 'Mat.* Fanny, Mel, and Gerri are three busy married mothers who all met one sunny Saturday morning last year while doing laundry at the Laundromat. They hit it off nicely with one another, so they coordinated their schedules in order to meet each Saturday

at the "'mat." There, they exchange the latest gossip and discuss what is going on in each other's lives.

→ *Scenario C. Jack in the Pulpit.* Jack is holding his weekly Bible study in his home this evening. Attending will be three members of his church, all of whom come almost every week; two other friends who attend different churches and who are also regulars; and a coworker from his factory who is skeptical about God and the truth of the Bible but who nevertheless finds it to be pretty interesting stuff. This will be the coworker's second time attending the Bible study.

Jack will lead the group in a forty-five-minute discussion of the nature of marriage based on the book of Genesis, and then they will spend about another thirty minutes praying for each other's needs. Most attendees wish to increase their knowledge of the Bible, get closer to God, and discuss answered prayers as well as receive prayer.

→ *Scenario D. The 5:15 for Fairyland.* In Fairyland, a group of ten people from several different local workplaces wait to catch the 5:15 P.M. commuter train home from work every Monday through Friday.

→ *Scenario E. Moms and the Seven Kids.* There is a group of seven women lingering in a pediatrician's waiting room as each awaits her child's visit with the doctor. Some moms are playing with their children, others are making small talk among themselves, and several are reading the available magazines (*Physicians' Quarterly* and other exciting rags).

→ *Scenario F. Middle Management on Break.* There are five middle management employees at Fonswick Corp. who meet every weekday for fifteen minutes in the morning in the executive dining room. Mostly they "talk shop" about managing employees and what is going on within the company.

3. For each of the ads in Exhibits 8.2 through 8.6:
   a. Explain whether you would expect reference group influence to be relatively strong or weak for the advertised product, given its nature (social visibility, relevance).
   b. Describe the type of reference person (or persons) in the ad: celebrity, common man, or expert. Discuss the effectiveness of using this person.
   c. Explain the nature of the reference group to which the ad appeals, according to the classification scheme in this exercise (aspiration group, primary group, disclaimant group, etc.). Then, discuss the effectiveness of this approach.

4. Whether or not virtual groups are truly social groups is debatable. Are "friends" on MySpace or Facebook "real" friends? Evaluate them on the three criteria for a social group.

WRITTEN APPLICATIONS

1. Answer Question 1 in the In-Class Applications.

2. Answer Question 3 in the In-Class Applications. Also, for one of these ads, propose another type of reference person and reference group to appeal to (aspiration group, primary group, etc.).

3. Find three more ads with a reference group appeal for which you can answer Question 3.

EXERCISE 8.2. TYPES OF REFERENCE GROUP INFLUENCE

OBJECTIVES

1. To observe and identify how marketers make use of the three types of reference group influences: informational, utilitarian, and value-expressive.
2. To describe critical characteristics of reference groups: values, norms, roles, and socialization.
3. To provide insight into how marketers use reference group characteristics to influence consumers.
4. To provide perspective on the characteristics of your reference group and the influence processes it uses and how marketers capitalize on this influence.

EXHIBIT 8.2   Claritan RediTabs Ad

TAKE CLEAR CONTROL.
TAKE CLARITIN.

What I can't control:
Bruises, scrapes, and cuts
Upper-management decisions
My rent
The pollen count

What I can control:
The miles I log
My career moves
How I live my life
Where and when I take
my allergy medication

Once-a-day
Claritin RediTabs
10mg (loratadine rapidly-disintegrating tablets)

Dissolves on your tongue without water for relief of seasonal allergy symptoms

Talk to your doctor about once-a-day, nondrowsy, mint-flavored CLARITIN® REDITABS® – for people ages 6 and up. One CLARITIN® REDITABS® tablet relieves your seasonal allergy symptoms all day without making you sleepy. CLARITIN® REDITABS® are safe to take as prescribed: one tablet daily. At the recommended dose, CLARITIN® REDITABS® are nondrowsy. *The most common side effects* occurred about as often as they did with a sugar pill, including headache, drowsiness, fatigue, and dry mouth. Please see next page for additional important information. *Available by prescription only.*

Call 1-888-833-0003 for more information and a $5.00 rebate certificate. Or visit www.claritin.com

EXHIBIT 8.3   Weber Grill Ad

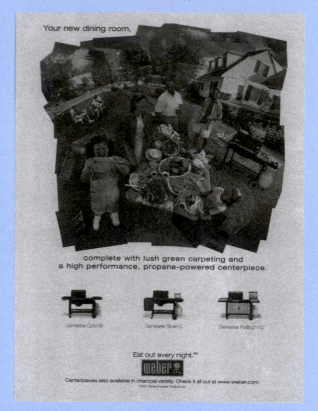

Your new dining room,

complete with lush green carpeting and
a high performance, propane-powered centerpiece.

Genesis Gold-B   Genesis Silver-C   Genesis Platinum-C

Eat out every night.™
weber

Centerpieces also available in charcoal variety. Check it all out at www.weber.com

EXHIBIT 8.4   Eckerd Pharmacy Ad

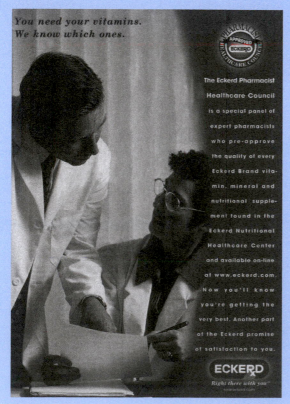

You need your vitamins.
We know which ones.

The Eckerd Pharmacist Healthcare Council is a special panel of expert pharmacists who pre-approve the quality of every Eckerd Brand vitamin, mineral and nutritional supplement found in the Eckerd Nutritional Healthcare Center and available on-line at www.eckerd.com. Now you'll know you're getting the very best. Another part of the Eckerd promise of satisfaction to you.

ECKERD
Right there with you

EXHIBIT 8.5   The Breast Cancer Research Foundation Ad

Breast Cancer Doesn't Just Affect Women

43,500 women will die from breast cancer this year. Sadly, they won't be the only casualties. Consider the families and friends who survive them. We cannot rest until we win the battle against breast cancer.

85% of your contribution will go directly to breast cancer research. Please make checks payable to The Breast Cancer Research Foundation, Box 9236-GPO, New York, NY 10087-9236, or visit our website at www.bcrfcure.org and make a donation online.

Name
Address
I'd like to give $100 $75 $50 $25   Other
Name of Publication
A not-for-profit organization.

EXHIBIT 8.6   Stouffer's Ad

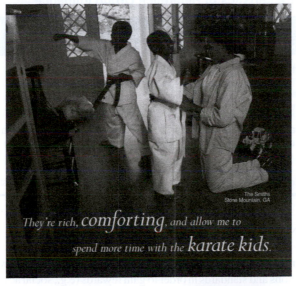

BACKGROUND

TYPES OF REFERENCE GROUP INFLUENCE

Reference groups and reference persons can influence consumers' thinking, attitudes, decisions, behaviors, and lifestyles. Reference group influences can involve one or more of the following types: informational; utilitarian (normative, instrumental); and value-expressive (identification, comparative). These three types of influence are summarized in Exhibit 8.7.

1. INFORMATIONAL INFLUENCE

Informational reference group influence occurs when the consumer uses the attitudes and behaviors of reference group members to gain information and advice. For example, if almost all marketing personnel in a firm read *Advertising Age,* a new marketer might infer that the magazine is essential to becoming an informed professional. Or, if the friends of an individual snack on Chippie Chips, the consumer could reason that the chips must be tasty. The consumer's objective in using group informational influence is to gain knowledge in order to make an intelligent buying decision.

Reference groups and their members can be useful sources of purchase information if they are *credible*— both knowledgeable and trustworthy information providers. Informational influence is especially potent where there is high perceived risk, since informational influencers can credibly reduce uncertainty, and if buyers lack product knowledge or experience that the credible informants can provide.

> ### EXHIBIT 8.7　Key Characteristics of Reference Group Influence
>
> | Nature of Influence | Consumer Objectives | Perceived Source Characteristics | Behavior | Social Power |
> |---|---|---|---|---|
> | Informational | Knowledge | Credibility | Acceptance | Expert |
> | Utilitarian (normative, instrumental) | Gain rewards, avoid punishment | Power | Compliance | Reward, coercive, or legitimate |
> | Value-expressive (comparative, identification) | Maintenance and enrichment of self-image | Similarity | Identification and internalization | Referent |
>
> *Source:* Based on Table 14.1 in Henry Assael, *Consumer Behavior: A Strategic Approach* (Boston: Houghton Mifflin, 2004), p. 413.

2. UTILITARIAN (NORMATIVE, INSTRUMENTAL) INFLUENCE

Utilitarian (normative, instrumental) reference group influence occurs when an individual decides to conform to group expectations and standards in order to gain rewards (e.g., social acceptance) or to avoid punishment (e.g., social sanctions). Consequently, the reference group has *power,* for example, one might wear the latest fashion to "fit in," or watch a certain popular TV show to take part in the "water cooler chatter" the next day at work. The person gains satisfaction, or utility ("utilitarian") from conforming to social group norms ("normative"). Conforming is instrumental to getting rewards.

An example of such conformity is purchasing the same products or brands or shopping at the same stores as other group members. Such conformity primarily takes the form of **compliance**, or consenting to a social group's expectations without accepting all its beliefs or behaviors. This contrasts with a more permanent form of conforming—**acceptance**—which occurs when a person actually changes his or her beliefs and attitudes to be consistent with those of the group (i.e., he or she internalizes the group's ideas). Acceptance is usually the result of informational influence rather than utilitarian influence.

Normative influence is most likely to occur when the person's behaviors are visible to the group, such as purchasing conspicuous products like clothing and furniture. Advertisements using utilitarian influence typically suggest either social approval for using a brand (e.g., guests "ooohhing" and "aahhing" over the taste of a hostess's coffee) or social punishment for not using the brand (such as a person offending others because she used the wrong brand of deodorant).

3. VALUE-EXPRESSIVE (IDENTIFICATION, COMPARATIVE) INFLUENCE

In **value-expressive (comparative, identification) reference groups,** members' attitudes and behaviors are guides for others. They serve as a **comparative reference group**, a yardstick against which people compare their own attitudes and actions.

The key group characteristic for comparative reference groups is *similarity*. Members are either perceived to be like the consumer or are the way he or she wishes to be. The buyer, so influenced, *identifies* with or feels he or she can relate to group members, internalizing group values, attitudes, and behaviors. The consumer's reasoning about products used by group members is: "If it's good enough and works for them, then it's good enough and will be fine for me!"

Value-expressive influence works best for products that are highly visible and have high social or ego risk. Advertising presenters with value-expressive influence can be either the common man with whom targeted customers identify, or celebrities, whom people wish to emulate.

CHARACTERISTICS OF REFERENCE GROUPS

There are several attributes of reference groups that are similar to cultual characteristics (Exercise 5.1) that enable the groups to sway consumers, such as material elements (a work group might use an internal social network and instant messaging to communicate); beliefs (a civic organization's members might believe that it is important to give back to the community); attitudes (individuals in an alumni group are likely sentimental about their alma mater); and language (many business organizations are notorious for having their own peculiar acronyms and invented words). Here we shall focus on the following reference group attributes: values, norms, roles, social status, and socialization.

Values

Recall that cultural values are widely shared ideals in society. **Social group values** are widely shared values within a social group. In either case, the ideals concern general goals and means for achieving those goals deemed desirable or undesirable. For instance, **corporate (organizational) cultures** consist of an organization's clearly defined, informally shared values, assumptions, and ways of doing business. The Hewlett-Packard Company is famous for "The HP Way," characterized by egalitarianism, decentralization, and community involvement.

The clear marketing implication is to understand the important values of your customers' social groups and to appeal to them through advertising and promotion.

Norms

Social group norms are informal rules or standards regarding socially acceptable boundaries of proper behavior in a social group (as opposed to cultural norms, which occur in the context of a culture). *Normative social influence* is based on group norms, which are largely derived from cultural and subcultural norms, although they can deviate somewhat.

These unwritten "rules" set the boundaries for what is socially acceptable social group behavior: ways to dress (e.g., workplace "casual"); how to address superiors (e.g., "Sir" or "Ma'am" in the military); how to eat (mess hall manners versus business dining etiquette); and ways to conduct oneself during meetings (above all: Do not fall asleep!). Thirty or so years ago, men and women who were interested in each other would go out on a "date." The guy would nervously, with sweaty palms, phone the gal to ask her out. This norm has been replaced with a more casual approach of hanging out together, meeting up as partners, or "hooking up" with strangers. And if you are still waving a Bic lighter instead of a cell phone or wearing a T-shirt you just bought at the rock concert you are attending, concert-goers will likely consider you geeky rather than cool.

Social group norms lead to group *conformity*, with those who conform to group expectations being rewarded through social approval, advancement within the group, and other desired outcomes. Those who refuse to conform are socially sanctioned through disapproval, teasing, embarrassment, and perhaps even ostracism.

As with social group values, marketers must be aware of targeted consumers' group norms and appeal to rather than violate them. In selling to social group members, marketers should "conform to the norm." Miller Lite beer ads played upon men's confusion about how to behave in certain beer-drinking situations. The ad campaign featured a secret society of men. Among the topics discussed were when it is acceptable to date a friend's ex-girlfriend and whether it's OK to stick one's fingers in beer bottles when carrying them from the bar to the table.

Roles

A **social group role** is appropriate behavior for a particular person or position within a social group. William Shakespeare observed, "All the world's a stage and all the men and women merely players." A **role set** consists of all the various social group roles a person plays in life, and it is an important determinant of the individual's *self-concept*, helping answer the all-important question, "Who am I?" You might simultaneously be a son or daughter, sibling, friend, student, part-time employee, and member of a knitting club.

Likewise, much CB resembles actors in a play, with products as props and clothing as costumes to play the roles. Your beverage of choice for guests may vary depending on whether you are playing the role of son or daughter in the presence of your parents as opposed to socializing with your pals.

Role-related product clusters (consumption constellations) are groups of related products used to fulfill a particular role. For example, the role of business executive requires proper clothing, an attaché case, a laptop computer, and various mobile communications devices. A parent of a toddler would own a child's car seat, a basement littered with toys, boxes of disposable diapers, a changing table, and picture books. Marketers selling to certain role players might develop and cross-promote complementary products. Students need notebooks, pens, and pocket calculators, so a seller could market these as a back-to-school bundle.

Gender (sex) roles are behaviors considered appropriate for either males or else females in society or within particular social groups. We are currently witnessing a blurring of sex roles. Men used to be seen as progenitors, providers, and protectors, while women were caretakers and nurturers. In the twenty-first century, there are blurred boundaries, "gender benders," and even role reversals that are acceptable, such as women fighting, men crying, and women becoming more sexually predatory.

Shifting family gender roles have led marketers to alter target markets and portrayals of husbands and wives in advertising. Old-fashioned stereotypes of women as weak, overly emotional, dependent on men, and happy housewives are avoided. Sex role changes also alter the way salespeople target and treat their customers. They must be careful not to patronize women (e.g., "Hey, honey, come back with your husband before you decide on which car to buy"). And, some formerly sex-typed products and brands are now taking a unisex position, such as Liz Claiborne, once an exclusively female brand, which has developed Claiborne for Men. Although men traditionally shunned diet beverages as effeminate, Diet Pepsi Max used a male name, potent ingredients (a double dose of caffeine and ginseng), and a bold selling proposition ("Wake up, people!) to appeal to male desk jockeys battling the midday blahs.

People are increasingly taking on multiple roles, thereby expanding their **role load**—the number of different roles they acquire in their various social groups. Manifold roles can lead to two negative states: role overload and role conflict.

Role overload means consumers feel they have taken on more role demands than time or energy allows. While your professor insists that you have that twenty-page term paper completed by Monday morning, your friends are asking you to party hardy all weekend, and your parents want you to come home for a weekend visit.

Role overload results in **role conflict**, in which there are competing role expectations because one has taken on two or more incompatible roles. Assuming multiple roles causes **inter-role conflict**—mutually incompatible demands among one's various roles, such as being expected to be in two different places at the same time or taking on too many tasks. For example, working mothers still end up doing most of the housework even though they come home from work exhausted.

To resolve inter-role conflict, people can cut back or cut out some of their roles. A more common solution is to **multitask (polychronic time use)**, or engage in two or more activities simultaneously in order to accomplish them all. As every parent well knows, today's teenagers are at this: with the TV blasting, they check their Facebook page, chat on IM, and listen to their iPod—all while doing homework.

Marketers can help resolve inter-role conflicts by developing and promoting **timesaving goods**. These products are designed to save consumers time and effort or allow them to multitask. Examples of timesaving goods for commuting drivers trying to achieve work-life balance include hands-free cell phones, books on CD or MP3 download, and the eMagin's EyeBud 800 viewer. This funky-looking pair of eyeglasses plugs into a PC, video iPod, or similar device, and projects a video image in front of one of the viewer's eyes. The other eye to remains uncovered so the viewer can see what's going on around him or her.

A second type of role conflict is **intra-role conflict**, in which a given role places competing demands on a person's time and energy. Parents must be disciplinarians one minute and their child's companion the next. Some professors wonder whether they should be their students' friend or an authority figure. Salespeople balance time spent prospecting for new customers with servicing current customers.

Marketers can show how their product fulfills one of a consumer's conflicting roles and why it is more important than the other roles, or they can demonstrate how they can help balance conflicting roles. For instance, books by child psychologists explain how to discipline children with love, thereby maintaining the parent-child friendship.

A **role model** is a person whose attitudes and behaviors others imitate because they want to be like the model. Parents, teachers, and friends all serve as **direct role models;** they have personal contact with their imitators. Dress-up is a role-playing game that lets children try out grown-up roles without any of the responsibilities. Children's metal lunchboxes of years ago had their inspiration in the metal lunch buckets blue-collar men carried to work in the early twentieth century, so that kids could imitate their dads. Mattel's Barbie doll was designed to be a role model for young girls play-acting various parts of adult life. A classic antismoking commercial showed a little boy mimicking his cigarette-smoking pop, closing with the tagline, "Like father, like son." Marketers use celebrities as role models in children's ads, Charles Barkley's classic refrain notwithstanding: "I don't believe professional athletes should be role models. I believe parents should be role models."

Even grown-ups can be influenced by role models, such as corporate mentors and "older and wiser" friends. Hence, marketers at times have opportunities to serve as role models. Salespeople teach prospects and customers about how to properly use their products, and advertisers use celebrities or other reference persons as **indirect (vicarious) role models**—role models lacking direct contact with the people who imitate or are influenced by them.

The life of a consumer can change in an instant, often with just a few words, such as "I do" or "You're fired," or the cry of a newborn baby. **Role acquisitions** occur as we take on important new roles. As we mature, key life transitions cause shifts in our lives and changes in our behavior, including CB. As people pick up new roles in life, they acquire new products to serve as props for these roles. The biggest buying binge ordinarily occurs when people marry. Other special spending spree occasions are the birth of a child or purchase of a starter home. For marketers, these change points create opportunities to sell products and even forge relationships that could last a lifetime.

This explains the need for bridal showers, baby showers, and housewarming parties. It also clarifies why many retailers establish bridal registries. Through customer databases, marketers can identify consumers entering these roles and be the first to offer buyers appropriate products, such as a diaper service for new or expecting parents or landscaping for first-time homeowners.

SOCIAL STATUS

Chapter 7 defined **social status** as the relative rankings of members of society with respect to prestige, respect, power, and influence. That chapter was concerned with **between-group stratification**, which entails ranking individuals or groups within society or a community as a whole, such as via social class and subculture.

Within the context of a social group, there is **within-group stratification**, or the esteem, status, and power accorded an occupant of a certain position or role within the group. **Social group status** is accorded to an occupant of a certain position or role within the group and is the relative ranking of members of a social group regarding prestige, respect, power, and influence within the group. In a college campus community, freshmen are at the bottom and seniors are at the top of the social totem pole. Sports team captains are the "big men on campus," as are class officers. Within each campus organization there is a hierarchy, with high-status officers, team captains, and other leaders.

One marketing application here is the selling of products as **status symbols**, which are visible, physical status-conveying representations of membership in or aspiration to a particular social class or status group. In the business world, an expensive gold pen, Armani suit, or fine dark brown leather attaché case can all communicate a high position, as they are luxurious and relatively exclusive in ownership. A seat in the first class section on an airline allows one to experience superior status as one boards and then watches other passengers parade by with envy. A Mercedes three-pointed star on the car hood conveys eminence.

SOCIALIZATION

Socialization is the process whereby people learn the social roles and behaviors required to effectively participate in society. Socialization occurs within society when people learn how to live in the culture, adopting its values, norms, and other cultural characteristics. Such learning occurs within *socializing institutions* and from the people within them. These include social groups and organizations such as families, schools, churches, and the media.

Social group socialization is the process by which values, norms, roles, and other characteristics of a social group are learned. Most group socialization occurs in the early years of childhood and adolescence as children learn how to get along with one another in playgroups, behave in a classroom, and interact with grown-ups.

Adults also become socialized when they join groups. After moving to a new neighborhood, a family experiences "newcomer socialization," discovering new norms such as how loud and long children can yell outdoors, whether dogs may run loose and bark, and how tall to let the grass grow.

Marketers are especially interested in **consumer socialization**, the process whereby children, teenagers, and young adults learn skills, knowledge, and attitudes necessary to function effectively in the marketplace. This includes learning to get good value for one's money, to be an efficient and effective shopper, to negotiate with a salesperson, and which Web sites are "safe" to visit.

REVIEW QUESTIONS

1. Cite and explain the three types of reference group influences, including the nature of influence, consumer objectives, perceived source characteristics, and behavior of influenced group members. Explain how marketers can tap into each type.
2. Cite and explain the five characteristics of reference groups and explain how marketers can tap into them.

IN-CLASS APPLICATIONS

1. For three of your own important social groups (e.g., those you discussed in Exercise 8.1):
   a. Describe each group's major values and norms, the role(s) you play in each group, status positions within the group (including the status of your positions), and any socialization processes you're aware the group uses to help members assimilate.

      How could a marketer of a product you would consider purchasing use knowledge of these reference group characteristics to persuade you and/or other group members to buy the product?
   b. Illustrate how each of the three groups named in In-Class Application 1a uses one or more of the reference group influences to change member behaviors. Have the groups ever successfully affected any of your attitudes and/or behaviors? Explain. What marketing opportunities can tap into these reference groups' influence processes?
2. Identify and explain which types of reference group influences are found in the following scenarios. (Note: Several influences can usually be found in a given scenario.)
   → *Scenario A. Johnny Wannabee—Closet Case.* Johnny Wannabee is a fourth grader who wants to be a cool kid. Even though his mom does not like it, he wears baggy pants and an untucked shirt to school because that is how his friends dress. If he were to put on the nerdy dress shirts and pants his mother wants him to wear, he fears his friends would tease and even shun him.
   → *Scenario B. Lou on the Learning Curve.* It is Louie's first day on the job at Gentron Corp. Wishing to adapt well and make friends quickly, he spends his lunch hour studying names and faces in the corporate directory and reviewing the rules of conduct in Gentron's policy manual.
   → *Scenario C. Candy Learns the Ropes.* Candy learned lots in the training course at Quazzimatic, Inc., to help her in her new role as assistant manager. She also constantly asked advice from her seasoned coworkers on the best ways to accomplish various tasks and motivate the worker bees.
   → *Scenario D. Sew Funny to Be with You.* Ms. Taylor wants more people in her sewing circle to like her, so she bought several joke books. She is learning as many jokes as possible so the women will think she is a "fun" person.
   → *Scenario E. Listen Up, Tim!* Tim likes to hear the ideas and advice given by his classmates in an Evening Division course he is taking at Quxntrvlyl College: Principles of Beehive Management. He enjoys listening because many of them are seasoned beehive managers and successful students speaking from experience.

→ *Scenario F. Barb Loosens Her Clothes.* Many of Barb Dwire's colleagues are now "dressing down" on Fridays in more casual, yet not sloppy, attire. Barb decides that she too should "loosen up" her attire on Fridays.

3. Evaluate each of the advertisements in Exhibits 8.8 through 8.11 for their appeal to social group characteristics. Describe the relevant social group each ad illustrates. For each ad you should be able to find at least one example of a social group characteristic: group values, norms, roles, status symbols, or socialization. Also, find at least one use of a reference group influence in each ad.

How effective do you believe each ad is in using these social group characteristics and reference group influences? Can you offer suggestions to improve any of the ads to better appeal to social group characteristics and influences?

4. Should marketers be allowed to supply public schools with free sponsored learning materials that integrate their brand names into lessons in order to help students' socialization? Is it ethical for schools to sell soda, candy bars, and other nutritionally challenged foods and beverages? Should schools permit advertising on schoolbook covers or on school buses?

WRITTEN APPLICATIONS

1. Answer Question 1 in the In-Class Applications. Alternatively, you can interview a friend or relative using these questions.

2. Answer Question 3 in the In-Class Applications.

3. Find three more ads, each containing at least one characteristic of reference groups and one use of a reference group influence. Answer Question 3 in the In-Class Applications for each of the ads you find.

EXERCISE 8.3. SOCIAL POWER

OBJECTIVES

1. To understand and recognize the many sources and uses of social power in marketing.
2. To acquire insight into your own social groups and how they use social power to influence your behavior.
3. To gain experience using social power as a marketer.

BACKGROUND

THE NATURE OF SOCIAL POWER

Social power is the degree to which someone can influence others' thinking, attitudes, or behaviors. In this exercise, we will delve into the details of various kinds of social power and see how marketers can use them to appeal to and persuade consumers.

Social power is held by **social agents**, individuals, groups, or organizations that can affect an individual's thinking, attitudes, and behaviors. Examples include parents, teachers, peers, and bosses. Social groups also function as social agents.

Marketing social agents include companies, salespeople, retailers, frontline service organization personnel, and the people and characters featured in advertising. Unfortunately, marketers' social power is rather restricted. The notion of consumer sovereignty reminds us that marketers can influence (but not control) their targeted prospects. Hence, it behooves marketers to understand the nature of social power at their disposal and become adept and creative at using that power. This exercise will enable you to do so.

The relation of each social power source to a particular reference group influence process (discussed in Exercise 8.2) is summarized in Exhibit 8.12. The first *three* types of social power—*reward power, coercive power*, and *legitimate power*—all tie into *utilitarian social influence*, which is the social agent's ability to

EXHIBIT 8.8   Budweiser Ad

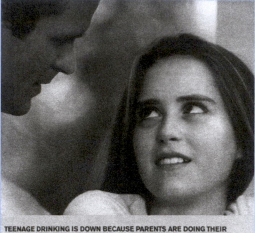

TEENAGE DRINKING IS DOWN BECAUSE PARENTS ARE DOING THEIR

HOMEWORK.

John knows if Sarah has all the facts, she'll make a better decision about any subject. Even underage drinking. So he took advantage of "Family Talk About Drinking," a free guide offered by Anheuser-Busch to help parents talk to their kids. In the past decade alone, Anheuser-Busch and its distributors have provided nearly 3.5 million guides. It's people like John and programs like this that have helped reduce teenage drinking by 45% since 1982.

For a free family guidebook, call 1-800-359-TALK, or download it at www.beeresponsible.com.

WE ALL MAKE A DIFFERENCE.

Budweiser
www.beeresponsible.com

EXHIBIT 8.9   Jockey Ad

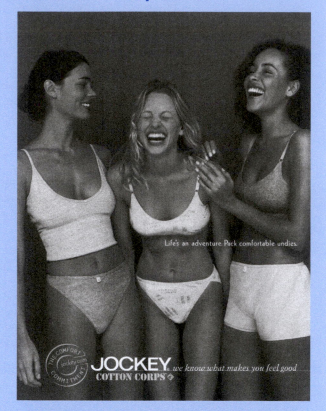

Life's an adventure. Pack comfortable undies.

JOCKEY *we know what makes you feel good*
COTTON CORPS

EXHIBIT 8.10   Destination ImagiNation by OM Association Ad

Think outside the box.

They can, you know. All they need is the opportunity—and a little help from volunteers and friends.

Through Destination ImagiNation, students work together in teams to come up with ingenious (and entertaining) solutions to complex challenges. The creative problem-solving process not only calls for divergent thinking, but also for technical, theatrical, scientific, even linguistic expertise. Projects range from building a weight-bearing structure out of ultra-light materials to telling a story using only the language of music.

Presented by OM Association, Inc., Destination ImagiNation offers creative, collaborative competition to thousands of students in 40 states and several nations.

For information, visit www.dini.org or call (856) 881-1603.

Copyright 1999, OM Association, Inc.

Help develop the next generation of innovative thinkers! Visit www.dini.org or call (856) 881-1603.

DESTINATION IMAGINATION.

EXHIBIT 8.11   Atria Assisted Living Ad

ATRIA ASSISTED LIVING

The Setting: Inviting.
The Menu: Tantalizing.
The Occasion: 3 Times A Day.

Call us for a tour, and discover Assisted Living at its most tasteful.

• Elegant dining, with meals by an expert culinary staff
• On-site libraries, exercise/game rooms, hobby shops, wellness clinics, and barber/beauty shops
• A calendar bursting with social events, outings, and activities
• Private apartments with your choice of floor plans
• Carefully integrated safety and security features with 24-hour staffing
• Customized personal service plans
• Scheduled transportation to designated shopping, healthcare centers, places of worship and special events
• The experience that comes from more than 30 years in senior residential service

Amenities and services may vary by community due to state legal restrictions.

Call toll-free today for the community nearest you.
1-888-287-4201

ATRIA
ASSISTED LIVING
www.atriacom.com

THE WISDOM OF EXPERIENCE

Social power	Social agent's ability	Influence process	Behavior
Reward power	Dispense rewards	Utilitarian/normative	Compliance
Coercive power	Dispense punishments	Utilitarian/normative	Compliance
Legitimate power	Establish social norms give approval/disapproval	Utilitarian/normative	Acceptance or compliance
Referent power	Induce imitation of the agent	Value-expressive (comparative identification)	Identification, emulation, and imitation
Expert power	Provide expert, objective evaluation	Informational	Acceptance

EXHIBIT 8.12 Sources of Social Power

offer rewards or inflict punishment. The desired behavior the agent wishes to cause is conformity, either in the form of compliance or acceptance. *Referent power* is associated with *value-expressive influence*, and it seeks to gain identification, emulation, or imitation. *Expert power* is affiliated with *informational influence* and also attempts to gain acceptance.

We shall survey the five sources of social power by defining each and giving everyday examples. Then, we will discuss the various marketing applications of each social power basis.

REWARD POWER

THE NATURE OF REWARD POWER

Because reward power and coercive power are flip sides of the same coin, they are sometimes lumped together as **reinforcement power (instrumental power)**, a social agent's ability to use instruments as rewards and punishments to affect attitudes and behavior.

Reward power and coercive power use the *utilitarian influence process* and seek to gain *compliance.* The motivation for influencing others is the external reward or punishment.

Reward power is the ability to gain compliance via administering rewards for desired actions. These rewards include material and psychological rewards. *Material rewards* are tangible, physical rewards, such as children receiving a treat for good behavior, professors doling out extra credit, and high-performing employees being granted a pay raise. *Psychological rewards* are nonmaterial rewards that are emotionally satisfying, such as obedient children receiving praise and attention, professors providing positive feedback on papers, and business organizations bestowing intangibles such as public recognition of high performers, social events, and extra time off. For instance, McDonald's uses both categories of rewards, recognizing the best crew members every month as outstanding employees, who receive an on-the-spot raise. The hardest-working managers, in turn, might win a vacation and even an opportunity to own their own McDonald's. And, the world's top McDonald's performers are given the President's Award along with stock options at an annual gala in Chicago.

MARKETING APPLICATIONS OF REWARD POWER

Since marketing is all about satisfying needs, the opportunities for rewarding customers are only limited by the marketer's creative imagination. Some general possibilities are:

- *Product quality.* Selling buyers something that fulfills their desires and expectations.
- *Sales promotions (promotions).* Short-term buying incentives in the form of indirect price cuts (e.g., coupons, rebates) or value added to the product (e.g., premiums, contests).

- *Advertising.* Advertising can be an intangible reward by providing customers information ("Sale this week!"), reassurance ("The pride of ownership"), a brand image ("I'm young and fun because I drink Fruitsee Tootsie"), sponsorship of buyers' favorite programs ("Hallmark Hall of Fame"), or even entertainment (Bud Light's humorous commercials).
- *Salespeople.* Effective sales associates provide intangible rewards by acting as the customer's consultant, offering assistance and honest feedback.

COERCIVE POWER

THE NATURE OF COERCIVE POWER

If reward power is the "carrot," coercive power is the "stick." **Coercive (punitive) power** entails dispensing sanctions for undesirable behavior. These penalties include punishments, either physical ("Spare the rod and spoil the child"), material (police officers issuing fines for moving violations; professors penalizing late papers), or psychological (giving an employee a verbal dressing down); and withholding rewards ("No dessert, Jimmy, unless you eat your asparagus and squash"; withholding a raise if the salesperson fails to achieve quota).

MARKETING APPLICATIONS OF COERCIVE POWER

Although marketers cannot spank or physically threaten their customers, there are several psychological ways for them to administer coercive power.

High-Pressure Selling. Although pressing the customer into buying might work in the short run, it is of dubious long-term effectiveness, not to mention ethically questionable.

Fear Appeals. Fear is anxiety created by anticipated negative consequences. **Fear (threat, problem-avoidance) appeal** creates worry by suggesting problems will arise or persist if the recommended course of action (e.g., brand purchase) is not taken. Due to *risk aversion*, the fear of loss is a far more powerful motivator than the hope of gain.

Two types of angst can be created: physical fear and social fear. *Physical fear* is based on physical risk, such as bodily harm that can come from a malfunctioning product. Marketing communications can suggest that not taking the seller's advice will result in an unwanted condition. ("Without our cholesterol-lowering wonder drug, you could suffer a heart attack!") The packaging for the SPOT Satellite Messenger, a GPS for outdoor enthusiasts, says "Live to tell about it!" and "Opening this box is the first step to making sure you don't come home in one." *Social fear* is associated with social risk. Examples of marketing messages related to social fear are "Use Brand X deodorant or you'll smell like a goat!" and "Serve an inferior cut of meat and your family will reject you."

Fear appeals work well for unsought goods that provide problem avoidance, such as life insurance, estate planning, health checkups, and car tires. Since consumers derive no immediate benefits from these products (but can suffer harm if they don't buy them), they tend to procrastinate and need a marketing kick in the butt to make a purchase. The American Legacy Foundation's "Truth" campaign targeted youth at the greatest risk for drug use. This campaign is an excellent example of effective, ethical (i.e., not exaggerated) use of the fear appeal. Ads such as one that showed teens unloading body bags in front of a tobacco company's headquarters appeal to kids' rebellious nature.

Aristotle's adage, "In all things, moderation," applies to choosing how frightening fear appeals should be. If the threat is too small, not enough tension is created and consumers are not motivated to take action. If the threat is too large, they either laugh it off as ridiculous or else mentally tune it out in psychological self-defense, resulting in a more negative brand attitude.

Stronger fear appeals can be used where the issue is more serious, the source (either the advertiser or the ad's presenter) is credible, a realistic solution to the threat is offered, and immediate action can be taken regarding this solution. However, there is the ethical issue of creating so much fear that it causes the buyer to act irrationally against his or her own self-interest.

Guilt Appeals. **Guilt** is a violation of one's internal standards (values, norms, etc.), which leads to lower self-esteem and/or remorse. Examples of guilt appeals include charities that use the classic "You-can-feed-this-famished-child-or-you-can-turn-the-page" approach, toy marketers who make parents feel they are cheating their kids if they do not buy the latest educational toy, and individual 100-calorie snack packs for cookies and crackers, which reduce guilt for snackers.

Shame Appeals. These are similar to guilt appeals in that they cause lower self-esteem and/or remorse, except rather than being inwardly focused, **shame appeals** center *externally* on other peoples' evaluation of one's behavior. For example: "If you don't buy Daintee dish detergent, you'll suffer the embarrassment of little spots on your glasses and plates."

Hard-Sell Advertising. Hard-selling is advertising derived from high-pressure personal selling ("Buy now, buy now!"), using hard-hitting, hyperactive, repetitive persuasion. This "yell-and-sell" school of advertising is typified by local car salespeople's TV commercials, with owners racing through the showroom like crazed madmen, breathlessly imploring us to "Come on dowwwnn!! Prices can't be beat!!"

Threatening to Withhold Rewards. This is the old-fashioned "It's-now-or-never" school of marketing, which focuses on what customers will lose if they do not purchase immediately. The salesperson's "standing-room-only" closing technique is a classic example, suggesting that if prospects do not buy now, the merchandise might be gone later. Advertisements add urgency by warning, "Offer expires at midnight tonight," or "Get one now while supplies last!"

LEGITIMATE POWER

THE NATURE OF LEGITIMATE POWER

Legitimate power is founded on an agent's ability to establish social norms ("What is the correct thing to do?" and "What is legitimate?") and then to approve of people who follow the norms and disapprove of those who do not. Legitimate power can be formal, to gain compliance, and informal, to garner acceptance.

FORMAL LEGITIMATE POWER

An agent with **formal legitimate power** has formal authority to set norms by virtue of position or role in the social group. These individuals have the ability to demand *compliance*. A judge, traffic cop, prison warden, and work supervisor all have legitimate authority. Professors determine what students study, what assignments they must complete, and what standards they must achieve.

Since marketers ordinarily lack legitimate authority ("Buy my product because I'm the salesperson!" doesn't wash), they must hitch themselves to someone or some organization with formal legitimate power, such as a medical expert ("Four out of five dentists surveyed recommend Trident sugarless gum"), a college professor ("Professor Glotz suggests you buy this educational book"), or an author ("Dr. Schlock says you should coddle your child"). The marketer could also seek the endorsement of a credible, neutral certifying authority, such as the Green Seal of environmental approval. Most such authorities are also experts (see section on expert power).

INFORMAL LEGITIMATE POWER

Informal legitimate power is an appeal to social values and norms in an attempt to gain *acceptance* by a society or group. For example, friends are often able to coax one another due to their informal legitimate power.

Some advertisers have crafted catchy advertising slogans based on existing norms. Labor unions have urged us to "Buy American" and "Look for the union label," Dry Idea deodorant implored us to "Never let them see you sweat," Nike demands us to "Just do it," and Wendy's suggests we "Do what tastes right." Public service advertisers also try to establish or reinforce group norms via **moral appeals** to do the right thing based on social norms, such as vote, do volunteer work, support a particular social cause, or "just say no" to drugs.

REFERENT POWER

THE NATURE OF REFERENT POWER

A **social referent** is a reference group or reference person. **Referent power** is the ability to induce imitation of the referent's attitudes and behaviors through getting group members to either *identify* with or *emulate* the social agent. The key social agent characteristic for referent power based on identification is either actual or ideal perceived *similarity* to target audience members. The agent serves as a *comparative reference group*, using *value-expressive social influence*. Referent power is used to help people establish and maintain their self-concept.

Two types of referent power are those based on identification and on emulation. **Identification** is the process of attributing the characteristics of another person or group to oneself. The social referent is perceived to be similar to the person being influenced, resulting in a feeling of oneness with the social agent. **Emulation** is the process of imitating someone else's behavior because they are deemed superior in appearance, taste, knowledge, or experience. The referent is similar to the influenced individual's ideal self. Perhaps you admire your professor, or at least positively regard her.

REFERENT POWER BASED ON IDENTIFICATION

Identification results in a feeling of oneness with the social agent. The individual can relate to the agent because the referent is perceived to be similar to the person influenced, either demographically, psychographically, or behaviorally. Identification occurs primarily at an emotional (versus rational) level, resulting from a close emotional association with the agent.

Referent power can be tapped by matching salespeople with their customers on relevant characteristics. Marketing research interviews are more likely to be granted and honest answers given by respondents who believe the interviewer is like them.

In advertising, the referent identified with is the *common man (typical person)* presenter. A satisfied user demonstrates to buyers that someone similar to them buys, consumes, and gains satisfaction from the product. This can be effective because consumers empathize with and relate to the presenter, the typical users are viewed as credible, and such presenters humanize the advertiser. For instance, in Apple computer's "Switchers" campaign, real-life consumers described how they abandoned their Windows PCs for the ease of using Apple Macs. Dove made a big splash with their "real women" featured in the genesis of their "campaign for real beauty." Ads for Nike featured women who were unapologetic about their "big butts" or "thunder thighs" in ads focusing on these body parts. Many male baby boomers remember Dockers' first ads featuring "guys just like us," in contrast to most fashion ads with impossibly hip and handsome models. Dockers told it straight: These were good-looking, casual slacks that could be confidently worn by pudgy, balding, graying guys.

REFERENT POWER BASED ON EMULATION

The second type of referent power is based on *emulation*. Emulated referents set standards of achievement for those being influenced. Emulation is based on the learning principle called **modeling**, in which people copy the behavior of an idealized social lifestyle model in order to be like (or appear to be like) him or her. The key social agent characteristic for referent power based on emulation is perceived physical or social attractiveness. Aspirational advertising uses celebrities whom people wish to emulate, including athletes, TV and movie personalities, musicians, authors, fashion models, politicians, and spiritual leaders.

EXPERT POWER

THE NATURE OF EXPERT POWER

An **expert** social agent has skill in or knowledge of the subject area through formal training, education, occupation, or experience. This power derives from the referent's ability to provide an authoritative, objective evaluation. **Expert power** is a form of social power based on the social agent's expertise.

Informational influence is at work here; that is, "knowledge is power." Marketers expect consumers to accept and internalize the information. The key expert social agent characteristic is *credibility*, i.e., the agent is seen as a trustworthy expert. So, when a favorite professor recommends reading a good book or a dentist suggests getting a tooth filled, we are likely to take action.

MARKETING APPLICATIONS OF EXPERT POWER

Although marketers have expertise, they are obviously highly biased information providers. Therefore, many marketers hitch their wagons to credible experts. Case in point: Hair care marketers strive to get their shampoos, conditioners, and the like distributed through hair salons.

There are several types of experts that advertisers can tap. The following frequently appear in ads.

• *Celebrities.* In tools-of-the-trade endorsements, experts have professional experience with the product, such as a hockey player endorsing a hockey stick or rock musician plugging a guitar.

• *Professional experts.* Max Factor has employed Hollywood makeup artists, The Club antitheft device has used police officers, and countless medical products have been promoted by health care practitioners.

• *CEOs and employee spokespersons.* Chief executive officers (CEOs) are obviously product experts. Many CEOs have helped to humanize otherwise impersonal corporations and to personify the firms' brands by capitalizing on a charismatic leader: Charles Schwab (discount brokerage), Michael Dell (computers), Wally Amos (Famous Amos cookies), Bill Ford (great-grandson of Ford Motor founder Henry Ford), and James Dyson (Dyson vacuum cleaners) all became "rock star CEOs" by serving as their companies' public face.

• *Employees/workers.* Employees have the double advantage of possessing expert and referent power since we can relate to them and they presumably know what they are talking about. Saturn ads feature the people who make and sell the cars. The geeky Verizon Wireless man who asked, "Can you hear me now?" was the personification of Verizon employees who drive around testing the reliability of Verizon's network. McDonald's runs commercials featuring counter workers merrily serenading and serving customers.

• *Expert third-party endorsements.* Examples of such unbiased, neutral sources of information include *Motor Trend* magazine's "Car of the Year"; the Insurance Institute for Highway Safety organization's crash test scores; and Morningstar Investment Guides ratings of mutual funds.

The third parties typically rank competing brands on one or more criteria. They then either award a "seal" of approval to certain brands (the Good Housekeeping Green Seal of Approval for meeting criteria such as energy efficiency and packaging reduction, and the U.S. Environmental Protection Agency and Department of Energy's joint Energy Star designation for energy-efficient appliances, electronics, lights, and heating products) or give a subjective favorable evaluation of the product. These ratings and approval seals are typically trumpeted in the high-ranking firms' advertising. It was the American Dental Association's Seal of Acceptance, issued to Crest with fluoride in 1960 and touted ever since in its advertising, that propelled Crest past Colgate as the toothpaste market leader.

• *Advertise in expert media.* Some media vehicles command high respect and authority. *Stereo Review* is a credible publication in which to place ads for a car stereo system, *Car and Driver* works well for almost any automotive product, and *Conservative Chronicle* could convince readers to join the Conservative Book Club.

• *Use a spokescharacter with perceived expertise.* **Spokescharacters** are animated "experts" who serve as endorsers. They can be created characters (Betty Crocker and Chef Boyardee) or celebrity cartoon characters (Dilbert for Office Depot and the Peanuts characters for Metropolitan Life Insurance). Not only do spokescharacters provide "expert" advice, they also usually have a likeable personality that rubs off on the brand.

• *Develop company expert power so that the firm becomes the voice of authority.* Via product excellence, heritage (being in business for many years), and promotion of expertise, some firms can stand on their own merits without needing outside experts. Examples include Weight Watchers, Coleman camping equipment, Midas Mufflers, and Xerox copiers.

REVIEW QUESTIONS

1. Describe five types of social power, the reference group influence process used, the type of behavior elicited, and the major ways marketers tap into each of them.
2. Describe the different forms that coercive power takes and how marketers use them.

3. Discuss two forms of legitimate power and their marketing uses.
4. Describe two bases for referent power and the forms that ads using each can take.
5. What are the specific forms marketing expert power can take?

IN-CLASS APPLICATIONS

1. Thinking about social groups to which you belong, identify how each form of social power has been used by one of these groups, either on you or other group members. Have marketers ever tried to influence you via any of these social groups? Explain.

2. Identify the type(s) of social power you believe are appealed to in each of the ads in Exhibits 8.13 through 8.17, being as specific as possible. For example, is reward power being based on material or psychological rewards, and what exactly is the nature of the reward? Which type of coercive power is being used (fear appeal, shame appeal, etc.)? Is the legitimate power formal or informal? Is referent power based on identification or emulation? Which type of expert produces expert power? Are the appeals effective in each ad? Could any of the ads be improved or incorporate additional forms of social power, either in addition to or in conjunction with the existing form of social power used?

WRITTEN APPLICATIONS

1. Answer Question 1 above. You may interview other members of your social groups to get some of your information.

2. Answer Question 2 above.

3. Find five ads, each of which appeals to one of the five types of social power (one for each power type). Then, answer Question 2 in the In-Class Applications section above for each ad you find.

4. Develop either your own advertisement or the script for a short personal selling presentation that incorporates at least three different types of social power.

EXHIBIT 8.13   Bayer Aspirin Ad

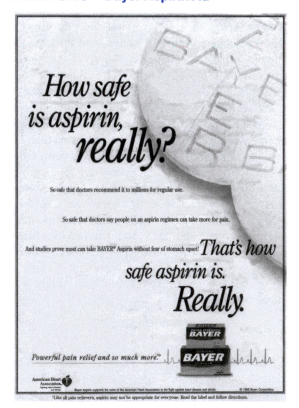

EXHIBIT 8.14   Finesse Ad

EXHIBIT 8.15   Sears HomeCentral Ad

EXHIBIT 8.16   BlueCross BlueShield Ad

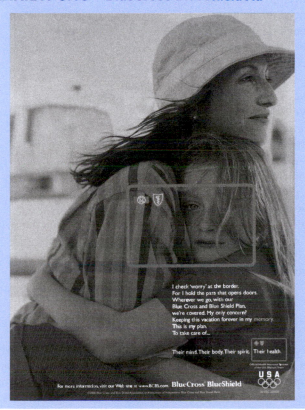

EXHIBIT 8.17   Procrit by Amgen Ad

KEY CONCEPTS

acceptance
anticipatory aspiration group
aspiration group
between-group stratification
brand communities
coercive (punitive) power
cohesiveness
commercially sponsored brand communities
comparative reference groups
compliance
conformity
consumer-driven brand communities
consumer socialization
contactual groups
corporate (organizational) cultures
demarketing (unselling, conversional marketing)
direct role model
disclaimant groups
dissociative groups (avoidance groups)
emulation
expert power
fear (threat, problem-avoidance) appeal
formal groups
formal legitimate power
gender (sex) roles
guilt
hard-sell advertising
identification
indirect reference groups
indirect (vicarious) role models
informal groups
informal legitimate power
informational reference group influence
inter-role conflict
intra-role conflict
legitimate power
membership groups
modeling
moral appeals
multitask (polychronic time use)
nonmembership groups
primary groups

reference group
reference person (reference person, reference other,
    reference figure, significant other)
referent power
reinforcement power (instrumental power)
reward power
role acquisitions
role conflict
role load
role model
role overload
role-related product clusters (consumption constellations)
secondary groups
social agents
social aggregate
social category
social group
social group norms
social group role
social group socialization
social group status
social group values
social networking sites
social power
social psychologists
social referent
social status
socialization
sociologists
spokescharacters
status symbols
symbolic reference groups
timesaving goods
utilitarian (normative, instrumental) reference
    group influence
value-expressive (comparative, identification) reference
    groups
virtual communities
virtual groups (virtual communities, online communities,
    cybercommunities, social media)
wikis
within-group stratification

SUMMARY

This chapter covered social groups. These sets of individuals regularly and interdependently interact with one another over time to satisfy common needs or accomplish individual or mutual goals and share some significant common ideology, which leads to group cohesiveness and conformity. Social groups differ from social aggregates and social categories. Social groups are studied by sociologists and social psychologists.

The focus of this chapter was reference groups and reference people. Reference people used by advertisers include celebrities, the common man or typical consumer, and experts.

Exercise 8.1 provided an overview of types of social groups that marketers can deploy. They are all important because they influence lots of purchases, many products are purchased to achieve a sense of belonging or to make a statement about social group membership, and group members sometimes make joint decisions.

Reference groups are especially influential for particular types of products: socially visible products, luxuries, products for which consumers lack buying confidence, and producer relevant to a social group. There are four classification criteria for social groups that are of particular usefulness to marketers. Classifying social groups by membership yields membership groups and nonmembership groups. Brand communities are a type of membership group. If the person wishes to belong to a nonmembership group, it is an aspiration group, which could be an anticipatory aspiration group. Marketers appeal to consumers' aspirations to join such groups by associating usage of their product with them. Symbolic reference groups are the basis for celebrity-studded advertising that plays upon peoples' aspirations to emulate the stars. Other ads playing off symbolic reference groups use idealized "everyday" people and situations.

Categorizing social groups by type of contact gives primary groups, secondary groups, and virtual groups, which result in indirect but usually frequent contact. Virtual groups are built via Internet tools such as blogs and chat rooms. There are two types of social networking sites: commercially-sponsored brand communities and consumer-driven brand communities. Indirect reference groups are used by marketers through celebrities, the "common man," and experts.

Groups are also classified by formality of structure, which results in formal groups and informal groups.

Finally, social groups can be categorized by nature of attraction into contactual groups, which marketers associate with their products; disclaimant groups, which marketers use in demarketing; and dissociative groups. Marketers affiliated with a negative group, product, or behavior can try to make the group glamorous. Also, many marketing public service campaigns try to maintain the negative image of harmful groups, saying, "Don't get started!"

Exercise 8.2 described how consumer DM is influenced through three types of reference group influence (summarized in Exhibit 8.7). Informational reference group influence can be a useful source of purchase information if viewed as credible. The consumer accepts the information, resulting in a change in beliefs and attitudes. The reference group is believed to possess expert power. Utilitarian reference group influence results in conformity, which takes the form of compliance. The social group uses either reward power or coercive power.

Value-expressive influence is based on similarity. The consumer identifies with group members and internalizes their values, attitudes, and behaviors. The group exerts referent power.

Five characteristics of reference groups that can be tapped into by marketers were examined:

1. *Social group values*, which marketers must understand and appeal to.

2. *Social group norms*, on which normative social influence is based and whose norms lead to group conformity.

3. *Social group roles*, including role sets. Role-related product clusters help consumers fulfill a particular role. Marketers must reflect changing gender roles. A high role load can lead to role overload and role conflict, resulting in marketing opportunities to reduce them.

Assuming multiple roles causes inter-role conflict, which consumers resolve by multitasking. Marketers can help resolve inter-role conflict by developing and promoting timesaving goods. Marketers can also help consumers resolve intra-role conflict.

Parents, teachers, and friends can all serve as direct role models. Salespeople can also serve as role models, and advertisers use celebrities or other reference persons as indirect (vicarious) role models. Role acquisitions lead to product acquisitions.

4. *Social group status* is based on within-group stratification, not between-group stratification, upon which social classes are founded. Often, products are sold as status symbols.

5. *Socialization* and *social group socialization*, whose subset—consumer socialization—marketers tap into.

Exercise 8.3 discussed five types of social power that marketers can use to appeal to and persuade consumers. Social power is held by social agents. Marketing social agents include companies, salespeople, retailers, and the people featured in advertising.

Exhibit 8.12 summarizes the nature of each type of social power, the reference group influence process each uses, and the type of behavior each elicits.

Reward power can be achieved through material rewards or psychological rewards. Marketing's use of reward power includes product quality; sales promotions; continuity programs; advertising that informs; reassures, or entertains; and helpful salespeople.

Coercive power can be achieved through doling out punishments that are physical, material, or psychological and (2) withholding expected rewards. Marketers use coercive power via:

- High-pressure selling;
- Fear appeals that create anxiety by suggesting problems if the branded product is not purchased. Fear appeals can be based on either physical fear founded on physical risk or social fear associated with social risk. Fear appeals work best for unsought goods;
- Guilt appeals. Guilt is the violation of one's internal standards, leading to lower self-esteem and/or remorse;
- Shame appeals. Rather than being inwardly focused as guilt appeals are, shame appeals focus on other peoples' evaluation of an individual's behavior;
- Hard-sell advertising. This is the aggressive, obnoxious, urgent school of advertising;
- Threatening to withhold rewards. This is the school of marketing that focuses on what customers will lose if they do not purchase immediately.

There are two types of legitimate power: (1) formal legitimate power, whereby marketers hitch themselves to an individual or organization with formal legitimate power, such as a doctor or certifying authority; and (2) informal legitimate power, whereby advertisers create their own social norms or appeal to existing norms, as with moral appeals.

The concept of a social referent gives rise to referent power. The key social agent characteristic is either actual or ideal perceived similarity to target audience members. Two bases for referent powers are (1) identification and (2) emulation. The key social agent characteristic is perceived physical or social attractiveness. Advertising using emulation employs celebrities.

Expert power uses a social agent who is an expert. The key social agent characteristic of expert power is expertise. Marketing experts include celebrities providing "tools-of-the-trade" endorsements, professional experts, CEOs and employees, expert neutral third parties, expert media, spokescharacters with perceived expertise such as Betty Crocker, and the company itself if viewed as a leader in its field.

REFERENCES

Alreck, Pamela. (1994). "Commentary: A New Formula for Gendering Products and Brands." *Journal of Product and Brand Management,* 3, 1, 6–18.

Assael, Henry. (2004). *Consumer Behavior: A Strategic Approach.* Boston: Houghton Mifflin.

Atkin, Charles, and Block, Martin. (1983). "Effectiveness of Celebrity Endorsers." *Journal of Advertising,* 23, 1, 57–61.

Bearden, William O., and Etzel, Michael. (1982). "Reference Group Influence on Product and Brand Purchase Decisions." *Journal of Consumer Research,* 9, 2, 183–194.

Bourne, Francis S. (1957). "Group Influence in Marketing." In R. Likert and S. Hayes, eds., *Some Applications of Behavioral Research.* Paris: UNESCO, 208–224.

Burnett, John, and Wilkes, Robert E. (1980). "Fear Appeals to Segments Only." *Journal of Advertising Research,* 20, 5, 21–24.

Burnett, Melissa S., and Lunsford, Dale A. (1994). "Conceptualizing Guilt in the Consumer Decision-Making Process." *Journal of Consumer Marketing,* 11, 3, 33–43.

Burnkrant, Robert E., and Cousineau, Alain. (1975). "Informational and Normative Social Influence on Buyer Behavior." *Journal of Consumer Research,* 2, 3, 206–215.

Dotson, Michael J., and Hyatt, Eva M. (2005). "Major Influence Factors in Children's Consumer Socialization." *Journal of Consumer Marketing,* 22, 1, 35–42.

Erdogan, B. Zafer, Baker, Michael J., and Tagg, Stephen. (2001). "Selecting Celebrity Endorsers: The Practitioner's Perspective." *Journal of Advertising Research,* 41, 3, 39–48.

Fischer, Eileen, and Arnold, Stephen J. (1994). "Sex, Gender Identity, Gender Role Attitudes, and Consumer Behavior." *Psychology and Marketing,* 11 (March-April), 163–182.

French, J.R.P., and Raven, B. (1959). "The Bases of Social Power." In D. Cartwright, ed., *Studies in Social Power.* Ann Arbor, MI: Institute for Social Research, 150–167.

Huhmann, Bruce A., and Brotherton, Timothy P. (1997). "A Content Analysis of Guilt Appeals in Popular Magazine Advertisements." *Journal of Advertising,* 26, 2, 35–46.

John, Deborah Roedder. (1999). "Consumer Socialization of Children: A Retrospective Look at Twenty-five Years of Research" *Journal of Consumer Research,* 26, 3, 183–213.

Kelley, Harold H. (1952). "The Two Functions of Reference Groups." In G.E. Swanson, T.M. Newcomb, and E.C. Hartley, eds., *Readings in Social Psychology.* New York: Holt, 410–414.

Kogan, Nathan, and Wallach, Michael A. (1967). "Risky Shift Phenomenon in Small Decision-Making Groups: A Test of the Information Exchange Hypothesis." *Journal of Experimental Social Psychology,* 3 (January), 75–84.

Moschis, George P., and Churchill, Gilbert A. (1978). "Consumer Socialization: A Theoretical and Empirical Analysis." *Journal of Marketing Research,* 15, 4, 599–609.

Muniz, Albert M., Jr., and O'Guinn, Thomas. (2001). "Brand Community." *Journal of Consumer Research,* 2, 4, 412–432.

Ostlund, Lyman E. (1973). "Role Theory and Group Dynamics." In Scott Ward and Thomas S. Robertson, eds., *CB: Theoretical Sources.* Englewood Cliffs, NJ: Prentice-Hall, 230–275.

Park, G. Whan, and Lessig, V. Parker. (1977). "Students and Housewives: Differences in Susceptibility to Reference Group Influence." *Journal of Consumer Research,* 4, 2, 102–110.

Petty, Richard E., Cacioppo, John T., and Schumann, David. (1983). "Central and Peripheral Routes to Advertising Effectiveness: The Moderating Role of Involvement." *Journal of Consumer Research,* 10, 2, 135–146.

Pitta, Dennis A., and Fowler, Danielle. (2005). "Internet Community Forums: An Untapped Resource for Consumer Marketers." *Journal of Consumer Marketing,* 22, 5, 265–274.

Ray, Michael L., and Wilkie, William L. (1970). "Fear: The Potential of an Appeal Neglected by Marketing." *Journal of Marketing,* 34, 1, 54–62.

Rubin, Vicki, Mager, Carol, and Friedman, Hershey H. (1982). "Company President versus Spokesperson in Television Commercials." *Journal of Advertising Research,* 22, 4, 31–33.

Sherif, M. (1953). "The Concept of Reference Groups in Human Relations." In M. Sherif and M.O. Wilson, eds., *Group Relations at the Crossroads.* New York: Harper and Row, 203–231.

Shibutani, Tamotsu. (1955). "Reference Groups as Perspectives." *American Journal of Sociology,* 60 (May), 562–569.

Solomon, Michael R. (1988). "Mapping Product Constellations: A Social Categorization Approach to Symbolic Consumption." *Psychology and Marketing,* 5, 3, 233–258.

———. (1983). "The Role of Products as Social Stimuli: A Symbolic Interactionism Perspective." *Journal of Consumer Research,* 10, 3, 319–329.

Stafford, James E. (1966). "Effects of Group Influence on Consumer Brand Preferences." *Journal of Marketing Research,* 3, 1, 8–75.

Sternthal, Brian, and Craig, Samuel C. (1974). "Fear Appeals: Revisited and Revised." *Journal of Consumer Research,* 1, 4, 22–34.

Till, Brian D. (1998). "Using Celebrity Endorsers Effectively." *Journal of Product and Brand Management,* 7, 5, 400–410.

Ward, Scott (1974). "Consumer Socialization." *Journal of Consumer Research,* 1, 2, 1–14.

FAMILY INFLUENCES

The most significant consumer social group is the **household (consumer unit, dwelling unit)**. This is any occupied housing unit, regardless of the relationships among the people living there. Examples of households include roommates sharing an apartment, unmarried couples dwelling together (cohabiting couples), same-sex couples, and two (or more!) couples sharing a house. In all of these situations, buying decisions are often based not just on one individual's needs but rather on the household's welfare. The most common type of household is the **family household (family)**, with two or more people related by blood, marriage, or adoption who reside together.

There are two basic types of traditional families.

1. The **nuclear (conventional, normal, limited, typical) family** consists of a heterosexual adult couple and their own or adopted children. This is the stereotypical loving husband, devoted wife, their 2.2 freckle-faced kids, plus the dog, Spot, and kitty, Fluffy. (Note: About 60 percent of all homes have a pet while only 35 percent have children, with nearly half considering the animals as part of the family.) The nuclear family one is born into is the **family of orientation (family of origin)**, so named because it provides an orientation toward values, norms, political and religious beliefs, and other cultural characteristics. The family established through marriage is the **family of procreation**.

2. The **extended family** includes the nuclear family plus one or more additional blood relatives, such as grandparents, uncles and aunts, nephews and nieces, and parents-in-law. It typically spans three generations.

When the "family" is discussed in the United States, it is usually the nuclear family, the primary emphasis of this chapter. In many countries, though, the extended family is the defining unit. In addition to traditional families there are two other types of rapidly growing consumer units of interest to marketers. **Nontraditional families** are families that do not include a married couple with children. They fall outside the normative nuclear family but do contain people related by blood, marriage, or adoption. They include single-parent households, created either by divorce, death of a spouse, or, increasingly, by women who bear children out of wedlock; married couples without children; and **blended families (stepfamilies, reconstituted families, aggregate families, second chancers)**, which consist of a married couple, one or both of whom were previously married, any children they produce as a couple, and offspring from previous marriages. **Nonfamily households** include combinations of unrelated people. These may consist of cohabiting couples, also known as persons of the opposite sex sharing living quarters (POSSLQ); friends sharing an apartment; and persons living alone.

SIGNIFICANCE OF FAMILY FOR MARKETERS

The family is an informal, primary, contactual, membership group: small in size, with regular face-to-face interaction. In general, families share ideology and have common goals. Families are the most influential of the many types of reference groups surveyed in Chapter 8.

Why else should this topic, studied by family sociologists, be singled out for special consideration by marketers? Let us count the ways.

FAMILIES ARE THE LARGEST CONSUMER MARKET

Family members make the majority of consumer goods purchases, and so the family is America's largest consumer market. Witness the numerous advertisers targeting families: Olive Garden restaurants ("When you're here, you're family"); Bertucci's restaurants ("Everybody eats when they come to our house"); Bounty paper towels ("Little kids, big spills"); Kodak ("Family moments"); and even Club Med, which repositioned itself from being a locale for finding one-night hookups to a family-friendly, family-fun place.

FAMILIES FORM SOCIETY'S BUILDING BLOCK

It is true that in 1960, almost half of all U.S. households fit the mold of a married couple with one or more children under age eighteen, whereas today less than a quarter of households fit this family model. Married-couple households have slipped from almost 80 percent during the 1950s to just 50 percent today. Nonetheless, traditional families still outnumber other types of household units, and the relative decline of the traditional family seen over the past several decades seems to have leveled off.

The family, as the central or dominant social institution, has been labeled the "building block of society," the "cradle of the culture," and a "God-ordained institution." Families provide emotional (love, nurture, and stable relationships) and economic resources, including allowances so kids can buy, buy, buy! Consequently, many products are pitched as promoting togetherness, such as food, video games, electronics, and cars.

Parents breed children and then socialize them regarding cultural characteristics. Families also play a key role in *consumer socialization*. Children's lifetime attitudes are heavily influenced by their parents and older siblings, not just toward religion, country, sex, politics, and apple pie, but also toward products, brands, and stores. We regard some marketplace alternatives favorably or unfavorably, depending on whether our parents swore *by* them or *at* them.

Noteworthy for marketers is that families establish a *lifestyle* for their members. In fact, believe it or not, even teens are primarily influenced by their parents' lifestyles and consumption patterns, although they will seldom admit it. Parents are often unaware of how much influence they have on their children (tastes in fashion and music excepted!). Families also perform a *mediating* function, with older members filtering and interpreting for the young 'uns the influences of other societal institutions, such as TV shows, movies, magazines, and . . . advertising!

Parents and their grown children often share brand preferences, which suggests that early family influences in the marketplace endure throughout one's lifetime via **intergenerational influence**. For example, a common decision heuristic is to buy the brand Mom always purchased, since mother was the expert household purchaser.

RENEWAL OF INTEREST IN THE FAMILY

There has been a revitalization of the family, hearth and home, and "family values," especially following 9/11. Consequently, households are feathering their nests with goods and services, and they are turning to an increasing number of magazines whose editorial matter zeroes in on family living and parenting. This is especially true for Generation Xers, many of whom were deprived of stable family lives due to skyrocketing divorce and having two full-time working parents. People of this generation display renewed enthusiasm for and commitment toward the family and crave establishing stable families of procreation. Panasonics's "Bring back family time" ad campaign is based on the premise that families do not spend enough time together even though they desperately want to.

In fact, many products are pitched as promoting togetherness, such as food, video games, electronics, and cars. For instance, baby boomers are playing Wii with their kids and Hasbro promotes family game night. Marketers increasingly position their wares as trusted family members, from Parkers Brothers board games to family soaps and deodorants. Campbell's Soup's ad campaign uses scrapbook-like scenes of moms using the soups in their everyday lives.

GROWING INFLUENCE OF WOMEN AND CHILDREN

The influence of women and children on major household purchase decisions is increasing. Both groups are becoming more important consumer markets. For instance, moms and kids are McDonald's core target market.

Women and Mothers Are Influential. During the 1920s, advertisers figured out that women were responsible for as much as 80 percent of household purchases. While men were in the "jungle" of the work world, women were in the stores making most buying decisions. As a result, most consumer marketers zeroed in on women as their primary target market.

With changing gender roles, men are no longer the sole breadwinners and women the bread buyers and bakers. Over the past several decades women have been doing more market work and less housework.

Consequently, women are not just buying household convenience goods, such as sponges and shampoo, but also big-ticket items such as cars, hi-tech toys, travel services, and golf equipment, all sans hubby's input. In fact, it has been estimated that women control about two-thirds of all consumer purchases and influence about 85 percent of major purchasing decisions for the home—they hold the family purse strings and manage the homestead. Furthermore, many men are at ease with this—when they are not in the workplace, these husbands follow their partner's lead. According to J.D. Power & Associates, women buy 40 percent of new vehicles, 51 percent of consumer electronics, and constitute 43 percent of investors. Knowing this, electronics retailer Best Buy added personal shopping assistants to explain "geek speak" to uninitiated women. Financial services, stereotypically a male-focused industry, have been modifying their advertising portfolio so that nearly every financial campaign now features women.

Research by Lowe's home improvement stores found that women initiate 80 percent of home improvement projects, so Lowe's retargeted their marketing efforts accordingly. Both Lowe's and Home Depot refashioned their stores to appeal to women by using brighter lighting, fewer products stacked to the ends of the aisles, and better signs, all to tone down the warehouse atmosphere.

Similarly, the target decision makers for appliances such as washers, dryers, and dishwashers tend to be women. Realizing this, Maytag redesigned its Maytag stores, which are more colorful, brightly lit, include children's play areas, and offer a higher level of customer service.

Not only do moms influence family members, some influence other mothers and families too. These so-called *alpha moms* are well-educated, high-income, type A, tech-savvy perfectionists striving to achieve mommy excellence and be wonderful, can-do wives. They are multitasking, kidcentric women who may or may not work outside of the home. They view motherhood as a job that can be mastered with diligent research. Influential leaders of the pack, they enthusiastically share their knowledge with other mothers. When they believe in a brand, they advocate it to their peers with conviction. Hence, marketers pursue this segment with a vengeance. Also, single women are on the rise and now constitute the second-largest group of home buyers in the United States, just behind married couples.

Kid Power. Children's purchase influence has also grown tremendously. This is a result of rising household incomes; fewer children per family (hence each has more household responsibility and increased spending power); busy full-time working or single parents who need help buying household goods; aggressive child-aimed marketing that makes youngsters consumer savvy; and more media-wise kids, especially regarding the Internet.

Another aspect of growing kid power is age compression (kids getting older younger [KGOY]). Today's children are more mature psychologically due to their increased independence and spending power, high purchase influence over their parents, and tech know-how. This is why marketers target nine-year-olds with apparel and accessories once considered appropriate only for teens. Eight- to twelve-year-olds are pitched with a dizzying array of music, movie, and cell phone choices, and preteen girls receive abundant attention from fashion, skin care, and makeup marketers. Sellers must walk a tightrope, appealing to these youngsters' sophisticated tastes while not turning off their folks. It's the parents after all who control both the purse strings and the transportation to the mall.

This rising kid power is evident in more purchasing independence and more sophisticated tastes in everything from sneakers to sporting goods to clothing. Many of today's young ones take charge of the home computer, control the TV, decide what to wear to school, shop alone, and fix their own meals. Marketers are responding to this by targeting promotions to teens, tweens, and tykes. They recognize that young consumers are really three types of markets: a present primary market, a future market, and an influential market.

A Present Primary Market. Children are a lucrative market for products they currently consume, such as toys, clothes, candy, snacks, breakfast cereal, and school supplies. Children's food products are nothing new—remember Chef Boyardee spaghetti and Franco-American SpaghettiOs? But food is fancier today. The food industry is wooing kids with colors and fun flavors: green, purple, and mystery—Heinz EZ

Squirt colored ketchup, Kraft's Blues Clues macaroni and cheese; and Yoplait Go-Gurt in fun flavors like Strawberry Splash and Cool Cotton Candy.

More youth-centric retail outlets are popping up. Claire's stores sell inexpensive baubles, bows, and bangles for teens and tweens. They launched an exclusive line of Mary-Kate and Ashley cosmetics and a line of costume jewelry handpicked by singer Mariah Carey. Other stores highlight sections targeting young consumers, such as Bath & Body Works' tweens sector with its American Girl line, which includes hair care products, lip gloss, and perfume.

A Future Market. Today's marketers consider kids when developing items that they will buy later in life, such as magazines and consumer electronics. Every product purveyor targets an age group to establish brand preferences early. For fast-food feeders, it is the Happy Meal set; for soft-drink sellers, it is preteens; and for beer brewers, it is the college crowd. To establish brand loyalty at an early age, marketers of such wares use gateway marketing, developing kids' versions of adult products, such as health and beauty aids (shampoos, soaps, and even cosmetics with fruity scents); clothing (Polo Ralph Lauren apparel and accessories for infants and children); magazines (*National Geographic for kids* and *Time for Kids*), and even consumer electronics (Nickelodeon's Npower SpongeBob SquarePants Flash digital camera and digital media player and Fisher Price's Disney Pix Jr. digital camera for kids as young as three years old).

Such gateway products are all part of the aspirational trend—kids want what their parents have and often role play as parents and other adults with such goods. The Disney Dream Desk is a PC with mouse ears and built-in parental controls for kids ages six to eleven. The Disney Mobile's family cell phone service for ten- to fifteen-year-olds lets parents monitor and control how their progeny use the service (e.g., spending limits and when and where it can be used). Disney also offers a colorful, whimsical line of TVs, DVD players, personal digital radios, and CD boom boxes with Disney characters that pop up with on-screen controls.

An Influential Market. The young ones act as influences on their parents' decisions for products used by most or all family members. Children and adolescents are especially influential on parents' choices of child-relevant items such as fast food. However, they also affect some family choices of leisure activities, such as family vacations, movies, and restaurants. Youngsters have the least effect on decisions related to durables like cars and appliances. Kids' influence is stronger in the earlier stages of family decision making (problem recognition and information search) than in the actual decision stage. Toyota, believing in kids' influence on parental car choices, launched a TV campaign in which kids helped redesign the Sienna minivan.

FAMILIES PROVIDE MULTIPLE TARGET MARKETS

Individual family members represent distinct target markets for many products based on the roles they play. Some products will have one group (e.g., parents) as the *primary target market*, another bunch (perhaps teens) as the *secondary target market*, and a third cluster (possibly children) as the *tertiary target market*. One ad can simultaneously appeal to some or all of these groups, most typically moms and kids. Alternatively, campaigns can be launched for each family segment under an integrated marketing communications program.

Accordingly, after promoting Pop-Tarts to children for many years, Kellogg's began running commercials aimed at moms, who also desire a great-tasting indulgent morning food. Campbell's soup discovered that soup interests youngsters because it is wet, juicy, and slurpy, so now they run commercials on TV programming for both kids and for adults. One campaign aimed at mothers depicted soup consumption in a variety of scenarios against the backdrop of contemporary music; another—Campbell's "mouth fun" ads—targeted kids and personified soup varieties as rock stars while a lively mix of rock and hip-hop played in the background.

On the other hand, ever since Jell-O gelatin was first advertised in *Ladies' Home Journal* in 1902, it has been aimed primarily toward moms as a convenient dessert for the family, as in TV commercials featuring Bill Cosby beseeching mothers with the message, "Kids love pudding." Now that youngsters' purchasing power is stronger than ever and the "nag factor" has become a critical success driver for children's products, the brand is aimed squarely at the little ones in ads for X-treme Jell-O Gel Sticks and Gel Cups. Meanwhile, ads claiming marketers offer the coolest clothing, the most fashion-forward backpacks, even the trendiest lunchboxes, are targeted not just to the youngsters but also toward upwardly mobile conspicuously consuming parents.

ORGANIZATION OF CHAPTER 9

Exercise 9.1 examines family decision roles during the family decision-making process, highlighting the individual influences of women, kids, and men on household purchases. It also illustrates marketers addressing all three groups in a single advertisement. Exercise 9.2 explores the use of the family life cycle for market segmentation and illustrates how advertisers target traditional nuclear families as well as non-traditional families. Exercise 9.3 allows you to ponder your own family roles and life cycle stages (present and future), think about how they affect your marketplace behavior, and contemplate how these roles and life cycle stages shape marketers' efforts to appeal to you.

EXERCISE 9.1. FAMILY DECISION-MAKING ROLES

OBJECTIVES

1. To recognize the multiple decision-making roles that go into purchasing family and household products and how marketers appeal to each role.
2. To analyze how marketers portray and target multiple roles in a single ad for a family product.
3. To increase understanding of family purchase roles by considering the decision-making roles taken by you and other family members during your college-choice process.

BACKGROUND

So far, this book has viewed consumer decision making primarily as an individual activity. However, many decisions are made in the context of social groups, notably families. To aid the group decision-making process, different group members adopt various **decision roles (consumption roles, purchase roles)**, which are appropriate behaviors for a particular person or position within the social group.

Family decision-making principles can often be generalized to other group decision-making contexts, such as nonfamily households and **buying centers**, which are decision-making units within organizations. A buying center is not a fixed, formally identifiable department within a firm but rather a network of people, including manufacturing engineers, purchasing specialists, and product managers. Each participant has a formal role in the organizational hierarchy (e.g., vice president of manufacturing, procurement officer). They typically meet in task forces or committees to make important organizational purchase decisions. Likewise, in informal social groups, there are usually several people who decide for the group, such as a group of mothers collectively deciding which park to visit with their children.

The roles that members play or the tasks they perform in the family (or household, including nontraditional and nonfamily households) decision-making process are known as **family (household) decision (consumption, purchase) roles.** These are not enduring roles, such as parent, son, daughter, or sister. Rather, they are short-term roles taken in the family consumer decision process for a particular product. For any given purchase decision, each of the family decision roles can have more than one family member taking that role and each family member can play more than one role.

Some decision roles are **instrumental (functional, economic) roles**. They relate to choosing functional products and to financial, performance, or other practical matters affecting the buying decision, such as when and how much to purchase, features and functions to consider, and budgeting. Others are **expressive roles**, which are predominant for hedonic products and express the family's aesthetic, social, or emotional needs through decisions on color, style, design, and so on. Traditionally, the husband fulfilled the instrumental role and the wife the expressive role. However, sex role evolution has changed these somewhat so that either role may be fulfilled by either partner.

EXHIBIT 9.1   Family Decision-Making Roles

Family role	Decision-making stage	Description
Initiator	Problem recognition	Suggests a need for the product to other family members
Gatekeeper	Information search	Collects and controls the flow of product information to others
Influencer	Information search and alternative evaluation	Provides others with information, advice, and opinions
		Goes beyond information to persuasion
Decider	Choice (decision)	Determines either unilaterally or jointly with others whether and what to buy
Buyer	Purchase	Purchases or physically acquires the product
Preparer	Postpurchase	Transforms the product into a form suitable for consumption by other family members
User	Postpurchase consumption	User(s) or consumer(s) of the product
Monitor	Postpurchase behavior	Regulates or controls consumption by others
Evaluator	Postpurchase evaluation	Evaluates product performance, either for self or others
Maintainer	Postpurchase behavior	Services or repairs the product so it continues to perform in a satisfactory manner
Disposer	Postpurchase behavior	Carries out the disposal or discontinuation of the product

FAMILY DECISION-MAKING ROLES

The following household decision-making roles are outlined in Exhibit 9.1.

PREPURCHASE ROLES

Initiator. The **initiator** first suggests that the family has a need or want for a particular product, triggering the *problem recognition stage*. The initiator tends to be the individual with the most urgent need, the heaviest user, or the one who derives the most consumption satisfaction. To spark the family decision-making process, marketers often target initiators, suggesting a need for the product.

Gatekeeper. During the *information search stage*, the **gatekeeper** gathers information, controls its flow to other family members, and might make a recommendation. The gatekeeper literally controls the information gate and can thereby influence product selection. This tends to be the person with easiest access to information or having the most interest and/or expertise. The gatekeeper could be the homemaker who discards junk mail, hangs up on the telemarketer, or gathers data online. Gatekeepers might be teens or children who become the designated family Internet researchers for things like travel while their parents are still trying to figure out e-mail. They could also be children who know about the latest and greatest toys "as advertised on TV." Marketers need to feed information to the appropriate gatekeeping party.

Influencer. The **influencer** provides information, advice, and persuasion during the *information search* and *alternative evaluation stages*. The influencer goes beyond the gatekeeper, who simply provides information and perhaps a recommendation, using information to persuade family members. The outcome of the decision is usually very important to influencers. Hence, moms are a big influence on their tweens' fashion choices. In turn, teenagers and even preteens are influential experts on technology products. Children are very likely to influence their parents ("pester power," "tug-on-the-pants factor"), suggesting everything from making a pilgrimage to McDonald's for the latest Happy Meal toy to what goes into the lunch box to what comes out of the microwave. Some marketers call this kidfluence. They can sway the influencer through persuasive marketing communications that discuss the importance of the criteria on which their brand performs particularly well.

The influencer sometimes is someone outside of the family. Microsoft Money personal finance software was unable to compete successfully against Intuit's Quicken software because the latter was widely used by accountants and financial planners, who recommended Quicken to their consumer clients.

Influencers' Conflict Resolution Strategies. Conflict often occurs as various family members attempt to influence one another, sometimes resulting in satisficing and extra time and effort to make decisions. There are several conflict resolution strategies that influencers can employ:

- *Problem solving or reasoning:* using a logical argument to win others over to one's viewpoint. Example: "We should buy the high-priced widget because, although it costs more, it is much better quality."
- *Bargaining:* trying to reach a compromise by making concessions. Spirited bargaining usually involves trading off people's less important preferences for their more strongly felt predilections. "If you do this, I'll do that," or "If you give up this, I'll surrender that." Example: "Mom, I like the more expensive jeans. If you pay half, I'll pay half."
- *Impression management:* misleading others by misrepresenting the facts in order to prevail. Example: "No brand of aspirin is better than this brand, dear" (when all brands are actually identical).
- *Use of authority or autocratic control:* claiming superior expertise or role appropriateness (legitimate power). Example: "As the head of this household, I'll make the decision."
- *Accommodation:* acquiescing to others' wishes. Example: "Okay, whatever. Have it your way, Sis."
- *Playing on emotions:* capitalizing on others' feelings. May include the silent treatment, getting angry, and sweet talking. Example: "Honey, I love your cooking, but you deserve a break. Let's go out to eat tonight."
- *Obtaining additional information:* gathering more data or getting a third-party opinion. This can be accomplished by someone playing both the gatekeeper and influencer roles.

Marketers' efforts to establish the relevant evaluative criteria, determine the alternatives to be compared, and evaluate the various brands' standings on attributes can all contribute to the influencer's cause. Sellers can sway the influencer through persuasive marketing communications that discuss the importance of the criteria on which their brand performs particularly well.

Decider. The family member who makes the ultimate decisions on whether and what to purchase, as well as related choices such as where and when to buy, take the **decider** role during the *choice stage*. The decision makers are usually those with some level of authority or power (financial, social, physical, etc.). Deciders also typically have expertise, interest, and involvement. Parents who exercise ultimate veto power over many of their youngsters' choices are deciders.

Role Dominance Among Deciders. Regarding husband-wife choices, one issue is **role dominance**, which is the extent to which husbands and wives influence the final decision relative to each other and additional family members. There are four types of decisions:

1. **Husband-dominant (patriarchal) decisions.** The husband largely controls the family decision, although the wife may have some input. Traditionally, husband-dominant decisions were for more task-oriented and instrumental products, such as cars, lawn mowers, tools, and gardening supplies. Today, fewer important decisions are husband dominant than a few decades ago, although modern hubbies now make decisions for less involving household purchases, such as food and laundry detergent.

2. **Wife-dominant (matriarchal) decisions.** The wife dominates the decision, perhaps with some input from her spouse. Traditionally, these decisions pertained to more aesthetic and expressive items, such as children's clothes, rugs, and draperies, as well as household items (e.g., food, cleaning sup-

plies, and toiletries) and appliances. As noted earlier, wives today have a more dominant role in major purchase decisions.

3. **Joint (syncratic) decisions.** Husband and wife decide together, which is especially likely where high perceived risk and high involvement exist, such as for houses, family cars, living room furniture, home electronic appliances, and financial planning services.

Increasingly, decisions that were once dominated by a particular spouse are being made syncratically. This is due to changing gender roles and the fact that more women now work outside of the home, giving them more economic household clout.

4. **Autonomous (autonomic, autocratic, individualized) decisions.** Either the husband or wife makes an individual decision. This occurs in cases where one spouse has more expertise in a decision area or if the decision is not important enough for both spouses to get involved (e.g., "Choosy mothers choose Jif").

There can also be *child-dominant decisions* or various combinations of husband, wife, and child joint decisions. The marketer should ascertain that deciders are provided with the information needed to make a choice, whether it comes from the firm, other family members, or other information sources.

Buyer. The **buyer (family purchasing agent)** is the family member who procures the product during the *purchase stage*. This is most often mothers, although increasingly fathers, teenagers, or even young children make purchases. Since deciding and buying often go hand in hand, the buyer is often the decider. For example, wives often select and purchase underwear, socks, and ties for their disinterested husbands as well as most food and drug items. Marketers must ensure their product is conveniently available to the purchaser and use in-store influences such as attractive point-of-purchase displays and coupon dispensers.

The following roles all occur during the *postpurchase consumption* stage.

POSTPURCHASE ROLES

Preparer. The **preparer** converts the product into a form consumable by family members. This is usually the person most skilled in the preparation task, such as baking cookies, putting together "easy-to-assemble" toys, or completing income tax forms online. Marketers should know who the preparer typically is and provide clear instructions for that person to follow.

User. The **user (end user)** is the ultimate consumer of the product. Although users might not have a role in the purchase process, marketers must ensure that the product ultimately appeals to and satisfies them.

Monitor. The **monitor** keeps an eye on what is consumed by family members. Usually one or both of the parents serve this role. For example, the cook watches the sugar, salt, and saturated fat in a recipe, parents regulate the amount of TV and computer time their kids have as well as what they're viewing, and children tell their parents how hopelessly out of fashion their clothing is. Marketers have an opportunity to educate or assist the monitor, such as television manufacturers installing V-chips so parents can screen out shows with violent or sexual content or software makers offering Web site filters to weed out the sites children should be avoiding.

Evaluator. All family users and some nonusers are **evaluators.** They assess the product's performance. Product designers must not neglect considering possible product evaluations by nonusers, and fashion the product to satisfy their expectations. For instance, wives ask their husbands, "How do you like my new dress?" (to which most men respond "How much did it cost?"), and children make unsolicited comments like "Gee, Mom, that dress makes you look fat!"

Maintainer. **Maintainers** keep a durable good in tip-top shape by checking it regularly, getting it serviced, and taking it to be repaired or doing the repairs and servicing themselves. For example, someone usually makes sure the family car gets oil and filter changes as well as tune-ups. Marketers need to remind maintainers when it is time to do maintenance work and make it convenient to have those tasks done. For instance, car service shops send postcard reminders for oil changes and tune-ups, and technology product sellers maintain toll-free help desks.

Disposer. The person who gets rid of the product by trashing, recycling, reselling, trading, or giving it away is the **disposer**. Marketers should assist in disposal where possible. Computer and electronics manufacturers are increasingly pressured to help with recycling of their products since most electronics contain lead, mercury, or other substances that are harmful if dumped in landfills.

TARGET MARKETING AND PROMOTION IMPLICATIONS

Although we have looked at specific applications of the family role concept, there are two general implications for target marketing and product promotion. First, because different family members can represent divergent target markets for the same product, marketing communications can be aimed toward multiple target markets within the family through multiple ads. An advertiser can simultaneously run a mom campaign, a dad campaign, and a kid campaign, with each emphasizing different decision-making roles, product attributes, and selling appeals. Happios corn chips could direct one ad campaign toward children as influencers, stressing taste and a "cool," fun image, while a second campaign targeted toward parents as deciders emphasizes nutrition and a reasonable price.

A second approach is to target more than one role in a given advertisement that likely will be exposed to multiple family members. Such broad exposure occurs in media such as television, radio, outdoor billboards and signage, and general interest magazines such as *People*. The ads you will evaluate in this exercise take the latter approach.

REVIEW QUESTIONS

1. In what sense is a family analogous to an organizational buying center?
2. Describe each of the family decision-making roles, the stage in the consumer buying process that corresponds to each one, which family member(s) are most likely to assume each role, and how marketers can tap into each role.
3. What are the target marketing and promotional implications of family decision making?

IN-CLASS APPLICATIONS

1. In Exercise 3.2, you thought about the consumer decision process you undertook for your college choice decision. However, such an important decision probably had input from other family members and outside parties. Discuss the different family decision-making roles that went into your college purchase decision, in which stage in the decision process each role occurred, who played each role, and college marketing efforts that either could have or did influence the player of each role.

2. For each of the ads in Exhibits 9.2 through 9.6, identify and describe the family decision-making roles targeted. Which family member will likely play each of these roles and why? How effective do you think each ad is in portraying each family role?

Are there any other family roles for each product's purchase decision process not appealed to in its ad? If so, who would play the role(s)? Should such role(s) be appealed to in this same ad or would a separate ad targeted to such role players be advised?

3. Describe whether each ad illustrates an instrumental role, an expressive role, or neither. Explain who in the family is taking each role.

4. What would you expect to be the role dominance pattern for the product featured in each ad? Does each ad appeal to this role dominance pattern?

5. Recently, Wal-Mart created a toy wish list featuring two elves who encouraged children to create a Christmas wish list to be e-mailed to their parents. "If you show us what you want, we'll send it straight off to your parents," promised one elf. When a toy appeared on the screen, kids could select "Yes" to add the item to their wish list, in which case they heard applause. If kids chose a "No" response, there was silence.

Critics contended Wal-Mart encouraged kids to nag parents for toys (influencer role). Wal-Mart said that

EXHIBIT 9.2   Goodyear Ad

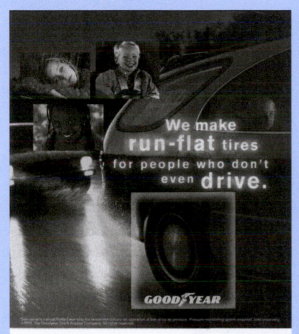

Goodyear Eagle Aquasteel Run-Flat Nobody looks out for your family better than you do. But Goodyear can help. With Eagle Aquasteel Run-Flat radials you can literally run over a hazard, lose all air pressure and keep driving for up to 50 miles at up to 55 miles per hour.* No more getting stuck in bad weather and having to get out of your car in emergency lanes or in the middle of nowhere to change a tire. Goodyear Run-Flat technology helps the tire keep its shape, so you can keep driving to safety. To learn more about Goodyear's innovative Run-Flat technology, visit our website at www.runflat.com. Or call 1-800-RUN-FLAT.

Goodyear. Number One in tires.

EXHIBIT 9.3   BBC's Video Language Course for Children Ad

Let the BBC teach your child a second language!

It's a scientific fact. A child naturally learns a language far more easily than an adult does. In Europe, kids commonly learn a *second* language at the *same* time as their *first* — in early childhood. Why? Because it will never be as easy again.

Start early. The window of opportunity.

New neurological research confirms that the prime time for learning a *second* language is from birth to age 10 or 12. NEWSWEEK calls it the "window of opportunity" for languages.

Breakthrough! MUZZY: The BBC's Video Language Course for Children.

Only the British Broadcasting Corporation has developed a complete language course for children. It has won awards and devoted families the world over. MUZZY, a delightful animated program, allows kids to pick up a *second* language the same way as a *first*. By seeing, hearing and learning.

MUZZY is fun. And it works.

MUZZY is a lovable space traveler who fascinates even the youngest child. Sophisticated 11-year-olds love him, too! The course introduces a language and provides months and years of instruction and enrichment. Videos, audios, CD-ROM and book combine to reach every child. Kids keep coming back. They grow up with MUZZY! Available in Spanish, French, Italian and German.

Powerful new edition. Videos & CD-ROM.

This brand new MUZZY edition is the best yet. Features 4 captivating story videos, 1 new vocabulary video, 2 audiocassettes for car or home, script book, and a new BBC CD-ROM filled with language activities.

Free Bonus.

You will receive the whole course in one shipment. You may pay in five monthly credit card payments of just $33.80 each. The vocabulary video — a $69 value — is your Free Bonus for ordering now. Satisfaction guaranteed. Let MUZZY give your child an Early Advantage for life!

Call Toll Free: 1-800-211-7775
Dept. 0004

— RESERVATION APPLICATION —

Early Advantage   FREE BONUS:
25 Ford Road   Vocabulary Video
Westport, CT 06880   for ordering now.

Call Toll Free: 1-800-211-7775
Dept. 0004

The BBC's *Video Language Course for Children*

YES, send me MUZZY. For each course ordered, please charge my credit card $33.80* a month for five months. Charge me $9.50* shipping/handling with the first installment. 30-day return privilege. Satisfaction guaranteed.

QTY Spanish   QTY French
QTY Italian   QTY German

Name _____

Address _____

City/State/Zip _____

Credit Card:
□ VISA □ MasterCard □ Am. Ex.

Credit Card Number _____ Exp. Date ____

Signature _____

□ I prefer to pay by check and am enclosing ($169 + $9.50) a total of $178.50* for each program ordered, payable to Early Advantage.
*CT residents, add 6% sales tax.

EXHIBIT 9.4   Pull-Ups Ad

I've been dry for 3 hours... and I can prove it!

Pull-Ups® training pants have magic flowers and stars that fade when they get wet, helping your child potty train.

Toddlers have minds of their own. They wander off in different directions. They say "no." And they need to feel ready before Mom can help them begin to potty train.

But no matter when they start, Pull-Ups® training pants can help. They assist your child in learning to potty train with magic flowers and stars that fade when wet. When used regularly, Pull-Ups® encourage toddlers to stay dry. It's a simple way to begin learning those important Big Kid™ skills.

You can even make a game of seeing how long your child can keep the magic flowers (for girls) or stars (for boys) from fading. So use Pull-Ups® to help your child achieve an important accomplishment – one to be truly proud of.

Pull-Ups®
I'm a Big Kid Now.®
www.pull-ups.com

EXHIBIT 9.5   JCPenney Ad

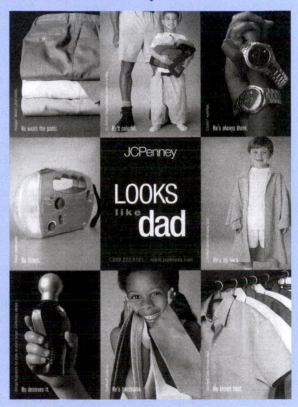

EXHIBIT 9.6   Honeywell Ad

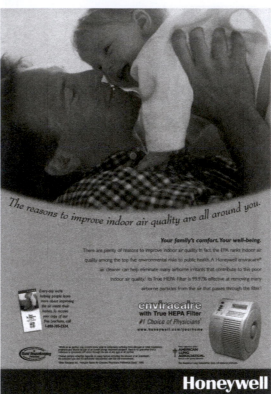

the Web site was simply a modern twist on the tradition of making a wish list and sharing it with parents. Do you think what Wal-Mart did was socially responsible? How do you think you'd feel and act as a parent presented with a Wal-Mart wish list?

6. Some child advocates are questioning whether electronics, such as digital cameras for tots, are appropriate for preschool play. To make a buck, they claim, toy marketers are simply lowering age targets for adult-oriented electronic gadgets. Further, they believe that this is the marketing world's push to drive children to digital screens and away from creative play. Toy makers strongly disagree, pointing out that this generation of kids is born with technology surrounding them, and kids want to use their parents' digital toys, so they are simply filling a marketplace need. What say you?

7. Victoria's Secret has launched the Pink line of "loungeware" (e.g., sweatpants, T-shirts, pajamas, bras, and panties) for eighteen- to thirty-year olds, but stronger interest exists among girls ages eleven to eighteen, raising critics' cries of promoting adolescent sexuality. Is this an ethical and socially responsible example of targeting children as a future market through gateway products?

WRITTEN APPLICATIONS

1. Answer Question 1 in the In-Class Applications, both for yourself and based on a personal interview with a classmate or friend.

2. Answer Questions 2, 3, and 4 in the In-Class Applications for three of the ads.

3. Find two other ads for products consumed by family members. For each ad, answer Questions 2 through 4 in the In-Class Applications.

4. Cite an example of a product for which two or more families might have two or more dissimilar family decision role structures. Describe these different structures.

If families exhibit various family role structures, what does this suggest for a marketer's advertising strategy to effectively reach all targeted family members?

EXERCISE 9.2. FAMILY LIFE CYCLE STAGES

OBJECTIVES

1. To become familiar with the stages in both a traditional and contemporary family life cycle (FLC) model; to describe the typical family in each stage in terms of demographics, needs, earnings, and spending patterns; and to identify effective marketing strategies for appealing to typical families in each stage.
2. To become aware of changes in family composition and lifestyle, how they relate to the stages in both the traditional Wells and Gubar and modernized Gilly and Enis FLC models, and to see how these changes affect marketing efforts.

BACKGROUND

OVERVIEW OF THE FAMILY LIFE CYCLE CONCEPT

A TV commercial for Volkswagen featured a deep male voiceover tracing the development of a family from marriage through the birth of children and the acquisition of pets and possessions. A growing family crossed the screen, getting a different Volkswagen (Beetle, Cabriolet, Jetta, Passat, and Eurovan) at each life stage. A Chase bank TV commercial promoted credit cards as appropriate for successive life stages. The ad depicted a man at his college graduation, on his first day of launching his career, on a date, on his honeymoon, and with his young family. The voiceover said, "The road of life takes many turns. Chase has over 900 credit cards to make the most of every one." These commercials show how marketers have successfully borrowed the sociological concept of **family life cycle (FLC; life stages, household life cycle, consumer life cycle)**, which describes the phases a family of procreation typically goes through in their process of formation, development, and ultimate dissolution.

FLC stages are based on critical transition points or life stage changes: marriage, birth of the first child, entry of that youngster into school, launching of the youngest child from the nest to college or full-time work, workforce retirement of the family breadwinner, and death of a spouse.

These pivotal events spur changes in consumers' lifestyles. Consequently, FLC can be used as a basis for market segmentation because lifestyle determines CB. Consider how having young children changes their parents' lifestyles: Instead of going out and whooping it up to all hours of the night they join baby-sitter clubs and enjoy *cocooning (nesting)*. The most important thing at this stage is keeping their wings of protection over their young ones and staying close to hearth and home. Your own purchasing patterns will be quite different once you earn your college sheepskin.

Car marketers have always understood this. General Motors' original market segmentation scheme was based on CEO Alfred Sloan's strategy of "a car for every purse and purpose." The idea was that your first car would be a Chevrolet, followed by Pontiac, then a Buick and Oldsmobile, and finally a Cadillac when you moved to Florida to retire. Likewise, Toyota will sell you a $12,000 Yaris economy sedan when you graduate college, offer you all types of family cars and trucks as you establish and grow a family, and help you celebrate success in your sunset years with a $120,000 Lexus.

Transition points are also times when consumers are more likely to switch brand preferences and be openly receptive to marketing efforts. For example, life events drive the insurance rates process: customers have kids, the kids turn driving age, and then they leave home. The parents, in turn, buy life insurance to protect their little ones; later load up on additional car insurance when the teens are ready to borrow the car keys; and still later sell the home, downsize, and become empty nesters, thereby reducing their home insurance needs.

DEMOGRAPHIC VARIABLES COMPOSING FLC

Although there are different schemes for measuring FLC, the following demographic variables are generally used as determinants of a family's FLC phase:

- *Age.* This is the age of the parents (usually the head of household) and/or, more important, the age of the youngest child. Age six is critical since mothers often return to the labor force on a part-time or full-time basis once the last child enters school.
- *Marital status.* The major distinction here is married versus single. Other possibilities include separated, widowed, and divorced.
- *Presence versus absence of children.* Children have a dramatic impact on lifestyle due to the expense, time, and physical and mental energy involved in raising them. The family's focus shifts from adults and their desires to the kiddies' wants and whims.
- *Residence of the youngest child.* This concerns whether any of the children are still in the nest or have left the comfort of the womb for the "cold cruel world."
- *Work status of the head of household.* Whether one, or both, or neither of the spouses are working outside of the home has an impact on discretionary income as well as available leisure time to support a desired lifestyle.
- *Whether or not both spouses are still alive.* Solitary survivors often either scale back their living standard or else go full speed ahead with an active lifestyle.
- *Relative income.* This is household income in relation to earlier and later stages in the family's FLC. Relative income is often inferred from knowledge of the FLC stage, especially from age and workforce status of the head of household. However, it is difficult to track a family's income over time, and so income is usually excluded when measuring FLC. Typically, occupational income peaks shortly before retirement, and total income then slowly declines for high savers living on investment and pension income and more rapidly for low savers.

Since absolute income—total annual family income—differs widely from family to family, it cannot be correlated meaningfully with FLC. However, in general, lower-income families are younger and in earlier FLC stages, while the well-to-do have been granted pay raises and have accumulated wealth over time and are therefore older and in later FLC phases.

FLC as a Composite Variable

Like social class, FLC is a composite variable. It is made up of several factors and can give richer descriptions than single, isolated variables can. FLC is also better able to predict future behavior. Hence, FLC better describes and predicts family buying behavior than single variables such as age of the parents or the children, or family income. Constituents of FLC, such as marital status, presence of children in the family, and workforce status, generally have more explanatory power than either age or household income. For example, age alone might not be a particularly good behavioral discriminator. A fifty-seven-year-old male could be a happy bachelor, a father (married or divorced) working to support his children, or a retired grandfather. Young adults who are married with a toddler are less likely to buy Lollapalooza tickets and more likely to be stocking up on Pampers.

Key FLC Stage Changes in Family Characteristics

The following are the key marketplace family variables that change through the FLC phases:
- *Needs, wants, and preferences.* Transition through the critical stages often means major buying binges. For example, nothing generates more sales than weddings (hence bridal showers), followed by the birth of a first child (baby showers) and the purchase of a new or upgraded home (housewarming parties).
- *Buying power.* Income is combined with accumulated wealth, and then debt service is subtracted to determine the household's buying power (state of wallet). The FLC consists of endless buying power cycles. Most college students operate in the red, but when they land their first job they go into the black. After marriage and children, heavy expenses are incurred, and so they might go into the red again. Following the kids flying the coop (and college debts and the mortgage being paid off) the couple goes back in black. After retirement, resources are often stretched thin again. (What a vicious cycle!)
- *Spending patterns.* Needs and buying power combine with the demographic characteristics of each FLC

EXHIBIT 9.7　Wells and Gubar Traditional Family Life Cycle Model

Life cycle stage	% of U.S. population*	Description
Bachelor	8.2	Young single people not living at home
Newly Married Couples	2.9	Young newly married couple without children
Full Nest I	24.2	Young married couple with youngest child under 6
Full Nest II	13.2	Young married couple with youngest child over 6
Full Nest III	14.7	Older married couple with dependent children (usually teens)
Empty Nest I	5.5	Older married couple with no children at home, husband employed
Empty Nest II	5.2	Older married couple with no children at home, husband retired
Solitary Survivor I	0.2	One remaining spouse, employed
Solitary Survivor II	2.0	One remaining spouse, retired

*As of 1966.

stage (marital status, presence of kids, etc.) to determine what consumers will buy with their hard-earned dollars. For example, college students spend heavily on CDs and digital music and movie downloads, frozen pizza, beer, books, entertainment, and junk food. Couples with young children purchase disposable diapers, children's clothing, ready-to-eat cereal, toys, snacks, and fruit drinks. Empty nesters spend on travel, entertainment, and health care.

THE WELLS AND GUBAR TRADITIONAL FLC MODEL

The 1966 Wells and Gubar Traditional FLC model, described by authors William Wells and George Gubar, describes family patterns as follows: people marry, have children, the kids leave home, the parents retire, and one partner loses a spouse. Exhibit 9.7 summarizes the stages and percent of the population Wells and Gubar found to be in each stage. What follows is a brief description of the family structure in each phase of the Wells and Gubar taxonomy (with minor updated adjustments). The description of each stage includes demographics, earnings, spending patterns, and effective marketing communications appeals.

BACHELOR

The **Bachelors (Young Singles) stage** consists of young single adults (mostly twenty to thirty years old) who have either graduated high school or college and are living on their own. They are establishing their independence, launching their careers, and enjoying recreational pursuits. Bachelors have moderate discretionary income and few financial obligations (other than repaying college debts).

Young singles' lifestyle focuses on socializing, dating, and other forms of instant gratification. They spend on clothing, cars, stereos, travel, recreation and entertainment (health clubs, sports clubs, and night life), restaurants, and basic equipment for their apartments. They save little.

Young singles read special-interest magazines: *GQ, Maxim,* and *Playboy* for men and *Cosmopolitan, Allure,* and *Glamour* for women. Bachelors respond to promotional appeals that emphasize status and fun.

NEWLY MARRIED COUPLES

The **newly married couples (Newlywed Game, Honeymooners)** segment consists of young couples (generally under age thirty-five) without children. They are relatively well-off financially because both earners' incomes are climbing. Honeymooners are likely to have paid off debts and incur economies from two people sharing one dwelling unit, plus they have no children to support.

Purchases at this stage are self-indulgent but also include start-up durables such as cars, furniture and furnishings, utensils, and small appliances. Honeymooners spend on clothing, travel, leisure-time activities, and high-tech toys. They save or invest surplus funds.

Appeals to enjoyment and togetherness work well in periodicals that offering buying advice, especially shelter magazines such as *Better Homes and Gardens* and *Metropolitan Home.*

FULL NEST I

The **Full Nest I (Expanding I, Parenthood I)** stage includes young married couples (usually ages thirty to forty) with the youngest child younger than six years old. Their discretionary income is doubly squeezed as the wife often exits the workplace or else cuts back to part-time status, while expenditures for the children and first home are incurred, resulting in dissatisfaction with their financial position.

Parenthood I people typically purchase their first home, furniture and furnishings for the children's rooms, major appliances, pharmaceuticals, baby items, toys, and day care. Appeals to economy, durability, and safety work well in magazines such as *Parents* and *Parenting.*

FULL NEST II

Full Nest II (Expanding II, Parenthood II) families are comprised of young couples (usually under age forty-five) with the youngest child six years old or more (school age) but still dependent. Family income rises as the wife often returns to work and because the husband's income continues to climb.

However, as the children grow, the family finds itself purchasing more and in larger quantities. Consumption is still heavily oriented toward the children: SUVs, school supplies, electronic toys, sports equipment, fast food meals, family vacations, extracurricular lessons, and larger-sized packages of food and cleaning supplies. The parents also invest money for college and retirement. Comfort and long-term enjoyment are viable selling appeals.

Primary school children can be reached through TV shows and publications such as *Humpty Dumpty, Scholastic Magazine, Boys' Life* and adult spin-off publications such as *Sports Illustrated for Kids, National Geographic Kids, CosmoGIRL,* and *Teen Vogue* (gateway products).

FULL NEST III

In the **Full Nest III (Contracting, Parenthood III)** phase, the older couple (late 30s through early 50s) still has one or more children at home, typically teens or very young adults. Family income continues to rise somewhat as the spouses climb their career ladders and their children work part-time. Parenthood III money is spent on furniture replacement, another automobile, luxury appliances, braces, additional PCs for older children, and the children's education.

Advertising appeals are to parents' concerns with comfort and luxury, while teen and post-teen girls look for fashion advice in magazines such as *American Girl* and *Seventeen,* teen boys read hobby magazines (*Hot Rod* and *Muscle and Fitness*), and both sexes peruse periodicals such as *Bop, Teen Beat,* and *Tiger Beat.*

EMPTY NEST I

In the **Empty Nest I (Postparental I, Childless I)** phase, the older married couple (mid-40s through mid-60s) no longer has children at home. One or both spouses continue to work, earning a relatively high income which, along with investments and lack of expenditures on their offspring or mortgage, put the family in their best financial position ever.

The large discretionary income goes toward indulgences such as a vacation abode, home improvements, luxury goods and services, travel, clothing, self-education, and recreation and entertainment. Ads appeal to self-gratification. This and all subsequent groups can best be reached via television and special-interest magazines such as *AARP—The Magazine.*

EMPTY NEST II

In the **Empty Nest II (Postparental II, Childless II)** stage, the children of older married couples (late 50s and older) have moved out and become financially independent. However, typically both spouses are retired or only work part-time, resulting in an earnings drop. Nonetheless, Americans over sixty-five years of age or older are the wealthiest age segment and have multiple income sources, such as pensions, social security, and investments. Also, many work past retirement age or do volunteer work. Often, the couple is still active and in good health, allowing them to spend time traveling, exercising, and volunteering.

Expenditures tend to downshift and are oriented toward health care, grandchildren, vacations, and recreation. Sales pitches focus on comfort at an affordable price.

SOLITARY (SOLE) SURVIVOR I

In the **Solitary (Sole) Survivor I (dissolution)** stage, one of the spouses has died and the other (usually the wife) continues or returns to work in order to live on earned income rather than savings and to remain socially active. Often, the home is sold and the survivor moves into a condo or assisted living community.

The good income enables spending on vacations, recreation, clothing, grandchildren, health care, and home services such as lawn care and house cleaning. Effective ads appeal to the productive citizen who also enjoys some leisure time.

SOLITARY (SOLE) SURVIVOR II

The **Solitary (Sole) Survivor II** is one spouse living on a lower retirement fixed income. This person sometimes feels futility, depending on whether there are substantial savings. These individuals have special needs for attention, affection, and security.

Expenditures tend to be scaled back, although health care costs continue to rise and money is still often spent on travel and leisure pursuits. Sole survivors respond to appeals to economy and social activity.

DEMOGRAPHIC AND LIFESTYLE MODIFICATIONS IN FAMILY STRUCTURE

The traditional Wells and Gubar FLC model fails to take into account most of the following important sociodemographic changes in family and household structures and family living arrangements. According to the 2000 U.S. Census, in today's fragmented family structure, only one-third of all households consist of traditional nuclear families. And, families of breadwinner dads and stay-at-home moms now make up just 10 percent of all households. Today, nonfamily households and nontraditional families comprise the majority of households. Marketers are responding to these cultural shifts in the family. For example, ten percent of Mother's Day cards are now designed for someone other than the sender's mother, such as a single mom or stepmother.

The following changes can be incorporated into traditional FLC models or relate to the contemporary Gilly and Enis FLC schema that follows.

DUAL-INCOME HOUSEHOLDS

Both spouses typically work outside the home, with women contributing a median of 35 percent to family income, although the decades-long rise of working women has recently leveled off and begun to reverse. Such **dual-income households (dual-career families)** exist not just before kids arrive on the scene and after all children are back in school, but even while the children are very young. They present a minor change from the original Wells and Gubar framework with its breadwinning husband and stay-at-home wife, requiring no change in the traditional FLC categories above. Cute acronym-based names for dual-income households and their children include DICKS (dual income, couple of kids), DIMPS (dual income, multiple progeny), and CHUMPS (children of upwardly mobile professionals). With their enhanced earnings, they are a lucrative market.

DELAYED MARRIAGES AND CHILDBEARING

Rather than marrying right after high school or college, the current trend is for young adults to first repay debts and/or save money while enjoying their independence and freedom for several years, with some also completing graduate school before contemplating marriage. This too necessitates a minor adjustment in the traditional FLC schema and has been reflected in the age brackets given for each FLC phase in the Gilly and Enis Modernized FLC Model (see p. 278), which are higher than in the Wells and Gubar model. This trend results in the creation of the Bachelor II and Delayed Full Nest stages in the Gilly and Enis Model. Couples delaying childbirth stress a quality lifestyle: "Only the best is good enough." Hence, they are a great market for high-priced, fine-quality merchandise.

SMALLER FAMILIES

"Honey, I shrunk the family!" Due to dual-career couples and delayed marriages, today's families are smaller, typically with two children who are born relatively late in the parents' lives. This trend does not require the addition or deletion of stages to the traditional FLC structure, but it results in the inclusion of the Delayed Full Nest stage in the Gilly and Enis model. Smaller families have more money to spend on each child as well as on the finer things. However, recently, more professional working women are having three kids instead of two, often either cutting back to part-time employment or taking time off from work.

CHILDLESS COUPLES

One of the fastest-growing types of households is couples without kids. These household are sometimes called DINKS or TINKS (double or two incomes, no kids). The adults in the family are often working professionals who have no time and/or desire for children. Contributing forces are dual-income homes and delayed marriages, as well as increased career emphasis by women as well as men. This phenomenon results in a childless couples category found in the contemporary FLC model. Due to high incomes from both spouses and no child care expenditures, people in this group do a lot of discretionary spending.

COHABITING COUPLES

A generation ago, unmarried couples who lived together were often derided for "shacking up," "playing house," or even "living in sin." Now, a **cohabiting couples (domestic partnerships, mingles, POSSLQ)** lifestyle arrangement precedes more than two-thirds of marriages. This is due to high housing costs and tight budgets, as well changing societal moral standards regarding marriage. This group largely overlaps with Childless Couples and could be added as an optional stage between the Bachelor and Newly Married couples in the conventional FLC model. Since both spouses typically work and there are usually no children for whom to provide, discretionary income tends to be higher than for married couples of a similar age, resulting in relatively high consumption of luxuries among unmarried couples.

DIVORCED PEOPLE

It is no longer necessarily "Till death do us part"—approximately one-half of all marriages eventually end in dissolution, although the late 1990s saw a leveling off of the rising divorce rate. Marital dissolution often leads to lifestyle changes that necessitate the purchase of new goods and services to help form a new identity and relieve stress. Childless divorce results in lifestyles similar to those of young singles, while married couples who divorce often create single-parent families and have tighter financial circumstances.

THE SINGLES SURGE

Due to later marriages, high divorce rates, and people living longer as solitary survivors, more people are "home alone." These are the Bachelor II and III stages in the contemporary FLC. The social stigma that singleness once had has been removed. The singles boom is reflected in individualized servings of packaged grocery items.

SINGLE PARENTS

Once called "troubled" or "broken" homes, single-parent families are now dubbed subnuclear families. Single-parent families are headed by a mom or dad (most often a mom) who is usually divorced, separated, or widowed. Increasingly, single-parent households are the consequence of out-of-wedlock births and adoptions. Most such families need to both earn an income and raise children. Consequently, they require convenient goods and services such as child care, easy-to-prepare foods, and recreation, all at affordable prices since single parents tend to have lower-than-average incomes.

THE BABY BOOMERANG

"They're baaackk!!" **The Baby Boomerang (Boomerangers, Boomerang Kids, Back-to-the-bedroom Kids, Returning Young Adults, Twixters)** is an emerging market of young adults, mostly in their twenties, who either return to or continue to live with their parents. Due to financial pressures, convenience, out-of-wedlock children, and an unwillingness to trade down their folks' affluent lifestyle for a more modest means of living, approximately one-half of college students and one-third of all adults between the ages of twenty and thirty-four, disproportionately men, are Boomerangers. They leave; and then they come back, sometimes more than once. This return to the parents' home does not only follow college but also occurs between jobs, before marriage, and after a divorce. The traditional FLC model can easily accommodate this change by adding it as an optional living arrangement within the Bachelor stage.

The Boomerang Kids create a wonderful marketing opportunity because all of the money ordinarily spent on independent survival in the Bachelor stage translates to discretionary income lavished on high-priced goodies. Twixters job hop, dress like teenagers, and expect instant gratification.

REVIVAL OF EXTENDED FAMILIES

Increasingly, grandparents and other relatives are taking up residence with the nuclear family, resulting in **multigenerational households**. The **Sandwich Generation** is composed of adults caring for their aging parents as well as their own children. This is a consequence of dual-income parents who can afford to help their parents and single parents who need help with child care. Other causal factors include divorce, higher housing costs, and aging parents who are living longer and require care.

STEPFAMILIES

Due to divorce and remarriage, wedlock is not the "lock" it once was. Today it is common to see blended families who, together with single-parent households, constitute the largest change in family composition. In fact, almost one-half of all divorces now involve at least one partner remarrying, which often creates families with children from one or both of the previous marriages, plus perhaps children from the new marriage. Market opportunities arise as children who travel between two families need duplicate supplies of clothing, personal care items, and toys and recreational items.

HOMOSEXUAL COUPLES

Same-sex monogamous partnerships are now more socially acceptable than just a few years ago. They are also acquiring legal legitimacy as civil unions and even as marriages following the 2003 Massachusetts Supreme Court ruling that permits same-sex couples to marry. Some gay couples today also have kids, typically adopted. While controversial among traditionalists, homosexual partners and families constitute a segment increasingly courted by marketers due to their high discretionary incomes.

EXHIBIT 9.8   Gilly and Enis Modernized Family Life Cycle Model

Gilly and Enis life cycle stage	% U.S. Population	Description	Wells & Gubar FLC stage	Corresponding societal shifts
Bachelor I	7.9	Unmarried, under age 35	Bachelor	
Bachelor II	13.3	Unmarried, 35 to 64		Delayed marriage, divorce, cohabitation, singles surge
Newlywed	17.4	Married w/o children, under 35	Newly Married couples	
Single Parent I, II, III	5.9	Single parents, under 65	Single parents	
Full Nest I	9.9	Couple with female under 35, children under 6	Full Nest I	
Delayed Full Nest	3.8	Couple with female over 35, children under 6		Delayed marriage, smaller families
Full Nest II and III	22.2	Couple with children over 6	Full Nest II, III	
Childless Couple	16.0	Couple 35 to 64 without children	Childless couples, cohabitation	
Older Couple	5.9	Couple over 64 w/o kids at home	Empty Nest I, II	
Bachelor III	7.4	Single, over 64	Singles surge, divorce	
Other	.5	Misc. other groupings, such as children staying with other relatives (especially grandparents)	Revival of extended families	

Source: Following Mowen and Minor, *Consumer Behavior*, 5th ed. (Upper Saddle River, NJ: Prentice-Hall, 1998), we collapse the original fourteen categories into eleven to reduce complexity.

INTERRACIAL MARRIAGES AND ADOPTIONS

We are witnessing more interracial marriages and more adoptions of children of a different race or nationality from that of their parents, including children from abroad. Woe to the marketer who only thinks in terms of targeting the bland, white-bread suburban husband and wife with two freckle-faced kids!

THE GILLY AND ENIS MODERNIZED FLC

To reflect these societal shifts, consumer researchers Gilly and Enis (1982) developed a modernized FLC model (see Exhibit 9.8). It has the advantage of including ages of all family members, with age six again a critical cutoff for children. Additionally, ages thirty-five and sixty-five are used as important transitional points for adults as they represent mid-life and traditional retirement age, respectively.

The details of the buyer behavior of consumers in each stage can be deduced from the earlier discussion on demographic and lifestyle family changes. Exhibit 9.8 relates some of these stages to the Wells and Gubar model and associates some of the stages with the structural changes in families that we just examined.

REVIEW QUESTIONS

1. What is the family life cycle (FLC) and how do consumer marketers use it?
2. Describe the nature of FLC as a composite variable. What single variables make up FLC? What are the advantages of using a multi-item variable?
3. Briefly describe each of the stages in the Wells and Gubar traditional FLC model regarding de-

mographics, needs, earnings, and spending patterns. Also, identify effective marketing strategies for appealing to typical families in each stage.

4. Outline the important sociodemographic changes in family and household structures that have necessitated modifications to the Wells and Gubar traditional FLC model. How can each change be accommodated in either the traditional FLC model or the Gilly and Enis modernized FLC model? What market opportunities arise from each of these trends?

5. Briefly describe each of the stages in the Gilly and Enis modernized FLC model.

IN-CLASS APPLICATIONS

1. For each of the advertisements in Exhibits 9.9 through 9.14, determine the target market's FLC stage. Use the Wells and Gubar model, Gilly and Enis model, or both, as appropriate for each ad.

2. For each ad, discuss the demographics, needs, buying power, and spending patterns of the target market that are especially relevant to the product, as well as any changes in family composition and lifestyle that are reflected in the ad.

Does each ad effectively appeal to its FLC target market? In which media vehicles should each ad run?

3. Are there any other stages in the FLC that could have been targeted by the product featured in each ad? If so, how, if at all, would this change the advertising appeal?

For the product in each ad, is the FLC the best way to segment the market? What other demographic variables, either in isolation or in conjunction with each other, could have been used to segment the market in each case?

WRITTEN APPLICATIONS

1. For five of the ads (Exhibits 9.9–9.14), answer Questions 1 through 3 in the In-Class Applications. Which of these FLC stages do you recall personally experiencing during your lifetime, and how did being in that stage influence you and/or your parents' buyer behavior?

2. Find three other ads for products consumed by families, each of which is targeted to a different FLC stage. Then, repeat Questions 1 through 3 in the In-Class Applications.

EXERCISE 9.3. FAMILY INFLUENCES AND YOU

OBJECTIVES

1. To give you insight into how your family role structure and family life cycle (FLC) stage have influenced your and/or your family members' buying behavior.

2. To help you recognize how advertisers attempt to influence you by appealing to your family roles and FLC stage.

3. To have you design an ad which appeals to people who take on the family roles you do and who are in the same stage of the FLC as you are.

BACKGROUND

See the Background sections for Exercises 9.1 and 9.2, which provide all the information you will need for this exercise. Although students can discuss answers in class, many might find it too personal. Therefore, instructor discretion is advised on using this as an in-class application.

WRITTEN APPLICATIONS

1. Select a product that is purchased and consumed within the context of your family. This could either be your family of orientation or, for those of you who have started your own family, your

EXHIBIT 9.9   Nestlé Ad

EXHIBIT 9.10   Ensure Ad

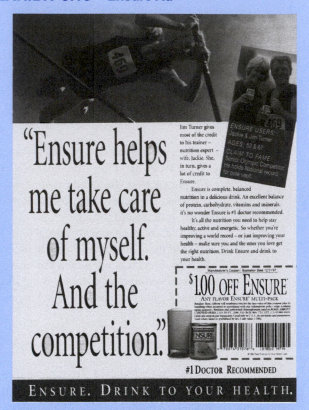

EXHIBIT 9.11   Taittinger Ad

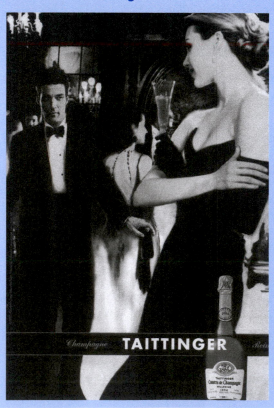

EXHIBIT 9.12   Stouffer's Ad

EXHIBIT 9.13 Pork: The Other White Meat Ad

Some children take their stand at bedtime. Others choose the dinner table.

EXHIBIT 9.14 Bluefly.com Ad

family of procreation. If you prefer, you can do this in the context of a household buying situation, such as roommates, in which case you should substitute "household" for "family" in the following questions.

Which family decision-making role (or roles) outlined in Exhibit 9.1 do you personally take for this product and why? Which roles do your other family members take for this item? Why?

Discuss any relevant instrumental and expressive roles and role dominance for this product within your family. Then, either find an ad for this product and describe how the advertiser is or is not effectively appealing to one or more of these roles or create an ad for this product and describe how it effectively appeals to one or more of these roles.

2. Describe which stage in the FLC your family is in, according to both the Wells and Gubar traditional FLC model (Exhibit 9.7) and the Gilly and Enis modernized FLC model (Exhibit 9.8). (If you are single and prefer to, you may just consider yourself in one of the Bachelor stages, in which case you alone are the family.)

In the context of a product your family has recently purchased, describe your family's demographics, needs, buying power, and some effective (or ineffective) advertising and personal selling appeals your family was exposed to for that product.

3. Find an ad targeting your FLC stage, using a stage found in either the Wells and Gubar or the Gilly and Enis model. How effective is the ad in appealing to families in that stage? Would it appeal to you and members of your family? Explain.

4. Create an ad to appeal to other families in your FLC stage for a product that interests you. Explain why you think your ad would be effective in appealing to people in that FLC stage and in which advertising media you would run your ad.

KEY CONCEPTS

alpha moms

autonomous (autonomic, autocratic, individualized) decisions

Baby Boomerang (Boomerangers, Boomerang Kids, Back-to-the-bedroom Kids, Returning Young Adults, Twixters)

Bachelors (Young Singles) stage

blended families (stepfamilies, reconstituted families, aggregate families, second chancers)

buyer (family purchasing agent)

buying centers

cohabitating couples (domestic partnerships, mingles, POSSLQ)

decider

decision roles (consumption roles, purchase roles)

disposer

dual-income households (dual-career families)

Empty Nest I (Postparental I, Childless I)

Empty Nest II (Postparental II, Childless II)

evaluators

expressive roles

extended family

family (household) decision (consumption, purchase) roles

family household (family)

family life cycle (FLC; life stages, household life cycle, consumer life cycle)

family of orientation (family of origin)

family of procreation

Full Nest I (Expanding I, Parenthood I)

Full Nest II (Expanding II, Parenthood II)

Full Nest III (Contracting, Parenthood III)

gatekeeper

household (consumer unit, dwelling unit)

husband-dominant (patriarchal) decisions

influencer

initiator

instrumental (functional, economic) roles

intergenerational influence

joint (syncratic) decisions

maintainers

monitor

multigenerational households

newly married couples (Newlywed Game, Honeymooners)

nonfamily households

nontraditional families

nuclear (conventional, normal, limited, typical) family

preparer

role dominance

Sandwich Generation

Solitary (Sole) Survivor I (dissolution)

Solitary Survivor II

user (end user)

wife-dominant (matriarchal) decisions

SUMMARY

This chapter explored family household and household decision making. The two basic types of traditional families are the nuclear family, including the family of orientation and the family of procreation, and the extended family. In addition to traditional families there are also nontraditional families, including blended families, and nonfamily households, including POSSLQ.

The family is of special interest to marketers for several reasons:

1. Families are the largest consumer market.
2. Families form society's building block. Parents socialize children, teaching them cultural characteristics and consumer socialization; provide for their members' emotional and economic well being; and perform a mediating function, with older members filtering and interpreting for the younger ones the influences of other societal institutions such as media and advertising. There is a renewal of interest in the family.
3. The influence of women and children is growing. Changing gender roles mean that women are buying big-ticket shopping and specialty goods. Alpha Moms influence other moms. Children's influence has also grown, reflected in age compression. Children and adolescents constitute a present primary market, a future market, and an influential market.
4. Families contain multiple target markets. Some products will have one group (e.g., parents) as the primary target market, another bunch (teens) as the secondary target market, and a third (children) as the tertiary target market.

Exercise 9.1 described the various roles different family members can take during the family decision-making process and how marketers can tap into each of these roles. Family purchases entail group decision making and, as such, are analogous to corporate purchases by buying centers. To aid the group decision-making process, different group members adopt various family decision roles. One way to classify these decision roles is as instrumental roles versus expressive roles.

Exhibit 9.1 defines each of the decision roles and in which stage of the family decision-making process each role occurs. The roles, listed chronologically as they occur during the family decision-making process, are initiator, gatekeeper, influencer, decider, buyer, preparer, user, monitor, evaluator, maintainer, and disposer.

Regarding the decider role, the decision makers are usually those with some level of authority or power. Husband-wife decision influence varies according to role dominance. Decisions can be husband-dominant, wife-dominant, joint, autonomous, child-dominant, and joint decisions between husband, wife, and child. Marketers should ascertain that deciders are provided with the information they need to make the decision.

The family decision role concept suggests that marketing communications can be aimed toward multiple target markets within the family through multiple marketing communications campaigns and can target more than one role in a given advertisement that is likely to be viewed or heard by multiple family members.

In Exercise 9.2, both a traditional and contemporary model of the FLC were described and applied to family target marketing. FLC is important for marketers because the FLC stages are based on critical transitions that modify role relationships and induce lifestyle changes. These lifestage passages give rise to major outlays for consumer goods and serve as a basis for market segmentation since lifestage determines lifestyle.

Family life cycle is a composite variable, composed of ages of parents and youngest child, marital status, presence versus absence of children, residence of the youngest child, workforce status of the head of household, and whether or not both spouses are still alive. Another consideration is relative income (but not absolute income). The key marketplace family variables that are dependent upon the family's life stage include needs and wants, buying power, and spending patterns.

One widely used FLC model was formulated by Wells and Gubar. The stages and descriptions of each phase in this model are summarized in Exhibit 9.7 as well as the background to Exercise 9.2.

Traditional FLC models such as Wells and Gubar's fail to take into account most of the following important sociodemographic changes in family and household structures, notably the increase in nonfamily households and nontraditional families that now make up the majority of homes. Key changes are as follows.

- *Dual-income households.* Both spouses usually work outside the home. This societal shift requires no change in traditional FLC categories above.
- *Delayed marriages.* This results in the creation of the Bachelor II and Delayed Full Nest stages in the Gilly and Enis modernized FLC Model.
- *Smaller families.* This trend results in the addition of the Delayed Full Nest stage in the modernized Gilly and Enis model.
- *Childless couples.* These are often working professionals who feel they have no time and/or desire for children. The result is a childless couples category in the contemporary FLC model, a group with very high discretionary incomes.
- *Cohabiting couples.* This lifestyle arrangement now precedes the majority of marriages. Cohabiting couples could be added as an optional stage between the Bachelor and Newly Married Couples in the conventional FLC model.
- *Divorced people.* Approximately one-half of all marriages eventually end in divorce.
- *The singles surge.* These are the Bachelor II and III stages in the contemporary FLC.
- *Single parents.* Also known as subnuclear families, these people are usually divorced, separated, or widowed.
- *The Baby Boomerang.* These are young adults who return home to live with their parents for a while. The traditional FLC model can accommodate this change by adding it as an optional living arrangement within the Bachelor stage.
- *Revival of extended families.* Grandparents and other relatives are once again taking up residence with the nuclear family, resulting in multigenerational households and the Sandwich Generation.
- *Stepfamilies.* Almost one-half of all divorces now involve at least one partner remarrying, creating

blended families that include children from one or both of the previous marriages, plus perhaps children from the new marriage.
- *Single-sex couples.* Monogamous homosexual partnerships are gaining both social and legal acceptance. These couples tend to have high discretionary incomes and sometimes adopt children.
- *Interracial marriages and adoptions.* Interracial marriages and adoptions of children of a different race or nationality from that of their parents are becoming more common.

To reflect such societal shifts, Gilly and Enis's modernized FLC model includes ages of all family members. This life stage model is summarized in Exhibit 9.8.

Exercise 9.3 applied your knowledge of family influences from Exercises 9.1 and 9.2 to understanding how your family role structure and family life cycle stage have influenced the buying behavior of you and your family members.

REFERENCES

Belch, Michael A., and Willis, Laura A. (2001). "Family Decision at the Turn of the Century: Has Changing Structure of Households Impacted the Family Decision-Making Process?" *Journal of Consumer Behavior,* 2, 111–124.

Burns, Alvin C., and Granbois, Donald H. (1980). "Advancing the Study of Family Purchase Decision Making." In J. Olson, ed., *Advances in Consumer Research,* vol. 7. Ann Arbor, MI: Association for Consumer Research, 221–226.

Coffey, Tim, Siegel, David, and Livingston, Greg. (2006). *Marketing to the New Super Consumer: Mom & Kid.* Ithaca, NY: Paramount Market Publishing.

Davis, Harry L., and Rigeaux, Benny P. (1974). "Perceptions of Marital Roles in Decision Processes." *Journal of Consumer Research,* 1, 1, 51–62.

Ferber, Robert, and Lee, Lucy Chao. (1974). "Husband-Wife Influence in Family Purchasing Behavior." *Journal of Consumer Research,* 1, 1, 43–50.

Gil, R. Bravo, Andres, E. Fraj, and Salinas, Martinez. (2007). "Family as a Source of Consumer-Based Brand Equity." *Journal of Product and Brand Management,* 16, 3, 188–199.

Gilly, Mary, and Enis, Ben. (1982). "Recycling the Family Life Cycle: A Proposal for Redefinition." In A. Mitchell, ed., *Advances in Consumer Research,* vol. 9. Ann Arbor, MI: Association for Consumer Research.

Isler, Leslie, Popper, Edward T., and Ward, Scott. (1987). "Children's Purchase Requests and Parental Responses: Results from a Diary Study." *Journal of Advertising Research,* 27, 5, 28–39.

Lackman, Conway, and Lanasa, John M. (1993). "Family Decision-Making Theory." *Psychology and Marketing,* 10, 2, 81–93.

Lee, Christina K.C., and Beatty, Sharon E. (2002). "Family Structure and Influence in Family Decision Making." *Journal of Consumer Marketing,* 19, 1, 24–41.

McNeal, James U. (1998). "Tapping the Three Kids' Markets." *American Demographics,* 3 (April), 737–741.

———. (1999). *The Kids Market: Myths and Realities.* Ithaca, NY: Paramount Market Publishing.

Moore, Elizabeth, Wilkie, William L., and Lutz, Richard J. (2002). "Passing the Torch: Intergenerational Influences as a Source of Brand Equity." *Journal of Marketing,* 66, 2, 17–37.

Murphy, Patrick E., and Staples, William A. (1979). "A Modernized Family Life Cycle." *Journal of Consumer Research,* 6, 1, 12–22.

Palan, Kay M., and Wilkes, Robert E. (1997). "Adolescent-Parent Interaction in Family Decision Making." *Journal of Consumer Research,* 24, 2, 159–169.

Razzouk, Nabil, Seitz, Victoria, and Prodigalidad Capo, Karen. (2007). "A Comparison of Consumer Decision-Making Behavior of Married and Cohabiting Couples." *Journal of Consumer Marketing,* 24, 5, 264–274.

Schaninger, Charles M., and Danko, William D. (1993). "A Conceptual and Empirical Comparison of Alternative Household Life Cycle Models." *Journal of Consumer Research,* 19, 4, 580–594.

Sheth, Jagdish N. (1974). "A Theory of Family Buying Decisions." In Jagdish N. Sheth, ed., *Models of Buyer Behavior.* New York: Harper & Row, 17–33.

Spiro, Rosann L. (1983). "Persuasion in Family Decision Making." *Journal of Consumer Research,* 9, 4, 393–402.

Ward, Scott, and Wackman, Daniel B. (1972). "Children's Purchase Influence Attempts and Parental Yielding." *Journal of Marketing Research,* 9, 3, 316–319.

Wells, William, and Goober, George. (1966). "Life Cycle Concept in Marketing Research." *Journal of Marketing Research,* 3, 4, 355–363.

Wilkes, Robert E. (1995). Household Life-Cycle Stages, Transitions, and Product Expenditures." *Journal of Consumer Research,* 22, 1, 27–42.

GROUP AND INTERPERSONAL COMMUNICATIONS FOR INNOVATIONS: ADOPTION AND DIFFUSION PROCESSES

DIFFUSION AND ADOPTION OF INNOVATIONS

An **innovation** is a commercially successful new product. Social groups and interpersonal influences are increasingly helpful to marketers' grassroots efforts in gaining consumer acceptance for new products, which are vital for marketing success and for society. In order to increase the likelihood of launching a successful new product, marketers must understand **diffusion**, in which new product information spreads throughout society and the product is accepted within a social system. A **social system** is defined as one or more groups of individuals who interact fairly frequently, ranging from a local neighborhood to an entire society.

Marketers also need insight into **adoption**, or the CB involved when potential users (individuals, families, or other social groups) decide whether or not to commit to regularly using a new product. For high-priced durable goods, adoption means product purchase. For nondurables and services, adoption entails a decision to regularly buy the product.

The framework for exploring consumer acceptance and the societal spread of new products is drawn from research on the **diffusion of innovations (DOI)**, the process whereby a new idea is communicated through certain channels over time among the members of a social system. Communication regarding new products across groups happens through this diffusion process. Within groups, one-on-one interpersonal influence occurs in the form of word-of-mouth (WOM) communication.

Diffusion theories suggest the following process: At first, products are adopted slowly due to consumer skepticism, risk aversion, and inertia. Then, as new items gain popularity, they are adopted at a rapid, escalating rate, like a disease spreading throughout the target population, as the number of adopters increasingly interacts with nonadopters, thereby influencing them to also adopt. Next a saturation point occurs, where there are more adopters than nonadopters, slowing the diffusion process (see Exhibit 10.1). Consequently, the adoption cycle tends to take the shape of a classic, bell-shaped normal curve: slow growth, followed by a rapid increase, and then a decrease in adoption.

Exhibit 10.2 shows the various adopter categories in this normal curve: innovators—the first to buy and use an innovation (e.g., young men for new technologies such video games, mobile devices, and online activities); a fast-following majority led by early adopters; a slow-following majority; and the laggards who do not adopt until the product is old hat. From innovators and early adopters come opinion leaders, a major focus of Exercise 10.1.

In this chapter we study several key elements that influence the adoption and diffusion of innovations. Innovations add value for society, buyers, and shareholders or business owners.

ORGANIZATION OF CHAPTER 10

This chapter focuses on three important influences in adoption and diffusion: the characteristics of the innovation, the communication channels used to promote the benefits of the innovation, and the social system in which the innovation diffuses. Exercise 10.1 shows that the degree of novelty and certain innovation characteristics influence the likelihood of consumer acceptance. Generally, the more novel the innovation, the longer it will take to be adopted and diffuse.

Skeptical, risk-averse consumers often turn to WOM communication from credible friends, relatives, neighbors, and others for the scoop on new products. Sometimes they rely on influential consumer adopters

EXHIBIT 10.1   **DOI Curve**

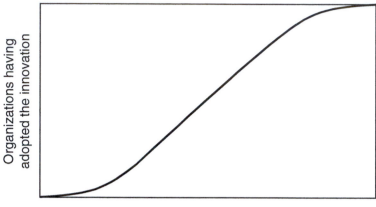

EXHIBIT 10.2   **Adopter Categories**

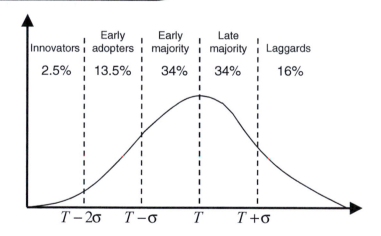

known as opinion leaders. Exercise 10.2 discusses opinion leaders and WOM communication as well as strategies marketers can use to take advantage of them.

EXERCISE 10.1. CATEGORIES OF INNOVATIONS AND PRODUCT CHARACTERISTICS THAT INFLUENCE ADOPTION AND DIFFUSION

OBJECTIVES

1. To understand the relationship between perceived product newness and the likelihood of new product adoption and diffusion.
2. To understand how perceived product newness is influenced by the extent to which the innovation alters CB, as described by Robertson's classification of innovations as continuous, dynamically continuous, and discontinuous.

EXHIBIT 10.3   Booz Allen Hamilton Classification Scheme for New Products

	Low ← Newness to Market → High
High Newness to Company	New product lines (30%) · · · New-to-world products (10%)
	Improvements and revisions to existing products (26%) · · · Additions to existing product lines (26%)
Low	Cost reductions(11%) · · · Repositionings (7%)

3. To appreciate the relationship between the degree of innovativeness in the Booz Allen Hamilton new product classification system and Robertson's scheme, and their implications for CB.
4. To become familiar with the characteristics of innovations that influence probability of adoption and diffusion: relative advantage, compatibility, complexity, trialability, and communicability.
5. To reflect on your own purchase behavior as well as that of your peers in light of the classification schemes for new products and innovation attributes discussed in this exercise.
6. To practice analyzing products and ads in light of these new product classification systems and innovation attributes.

BACKGROUND

Product innovation is the driving force of business, the economy, and of societal progress, with consumer advertising providing the fuel that propels new products into the marketplace. Product innovations are considered the "lifeblood of business" because most companies depend on them for a significant share of their sales, market share, profits, and growth. An old adage declares: "Innovate or die!"

CATEGORIES OF INNOVATIONS BASED ON NEWNESS TO THE COMPANY, NEWNESS TO THE MARKET, AND BEHAVIORAL CHANGE

The most important product factor determining whether a product will be perceived by buyers as new is the extent to which the innovation alters CB. New products can be classified into three categories of innovation based on degree of behavioral change. They can also be classified by "newness" from the firm's as well as the consumer's perspective.

In this discussion, we will integrate two categorization schemes for innovations: Thomas S. Robertson's threefold classification of innovations based on degree of behavioral change and Booz Allen Hamilton's (BAH) six types of new products from the firm's and consumer's perspective. Both of these categorization methods range from least to most innovative, that is, from least to most disruptive of CB.

BOOZ ALLEN HAMILTON'S NEW BRANDS CLASSIFICATION: NEWNESS TO FIRMS AND CONSUMERS

Exhibit 10.3 shows six categories of new products according to the BAH scheme, which classifies innovations according newness to the company and newness to the market.

In Exhibit 10.3, newness to the company concerns whether the business organization has ever produced and marketed the product, regardless of other companies having already done so. For example, although bottled water has been popular since Perrier debuted in the 1970s, it was not until 1999 that Coca-Cola Corp. launched Dasani bottled water. Such a company must complete a learning process before launching a new product. First, they must study the product's underlying **technology**, defined as a body of knowledge, tools, and techniques derived from science and practical experience, which is used in the development, design, production, and application of products, processes, systems, and services. Second, a firm must learn about a new marketplace—consumers, competitors, suppliers, and channels of distribution.

Newness to the market concerns whether the target market believes that the product is new and will entail some behavioral change on their part. From this perspective, an innovation can be defined as any product (good, service, or idea) perceived by the potential adopter to be new. Perceived newness determines the extent of consumer learning and possible **innovation resistance**, or preference for existing, familiar products and behaviors over less familiar ones.

The percentages next to each category label in Exhibit 10.3 show the approximate proportion of new products in each group. The more innovative products appear in the upper right corner of the figure, and the less innovative are found in the lower left portion.

ROBERTSON'S CLASSIFICATION OF INNOVATIONS BASED ON BEHAVIORAL CHANGE: CONTINUOUS, DYNAMICALLY CONTINUOUS, AND DISCONTINUOUS

Thomas Robertson's taxonomy is based on the consumer's perceived degree of product novelty and the extent to which the product changes individual CB as well as the degree to which it affects behavior in the social structure. Robertson presents three discrete new product categories arranged from incremental new products to radical innovation: continuous innovations, dynamically continuous innovations, and discontinuous innovations.

Robertson's Continuous Innovations. Least likely to encounter consumer resistance are **continuous innovations**. These new products are perceived as having the least disrupting influence on established patterns of CB. They are used in basically the same way as their predecessor products. For example, herb-enhanced beverages do not change the way people consume drinks. Most continuous innovations, such as angled toothbrushes, entail little technological change. They involve modification of the taste, appearance, performance, or reliability of an existing product rather than establishment of a totally new product.

The majority of new products are continuous innovations. Consequently, they require less marketing effort and have a lower risk of failure than Robertson's other two types of innovations, which are more disruptive of established behavioral patterns. However, continuous innovations' expected profitability is also limited; as you'll recall from Finance 101, "With risk goes reward."

Booz Allen Hamilton Continuous Innovations. Continuous innovations include the following categories of new product types according to the BAH classification scheme, organized from least to most "new."

➢ *Cost reductions.* The primary benefit of these new products is that they are lower-priced than most (or all) competitors, due to lower manufacturing and/or marketing costs. For instance, Scott towels "with ridges" require 20 percent less paper pulp, thereby reducing production costs.

➢*Repositionings.* Psychological positioning entails differentiating a brand from competitive offerings in the buyer's mind by locating the brand in that customer's memory relative to (a) alternative product uses (e.g., cola as a rust remover); (b) target market users or user imagery (Mountain Dew for young hipsters instead of old hillbillies); or (c) competitive products and brands (raisins as "nature's answer to candy"). **Repositioning (relaunching, restaging, remarketing)** means staking out a new position for the brand due to marketplace changes, such as values and norms, demographics, competitive positioning, and technology. Thus, long ago, Ivory soap was restaged as all-family soap rather than strictly for sensitive baby skin. Many "recycled" old products are repositioned. Ceiling fans, fountain pens, and wood-burning stoves were all relaunched from being purely utilitarian to fashionable items. ("Everything old is new again.")

➢ *"New-and-improved" (next-generation) products.* **"New-and-improved" (next-generation) products** are modifications of existing products that lead to the replacement of a previous version of the product. This can be done by a quality improvement (e.g., Energizer enhances battery durability), design change (the redesigned *Wall Street Journal* with subdued colors and a new layout), an improved formula (General Mills cereals converted to whole grain), a revision or upgrade (software version X.1), and a functional enhancement (Dutch Boy paint's easier-to-open-and-pour Twist & Pour container).

> *Additions to existing product lines.* These supplement or round out a current product line rather than replace it, as do "new-and-improved" products. **Additions to existing product lines** are derivatives of or variations on a firm's existing product, usually the **core (anchor, flagship) product**—a firm's mainstream product. Examples of product line additions are Coca-Cola launching Cherry Coke and Tide detergent introducing Tide Free. Such additions include new forms (e.g., "lite" food and beverage products) and more variety (styles, scents, colors, flavors, sizes, shapes, packaging options, etc.).

When additions to a product line carry a new brand name, they are known as **flankers** (e.g., Procter and Gamble introduced Cheer detergent as an alternative to Tide, and PepsiCo added Mountain Dew). When firms use one of their existing names on an addition to a product line, the new product is dubbed a **product line extension (line extension)** (e.g., Oreo Big Stuf, Mini Oreos, single-serve Oreo Packs 2 Go!, and Oreos with chocolate creme).

> *New product lines (new category entries).* Such products are already established in the marketplace but are new to the firm launching them. Because consumers do not associate the particular product with the individual company, they might view the products as "new" (e.g., Microsoft's Xbox videogame console, Tom's of Maine herbal remedies, and energy drinks from major soft drink companies competing with Red Bull).

When a firm's new line includes their well-known and trusted brand or corporate name, they are known as **brand franchise extensions (brand extensions)** (e.g., Starbuck's ice cream, Nike sportswear, Creamsicle candy twists). Like product line extensions, brand franchise extensions capitalize on **brand equity**—the value of the brand name to consumers over and above its functional characteristics. Mr. Clean traded on its tough dirt-fighter image in launching Mr. Clean Magic Eraser cleaner-sponge combo and Mr. Clean AutoDry for washing cars without water.

Dynamically Continuous Innovations. Second among Robertson's three innovation types are **dynamically continuous innovations.** Consumers view such new products as somewhat new since they require more behavioral change than continuous innovations, although the degree of change in customer buying and product use is modest and usually makes buyers' lives easier. This was so for FluMist nasal flu vaccine, for the needle-shy who dread traditional flu shots. Likewise for TiVo, the first digital video recorder, which, like its predecessor the VCR, made it fairly simple to record TV shows, which resulted in less channel surfing and more time shifting. "Bucketless mops," such as the battery-powered Swiffer WetJet, which eliminate mess, elbow grease, and heavy lifting of floor cleaning materials, also fill the dynamically continuous bill.

BAH Dynamically Continuous Innovations. These generally are of the following two kinds, the sixth and seventh product types in the BAH classification taxonomy.

> *Major additions to existing product lines and significant new product lines* are both key modifications of existing product classes. Examples of major changes to existing product lines include instant pudding, electric carving knives and toothbrushes, disposable extended contact lenses, instant cameras, registerless supermarket checkouts, and on-line banking.

> *New-to-the-world products (new product categories).* These innovations either revolutionize existing product categories (electric cars) or define wholly new categories (air conditioning, frozen vegetables, premoistened towelettes, and satellite TV and radio). Dynamically continuous new-to the-world products, while very new in form and perhaps technology, nonetheless only somewhat alter CB.

Discontinuous Innovations. **Discontinuous innovations** are innovations perceived by customers to be radically new, causing buyers to significantly alter their behavioral patterns, and also usually entailing extensive technological breakthrough. Digital movie downloads are purchased and consumed much differently than DVDs that are bought or rented. Electric cars, requiring recharging the battery, are discontinuous innovations, while hybrid autos, whose batteries recharge while driving, are dynamically continuous.

BAH Discontinuous Innovations. In the BAH scheme, discontinuous innovations include new-to-the-world products (new product categories). Unlike dynamically continuous new-to-the-world products, these have a major impact on CB and lifestyles. Examples of such revolutionary, life-altering products include wheels, tools, and weapons in prehistoric times; the steam engine, electricity, and spinning jenny during the Industrial Revolution; and automobiles, telephones, radio and TV, xerography, personal computers, fax machines, and e-mail in the twentieth century.

MARKETING IMPLICATIONS FOR CATEGORIZING INNOVATION BY BEHAVIORAL CHANGE

General strategy implications for the BAH and Robertson new product classification schemes are as follows.

- Moving from incremental to radical innovations, the marketing job of educating and persuading consumers looms larger because highly innovative products are more likely to meet innovation resistance since they tend to be higher in perceived risk.
- Proceeding from evolutionary to revolutionary innovations, the adoption cycle becomes longer since there is more innovation resistance due to consumer skepticism and perceived risk.
- The probability of large-scale adoption within the target market, and hence of ultimate marketing success, is inversely proportional to the degree of product innovativeness. But, when innovative products succeed, they tend to succeed big (high risk, high expected return).
- The extent of immediate competition is inversely related to the degree to which a product is "really new" since more groundbreaking products are tougher to imitate technologically.
- Incremental innovations require selective (secondary) demand stimulation, especially among current customers, while "really new" products mandate primary demand creation, often among new target markets such as technophiles.

INNOVATION ATTRIBUTES: PRODUCT CHARACTERISTICS INFLUENCING LIKELIHOOD OF ADOPTION AND DIFFUSION

The probability of individuals' adoption and subsequent diffusion of an innovation throughout a social system depend not only on perceived newness and the degree of behavioral change required, but also on certain innovation attributes (product characteristics) influencing adoption. If a marketer is aware of which innovation characteristics are likely to either help or hinder adoption, that seller can plan appropriate marketing strategies to overcome resistance barriers.

The following are the five key product factors affecting the rate of innovation adoption and diffusion as well as the likelihood of marketplace success, along with strategy recommendations for each.

RELATIVE ADVANTAGE

Relative advantage is the degree to which consumers perceive the innovation as superior to existing products in satisfying their needs and solving their problems. A new product must have a discernible, meaningful (vs. merely gimmicky) difference along one or more determinant buying criteria. It should be unique and competitively superior. For example, e-mail is much more convenient and less expensive than faxing, which had time and money advantages over snail mail.

Relative advantage is the key success/failure factor for new products because innovation success boils down to effectively satisfying customer needs and wants better than do competitors. Therefore, creating products based on knowledge of unsolved consumer problems and unsatisfied needs via problem-based ideation is essential, as discussed in Exercise 4.1. Unfortunately, too many inventions lack a "reason for being." How many varieties of microwave popcorn or salad dressing do you think can make the cut on the supermarket shelf?

Advertising and selling should educate buyers on the product's relative advantage. Alternatively, promotion can create a psychological point of difference such as a unique brand image.

COMPATIBILITY

Compatibility is the extent to which consumers believe that a new product is consistent with their current ways of thinking and behaving. Continuous innovations in Robertson's classification are high in compatibility and therefore meet little innovation resistance, while discontinuous innovations are low in compatibility and often meet significant consumer hesitation. The first automobiles were fiercely resisted—car drivers were exhorted by skeptics to "hire a horse!" So, marketers positioned the first cars as a "horseless carriage" in an attempt to minimize the psychological newness.

Research finds that compatibility ranks second in importance to relative advantage among these five factors in influencing adoption. Consequently, it behooves marketers to (a) know the values, norms, and other characteristics of the targeted consumer's culture, subculture, social class, and social groups; and (b) to develop and market the product to be consistent with these societal components. Whenever possible, new products and their marketing should not "go against the grain" but rather "go with the flow." Additionally, consumer education might be required to change misperceptions of compatibility, as the first refrigerator manufacturers had to do for people who thought the only way to keep lettuce fresh was to keep it on ice.

COMPLEXITY

Complexity (converse is **simplicity**) concerns the innovation's perceived usability (ease of use). (It does not concern complexity of technology.) Personal video recorders by TiVo and ReplayTV took time to catch on because they were difficult to deploy. On the other hand, television was a rapid hit in part because the first TVs were easy to use (unlike today's sophisticated sets with remote controls having more buttons than there are channels!). Sales of digital cameras spiked when "point-and-shoot" versions were launched. In short, products should be designed to be user friendly.

TRIALABILITY

Trialability (divisibility) entails the extent to which the new item can be sampled or evaluated on a limited basis prior to adoption. For nondurables, trial can be accelerated via sales promotions such as samples and coupons or through offering small "trial" sizes. For durable goods, a *surrogate trial experience* without commitment can be provided, such as showroom demonstrations, trial runs (e.g., an automobile test drive), or even loaning or leasing the product. Many Maytag stores allow shoppers to do a load of laundry to test out their washers and dryers, to bake a sheet of cookies in a range, or listen to a dishwasher to see if it is really quiet.

COMMUNICABILITY

Communicability (observability) concerns how readily visible the product and its benefits are to potential adopters, as well as how easy it is for users and marketers alike to explain the nature and relative advantages of the product to prospects. Products high in visibility, such as new model cars, hairstyles, and clothing styles, are more communicable than private items such as a new medicated shampoo, garbage disposal system, or ice maker.

Marketers should find ways to make new products more visible, such as by pushing for adoption in public places (service establishments, social organizations, etc., as with the first TVs, which were initially adopted by taverns where patrons could experience them). Sellers can also raise consumer interest via publicity and massive doses of advertising so that users are willing to discuss the product with others.

REVIEW QUESTIONS

1. What is the relation between adoption and diffusion of innovations? Describe the diffusion process.
2. What is an innovation? Why are innovations important to firms?
3. Describe the two dimensions of product newness. Then, explain each of the six types of new products in the BAH classification scheme and how each can be described on these two dimensions.

4. Cite and discuss the three categories of innovations according to Robertson's classification system regarding degree of behavioral change and perceived degree of product novelty. Which types of BAH innovations fall into each category?
5. What are the marketing implications of the BAH and Robertson classification schemes?
6. Describe each of the five innovation characteristics that influence probability of adoption and diffusion and the marketing implications of each.

IN-CLASS APPLICATIONS

1. Think of a product that you consider to be an innovation but you have yet to purchase. Classify it according to both the Robertson and the BAH new product categorization systems.

   Do you plan to purchase this product? Explain why or why not, considering benefits to you as well as the five innovation characteristics influencing likelihood of adoption and diffusion.

2. Choose a well-known brand name that you are personally familiar with and complete the following.
   a. Develop three ideas for innovations that could be branded with this name (they need not all be technologically feasible). You should have one new product for each of Robertson's three innovation types. Briefly describe each product in terms of features and benefits as well as reasons that using the existing brand name would be a good idea.

      Classify each of these new product concepts according to the BAH taxonomy.
   b. Describe how each of these innovations will affect the behavior and lifestyles of existing users of that brand.

      Which of these products will attract a new target market? Describe that market and identify the innovation attributes that attract them to each of these products.

3. According to www.productscan.com, some of the top domestic innovations of 2000 were:
   • General Mills's Milk 'n Cereal Bars: convenient breakfast bars made with real milk and cereal
   • StarKist premium tuna in a pouch: fresh, easy-open packaged tuna with no liquid
   • Saran QuickCover Food Storage Lids: varied size elastic lids that ensure a snug fit and freshness
   • Crest Whitestrips dental whitening system: innovative plastic strips that guarantee whiter teeth in less than two weeks

   For the year 2001, the Productscan top innovations included:
   • P J Squares peanut butter and jelly slices: combined peanut butter and jelly slices packaged like American cheese slices
   • Campbell's Soup to Sip microwaveable soup: easy-to-sip soup in a mug-shaped cup that snuggly fits in a car's cup holder
   • Parkay Fun Squeeze Colored Margarine: doodle-friendly margarine to make any meal fun for kids
   • American Woman Tri-Color 3-in-1 nail color: nail polish that changes color with the user's mood swings and sunlight exposure

   For each of these products, answer the following:
   a. Have you purchased or used this product since its release? If so, describe your level of satisfaction or dissatisfaction and why. If not, how do you think you would like this product?
   b. Which innovation attributes of this product have probably influenced the success or failure of its adoption and diffusion? Have any of those characteristics possibly hindered its success or failure?
   c. Considering these innovation attributes, what suggestions for marketing strategy can you offer for causing a quicker adoption of this innovation?
   d. The ads in Exhibits 10.4 through 10.7 feature new product innovations. Briefly explain which of Robertson's degrees of innovativeness each product displays and why. Also, classify each new product according to the BAH scheme. Discuss any implications of your classifications of innovativeness for each product's marketing program.

      Finally, describe each product in terms of the five innovation attributes. What does your discussion suggest for each product's probability of adoption and diffusion?

EXHIBIT 10.4   Kodak Ad

EXHIBIT 10.5   Charmin Ad

EXHIBIT 10.6   Orajel Ad

EXHIBIT 10.7   Symantec Ad

WRITTEN APPLICATION

1. Complete Questions 1 through 4 in the In-Class Applications. For the first question, take a survey of ten peers (or other members of the likely target market) and summarize their answers to all of its questions. Do they discuss any of the five innovation attributes? Summarize your findings, along with recommendations for how the marketer of this product can minimize any innovation resistance barriers. For the fourth question above, find three more ads, each of which exhibits one of Robertson's innovation types. Answer all of the parts of Question 4 for each ad you find.

EXERCISE 10.2. WORD-OF-MOUTH COMMUNICATION AND OPINION LEADERS

OBJECTIVES

1. To become aware of the important role of WOM communication in new product adoption and diffusion.
2. To understand the types of goods and services for which WOM and opinion leaders are most influential on CB.
3. To understand the significance of opinion leaders (OLs) and the nature of the various information flows involving OLs.
4. To learn about the different research techniques used to identify OLs in a local community and to gain practice in using one of those methodologies.
5. To become familiar with, identify, and experience developing creative marketing strategies using WOM communication and OLs.

BACKGROUND

THE NATURE OF WORD-OF-MOUTH, INTERPERSONAL COMMUNICATION, AND INTERPERSONAL INFLUENCE

WORD-OF-MOUTH COMMUNICATION

An important factor in the adoption and diffusion of innovations is the social system through which individuals influence their fellow consumers. This exercise investigates non-marketer-controlled, independent, personal sources of informal consumer information in the social system, with an emphasis on WOM communication and on using OLs to encourage new product adoption and diffusion. For example, when Mountain Dew was repositioned as a "hip," youthful drink, WOM had a large role to play as members of Generation Y learned from one another (rather than from Gen-Y–targeted advertising) that this drink is loaded with caffeine and sugar to give the quick "buzz" they sought.

Although such personal sources are non-marketer controlled, we shall see how clever, creative marketers can influence them. As the twenty-first century gets into full swing, creating and capitalizing on consumer "buzz" is turning out to be the next wave of consumer marketing.

Word-of-mouth communication (interpersonal search, buzz) is unpaid and unsponsored transmission of personal messages between consumers, usually via reference persons and reference groups. While traditionally WOM occurred in person, increasingly e-mail, instant messaging, blogs, podcasts, and other electronic communications are also being used to "spread the word." For new products, WOM is usually most influential after consumers have been exposed to mass media advertising and publicity, which perform an informing function, while WOM executes a legitimizing role, putting a trusted person's "stamp of approval" on the product.

INTERPERSONAL COMMUNICATION

Interpersonal communication is the personal exchange of information between two or more individuals. It usually occurs in a face-to-face situation, although it can also be by written correspondence, personal electronic communication (e.g., instant messaging), and telephone conversation. Most interpersonal communication is verbal communication as people discuss matters. However, interpersonal communication can also be nonverbal or observational in nature, such as one neighbor observing another driving a "hot" new sports car or sporting a new style. In fact, the new Volkswagen Beetle was a success, in part, due to its unique styling. Every time the very round Beetle drove down a street filled with boxy SUVs, it was marketing itself.

While some interpersonal communication entails personal selling, the discussion here will be confined to WOM. We focus on **social channels**, channels of communication between friends, family members, neighbors, work associates, and acquaintances, rather than **advocate channels**, which are biased marketer-controlled sources.

Much interpersonal communication is **referral communication**, in which one consumer recommends a particular good or service to another. Great brands are best built by referral—for example, your parents, friends, wife, child, or neighbor saying, "You have to try this." They, in effect, become *product proselytizers* or *brand evangelists*.

WOM referral communication has become more influential in recent years. The majority of people rely more than ever on friends and family, rather than advertising or editorials when selecting places to visit, prescription drugs to buy, car repair personnel to consult, and videos to rent. This is likely due to heightened distrust of institutions and increasing self-reliance. Also, there are now customer review sites online. Consumers now prowl the Web in search of recommendations or warnings by other consumers. For example, the music-recommendation site iLike, steers customers to tunes they are likely to enjoy.

INTERPERSONAL INFLUENCE

Interpersonal influence occurs when a consumer's attitude and/or behavior changes as a consequence of interpersonal communication. Generally, personal influence has greater impact than nonpersonal consumer information sources such as advertising and personal selling. Interpersonal influence tends to be more powerful where individuals have *strong ties*—a close, intimate social relationship—or in social groups.

The growing popularity of the Internet as a communication forum has led to new electronic channels for facilitating the sharing of consumer-to-consumer information. Today, in addition to talking over the picket fence to a neighbor about food, travel, and technology, consumers are also discussing products on line with "neighbors" who might live in another state or even another country. For instance, teens tell each other what to purchase through podcasts and playlists posted on MySpace. Consumer reviews appear at shopping sites such as Amazon.com and BarnesandNoble.com. Internet-mediated WOM has primarily taken two forms: (1) dedicated consumer opinion Web sites and (2) corporate Web sites.

Dedicated Consumer Opinion Web Sites and Blogs. Epinions.com and ecomplaints.com are popular consumer-controlled spaces offering a forum for consumers to write and archive their consumption experiences with any good or service. They sometimes provide a powerful search engine for consumers relying on the "wisdom of the crowds" to find and read opinions expressed by others.

Some blogs are managed by consumers or brand enthusiasts to promote a brand or kind of product. However, others are run by groups or individuals to promote a negative view of a firm and its offerings. Consequently, marketers should monitor Web sites, blogs, and social media such as Twitter to see what people are saying about the firm. Many firms have specialists whose job it is to put into Google and blog search engines the name of the company or brand, followed by the words "complaints," "sucks," "I hate," and other unflattering terms, just to see what consumers are saying. There are also firms such as BuzzLogic that track who is saying what about firms and brands. Some of these sites reveal legitimate gripes that should be addressed. Others are vindictive attempts to unfairly sully brand and corporate reputations.

Corporate Web Sites and Blogs, and Social Media Outlets. Some commercial sites allow consumers to express their opinions regarding the products sold on the marketer's Web site. Amazon.com famously encourages consumers to write reviews about books, music, and other products traded on their site. Other forms of Internet-facilitated consumer-to-consumer communication continue to evolve, such as online communities, chat rooms, message boards, opinion forums, listservs, social networks, podcasts, and blogs.

Hasbro's Playskool toys division sponsors CafeMom. The company sent Kid Motion toy kits to five thousand site members, suggesting that they talk up the kit on CafeMom while swapping tips about "how to make play fun and enriching."

Unfortunately for some marketers, there is a **negativity bias**. Bad news travels faster and further than good news, and it has greater priority and influence in decision making than does positive communication. Conversely, when customer experiences are favorable, positive recommendations tend to snowball. It is axiomatic that "a good product sells itself" and "a satisfied customer is your best salesperson."

PRODUCTS FOR WHICH WOM COMMUNICATION IS IMPORTANT

Regarding new products, interpersonal communication is likely to be more important for discontinuous innovations such as mobile communication devices, and mass media communication is more consequential for continuous innovations such as perfumed toilet tissue, which people are less likely to discuss.

Exercise 8.1 explained that reference groups are more influential for certain types of products. Since WOM referrals are a subset of reference group influence, most of those same product criteria apply. They are:

- Socially visible or conspicuous products, especially hedonic goods such as entertainment
- Products for which buyers lack self-confidence in decision making, such as credence goods
- Products that are relevant to a social group or individuals engaged in discussion (e.g., golfing buddies discuss golf clubs)
- Products associated with high involvement and high perceived risk (e.g., discontinuous innovations)
- Products for which alternative information sources lack credibility (e.g., used car dealers)

OPINION LEADERS

Opinion leaders (OLs) (influentials, tastemakers, trendsetters, thought leaders, pioneer consumers, product enthusiasts) are influential individuals who are knowledgeable about products in a particular field and whose advice others take seriously. Examples include wine connoisseurs, audiophiles, fashionistas, cigar aficionados, chess champs, and computer jocks.

OLs act as change agents, providing favorable product information and advice to peers to encourage them to adopt a new product. OLs are often motivated by needs for power and affiliation. A person's opinion leadership is the extent to which that individual directly (via verbal WOM) or indirectly (by being observed) changes others' attitudes and behaviors.

While the sender of information and opinions is known as the opinion leader, the receiver of such influence is called the **opinion follower**, who is called an **opinion receiver** when passively accepting the information and advice from an OL without having requested it, and an **opinion seeker** when actively pursuing guidance from the OL.

Opinion leadership tends to be category specific—there are few **generalized opinion leaders** who are know-it-all jack-of-all-trades. One example is high school athletes, whose usage of certain brands of products ranging from sneakers to bottled water is mimicked. Usually, however, an OL for one product might become an opinion seeker or receiver for another unrelated item.

Nonetheless, there is some **opinion leadership overlap (quasigeneralized opinion leadership, polymorphic opinion leadership)**. OLs in one product class are often OLs in one or more related categories. So, a person might be an OL for cosmetics and fashion, but probably would not be an OL for large appliances and cosmetics.

There are several categories of OLs. **Purchase pals** are OLs who accompany buyers on their shopping trips in order to provide information on and advice for their on-site purchase decisions. Inexperienced consumers who lack confidence in their ability to evaluate products and brands are more likely to take a pal along when they shop, to reduce perceived risk. **Surrogate buyers (shoppers, consumers)** are professionals who are hired and paid to give information and recommendations, as well as to buy on behalf of their clients, such as wardrobe consultants, financial advisers, and interior decorators.

Consumers who have general marketplace information about many different types of products, places to shop, and brands to buy, rather than expertise on any particular product categories, are called **market mavens**. They exhibit opinion leadership overlap, as they are two to five years ahead of the curve in their involvement with new products, trends, and lifestyle choices. Market mavens tend to be aware of new products before most other people and are more "plugged in" to various sources of consumer information.

Innovators (pioneers) are consumers who are among the very first (technically the first 2.5 percent) to adopt an innovation. They are influential because of their early product experience and expertise (and, hence, are often called "geeks"). Although innovators tend to be OLs, only approximately one-half of OLs are innovators. Also, some innovators tend to be isolates who do not interact much with members of their local community, preferring to stay in touch with the outside world through general and specialized media.

INTERPERSONAL INFLUENCE PROCESSES

Interpersonal influence usually flows in conjunction with mass media publicity and/or advertising communication. It can occur either through one-step, two-step, or multistep communication flows.

PUBLIC OPINION LEADERS, TOP-DOWN SOCIAL CHANGE, AND ONE-STEP COMMUNICATION FLOWS

Opinion leaders can be either public or private. The **public opinion leader** is an influential celebrity or person in the public limelight, various aspects of whose CB are reported by the media, thereby influencing the masses (especially younger consumers) to follow suit. Public OLs include actors, sports stars, musicians, authors, editors, politicians, critics and reviewers of entertainment products, financial and industry analysts, scientists, academics, and etiquette "experts" like Emily Post. For instance, impressionable teens are more apt to take up the habit when their film idols smoke. The cars driven by "hot" sports and music stars influence others. Cohabitation is popular in part because an increasing number of celebrities live together. Mascara demand was shaped by cosmetologists, allergists, eyeglass makers, and optometrists, as well as well-known make-up artists. For years, swimsuit makers mostly relied on fashion magazines such as *Vogue* or *Glamour* for exposure. Now it is as important to be on the cover of the *Sports Illustrated* swimsuit issue, in Teen People.com, in a Britney Spears music video, or worn by the world's top male and female surfers. Marketers need to monitor TV, movies, celebrity magazines, and other aspects of popular culture so as not to miss out on the next big thing.

Examples of the influence of public OLs include the following:

- Oprah Winfrey popularized powdered protein mixes when she announced that she lost 67 pounds by using them. Oprah's Book Club endorsements launched many best sellers.
- When Jennifer Lopez started spray tanning in the early 2000s, she made the practice not just acceptable but fashionable.
- Various trendy celebrities, including the "Brit Pack"—Britney Spears, Paris Hilton, and Lindsay Lohan—sporting fingerless gloves during the mid-2000s resulted in a comeback in the palm warmers from an earlier sales peak two decades earlier.
- When Alaska governor Sarah Palin was nominated as John McCain's running mate in 2008, the rimless, rectangular-lensed Kawasaki-brand eyeglass frames she sported became an overnight sensation.
- Clothing retailer Chico's became especially fashionable after Olympic swimmer Michael Phelps's mom, Debbie, was seen on TV throughout the 2008 Olympics in Chico's garb.

Public opinion leadership is an example of **top-down social change (trickle-down influence, downward diffusion)**, social change flowing from society's leaders to the masses, or from the upper to lower social strata. Members of the lower status groups seek to emulate the behavior of members of the higher societal echelons. This top-down communication pattern is also known as the **one-step flow of communication theory (top-down model, direct flow model, hypodermic needle model)**. Shown in Exhibit 10.8A, this suggests that mass media have a direct, immediate, and powerful effect on a mass audience. For example, in the early days of rock and roll, radio disc jockeys were enlisted to hype the latest record releases.

EXHIBIT 10.8 Theories of Communications of Information Flows

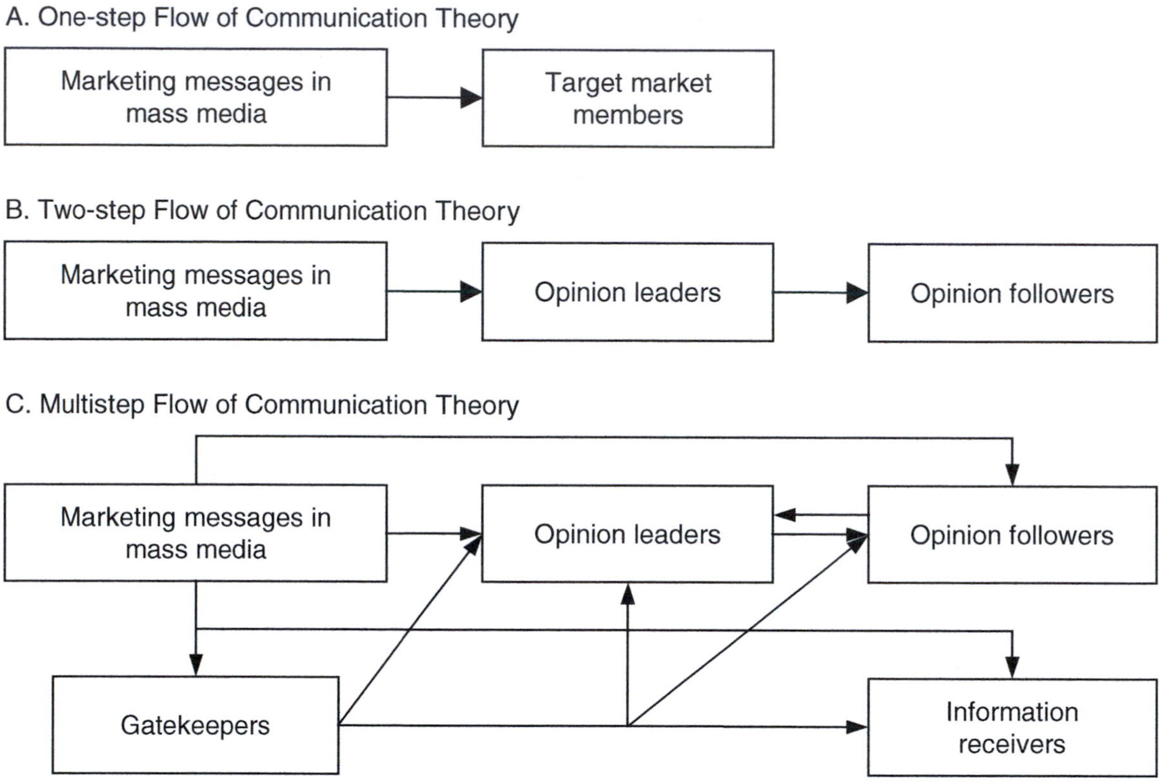
A. One-step Flow of Communication Theory
Marketing messages in mass media
Target market members
B. Two-step Flow of Communication Theory
Marketing messages in mass media
Opinion leaders
Opinion followers
C. Multistep Flow of Communication Theory
Marketing messages in mass media
Opinion leaders
Opinion followers
Gatekeepers
Information receivers

Two-Step Communication Flows and Private Opinion Leaders

A polar opposite of trickle-down information flow is the **bottom-up (trickle-up, upward diffusion) model.** Here, social change moves from the bottom rungs of the social ladder (or even from a counterculture) to mainstream society, perhaps even reaching the upper echelons. Much of this is mainstreaming (crossover sale), as has happened with Mexican and Asian foods. Ethnic groups frequently start trends in entertainment (break dancing, black cinema); music (rap, hip-hop, and R&B); and fashion (grunge, baggy clothes, "urban" fashion, new hairstyles).

Since they are less concerned with maintaining the status quo, those of lower societal status feel freer to innovate and take risks. Years ago, prostitutes made high heels, rouge, and lipstick fashionable. Professional wrestling and pickup trucks were popular with blue-collar country bumpkins before they went mainstream. Trucker chic (the dressed-down, rough-and-tumble look) caught on with celebrities and other high-society types during the early 2000s.

Prone to experiment, teens often originate or popularize street-cool trends in fashion (expensive sneakers, the punk look, body piercing, Vans slip-on sneakers, and trucker hats); music (1950s beat, 1970s punk music, and 1990s boy bands); and even sports (extreme sports). Young males help set the standard for what is "in" in videogames. Teens are the early adopters and influencers for portable mobile devices such as cell phones and digital MP3 players. Many youth were horrified as their parents and other adults invaded their turf on Facebook in the late 2000s.

From the bottom rungs of the social ladder, the innovations then percolate up to the general culture through media such as teen magazines and MTV. Accordingly, white suburban teen males now represent a bigger chunk of hip-hop expenditures than the black community. Sometimes the adoption of such upwardly diffused products takes the form of **parody display**, whereby the well-to-do deliberately mock status symbols by adopting items that originally skewed downscale, such as ripped jeans, Jeeps, and tattoos.

With both trickle-up and trickle-down communication flows, influence travels between different social groups, usually aided by the mass media (including advertising and publicity) but often without WOM.

TWO-STEP FLOW OF COMMUNICATION THEORY

Much WOM occurs through **private opinion leaders**, those who have personal contact with the people they influence. Like public OLs in the trickle-down model, these private OLs also serve as gatekeepers, controlling the flow of product information to others. Traditionally, this information movement was explained by the **two-step flow of communication theory** (see Exhibit 10.8B). This two-step model says that (1) information flows from the impersonal mass media to OLs, who have high media exposure and (2) OLs operate as filters, interpreters, and transmitters of this information, which they pass on to the opinion followers. In effect, OLs act as information middlemen for their friends, relatives, neighbors, and acquaintances who constitute the "masses."

For example, pharmaceutical manufacturers often first promote their new drugs to the most influential doctors who, in turn, let their colleagues and patients know about the medication. High-tech marketers focus their first efforts on technophiles, who then enlighten technophobes.

The original two-step flow model was one of **trickle-down diffusion**, with marketers relying on mass media and public OLs to spread product information. Today, however, it is believed that most two-step communication flow is **trickle across (lateral diffusion)**, in which communication occurs horizontally within social groups (rather than vertically between individuals of unequal social status), typically between an OL and an opinion follower. There exists **homophily**, the "like-me" principle that says people mostly interact with and discuss issues with similar others regarding sex, age, and socioeconomic status as well as beliefs, attitudes, and values.

MULTISTEP COMMUNICATION FLOWS

However, the two-step model has been largely supplanted by the **multistep flow of communication model (multistage interaction model)**, which suggests that not only do OLs get media information, but so do opinion followers (see Exhibit 10.8C). In fact, some information receivers get marketplace information solely from the mass media rather than from OLs.

Also, according to this model, two-way flows of communication occur whereby OLs both influence and are influenced by opinion receivers. Such communication is less a lecture by the OL and more a conversation between two or more parties. Hence, perhaps a better name than opinion *leader* is opinion *giver* or *guide*, since such OLs are not formal leaders but rather informal influentials.

This model also includes **gatekeepers**, who do not influence and are not influenced by others, but merely pass along information they obtain from the media and personal sources to OLs and opinion followers (as family members often do for one another, for example).

Because of all of these possible information channels, it is important for marketers to monitor the various flows of influence for their product (discussed next). This can be done through surveys that ask, "Where did you first learn about this product?" with answers being linked to demographics such as age, income, education, and to media habits. Marketers can also monitor the various Internet communication channels to see who is buzzing.

IDENTIFYING OPINION LEADERS AND INTERPERSONAL COMMUNICATION FLOWS

If marketers can identify OLs and understand the nature of marketing communication flows between OLs and opinion followers, they can make strategic use of OLs, targeting their efforts accordingly. The following are various methods used to identify OLs.

CHARACTERISTICS OF OPINION LEADERS

In order to conduct research on and strategically use OLs, they must first be identified. Generally, the most important characteristic of OLs is their high degree of enduring involvement with a particular product category, resulting in high knowledge about and experience with that product. Typically, OLs are innovators, giving them a high degree of product experience to discuss with others. And OLs and opinion receivers often share similar demographic and socioeconomic characteristics and lifestyles, that is, they are **homophilous**, resulting in lateral (peer) influence (referent power). OLs also tend to have the following observable traits.

- *Demographic characteristics.* Generally, OLs tend to be younger and of slightly higher socioeconomic status. College students are often trendsetters for fashion and electronic devices.
- *Social characteristics.* OLs are typically socially active; more involved in community organizations and affairs; friendly, outgoing, and "sociable," with a large circle of friends; cosmopolitan, or "plugged in" people who are attuned to the world at large; and socially mobile, or willing to change their position socioeconomically, geographically, and within social groups.
- *Personality characteristics.* OLs are characteristically confident in their appraisal of the product category; independent decision makers; inner directed, marching to the beat of their own drummer rather than trying to please others; and variety seekers.
- *Behavioral characteristics.* OLs are innovative—more open to change, experiential and experimental, and more favorably disposed toward innovations overall, especially in their arena of interest and expertise; willing to talk, share information, and seek others' opinions; more exposed to both general and special interest media; and venturesome, having a high tolerance for risk.

RESEARCH TECHNIQUES TO IDENTIFY OPINION LEADERS AND MONITOR INTERPERSONAL COMMUNICATION FLOWS

Sociologists have developed the first three of the following approaches to identifying OLs.

Self-Designating Method. In the **self-designating method,** respondents are asked a series of survey questions to determine whether they are more or less likely than others to be asked advice about some general product categories and whether others view them as a good information source for these products. For example, interviewees might be given a five-point Likert scale ("strongly agree" to "strongly disagree") with the statement, "Friends and neighbors often come to me for advice on buying clothes."

Sociometric Method. With the **sociometric method,** members of a social system are asked to identify to whom they give advice and to whom they go for information and guidance about various products. Marketers can also monitor the various Internet communication channels to see who is buzzing, and creating digital maps of social influence. For instance, Facebook popularized the term "social graph," referring to a Facebook user's friends, their friends' friends, and so on.

Key Informant Method. The **key informant method** relies on **key informants**—people who frequently engage in WOM communications within a social system. They are asked to identify OLs for a particular product or situation through surveys that ask questions such as "Where did you first learn about this product?" Who are the most influential people in this group?" or "Who do you turn to for advice about this service?" Answers can be linked to demographics such as age, income, education, and to media habits. These informants need not be OLs or members of the social group themselves. For instance, professors or student activities personnel could be asked to identify social leaders on campus.

Objective Method. Instead of these three sociological research approaches, marketers have also used the **objective method**. Here, a "controlled experiment" is run in which a new product or information about an innovation is placed with selected persons. Then, the resulting chain of WOM communication is tracked by asking people if they received the information on and/or tried the new product and from where they received their product knowledge.

Other Methods to Identify Opinion Leaders. The following relatively quick-and-easy methods to identify OLs for a product category are also more likely to be used by marketing practitioners than the sociological approaches.

- Using company purchase records (e.g., credit card information, warranty card returns, direct response purchases) to locate early and/or frequent product purchasers, many of whom are likely to be OLs
- Keeping tabs on individuals who are frequent or early responders to offers for additional information, contests, samples, and so on; response devices include business reply cards, toll-free numbers, links to Web site surveys, and e-mail addresses
- Obtaining mailing lists from commercial list houses for special interest groups, magazine subscribers, club members, and knowledgeable experts (e.g., tennis pros and pharmacists)
- Finding out who community leaders are, especially in relevant areas of interest such as local politicians, civic group leaders, community organization volunteers, and church elders

WOM MARKETING STRATEGIES

WOM marketing uses person-to-person consumer communication to raise awareness of an organization's offerings and generate sales. WOM is regarded as a credible, hence particularly influential, cost-effective, and speedy means of disseminating marketplace information. If marketers discover that WOM and opinion leadership play an important role in influencing consumers about their products and they can identify OLs, one or more of the following marketing strategies can be planned and deployed. Such WOM marketing began in earnest in the late 1990s, when brand marketers began grappling with fragmented and cluttered media. Some companies, such as Advanced Media Productions, specialize in starting and spreading brand-oriented chatter. There are research companies devoted to measuring and tracking electronic WOM on Web sites, blogs, message boards, and other social or traditional media (e.g., Nielsen's BuzzMetrics, CyberAlert, and TNS Cymfony). The Word of Mouth Marketing Association is the official trade association for the WOM marketing industry.

USE BUZZ MARKETING TECHNIQUES

Buzz marketing entails efforts to gain awareness and trial of new products by stimulating WOM communication. Used as a verb, the word "buzz" means seeding the media with news and information about a brand with the objective of creating favorable WOM. As a noun, buzz means an intense and interactive form of WOM referral that occurs both on and off line.

Buzz marketing often targets OLs as **product missionaries**, well-connected people at the hub of social networks who can serve as "seeding points" to spread the word about a product with evangelical zeal, converting unreached unbelievers into enthusiastic customers. Often, they are community influentials (journalists, civic leaders, small business owners, and the like). Buzz marketers relay information directly to OLs and encourage them to spread the good word.

A growing number of marketing agencies specialize in the development of buzz campaigns for companies. For instance, BzzAgent, Inc., recruits "agents" to participate in an organization's campaign, locates agents through its database, and matches members' profiles with that of the firm's target market.

For the most part, these are **grassroots (guerrilla) marketing tactics**, low budget marketing efforts executed, often in unconventional ways, in local communities to deliver marketing messages to target audiences where they live, work, or play. Such techniques work especially well within the youth culture, since teens and young adults like to discover brands on their own rather than having them forced down their throats by slick marketers.

The following are specific types of buzz marketing tactics.

Targeting Advertising and Other Marketing Communications Directly to OLs. Targeted media include trade shows, direct mail, e-mail and other online media, telemarketing, and advertising in niche channels such as special interest magazines.

Stimulating WOM Through Product Trial by Loaning, Giving, or Selling the Product at a Reduced Price to OLs for Use and Demonstration to Others. Professionals and other tastemakers are sometimes given (are seeded with) free samples they can demonstrate to others. Dentists dispense Oral-B brand toothbrushes and dental floss, and physicians offer patients samples of medications. Travel agents are given free trips and travel accommodations so that they will aggressively market the travel destinations and services to their clients. Ebsco Faculty Subscription Services sells discount magazine subscriptions to college professors because of the influence they have in the classroom and their local communities. At trade shows, aerobics trainers are given free athletic shoes. The Snickers energy bar was sampled to marathoners and nutrition specialists. Pepsi shipped free cases of Mountain Dew Code Red to hip-hop DJs and rap celebrities. Hewlett-Packard sent free printers to targeted moms to help them scan photos. And, Ford enlisted an army of one hundred blogging social media trendsetters to drum up buzz by loaning the 2010 Fiesta to them for six months, counting on them to drive the Fiesta and chat about their driving experiences. The one hundred "Fiesta agents" were selected from 4,000 online applications based on how many followers they had online. Agents posted videos and updated their friends and followers on their blogs, YouTube, Facebook, and Twitter.

A rapidly growing tactical variation is **stealth marketing**, a form of buzz marketing whereby companies lure key customers with coveted items that are deliberately kept in short supply, such as cool gadgets or free products. The tastemakers use their influence to diffuse the idea that the firm's brand has pop cultural value (i.e., it's "cool"). Specialized agencies with names like Tribal DDB, Brand Buzz, Sputnik, and the Dream Team have organized armies of in-the-field or on-the-street teams to execute these underground assignments.

Stimulating WOM Through Targeting Business Organizations. Here, the initial target of information is service organizations whose customers a marketer wishes to reach. Color TV manufacturers sell their sets to hotels and motels at discounted prices, in effect buying customer experience. The producers of the film *The Passion of the Christ* enlisted church leaders to encourage group sales of tickets and even rent out movie theaters showing the flick, providing them with free posters and other marketing materials promoting the movie.

Hiring OLs to Promote the Brand. Some retailers employ popular and attractive high school and college students as sales clerks and sometimes offer them product discounts. Red Bull created buzz on college campuses by seeking student representatives who talked up the brand and threw parties, sometimes using Red Bull as a mixer.

Another strategy is to encourage OLs to host product presentations in their homes, such as the classic Tupperware or Pampered Chef parties. To help launch Xbox Live Internet-based games and services, Microsoft hired women to host Xbox parties. They located the ladies from consumer-facing professions such as hairdressers and guidance counselors, as well as IT technicians, through a service called House Party. This firm has a database of 100,000 consumers who have provided a profile of personal information and who wish to be "brand advocates." Based on the profiles, House Party selects people most prone to discuss a good or service. Other firms hire **brand ambassadors**, buzz marketing teams usually consisting of young adults planted in visible locations such as bars and city street corners. They are clad in outfits to promote and demonstrate products and may land on the local TV news or in the newspapers.

Some firms pay nonemployees called buzz agents to promote their brands personally. For instance, Tremor is Procter & Gamble's WOM marketing program, which uses a panel of 250,000 teens who are asked to talk with friends about new products or concepts that P&G sends them from other companies that pay P&G to participate. Tremor panelists are not paid cash but instead receive free samples or other items. BzzAgent gives their agents a sample product and a training manual describing buzz-creating tactics, such as discussing the brand with friends or e-mailing influential people regarding the product. Although such systems are legal, the ethics of paying nonemployees to promote a brand via WOM have been questioned, and regulators have cried foul unless the product missionaries reveal to consumers that they are being paid to spread the good word. Nondisclosure violates a tenet of the Word of Mouth Marketing Association.

USE ADVERTISING THAT SIMULATES WOM COMMUNICATION

Ed Keller, co-author of the seminal tome *The Influentials,* discovered in a separate study that 22 percent of WOM conversations were fueled directly by advertising and that those 22 percent were much more likely to include brand recommendations than the remaining 78 percent of brand-related conversations that weren't initiated directly by an ad. Keller's study also found that 30 percent of online buzz was initiated by ads. By portraying product discussions among consumers, advertising can imitate WOM communication. The approaches are as follows.

- Testimonials from typical satisfied users extolling the brand's virtues based on their personal experiences. Scotts Turf Builder's neighbor-to-neighbor campaign cast real-life Scotts customers who proudly showed off their great-looking lawns in TV commercials.
- In slice-of-life advertising, the typical formula is: Person A, with an unsolved consumer problem, meets person B. Person B offers the perfect solution—the branded product. Later, A tries the brand, and still later, B meets the now ecstatic A, who loves the product and is indebted to B for life.
- Use of an expert public OL (e.g., a well-known professional) who stars in advertising and/or makes grassroots personal appearances.
- Ads that report favorable findings of consumer surveys (e.g., "favored by mothers 4 to 1") can be surrogates for WOM.

STIMULATE WOM COMMUNICATION THROUGH ADVERTISING AND PROMOTION

The following are other ways to generate water-cooler conversation about a brand by creating advertising and promotion with "talk value."

- *Run advertising that portrays people engaged in informal communication.* Such depictions suggest the appropriateness of discussing the product and either encourage brand users to share their experience with prospects or else persuade nonusers to discuss the brand with current users. Daffy's, an off-price NYC retailer, used a transit poster beseeching readers, "Friends don't let friends pay retail." Days Inn implored consumers to "Pass the word . . . save money at Days Inn."
- *Employ very entertaining or deliberately vague and intriguing ads.* Examples of the former include the Energizer Bunny; the Budweiser frogs; and Terry Tate, the office linebacker. An example of vague and intriguing ads was Nissan's launch ads for Infiniti, which featured rocks, trees, and pussy willows, not the car, which got people talking and speculating.
- *Run "teaser" ads.* **Teaser advertising** involves planned secrecy for new products, new events, and other novelties, deliberately leaking bits of information over time in ads to keep people guessing and talking. For example, prior to the launch of Trouble cologne, billboard ads ran asking, "Are you looking for Trouble?" At the time of its debut, Oldsmobile Intrigue marketers drove vehicles to toll plazas where they would tell the toll-taker, "I'm paying for me and the ten vehicles behind me." When those motorists reached the tollbooth, they were given a card saying, "Compliments of Intrigue" with a picture of the new model and where to get more information on it. Intriguing indeed!
- *Use product publicity.* For example, a new product can be displayed at large national trade shows attended by the press, which then generates buzz. Also, newsworthy happenings can be manufactured to be reported in the news and get people talking. Pontiac garnered enormous amounts of publicity when it gave away 276 of its new G6 sedans to an audience attending the TV show "Oprah."
- *Use planned secrecy with carefully timed leaks to the media.* This can also keep consumers guessing and discussing. Apple kept the iMac computer under wraps until founder Steve Jobs unveiled it to the press just before market launch. The result: Massive media coverage preceded the appearance of iMac in stores, plus it received plenty of consumer buzz.
- *Employ sales promotions.* Sweepstakes, contests, and giveaways work well to stimulate buzz. M&Ms has held several contests in which consumers voted on the next color for the candy.
- *Hold special events.* Because of their uniqueness and enjoyment value, special events can get people gabbing. Harley-Davidson creates family-oriented gatherings to get Harley owners together to swap stories about their motorcycle adventures. The more outrageous the event the better. During the Texas sesquicentennial, the world's largest cake (76,000 pounds) was baked with Duncan Hines cake mix.
- *Use repeatable advertising slogans or advertising that has high "conversation value."* Quotable slogans can become **catch phrases**—words, phrases, or expressions that are so attention-grabbing

and memorable they become recognizable by their repeatable utterance, thereby becoming part of the cultural landscape and national vernacular. Repeatable ad phrases include Nike's "Just do it"; the California Milk Processor Board's "Got Milk?"; the Verizon Wireless Test Man's "Can you hear me now?"; Las Vegas's "What happens in Vegas stays in Vegas"; and Disney's "I'm going to Disney World."

- *Put short films online.* These are known as **webisodes (video webcasting)**, original animated mini-video episodes for the Internet similar to TV shows with recurring episodes. Such short films use streaming audio and video. They have the cool quotient to generate buzz among younger consumers. An innovator was BMW automobiles, which featured its car involved in chases and plot twists and ran shorts featuring Madonna and soul singer James Brown. A five-minute Web-only commercial starring Tiger Woods was another early hit. More recently, Ikea's "Easy to Assemble, "a comedy series starring Illeana Douglas as a Hollywood actor looking to quit acting and work at the local IKEA furniture megastore, has received widespread online exposure.

CREATE OPINION LEADERS

Companies sometimes take people who are not necessarily OLs, but who are visible and "get around," turning them into leaders by getting them involved with and enthusiastic about the brand. This can save on the time and expense of first trying to identify who the product's OLs might be. Suburban homeowners who are centrally located within their neighborhood are given lawn care products gratis or at cost. Movie marketers for *My Big Fat Greek Wedding* held private screenings and doled out free T-shirts, Frisbees, and other souvenirs at Greek organizations, churches, and dance festivals.

USE STAR PERKS

Using **star perks (celebrity seeding, celebrity placements)** entails giving public OLs various perquisites, ranging from special treatment (as in the best restaurants), to product giveaways (cars, clothing), to endorsements with lucrative incentives. The purpose is to have the famous folks seen using the product. Nike gives free clothes and shoes to such pop heroes as Jack Nicholson and Sting, and Breathe Right nasal strips sent a case to all NFL trainers, whose players were seen wearing them on games broadcast on TV. TiVo doled out units to celebrities, leading to mentions on talk shows, which built the brand via WOM. Gift bags containing swag like jewelry, laptops, and handbags are lavished on Emmy and Oscar Award nominees at the shows. Participating vendors expect stars to provide publicity when they appear with their wares. A recent controversial practice is to pay (in cash or in kind) celebrities to tweet and blog about a product. Critics allege that there should be full disclosure of the payment. Proponents argue that for years public relations professionals have used this practice with journalists.

EMPLOYEE REFERRAL INCENTIVE PROGRAMS

Referral systems (customer referrals, pyramiding schemes, member-get-a-member programs, peer-to-peer marketing) recruit satisfied customers to encourage others to sign up, check out, or buy the product by offering those customers incentives such as product discounts or even cold cash. For years, charities have suggested that donors "get a friend to help." American Express once offered free airline travel tickets to consumers who persuaded three friends to sign up for the credit card. In a variation known as **multi-level marketing,** salespeople (distributors) earn extra commissions by convincing their customers to also become distributors.

GENERATE BUZZ ON THE INTERNET

Increasingly, marketers are feeding consumers information and marketing materials on Web sites, via e-mail, and in chat rooms, so that they will spread their newfound knowledge to others as though it was news of the second coming using *word of mouse* (*word of Web, word of blog*). **Viral marketing** facilitates and encourages current and potential customers to pass along a marketing message or to tell others about the company's products and services, encouraging those people to tell yet others. For instance, Christina Aguilera makes information regarding concert dates and song lyrics available in chat rooms and on bulletin boards. However, viral marketing usually entails creating an ad that is so informative or entertaining that consumers will want to pass it along to others, usually via e-mail, so that it rapidly spreads like the flu. When an e-mail comes from a friend, the recipient is much more likely to open and read it than if it came from a marketer. Popular here are TV commercials rejected by the television networks as too risqué.

Via *user-generated content*, companies get consumers to create videos about their products and then share them by e-mail with family and friends. Pizza Hut rallied consumers to spread praise for their pizza via videos. Contest entrants uploaded videos to the firm's Web site. Pizza Hut then named finalists and asked online consumers to vote for a winner.

REVIEW QUESTIONS

1. What is WOM communication, what are its limitations from a marketing perspective, for what reasons is WOM important to marketers, and for what types of products is it most important?
2. What are OLs? Describe the different categories of OLs (purchase pals, surrogate buyers, market mavens, and innovators) and explain why OLs are important as part of the WOM communication process for new products.
3. What is the difference between public OLs and private OLs? Between trickle-up and trickle-down social change? Between the one-step, two-step, and multistep flow of communication models?
4. Describe the roles of gatekeepers and innovators in opinion leadership.
5. Cite, describe, and explain the three sociological research approaches as well as the objective method for identifying OLs. What other methods besides sociological approaches can be used to identify OLs?
6. Describe the major marketing strategies that are available to capitalize on opinion leadership.

IN-CLASS APPLICATIONS

1. For each of the following new product advertisements (Exhibits 10.9–10.12), explain to what extent WOM communication and OLs would be an important influence on consumer adoption and diffusion of the innovation featured in the ad and why.

2. For products in these ads that would be heavily influenced by WOM and OLs, suggest and describe three potentially effective creative strategies for capitalizing on WOM and/or OLs. Do any of these ads use one of these strategies?

3. Before class, go on line and visit a consumer-oriented Web site such as www.epinions.com. How does this Web site enable WOM communication and capitalize on opinion leadership? How does this site help consumers make informed buying decisions?

4. As discussed, sometimes WOM communication comes in a negative form. This could happen with any product. But does the company know about this negative WOM communication? Before class, visit www.ewatch.com and see how this site helps companies beat the buzz. How does eWatch assist companies in tracking online chatter about their products? At the same time, how does this site use OLs to sell itself?

5. Whom do you rely on as a WOM information source, why, and for which products? How do these individuals rate on the various characteristics of OLs? Explain whether these are the types of products for which WOM would be expected to be important.

6. Are you an OL for any products? If so, for which ones and why? Where do you get your information on these products and to whom do you give it? Why do you do so? Does the information flow process here resemble any of those in Exhibit 10.8?

7. How do you rate yourself on the various characteristics of OLs? Select a classmate or friend (especially one you believe is an OL for one or more products) and rate that person on these characteristics. Does the individual agree with your assessment that the person is an OL?

8. How do you feel about the ethics of firms paying nonemployees to promote a brand via generating WOM as in the cases of BzzAgent, Tremor, and VocalPoint? Would you participate in such programs as

EXHIBIT 10.9   Northwest Airlines Ad

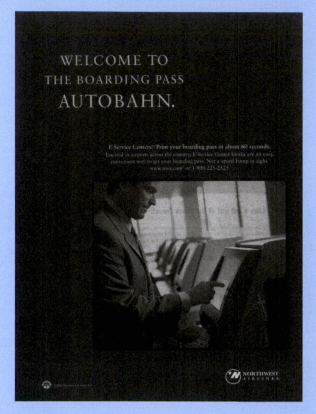

EXHIBIT 10.10   Clarinex Ad

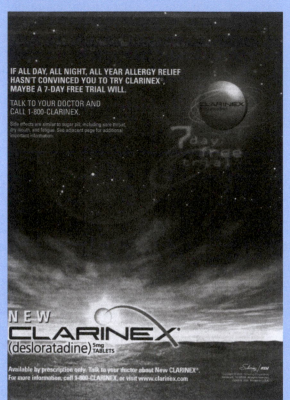

EXHIBIT 10.11   Bose Ad

EXHIBIT 10.12   Diet Coke Ad

an information sender if firms compensated you with free samples and coupons? Why or why not? How would you feel if you found out one of your friends was giving you product information in return for compensation by a marketer?

9. Have you ever been the sender or receiver of a viral marketing campaign? Describe the campaign, your role in it, and how effective you believe it was.

WRITTEN APPLICATIONS

1. Answer In-Class Applications Questions 1 and 2 for products featured in three of the ads (Exhibits 10.9–10.12). Select the products you believe are most heavily influenced by WOM and OLs. Then, find three more ads for new products that you suspect are also subject to these influences. Repeat Question 1 and 2 for the products featured in these ads.
2. Choose a good or service that interests both you and others on your university campus (or in your home neighborhood) and that you think is subject to significant WOM communication and opinion leadership.
   a. Explain why you believe the product is likely to be heavily influenced by WOM and OLs. Describe the likely pattern(s) of communication flow.
   b. Choose one of the research methods used to identify OLs for the product. For example, you could use the self-designating method and give a short survey to between one and two dozen people in the community to see if they classify themselves as OLs. You could make part of this a purposive sample in which, instead of randomly selecting respondents, you select those you suspect will be OLs, such as friends you know are very interested in the product, very popular people, or individuals in positions of influence. Or, you could use the key informant method to get information on people's opinions on the OLs. Alternatively, you could try the sociometric technique to trace conversations among a group of a dozen or so people who know each other.

    c. Describe characteristics that differentiate the OLs from the non-OLs (you might want to gather some basic demographic and media exposure data from your respondents). Do the OLs' traits match the characteristics described in this exercise?

    d. Devise at least two marketing strategies that employ the OLs you identified, which could be used on your campus or in your community to market the product.

        Answer In-Class Applications Questions 5, 6, 8, and 9.

KEY CONCEPTS

additions to existing product lines
adoption
advocate channels
bottom-up (trickle-up, upward diffusion) model
brand ambassadors
brand equity
brand franchise extensions (brand extensions)
buzz
buzz marketing
catch phrases
communicability (observability)
compatibility
complexity
continuous innovations
core (anchor, flagship) product
cost reductions
diffusion
diffusion of innovations (DOI)
discontinuous innovations
dynamically continuous innovations
flankers
gatekeepers
generalized opinion leaders
grassroots (guerrilla) marketing tactics
homophilous
homophily
innovation
innovation resistance
innovators (pioneers)
interpersonal communication
interpersonal influence
key informant
key informant method
market mavens
multi-level marketing
multistep flow of communication model (multistage interaction model)
negativity bias
"New-and-improved" (next-generation) products
new-to-the-world products (new product categories)
new product lines (new category entries)
objective method

one-step flow of communication theory (top-down model, direct flow model, hypodermic needle model)
opinion follower
opinion leaders (influentials, tastemakers, trendsetters, thought leaders, pioneer consumers, product enthusiasts)
opinion leadership overlap (quasigeneralized opinion leadership, polymorphic opinion leadership)
opinion receiver
opinion seeker
parody display
private opinion leaders
product line extension (line extension)
product missionaries
public opinion leader
purchase pals
referral communication
referral systems (customer referrals, pyramiding schemes, member-get-a-member programs, peer-to-peer marketing)
relative advantage
repositioning (relaunching, restaging, remarketing)
self-designating method
social channels
social system
sociometric method
star perks (celebrity seeding, celebrity placements)
stealth marketing
surrogate buyers (shoppers, consumers)
teaser advertising
technology
top-down social change (trickle-down influence, downward diffusion)
trialability (divisibility)
trickle across (lateral diffusion)
trickle-down diffusion
two-step flow of communication theory
viral marketing
webisodes (video webcasting)
WOM communication (interpersonal search, buzz)
WOM marketing

SUMMARY

This chapter covered the role of social group and interpersonal influences in the adoption and diffusion of innovations. Diffusion occurs within a social system. Adoption means purchase of a durable good or a decision to regularly buy a nondurable item. During the diffusion of innovations process, the distribution of adopters is expected to take the shape of a normal curve until the end of the adoption cycle. OLs are largely innovators and early adopters.

Exercise 10.1 concerned innovation characteristics that influence adoption and diffusion. Product newness can be classified along two dimensions: (1) newness to the company and (2) newness to the market. Perceived newness determines the extent of consumer learning and possible innovation resistance.

The most important product factor determining whether a product will be perceived as new is the extent to which the innovation alters CB. Robertson's classification of innovations divides new products into three types based on degree of behavioral change and perceived degree of product novelty. Exercise 10.1 combined Robertson's classification scheme with Booz Allen Hamilton's categorization of new products in terms of their degree of newness to the firm and newness to the market, as shown in Exhibit 10.3.

Least likely to encounter consumer resistance are continuous innovations, which include the following BAH categories of new product types, arrayed from least to most "new": cost reductions, repositionings, "new and improved" products, additions to existing product lines that are variations on a firm's core product (including flankers and product line extensions), and new product lines (including brand franchise extensions). Second, dynamically continuous innovations include the following BAH categories of new product types: major additions to existing product lines and significant new product lines, and new-to-the-world products. Robertson's third category of new products is discontinuous innovations, which in the BAH scheme include some new-to-the-world products.

The BAH and Robertson new product classification schemes suggest:

- Moving from incremental to radical innovations, the marketing job of educating and persuading consumers looms larger due to consumer resistance caused by perceived risk.
- Proceeding from evolutionary to revolutionary innovations, the time period for diffusion lengthens due to more consumer skepticism and uncertainty.
- The probability of large-scale adoption within the target market is inversely proportional to the degree of product innovativeness.
- The extent of immediate competition is inversely related to the degree to which a product is "really new," since more groundbreaking products are tougher to imitate.
- Incremental innovations require selective demand stimulation, while "really new" products mandate primary demand creation.

Whether or not a product will be widely adopted and diffused throughout the target market also depends on the following innovation attributes (product characteristics), each of which has particular marketing implications: relative advantage, compatibility, complexity (converse is simplicity), trialability, and communicability.

A second important influence in adoption and diffusion is WOM communication about the product within the social system. Skeptical, risk-averse consumers turn to OLs. Exercise 10.2 discussed OLs and strategies marketers can use to take advantage of OLs and WOM communication to stimulate new product adoption and diffusion.

WOM communication is a form of interpersonal communication that occurs through social channels, not advocate channels. While some interpersonal communication is nonverbal, most of it is verbal, often referral, communication. This can result in interpersonal influence, as occurs on customer review sites.

Internet-mediated WOM occurs on: (1) dedicated consumer opinion Web sites and (2) corporate Web sites. The power of WOM communication highlights the importance of customer satisfaction: Dissatisfied customers complain much more to other people than they do to the marketer. A negativity bias exists.

WOM communication is most important for products for which reference groups are most influential: products that are socially visible or conspicuous, for which buyers lack self-confidence in decision making, that are relevant to the group or individuals engaged in discussion, that are associated with high involvement and high perceived risk, and for which alternative information sources lack credibility.

OLs are key to generating consumer "buzz." OLs can act as change agents by exercising their opinion leadership over opinion followers, who can be either opinion receivers or opinion seekers. Opinion leadership tends to be category specific; there are few generalized OLs. Nonetheless, there is opinion leadership overlap. Types of OLs include purchase pals, surrogate buyers, market mavens, and innovators. Not all market mavens and innovators are OLs, however.

Interpersonal influence is transmitted through one-step, two-step, and multistep communication flows, usually in conjunction with mass media publicity and/or advertising communication (see Figure 10.8).

OLs can be either private or public. Public opinion leadership is an example of top-down social change, with leaders functioning as cultural gatekeepers. This communication pattern is also known as the one-step flow of communication theory (Exhibit 10.8A). In the bottom-up model, from the lower levels of the social ladder, the innovations usually percolate up to the general culture, sometimes taking the form of parody display. Private opinion leadership is explained by the two-step flow of communication theory (Exhibit 10.8B). Whereas the original two-step flow model was one of trickle down, today it is believed that most two-step communication flow trickles across with a high degree of homophily.

The simple two-step model has been largely supplanted by the multistep flow of communication model (Exhibit 10.8C). This model is more complex in several ways, including the addition of gatekeepers.

There are some general characteristics typical of OLs. They are homophilous with their followers, have a high degree of product involvement, and tend to be innovators. They also differ in particular ways demographically, socially, regarding personality traits, and behaviorally.

Sociologists have developed three approaches for identifying OLs: the self-designating method, the sociometric method, and the key informant method. Marketers also use the objective method to identify OLs.

Some other quick-and-easy methods to locate OLs include using company purchase records to identify early and/or frequent product purchasers; tracking individuals who are frequent or early responders to direct marketing efforts; obtaining mailing lists for special interest groups, magazine subscribers, club members, and knowledgeable experts; discovering community leaders; and enlisting retailers' and e-tailers' cooperation in determining who are frequent browsers in their stores and on their Web sites.

Once OLs have been identified, they can be strategically used in one or more of the following ways:

- Using buzz marketing techniques. Buzz marketing targets OLs as product missionaries using grassroots (guerrilla) marketing tactics. There are many methods, including using stealth marketing and brand ambassadors.
- Creating advertising that simulates WOM communication. This includes consumer testimonials, slice-of-life advertising, and using expert OLs.
- Stimulating WOM communication through advertising and promotion. Methods include running teaser advertising and using catch phrases in advertising, among many others.
- Creating OLs.
- Using star perks.
- Employing referral incentive programs, including multilevel marketing.
- Generating buzz on the Internet, including viral marketing.

REFERENCES

Arndt, Johan. (1968). "Profiling Consumer Innovators." In J. Arndt, ed., *Insights into Consumer Behavior.* Boston: Allyn and Bacon, 71–83.

Brown, Jaqueline Johnson, and Reingen, Peter H. (1987). "Social Ties and Word-of Mouth Referral Behavior." *Journal of Consumer Research,* 14, 3, 350–362.

Cesvet, Bertrand, Babinski, Tony, and Alper, Erik. (2009). *Conversational Capital: How to Create Stuff People Love to Talk About.* Upper Saddle River, NJ: Pearson Education.

Chan, Kenny K., and Misra, Shekhar. (1990). "Characteristics of the Opinion Leader: A New Dimension." *Journal of Advertising,* 19, 3, 53–60.

Engel, James F., Kegerreis, Robert J., and Blackwell, Roger D. (1969). "Word-of-Mouth Communication by the Innovator." *Journal of Marketing,* 33, 15–19.

Feick, Lawrence F., and Price, Linda L. (1987). "The Market Maven: A Diffuser of Marketplace Information." *Journal of Marketing,* 51, 1, 83–87.

Gatignon, Hubert, and Robertson, Thomas S. (1985). "A Propositional Inventory for New Diffusion Research." *Journal of Consumer Research,* 11, 4, 849–867.

Gladwell, Malcolm. (2000). *The Tipping Point: How Little Things Can Make a Big Difference.* Boston: Little, Brown.

Gloor, Peter A. (2007). *Coolhunting: Chasing Down the Next Big Thing.* New York: AMACOM.

Hartman, Cathy L., and Kiecker, Pamela. (1994). "Buyers and Their Purchase Pals." In Ravi Achrol and Andrew Mitchell, eds., *Enhancing Knowledge Development in Marketing.* Chicago: American Marketing Association, 138–144.

Hirunyawipada, Tanawat, and Paswan, Audhesh K. (2006). "Consumer Innovativeness and Perceived Risk: Implications for High Technology Product Adoption." *Journal of Consumer Marketing,* 23, 4, 182–198.

Hollander, Stanley C., and Rassuli, Kathleen M. (1999). "Shopping with Other People's Money: The Marketing Management Implications of Surrogate-Mediated Consumer Decision Making." *Journal of Marketing,* 63, 2, 102–118.

Howe, Jeff. (2008). *Crowdsourcing: Why the Power of the Crowd Is Driving the Future of Business.* New York: Crown Business.

Katz, Elihu, and Lazarsfeld, Paul F. (1955). *Personal Influence.* Glencoe, IL: The Free Press.

Keller, Ed, and Berry, Jon. (2003). *The Influentials.* New York: The Free Press.

Kelley, Lois. (2007). *Beyond Buzz: The Next Generation of Word-of-Mouth Marketing.* New York: AMACOM.

Kerner, Noah, and Pressman, Gene. (2007). *Chasing Cool: Standing Out in Today's Cluttered Marketplace.* New York: Atria Books.

King, Charles W., and Summers, John O. (1970). "Overlap of Opinion Leadership Across Consumer Product Categories." *Journal of Marketing Research,* 7, 1, 43–50.

Kirby, Justin, and Marsden, Paul, eds. (2006). *Connected Marketing.* Burlington, MA: Butterworth-Heinemann.

Lazarsfeld, Paul. F., Berelson, Bernard, and Gaudet, Hazel. (1944). *The People's Choice: How the Voter Makes Up His Mind in a Presidential Campaign.* New York: Columbia University Press.

Mancuso, Joseph R. (1969). "Why Not Create Opinion Leaders for New Product Introduction?" *Journal of Marketing,* 33, 3, 20–25.

McConnell, Ben, and Huba, Jackie. (2007). *Citizen Marketers: When People Are the Message.* New York: Kaplan Publishing.

Myers, James H., and Robertson, Thomas S. (1972). "Dimensions of Opinion Leadership." *Journal of Marketing Research,* 9, 2, 41–46.

Nabith, M.I., Bloem, S.G., and Poiesz, T.B.C. (1997). "Conceptual Issues in the Study of Innovation Adoption Behavior." In M. Bruck and J. MacInnis, eds., *Advances in Consumer Research,* vol. 24. Provo, UT: Association for Consumer Research, 190–196.

Ostlund, Lyman E. (1974). "Perceived Innovation Attributes as Predictors of Innovativeness." *Journal of Consumer Research,* 1, 23–29.

Petty, Ross D., and Andrews, J. Craig. (2008). "Covert Marketing Unmasked: A Legal and Regulatory Guide for Practices That Mask Marketing Messages." *Journal of Public Policy and Marketing,* 27, 1.

Robertson, Thomas S. (1967). "The Process of Innovation and the Diffusion of Innovation." *Journal of Marketing,* 31, 1, 14–19.

———. (1971). *Innovative Behavior and Communications.* New York: Holt, Rinehart, and Winston.

Robertson, Thomas S., and Myers, James H. (1969). "Personality Correlates of Opinion Leadership and Innovative Buying Behaviors." *Journal of Marketing Research,* 6, 2, 164–168.

Rogers, Everett M. (1962). *Diffusion of Innovations.* New York: The Free Press.

Salzman, Marian, Matathia, Ira, and O'Reilly, Ann. (2003). *Buzz: Harness the Power of Influence and Create Demand.* Hoboken, NJ: John Wiley & Sons.

Silverman, George. (2001). *The Secrets of Word-of-Mouth Marketing: How to Trigger Exponential Sales Through Runaway Word of Mouth.* New York: American Management Association.

Solomon, Michael R. (1986). "The Missing Link: Surrogate Consumers in the Marketing Chain." *Journal of Marketing,* 50, 4, 208–218.

Stokburger-Sauer, Nicola E, and Hoyer, Wayne D. (2009). "Consumer Advisers Revisited: What Drives Those with Market Mavenism and Opinion Leadership Tendencies and Why?" *Journal of Consumer Behaviour,* 8, 2–3, 100–115.

Sundaram, D. S., Mitra, K., and Webster, C. (1998). "Word-of-Mouth Communications: A Motivational Analysis." *Advances in Consumer Research,* 25, 1, 527–531.

Tinson, Julie, and Nancarrow, Clive. (2007). "Teen Perceptions of Disclosure and Ad Involvement on Consumers in DTC Advertising." *Journal of Consumer Marketing,* 24, 3, 151–159.

Williams, Terrell G., and Slama, Mark E. (1995). "Market Mavens' Purchase Decision Evaluative Criteria: Implications for Brand and Store Promotion Efforts." *Journal of Consumer Marketing,* 12, 3, 4–21.

Zaltman, Gerald, and Wallendorf, Melanie. (1973). "Theories of Diffusion." In Scott Ward and Thomas S. Robertson, eds., *Consumer Behavior: Theoretical Sources.* Englewood Cliffs, NJ: Prentice-Hall, 416–468.

EXTERNAL SOCIOCULTURAL FORCES VERSUS INTERNAL PSYCHOLOGICAL INFLUENCES

Sociocultural forces (Part III) entail the consumer's external cultural and social environment. Socioculturally, consumers are described in terms of *external* states-of-being variables. These visible demographic characteristics can serve as bases for target marketing.

Psychological influences (Part IV) involve the consumer's *internal* world. Buyers are described via states-of-mind variables, which are mental states or the way consumers think, and states-of-action variables, behavioral variables or the way consumers act.

These two sets of psychological variables are also used for market targeting. State-of-mind segmentation criteria include personality, psychographics, buyer learning states (degree of awareness, interest, information, experience, etc.), perception (creating "male" vs. "female" products such as his or hers deodorant), and attitudinal segmentation (such as targeting women who feel marriage is a trap and intend to remain single). Second, state-of-action (behavioristic) variables include benefit segmentation, brand loyalty status, and marketing factor sensitivity.

PSYCHOLOGY AND CONSUMER BEHAVIOR

An understanding of the consumer's states of mind and action comes from **psychology**, which is the scientific study of the processes of thinking (states of mind) and behavior (states of action). Psychology uses the **scientific method**, a systematic process for analyzing empirical evidence in an objective and accurate manner, to confirm or dispute prior conceptions (hypotheses) in an ongoing, open-minded fashion.

Psychological factors can be used to yield a psychological target market profile. For instance, targeted customers might be introverted, esteem-driven, innovative wine connoisseurs, who are very class conscious.

THE STIMULUS-ORGANISM-RESPONSE MODEL

Sociocultural approaches to consumer behavior (CB) study people in their natural social context. Psychologists, however, isolate psychological influences, often in a laboratory

313

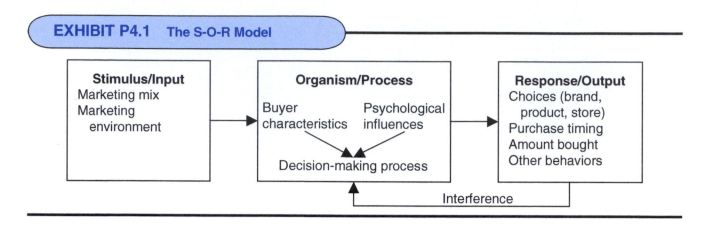

EXHIBIT P4.1   **The S-O-R Model**

Stimulus/Input	Organism/Process	Response/Output
Marketing mix Marketing environment	Buyer characteristics Psychological influences Decision-making process	Choices (brand, product, store) Purchase timing Amount bought Other behaviors

Interference

environment. A useful organizational framework for the study of these psychological influences on CB is the **stimulus-organism-response (S-O-R) model (input-process [throughput]-output model)**, shown in Exhibit P4.1. The S-O-R model illustrates how CB is studied within the context of psychology using its three elements: stimulus, organism, and response.

Stimulus. The stimuli (inputs) are the antecedents (preceding events) to CB. There are two general classes of stimuli: (1) the marketing mix and (2) the marketing environment. The marketing mix of product, price, place, and promotion ("four Ps") constitutes the marketing manager's tool kit of controllable decision variables. They answer the manager's question, "What should we do?"

The marketing environment or situational variables answer the query, "What will conditions be like outside the firm?" Situational variables include all of the forces that influence the effectiveness of marketing decisions as well as the nature of consumer decision making. These factors include:

1. The firm's immediate microenvironment (operating environment, task environment): the organization's value-delivery system, which includes customers, competitors, suppliers, distributors, partners, and any other parties who can affect or are affected by the firm's actions.
2. The broad macroenvironment (general environment): universal societal forces that affect all actors in the microenvironment, including economic, technological, political/legal, natural, demographic, and the sociocultural forces studied in Part III.

Organism. Psychologists refer to all living creatures as "organisms," which include consumers. Marketers need to understand how the consumer takes in stimuli and decides whether or not and how to act on the marketing and environmental cues. Factors here include the customer's characteristics or states of being, through which marketers derive a sociocultural profile, and the buyer's psychological influences or psychological profile—the states-of-mind factors we will be investigating.

Together, the customer's demographic and psychological makeup, plus the marketing program and environment, determine the nature of the consumer's decision-making process.

Response. The consumer's response (output) involves the buyer's reactions to the stimuli based on that person's decision-making process. Responses answer the question, "What happens?" as a reaction to the marketing program in a given environment. Response variables involve all aspects of CB. Such states of action include all consumer decisions (regarding products, brands, purchase venues, etc.); storing, preparing, using, evaluating, and disposing of the product; and giving word-of-mouth referrals on (or warnings about!) the product. Such outcome variables are often aggregated across consumers and translated into marketing objectives such as sales volume and sales dollars, customer inquiries, buyer satisfaction levels, customer acquisition and retention rates, and brand loyalty rates.

INDEPENDENT, DEPENDENT, AND INTERVENING VARIABLES

For conducting consumer research, the stimuli are conceptualized as *independent (predictor, causal, explanatory) variables*, which influence or cause changes in the behavioral response variables. The responses are *dependent (predicted, criterion) variables*—outputs predicted or explained by one or more independent variables. We say that the dependent variable is a function of the independent variables. Cryptically, we write: dependent variable = f (independent variables).

The consumer's characteristics and psychological influences intervene between stimuli and response, and are therefore referred to as *intervening variables*. This is represented as the center box in Exhibit P4.1. The consumer's internal influences and processes are sometimes referred to as the *black box*, since we do not fully understand them. Perhaps instead of thinking "outside the box," more marketers need to think inside the box! In so doing, they must draw heavily upon the cognitive perspective in psychology, which studies the human mind and mental processes of perception, memory, problem solving, thinking, and forming beliefs. (The word *cognitive* comes from the Latin word for "to know.") In short, marketers wish to know what in the world is going on inside of consumers' heads!

MAKING INFERENCES ON HYPOTHETICAL CONSTRUCTS

To fully comprehend the buyer's cognitive realm is extremely difficult because we cannot directly observe it. We cannot locate the buy button in consumers' brains. Therefore, explanations of what transpires within the psychological field during consumer decision making are inferences (educated guesses) on what most likely occurred, based on research observations of consumers' behavioral responses to the stimuli.

Because we cannot directly see psychological variables, these intervening variables are **hypothetical constructs**. They are not physical entities but rather unobservable, theoretical, postulated states, conditions, or processes. These concepts exist in the abstract, rather than being concrete, as demographic characteristics are. These hypothetical constructs have also been termed *latent (hidden) variables*, as opposed to *manifest (observable) variables*.

Consider learning: We cannot look into people's brains to see new connections being made, so we must infer (deduce) what they have learned by observing their actions. For example, one-on-one, a teacher can ask, listen, and observe a pupil's changes in performance. With a classroom full of students, however, the most efficient way to infer learning is to administer tests and observe the results.

So, we must indirectly infer latent variables from behavior. You can do so when you see someone ponder over a textbook (learning) or when a person makes a face of disgust in response to something you say or do (indicating disapproval). What you are really observing in these situations are a person's responses to various stimuli (i.e., expressions of the intervening variables). Unfortunately, your inference could be dead wrong! For example, perhaps a fellow student was daydreaming while looking at his textbook, rather than studying its content.

MEASURING PSYCHOLOGICAL VARIABLES

Consumer research helps marketers to understand what is going on in the buyer's head. However, since psychological variables such as motives and perceptions are not directly observable, what marketers measure are observable personal responses, such as purchase behavior and verbal expressions of those psychological variables. For instance, your instructor cannot directly know how much of this material on psychology you are learning. But he or she can measure it by an indirect means, such as a test. Likewise, marketers are unable to directly see their consumers' attitudes, but they can measure preferences via attitude questionnaires or customer satisfaction surveys.

A "SOFT" SCIENCE LACKING CONSENSUS

A complicating factor is the numerous and sometimes conflicting theories about each of the areas of investigation, which leads to disagreements on how to measure (operationalize) a given construct. This clearly threatens the research's **validity**, or the degree to which research is correctly measuring the concept it should

EXHIBIT P4.2   Perception and Learning in the Information Search Stage

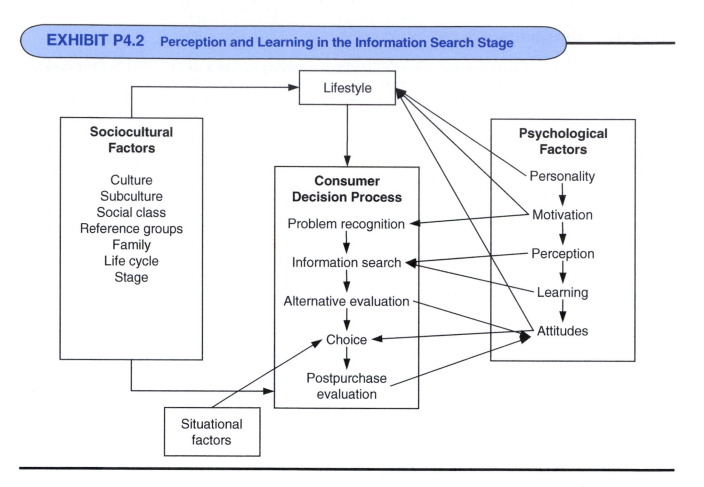

be measuring, and **reliability**, the ability to obtain repeatable, consistent results when research studies are replicated. Different concepts, theories, and research perspectives will predict best in various situations, for distinct products, and for different consumers. Thus, we view the various psychological perspectives on a given concept as complementary, not competing. To get the entire picture, we should explore multiple perspectives, which we shall do for the topics in this part of the book.

ORGANIZATION OF PART IV

We have arranged the discussion of the psychological influences in the order in which they affect the consumer decision process (see Exhibit P4.2). Chapter 11 discusses personality, which, combined with sociocultural factors and motivation, shapes lifestyles. Personality and lifestyle will be studied first because they have the greatest influence on CB, are closely related to many of the sociocultural factors, and are the most observable and hence understandable of the psychological variables.

Chapter 12 investigates motivation, which is tied most closely to the problem recognition stage in the decision process. Also, motivation is a major determinant of perception. Perception, taken up in Chapter 13, serves as the gateway to the learning process, which is the procedure whereby memory and behavior are changed as a result of perception and information processing, the subject of Chapter 14.

Finally, Chapter 15 explores attitudes, which are formed during the alternative evaluation phase and are based on the learned information. Attitudes and situational factors result in a purchase made in the buying decision stage of the consumer decision process. These attitudes might be changed during the postpurchase behavior stage as a result of product usage and evaluation, leading to satisfaction or dissatisfaction, another attitude variable.

PERSONALITY AND LIFESTYLE

"You are what you own." While this might be a rather shallow philosophy of life and we are certainly much more than the sum of our possessions, it is nonetheless true that, at least for certain products, we consciously or subconsciously buy things that reflect our **personality**, our relatively enduring, consistent, and distinguishing characteristic traits that differentiate us from others. These differentiating **personality traits** are characteristic behavior and thought patterns—any distinguishing, relatively enduring way that one person differs from another regarding the individual's typical responses to environmental stimuli. Personality is essentially a bundle of many traits. A given individual might be described by the traits shy (vs. bold), trusting (vs. suspicious), self-assured (vs. apprehensive), and conservative (vs. experimenting). Personality has elements that are both innate (known as temperament) and learned; it is a combination of both nature and nurture.

A person's personality traits tend to be consistent with one another. It is doubtful that a person would be both aggressive and shy or happy-go-lucky and apprehensive. For example, people are often classified as either Type A or Type B personalities, where each type is a bundle of correlated traits. These two personality types differ from one another in their desires for achievement, perfectionism, competitiveness, and ability to relax. Type A traits include high need for achievement, perfectionism, competitiveness, restlessness, impatience, aggressiveness, and nervousness. In contrast, Type Bs are less achievement oriented, nor perfectionists, relaxed, easy going, and they tend to "take it slow." Their motto is, "What? Me worry?"

ORGANIZATION OF CHAPTER 11

The four exercises in this chapter examine three aspects of personality theory that have been widely applied in consumer marketing. Exercise 11.1 looks at one of the earliest and most enduring personality theories—Freudian personality theory—with its emphasis on the subconscious elements of personality and motivation. Exercises 11.2 and 11.3 delve into brand image, an extension of Freud's concept of the ego. Many consumers believe their self-image (self-concept) is determined by brand images of the products they own. The brand image a marketer forges should be consistent with the actual or desired self-image of target market members.

Exercise 11.2 inspects the nature of personality and self-image and how a marketer can craft a brand image to appeal to particular self-images. Exercise 11.3 discusses how both an individual's personality and a brand's image can be measured to ensure that they are consistent with one another.

Finally, Exercise 11.4 looks at psychographics as a psychological market segmentation tool that is an extension of personality theory. The focus will be on the Values and Lifestyles System 2 (VALS2™) lifestyle segmentation scheme, which is the most widely adopted of the lifestyle segmentation techniques.

EXERCISE 11.1. FREUDIAN PERSONALITY THEORY

OBJECTIVES

1. To understand the elements underlying Sigmund Freud's psychoanalytical theory of personality and how marketers apply them.

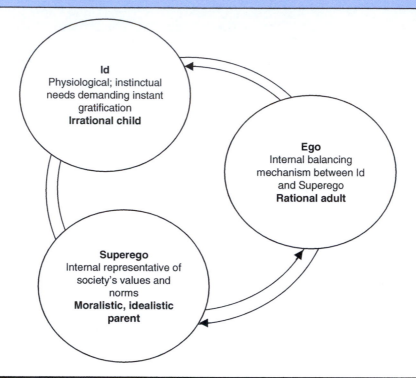

EXHIBIT 11.1   Dynamics of Freud's Subconscious Conflicted Motivational System

Id
Physiological; instinctual needs demanding instant gratification
Irrational child

Ego
Internal balancing mechanism between Id and Superego
Rational adult

Superego
Internal representative of society's values and norms
Moralistic, idealistic parent

2. To practice recognizing and evaluating ads using Freudian psychoanalytical components.
3. To become familiar with and practice using the motivational research techniques of in-depth interviews and focus group interviews, which are based on Freud's psychoanalytical system.

BACKGROUND

Sigmund Freud's explanations of human psychology, although largely discredited, have greatly affected our way of thinking about personality and motivation as well as marketing and consumer behavior (CB). This exercise reviews the major elements of Dr. Freud's theories and how modern marketers apply them in advertising and marketing research. Freud's **psychoanalytical theory of personality** suggests that subconscious (unconscious needs) or drives (especially biological drives) underlie most human motivation, personality, and behavior. Many of these are urges that people repress (push into the subconscious) while growing up. However, the urges are never eliminated, and they emerge in dreams, slips of the tongue, or in abnormal behaviors.

ELEMENTS OF THE FREUDIAN PSYCHOANALYTIC SYSTEM

THE CONFLICT SYSTEM: ID, SUPEREGO, AND EGO

According to Freud, the unconscious nature of personality and motivation is explained by childhood conflicts among three interacting energy systems of the personality or psyche. Two of these theoretical sectors or agencies of the mind are unconscious and one is conscious: the id (representing biological forces), the superego (internalizing societal forces), and the ego (embodying human consciousness). Therefore, human behavior is determined by biology, society, and the self. These three sectors are summarized in Exhibit 11.1.

These three psychological components are purely theoretical in nature. They are hypothetical constructs, or concepts that are abstract and presumed (but cannot be proven) to exist. They do not have physical, biological counterparts in the human brain. Nonetheless, these three concepts do yield important insights into CB.

The Id. Part of the unconscious mind is the **id**, a "warehouse" of primitive instincts and impulses that exist at birth. It encompasses basic physiological drives such as thirst, hunger, sex, and self-preservation. The id seeks immediate gratification of these biological instincts as people strive to achieve pleasure and avoid pain. For instance, people crave sweetness because mother's milk is sweet, and they often substitute sweets for love because eating and sex are among the few arenas wherein individuals act on animal instincts. Hence, heart-shaped Valentine's Day candy boxes are appealing. Operating on the pleasure principle, the id desires positive feelings and emotions and is likened to the child inside us: impulsive, carefree, selfish, and demanding.

Many marketing appeals are designed with the id in mind, especially for hedonic products. Ads implore us to "eat this," "drink that," and "enjoy the other" to be satisfied. Appeals to seek immediate gratification abound, with the airline industry's "Fly now, pay later" and Nike's "Just do it!" as classic examples. Impulse purchasing seems to be rooted in the id.

The Superego. Another subconscious mind sector is the **superego**—a person's conscience or internal representative of societal and parental values and norms. Whereas the id exists at birth, the superego develops during childhood through interactions with parents and other adults who transmit society's values, morals, norms, and laws.

Hence, the superego is likened to the parent—it nags the id not to act on its impulses and desires, in effect exclaiming "You can't do that!" The superego serves as the individual's moral monitor and demands self-control, to which the id does not wish to yield. The superego punishes unacceptable behavior through a sense of guilt.

Marketing appeals aimed at the superego are either moralistic in tone, use guilt appeals, or strongly appeal to cultural values and norms. Public service advertising admonishes us to do socially desirable things, such as using our seat belts and recycling our trash.

The Ego. Operating on the reality principle, the **ego** attempts to resolve the id-superego dispute by allowing the id's desires to be satisfied practically and sensibly in a manner socially acceptable to the superego. Unlike the unconscious id and superego, the ego is conscious and is therefore controllable. Accordingly, a basic need to be aggressive might be channeled away from beating up on other people and toward buying a powerful sports car. Sometimes likened to the adult, the ego, as the "voice of reason," acts as the referee or mediator, patiently and logically resolving the conflict between the id and the superego.

Marketers appeal to the ego with ads that help to rationalize an expensive purchase by describing the product as an acceptable solution to the id-superego conflict. Common appeals are "You're worth it," "You've earned it," or "You deserve a break today."

OTHER ELEMENTS OF THE UNCONSCIOUS MIND

The following elements of the unconscious mind tie into the id, ego, and superego and the conflict among them.

Symbolism. **Symbolism** is the use of tangible representations of abstract concepts. Freud viewed many objects and behaviors as having symbolic overtones. For example, Freud viewed a cigar as a phallic symbol. However, it also symbolizes success and celebration.

Brand symbols include almost any marketing element, such as trade characters (Mack trucks' bulldog implies that its trucks are bulldog tough), brand names (Sears Diehard battery and Camel cigarettes both signify long-lasting brands), brand colors (the brown and red colors used in Marlboro's advertising and packaging are masculine), and package shape (Coke's hourglass bottle resembles a woman).

Product symbolism can be used as a surrogate for the actions inhibited by the consumer's superego. By acquiring the product, the buyer vicariously or symbolically experiences the forbidden fruit and fulfills his innermost urges and desires. So thinking, motivational researchers said that a sporty convertible serves as a substitute mistress for some men and that the repressed need for oral gratification might be manifested in cigarette smoking and lollipop sucking.

Libido (eros, sex). Freud famously fixated on **libido (eros, sex),** the life-seeking sexual drive. Sexual imagery abounds in advertising ("Sex sells!" is some advertisers' maxim). While sex appeal is a powerful technique for gaining attention and interest, too often it is a source of borrowed interest irrelevant to the purchase proposition (e.g., useful for selling perfume, not insurance policies). Also, the use of sex to sell runs the risk of offending people.

Primary Process Thinking (Fantasy). **Primary process thinking**, Freud's term for **fantasy**, is a self-induced shift in consciousness to compensate for lack of permissible external stimulation. The subconscious mind satisfies the id's longing for pleasure by fantasizing, enjoying thoughts about unrealized pleasures and forbidden fruits, thereby allowing daydreamers to gratify the id in an acceptable fashion.

Marketers sometimes develop products and promotional appeals that draw on wish fulfillment, dreams and aspirations, and people's fantasy lives. Disney's fantasy theme parks are popular among adults and children alike. Fanciful trade characters such as the Pillsbury Doughboy and the Jolly Green Giant are popular in part because they appeal to buyers' idealized worlds. Video games permit players to enter a dream world where they can fly jet fighters, slay dragons and save damsels, and control every inch of the universe.

Many diversionary activities enable people to fantasize and take a break from reality. We escape into a good book, movie, TV show, or fantasy sports. Consequently, escape themes are common in advertising for such pleasures as motorcycles ("Escape on a Honda") and vacations ("Get away from it all"). Marketers can, indeed, help us turn our dreams into reality! However, sometimes the dream is illusionary, such as when advertisers suggest that if we wear a certain brand of cologne we will be irresistible, or that consuming an energy drink will make us invincible.

Thanatos (Death Wish, Death Instinct). **Thanatos (death wish, death instinct)** represents a primitive impulse for destruction, decay, death, misery, aggression, and self-hatred. Freud suggested people possess a subconscious death wish and a primal urge to kill, driving people to destructive acts and self-destructive behaviors.

The Thanatos concept might help explain the popularity of Halloween and people's tendency to flirt with death and danger. Some people enjoy the rush of horror movies, dark themes, and brutal video games, and they seek thrills through roller coasters, high-risk sports such as hang gliding and rock climbing, and even taking illegal and potentially life-threatening drugs.

Advertisers sometimes appeal to this dark side of human nature. Witness commercials for Combat insecticide featuring the Grim Reaper pursuing ants and roaches, the Slim Jim guy exclaiming "eat me!" and Bauer in-line skates, proclaiming that "it's fun in the same twisted way that having a near death experience is fun."

APPLICATIONS OF PSYCHOANALYTICAL THEORY: MOTIVATIONAL RESEARCH

THE NEED FOR MOTIVATIONAL RESEARCH

Freud taught that id-ego-superego conflicts that are not resolved in a satisfactory manner during childhood result in **defense mechanisms**—unconscious, irrational strategies the ego uses to reduce tension, maintain self-image, or falsify an unpleasant reality (instead of employing rational, problem-solving methods). Repression is one example. Three defense mechanisms relevant to marketing are *denial* of reality, **projection**, a means by which people attribute their own thoughts and feelings (conscious and unconscious) to the external world, and *rationalization*, in which the ego finds an excuse to do something that is unacceptable to the superego. (Some would say that to "rationalize" is to tell oneself "rational lies.") All of these are based on **repressed needs (latent motives)**, desires pushed into the subconscious mind.

Denial, projection, and rationalization are applied in **motivation (motivational) research,** which is based on Freud's notion of latent, subconscious motives and instincts that people are unable and/or unwilling to express. Ernest Dichter, Pierre Martineau, Louis Cheskin, and other motivational 1950s researchers convinced major advertisers and their ad agencies to hire their research services in order to tap into customers' deep unconscious worlds. This research usually uses detailed analysis of the responses of a limited number of interviewees.

Such investigation is designed to overcome the limitations of survey research, which is inadequate if researchers are dealing with repressed needs, which in turn are especially likely for hedonic, emotional, socially sensitive, or embarrassing products. When discussing these, people rely on defense mechanisms such as denial ("No, I don't watch reality TV shows") and rationalization ("I exercise to stay healthy, not so I can eat more"), thereby limiting survey research validity.

METHODOLOGIES FOR MOTIVATIONAL RESEARCH

To uncover repressed needs, motivation researchers ask questions that either probe, based on Freud's notion that hidden motives can be uncovered via conversation and free association, or are disguised so that the interviewee uses the projection defense mechanism, rather than denial or rationalization. Methodologies used to crawl inside consumers' heads include depth interviews, focus groups, and projective techniques.

Depth Interviews. In order to probe and uncover deep-seated purchasing motives, motivation researchers conduct **depth interviews (in-depth interviews, one-on-ones, extended interviews).** Based on Freud's clinical psychological technique, these are unstructured (flexible and nondirective), probing, conversational personal interviews lasting from thirty minutes to two hours each. Similar to Freud's patients lying on his couch freely associating, consumers are encouraged to talk freely to reveal their "real" purchasing motives and inhibitions. For example, in a study conducted for the Daimler-Chrysler PT Cruiser, interviewees were asked to "drift back to childhood" and list memories triggered by the car's appearance in an attempt to uncover the emotions and associations a family car elicits.

Depth interviews use a very loose, informal discussion (question) guide rather than a strict set of questions to be asked in a predetermined order as in a survey questionnaire. From this guide, the interviewer drills down deep to uncover the unconscious motives, beliefs, and attitudes underlying people's actions. Follow-up questions are often formulated on the fly by the interviewer in response to the interviewee's answers.

Unfortunately, depth interviews have their limitations: They are expensive and time-consuming; they use small sample sizes (typically ten to twenty per demographic group) that might not be representative of the target market; interpretation of respondents' answers by the analyst is highly judgmental and sometimes questionable (suspenders were interpreted to be worn as a reaction to an unresolved castration complex rather than to hold up one's pants); and, as qualitative research, they produce mountains of data: transcripts or audio or video recordings of the interviews, rather than quick, easy-to-digest bottom-line statistics of quantitative research.

Nonetheless, depth interviews are especially useful where detailed probing of needs, attitudes, or behaviors is required, or where the subject matter is of a very personal, confidential nature (e.g., incontinence products, extramarital affairs, watching NC-17 movies), and probing is required to get people to "open up." Highly detailed (step-by-step) understanding of consumer decision making (e.g., planning the family vacation) can also be gained through depth interviews.

Focus Group Interviews. A variant of the depth interview is the **focus group interview (group depth interview).** Here, a **moderator (interviewer)** leads a one- to two-hour discussion involving about six to twelve consumers. Participants are encouraged to freely talk about their feelings or thoughts regarding a particular topic, in effect probing one another.

The focus group moderator works off of a loosely structured discussion guide (discussion outline). This is similar to the depth interview question guide in that it supplies general topics and questions to address and explore without providing specific, detailed questions.

There are two main ways focus groups differ from depth interviews:

1. They clarify attitudes and feelings through a give-and-take group discussion, where group members explore and build off of one another's ideas. In fact, brainstorming new ideas for products, slogans, brand names, and the like is often encouraged in focus groups.

The group dynamics yield richer insights than individual interviews since focus group sessions are usually more stimulating and interesting. People tend to be more candid when they sense others are being open and sharing their answers. Also, focus groups can be less intimidating since the focus is on the group, not the individual.

2. Focus groups are less time-consuming and hence less expensive than depth interviews since information is obtained from several respondents simultaneously.

As with the extended interview, a trained questioner is necessary. Some of the skills of an effective focus group moderator include:

- Establishing rapport with group members;
- Clearly and concisely communicating;
- Not dominating but rather letting the group carry the conversation;
- Not leading the group to give certain answers, i.e., keeping an objective, nonvested viewpoint;
- Keeping the discussion focused and not letting the group digress. Interviewers should make sure all key points on the discussion guide are covered;
- Probing participants to gain deep insight;
- Getting all members involved, dealing with both dominant individuals and quiet types;
- Being patient and able to tolerate diverse viewpoints as well as lack of consensus;
- Blending into the group and varying the approach, based on participants' demographics, psychographics, and behavioral experiences;
- Attending to various levels of nonverbal communication, such as facial expressions, eye movements, and fidgeting;
- Being flexible—an ability to go with the flow;
- Reinforcing answers to encourage further discussion;
- Knowledge of the subject matter;
- Being a good listener, rather than an informer. The moderator should refrain from acting as "expert," but rather "play dumb" in order to elicit information from participants.

Many of the limitations of depth interviews also apply to focus groups: they are expensive and time-consuming (although less so); they use small sample sizes, yielding possibly atypical respondents; an analyst's interpretive bias can threaten validity; and reams of data are generated that must be boiled down. Additionally, focus groups have their own unique problems: there is a tendency for some individuals to conform to group members due to peer pressure; a violation of strong social norms would not be revealed in a focus group discussion (e.g., racial prejudice, littering); and "group hogs" can dominate the discussion.

Nonetheless, focus groups are quite useful in the following ways:

- Identifying new ideas for products, positioning statements, ads, sales promotions, and other marketing strategies and tactics.
- Assessing consumers' reactions to such ideas.
- Learning about consumers' vocabulary used in discussing the product. This is accomplished by recording **verbatims**, word-for-word consumer quotations from interviews. Consumers' language is useful for designing surveys, advertising copy, product instructions, and so on.

Projective Techniques. Whereas depth and focus group interviews are based on the *probe*, projective techniques are founded on the Freudian defense mechanism *projection*. Hence, instead of saying, "I hate him," a person might say, "He hates me." The projective questions usually are embedded in a focus group discussion or in one-on-one interviews.

These are **indirect questions (disguised questions)**, queries designed to conceal their true purpose, making them less threatening than asking a person potentially embarrassing direct questions, such as whether they find sex appeal to be an important toothpaste benefit. The questions get beyond surface answers and discover the respondent's innermost thoughts and feelings. Projective questions allow respondents to project (transfer) their values, motives, beliefs, and feelings onto someone or something else. These questions use projectives—ambiguous, nonpersonal stimuli (questions or situations) that a person is asked to describe, expand on, or respond to.

One popular approach is **word association**, in which the respondent is given a word or phrase and asked to respond with the first word or phrase that comes to mind. If the interviewer says "homer," the respondent could answer with "author of *The Iliad* and *The Odyssey*," suggesting that he or she likes the classics. The response, "Bart Simpson's father," reveals that he or she enjoys TV cartoons. "Going, going, gone" shows that the respondent is a baseball fan.

Another popular projective technique is **third-person (referent other) questioning**, asking about other people rather than inquiring about the respondent. This allows the interviewee to transfer feelings, motives, and other mental baggage onto those people. Instead of asking "Do you visit chat rooms on the Internet at work?" the interviewer could ask, "Do your colleagues visit chat rooms on the Internet at work?"

Projective techniques are especially useful for learning about sensitive or embarrassing topics and products. Respondents generally find them interesting, involving, and fun.

However, projective techniques suffer the same limitations of other qualitative research methods. Additionally, they are ethically suspect, as respondents are, in effect, tricked into revealing their true selves, a violation of privacy rights.

REVIEW QUESTIONS

1. What does Freud's psychoanalytical theory suggest about the nature of human personality and motivation?
2. Describe each of the three elements of the Freudian motivational conflict system, how they interrelate, and marketing implications of each component.
3. Cite and describe the other parts of the unconscious mind according to Freud, as well as marketing implications of each.
4. What are the problems inherent in survey research that can be overcome by using motivational research?
5. Describe each of the three major methodologies for motivational research, the types of situations in which each is best used, and the advantages and disadvantages of using each.

IN-CLASS APPLICATIONS

1. How much do you really know about Freud? Visit "A Science Odyssey: That's My Theory: Freud" at http://www.pbs.org/wgbh/aso/mytheory/freud/menu.html and see if you can identify the special guest! Be prepared to discuss your experience in class.

2. Would you enjoy a vacation of tornado chasing? Point your browser toward the Storm Chaser's home page at http://www.stormchaser.com/ to meet people who actually do! To which appeal(s) of Freudian personality theory might storm chasers be attracted? Identify some products that this personality type would be inclined to purchase. Be prepared to compare notes with your classmates.

3. "It was only in my dreams," sang the 1980s pop-star Debbie Gibson. But, what can dreams really tell us? According to Freud, dream analysis technique interprets our dreams and applies them to our conscious everyday lives. Do you remember your dreams? What do they imply about your conscious world?

In attempting to answer these questions, keep a log of your dreams for about a week or so. Then visit iVillage (http://quiz.ivillage.com/health/tests/dreams.htm) and take the Dream Interpretation Quiz. Be ready to share your experiences in class.

4. For each of the advertisements in Exhibits 11.2 to 11.6, determine which elements of Freudian personality theory are being applied: id (hedonic appeals), ego (rational appeals), superego (forgiveness appeals, moral appeals), symbolism (symbolic appeals), eros (sex appeals), primary process thinking (fantasy appeals), and Thanatos (death appeals). For each ad, are the Freudian elements used being effectively deployed? If not, which of the other Freudian components, if any, would be more appropriate in stimulating consumer desires?

5. Either your instructor or a student in your class will lead another student in an in-depth interview on a subject of interest to students, such as music, fashion, sports, or weekend activities. The interview should last approximately ten to fifteen minutes (admittedly shorter than a "real-world" interview).

Class members will evaluate how skillfully the interview was conducted and how cooperative the

EXHIBIT 11.2   Kudos Ad

EXHIBIT 11.3   Häagen-Dazs Ad

EXHIBIT 11.4   Crown Royal Ad

EXHIBIT 11.5   Benson & Hedges Ad

EXHIBIT 11.6   Jōvan Ad

respondent was in revealing personal information. They will also summarize information learned and insights for marketing strategy.

6. Some class members will participate in a focus group. The entire class will select a general topic area, such as a product category (like automobiles or a vacation) or activity area (such as washing the car or packing for Spring Break), and specific alternatives within that product class, such as brands, uses, or modes of preparation (like washing the car yourself versus hiring the neighbor kids to do it versus taking it to a car wash).

Attitudes, behaviors, and likes/dislikes are all open for discussion. The class will develop research objectives (e.g., to develop or evaluate ideas) and a discussion guide (perhaps working in smaller groups). The instructor will either take the role of the moderator or ask for a volunteer to do so, and will ask six to twelve students to take the part of focus group members.

Remaining students will take the role of client observer and evaluate the moderator's skills plus the cooperativeness of focus group members. Observing students should also write down any potentially useful verbatims (consumer quotations) and explain how these can be used for marketing strategies. Students should also summarize the information they've gained from watching the focus group interview and insights for marketing strategy.

The session should last for approximately fifteen to twenty minutes (again, shorter than a "real-world" interview).

WRITTEN APPLICATIONS

1. Answer Question 4 in the In-Class Applications for five of the ads. Then, find examples of four other ads each using several Freudian concepts. How effective is each ad?

2. What are some of the difficulties or potential pitfalls in applying Freud's theories and concepts to product development, promotion, and marketing research?

3. Conduct either your own in-depth interview (about three respondents for about ten to fifteen minutes each) or focus group interview (about six to eight participants for about twenty to thirty minutes) on a marketing topic of your choosing.

After each interview have respondents evaluate your interviewing skills. You should also assess how you felt the interview(s) went. Summarize what you learned and its potential marketing applications.

EXERCISE 11.2. BUILDING A BRAND IMAGE

OBJECTIVES

1. To understand the concept of self-image and its relevance to consumer brand marketing.
2. To experience how marketers relate brand image to their target market's self-image based on the ideas of the extended self and the image congruence hypothesis.
3. To become familiar with the sociocultural dimensions that constitute brand image, and to practice recognizing their use in ads and the use of marketing elements to create brand images.
4. To conduct a critical self-assessment analyzing your personal brand image.

BACKGROUND

CB AND SELF-IMAGE

"Brand, brand, on the wall, who's the fairest buyer of all?" Many brands are created to reflect either the purchaser's actual or desired personality—who the individual is or aspires to be. Self-expression starts early in life. In high school, kids put stickers on their lockers to let others know what is important to them. This principle applies to people of all ages with widgets they consider as an extension of their personality. Mobile devices, which are very personal items, are mini-reflections of their owners' personalities—witness the variety of ringtones. If you own an iPod or have an iPhone, you are part of a group that's "cool" and "up and coming." Coke is real and honest; Dr Pepper is nonconformist and fun.

Cars are perhaps the most-used expressions of users' personalities and self-image. Consumers think "I am what I drive." In response, Ford offers created brands for various personalities: Taurus is a family-oriented car, Mustang is a sporty brand, Ranger is youthful, and F-Series is tough. The Toyota Scion is youthful, marketed to young influencers and the hipster underground culture. Buying a hybrid car is not just a way to economize on gas, it is also a statement about how green consumers are. Expensive, fast cars indicate that one has made it to the top. Old cars signal that owners are frugal (or else broke)!

Buyers also believe "I am what I wear" and "Clothes make the man" (to which others would respond that what you wear, pardon the expression, is immaterial). Rather literally people think, "I am what I eat," and so Wheaties has long been the "Breakfast of Champions!"

Hence, our working assumption is: Much CB is a function of personality. This makes sense in light of the fact that personalities are manifested in behaviors, including buyer behavior. Traditionally, people identified themselves with social categories, in ethnic, regional, religious, or political terms. Today, Americans less frequently think of themselves in demographic terms (e.g., I am a married Asian American Midwestern Republican Methodist). Instead, they perceive themselves more on the basis of what they consume (e.g., "I am an Absolut-drinking, Mercedes-driving, *Vanity Fair* reader").

To understand how to connect the brand's personality with the personality of the seller's target market, we first need to clarify the concept of the self. The **objective (actual, real) self** is who a person actually is—the "real you." It can be objectively identified through a standardized personality test.

A person's **self-image (self-concept)** is one's conscious feelings and attitudes about himself or herself as a person, that is, who a person believes he or she is at a given time. As such, self-image is subjective in nature and so might deviate somewhat from one's personality as objectively measured. In fact, whereas personality is relatively stable, self-image is subject to change as social roles and interactions with others alter. The self-image answers the questions, "Who am I?" and "What am I like as a person?" For instance, a guy could be a macho man or a metrosexual.

Several types of self-image are relevant to CB:

1. **Actual (real) self-image** is how consumers view themselves or think they really are.
2. **Ideal (desired) self-image** is how consumers would like to see themselves or would like to be.
3. **Social (public, others, looking glass, apparent) self-image** is how consumers believe others see them.
4. **Ideal social self-image** is how consumers would like others to see them. (Some observers suggest that people represent their ideal selves via the avatars they create to reside in virtual worlds.)
5. **Expected self-image** is how consumers expect to see themselves at some identified future time, as they plan to move from their actual self-image to their ideal self-image.

The question is: Which self-image should the marketer appeal to in creating a brand image? While this is controversial, some argue that because the expected self-image provides consumers with a realistic benchmark to strive for (as opposed to the ideal self-image, which might be unobtainable), expected self-image is the best self-image to use in crafting a brand's image.

BRAND IMAGE, THE EXTENDED SELF, IMAGE CONGRUENCE, AND SOCIOCULTURAL BRAND IMAGE

To appeal to the consumer's self-image, marketers design a **brand image (brand personality, brand character)**, a set of associations that reflect the brand's personality. Brand image is consumers' perception of a brand, including its personality or character and the associated emotions and associations stored in the consumer's mind. It is what the brand would be like if it were a person, the brand's "soul," as it were. This can serve as a brand-positioning basis.

A brand can be given whatever image the marketer desires: sincere and down-to-earth, daring and spirited, intelligent and successful, sophisticated and charming, rugged and outdoorsy, or any combination of personality traits. While Calvin Klein's Eternity and Celine Dion perfumes are romantic, Adidas and Jovan are sportive and sexy fragrances. Similarly, firms can create corporate images and retailers can fashion store images. General Electric is innovative and forward-looking. Home Depot is a down-home, honest, thrifty, friendly, working-class store.

Such brands can become part of the **extended self**—the self, plus a person's possessions and social network. The extended self includes belongings and people we consider as part of us. Possessions comprise primarily personal belongings and family residence and furnishings. A house becomes a "home" because it is a central part of consumers' identities, personalized with furniture, decor, landscaping, and so on, not to mention a library of family memories. Another part of our extended self is anything we collect: trading cards, DVDs, books, and even iPod playlists. People's extended self also includes community and social groups, and profession and workplace. The young person's self-image is given a boost when he or she logs onto Facebook and reads the posts of fifty people who have made comments. Finally, part of our extended self is the various social roles we play in our families, houses of worship, social organizations, and communities.

The basic idea underlying the crafting of a brand image to become part of the extended self is the **image congruence hypothesis**. There should be a match between the brand's image and the consumers' self-image. Consumers usually have more favorable attitudes and purchase intentions toward brands they believe are consistent with their self-image. A marketer should construct a brand image that people can either identify with (actual self-image or expected brand image) or aspire to and wish to emulate (ideal self-image).

This can be accomplished by imbuing a brand with one or more personality traits. Hallmark and Kodak are loving and caring, Volvo and Michelin are trustworthy and competent, and Mercedes and Rolex are smart and sophisticated. Exhibit 11.7 illustrates brand image congruence.

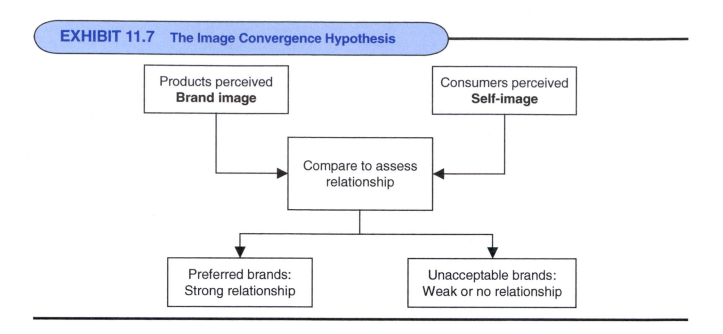

EXHIBIT 11.7   The Image Convergence Hypothesis

In addition to endowing a brand with personality traits, marketers can also base the brand's image on factors related to elements in the sociocultural environment:

- *Age.* Age is more than just a matter of chronology; it is also an attitude. Pepsi is a youthful brand and "Trix is for kids!"
- *Gender.* There are variations in disposition between males and females. For example, men tend to be aggressive and competitive, while women are inclined to be nurturing and caring. Coffee is seen as strong and masculine; tea as weak and feminine. Marlboro was positioned as a rugged male brand, and Virginia Slims as an assertive female brand. Barbie is for girls, while G.I. Joe (an "action figure," not a "doll,") is for boys. Even paper towels are gendered: Scott is definitely a guy's name, and those bold, manly package graphics leave little doubt. Viva, however, is girlish and soft. Brawny is manly, albeit sensitive (embodied in the beefcake, barrel-chested Brawny Man.)
- *Culture/subculture.* Coca-Cola is the all-American, patriotic cola. Doritos chips are Hispanic, especially newer flavors such as Queso Grande and Fiery Ranch. Samuel Adams beer is patriotic, with strong New England Yankee roots.
- *Social class/social status.* Many of the attributes that determine a person's social class can be built into a brand: occupation, education, social groupings, location of residence, activities, etc. Grey Poupon mustard, an upper-crust gourmet condiment, is seen in ads featuring upscale venues such as limousines and yachts. It comes across as sophisticated, educated, and urbane. On the other hand, Mr. Clean is a friendly and caring blue-collar guy.
- *Social groups (including family).* Campbell's soup is a family brand. Budweiser is for the "Whassup?" guys just hanging out. "Soccer moms" drive minivans.
- *Lifestyles.* A brand can be active and sociable, passive and stay-at-home, a man-about-town, or whatever the marketer wishes. Greeting cards and long-distance telephone service have always been shown in advertising in the context of family-oriented lifestyles, and Timberland gear is affiliated with active outdoor living.

WHEN IS BRAND IMAGE IMPORTANT TO PRODUCT POSITIONING?

There are several general types of products for which creating a brand personality is significant. These are sometimes called badge products since some consumers wear brands on their sleeves like badges to communicate their self-image.

- *Socially visible (conspicuous) products* consumed with others. Examples are anything served to guests (e.g., alcoholic beverages, soda, and munchies), items attached to one's self (e.g., jewelry, cosmetics), and objects associated with the home (e.g., home furnishings, furniture).
- *Luxuries (exclusive products)* that many people cannot afford and that consequently connote status. People identify their personalities with brands such as Jeep and PT Camaro, but they do not go around saying, "I'm a Bounty paper towel kind of guy."
- *Value-expressive products* that are symbols of who people are and what their values are. People suggest they are successful by owning luxury cars, split-level homes, and expensive brands of clothing. Men tell us they are virile by driving muscle cars and wearing muscle shirts. Women indicate they are beautiful with revealing clothing, decorative jewelry, and heavy makeup. Teens testify they are cool by sporting tattoos and getting body piercings. A college student's backpack expresses something about him or her—North Face is "in" while Land's End is not as fashionable. The guy who drives a Harley-Davidson is suggesting that he is edgy, a bit naughty, hard-edged, rebellious, and macho.
- *Parity products* lacking physical brand distinctions. Instead, psychological differences are created such as through brand imagery, which results in added psychological value. A brand personality helps such products avoid having a bland personality. The focus is less on the product and more on the user and usage situations. Some consumers will be more likely to choose a brand of baby powder if it conveys an image of "nurturing parent." They will select a kind of cola when it is affiliated with the hip crowd or a style of running shoe that suggests athletic prowess.

CRAFTING A BRAND IMAGE

To create a brand image, a marketer simply needs to don his or her creative thinking cap to imaginatively put together the various pieces of the marketing puzzle, notably the following.

BRAND NAME

The brand's name can be that of a person, real (Mrs. Fields cookies, Mama Celeste pizza, Uncle Ben's rice, Duncan Hines cake mix, Orville Redenbacher popcorn) or fictional (Mr. Clean, Mrs. Butterworth, Aunt Jemima, Betty Crocker). It can also be a suggestive name. Charlie perfume is for the take-charge woman (it would not seem so if named "Ethel"). Scoundrel perfume, Brut cologne, Beautyrest mattresses, and La-Z-Boy recliners all connote personal qualities.

PACKAGING

Elements of the package used to craft brand image include:

- *Shape.* Round is female and square is male. Mrs. Butterworth's pancake syrup comes in a bottle fashioned like a grandmother dressed in her apron.
- *Graphics.* Typefaces can be old-fashioned versus modern, masculine versus feminine, bold versus timid.
- *Colors.* United Parcel Service uses masculine brown trucks, Mary Kay cosmetics' delicate pink packages are for ladies, and Ivory Soap's white package and product reinforce its purity positioning.
- *Labeling.* Information on ecologically safe materials can make the brand's image environmentally correct. Palmolive dishwashing detergent's label notes that it "Soften hands while you do the dishes," appealing to women's feminine side.

RETAIL DISTRIBUTION

Retail images can rub off on a brand's image. Neiman Marcus connotes sophistication and status, Frugal Fannie's suggests frumpiness and lack of social grace, and Foot Locker is obviously for athletes.

PRICE POINTS

A high price supports an image of class and snob appeal (Godiva chocolates), while a moderate price connotes an everyman image (Hershey's) and a low price suggests a pedestrian image (store brand chocolate). Bic perfume failed because the low price point, along with the Bic brand name, suggested cheap and disposable, which no woman wants to be considered!

ADVERTISING

The following elements of an advertisement help build the brand's image.

- *People.* Camel cigarettes portrays macho, self-reliant guys. McDonald's features friendly employees and happy families.
- *Trade characters.* The dignified Mr. Peanut character helped transform the image of a crude peanut into an elegant party snack. The Maytag Repairman suggests reliability.
- *The settings in which the people or characters appear.* The original Miller Lite ads featured tough and rugged he-men drinking Miller beer in bars and other manly locales to build a macho image for the low-calorie beer, while Mercedes Benz automobiles grace country clubs.
- *The lifestyles portrayed.* Sodas are often found at parties. Beer facilitates male bonding. SUVs allow family bonding.
- *The musical background.* Jazz and classical music connote sophistication, country suggests down-to-earth, and rock connotes active, rebellious, and hip.
- *The slogan.* State Farm's "Like a good neighbor" evokes an image of a helpful, trustworthy insurer. BMW is reliable and powerful as the "ultimate driving machine."

EVENT MARKETING

Most events are associated with a lifestyle. Different images can be built depending on whether a brand is tying in with sports events, music concerts, charity events, or art events. In each case, the sponsor's image rubs off on the brand's image.

FRONT-LINE EMPLOYEES

Front-line employees are personnel who have customer contact responsibilities, such as service representatives, call center workers, and store clerks. They all have personalities that can rub off on the company and its brands. To many consumers, such workers *are* the firm.

REVIEW QUESTIONS

1. What is the self and what are the two principal types of self? What is self-image, how does it relate to brand image, and which types of self-image are most relevant to brand image?
2. What is brand image and for what types of products is it most important to product positioning? How do such products relate to the extended self?
3. Explain the image congruence hypothesis.
4. Describe the various sociocultural dimensions of brand image.
5. Outline the marketing mix elements that are most important to crafting a brand image, and explain how each can be used in brand image creation.

IN-CLASS APPLICATIONS

1. Based on what you know regarding brand image and its reflection of a consumer's self-concept, which commercially available brand best represents your personality? That is, for which brand do you feel the greatest brand image congruence?

EXHIBIT 11.8 Armstrong Floors Ad

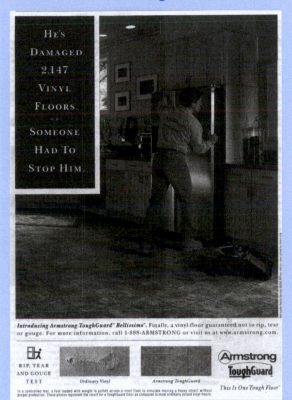

EXHIBIT 11.9 Mootsies Tootsies Ad

EXHIBIT 11.10 Oshkosh Ad

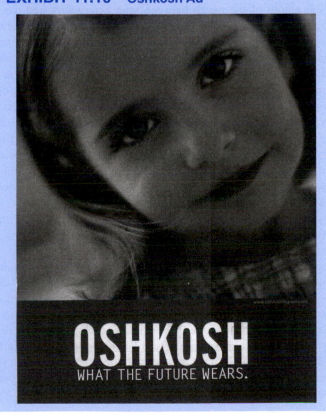

EXHIBIT 11.11   Bombay Company Ad

EXHIBIT 11.12   Jaguar Ad

Describe the nature of the match between your personality and the brand's personality in terms of personality traits and/or sociological traits. (Representative responses are, "I'm like Maytag because I'm practical and dependable," "I'm similar to Charmin toilet tissue: soft and squeezable," "I resemble Ford Bronco: tough, bold, strong, aggressive, fast-paced, and dependable," and "I identify with Pepsi: sweet, bubbly, youthful, and fun.") The more adjectives you can think of to link the brand with you, the better.

Has this image congruence influenced your purchase behavior? Why or why not? If so, do you feel you are basing your purchase decisions on your objective self or your self-image? If self-image, which type?

2. What products or personal belongings do you consider part of your extended self? Examples of such items include a watch, childhood blanket, and eyeglasses. Why are they important to you?

Identify the product attributes in these items most congruent with your personality. (Many of these attributes could be quite intangible and subjective, such as a childhood blanket being cuddly and cute.)

What social connections help define part of your extended self? How could a marketer capitalize on knowledge of your extended self to entice you to purchase a product?

3. If each of the brands in the ads from Exhibits 11.8 through 11.12 was a person, how would you describe each "personality" in terms of the various sociocultural dimensions of brand image: sex, age, culture, subculture, social class, social groups, family situation, and lifestyle?

4. Many companies use T-shirts and caps as promotional tools for their brand. At every concert event, fundraiser, and movie debut, dozens and sometimes hundreds of free T-shirts and/or caps are handed out.

In class, look around you to see how many peers are wearing T-shirts or caps with logos, slogans, and the like. What are some of the brands featured on these apparel items? Can a T-shirt or cap suggest anything about someone's personality? Do any of these items correspond to any of your classmates' personalities?

5. During the 1990s management guru Tom Peters wrote a seminal article entitled "The Brand Called You." Brand You encompasses both your outer self (the clothes you wear, your haircut, even your piercings) and your inner self (feelings, character, and purpose in life). Describe your brand, and include a slogan for your brand campaign.

WRITTEN APPLICATIONS

1. Answer Questions 1 and 2 in the In-Class Applications.

2. Answer Question 3 from the In-Class Applications for two of the ads. Then find two more ads and answer the same question for those ads.

3. Select a packaged good product category where real physical brand differences are virtually nonexistent (e.g., cake mixes, margarines, dishwashing detergents, canned peas, antacids, scouring pads, pain relievers, etc.). Create an appealing brand image for a branded product in this category using as many of the elements of the marketing mix as you choose. Explain how the psychological characteristics you have endowed your brand with differentiate your brand.

Who would be the target market for your product? How would its brand image match the typical target market member's self-image?

4. *Marketing News* columnist Bob Lamons wrote, "Do individuals have brand images? Absolutely. Brand images define expectations, and a person's name (or nickname) is his or her brand. When you hear or see any person's name, you immediately think of certain attributes associated with that person. He's funny. She's smart. He's always working. She's someone you can count on. And so on."

Lamons asks some good questions for you to consider regarding your personal image: How do people see you? What attributes spring to mind when they recall your name? And how should you go about refining or reemphasizing those attributes to create expectations that are more suited to your goals in your personal life, college life, or future career?

It is important that you size up the way your personal style is being perceived by others. You can start by asking yourself the question raised by Rick Warren in his best-selling *The Purpose Driven Life*—what is your life purpose? Is it money? Knowledge? Recognition? Status? Power? The opportunity to interact and have relationships with others? Be assured that what drives you is probably front and center to the image you convey. And if you're not careful, it can result in a negative image ("He's a money-grabber," "He always takes all the credit," "Mr. Know-it-all," and so forth).

Write two brief brand statements: one that describes the way you are perceived and another on how you would like to be known by others (if it differs from how you think you are perceived). Use your one or two strongest characteristics. Then, do a critical self-assessment of your strengths and weaknesses. Do they fit the brand statement? If not, decide which ones need attention. How will you go about "fixing" any weak areas?

Finally, recruit several trusted friends to get feedback from others on how people see you. Don't try to do this yourself, because people will generally tell you what they think you want to hear. Another person can solicit their true feelings much more successfully.

EXERCISE 11.3. MEASURING PERSONALITY AND BRAND IMAGE

OBJECTIVES

1. To become familiar with some of the major personality traits as well as several personality inventories that measure personality.

2. To understand the Hippocratic personality classification scheme, to discover your personality type using this taxonomy, and to apply it to brand image.

3. To further learn about your own personality by taking some personality tests, allowing you to identify personal strengths on which to capitalize and weaknesses to try to rectify.

4. To realize why standardized psychological personality tests are poor predictors of CB, and to recognize personality traits more directly related to buyer behavior that advertisements can appeal to.

5. To gain experience in conducting consumer research to measure both brand image and self-image using semantic differential scales and Freudian projective techniques.

6. To use brand image questionnaires to describe the personalities of some well-known brands.

BACKGROUND

In this exercise, you will gain personal experience in research measuring buyers' personalities, using both general-purpose personality tests and particular personality traits that more closely relate to CB. You will learn how to measure brand images using both quantitative semantic differential scales and qualitative Freudian projective techniques. The underlying theory in all of this is that a buyer's decisions are often an expression of that purchaser's personality, expressing some aspect of self-concept.

PERSONALITY INVENTORIES

Trait theory considers one's personality as comprised of a constellation of personality traits that describe that person's general response predispositions. For example, the often-used "big five" traits model suggests five significant factors: (1) conscientiousness, which is linked to organization and disciple; (2) agreeableness, connected to worrying and instability; (3) openness, associated with trying new experiences; (4) neuroticism, also connected to trying new experiences; and (5) extraversion, affiliated with seeking social support.

Based on this trait, quantitative personality research studies are conducted using a large sample of consumers who are administered a standardized **personality inventory**, an extensive list of statements with scales expressing likes or dislikes for certain objects, people, or situations, used to measure respondents' personality traits. Interviewees are asked to what degree they agree or disagree with each statement. Examples include the Edwards Personal Profile Scale, Cattell's Personality Factor Questionnaire, the California Psychological Inventory, the Gordon Personal Profile, and the Thurstone Temperament Scale.

THE HIPPOCRATIC TEMPERAMENT SURVEY

According to ancient Greek physician Hippocrates, people can be classified into four basic temperaments (personality types). Accordingly, the **Hippocratic Temperament Survey** categorizes people in terms of strengths and weaknesses for each personality trait.

- **Doers (choleric).** Strengths: Take-charge, self-reliant leaders who like to make quick decisions, solve problems, and get immediate results. Weaknesses: They tend to be impatient, insensitive to others, inflexible, too risk-taking, and overly demanding of others. Typical positions: managers, producers, builders, and organizational leaders.
- **Influencers (sanguine).** Strengths: Personable, helpful, enthusiastic, verbally articulate optimists. Weaknesses: Inclined to be impulsive, too talkative, overreaching, and over-committing. Typical occupations: actors, salespeople, and speakers.
- **Relaters (phlegmatic).** Strengths: Loyal, agreeable, supportive team players who perform established work patterns and get along with virtually everybody. Weaknesses: They resist change, procrastinate, are overly lenient, and lack initiative. Typical careers: diplomats, accountants, teachers, and technicians.
- **Thinkers (melancholy).** Strengths: Thorough, analytical, orderly, and conscientious planners and creators. Weaknesses: They can be indecisive, too detail-oriented, rigid, hesitant to try new things, and pessimistic. Typical jobs: artists, musicians, inventors, philosophers, and professors.

Exhibit 11.13 shows specific personality traits for each of these four personality types. The left column exhibits their strengths or positive traits (+), which they should use to their own and others' advantage. The right column indicates their weaknesses or negative traits (−), which they should be aware of and attempt to overcome. As is true of many personality classification schemes, most people have both a *primary personality type* (most characteristic of them) and a *secondary personality type* (less descriptive of them than their primary type).

EXHIBIT 11.13   Hippocratic Personality Types

Extroverted			
(+)	**(-)**	**(-)**	**(+)**
Influencers	**Sanguine**	**Doers**	**Choleric**
Outgoing	Emotional	Crafty	Strong-willed
Personable	Disorganized	Unemotional	Determined
Responsive	Undisciplined	Self-sufficient	Independent
Carefree	Restless	Unsympathetic	Visionary
Compassionate	Unproductive	Impetuous	Optimistic
Friendly	Weak-willed	Proud	Practical
Warm	Loud	Domineering	Productive
Talkative	Egocentric	Inconsiderate	Decisive
Enthusiastic	Undependable	Unappreciative	Courageous
Like to please	Exaggerative	Unforgiving	Leader
Gifted	Moody	Indolent	Calm
Analytical	Negative	Blasé	Quiet
Sensitive	Rigid	Unmotivated	Easy-going
Artistic	Self-centered	Spectator	Dependable
Perfectionist	Touchy	Self-protective	Efficient
Conscientious	Revengeful	Selfish	Conservative
Aesthetic	Theoretical	Stingy	Organized
Musical	Impractical	Indecisive	Objective
Idealistic	Persecution-prone	Fearful	Practical
Loyal	Unsociable	Tease	Leader
Self-sacrificing	Critical	Indolent	Likeable
Self-disciplined		Blasé	Diplomatic
Thinkers	**Melancholy**	**Relaters**	**Phlegmatic**
(+)	**(-)**	**(-)**	**(+)**
Introverted			

THE MYERS-BRIGGS TYPE INDICATOR PERSONALITY INVENTORY

The most widely used psychological test is the **Myers-Briggs Type Indicator Personality Inventory**. It describes peoples' characteristic decision-making styles: Extroverts versus Introverts, Sensors versus Intuiters, Thinkers versus Feelers, and Judgers versus Perceivers. People taking the test are asked more than 100 questions to discover how they react or feel in certain situations.

The Myers-Briggs inventory measures **cognitive style**—how consumers process information and make decisions. From the answers, the Myers-Briggs test classifies a person along each of the following four dichotomous dimensions of personality traits, yielding sixteen possible personality types.

Extroverts Versus Introverts. This is an individual's preferred attitude or orientation toward the world as well as preference for talking and being around others, that is, whether someone's energy is inwardly or outwardly directed.

- **Extroverts** (75 percent of the U.S. population) are oriented toward people and their external environment. They are highly communicative. With high energy, they are talkative, think out loud, enjoy being with people, are easily distracted, make decisions only after consulting others, and are aware of the environment, relying on it for stimulation and guidance.
- **Introverts** (25 percent) are oriented internally toward the pursuit of concepts and ideas, being less communicative. They tend to have quiet energy, talk less, think before they act, be comfortable spending time alone, have good concentration, and make decisions by internally processing information before asking others.

The introvert-extrovert personality dimension is most useful for segmenting a market concerning how consumers gather data in the external search stage of the consumer decision process. Extroverts prefer personal sources such as salespeople and word-of-mouth, whereas introverts opt for nonpersonal sources such as advertising and news reports.

Sensing Versus Intuiting. This indicates whether people rely more on their external five senses or their internal "sixth sense" in gathering data.

- **Sensors** (75 percent) are prone to depend on their senses, to focus on the facts and concrete information, and to have a concern for specifics and details. They are practical and patient, have straightforward speech, are realistic, notice the "big picture," are present-oriented with a strong sense of what is currently happening, dislike new problems unless there are old ways to solve them, enjoy established routines, and are patient with the decision-making process.
- **Intuiters** (25 percent) rely on their "sixth sense" or "gut feeling" when deciding, operate on hunches and possibilities, are creative, focus on ideas and the big picture, are theoretical, have roundabout thoughts, are imaginative, see possibilities, look for patterns and relationships, enjoy solving problems, dislike repetitive tasks, are future oriented, and are less patient with the decision-making process, although they are more tolerant of complicated situations.

Sensors prefer detailed, informative marketing communications, while Intuiters are attracted to more "bottom line," holistic communications. The sensing-intuiting dimension helps consumer researchers understand the data gathering during the external search stage and alternative selection during the decision stage.

Thinking Versus Feeling. This dimension offers insight into how individuals prefer to decide.

- **Thinkers** (50 percent) are objective, make decisions based on facts and logic, have a high need for cognition (they enjoy and engage in thinking), and are cool and reserved, honest and direct, naturally critical, and motivated by achievement.
- **Feelers** (50 percent) are concerned with choosing based on their emotions and values. Feelers consider how their decisions will make them feel or others feel. They also make decisions grounded in personal beliefs and personal and group values. These individuals are warm and friendly, get their feelings hurt easily, are sensitive and diplomatic, try hard to please others, and are motivated by being appreciated.

This trait offers insight into the alternative evaluation phase of consumer decision making. Thinkers prefer marketing communications that contain analytical arguments, while Feelers favor promotion that is emotional and expresses the interpersonal dimensions of a product.

Perceiving Versus Judging. This describes the preferred attitudes when dealing with the outer world and the kind of environment in which people are most comfortable.

- **Judgers** (55 percent) favor being organized and systematic, living in a planned and orderly way, making quick decisions, and being serious and formal. They are time-conscious, work first and play later, and prefer to finish projects, although they might experience trouble starting them.
- **Perceivers** (45 percent) like to live life flexibly and spontaneously, are open to new events, tend to wait for more information and procrastinate in decision making, are playful and casual, are unaware of time, prefer to wait and see, play first then work later, and like to start projects.

The perceiving/judging factor is most relevant to the decision/choice stage.

CONSUMER RESEARCH USING PERSONALITY INVENTORIES

In consumer research using personality inventories, consumers' responses to personality inventories are statistically analyzed to reduce their replies to a few basic personality dimensions. People are thereby described by a series of adjectives profiling their personality traits, such as docile versus aggressive, trusting versus suspicious, and relaxed versus tense. They are also asked questions about their CB, including choice behavior (e.g., product, brand, and store selection) as well as more general consumer activities (innovativeness, opinion leadership, and the like). Multiple regression equations are then run to see if any personality traits can predict these behaviors.

Some studies have been successful in using personality traits to forecast CB and thereby segment markets by personality type. For example, studies have found that smokers rate high on rebelliousness, sensation seeking, and extroversion but low on self-esteem. Male owners of Fords were independent, impulsive, and masculine, whereas buyers of Chevrolets were conservative, thrifty, and less masculine. Women who purchased private label brands were enthusiastic, sensitive, and submissive. And, Hershey's knows that consumers who prefer dark chocolate are more sophisticated and indulgent (and demographically are more upscale).

PROBLEMS WITH PREDICTING CONSUMER BEHAVIOR FROM STANDARDIZED PERSONALITY INVENTORIES

Unfortunately, most studies have been less successful, typically finding that personality traits divine at most 10 percent of the variance in CB. There are a number of reasons why standardized personality inventories usually poorly predict CB.

- Buyer behavior is a function of many factors besides personality, primarily sociocultural and multiple psychological variables.
- Researchers too often try to forecast very specific behaviors, such as brand preference, from general response dispositions. Personality tests tend to predict better for very broad aspects of CB, such as whether someone will buy colonial versus modern furniture or sport utility vehicles versus minivans. Personality traits do a poorer job foretelling what specific brands buyers will purchase or particular stores they will patronize.
- Behavior is often highly situation-specific, being dependent on the purchase and/or usage situation. For instance, a conservative businessperson might occasionally enjoy avant-garde cuisine or sport the latest wild fashion on "casual Friday." Or, consider that you behave one way with professors, another with parents, and yet another with peers. Hence, personality is better used in conjunction with the situation in which a product is purchased and used. For example, a sociable person might buy a fine wine or bourbon to serve to guests but settle for a more pedestrian brand like "Old Rotgut" when relaxing alone. Or, consider that even gourmets take their kids to Burger King now and then.
- Personality tests tend to measure the objective self rather than self-image, which is more relevant to choices based on brand image.
- Many of the personality scales lack validity. It is easy to "cheat" to make oneself seem desirable. For example, a man might wish to appear aggressive, not passive.
- Some research has been conducted without a priori hypotheses regarding what types of personality traits should logically predict which kinds of CBs. For example, cosmetics might be anticipated to appeal to narcissists or a book club to people with a high need for thinking and knowledge. Instead, researchers have gone on fishing expeditions, hoping that a slew of personality data will correlate with some sort of CB, regardless of whether it intuitively makes sense.
- People who are similar in terms of personality might not be identifiable. For example, how would you locate self-conscious people for purposes of advertising or personal selling? Since most media commonly describe their target audiences using demographics, one solution is to first segment the market on the basis of demographics, such as young women who are homemakers. Then, within the demographic group, a marketing strategy can be formulated that will attract one particular personality type. As an example, a home cleaning item could be targeted at young women homemakers who are compulsive cleaners.
- Many personality scales were developed for clinical psychology to ascertain personality disorders rather than to predict CB. Consequently, tailor-made inventories can be created to measure personality traits specifically related to CB.

CUSTOMIZED CONSUMER PERSONALITY RESEARCH

Custom-made personality inventories measure various consumer-relevant personality traits.

Traits Related to Being an Innovator or Early Adopter of a New Product. New product marketers can appeal to the following personality traits in their communications to attract early-bird consumers.

- **Consumer innovativeness**—how receptive a person is to new products, services, practices, or experiences. Innovative consumers are open to novelty.
- **Dogmatism**—whether an individual is open-minded or closed-minded. Consumers who are less dogmatic (more open-minded) are more receptive to new ideas and experiences, prefer innovative products, and are innovators, early adopters, and opinion leaders.
- **Social character**—the degree to which an individual is inner-directed versus outer- (other-) directed. **Inner-directed** people are introverted and individualistic, self-sufficient, self-disciplined, and indifferent to group standards and opinions. They are more likely to be consumer innovators, prefer products that please them and perform functionally, and favor ads that stress product features and personal benefits. Examples of appeals to inner-directed consumers include Apple computer's "Think different," Saab's "Find your own road," and Saturn's "A breed apart."
- **Outer- (other-) directed** people are extroverted and conformists. Concerned with what others will think of them, they tend to yield to peer pressure and reference group influences and are thus less likely to be consumer innovators. They prefer to wait until other people are regular product users. Outer-directeds also perceive high social risk in many products, are more social class/status conscious, and hence are into conspicuous consumption. They prefer ads that feature an approving social environment or social acceptance.
- **Optimal stimulation level (OSL)**—people's preference for a simple, uncluttered, and calm life as opposed to a novel, complex, and everchanging existence. People have different OSLs, which are desired levels of environmental arousal. Stimulation can be physical (bodily exercise), psychological (studying CB!), or emotional (watching a romantic movie).

Consumers with high OSLs (high sensation seekers) prefer situations, activities, and ideas that are novel, complex, exciting, surprising, and intense, while low OSL consumers (low sensation seekers) do not. High OSL customers are creative and are more likely to be new product innovators and early adopters, impulse buyers, and risk takers, plus they enjoy shopping in malls featuring variety.

Traits Related to Information Processing. The following personality factors are relevant for developing creative and media advertising strategies.

- **Need for cognition (NC)**—the extent to which a person enjoys thinking, challenging information processing, and problem-solving activities. High NC consumers enjoy thinking and are therefore responsive to rich product-related information and strong, rational arguments. Low NC consumers are more attracted to ads with little information and to the peripheral aspects of an ad, such as music, celebrity presenters, or pretty pictures. They are also more likely to use easy decision heuristics such as "Buy the brand your friend recommends." Since print media tend to be information intensive, they are more effective with high NC consumers, while broadcast media, being limited in information content, work best for low NC customers.
- **Visualizers versus Verbalizers**—an individual's preference for information presented pictorially versus with words. Visualizers prefer broadcast media while verbalizers opt for print.

OTHER TRAITS RELEVANT TO CB

- **Consumer materialism**—the extent to which consumers are attached to worldly belongings and see possessions as central to their lives. Consequently, brand image congruence is especially relevant to them.
- **Locus of control**—whether an individual believes that events in his or her life are caused more by factors under his or her own control and actions (internal locus of control) or by uncontrollable conditions, that is, other people or events (external locus of control). Internalizers believe they control their own lives and actions, taking responsibility for their decisions and behaviors. Externalizers believe that events are beyond their control and that others manipulate their lives, tending to blame the environment rather than themselves for their failings.

MEASURING BRAND IMAGES

A brand image embodies the personality traits that consumers believe a particular brand possesses. Once a brand's image has been constructed and communicated to the target market, the marketer should use consumer research to ensure that the desired brand character has been burnished in buyers' minds. This can be done using either quantitative research, which employs surveys containing semantic differential attitude scales, or qualitative research, which uses Freudian projective techniques.

SEMANTIC DIFFERENTIAL SCALES

The **semantic differential scale** measures consumer attitudes using a series of seven-point rating scales. Bipolar (opposite) adjectives anchor the poles, that is, the ends of each scale item (e.g., masculine-feminine, youthful-mature, and modern vs. old-fashioned).

Typically, the self-administered attitude questionnaire has twenty to thirty adjective pairs on which both the marketer's and competitors' brands are evaluated. One challenge is to represent all relevant dimensions of the brand's personality and users' self-concepts. Another is to come up with adjectives that are truly opposites. For example, is the opposite of youthful, "mature" or "old"? (Checking the antonyms in your word processor's thesaurus can help.) The same questionnaire can also be used to record consumers' self-images to be compared against the brand's image.

Exhibit 11.14 gives an example of a series of bipolar adjectives from which such a semantic differential brand image questionnaire has been constructed. A brand has a sharper image on a given set of adjectives the closer to either end of the scale consumers rate it. Being rated a 4 indicates little-to-no image. Ratings on these dimensions are combined to create an overall brand image profile. Accordingly Caterpillar, the construction equipment manufacturer, was described by consumers with adjectives such as "strong," "reliable," "genuine," and "serious." The closeness of a brand-image profile to the targeted consumer's self-image profile tells the degree of congruence between the consumer's self-image and the brand image.

FREUDIAN PROJECTIVE TECHNIQUES

Qualitative research techniques using projective questioning are also popular for measuring brand personality. They are useful when researchers suspect respondents are *unable* (due to subconscious thoughts and feelings) or *unwilling* (because they feel embarrassed or threatened) to answer more straightforward questions, such as those of a semantic differential scale.

In projective questioning, consumers are asked to respond to an ambiguous, nonpersonal situation. Alternatively, projective (indirect, disguised) questions are asked, usually either as part of a depth interview or a focus group discussion. The theory is that people will project their own beliefs, feelings, and behaviors onto the stimulus object.

For example, if you ask why a person drinks Pepsi, she would find it hard to say, "I think it's a reflection of who I am as a person and the values that define my life." Instead, she would give a more "rational" answer, such as "I prefer Pepsi's flavor." Researchers need to uncover the *real reason*—that it reflects her self-image and values.

The following are projective methods that have been applied to brand image research.

Word Association. Using word association, respondents are asked to name the first word that comes into their mind when they hear the brand name. Example: "Tell me the first word that you think of when you hear each of the following brand names: Tide detergent . . . ; Southwest Airlines . . ."; Tide detergent might be described as "tough" or "All-American," and Southwest Airlines as "friendly" or "frugal." Consumers are also sometimes requested to associate the brand with a famous personality.

Sentence Completion. With **sentence completion**, interviewees finish incomplete sentences with the first word or phrase that comes to mind. Example: "Women who bathe with Camay soap are _____."

EXHIBIT 11.14   Semantic Differential Scale for Brand- and Self-Image

#	Left	1	2	3	4	5	6	7	Right
1.	Rugged	1	2	3	4	5	6	7	Delicate
2.	Exciting	1	2	3	4	5	6	7	Calm
3.	Comfortable	1	2	3	4	5	6	7	Uncomfortable
4.	Masculine	1	2	3	4	5	6	7	Feminine
5.	Dominating	1	2	3	4	5	6	7	Submissive
6.	Emotional	1	2	3	4	5	6	7	Rational
7.	Youthful	1	2	3	4	5	6	7	Mature
8.	Formal	1	2	3	4	5	6	7	Informal
9.	Modest	1	2	3	4	5	6	7	Vain
10.	Thrifty	1	2	3	4	5	6	7	Indulgent
11.	Colorful	1	2	3	4	5	6	7	Colorless
12.	Pleasant	1	2	3	4	5	6	7	Unpleasant
14.	Contemporary	1	2	3	4	5	6	7	Noncontemporary
15.	Strong	1	2	3	4	5	6	7	Weak
16.	Conservative	1	2	3	4	5	6	7	Liberal
17.	Organized	1	2	3	4	5	6	7	Unorganized
18.	Simple	1	2	3	4	5	6	7	Complex
19.	Graceful	1	2	3	4	5	6	7	Awkward
20.	Popular	1	2	3	4	5	6	7	Unpopular
21.	Extravagant	1	2	3	4	5	6	7	Economical
22.	Successful	1	2	3	4	5	6	7	Unsuccessful
23.	Informed	1	2	3	4	5	6	7	Uninformed
24.	Interesting	1	2	3	4	5	6	7	Dull
25.	Conformist	1	2	3	4	5	6	7	Nonconformist
26.	Modern	1	2	3	4	5	6	7	Old fashioned
27.	Extrovert	1	2	3	4	5	6	7	Introvert
28.	Athletic	1	2	3	4	5	6	7	Smooth
29.	Adventurous	1	2	3	4	5	6	7	Timid
30.	Leader	1	2	3	4	5	6	7	Follower
31.	Active	1	2	3	4	5	6	7	Passive
32.	Plain	1	2	3	4	5	6	7	Ornate
33.	Confident	1	2	3	4	5	6	7	Apprehensive
34.	Relaxed	1	2	3	4	5	6	7	Tense
35.	Hard	1	2	3	4	5	6	7	Soft
36.	Sophisticated	1	2	3	4	5	6	7	Unsophisticated
37.	Bold	1	2	3	4	5	6	7	Shy
38.	Sporty	1	2	3	4	5	6	7	Businesslike
39.	Impulsive	1	2	3	4	5	6	7	Deliberate
40.	Clean	1	2	3	4	5	6	7	Dirty
41.	Changeable	1	2	3	4	5	6	7	Stable
42.	Urban	1	2	3	4	5	6	7	Rural
43.	Formal	1	2	3	4	5	6	7	Informal
44.	Aggressive	1	2	3	4	5	6	7	Defensive
45.	Honest	1	2	3	4	5	6	7	Dishonest
46.	Self-confident	1	2	3	4	5	6	7	Not self-confident
47.	Enthusiastic	1	2	3	4	5	6	7	Unenthusiastic
48.	Intelligent	1	2	3	4	5	6	7	Unintelligent
49.	Competitive	1	2	3	4	5	6	7	Cooperative
50.	Friendly	1	2	3	4	5	6	7	Unfriendly
51.	Likeable	1	2	3	4	5	6	7	Not likeable

Third-Person (referent other) Questioning. **Third-person (referent other) questioning** asks respondents what another person (a friend, neighbor, colleague, etc.) or people in general think or do, rather than directly asking the interviewees about themselves. Example: "What do your friends think about Lincoln Continentals?" Respondents presumably transfer their own thoughts or feelings onto others.

Role playing. With **role playing**, consumers act out the role of someone else in a particular situation. Example: "Pretend you are a husband and have just discovered that your wife has replaced your favorite brand of potato chip, Ruffles, with another, Wise . . ."

Consumer Drawings (psychodrawings). Using **consumer drawings (psychodrawings)**, buyers are requested to express their perceptions of or feelings about the brand or its usage in pictorial format. Example: "Draw a picture of men who drive Porsches."

Personification (anthropomorphism). With **personification (anthropomorphism)**, consumers are asked to imagine that the brand comes to life as a person and are asked what the brand is like in terms of its demographic characteristics, lifestyles, likes and dislikes, and so on. Example: "Write a letter to Kodak as though it were your friend."

Personification once revealed that consumers were intimidated by the American Express green card. One respondent imagined the card sneering at him, "You're not my type—you can't keep up," apparently because commercials featured high-powered business executives using the credit card. In another case, focus group participants asked to attribute female characteristics to islands likened Jamaica to "a slightly dangerous (but nonetheless tantalizing) slut you probably wouldn't take to the country club"—clearly an image problem!

Direct Analogies and Symbolic Analogies. Using **direct analogies** and **symbolic analogies**, consumers are asked to describe the brand as another object. Examples: "What kind of a day would a Lux day be?" or "What kind of an animal is Wal-Mart?"

Personal Analogies. Using **personal analogies,** respondents are requested to imagine and describe themselves as the product. Example: "If you were a can of Ajax cleanser, what would you be like? How old would you be? Would you be a man or woman?"

Fantasy Solutions and Future Scenarios. With **fantasy solutions** and **future scenarios,** interviewees are presented with a consumer problem and asked to present their ideal solution or to otherwise imagine a fanciful situation. Example: "Imagine you are at a tenth college reunion of beers. Describe their occupations, marital status, what they discussed, and how they acted."

Picture Sorting. With **picture sorting**, respondents are given a deck of cards showing photos of different kinds of people who vary by gender, ethnicity, dress, etc. To enable researchers to learn about brand image, interviewees are asked to identify the brands in a particular product category that each person uses. Also, to reveal their own self-images, respondents are requested to identify pictures of people most like them. Using this technique, the Della Femina advertising agency found that Iron City beer drinkers were perceived as "blue collar steel workers stopping at the local bar."

Storytelling. In **storytelling**, consumers are requested to tell a story related to a setting or situation. For example, "Let's pretend you are in the supermarket. The woman next to you has Brand X in her cart. Tell me about that woman. What else does she have in her cart? How is she dressed? Where does she live? What does her house look like—inside and outside? What kind of car does she drive?"

REVIEW QUESTIONS

1. Describe the Hippocratic Temperament Survey and the Myers-Briggs Type Indicator Personality Inventory as well as the various personality types according to each. Explain how each of these personality inventories can be applied to CB.
2. Why have traditional standardized personality tests done a poor job predicting CB? How have consumer-relevant personality traits been more successfully applied to predicting buyer behavior? Describe some of these traits.
3. Discuss how marketers use consumer research to ensure that the desired brand image has been built in buyers' minds via semantic differential attitude scales and through Freudian projective techniques. In what kinds of situations might the latter be more appropriate than the former for measuring brand image?

IN-CLASS APPLICATIONS

1. For each of the following ads (Exhibits 11.15–11.18) describe the personality traits of the target market to which the ad seems to be appealing using each of the following: a) the Hippocratic personality types, b) the Myers-Briggs Type Indicator personality types, and c) one or more of the consumer-relevant personality traits.
2. Before coming to class, take the following Temperament Survey based on the Hippocratic classification scheme below to see into which personality category you fall.

    Directions: Circle ONE word in each row that you feel describes you BEST.

	A	B	C	D
1.	Restrained	Forceful	Careful	Expressive
2.	Pioneering	Correct	Emotional	Satisfied
3.	Willing	Animated	Bold	Precise
4.	Stubborn	Bashful	Indecisive	Unpredictable
5.	Respectful	Outgoing	Patient	Determined
6.	Persuasive	Self-reliant	Cooperative	Gentle
7.	Cautious	Even-tempered	Decisive	Life-of-the-party
8.	Popular	Assertive	Perfectionist	Generous
9.	Unpredictable	Bashful	Indecisive	Argumentative
10.	Agreeable	Optimistic	Persistent	Accommodating
11.	Positive	Humble	Neighborly	Talkative
12.	Friendly	Obliging	Playful	Strong-willed
13.	Charming	Adventurous	Disciplined	Consistent
14.	Soft-spoken	Dry-humor	Aggressive	Attractive
15.	Enthusiastic	Analytical	Sympathetic	Determined
16.	Bossy	Inconsistent	Slow	Critical
17.	Sensitive	Forceful	Spirited	Laid-back
18.	Influential	Kind	Independent	Orderly
19.	Idealistic	Popular	Cheerful	Out-spoken
20.	Impatient	Moody	Aimless	Show-off
21.	Competitive	Spontaneous	Loyal	Thoughtful
22.	Self-sacrificing	Considerate	Convincing	Courageous
23.	Fearful	Changeable	Pessimistic	Tactless
24.	Tolerant	Conventional	Stimulating	Resourceful

    On the scoring sheet on p. 344, circle the answer you gave for each question. Then add up the number of answers you circled for each temperament. Which is your primary temperament (highest score) and secondary temperament (second highest score)? How accurate do you think this personality test is? Explain.

    According to your knowledge of your Hippocratic personality type and insight into yourself, what are strengths that you can build on in your life, including in your relationships with your family and friends, school life, and (present and future) work life? What weaknesses do you need to be aware of and should you work to improve? How can you do so? What does your Hippocratic personality type suggest about your CB?

    What do you think your instructor's Hippocratic personality type is—a Thinker? Why? What would this suggest about your professor's CB?

EXHIBIT 11.15   Grey Poupon Ad

EXHIBIT 11.16   Canon Ad

EXHIBIT 11.17   Wish-Bone Ad

EXHIBIT 11.18   Singulair Ad

SCORING SHEET

	Doer	Influencer	Relater	Thinker
1.	B	D	A	C
2.	A	C	D	B
3.	C	B	A	D
4.	A	D	C	B
5.	D	B	C	A
6.	B	A	D	C
7.	C	D	B	A
8.	B	A	D	C
9.	D	A	C	B
10.	C	B	C	A
11.	A	D	C	B
12.	D	C	A	B
13.	B	A	D	C
14.	C	D	B	A
15.	D	A	C	B
16.	A	B	C	D
17.	B	C	D	A
18.	C	A	B	D
19.	D	B	C	A
20.	A	D	C	B
21.	A	B	C	D
22.	D	C	B	A
23.	D	B	A	C
24.	D	C	A	B

3. Personality type is very important in forecasting CB, especially brand and store choices. Complete the following personality tests to discover more about yourself. How accurate do you believe each test was in predicting your personality type? What are the marketing implications of classifying consumers by each of these personality types?

   a. The Meyers-Briggs Type Indicator (MBTI): See HumanMetrics at http://www.humanmetrics.com/cgi-win/JTypes2.asp.

   b. Type A or Type B? See Type A Personality Test at http://discoveryhealth.queendom.com/type_a_personality_access.html.

   c. (Optional) You've probably heard the radio commercials with founder Dr. Neil Clark Warren touting his matchmaking site, eHarmony.com, where you can find your soulmate. It is a forty-five-minute-long personality quiz containing 436 questions. Try it out at www.eHarmony.com.

   d. (Optional) If you'd rather click on pictures than read through questions, check out Youniverse at http://www.youniverse.com/. Here, you can take a personality quiz to determine your "VisualDNA." You will be asked to click on beautifully arranged photographs to answer questions about yourself.

   e. Looking for a movie to rent tonight? Try What to Rent? at http://www.whattorent.com/. The site administers a personality test to visitors and recommends DVDs based on the findings. Were their recommendations good ones for you?

4. From the following list of brands, choose three brands and list five personality traits associated with each: Pepsi, Oscar Mayer, Tylenol, Ben & Jerry's, Calvin Klein, Volkswagen, Nike, Budweiser, Campbell's, IBM, Marlboro, Hush Puppies, Abercrombie & Fitch, Miller Beer, Cadillac. What are the marketing implications of the personality traits of these brands?

5. Make five photocopies of the semantic scale below. Then, rate the following brands: Ford, Oil of Olay, Charmin, Dell, and Sketchers.

   In class, compare your ratings with your fellow classmates. Are there similarities or differences? What is the overall impression of each brand image? What are the marketing implications of measuring brand image?

1.	Rugged	1	2	3	4	5	6	7	Delicate
2.	Exciting	1	2	3	4	5	6	7	Calm
3.	Uncomfortable	1	2	3	4	5	6	7	Comfortable
4.	Dominating	1	2	3	4	5	6	7	Submissive
5.	Thrifty	1	2	3	4	5	6	7	Indulgent
6.	Pleasant	1	2	3	4	5	6	7	Unpleasant
7.	Contemporary	1	2	3	4	5	6	7	Uncontemporary
8.	Organized	1	2	3	4	5	6	7	Unorganized
9.	Rational	1	2	3	4	5	6	7	Emotional
10.	Youthful	1	2	3	4	5	6	7	Mature
11.	Formal	1	2	3	4	5	6	7	Informal
12.	Orthodox	1	2	3	4	5	6	7	Liberal
13.	Complex	1	2	3	4	5	6	7	Simple
14.	Colorless	1	2	3	4	5	6	7	Colorful
15.	Modest	1	2	3	4	5	6	7	Vain

WRITTEN APPLICATIONS

1. Answer parts a, b, and c of Question 1 from the In-Class Applications for two of the ads. Then, find two more ads and answer parts a through c for each ad.
2. Answer Question 2 from the In-Class Applications.
3. Conduct your own consumer research to measure the brand image of a brand that interests you. You may choose one of the following two research approaches.
   a. Administer a semantic differential survey using about a dozen of what you believe are the most relevant pairs of adjectives in Exhibit 11.14. Gather a sample of about a dozen people who you believe are target market members. Use the same scale to measure their self-image. Is there a match between the brand image and each target buyer's self-image? Then, design a print ad to appeal to the target market using this brand image.
   b. Choose two of the qualitative projective techniques for measuring brand image. At least one of these should use either individual interviews or a focus group of six to eight target market members. Describe the brand's image according to each of these methodologies. Then, design a print ad to appeal to the target market using this brand image.
4. Use the rating scales for six of the fifteen attributes of your choice found in Question 5 of the In-Class Applications to measure the brand image of three different brands in a socially visible product category, such as cars, clothing, sporting goods, and so on. One should be a brand you own or regularly consume. Then, use the same rating scales to measure your self-image.

   Does there appear to be congruence between your self-image and the brand image? If yes, describe on which dimensions. If not, why not? What problems do you see with using these scales?

EXERCISE 11.4. PSYCHOGRAPHICS: VALS2 AND CLARITAS PRIZM LIFESTYLE SEGMENTATION

OBJECTIVES

1. To comprehend the nature of psychographic (lifestyle) research and to be able to conduct your own psychographic study.
2. To create a psychographic profile for a consumer, as well as positioning and promotional strategies appealing to that buyer.
3. To understand the nature of standardized psychographic research services and to gain experience in using the VALS2 segmentation system.
4. To learn about your own VALS2 type as well as those of your classmates and instructor.

5. To analyze the use of VALS2 lifestyle marketing by various types of marketers.
6. To become familiar with geodemographic segmentation using the Claritas PRIZM system and to learn about your own neighborhood's PRIZM-based lifestyle characteristics.

BACKGROUND

In this exercise, we will explore a means for segmenting and targeting consumer markets. It incorporates multiple segmentation bases using several marketing research methodologies. The result is a highly effective and sophisticated means for market segmentation known as lifestyle segmentation. The associated lifestyle research is known as psychographics.

ORIGINS OF PSYCHOGRAPHICS: MARKETING RESEARCH FOR SEGMENTING MARKETS

THE QUANTITATIVE ERA: DEMOGRAPHIC RESEARCH

The earliest market segmentation was demographic segmentation, which premiered in the early twentieth century, the quantitative era in consumer research. Survey research employed questionnaires administered to large, representative samples of consumers to discover demographic characteristics of purchasers of particular products or brands or certain store shoppers' demographics.

The overriding advantage of demographic measures of markets is that the requisite information is readily available from secondary data sources. These include the U.S. Commerce Department's Census Bureau, media companies, and syndicated (prepackaged) research firms such as Simmons and MediaMark that sell data on consumption and media exposure habits broken down by demographic variables. Such information is free (from the Census Bureau and media companies) or relatively low in cost (from syndicated data). Also, demographics provide easy-to-digest, quantified summary data.

Unfortunately, demographics only provide a superficial description of *who* buys, not an explanation of *why* they buy. What insights do marketers gain from knowing that their typical target buyer is a male eighteen to thirty-four who earns $50,000 to $64,000 per year and is married and living with a wife, 2.3 children, and a pet? Demographics merely describe statistical averages and ranges within large groups, yielding little understanding of targeted individuals.

In reality, there is generally great lifestyle diversity within any particular segment. For example, not all senior citizens are alike—some are more mentally and physically active than your typical college student, while others are retired and glued to the rocking chair in their dark, dingy apartments. Some drive BMWs to the country club and others drive Kias to the local pharmacist.

The fact is that consumers do not usually buy a product simply because they are 50-plus white-collar workers who graduated from Cornell, live in the 'burbs, and earn $75,000 a year. Consumers make purchases to enhance their **lifestyles**, the distinctive or characteristic modes of living of groups or individuals in society, including how they spend the valuable resources of time and money. Thus, demographics offer poor explanations for the "real reasons" people purchase.

THE QUALITATIVE ERA: MOTIVATIONAL RESEARCH

In order to better understand consumers as complex, flesh-and-blood beings rather than dry, dusty statistics, marketers entered the qualitative era of research, primarily motivational research. Whereas demographic measures reveal states of being, motivation research uncovers states of mind and the unconscious "real reasons" why people buy. By the 1950s big advertising agencies were tapping psychologists to get this information.

Although the information garnered can be quite detailed and revealing, there are severe shortcomings of motivational research techniques (see Exercise 11.1): They are expensive, time-consuming, have small sample sizes not representative of the target market, are of dubious validity, and yield lengthy transcripts and videotapes of interviews that are hard to summarize.

Disillusioned with motivational research, consumer researchers attempted to link consumer choices to personality traits by gathering attitudinal and behavioral data on people who completed personality inventories (see Exercise 11.3). Like motivation research, personality research was designed to yield insights into buyers' states of mind, which were felt to be better explanatory variables for customer behavior than states of being while retaining their quantitative nature. Although there were some modest successes, most studies conducted during the late 1960s and 1970s found little association between personality and buyer behavior, despite the intuitive appeal of this approach.

CONSUMER LIFESTYLES AND PSYCHOGRAPHIC RESEARCH

Still determined to uncover the Holy Grail of consumer insight, during the late 1960s into the early 1970s researchers unveiled a new concept that was **psychosocial (sociopsychological)**—of a nature relating to or combining social and psychological factors (i.e., concerned with psychological development and interaction with a social environment). Known as consumer lifestyles, this idea tied together many sociological and psychological ideas, including the personality and self-concept constructs.

CONSUMER LIFESTYLES

Examples of lifestyle groups abound. There are the Joe Six-Pack and Harriet Homemaker ways of life. We have couch potatoes and bookworms, barflies and party animals, swinging singles and mall rats. You might know some hipsters, country bumpkins, city slickers, church ladies, rednecks, NASCAR guys, and "wired" Web heads. We encounter soccer moms, weekend warriors, surfer dudes, and techno-geeks.

Admit it—even in high school and college you pigeonholed fellow students into amateur psychographic groups such as jocks, cheerleaders, slackers, preppies, freaks, geeks, straight edges, Goths, ravers, headbangers, jarheads, surfer dudes, metal heads, rebels, and skate punks. What other names are there for student clusters on your campus? Regardless, besides academics, the contemporary youth and college lifestyle revolves around part-time jobs, college activities and sports, music, action sports, and video gaming.

In American society, first there were hippies, followed by preppies, then yuppies (young upwardly mobile professionals). Several lifestyle groups have more recently come under the marketing microscope:

- *Metrosexuals:* straight, affluent, sophisticated, hip urban men, age twenty to fifty, who are in touch with their feminine side and love to shop and preen, buying $100 haircuts and chemical tans. They have the good taste of gay men, but they are straight.
- *Retrosexuals:* macho "guy's guys" who reject metrosexuality and feminism and instead happily wallow in traditional male behavior. They star in sophomoric beer ads.
- *Ubersexuals:* guy's guys who embrace the positives of masculinity—self-confidence, leadership, passion, and compassion—without succumbing to the negatives. They have a feminine side but neither fear nor flaunt it. "Uber" is German for "above," meaning these guys are above being merely sexy and need to be complete gentlemen too. They seek quality products, such as fine wine and yellow Labs.
- *Alpha Women:* females who try to have it all: family, career, and a nice social circle. Many are alpha moms balancing husband, family, home, and job.
- *Scuppies:* socially and ecologically conscious upwardly mobile persons. They eat, drink, and sleep organic; think it is easy being green; and wish to live well while doing good, including buying from firms that practice corporate social responsibility.

If we can slot people into partitions like these, does it not follow that we can make some pretty safe predictions regarding their CB? Designers such as Calvin Klein and Ralph Lauren sell lifestyles as much as clothes and cologne.

Exhibit 11.19 summarizes the nature of the many sociocultural and psychological influences on lifestyle, which, in turn, becomes an important determinant of CB.

EXHIBIT 11.19   **Determinants and Consequences of Consumer Lifestyles**

Sociocultural and Psychological Factors Influencing Lifestyle	Elements of Lifestyle (AIOs)	Consumer Behaviors Influenced by Lifestyle
<u>Sociological factors</u> Demographics Culture Subculture Social class Reference groups Family lifestyle stage <u>Psychological factors</u> Personality Personal values Motives and emotions	<u>Activities</u> Hobbies, social events, vacations, entertainment, community, shopping, sports <u>Interests</u> Family, home, job, recreation, fashion, food, media, achievements <u>Opinions</u> Themselves, social issues, politics, business	• Benefits sought • Consumer decision-making style • Shopping style <u>Choices</u> Goods, services, brands, stores, and media • Product usage patterns

---

THE NATURE OF PSYCHOGRAPHIC RESEARCH

Psychographic (lifestyle, values) research is the quantitative research method used for measuring consumer lifestyles. It captures buyers' activities, interests, and opinions (**AIOs**; see the center box in Exhibit 11.19).

To paint a rich portrait of consumers, psychographic questionnaires collect data on various sociological and psychological determinants of lifestyle (see the left box in Exhibit 11.19). These include basic demographic and behavioral characteristics, especially products and brands used and media exposure habits (see the right box in Exhibit 11.19). Media usage patterns are included so marketers know where to advertise to reach targeted lifestyle groups and because media habits are part of people's lifestyles. From such data, Ford decided to advertise the Escape hybrid SUV in ultraliberal *Mother Jones* magazine, as well as *Organic Gardening* and *Green Car Journal,* and to be a National Public Radio sponsor.

In short, psychographics includes demographic states of being (sociological factors), states of mind (psychological factors), and states of action (as embodied in lifestyle activities and selected CBs). Consequently, psychographics is superior to demographics, motivation research, and personality research because it combines the best elements of all three to provide richer insights into CB. In fact, similar to personality segmentation, lifestyle segmentation often starts with broad demographic groups and then divides them psychographically. Most firms work with secondary research suppliers, such as SRI International and Nielsen Claritas Corp., who specialize in psychographic research.

THE PROCESS OF PSYCHOGRAPHIC RESEARCH

Typically, survey research is undertaken on a large sample (typically 500-plus) of targeted customers or product/brand users to get information on their AIOs, demographics, and behavior. In the more thorough studies, rather lengthy questionnaires are used, sometimes consisting of two-hundred questions or more,

> ## EXHIBIT 11.20   Classification Scheme for Psychographic Questions
>
> **Individual/Personal** _____
>
> *General/Generic*
> I feel that my life is moving faster and faster, sometimes just too fast.
> I think about my safety and security when planning a trip.
> Given my lifestyle, I suffer more from a shortage of time than of money.
> I would rather spend a quiet evening at home than go out to a party.
> I have personally worked in a political campaign for a candidate or an issue.
> I prefer to participate more in team sports than in individual sports.
>
> *Product-specific/Marketplace*
> I always look for the manufacturer's name on the package.
> I prefer to buy things that my friends or neighbors would approve of.
> All products that pollute the environment should be banned.
> When in the store, I often buy a product on the spur of the moment.
> I like to try new and different products.
> I usually have one or more outfits of the latest style.
> I shop a lot for "specials."
>
> **Family/Household** _____
>
> *General/Generic*
> Television is our primary source of entertainment.
> When the children are in bed I drop almost everything else to see to their comfort.
> Our family likes to do volunteer work in the community together.
> We attend church almost every week.
> We have one or more pets as an important member of the family.
> Spending time with my children is very important to me.
>
> *Product-specific/Marketplace*
> Our family really appreciates the peace of mind that traveler's checks bring.
> Our family frequently switches food brands in order to get variety and novelty.
> We caution our children not to believe everything they see in advertising.
> Our family generally plans far ahead when buying expensive things such as automobiles.
> We shop a lot together as a family.
> We do not often go out to dinner or the theater together.

although they can be answered quickly. These surveys are administered using any standard interview medium: self-administered pencil-and-paper, on line, via telephone, or in person.

AIO Items. AIO questions usually appear as 5- or 7-point Likert scales that use statements with which respondents indicate their extent of agreement (strongly agree to strongly disagree). AIO statements can be classified in twofold fashion, as shown in Exhibit 11.20.

- *Individual* (personal) lifestyle statements concern the individual respondent. *Family* (household) lifestyle statements are useful in light of the importance of family/household purchase behavior.
- *General* (generic) lifestyle statements are about living life in general. *Product-specific* (marketplace) lifestyle statements deal with various aspects of an individual's or household's CB. Exhibit 11.20 gives some examples of each.

Naming Market Segments. Based on the data analysis, psychographic segments are then described with colorful labels such as Value Seekers, Voluntary Minimalists, Sophisticates, Friendlies, and Reassure-Mes. Brief portraits (descriptions) that capture the essence of each group's lifestyle are also provided. Every segment should be described using several dimensions from each column in Exhibit 11.19: sociodemographics, lifestyle, and behavior. For example, there is no denying that a "fifty-five-year-old NASCAR enthusiast/

six-pack/fishing-boat/rod'n reel/RV-drivin' fella" differs from a "fifty-five-year-old cruise-travel/white wine/sailboat/beach house dweller."

STANDARDIZED PSYCHOGRAPHIC RESEARCH SERVICES

Most firms obtain psychographic data from various syndicated research services or their advertising or media agency. Some of the best-known and most widely adopted syndicated research typologies include the Yankelovich MindBase, the List of Values (LOV), VALS2, and PRIZM.

The typical system segments the U.S. population into five to fifteen major segments, sometimes with finer breakdowns. Each group is given a descriptive label and a profile of the typical member. Using this psychographic data, marketers can identify the heavy, light, and nonusing segments for their product category and for their brand, and then they target their efforts appropriately.

VALS2™

The most popular standardized lifestyle research service is the **Values and Lifestyles 2 (VALS2™) System,** developed by SRI Consulting Business Intelligence (SRIC-BI). VALS2 is a psychographic tool that measures demographic, lifestyle, value, and attitude variables.

The VALS2 survey consists of thirty-five Likert lifestyle indicator statements, plus four demographic questions. Sample statements include: "I often crave excitement," "I would rather make something than buy it," "I consider myself an intellectual," "I must admit that I like to show off," and "I like to dress in the latest fashions." An individual's responses to these lifestyle statements are used to classify that person into one of eight groups or "VALS Types" as defined by two key variables: primary motivation and resources.

Details of the VALS2 system are available at "The VALs Segments" (http://www.strategicbusinessinsights .com/vals/ustypes.shtml).

VALS2 Dimensions. The first key dimension, **primary motivation**, determines what in particular about an individual or the world is the meaningful core governing that individual's activities. The following three primary motivations are very effective predictors of CB:

1. **Ideals-inspired consumers** are guided in their choices by abstract, idealized knowledge and principles, rather than by feelings, events, or desire for approval and opinions of others. They tend to be inner-directed.
2. **Achievement-inspired consumers** are heavily influenced by the actions, approval, and opinions of others. These outer-directed consumers look for products and services that demonstrate their success to peers.
3. **Self-expression-inspired consumers** are guided by a desire for social or physical activity, variety, and risk taking. They are typically high sensation seekers and the "movers and shakers" who buy products to influence the world around them.

The second key dimension underlying the VALS2 typology is **resources**—peoples' full range of psychological, physical, demographic, and material means and capacities to draw upon. These encompass socioeconomic factors such as education and income, as well as psychological constructs including self-confidence, health, eagerness to buy things, intelligence, and energy level. The resources dimension is arrayed on a continuum from "minimal" to "abundant."

VALS2 Types (Segments). Combining the primary motivation and resources dimensions, VALS2 defines eight psychographic segments. Exhibit 11.21 provides a thumbnail sketch profile of each VALS2 segment.

• **Innovators** are achievement-oriented with abundant resources. They are successful, sophisticated, active, "take-charge" people with high self-esteem. These individuals are interested in growth and seek to develop, explore, and express themselves in a variety of ways—sometimes guided by principle and sometimes by a desire to have an effect or make a change.

EXHIBIT 11.21   SRI Consulting's Values and Lifestyles (VALS2™) System

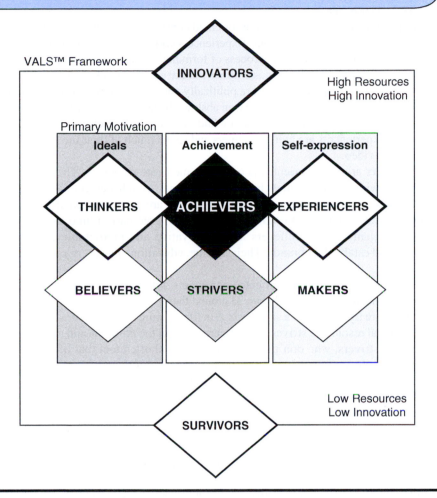

Image is important to Innovators, not as evidence of status or power, but as an expression of their taste, independence, and character. Innovators are among the established and emerging leaders in business and government, yet they continue to seek challenges.

Innovators have a wide range of interests, are concerned with social issues, and are open to change. Richness and diversity characterize these folks' lives. Possessions and recreation reflect a cultivated taste for the finer things in life.

• **Thinkers** are ideals-oriented people with high resources. They are mature, satisfied, comfortable, reflective people who value order, knowledge, and responsibility. Most are well educated and in (or recently retired from) professional occupations. These people are informed about world and national events and are alert to opportunities to broaden their knowledge. Content with career, family, and station in life, thinkers' leisure activities tend to center around the home.

Thinkers have a moderate respect for the status quo institutions of authority and social decorum but are open-minded to new ideas and social change. Decisions are based on firmly held principles and, consequently, thinkers appear calm and self-assured. While their incomes allow them many choices, thinkers are conservative, practical consumers, seeking durability, functionality, and value in the products they buy.

• **Achievers** are achievement-oriented people with high resources. Successful in their work life, they like to, and generally do, feel in control of their lives. They value consensus, predictability, and stability over risk, intimacy, and self-discovery. Achievers are deeply committed to work and family. Work provides a sense of duty, material rewards, and prestige. Their social lives reflect this focus and are structured around family, church, and career.

Achievers lead conventional lives, are politically conservative, and respect authority and the status quo. Image is important to them. They favor established, prestige products and services that demonstrate success to their peers.

• **Experiencers** are self-expression-oriented consumers with high resources. They are young, vital, enthusiastic, impulsive, and rebellious. Experiencers seek variety and excitement, and they savor the new, the offbeat, and the risky. Still in the process of formulating life values and patterns of behavior, they quickly become enthusiastic about new possibilities but are equally quick to cool.

At this stage in their lives, they are politically uncommitted, uninformed, and highly ambivalent about what to believe. Experiencers combine an abstract disdain for conformity with an outsider's awe of others' wealth, prestige, and power. Their energy finds an outlet in exercise, sports, outdoor recreation and social activities. Experiencers are avid consumers and spend much of their income on clothing, fast food, music, movies, and video.

• **Believers** are ideals-oriented people with moderate resources. They are conservative, conventional individuals with concrete beliefs based on traditional, established codes: family, church, community, and the nation. Many believers express moral codes that are deeply rooted and literally interpreted.

They follow established routines, organized in large part around their home, family, and social or religious organizations. Believers are conservative and predictable consumers, favoring American products and established brands. Their income, education, and energy are modest but sufficient to meet their needs.

• **Strivers** are achievement-oriented consumers with moderate resources. They seek motivation, self-definition, and approval from the world around them.

Strivers are trying to find a secure place in life. Unsure of themselves and low on economic, social, and psychological resources, strivers are concerned about the opinions and approval of others. Money defines success for strivers, who don't have enough of it and often feel that life has given them a raw deal.

These people are impulsive and easily bored. Many of them seek to be stylish. Strivers emulate those who own more impressive possessions, but what they wish to obtain is often beyond their reach.

• **Makers** are self-expression-oriented individuals with moderate resources. These practical people have constructive skills and value self-sufficiency.

Makers live within a traditional context of family, practical work, and physical recreation, having little interest in what lies outside that context. These individuals experience the world by working on it—building a house, raising children, fixing a car, or canning vegetables. Makers have enough skill, income, and energy to carry out their projects successfully.

Although politically conservative, suspicious of new ideas, and respectful of government authority and organized labor, Makers are resentful of government intrusion on individual rights. They are unimpressed by material possessions other than those with a practical or functional purpose, such as tools, utility vehicles, and fishing equipment.

• **Survivors** are achievement-oriented folks with minimal resources. Their lives are constricted. Chronically poor, ill-educated, low-skilled, without strong social bonds, elderly, and concerned about their health, survivors are often resigned and passive.

Because they are limited by the need to meet the urgent needs of the present moment, they do not show a strong self-orientation. These cautious consumers' chief concerns are security and safety. Survivors represent a very modest market for most products and services but are loyal to favorite brands.

PRIZM GEODEMOGRAPHIC ANALYSIS

The Nature of Geodemographic Segmentation. **Geodemographic segmentation (geodemography)** is a micromarketing system that combines data on geography, demography (primarily age, degree of urbanity, and socioeconomic data such as education, occupation, income, and household type), lifestyle, and buyer behavior (notably consumption and media usage data). This segmentation tool describes micro-regions, based on the notion that people of similar economic and cultural backgrounds tend to cluster together geographically—"Birds of a feather flock together." People live in bedroom communities, trailer parks, "hoods," "burbs," and so on. Those who live near one another are likely to have similar lifestyles, demographics, and CB. However, unlike VALS2, PRIZM does not measure values or attitudes.

EXHIBIT 11.22   The PRIZM Geodemographic System

Social Groups: Linking affluence factors and
urbanization to PRIZM

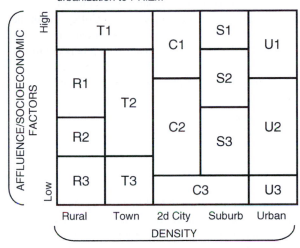

When these two concepts—Urbanization and Affluence—
are pushed through the PRIZM filter, some very distinct
and recognizable pools of people come into view.

Several syndicated research firms specialize in the ongoing collection and analysis of **geodemographic data**. This information marries geographic location, demographic/socioeconomic statistics, and lifestyle data to describe microregions.

The statistical technique for identifying groups of neighborhoods with households that are demographically similar is called **cluster analysis**. Each geographic cluster is comprised of similar consumers, consisting of one of a number of predetermined lifestyle groups with common demographic characteristics, lifestyles, values, and buyer behaviors.

Such data is most useful for efficient **micromarketing**, the geographic targeting of a community down to the zip code and neighborhood levels. It is primarily used by direct marketers, retailers, and local businesses, with the latter two also employing this information to pinpoint the best locations for their firms. Geodemographics is also often used to identify social class target markets since it is so rich in socioeconomic data. Some magazines, such as *Time* and *Newsweek*, sort their mailing lists by clusters so that an ad run by a national advertiser can be seen by specific neighborhoods. Different neighborhoods receive the same editorial matter, but the ads vary somewhat.

The Nature of the PRIZM System. One of the most popular geodemographic segmentation systems is the **PRIZM** system developed by Nielsen Claritas. PRIZM stands for Potential Rating Index by Zip Market. PRIZM has identified sixty-two major types of neighborhoods or clusters, which can be grouped into fifteen larger social groups based on degree of urbanization and socioeconomic status (see Exhibit 11.22).

Each of the more than 36,000 zip codes and 500,000-plus neighborhoods in the United States can be slotted into one of these cluster types. Marketers use PRIZM to identify which clusters perform at, above, or below average usage rates for their products and services.

The PRIZM Clusters. Clusters have descriptive labels ranging from the best-off Blue-Blood Estates to the least affluent Hard Scrabble. Exhibit 11.22 shows how the fifteen PRIZM social groups are derived from the two classification variables: urbanization and socioeconomic status. A record of the fifteen social groups, plus the sixty-two neighborhood cluster numbers, labels, and capsule descriptions can be found at PRIZM NE: The New Evolution Segment Snapshots, available at http://www.tetrad.com/pub/prices/PRIZMNE_Clusters.pdf.

PRIZM Cluster Differences. Dramatic disparities in consumption behavior have been found among clusters. For example, the author's institution, Stonehill College, is in the 02357 zip code, which is in PRIZM Cluster 3, Executive Suites. This cluster contains upscale, professional white-collar couples, age 45–64, with household income of $68,500. This cluster's members are most likely to belong to a health club, visit Japan/Asia, have an airline travel card, and read *Entrepreneur.*

On the other hand, people who reside in zip code 63763 in McGee, Missouri, are members of the Cluster 62, Hard Scrabble. Such families are in poor isolated areas, age 6–17 and 65+, blue-collar/farming/service jobs with household income of $18,100. CB patterns include entering sweepstakes, adding a bathroom, watching auto racing on TV, and reading *True Story.*

REVIEW QUESTIONS

1. What are the various research and market segmentation techniques that psychographic segmentation builds upon? What are the weaknesses of each of these other research and segmentation approaches, and how does psychographics overcome these?
2. What is lifestyle? Describe lifestyle research, including the nature of the questions and the market segments and profiles produced.
3. Discuss the nature of standardized psychographic research services in general and that of VALS2 in particular, including its dimensions and segments.
4. Explain the nature of geodemographic segmentation in general and of the PRIZM system in particular, including its dimensions and examples of PRIZM clusters.

IN-CLASS APPLICATIONS

1. Form groups of three to four students each. Your task is to identify, describe, and develop a product and marketing strategy for a psychographic segment. Create your own segment and choose a product category you know well (or make one up). Specifically, answer the following:
   a. Identify and briefly describe the portrait for a stereotypical psychographic person. Examples:
      - A rebellious, party-hearty, pleasure-seeking teenage girl.
      - A young adult who likes material simplicity and helping to "save the environment."
   b. Develop a psychographic group label that captures the essence of this segment. Examples:
      - Kerry Kool, Peggy Punky, Terri Teenybopper
      - Edie Ecology, Simple Simon, Nick Natural
   c. Describe the segment's demographic characteristics and sociological factors. Include several of the following: subculture(s), social class, reference groups, and family structure/family life cycle stage. Examples:
      - Kerry Kool—Age and gender: A just-turned-teenage girl. Subculture: Generation Y. Social class: Upper-middle class, lives in a well-to-do neighborhood in the suburbs. Reference groups: Other thirteen-year-old girls and the young teen boys they secretly admire and pursue. Family structure: Lives with nagging middle-aged parents and annoying younger brother.
      - Edie Ecology—Age and gender: A young (20s–30s) female. Subcultures: Generation X, urban living. Social class: Upper-middle class to upper class. Reference groups: Like-minded young adults who are into a totally "natural," "less-is-more," "small-is-beautiful" lifestyle. Family structure: Either single or married with at most one child.
   d. Discuss important psychological factors for segment members. Include one or more of the following: personality, personal values, and motivation.

Examples:

- Kerry Kool—Personality: Self-absorbed, showoff, moody, stubborn, and excitable. Personal values: Social recognition, pleasure, being in style, impressing others, and comfort. Motivation: "Girls just wanna have fun," social recognition, fitting in.
- Edie Ecology—Personality: Open-minded, politically liberal, straightforward, outspoken, and sincere. Personal values: Inner harmony, a world at peace, sense of accomplishment, self-respect. Motivation: Being true to self and others, doing one's part to keep the earth "green."

e. Psychographics/AIOs. Describe this person's lifestyle and any relevant activities, interests, and opinions.

Examples:

- Kerry Kool—Lifestyle: Thinks she is hot stuff and acts accordingly. Activities: Likes to go where the crowd is and "where the boys are," enjoys hanging at the mall with her friends, likes listening to the latest boy bands and pop music, lives for summer vacation when she can work on her tan at the beach with her girlfriends. Interests: The latest music, movies, and fashions. Opinions: Has a somewhat rebellious "attitude" toward parents, teachers, and other authority figures.
- Edie Ecology—Lifestyle: Lives a life of moral and spiritual growth by being concerned with ecological responsibility, self-sufficiency, and low consumption; prefers to lead a relatively simple life unencumbered by material possessions. Activities: Volunteers for various eco-logical groups that spend weekends helping to clean up state parks and natural habitats; does fundraising and "get-out-the-vote" drives for "green" politicians. Interests: The environment, outdoor pursuits such as gardening and hiking. Opinions: Believes everybody should recycle, despises litterbugs.

f. Discuss CB patterns for segment members. Describe several of the following: benefits sought, decision-making style, shopping behavior, product usage, media habits.

Examples:

- Kerry Kool—Benefits sought: Thrills, fun, excitement, pleasure, being "ahead of the curve," making friends jealous of what she has or does, annoying her parents. Decision-making style: Relies heavily on friends' advice and follows the bandwagon, impulsive, seeks variety and the Next Big Thing. Shopping behavior: Trolls the mall to find the latest music and fashions, hangs out for hours with her friends, does more "window shopping" than buying. Product usage: Consumes most things (food, entertainment, etc.) with her friends (not her parents), flashily displays her possessions where possible, is often wasteful and discards products that still have a "useful life."
- Edie Ecology—Benefits sought: Durability, economy, energy efficiency, peace of mind, tranquil-ity, harmony with nature, oneness with the universe, feeling good about the contributions she has made to society. Decision-making style: Cautious and deliberate, shops around to get the best deal. Shopping behavior: Carefully plans shopping trips, purchases at no-frills stores and flea markets, likes to bargain with sales clerks to get the most for her money, buys and consumes only what she needs, purchases smaller and fewer products. Product usage: A minimalist in all regards, holds onto products for as long as possible, consumes slowly and cautiously only on an as-needed basis, is into handcrafted items and do-it-yourself services.

g. Choose a product category for which you will develop positioning and promotional (message and media) strategies.

Examples:

- Kerry Kool—Product: A new fashion in tongue rings: "Totally Tongue," with diamond studs and gold plating. Positioning: For the antiestablishment gal who's going places. Message: "Tell them you're totally cool with Totally Tongue." Media: MTV, *Sassy, Cosmo GIRL!, Teen,* and *YM.*
- Edie Ecology—Product: Universal Springs, a water purification appliance that gets rid of all the nasty stuff in your city tap water and leaves you feeling healthier and more energetic. Position-ing: For healthy naturalists, makes your water as natural as spring water. Message: "Do your body a favor, keep your organs clean with natural, springlike water from Universal Springs." Media: *Mother Jones, New Republic,* National Public Radio, Public Broadcasting System.

2. Before class, based on the VALS2 segment descriptions, try to figure out what you believe are your primary and secondary VALS types. Describe in what ways you fit these VALS segments.

    Now, see if you were right! Visit VALS Survey at http://www.strategicbusinessinsights.com/vals/presurvey.shtml and take the survey (which takes about five to ten minutes). You will receive your primary and secondary VALS types within about five to ten seconds.

    Did you guess correctly? Click on each of your types to find out more about your VALS types. Are they accurate descriptions of your lifestyle? Of your CB? Also, try to guess what your instructor's primary and secondary VALS types might be and ways in which he or she seems to fit these VALS segments.

    Pick a product category of interest to those of your primary VALS type and describe how you would position and promote it to appeal to that group.

3. Visit and browse the Web pages for three radio stations of your choosing. Alternatively, your instructor might assign you three radio stations. You can locate radio stations by format and zip code at radio-locator (http://www.radio-locator.com/) or by station, country, and category at Radio Tower (http://www.radiotower.com/).

    Which VALS2 segment does each station seem to be targeting? Explain. Try to identify each market's secondary VALS type as well. (Listen to the music playing and any other programming, and/or to the commercials, if necessary.) Compare notes with your classmates.

4. Precision marketing company Nielsen Claritas confidently claims "You are where you live!" This firm has designed a lifestyle segmentation system that encompasses the entire United States. See how it works by visiting MyBestSegments.com at http://www.claritas.com/MyBestSegments/Default.jsp. Go to "zip code look up" and search your own zip code to find out about your town's lifestyle(s). Do you agree with how your town or city was categorized? Is it accurate or even fair to make assumptions about consumers based solely on where they live? What variables does PRIZM use in measuring and segmenting the population based on lifestyle?

    Choose any number/cluster you wish and make a list of products you would market to that group. Then, select one of those products and describe how you would position and promote it to appeal to members of that cluster.

5. Describe the AIOs (Activities, Interests, and Opinions) of consumers who watch each of the following television shows: *The Simpsons* (http://www.thesimpsons.com/index.html), *The Oprah Show* (http://www.oprah.com/index), and *Survivor* (http://www.cbs.com/primetime/survivor/). Are your AIO descriptions a form of stereotyping or are they simply market segmentation?

6. Marketers use lifestyles and AIOs to segment current markets, but what about future markets? Faith Popcorn is a futurist who claims to accurately predict CB trends. She bases these predictions on what she thinks future consumer lifestyles will be. Is this legitimate?

    Check it out on Ms. Popcorn's website at http://www.faithpopcorn.com/. Peruse her site to discover her ideas for the future. Are there any predictions you think probably will come true and any you think will not? Why or why not? How should marketers respond to Ms. Popcorn's predictions?

7. The background for this exercise listed some high school lifestyle segments. What are or could be the names of some the groups on your university campus? Describe the typical member of each segment. What types of advertising and selling appeals would be effective for each campus lifestyle group? In which segment do you fit, and which appeals effectively entice you?

Written Applications

1. Answer Questions 1 (individually, not in groups), 2, and 4 in the In-Class Applications.

2. Construct and administer your own psychographic questionnaire to learn more about particular target market users of a product of your choice. Use a sample of about twelve consumers you think live similar lifestyles. Be sure to include several AIO questions of the type shown in Exhibit 11.20. You should measure all three major groups of variables shown in Exhibit 11.19, and several of your questions should be specific to the product category.

    Tabulate and summarize your results. Then, come up with a descriptive label and brief portrait of your psychographic group. Finally, give several suggestions for marketing strategy to reach your targeted group for a product of your choosing.

KEY CONCEPTS

achievement-inspired consumers

Achievers

actual (real) self-image

AIOs

Believers

brand image (brand personality, brand character)

cluster analysis

cognitive style

consumer drawings (psychodrawings)

consumer innovativeness

consumer materialism

defense mechanisms

depth interviews (in-depth interviews, one-on-ones, extended interviews)

direct analogies and symbolic analogies

Doers (choleric)

dogmatism

ego

expected self-image

Experiencers

extended self

extroverts

fantasy solutions and future scenarios

Feelers

focus group interview (group depth interview)

geodemographic data

geodemographic segmentation (geodemography)

Hippocratic Temperament Survey

hypothetical constructs

id

ideal (desired) self-image

ideal social self-image

ideals-inspired consumers

image congruence hypothesis

indirect questions (disguised questions)

Influencers (sanguine)

inner-directed

Innovators (a VALS2 type)

introverts

Intuiters

Judgers

libido (eros, sex)

lifestyle

locus of control

Makers

micromarketing

moderator (interviewer)

motivation (motivational) research

Myers-Briggs Type Indicator Personality Inventory

need for cognition (NC)

objective (actual, real) self

optimal stimulation level

outer-directed (other-directed)

Perceivers

personal analogies

personality

personality inventory

personality traits

personification (anthropomorphism)

picture sorting

primary motivation

primary process thinking (fantasy)

PRIZM

projection

projective techniques

psychoanalytical theory of personality

psychographics (lifestyle, values) research

psychology

psychosocial (sociopsychological)

Relaters (phlegmatic)

reliability

repressed needs (latent motives)

resources (in VALS2)

role-playing

scientific method

self-expression-inspired consumers

self-image (self-concept)

semantic differential scale

Sensors

sentence completion

social character

social (public, others, looking glass, apparent) self-image

stimulus-organism-response (S-O-R) model (input-process [throughput]-output model)

storytelling

Strivers

superego

Survivors

symbolism

Thanatos (death wish, death instinct)

Thinkers (both a Myers-Briggs Indicator Personality Inventory type and a VALS2 type)

Thinkers (melancholy)

third-person (referent other) questioning

trait theory

validity

Values and Lifestyles 2 (VALS2™) System

Verbalizers

verbatims

Visualizers

word association

SUMMARY

Chapter 11 commenced Part IV's investigation of internal individual psychological influences on CB, which involve the consumer's internal world of personality and self-image, motivations, perceptions, learning, and attitudes. Regarding their external world, consumers have a sociocultural profile described in terms of external states-of-being variables. Psychologically, buyers are described via states-of-mind variables and states-of-action (behavioral) variables. Both categories provide specific variables on which to segment markets that can be combined into a psychological profile of targeted customers.

Psychology's influences on CB are investigated via the stimulus-organism-response model (see Exhibit P4.1). Inferences are made concerning what transpires within the psychological field regarding hypothetical constructs during consumer decision making. These inferences are based on observations of consumers' behavioral responses to the stimuli discovered through marketing research.

This chapter covered personality and lifestyle. Exercise 11.1 investigated Freud's psychoanalytical theory of personality. Freud suggested that personality and motivation are the result of interplay between the id, superego, and ego (see Exhibit 11.1). He also discussed several other unconscious mind elements: symbolism, libido, primary process thinking, and Thanatos. Freud also identified defense mechanisms such as identification, denial, projection, and rationalization, which were applied during the qualitative era in consumer research using motivational research. These were based on Freud's notion of latent, subconscious motives, and instincts that people are unable and/or unwilling to express.

The three principal methodologies used in motivational research are depth interviews, focus group interviews, and projective techniques, the latter based on projection. Each method is appropriate to particular types of situations, and each one has certain research advantages (e.g., collection of verbatims) and limitations (e.g, nonrepresentative samples).

The focus of Exercise 11.2 was how to build a brand image based on self-concept (self-image), which is of two types: the objective self and the self-image. The most useful types of self-image are actual self-image, ideal self-image, and expected self-image. Other types are social self-image and ideal social self-image.

To appeal to the consumer's self-image, marketers design a brand image, which is especially significant for conspicuous badge products, luxuries, value-expressive products, and parity products. Products meeting one or more of these criteria become part of the extended self.

The image congruence hypothesis suggests consumers should have more favorable attitudes and purchase intentions toward brands they believe are consistent with their self-image.

Brand image can be based on elements in the sociocultural environment (age, gender, culture, subculture, social class, social groups, family, and lifestyles). Brand image can also be founded upon marketing mix elements, notably brand name, packaging, retail distribution, price points, advertising, and event marketing.

Exercise 11.3 examined how to measure targeted consumers' personalities and a brand's image to ensure a match exists between them, as suggested by the image congruence hypothesis.

Consumer researchers sought to predict CB during the 1960s quantitative era in consumer personality research, relying on trait theory and measuring personality via personality inventories such as the Hippocratic Temperament Survey (see Exhibit 11.13). The four Hippocratic personality types are Doers, Influencers, Relaters, and Thinkers. Another personality inventory is the Myers-Briggs Type Indicator Personality Inventory, which describes peoples' cognitive styles. The four basic dimensions are: Extroverts versus Introverts, Sensors versus Intuiters, Thinkers versus Feelers, and Perceivers versus Judgers.

Some studies have been successful in their attempts to use personality traits to predict CB and thus to segment markets by personality type. But most studies have been less fruitful, typically finding that personality traits predict at most 10 percent of the variance in CB. A number of reasons for this lack of success have been outlined in this chapter.

Tailor-made inventories, which are usually single-trait inventories, are better to measure personality traits for marketing purposes rather than standardized personality inventories. These consumer-relevant personality traits include consumer innovativeness, dogmatism, social character (inner-directed versus other-directed), optimal stimulation level, need for cognition (NC), Visualizers versus Verbalizers, consumer materialism, and locus of control.

Marketers should use consumer research to ensure that the desired brand image has been built in buyers' minds via quantitative research employing surveys that contain semantic differential attitude scales or through qualitative research that uses Freudian projective techniques. The semantic differential scale is shown in Exhibit 11.14. Brand images and consumers' self-images can be measured using these scales to ensure a match between the two.

Qualitative research techniques using projective questioning are also popular for measuring brand personality when researchers believe respondents will not answer more straightforward semantic differential questions. Either an ambiguous, nonpersonal situation is created to which consumers are asked to respond, or else indirect, disguised questions are asked.

Projective methods that have been applied to brand image research include word association, sentence completion, third-person (referent-other) questioning, role playing, consumer drawings (psychodrawings), personification (anthropomorphism), direct analogies and symbolic analogies, personal analogies, fantasy solutions and future scenarios, picture sorting, and storytelling.

Lifestyle segmentation and its associated research—psychographics—were explored in Exercise 11.4. These blend several other major market segmentation bases and marketing research methodologies. Psychographics builds on and overcomes the limitations of demographic segmentation, motivational research techniques, and segmentation based on personality traits. All of these research and segmentation techniques are combined in a new psychosocial concept known as consumer lifestyles. Psychographics research captures consumer lifestyles in their activities, interests, and opinions (AIOs). Additionally, psychographics gathers demographic and behavioral data to paint a rich portrait of consumers.

Hence, psychographics goes beyond demographic states of being to include states of mind and states of action. Consequently, psychographics is superior to demographics, motivation research, and personality research because it combines the best elements of all. However, secondary psychographic information is not as readily and inexpensively available as is secondary demographic information, and it is more difficult to obtain primary psychographic data.

Psychographic research consists of large-scale surveys to get information on consumers' AIOs plus basic demographic and perhaps behavioral data. AIO items usually appear as five- or seven-point Likert items that can be classified in twofold fashion (see Exhibit 11.20): (1) general lifestyle statements versus product-specific statements and (2) individual lifestyle statements versus family lifestyle statements. Market segments are thereby described with colorful group labels, along with brief portraits that capture the essence of each group's lifestyle.

Most companies rely on one of several major syndicated research services that provide ongoing standardized psychographic typologies. The typical system breaks the U.S. population into about five to fifteen major segments, and each is given a descriptive label and a profile of the typical member. The most popular marketing application of lifestyle research is the Values and Lifestyles 2 (VALS2™) System, which classifies people into one of eight VALS Types as defined by two key variables: (1) primary motivation (ideals-inspired consumers, achievement-inspired consumers, and self-expression-inspired consumers) and (2) resources, arrayed on a continuum from "minimal" to "abundant."

Combining the primary motivation and resources dimensions, VALS2 defines eight psychographic segments (see Exhibit 12.17). Everyone who takes the VALS survey is assigned both a primary VALS type and a secondary VALS type from the eight groups: Innovators, Thinkers, Achievers, Experiencers, Believers, Strivers, Makers, and Survivors.

Geodemographic segmentation provides geodemographic data by combining information on geography, demography, lifestyle, and buyer behavior using cluster analysis. It describes microregions based on the notion that people of similar economic and cultural backgrounds tend to cluster together geographically and have similar lifestyles, demographics, and CB.

Such data is most useful for efficient micromarketing. A popular approach is Nielsen Claritas's PRIZM geodemographic system, using sixty-two major types of neighborhoods or clusters, which can be grouped into fifteen larger social groups based on degree of urbanization and socioeconomic status (see Exhibit 11.22). Marketers use PRIZM to identify which clusters perform at, above, or below average usage rates for their products and services. Clusters have descriptive labels from the most well-off Blue-Blood Estates to the least affluent Hard Scrabble (see http://www.tetrad.com/pub/prices/PRIZMNE_Clusters.pdf).

REFERENCES

Aaker, Jennifer L. (1997). "The Dimensions of Brand Personality." *Journal of Marketing Research,* 34, 3, 347–356.

Ahuvia, Aaron C. (2005). "Beyond the Extended Self: Loved Objects and Consumers' Identity Narratives." *Journal of Consumer Research,* 32, 1, 171–184.

Alpert, Louis, and Gatty, Ronald. (1969). "Product Positioning by Behavioral Life Styles." *Journal of Marketing,* 33, 2, 65–69.

Ataman, M. Berk, and Ulengin, Burc. (2003). "A Note on the Effect of Brand Image on Sales." *Journal of Product and Brand Management,* 12, 4, 237–250.

Belk, Russell W. (1988). "Possessions and the Extended Self." *Journal of Consumer Research,* 15, 2, 139–186.

———. (1989). "The Role of Possessions in Constructing and Maintaining a Sense of Past." In Thomas K. Srull, ed., *Advances in Consumer Research,* Vol. 16. Provo, UT: Association for Consumer Research, 669–678.

Bhargava, Rohit. (2008). *Personality Not Included: Why Companies Lose Their Authenticity and How Great Brands Get It Back.* New York: McGraw-Hill.

Birdwell, A.L.E. (1968). "A Study of Influence of Image Congruence on Consumer Choice." *Journal of Business,* 41, 1, 76–88.

Boote, Alfred S. (1980). "Psychographics: Mind Over Matter." *American Demographics,* April.

———. (1992). "What's in an Image?" *Journal of Product and Brand Management,* 1, 2, 54–60.

Brody, Robert P., and Cunningham, Scott M. (1968). "Personality Variables and the Consumer Decision Process." *Journal of Marketing Research,* 5, 1, 50–57.

Burnett, John J., and Bush, Alan J. (1986). "Profiling the Yuppies." *Journal of Advertising Research,* 26, 2, 27–35.

Dolich, Ira J. (1969). "Congruence Relationship Between Self-Image and Product Brands." *Journal of Marketing Research,* 6, 1, 80–84.

Durgee, Jeffrey F., and Stuart, Robert W. (1987). "Advertising Symbols and Brand Names That Best Represent Key Product Meanings." *Journal of Consumer Marketing,* 4, 3, 15–24.

Horton, Raymond L. (1973). "On the Appropriateness of Brand Loyalty and Brand Choice as Dependent Variables in Consumer Personality Studies." *Proceedings of the Southern Marketing Association,* 147–151.

———. (1979). "Some Relationships between Personality and Consumer Decision Making." *Journal of Marketing Research,* 16, 2, 233–246.

Kassarjian, Harold. (1971). "Personality and Consumer Behavior: A Review." *Journal of Marketing Research,* 8, 11, 409–418.

Kassarjian, Harold, and Sheffet, Mary Jane. (1975). "Personality and CB: One More Time." *Combined Proceedings of the American Marketing Association.* Chicago: American Marketing Association, 197–201.

Landon, E. Laird. (1974). "Self-Concept, Ideal Self-Concept, and Consumer Purchase Intentions." *Journal of Consumer Research,* 2, 2, 44–51.

Mizerski, Richard W., and Settle, Robert B. (1979). "The Influence of Social Character on Preference for Social Versus Objective Information in Advertising." *Journal of Marketing Research,* 26, 4, 552–558.

Onkvisit, Sak, and Shaw, John. (1987). "Self-Concept and Image Congruence: Some Research and Managerial Implications." *Journal of Consumer Marketing,* 4, 1, 13–23.

Peters, Tom. (1997). "The Brand Called You." *Fast Company,* December 18. http://www.fastcompany.com/magazine/10/brandyou.html.

Plummer, Joseph T. (1974). "The Concept and Application of Life Style Segmentation." *Journal of Marketing,* 38, 1, 33–37.

———. (1985). "How Personality Makes a Difference." *Journal of Advertising Research,* 24, 6, 27–31.

Raju, P.S. (1980). "Optimum Stimulation Level: Its Relationship to Personality, Demographics, and Exploratory Behavior." *Journal of Consumer Research,* 7, 3, 272–282.

Reisman, David. (1969). *The Lonely Crowd: A Study of the Changing American Character.* New Haven, CT: Yale University Press.

Sirgy, M. Joseph (1982). "Self-Concept in CB: A Critical Review." *Journal of Consumer Research,* 9, 287–300.

Soley, C., and Smith, Aaron Lee, eds. (2008). *Projective Techniques for Social Sciences and Business Research.* Milwaukee, WI: Southshore Press.

Steenkamp, Jan-Benedict E.M., and Baumgartner, Hans. (1992). "The Role of Optimum Stimulation Level in Exploratory CB." *Journal of Consumer Research,* 19, 3, 434–448.

Wells, William D. (1974). *Life Style and Psychographics.* Chicago: American Marketing Association.

———. (1975). "Psychographics: A Critical Review." *Journal of Marketing Research,* 12 (May): 196–213.

Wells, William D., and Beard, Arthur D. (1973). "Personality and CB." In Scott Ward and Thomas S. Robertson, eds., *CB: Theoretical Sources.* Englewood Cliffs, NJ: Prentice-Hall, 141–199.

Wells, William D., and Tigert, Douglas J. (1971). "Activities, Interests, and Opinions." *Journal of Advertising Research,* 11, 4, 27–36.

Wright, Newell D., Claiborne, C.B., and Sigy, M. Joseph. (1992). "The Effects of Product Symbolism on Consumer Self-Concept." In John F. Sherry, Jr., and Brian Sternthal, eds., *Advances in Consumer Research,* Vol. 19. Provo, UT: Association for Consumer Research, 311–318.

Motivation is the most fundamental of all of the psychological influences on consumer behavior since it seeks to answer the most basic question about the human condition: "Why do people do the things they do?" For the marketing manager, this question translates to "Why do consumers buy and consume the products that they do in the way that they do?" Rooted in *personal values*, motivation is the "why" behind the buy. Motivation is an important psychological determinant of lifestyle (see Exhibit 11.19) as well as of perception, which is investigated in Chapter 13.

MOTIVATION DEFINED

Motivation is an activated internal need state leading to goal-directed behavior to satisfy that need. Accordingly, **motives** can be defined as relatively enduring, strong, and persistent internal stimuli that arouse and direct behavior toward certain goals. The terms "motive," "need," and "drive" are often used synonymously.

In a marketing context, motivation is the internal drive that influences consumers to seek out, evaluate, and purchase goods and services. Such "reasons why" people make purchases include health, popularity, security, freedom, and comfort. To effectively develop products and communicate their benefits to customers, marketers must hit these hot buttons and stroke these responsive chords. Motives provide the hook upon which to hang the sale. Axe deodorant knows what goal young men seek from deodorant: to get an edge in the mating game. Effective marketing is all about hitting the consumer's so-called sweet spot.

In the **motivational process,** internal forces move people from an actual or existing state of being toward a desired or ideal state (see Exhibit 12.1).

KEY ASPECTS OF MOTIVATION

The following are important facts about motivation suggested by the definitions of motivation and the motivational process diagram.

1. *Motivation is an internal state.* Like all psychological hypothetical constructs, motivation is an internal state, hidden from our direct observation. Hence, it is incorrect to say that friends are a motive; rather, they are a goal. The internal motive satisfied by friends is the need for companionship. Likewise, a sports car is not a motive. Instead, it satisfies motives such as feeling popular or secure (or in a hurry to get places!).

As for all psychological intervening variables, the nature of motivation can be inferred from survey research or observing behavior in the context of environmental stimuli. Watching someone work hard for money (a goal), we might conclude that person has a need for attaining financial security, feeling successful, being comfortable, and so on.

2. *Motivation endures.* These relatively enduring motives are the long-term reasons why people behave and buy. Motives known as *innate needs* are present at birth and last until death, while *acquired needs* are learned later in life and then persist. Innate versus acquired needs will be further discussed in Exercise 12.1.

3. *Motivation underlies needs and wants as well as problem recognition.* Long-term motives underlie short-term needs and wants as well as unsolved problems. Recall that in the problem recognition stage in the consumer decision process there is a gap between an individual's short-term actual state of affairs and that person's long-term desired state of being (signified by the goal or need fulfillment; see Exhibit 12.1).

Both long-term motivation and short-term problem recognition help answer the fundamental question,

EXHIBIT 12.1   Model of the Motivation Process

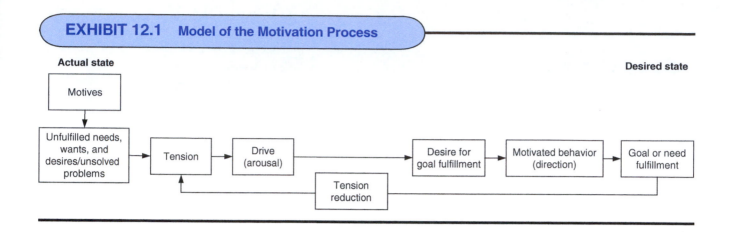

"Why do consumers buy?" Problem recognition arises when long-term motives are not being fulfilled. For example, a consumer's motives for purchasing a home might be shelter and security. As this person is commuting to work one day, he or she could suddenly realize that the iron might still be on at home. This creates a short-term problem that is rooted in the motives of security and having shelter. Thus viewed, motives are forces or drives that move people from an actual state to a desired state of existence.

4. *Unsatisfied needs and wants create tension, causing consumers to be driven.* A state of tension is created by unsatisfied desires (the gulf between the actual and desired states). This tension results in a **drive**, an activated need, aroused energy state, or degree of internal tension that causes the consumer to attempt to reduce or eliminate the need.

This internal drive creates a desire to achieve a goal that will fulfill the need, thereby reducing the drive. For a consumer, the desire would be for a product, service, or experience that satisfies unfulfilled consumption needs. The commuting woman worrying about her house burning because she fears she left the iron on might wish she had purchased an iron that shuts off automatically.

5. *Very driven consumers have high motivational strength and are highly involved.* The magnitude of the tension and the size of the gap between the actual and desired states determine the urgency of satisfying the need. The level of urgency is known as **motivational strength**—the degree to which a person is willing to expend energy to achieve the goal.

Motivational strength relates to *involvement*, which is based on a person's needs, values, and interests. **Involvement** can be considered as the psychological outcome of motivation, resulting in interest in searching for and processing buying information and otherwise exerting effort to acquire the product. For any given product there are individual differences in motivational strength and, hence, in degree of involvement in purchasing. For example, the need for sex is very strong in some people and much weaker in others, meaning that a sex appeal approach to selling might work for some consumers but not others.

6. *Driven consumers engage in motivated behavior.* If there is sufficient motivational strength, the drive and desire induce **motivated behavior**, meaning taking part in activities to satisfy needs and wants. The word *motivation* derives from the Latin *movere*, which means "to move." Therefore, motivation is a force that moves consumers from an actual to a desired state of existence. Unsatisfied motives have **motivational direction**. They direct people's actions toward a particular goal used to reduce the motivational tension and satisfy a desire.

7. *Motivation seeks goals (need) fulfillment.* **Goals (need fulfillment)** are the objects, activities, or conditions toward which motivated behavior is directed, that is, goals are the desired states of affairs. Once the goal is achieved, tension is reduced, motivation dissipates for the time being, and the marketer has a satisfied customer.

For consumers, the goal object is the product that satisfies their desires and solves their consumption-related problems. However, the ultimate goal is not just the product; it is the satisfactions of using the product—consumer benefits! Consumers do not just purchase products; they buy need satisfiers or problem solutions. People buy an unclogged drain, not a can of Drano; fresh breath, not Dentyne gum. But, again, underlying all of these short-term benefits are the long-run motivations. So, a desire for fresh-smelling breath might be motivated by a need for health, for friends, or perhaps both, or even something else.

For consumers, there are two types of goals: generic and product specific.

Generic goals are the general product categories that consumers see as satisfying their desires. For example, if someone wants a snack, generic goals could be chips, fruit, or ice cream. The following types of marketers would want to promote generic goals, that is, to build **generic (primary) demand** for the product category:

- *Industry trade associations.* Examples: "Got milk?"; "Wine, since 6000 B.C."
- *Market leaders* who stand the most to gain from increased product class consumption coming from light users, lapsed buyers, and nonusers. Kellogg's suggests, "Cereal. Eat it for life." Microsoft might want to promote PC ownership among laggards who have not yet purchased a home computer.
- *New product marketers.* Sony touted the advantages of personal stereos when launching the Walkman so that the brand name became synonymous in the consumer's mind with the product name; people referred to a "Walkman," not a "personal portable stereo."

Product-specific goals. These are branded products that consumers seek to fulfill their needs. Most marketers work to build **selective (secondary) demand**, or demand for their specific branded product. Such a brand seller is Kellogg's, encouraging us to buy Rice Krispies because it goes, "Snap, crackle, pop."

8. *Goals have valence.* Goals and their underlying motives have **valence (direction)**, meaning they can be either positive or negative. Positive motives are referred to as needs, wants, or desires. Positively valenced **approach objects** are the ideal (desired) state consumers seek, such as achievement, affiliation, or prestige. The **approach goal** is the customer's desire to achieve the approach object because it either satisfies functional needs and wants or fulfills hedonic desires for pleasure. Most products are marketed as approach objects, such as attractiveness-enhancing goods like nice clothing, good-looking jewelry, and colorful cosmetics.

On the other hand, negative motives are called negative drives, fears, or aversions. The consumer wishes to overcome an **avoidance object**. This is a consumer problem to be solved or a negative state of existence, such as social disapproval, anxiety, or discomfort. Consumers wish to stay away from or get rid of avoidance objects such as a runny nose or a flaky scalp. Consumers' **avoidance goal** is their objective to avoid this bothersome object. We want the avoidance goals of freedom from graying hair, a balding head, pimples, sweaty armpits, and other unpleasant personal conditions. Marketers can develop products that remove or help alleviate the avoidance object, such as deodorants, pain relievers, and mouthwash.

Exercise 12.2 illustrates that conflicting approach and/or avoidance goals can sometimes lead to an undesirable state known as motivational conflict.

9. *There are two types of relationships between motives, motivated behavior, and goals.* Since motivation is an unobservable construct, we must always be careful when making inferences about the nature of consumer motivation in a given situation. This is best explained by noting the relationship between motives, motivated behavior, and goals, as summarized in Exhibit 12.2. Two relationships are noteworthy here.

First, a given motivated behavior (e.g., purchase of a product) could be seeking one or more possible goals, each pursued because of a different relevant motive (see Exhibit 12.2, Part A). For example, suppose a person reads a book (motivated behavior). This could be to alleviate boredom, to relax, to learn and grow intellectually, to escape, to pass a test, or to get to sleep (the goals). Or, consider the reasons why someone might eat a sandwich: hunger, boredom, nervousness, sociability, or simply because it is time to eat. The implication is that using observational research (watching consumers in action) to infer motives is highly tenuous. (Remember what your parents taught you: "Don't judge people's motives.")

Second, a given motive leading to pursuit of a goal could result in many different behaviors to achieve that goal (see Exhibit 12.2, Part B). For example, in order to alleviate hunger (goal), someone could seek bean sprouts or baked beans; might procure baked ham or hamburger; and could settle in for a home-cooked meal, grab some quick takeout fare, go to a restaurant, or even mooch a meal at a friend's house (behaviors). Or, consider that the need for socialization could be met by getting together with a friend, talking with a pal on the phone, instant messaging a buddy, visiting a social networking site, joining a social club, or taking an evening course. This has important implications for defining one's competition, that is, the competitive set. It suggests that different goal objects could represent indirect (secondary) competitors for one another, even though they might not compete head-to-head as direct (primary) competitors. This is because they nonetheless satisfy the same needs and wants.

EXHIBIT 12.2   The Relationship Between Motives, Behavior, and Goals

A. Behavior Caused by Multiple Motives and Goals

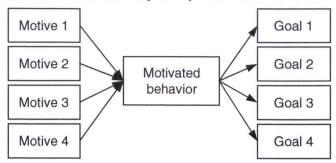

B. Multiple Behaviors Caused by a Single Motive and Goal

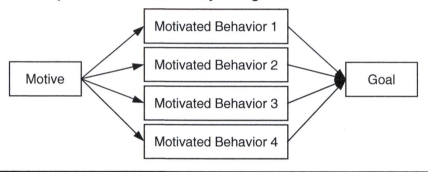

For instance, beer marketers were concerned with besting each other as direct competitors, and so Miller went head-to-head with the likes of Budweiser and Molson. However, when the beer industry lost ground to wine and spirits, the emphasis shifted somewhat to building primary demand for beer against indirect competitors, such as promotion of the U.S. Beer Drinking Team by the beer industry. Concern is for "share of throat," which includes other thirst-quenchers such as soft drinks, tea, and bottled water, as well as competitive beer brands.

New products can become competitive threats if they appeal to the same motives as existing products. The mechanical adding machine made the abacus obsolete, and the automobile replaced the horse-and-buggy carriage. YouTube is taking over for videos, Skype Internet phone service for landline long distance, and Wikipedia for traditional encyclopedias. Marketers must avoid **competitor myopia**, defining the competitive set too narrowly, thereby leaving the product vulnerable to new, unexpected indirect competition.

CLASSIFYING NEEDS AND WANTS

Consumer needs and wants can be categorized as innate versus acquired needs, utilitarian versus hedonic needs, or as defined by McClelland's trichotomy (trio) of social needs.

INNATE VERSUS ACQUIRED NEEDS

Innate (physiological, primary, biogenic) needs are biological and inborn. Sometimes simply called *needs,* they include requirements for survival, such as food, water, shelter, sleep, oxygen, relief from pain, waste elimination, a relatively constant body temperature, and sexual release. People learn **acquired (psychological, secondary, psychogenic) needs** in response to their culture (reflecting its priorities) or environment (reflecting its demands). Sometimes termed *wants,* desires such as self-esteem, power, affection, individualism, and pride are primarily psychosocial in nature and are of secondary importance to the more basic biological needs.

For marketers, wants are sometimes considered as the particular form of consumption capable of satisfying an underlying need. Thirst is a need and Coke is a want; shelter is a need and a four-bedroom colonial house is a want. The same product can satisfy both innate and acquired needs. For example, a meal could be served to provide physiological sustenance as well as to impress guests with the chef's gourmet skills, thereby bolstering self-esteem. Generally, people are more aware of their physiological than their psychological needs. Since some of the latter operate at a subconscious level, motivation research might be necessary to discover them.

Utilitarian Versus Hedonic Needs

Recall that **utilitarian (functional, instrumental) needs** entail a desire to achieve some practical (utilitarian) or functional benefit; that is, the product is instrumental in getting the job done. Vegetables might be eaten for their nutritional value or blue jeans worn because they are durable.

Utilitarian needs suggest that consumers focus on objective, tangible, measurable "rational" product criteria such as quality, reliability, workmanship, and ingredients. These relate to the rational motives to be discussed in Exercise 12.1.

Hedonic (experiential, transformational) needs involve desires for pleasure (hedonic), new experiences (experiential), or emotional satisfaction. They are abstract, symbolic, sensory, and aesthetic needs.

Buyers driven by hedonic needs focus on product criteria that are subjective, intangible, and nonrational, such as excitement, self-confidence, status, fun, and fantasy. Often, hedonic needs help express a person's self-concept. For example, Calvin Klein cologne might make one feel sensual or romantic. The brand image transforms the experience of buying and using the product (transformational needs). Hedonic needs are associated with emotional motives, also discussed in Exercise 12.1.

Of course, a product could simultaneously satisfy both utilitarian and hedonic needs. For example, most food products are consumed to provide nutrition and also pleasure.

McClelland's Acquired Needs

A popular classification of social motives is found in David **McClelland's trichotomy (trio) of social needs**. He identified three acquired needs that inform social dynamics between individuals, groups, and even entire nation-state societies:

- *Affiliation*—The need to associate with others for friendship, acceptance, and belonging.
- *Achievement*—The need to accomplish personal goals, improve performance, and succeed.
- *Power*—The need for control over resources, the environment, and others.

Marketing Applications of Motivational Concepts

The following suggestions follow from the previous discussion.

1. *Discover dominant buying motives.* Marketers must know what motivational forces underlie a product's purchase to develop products (goals) that fulfill those motives and to promote products by speaking to the buyer in terms of benefits that will satisfy the motives.

So what are the major motives underlying CB? There is no standard list. Instead, there are many widely known classification schemes for motives because there are many ways to conceptualize and research motivation.

2. *Use motivational research to uncover hidden consumer motives.* Unfortunately, whether we are examining private behavior, social behavior, or market behavior, one of the most difficult questions for a person to answer on a survey is "Why?" especially in the case of psychological needs. This is because many psychological needs are **latent (subconscious, covert) needs (problems)**, which are unknown by the person and therefore unable to be expressed. Easier for consumers to discuss are **manifest (expressed, overt) needs**, those psychological needs respondents are conscious of and will freely discuss.

A standard marketing research survey would be unlikely to reveal latent motives because people are unaware of them or, if they are aware, they will not admit to them. In such cases, we must rely on motivation research methods such as depth interviews and projective techniques.

3. *Use survey research to discover consumer goals.* It might be easier for survey researchers to ask consumers about their tangible goals rather than their intangible motives, which they are less aware of. Instead of asking someone why she purchased a particular book (vague response: "It looked interesting"), a researcher could inquire as to what the buyer expects to gain from reading it (specific goal-oriented responses: "It looked like a book I could relax with," or "I thought it would help me better understand my husband"). From these goals the researcher can infer the underlying motives. If our consumer wanted relaxation, her motive was probably stress reduction. If her objective was to be in better touch with her husband, the underlying motive could have been tranquility and security within the home.

4. *Use motives to segment markets.* Motivation, like many other psychological variables, can serve as a market segmentation basis. For example, kids might choose a breakfast cereal such as Wheaties for perceived athletic prowess or to express adulthood, while grownups might select it for energy or good health. Benefit segmentation is a popular form of motivational segmentation (see Exercise 2.3).

5. *Use promotional appeals based on consumer motivation.* To illustrate the application of motivation for promotional messages, here are some classic advertising slogans, followed by the motives they apparently appealed to:

- Listerine—"Even your best friends won't tell you." (social fear of offending, self-confidence)
- United Airlines—"Fly the friendly skies." (affiliation, safety, comfort)
- Liberty Bonds (during World War II)—"Buy till it hurts." (patriotism, guilt, self-sacrifice)
- Wisk detergent—"Ring around the collar!" (cleanliness, beauty)
- Hallmark cards—"When you care enough to send the very best." (love, friendship)

ORGANIZATION OF CHAPTER 12

The exercises that follow look more closely at three areas of motivation that have received widespread attention from marketers. Exercise 12.1 revisits the idea of functional needs and hedonic needs in the classic distinction between rational and emotional motives. Exercise 12.2 shows how motivational valence (motivational direction) can give rise to motivational conflict. Finally, Exercise 12.3 investigates the most widely applied classification system of motives in both management and marketing: Maslow's Hierarchy of Needs.

EXERCISE 12.1. RATIONAL AND EMOTIONAL MOTIVES

OBJECTIVES

1. To recognize the use of rational and emotional appeals in advertising and where each approach is most effective.
2. To understand the appropriate use of popular emotional advertising appeals such as fear, humor, and sex.
3. To recognize McClelland's social motives of affiliation, achievement, and power in marketing situations.
4. To form an opinion on the controversial issue of advertising to children.

BACKGROUND

THE NATURE OF RATIONAL AND EMOTIONAL APPEALS

RATIONAL (COGNITIVE) APPEALS

One of the most general ways to categorize motives is as rational and emotional motives. These motives underlie a marketing communication's **motivational appeal**—the nature of the driving force used to convey the advertiser's or salesperson's message. This **message (theme, selling premise, selling appeal)** is the major point about the brand communicated to the target audience. For example, for over a century, advertising has proclaimed that Ivory soap is gentle, mild, and pure.

As far back as 1924 in his classic *Principles of Merchandising,* Melvin Copeland observed that both rational and emotional motives stimulate consumers. **Rationality** entails reason, thought, logic, and physical control. Economic rationality suggests that consumers carefully consider and evaluate all alternatives on the important buying criteria and choose those they expect will give them the greatest satisfaction for the money they spend.

Rational (cognitive) appeals, then, are communication messages directed toward the message receiver's logic and self-interest, emphasizing hard facts, presenting reasoned arguments to buy, and focusing on informational needs. The appeal is *cognitive*—to the head or intellect. The sales pitch is heavily factual and information intensive, describing product features and benefits, functions and uses, claims about product performance, and other objective information about tangible product attributes such as value, performance, size, weight, ingredients, efficiency in operation, and dependability in use.

The rational appeal is directed toward utilitarian (instrumental) needs; that is, the product maximizes the consumer's satisfaction, performs a useful (utilitarian) function, and is instrumental in meeting the buyer's needs or in achieving her goals. The product's purpose is to either satisfy basic needs and wants or remove or avoid a problem.

Generally, rationality prevails for high-involvement "considered" purchases with real physical brand differentiation, such as appliances, tools, furniture, consumer electronics, and medicine. Print media and online media allowing shoppers to drill down deep are most heavily used, as they allow for detailed, informative copy and can be reread and studied, if necessary.

EMOTIONAL (AFFECTIVE) APPEALS

Emotional (affective) appeals are communication messages directed toward the consumer's *affect*—feelings of like or dislike. **Emotions** are feelings that are not physically controllable, such as fun, excitement, pride, affection, social enhancement, sensory pleasure, and vanity.

The emotional appeal aims at the heart and concentrates on subjective, intangible, unverifiable product criteria (difficult to objectively measure and, hence, subjectively evaluated). Such emotionally based personal criteria include status, expression of artistic taste, satisfaction of the appetite, securing personal comfort, pleasure of recreation, and warm memories.

Emotional appeals work to establish a bond or relationship between the customer and product. Angel Soft toilet paper bonded with consumers through a series of TV commercials called "Bathroom Moments": a little boy peeing on the floor, a family holding a funeral and flushing their goldfish, and a woman gingerly approaching the moment of truth on her bathroom scale. In these spots, consumers connected to experiences they could relate to.

This information is best communicated symbolically via pictures and aurally through means such as music and tone of voice. Hence, emotions are best expressed through sight, sound, and motion, suggesting that they lend themselves especially to TV and radio commercials, Internet video, and outdoor media, none of which are copy intensive.

Emotional appeals are to hedonic, experiential, transformational, or value-expressive needs. The chosen product typically provides pleasure (hedonic needs); creates feelings or experiences or provides stimulation (experiential needs); transforms the experience of buying and using the brand by associating it with a particular emotional experience, such as romance or an exciting sports event (transformational needs); provides social or aesthetic utility; or tells others about the user's self-image (value-expressive needs). Emotional purchases seldom entail real physical brand distinctions but, rather, psychological differences "induced" by advertising. For years Betty Crocker has implored buyers to "Bake someone happy," as almost sinfully sensual "beauty shots" of a home-baked tray of golden-brown muffins are displayed, promoting the product in a relaxing, enjoyable manner—persuading by suggestion rather than arguments. Ad agency Saatchi & Saatchi recently popularized this approach in their Lovemarks philosophy: create emotional connections between consumers and brands that become lasting, loving relationships.

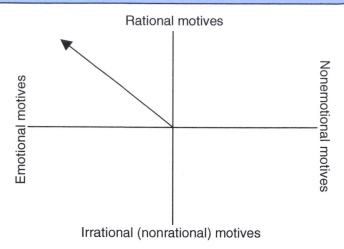

> **EXHIBIT 12.3   Fallacy of the Rational-Emotional Motives Dichotomy**

Note: The axes in Exhibit 12.3 are orthogonal—statistically independent—suggesting two different but possibly simultaneously existing motives. The axes are not two mutually exclusive ends of a continuum of motivation.

ATTITUDE-BASED VERSUS ATTRIBUTE-BASED EMOTIONAL CHOICES

Emotional advertising usually appeals to consumers making an *attitude-based (affective, hedonic) choice*, founded on feelings and global impressions, not specific attributes. However, emotional advertising can also include emotional benefits resulting from product use. Advertising featuring emotional benefits appeals to buyers making *attribute-based choices*, which are decisions founded in this case on specific emotional attributes.

RATIONAL AND EMOTIONAL APPEALS CAN BE USED SEPARATELY OR TOGETHER

Contrary to popular misconception, subjective or emotional criteria are not irrational! This is because **irrationality (nonrationality)** implies a failure to maximize utility or to shop wisely. However, it seems reasonable to assume that consumers almost always select alternatives that, in their estimation, maximize their satisfaction. In fact, a rational choice might very well include emotional criteria. For example, a brand could be selected on the basis of its promise to enhance the user's sex appeal. If this boosts the consumer's confidence, this is a perfectly rational purchase. What might appear to be irrational to an outside observer could nonetheless be rational in the buyer's own mind.

Thus, both rational and emotional motives can underlie a given purchase. As shown in Exhibit 12.3, the opposite of rational is not emotional but irrational. The opposite of emotional is not rational but rather nonemotional (i.e., lacking feelings). The arrow in Exhibit 12.3 suggests that in many cases an appeal that is both highly rational and emotional might work best. So, a fear appeal could speak to the emotion of fright while giving people solid reasons to be scared. The MasterCard "Priceless" ad campaign doesn't strictly focus on the things you can purchase with their credit card but also on the emotional benefits the credit allows users to experience, such as the quality time shared by a father and son at a baseball game.

Hence, an ad or sales pitch can include both a rational appeal and an emotional appeal. An old advertising adage says, "People buy emotionally and then justify their purchase with rational 'reasons why.'" Effective ads capture both the hearts and minds of their target audience, hitting both intellectual and emotional buttons. Phone companies' TV spots show emotion-laden shots of loved ones in long-distance communication but also include rational appeals of low price and quality transmission.

PARTICULAR EMOTIONAL APPEALS

A POTPOURRI OF EMOTIONAL APPEALS

While rational appeals are fairly straightforward presentations of information, emotional appeals are more complex. Earlier in the book we discussed guilt appeals, shame appeals, moral appeals, and fantasy appeals. The following are other types of popular emotional appeals.

- *Human interest appeals.* These play upon our interest in people. Examples are ads featuring reunions of long-lost loved ones or children adopting a puppy from the local dog pound.
- *Agony appeals.* Such ads feature people suffering pain that the product can alleviate, such as heartburn after overindulging. (Alka Seltzer to the rescue!)
- *Sensual appeals.* Sensory enjoyment is the focus here. "Do not lick this page," kidded a classic ad for LifeSavers featuring oversized pictures of the candy.
- *Nostalgia appeals.* Through old-time imagery and music, the ad associates the brand with the "good old days," bringing back warm, pleasant memories of yesteryear.
- *Bandwagon appeals.* The message here is, "Follow the crowd," "Do what is popular," or "Don't be the last on your block to buy this fabulous item."

THREE POPULAR EMOTIONAL APPEALS

The following three common emotional appeals play on very strong emotions.

1. Fear Appeals. **Fear (threat, problem-avoidance) appeals** create worry by emphasizing the negative outcomes that could arise if the consumer does not buy the product or take the recommended course of action. Two types of fear can be appealed to in promotional messages: (1) *physical fear,* such as loss of life or limb, and (2) *social fear,* such as losing the respect of friends or neighbors due to such social maladies as yellow teeth or cellulite.

2. Humor Appeals. The **humor appeal** is a promotional appeal relying on *incongruity*—deviation from expectations—and resolution of that incongruity. The result is surprise, such as when a toddler giggles when you play "Peek-a-boo."

Humor has many advantages. It grabs attention and awareness, is memorable, associates the product with positive emotions, can get past a person's conscious defenses, inhibits the receiver from *counterarguing*—thinking of reasons to disagree with the message—thereby increasing persuasion, and distracts people, causing them to put down their guard. Also, people are more receptive to ideas when laughing.

However, humor has potential problems. It might hinder comprehension of the selling message (unless that message is very simple); it must be compatible with the target audience's sense of humor (what one person finds funny another finds offensive and a third person is left clueless); and it can interfere with persuasion and recall (people remember the joke but not the brand). Therefore, humor works best when it relates to the product rather than being a source of borrowed interest.

To effectively deploy humor, it should be harmonious with the product, that is, it is best used with fun and pleasurable products such as soda and entertainment venues but not with serious items such as funeral or hospital services. Humor should be subtle since subdued humor is less likely to rapidly wear out than belly laugh, wet-your-pants, laugh-out-loud humor. It is most effective on radio and TV, but often falls flat in print media. And humor should never make fun of either the product or the consumer.

3. Sex Appeals. The **sex appeal** is a selling appeal based on sexual imagery. Since sex is such a powerful human motive, the steamy stuff does get awareness of, interest in, and favorable attitudes toward the ad.

Conventional wisdom says, "Sex sells." However, as with humor, sex can overpower the message (especially when the message is complex) and fail to register the brand in the buyer's mind because the visual elements in such ads detract from the verbal content.

And, as with humor, sex is most effective when it pertains to the product, such as goods associated with romance or pleasure. Sex probably sells perfume, lingerie, and jewelry but not mortgage financing or mortuary services. Also, as with humor, sex can offend people who view it negatively (as sexist, demeaning, or vulgar).

Finally, there are social responsibility issues related to appealing to promiscuity; sexy ads might fan the flames of young lust. An ethical issue is that too often women (and increasingly men) are degraded and treated as sex objects.

REVIEW QUESTIONS

1. Explain the distinction between rational appeals and emotional appeals, and explain for which kinds of products each is most effective.
2. Why is it wrong to believe that emotional appeals are irrational? Explain how it is possible to simultaneously use a rational appeal and an emotional appeal.
3. Describe the nature of fear appeals, humor appeals, and sex appeals, citing examples of each from ads you have seen. What are the advantages and disadvantages and potential problems of each? For what kinds of products is each most effective? What other types of emotional appeals can be used besides these three?

IN-CLASS APPLICATIONS

1. For each of the following advertisements (Exhibits 12.4–12.8), which motive(s) does the ad appeal to? Is it an innate need or an acquired need? Is the appeal to this motive being made effectively?
2. For each ad, identify which type(s) of motive is being appealed to: rational (utilitarian needs); emotional (hedonic needs); or both. Is this an effective approach for the product's target market?

   If an emotional appeal is used, which type of appeal (fear, humor, sex, human interest, etc.) is employed? Is the appeal being used in an effective and appropriate manner?

   Is each emotional appeal attitude-based or attribute-based? Is this an effective approach, given the consumer's likely decision-making style?
3. Advertising to children has received a lot of attention as an unethical marketing strategy. What is your viewpoint on this? Are children capable of identifying rational uses for a product despite their emotional motives? Should unhealthy snack foods be marketed to kids using emotional appeals like fun and sensory enjoyment?

   Take a look at the following Web sites to assist your perspective on this issue: Nesquik at www.nesquik.com, McDonald's at www.mcdonalds.com, and Kellogg's at www2.kelloggs.com. You can also try locating other kid-targeted sites.
4. For each of the following scenarios, identify which of McClelland's need(s) is applied.
   → *Scenario A. See Cindy's Noticeable Necklace.* Cindy was browsing through Perfectionist Plus department store when she came across a beautiful pearl necklace. Since she just got a promotion at work, she decided to buy it! The next day she made sure all of her coworkers noticed her necklace, signifying what wonderful work she did.
   → *Scenario B. Sara Is Sold a Cell Plan.* Sara really likes to keep in touch with her friends and family, but she recently moved out of state where long distance calls get expensive. She was searching on line when a pop-up ad for a cell phone plan came up. The ad claimed they had the lowest rate for unlimited long-distance minutes. Sara was hooked and ordered it right away.
   → *Scenario C. Hot Rod Rob.* Rob is a sports car fanatic! He always needs the latest and greatest model and the fastest on the road. While zipping down the highway one day, Rob spotted a billboard for Mercedes' new roadster, the Bullet. He drove right to the dealership and made a trade. Now he will show everyone who is king of the speedway!
   → *Scenario D. Summa Cum Laude or Bust.* Anita is a stickler about her grades! Every times she gets a paper or an exam back, she calculates her updated GPA. She must, must, must graduate summa cum laude and get into her number one choice of graduate school. If she doesn't, she will feel she has failed as a student.

EXHIBIT 12.4 The Shops at Prudential Center Ad

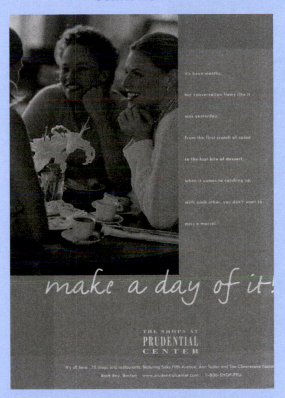

EXHIBIT 12.5 Jergens Ad

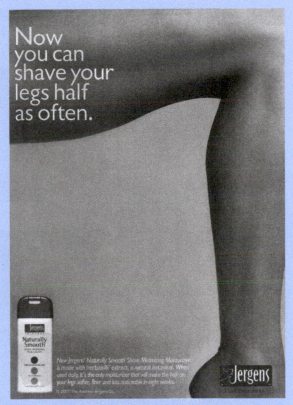

EXHIBIT 12.6 Huggies Little Swimmers Ad

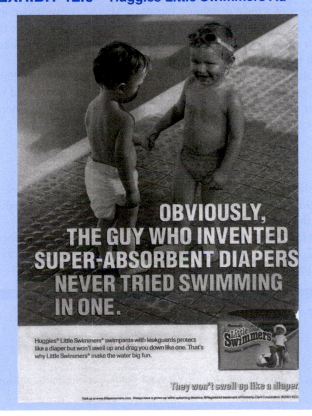

EXHIBIT 12.7 Children, Inc. Ad

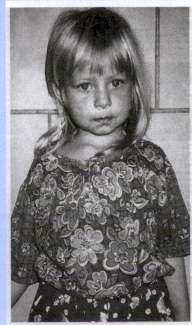

EXHIBIT 12.8   LOOP-LOC Pool Covers Ad

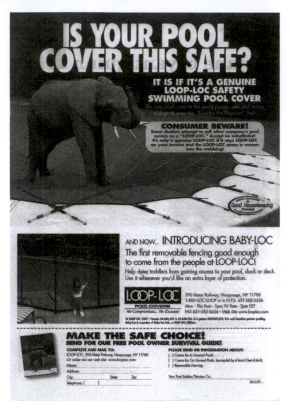

→ *Scenario E. Max Is the Man.* The manager of a huge restaurant business, Max is always breathing down the backs of his staff. If a worker is not doing something right, he will fire that person on the spot. If an employee doesn't listen, he or she will know who is boss! Our man Max is not well-liked by the staff, but he is quite popular with the ladies, who admire his authority.

→ *Scenario F. She Feels Their Pain.* Ophelia Payne is quite the couch potato! But, when those "Save the Children" ads come on, she can't help but pick up the phone and adopt one. She feels so bad for the little tykes and wants to help, but her underlying reason for adopting is the letter she gets once a month from each of her orphans (all twenty-seven of them).

WRITTEN APPLICATIONS

1. Answer Question 1 in the In-Class Applications for two of the ads, one illustrating an innate need and one an acquired need. Then, find two more ads, one of which illustrates an innate need and the other an acquired need, and answer Question 1 for those ads.

2. Answer Question 2 for four of the ads. At least two of these should illustrate emotional motives. Then, answer Question 2 for four more ads you find, at least two of which should include emotional motives.

3. Answer Question 3 from the In-Class Applications, p. 370.

EXERCISE 12.2. MOTIVATIONAL CONFLICT

OBJECTIVES

1. To understand the relationship between the valence of motivational goals, problem recognition, and motivational conflict.

2. To describe and recognize each of three motivational conflict situations and the marketing strategies used to resolve the conflict for consumers in each type of situation.

3. To think about motivational conflicts you have experienced and describe how a marketer could have or did resolve them.

BACKGROUND

THREE TYPES OF MOTIVATIONAL CONFLICT

Recall that motivational goals have valence; they can be either positive or negative. Consumers are motivated to achieve an *approach object*, that is, a positive state of affairs that fulfills their needs, such as a refreshing drink or an enjoyable TV show. Conversely, buyers want to steer clear of *avoidance objects*, that is, negative states of affair that hinder need fulfillment, such as a runny nose or a flaky scalp. Marketers can help consumers achieve their avoidance goals by producing and marketing products that alleviate negative outcomes.

Conflicting approach and/or avoidance goals can sometimes lead to an undesirable state of **motivational conflict**, which is a clash concerning positively and/or negatively valenced objects. Here, the consumer's misfortune can be the marketer's good fortune! Where consumers experience motivational conflict, marketers can reduce or resolve motivational conflict, thereby becoming problem-solving heroes!

There are three general motivational conflict scenarios summarized in Exhibit 12.9. Each suggests one or more general marketing opportunities for providing a solution to the conflict.

APPROACH-APPROACH CONFLICT

The Nature of Approach-Approach Conflict. In an **approach-approach conflict** situation (see Exhibit 12.9A), the consumer's choice is between two or more desirable alternatives (approach objects). The conflict arises because people cannot "have it all" or, at least, they cannot "have it both ways" or experience "the best of both worlds." Such conflict arises in any situation where someone has clashing opportunities, such as spending time with a good friend as opposed to relaxing at home. Should the choice be made to stay home and relax, there could be another approach-approach conflict between reading an enjoyable book and watching a good movie.

Consumers also become conflicted. For example, a graduating senior might like to take one last spring break fling but knows he should spend money and time buying a new suit and going on job interviews. And, if he has yielded to that little devil with a pitchfork prodding him to vacation rather than the little angel with a halo encouraging him to go interviewing, he must then decide whether to spend the time and money in a warm climate in the sand and surf or in a cold locale on the snowy ski slopes!

Generally, the more equal the alternatives in terms of overall desirability, the greater the conflict. Hence, the more likely the consumer is to vacillate and do nothing, delaying the decision either temporarily or indefinitely.

Marketing Solutions for Approach-Approach Conflict. There are three general solutions marketers can offer to resolve the consumer's approach-approach conflict.

1. Demonstrate brand superiority. Marketing communications can show how the marketer's offering is superior to that of the other alternative(s). Suppose our student is deciding between spending spring break on the warm beach versus snowy ski slopes. The purveyor of a spring-break-in-Cancun travel package must make sure the product is truly better than a week in the Great White North and promote it as such (the classic, "It's better in the Bahamas" approach).

Such "we're superior" promotion points out the marketer's positive attributes. ("Impress your friends with your deep tan.") It can also show the negatives in the alternative(s). ("Why freeze your buns off during spring? Spring is supposed to be about warm weather!")

2. Reduce dissonance. Such "we're-better-than-them" marketing might even need to continue after the purchase to reduce any cognitive dissonance (postpurchase doubt) arising from the fact that the chosen alternative has some foregone positive features (the excitement of snow skiing) and the selected alternative has some negative attributes (sunburn pain).

Accordingly, marketers of high involvement products should target marketing communications to recent

EXHIBIT 12.9   Three Motivational Conflict Situations

A. Approach—Approach Conflict

B. Approach—Avoid Conflict

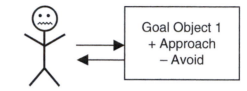

C. Avoid—Avoid Conflict

buyers, reassuring them of the wisdom of their decision. A beach resort could send a brochure to former guests featuring photos of people enjoying the resort and offering a discount on a future vacation there.

3. Combine the best of the conflicting alternatives. Marketers can provide consumers with a product that merges the best features of the two conflicting choices. In effect, the marketing message becomes, "You can have your cake and eat it too!" In the sunny vacation versus snowy conflict scenario, a travel agency could offer a package vacation deal: three days and nights in the mountains and four more at the shore. Consider that historically consumers had to choose between the "therapeutic" benefits of strong-tasting Listerine and the good taste of less medicinal, "cosmetic" mouthwashes like Scope. Along came Cool Mint Listerine, which promises to kill germs and fight plaque and gum infection like Listerine and to taste good like Scope.

APPROACH-AVOID CONFLICT

The Nature of Approach-Avoid Conflict. In the **approach-avoid conflict** situation the goal object is a mixed blessing, having aspects that are both positive (approach object) and negative (avoidance object; see Exhibit 12.9B). A person has a love-hate relationship with the goal object—he must take the bad with the good.

Students want good grades (approach) but do not want to have to study hard to get them (avoid). You wish to eat, drink, and be merry at the party, but you do not want to suffer any physical ailments afterward. Employees want to work extra hours to boost their pay and career, but they wish to avoid neglecting their families and friends.

Consumers must sometimes choose from alternatives, each of which has both positive and negative dimensions. High-quality products usually cost more: choose the organic fruits and vegetables, which are healthier and promote green farming practices but are pricier and remain fresh for only a short time. However, the latter, while cheaper and longer lasting, may contain chemicals and pesticides. Many medicinal drugs cure ailments but also cause unwanted side effects. Ice cream tastes yummy but is high in butterfat and cholesterol. You wish to devour a chocolate bar without breaking out in pimples.

Marketing Solutions for Approach-Avoid Conflict. Like the Freudian ego, marketers can settle a conflict, in this case between a product's positive and negative features. There are three approaches.

1. Highlight the good and minimize the bad. Here, sellers resolve approach-avoid conflict by providing customers with a product that offers the positives but minimizes or even eliminates the negatives and by promoting it as such. The airlines and American Express credit card have each proclaimed, "Fly now, pay later." Many convenience food products offer almost the same great taste as home-cooked meals or baked goods without all the fuss and muss. Buffered aspirin (Bufferin) alleviates pain yet also reduces the stomach-upset side effect of aspirin. ("Why trade a headache for an upset stomach," ads once asked.) Items such as ice milk, light beer, fat-free cookies and crackers, and low-tar cigarettes all minimize their "bad stuff." Technology products ultimately make our lives easier, but there is often a learning curve in the process. Hence, marketers develop "user-friendly" versions. For many parents, the idea of wireless phones for tweens is appealing because it helps them to reach their youngsters in emergencies or just tell them they are running late. However, cell phones can also be an opportunity for mischief and sky-high bills. Hence, a slew of cell phones allow parents to control how much and to whom their kids talk.

2. Eliminate negative emotions or thoughts caused by the product. Sometimes, marketers focus on eradicating guilt, shame, fear, and the like associated with product use by helping consumers to rationalize that "You're worth it" or "You've earned it," or by demonstrating that the negatives are not as bad as consumers believe or perhaps are even nonexistent (e.g., Yes, bananas are very nourishing but, no, they are not fattening).

3. Add an alternative to replace the negative option. For instance, self-service kiosks in hotels, airports, car rental outlets, and auto dealerships help customers avoid the hassles of dealing with rude or incompetent service or sales personnel.

AVOID-AVOID CONFLICT

The Nature of Avoid-Avoid Conflict. **Avoid-avoid conflict** buyers must choose between two or more undesirable alternatives (avoidance objects; see Exhibit 12.9C). It is the classic "Your money or your life," "You choose, you lose," "Heads you win, tails I lose," decision. A student on academic probation could either study hard or get booted out of college. In political elections citizens sometimes hold their noses and vote for the lesser of two evils; hence, third-party candidates at times enter the fray.

Consumers, too, face such no-win decisions. An urban commuter's choices are either to fight downtown traffic or to take the smelly, crowded, unsafe subway. Someone could spend several hundred dollars getting his television repaired or spend even several hundred more to get a new set. Either visit the dentist for the unpleasant, expensive fussing inside of your mouth or suffer gum disease.

Unsought goods entail avoid-avoid conflict. Shell out big bucks for life insurance to protect your loved ones or else worry that they will be destitute should you expire. Go through the headache of estate planning or suffer a confiscatory tax bill down the road. Buy a new set of tires or drive on unsafe, balding tires, perhaps ending up wrapped around a tree.

The closer the alternatives are in undesirability, the more difficult the decision is to make and the longer the person procrastinates.

Marketing Solutions for Avoid-Avoid Conflict. There are three general marketing strategies to solve avoid-avoid dilemmas.

1. Promote the product as a reasonable alternative. The marketer can show that the product is not so awful—it is, indeed, the "lesser of two evils" or not evil at all! Accordingly, dentists provide Novocaine to ease the pain, video games to play, and pleasant music to soothe the patient's soul. Mass transit systems in some major cities have literally cleaned up their act and become more sanitary and safe to ride. "Easy payment plans" relieve the financial burden of expensive goods.

2. Turn a disadvantage into an advantage. Psychologically, a product promoter can turn a shortcoming into a strength. Listerine told consumers that its bad taste was a good thing since it means it was destroying germs and fighting bad breath. The U.S. Army insisted that "it's not just a job, it's an adventure."

3. Minimize or eliminate the negatives. A marketer can offer an alternative that diminishes or eradicates both of the negatives. Hence, a teenage girl worried about being pregnant, whose choice traditionally was

to worry or go to a doctor, can now use a pregnancy self-testing kit. Murine Wet & Clean Contact Lens Eye Drops offers their product as a third alternative to unattractive eyeglasses or suffering burning, stinging eyes from wearing contact lenses.

REVIEW QUESTIONS

1. Explain the nature of approach objects and avoidance objects, and their relationship to valence of motivational goals, problem recognition, and motivational conflict.
2. Describe each of the three motivational conflict situations, and discuss marketing strategies that can be used to reduce the consumer's conflict in each situation.

IN-CLASS APPLICATIONS

1. For each of the following ads (Exhibits 12.10 through 12.15), describe the type of motivational conflict the product is attempting to solve: approach-approach, approach-avoid, or avoid-avoid. Does each appeal seem to offer an effective resolution of the problem for the consumer?
2. For each of the following purchase decisions, identify how a consumer could encounter all three types of motivational conflict:
   a. New house
   b. Used car
   c. Facial tissues
   d. Used schoolbooks
3. Describe the last time you experienced a state of motivational conflict. Which type of conflict situation was it? Did you find a solution or did you procrastinate? Did marketing strategies contribute to your decision? Why or why not?
4. For each of the following (extremely brief!) scenario choices, describe the motivational conflict at hand and how you would resolve the conflict if it was important to you.
   a. Candy bar or diet?
   b. Pain or anesthesia?
   c. Roller coaster or bungee jump?
   d. Rolex or Movado?
   e. Fix car or remain broken down?
   f. Hawaii or St. Thomas?
   g. Study or sleep?

WRITTEN APPLICATIONS

1. Answer Question 1 in the In-Class Applications above for five of the ads. Then, repeat Question 1 for three other ads that you find. Note: You should find an example ad for each of the three types of motivational conflict situations.
2. Answer Question 2 above for two of the products.
3. Answer Question 3 above.

EXERCISE 12.3. MASLOW'S HIERARCHY OF NEEDS

OBJECTIVES

1. To understand Maslow's classification of motives as a hierarchical ladder and an influential system for explaining human and consumer motivation.
2. To learn how to appropriately appeal to the various levels in Maslow's hierarchy through marketing communications.
3. To practice creatively applying Maslow's hierarchy in advertising.

EXHIBIT 12.10   Orbitz Ad

EXHIBIT 12.11   Dove Ad

EXHIBIT 12.12   Lactaid Ad

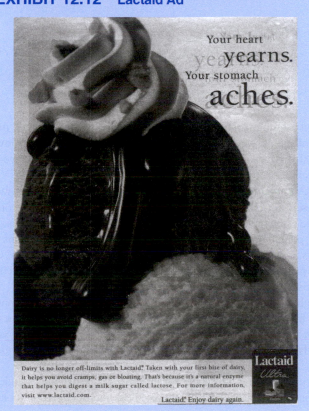

EXHIBIT 12.13   Nasonex Ad

EXHIBIT 12.14   **Atrovent Ad**

BREAK FREE FROM YOUR RUNNY NOSE.

Ask your doctor about an exciting advancement for treating runny noses, ATROVENT® Nasal Spray. [NOT A STEROID] It's the first in a unique class of nasal sprays that actually stop runny noses where they start. [NOT AN ANTIHISTAMINE] ATROVENT Nasal Spray's special inhibitors provide effective relief without insomnia [WON'T KEEP YOU AWAKE] or drowsiness. [WON'T PUT YOU TO SLEEP] And it can be safely used by children 12 years and older. ATROVENT Nasal Spray is available exclusively by prescription. Only your doctor knows if it's right for treating your runny nose. Though most ATROVENT Nasal Spray users experience trouble-free relief, nasal dryness (approximately 1 in 20 patients) and mild nose bleeds (approximately 1 in 10 patients) are potential side effects.* So ask your doctor about ATROVENT Nasal Spray, or call toll-free 1·888·ATROVENT (287·6836) for a free brochure and money-saving coupon.

STOP IT FROM THE START.

ATROVENT®
NASAL SPRAY
(ipratropium bromide)

* See following page for additional important information.
AN-6547R

http://www.atrovent.com

EXHIBIT 12.15   **National Flood Insurance Program Ad**

BACKGROUND

OVERVIEW OF MASLOW'S NEED HIERARCHY

NEEDS ARRAYED IN A HIERARCHY

To explain the nature of human motivation, psychologist Abraham Maslow organized human needs into a fixed sequential progression, or **hierarchy of needs.** Maslow's need hierarchy ranges from lower-level physiological needs to complex psychological motives. Maslow believed that people naturally strive to travel up through the five levels of this hierarchy.

This hierarchic theory is often represented as a pyramid with the larger, lower levels signifying the lower needs and the upper point being the need for **self-actualization**, which is self-initiated striving to become whatever one is able to become or whatever one is meant to be (see Exhibit 12.16). Such needs relate to self-fulfillment and maximization of one's unique potential. Self-actualization explains people's aspirations to become celebrity CEOs (with their mug on *Business Week*), renowned scientists, or best-selling authors.

The ladder of needs is arranged in order of **prepotency**, or relative predominance. A prepotent need has the greatest influence over people's actions, given where they are in the hierarchy.

Lower-level needs must be largely, although not entirely, satisfied before higher-level needs dominate. For example, a starving garbage picker cares little about the healthiness or safety of his food. Nor does a philosophy professor whose wife just left him for another man think too deeply about his theories. If you are very tired, you probably are not particularly interested in attending your CB class or reading this book (as exciting and fulfilling as both are)!

In a marketing context, an extremely hungry customer cares little about the ambience of a restaurant. A student searching for basic, reliable yet affordable personal transportation hardly thinks about how "cool" a car looks.

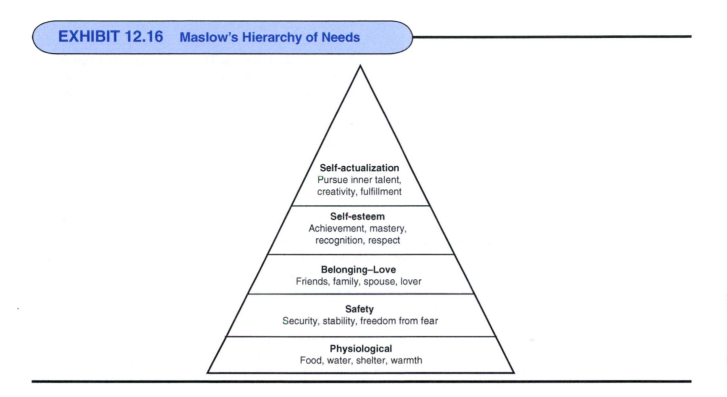

EXHIBIT 12.16   Maslow's Hierarchy of Needs

Self-actualization
Pursue inner talent,
creativity, fulfillment

Self-esteem
Achievement, mastery,
recognition, respect

Belonging–Love
Friends, family, spouse, lover

Safety
Security, stability, freedom from fear

Physiological
Food, water, shelter, warmth

The first two levels—physiological and safety needs—are mostly innate needs. The next three levels—social, esteem, and self-actualization—are primarily acquired needs.

APPLYING MASLOW'S HIERARCHY

Published in Maslow's 1954 book *Motivation and Personality,* the hierarchy was picked up by corporations, taught at business schools, and used in management training seminars. The basic idea is that employees will not be fulfilled in their work unless all five need levels are satisfied by their job. One's work will not be satisfying if it is done merely to pay the bills.

The hierarchy also helps marketers think about the types of motives their products can satisfy. One product can meet multiple needs levels in the hierarchy. For example, a house can be purchased for shelter (level 1), for safety from crime (2), for family togetherness (3), as a symbol of one's wealth (4), and to help fulfill one's ambition as an interior decorator (5).

The marketer's tasks regarding Maslow's hierarchy are to discover which level of needs a product primarily fulfills for a target market and to persuasively communicate how the product fulfills those needs.

THE FIVE BASIC LEVELS IN MASLOW'S HIERARCHY

1. PHYSIOLOGICAL NEEDS

Physiological (innate) needs are basic biological requirements for living. They are the strongest needs because, if deprived of their satisfaction, a person could experience sickness, irritation, pain or discomfort, or even die. These feelings motivate people to alleviate these needs quickly. Once physiological needs are met, individuals begin to think about higher-level needs. For most Americans, physiological needs are regularly and easily satisfied; hence, they are not prepotent. In the workplace such needs can be met through a "living wage" and health care benefits.

Products providing "creature comforts" to fulfill physiological needs include food, beverages, and pain relievers. For such products, appeals to physiological needs can be potent. Witness, for example, the many appetizing food product shots on TV commercials.

2. SAFETY NEEDS

Safety (security) needs involve physiological and psychological needs. They are concerned with establishing stability and consistency in one's life in a chaotic world. These needs include physical safety, physical and psychological security, protection from the physical environment, and freedom from anxiety. For instance, young children take comfort in established mealtime rituals and bedtime routines.

Although safety needs are fairly well met for most Americans, gaps are occasionally experienced. Employers provide for safety needs by offering pension funds and allowing workers to join a union.

Products that provide a security blanket include financial instruments, insurance, deadbolt locks, baby monitors, emergency generators, burglar alarms, cell phones, and radial tires.

3. SOCIAL NEEDS

Social (love and belonging, affection, affiliation) needs are oriented toward loving and being loved by others, affiliation, social recognition, and being accepted by people despite one's flaws. Individuals have needs to escape feelings of loneliness and alienation and to give and receive affection. All of these needs are satisfied through intimate relationships, social groups, friends, acquaintances, and advisors.

Whereas the first two motivation levels are primary and inward-focused, social needs are largely secondary and outer-directed. For example, performers appreciate applause. Companies help their employees to meet social needs through work teams, organized sports, meal rooms, and work break lounges.

Social motives are not adequately met for many Americans because of a highly geographically and socially mobile society. Often, families are physically separated and people are too busy to take time to get to know their neighbors.

Many marketing appeals show how a product will help win the love and approval of others. Typical goods that satisfy social needs include anything bought in a family context (from food to household furnishings) and products used in a social setting (from deodorant to perfume). Beer commercials often show how a brew makes for camaraderie such as male bonding. When was the last time you saw a beer commercial with someone drinking alone?

4. ESTEEM NEEDS

Esteem (ego, egotistic) needs are for self-worth, self-confidence, and self-respect. There are two types: (1) *inner-directed needs* toward competency and self-confidence resulting from mastery of a task and (2) *outer-directed needs*. In the latter, the attention and recognition comes from others, including respect, prestige, and status. If esteem needs are not met, the person feels inferior, weak, helpless, and worthless.

Many people in modern societies strive to meet their esteem needs. Employers satisfy these needs through public recognition of high performers, prestigious job titles (it seems that everyone is a vice president of something), and granting more personal responsibility.

The marketplace is flooded with self-help books and CDs designed to bolster consumers' inner-directed esteem needs. Products marketed on the basis of brand image and conspicuous consumption appeals draw on outer-directed esteem needs.

5. SELF-ACTUALIZATION NEEDS

Self-actualization needs relate to the idea that "what a man can be, he must be." Maslow believed that humans differ from the lower animals in that people have a capacity for self-actualization. Maslow described self-actualization as an ongoing process. Self-actualizing people are usually involved in a cause apart from themselves, are devoted, and work at something very precious to them, to fulfill their personal potential.

These needs are relatively unsatisfied for most people. Consequently, the workplace has changed from being simply a means of satisfying one's physiological needs to providing personal fulfillment. Employees look for opportunities to advance up the career ladder, to successfully complete challenging assignments, and to "make a difference." Self-actualization also explains why so many people write a blog—because they want their lives to count. Entrepreneurs attempt to build business empires and professors try to publish a groundbreaking article or book. The U.S. Army, inspired by Maslow's theory, told young adults, "Be all that you can be." Products to help people be productive in their careers or to excel in their hobbies appeal to self-actualization needs.

THREE ADDITIONAL LEVELS

Later in his career, Maslow expanded on the growth need of self-actualization. He named two lower-level growth needs prior to the general level of self-actualization and added one additional level at the top of the hierarchy. Arrayed according to prepotency and following from esteem needs (level 4), these highest-level needs are as follows:

Level 5. **Cognitive needs.** Desires to know, to understand, to explore, to experience new things, to achieve, and to find meaning are Maslow's cognitive needs. They also include a desire to systematize, organize, and construct a value system. Educational products, experiential services such as adventure travel, and products that provide uniqueness and variety, such as product line extensions and flankers, satisfy cognitive needs.

Level 6. **Aesthetic needs.** Aesthetic needs are desires for symmetry, order, and beauty. Products appealing to these requirements are found in the artistic arenas of music, art, and poetry. Items designed to make people and their homes more attractive, such as furniture and other furnishings, also appeal to aesthetic needs.

Level 7. **Self-actualization needs.** Note that the placement of these needs in the hierarchy now occurs above the cognitive and aesthetic needs.

Level 8. **Transcendence needs.** The very highest-level needs to help others find self-fulfillment and realize their potential are called transcendence needs. Volunteer activities that involve "giving back" to society, such as tutoring inner-city kids, can satisfy transcendence needs. Some firms appeal to this level in their employees by involving them in their corporate social responsibility activities, which involve good works in the community and the world.

SHORTCOMINGS OF MASLOW'S HIERARCHY

Maslow's theory has been criticized on at least four counts.

1. It was based on intuition rather than an empirical foundation. Research investigators have found that the order of motives in the hierarchy is an individual difference variable. For some people, the need for love, security, and safety will dominate, while for others the desire for esteem or achievement will rule, regardless of whether "lower-level" needs have been satisfied. For instance, someone who has taken a religious vow of celibacy and poverty would disagree that physiological and social needs must be satisfied before self-fulfillment can be achieved.

2. The hierarchy is more descriptive of typical people in individualistic Western culture, which places more weight on individual accomplishment, self-esteem, and self-fulfillment. Eastern culture is more collectivist, emphasizing the primacy of group needs over individual needs.

3. Maslow's hierarchy suggests that self-actualization rather than concern for others should be the highest good, suggesting selfishness is a virtue. However, the modified version puts transcendence needs at the top.

4. The hierarchy neglects spiritual needs. However, most, if not all, major religions place spiritual needs on a level equal to or greater than most other categories of needs. For example, the Judeo-Christian tradition teaches that people's greatest need is for a personal relationship with God, and Buddhism preaches spiritual enlightenment through the cessation of earthly desires and needs.

Nonetheless, Maslow's hierarchy is useful for marketers in pointing out basic consumer motives that vary with individuals' different stages in development and/or environmental conditions. These are needs that sellers can creatively tap into, as you are about to do.

REVIEW QUESTIONS

1. Explain the nature of Maslow's need hierarchy, relating it to the concepts of self-actualization and the prepotency of needs.
2. Describe each of the five levels in Maslow's original hierarchy, provide examples of specific needs at each level, and give examples of typical products satisfying each level of needs.

3. Cite and explain the three additional levels Maslow later added to the hierarchy and where they fit into the original hierarchy. Then, offer examples of typical products that satisfy each of these need levels.

IN-CLASS APPLICATIONS

1. To which levels of Maslow's hierarchy could an ad for a Ford truck appeal? Which of these would be most effective in an advertising appeal and why? How does the efficacy of the appeal depend on the target market and its situation?
2. Using each level in Maslow's hierarchy of needs, describe effective advertising messages, along with the appropriate target market, for each of the following marketers.
   a. M.A.D.D. (Mothers Against Drunk Driving)
   b. Crest toothpaste
   c. A student running for class president
3. For each of the following advertisements (Exhibits 12.17–12.21), identify which level(s) in Maslow's hierarchy of needs the ad is attempting to satisfy. Are there any other levels on Maslow's ladder that each product satisfies and that could be appealed to? (Consider including the more recently added cognitive, aesthetic, and transcendence needs.) If so, would appealing to that (those) need(s) be a more effective approach than the one taken in the ad?

WRITTEN APPLICATIONS

1. Answer Questions 1 and 2 in the In-Class Applications.
2. Answer Question 3 for three of the ads. Then find five more ads, each of which appeals to a different need/motive in Maslow's hierarchy. (Your five ads should collectively cover all five levels in the hierarchy.) Answer Question 3 above for each of these ads as well.

EXHIBIT 12.17   Tylenol Arthritis Pain Ad   **EXHIBIT 12.18   Mercedes-Benz Ad**

EXHIBIT 12.19   New York Palace Hotel & Towers Ad

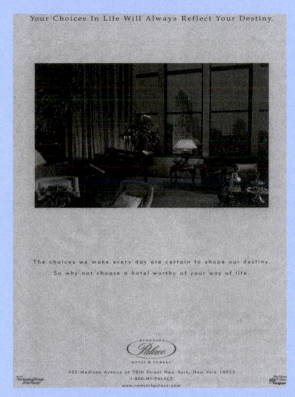

EXHIBIT 12.20   Hop.com Ad

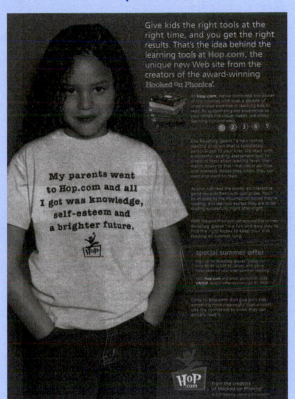

EXHIBIT 12.21   Eternity Ad

KEY CONCEPTS

acquired (psychological, secondary, psychogenic,) needs
aesthetic needs
approach-approach conflict
approach-avoid conflict
approach goal
approach object
avoidance goal
avoidance object
avoid-avoid conflict
cognitive needs
competitor myopia
drive
emotional (affective) appeals
emotions
esteem (ego, egotistic) needs
fear (threat, problem-avoidance) appeals
generic goals
generic (primary) demand
goals (need fulfillment)
hedonic (experiential, transformational) needs
hierarchy of needs
humor appeals
innate (physiological, primary, biogenic) needs
involvement
irrationality (nonrationality)

latent (subconscious, covert) needs (problems)
manifest (expressed, overt) needs
McClelland's trichotomy (trio) of social needs
message (theme, selling premise, selling appeal)
motivated behavior
motivation
motivational appeal
motivational conflict
motivational direction
motivational process
motivational strength
motives
physiological (innate) needs
prepotency
product-specific goals
rational (cognitive) appeals
rationality
safety (security) needs
selective (secondary) demand
self-actualization
sex appeals
social (love and belonging, affection, affiliation) needs
transcendence needs
utilitarian (functional, instrumental) needs
valence (direction)

SUMMARY

Motivation seeks to answer the fundamental question: "Why do consumers buy and consume products?" The motivational process is outlined in Exhibit 12.1.

Key aspects of motivation are as follows:

1. Motivation is an internal state, hidden from direct observation; it can be inferred.
2. Motivation endures. Motives are the long-term reasons why people behave and buy.
3. Motives underlie short-term needs and wants as well as problem recognition.
4. Unsatisfied needs and wants create tension, resulting in a drive. This creates a desire to achieve a goal (a product) that will fulfill the need, thereby reducing the drive.
5. Very driven consumers have high motivational strength and experience high involvement.
6. Driven consumers engage in motivated behavior. Unsatisfied motives have motivational direction, guiding people's actions toward a particular goal.
7. Motivation seeks goals, that is, the desired state of affairs. The goal object is the product that satisfies desires and solves problems or that delivers consumer benefits. There are two types of goals for marketers to appeal to: (1) generic goals, thereby building generic demand, as do industry trade associations, market leaders, and new product marketers, and (2) product-specific goals, thereby building selective demand for a brand.
8. Goals and the underlying motives have valence. A positively valued goal is an approach object, such as achievement, affiliation, or prestige. The approach goal is the customer's desire to achieve the approach object. A negatively valued goal is an avoidance object, leading to an avoidance goal where the objective is to evade it.

9. There are two types of relationships between motives, motivated behavior, and goals (summarized in Exhibit 12.2). First, a given motivated behavior, such as purchase of a product, could be seeking multiple goals, each due to a different motive (Exhibit 12.2A). The implication is that using observational research (watching consumers in action) to infer motives is highly tenuous. Second, a given motive could result in many different behaviors to achieve a particular goal (Exhibit 12.2B). This suggests that different goal objects represent indirect competition.

Needs and wants can be classified as innate needs versus acquired needs and utilitarian needs versus hedonic needs. Utilitarian consumers focus on objective, tangible, measurable, "rational" product criteria relating to rational motives. Hedonic buyers focus on product criteria that are subjective, intangible, and nonrational. Hedonic needs relate to emotional motives. Another classification scheme is McClelland's trichotomy of social needs (power, affiliation, and achievement).

There are several significant marketing applications of motivational concepts:

1. Discover dominant buying motives.
2. Use motivational research to uncover hidden (latent) motives, which are often psychological needs. Manifest needs are easier for consumers to discuss.
3. Use survey research to discover consumer goals. It might be easier to ask consumers about their tangible goals rather than their intangible motives, of which they are less aware. From these goals the researcher can deduce the underlying motives.
4. Use motives to segment markets (e.g., benefit segmentation).
5. Use promotional appeals based on consumer motivation.

Exercise 12.1 focused on rational and emotional motives, which underlie the motivational appeal (i.e. message). Rational appeals are cognitive such as economic rationality. The sales pitch describes objective information, and it focuses on logical, objectively verifiable, tangible product attributes, appealing to utilitarian needs. Generally, rationality prevails for "considered purchases" with physical brand differentiation. Rational buyers carefully pass through the five-stage decision process. Print media are most heavily used.

Emotional appeals are directed toward the consumer's emotions, aiming at the heart and concentrating on subjective, intangible, unverifiable product criteria and appealing to hedonic needs. Emotional motives dominate where there are few real physical brand distinctions but where psychological differences exist. Emotions are conveyed especially well in TV and radio commercials as well as in outdoor media. Emotional advertising usually appeals to consumers who make an attitude-based choice. At other times emotional ads appeal to buyers making attribute-based choices using emotional attributes.

Rational and emotional appeals can be used separately or together because subjective or emotional criteria are not irrational. A rational choice might include emotional criteria to maximize one's satisfaction. Thus, rational and emotional motives can both motivate a given purchase. The opposite of rational is not emotional but irrational, while the opposite of emotional is not rational but rather nonemotional (see Exhibit 12.3).

There are several types of popular emotional appeals, including guilt, shame, morality, fantasy, human interest, agony, sensuality, nostalgia, and hopping on the bandwagon. Exercise 12.1 focused on three especially potent emotional appeals—fear appeals, humor appeals, and sex appeals—each of which has its advantages and disadvantages and is most appropriate for particular types of products.

Motivational conflict was the subject of Exercise 12.2. Motivation, as goal-seeking behavior, often involves one of three types of conflict, summarized in Exhibit 12.9. Three marketing solutions to approach-approach conflict are as follows:

1. Demonstrate brand superiority by pointing out the marketer's positive features and/or showing the negatives in the alternative(s).
2. Reduce cognitive dissonance by targeting marketing communications to recent buyers, reassuring them of the wisdom of their decision.
3. Combine the best of the conflicting alternatives in one product.

Marketing solutions for the approach-avoid conflict situation include highlighting the good and minimizing the bad, eliminating negative emotions about the product by helping consumers to rationalize that "You're worth it" or "You've earned it," and adding an alternative to replace the negative option.

The avoid-avoid conflict situation is likely for unsought goods. Marketing strategies to resolve avoid-avoid dilemmas include promoting the product as an acceptable alternative, turning a disadvantage into an advantage, and minimizing or eliminating the negatives.

Exercise 12.3 reviewed Maslow's hierarchy of needs, summarized in Exhibit 12.16. Maslow believed that humans differ from the lower animals in their capacity for self-actualization.

Maslow organized human needs into a fixed sequential progression or hierarchy of needs ranging from lower-level physiological needs to complex psychological motives. The hierarchy is arranged in order of prepotency. Lower-level needs must be largely, although not entirely, satisfied before higher-level needs dominate.

The first two levels—physiological and safety needs—are mostly innate needs, while the next three levels—social, esteem, and self-actualization—are primarily acquired needs. One product could satisfy multiple levels of needs in the hierarchy.

The five basic levels in the original Maslow hierarchy are as follows:

1. Physiological needs. When these needs are not satisfied, a person might feel sickness, irritation, pain, or discomfort, motivating that individual to alleviate them quickly. Products providing "creature comforts" to meet these needs include food, beverages, and pain relievers.
2. Safety needs. These include motives for physical safety, security, protection from the physical environment, and freedom from anxiety. Products that appeal to safety needs include financial instruments, insurance, deadbolt locks, burglar alarms, cell phones, and radial tires.
3. Social needs. Social needs are largely secondary and outer-directed. Many marketing appeals show how a product will help win the love and approval of others, especially anything bought in a family context or in a social setting.
4. Esteem needs. These include inner-directed needs toward competency and self-confidence and outer-directed needs toward the attention and recognition that comes from others. Self-help/improvement books and CDs bolster consumers' inner-directed esteem needs, while products marketed on the basis of brand image and conspicuous consumption draw on outer-directed esteem needs.
5. Self-actualization needs. Products to help people to be productive in their careers or to excel in their hobbies appeal to self-actualization needs.

Maslow later revised his hierarchy, adding higher-level needs to follow esteem:

6. Cognitive needs. Educational products, experiential services such as adventure travel and products that provide novelty and variety satisfy such desires to know.
7. Aesthetic needs. Products satisfying these include music, art, poetry, and items enhancing personal and home beauty.
8. Self-actualization needs. These were in the original hierarchy.
9. Transcendence needs. These can be fulfilled, for example, via volunteer activities.

REFERENCES

Bagozzi, R. P., Gopinath, M., and Nyer, P. U. (1999). "The Role of Emotions in Marketing." *Journal of the Academy of Marketing Science, 27*, 2, 184–207.

Chaudhuri, Aujun. (2006). *Emotion and Reason in Consumer Behavior.* Amsterdam: Elsevier.

Copeland, Melvin T. (1924). *Pinnacles of Merchandising.* Chicago: A.W. Shaw Company.

Danziger, Pamela N. (2002). *Why People Buy Things They Don't Need.* Ithaca, NY: Paramount Marketing Publishing.

Dichter, Ernest. (1964). *The Handbook of Consumer Motivation.* New York: McGraw-Hill.

Gulas, Charles S., and Weinberger, Marc G. (2006). *Humor in Advertising: A Comprehensive Analysis.* Armonk, NY: M.E. Sharpe.

Haire, Mason. (1950). "Projective Techniques in Marketing Research." *Journal of Marketing,* 14 (April), 649–656.

Madden, Thomas J., and Weinberger, Marc G. (1984). "Humor in Advertising: A Practitioner View." *Journal of Advertising Research,* 24, 4, 23–29.

Maddock, Richard C. (2000). *Motigraphics: The Analysis and Measurement of Human Motivations in Marketing.* Westport, CT: Quorum Books.

Maslow, Abraham. (1970). *Motivation and Personality,* 2nd ed. New York: Harper and Row.

Norman, Donald A. (2004). *Emotional Design: Why We Love (or Hate) Everyday Things.* New York: Basic Books.

Packard, Vance. (1957). *The Hidden Persuaders.* New York: D. MacKay.

Roberts, Kevin. (2005). *Lovemarks: The Future Beyond Brands.* New York: Powerhouse Books.

Robinette, Scott, and Brand, Claire. (2001). *Emotion Marketing: The Hallmark Way of Winning Customers for Life.* New York: McGraw-Hill.

Stern, Barbara B. (2004). "The Importance of Being Ernest: Commemorating Dichter's Contribution to Advertising Research." *Journal of Advertising Research,* 44, 2, 165–169.

Sternthal, Brian, and Craig, C. Samuel. (1973). "Humor in Advertising." *Journal of Marketing,* 37, 4, 12–18.

———. (1974). "Fear Appeals: Revisited and Revised." *Journal of Consumer Research,* 1, 3, 22–34.

Weinberger, Marc G., and Gulas, Charles S. (1992). "The Impact of Humor in Advertising: A Review." *Journal of Advertising Research,* 21, 4, 35–60.

Wolfe, David B., and Sisodia, Rajendra. (2003). "Marketing to the Self-Actualizing Customer." *Journal of Consumer Marketing,* 20, 6, 555–569.

Zaltman, Gerald M., Hong, Jae W., and Lawson, Robert. (1990). "Achievement and Affiliation Motivation." *Journal of Business Research,* 20 (March), 135–143.

PERCEPTION AND INFORMATION PROCESSING

Perception is the process whereby individuals receive, select, organize, and interpret sensory stimuli to produce a meaningful picture of their world. This definition suggests that the perceptual process includes three key stages:

1. *Exposure:* Consumers receive or sense sensory stimuli (cues) through their senses.
2. *Attention:* Consumers attend to or allocate information-processing capacity to selected stimuli, allowing the resulting sensations to enter their brain for information processing.
3. *Comprehension (interpretation):* Buyers organize and interpret information to derive meaning from or make sense of it.

Information processing entails as the series of activities whereby sensory stimuli are perceived, transformed into information, and stored in a person's memory to be retrieved for later use. Hence, information processing is a broader term than perception in that it includes perception plus the transformation and storage of that information in memory as part of the learning process.

Information processing adds a fourth stage beyond the perceptual process of exposure, attention, and comprehension. This stage is **retention**, the storing of information in short-term and long-term memory at the conclusion of the information processing process.

Exhibit 13.1 captures the essence of the perceptual and information processing procedures. Note that the arrow underneath "information processing" on the right side of the figure extends through the retention stage, whereas the arrow under "perception" only goes through the comprehension phase.

The degree of motivation to process information, that is, the consumer's level of involvement, helps establish whether he or she will be exposed to information. Highly motivated, actively involved consumers engaged in deliberate search will intentionally expose themselves to relevant information input and **perceptual (informational) cues**, which are characteristics of stimulus objects as consumers perceive them. However, a less motivated and involved buyer will primarily be randomly exposed to information during accidental search, such as online pop-up ads. A more involved consumer is more likely to move through all information processing stages—exposure, attention, comprehension, and retention—rather than terminating before the process is complete.

CHARACTERISTICS OF PERCEPTION

Perception is a three-stage process consisting of reception of, attention to, and interpretation of sensory information.

SENSORY STIMULI ARE PERCEIVED

Individuals perceive **sensory stimuli (cues, sensory inputs)**: sights, sounds, smells, tastes, and feelings. The **stimulus object** is the physical object in the environment that is the source of the stimuli experienced through the five senses. This stimulus includes any marketing program elements (product package, brand name, storefront, advertisement, salesperson, and the like). People's **sensory receptors (sensory organs)** are their human organs (eyes, ears, mouth, nose, and fingers and skin)—"windows on the world" that receive sensory stimuli.

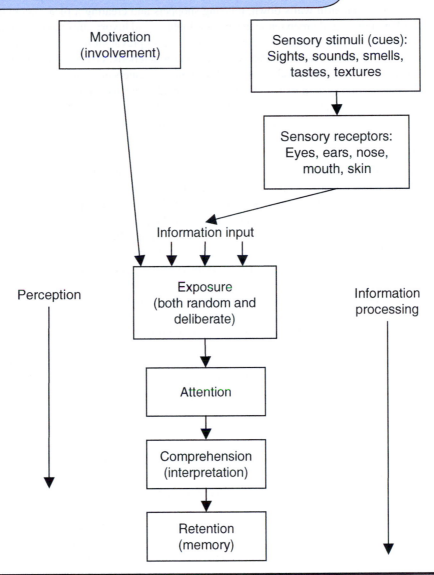

EXHIBIT 13.1   Consumer Information Processing Model

Stimuli are experienced through **sensory systems (sensory functions)**—vision, hearing, smell, taste, and touch. The sensory systems permit **sensation**, which is the immediate and direct reception of sensory stimuli by the sensory receptors. Here, humans organize raw stimuli (light waves, levels of temperature, etc.) into **information input** whereby content of sensory stimuli is adjusted so it is *meaningful*. For example, people experience sound waves but hear words. Consequently, **perception** can also be defined as "the interpretation of sensations to produce meaning."

Starbucks takes advantage of all five senses through their **sensory marketing (branding)**, which appeals to the five senses through the marketing program. When you enter a Starbucks store, you smell the coffee (since they grind in their stores for the purpose of creating the coffee aroma), hear the coffee grinding and the background music, see the store's unique look, touch the smooth tables and wood grain, and, of course, taste the coffee.

Smell seems to be the new frontier in sensory marketing. Smell is a very powerful sense for making emotional connections and enhancing peoples' experiences. Fast food restaurants and supermarket bakeries use artificial fresh-cooked food aromas. Many retailers and service firms use custom-made "signature scents" that you smell only in their shops to create unique associations. At Sony Style stores, the subtle fragrance of vanilla and mandarin wafts down, relaxing shoppers and creating a pleasant environment. Omni Hotels spritzes lemongrass and green tea scents in their lobbies, and luxury shirtmaker Thomas Pink pipes the smell of clean, pressed shirts into its stores. Scent strips are so prevalent in women's magazines that some smell like French bordellos. The ThinkPad Reserve Edition notebook, covered in leather, was designed to be the first computer that smelled good. Some European movie theaters now pump a barely detectable aroma though the air conditioning system to accompany on-screen ads, such as one for Nivea Sun lotion, accompanied by a faint whiff of the brand and the words "The Scent of Summer" splashed across the screen.

Lighting also works on an emotional level to influence buyers' moods. Bright lighting creates excitement, while softer lighting induces a mellow mood. This can also affect the pace at which patrons move and shop.

Sounds also affect buying. Audio chips are placed in magazine ads for new movies so music from the soundtrack plays when you open to the page, and some dog food packaging features a barking dog. One study demonstrated that shoppers bought French or German wine depending on which nationality's music was played on store speakers. Cell phone marketers help consumers brand themselves with ringtones.

Taste is also used in sensory marketing. First Flavor Inc.'s Peel 'n Taste strips are used to allow consumers to sample new foods and beverages advertised in magazines.

People differ in their reception of these sensory stimuli due to physiological and psychological differences. Physiological differences are primarily caused by nature, that is, differences in the quality of people's sensory receptors. Therefore, people vary in their physical sensitivity to stimuli. Hay fever sufferers cannot smell very well, heavy smokers have trouble tasting, and many senior citizens cannot see well and require a larger typeface. A blind person might compensate for lack of sight by having a more highly developed sense of hearing.

Psychological differences are mostly due to nurture, although some are caused by nature. These distinctions result from varying interests, characteristics, backgrounds, and sensory preferences. Consequently, individuals favor some sights, sounds, tastes, smells, and feelings over others.

PERCEPTION IS SELECTIVE AND SUBJECTIVE

Perception is a *selective* process. People consciously and subconsciously determine the sensory stimuli to which they will attend. This selectivity occurs at each and every stage of information processing.

Perception is also *subjective*. People comprehend things differently. The manner in which consumers organize and interpret information is individualistic and biased. That is, people experience **subjective perception**; perception deviates from reality due to individual differences in the perceptual process.

Perceptual organization suggests that to produce meaning, consumers must integrate new information with what they already know. Perceptual interpretation is the assignment of meaning to this organized information. People give meaning to sensory inputs based on expectations and familiarity. Therefore, when changing logos, package designs, and other marketing elements, sellers should proceed with caution in light of consumers' existing associations for these stimuli.

Subjective perception suggests that two people might be exposed to the same stimuli under identical circumstances, and yet each of them organizes and interprets the cues in different ways based on each individual's unique needs and wants, interests, values, and expectations. To the optimist the glass is half full, but to the pessimist it is half empty. Do you win a silver medal or lose a gold medal?

Consequently, because marketers are so close to their products and marketing communications, they can easily lose perspective. They may fall into the trap of believing that their customers view their products and communications as they do. While the Atkins diet sellers viewed their offering as a healthy, effective, and safe way to lose weight, many consumers saw it as an all-meat, fatty, unhealthy fad diet.

Marketers cannot be sure that people will interpret information the way the sellers assume they will. Consumer research must be used to check this assumption. The word *communication* comes from the Latin word *communicare* (to impart, share, or make common). A popular definition of communication is "the act of conveying meaning between people." Effective marketing communication, therefore, entails a sharing of meaning. To ensure a mutually understood meaning, the marketing communicator must *encode* (develop and send) the message using a series of signs or symbols representing concepts. Consumers must then *decode* (receive and interpret) these signs or symbols into concepts. Miscommunication occurs when something is lost in transmission and incorrect concepts are assigned by consumers to the signs and symbols.

The decoded concepts become peoples' perceptions. A basic law of human nature is that people act on the basis of what they perceive (believe) to be true, whether their beliefs square with reality or not! Is a larger car safer than a smaller car? Does a bad-tasting mouthwash kill more germs than a good-tasting one? Is a loud engine more powerful than a quiet one? In reality the answer in each case might be "no," yet in the consumer's mind the answer to each might be "yes."

Together, selective and subjective perception suggest that merely attempting to communicate with someone through marketing messages is no guarantee that successful communication has occurred!

ORGANIZATION OF CHAPTER 13

Exercise 13.1 delves deeper into the selective and subjective nature of perception. It looks at the underlying reasons for selective and subjective perception, and offers marketing strategies to overcome such perceptual limitations and to capitalize on them. Exercises 13.2 through 13.5 investigate some selected aspects of individual cognitive differences in information processing, working through the stages of selective exposure, attention, and comprehension.

Exercise 13.2 looks at one aspect of the selective exposure stage, the controversial topic of subliminal advertising in which hidden images and messages are snuck into in ads. Exercise 13.3 investigates a related aspect of the selective exposure stage—stimuli that are (or are not) barely detected. Weber's law describes this just noticeable difference.

Exercise 13.4 delves into an example of selective comprehension, which is the use of sometimes misleading surrogate (substitute) indicators of product quality, such as color, odor, and sound. Finally, Exercise 13.5 shows how various aspects of the stimulus object influence how it is viewed and investigates the gestalt school of psychology's principles for how people perceptually organize the various aspects of the stimulus.

EXERCISE 13.1. MARKETING TO SELECTIVE AND SUBJECTIVE PERCEPTION

OBJECTIVES

1. To understand the reasons for and nature of selective perception and subjective perception.
2. To become familiar with some of the basic marketing strategies to overcome the problems posed by selective and subjective perception and how marketers can take advantage of the opportunities they present.
3. To become aware of your own tendencies toward selective and subjective perception and how they restrict your understanding of the world around you.
4. To illustrate how advertisers effectively deal with the limitations and opportunities posed by perception's selectivity and subjectivity.
5. To experience how Internet marketers take advantage of selective and subjective perception.

BACKGROUND

The perception process is one of the most significant barriers to effective communication because it is both *selective* (people do not perceive a lot of the sensations that surround them) and *subjective* (they perceive many of these sensations in a distorted, biased manner).

SELECTIVE PERCEPTION

Selective perception (perceptual selection) suggests that people will consciously or subconsciously process only a fraction of the sensory stimuli to which they are exposed during each of the stages of the

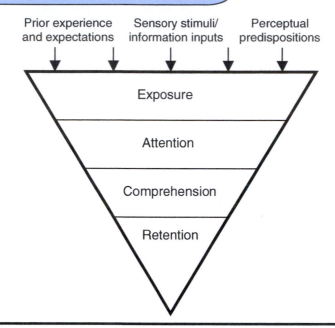

EXHIBIT 13.2   Selective Information Processing

Prior experience and expectations   Sensory stimuli/ information inputs   Perceptual predispositions

Exposure

Attention

Comprehension

Retention

perceptual process. We filter these stimuli through our perceptual screens, "turning off and tuning out" many of them.

Exhibit 13.2 shows that at each phase of consumer information processing, fewer and fewer stimuli survive this weeding-out process. Selective perception is most likely to occur during the first two stages (exposure and attention), while subjective perception most probably happens during the comprehension (interpretation) stage.

People are selective in their information intake due to **information overload (sensory saturation)**. They are constantly bombarded with myriad stimuli: e-mail, voicemail, IMs, Facebook pokes, RSS feeds, Twitter tweets, text messages, and so on. There are limits to people's ability to absorb and process this data deluge.

FACTORS DETERMINING THE NATURE OF SELECTIVE PERCEPTION

Two things determine which stimuli pass through individuals' perceptual barriers and enter into their memory banks, as shown at the top of Exhibit 13.2: prior experiences and expectations and perceptual predispositions.

People's prior experiences affect their expectations regarding what they shall experience. Individuals are likely to notice some things more than others because they generally see what they expect to see and hear what they anticipate they will hear. For instance, municipalities know that if they install a new traffic light, they must use flashing yellow lights for several weeks because many people do not "see" the new light and drive right through it. Americans still think of diesel vehicles as slow, smelly, and loud, even though today's models feature more powerful, clean, and quiet engines.

Stimuli that deviate markedly from expectations are more likely to be noticed: Novelty grabs attention. For example, if your professor were to use a four-letter profanity in class, would you not sit up and take notice?

Perceptual predispositions are a person's needs, wants, interests, values, and beliefs and attitudes. **Perceptual vigilance** means that people are more likely to notice stimuli relevant to these five factors. On the other hand, **perceptual defense** is an individual's tendency to ignore cues he or she finds psychologically threatening or that contradict that person's value, beliefs, or attitudes. Consequently, very strong fear appeals often fail to persuade because people ignore them. In fact, research verifies that people look the other way to avoid seeing what makes them uncomfortable. The following lists and illustrates each of the five perceptual predispositions.

1. *Physical needs.* People who are hungry and thirsty while driving down the highway will be more likely to catch signs for restaurants than for home improvement centers.
2. *Psychological wants.* People who feel lonely at a public event will keep their eyes peeled for a friend to hang with.
3. *Interests.* A fishing enthusiast will readily spot the fishing gear in a sporting goods store or a *Fishing Today* magazine on a newsstand.
4. *Values.* If listeners agree with the ideology being spouted by a politician, they are more likely to stick around and listen to a speech than if they do not agree.
5. *Beliefs and attitudes.* People have a need for cognitive consistency. Consequently, a smoker is likely to tune out a message from the American Cancer Society warning about the dangers of smoking.

MARKETING IMPLICATIONS OF SELECTIVE PERCEPTION

Consumers exposed to advertising and promotion do experience information overload. However, consumers will be more attuned to marketing messages that are clearly communicated, either conform to or sharply deviate from target customers' expectations and experience, are consistent with their perceptual predispositions, and appear in uncrowded media.

Use Clear Communication. Miscommunication by ads and salespeople is a problem. Advertisements should be copy tested to ensure that consumers "get it." Things to avoid include incorrect understanding of imagery, inappropriate humor, and double entendre or sexual allusion. Also, lengthy communications are less likely to pass through consumer' mental filters.

Conform to or Sharply Deviate from Consumers' Expectations and Experiences. Consumers tend to select stimuli that "break the mold" by deviating from their expectations shaped by prior experiences. Consequently, advertisers should use attention-getting elements in their advertising. The following ad aspects get engagement—interest in and involvement with products and advertisements.

- Unique and unexpected. For example, print ads that run upside down or radio commercials using strange voices or garbled speech. Heinz Easy Squeeze Ketchup and Kraft barbecue sauce both pop off supermarket shelves because they are packaged in upside-down bottles.
- Large. For example, a two-page magazine ad.
- Intense. For instance, loud sounds and bright colors such as neon yellow and bright orange grab car shoppers' attention.
- Moving. For example, in-store motion-activated displays (a shelf display for Bullfrog Waterproof sunblock croaks when a shopper passes by) and rapid scene changes in TV commercials.
- Colorful. Vivid and contrasting colors, such as black on yellow.
- Attractive. Gorgeous models and beauty shots (visually attractive pictures) of products such as cars and food.
- Simple, not complex. Brevity is beautiful. (Notice how short that last sentence was?)

Conform to Consumers' Perceptual Predispositions. Effective ads must appeal to consumer needs and desires in an interesting way. To get consumers' interest, it is important to know what they are interested in (e.g., for the typical teenage girl, that would be handsome teenage boys!). This is the idea behind **keyword search (contextual) advertising**, a system through which ads get served up on line to an individual viewer of a Web page based on the content the viewer is reading. Advertisers purchase **keywords** from search engines. These are words and phrases that will trigger the advertiser's banner ad, known as a keyword ad, to appear whenever users select that keyword for an online search.

It is also important to be consistent with the values of the culture, subculture, social class, and reference group targeted.

Use Uncrowded Media. It is usually wise to avoid cluttered media (e.g., Sunday newspapers), especially those where many direct competitors appear (skiing gear in a skiing magazine). Instead, marketers are smart to run ads in less crowded media, emerging media (e.g., mobile media such as cell phones and video MP3 players), or to become exclusive sponsors of a media vehicle (e.g., *Hallmark Hall of Fame*).

SUBJECTIVE PERCEPTION

"Beauty is in the eye of the beholder." "I call them as I see them." "Love is blind." "You're only as young as you feel." People's *cognitive age*—the age they perceive themselves to be (an element of self-concept)—is less than their chronological age. Subjective perception refers to individual differences in the organization and interpretation of sensory stimuli. This occurs primarily at the comprehension (interpretation) stage of information processing. Individuals differ in the meaning that they assign to environmental cues.

For example, selective perception, subjective perception is the result of prior experience and expectations and perceptual predispositions. Due to TV home shopping's roots in hawking the likes of Slim Whitman albums and Slicer Dicer mixer blenders, many people still view direct response TV as lowbrow, even though QVC sells brand-name goods, sophisticated electronics, and couture designer fashions. During the O.J. Simpson trial, most whites saw a murderer while many blacks saw a victim of police racism. Consider that some people believed Mel Gibson's movie *The Passion of the Christ* was a brilliant portrayal of Jesus' suffering, while others saw the film as anti-Semitic and overly violent.

Our expectations are grounded in previous experience and what is familiar. The result is perceptual distortion of information. Hence, if a customer has had a bad experience with a restaurant, he or she might expect and perceive the service to be poor, regardless of whether or not it really is.

THREE GENERAL FACTORS DETERMINING THE NATURE OF SUBJECTIVE PERCEPTION

The nature of subjective perception is influenced by three general "it depends" mediating factors: (1) the environment in which perception occurs, (2) the consumer's desires, expectations and other perceptual predispositions, and (3) the marketing stimulus object.

Factor 1. The Environment (Situation, Context). Subjective perception is shaped by the environment, situation, or context in which a stimulus object is perceived. Consider the expressions, "It was so quiet, I could hear a pin drop," and "You're seeing things through rose-colored glasses." A bikini on an attractive woman would look appropriate on the beach but not at the opera or on an unattractive woman.

Likewise, the marketing environment can influence consumer perceptions. As they say, a hot dog at the ballpark tastes better than a steak at the Ritz. On the other hand, studies have shown that the same food served in an uptown restaurant would not taste as good if eaten in a downtown dive.

➤ *The media environment.* Advertising agency media buyers consider the editorial (media) environment of the media vehicle when deciding where to run an advertisement. This "environment" refers to its credibility, respectability, feel, look and sound, and image. A mutual fund would be wiser to advertise in *Money* magazine than in the *National Tattler,* and an ad for *The Life Application Bible* would fit well in *Christianity Today* but not in *Hot Babes.*

➤ *The retail environment.* Research has proven that store image matters: Consumers will evaluate a blouse more positively if it is displayed in Bloomingdale's or Macy's, rather than in a no-frills outlet, such as Pick 'N Save or Frugal Fanny's. Also, the section of the store in which an item is displayed can influence perceptual product category positioning. When Ocean Spray Craisins (cranberry raisins) were test marketed, managers debated whether they should be stocked in the supermarket produce aisle (where consumers would think of them as a fresh fruit), in the dried fruits section (like raisins), in the baking ingredients aisle (with chocolate chips), or in the snack food area. If placed in the electronics aisle, shoppers would believe a Nintendo game was for adults, whereas if placed with children's toys they would view it as a kids' game.

➤ *The economic environment.* During periods of rapidly rising fuel prices, instead of raising fares, airlines institute "fuel surcharges," shifting the blame to the "greedy" oil companies. Throughout the financial crisis and recession of 2008–2009, even wealthy consumers held back on buying luxury items such as BMWs and Louis Vuitton handbags, not wanting to be perceived as spendthrifts who were unsympathetic to their economically struggling neighbors. Purchasing these brands in a bull market, however, would simply be seen as an expression of the consumer's newly gained wealth and acumen in investing.

Factor 2. The Stimulus Object. Exercise 13.5 demonstrates how stimulus object factors such as size, color, and novelty influence how the stimulus is viewed according to the Gestalt school of psychology's principles of perceptual organization.

Factor 3. The Individual Consumer. Each consumer shapes her own perceptions. The **cognitive school of psychology** studies how the human mind works when processing information. The basic idea is that the same stimulus can have different psychological meaning to different people.

Chapter 6 explained that people of different generations have diverse musical preferences, depending on what music was "hot" when they were children and that people from different ethnic and geographic subcultures have varying tastes in food. Women are more prone than men to notice pictures of babies, are more sensitive to loud sounds (fewer women like hard rock music), and are more apt to notice dirt and dust.

MARKETING IMPLICATIONS OF SUBJECTIVE PERCEPTION

Marketers must make a conscious effort to have biased perceptions work in their favor rather than against them. They can do this by overcoming and managing negative false perceptions, using subjective perceptual cues, avoiding deception, and using impression management.

Overcome and Manage Negative False Perceptions. Subjective perception can work against marketers if it leads to negative impressions. Men consider diet beverages feminine, working class drinkers deem wine too snooty, and young consumers regard coffee (Starbucks excepted) as unhealthy. Marketers of such products must set the record straight via tactics such as effective positioning, exceptional product experiences, and credible word-of-mouth communication that corrects misperceptions.

Pittsburgh had an image problem as a dirty, grimy, blue-collar steel town where people choked on air pollution and you could light a fire on the river. So, the town leaders ran an ad campaign to attract businesses by portraying the city as the high-tech, modern, and prosperous place it really is. Despite its state motto, "The Garden State," New Jersey officials fight the perception that it is as scenic as the rest stops along the New Jersey Turnpike and that it smells like one giant rump. MySpace was perceived as a teenage refuge where provocative photos are shared, even though almost half the site's members are thirty-five and older. Accordingly, MySpace gave itself a facelift to appear more polished and professional.

Employ Subjective Perceptual Cues. Marketers should be aware of the nature of subjective perception regarding the following perceptual stimuli, and use it to their advantage to enhance perceptions of their brands.

➤ *Colors.* Colors have particular connotations. Some of these meanings are *cultural*, such as pink being for girls, associated with frilliness and warmth, and blue being for boys, affiliated with efficiency and productivity. Blue is correlated with the corporate world, especially high-tech industry, and black conveys luxury, power, sophistication, and authority.

Other color connotations are believed to be *biological*, due to a color's inherent qualities for exciting people's nervous systems. Light blue and pink taste sweet, and therefore these are the color of packets, respectively, for Domino's sugar and Sweet'N Low artificial sweetener. Red is inherently an attention-getting color, but culturally it is also a warning signal (e.g., a stop sign or fire truck). Orange is a high-energy color, and it is used in Tide detergent's packaging to represent energy and cleaning power.

There are also demographic color preferences. Purple is popular with women and brown with men.

Regarding product colors, cream-colored ice cream tastes creamier. Brown connotes strength, stability, and dependability, and is therefore used on UPS trucks. A clear color in soaps and many personal care products signals purity and freedom from unnatural ingredients.

Concerning packaging colors, the bright orange Wheaties box has appetite appeal, blue on frozen food packages means icy, and Wrigley's gum comes in white packaging suggesting a "cool, clean" flavor. Meat and bread are rarely packaged in green wrappers due to the association of green with mold.

Colors featured in advertising also affect customers' impressions. Some cigarette ads feature lots of lush green to imply healthiness and freshness, an obvious, perhaps unethical, deviation from reality. Green is used in ads for drugs and medical products to suggest safety.

➤ *Shapes.* Round and curvy figures seem soft, feminine, serene, assured, sensuously relaxed, and optimistic. Circles are viewed as warm and protective, and their continuity is comforting. Ovals are the most aesthetically pleasant shape, offering balance and gentleness. Rectangular and angled forms connote masculinity and harshness. Squares suggest solidity, unity, straightforwardness and honesty, and stability. Triangles appear lively and imply spirit, animation, agitation, conflict, tension, and aspiration.

A slim bottle of salad dressing suggests it is low fat and will help you become slender. Coast soap combined color (blue-and-white swirl patterns) and shape (oval) to connote freshness. Car designers make vehicles appear large inside by using light upholstery shades and lots of glass. Rounded corners on the outside make the vehicles appear more compact.

➤ *Words.* People sometimes use **euphemisms**—the substitution of inoffensive, more pleasant-sounding, words for offensive, harsh, unpleasant, or embarrassing terms. We say that someone "passed away" rather than "died"; people live in "mobile homes," not "trailers"; and guys are "getting in shape" rather than "going on a diet." You live in a "residence hall," not a "dorm."

Advertisers are notorious for their use of euphemistic language. The following are examples of word pairs that can be respectively filled into the two blanks in the following statement: "Instead of saying _____, say _____." Word pairs for the blanks include: toilet paper . . . bathroom tissue; constipation . . . irregularity; used car . . . previously owned automobile; gambling . . . gaming; fast food joint . . . quick-serve restaurant; cheap . . . low (or bargain)-priced; sneakers . . . athletic shoes; liquor store . . . package store; war toys . . . action figures; sweaty armpits . . . underarm wetness; and interest charge . . . convenience fee.

Even the term "minivan" now has a dorky image since for most people it is a kid hauler, so car marketers call the vans "family utility vehicles" and "multipurpose vehicles." And only advertisers could cement "erectile dysfunction" in Middle America's vocabulary as a replacement for "male impotence."

Brand names can also be selected or changed with nicer meanings in mind. Because sugar is viewed as unhealthy, Sugar Crisp cereal became Golden Crisp, and Sugar Smacks cereal was rechristened as Honey Smacks. Kentucky Fried Chicken was reborn as simply KFC, as though that magically got rid of all the grease and cholesterol in fried chicken. (It did not; KFC has been reborn as Kentucky Fried Chicken.)

Avoid Deceptive Tactics. **Deception** is a form of impression management that entails deliberately creating perceptions that deviate from reality to mislead consumers acting rationally. The Federal Trade Commission defines **deceptive advertising** as an ad that contains a material misrepresentation, omission, or other practice that can mislead a significant number of rational consumers to their detriment. This issue is whether the ad conveys a false impression even if it is literally true. For instance, the omission of negative information (a food is high in sodium content) in an ad making positive claims (the food is "heart healthy") can be deceptive if it causes consumers to believe the food product is entirely healthy.

However, there are times when it is in a marketer's self-interest to reinforce false positive perceptions, although this might be difficult to do without being deceitful. The pet supply industry plays on pet owners' beliefs that their pets need outfits (25 percent believe this), enjoy souvenirs from family vacations (44 percent), and want their birthdays celebrated (63 percent). Retailers often place products at the end of an aisle in end cap displays or feature them in a grocery store newspaper circular to make it appear they are on sale. Buyers beware: Such items aren't always marked down.

Use Impression Management. **Impression management (spin control)** involves selectively and positively reporting information to make one's self or firm look good; accentuating the positive and downplaying any negative. In a job interview, candidates are counseled to look authoritative and confident by standing straight and striding right into the interview room without any hesitation. They should stand straight, look the interviewer directly in the eye, and shake hands firmly with knuckles popping. In the office at work, impression-conscious employees make sure they get plenty of "face" time with the boss.

Many consumers viewed Perrier as a yuppie country-club drink. To counter this, Perrier launched ads featuring a cross section of real places and people across America to depict it as a natural and common part of everyday life, using the tagline, "Perrier. Part of the local color."

THE BOTTOM LINE ON SUBJECTIVE PERCEPTION

The overriding lesson for marketers is to learn to view things through their customers' eyes. Businesspeople often assume that their customers perceive the world as they do. A lot of American business is run under the fallacious assumption that everyone sees things in pretty much the same way. Thus, technical people build products they like (usually too complex for us mere mortals to operate) and copywriters write ads they find amusing and convincing (but the rest might find insipid).

It has been said, "The downfall of a magician is belief in his own magic." The solution to the problem of misgauging consumer perceptions is simple: Marketers must consult their customers to learn of their interests, interpretations, and viewpoints. Then, sellers can market to the perception, not the reality!

REVIEW QUESTIONS

1. What is the difference between perception and information processing? Outline the stages in the processes of perception and information processing and define each step.
2. Describe the relationship between the degree of motivation (involvement) and the nature of information exposure.
3. Explain the role of each of the following in providing information inputs into the perceptual process: sensory stimuli, sensory receptors, sensory systems, and sensations.
4. Discuss the nature of selective perception and the process involved.
5. Explain the nature of subjective perception. Describe how each of the three general mediating ("it depends") factors influences the nature of subjective perception.
6. Describe two general factors determining the nature of selective perception as well as reasons why people experience subjective perception.
7. Discuss important marketing implications of both selective perception and subjective perception.

IN-CLASS APPLICATIONS

1. Fun times with selective perception:
   a. Give yourself a break—don't review this part before class! Skip part (b) also—go right to part (c) of this question.

   In class, your instructor will have you pair up. One student will read the following passage aloud and another person will carefully listen (with this book closed).

   "You are a bus driver. You pick up a nineteen-year-old girl and her mother, who is fifty-two. A young man of twenty-two named Charlie gets off the bus with his sixty-eight-year-old grandfather. At the next stop, a three-year-old, nineteen-year-old, and thirty-six-year-old get on the bus. They all sit near the front of the bus, where a twenty-eight-year-old woman is holding her baby of three months. The final stop comes and everyone gets off the bus. How old is the bus driver?"
   b. Don't look at this one before class, either.

   While staring at the X below, notice what surrounds your book on your desk, and even what surrounds your desk and yourself.

   Did you notice the colors or items around your book before, such as the shoes on the person next to you? Now, without glancing up, what is the color and texture of the ceiling of the room you are in right now? Look up to see if you were correct.
   c. Your instructor and/or a student will scan the room for one minute, and then leave the room for two minutes. You and your classmates are to change five things about the room (e.g., seating arrange-

ments, clothing swap, shoes off, and the like). The instructor and/or student will return to the room and attempt to identify the five changes. Did he or she find them all?

   d. The instructor will randomly hand out pieces of paper to every class member. Each strip of paper will contain a different number, starting from one and going up to the number of students in class. Then, at the count of "three," the entire class will proceed to read their numbers aloud over and over, all at the same time. The instructor will then attempt to identify the person saying the number "one."

   e. Pick a card, any card . . . Visit www.niehs.nih.gov/kids/cardtr.htm and follow the directions. How does this card trick use selective attention to fool you?

   f. Time for another fun trick, this time with subjective perception! Hold your two index fingers about four inches in front of your eyes, with your fingertips about a half-inch apart. Now look over and beyond your fingers at the other side of the room. What happens to your fingers? While looking out into the distance, move your fingers farther apart. What happens to the "floating sausage?"

2. Remember that silly childhood game of "telephone?" Now it's time to recreate the memories! Your instructor will hand out two pieces of paper, each containing a story, to the two people in the front and back corners of the room. Both students will tell the story to their fellow classmates via whispering, one person at a time going around the classroom.

    When the two storytelling chains meet at the middle of the room, those two students will each write down their "version" of each story. When they are done, each of the first storytellers in the corners will read the original story aloud to the class. Then, each middle storyteller will then share his or her version of the story.

    How well did you all do? Was each story passed down accurately? What does this exercise say about selective perception and subjective perception?

3. For each of the first five ads (Exhibits 13.3–13.7), identify how the advertiser is attempting to either combat or take advantage of selective attention, either by using attention getters such as size of stimulus, movement, color, novelty, attractiveness, celebrity, sex, and humor, or by appealing to consumer predispositions, such as needs and wants, interests, values, beliefs, and attitudes. How effective do you believe each ad is in its attempt to "cut through the clutter"?

4. In each of the last five ads (Exhibits 13.8–13.12), describe how the advertiser has employed the concept of subjective perception through the following devices.

   • Impression management
   • Trying to correct negative false perceptions
   • Using perceptual cues such as colors (imagine what the colors would be), shapes, and words.

   Do any of the ads reveal good insight into consumers' subjective perceptions (or lack of insight therein)?

5. Fun times with the Internet.

   a. Visit www.nielsenmedia.com/nc/portal/site/Public/ and peruse the Web site. Be sure to pay special attention to how the data are collected. Based on your knowledge regarding selective perception, how accurate could Nielson ratings actually be?

   b. Point your browser to http://www.hotelsetc.com/images/public/rest_cert/restaurant_logos.jpgnd (look at each logo created for the food industry). Which restaurant or food service would you most likely patronize? Is this decision based on your subjective perception of the logo?

   c. What is your name? Do people see you differently after hearing your name? Does "Josephine" conjure up different images than "Monica"? Why does "Butch" sound like the name of a tough guy but "Percy" sounds like a little girlie-man?

    Apply this idea to brand names and visit www.ivarson.com to view what it takes to name a brand. (Click on Brand Vision to begin.). How do selective perception and subjective perception affect how consumers view brand names?

EXHIBIT 13.3   Campbell's Soup Ad

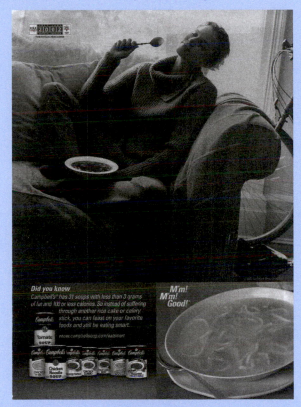

EXHIBIT 13.4   Budweiser Ad

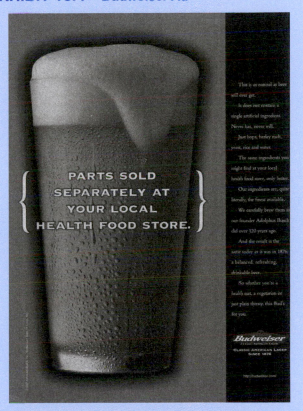

EXHIBIT 13.5   Got Milk? Ad

EXHIBIT 13.6   Max Factor Ad

EXHIBIT 13.7   Miracle Whip Ad

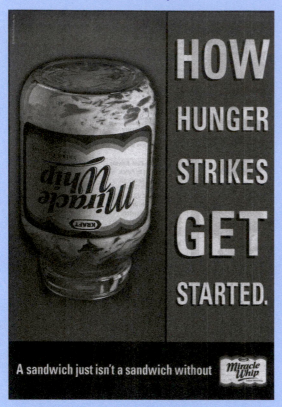

EXHIBIT 13.8   Crest Whitestrips Ad

EXHIBIT 13.9   Lever 2000 Ad

EXHIBIT 13.10   Endust Ad

EXHIBIT 13.11   Post Cereal Ad

EXHIBIT 13.12   Kmart Ad

6. Color Quiz: Let's see how well you know your colors. Using the chart below, try to match the colors in the Color Column with the Color Description (attributes and general appearance, mental associations, and effects or impressions they give the viewer).

Color Description

Color Column		Attributes/ Appearance	Mental Associations	Effects/Impressions
1. Red	a.	Sunny, radiant, warmth, cheerful, happy	Sunlight, creativity, imagination, optimism, futuristic, spirituality, newness, low prices	Cheerful, inspiring, vital, healthy
2. Orange	b.	Clean, fresh, pure, modern, neat	Purity, sterility, calm, brides, cool, snow	Brightness of spirit, normality, attention-getting
3. Yellow	c.	Warm, cheerful, simple, uncomplicated	Romance, sweetness, delicacy, subduing, flattering	Tenderness, refinement, femininity, innocence
4. Green	d.	Exciting, daring, dynamic, sexy, brilliant, intense	Blood, fire, competition, optimism, life, violence, communism	Passionate, exciting, arousal, activity, increases heart and respiration rates
5. Blue	e.	Comfortable, reliable, steady, simple	Earth, stability, harmony, hearth, home, neutrality	Comforting, soothing
6. Purple/ Violet	f.	Bright, luminous, glowing, vibrant, warm	Warm, metallic, autumnal, extroversion, adventure, celebration	Jovial, lively, energetic, forceful, stimulating, triggers alert
7. White	g.	Exciting, mysterious complex, intriguing	Passion, spirituality, art, creativity, wit, sensitivity, vanity, royalty, homosexuality	Dignified, pompous, mournful, inspiring, thought-provoking

(continued)

| | | Color Description | |
Color Column	Attributes/ Appearance	Mental Associations	Effects/Impressions
8. Black	h. Safe, secure, practical, dependable, elegant	Neutrality, boredom, conservatism, ashes	Reassuring, dulling
9. Pink	i. Fresh, clean, restful, peaceful, clear, moist	Cool, nature, water, ecology, fertility, spring	Quieting, refreshing, innocent, stabilizing
10. Brown	j. Transparent, wet, calm, tranquil, holy	Cold, sky, water, sky, dependability, protection, loyalty, sadness, hope	Calming, cleansing, cooling, subdued, melancholy, sober
11. Gray	k. Mysterious, elegant, sophisticated, worldly	Death and mourning, bad luck, night, power, evil	

WRITTEN APPLICATIONS

1. Answer Question 3 in the In-Class Applications. Then find four more ads that use several techniques to capitalize on or else battle selective attention. Evaluate the effectiveness of each ad in using consumer perceptions.

2. Answer Question 4. Then find four more ads, each of which employs one or more devices related to subjective perception. Answer the set of questions found in Question 4 for each ad.

3. Euphemisms abound to make us feel better about things and ourselves. We no longer have poor people—they are economically disadvantaged (underprivileged). Old people are senior citizens (or—pardon our regurgitation—Golden Agers). And those with a handicap are mentally or physically challenged. Job titles have changed: Secretaries are now administrative (executive) assistants, undertakers are funeral directors, janitors are either custodians or sanitary engineers, strippers are exotic dancers, mechanics are service technicians, checkout clerks are store associates, and manicurists are nail technicians.

To find out just how powerful the impact of each of these pairs of terms for people is, conduct a qualitative study, interviewing a dozen people. Ask half of them to briefly describe a person you label with each of the less flattering labels above (e.g., "a poor person") and half of them to briefly describe a person you label with each of the more pleasant labels (e.g., "an economically disadvantaged" person) above.

Summarize your results. What does this teach you about the power of words?

EXERCISE 13.2. THE ABSOLUTE THRESHOLD LEVEL AND SUBLIMINAL MESSAGES

OBJECTIVES

1. To recognize the relevance of the absolute threshold level concept to marketing.
2. To understand subliminal messages in light of the perceptual process and of the absolute threshold level.
3. To become more informed on the controversial issue of subliminal advertising.
4. To analyze the usefulness and limitations of subliminal messages.
5. To gain experience in evaluating ads that could be perceived as subliminal and to assess your personal experiences with subliminal messages.
6. To determine whether subliminal messages are immoral.
7. To learn about and experience subliminal messages by visiting Web sites.

BACKGROUND

Recall the consumer information-processing model outlined in Exhibit 13.1 for this chapter with its stages of exposure, attention, comprehension, and retention. This and the following three exercises investigate several phenomena related to the attention and comprehension phases of the process shown in Exhibit 13.13. We look briefly at the three stages constituting the perceptual process.

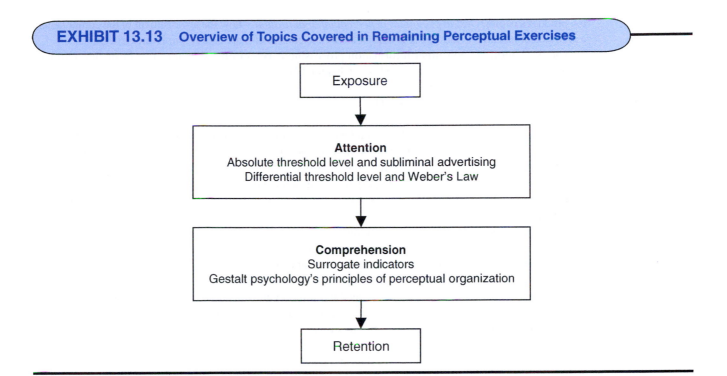

EXHIBIT 13.13   Overview of Topics Covered in Remaining Perceptual Exercises

Exposure

↓

Attention
Absolute threshold level and subliminal advertising
Differential threshold level and Weber's Law

↓

Comprehension
Surrogate indicators
Gestalt psychology's principles of perceptual organization

↓

Retention

EXPOSURE

Exposure occurs when a consumer confronts (or is confronted by) a stimulus so that one or more sensory organs are activated and information processing can begin. Exposure can be either random or involuntary, such as with broadcast commercials and outdoor billboards, or deliberate and voluntary, as with online searches and print media.

The key consideration for the advertiser is matching characteristics of the target market with those of a medium's target audience so that the right consumers are potentially exposed to marketing communications in the proper medium. Advertisements are then placed in locations within media vehicles where they are most likely to be encountered, such as next to interesting editorial matter in a magazine or in a relevant section of the newspaper, as with sporting goods ads positioned in the sports pages.

ATTENTION

Next, **attention** occurs, in which the consumer focuses on an incoming stimulus, thereby allocating information processing capacity to it so that the sensations enter his brain for processing. Job number one for any promotional effort is to grab the prospect's attention!

Exercises 13.2 and 13.3 focus on two aspects of the attention phase: absolute threshold level and just noticeable difference (jnd). The *absolute threshold level* is the minimum level of stimulus intensity that is noticeable. Exercise 13.2 is concerned with the absolute threshold level and *subliminal advertising*. The latter is when advertising elements are supposedly snuck in below the consumer's absolute threshold level in an effort to covertly influence CB.

Exercise 13.3 investigates the *jnd (differential threshold)*, which is the level of stimulus intensity change that can just barely be detected by a consumer, such as a slight price hike or miniscule cut in product quality.

COMPREHENSION (INTERPRETATION)

Exercises 13.4 and 13.5 involve the stage of **comprehension**, or the consumer's level of understanding and interpretation of the stimulus. Exercise 13.4 investigates consumers' use of *surrogate indicators*—shorthand signals of product quality or performance, such as price and brand name, which may or may not be valid indicators of the product's nature. *Gestalt principles of perceptual organization*—how the arrangement of the components of a stimulus object affects the way it is interpreted by the consumer—are covered in Exercise 13.5.

The final hurdle in consumer information processing is **retention**—the entry if information into long-term memory so that it can be recalled (see Chapter 14).

PSYCHOPHYSICS AND THE ABSOLUTE THRESHOLD LEVEL

Whether or not a consumer actively pays attention to a stimulus is determined in large part by its level of intensity. **Psychophysics** is the study of the how the physical environment is related to people's subjective (psychological) experience, that is, the relationship between the nature and amount of a stimulus and the sensation that it produces. This discipline investigates the absolute threshold level and the differential threshold.

The lowest level at which a person just barely detects a stimulus is known as that cue's **absolute (lower, detection) threshold level (ATL).** The ATL is the minimum level of stimulus intensity that the individual can perceive, or the point at which a person just barely notices that "something" is there. The tone you could just barely hear in the hearing tests given in grade school was your ATL for hearing.

For example, a typical person can see a candle flame at thirty miles on a dark clear night and can also taste one teaspoon of sugar in two gallons of water and smell one drop of perfume diffused throughout a three-bedroom apartment (therefore, you need not dowse yourself with cologne for people to notice).

Of course, there are individual differences in such ATLs, so these are only averages. Furthermore, one person might vary somewhat in sensitivity to stimuli from day to day or from one situation to another.

Generally, our senses can only perceive a rather narrow range of stimulus intensity. For instance, humans cannot see ultraviolet rays but bees can. Bats and porpoises can hear sounds two octaves beyond our range. You cannot notice radar, but a radar detector can.

Firms sometimes hire professionals with relatively low ATLs as taste testers or to determine the efficacy of personal care products such as deodorants (testers actually smell peoples' armpits to detect if deodorant eliminates odor) and mints (they smell people's breath).

THE ADAPTATION LEVEL: A CHANGING ABSOLUTE THRESHOLD LEVEL

Sometimes people's ATLs change over time. **Adaptation (sensory adaptation, habituation)** is the process of adjusting to or growing accustomed to a frequently occurring stimulus so that it is no longer noticed. Recall how the first chilly day of winter that comes along feels quite cold, but after several days of cold you "get used to" the chill so that it is no longer so uncomfortable.

Likewise, stepping into an air-conditioned store on a very hot day feels great at first. But after several minutes, you adapt to the cooler air and no longer notice it. When you enter a locker room, at first you choke on the odor of "eau de locker room," but after awhile it no longer bothers you. Although when you turn on a car's ignition, you hear the "ding, ding, ding" of the car safety belt reminder to buckle up, after awhile you ignore it.

The **adaptation level**, then, is that amount of stimulus intensity to which a person becomes accustomed. It serves as a reference point or standard of comparison for changes in the level of the stimulus. Consequently, someone coughing at a noisy party would not be heard, but in a quiet room where students are taking a test this same sound would be startling.

For marketers, the implication is to make sure consumers do not become adapted to their marketing stimuli, such as advertising or packaging, so that they tune them out. This is accomplished by offering change or variety in marketing cues. Consequently, most advertising campaigns, while featuring similar messages and creative executions of that message, present variations in individual ads so that consumers do not grow bored. Although Wheaties remains the "Breakfast of Champions," the individual sports stars featured in the ads and on the package continually evolve. In the area of product development, new and improved versions as well as line extensions (new flavors, scents, styles, etc.) keep a product fresh and interesting for consumers and provide variety. In short, consumers should "expect the unexpected."

However, marketers must be cautious in making radical changes, such as altering ingredients in food or drink items or rapidly raising prices. Often the adaptation level is preferred, and so customers might better receive evolutionary change than revolutionary change. When the Tropicana orange juice carton was redesigned in 2009 with a new, bold graphic of a glass filled with orange juice, there arose a firestorm of dissatisfied loyal customers who wanted the original orange-and-straw motif and complained about the change on blogs. Similarly, when H.J. Heinz replaced the gherkin from their ketchup label logo with a tomato on the vine in an attempt to appear healthier, consumers fought back with the Facebook page, "Save the Heinz pickle!" On the other hand, when gasoline prices rose rapidly in the late-2000s, at first consumers experienced sticker shock. However, the shock did not last forever, and people got used to paying $3 to $4 per gallon rather than $2.

Following its merger with Cingular Wireless, AT&T Wireless decided to phase out the Cingular name. However, they did so gradually over several months. They began by using a tagline in commercials, "Cingular is now part of AT&T." The next phase made the AT&T name more prominent. And eventually the Cingular moniker was dropped altogether.

MARKETING STIMULI AND THE ABSOLUTE THRESHOLD LEVEL

STIMULI ABOVE AND BELOW THE ATL

Of course, marketers need to make sure that their important stimuli (advertising elements, reduced prices on packages, etc.) are above the consumer's ATL in order to get noticed and arouse interest, which is a big challenge in cluttered commercial environments. Marketers must resort to tactics such as large sizes and loud sounds to get consumer attention, as demonstrated in Exercise 13.5.

There are also instances in which marketers do not wish for consumers to detect certain stimuli; they prefer to remain below the consumer's ATL radar. You have heard of the "fine print" in advertising disclosures, packages, and other written materials. This is made almost too small to read to avoid catching the consumer's attention. Similarly, the legally required audio disclosures in radio commercials ("Offer void where prohibited") usually run at warp speed and at low volume so that consumers cannot really understand them.

SUBLIMINAL ADVERTISING

OVERVIEW OF SUBLIMINAL INFLUENCES

A much-discussed tactic whereby marketers allegedly lurk below the ATL is the case of subliminal advertising. The word subliminal comes from combining two Latin words: the prefix *sub* (meaning "below") with *limen* ("threshold" or "limit").

Subliminal, then, literally means "below the threshold of conscious perception (ATL)," that is, people cannot perceive the stimulus object at all. Consequently, **subliminal stimuli (subliminal messages)** are cues that activate one or more sensory receptors but are below the ATL.

A person's subconscious perception of subliminal cues is called **subliminal perception**. The belief is that one can influence CB by secretly appealing to the subconscious mind with words, images, or sounds. Critics claim that advertising agencies who use these subliminal stimuli in **subliminal advertising (subliminal seduction)** are trying to manipulate consumers by placing hidden images, words, or sounds in print, audio, or video advertising media. The theory is that, although the stimulus is below the consumer's level of conscious awareness, the subconscious mind nonetheless processes the stimulus. This leads to attitude change (e.g., brand preference) followed by behavioral change (e.g., a product purchase or a store visit).

TYPES OF SUBLIMINAL MESSAGES

During the 1950s, the United States experienced what became known as the "red scare." This was the fear of communism and its "mind control." In this environment of alarm, stories began circulating about advertising agencies doing motivation research, using their findings to seduce customers into buying unwanted merchandise with subliminal messaging.

We now investigate five different types of subliminal stimuli: subvisual messages, embeds, incongruities and suggestiveness, subaudible messages, and backward masking. While subliminal stimuli perhaps occasionally exist, subliminals cannot be effectively used to persuade or alter CB. Years of research have shown very limited emotional effects from subliminal stimulation, and there has been no support for its effectiveness in behavior modification. Nonetheless, at least three-fourths of the general adult American population believes that subliminal advertising is purposely created and used to sell products.

Bottom line: If some marketers do use subliminal stimuli, they are wasting their efforts and being unethically sneaky in the process.

Subvisual Messages. The brouhaha over subliminal advertising began in 1957, when a movie theater hired Subliminal Projection Company, run by the originator of the term subliminal advertising, James Vicary. The firm had developed a subliminal projection machine that delivered **subvisual messages** by implanting single-frame visual images or words, each only milliseconds in duration, into a film. These messages were repeatedly flashed every few seconds. For a six-week test run in the movie theater, Vicary alternated the subliminal messages, "Hungry? Eat popcorn" and "Drink Coke," exposing 45,699 patrons.

Vicary held press conferences claiming that the subliminals had increased sales of Coke by 18 percent and of popcorn by 58 percent. However, he never released a detailed description of his study. Nor has there ever been any independent evidence to support his claims—all attempts at replication failed. Moreover, in an interview with *Advertising Age* in 1962, Vicary admitted that the original study was a fabrication designed to help his struggling business. And, despite the notoriety, no regulation or legislation has ever been enacted against subvisual communication.

Nonetheless, there are occasional reports of efforts to use subliminal messages in TV commercials. Film companies have also been accused of planting subvisuals, such as a death mask flashed on screen to give audiences an extra scare in *The Exorcist,* a suspect bulge on a character that appeared to be an erection in *The Little Mermaid,* and a wispy S-E-X spelled out in the clouds in a scene from *The Lion King.* Subvisual messages have also been used by self-improvement software such as InnerTalk, with managers programming computers to flash messages such as "work faster."

Subliminal Print Ads: Embeds. During the 1970s and 1980s, Dr. Wilson Bryan Key published a series of books that investigated print media **embeds**. These are hidden words and images, most of which appeal to subconscious drives such as sex and the Freudian death wish (Thanatos). Key alleged that these faint visuals were being placed in magazine ads via techniques such as high-speed photography and airbrushing. Today, digital manipulation is supposedly used as well. Allegedly, viewers subconsciously perceived the embeds, which could elicit drives such as sexual arousal. This, in turn, supposedly made the products more attractive to consumers, thereby positively influencing their attitudes and provoking sales.

Key found embeds including women's breasts, male and female genitalia, and death masks in the ice cubes of liquor ads. He famously found the word "sex" as well as many unprintable four-letter words emblazoned on people's hair and beards, plus couples in compromising positions in floral designs. He even claimed that the word "sex" was formed by the holes in Ritz crackers, making this delicacy taste even better!

However, conceptually, Key offered no conceptual explanation for exactly how subliminal advertising works. Key backed up his case with a hodgepodge of theories from the fields of communication studies, media criticism, and Freudian psychology, most of which is dismissed by the modern scientific community. For instance, drawing on Freudian thinking, he claimed that when we perceive these images subliminally but repress them, we are irrationally attracted to the ad.

Empirically, there is virtually no experimental support for the efficacy of subliminal embeds. Key's own "research" with his students lacked proper scientific controls. He simply asked how many of his students saw particular alleged embeds in ads, considering their acquiescence as evidence.

Some psychology experiments have shown that subliminal stimuli can influence high-level cognitive and affective processes (e.g., recognition of and preferences for geometric shapes), although these are fleeting in nature. Some studies suggest that human sensory organs pick up stimuli presented below the threshold of consciousness and that people can process information without being aware of it. More recent research also suggests that subliminally presented stimuli can influence behavior.

However, these studies were conducted in artificial laboratory situations. And, the effects are generally so small and short-lived as to be useless in altering CB. Investigations have failed to show conclusive results in an advertising context.

The key (pun purely coincidental) issue is whether subliminal stimuli provide advertisers with a tool to bypass buyers' defenses without their awareness, so that consumer exposure to subliminals results in effective persuasion and manipulation of CB. The nearly universal consensus is that this is not possible.

Other questions remain unanswered by Key:

• Where is his documentation for the cognitive, affective, and behavioral effects of subliminal advertising? All he offered was anecdotal evidence based on what he and his students "discovered" in print ads. As the ad industry has pointed out, such "findings" seem to be the product of hyperactive imaginations. Whether or not erotic imagery has been deliberately planted, a diligent search for a phallic symbol will probably uncover it. All of us are able to "see" all sorts of things in clouds, mountaintops, trees, and other objects.

• Why are there no witnesses to the preparation of embeds? If subliminals are used by so many advertisers, why was Key unable to quote just one of them on how they employ the tactics? Is there not one unemployed ex-stimulator who can come forward with the truth, perhaps writing an exposé or even a how-to book? Professor Jack Haberstroh of Virginia Commonwealth University surveyed more than 100 U.S. ad directors, and not a single one claimed to have ever worked on a subliminal ad!

• If subliminal stimulation is rampant and urges people to buy, why do the government and other public service advertisers not use subliminal ads to make people stop taking drugs, abusing children, and driving drunk? College professors could even use subliminal messages in the slides and videos they show their classes to encourage students to study hard, stop going to wild parties and staying up late, give up smoking and excessive drinking, and be courteous and attentive to and absolutely idolize their instructors!

The academic community, the advertising establishment, and even government regulators all nearly unanimously pooh-poohed the notion of subliminal advertising during the Vicary and Key eras. But the legend lives on.

SUBLIMINAL PRINT ADS: INCONGRUITIES AND SUGGESTIVENESS

Incongruities and suggestiveness are two other types of print advertising sometimes described as subliminal that do not technically meet the definition of this term because people often are aware of them. Nonetheless, they can at times operate at a low level of awareness, perhaps even subconsciously.

Incongruities are portions of an ad containing an inconsistency, that is, two or more of its elements do not logically fit together. For example, an ad for Jantzen swimsuits included a female whose trunks were unusually loose and contained a zipper fly. The man with her wore swim trunks matching her brassiere, implying crossdressing. Benson and Hedges cigarettes ran an ad that featured a protruding right hand placed so it could not belong to any of the characters in the ad. Several advertising researchers have suggested that such ads lead to more information processing as well as arousal, and consequently more favorable ad evaluations.

Some print ads contain **suggestiveness**, that is, the advertisement implies more than the written copy states. The message is not spelled out explicitly in words but rather is subtly implied via use of verbal language, body language, color, and other perceptual devices, often including sexual innuendo, or subtle sexual messages. For example, a Levitra TV commercial featured a fortyish woman sporting a man's dress shirt, suggesting to some observers that she had just engaged in sexual relations. However, suggestiveness is *not* subliminal because we are supposed to notice the suggestive ad elements.

Subaudible Messages. **Subaudible messages (subaudible communications, audio conditioning, threshold messaging, psychoacoustic persuasion)** consist of accelerated (time-compressed) and/or garbled speech played at a low volume and masked under a "carrier," such as music or ocean waves, so that the message cannot be consciously heard. The claim is that while the message is unintelligible and therefore goes consciously unnoticed, it is subconsciously processed, leading to affective and/or behavioral changes.

Department stores in both the United States and Canada have reportedly reduced shoplifting by fusing bland "elevator music" with subliminal antitheft messages, such as "I am honest. I will not break the law and steal." Sales organizations and athletic teams have employed subliminal motivational tapes to rally the troops, doctors have used them to calm patients in waiting rooms, and subaudible messages in rock music have been blamed for encouraging Satan worship and suicide.

While there is mixed evidence of the effectiveness of such messages, researchers note that only individuals who are predisposed toward what the subaudible messages advocate will accept them. Hence, a normally honest person tempted to take a five-finger discount will respond to the suggestion "I don't want to go to jail for stealing," but a professional shoplifter will not.

Subaudible messages seem to work in a manner similar to hypnotism. You can subconsciously encourage people to avoid or undertake certain behaviors only if they are so inclined. Also, many researchers believe that subaudible communications work due to the placebo effect, that is, people expect them to work, and so they do.

While there are no reported advertising applications of subaudible messages, the evidence suggests that this is for good reason: They would be impotent in altering CB.

Backward Masking. Also known as **backmasking** and **audio reversal, backward masking** entails inserting a message in reverse into an audio medium (e.g., record, tape, CD, or DVD). Although the words cannot be consciously perceived when the audio is played in its normal, forward manner, the claim is that these imperceptible communications are heard at an unconscious level, thereby influencing attitudes and behavior.

Reported applications have occurred in rock music. The Beatles were among the first to employ the technique in their music with backward messages including "Paul is dead," "Turn me on dead man," and "I buried Paul." However, this turned out to be a public relations ploy to revitalize the group's waning dominance. The 1970s and 1980s saw an explosion in backward masking in rock music, some of which carried satanic messages.

One theory underlying backward masking is that selective cognitive processes ordinarily screen out unwanted information. However, when data enters our brain backward, it is not filtered, and somehow the subconscious can translate it to become meaningful. Supposedly, when hearing these songs forward, the brain picks up the backward messages subliminally. Consequently, they can affect one's mind, actions, and personality.

However, researchers have shown this theory to be untrue. Humans simply do not have a subconscious speech perception mechanism that can decode a reversed signal. It appears that backward masking is ineffectual in influencing people and of no value for marketing, other than stirring up word of mouth and publicity for rock groups and sensationalistic critics!

CONCLUSION ON SUBLIMINAL ADVERTISING

The public continues to believe subliminal messaging is a civic menace due to the negative image of the advertising profession, the fact that sensationalism sells, and because people dislike the fact that advertising conspicuously attempts to influence (not manipulate) them. If folks cannot explain certain emotions or purchases, or if they experience postpurchase regret, it is more comfortable to blame mysterious forces at work than to take personal responsibility. However, the evidence suggests that subliminal advertising does not work, although it does apparently exist since there will always be fraudulent people doing deceitful things, such as sneaking hidden messages into ads. The deliberate use of subliminal communication is immoral because it is insidious, violates the consumer's right to know, and tries to control human behavior in violation of free will.

In those rare cases where it is used, subliminal communication is relatively ineffectual. Subliminals only work to some degree in the case of constant message repetition (as with subvisual messages and subaudible messages) and where audience members are predisposed toward the message (i.e., their free will cannot be violated).

It is true that in tightly controlled lab settings, subliminals have produced mild but fleeting emotional reactions and heightened existing drives. However, there is virtually no research evidence supporting their effectiveness in altering CB. A big gap exists between perception and persuasion when it comes to subliminal advertising's efficacy.

Furthermore, there are quite a number of practical difficulties in using subliminal messages:

- Needs and wants cannot be created. Instead, marketers should appeal to and satisfy existing drives, which they can heighten and influence only at a general level. While a subliminal message saying "Drink Coke" might induce thirst, it could trigger a desire for Pepsi or even for water. Therefore, to change CB against sovereign consumers' free will is impossible.
- Supraliminal stimuli (ordinary stimuli, above the threshold level) tend to overpower or nullify subliminals (hidden below the threshold level). Indeed, psychological studies demonstrate that a strong stimulus produces a strong response and a weak stimulus a weak response.
- Perceptual thresholds vary across persons and over time for any one individual. Consequently, what is subliminal for some will be supraliminal for others, and what is subliminal for you today could be supraliminal for you tomorrow. To go undetected by virtually everyone, subliminal stimuli would need to be at an extremely low threshold level, perhaps too low to have even a subconscious effect on most people.
- People selectively screen out supraliminal stimuli not consistent with their predispositions, and probably do so for subliminal stimuli as well.
- In their normally busy, mutitasking worlds, individuals do not typically give undivided attention to a stimulus as subjects in subliminal experiments do.
- Since consumers subjectively interpret stimuli, misinterpretation is likely. Was that message "Drink Coke," "Drink Cola," "Drink Pepsi," "Drink cocoa," or "Stink Coke"?

Please—lose no sleep tonight over being subliminally seduced by Madison Avenue.

REVIEW QUESTIONS

1. Explain the absolute threshold level.
2. Explain the relationship between subliminal stimuli, subliminal perception, and subliminal advertising.
3. Describe each of the five types of subliminal messages, how each one has been used, and the limitations of each.
4. Discuss the practical difficulties in using subliminal messages.
5. What are the ethical problems with subliminal advertising?

IN-CLASS APPLICATIONS

1. For each of the advertisements in Exhibits 13.14 through 13.18, identify any evidence or possibilities of subliminal advertising based on the three types of subliminal elements used in print ads: embeds, incongruities, and suggestiveness. Are these ads more effective through the use of such possible subliminal elements or would they be just as effective without hidden messages? Note: For more information (or, at least, opinion) on how these ads are manipulated, check out "Subliminal Smokes: Part 1," at http://www.angelfire.com/rock/cpar/p2k/2ksep17paperless.html.

2. Consider the following quotation from the U.S. FCC Broadcasting and Advertising Regulations (June 1999): "We sometimes receive complaints regarding the alleged use of subliminal techniques in radio and TV programming. Subliminal programming is designed to be perceived on a subconscious level only. Regardless of whether it is effective, the use of subliminal perception is inconsistent with a station's obligation to serve the public interest because the broadcast is intended to be deceptive."

After reading the background for this exercise and this quotation, what is your impression of subliminal advertising? Could it be effective in changing CB? Could it ever be used as an ethical practice? Is limiting the use of subliminal messages a violation of an advertiser's right to free speech?

3. Visit the following Web sites and see how subliminal messages have been used in other forms of media: Snopes, "Hidden Persuaders," at http://www.snopes.com/business/hidden/hidden.asp; Snopes, "Disney films," at http://www.snopes.com/disney/films/films.asp; "Subliminal Messages Pathfinder" at http://www.sdst.org/shs/quest/pathfinder/submes.htm; Mindfit Hypnosis, "What Are Subliminal Messages?" at http://www.hypnoticmp3.com/about_subliminals.htm; and The Paly Voice, "Subliminal Messages Are Everywhere

EXHIBIT 13.14   Paul Mitchell Ad

Instant Moisture. *Instant* Shine.

Instant Moisture™ Daily Shampoo
Instant Moisture™ Daily Treatment
• Provides deep moisture and conditioning
• Repairs and helps prevent split ends
• Creates brilliant shine

EXHIBIT 13.15   Absolut Vodka (Citron) Ad

ABSOLUT CITRON.

ONLY REAL CITRUS JUICES. ONLY ABSOLUT CITRON

EXHIBIT 13.16   Bacardi Rum Ad

EXHIBIT 13.17   Maker's Mark Ad

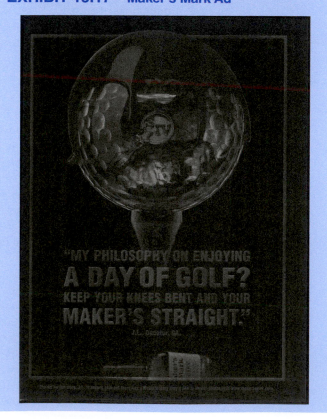

EXHIBIT 13.18   Crown Royal Ad

The end of a perfect day.

Crown Manhattan, Crown on the rocks, Crown and ginger. The perfect mix.
Enjoy our quality responsibly • Visit crownroyal.com

in Pop Culture" by Galin Cook, at http://voice.paly.net/view_story.php?id=2399. What is your opinion on what you have read and viewed on these sites? Were these subliminal effects strategically manufactured, or are they simply "in the eye of the beholder"?

4. Although subliminal messages have been declared an unsuccessful attempt at significantly altering CB, many Americans still believe in their existence. This is evident in the purchases of subliminal self-help products, based on the notion of subaudible messages, which can be further explored at www.infinn.com/subliminal.html and www.infinn.com/subliminaldownload.html. Have you ever purchased or used one of these products? If so, did it alter your behavior and/or mindset? Do you think these products actually have an effect on people or are buyers just convincing themselves that they work to ease the pain of cognitive dissonance?

5. Do you recall any ads that were subliminally stimulating? Do you believe the ads were effective? Were they ethical?

6. Do you know anyone who has ever claimed to be the "victim" of subliminal advertising? Do you or does anyone you know have any experience with any of the types of subliminal messages discussed in the exercise?

WRITTEN APPLICATIONS

1. Answer Question 1 in the In-Class Applications for four of the ads.

2. Find three more ads that someone might believe contain subliminal messages and repeat the analysis in Question 1.

3. Answer Questions 2 and 3.

4. Answer either Question 4, 5, or 6 above.

EXERCISE 13.3. WEBER'S LAW: THE JUST NOTICEABLE DIFFERENCE

OBJECTIVES

1. To understand the usefulness of Weber's law regarding the just noticeable difference (jnd) for decisions on altering marketing mix variables.
2. To recognize situations where marketers apparently made changes to marketing mix variables below the consumer's jnd and scenarios where they made modifications above the customer's jnd.
3. To decide on the ethicality of sneaking in changes deemed undesirable by consumers so they will not be noticed.
4. To experience the jnd phenomenon through visiting Web sites and to calculate the jnd by conducting consumer experiments.

BACKGROUND

THE DIFFERENTIAL THRESHOLD

In this exercise you will gain experience with another type of threshold level, which, like the absolute threshold level (ATL), relates to the attention stage during information processing. This phenomenon is known as the **differential (difference) threshold** or the **just noticeable difference (jnd).** The jnd is either the minimum amount of change in the intensity of a stimulus that can barely be detected by an individual or by the average person, or a barely noticeable difference between two similar stimuli by one person or the typical individual.

A person's ability to distinguish between slightly changing or similar stimuli is known as **stimulus discrimination (sensory discrimination)**. For instance, how much must a light be dimmed before you notice it? By what amount can you crank up the volume on your favorite music without your parents or dorm-mates noticing and complaining?

In a marketing context, stimulus discrimination involves things such as noticing differences or improvements in the quality of sound in various stereo systems, the clarity of display screens, and the taste of foods and drinks.

WEBER'S LAW

German psychophysicist Ernst Heinrich Weber discovered that the amount of change to a stimulus that is necessary for someone to notice it is related to the intensity of the original stimulus. It is the relative or percent variation in the stimulus that matters (whereas the ATL concerns the absolute or total minimum amount of a stimulus that is discernable). You could, for example, more securely whisper a secret to a friend on a busy city street than you could in a quiet library.

Hence, the stronger the intensity of an initial stimulus, the greater a change in intensity must occur for it to be noticed as different from the original stimulus. The formula for **Weber's law** is:

$$jnd = K = \frac{\Delta I}{I}$$

where K = a constant, given a person's particular sense and the stimulus
I = the initial intensity of the stimulus before the change occurs
ΔI = the minimal change in intensity of the stimulus that can be detected relative to the stimulus's initial intensity.

In a marketing situation, the actual value of K depends on the consumer (and which senses are being measured), the nature of the marketing stimulus, and the environment in which the consumer perceives the stimulus.

MARKETING APPLICATIONS OF WEBER'S LAW

Marketers should determine the jnd for key elements of their marketing program so that:

1. Changes that consumers consider undesirable (e.g., price hikes) are not readily detectable by them (i.e., they remain below the jnd).
2. Modifications desired by consumers (e.g., price decreases) are noticed (i.e., they are just at or slightly above the jnd).

NONDETECTION OF UNDESIRABLE MARKETING CHANGES

There are several types of marketing mix adjustments consumers disfavor and that marketers try to ensure they will not notice:

• *Price hikes.* The amount of a price spike that can go undetected is relative to the original price point. So, if an automobile manufacturer raises the price of a car $20, most consumers will be unlikely to detect it, but if the price of a gallon of gasoline for that vehicle goes up by just twenty cents, they surely will notice!

• *Package or product downsizing.* Because consumers are very sensitive to small price increases, especially on inexpensive products, marketers sometimes try to institute indirect price rises, such as **package downsizing (package shorting, weight out)**. This decreases the amount and/or weight of package contents while the price is held constant. (Box sizes sometimes remain constant in the face of reduction of their contents because boxes serve as billboards on store shelves and suggest more content.) Frito-Lay decreased some 12-ounce bags of chips to 10 ounces, Hellman's reduced the mayo from 32 to 30 ounces, and Bounty chopped the number of towels on a roll from 60 to 52. Similarly, in the face of escalating paper and printing costs, some magazine publishers trim the page size and/or the number of pages. You may have noticed some restaurants trying to beef up profits by replacing 16-ounce glasses with 14-ouncers and cutting back on portions (usually a recipe for disaster!).

• *Quality cuts and inferior ingredients substitution.* Another option to raising a product's price is decreasing its quality, such as introducing inferior coffee beans into ground coffee or substituting less expensive for more expensive oil in a food product. Ingredient alterations are sometimes made in food or beverage items due to factors such as changing raw ingredient costs, consumer concerns for more healthful ingredients, shortages of ingredients, or government regulations. For instance, food manufacturers at times exchange one cooking oil for another as relative oil prices fluctuate. McDonald's, as well as various chips manufacturers, now use "healthy" oil rather than unhealthy trans fatty acids in their products. Marketers hope that loyal customers will not notice the effects of such changes on taste.

Sneaking negative changes under consumers' radar screens is ethically suspect, since it violates their right to know.

DETECTION OF DESIRED MARKETING CHANGES

There are also several kinds of marketing mix modifications consumers appreciate, which marketers need to ensure are large enough for buyers to notice.

• *Price decreases.* Although the percentage price cut needed to stimulate buying varies by product category, a general rule of thumb used by retailers is that a markdown should be at least 20 percent. Coupons must usually offer at least a 15 percent discount.

• *Quantity, weight, and size increases.* Such improvements must all be discernable to customers, whether more scoops of raisins are added to raisin bran, extra sheets are added to a roll of toilet paper, or more product is offered ("2 free ounces!").

• *Quality improvements.* Quality enhancements must be large enough to matter, whether it is making a product that lasts longer (e.g., batteries, cough suppressant), produces better results (e.g., popcorn pops bigger and better), is stronger (nail polish will not chip as easily), or works faster ("Unclogs nasal passages in half the time!"). New-and-improved products must seem discernibly better to customers, and buyers should view products claiming to be superior to competitors as such.

• *Other positive marketing changes.* Other desirable changes for consumers that marketers want to be above the buyer's jnd include making a package more attractive, spiffing up a logo to make it more contemporary, and reengineering trade characters to make them more contemporary. Sometimes, however, it is preferable to make such changes below customers' radar screens because consumers might perceive some changes to be too radical, upsetting, or shocking. Noticeable modifications can also cause loss of brand equity. Hence, Camel cigarettes was careful to give the camel on its package a more modern look and feel while not losing sight of the brand's rich heritage.

REVIEW QUESTIONS

1. Explain the nature of the just noticeable difference. How is it formulated according to Weber's law?
2. What are the two general applications of Weber's law for marketing purposes regarding detectable and unnoticeable changes in a marketing mix variable? Give some specific examples of both generally desirable and undesirable changes.
3. What is the ethical issue involved in negative changes?

IN-CLASS APPLICATIONS

1. It's color time! See how well your brain perceives differences in color by visiting "Mix & Match: The Exploratorium's Online Exhibits" at http://www.exploratorium.edu/exhibits/mix_n_match/. Follow the instructions and "mix 'n match!" What are the marketing implications of this exercise?

2. It's time for a taste test. Are national brands (manufacturer brands) such as Coca-Cola and Whirlpool appliances better in quality than private label brands (store brands), such as Sam's Choice cola (from Wal-Mart) and Kenmore appliances (from Sears)? While it would be difficult to compare durable goods such as appliances in class, your instructor might bring in a national brand and private label food or beverage product and run a "taste test." You and some fellow students will be asked to compare the two brands without knowing which is which to see if you can discern the difference and which is of better quality. Are you up to the challenge?

3. Quickly jot down how much of a price cut would be necessary to get you to buy a product you planned to postpone purchasing until a possible future markdown at each of the following original price points: $1.00, $5.00, $25.00, $100.00, $500.00, and $2,500. Was your relative change the same in each instance, that is, was there a constant (K) in the Weber's law formula? Compare notes with your classmates.

4. Discuss the results of the written fieldwork from the Written Applications exercises that follow.

WRITTEN APPLICATIONS

1. Choose one of the two laboratory experiments described below to conduct and write up. Each involves using the *constant stimuli method* to find the consumers' jnd. In this procedure, an individual is asked to compare increasingly intense or successively more different stimuli with a standard stimulus until she reports a difference between the standard stimulus and changing stimulus. The point at which she can detect the difference is her jnd. Questions you should answer in writing up either experiment appear at the end of Experimental Scenario B on p. 415.

→   *Scenario A. The Watered-Down Soft Drink Experiment.* How much change would it take for consumers to realize a glass of Coca-Cola has been watered down? See for yourself! Conduct this experiment with about ten individuals (friends, relatives, coworkers, etc.), who will serve as your experimental subjects.

For each subject, fill a cup three-fourths of the way with Coke (or any other soft drink), counting the number of teaspoons it takes to fill the cup. Then, blindfold each subject and ask him or her to taste the Coke.

Next, ask your subject to leave the room for a moment so you can pour one teaspoon of water into the cup (without telling the individual what you are doing). Invite the person back into the room, and have the subject taste the diluted Coke. Can he or she tell any difference in taste? If so, what does the person believe to be the nature of the difference? Could the subject tell that you watered down the Coke or perceive that you did something else?

If the person believes you did something else, record the nature of this perceived difference and (unless the subject detected that you added water to the Coke) continue this process. Add one more teaspoon at a time with the subject out of the room each time (making sure the cup is still filled three-quarters of the way with Coke), and record the point at which the consumer can tell that you are watering down the drink.

After you have conducted the experiment with ten different subjects, look at your results to see at which point the majority of consumers noticed the actual difference. How many teaspoons of water determine the jnd? Calculate the relative amount using Weber's law. You measured the number of teaspoons of Coke in the cup to serve as the denominator in the Weber's law formula. Answer all questions that follow Experimental Scenario B.

→   *Scenario B. The Incredible Shrinking Candy Bar Experiment.* Ever notice how the prices of candy bars and many other packaged foods keep creeping up, just as size and/or net weight constantly inches down, and quality sometimes suffers in the process?

Until 1946, the typical single American candy bar sold for a nickel (and when the price ascended to six cents in that year, the nickel's existence was threatened, according to marketing folklore). By 1950, a candy bar typically retailed for ten cents; in 1974, it was fifteen cents; and by the early 1980s, it was thirty-five cents. Today, we expect to pay about 85 cents for a candy bar that is no larger (and probably smaller!) than in years gone by. In fact, over time, it seems that candy bars have been shrinking while their cardboard backing has stayed constant in size. Perhaps we will open up a four-inch wrapper one day and find an M&M-sized candy nugget inside!

This is because, when faced with rising costs, candy manufacturers elect to lower the net weight and/or size of the candy rather than raise its price. Can you guess why this is so? It is because consumers are more likely to detect a small price change than a small weight/size change. After all, are you not more aware of how much you pay for your favorite candy bar than you are of its size and weight?

This brings us to this experiment. Although you may conduct it using any candy bar brand you wish, it will work especially well for a bag of equal-sized candy pieces such as M&Ms, Reeses's Pieces, Skittles, or Junior Mints. You will be successively subtracting small amounts from the original bar or bag of candy to detect your subject's jnd level.

You will carry out this experiment with about ten subjects. If you decide to use candy bars, you will prepare in advance by shaving increasingly large amounts off of five of the six bars. Place an equal size, equal weight piece of cardboard (preferably from the original wrapper) underneath each candy bar. Rewrap them so they appear identical, and label them "1" through "6," the latter being the original candy bar with nothing shaved off. Record the weight of each candy bar (your college mailroom probably has a scale you may use to weigh the candy bars). If you use a bag of equal-sized candy pieces, you just need to remove one piece each time until your subject notices a difference between the full bag and the bag with pieces removed.

Have each subject compare the original candy bar to the largest of the experimental bars, placing the original bar in one hand and the experimental bar in the other hand. Ask each subject if he or she can detect a difference in weight between the two candy bars. If a subject cannot, ask this person if he or she notices a difference between the original candy bar and the second (smaller) experimental bar. Keep going through the successively smaller experimental bars until the subject is able to perceive a difference in weight. This is that subject's jnd.

If you use a bag of equal-size candy pieces such as M&Ms, before running the experiment, weigh the candy bag and record the weight of an individual piece. (You might want to weigh several pieces to see if they differ at all in weight. If so, use the average weight in your calculations). You just need the original candy bag and one experimental bag, from which you can successively take out one piece of candy at a time. Ask each subject if he or she can detect a difference in weight between the two bags of candy as you sequentially remove one piece of candy at a time from the experimental bag. When a subject is able to perceive a difference in weight, this is that subject's jnd.

QUESTIONS FOR WRITE-UP OF EXPERIMENT

1. a. Regardless of which experiment you performed, describe your experiment: the nature of your consumer sample, subjects' reactions to the experiment, the experiment's validity (do you think it is giving an accurate

measurement of the jnd?), and its methodological shortcomings (e.g., artificial testing environment, sample size, and sample composition limitations).

Also, discuss your findings: Calculate each subject's jnd as well as the average jnd for your entire sample of subjects using the Weber's law formula (a percentage). You can also plot a frequency and/or percentage distribution showing the number and/or percentage of subjects at each jnd level.

b. Discuss the strategic and ethical marketing implications of your results. Are there any practical problems in implementing such a size-reduction strategy?

2. Answer Question 1 in the In-Class Applications.

EXERCISE 13.4. SURROGATE INDICATORS

OBJECTIVES

1. To explain the relationship between surrogate indicators and subjective perception.
2. To understand the relationship between surrogate indicators and various types of perceptual cues, such as intrinsic cues versus extrinsic cues and performance attributes versus nonperformance attributes, as well as perceptual cues classified by their predictive value and their confidence value.
3. To become familiar with the types of situations in which buyers are likely to use surrogate indicators and the general types of surrogate indicators employed by marketers, and to enable you to cite examples of each, knowing when each one is likely to be a performance versus a nonperformance cue.
4. To experience consumers' use of surrogate indicators through conducting an experiment and analyzing advertisements.
5. To judge the ethicality of using certain surrogate indicators to indicate product qualities that might not exist.

BACKGROUND

THE NATURE OF SURROGATE INDICATORS

This topic relates to the comprehension stage of information processing, where consumers organize and interpret information to derive meaning from it. For example, what does a high price mean to buyers? They could interpret it to signify that the product has a "high quality," is a "great deal," or is an "unfair price."

Whereas absolute threshold level and differential threshold are examples of the selective nature of perception during the attention phase of the perceptual process, surrogate indicators illustrates the subjective nature of perception at the comprehension stage.

Surrogate (proxy) indicators (market signals) are readily observable product attributes that consumers use, often wrongly, to make probabilistic inferences on product characteristics unknown to them because they are not easily discerned. Examples of such difficult-to-define product attributes that consumers are especially ultimately concerned with are a product's nature, composition, quality, performance, durability, and reliability, which we shall collectively call "performance." Surrogate indicators are also named **proxy indicators** since both the words "surrogate" and "proxy" denote a substitute. Proxy indicators are used instead of a possibly more accurate gauge of the product's performance. Sometimes surrogate indicators are known as **market signals** because they send a signal, indicating or suggesting to the marketplace of consumers something about the product's performance that might not otherwise be known. The use of surrogate indictors gives rise to **market beliefs**, assumptions about how product signals connote quality or performance.

Factors consumers use as surrogate indicators include price, brand name, color, size, and shape, which are all readily perceptible. Such attributes can provide shorthand signals of performance, although they may or may not be valid indicators of the product's performance. Hence, using market signals can lead to perceptual distortion, a type of subjective perception.

Such easy-to-use but potentially misleading criteria are applied in all walks of life. College admissions boards employ high school grades and SAT or ACT test scores to predict academic success in college. Employers utilize college grades and relevant job and extracurricular experiences to forecast job success, setting starting salaries for graduating seniors accordingly.

In both of these cases, the attributes used have fairly high predictive value; they are reasonably accurate predictors of unknown human performance. However, many marketing surrogate indicators have low predictive value, meaning they do not accurately forecast a product's performance that is unknown to consumers.

CATEGORIZING PERCEPTUAL CUES

To better understand the nature and use of surrogate indicators, it is helpful to understand cue utilization theory, which categorizes different types of perceptual cues. This theory suggests that surrogate indicators are perceptual cues used either correctly or incorrectly to categorize an object regarding performance. Performance is often difficult to understand or discern, and so surrogate indicators are used to try to detect it.

PERCEPTUAL CUES CATEGORIZED PHYSICALLY

Perceptual cues can be classified physically into intrinsic and extrinsic cues.

Intrinsic cues (direct indicators, product-related attributes) are product characteristics that are part of the tangible product. They are inherent in the product's physical composition and are consumed, used up, worn out, or destroyed during the product's use. For instance, a soft drink has a certain level of sugar, amount of carbonation, and a particular color.

Extrinsic cues (indirect indicators, non-product-related attributes) are product characteristics that are external to the physical product but are nonetheless closely associated with it. As non-product-related attributes, they are not consumed in use, and they can be changed without altering the product's nature. Extrinsic cues entail elements of the marketing mix other than the physical product. They include intangible product elements, such as brand name, packaging and labeling, manufacturer, country of origin (e.g., USA, Mexico), and brand image. Extrinsic cues also include other marketing program factors such as price, retail or virtual distribution, amount and nature of advertising, and salespeople.

Most surrogate indicators are extrinsic cues because they do not directly affect the product's performance. However, due to their visibility, surrogate indicators are easily (albeit often erroneously) used in evaluating a product. Proxy indicators can also be intrinsic cues when these are easy to detect and consumers believe (rightly or wrongly) that product attributes such as color and size do predict a product's performance.

PERCEPTUAL CUES CATEGORIZED BY PREDICTIVE VALUE

A perceptual cue's **predictive value** is its relevance or validity in predicting product performance. Of bearing here are performance attributes and nonperformance attributes.

Performance (functional) attributes are relevant traits for judging product performance. They have high predictive value. For the most part, performance attributes are intrinsic cues since these directly affect product performance.

For instance, to know whether a soft drink will be tasty, we can read about its ingredients on the label, listen to the "fizz" as we open it to ensure it is fresh, and look at the bubbles to make sure it is not flat. To discover whether "fresh" vegetables are truly fresh, we can inspect them to see if they are a lush green (not brown) and firm (not wilted).

However, functional attributes can also be extrinsic cues if these have high predictive value. For example, well-known brand name products generally are of high quality. So are items with a longer and more inclusive warranty, as are goods bearing third-party certification, such as the Good Housekeeping Seal of Approval or Morningstar Investment Guide mutual fund ratings.

On the other hand, **nonperformance (nonfunctional) attributes** are irrelevant for judging a product's performance. They have low-to-no predictive value for understanding the difficult-to-discern product elements. Nonperformance attributes are primarily extrinsic cues since elements outside of the product are less likely to directly correlate with its performance. However, intrinsic cues such as styling, color, and size can also be nonperformance attributes if they are more for form and style than function and substance.

Most (but not all) surrogate indicators are nonperformance attributes since most of them are extrinsic cues, and such stimuli are generally less likely to validly predict product performance. You have heard it said: "Don't judge a book by its cover," "Clothes don't make the man," and "All that glitters is not gold."

PERCEPTUAL CUES CATEGORIZED BY CONFIDENCE VALUE

A perceptual cue's **confidence value** concerns the consumer's self-perceived ability to use a product's attributes to correctly assess and thereby distinguish among brands. A shopper might believe that food and beverage ingredients have high predictive value for the product's nutritional value yet not use them as evaluative criteria due to that buyer's lack of self-confidence in using nutritional information to judge nutritional worth.

Generally, extrinsic cues are high in confidence value because they are simple to use and readily observable, whereas intrinsic cues are low in confidence value because they are often more complex and not so easily discernable.

SUMMARY OF TYPES OF PERCEPTUAL CUES

In short, surrogate indicators tend to be: (1) extrinsic cues, (2) low in predictive value (i.e., nonperformance attributes), and (3) high in confidence value.

Exhibit 13.19 summarizes this discussion. Consumers' use of proxy signals is the "kicking-the-tires, slamming-the-door" syndrome: Some shoppers presumptuously judge a car's quality by stomping the tires and banging the door to see if it "seems" solidly built, with a nice muffled thump signifying quality construction in a luxury car and a tinny rattling sound suggesting a flimsy economy car. Further, used car dealers often spiff up a car's exterior and interior, and they then tout it as a "clean car," as if that means it runs well.

CONDITIONS UNDER WHICH CONSUMERS USE SURROGATE INDICATORS

Consumers use these false prophets under the following marketplace conditions.

1. Where they lack knowledge, experience, expertise, or alternative information sources. This happens, for example, during extended decision-making situations where buyers know little about the product category or its brands, especially for new products, or by people who are purchasing a particular product for the first time (e.g., new parents buying baby accessories). Consumers lack pre-purchase knowledge for experience goods such as food and perfume that are rich in sensory experiences and are therefore difficult to evaluate without personal experience.
2. Where buyers have low self-confidence, lacking assurance in their decision-making ability. This is especially true for complex products such as high-ticket goods (e.g., cars or professional services, such as lawyers and accountants). This also applies with credence goods. These products contain attributes that are difficult to evaluate even after consumption, such as a vitamin pill's health-enhancing qualities or a motor oil's lubricating efficacy. Professional service providers' intangible (unobservable) and often complex nature (e.g., auto mechanics and lawyers) results in low buyer confidence. Consequently, many consumers judge service quality based on surrogate indicators such as the size and architecture of the building housing the service, signage on the outside of that building, framed degrees and certificates on office walls, and quality of furniture and furnishings (e.g., marble pillars in banks indicate security).
3. Where purchasers believe that quality variations exist among brands but are difficult to detect.

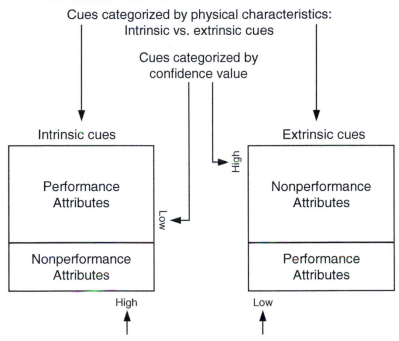

EXHIBIT 13.19   Categorizing Perceptual Cues

Cues categorized by physical characteristics:
Intrinsic vs. extrinsic cues

Cues categorized by
confidence value

Intrinsic cues   Extrinsic cues

Performance   Nonperformance
Attributes   Attributes

High

Nonperformance   Performance
Attributes   Attributes

Low

High   Low

Cues categorized by predictive value:
Performance vs. nonperformance attributes

Note: Surrogate indicators tend to be those on the right-hand side of the figure: extrinsic cues that are nonperformance attributes but that nonetheless have high confidence value for consumers.

Even parity products that are virtually indistinguishable from competitive brands try to differentiate themselves via surrogate indicators. Therefore, one dish soap smells like lemon and another like lime, or one scouring pad is blue and another is pink, even though they perform equally well.

4. Where consumers are lazy, rushed, or otherwise wish to simplify decision making. Here, surrogate indicators serve as easy-to-use, shorthand decision heuristics, such as "Buy only high-priced brands because they are of better quality."

5. Customers have low involvement and therefore do not wish to take the time or effort to use more complex performance attributes.

6. Customers have high involvement and wish to use a risk reduction strategy (such as relying on a brand name).

TYPES OF SURROGATE INDICATORS

We now briefly scrutinize commonly used surrogate indicators and provide specific examples of each. Where possible, we will generalize as to whether or not a particular market signal tends to be a performance attribute with high predictive value.

The first two market signals discussed—price and brand name—are the most commonly used proxy indicators, with well-known brand names often sporting premium prices.

PRICE

Due to its high confidence value, price is probably the most widely employed surrogate indicator. A widely held market belief is that "you get what you pay for." People believe in strong price-quality relationships—

if you pay a king's ransom, you get performance fit for a king. This would seem to be a rational belief for two reasons.

First, price is partly determined by production costs. Higher manufacturing expenses suggest more costly factors of production and hence higher product quality. As L'Oreal advertises, "We cost a little more because we're worth it." A Rolls Royce costs more than a Kia, and Häagen-Dazs ice cream is more expensive than Breyers.

Second, price is partially due to demand. The law of demand says that as demand increases, marketers can set a higher price to sell a given quantity. One reason for demand to be high is the product's superior performance. In short, the market "works": High price is a consequence of buyers' willingness to pay more for a better product.

However, "Buyer beware": This reasoning is not foolproof. Higher demand could also simply be the result of false product perceptions. A high price might cause people to erroneously believe a product has fine quality. Or, people might be willing to pay a high price for the "snob appeal" generated by a product's advertising and distribution in "finer stores." Additionally, brand demand could be strong because of few competitive alternatives since strong competition serves to keep prices low (just ask the antitrust regulators!).

So, does high price mean you're getting high quality or not? This discussion suggests that price might be a performance attribute, but, then again, it might not be! Consequently, consumers using price as a proxy indicator for quality might end up making suboptimal purchases. Consider, for example, that many generic drugs are chemically identical to their branded counterparts, yet they sell for much less.

Research evidence concerning an actual generalized price-quality relationship is mixed, varying by product category. It has been found that for many products, the association between quality and price appears to be weak, with frequently purchased items displaying weaker relations than less-often-bought items (perhaps because less frequently purchased goods are generally more expensive and so shoppers put more effort into acquiring valid information on them). Hence, for many products, higher prices appear to be false signals of higher quality.

BRAND NAME AND MANUFACTURER NAME

Like price, names are very powerful proxy indicators. People generally believe that so-called name brands are of better quality. As Zenith electronics once advertised, "The quality goes in before the name goes on." The jam and jelly purveyors informed buyers, "With a name like Smuckers, it has to be good."

As is true of a high price, a well-known and respected brand or producer's name can add psychological product value. In fact, part of brand equity is the positive associations the name has in buyers' minds. Tests over the years have shown that cigarettes, food, and beverages taste better when they are identified as brands that people know or to which they relate. Even preschoolers prefer brands they recognize. A Stanford University study found that youngsters favor food (a hamburger, French fries, and chicken nuggets) by a whopper (oops . . . wrong brand!) of a majority when they believed the goodies came from the Golden Arches (McDonald's box) rather than an unknown source (plain brown wrappers).

Even with products such as automobiles, where the benefits should be primarily rational, the imagery built for a prestigious or youthful car is very much a part of the satisfactions that the driver derives from the product. A Porsche has cache that translates to higher perceived performance and quality.

Is a well-known marketer's name high in predictive value? Generally yes, but again: "Buyer beware"— there is no guarantee, since marketers can create inaccurate impressions. However, a brand name is a promise that a manufacturer must live up to since its reputation is on the line. This suggests that well-known brands have an interest in maintaining high quality standards so that consumers can trust them.

NATURE AND AMOUNT OF ADVERTISING AND PROMOTION

Well-known brands are more heavily advertised, and research has shown that in general, highly promoted brands are of better quality. There is truth to the advertising adage, "The best way to quickly kill a poor product is with good advertising." A poor product's clever advertising will induce trial purchases, leading to consumer disappointment, resulting in no repurchases and negative word of mouth. Also, promotable products are those with a significant point of ("promotable") difference the advertising can discuss. Despite all this, the gap in quality between private labels and national brands closed significantly during the 1990s and varies widely from product category to product category. Brand positioning, endorsers, and advertising messages can all influence buyers' perceptions of quality. Celebrities lend cache (albeit an expensive one) to the products they endorse.

COLOR

Our perceptions can literally be colored by color. It is said that people "taste with their eyes." The color of a food or beverage item might make it seem more delicious. Hence, when light-colored beer gets a golden amber shot of food coloring, consumers describe it as heartier and better tasting. Some people are repulsed by green beer sold on St. Patrick's Day while others believe the artificial coloring makes it more festive. Mint ice cream is naturally white, but it is colored green to make it "taste" mintier. Purdue chickens are fed marigold petals to enhance their yellow color, making them taste more succulent. Fresh meat is sometimes packaged with a harmless dose of carbon monoxide since the gas keeps the meat an appetizing red for more days, far longer than the few days unwrapped meat stays red in a butcher's case.

Nonfood examples of color-quality connotations also abound. Black, silver, and gold all lend an upscale aura to a product's packaging or labeling. Clear-colored products such as soda (Crystal Pepsi), dishwashing liquid (Clear Ivory and Palmolive), dental rinse (Plax and Scope), and deodorant (almost all major brands) blossomed during the 1990s since clear connotes purity and absence of unnatural ingredients.

AROMA

A product's scent can suggest quality. During the 1970s, lemon was added to a whole pantry of household cleaning products to suggest an ability to cut through grease and grime as well as freshen up the item being cleaned. Although a brand of soap might smell "springlike," its cleansing power is not really affected. An odorless mouthwash once failed because people thought it should either smell like medicine or mint to work.

Manufacturers of fancy new vehicles use higher-quality materials, such as leather, that might be more pleasing to a customer's nose, thereby signaling a quality automobile. That new-car smell that comes with a car's purchase originates from an aerosol container sprayed into the car's cabin as it leaves the factory, lingering for about six weeks. Aroma has even been used to sell houses: The scent of bread or cookies baking, or perhaps beef roasting, makes a house seem homey and therefore more desirable.

TEXTURE AND FEEL

For many years, Prell shampoo advertised its thickness in commercials featuring a pearl (which in itself implies quality) very slowly falling to the bottle's bottom. Heinz ketchup was promoted as the "slow" ketchup because its thickness means it is a better product. Similarly, a milk shake that is "so thick it can stand up to a straw" supposedly is good. Carpet and bedding manufacturers know that their wares must feel plush since many consumers "see" with their hands. Crest Rejuvenating Effects toothpaste leaves a slight tingling sensation in the mouth to suggest that it is freshening one's breath. When Bactine antiseptic removed the stinging sensation, sales plummeted because consumers thought it had to sting to heal. And, men's after-shave lotion stings to offer proof that something is happening (and to help wake users up in the morning!).

Ingredients and Materials. All-natural ingredients seem to guarantee better quality. When first invented, plastics lent a high-tech space-age aura to some products but later on suggested a cheap image. Gel became the ingredient of choice in many products during the 1990s, such as toothpaste, shaving cream, and deodorant, since it implies product purity.

Sound. Motorcycle makers know that a certain timbre in the engine's roar suggests power. Mazda Miata designed its exhaust system to sound like a "hot" sports car. Ford put a new latch system into the Taurus that makes a vaultlike (rather than a rickety) sound when the door closes. A lawn mower with a low-noise muffler and a food mixer that made no sound both flopped because consumers wrongly assumed they lacked power. Crunchiness makes cereal and chips taste better. And, United Airlines research found that longtime use of a snippet of George Gershwin's *Rhapsody in Blue* translates into consumer trust.

Size. Size is often used to "size up" goods, although both a large and a small size can connote quality, depending on the product. In an era of miniaturized electronics, most consumers realize that it is false that "bigger is better," and true that often "good things come in small packages."

Big can be beautiful. Although larger tires are generally more rugged, they add extra weight to a car, giving it poorer miles per gallon. And audiophiles are no longer content with their tiny, white, plastic iPod earbuds, but are instead trading up for big, higher-quality headphones that can cost as much as $1,000.

Packaging. Ever notice how food items look better on the package or wrapper (as well as in advertisements) than they do in reality? Food stylists carefully touch up food products before photographing them so that the packages suggest superior-tasting vittles.

Packaging material can also influence quality perceptions. Bread wrapped in plastic wrap is perceived as fresher than when in waxed paper. Foil packaging for chocolates indicates superiority delicacy. Grey Goose vodka comes in frosted bottles that are packaged in wooden boxes like expensive French wines to convey its premium position.

Country of Origin. Back in the 1950s, "Made in America" was associated with high quality and "Made in Japan" suggested junk. Now, many American manufacturers are fighting to regain the image of superiority that they lost to Asian and European manufacturers. Japanese and Korean electronics manufacturers have built big brand equity with names such as Sony, Samsung, and Sanyo. Many imported autos also have a quality halo.

Imported beer has a quality cache: Molson's comes from "Canada—the land where ice was born," and some people will argue that Belgium's beer is best. Barilla pasta was touted as superior via the slogan, "It must be good because it's Italy's number one pasta."

Would you rather buy a car made in Afghanistan or in Japan? A suit from Italy or the Ukraine? If the wine is from France and the vodka from Russia, it must be good, no? Watches from Switzerland? Check. Toys from China? Could be a problem!

Age and Heritage. Ever notice how (so unlike most adults) marketers like to brag about how old they are? A store or service provider will boast that it was "established in 1869," that it has "been proudly serving you for fifty years," or that it is celebrating a "century of excellence." During the 2008 financial crisis, financial institutions reassured their customers by emphasizing how long they had been in business. Patrons assume (probably correctly) that if a firm has been around a while, they probably know what they are doing and are good at doing it.

Channels of Distribution. Having a product sold in upscale venues affects its perceived elegance. Display quality, salesperson courtesy and knowledge, and store atmospherics (music, lighting, etc.) all "rub off" on a brand's quality image.

Amount of Retail Shelf Space. Similar to the volume of advertising, the number of retail shelf facings allocated to a brand shapes quality perceptions. Consumers figure, "With all that shelf space, they must be selling like hot cakes" and so it must be better. When asked how much shelf space he wanted for his then-new Purdue Chicken Franks, CEO Frank Purdue quipped, "Oh, about all of it."

Market Share and Sales Volume. Why do best sellers boast that they are unsurpassed in sales? Why does McDonald's tout its billions of hamburgers sold? Why is Budweiser so enamored with the fact that it is "The king of beers"? Why did Taurus toot its horn that it was "America's best-selling car—again"? Mail-order marketers know that if they promote an item as a "best seller," sales head north. Buyers can probably safely assume that market leaders are pretty competent at what they do.

Warranties and Guarantees. If a firm backs up its product promise, that pledge is probably true since a company would otherwise rapidly lose money as buyers would demand a replacement product or else their money back. Hyundai, known in the 1990s for shoddy cars, communicated its much-improved quality at the turn of the twenty-first century by advertising its ten-year warranty, and sales skyrocketed. But beware: These selling tools might create exaggerated perceptions of product quality.

Words. Advertising and selling buzz terms, such as "slow-roasted," "tender," grilled," "spicy," and "fresh-cut," give quality cues for fast-food feeders, which use them to make people think their fare is healthy.

REVIEW QUESTIONS

1. How do surrogate indicators relate to subjective perception? Into which stage of the perceptual process do these proxy indicators tie?
2. Describe the relationship between surrogate indicators and each of the three classification schemes for perceptual cues.
3. Under what types of marketplace conditions are consumers likely to use surrogate indicators?
4. Are price and brand or manufacturer name performance or nonperformance cues? Explain. Cite other examples of other surrogate indicators often used by consumers and the logic behind their use.

IN-CLASS APPLICATIONS

1. When buying a car, which surrogate indicators might affect a consumer's purchase decision? Do these attributes have anything to do with the vehicle's true performance, i.e., could they actually be performance cues?

Think of an example of another product that meets many of the conditions under which buyers use surrogate indicators. What are those marketplace conditions, and which specific proxy cues do consumers use for this product?

2. For each of the following ads (Exhibits 13.20–13.24) identify perceptual cues (i.e., brand name, product attributes, endorser, etc.) that each ad suggests might serve as surrogate indicators for consumers. Were these factors intended by the marketer to be the product's selling point? Are any of the proxy cues accurate performance indicators?

3. If a product is of about the same quality as its competitors, is it ethical to charge a higher price just to create a higher-quality image? Might the marketer be implying a level of quality that might not exist? Is added psychological value relevant here? In general, do you believe it is ethical for marketers to promote brands by using surrogate indicators?

4. Discuss the results of your written fieldwork from the Written Applications that follow.

WRITTEN APPLICATIONS

1. Choose and perform one of the following two laboratory experiments. The first study tests whether a brand name can serve as a surrogate indicator for candy quality. The other experiment assumes that sometimes consumers do taste with their eyes, with color used as a surrogate indicator in judging the taste and quality of foods and beverages. Questions you should answer in writing up either experiment appear following the description of Experimental Scenario B.

→   *Scenario A: The Quality Brand Candy Experiment.* How much importance do consumers put on brand name when evaluating boxed chocolates? Do you really need to buy expensive chocolate for that special someone? Now it's time to find out!

You will need three pieces of chocolate for each of about ten subjects. One piece of chocolate will be labeled with a very prestigious brand name (e.g., Godiva, Cadbury), one with a somewhat upmarket name (e.g., Russell Stover), and one with a mass market or popular brand name (e.g., Whitman's,) or perhaps even a low-end private label (e.g., Sam's Club). However, in reality, they will all be mass market brand chocolate. The experiment should be conducted on a one-on-one basis (rather than in a group).

Tell each subject that the study's purpose is to find consumer preferences for various chocolate brands. Have each sampler taste all three candies and then state rank order preference (numbers 1, 2, and 3) and reason(s) for that ordering. Probe for reason(s) for their preferences; for instance, if a person says, "taste," ask exactly how one brand tastes better than another.

Next, reveal that the three "brands" are all the same chocolate! Note each subject's reaction to this news, and then ask why each subject believed he or she nonetheless "noticed" a difference.

How many participants perceived a distinction between the three samples? Tabulate how many subjects believed that each of the three brands tasted best. Regarding reasons for their preferences, how many admitted to being influenced by the brand name, either before or after you revealed the true nature of the experiment? What other cues did they use and how often? (You can tabulate all of these results, too.) What are the marketing implications of your results?

EXHIBIT 13.20   Pepperidge Farm's Goldfish Snacks Ad

EXHIBIT 13.21   Butterfinger Ad

EXHIBIT 13.22   Rolex Ad

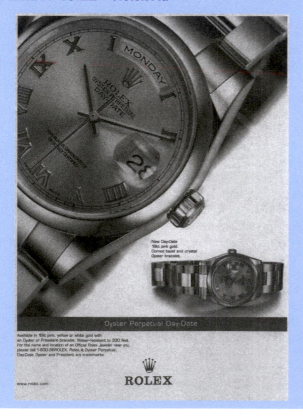

EXHIBIT 13.23   Absolut Vodka (Mandrin) Ad

EXHIBIT 13.24   Mr. Clean Ad

He'll bring you a bouquet of spring flowers...

whisk you off to the crisp mountain air...

and wait till you see what he does with a twist.

Antibacterial Mr. Clean. In Springtime Fresh, Mountain Falls, and Lemon Fresh. Three easy ways to make sure your home smells as clean as it looks.

Tough on Dirt & Germs, Easy on You!

→   *Scenario B: The Chocolate Pudding Experiment.* To what extent does a food product's color influence its taste? Do consumers use the color of pudding to infer its other attributes? Let's investigate!

You will need to prepare three bowls of pudding from commercial chocolate pudding mix. There should be enough pudding in each bowl so that about ten subjects can sample from each. Label each one with a neutral letter: C, M, or D.

You will also need three small bottles of food coloring: light brown, medium brown, and dark brown. (Brown food coloring can be made by mixing blue, red, and yellow, with the lighter shades made by adding more yellow.) The experiment can either be conducted on a one-on-one basis or in a group.

Tell each participant that the study is being conducted to determine consumer preference for a new variety of chocolate pudding. Hand each subject a spoon and a sample cup for each of the three puddings. Ask each person to taste every pudding sample successively. (You should rotate the order so that each color is first about one-third of the time, second one-third of the time, and third one-third of the time. This controls for possible order bias.) Then, ask each subject to rank order the three pudding samples along each of the following eight dimensions: overall preference, perception of amount of chocolate, judgment of smoothness, judgment of consistency, texture preference, thickness, creaminess, and buying intentions. Summarize your findings.

QUESTIONS FOR WRITE-UP OF EXPERIMENT

1. a. For either experiment, describe the nature of your consumer sample, subjects' reactions to the experiment, the study's validity, and any methodological shortcomings (artificial environment, sample limitations, etc.). Then, discuss your findings by answering the specific questions above for the experimental option you chose. Limit your data presentation to tabulations, rank orderings, and percentages.

    b. What are the marketing implications of your results?

2. Think of at least three other goods or services for which either you or others use different surrogate indicators to judge product quality or performance. Describe these surrogate indicators, why you believe consumers use them, and whether they are really accurate performance indicators, and discuss the marketing implications.

EXERCISE 13.5. GESTALT PSYCHOLOGY'S PRINCIPLES OF PERCEPTUAL ORGANIZATION

OBJECTIVES

1. To demonstrate how various properties of a stimulus object influence peoples' subjective perception of that object.
2. To become familiar with the basic Gestalt principles of perceptual organization and their effects on perception.
3. To apply these Gestalt psychology principles in analyzing visual puzzles and the effectiveness of print ads.

BACKGROUND

THE NATURE OF GESTALT PSYCHOLOGY

This exercise is concerned with people's subjective comprehension of a stimulus object, specifically how the physical arrangement of the elements of that object and of surrounding stimuli affect consumers' perceptions of the object. Relevant here is the **Gestalt school of psychology**, an early twentieth-century approach to studying perception, which suggests that people acquire meaning from the totality of a group of proximate stimuli rather than from any one individual stimulus. The Gestalt school investigates how humans arrange discrete stimuli or bits of information into holistic perceptions.

The underlying idea is that stimuli are perceived as an organized whole, not as unrelated or disjointed pieces, that is, the whole is greater than the sum of the parts. The **Gestalt principles (laws) of perceptual organization** concern the process whereby people categorize and organize stimulus information into meaningful units to make sense of the stimuli.

For instance, people recognize a familiar tune but do not ordinarily hear each distinct note or even every musical instrument playing the song. They identify a person's face but do not usually pay attention to each eye, eyebrow, nostril, and so on.

This exercise examines the Gestalt perceptual organization principles of most interest to marketers —those of **form (shape) perception**, which deal with how individual stimuli work together to create perceptions of one or more objects. They consist of principles of grouping, or how people organize individual stimuli into groups or chunks of information, and **principles of context**, how the surrounding environment (context) helps determine individuals' perceptions of stimuli in that environment.

PRINCIPLES OF GROUPING

Gestalt psychology explores how people tend to group stimuli to form a unified impression. **Grouping** is a process whereby individuals are inclined to perceive stimuli as groups or chunks of information rather than as discrete bits of data. This grouping process facilitates recognition and recall of those cues as a whole. Five of these principles are similarity, proximity, continuity, closure, and simplicity.

SIMILARITY

The Similarity Principle. The **similarity principle** says that things that are physically similar are perceived as belonging together or as forming a whole figure (gestalt). Therefore, "XXOO" is seen as two groups, with the XX as one group and the OO as another group.

In the following illustration, people tend to see alternating columns of circles and squares, grouping all circles together into columns and chunking all squares together into columns.

Marketing Applications of the Similarity Principle. Marketers want their customers to see their various marketing entities as belonging together in an integrated marketing program, and so they create them to be similar. The following are some examples.

  • An advertising campaign consists of a series of ads that are similar, such as sharing a common theme or slogan, presenter, graphic design elements, presentation format (e.g., drama, cartoon, etc.), and overall "look and feel" (e.g., Absolut vodka's playfulness with the brand name and bottle).

  • Department stores group similar items together to facilitate the shopping process. You would not look for scarves among hammers and screwdrivers.

  • Sometimes marketers want to avoid being perceived as similar to familiar images. Zipper, a packaged shot of gelatin and alcohol, came under fire because it too closely resembled children's Jell-O gelatin dessert. Starbucks pulled a poster that featured side-by-side tea drinks below the headline "Collapse into cool" because someone complained that the image evoked New York's Twin Towers. Some community and law-enforcement leaders were concerned with the thumb-sized pouches and white powder form of Ice Breakers Pacs, fearing they could be mistaken for illicit items.

The Proximity Principle. The **proximity (contiguity) principle** suggests that things that are in close proximity to one another are perceived as belonging together or as forming a gestalt. In your clothing drawers you probably put things together that logically go together; undergarments in one drawer, shirts or blouses in another, and so on. You would not expect to find canned peas in someone's medicine cabinet.

As a visual example of the principle of proximity, what you are likely to notice in the following illustration is that this is not just a square pattern of dots but rather is a series of rows of dots. You do so because you group together dots that are close to one another.

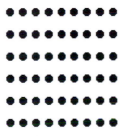

Marketing Applications of the Proximity Principle. The basic idea in all of the following cases is to "group like with like."

  • As a form of silent cross (suggestion) selling, stores often feature complimentary items near each other, such as a table and chairs in a furniture shop, or dressing a mannequin in a dress shirt, sport coat, and tie that all look fabulous together.

  • Bundling similar items and selling them as a unit is done for the likes of vacation packages (airfare, hotel, nightclubs, etc.), fast food "extra value" combo meals (sandwich, fries, and drink), and telecommunications services (phone, cable TV, and Internet access services).

  • Marketers are careful to associate their product with appropriate symbols, imagery, endorsers, and other stimuli. Having a goofy comedian dressed as a slob endorsing a stock mutual fund would be ludicrous.

- In laying out print advertisements, there is an axiom: "Keep things together that belong together, and keep things apart that belong apart." So, captions are placed near the pictures they describe, headlines lead into subheadlines or body copy, and white space and boxes are used to separate elements that are meant to be kept apart (such as two different pictures).
- A trend is for merchants such as Target to organize their wares based on usage contexts. Items needed for a barbecue (e.g., hamburger buns, lighter fluid, and potato chips) might be all found in the same aisle. Hertz groups its cars online not just by size but also by use, such as "fun," "prestige," and "green."

CONTINUITY

The Continuity Principle. The **continuity principle (law of good continuation)** holds that people categorize stimuli into smooth, uninterrupted, continuous forms, rather than into discontinuous patterns. Therefore, in the following illustration, we are more likely to identify lines a–b and c–d crossing than to see a–d and c–b or a–c and d–b as continuous figures.

MARKETING APPLICATIONS OF THE CONTINUITY PRINCIPLE

- Companies with a long-running, continuous ad campaign are better at building brand equity than those that are short-lived. Pepsi Cola has always been for the younger generation and the young at heart. However, Coca-Cola has had too many ad themes over the years: Quick—what is their current slogan or theme?
- Department stores do not want sharp breaks between departments, with radically different layouts, lighting, music, and so on. Transitions between sections should be more or less continuous.
- Exercise 13.3 pointed out that updates to visual marketing elements, such as trade characters and logotypes, should usually be made gradually because a discontinuous change would be too confusing and disruptive for most consumers, resulting in a loss of brand equity.

CLOSURE

The Closure Principle. The **closure (mental completion) principle** states that people tend to perceive incomplete patterns as being complete, "filling in the blanks" based on prior experiences. A triangle with a small part of its edge missing will still be seen as a triangle. Consider the annoyance that arises from having a missing element or two from a collection, such as magazines or CDs by a particular musical group. And, soap operas keep viewers hanging on with "cliffhanger" endings.

In the following illustration, people are inclined to see three broken rectangles (and a lonely shape on the far left) rather than three "girder" profiles (and a lonely shape on the right).

MARKETING APPLICATIONS OF THE CLOSURE PRINCIPLE

- Some advertisers teach consumers a jingle or slogan through frequent repetition, and then in subsequent ads delete part of the jingle or slogan. This requires the audience to get involved with the message and complete it in their mind. For instance, an ad with Smokey the Bear said, "Repeat after me, 'Only you . . .' "

- Headlines phrased as questions in print ads demand an answer, thereby encouraging audience participation.
- Marketers at times crop an object into an ad so that it appears ambiguous, encouraging consumers to surmise what the item is.
- Radio is called the "theater of the mind" because listeners must achieve closure by imagining in their mind's eye what is happening.

SIMPLICITY

The Simplicity Principle. The **simplicity principle (pragnänz)** suggests that individuals opt for relatively simple perceptions even when more complex perceptions can be derived. That is, every stimulus pattern is seen in such a way that the resulting structure is as simple as possible.

Marketing Applications of the Simplicity Principle. The law of simplicity is vital to marketing communications, where the KISS formula rules: Keep it short and sweet (or, as the military instructs, "Keep it simple, stupid!"). Uncomplicated illustrations, straightforward language, use of symbols for abstract concepts (e.g., a heart shape for "love"), lots of white space, and simple messages all help consumers process advertising and packaging communications.

PRINCIPLES OF CONTEXT

The principles of context consider how perception of a stimulus object is influenced by its surroundings. Two principles of context relevant to CB are figure and ground and contrast.

FIGURE AND GROUND

The Principle of Figure and Ground. The **figure and ground (figure-ground) principle** says that people interpret a stimulus in the context of its background. They tend to distinguish a prominent and well-defined stimulus in the foreground (the figure) from less prominent, indefinite stimuli in the background (the ground). The figure becomes the focal point of attention and interest. For instance, most people can easily pick out a familiar face in a crowd, with the recognizable person becoming the foreground and everyone else lurking in the background.

The classic illustration of the figure-ground principle is the following ambiguous or reversible picture—the part that is the figure and the portion that is the ground can be reversed, resulting in two very different interpretations of the stimuli.

Is the figure a white vase (or goblet, or birdbath) on a black background, or is it two silhouetted human profiles on a white background? The answer depends on the individual's **perceptual (mental) set**—what a person expects to perceive or is used to perceiving. Most Americans see the two faces rather than a goblet or birdbath since the former is more familiar in their culture.

Marketing Applications of the Figure-Ground Principle. It is important to make sure that the most important stimuli, such as the product and selling theme, stand out as the figure and do not fade to the background!

Unfortunately, the product and message can get lost in the shuffle when ads use potentially irrelevant sources of borrowed interest to grab consumers' attention, such as entertainment, celebrities, humor, and sex.

The following are several attention-getting devices that can cause a stimulus to be perceived front and center. Each one makes a stimulus more salient (noticeable).

- *Size.* Important is relative size—the size of the stimulus in relation to its surroundings. Products, packages, brand names, and other important ad elements should be relatively large.
- *Movement.* People are attracted to anything in motion, such as interactive point-of-purchase displays, blinking lights and moving fixtures on outdoor ads, and animated banner ads.
- *Color.* Colors, especially bright ones, attract attention. Web sites often use bright colors but sometimes overdo it with too many bright colors, making the site difficult to read.
- *Isolation.* An object that is separated from other surrounding objects (as by white space in a print ad) is more likely to be noticed.
- *Shapes.* Unusual shapes stand out. An advertising model with distorted body proportions (as in a fun house mirror) would attract the eye.

CONTRAST

The Contrast Principle. The **contrast principle** says that a stimulus that stands out from its surroundings is more likely to be noticed. To be readily discerned, a sound must be much softer or louder, a color brighter or paler, or an object larger or smaller than others near it.

Marketing Applications of the Contrast Principle. Marketers must "differentiate or die!" Sellers should create unique brand names (not "Acme" or "Ajax"), packaging styles (Janitor in a Drum), and advertisements (scent strips and pop-ups were once novel but are no more). The first TV commercials shot in 3D were unique.

IN-CLASS APPLICATIONS

1. Let's have some fun with Gestalt psychology principles! Several of the following concepts were not discussed in this section but are easily explained using the illustrations for each that follow.
   a. *Relative size and context.* Are the ovals in the centers of these two squares the same size? Guess first and then see if you are right by measuring them with a ruler.

   0 0 0 0 0   0 0 0 0 0
   0 0 0 0 0   0 0 0 0 0
   0 0 0 0 0   0 0 0 0 0

   b. *Continuity and context.* What is the second symbol in each line? How do you interpret it differently in each case due to the need for continuity and the surrounding environment?

   A /3 C D

   12 /3 14 15

   c. *Relative brightness.* Which of the two gray squares is darker?

d. *Negative after-image.* Stare at the center dot in the middle of the circle for at least twenty seconds. Then shift your gaze to a white surface . . . what do you see?

e. *Proximity.* How do you view each of the four following patterns (columns, rows, etc.)?

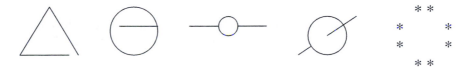

f. *Closure and continuity.* Describe what you see in the following five patterns.

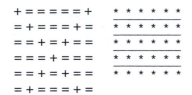

g. *Similarity.* How would you describe the following patterns?

```
+ = = = = = +        * * * * * *
= + = = = + =        * * * * * *
= = + = + = =        * * * * * *
= = = + = = =        * * * * * *
= = + = + = =        * * * * * *
= + = = = + =
```

h. *Linear perspective.* Which of the two lines is longer, the top or bottom?

i. *Figure and ground.* Which part of the picture do you notice first?

j. *Relative height.* Does the vertical line appear longer, shorter, or equal to the horizontal line?

2. Time to explore websites featuring Gestalt perceptual organization principles.
   a. Visit Magic Eye at http://www.magiceye.com/. Can you see the hidden 3-D image? Hint: Focus your eyes beyond the image and be patient. Click on the illustration to see what is behind it. For more Magic Eye fun, enter the site and browse the image of the week's (and past weeks') winners. Which Gestalt principle does Magic Eye bring to life?
   b. Can we see everything before us? While we favor complete images versus incomplete images, we do not actually see a complete image when it is not there . . . or do we? See how our brains actually live out the closure principle at Serendip's website, "Seeing more than your eye does," at http://serendip. brynmawr.edu/bb/blindspot1.html.
3. For each of the following ads (Exhibits 13.25–13.29), identify which principles of perceptual organization according to Gestalt theory are being used. Consider: Grouping—similarity, proximity, continuity, closure, and simplicity; Context—figure and ground, and contrast; and Attention Getters—size, movement, color, isolation, position, and shapes. Does each ad use the principles effectively to gain attention, interest, comprehension, and/or retention of the brand and its selling message?

WRITTEN APPLICATIONS

1. Answer Question 3 in the In-Class Applications for five of the following ads.
2. Find three additional ads and repeat the analysis for Question 3 in the In-Class Applications.

EXHIBIT 13.25   **ViewSonic Ad**

EXHIBIT 13.26   **Nike Ad**

EXHIBIT 13.27   Lexmark Ad

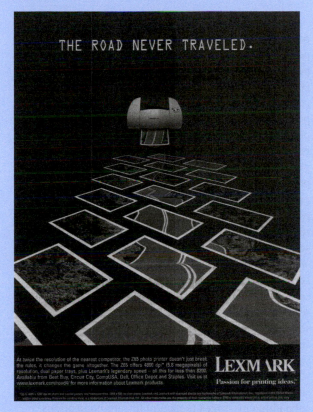

EXHIBIT 13.28   Breitling Ad

EXHIBIT 13.29   United Way Ad

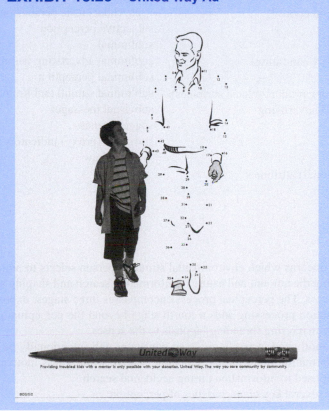

KEY CONCEPTS

absolute (lower, detection) threshold level (ATL)
adaptation (sensory adaptation, habituation)
adaptation level
attention
backward masking (backmasking, audio reversal)
closure (mental completion) principle
cognitive school of psychology
comprehension
confidence value
continuity principle (law of good continuation)
contrast principle
deception
deceptive advertising
differential (difference) threshold (just noticeable difference [jnd])
embeds
euphemisms
exposure
extrinsic cues (indirect indicators, non-product-related attributes)
figure and ground (figure-ground) principle
form (shape) perception
Gestalt principles (laws) of perceptual organization
Gestalt school of psychology
grouping
impression management (spin control)
incongruities
information input
information overload (sensory saturation)
information processing
intrinsic cues (direct indicators, product-related attributes)
keyword search (contextual) advertising
keywords
market beliefs
market signals
nonperformance (nonfunctional) attributes

package downsizing (package shorting, weight out)
perception
perceptual (informational) cues
perceptual defense
perceptual (mental) set
perceptual predispositions
perceptual vigilance
performance (functional) attributes
predictive value
principles of context
proximity (contiguity) principle
psychophysics
retention
selective perception (perceptual selection)
sensation
sensory marketing (branding)
sensory receptors (sensory organs)
sensory stimuli (cues, sensory inputs)
sensory systems (sensory functions)
similarity principle
simplicity principle (pragnänz)
stimulus discrimination (sensory discrimination)
stimulus object
subaudible messages (subaudible communications, audio conditioning, threshold messaging, psychoacoustic persuasion)
subjective perception
subliminal
subliminal advertising (subliminal seduction)
subliminal perception
subliminal stimuli (subliminal messages)
subvisual messages
suggestiveness
surrogate (proxy) indicators (market signals)
Weber's Law

SUMMARY

Perception concerns which environmental stimuli a person selects to notice and how he or she interprets them, affecting the amount and nature of information search and shaping alternative evaluation during the learning process. The perceptual process encompasses three stages: exposure, attention, and comprehension. Information processing adds a fourth stage beyond the perceptual process—retention (see Exhibit 3.1). Sensory marketing (branding) appeals to the senses.

A highly motivated, actively involved consumer will intentionally be exposed to relevant perceptual cues and information input during deliberate search, while a less motivated and involved buyer will be randomly exposed to information during accidental search.

There are several key characteristics of perception:

What is perceived are sensory stimuli that are received by people's sensory receptors and are experienced through their sensory systems, permitting sensation. During the perceptual process, people organize raw stimuli into information input. Individuals differ in their reception of sensory stimuli due to physiological differences, primarily nature (e.g., sensitivity to stimuli), and psychological differences, mostly nurture. Hence, attempting to communicate with someone is no guarantee that successful communication has occurred.

Perception is subjective. Consequently, marketers cannot be sure that people interpret information the way the marketers assume they will.

The nature of selective and subjective perception was investigated in Exercise 13.1. Selective perception involves selective exposure, selective attention, selective comprehension, and selective retention (Exhibit 13.1). Selective perception typically occurs during exposure and attention, whereas subjective perception mostly happens during the comprehension stage.

Selective perception is primarily caused by information overload. Two factors contribute to the nature of selective perception: prior experiences affecting people's expectations and perceptual predispositions, which explains perceptual vigilance and perceptual defense.

There are four primary marketing implications of selective perception:

1. Clearly communicate so consumers do not tune out the message.
2. Either conform to or sharply deviate from consumers' expectations and experiences. Advertisers should use attention-getting advertising elements.
3. Conform to buyers' perceptual predispositions, especially by selecting the appropriate target market and placing advertising in media, stores, and Web sites frequented by targeted customers. Effective ads appeal to consumer needs and desires in an interesting way and are consistent with their values. To attract customers to a Web site, an advertiser can purchase keywords from a search engine, a practice known as keyword search advertising.
4. Use uncrowded media.

Like selective perception, subjective perception is also a result of prior experience and expectations and perceptual predispositions, resulting in perceptual distortion of information. The message decoded is not the same as the message encoded.

Marketing ramifications of subjective perception are to overcome and manage negative impressions, correcting any false beliefs; employ subjective perceptual cues such as colors, shapes, aromas, sounds, and words (e.g., euphemisms); use impression management; and avoid deception and deceptive advertising.

Subjective perception suggests that marketers must learn to see things through the customers' eyes by consulting them to learn of their interests, interpretations and viewpoints. Then, marketers can market to the perception, not the reality.

Exercise 13.2 on the absolute threshold level (ATL), studied by psychophysics, tied in to the attention phase of the perceptual process. Adaptation concerns a changing adaptation level. Marketers must ensure that consumers do not become adapted to marketing stimuli, growing bored or tuning them out, by offering changes or variety in marketing stimuli while avoiding radical change that could upset consumers.

Marketers should ascertain that their important stimuli are above the consumer's ATL by using attention-grabbing techniques. There are also instances in which marketers do not wish for consumers to detect certain stimuli, preferring to remain below the ATL. Some of these tactics, such as subliminal advertising, are ethically questionable. This advertising uses subliminal stimuli to create subliminal perception, trying to manipulate CB via placing hidden stimuli in advertising media so as to cause them to change their attitudes and/or behaviors. Although research shows that subliminals cannot be effectively used to persuade people or alter CB, many people believe that it does.

There are five types of subliminal messages: subvisual messages, embeds, incongruities and suggestiveness, subaudible messages, and backward masking. Although subliminal advertising is rare and ineffective, the public continues to view it as a menace since the advertising industry suffers a negative image as manipulators, consumer sovereignty not withstanding; sensationalism sells; and people dislike the fact that advertising conspicuously attempts to influence (not manipulate) them.

Although a certain amount of subliminal advertising exists, to sneak hidden messages into ads is immoral because it is deceptive, violates the consumer's right to know, and tries to control human behavior in violation of free will. Subliminals only work to some degree in the case of constant message repetition (as with subvisual and subaudible messages) and where audience members are predisposed toward the message. Otherwise, there are a number of practical difficulties in using subliminal messages:

- Needs and wants cannot be created.
- Supraliminal stimuli tend to overpower or nullify subliminal stimuli.
- Perceptual thresholds are variable across persons and over time for any one individual.
- People selectively screen out supraliminal stimuli not consistent with their predispositions and probably do so for subliminal stimuli, too.
- Misinterpretations of subliminal stimuli are highly likely.

Another phenomenon at the attention phase of the perceptual process was covered in Exercise 13.3: the differential threshold or the just noticeable difference (jnd). This relates to sensory discrimination and is explained by Weber's law. The Weber's law formula is

$$jnd = K = \frac{\Delta I}{I} \, ,$$

where the value of K varies as the function of the consumer, the marketing stimulus, and the environment.

Marketers need to determine the jnd for key elements of their marketing program so that changes considered undesirable remain below the jnd and modifications desired by consumers are just at or slightly above the jnd. The changes can be between a marketer's old and new marketing programs or they can be differences between the marketer's and competitors' offerings.

Types of marketing mix adjustments consumers deem undesirable and that marketers hope they will not detect include price hikes, package downsizing, and quality cuts and inferior ingredients substitution. Some such changes might be considered unethical. There are also several kinds of marketing mix modifications consumers like and that marketers need to make sure are large enough so that buyers notice them: price decreases; quantity, weight, and size increases; and quality improvements. Also to be noticed are changes in packages, logos, company names, or trade characters. Although many of the latter modifications can contemporize a brand, some changes might be perceived as upsetting to consumers.

The topic of surrogate indicators, which ties into the comprehension stage of information processing, was covered in Exercise 13.4. Surrogate indicators are often inaccurate indicators of product performance, and so the use of market signals can lead to perceptual distortion.

Surrogate indicators can be classified physically into intrinsic cues and extrinsic cues. Most surrogate indicators are extrinsic cues because, due to their visibility, they are easily (but often erroneously) used in product evaluation.

Perceptual cues can also be categorized by their predictive value as performance attributes and nonperformance attributes. Performance attributes have high predictive value and, for the most part, are intrinsic cues since these directly influence performance.

Nonperformance attributes have low-to-no predictive value for understanding product performance and are primarily extrinsic cues since elements outside of the product are less likely to directly correlate with its performance. However, intrinsic cues can also be nonperformance attributes if they are more for form and style than function and substance. Most (but not all) surrogate indicators are nonperformance attributes since most proxy indicators are extrinsic cues, and extrinsic cues are generally less likely to have high predictive value.

Perceptual cues can also be classified by their confidence value. Generally, extrinsic cues are high in confidence value because they are simple to use and readily observable, whereas intrinsic cues are low in confidence value because they are often more complex and not so easily discernable. However, just because a consumer has high confidence in an attribute's predictive ability does not mean that it is an accurate product performance predictor.

In short, surrogate indicators tend to be extrinsic cues, low in predictive value (nonperformance attributes), and high in confidence value. Figure 13.19 summarizes these relationships.

Buyers use surrogate indicators where they lack marketplace knowledge or experience (e.g., extended problem solving, credence goods); have low self-confidence (e.g., complex products, credence goods);

believe that difficult-to-detect quality variations exist among brands; are lazy, rushed, or otherwise wish to simplify decision making (e.g., decision heuristics); have low involvement and therefore do not wish to use more complex performance attributes; or have high involvement and wish to use a risk reduction strategy. Often-used surrogate indicators include:

- *Price.* People believe in price-quality relationships, rationally figuring that high price suggests high production costs and high demand. However, high price does not guarantee high quality, since price could be high due to other factors like demand based upon false product perceptions and absence of competition.
- *Brand name and manufacturer name.* Like a high price, a brand name can add psychological value. Part of brand equity is the positive associations the name has in buyers' minds. While usually well-known brand names are of higher quality, this is not always so.
- *Color.* People often "taste" with their eyes. Certain colors, such as black, gold, and silver, are associated with quality, while clear is affiliated with purity and natural ingredients.
- *Aroma.* A product's scent can suggest quality, such as lemon in cleaning products.
- *Texture and feel.* Thickness in many products connotes quality, and a stinging sensation in certain medicinal products suggests effectiveness.
- Other surrogate indicators include ingredients and materials, sound, size, packaging, country of origin, age and heritage, nature and amount of advertising, channels of distribution, amount of shelf space, market share and sales volume, warranties and guarantees, and words.

Another subjective perception phenomenon was investigated in Exercise 13.5—the Gestalt principles of perceptual organization formulated by the Gestalt school of psychology. This exercise focused on concepts related to form perception.

There are five principles of grouping as follows. The similarity principle explains the existence of advertising campaigns and department stores. The proximity principle accounts for cross selling, bundling, association strategies, advertising layout, and organization of wares on websites by usage context. The continuity principle explains long-term ad campaigns, department store transitions between departments, and gradual changes in visual marketing elements. The closure principle suggests letting consumers mentally "fill in the blank" in advertisements, using question headlines, cropping visuals, and using radio as the "theater of the mind." The principle of simplicity suggests the KISS principle.

The principles of context—figure and ground and contrast—consider how perception of a stimulus object is influenced by its surroundings. The figure-and-ground principle suggests that what is perceived as the figure and what is viewed as the background depends, in part, upon on the individual's perceptual set. This suggests that marketers must make sure that the most important marketing stimuli stand out as the figure and do not fade to the background. Attention getters such as celebrities, humor, and sex should not drown out the selling message. There are several attention-getting devices that can cause a stimulus to be noticed, including relative size, movement, color, isolation, position, and unusual shapes.

The contrast principle suggests that a marketer must "differentiate or die."

REFERENCES

Alpert, Frank, Wilson, Beth, and Elliot, Michael T. (1993). "Price Signaling: Does It Ever Work?" *Journal of Product and Brand Management,* 2, 1, 29–41.

Aqueveque, Claudio. (2006). "Extrinsic Cues and Perceived Risk: The Influence of Consumption Situation." *Journal of Consumer Marketing,* 23, 5, 237–247.

Bettman, James R. (1979). *An Information Processing Theory of Consumer Choice.* Reading, MA: Addison-Wesley.
———. (1970). "Information Processing Models of Consumer Behavior." *Journal of Marketing Research,* 7, 3, 370–376.

Boulding, William, and Kirmani, Amna. (1993). "A Consumer-Side Experimental Examination of Signaling Theory: Do Consumers Perceive Warranties as Signals of Quality?" *Journal of Consumer Research,* 20, 1, 111–123.

Britt, Stuart Henderson, and Nelson, Victoria M. (1976). "The Marketing Importance of the 'Just Noticeable Difference.'" *Business Horizons* (August), 38–40.

Dawar, Niraj, and Parker, Philip. (1994). "Marketing Universals: Consumers' Use of Brand Name, Price, Physical Appearance, and Retailer Reputation as Signals of Product Quality." *Journal of Marketing,* 58, 2, 81–95.

Duncan, Calvin P. (1990). "Consumer Market Beliefs: A Review of the Literature and an Agenda for Future Research." In Marvin E. Goldberg, Gerald Gorn, and Richard W. Pollay, eds. *Advances in Consumer Research,* 17. Provo, UT: Association for Consumer Research.

Gardner, Gerald M. (1973). "Is There a Generalized Price-Quality Relationship?" *Journal of Marketing Research,* 8 (May), 241–243.

Gerstner, Eitan. (1985). "Do Higher Prices Signal Higher Quality?" *Journal of Marketing Research,* 22, 2, 209–215.

Gorn, Gerald J. (1982). "The Effects of Music in Advertising on Choice Behavior: A Classical Conditioning Approach." *Journal of Consumer Marketing,* 46, 1, 94–101.

Haberstroh, Jack. (1994). *Ice Cube Sex: The Truth about Subliminal Advertising.* Notre Dame, IN: Cross Cultural Publications.

Haley, Russell I., Richardson, Jack, and Baldwin, Beth M. (1984). "The Effects of Nonverbal Communications in Television Advertising." *Journal of Advertising Research,* 24, 4, 11–18.

Harris, Richard Jackson, Garner-Earl, Bettina, Sprick, Sara, and Carroll, Collette. (1994). "Effects of Foreign Product Names and Country-of-Origin Attributions on Advertisement Evaluations." *Psychology and Marketing,* 11 (March–April), 129–145.

Hoegg, JoAndrea. (2007). "Taste Perception: More Than Meets the Tongue." *Journal of Consumer Research,* 33, 4, 490–498.

Irmani, Anna, and Wright, Peter. (1989). "Money Talks: Perceived Advertising Expense and Expected Product Quality." *Journal of Consumer Research,* 16, 3, 344–353.

Kassarjian, Harold H. (1971). "Personality and Consumer Behavior: A Review." *Journal of Marketing Research,* 8, 4, 409–418.

Kelly, Steven J. (1979). "Subliminal Embeds in Print Advertising." *Journal of Advertising,* 8, 3, 20–24.

Key, Wilson Bryan. (1973). *Subliminal Seduction: Ad Media's Manipulation of a Not So Innocent America.* Englewood Cliffs, NJ: Prentice-Hall.

———. (1977). *Media Sexploitation.* Englewood Cliffs, NJ: Prentice-Hall.

———. (1980). *The Clam-Plate Orgy and Other Subliminals the Media Use to Manipulate Your Behavior.* Englewood Cliffs, NJ: Prentice-Hall.

———. (1990). *The Age of Manipulation: The Con in Confidence, the Sin in Sincere.* Englewood Cliffs, NJ: Prentice-Hall.

Kirmani, Amna, and Rao, Akshay R. (2000). "No Pain, No Gain." *Journal of Marketing,* 64, 2, 66–79.

Lindstrom, Martin. (2005). "Broad Sensory Branding." *Journal of Product and Brand Management,* 14, 2, 84–87.

———. (2008). *Buyology: Truth and Lies About Why We Buy.* New York, NY: Doubleday Business.

McSweeney, Frances K., and Bierley, Calvin. (1984). "Recent Developments in Classical Conditioning of Preferences for Stimuli." *Journal of Consumer Research,* 11, 2, 619–631.

Merikle, Philip M. (1988). "Subliminal Auditory Messages: An Evaluation." *Psychology and Marketing,* 5, 4, 355–372.

Miyazaki, Anthony D., Grewal, Dhruv, and Goodstein, Ronald C. (2005). "The Effect of Multiple Extrinsic Cues on Quality Perceptions: A Matter of Consistency." *Journal of Consumer Research,* 32, 1, 146–153.

Moore, Timothy E. (1982). "Subliminal Advertising: What You See Is What You Get." *Journal of Consumer Marketing,* 46, 2, 38–47.

Pullig, Chris, Simmons, Carolyn J., and Netemeyer, Richard G. (2006). "Brand Dilution: When Do New Brands Hurt Existing Brands?" *Journal of Marketing,* 70, 2, 52–66.

Rao, Ashkay R., and Monroe, Kent B. (1989). "The Effect of Price, Brand Name, and Store Name on Buyers' Perceptions of Product Quality." *Journal of Consumer Research,* 16, 3, 351–357.

Rogers, Martha, and Seiler, Christine A. (1994). "The Answer Is No: A National Survey of Advertising Industry Practitioners and Their Clients About Whether They Use Subliminal Advertising." *Journal of Advertising Research,* 34, 2, 36–45.

Sacharin, Ken. (2001). *Attention! How to Interrupt, Yell, Whisper, and Touch Consumers.* New York: John Wiley & Sons.

Tom, Gail, Barnett, Teresa, Lew, William, and Selmonts, Jodean. (1987). "Cueing the Consumer: The Role of Salient Cues in Consumer Perception." *Journal of Consumer Marketing,* 4, 2, 23–27.

Venkataraman, V. K. (1981). "The Price-Quality Relationship in an Experimental Setting." *Journal of Advertising Research,* 21, 4, 49–51.

Volckner, Franziska, and Sattler, Hernrick. (2006). "Drivers of Brand Extension Success." *Journal of Marketing,* 70, 2, 18–34.

Wheatley, John J., and Chiu, John S. (1977). "The Effects of Price, Store Image, and Product and Respondent Characteristics on Perceptions of Quality." *Journal of Marketing Research,* 14, 2, 181–186.

Zajonc, R. B., Markus, H. M., and Wilson, W. (1974). "Exposure Effects and Associative Learning." *Journal of Experimental Social Psychology,* 10, 248–263.

CHAPTER 14

LEARNING AND MEMORY

LEARNING DEFINED AND RELATED TO THE CONSUMER DECISION PROCESS

"There is always something to learn about learning," an educator once mused. A major activity of our lives is learning—we are "lifelong learners." This chapter will lead you to discover how you acquire and retain information. The material herein will also aid you as a marketer. One of the major tasks of marketers is to educate potential and current customers about products and brands.

Learning is the procedure whereby memory and behavior are changed as a result of perception and conscious and unconscious information processing. Learning follows from the nature of perception and information processing (Chapter 13). Learning is also conceptualized as a process in which behavioral tendencies are changed as a result of experience, provided they cannot be accounted for by instincts, maturation, temporary states of the organism, or reflex actions. Per this second definition:

1. Learning can be evidenced by *behavioral tendencies* rather than behavior per se. Example: Positive purchase intentions arise from favorable attitudes as a result of exposure to marketing promotion.

2. Experience is the key learning source. *Experiences* are physical, cognitive, and emotional interactions with a cultural and social environment. This includes both personal direct experience (experiential learning, such as postpurchase usage) and indirect experience, which encompasses learning from others' experiences (vicarious learning, such as ads featuring people shown using a product) and information acquisition from sources of prepurchase information. Usually, direct experience provides the best learning. Compared to indirect learning, it is more motivated, involving, vivid, credible, concrete, sensory, and under the consumer's control.

3. Not all behavior is learned, such as that which is innate due to maturation or caused by temporary conditions.

The topic of learning is important because one of the chief determinants of human behavior is learning. CB is primarily learned behavior. Virtually all of the phenomena you study in this course—values, symbolic meanings, lifestyles, tastes and preferences, attitudes, brand images, and so on—are acquired through the learning process. Learning experiences are provided by various sociocultural phenomena such as the culture, societal institutions such as schools and mass media, subcultural groups, social classes, social groups and friends, and, especially, family.

Recall from the discussion concerning Exhibit P4.2, reproduced in modified form here as Exhibit 14.1, that a motivated consumer experiencing problem recognition will usually expose him- or herself to relevant information during information search. This type of prepurchase learning is **intentional (directed, purposive) learning**, or based on an information search wherein highly involved consumers actively seek out and consciously process information in a goal-directed fashion.

The other type of prepurchase learning is called **incidental (accidental, passive, iconic rote, associative) learning**. This is low-involvement learning that occurs by accident, without deliberate effort, when the consumer passively encounters unsought information, such as walking past and noticing in-store signs and displays or being exposed to TV commercials and billboards. For instance, you didn't learn most of the jingles you can hum and brand names you know through your own conscious efforts. Incidental learning is also called associative learning because people learn associations or connections between stimuli this way. The process entails simple stimulus-response learning via repetition and association, much of it being classical conditioning when an unconditioned stimulus is involved (see Exercise 14.3). Much incidental learning occurs almost unconsciously through sheer repetition. Intentional learning, on the other hand, entails higher-level learning modes such as instrumental conditioning and cognitive learning (see Exercise 14.3).

EXHIBIT 14.1   The Place of Learning in the Learning and Perceptual Processes

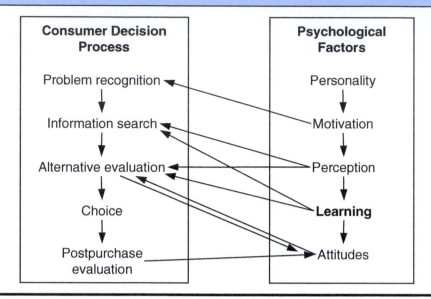

The different ways that knowledge can be acquired suggest that there are various modes whereby people learn, ranging from simple, reflexive responses to purposeful problem solving. Various learning theories explain certain types of consumer learning process.

Regardless, consumer perceptions of this information serve as the gateway to the learning process, which occurs in conjunction with the information search and alternative evaluation phases of the consumer buying process. Following consumer learning, prepurchase attitudes are formed during the alternative evaluation phase, leading (all else equal) to a purchase. These attitudes might be changed as a consequence of personal experience and consequent learning during the post-purchase behavior stage. The formation of and changes in these attitudes are the focus of Chapter 15.

ORGANIZATION OF CHAPTER 14

Exercise 14.1 investigates memory, retention of information in memory, and retrieval of information stored in memory. Techniques marketers can use to enhance memory, retention, and retrieval are illustrated. Such tricks of the trade often entail getting consumers more involved in the learning process.

Exercise 14.2 reviews four basic elements of the learning process—drives, cues (stimuli), responses, and reinforcement—that most learning theorists believe are necessary for effective learning to occur. You will see how each of these elements explains different types and aspects of consumer learning and how marketers tap into each element to ensure more effective learning.

Finally, Exercise 14.3 describes the various theories of learning and shows how and when each is applicable to certain types of consumer behavior (CB).

EXERCISE 14.1. MEMORY, RETENTION, AND RETRIEVAL

OBJECTIVES

1. To gain insight into techniques for enhancing consumers' retention of information by explaining short-term memory and long-term memory, and to practice recognizing and using these techniques.
2. To demonstrate some methods of aiding consumers' information retrieval.

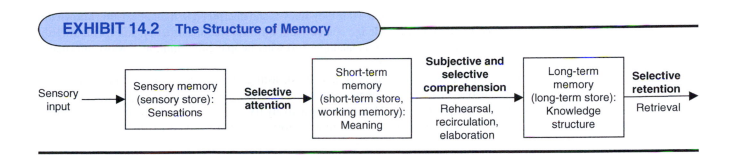

EXHIBIT 14.2   The Structure of Memory

3. To test your own consumer learning and gain insight into how you learned this marketplace information.

BACKGROUND

THE NATURE OF MEMORY

Memory is the outcome of the learning process, providing a storehouse of information. Someone's memory is the total accumulation of **memories**, which are key elements from prior learning experiences. **Retention** refers to the act of storing information in short-term and long-term memory at the conclusion of information processing so that it can be recalled. **Retrieval** is the process whereby people recover (access) information from long-term memory, that is, the process of remembering. And **forgetting** is loss of previously learned material over time due to lack of repetition of the stimulus or message.

This exercise will help you understand conceptually what memory, retention, and retrieval each entail and provides some tools for enhancing consumers' retention and retrieval of important marketing information from their memory. It is hoped that you will remember and be able to apply this material through experiences provided in the applications questions for each exercise!

MEMORY STRUCTURE

Cognitive psychologists have developed **multiple store theory**, suggesting there are three interrelated **memory stores**, or processing areas in memory: sensory memory, short-term memory, and long-term memory. Exhibit 14.2 summarizes these three hypothetical constructs.

SENSORY MEMORY

When sensory stimuli first enter the brain as information inputs, they are captured by **sensory memory** in a storage area known as a **sensory store**, where information might register as no more than a fleeting sensation of size, shape, texture, or other stimulus. Hence, processing is shallow and does not require active attention to the stimulus in order to remember it.

If the sensation seems relevant or of interest, consumers will be motivated to interpret what it means, or process it, moving the sensation into short-term memory. However, if the information is not deemed relevant or interesting, it is not further processed or analyzed and disappears from the sensory store and is forgotten (selective attention).

Echoic memory is a type of sensory memory that holds audio information very briefly. This information includes words, jingles, and background music. These can catch attention and convey meaning congruent with the message, thereby increasing learning. In **iconic memory**, visual information is briefly retained and recollected.

SHORT-TERM MEMORY

Short-term memory (short-term store, working memory) is a memory store that analyzes the sensations and information from sensory memory and assigns meaning to them based on prior knowledge. Individuals use short-term memory to hold information while they analyze and interpret it in light of existing **knowledge**, or information stored in memory (knowledge content) and form for that information storage (knowledge structure). Basically, short-term memory is analogous to what people call "thinking." Most information processing occurs in short-term memory.

Like sensory memory, short-term memory is short-lived, lasting a few minutes at most. This explains why you might forget someone's name just moments after being introduced or cannot recall a phone number right after looking it up in a telephone book. Unless people actively try to remember information using working memory, thereby transferring it to long-term memory, information will evaporate from their minds.

Short-Term Memory Capacity Limitations: Chunks and the Span of Recall. Short-term memory's capacity is limited to a finite number of **chunks**, or units of memory. Each chunk stores a group of similar or related items that can easily be processed together to give it meaning. Chunking related information together helps to ensure the information will not be lost from short-term memory.

Span of recall is the number of discrete items or bits of information that can be held at one time in short-term memory. It was long believed by psychologists that most people can hold between five and nine chunks at a time. This limited span of recall explains why U.S. telephone numbers (excluding area codes) are seven digits long.

Recent research has revealed that only three to four information chunks can be held in short-term memory. This explains breaking a phone number into a three-digit area code, three-digit exchange, and four-digit individual number (e.g., 508–565–1205). A zip code plus four digits is too many bits of information for most people to remember. However, separating it into two chunks (07060–1536) facilitates memory chunking. Social security numbers are likewise broken into three chunks with two dashes.

Marketers can assist consumers' ability to hold information in short-term memory and transfer it to long-term memory by presenting it in chunks. 1–800-FLOWERS built its business around its memorable name. IBM presents one chunk from the longer International Business Machines, as does KFC (Kentucky Fried Chicken).

It follows that ads and sales presentations should be built around one or a few key ideas at most. Consumers can usually only remember three to five chunks of information from package labels (typically brand name, logo, and any picture or key image), so package designers are warned to keep it simple. In fact, visuals are a great idea for any marketing communication since visual information is more efficiently chunked than verbal material and is therefore better retained. Aural chunking is also possible and is one reason for the popularity of rhymes and jingles. Brand and organizational name acronyms (e.g., Nabisco for National Biscuit Company, Mothers Against Drunk Driving [MADD], the "Four As" [American Association of Advertising Agencies], and SPELL [Society for the Preservation of English Language and Literature]) also aid chunking, as do simple descriptors such as "healthy," which chunks more complex information (i.e., low in calories, cholesterol, and fat, and high in protein and in vitamins and minerals).

Information Processing Activities in Short-Term Memory. The meaning of information stored in short-term memory can be retained if is subjected to one or more types of short-term memory information processing activities: maintenance rehearsal, recirculation, and elaborative activities. These activities are most likely to occur for information that is relevant, interesting, meaningful, and/or familiar.

Maintenance rehearsal (rehearsal) is the silent, mental repetition of a piece of information in short-term memory. It is a form of inner speech, essentially talking to oneself. For example, you might rehearse a telephone number so that you remember it. Following rehearsal, the information is then transferred to long-term memory.

Rehearsal happens only if an individual is motivated to process and remember information, i.e., there is fairly high-involvement learning. If motivation is low, marketers should use tactics to heighten motivation and involvement, such as appealing jingles and interesting slogans.

Another way to transfer information to long-term memory is through **recirculation**, the process whereby information is remembered when a person is repeatedly exposed to information without active rehearsal. This is low-involvement learning in that consumers make no active attempt to learn information. Consequently, marketers must repeat information over and over, banging it into consumers' memory banks, like beating a nail into a board with a hammer.

Rehearsal or recirculation leads to **surface-level processing (sensory processing)** in which information is stored in long-term memory without being analyzed for meaning. For instance, a food shopper might learn that Junko chocolate candy has 17 grams of fat, including 9 grams of saturated fat per 1.5 ounces. However, he or she fails to ponder the health implications such as whether this is a very fatty food or a food relatively high in saturated fat.

Elaborative (meaning-level, semantic) processing is the storage of meaning (rather than raw data) in long-term memory. In the candy bar example, it would involve remembering that Junko is very high in fat, especially saturated fat. Although this type of short-term information processing takes longer than surface-level processing, it is less likely to result in judgment errors leading to poorer decision making.

Elaborative activities occur during elaborative processing and entail relating or integrating new information with existing knowledge and prior experiences. They involve deep processing of the information, making connections between the stimulus and one's knowledge base to interpret and evaluate the stimulus. For instance, "The car gets thirty miles per gallon" might be translated to "The car gets great gas mileage." This is high-involvement learning.

An elaborative activity that involves the process of labeling or identifying an object based on what someone already knows is called **categorization** (discussed in Exercise 14.2). Elaborative processing results in the formation of **concepts**, which are abstractions of or generalized ideas about reality, such as objects (brands, stores, endorsers, etc.) and their attributes. Concepts enable us to understand the meaning of things. For example, the brand name Beautyrest might help consumers associate the mattress with a good night's sleep.

LONG-TERM MEMORY

Information that is rehearsed, recirculated, and/or elaborated is transferred to **long-term memory**, which stores unlimited learned information over a long period. Learning can therefore be defined as a change in the content of long-term memory.

There are several types of long-term **knowledge structures** by which information can be stored in long-term memory: semantic memory, episodic memory, and schematic memory.

Semantic Memory. **Semantic memory** is a person's general knowledge and feelings about a concept, that is, what the concept means to that individual, and is not tied to any particular object or event. For example, you know that stop lights are found at busy intersections, have three lights, and the order of lights from top to bottom is red, amber, and green. The marketing admonition is to know the meaning consumers give to the product category and marketplace.

Episodic Memory. Another knowledge structure is **episodic memory**, in which a person remembers a particular sequence of events in which he or she participated. Information is stored sequentially by episodes or events, such as shopping trips, meal preparation, and packing for a vacation.

An episodic memory of how an action sequence should occur is known as a **script**. For instance, shopping for a car once entailed visiting several dealers, test-driving preferred cars, and then haggling with the dealer concerning price, options, and so on. Now, many car dealers have changed the script by offering "no-dicker stickers," which eliminate bargaining. Although many car sellers have been successful, marketers should proceed with caution. It is often difficult to change engrained scripts unless (as with the car-buying script) consumers are not happy with them. Therefore, since the mid-1990s most automobile buyers have added the car-buying script of comparison shopping online since it bolsters their confidence in dealing with car salespeople.

Scripts for low-involvement products occur almost effortlessly and without a lot of careful thought, such as grocery shopping. Rituals for high-involvement products, such as shopping for a car, entail more thought, so it is more likely the participants will deviate from the script.

One particular type of episodic memory is **autobiographical memory**, an episodic memory about a person's past. Such memory is of an important, personal event that lasts for a long period of time and becomes part of someone's personal history. It includes prior experiences as well as the emotions and sensations affiliated with these experiences. You might remember the sequence of events concerning your first day in school or your first date.

Ads often generate good feelings by helping audience members recall autobiographical experiences or by appealing to nostalgia. An ad for Hershey's asked, "Remember your first Hershey's bar?"

Schematic Memory. Information can also be stored in long-term memory as **schematic memory**, a knowledge structure in which concepts and episodes acquire a depth of meaning by becoming associated with other concepts and episodes.

Psychologists suggest that schematic memory consists of **schema**, which are organized categories of knowledge (beliefs and feelings) held in memory that are structured around a focal concept and that determine how new stimuli will be processed. Schema are patterns of association among concepts and episodes that are brought to mind when a cue is activated. They are organized and stored in long-term memory as an **associative (semantic) network**. This knowledge representation system is composed of concepts organized around a particular concept or event. The network consists of various **nodes**, which are beliefs, concepts, or objects in memory. These are joined to other nodes through connections called **links,** which are of varying strengths.

For instance, a *brand image*—a set of associations reflecting a brand's personality—is the schematic memory for a brand. Associations for Home Depot include down-home, honest, thrifty, friendly, and working class. The various marketing elements (e.g., packaging, brand name, trade characters) constitute the nodes contributing to a brand's image.

When one concept is activated, others might also become activated via the links. **Memory trace strength** is the extent to which an association or link is strongly or weakly joined to a concept in memory. Some links are strong, that is, they are firmly established in memory. Concepts associated via strong links are more likely to activate one another than those joined by weak links. Some of these links represent semantic memory, while others signify episodic memory.

ENHANCING LONG-TERM MEMORY THROUGH REPETITION

Exhibit 14.2 and the previous discussion suggest that to move information from short-term memory to long-term memory, it must be rehearsed, recirculated (repeated), and/or elaborated. As already noted, rehearsal and elaboration presuppose consumer motivation. While this is likely for high-involvement products, for low-involvement items marketers must motivate consumers to learn through techniques such as contests, interesting advertising story lines, and the like. Low-involvement consumers can also learn through recirculation as the marketer goes for high frequency in message presentation and/or repetition of key points within each message.

The following discussion focuses on *recirculation*—teaching consumers through sheer force of repetition—and techniques to encourage deep **elaboration**: the extent of effort consumers exert in learning about and forming an attitude for a given attitude object, i.e., how deeply they process information for meaning, such as by integrating new information with their existing knowledge and previous experiences.

RECIRCULATION THROUGH REPETITION: LEARNING AS A FUNCTION OF INFORMATION EXPOSURE

It is well known that learning improves when the material to be learned is repeated. Repetition (or practice) increases the strength and speed of learning. This suggests that, rather than waiting until the night before an examination to begin cracking open books and cramming in material, students should peruse their assigned reading before class; have that material reinforced by classroom lectures, discussions, and presentations; and then review and integrate assigned reading and corresponding class notes before moving on to the next assigned chapter and new material. The more times you review your notes, the more familiar you will become with the material and the better it will "stick."

Learning increases with repeated exposure to the same information, sooner or later at a decreasing rate, that is, there are usually diminishing returns to repetition. This results in the classic **learning curve**. This is represented in Exhibit 14.3, which shows two different possible shapes for the learning curve.

The Y axis represents the amount of material learned and remembered (i.e., the degree of retention), which can be measured using indicators such as recognition and recall, comprehension or "getting it" (e.g., correct interpretation of imagery or puns), and attitude. Learning is plotted as a function of the number of

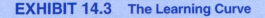

EXHIBIT 14.3   The Learning Curve

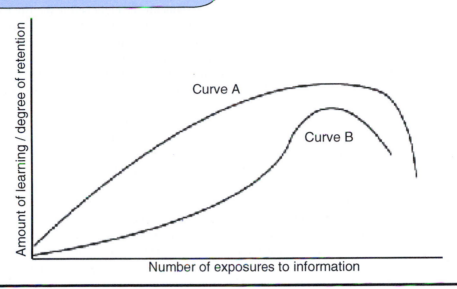

exposures to information, indicated on the X axis. Observing Exhibit 14.3, you can surmise the origin of the expression, "marching up the learning curve."

STRENGTH OF LEARNING

Strength of learning refers to how completely and rapidly learning occurs with repetition and how permanent the learning is. Curve A in Exhibit 14.3 illustrates stronger learning than curve B since it occurs more rapidly (assuming that it is not forgotten quicker than curve B learning). With stronger learning, there will be a slower rate of forgetting.

Curve A shows diminishing returns throughout, whereas curve B—an S-shaped curve—demonstrates increasing returns to repetition after which there is an inflexion point, followed by declining returns. In both cases, saturation eventually occurs as the learning curves flatten out, that is, learning ceases with further repetition, and it might even start to decline with additional repetition for reasons such as "wearout."

INFORMATIONAL AND CONSUMER CHARACTERISTICS INFLUENCE STRENGTH OF LEARNING

Which shape will the learning curve take—that of curve A or of curve B? The answer depends on characteristics of the information and the consumer.

Informational Characteristics Influencing Learning Strength. Generally, curve A (strong learning) will prevail where the following informational characteristics exist:

- The material to be learned is simple and straightforward (rather than complex and ambiguous). If a marketer wants customers to quickly absorb the message, the message should be kept short and simple.
- The information to be learned is unique, causing learners to pay attention. This argues in favor of avoiding clichéd advertising and sales presentations and being daringly different from competitors in communication tactics.

Consumer Characteristics Influencing Learning Strength. Curve A (strong learning) is more likely where the following consumer characteristics prevail. Some involve not just being exposed to repetitive information but also being actively engaged with it through elaborative activities.

- Consumers are highly involved and therefore motivated to learn, which results in more effort invested in learning. When the information is seen as important, more elaboration, categorization, and deeper processing are likely to occur. For instance, suddenly the night before the Big Exam, the information in this chapter will become very important to you and you will be deeply driven to learn it quickly. (However, we do not recommend a cramming strategy if you wish to recall the information in the long term, such as for the final exam, future marketing courses, or your career).

  Motivated consumers retain information longer and more accurately. Therefore, it behooves marketers to use some of the principles presented in this discussion to aid the elaboration process and cause consumers to become more involved with an ad.
- The material to be learned is highly meaningful and relevant to consumers, thereby enhancing motivation and involvement. In this book, we try to assist your learning by making material relevant to you, not just as a future marketer, but also in your current roles of student and consumer. Promotional activity should relate the product to consumers' lives and point out meaningful, significant benefits.
- Consumers already have some general familiarity with the material or ability to work with the information to be learned. This results in stronger learning because experienced learners are better able to process additional information at deeper levels and are therefore more involved with it, relating it to what they already know. Hence, consumers who are familiar with a product category (limited problem-solving learning stage) are more likely to effectively learn new information.
- Consumers are in a positive mood, since a good mood during information reception seems to enhance its elaborative processing. This suggests that advertisers should place their ads on shows and in publications that leave audience members feeling upbeat. In fact, recent research demonstrates that advertising during violent programs results in lower recall.

Curve B (weak learning) is more likely to describe the pace of learning where:

- The material to be learned is ordinary and dull. Therefore, marketers must keep the presentation interesting for their audience. Very creative ads have the advantage that they need to be repeated less often.
- The material to be mastered is complex, causing the learner to pour over the material awhile before "getting" it. Difficult material is also harder to retain. Think about how long it takes you to understand subjects such as calculus and organic chemistry as opposed to, oh, say, CB. The marketer selling high-tech gear needs more patience with customers understanding the message than the one selling pedestrian packaged goods.
- The consumer has a low level of involvement. If there is little motivation, why bother to put effort into learning?
- The learner does not relate well to the material. If the information does not seem relevant and meaningful, the learner feels less motivated to be taught.
- The learner is less familiar and therefore less able to deal with the topic to be learned, such as during extended problem solving. Such consumers lack the skills to process the information at deep levels.
- Consumers are in a neutral or negative mood.

A marketer or salesperson who is enthusiastic about the product can help raise the consumer's motivation quotient (MQ). Elevating the level of consumer involvement and interest, such as through special events, can also raise consumer MQ. The Holiday Inn hotel chain accomplished heightened involvement, and hence recall, through a "Towel Amnesty Day" for customers who had "borrowed" the hotel's towels. They set up cabanas at vacation spots, offering customers who returned linens a limited edition Holiday Inn embossed towel as a gift. This was a memorable event for consumers, who were continually reminded of it by the presence of the towels in their bathrooms and chatting it up among friends.

Usually, however, the best way to teach consumers in a state of low involvement is through high levels of repetition. This can be accomplished in two ways in advertising. First, is by repeating the brand name and any important points repeatedly throughout the ad, especially when using low-involvement media like radio and TV. Repetition burnishes the brand name into the consumer's consciousness. (We suppose that's why they call them brands.) Perhaps the all-time record for most brand mentions in a single ad is either

"Kibbles and Bits, Kibbles and Bits, I gotta get me some Kibbles and Bits" repeated over and over in a dog food commercial or the never-ending "Meow, Meow, Meow, Meow" for Meow Mix cat food.

Second, the advertiser of a low-involvement item can achieve high levels of repetition in the advertising schedule by repeatedly rerunning the ad or variations on it, using high media frequency. That explains why you will sometimes be exposed to a commercial message and then be re-exposed to it on the same broadcast station just minutes later (sometimes again and again and again and . . .).

MESSAGE WEAROUT: TOO MUCH REPETITION

Although retention can be aided by *overlearning*—repetition beyond what is necessary for learning—at some point a person can be overexposed to a message. This explains why the learning curve, after reaching the saturation point where the consumer has learned all that can be learned, might actually start to turn downward as the consumer becomes satiated with too much repetition, a phenomenon known as **message wearout (wearout, advertising wearout** [in an advertising context]). Wearout is the result of either habituation or counterarguing, or both.

Habituation is the process of adjusting to or growing accustomed to a frequently occurring stimulus to the point where it is no longer noticed, caused by fatigue, boredom, or even irritation. Audience members get sick of the ad (it "gets old"), and consequently they mentally tune it out.

Counterarguing occurs when overexposed consumers begin arguing against whatever the message is advocating because they experience attitude wearout (i.e., their attitude toward the ad becomes negative). If the ad asks, "Did somebody say McDonald's?" they might sarcastically think to themselves "Not really" and proceed to dine at Wendy's.

Advertisers should be aware that wearout is more likely to occur where there is very high message frequency in a short time frame; there are few different executions of the message during the promotional campaign; and the message invites rapid wearout by being uninteresting or annoying, or using belly-laugh humor.

OTHER BENEFITS OF REPETITION

One benefit of frequent exposure is the **mere exposure effect**, in which frequent exposure to a stimulus creates liking for it. One possible explanation is that familiar stimuli are more easily processed, causing people to like them. It is the "I've grown accustomed to her face" phenomenon experienced by Professor Henry Higgins regarding flower girl Eliza Doolittle in the classic play *My Fair Lady*.

Another possible by-product of frequent repetition is the **truth effect**, in which exposure to repeated claims leads to increased belief in those claims. Research shows that marketing claims believed by audience members to have been frequently repeated were given more credence than claims believed to be new.

THE LENGTH AND PATTERN OF INFORMATION EXPOSURE DURING REPETITION

Another issue affecting how effectively information is learned via repetition is the length (massed versus spaced learning) and pattern (continuity, flights, and pulsing) of repeating information over a time frame such as an advertising campaign period. The decision between these strategies hinges on consumer buying patterns and consumer learning patterns.

Massed Advertising: Flights and Pulsing. In **massed advertising**, ads are bunched together in one or more short time periods during the entire ad campaign, often coinciding with peak buying periods, such as chocolates during Halloween, Christmas, and Easter.

Massed advertising can be in either flights or in pulses. **Flights** are heavy periods of advertising followed by intervals of no advertising, such as during seasonal sales periods, special events, and sales promotions. The flighting pattern assumes *advertising carryover*—residual remembrance of prior advertising during the advertising hiatus. However, forgetting eventually sets in and consumers need reminders.

Pulsing refers to periods of high levels of advertising (pulses) followed by intervals of minimal advertising. However, whereas during flights the ad spigot is turned off at times, with pulsing it always at least drips, although perhaps at relatively low levels. Pulsing is used where it is believed that consumers need continual advertising exposure lest they forget, but extra weight is needed for reasons such as seasonal buying, special events, and sales promotions.

Spaced Advertising: Continuity. In **spaced (continuous, distributed) advertising**, the ads are distributed fairly evenly throughout the campaign's duration. This is known as continuity in an advertising schedule. Spaced advertising is most typically used in the following scenarios: for products without seasonal sales patterns; if consumers easily forget in the absence of any advertising; where there is rapid buyer turnover (e.g., maternity dresses); if rivals continuously advertise; and if constant reminders are necessary to avoid brand switching in high-frequency categories.

PRINCIPLES OF LEARNING TO AID IN THE ELABORATIVE PROCESS

Several tactics are available for marketers to use in their marketing communications to increase the probability that consumers will elaborate on information and hence remember it. The goal of all of the following techniques is to make the advertising interesting for audience members so that they spend time thinking about it, often by making it novel or unexpected.

ASSOCIATION

Association refers to pairing stimuli repetitively to establish linkages between them. Associative learning is a mechanism whereby links or relationships between stimuli are established within the associative network consisting of linked nodes. Why is ice cream so universally loved? Because, for almost everyone, ice cream has strong ties to childhood. You ate it at birthday parties, family picnics, and just for fun (perhaps when Mom wasn't looking!).

Association Through Repetition. The associations are usually created through sheer repetition during low-involvement incidental learning. This is how people learn to associate brand names with slogans, logos, package designs, trade characters, and jingles. Campbell's is linked with the slogan "M'mm! M'mm! Good!" as well as its red and white package colors; Kodak and Cheerios are burnished in our brains as yellow; Apple is white; UPS has brown; and Target owns red. The Poppin' Fresh doughboy immediately triggers the Pillsbury name, and Snap, Crackle, and Pop are known as the Rice Krispies Guys.

Association Through Elaboration. An association technique calling for elaboration rather than sheer repetition is **analogy (analogical learning)**, in which a connection is established between things otherwise not affiliated. However, analogy goes beyond mere repetitive association. It gets people involved in learning by getting them to think about the connections. This aids the learning process, because when people are actively involved in learning they exert effort, which in turn leads to better retention.

There are two analogy techniques: simile and metaphor. A **simile** is a figure of speech using an explicit comparison in which two essentially unlike things are compared. Typically, simile uses a phrase including the words "like" or "as." Examples: "I'm as hungry as a bear," "Her skin was soft like satin," or "He is sly as a fox." Similes are popular with advertisers. Mennen promised "skin as soft as a baby's behind," laundry detergents assure they will leave laundry "white as snow," and numerous brands in countless categories have claimed to be "springtime fresh."

A **metaphor** is a figure of speech using an implicit comparison suggesting two objects or experiences are alike, related, or identified with each other. A metaphor transfers a term or characteristic from the object it ordinarily designates to another object. It says, "A is to B as C is to D." This helps to make an unfamiliar or abstract idea more concrete by connecting it with something familiar.

Typically, marketers transfer the qualities of familiar objects to their advertised product. When introduced, cars were called "horseless carriages." During the late 1990s, Lycos used a black Labrador retriever that fetched things as a way of explaining how a search engine works. American Airlines dubbed itself the "on-time machine," in effect saying that American is to business travel what a machine is to reliability and performance.

Advertisers use trade characters as visual metaphors. Tony the Tiger equates Frosted Flakes cereal with strength, Betty Crocker suggests home-baked goodness, and the Jolly Green Giant suggests that his vegetables are healthy and will help kids to grow up big and strong.

Logotypes (logos) and other brand symbols also serve as frequently repeated visual metaphors. The "missing bite" from Apple computer's logo conveys the idea that you can expect something unusual from them, plus it is a play on the computer term "byte." Moreover, the apple is a warm, friendly, relaxing everyday kind of object that is not only user-friendly but also good for you. Apples have symbolized knowledge since the Garden of Eden.

Even audio symbols can represent special meanings. Sprint's clever use of a pin dropping promotes sound transmission quality and Memorex's shattering glass represents high-quality audio reproduction.

MENTAL COMPLETION

Mental completion (closure) is the human tendency to remember incomplete patterns better than complete patterns. Omitting details aids the learning process by getting people actively involved in learning as they mentally add their own information, such as the slogan "I ♥ New York."

COVERT INVOLVEMENT

Covert involvement refers to the mental or emotional feelings that stimuli evoke. The feelings follow from the consumer thinking about the stimuli and thereby getting involved with them.

Ads use this principle by encouraging consumers to imagine how it feels to buy or use the branded product, causing the consumer to imagine interacting with the brand. The purpose of showing scenes of a product or products being consumed in ads is to create a vicarious consumption experience. For example, a Sierra Mist commercial featured two guys plunging into a lake, followed by the tagline, "Yeah, it's kinda like that." Ads for Gatorade depicted hot, sweaty athletes chug-a-lugging the sports drink after a workout.

SEMANTIC GENERALIZATION

Semantic generalization is the process of establishing meaning for words that essentially have no meaning. Brand names can employ this principle by being similar or identical to words that are meaningful. Gleem toothpaste proclaimed, "Teeth aren't white until they Gleem." Coffee-mate's ad tagline is, "Coffee's perfect mate."

Often, semantic generalization entails a play on the brand name by inserting the brand name into the advertising theme mnemonically. Shout stain remover asked, "Want a tough stain out? Shout it out"; Spam processed meat spread suggested using it to make a "Spamwich"; Zest soap asked for "Zestimonials from satisfied users"; and Blockbuster video explained that you can "Make it a Blockbuster night" by renting their videos.

Some brand names have been given meaning and made memorable by being used as verbs and adjectives: You can "Midasize" your car with Midas mufflers; "Nutrisize your life" with Nutrisystem; and get "Comcastic" service with Comcast.

VISUAL IMAGERY (MENTAL IMAGERY)

Elaborative processing can also take the form of **imagery**. This is information stored in sensory form, representing an object in terms of its tangible sensory attributes: taste, feel, look, sound, or smell.

Visual (mental) imagery refers to the imagery that is associated with visual, verbal, or aural material.

Visual Images. Visual material can be used to create visual imagery. Pictures enhance visual imagery by allowing people to "see" information in pictorial form. For example, an ad for Carefree gum showed a pack of the gum floating through an hourglass, accompanied by the headline, "The flavor lasts."

Verbal Images. Verbal material, such as brand names and slogans, can conjure up verbal images. Words that are high in imagery are much easier to learn and remember than low-imagery words. For example, brand names that describe a brand feature, function, or benefit are highly memorable. Dustbuster describes what the product accomplishes, EASY-OFF expresses how the oven cleaner works, Coffee-Mate tells what the creamer is for, and La-Z-Boy depicts the recliner's comfort.

Aural Images. Visual imagery can also be achieved through aural stimuli such as the human voice, music, and sound effects. Music evokes moods, and popular tunes often have distinct associations. Sound effects can also be used to craft visual images, such as a can of soda being cracked open, followed by the distinctive whisper of escaping bubbles, the glug-glug of the pour, ice clinking cheerfully in a glass, and, of course, a satisfied human "Ahhhh."

LUDICROUS JUXTAPOSITION

Ludicrous juxtaposition entails placing two objects side by side that normally are not found near each other. This creates an *incongruity*—something inconsistent with expectations—thereby inviting evaluation and involvement, leading to better retention.

The National Fluid Milk Processor Promotion Board ads featured celebrities sporting milk mustaches. An ad for Norelco showed a man with bees all over his face, along with the headline "Abuzz over new razor."

MNEMONICS

Mnemonics involves imposing a structure or organization upon material to be learned to give it meaning so that it can be better remembered. Mnemonic devices popular in advertising include rhymes; alliteration which uses the same consonant in two or more adjacent words (Lexus: "The passionate pursuit of perfection"); assonance, the repetition of the same vowel sound "Nobody knows like Dominoes"; "Do you Yahoo?"); and onomatopoeia, in which the sound of a word imitates what the word denote ("Campbell's soups are m'mm, m'mm good!").

RETRIEVAL OF INFORMATION FROM LONG-TERM MEMORY

Retrieval entails **recall**—the ability to retrieve information from memory—and it is more likely to occur where there has been rehearsal, recirculation, or elaboration.

LEVELS OF RECALL AND RETRIEVAL CUES

Retrieval cues are stimuli to aid remembering information stored in long-term memory. Marketers can jog consumers' minds with retrieval cues such as point-of-purchase displays featuring trade characters and packaging displaying colors associated with the brand, a logo, and the like.

There are several levels of retrieval, depending on the nature of retrieval cues provided by the marketer. **Unaided (free) recall** involves remembering in the absence of retrieval cues. If, on a shopping trip, a consumer can remember a particular product or brand he or she wanted to purchase or the "correct" price to pay for an item, this is unaided recall. Such awareness is important since, for many low-involvement categories, the first brand remembered is the most apt to be bought. Also, consumers might infer popularity and quality from the ease with which they recall brands.

Aided (cued) recall entails providing the consumer with various amounts of retrieval cues. To help you remember what you had for lunch yesterday, I could ask whether it was a sandwich or a hot meal and whether or not it contained meat. Marketing stimuli that can act as retrieval cues include brand names, logos, and packages.

Recognition occurs when a consumer remembers having previously encountered a visual stimulus shown to him, such as pictures of brand identity elements including logotypes, packages, brand names, trade characters, and advertisements. Young children can easily recognize logos such as the McDonald's golden arches.

CHARACTERISTICS OF STIMULI TO ENHANCE RECALL

Generally, information is better remembered where it exhibits salience, prototypicality, and/or redundancy. **Salience** refers to the prominence of the information—how well it stands out from other information surrounding it. It is easier to gain consumer attention, interest, and hence recall where stimuli are unique, large, intense (loud or bright), moving, or colorful.

Prototypical information is specific information that is exemplary or representative of a more general category. A category **prototype** is considered to be the best example of that category. When you think of birds, you most likely first think of robins, and thinking about salty snack foods probably brings to mind potato chips.

In terms of the structure of memory, prototypical information consists of nodes in the associative network (e.g., slogans, logos, endorsers, or brand names) that are similar to others, are linked to many other concepts in memory, which makes their activation high, and can be considered good representatives of the category alternatives. Also, prototypical members are frequently encountered, such as the ubiquitous Coca-Cola and Google.

Prototypical (master) brands are viewed as the best examples of a product category. Prototypical brands are similar to other brands in the product class, are encountered frequently, and often are the innovator and/or market leader brand in the product category, such as Sweet'N Low sugar substitute. They also tend to be heavily advertised. Think of camera and film and you probably recall Kodak, peanuts brings to mind Planters, and grape juice or jelly conjures up Welch's.

Redundancy does not entail repetition of identical information. Instead, it means to repeat information but in a different manner than previously presented, such as by providing similar information or cues, or by presenting the information in a different communication channel. A popular promotional strategy that employs redundancy is **integrated marketing communication (IMC)**, using multiple promotional tools (advertising, sales promotion, publicity, packaging, etc.) that contain common elements, such as the same selling message, graphic design, and trade character. When General Motors launched Saturn cars, advertising, dealer promotions, direct mail pieces, and salespeople all touted the idea of "A different kind of company, a different kind of car."

FORGETTING

Forgetting is the loss of memory (stored information) over time. This failure to retain previously learned material is either due to lack of repetition of the stimulus or message (decay) or because of interference caused by similar information.

Decay. **Decay** is a form of forgetting that occurs when memory or trace strength fades over time due to lack of refreshment via rehearsal, recirculation, or elaboration. Memory links eventually decay if they are not used.

This is what we usually mean when we talk about forgetting, and it is illustrated in the **forgetting (decay) curve**, which is usually a logarithmic function of time elapsed since information was learned: Learning generally decays rapidly at first ("How soon they forget!") and then the rate of decay slows. This is shown by curve C in Exhibit 14.4.

This tendency to forget in the absence of repetition suggests the critical importance of **reminder advertising**. The sole function of these ads is to keep the brand name, slogan, important visuals such as the logo and package design, and other significant marketing stimuli in the target market's mind. Such ads are typically devoid of persuasive arguments.

Curve C, the rapid forgetting curve, usually follows from the "S-shaped" slow-learning curve (Exhibit 14.3, curve B). We forget quickly in the following circumstances:

- Information is boring (e.g., side effects information for prescription drugs)
- Information is not unique (an ad with a new car trudging through muddy, windy roads)
- Information is complex (chemical makeup of over-the-counter drugs)

EXHIBIT 14.4   The Forgetting Curve

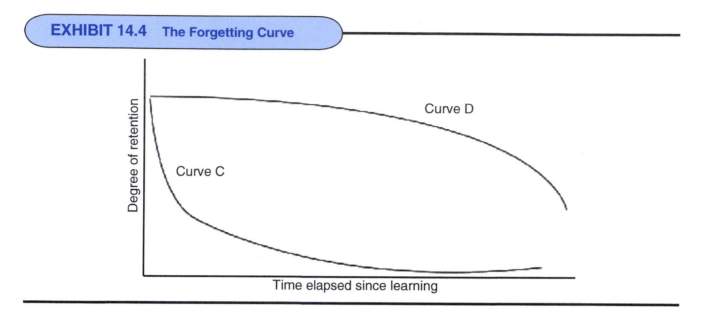

Curve D

Curve C

Degree of retention

Time elapsed since learning

- We are not very involved (what is Aunt Matilda's favorite scent of perfume?)
- We find information irrelevant or not meaningful (what does GR-78–14 mean on a car tire?)
- We are less familiar with the information (options in a DVD player, such as S-video, component video, digital video interface, and FireWire)
- We are in a bad mood

All of these conditions would apply if, for instance, you were learning a foreign language for a course that you considered deadly dull, could not care less about (other than getting a good grade), find "It's Greek to me," and are consequently in a lousy mood.

Also, the level of recall will influence the shape of the decay curve. Since recognition is an easier task than aided recall, it is likely to decay more slowly. For the same reason, aided recall will decay more slowly than unaided recall.

Forgetting curves, regardless of their exact shape, remind us that a person is less likely to remember an event that happened long ago. As a result, you can probably recollect where you were this morning but not where you were at the same time on a morning three weeks ago.

Curve D in Exhibit 14.4 is the gradual forgetting curve, and it is likely to follow the rapid learning curve (curve A in Exhibit 14.3). Generally, decay of events occurs more slowly in the following instances:

- *Important events.* If you are a sports fan or are from a winning team's hometown, you are more likely to recollect who won the Super Bowl or the World Series last year than someone disinterested in sports. Few consumers can recall the brand of canned peas they bought three years ago, but they can recollect the make and model of car they purchased around the same time.
- *Personal events.* Experience is the best teacher. People remember things that they personally experience versus things they read about or events other people tell them about. (This is why we wrote this experiential textbook—to help you to learn through personal involvement with the material!) Likewise, wise marketers teach consumers through personal experiences, such as providing free samples, offering test runs, and through sensory marketing techniques such as singing print ads that contain musical microchips.
- *Unique events.* Since they are extraordinary, very pleasant and very unpleasant experiences are more likely to be recalled. A consumer who has a very negative experience with a hotel or restaurant or who is very dissatisfied with a product is unlikely to soon forget.
- *Frequently occurring events.* The details of rote, habitual activities, such as one's workday morning

routine, tend to be forgotten. However, because they are frequently encountered, the overall activities are generally remembered since, each time someone is exposed to information, there is either rehearsal or recirculation, thereby halting decay.

- *Recently occurring events.* The decay curve suggests that the more time that has elapsed since something happened or information was learned, the more the likelihood of forgetting it increases.

Inability to recall is a major issue in survey research. Consumers usually do not know how many cans of soda they consumed last week or what brand of spaghetti sauce they last purchased (unless they are highly involved or brand loyal). To bolster recall, researchers are advised to ask about important, personal, and/or unique events; frequently occurring happenings; and more recent events (e.g., their most recent purchase).

Interference. A second major cause of forgetting is **interference**, in which similar information subsequently or previously learned hinders recall or learning of new information. For instance, when a celebrity endorser appears in ads for many different products, consumers lose track of the star's brand affiliation. Competitive clutter can also cause interference; the more advertising done by rivals and the more similar competitors' ads are to a marketer's, the more interference will occur. This suggests using a unique creative strategy that avoids formulaic advertising, such as telecom company ads featuring pictures of guys climbing poles and working. A cluttered advertising landscape also suggests a unique media strategy (e.g., tire ads are too often on sports shows and in the newspaper's sports pages).

Interference can be either retroactive or proactive. **Retroactive inhibition** occurs when newer information interferes with recollection of information previously learned. For example, following exposure to a particular car's TV commercial, a consumer might have difficulty recalling selling points or the nameplate of a car featured in a commercial seen minutes earlier.

Proactive inhibition happens when earlier learned information hinders later learning of similar information. Ever wonder if you could remember things better if your head was not stuffed with so much trivial information?

In attempting to recall a long list of items, the first few are fairly easy to recollect, but it becomes increasingly difficult to remember additional items. This occurs because in attempting to remember the later items you keep recalling those you have already remembered. Therefore, trying to keep an earlier car ad's message in mind might interfere with learning about a different auto featured in a more recent commercial. Proactive interference helps explain why launching a new brand in an existing product category is such a difficult task and why marketers use their existing brand names to aid learning about the new brand.

For either proactive or retroactive inhibition, the more similar two objects are, the more likely interference will occur. Consequently, if the car in the first ad is a large luxury vehicle and that in the second commercial is a small, ordinary car, interference is less likely and less severe than if both were big luxury models.

Interference Due to Serial Position Effects: Primacy and Recency. Interference can be caused by **serial position effects (order of presentation)**. The order of presentation of information within a marketing communication influences someone's ability to remember that information as illustrated by the primacy and recency effects.

The **primacy effect** is the inclination to better recall information that occurs first or early in a sequence of information. The **recency effect** is the tendency to better remember information that comes last or later in an information series. For instance, you typically best remember the first and last information you study. These effects logically follow from the existence of decay and interference as well as several other factors.

The primacy effect occurs because there was no earlier information to cause proactive inhibition and since people generally pay closer attention to early items in a list.

You are also likely to recall the last piece of information since it has had less time to decay, although people tend to pay less attention to later items on a list and later items are subject to proactive inhibition from the previous information. All of this suggests that the initial items in a series are usually better recalled than the last ones—primacy generally dominates recency. Another reason the first and last information pieces are remembered best is that early and late positions are more distinctive and serve as anchors (points of reference), thereby garnering higher attention.

Recency and primacy effects suggest that in scheduling commercials within a commercial pod—a string of commercials—preferred spots are the first and last. Primacy and recency effects also indicate that the strongest positions within a print ad are its beginning and end. Hence, important ad elements such as headlines and illustrations are typically strategically positioned at the top, and taglines (usually slogans) are placed at the bottom of the advertisement.

In oral presentations and sales talks, not to mention important written documents such as term papers and research reports, it is also wise to insert the key points in the introduction and conclusion. In *anti-climax messages*, the most important information is presented first, in climax presentations it appears last, and in *pyramidal messages* the strongest points occur in the middle. In retail store layouts it is advised that managers place the most lucrative or highest-selling products in the prime real estate locations, that is, near the entrance (a customer's first encounter within the store) and close to cashiers (the shopper's last opportunity to purchase).

REVIEW QUESTIONS

1. What does the term *learning* mean? Why is learning such an important topic? How does learning fit in with the consumer decision process and the perceptual process?
2. Describe the structure of human memory, including an explanation of the relationships between the three memory stores. Also, explain the activities in short-term memory as well as the three types of long-term memory.
3. Discuss the nature of the learning curve. What is meant by the strength of learning and what are the major determinants of the strength of learning?
4. What causes message wearout and what can advertisers do to minimize this problem?
5. Describe the nature of massed advertising (including both flighting and pulsing strategies) and spaced advertising, as well as conditions under which each of these media scheduling options is most appropriate.
6. Explain each of the principles of learning used to aid the elaboration process.
7. Describe the three levels of recall and how each relates to conducting marketing research.
8. Discuss the characteristics of stimuli that can make them easier to recall, relating them to marketing tactics.
9. Describe the nature of the decay curve and the factors that influence its shape.
10. Describe the two serial position effects and how each relates to either proactive inhibition or retroactive inhibition. What are the implications for advertising and for marketing research?
11. Discuss the three types of memory errors: decay, interference, and the serial position effect.

IN-CLASS APPLICATIONS

1. In your classroom, what kinds of sensations—sights, sounds, smells, and tactile stimulations (even tastes)—are available? Which sensations best aid the in-class learning process, and which ones are most distracting? Which are most likely to enter your short-term memory and why? Are any past sensations you previously encountered in this classroom now part of your long-term memory? (Your instructor certainly hopes so!) Why or why not?
2. This question is designed to test your span of recall. Do not look at the rest of this question before class!

   In class, pair up with another student (if there are an odd number of students, one can pair up with the professor). Now, see how many information bits each of you can hold in your short-term memory at one time by doing the following.

   The first student in each pair will read aloud to the second student each of the following successively longer groups of numbers. The second student will then repeat the list of numbers. Continue until the other student is unable to repeat a group of numbers. The last line successfully repeated is that student's span of recall. The process can then be repeated with the next batch of numbers for the first student to play back.

   Note: It is important when reading a group of numbers to keep the time between each number spoken the same (otherwise chunking will be facilitated, making the task much easier).

Number sequences for the second student:

6382
95831
852196
4285713
84620741
729158302
5916370427
62862740716
317394069218
5275397031842
41836063649219
9428501742737515

Number sequences for the first student:

3818
52716
739204
4297361
58629714
284736496
1746206843
73926491537
417538692174
3175973523610
73927405218620
483062529716528
6285972937218536

Next, repeat this exercise, but facilitate each other's memories via chunking. Read each group of digits, chunking two at a time (e.g., "531804 would be read as "53–18–04"). If there is an odd number of digits in a given number sequence, the last chunk will just consist of one digit. See how much longer your span of recall is now. How many chunks of information could each student remember?

Now repeat the process chunking three numbers at a time (the last chunk can consist of one or two numbers). Then, try chunking four numbers at a time. Compare results for each person over the different chunk sizes and compare between the two of you.

If time permits you can also repeat the exercise with successively longer groups of numbers you randomly make up, following the pattern above.

The instructor will then poll the class members to see how large each student's span of recall is with chunks of one, two, three, and four numbers. Alternatively, the professor might choose to be the reader of the groups of numbers, with each student repeating each group by writing it down. Or, the entire class can attempt to repeat each list in unison.

Finally, think of ways other than those mentioned in the background discussion or specific examples you recall when marketers effectively enabled consumers to remember information sequences, perhaps via the chunking process.

3. Identify the company/brand associated with the following well-known slogans and lines from commercial jingles.
   a. "Be all you can be."
   b. "Strong enough for a man, pH balanced for a woman."
   c. "It is everywhere you want to be."

d. "I love what you do for me _____."
e. "The best part of waking up is _____ in your cup."
f. "Just do it."
g. "Have it your way."
h. "Don't leave home without it."
i. "M'mm, m'mm good."
j. "Everybody eats when they come to our house."
k. "Nothing comes closer to home."
l. "It's where the pets go."
m. "You deserve a break today."
n. "Melt in your mouth, not in your hand."
o. "Double your pleasure, double your fun."
p. "For those who think young."
q. "Breakfast of champions."
r. "When you care enough to send the very best."
s. "We bring good things to life."
t. "A fragrance for a man or a woman."
u. "The fresh deodorant clean with moisturizer for our 2000 parts."
v. "The ultimate driving machine."
w. "Get Met. It pays."
x. "The best tires in the world have _____ written all over them."
y. "Do the Dew."
z. "A diamond is forever."

How did you learn, and how do you remember, these associations? Do you recall reading any in this or other marketing textbooks? If so, did you learn them differently from those you encountered in advertising?

How many familiar slogans are for brands you have purchased? How many are for brands you have not bought but consumed? For how many of the brands with which you are unfamiliar with the slogan do you have purchase experience? Usage experience? Are you more likely to purchase and/or consume brands with familiar slogans?

Which level of recall is this slogan/jingle task asking for—unaided recall, aided recall, or recognition?

4. Now it is time to use your eyes in applying incidental learning. Which of the following logotypes do you recognize? Try to identify the company behind each of these images. How did you come to learn each of these you successfully identified? Which level of recall is this task asking for?

You can also go to Guess the Logo at http://www.guessthelogo.com/ to try your hand at more logos. How did you do with these? Additionally, you can test your knowledge of icons, slogans, mascots, and audio trademarks at CramerSweeney's Smart Marketing test at http://www.cramersweeney.com/smartmarketing.html.

5. Can you cite any advertisements for which you've experienced advertising wearout? Has your response been either habituation or counterarguing? If the latter, describe how you counterargued. Has your counterarguing influenced your purchase behavior at all?

6. For each of the following advertisements (Exhibits 14.5–14.9), identify the learning principle(s) used to aid the elaboration process: association (is it through repetition or elaboration?), mental completion, covert involvement, semantic generalization, visual imagery, ludicrous juxtaposition, and mnemonics. Do any of these ads use salience or prototypicality to enhance recall?
Which learning principles does each ad apply and how effectively do they aid learning?

EXHIBIT 14.5   Pedigree Dog Food Ad

EXHIBIT 14.6   Partnership for a Drug Free America Ad

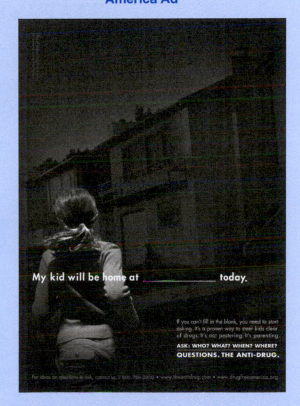

EXHIBIT 14.7   Lever 2000 Ad

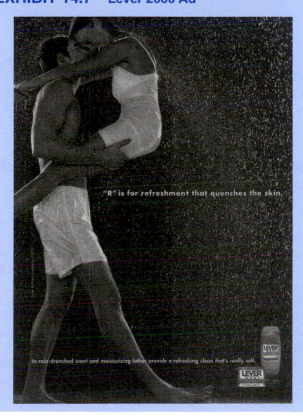

EXHIBIT 14.8   Absolut Ad

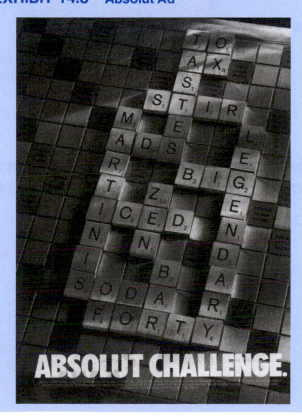

EXHIBIT 14.9   **Clairol Herbal Essences Ad**

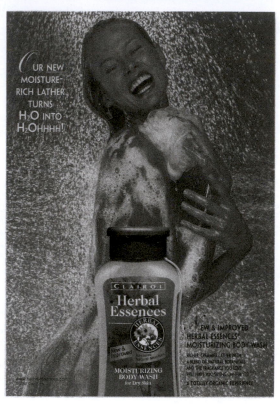

WRITTEN APPLICATIONS

1. Conduct In-Class Applications Question 2 as an out-of-class experiment, using at least ten subjects. Summarize the results, and answer all related questions.

2. Answer Question 5 for the ads in Exhibits 14.5 through 14.9. Then find four additional ads, each of which uses several different learning principles described in this exercise. Answer Question 5 for each of these ads as well.

EXERCISE 14.2. ELEMENTS OF THE LEARNING PROCESS

OBJECTIVES

1. To understand the four essential elements of the learning process—drives, cues, responses, and reinforcement—realize the interrelationships between these components, and recognize and evaluate marketing applications of each element.

2. To become aware of, recognize examples of, personally experience, and search out applications for advertising, branding, and packaging in the marketplace; learning principles related to marketing cues (verbal and nonverbal cues); and learned marketing stimuli, including advertising retrieval cues, stimulus generalization, and stimulus discrimination.

3. To recognize, explain the use of, and critically evaluate each of the major marketing applications of stimulus generalization: guilt by association and cachet by association (including stereotyping); product generalization and copycat products (imitative brands, value brands, and trade

dress infringement, including confusingly similar brands, package knockoffs, and counterfeit merchandise); branding generalization, including brand franchise extensions, product line extensions, and family branding (sometimes in conjunction with family packaging); and advertising generalization.

4. To understand the role of reinforcement and schedules of reinforcement in consumer learning, the related operant learning principles of punishment and extinction, and to distinguish and evaluate marketing uses of these concepts.

BACKGROUND

LEARNING ELEMENT 1: DRIVES (MOTIVES)

A **drive** is internal tension that causes the consumer to attempt to reduce or eliminate a need. The term *drive* is narrower than the word *motivation,* because the latter also includes goal-directed behavior, however, we use the two concepts interchangeably. CB is initiated by motivation because an unsatisfied drive gives rise to problem recognition, which is the launching point for the consumer decision process. Drives are therefore the origins for the learning process during the search and alternative evaluation stages. Hence, low-involvement circumstances excepted, motivation precedes learning. For example, if you wish to pass this course (or, better, to earn a good grade) you will be motivated to learn the assigned information and to apply it correctly.

LEARNING ELEMENT 2: CUES (STIMULI)

A driven individual will search for **cues (stimuli)**. These are environmental signals (sights, sounds, smells, flavors, and tactile stimuli) received through our five senses that are associated with need-satisfying products. For instance, the traveler who drives along the highway and becomes fatigued will search for signs for a rest stop or, if really exhausted, signs for a motel. Stimuli are perceived, transformed into information, and stored in a person's memory during information processing.

VERBAL AND NONVERBAL CUES

Most cues used in human communication are transmitted either as **verbal cues**—spoken or written words— or as **nonverbal cues**—stimuli other than words.

Auditory communication is one form of verbal communication, and spoken words can be powerful motivators to learn. Effective salespeople realize that words of appreciation, affirmation, or encouragement communicate to customers, "I know, I care, I want to help you." The way a salesperson and customer speak to each other communicates a multitude. The same sentence can have two different meanings, depending on how it is spoken. The listener will usually interpret the speaker's message by tone of voice more than by the words used. "That's just great" can be said positively and enthusiastically or negatively and sarcastically. Expressiveness, word choices, pacing, and loudness of voice can also speak volumes. One problem with electronic messaging is that such "social cues" (except for emoticons) are absent.

Marketers also use nonverbal auditory cues to enhance learning. Commercial jingles serve as "musical logotypes" and are much more readily recalled than if the lyrics were merely spoken. Distinct musical trademarks (soundmarks) include the AAMCO Transmissions horn honk, the Metro-Goldwyn-Mayer lion's roar, and the NBC chimes.

Communication experts know that the vast majority of human communication is nonverbal in nature. Some nonverbal cues are obvious, such as thumbs-up, thumbs down, or thumbing of the nose, although these symbolic gestures can differ markedly from culture to culture. The thumbs-up signal means "up yours" in Australia, the number 1 in Germany, the number 5 in Japan, and "I'm winning" in Saudi Arabia, while in many countries the thumbs-down sign signifies something is wrong or bad. Most nonverbal communication is unconscious and not so obvious. Since such nonverbal signals are regarded as less controlled and guarded than most verbal cues, they are perceived by recipients as more genuine.

Three forms of nonverbal communication are kinesic, polemic, and tactile communication. **Kinesic**

communication occurs through the movement of body parts such head nods, eye glances and winks, and movement of the hands, arms, legs, and torso. Such body language can be very revealing, especially when it is unconsciously transmitted. Wide eyes show you are interested, and failure to make eye contact decreases credibility and the chance to connect. Open palms suggest trustworthiness. Tilting your head and leaning in indicate concern and interest, whereas slouching is off-putting because it gives an "I don't care" impression. Marriott Hotels believes so much in the importance of body language that they give their employees classes on reading body language. (You can find a quick primer at The Romance Bible's "Body Language" at http://www.romancebible.com/articles/body-language.)

Salespeople must be alert to sending and receiving kinesic communication during sales presentations. Not only should they be careful to transmit warm and confident signals, they must also learn to read their prospects' nonverbal cues and adjust their sales pitches accordingly. For instance, if customers are leaning back in their seats, they are relaxed and comfortable. If a prospect raises her eyebrows, she is either skeptical or surprised. If she keeps glancing at her watch she is either bored and the salesperson should enliven his presentation, or she is rushed, in which instance the seller should speed up or shorten the discourse. Body language of people in advertisements also communicates meaning. For instance, models who direct their gaze away from the ad viewer can suggest brand users' rugged individualism.

Proxemic communication occurs by varying the physical distance in face-to-face interactions. For example, when a client backs away from a salesperson, this indicates that he or she is either disinterested or dislikes the salesperson (or, perhaps the seller has bad breath or body odor).

Tactile communication occurs via touching and can be a very powerful communication tool. Positive characteristics such as closeness, awareness, and liking are usually attributed to the toucher. Salespeople who gently touch their prospect communicate, "I like you and care about you." Restaurant waitstaff receive larger tips when they touch patrons and marketing research interviewers are more likely to get more respondents if they lightly touch them.

ADVERTISING RETRIEVAL CUES

Marketing communications tools such as advertisements, point-of-purchase displays, and packaging can serve as retrieval cues that jog consumers' memories. **Advertising retrieval cues** are visual or verbal stimuli uniquely associated with an ad and its brand that are also available when and where consumers make decisions. These advertising stimuli might consist of a key visual from a print ad or key frame (scene) from a TV commercial, a catchy slogan, an instantly recognizable logo or package, an ad character or presenter, a jingle, or any other unique advertising element. The cue can appear on a package, in-store signage, a billboard seen on a shopping expedition, a sweepstakes or contest offer, a Yellow Pages directory listing, a Web site, an in-store public address system, or any other consumer touchpoint—locale where consumers come into contact with the brand and might make a decision. In all cases, the cue's purpose is to maximize the likelihood that consumers who have seen or heard the ad are able to recall the information created in memory by that ad and then act upon it by purchasing the brand, calling for more information, or entering a contest.

OVERVIEW OF STIMULUS GENERALIZATION

Stimulus generalization occurs when an organism's response or reaction to a given stimulus is also evoked by a similar but nonidentical stimulus. Simply, stimulus generalization occurs when people respond in like fashion to similar stimuli. We see this even in toddlers who label all men as "daddy" and all women as "mommy." Small children who see a goose might say "Quack, quack," confusing it with a duck (clueless city slickers might do likewise).

This so-called ruboff effect is explained by the principle of *categorization*, an elaborative process of labeling or identifying an object based on what a person already knows. A new stimulus is classified using familiar concepts or an existing structure of meanings, known as a *schema*. For instance, both JCPenney and Sears fought an uphill battle in trying to convince consumers that they carried fashionable apparel, because Sears is associated with tools, appliances, car batteries, and tires and JCPenney is categorized as a purveyor of home goods such as sheets, towels, and window treatments.

At times, marketers commit unfortunate, unanticipated stimulus generalization. A Dunkin Donuts online ad was pulled after there were complaints that the paisley scarf Rachael Ray wore resembled the Arab head-dress. Hershey discontinued Icebreaker Pacs, white powder mints that came in blue pouches and dissolved on the tongue, after law enforcement personnel complained the candy resembled cocaine.

The following are common marketing applications of stimulus generalization.

GUILT BY ASSOCIATION AND CACHET BY ASSOCIATION

In **guilt by association**, if one of two similar cues is considered negatively, so is the second stimulus. When a ValuJet Airlines airplane crashed a few years ago, other small airlines were also perceived as unsafe. Marketers must avoid creating impressions of guilt by association and be ready to persuade people that false perceptions of guilt by association are misguided.

With **cachet (upgrading) by association**, if one of two similar stimuli is perceived positively, so is the second cue. This explains the **upward stretch strategy (step-up extensions)**, in which classier or higher-end brands are added to a product line with the hope that its fine image will rub off onto the entire line. Corporate images and profit margins were enhanced when Toyota added the Lexus, Honda the Acura, and Nissan the Infiniti to their lines as luxury "halo brands" to cast a glow across their product lines. Apple Mac sales got a shot in the arm when the Apple iPod was launched, and the introduction of the iPhone and iPad further boosted Apple's image. To achieve cachet by association, comparison advertising is almost always done by the number two or lesser brand, which compares itself with the market leader (e.g., Burger King compares itself to McDonald's or Pepsi goes head-to-head against Coke).

STEREOTYPING

Stereotyping attributes characteristics, attitudes, or behaviors to someone based on the social category (especially subculture) or social group to which the individual belongs. It is a special case of both guilt by association (negative stereotyping) and cachet by association (positive stereotyping). Examples include the jolly fat man, the ascetic skinny person, and the dumb blonde.

Television advertisers employ stereotypes—harried mothers, absent-minded fathers, slacker teens, annoying office guys—because they serve as cultural shorthand in messages. Marketers of products with national origins or associations, such as Italian clothing manufacturers and French restaurants, sometimes play off of positive stereotypical characterizations in their promotional materials.

Unfortunately, marketers are sometimes guilty of reflecting negative stereotypes, thereby offending one or more of their constituencies. Mattel came under fire when they launched a Barbie doll who proclaimed, "Math is tough," playing off the image of girls being poor at math and science. African Americans are some-times depicted in TV commercials dancing to a heavy urban beat, or hunters and fishers are characterized as down-market, rural rednecks. An Energizer battery ad showed a Hispanic man, with an arm transplanted from a Japanese man, who could not stop taking pictures with his new hand.

Advertisers must be careful to avoid portraying their customers in stereotyped, negative ways. Too often they show beer drinkers as young guys overly interested in sex, sports, and bathroom humor. Video gamers are represented as social isolates with their faces glued to their screens. Dove, on the other hand, was widely hailed for debunking stereotypes of female beauty with images of ordinary-looking girls and women.

PRODUCT GENERALIZATION: COPYCAT PRODUCTS

Product generalization occurs when consumers generalize from one product or brand to similar ones. It occurs because **copycat products** appear similar to one of their major (usually larger) competitors. The purpose of all these might be to fool consumers into believing that the impersonator is the "real McCoy."

Another objective in selling copycat items is to make consumers perceive (correctly or incorrectly) that the marketer's merchandise is the same or just as good as the bigger brand. The copycatter piggybacks off the good reputation of a competitor, possibly tarnishing or diluting it.

We now examine several types of copycat products: imitative brands, value brands, and trade dress infringement, which can include package knockoffs and counterfeit merchandise.

Imitative Brands. **Imitative (emulative) brands** are "me-too" alternatives that mimic successful brands. These often succeed because consumers confuse imitators with brands they have previously purchased or seen advertised. For example, Burger King's Chicken Tenders closely followed McDonald's launch of Chicken McNuggets, and PepsiCo's FruitWorks nipped on the heels of Coca-Cola's Fruitopia. Emulative products can succeed since the imitator saves on significant pioneering costs, such as research and development and stimulating primary demand, and because imitators avoid the high risk of entering unchartered territory. Due to such market uncertainty, pioneers often end up with arrows in their backs.

Value Brands. **Value brands** are similar to the market leaders but cost less due to low-cost manufacturing or minimal marketing expenditures, notably advertising and packaging. Examples include Suave shampoo, Sally Hansen cosmetics, and Purex laundry detergent. The sales pitch is basically, "Why pay more for a premium brand when ours is just as good?" These brands are most successful in categories where shoppers are especially price sensitive and brand distinctions are minimal, and when the economy is in the doldrums.

Trade Dress Infringement. **Trademarks** are words, symbols, devices, or any combination thereof, adopted and used by a manufacturer or merchant to identify a product's source and distinguish the product from those manufactured or sold by others. **Trade dress** is a type of trademark encompassing the nonfunctional physical detail and design (color schemes, textures, sizes, designs, shapes, and placements of words, graphics, and decorations) of a product or its packaging. The general appearance or total image of a product constitutes its trade dress. An important part of trade dress is the **brand mark (logotype [logo]),** an identifying graphic design, symbol, or brand name written in a distinctive typestyle.

Trade dress is a form of **intellectual property**, or any product of human intellect that is unique and not obvious, with some value in the marketplace. Intellectual property laws protect ideas, inventions, literary creations, unique names, business models, industrial processes, computer program code, and other intellectual works from appropriation by others. Marketers of copycats might be accused of **trade dress infringement**, which is unlawful copying of a marketer's trade dress. The likelihood of consumer confusion regarding the product's source is the legal test used for trademark infringement.

Confusingly Similar Brands. Sometimes marketers attempt to piggyback off of well-known brands produced by other firms. They launch a brand that is so similar to an existing brand that shoppers may believe that the new item is the other more familiar product.

The courts generally rule that new brands must be different from existing brands in sound and significance (meaning). Otherwise, they can dilute (blur or weaken) the original trademark. The test of confusion is not merely whether the new brand appears to be similar to an existing brand but whether consumer surveys (or common sense guidelines) demonstrate that the like name causes buyer confusion.

Such mistaken identity is less likely to arise if the two brands are in different product categories. Lemon-Up lemon-lime soda might be ruled as confusingly similar to 7UP, but not if Lemon-Up is a hair conditioner or furniture polish. Although a brand of breakfast cereal was first to use the "Total" moniker, Colgate was also able to slap this name on their toothpaste.

Package Knockoffs. **Package knockoffs (look-alike packaging)** are a potential form of trade dress infringement wherein aspects of a brand's unique packaging are imitated by another manufacturer. Typically, the packaging of a **national brand**, a well-known manufacturer's brand (not necessarily sold nationwide), is mimicked by the package of a **private (house, store, dealer) brand (own label)**, a wholesaler's or retailer's brand (typically a supermarket, drug store, or mass merchandiser brand). With a package knockoff, the private label attempts to hitchhike off the advertising and fine reputation of the national brand. For example, in your local supermarket, yellow boxes of a house brand of oat rings cereal sit next to the yellow Cheerios box and colas in red-and-white cans are by the Coca-Cola.

Retailers will often *sell against the brand*—stock their brands next to those of the higher-priced national brands, with signage encouraging consumers to compare and save. Likewise, they will run price-and-item ads in local newspapers showing side-by-side comparisons of the two brands, encouraging consumers to save money by buying theirs.

Is using knockoff packaging an ethical retail practice? Manufacturers charge private labelers with hitching a "free ride" on their brand investments, thereby harming them as well as causing customer confusion. However, private label producers' claim they are benefiting shoppers, who realize that many private label products are very similar, if not identical, alternatives to national brands at lower prices. Furthermore, blind (unbranded) tests have shown that consumers have difficulty distinguishing between unlabeled private label and national brands in many grocery, drug, and household goods categories. The Private Label Manufacturers Association asserts that private label ingredients are generally as good as if not better than those of national brands. And U.S. Food and Drug Administration regulations require that store brand ingredients must be of competitive quality to national brands. Courts have been persuaded that the prominent presence of a private brand name on the label alleviates consumer confusion.

Counterfeit Merchandise. **Counterfeit (knockoff) merchandise** is an unauthorized copycat product claiming to be a well-known brand. Examples include watches, designer handbags, and even promotional T-shirts. Haute couture apparel created by top designers is frequently "knocked off" by rivals and sold to the mass market.

Counterfeit merchandise is pure piracy, and it is immoral because it deceives consumers who have trouble distinguishing the fakes from the genuine items; harms competitors by cannibalizing their sales and tarnishing their image through the lower-quality counterfeit merchandise; and is illegal.

BRANDING GENERALIZATION (BRAND LEVERAGING)

A **brand** is a name, term, symbol, or design, or a combination of them, that identifies the goods or services of one seller or a group of sellers and distinguishes them from those of competitors. A **brand name** is the part of a brand that can be vocalized, including letters, words, or numbers. A **corporate (trade, umbrella) name** is the name under which a corporation conducts its business.

Marketers create a variety of stimulus generalization strategies using brand names and corporate names. They do this via **branding generalization (brand leveraging)**. Sellers attempt to get buyers to generalize from the reputation of a marketer's brand and corporate names by employing brand franchise extensions and product line extensions.

Branding Generalization (Brand Leveraging) Through Brand Names. A **brand franchise extension (brand extension)** is a new-to-the-company product dubbed with an existing brand name. Cases in point: Crest Whitestrips dental whitening system and SpinBrush toothbrush. Starbucks has successfully extended its quality name to products such as bottled Frappuccino drinks, ice cream, and liqueur.

An existing product that carries an existing name is a **product line extension (line extension)**. Line extensions apply a firm's well-known brand name to additional items in an existing product line. Example: Dannon Light & Fit yogurt for dieters and Danimals for kids.

With such extensions, consumers are likely to generalize and attribute the characteristics of the *core (anchor) product* to the new item. Hence, when diet or light versions of products are launched, the advertising typically touts the "same great taste."

Family Branding: Brand Leveraging Through Corporate and Brand Names. **Family (umbrella) branding** entails tagging a parent corporate (umbrella, trade) name or a brand name on a group of the firm's products. This practice often employs similar packaging graphics (family packaging) on different products in the firm's product mix. There are two options.

1. Product identification can be added to the parent corporate name. The RCA name is found on a wide range of consumer electronics such as televisions and clock radios, and Kraft brands their corporate name on their food products, such as boxed macaroni and cheese, mayonnaise, and salad dressing. This works best when items in the product mix are similar. Corporations making a disparate portfolio of products typically avoid family branding and stick to brand name extensions. Therefore, General Foods plays up the Jell-O name rather than the corporate name on gelatin, pudding, and frozen pops.
2. A brand name can follow the corporate name, as is done by automotive manufacturers (Ford Aerostar, Bronco, and Escort). This strategy also capitalizes on corporate reputation, while individual brand names permit brand distinctions, such as Gillette MACH 3 and Venus razors.

The Limits of Extending Brands. This policy of tagging the corporate or existing brand name onto a new category entry works best if the innovation is not too far afield from the current product, since consumers are more likely to generalize for similar stimuli. Accordingly, Starbucks had a hit with coffee ice cream but flopped with Mazagran carbonated coffee (Starbucks soda, anyone?). PepsiCo decided that the Aquafina name would work better on its bottled water than the Pepsi moniker, even though Pepsi is a well-respected brand. However, a successful name will not breed success for a poor product, as Pepsi discovered with Pepsi Blue "berry cola fusion." Honey mustard flavored Popsicles probably would not fly either, despite the strength of the Popsicles brand.

The key in extending a brand name lies in *learned associations.* Some brands have broad connotations and can be widely extended, while others do not. Campbell's is most closely associated with tomato soup, so extending into tomato-based spaghetti sauce seemed a natural. However, the product failed because spaghetti sauce is much thicker than tomato soup; hence, Campbell's tomato sauce was perceived as thin and runny.

When a brand is most closely tied to a particular product class, its potential to extend is limited. Other brands have broader, intangible associations and so can be extended to quite different categories. Kingsford succeeded in branding barbecue sauce with the Kingsford label because Kingsford was more closely affiliated with the barbecue occasion than with charcoal briquettes. Other brands with such broad commutations include Weight Watchers (weight control) and Healthy Choice (healthy eating).

Family Packaging. When used in conjunction with family branding, **family (look-alike, umbrella) packaging** is the use of a package whose graphics resemble those on other products sold by an enterprise. Coca-Cola cans and bottles are distinctly red, while Pepsi's are invariably blue. Tide detergent packages and bottles all come in bright orange containers bearing the highly recognizable circular "bull's eye" logo encompassing the Tide name.

Advertising Generalization. A potential misuse of stimulus generalization is **advertising generalization,** or uninspired copycat advertising that mimics competitors' ads. Ever notice how a lot of advertisements in a given product arena tend to be very similar? Most cosmetics companies run nearly indistinguishable ads featuring "just another pretty face" of cheek-to-cheek models in the same glossy women's magazines. Life insurance TV commercials all seem to show teary, tug-at-the-heart vignettes with people talking about how much they loved and miss the deceased, wishing they had purchased the proper coverage. Contrast this with the Aflac insurance ads, which feature a popular, humorous spokesduck with an attitude, quacking "Aflaaaac," to register the brandname. Unfortunately, copycat advertising seems quite common, leading to dull, predictable, look-alike, sound-alike, act-alike and hence, forgettable ads.

STIMULUS DISCRIMINATION

It seems paradoxical that, while marketers at times practice stimulus generalization to enable consumers to perceive a *similarity* between their stimulus and another cue, at other times they prefer to do the opposite, enabling people to discern a *distinction* between the marketer's stimulus and another (usually a competitor's) stimulus. They do so by using the principle of **stimulus discrimination,** which occurs when an organism learns to distinguish between similar but not identical stimuli. Marketers want shoppers to perceive their product, ads, and other marketing stimuli as providing a discernable, meaningful difference. Above all else, competitive marketing is about having a clear-cut, positive distinction compared to what rivals offer. It is almost axiomatic that a marketer must "differentiate or die"!

Die, indeed, is what happened to Pets.com, the online pet store featuring the irascible Sock Puppet. Although this product mascot helped distinguish Pets.com in the dog-eat-dog world of online pet stores, there were too many vendors with similar names (Petstore.com, PetPlanet.com, PetQuarters.com, and Petopia .com) offering identical services using similar Web designs. On the other hand, Subway bolstered sales by daring to violate one of marketing's commandments: "Thou shalt not market fast food as healthy." They emphasized that not only were their sandwiches good for you ("Eat fresh") but that they taste good, too.

Usually, stimulus discrimination is practiced by market leaders and stimulus generalization by market followers. An imitator wishes for consumers to view its products as similar to those of the more popular market leader, often using comparison advertising to demonstrate this. However, market leaders want to clearly stand head and shoulders above the followers, in effect, saying, "Don't be fooled by imitators."

By virtue of being an innovator (pioneer)—first to market—a firm can automatically gain a distinction and be perceived as the market leader. The earliest brand out of the new-product gate is typically dubbed the better horse. Examples include Tide, the first synthetic laundry detergent, McDonald's, the initial franchised fast food chain, and eBay, the original online auctioneer.

Another marketing strategy to create marketing points of difference is positioning. If the product itself does not contain superior points of difference, a marketer's task is to create induced differences, such as through a unique brand image. Other marketing stimuli used to create brand differentiation include the following.

- *Breakthrough advertising.* Such ads dare to break the advertising mold and "cut through the clutter." OfficeMax's Rubberband man character—the Afro-sporting office supply guy who passed toner and towels to coworkers—distinguished this office supply chain from larger competitors.
- *Brand names.* Effective brand names are distinctive. Examples: Smucker's jams and jellies, Right Guard deodorant, and Bounce fabric softener.
- *Packages.* In a cluttered store, the package must stand out from the crowd. Heinz was the first to offer an upside-down squeezable ketchup container. Campbell's Soup At Hand comes in a portable plastic container with a pop-top resembling a mug that is microwaveable and fits in a car's cup holder.
- *Logos.* Every two-year-old recognizes the distinctive Nike "swoosh." The NBC peacock and CBS eye both help give identity to these broadcast TV networks, and Betty Crocker's distinctive red spoon is plastered across all packages in her pantry.
- *Trade characters.* The Dutch Boy, Aunt Jemima, the Cream of Wheat chef, the Morton salt girl, and Mr. Peanut all help to distinguish what otherwise might be viewed as parity products. In fact, Betty Crocker is the brand incarnate!
- *Slogans.* A slogan provides a unique, memorable way to communicate the brand's point of difference: Taco Bell says, "Think outside the bun"; KFC insists, "It's not fast food, it's KFC"; and Apple admonishes users to "Think different."

LEARNING ELEMENT 3: RESPONSES

A consumer's **response** is that person's reaction to the drive or stimulus in an effort to reduce the drive. Reactions can be either observable or unobservable. Observable (overt) reactions entail physical reactions to reduce the learner's drive and satisfy her need, such as a thirsty person getting a drink of water. Unobservable (covert) responses are changes in elements within the consumer's mind, i.e., hypothetical constructs such as learning about products that can satisfy a need and therefore reduce a drive. Examples include acquisition of brand information in order to determine whether buying that brand can reduce the drive, brand attitude change, and brand image formation. Because achieving an immediate sale (observable response) following a marketing communication is not always realistic, valid marketing objectives often include these intermediate unobservable responses that precede the sale.

LEARNING ELEMENT 4: REINFORCEMENT

Reinforcement is the satisfaction of the learner's drive resulting from response to a cue, leading to a reduction in the drive's strength. Reinforcement is also defined as an environmental event (stimulus, reinforcer) that increases the probability of generating a particular response in the future because it is desired by learners. Exhibit 14.10 summarizes reinforcement and related operant conditioning (see Exercise 14.3) methods to increase or decrease the likelihood that a behavior will occur in the future.

POSITIVE REINFORCEMENT

Positive reinforcement is a form of reward that provokes the desired learned response by generating wanted consequences following performance of the preferred behavior in response to a stimulus. Remember how

	EXHIBIT 14.10	Reinforcement and Other Operant Conditioning Techniques for Changing the Probability of a Response Happening in the Future		

Technique	Definition	Example	Response
Positive reinforcement	Giving a reward following performance of a desired response.	Offering a customer a cash discount for prompt payment.	Increases the likelihood of a response occurring again.
Negative reinforcement	Removing or helping avoid an undesirable condition following performance of a desired response.	Eye drops help ease a burning, stinging sensation.	Increases the likelihood of a response occurring again.
Punishment	Presenting an undesirable condition following performance of a desired response.	A software program repeatedly causes a computer to crash.	Decreases the likelihood of a response occurring again.
Extinction	Presenting no reinforcement or removing previously offered reinforcement following performance of an undesirable response.	Terminating a customer loyalty program.	Decreases the likelihood of a response occurring again.

warm and fuzzy you felt in first grade when Miss Hall glued a gold star or smiley face onto your assignments? She was providing you with positive reinforcement for performing well.

Psychologists refer to these rewards as **reinforcers**, distinguishing primary reinforcers from secondary reinforcers. **Primary reinforcers** are rewards that satisfy *primary motives*, or biological needs. Food is a primary reinforcer gratifying the primary motive, hunger. A sleeping aid is a primary reinforcer fulfilling the primary motive, need for rest. Sellers of food, beverages, and medications offer primary reinforcers.

Secondary reinforcers are rewards that gratify *secondary motives*, or wants acquired over time. Praise can serve as a secondary reinforcer to gratify the acquired need for esteem, and a job promotion might help fulfill secondary needs for recognition and power. Marketers of entertainment services such as vacation spas and nightclubs offer secondary reinforcers.

Marketers provide their customers with positive reinforcement in terms of the utilities of the marketing mix: a want-satisfying product, prices that offer a good value, convenient distribution, informative and entertaining ads, sales promotional incentives, and helpful salespeople. According to the marketing concept, by satisfying customers better than rivals, marketers receive their own reward—profits!

Generally, immediate rewards are more effective than delayed rewards. It is unfruitful to offer nine-year-old Kayla a car when she turns sixteen if she will take out the trash every week for the next seven years. Likewise, most consumers want immediate gratification, not deferred fulfillment. Therefore, sellers should reward customers on the spot whenever possible. Witness the popularity of instant coupons and immediate refunds. On the other hand, rebate checks and proof-of-purchase refunds typically take weeks (if not months) after the buyer mails in the rebate offer to arrive in the mail, and so are less motivating.

SCHEDULES OF REINFORCEMENT

Schedules of reinforcement concern the regularity and timing of rewards. Because the following discussion can be a bit confusing to follow, Exhibit 14.11 summarizes the types of reinforcement schedules.

Continuous Versus Partial Reinforcement. The most rapid learning happens with **continuous (total) reinforcement**, a reward schedule in which reinforcement is given each and every time the desired response occurs. The learner quickly catches on that rewards will occur for making the correct response. Example: A mint placed on your pillow every time you visit a hotel.

However, learning will be more permanent with **partial reinforcement**, a reward schedule in which reinforcement is given for some but not all correct responses. However, it takes longer for the learner to make the association between the response and the reward with partial reinforcement; hence, it takes

> **EXHIBIT 14.11　Schedules of Reinforcement**
>
> **Continuous (total) reinforcement**—Each desired response is reinforced whenever it occurs.
>
> vs.
>
> **Partial reinforcement**—Only some desired responses are rewarded.
>
> Partial reinforcement can be:
>
>   **Variable (random) reinforcement**—When and how often reinforcement occurs is purely random or by chance.
>
> vs.
>
>   **Fixed (systematic) reinforcement**—Rewards are regularly given, but only for some responses.
>
>   Variable reinforcement can be:
>
>   **Variable interval reinforcement**—The time between successive reinforcements varies around some mean value.
>
> vs.
>
>   **Variable ratio reinforcement**—A reward is given after a set number (or proportion) of responses, but the learner is unaware of how many (or what proportion of) responses are necessary.
>
>   Fixed reinforcement can be:
>
>   **Fixed interval reinforcement**—A specific time lapse or interval occurs between rewards with several responses happening between each reward.
>
> vs.
>
>   **Fixed ratio reinforcement**—Rewards are given after a certain number of correct responses. Reinforcement is given every "nth" time.

longer to catch on. Nevertheless, even though a given response is not reinforced, the learner will persist in responding to the stimulus in hopes that perhaps the next time a reward will be administered. Gamblers usually lose in the long run, but, as the TV commercials for the New York State lottery once said, "Hey, you never know!" Fishing hunting, and beachcombing are similar—you spend a lot of time "drilling dry holes" without anything to show for your efforts, but once in a while you get lucky. Entrepreneurs often doggedly persist with their ventures in the face of adversity for the same reason.

Partial reinforcement has its advantages. It is harder to extinguish (undo) than continuous reinforcement; can be less expensive for the reward dispenser since rewards need not always be bestowed; and is less likely to lose its novelty compared with continuous reinforcement, which can soon become old hat.

The use of total versus partial reinforcement depends on several factors. Naturally, product quality (the major reward) must be maintained. The same is true of courteous service, availability of a product in the store, and any other values the customer expects and desires.

If an advertiser wishes to teach a message quickly to consumers (such as the availability of sale events or short-term promotional offers), continuous reinforcement is necessary during the relevant time frame. Accordingly, advertisers run continuous media schedules in which ads appear frequently and regularly for a short duration. If advertisers are more concerned with educating buyers for the long haul, they schedule advertising at different levels of media intensity over time (pulsing media schedules) or even have periods of advertising activity followed by periods of running no advertisements (e.g., ads run every other week or every third month [flighting media schedules]).

To build long-term loyalty, marketers periodically dispense rewards that are not essential to customer satisfaction, such as a free T-shirt with purchase. Never knowing for sure whether a reward will be given on a particular purchase or usage occasion keeps the shopping and consuming games exciting and novel, causing customers to come back for more. This explains the popularity of periodic sweepstakes, contests, and "instant winner" promotions.

Fixed Versus Variable, and Interval Versus Ratio Partial Reinforcement. Partial reinforcement can be administered in fixed (systematic) or in variable (random) fashion, and each can be given either per interval or ratio schedules.

With **variable (random) reinforcement**, when and how often rewards are dispensed is determined purely by chance. There are two types of variable reinforcement: variable interval and variable ratio reinforcement. In **variable interval reinforcement**, the time that must pass before the learner is rewarded varies around an average. Since the learner is unaware of exactly when the reward will occur, that individual must consistently respond. Example: Some retail store managers continually strive to excel in customer service because they never know when corporate headquarters will send a "mystery shopper" to snoop on them to report back on their service performance.

In **variable ratio reinforcement**, a certain percentage or number of responses is rewarded, but the individual does not know what this reward ratio or number is. This causes learners to respond at very high and steady rates.

Variable reinforcement contrasts with **fixed (systematic) reinforcement**, a reward schedule in which reinforcement is only given occasionally when the correct response occurs. Rewards are bestowed regularly (not randomly) but only for some responses. A gambling casino patron never knows whether he will hit the jackpot with a slot machine. It happens unexpectedly but often enough to keep the gambler hooked. Under-the-cap instant winner promotions work in like fashion.

The regular period can either be a fixed interval or a fixed ratio. With **fixed interval reinforcement**, rewards are bestowed after a certain time interval elapses, even though several correct responses might have occurred during the time interval. Examples: An annual Christmas bonus or holding a retail sale every Presidents' Day. The problem is that people tend to respond more or only act as the known time for reward draws near.

To overcome this problem, a seller can instead use **fixed ratio reinforcement** in which rewards are given after a certain number of responses. The person is reinforced every "nth" time behavior occurs, e.g., every fourth time. Examples: compensation to a patron for every five customer referrals given (e.g., PetCo's loyalty club members get a bag of free pet food after every ten purchases). This motivates people to repeatedly engage in the behavior.

NEGATIVE REINFORCEMENT

Negative reinforcement is a reward that induces a desired reaction by removing or helping the learner to avoid adverse stimulus or unpleasant consequences following performance of that response. As with positive reinforcement, negative reinforcement increases the likelihood that a particular action will be repeated in the future. However, it works by establishing a link between elimination of a stimulus and a response. Example: Use an acne cream and your face will be clear of zits.

PUNISHMENT

Punishment Versus Reinforcement. Whereas both positive and negative reinforcement *increase* the probability of a desired response, either by offering something good (positive reinforcement) or by removing or averting something bad (negative reinforcement), **punishment** is an environmental event that *decreases* the probability of an undesirable response and is therefore avoided.

Like reinforcement, punishment works by creating a stimulus-response link. However, the stimulus is no longer something desirable but, rather, something unpleasant (the punishment), and the response is to avoid an undesirable behavior and therefore avoid the stimulus.

Positive Versus Negative Punishment. There are two types of punishment: positive punishment and negative punishment. **Positive punishment** is a form of punishment in which a negative stimulus (punishment) is administered for bad behavior. Example: If you do not tip the parking valet well, he will scratch up your car.

Negative punishment is a form of punishment in which a wanted stimulus (reward) is removed as a result of undesirable behavior. Example: You do not receive the free makeup bag because you did not order three or more bottles of perfume. Another example: "The offer expires at midnight."

Note: The terms *negative reinforcement* and *positive punishment* are confusing because we have all learned to associate the word "positive" with good and "negative" with bad. In psychological terms, however, positive simply means adding to the environment, while negative means taking away from the environment. Therefore, negative reinforcement is almost always confused with positive punishment, because people think negative means something unwanted (like a smack in the face) and positive means something good (like getting candy).

Using Punishment Effectively. According to psychologists, punishments are not as effective as rewards. Reinforcement is usually better because you learn what to expect after behaving a certain way. Punishment can result in more unwanted behavior due to resentment of the punisher, and so it might not actually solve the problem. Rather than punishing their customers, most marketers are interested in ensuring that they only experience desirable outcomes in buying and using a product (i.e., rewards).

Nonetheless, punishment does have its place. If it does not affect behavior, then why is the issuance of speeding citations so effective in controlling traffic on a busy street? Why do tax filers rush to get their taxes done on time to avoid paying late fees? The marketing applications of punishment, however, are limited. For instance, public service ads use fear appeals to administer a psychological punishment, such as generating anxiety about undesirable behaviors such as smoking or doing drugs. Many fear-laden ads or products also suggest punishment, such as embarrassment or ridicule, if you do not purchase the marketer's brand.

EXTINCTION

Extinction is when a previously established link between a stimulus and response is broken. Extinction constitutes inhibitory learning resulting from either lack of reinforcement following the undesired behavior or removing or withholding a reward that was previously given after an action was taken. Alternatively, a reward that was previously dispensed is replaced with a new, incompatible stimulus. The purpose is to reduce the likelihood that the behavior will be repeated. The learner discovers either that responses no longer lead to a desirable outcome or that behavior now results in an undesirable outcome.

If a consumer once but no longer gains positive outcomes from buying and using a brand, the association between the stimulus (the brand) and the response (purchasing and consuming the brand) is no longer reinforced. Consequently, the buying behavior will eventually cease. For low-involvement, frequently purchased items, a single unsatisfactory experience may be perceived as a fluke and the consumer will nonetheless buy again. However, after one or several more bad experiences, the buyer's purchase behavior will become extinguished—in effect "unlearned."

Punishment is generally more rapid than extinction in halting an unwanted action. This is because extinction tends to be subtler to the learner. However, punishment also more likely induces negative feelings and resentment toward the punishment's administrator because it is more obvious.

Unintended Marketing Extinction. Extinction differs from forgetting in that forgetting is the loss of retention of previously learned material due to lack of repetition of the stimulus-response linkage. Extinction happens because a response is not reinforced.

Marketers can combat forgetting through repetition of stimuli, such as high-frequency advertising or intensive distribution, where the product is constantly front and center at retail. However, the primary way to fight unwanted extinction is to continuously provide a satisfactory customer experience.

Marketers must be cautious in making radical changes to their marketing mix elements, which can extinguish buyer behavior. A "new and improved" product that loyal users do not perceive as such will cause the loyalists to abandon ship. For example, Ovaltine, a classic malt-flavored milk additive from the 1950s, was "contemporized" in the late 1980s with new packaging in stylish canisters instead of the original glass jar. Many Ovaltine loyalists wanted back the original taste and jar.

Intended Marketing Extinction. There are times when a marketer desires to achieve extinction of an undesirable behavior. A purveyor of breath mints might position the candies as an effective smoking deterrent. Popping a mint becomes the consumer's new response to satisfying the smoking urge—the old smoking desire–cigarette indulgence link becomes broken and replaced with a new smoking urge–mint linkage. Likewise, a marketer of low-fat or low-carb food can suggest the product as a new, healthier reward to satisfy the hunger stimulus.

If consumers have previously had poor brand experiences that the marketer would like to reverse, it might be appropriate to institute a **mea culpa strategy**, which involves admitting a marketing program shortcoming, apologizing for it, and assuring the audience that the problem has been rectified. The marketer is in effect saying, "We're sorry you got burned. We've cleaned up our act and promise it won't happen again." The seller is pledging to replace the old stimulus-response (bad experience with brand usage) with a new one (a good brand outcome). Blockbuster did this by very publicly abandoning its late rental returns fee policy. Ford did likewise subtly when they asked, "Have you driven a Ford . . . lately?" implying that they had previously taken their eye off the quality ball but had now fixed things.

REVIEW QUESTIONS

1. Explain the relationship between motivation, drives, and learning.
2. Cite examples of verbal and nonverbal communication tools and how sellers and buyers use them to communicate with one another.
3. Cite marketing applications of each of three learned marketing cues: advertising retrieval cues, stimulus generalization, and stimulus discrimination.
4. Clarify the relationship between stimulus generalization and each of the following: positioning, guilt and cachet by association (including stereotyping); product generalization and copycat products (imitative brands, value brands, and trade dress infringement, including confusingly similar brands, package knockoffs, and counterfeit merchandise); branding generalization or brand leveraging (brand franchise extensions, product line extensions, and family branding [sometimes in conjunction with family packaging]); and advertising generalization. Describe how marketers use each of these concepts to assist consumer learning.
5. Describe the reasons for and limitations of a branding generalization strategy.
6. Can confusingly similar brands and advertising generalization ever be of value to a marketer? Explain.
7. Some marketers use cues to achieve stimulus generalization while others employ stimuli to create stimulus discrimination. Explain this apparent paradox.
8. Describe common marketing techniques to achieve stimulus discrimination.
9. Cite and explain marketing examples of each of the following techniques for changing the probability that a response will occur in the future: positive reinforcement, negative reinforcement, punishment, and extinction.
10. Distinguish between each of the following schedules of reinforcement, and explain when each is most appropriate for a marketer to use: continuous versus partial, variable versus fixed, and interval versus ratio.

IN-CLASS APPLICATIONS

1. Without letting yourself become distracted from taking notes and participating in discussion during your classroom session, be observant of verbal cues and nonverbal cues sent by both your professor during her lecturing and leading of the class discussion, as well as by your classmates as they listen, take notes, and contribute to class discussion.

   Your instructor may choose to hold a discussion on this near the end or at any other point during the class session or ask you to raise your hand and point out your observations on these cues whenever you spot them during the class meeting.

   Be on the lookout for the following:
   - Auditory verbal communication: tone of voice, enthusiasm of speech, loudness of voice, expressiveness, word choices, and pacing
   - Kinesic nonverbal communication: body language, such as head nods, eye glances and winks, facial expressions, and movement of the hands, arms, legs, and torso
   - Proxemic nonverbal communication: physical distance between the instructor and students, and physical distance students maintain between each other
   - Tactile nonverbal communication: physical touch

How much additional information do you glean from these cues compared with simply the words spoken? Does any of it conflict with the verbal messages?

2. Evaluate each of the ads in Exhibits 14.12 through 14.14 to see how many examples of cues you can find. Be on the lookout for verbal and nonverbal communication tools and learned marketing cues: advertising retrieval cues and methods to achieve stimulus discrimination.

   How effective do you believe use of each of these tools is in communication with readers and helping them to learn favorable information about the brand?

3. Evaluate each of the ads in Exhibits 14.15 through 14.17 to see how many examples of each of the following applications of stimulus generalization you can find: cachet by association, stereotyping, copycat products (imitative brands, value brands, and confusingly similar brands); branding generalization (brand franchise extensions, product line extensions, family branding, and family packaging); and advertising generalization.

4. What do you think about the ethics of selling against the brand by private label retailers? Is it in the consumer's best interest? Does the answer to whether this is ethical depend in part on whether consumers can discern differences?

   To help you decide, your instructor will bring in two bags or boxes of a food product, such as a snack cracker, cookie, or breakfast cereal. One will be a national brand while the other will be a private label brand. The professor will perform a blind (masked) taste test, asking several students to sample from both brands, not knowing which is which. Do you think you will be able to tell the imitator from the "real McCoy"?

5. Try to guess why each of the following attempts at extending a brand name failed:
   a. Gillette Silkience facial moisturizer
   b. Country Time apple cider
   c. Arm & Hammer deodorant
   d. Crystal Pepsi (clear, like water)
   e. Sara Lee Chicken and Noodles Au Gratin
   f. Bic perfume
   g. Ivory scouring pads
   h. Betty Crocker breakfast cereal
   i. Osh Kosh maternity clothes

6. Time for you to be the judge! Give a ruling on whether each of the following attempts to achieve stimulus generalization should be ruled as a confusingly similar brand name. Justify your verdict in each case.
   a. Breyer's Creme Savers yogurt
   b. Ritz designer cigarettes
   c. Country Daze drink mix
   d. Promise furniture polish
   e. Ball Game wieners
   f. Quick Tips manicure finishing spray
   g. Creamy Wheat farina
   h. Toyota Lexus
   i. Whoppaburger sandwiches

7. Browsing through a supermarket can be quite a strenuous adventure—so many brands to choose from! How do manufacturers and retailers use their knowledge of stimulus generalization and stimulus discrimination to get you, the shopper, to notice (and hopefully buy) their product? Think about this question in terms of packaging, brand name, shelf position, in-store placement, in-store displays, and merchandising.

8. Time to put on your creative thinking cap. (You did bring it to class with you today, didn't you?) Your job is to market a new brand of toothpicks—not an easy task! After all, this is a commodity—toothpicks are toothpicks! Plus, the market is dominated by Diamond Brands, the manufacturer of other wood-based products such as matches and clothespins.

   But, you won't let that deter you. Assuming you have enough financial capital to do battle against Diamond Brands, how will you use stimulus discrimination techniques to differentiate your toothpick so you don't lose your shirt? Think of as many possibilities as you can.

EXHIBIT 14.12   Prilosec Ad

EXHIBIT 14.13   Viagra Ad

EXHIBIT 14.14   Northwestern Mutual Ad

EXHIBIT 14.15   Nestlé Crunch Ad

EXHIBIT 14.16   **Tide Ad**

EXHIBIT 14.17   **EarthLink Ad**

9. For each of the following scenarios, identify the reinforcement schedule being implemented: continuous, fixed ratio, variable ratio, fixed interval, or variable interval.
   a. Benny is always looking out for the best deal around. Since he travels a lot, he is a sucker for frequent flyer plans—the more he flies, the more free trips he gets!
   b. Dixie is an avid grocery shopper. She loves the deals she gets when checking out at the cashier. One day she will get half-off of all bread items, while another time she gets a free soda with any frozen food. She shops frequently because she never knows when the discounts will be given!
   c. Cassy is an avid gambler. She knows that after so many pulls on the slot machine, she is bound to win. Some days she must pull more than thirty slots to see the coins flow; other days it only takes five (lucky gal!).
   d. Cliff is a smart shopper when it comes to his favorite clothing store, Promises. He realizes that every time he spends fifty dollars, he gets 10 percent off of his purchase. Cliff knows to buy in bulk now.
   e. Earl E. Riser is a diligent worker, but only when he knows his boss is coming. Every day at ten minutes before the hour, Earl's boss comes strolling through the office. In between those times, Earl just kicks back and relaxes or surfs the Web for fun, waiting for that hour to pass until the next time he will look like a hard worker.

WRITTEN APPLICATIONS

1. Keep a diary for one day (or another relevant time period to give you enough data) of all (or else the more interesting) verbal and nonverbal cues you encounter in your interactions with people. (You may use the summary list of such communication from Question 1 in the In-Class Applications.)

How much communication seems to be nonverbal relative to verbal? Evaluate the effectiveness of some of this communication. Does the nonverbal communication ever conflict with the verbal communication? If so, which seems to tell you more and which do you trust more?

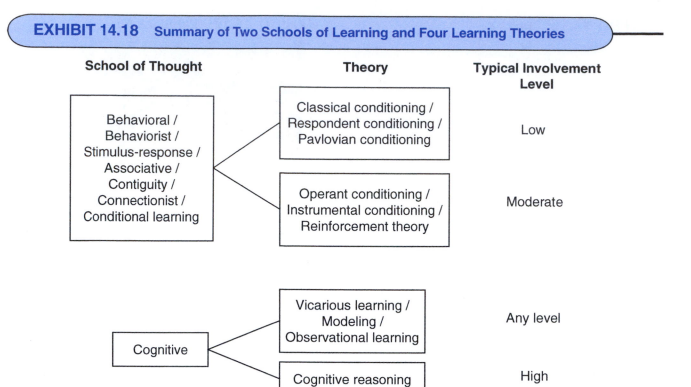

EXHIBIT 14.18   Summary of Two Schools of Learning and Four Learning Theories

2. Answer Questions 2 and 3 regarding three ads in Sections A and B respectively. Then, find two more ads for each question (four ads total) and repeat the analysis for these ads.

3. Answer Question 7 based on a visit to any major supermarket. Cite and explain examples in the supermarket of stimulus generalization and stimulus discrimination you find particularly effective as well as especially ineffective.

4. Answer Question 8.

EXERCISE 14.3. THEORIES OF LEARNING

OBJECTIVES

1. To understand the two schools of learning and four learning theories, as well as the various applications of each learning theory for consumer marketing.
2. To evaluate the type of learning theory that most likely is at work in any given marketplace situation, considering consumer involvement and incidental versus intentional learning.
3. To gain insight into the type of learning processes you went through for various types of products and brands you have learned about.
4. To further explore learning theories by visiting several Web sites devoted to these.

BACKGROUND

LEARNING UNDER HIGH- AND LOW-INVOLVEMENT CONDITIONS

Exhibit 14.18 provides an overview of two schools of learning and four affiliated learning theories covered in this exercise, including the synonymous names for each (separated by slashes in the exhibit) and level of involvement most typical of people learning in accordance with each theory.

The degrees of product involvement, purchase involvement, and message involvement are key determinants of how much and the nature of how people learn. The involvement level determines how motivated a consumer is to search out and to learn marketplace information. Because the nature of learning varies contingent on involvement level, different theories regarding the learning process will hold under various levels of involvement.

Generally, classical conditioning happens under low-involvement circumstances, whereas operant conditioning operates under moderately involving circumstances, and cognitive reasoning occurs under high-involvement circumstances. Vicarious learning can take place under any level of involvement. We will now describe and illustrate both of the schools of thought and each of the four learning theories outlined in Exhibit 14.18.

BEHAVIORAL LEARNING THEORIES

Psychologist John B. Watson in 1913 established the learning school of **behaviorism**. The focus is not on the internal psychology (hypothetical constructs, unobservable responses) of the learning process, that is, people's inner beliefs, ideas, motives, perceptions, and attitudes. Rather, behaviorists believe that psychology should study how organisms respond to environmental stimuli. Emphasis is on observable behavior.

The belief underlying behaviorism is *determinism,* that is, we are products of our environment. According to this **behavioral (behaviorist, stimulus-response, associative, contiguity, connectionist, conditioning) learning school**, the emphasis is on how individuals learn by making simple stimulus-response associations. Observable reactions to external stimuli indicate that learning has occurred. In effect, habits (routine responses to one's surroundings) are learned.

Associative learning is based on **conditioning**, a passively learned, low-involvement process of automatic responses or habits produced primarily by repetitive association of either two stimuli (classical conditioning) or of a stimulus and a response plus reinforcement of the response (operant conditioning). This learned response is an automatic, unthinking, knee-jerk reaction built up through repeated exposure to environmental stimuli. The response can be either an observable behavior or an unobservable thought or feeling. For instance, if a student feels fear every time he or she walks into math class, this is a conditioned mental reaction to frequent negative experiences in this course, such as being embarrassed by the teacher or regularly failing quizzes.

The behaviorist school, then, studies associative (incidental) learning, which entails the discovery that two events go together through a process of simple-stimulus-response learning via repetition and association. The events might be two stimuli, as in classical conditioning, or a response and its consequences (rewards and punishments), as in operant conditioning. Hence, consumers learn associations between marketplace stimuli such as brand names, packages, slogans, jingles, and other frequently repeated cues (classical conditioning), or between their buying behavior and the rewards that follow (operant conditioning).

For many people, the term *conditioning* has an onerous association with mind control and robotic behavior (as in Aldous Huxley's classic book *Brave New World,* in which neo-Pavlovian conditioning was used to create happiness and ability in a whole new society). However, conditioning simply means that people learn to associate two stimuli or else a stimulus and a subsequent response.

CLASSICAL (RESPONDENT, PAVLOVIAN) CONDITIONING

The Classical Conditioning Paradigm. **Classical (respondent, Pavlovian) conditioning** considers behavior as learned through making a close connection (contiguity) between two stimuli. We learn that a flash of lightning will be followed by a loud peal of thunder, and we brace ourselves for it. More specifically, classical conditioning is the process of using an existing stimulus-response relationship to create the learning of the same (or a very similar) response to a different stimulus. This learning procedure is also called *respondent conditioning* since it involves respondent behavior, or behavior that occurs as an automatic response to a stimulus. It is called *Pavlovian conditioning* after its founder, Russian psychologist Ivan Pavlov, a Nobel Prize winner in physiology.

Exhibit 14.19 diagrams the classical conditioning process. A primary cue, or **unconditioned stimulus**

EXHIBIT 14.19   **The Classical Conditioning Paradigm**

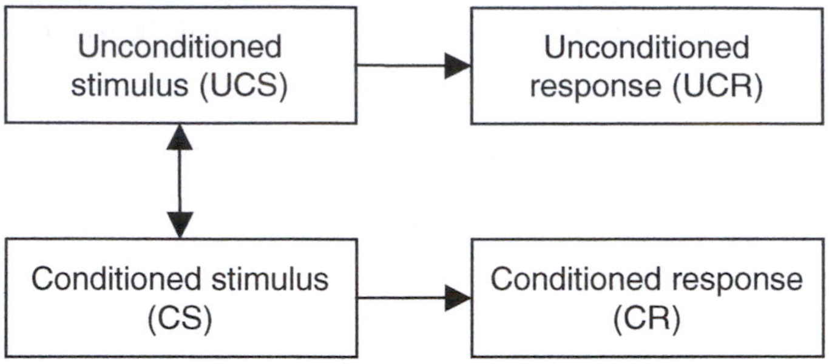

```
┌─────────────────────┐        ┌─────────────────────┐
│   Unconditioned     │───────▶│   Unconditioned     │
│   stimulus (UCS)    │        │   response (UCR)    │
└─────────────────────┘        └─────────────────────┘
          ▲
          │
          ▼
┌─────────────────────┐        ┌─────────────────────┐
│ Conditioned stimulus│───────▶│ Conditioned response│
│        (CS)         │        │        (CR)         │
└─────────────────────┘        └─────────────────────┘
```

(**UCS**), is followed by a natural or instinctual reaction, or **unconditioned response (UCR)**. That is, there exists a natural relationship between an UCS and an UCR. In Pavlov's famous experiment with salivating dogs (see Exercise 1.4), Pavlov placed meat powder, a UCS, under the nose or on the tongue of a hungry (driven) dog, who then automatically salivated, a UCR.

During the conditioning process, the UCS is repeatedly associated with a **conditioned stimulus (CS)**, a secondary cue that will alter enough repeated UCS-CS pairings, result in a **conditioned response (CR)**, an unnatural, involuntary, reflexive reaction. The CR is the same (or a very similar) response as the UCR naturally given to the UCS. Originally, the CS was a **neutral stimulus (NS)**, a cue that naturally would not produce any response on its own. Following the conditioning process where the UCS and CS are respectively paired, there is a post-conditioning relationship between the CS and CR.

Pavlov repeatedly rang a bell (NS) before presentation of the meat powder (UCS) and a feeding of meat to the dogs. Eventually a new association was created between the meat powder and the bell, so that the dogs would drool upon hearing the bell even in the absence of the meat powder. At this point, the bell had changed from being an NS to a CS to which basically the same response, salivation, had been learned as a CR. So, during post-conditioning, the bell (CS) evoked salivation (CR). Pavlov's pooches became conditioned to salivate upon hearing a ringing bell.

You might have observed the respondent conditioning process at home if you have a house pet. The family dog knows that it is going to be taken for a stroll and begins excitedly wagging its tail (CR) when the master walks to where the leash (CS) is kept. Or, when you open a can of cat food (CS), chances are Fluffy comes scurrying (CR). And, when Mom rings the dinner bell (CS), you probably do likewise (CR)!

Four Types of Associations. Marketers, however, are more interested in emotional and cognitive responses than in the behavioral responses demonstrated by Pavlov. Especially effective for conditioning CB is creating the right connections between a brand and needs, emotions and moods, information (cognitions), or cues.

➤ *1. Need association.* **Need association** is a classical conditioning process that repeatedly links a brand to a particular need or drive. The stronger the drive with which a brand is associated, the more effective the learning is likely to be.

Timing is everything. Marketers can be most effective in stimulating a purchase if they run their ads at a time of day, week, month, or year when consumers are strongly driven. Supermarkets wisely distribute food samples shortly before or during mealtimes and beverage samples on hot, humid days. If Porky's Pizza Joint always advertises on afternoon drive time radio when hungry commuters are driving home hungry, Porky's will become associated with the hunger drive. Consequently, the mere mention of the Porky's name could induce hunger (preferably for Porky's pizza) and association of Porky's as *the* place to grab some dinner to satisfy the hunger drive.

➤ *2. Attitudinal association.* Attitudes (evaluations of objects) can develop primarily via the repeated pairings of objects with positive and negative reinforcers. What consumers typically learn from marketing communications is not an involuntary, reflexive behavioral response such as salivation but rather emotional (affective) reactions, which are also more or less automatic, involuntary behaviors.

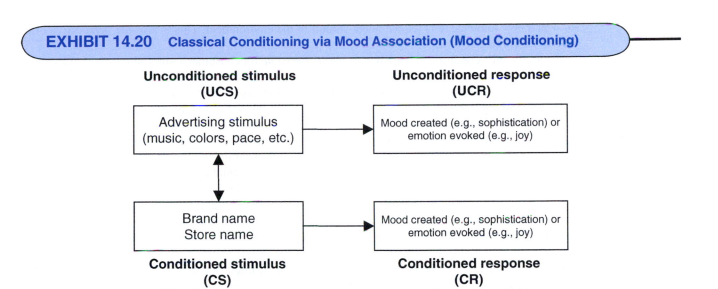

EXHIBIT 14.20   Classical Conditioning via Mood Association (Mood Conditioning)

Consequently, some marketers use **attitudinal (emotional, affective) conditioning (mood association)**, a form of classical conditioning in which, due to the constant S-R pairing, learners attribute whatever feelings they have about the UCS to the CS. Attitudinal conditioning is employed in forming emotional responses to the advertisement or other marketing stimulus that will rub off on the brand featured in the ad or otherwise associated with the stimulus. In the case of advertising, the idea is that the consumer's attitude or emotional responses toward an ad will rub off on the brand featured in the ad, a phenomenon known as **affect transferal**. Rather than conveying favorable brand-attribute information, the advertiser simply connects the brand with good feelings.

For instance, if a well-liked celebrity is featured in an ad campaign, the fondness for the celebrity should transfer to the brand. Or, with humor or music, the enjoyable feelings created by the comical or musical ad will rub off on the brand. Fun ad scenarios will make the brand seem like it is all about good times. An ad featuring scenes of loved ones enjoying each other's company will induce warm feelings toward the brand. If a product is shown being used by sports team players, loyalty to the team, or perhaps the excitement experienced by watching the team in action, could result in loyalty toward the brand. If a product is associated with a color, that color's perceptual meaning can transfer to the brand (e.g., blue is associated with trust and stability, while green is affiliated with nature and health). Pacing of commercials and some online ads can also build emotional connections: These ads can be rapid-fire and intense at one extreme or slow and easygoing at the other, creating a corresponding mood or feeling for the brand.

Whatever emotional appeal is used will become associated with the brand: Sex appeal will affiliate the brand with pleasure. A sentimental appeal will endow the brand with romantic overtones. In all cases, consumers will respond at an emotional level when presented with the brand.

As shown in Exhibit 14.20, each of these mood-developing advertising devices is a UCS. This UCS naturally evokes an unconditioned emotional response (UCR) such as happiness or excitement. The brand, company, or store name serves as the CS. By continually being linked with the advertising cue (UCS), eventually the marketer's name will evoke an emotional response (CR) similar to the UCR.

➤ *3. Cognitive associations (cognitive associative learning).* Attitudinal conditioning is generally most effective for look-alike, act-alike parity products lacking persuasive points of difference for an advertiser to convey. However, where there are brand distinctions people can learn information about these differences through classical conditioning. In fact, contemporary behavioral scientists view respondent conditioning as the learning of associations among events (stimuli) that permit organisms to anticipate the environment.

So viewed, the association between the CS and the UCS in Pavlov's experiment affected the dogs' expectations, which in turn influenced their responses (salivation). According to this perspective, classical conditioning is not an involuntary reflexive action but rather entails **cognitive associative learning**, in which new knowledge is gained about stimuli in the environment. This is also the perspective of the cognitive learning school.

Consequently, conditioned stimuli have *predictive value* for consumers—they allow them to anticipate results of a purchase decision, just as the ringing bell alerted Pavlov's dogs that it was chow time. For instance, the chiming bells on an ice cream truck alert kids that a special snack time is coming. Ringing bells and flashing lights in a video arcade can mean that someone just won a game.

➤ *4. Cue association.* **Cue association** is a classical conditioning technique that uses either unique marketing stimuli or else familiar environmental cues to identify and differentiate brands by linking the brands to these cues. Distinctive marketing cues include logos, jingles, slogans, trade characters, package graphics, and other easily recognized stimuli. Familiar environmental cues, such as sirens sounding (excitement), bustling offices (stress and business), or telephones or doorbells ringing (sense of attentiveness or urgency), can likewise be linked to the brand. Popular tunes sometimes evoke memories, which can become linked with a brand. Certain smells can operate in like fashion. For instance, a vanilla-scented cologne might remind users of baking cookies as a child and all the attendant warm memories.

Limitations of Classical Conditioning. Pavlovian conditioning might not effectively educate consumers about a brand because this theory assumes low involvement on the part of learners, who will learn in a passive, involuntary fashion. However, more involved consumers actively engage in voluntary, prepurchase (deliberate) search. Such motivated learning probably will be strongest if there is a reward for it. Operant conditioning theory addresses these two issues by incorporating active trial-and error learning and reinforcement (reward).

OPERANT (INSTRUMENTAL) CONDITIONING (REINFORCEMENT THEORY)

The Operant Conditioning Paradigm. **Operant (instrumental) conditioning (reinforcement theory)** suggests that responses are best learned if followed by reinforcement (either positive or negative) or weakened if followed by punishment. Through active, conscious, and voluntary trial-and-error learning, the learner discovers which stimuli are associated with the best rewards.

This describes *operant behavior*—the organism operates on the environment to elicit rewarding or punishing stimuli or consequences. It is called instrumental conditioning because the learner's response is the instrument whereby he or she is rewarded; the organism plays an instrumental role in either producing rewards or escaping punishment. Operant conditioning is also known as reinforcement theory because if the learner takes the desired action, he or she is rewarded.

With classical conditioning, an organism learns associations between events it cannot control and responds involuntarily. In operant conditioning, the learning involves making a connection between behavior and consequent reward or punishment and the response is volitional.

Whereas classical conditioning is most useful for explaining simple, low-involvement purchases, instrumental conditioning better accounts for more complex, goal-directed behavior under conditions of at least moderate involvement, since the learner actively gets involved in trial-and-error learning.

The operant conditioning learning process is outlined in Exhibit 14.21. First, the learner takes a specific action. If the consequences are favorable, entailing a reward or reinforcer (positive or negative reinforcement), the probability of the same response being elicited again or the frequency with which that behavior occurs is increased. Conversely, if the action's outcome leads to a punishment or punisher, the probability or rate of recurrence of that behavior is lessened.

At the turn of the twentieth century, while Pavlov was experimenting with his dogs, psychologist Edward Thorndike pioneered operant conditioning theory with his *law of effect*, in which consistently rewarded behavior is more likely to recur and repeatedly punished behavior is less likely to happen again. Thorndike used a "puzzle box" or wooden box in which he placed hungry cats. Outside the cage he positioned food where the cats could see and smell it. To get the food, they had to figure out how to open the cage door's latch. The cats learned to make the necessary response more rapidly as the number of trials increased.

Following up on Thorndike's work, behavioral psychologist B. F. Skinner designed his Skinner box, a soundproof chamber with a bar or key that rats or pigeons pressed or pecked to release premeasured food pellets or a drink of water. On the initial trial, due to random movement, the critter eventually made the desired response and was rewarded. After several more trials, the animal caught on and made the connection between

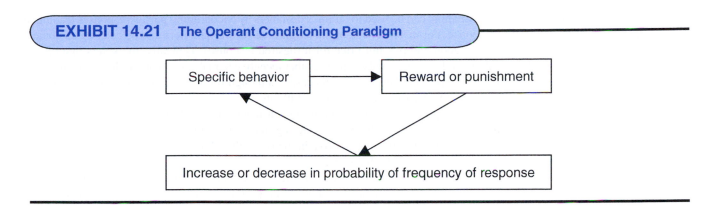

EXHIBIT 14.21   The Operant Conditioning Paradigm

| Specific behavior | → | Reward or punishment |

Increase or decrease in probability of frequency of response

its behavior and obtaining the reward. Skinner was thereby able to teach rats to take the desired action to get their goodies. In later experiments, Skinner delivered a shock (punishment) to the animals through the box's floor when they took the same actions, and they soon learned *not* to peck the bar or press the lever.

In more elaborate experiments, Skinner taught pigeons to play the piano and Ping-Pong, and even to do figure eights. Such complex learning, where the probability of getting a desired response initially through spontaneous occurrence is very low, can be achieved through **shaping**, in which successive approximations of a complex desired behavior are rewarded. Rewards are administered before the desired response occurs using a multistep process. The preferred behavior is learned over time because intermediate reactions are rewarded as they more closely approximate the final desired action.

Instead of rewarding the rat for lever pressing, Skinner reinforced the rodent whenever it performed a behavior similar to lever pressing, such as moving in the direction of the lever. The rat eventually touched the lever with the front half of his body and finally actually pressed the lever.

The apparently apocryphal story goes that Skinner's students used his shaping strategy on him and had him lecturing in the corner of the classroom by semester's end! They allegedly did so by being attentive and participative every time he moved in the direction of that corner, but they were unresponsive and inattentive every time Skinner moved away from the corner.

Today's animal trainers use shaping to get their creatures to do elaborate tricks such as jumping through fiery hoops. Shaping also works on humans. Workplace supervisors "train" tardy employees to eventually be prompt by praising them each time they are less late than the previous time. Perhaps a professor has encouraged you to work a bit harder on each successive assignment throughout the semester in order to keep earning the same grade, until finally she has you performing monumental work just to pass the course!

MARKETING APPLICATIONS OF OPERANT CONDITIONING

➤ *1. Rewarding customers.* Whereas classical conditioning is most useful for explaining simple, low-involvement purchases, instrumental conditioning better accounts for more complex, goal-directed behavior under at least moderately involving conditions. Where consumers are concerned with the buying decision, learning often takes place through a trial-and-error process of experiencing various brands to see which one a person likes best. Here, brand habits are acquired as a consequence of receiving rewards for purchasing and consuming. A favorable consumption experience, such as a first product trial, encourages repeat patronage, but if the experience is unsatisfactory (if bad enough it is punishment!), repurchase is less likely. If teenage girl Sally Mander gets favorable attention from the teen lads when she wears a new outfit from Old Navy, she is likely to shop there again for her other wardrobe needs. As long as the boys admire her new duds, she will probably continue shopping there.

The marketing implication is clear—be sure to reward and satisfy your customers! This is achieved via product quality, postpurchase reinforcement through dissonance-reducing communications and follow-up service, stores and services that provide rewarding experiences such as entertainment and special events, and many other means used to achieve customer satisfaction and loyalty.

➤ *2. Shaping CB.* Shaping can be used to "train" consumers by encouraging partial responses leading to the final desired response. For instance, one of the toughest tasks for marketers can be coaxing customers to try a new packaged good and pay full price for it (desired response). Typically, marketers first offer a free sample, usually including a discount coupon or other incentive to make a repeat purchase. The package so bought might then include another discount incentive, although for a lesser amount than the first one. Eventually, the satisfied buyer will be willing to pay full fare.

For durable goods, the process is a bit different. For instance, an automobile merchant might entice shoppers to "come on down" to the dealership by offering free coffee and donuts. Once in the showroom, patrons might be given $10 just to take a test drive in the new JalopyMobile. And, to nudge them to buy, the dealer might then tender a $1000 rebate check.

Holding special events works in a similar fashion. New outlets offer "grand openings" with free door prizes and other enticements such as free balloons for the kids to stop by. In the store, merchandise discounts are offered, as are gifts for applying for a store charge card to encourage continuing patronage.

Another application of shaping involves **multiple request techniques**, in which compliance is gained by making "critical" requests of the customer. Multiple request methods include both foot-in-the-door and door-in-the-face techniques.

Using the **foot-in-the-door compliance technique**, the requester first gets the learner to agree to fulfill a small favor. Later, the learner is consequently more likely to carry out a larger demand (the desired response). For instance, a salesperson who can get the prospect to take some small action, such as trying on an article of clothing or taking a test drive in a car, gets his or her foot in the proverbial door. The prospect is later more likely to make a larger commitment to the seller, such as buying the product. Charities will often ask for a very small donation the first time and later request a larger contribution.

With the **door-in-the-face compliance technique**, the consumer is asked for a big favor that he or she is expected to refuse. Then, a second smaller request is posed, which the consumer will then more likely grant than if not first requested to fulfill the large favor. Accordingly, a salesperson might begin by asking a prospect to buy the expensive, deluxe model. The consumer either figuratively or literally slams the door in the sales rep's face. The seller then suggests that the prospect purchase the lower-end model, which she is more likely to do than if she had not been initially approached.

Limitations of Operant Conditioning. There are several shortcomings of reinforcement theory that restrict its marketing applicability. Like classical conditioning, operant conditioning is of the behaviorism school, focusing only on the environment and how it influences learning and behavior. It is limited to learning fairly simple, mechanistic S-R linkages.

Also, this theory assumes that rewards or punishments are necessary for learning to take place, which might not be the case. Sometimes we learn for reasons such as satisfying our curiosity or solving problems (cognitive learning), or, the learning might be inadvertent (classical conditioning).

Another issue is that humans are seen as manipulable machines who are products of their environment and pushovers for manipulators. Consumerist critics take a deterministic view, alleging that buyers are passive puppets in the hands of Machiavellian master marketers rather than sovereign beings.

Further, with the behaviorist school, new behavior is considered to be evidence of learning. However, learning can occur without behavior. As you soak up the valuable knowledge from this book, you probably do not immediately jump out of your seat and do something with it (although the applications exercises are designed to eventually get you to do so!). In the marketplace, you might become aware of some new brands, but this does not mean that you will run out to purchase and experience them all.

Furthermore, behavior can occur without learning, including actions that are instinctual (salivating when hungry); due to temporary circumstances (a hungry person's stomach growls or a sleepy individual yawns); or are simply reflex actions (jumping when startled). For instance, a totally uninformed buyer could make an impulse purchase. Behavior (or nonbehavior) does not necessarily indicate that learning has or has not occurred.

Also, behaviorism ignores the "ghost in the machine"—people's thoughts, reasoning, feelings, evaluation, and other unobservable responses. But these are often an even more important part of much of our learning. In fact, the effectiveness of most marketing communications is measured via learning metrics such as awareness (of brand names, slogans, etc.) and information (such as sales or copy points), not by

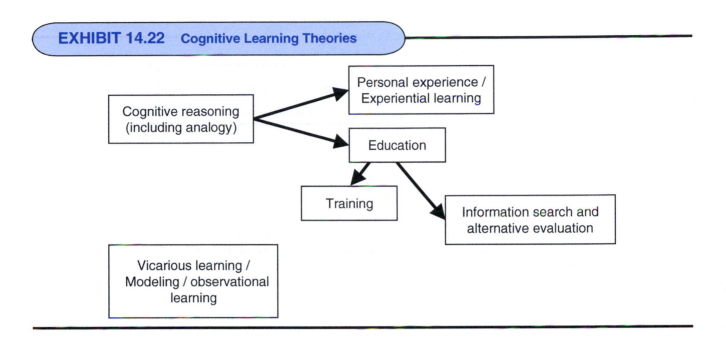

EXHIBIT 14.22   Cognitive Learning Theories

behavioral measures such as a spike in sales or market share. This is because the latter could be due to other marketplace factors such as improvements in the competitive situation or the economy.

COGNITIVE LEARNING THEORIES

The **cognitive learning school** centers on **cognitions**, peoples' mental activities associated with thinking, processing information, knowing, remembering, and communicating, and how they are fully engaged in the learning process. The focus is on actively thinking about acquired information, reasoning, and problem solving rather than doing.

Cognitive learning involves purposeful and goal-directed learning by interpreting environmental information and creating new knowledge or meaning from it. Often cognitive learning entails discovering cause-and-effect relationships between associated environmental stimuli. Thereby, young children "discover" that by flicking on a light switch, they can brighten a room, or that by pressing an elevator button, they can command an elevator to appear.

There are two principal types of cognitive learning: (1) cognitive reasoning (thinking about information and problem solving with it) and (2) vicarious learning (modeling) by observing others. Exhibit 14.22 overviews the cognitive learning techniques.

COGNITIVE REASONING THEORY

The Cognitive Reasoning Paradigm. **Cognitive reasoning (reasoning) theory** proposes that much human learning is the product of thinking and problem solving. The solution to a problem can come in a flash of brilliance based on personal experience ("Eureka!"), or it can result from education. In either case, due to the learner's active involvement, cognitive learning results in better long-term learning than do simpler forms of learning such as rote memorization (associative learning). That is why many instructors prefer teaching pedagogies such as the case study approach and the Socratic questioning method over rote learning. It is also why this book emphasizes active learning exercises, which, we hope, help you to engage in cognitive reasoning via analysis and evaluation rather than simple stimulus-response learning or rote memorization (recognition and recall).

Consumers are most likely to undertake complex cognitive reasoning under conditions of high involvement. Cognitive reasoning is an active process in which people deliberately seek out and ap-

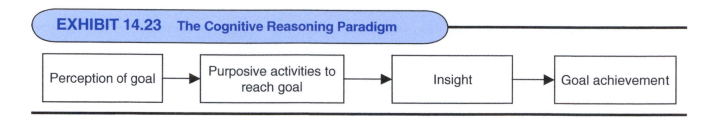

EXHIBIT 14.23 **The Cognitive Reasoning Paradigm**

| Perception of goal | → | Purposive activities to reach goal | → | Insight | → | Goal achievement |

ply information. The cognitive learning paradigm, therefore, is perfectly consistent with the consumer decision-making process perspective of this course, which envisions most buyer decisions as a result of a problem-solving process.

Exhibit 14.23 outlines the cognitive reasoning model. The learner begins with an unrealized goal. In the consumer decision process, this is problem recognition. Next, the learner engages in purposive activities to help achieve the goal, as occurs during the information search and alternative evaluation decision-making stages. In thinking about this acquired information, the learner has an insightful "eureka" experience, through which the person suddenly hits on a solution to the problem, i.e., the best alternative. Finally, the goal (product) can then be obtained (purchased).

One implication is that marketers must get prospects to perceive their products as solutions to their problems and as satisfiers of their needs. Should a low-carb food be marketed as an aid to looking good, feeling good, or both? It depends on who the target market is and what their problem or desire is.

Another suggestion is that marketers develop ads where insightful learning occurs. For example, an advertisement could feature a mom trying to put a cloth diaper onto her child that just will not stay on. Then, she has a "eureka" moment: A safety pin would do the trick! Then the voice-over would talk about the safety pin brand while the mom fastens the diaper and the baby coos and smiles.

The Cognitive Reasoning Process. Reasoned learning entails creative thinking to restructure and recombine existing and/or new information in order to form different associations and concepts, solve problems, and gain insights. During this active learning process consumers intuitively test hypotheses about products and adapt their beliefs in light of the data they acquire. This **cognitive reasoning process** consists of three steps: hypothesis generation, hypothesis testing, and hypothesis revision.

➤ *Stage 1: Hypothesis generation.* During **hypothesis generation**, the consumer formulates specific testable hypotheses or prior beliefs—assumptions about marketplace alternatives such as products, brands, and stores. For example, Sue might believe that high-priced headache remedies are no more effective than their store brand counterparts.

➤ *Stage 2: Hypothesis testing.* During **hypothesis testing**, the buyer gathers information relating to the hypothesis either through education or personal experience. He or she then evaluates the data to determine if the hypothesis is true or false.

Learning through education entails acquiring information from the environment. This can be accomplished through either formal instruction or informal education. Education through training entails accepting direction and guidance from others. Training can be formal, as in school or a corporate training program, or informal, as when parents teach their youngsters how to get dressed, tie a shoe, or prepare a sandwich. Marketers can also offer consumer training via methods such as videos, in-store demonstrations and instruction, brochures, and owner's manuals.

The consumer generally initiates informal consumer education, which entails information search and alternative evaluation. Marketers can supply searching shoppers with information via various consumer information sources. Additionally, consumers seek out nonmarketer information sources such as word-of-mouth, professional advice, and news stories, which marketers can try to influence (see Exercise 4.2).

Experiential learning is learning through personal experience. Marketers encourage prepurchase learning through offering "test runs" with durables and samples of nondurables. Providing dressing rooms in clothing stores and allowing consumers to sit on couches and lie on beds in furniture stores also allow experiential learning prior to buying.

Additionally, experiential learning occurs after the product is purchased and consumed (postpurchase learning). If someone buys a headache pain reliever, he or she could get a national brand and see how it works. Then, when the medicine runs out and the consumer needs to buy more, the person could procure a private label brand to see how it compares, thereby testing the hypothesis regarding the relative efficacy of store versus national brands.

Generally, experiential learning is superior, especially for experience goods. Experience-based learning results in better retention because it is a very active learning process, and the acquired information is more vivid and concrete.

➢ *Stage 3: Hypothesis revision.* During **hypothesis revision**, after exposure to and evaluation of the marketplace information, the consumer's prior beliefs (hypotheses) are either confirmed or revised if the information shows prior perceptions to be false.

Analogy. A particular type of cognitive reasoning uses **analogy (analogical learning)**, whereby the consumer transfers knowledge from one domain to learn about a similar arena. The consumer figures out how to apply what is already known to something new.

After graduation, for example, a college varsity baseball player might be introduced by friends to the British sport, cricket. Noticing that it is quite similar to baseball in many ways (there is batting, fielding, catching, innings, etc.), he is then able to transfer many of his baseball skills to learning how to be a good cricket player. Likewise, roller skating skills could be used to learn how to ice skate. Or, if someone knows that paint thinner is flammable, she might figure out that when she runs out of charcoal fluid she can substitute some paint thinner instead.

Many products develop **secondary uses**, or new uses for a product, through consumers' or marketers' analogical reasoning. If baking soda gets rid of the refrigerator's "bad breath" effectively, perhaps it can remove odors from pet litter boxes and other smelly areas too.

VICARIOUS LEARNING (MODELING, OBSERVATIONAL LEARNING) THEORY

With **vicarious learning (modeling, observational learning, imitation, imitative behavior)**, the outcomes of others' behaviors, not one's own actions, are scrutinized, and learners then modify their own responses accordingly. That is, they imitate or model the other person's reinforced behavior.

Much vicarious learning differs from reasoning in that it is of low or moderate involvement. Vicarious learning is likely during incidental search, where people happenstance observe others using a product, such as friends sporting a new fashion, thereby garnering admiring looks. However, vicarious learning can also occur during intentional search where involvement is high, such as deliberately tracking what kinds of cars "successful" people drive. Observational learning is most apt to occur where the learner wishes to emulate a role model. For instance, a youngster might notice how popular another kid is because he just bought the latest WonderGizmo and everyone wants to try it out. So, the youngster runs out to Games R Us to get a WonderGizmo, too.

There are several pragmatic consumer advantages to using vicarious learning.

- Modeling helps avoid the mistakes of trial-and-error operant conditioning. Rather than sampling all of the different possibilities, new residents in a community often simply ask their new neighbors to recommend a bank, dentist, supermarket, and other local service providers.
- Vicarious learning can be quicker and easier than trying to learn on one's own through reasoning and self-guided instruction. To discover how to work a mobile telecommunications device, would you rather read through a clunky manual or have a friend explain the basics to you?
- Imitation can be safer than learning on one's own through instruction or reasoning. In fact, modeling can teach safety procedures for products with safety risks, such as power tools, by demonstrating unsafe practices.

Chapters 9 and 10 how showed how marketers can enlist *direct role models*, through family and word-of-mouth influence techniques, to influence their followers. Salespeople can also serve as direct role models by demonstrating products and otherwise assisting customers to see firsthand the benefits that products provide. Chapter 9 also discussed how advertising uses celebrities and the "common man" as *indirect (vicarious) role models*. Additionally, marketers can make their products or the consequences of product use readily observable. For instance, manufacturers of new car models sometimes park demonstration models in shopping malls and motorway service stations rather than shelling out big bucks for glossy magazine ads.

REVIEW QUESTIONS

1. Describe, compare, and contrast the two schools of learning and the four learning theories discussed in this exercise. Which theories correspond with which schools? What typically is the involvement level of someone learning in accordance with each of the theories? What are the major marketing applications of each of the learning theories? What are the limitations of each of the theories?
2. Explain the influence of consumer involvement and use of intentional versus incidental learning on which learning theory is most likely to be operative in a given marketplace situation.
3. Describe and explain the marketing usages of attitudinal conditioning and cognitive associative learning.
4. Explain the marketing applications of need association, attitudinal association, cognitive association, and cue association.
5. What is shaping, which learning theory does it relate to, and how is it used to influence CB?
6. What are the two multiple request techniques and how can they be used to affect buyer behavior?
7. Outline the cognitive reasoning process.
8. Describe analogical reasoning and explain its relationship to cognitive reasoning.
9. Explain vicarious learning, its advantages for learners, and its marketing applications.

IN-CLASS APPLICATIONS

1. Each of the ads in Exhibits 14.24 through 14.28 probably taught people about the brand, either by creating awareness of a brand name, gaining belief in a brand claim or purchase proposition, providing knowledge about a brand and its attributes, encouraging recognition and recall about various aspects of the brand, building a brand image, or forming a brand attitude.

   Identify the learning theory (or theories) that each ad seems to be tapping into. Explain exactly how each ad appears to be using that theory. Be as specific as possible. For example, if there is classical conditioning, is it need association, attitudinal association, or cue association?

   Does the theory used by each ad make sense, given the level of involvement and the way consumers typically learn about the product category and its brands (e.g., intentional versus incidental learning)? Can you suggest any improvements in the ad or a different learning theory the advertiser could draw on to effectively teach audience members?

2. For each of the following scenarios, identify and explain the type of learning theory that best explains the learner's information acquisition according to the marketing approach used. Given the nature of the typical consumer's product and/or purchase involvement and use of incidental versus intentional learning, did the marketer use an appropriate learning theory in each case? If not, what suggestions could you offer for educating the marketer's consumers?

   → *Scenario A. Sexy Sherri Sings the Soda.* Sweet 'n Delicious soft drinks have been using hottie singer Sherri Cola to plug their new line of Xtreme Sour flavors. She croons the name of Sweet 'n Delicious Xtreme Sour soda on TV and radio commercials, and her mug is splashed on billboards across the nation.

   → *Scenario B. Slick Billy Moves the Sheet Metal.* When it comes to selling, Billy Baily is one Slick Willie. He is the quintessential new car salesman at Road Apple Motor Works. Mr. Baily butters up his prospects with compliments, pats them on the back, and flatters them with a big, toothy grin. Not only does he offer test drives, Billy lets serious shoppers take the vehicle home for a day or two. If he thinks it will help close a deal, Billy even takes folks out for a nice meal. And, to clinch the sale, a rebate or zero-percent financing can work wonders.

   And it all works for him! Billy was Road Apple's number one car salesperson last year!

EXHIBIT 14.24   Cialis Ad

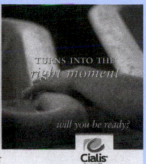

EXHIBIT 14.25   State Farm Insurance Ad

EXHIBIT 14.26   Total Gym Ad

EXHIBIT 14.27   The Vanguard Group Ad

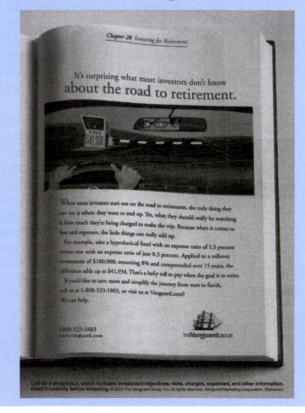

EXHIBIT 14.28   Sure Ad

→ *Scenario C. Candice Gears up First.* When it comes to buying pioneering new products, Candice is the trailblazer. She was the first in her circle of friends to buy a portable MP3 player, a DVD player, a Wi-Fi-enabled PC, an iPhone—you name it, she was there first! Because she is so knowledgeable about tech gear, Candy is the opinion leader within her clique. She tells her pals the ins and outs of shopping for high-tech goodies, and she never hesitates to make brand recommendations. Little do her buds know that the Swatchamacallit Corp. has enlisted Candice as a paid brand evangelist!

→ *Scenario D. A Byrd in the Hand Costs Less.* At his own retail establishment, Earl's Emporium, Earl E. Byrd sells major home appliances, such as washers, driers, refrigerators, and air conditioners. He lists all his products at very premium prices that almost no one will pay.

But word has gotten out: Shoppers can easily talk Earl down on price. For instance, he might advertise a stainless steel refrigerator for $1999. But when a buyer comes in and talks price, Earl E. will quickly relent with an excuse like, "It's a discounted model, so I'll knock $500 off for you."

→ *Scenario E. Everything's Fine and Dandy at Dandy's.* Dandy's Men's Clothiers treats its customers like royalty. The owner, Jim Dandy, encourages shoppers to try on clothes before they buy to ensure that the attire fits comfortably and looks right. He compliments them on how good they look in the garments. Plus, free cookies, coffee, and sodas are always on tap.

Jim insists that all salespeople treat customers like kings and queens. He also personally follows up after each sale to thank patrons and to make sure they are happy with their purchase.

→ *Scenario F. Problem-free Packaging.* Packaging Innovations, Inc., sends marketing researchers into consumers' homes to observe how they use nondurable packaged goods. The researchers are especially alert for problems people experience with packaging, such as difficulties in opening or resealing, troubles in storing, perceptions of unattractiveness, gripes about weight or size, and complaints about leakage, spillage, or breakage.

The researchers then inform their package designers about the consumer problems, which the design team sets about rectifying. Once a product is perfected, Packaging Innovations tries to sell it to one or more major manufacturer.

→ *Scenario G. You Can Teach an Old Connie New Tricks.* New technologies have always intimidated Connie. As a teenager during the 1960s, she had to learn to write papers on a typewriter in addition to using pen and paper. Just when she felt comfortable with a manual typewriter, during the 1970s she was given an electric typewriter. Although reluctant to use it at first, once she got the hang of it she found that it was very similar to using an old-fashioned typewriter, only faster and easier.

Not long after Connie had mastered the electric typewriter, her boss told her that she'd need to type her memos and reports on one of the new models launched during the 1980s. Although the idea of a typewriter having memory was scary at first, Ms. Fusion found that her keyboarding skills by and large transferred to the new machine.

Then, in the 1990s, Connie had to bite the bullet and convert to a personal computer (PC) with word processing. She was delighted to find that becoming comfortable with an electric typewriter enabled her to use a PC with confidence.

Just when she felt she was a whiz with the PC, along came the tablet PC in 2010. Connie could now do her typing with either a stylus pen or touchscreen while on the go. Although that little doohickey has taken a bit of getting used to, she now feels pretty comfy with it.

"What'll come down the typing pike next?" Connie wonders. Stay tuned! Mobile computing and voice recognition software continue to evolve.

3. Which learning theory best explains how you became familiar with each of the following product categories as well as one or more brands within that product category? What does that suggest for the marketing communications strategies used by marketers of that product?
   a. Pocket calculators
   b. Video game consoles
   c. Cough and cold medications
   d. Personal computers
   e. Sports equipment (pick your favorite sport)
   f. Cameras
   g. Cake mixes
   h. Smart cell phones

4. For each of the following scenarios, identify the five components of classical conditioning: UCS, unconditioned stimulus; UCR, unconditioned response; NS, neutral stimulus; CS, conditioned stimulus; and CR, conditioned response. Then, outline the following three stages of conditioning: the preconditioning relationship between the UCS and UCR, the conditioning pairing of the NS with the UCS and their association with the UCR, and the postconditioning relationship between the CS and the CR.

→ *Scenario A. Anna Mull's Dog Days.* Anna Mull was always a dog lover. Every time she saw someone walking a dog, she would run up and pet it, kiss it, and hug it, as though it was her own.

One day, Anna was walking to the store, and she saw the cutest little beagle. She ran up to it, but as she reached down to pet it, the dog bit her hand. She was immediately terrified of the dog because of the pain she was in.

The following day, she was walking home and spotted a friendly, loveable golden retriever. However, she would not go near the dog.

→ *Scenario B. Will Brighton Be Leaving?* Brighton was a hard worker who loved his job. He would always arrive on time for work with a smile on his face. Early one morning, his boss, Mr. Leeving, entered his office, called Brighton in, and told him that he was disappointed in how Brighton was performing and that he would be keeping an eye on him. Brighton did not take the news well.

Every day following that incident, when Mr. Leeving came in the office, Brighton would feel ashamed that he wasn't good enough, even without his boss saying another word.

→ *Scenario C. Giselle Pigs Out.* Giselle Pigg loves ice cream! Each afternoon, she waits for the ice cream man to come down her street ringing his bell so that she can get her favorite mouth-watering Drumstick novelty.

One day, Giselle was sitting around the house watching for the ice cream truck, and she heard the bell ring. Immediately her mouth started watering, even without having had any ice cream.

→ *Scenario D. Jane Salutes Sudso.* Jane never paid much attention to those TV commercials for Sudso detergent starring a happy homemaker delighting in her clothes being made clean and white from a wash in Sudso.

Recently, however, Sudso began a new ad campaign featuring patriotic songs in the background, such as "The Star Spangled Banner" and "America the Beautiful," with people dressed in clean red, white, and blue clothes. Even the Sudso box is now decked out in those three all-American colors.

Nowadays, when she sees a Sudso commercial, Jane feels so proud to be an American. And, when she passed by the Sudso section of the detergent aisle in the supermarket, she saluted the soap.

→ *Scenario E. Warren Loses the Peace.* Warren Piece always felt so stressed in the fast-paced, get-it-done-yesterday, war-zone environment at Brutus Brothers, Inc., where he works as an assistant vice co-president of Widget Polish. He loved to go home at 5 P.M. and chill out after hours by going to his refrigerator and grabbing a cold can of Fruit Blast soda.

A few weeks ago, however, Brutus Brothers installed a new vending machine loaded with Fruit Blast. Now, when Warren opens up the fridge at home and sees the soda, that peaceful feeling dissolves, and he turns into a mass of jagged nerves.

5. Think about a restaurant that you absolutely abhor. Why do you dislike this restaurant? Did you have a bad experience there? What makes you not want to try that restaurant again? Use the components of the classical conditioning model to explain.

6. Have you ever heard of claustrophobia? Or, how about arachnophobia? Check out a list of phobias on The Indexed Phobia List at http://www.phobialist.com/reverse.html and see how many there are! Why is this list so long? What has caused all of these fears? Do you suffer from any phobias? Do you believe you learned any of them?

   Apply the theory of classical conditioning to the root of phobias. A great example of creating fears is the "Little Albert" case. Here is your chance to see how classical conditioning can turn to horrible consequences. Visit *Classics in the History of Psychology: Conditioned Emotional Reactions* by John B. Watson and Rosalie Raynor at http://psychclassics.yorku.ca/Watson/emotion.htm. What do you think of this story? Is this experiment ethical?

7. What is your worst habit? Use principles of operant conditioning to devise a plan for stopping this bad habit. Make sure to identify the reinforcement schedule to be used and a specific reinforcer or punisher. If you are up for the challenge, see if you can eliminate this bad habit! If you do so, which learning theory did you use? (If you conquer your bad habit, congratulations! Be sure to tell your professor: Perhaps she'll give you extra credit!).

8. Do you think the practice of shaping CB is ethical? Can you identify any ethical issues with multiple request techniques?

9. Visit "Social Learning Theory" at http://tip.psychology.org/bandura.html to obtain information regarding cognitive psychologist Albert Bandura's social learning theory. Now, explore how his theory was put into action by reading the case study done on the infamous Bobo doll (*Classics in the History of Psychology: Transmission of Aggression Through Imitation of Aggressive Models* by Albert Bandura et al. at http://psychclassics.yorku.ca/Bandura/bobo.htm). Be sure to read the discussion section that pinpoints the study's importance and application. What do you think about the results of this experiment? How can media (especially television) take advantage of or (hopefully) learn from these results with regard to violence on television? Knowing about this experiment, how can marketers take advantage of or change their marketing strategies through products and advertising?

10. A psychologist named Edward Tolman explored behavioral psychology a bit further and discovered the idea of *latent learning*—the subject does not reveal that anything has been learned until a delayed period of time. Read through the study done by Tolman (*Classics in the History of Psychology: Cognitive Maps in Rats and Men* by Edward C. Tolman at http://psychclassics.yorku.ca/Tolman/Maps/maps.htm) and form an opinion on the topic of latent learning. Apply this concept (including the use of a cognitive map) in explaining how consumers know (a) how to get from their home to the mall, (b) how to find their way around in the mall, and (c) exactly locate where the sale racks are in one of the mall's stores.

   After doing so, apply the idea of a cognitive map to your own college or university campus—how did you learn your way around?

   How could a retailer or service establishment apply the results of this concept?

WRITTEN APPLICATIONS

1. Answer Question 1 in the In-Class Applications for four of the ads (Exhibits 14.24 through 14.28). Then, find four other ads, each of which uses one or more additional learning theories, and repeat the analysis for Question 1 in the In-Class Applications.

2. Answer Question 3 for three of the products listed in the question. Then, think of a product you learned about through either shaping or training, and another one you gained knowledge about through either analogical learning or vicarious learning. Describe your learning in each case, and analyze how effective you believe each marketer was in helping you to learn.

KEY CONCEPTS

advertising generalization
advertising retrieval cues
affect transferal
aided (cued) recall
analogy (analogical learning)
association
associative (incidental) learning
associative (semantic) network
attitudinal (emotional, affective) conditioning (mood association)
autobiographical memory
behavioral (behaviorist, stimulus-response, associative, contiguity, connectionist, conditioning) learning school
behaviorism
brand
brand franchise extension (brand extension)
brand mark (logotype [logo])
brand name
branding generalization (brand leveraging)
cachet (upgrading) by association
categorization
chunks
classical (respondent, Pavlovian) conditioning
cognitions
cognitive associative learning
cognitive learning
cognitive learning school
cognitive reasoning process
cognitive reasoning (reasoning) theory
concepts
conditioned response (CR)
conditioned stimulus (CS)
conditioning
continuous (total) reinforcement
copycat products
corporate (trade, umbrella) name
counterarguing
counterfeit (knockoff) merchandise
covert involvement

covert involvement advertising
cue association
cues (stimuli)
decay
door-in-the-face compliance technique
drive
echoic memory
elaboration
elaborative activities
elaborative (meaning-level, semantic) processing
episodic memory
experiential learning
extinction
family (look-alike, umbrella) packaging
family (umbrella) branding
fixed interval reinforcement
fixed ratio reinforcement
fixed (systematic) reinforcement
flights
foot-in-the-door compliance technique
forgetting
forgetting (decay) curve
guilt by association
habituation
hypothesis generation
hypothesis revision
hypothesis testing
iconic memory
imagery
imitative (emulative) brands
incidental (accidental, passive, iconic rote, associative) learning
instrumental conditioning (operant conditioning, reinforcement theory)
integrated marketing communication (IMC)
intellectual property
intentional (directed, purposive) learning
interference

(continued)

KEY CONCEPTS *(continued)*

kinesic communication
knowledge
knowledge structures
learning
learning curve
links
long-term memory
ludicrous juxtaposition
maintenance rehearsal (rehearsal)
massed advertising
mea culpa strategy
memories
memory
memory stores
memory trace strength
mental completion (closure)
mere exposure effect
message wearout (wearout, advertising wearout in an advertising context)
metaphor
mnemonics
multiple request techniques
multiple store theory
national brand
need association
negative punishment
negative reinforcement
neutral stimulus (NS)
nodes
nonverbal cues
operant (instrumental) conditioning (reinforcement theory)
package knockoffs (look-alike packaging)
partial reinforcement
positive punishment
positive reinforcement
primacy effect
primary reinforcers
private (house, store, dealer) brand (own label)
proactive inhibition
product generalization
product line extension
prototype
prototypical information
prototypical (master) brands
proxemic communication
pulsing
punishment
recall
recency effect

recirculation
recognition
redundancy
reinforcement
reinforcers
reminder advertising
response
retention
retrieval
retrieval cues
retroactive inhibition
salience
schedules of reinforcement
schema
schematic memory
script
secondary reinforcers
secondary uses
semantic generalization
semantic memory
sensory memory
sensory store
serial position effects (order of presentation)
shaping
short-term memory (short-term store, working memory)
simile
spaced (continuous, distributed) advertising
span of recall
stereotyping
stimulus discrimination
stimulus generalization
strength of learning
surface-level processing (sensory processing)
tactile communication
trade dress
trade dress infringement
trademarks
truth effect
unaided (free) recall
unconditioned response (UCR)
unconditioned stimulus (UCS)
upward stretch strategy (step-up extensions)
value brands
variable interval reinforcement
variable (random) reinforcement
variable ratio reinforcement
verbal cues
vicarious learning (modeling, observational learning, imitation, imitative behavior)
visual imagery

SUMMARY

The topic of learning is important because learning is one of the chief determinants of human behavior, and CB is primarily learned behavior. Prepurchase learning can be either intentional or incidental. The latter is also called associative learning because people learn associations between stimuli during a simple stimulus-response process via repetition and association, much of associative learning being classical conditioning. Motivated, high-involvement consumers engage in intentional learning, not incidental learning, and they actively seek out and consciously process information in a goal-directed fashion during prepurchase information search. Incidental learning is low-involvement learning.

There are various modes whereby people learn, ranging from simple, reflexive responses to purposeful problem solving. The various learning theories each explain a certain type of consumer learning process.

Exercise 14.1 investigated the structure of memory, retention of information in memories, and retrieval of that information from memory as well as forgetting.

Multiple store theory suggests that there are three interrelated memory stores, summarized in Exhibit 14.2. Sensory stimuli are captured by sensory memory in its sensory store. From here, the sensory information is either moved into short-term memory or is forgotten due to selective attention. Most important to most marketers in the sensory store are echoic memory (e.g., words, jingles, and background music, which can catch attention and convey meaning congruent with the message, thereby increasing learning) and iconic memory, such as visual images.

Short-term memory analyzes sensations and information from sensory memory and assigns meaning to them based on prior knowledge. Short-term memory's capacity is limited to a finite number of chunks and has a limited span of recall.

Although information might last for less than a minute in short-term memory, its meaning can be retained if it is subjected to one or more types of short-term memory information processing activities, that is, maintenance rehearsal, recirculation, and elaborative activities. Maintenance rehearsal presupposes consumer motivation. For low-involvement items, marketers must motivate consumers to learn or else use recirculation, a form of low-involvement learning.

To store information in their memories people can use either surface-level processing, which can occur through rehearsal or recirculation, or elaborative processing with its elaborative activities, including categorization and comprehension. Elaborative activities form a concept.

Information that is rehearsed, recirculated, and/or elaborated is transferred from short-term memory to long-term memory. Long-term knowledge structures include semantic memory; episodic memory (remembering a script); and schematic memory, where schema are organized and stored in long-term memory as an associative (semantic) network consisting of nodes connected through links. Memory trace strength is the extent to which an association or link is strongly or weakly joined to a concept in memory. Regarding recirculation, repetition increases the strength and speed of learning. With repeated exposure to the same information, learning increases, as shown by the learning curves in Exhibit 14.3. Strength of learning is greater with curve A than with curve B in this figure since it shows learning occurring more rapidly. With stronger learning there is a slower rate of forgetting.

The shape of the learning curve depends upon various informational and consumer characteristics. The more rapid learning of curve A will occur where the material to be learned is simple, straightforward, and unique, where the consumer is highly involved and therefore motivated to learn, the material to be learned is highly meaningful and relevant, the consumer already has some general familiarity with the material, and he or she is in a positive mood.

Although retention can be aided by overlearning, at some point there is message wearout, which occurs due to habituation and counterarguing. However, repetition can get consumers to like the marketer due to the mere exposure effect.

Regarding length of time for repetition, there are two general possibilities: massed versus spaced advertising. Regarding pattern of repetition, three possible media scheduling strategies are continuity, flights, and pulsing. Massed advertising can be in either flights or pulsing. The flighting pattern assumes that during the advertising hiatus there is advertising carryover but that forgetting eventually sets in and consumers need reminders. Pulsing is used in continuity patterns where it is believed that consumers need continual advertising exposure lest they forget, but extra weight is needed at times.

Spaced advertising is used for products with little or no seasonal sales patterns, if consumers tend to forget quickly if not reminded by advertising, where there is rapid buyer turnover, if competitors continuously advertise, and if constant reminders are necessary to avoid brand switching in high-frequency categories. If the advertiser wants consumers to learn rapidly, massed advertising is preferred. However, if more permanent learning is desired, spaced advertising is superior.

Principles of learning to aid in the elaborative process include:

- *Association.* Associative linkages are learned through either repetition (associative learning) or elaboration (analogy), using either simile or metaphor.
- *Mental completion.* Exercise 13.5 discussed closure techniques.
- *Covert involvement.* This often taps into episodic memory, or recalling events that involve the rememberer in order to create a vicarious consumption experience.
- *Semantic generalization.* Brand names can be words similar to words that are meaningful. Semantic generalization can entail a play on the brand name. Some brand names have been given meaning and made memorable by being used as verbs.
- *Visual imagery.* Elaborative processing can take the form of imagery, including visual imagery in the forms of visual images, verbal images, and aural images.
- *Ludicrous juxtaposition.* This creates an incongruity, which invites evaluation and involvement.
- *Mnemonics.* Techniques include alliteration, assonance, and onomatopoeia.

Learned information must be accessed from memory via retrieval. Recall requires extensive activation of the links in memory. Retrieval cues can be used to evoke three levels of recall: (1) unaided recall, (2) aided recall, and (3) recognition.

Another factor affecting degree of retrieval is the characteristics of the external stimulus to be remembered. The following traits help recall: salience, prototypicality (e.g., prototypical brands), and redundancy (e.g., integrated marketing communication).

Forgetting can occur due to decay, illustrated in the forgetting curve. This tendency to forget in the absence of repetition suggests the critical importance of reminder advertising. People forget quickly where information is boring, is not unique, and is complex. They also forget when they are uninvolved, find the information to be irrelevant or not very meaningful, are less familiar with the information, or are in a bad mood.

Generally, decay of events is less likely to occur or happens more slowly for happenings that are important, personal, unique, frequently occurring, and recently occurring.

Forgetting also occurs because of interference, which is either retroactive inhibition or proactive inhibition. Interference can be caused by serial position effects, which include the primacy effect and the recency effect, suggesting that the strongest positions within a commercial pod as well as within a print ad are the first and last places.

Exercise 14.2 investigated the four constituents of the learning process, emphasizing the interrelationships between them and their applications in helping consumers learn during the search and evaluation stage. The first element is drives and motives, which initiate the consumer decision-making process with problem recognition. Drives can be innate (inborn) or acquired (learned).

The second constituent of the learning process is cues, which can be classified either as verbal cues or nonverbal cues. Auditory communication is one form of verbal communication, such as tone of voice. Most human communication, however, is nonverbal in nature: kinesic, proxemic, and tactile communication. Advertising retrieval cues are found in ads as well as on packages, in-store signage, or any other locale where promotion can be found.

Stimulus generalization suggests that the more alike stimuli are, the more likely they are to be classified together, and hence the higher the probability that the same or a similar response will be elicited by both. Stimulus generalization entails categorization. There are a number of marketing applications of stimulus generalization:

• Marketers must avoid creating impressions of guilt by association and be ready to persuade buyers that false perceptions of association are misguided. Cachet by association explains the upward stretch strategy. One application of both guilt and cachet by association is stereotyping. Marketers should use upbeat stereotypes while avoiding potentially offensive negative characterizations.

• Product generalization or copycat products are cases where generalization occurs from one brand to another rival brand. Copycat products, which include imitative brands, may be confused with brands consumers have previously purchased or seen advertised. Copycat products also include value brands. Marketers of copycats might be setting themselves up for a trade dress infringement lawsuit. Trade dress is a type of trademark. Part of trade dress is the brand mark. Trade dress is a form of intellectual property. The likelihood of consumer confusion is the legal test used for trademark infringement. Marketers capitalizing on stimulus generalization sometimes imitate a rival's brand name, often in conjunction with package knockoffs, resulting in confusingly similar brand names. This causes shoppers to mistakenly believe that the new item is the rival's.

Package knockoffs are also a common form of trade dress infringement. Usually, the packaging of a national brand is imitated by the package of a private brand, often used in conjunction with selling against the brand. Counterfeiting merchandise is immoral and illegal.

Branding generalization entails a variety of stimulus generalization strategies using brands, brand names, and corporate names. Here, marketers attempt to get buyers to generalize from the reputation of their brand names through brand franchise extensions and product line extensions.

Sellers take advantage of the goodwill in their corporate names by using family branding, such as adding product identification to the corporate name (e.g., Kraft macaroni and cheese), and appending a brand name to the corporate name (e.g., Ford Aerostar). Sometimes family branding is implemented in conjunction with family packaging.

Advertising generalization is uninspired copycat advertising mimicking competitors' ads.

Opposite to stimulus generalization is stimulus discrimination, usually practiced by market leaders. Many marketing stimuli can be used to create brand distinctions, including breakthrough advertising, brand names, packaging, logos, trade characters, and slogans.

The third basic element of the learning process is the learner's response to the drive or stimulus, which can include overt and covert reactions.

The final learning component is reinforcement. Exhibit 14.11 summarizes positive reinforcement, negative reinforcement, punishment, and extinction.

Positive reinforcement occurs through primary and secondary reinforcers. Most marketers provide their customers with positive reinforcement, such as a want-satisfying product, informative and entertaining ads, or sales promotional incentives.

Marketers must choose from among schedules of reinforcement. Exhibit 14.12 summarizes the options. The most rapid learning happens with continuous reinforcement. However, learning will be more permanent but slower with partial reinforcement. This encourages people to keep trying, in hopes that maybe next time they will be reinforced. Partial reinforcement is harder to extinguish than continuous reinforcement.

Continuous reinforcement is critical regarding product quality, courteous service, and other consumer desires and expectations. Continuous reinforcement during the relevant time frame is also appropriate for messages to be learned quickly. Continuous reinforcement can be achieved through a continuous media schedule.

Regarding partial reinforcement, the possibilities are variable interval reinforcement and variable ratio reinforcement. Fixed reinforcement includes fixed interval reinforcement and fixed ratio reinforcement.

Negative reinforcement, like positive reinforcement, increases the probability of response. However, punishment decreases the probability of response and is avoided. Extinction's purpose is to reduce the likelihood that the behavior will be repeated. Punishment is generally more rapid than extinction in its ability to halt an unwanted action, although it is more likely to induce negative feelings and resentment. Extinction differs from forgetting in that it happens because a response is not reinforced. Marketers must be cautious in making radical changes to their marketing mix elements, for such modifications can also extinguish buyer behavior. An application of extinction is the mea culpa strategy.

Exercise 14.3 described and explained two different schools of thought and four associated learning theories regarding how people acquire and remember information. The relationships between the schools of thought and the theories are outlined in Exhibit 14.18. A key determinant of how much and the nature of how people learn is their degree of involvement (see Exhibit 14.18).

The major contrast is between the behavioral and the cognitive learning schools. The older behavioral school studies how organisms respond to environmental stimuli by focusing on observable behavior.

The underlying belief is determinism. However, the cognitive school focuses on understanding a person's mind.

According to the behavioral learning school, observable reactions to external stimuli indicate that learning has occurred. Such learning is conditioning, a form of associative learning, which also occurs in both classical conditioning and operant conditioning.

Classical conditioning theory uses an existing stimulus-response relationship to create the learning of the same or a similar response to a different stimulus. Learners relate an unconditioned stimulus (US) (which was originally a neutral stimulus [NS]), which results in an unconditioned response (UCR), with a conditioned stimulus (CS), which leads to a conditioned response (CR). Classically conditioned learning is passive; it is unconscious, automatic, and involuntary. Stimulus-response linkages are learned through a process of repetition, contiguity, and association. Exhibit 14.19 diagrams the classical conditioning process.

With attitudinal conditioning, emotional responses to the advertiser's brand are formed (see Exhibit 14.20) through affect transferal. The advertiser connects the brand with good feelings, such as those generated by the ad's music, celebrities, and emotional appeals. Attitudinal conditioning is generally most effective for parity products lacking persuasive points of difference. However, where there are brand distinctions, marketing communications can teach people about these differences through cognitive associative learning.

Especially effective for conditioning CB is creating the right connections between the brand and needs, moods and emotions, and cues. Tools include need association, attitudinal association, and cue association. A limitation of classical conditioning is that it assumes low-involvement consumers.

The second behaviorist theory, operant conditioning, suggests that responses are best learned when they are reinforced by stimuli. Such learning is active, conscious, and voluntary, suggesting a higher level of involvement than that found in classical conditioning situations. Response-stimulus links are taught via rewards and punishments obtained through trial and error. The main distinction between classical and operant conditioning is that with classical conditioning, an organism learns associations between events it cannot control and responds involuntarily, whereas with operant conditioning, the learning involves making a connection between behavior and consequent rewarding or punishing events, and the response is volitional. Exhibit 14.21 outlines the operant conditioning learning process.

While classical conditioning is most useful for explaining simple, low-involvement purchases, instrumental conditioning better accounts for more complex, goal-directed behavior under conditions of at least moderate involvement. Here, consumers must be willing to make the effort to undergo trial-and-error learning. Brand habits are acquired as a consequence of receiving rewards for purchasing and consuming. Customer satisfaction is crucial! Also, shaping can be used to "train" consumers by encouraging partial responses leading to the final desired response, such as offering a free new product sample followed by a coupon offer. Another application of shaping involves multiple request techniques: the foot-in-the-door and door-in-the-face compliance techniques.

Reinforcement theory has its limitations. It assumes that rewards or punishments are necessary for learning to take place. Like classical conditioning, it is limited to observing simple, mechanistic S-R linkages. Furthermore, humans are seen as manipulable products of their environment and not as sovereign. Behaviorism ignores people's thoughts, reasoning, feelings, evaluation, and other unobservable responses, even though these are often an important part of learning.

The newer cognitive learning school, summarized in Exhibit 14.22, centers on these unobservable cognitions. This approach proposes that people learn by acquiring information and then using it for problem-solving purposes in an active thinking and reasoning process.

Cognitive reasoning theory, the first cognitive theory, says that learning entails creative thinking to restructure and recombine existing and/or new information to form new associations and concepts. Cognitive reasoning is an active, high-involvement process in which people deliberately seek out and apply information. Exhibit 14.23 outlines the cognitive reasoning model: the learner perceives a goal (need satisfaction), engages in purposive activities to help achieve the goal (information search and alternative evaluation), has an insightful "eureka" experience (insight learning), and achieves the goal (buys a brand). Cognitive learning theory suggests marketers must get prospects to perceive their products as satisfiers of their needs.

The cognitive reasoning process consists of three steps:

1. Hypothesis generation.
2. Hypothesis testing, gathering information through either education, including training, or through personal experience. Consumers generally initiate informal consumer education through information search and alternative evaluation activities.

   Learning through personal experience (experiential learning) involves using products. Marketers encourage prepurchase learning through offering "test runs" with durables and samples of nondurables. Later, postpurchase experiential learning occurs.
3. Hypothesis revision. After exposure to and evaluation of the marketplace information, the consumer's prior beliefs (hypotheses) are either confirmed or revised if the information shows prior perceptions to be false.

   A particular type of cognitive reasoning uses analogy. Many products develop additional usages (secondary uses) through analogical reasoning.

   Vicarious learning, the second cognitive theory, concerns modeling, which can be either incidental search or intentional search. Observational learning is most apt to occur where the learner wishes to emulate a role model. People model others' behavior for several reasons: It helps one avoid the mistakes of trial-and-error learning, it is quicker and easier than reasoning and self-guided instruction, and it can be safer than learning on one's own.

REFERENCES

Allen, Chris T., and Madden, Thomas J. (1985). "A Closer Look at Classical Conditioning." *Journal of Consumer Research,* 12, 3, 301–315.

Atkinson, R. C., and Shiffrin, I. M. (1968). "Human Memory: A Proposed System and Its Control Processes." In K. W. Spence and J. T. Spence, eds., *The Psychology of Learning and Motivation: Advances in Research and Theory,* 2. New York: Academic Press.

Bergiel, Blaise J., and Trosclair, Christine. (1985). "Instrumental Learning; Its Application to Customer Satisfaction." *Journal of Consumer Marketing,* 2, 4, 23–28.

Cohen, Dorothy. (1972). "Surrogate Indicators and Deception in Advertising." *Journal of Marketing,* 36, 3, 10–15.

Du Plessis, Erik. (1994). "Recognition Versus Recall." *Journal of Advertising Research,* 34, 3, 75–91.

Feldwick, Paul. (1996). "What Is Brand Equity Anyway, and How Do You Measure It?" *Journal of the Market Research Society,* April, 85–104.

Gaidis, William, and Cross, James. (1987). "Behavior Modification as a Framework for Sales Promotion Management." *Journal of Consumer Marketing,* 4, 2, 65–74.

Gorn, Gerald J. (1982). "The Effects of Music in Advertising on Choice Behavior: A Classical Conditioning Approach." *Journal of Marketing,* 46, 1, 94–101.

Gregnan-Paxton, J., and John, D. R. (1997). "Consumer Learning by Analogy: A Model of Internal Knowledge Transfer." *Journal of Consumer Research,* 24, 3, 26–285.

Hawkins, Scott A., and Hoch, Stephen J. (1992). "Low-Involvement Learning: Memory Without Evaluation." *Journal of Consumer Research,* 19, 2, 212–225.

Krugman, Herbert E. (1965). "The Impact of Television Advertising: Learning Without Involvement." *Public Opinion Quarterly,* 29, 309–313.

Mao, Huifag, and Krishnan, H. Shanker. (2006). "Effects of Prototype and Exemplar Fit on Brand Extension Evaluations: A Two-Process Contingency Model." *Journal of Consumer Research,* 33, 1, 41–49.

Martinez, Eva, and de Chernatony, Leslie. (2004). "The Effect of Brand Extension Strategies upon Brand Image." *Journal of Consumer Marketing,* 21, 4, 39–50.

McSweeney, Frances K., and Bierley, Calvin. (1984). "Recent Developments in Classical Conditioning." *Journal of Consumer Research,* 11, 2, 619–631.

Miller, George A. (1956). "The Magical Number Seven, Plus or Minus Two: Some Limits on Our Capacity for Processing Information." *Psychological Review,* 63, 81–97.

Nord, Walter R., and Peter, J. Paul. (1980). "A Behavior Modification Perspective on Marketing." *Journal of Marketing,* 44, 2, 36–47.

Peter, J. Paul, and Nord, Walter R. (1982). "A Clarification and Extension of Operant Conditioning Principles in Marketing." *Journal of Marketing,* 46, 3, 102–107.

Pitta, Dennis, and Katsanis, Lea Prevel. (1995). "Understanding Brand Equity for Successful Brand Extension." *Journal of Consumer Marketing,* 12, 4, 51–64.

Ray, Michael. (1973). "Psychological Theories and Interpretations of Learning." In Scott Ward and Thomas S. Robertson, eds., *Consumer Behavior: Theoretical Sources.* Englewood Cliffs, NJ: Prentice-Hall, 45–17.

Rotfeld, Herb. (2007). "Theory, Data, Interpretations and More Theory." *Journal of Consumer Affairs,* 41 (Winter 2007), 376–379.

Rothschild, M., and Gaidis, William C. (1981). "Behavioral Learning Theory: Its Relevance to Marketing and Promotions." *Journal of Marketing,* 45, 2, 70–78.

Skinner, B. F. (1953). *Science and Human Behavior.* New York: Macmillan.

———. (1971). *Beyond Freedom and Dignity.* New York: Bantam/Vintage Books.

Staats, Arthur. W., and Staats, C. K. (1958). "Attitudes Established by Classical Conditioning." *Journal of Abnormal and Social Psychology,* 57, 37–40.

Stuart, Elnora W., Shimp, Terence A., and Engle, Randall W. (1987). "Classical Conditioning of Consumer Attitudes." *Journal of Consumer Research,* 14, 3, 334–349.

Till, Brian D., and Priluck, Randi Lynn. (2000). "Stimulus Generalization in Classical Conditioning: An Initial Investigation and Extension." *Psychology and Marketing,* 17, 1, 5–72.

Trout, Jack, and Rivkin, Steve. (2000). *Differentiate or Die.* New York: John Wiley and Sons.

Urdem, Tulin. (1998). "An Empirical Analysis of Umbrella Branding." *Journal of Marketing Research,* 35, 3, 339–351.

Young, James Webb. (1965). *A Technique for Producing Ideas.* Chicago: Advertising Publications.

Zaichkowsky, Judith Lynne. (2006). *The Psychology Behind Trademark Infringement and Counterfeiting.* Mahwah, NJ: Lawrence Erlbaum Associates.

CHAPTER 15

ATTITUDE FORMATION AND CHANGE

THE PLACE OF ATTITUDES AND ATTITUDE MODELS IN CONSUMER PSYCHOLOGY AND THE BUYER DECISION PROCESS

Attitudes, which are positive or negative evaluations of marketplace phenomena, develop during the alternative evaluation stage of the consumer decision-making process. An attitude is based on a person's perceptions of a stimulus and the consequent information learned regarding the stimulus. During alternative evaluation, buyers develop beliefs about (perceptions of) and preferences for (favorable predispositions toward) a marketplace option, i.e., the **attitude object (AO),** the entity toward which the attitude is held. These beliefs and preferences are based on the information a consumer has processed and learned about the AO and they form the foundation for a prepurchase attitude toward the AO. A postpurchase attitude toward this same AO might be altered during the postpurchase evaluation stage due to possible dissonance and changes in buyer satisfaction/dissatisfaction.

There are four basic marketing objectives related to consumer attitudes.

1. *Adapt to attitudes.* Make the brand (the AO) and its marketing program fit already existing attitudes rather than vice versa. If many consumers want a low-calorie version of a marketer's goose grease, the seller should figure out a way to formulate one.
2. *Reinforce attitudes.* Encourage customers to maintain their favorable brand attitudes.
3. *Form attitudes.* Shift people from lacking a brand attitude to having one via informing and persuading them.
4. *Change attitudes.* Transform people's brand attitudes from less to more favorable (or vice versa for a competitor's brand).

Objectives 1 and 2 are easier to achieve than are goals 3 and 4. Ordinarily, a firm could try to fit its products into existing attitudes rather than try to alter attitudes. Accordingly, Coca-Cola's Fuze is a tasty line of "healthy infusion" beverages brimming with vitamins, minerals, and antioxidants but lacking artificial preservatives, sweetener, or colors.

Points 3 and 4 are the more difficult marketing objectives to achieve. They are related to **attitude molding**, or attitude formation and change. Favorable attitude molding is what much marketing activity tries to achieve via launching new or improved products, offering wallet-friendly prices, distributing through preferred channels, or providing informative and entertaining marketing communications. In promotional activity, attitude molding involves **persuasion**, an explicit attempt to influence people's beliefs, attitudes, and/or behaviors, that is, to change their minds. Persuasion occurs when an attitude is initially formed (i.e., a position is first formed regarding an attitude object [AO]; point 3) or an existing attitude is changed (i.e., a position is altered regarding an AO; point 4).

In order to understand how to shape attitudes, psychologists have devised various **attitude models**. These theories portray the underlying dimensions of attitudes in order to help marketers mold attitudinal dimensions. Each model offers a somewhat different outlook on the number of attitude dimensions and their interrelationships.

THE NATURE OF ATTITUDES

An attitude is an overall evaluation of an AO, which expresses a degree of favor or disfavor toward it. Attitudes represent what we like and dislike about an AO; they are an evaluative reaction to it. The AO can be abstract or concrete, individual or collective. It can be an object (person, group, place, or thing), issue, situation, activity, or behavior. For marketing purposes, common AOs include products, brands, services, retailers, organizations, media, Web sites, possessions, people, oneself (self-image or self-esteem), advertisements, salespeople, causes, issues, and product uses. All of these AOs fall within the realm of the **attitude-toward-the-object model**, which measures attitudes toward AOs. This model is most commonly used by marketers to measure attitudes toward a product (or service) category or toward a specific brand.

In this chapter we shall usually assume that the AO is a brand since the type of attitude of greatest concern to marketers is **brand attitude** (A_b), consumers' learned tendencies to evaluate brands in a consistently favorable or unfavorable manner. A_b is typically determined by consumer evaluation of a brand's performances on evaluative criteria. For example, if Papa Razzi's potato chips are spicy and salty and you like chips that are spicy and salty, you probably will have a positive attitude toward Papa Razzi's. However, if you do not care for spicy, salty chips, your brand attitude toward Papa Razzi's will likely be negative. Brand attitude can also be based on *affect referal,* i.e., emotions associated with the brand.

Another common AO is **attitude toward the ad** (A_{ad}), whether or not a message recipient likes a particular advertisement during a particular exposure occasion. A_{ad} is a function of the advertiser, the message, the creative execution, the medium in which the ad appears, and emotions aroused by the ad. If there is affect transferal, A_{ad} will influence the consumer's A_b.

Additionally, there is the **attitude-toward-the-behavior model** (attitude towards the act, A_{act}), which concerns behavior regarding an AO (such as purchasing a brand or patronizing a store) rather than the attitude toward the AO itself. Generally, this model correlates more closely with CB than does the attitude toward the object model because unanticipated circumstances such as stockouts or price increases sometimes prevent shoppers from procuring their preferred brand. Thus, situational factors influence the relationship between an attitude and a behavior. A specific situation can cause buyers to behave in seemingly disparate ways vis-à-vis their attitudes. You might believe Wendy's is a great place to take your spouse and kids for a nice family meal, but you would not dare darken their door with clients or your boss for a business lunch.

Although attitudes are typically held toward objects or behaviors, they can also exist at a very general abstract level as **cultural attitudes**, such as the importance of family, punctuality for appointments, and proper dress for various occasions as taught by society.

ATTITUDE'S KINDRED CONCEPTS

The concept of an attitude should be distinguished from several closely related constructs. An **opinion** is a verbal (spoken or written) expression of an attitude. Attitudes are measured either by requesting people's opinions or by observing their overt behavior. Since interviewees are sometimes unwilling or unable to offer their opinions, one must instead observe what they do to infer their attitudes. For instance, if Abbie Birthday drinks a can of Bullmoose Soda, we can reasonably assume she likes Bullmoose (although this assumption might be false if, for instance, she consumes it because a friend serves it to her, unaware that Abbie dislikes Bullmoose).

A **preference** represents someone's attitude toward one AO in relation to another. Brand preferences can be measured by asking respondents to rank order several brands in a product category.

A **belief** is a perception of or subjective judgment linking an AO to a particular attribute of that object (e.g., "I think that the Smasher Gasher video game is challenging"). As such, a belief is emotionally neutral. According to the multi-attribute attitude mode, beliefs about an AO's ratings on various attributes, along with the person's weighting or evaluation of those attributes, form an attitude.

Central beliefs are strongly held and lie at the core of a person's cognitive structure (e.g., "God is the Creator of life"). Beliefs regarding oneself tend to be central (e.g., "I am an honest person"). **Peripheral beliefs** are less important than central beliefs, are not centrally held, and are anchored (tied) to central beliefs. For instance, the peripheral belief, "Smitty's seafood is the best" could be tied to more central beliefs about the importance of healthy and tasty foods to one's lifestyle and diet.

Values are relatively enduring, general, abstract ideals, positive or negative, not tied to any specific object or situation. They concern what is desirable regarding goals and the means for accomplishing them. Relative to attitudes and beliefs, values are:

- More general (not tied to specific AOs)
- More centrally held, and hence more enduring and difficult to change
- More widely accepted by most members of society
- Fewer in number

Cultural values relate to attitudes in that they govern which evaluative criteria or attributes buyers look for in products. Someone who values health will prefer food and drink high in nutritional value.

CHARACTERISTICS OF ATTITUDES

The following aspects of attitude determine the nature and degree of their influence on consumer behavior (CB).

ATTITUDE AVAILABILITY AND ACCESSIBILITY

In order to know what consumers' attitudes toward the marketer's brand are, those attitudes need to be measured. Two factors that are prerequisites for valid attitude measurement are **attitude availability**, that is, whether consumers have an evaluation of an object in their memory stores, and **attitude accessibility**, whether people can retrieve an available attitude from memory at any given moment. Accessible attitudes are "top of mind."

It is critical that attitude questionnaires tap into accessible attitudes. Attitudes are more accessible for AOs that are:

- *Important.* Few people can recall their attitude toward the brand of frozen peas they bought three years ago, but they do remember how they felt about the make and model of automobile that they purchased around the same time.
- *Unique.* You are more likely to recollect your feelings during your commute to work on a day of gridlock caused by a five-car accident than on the typical, ho-hum day. Likewise, consumers are more likely to recall how they feel about a brand they find extremely satisfactory or unsatisfactory.
- *Frequently encountered.* Rusty Carr can better discuss his attitude toward Donut Dive, where he goes every day for a coffee break, than toward Hamburger Heaven, where he has only eaten twice.
- *Recently encountered.* Winnie DiPoo is probably more aware of how she likes *Reality Sets In,* a TV program she watched yesterday evening, than *The Adventures of Alec Tricity,* a show she has not viewed in six months.

ATTITUDE FAVORABILITY (DIRECTION, VALENCE)

Attitude favorability (direction, valence) entails to what extent people like or dislike an AO. As is true of motives, attitudes have **valence (direction)**, ranging from very positive to very negative.

An important issue to measurement of attitude direction is whether attitudes, as a hypothetical construct, are conceptualized as unidimensional or multidimensional. **Unidimensional attitudes** are viewed as a position on a continuum along one general dimension regarding an AO, ranging from very favorable to very unfavorable. Taking a unidimensional view, we could ask patrons to rate their overall experience in shopping at Penny Pincher's Clothiers on a scale ranging from "excellent" to "horrible."

A **multidimensional attitude** perspective, as is represented in most surveys, considers the evaluation of an AO as occurring along several dimensions. Here, we would enquire about shoppers' opinions regarding Penny's selection, prices, salespeople, location, and the store's performance on other relevant evaluative criteria, each evaluated along a scale (low to high).

A person's attitude is ambivalent if he or she rates an AO favorably on some criteria and unfavorably on others. Such attitudes are less stable and balanced, and, hence, are easier to modify. This suggests that marketers should ensure that their products perform well on all important dimensions. It also implies that marketers will find it easier to persuade rivals' customers if they hold ambivalent attitudes toward the rivals' brands.

ATTITUDE STRENGTH

Like motives, attitudes have strength. **Attitude strength (importance, intensity)** concerns the degree of influence an attitude has on someone's behavior. **Strong (central) attitudes** are highly accessible and strong, or held with high confidence and commitment. Strong attitudes are based on *central beliefs*, while **weak (peripheral) attitudes** are founded on *peripheral beliefs*. Strong attitudes are those that people are more deeply committed to, are able to easily access, and of which the individual is quite confident. Compared with weak attitudes, strong attitudes are more resistant to subsequent change. For example, most college professors have strong attitudes regarding the importance of higher education and would oppose attempts to alter them.

Such centrally held attitudes serve as anchoring points for other related **peripheral attitudes**, or attitudes that are less important and weaker than central attitudes. Hence, a person who strongly believes that "men are insensitive" might also believe that "men are lousy gift givers because they don't care much." A woman might view herself as a competent hostess. Consequently, her attitude toward a brand of coffee, while not as strong as her feelings about herself, would nonetheless be somewhat important if she believed that serving good coffee reflected on her hospitality skills.

Although there is sometimes a disconnect between attitudes and behavior due to situational influences, stronger attitudes toward an AO are more likely than weaker attitudes to correlate with future behavior toward that AO, that is, they are high in predictive validity.

Attitudes formed as a consequence of direct personal experience (e.g., product usage) tend to be stronger than those resulting from indirect personal experience (e.g., advertising, word of mouth, and watching others use a product). This again highlights the importance of "buying customer experience" through free samples, low-cost trial offers, and "test runs."

Informed attitudes are more strongly held. Marketers should therefore ensure that buyers are well informed about the marketer's brand as well as the marketplace in general.

As is true of motivational strength, attitudinal strength correlates with consumer involvement. The more that a product purchase is involving, i.e., has perceived personal importance and relevance, the stronger the buyer's attitude toward that product will be.

Clearly, marketers prefer to create strong, favorable brand attitudes. However, brand attitudes are often weak and are therefore relatively easy to shift, unless consumers are brand loyal, in which case there is attitudinal loyalty.

Marketing communicators should not attack central beliefs and attitudes since this will usually be futile. Rather, they should tie their brands into central attitudes, i.e., adapt to and reinforce central attitudes rather than mold them. If targeted customers are highly patriotic, the product could be pitched as "made in America." Likewise, marketers of edutainment toys and games take advantage of parents' central attitudes regarding the importance of a good education.

It is, however, easier for sellers to alter peripheral beliefs and attitudes. If you launch a new brand into a market where brand loyalty is nil, you stand a better chance of making sales than if you try to break into a market filled with brand loyalists.

ATTITUDINAL STABILITY

Attitudes that are not prone to waver, even in the face of attempts to change them, are said to have **attitudinal stability**. We have just seen that stability correlates with attitude strength, and, therefore, involvement. Stability is also directly related to a person's confidence in his or her judgment.

ATTITUDINAL SALIENCE

Attitudinal salience refers to an attitude's relevance in a particular situation. Attitude salience varies across times and places. One's attitude toward Campbell's soup is not as relevant at breakfast time as at lunchtime, unless an individual is grocery shopping during the breakfast hour.

Also, the salience of one's evaluative criteria differs among products. A low price might be critical to the purchase of a new PC but not as important for buying a flash drive for that PC.

ATTITUDE COMPONENTS (DIMENSIONS)

An **attitude structure** consists of the attitude's various components and their relationships to one another. Based on the three attitudinal components, an attitude can be defined as a predisposition to think, feel, or behave in a positive or negative way toward an AO. The three attitudinal components are cognitive (think), affective (feel), and conative (behave).

1. **Cognitive attitude component.** This is the thinking, knowledge, or intellectual dimension. It consists of **cognitions**, or the manner in which the AO is perceived. These bits of knowledge, ideas, and perceptions about an AO acquired through information acquisition are referred to as descriptive (existential) beliefs or only beliefs. Cognitions are nonevaluative statements about an object's performance on various attributes. Example: Brite 'N White toothpaste has a refreshing, minty flavor and leaves teeth sparkling white.

2. **Affective attitude component.** This is the feeling, emotional, and mood component. **Affect** concerns evaluations, feelings, emotions, and moods regarding either an AO or its performance on specific criteria. The affective dimension entails **evaluative beliefs** about how good or bad an AO is, as well as an evaluation of its performance on evaluative criteria. Example: "Brite 'N White toothpaste tastes good (linked to the 'minty' descriptive belief) and makes my teeth look great (due to the belief that it whitens teeth)."

3. **Conative attitude component.** This component lies within the realm of the will (volition). It concerns people's behavioral intentions, that is, their attitude toward the behavior or how likely they are to act upon their knowledge or feelings. It also concerns their overt behaviors, that is, whether they do, indeed, act on their attitudes and intentions.

The conative dimension involves what one will or should do, based upon the cognitive and affective dimensions. Example: "The next time I go shopping, I should pick up a tube of Brite 'N White toothpaste because it has a refreshing minty flavor that makes it taste good."

ORGANIZATION OF CHAPTER 15

There are a number of models of persuasion and consequent attitude transformation strategies. Attitude models and attitude molding strategies can be classified according to two dimensions: 1) which of the three *attitude components* (cognitive, affective, or connative) they are linked to, and 2) whether the consumer's *elaboration likelihood* (motivation to process information) is high-effort (central route) or low-effort (peripheral route) information processing, as affected by the degree of consumer involvement and as reflected by how deep that information processing is. These two dimensions give us the classification scheme shown in Exhibit 15.1.

Exercise 15.1 discusses the two dimensions shown in Exhibit 15.1, the first being the tricomponent (ABC) model, which breaks attitudes into their cognitive, affective, and conative (ABC) components. Also investigated are the marketing research methodologies appropriate for measuring each of the components in order to determine whether marketing efforts have either formed or modified attitudes in accordance with marketing objectives.

Second, Exercise 15.1 explains the elaboration likelihood model that suggests there are two distinctly different routes to persuasion that depend on consumers' motivation (involvement), ability, and opportunity (MOA) to process information and make decisions These persuasion routes are central-route processing, when MOA is high and consequently much effort is put into information processing and decision making, and peripheral-route processing, where MOA is low and consumers expend little energy on processing information and making choices.

The last two exercises look at specific attitude models and related attitude molding strategies, each of which corresponds to one of the three elements in the tricomponent model. Exercise 15.2 tackles the more traditional and commonly used models and strategies related to the cognitive component. This is the decision-making perspective, which suggests that the persuasion process begins with a change in beliefs.

Exercise 15.3 discusses the experiential perspective, which relates to the affective component and entails altering attitudes emotionally or experientially, and the behavioral influence perspective, which corresponds to the conative component. With regard to the latter, Exercise 15.3 covers strategies to get consumers to take action, such as trying or buying a product, thereby inducing attitude transformation. Exercise 15.3 concludes by tying together the three persuasion perspectives, relating them to the hierarchy of the effects communication model.

EXHIBIT 15.1   General Approaches for Attitude Formation and Change

Attitudes are based on:

		Cognitions (thoughts, beliefs)	Affect (feelings/emotions)	Connation (intentions and actions)
		Decision-making perspective	Experiential perspective	Behavioral influence perspective
Degree of consumer elaboration	High effort central-route processing	Cognitive response model Multiattribute models Functional theory Balance theory	Emotional appeals Attitude toward the ad	Operant conditioning Cognitive dissonance theory Attribution theory
	Low effort peripheral-route processing	Simple beliefs	Mere exposure effect Classical conditioning Attitude toward the ad Mood	Passive learning

Source: This diagram is a variation of one found in Wayne D. Hoyer and Deborah J. MacInnis, *Consumer Behavior,* 3d ed. (Boston: Houghton Mifflin Company, 2004), p. 131.

EXERCISE 15.1. THE TRICOMPONENT (ABC) ATTITUDE MODEL AND THE ELABORATION LIKELIHOOD MODEL

OBJECTIVES

1. To understand the nature of the two dimensions that determine appropriate models and strategies for attitude molding: the tricomponent model and the elaboration likelihood model.
2. To understand the nature of each of the three dimensions in the tricomponent model—cognitive, affective, and conative—and to recognize, explain the use of, and critically evaluate appeals to each of these three attitude components in advertisements and how these appeals relate to advertising objectives.
3. To recognize appeals to central- versus peripheral-route processing.
4. To gain experience in recognizing and creating questions using the various types of attitude scales and other questioning techniques for learning about attitudes.

BACKGROUND

THE TRICOMPONENT (ABC) ATTITUDE MODEL

According to the **tricomponent (ABC—affect, behavior, cognition) attitude model**, attitudes toward objects (AOs) consist of three major dimensions: cognition, affect, and connation. Attitudes founded on cognitions (thoughts, beliefs) are based on information received from an external information source. Attitudes grounded in affect (feelings) are emotionally based, that is, the AO is liked simply because it feels

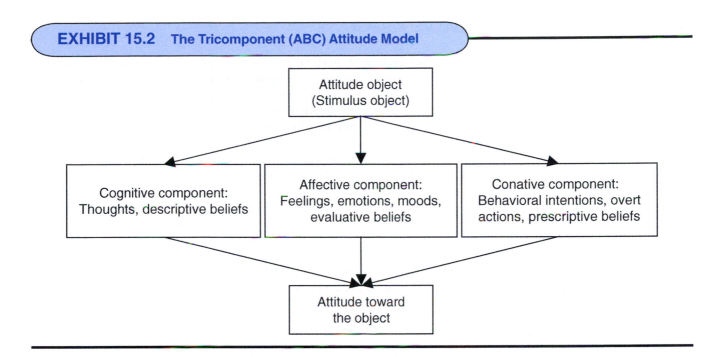

EXHIBIT 15.2   The Tricomponent (ABC) Attitude Model

good or seems right. Attitudes based on connation (intentions and actions) usually result from personal experience or behavioral intent. Exhibit 15.2 summarizes the tricomponent model.

We now investigate each of these attitude components, how to mold attitudes using each of them, and how each can be measured using marketing research.

THE COGNITIVE COMPONENT: BELIEFS

The first attitude dimension is cognition. This information is organized as **descriptive beliefs (beliefs)**, or nonevaluative perceptions about how an AO rates or performs on various product criteria. The total configuration of descriptive beliefs comprises a brand's cognitive component. These beliefs usually concern physical product features and psychological consumer benefits (i.e., satisfactions delivered by the features).

For example, Rhoda Dendren has objective beliefs that the Plummeting Prices DVD player costs $60, plays both Super Audio CDs and DVD-Audio disks, and has a 400-disc megachanger. Resulting benefits are that the low price of $60 will save her money, and the 400-disc megachanger will mean Rhoda need not load disks as often.

THE AFFECTIVE COMPONENT: FEELINGS

The second type of attitude component is affect. Affective components entail subjective beliefs containing evaluations of like or dislike—perceptions influenced by personal taste, such as picture and sound quality produced by a DVD player. Affect also consists of emotional benefits. Statements such as "I enjoy jazz music" or "I can't stand the taste of diet soda" reflect emotional benefits.

These subjective beliefs and emotional benefits are also known as *evaluative beliefs*. That is, affect is made up of the way people feel about or evaluate their descriptive beliefs. Additionally, emotional states of mind need not be rooted in cognitive beliefs. They might simply reflect a vague, general feeling or mood. The entire package of evaluative beliefs constitutes a brand's affective component.

For instance, Rhoda has subjective beliefs that the DVD player has an ultra-low price, gives crisp picture quality, yields excellent sound quality, and carries a trusted brand name. Owning a Plummeting Price DVD player will help Rhoda experience emotional benefits, such as feeling technologically on top of things, and the brand's downscale image will help her feel humble.

THE CONATIVE COMPONENT: INTENTIONS AND BEHAVIOR

The third attitude component is **conation**—behavioral intentions toward and actions taken concerning an AO. **Behavioral intentions (behavioral tendencies, response tendencies)** involve the likelihood that someone will undertake a specific behavior or act in a particular way regarding the AO, based on that person's knowledge and feelings. They are **prescriptive (normative) beliefs**—they prescribe what one will or should do, based upon the cognitive and affective dimensions. This behavioral component is usually an intention to buy (e.g., "I should shop at Marty's market and buy Marty's marinade sauce").

Intention to buy is an intervening variable between attitudes and behavior. Marketers and economists alike use buying intentions to forecast future behavior. Sellers want to know the potential sales success of proposed new product concepts, prototypes, and finished products, as well as the likelihood of ad concepts and completed ads to motivate people to buy the advertised brand. Economists use intentions to predict macroeconomic variables such as buying trends and consumer confidence.

Just as the cognitive dimension often informs the affective component, both the cognitive and affective components usually influence the conative constituent. For example, informing a consumer of a price cut or sales promotion offer (cognitive) or associating a brand with a relaxing luxurious lifestyle (affective) might induce a consumer to buy it (behavior) or to plan to purchase it in the near future (behavioral intention).

CONSISTENCY AMONG THE THREE ATTITUDE COMPONENTS

Any two attitude components will either be consonant (harmonious), dissonant (conflicting), or irrelevant to each other. Individuals strive to maintain consistency among the three components of their attitude structures. Inconsistencies cause psychological tension, which is uncomfortable and even disturbing. Such tension motivates people to modify one or more of these elements so as to restore attitude component consonance (consistency), which includes both intra-attitude consistency and inter-attitude consistency.

INTRA-ATTITUDE CONSISTENCY

Intra-attitude consistency suggests that the three internal attitude domains tend to be interrelated, mutually influential, and mutually consistent. This need for a balanced, stable relationship among attitude components is due to the need for *cognitive consistency*, i.e., cognitions need to be harmonious.

Most individuals can only tolerate minimal intra-attitude inconsistency because without intra-attitude consistency there is *cognitive dissonance*—psychological discomfort caused by discrepancies among beliefs, feelings, and/or actions. This conflict causes tension, making a person feel uncomfortable and leading to reappraisal of one of the conflicting dimensions in order to reduce the dissonance. Have you ever heard a person say, "I love Pepsi! It tastes terrible!"?

If Roc Bottom knows that eating Mississippi Fried Crawfish ("Thumb suckin' good!") is unhealthy, yet he loves them and buys them by the bucket, he will probably feel uneasy and be motivated to ease his psychological pain. It will likely be easier for him to just change the belief component and somehow convince himself that MFC are not unwholesome than to start to dislike them and give up eating them.

Intra-attitude consistency exists along both attitudinal direction and strength. Regarding direction, thoughts, feelings, and behaviors toward a given AO tend to be in harmony, that is, they are all positive, neutral, or negative. Someone who finds that a brand does not rate favorably on most dimensions will tend not to like it and will avoid purchasing it.

This suggests that if one attitude component is changed, the other two dimensions will tend to vary in the same direction. If an ad for Howie's frozen corn dogs, which you once tried and did not enjoy, explains that they have markedly improved the flavor through a new secret formula, you might think more kindly about Howie's and even plan to pick up a package at the supermarket. The marketing implication is that if you can alter just one attitude component, you can modify the entire package of attitude components!

The second characteristic on which components for a given AO are usually congruent is strength. If beliefs about an object are strong and positive, the corresponding feelings will tend to run deep, and the strong inclination will be to behave positively toward that object.

If Jeanie O'Logy has a strong belief in the trustworthiness of the Phara's Pharmaceuticals Firm and their medicinal products, she will likely feel very positive about the company and purchase their products or recommend them to others. She is being consistent in expressing her commitment to the firm.

Intra-attitude consistency suggests that you can measure one of these three components and then predict the other two dimensions. However, to confirm the validity of one type of measure, it is good practice to compare it to another sort of attitude measure to see whether they agree.

INTER-ATTITUDE CONSISTENCY

Inter-attitude consistency occurs when a person's overall system of attitudes is in balance. So, if Spanky's is a brand of frozen potato pancakes, and if Pearl E. Gates cannot stomach potato pancakes, it should be no surprise that Pearl dislikes Spanky's.

Central attitudes, you will recall, serve as the anchors for peripheral attitudes. So peripheral attitudes tend to be consistent with central attitudes. The former are more likely to change to be consistent with the latter than vice versa.

ATTITUDE MOLDING STRATEGIES USING THE THREE ATTITUDE COMPONENTS

Marketing efforts can create or transform attitudes by shaping one or more of the attitude components.

ATTITUDE MOLDING THROUGH THE COGNITIVE COMPONENT

If people either put much thought into buying (high-effort central-route processing) or rely on simple beliefs (low-effort peripheral-route processing, e.g., buying the brand recommended by a trusted expert), the cognitive component is key.

The cognitive approach is information based. Marketers create or modify descriptive beliefs about brand features and benefits. Providing favorable or useful information via a rational appeal, using logic and argumentation, generally works well for functional products such as household cleaners and medicines.

ATTITUDE MOLDING THROUGH THE AFFECTIVE COMPONENT

When people form attitudes mainly on the basis of emotion, the affective dimension should be the focus of marketing communications. In high-effort central-route processing situations, emotional appeals, such as romance, fear, and nostalgia, work well, especially for hedonic products such as perfume and entertainment.

Under low-effort peripheral-route processing conditions, affective approaches, such as creating likeable ads, using cute trade characters, or associating the brand with a pleasant mood, work well. Transformational advertising that links the brand to a particular experience, such as attending a backyard barbecue or going out on a date, can be effective under such conditions.

ATTITUDE MOLDING THROUGH THE CONATIVE COMPONENT

If people form their attitudes following experience with a product, as with sensory goods such as fragrances and music, a change in behavior should be induced to provide prospects with brand experiences. Auto dealers offer test drives to gain favorable attitudes. The same is true for free samples, trial offers, music download samples, and scent strips in magazines. For instance, free trial kits are available from doctors for all three male impotence drugs: Viagra, Levitra, and Cialis. Try Cialis, and if you do not like it, the doctor will mail you a voucher for a prescription of Viagra or Levitra.

Alternatively, marketers can suggest a purchase intention ("Be sure to pick up a six-pack of Plutz Stuff the next time you stop by the dairy case"). Yet another conative strategy is to reduce dissonance for those who have already made a purchase.

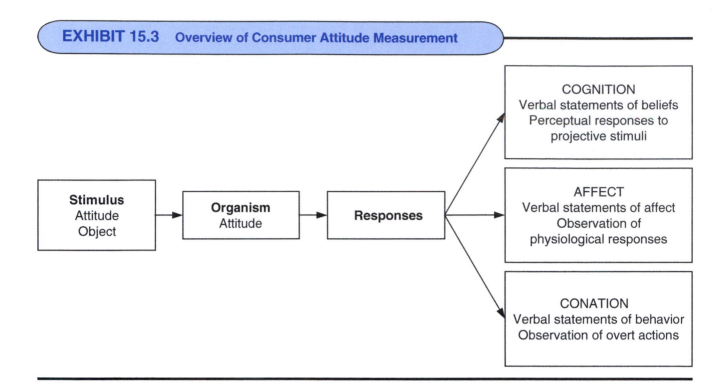

EXHIBIT 15.3   Overview of Consumer Attitude Measurement

RESEARCH TECHNIQUES FOR MEASURING ATTITUDES

In order to mold attitudes, marketers should measure attitudes via consumer research to to determine baseline or benchmark (initial) attitude levels and ascertain the extent to which subsequent marketing efforts change these baseline attitudes. This type of research uses questioning techniques such as surveys, focus groups, and depth interviews.

A MODEL OF THE ATTITUDE MEASUREMENT PROCESS

Usually, respondents are questioned regarding the cognitive and affective dimensions, that is, their descriptive and evaluative beliefs, and behavior is predicted from these. However, at times the conative component is measured, either through questions concerning behavioral intentions or by directly measuring behavior. Therefore, we shall discuss attitude measurement methodologies in general, followed by explanations of how to gauge each of the three attitude dimensions.

Exhibit 15.3 frames the discussion in terms of a stimulus-organism-response model of attitude measurement. The stimulus is the AO, the organism's unobservable hypothetical construct is the consumer's attitude, and the response is the measurement taken of one or more of the attitude components.

INTERVIEWING TECHNIQUES

Rating Scales. Measures of attitude most typically consist of self-report attitude rating scales given during self-administered interviews. A **rating** is a measurement task presenting the respondent with a statement or question regarding an AO's characteristic. The respondent is asked to estimate the magnitude or favorability of that characteristic along a numerically valued continuum or in one of a numerically ordered set of categories. Individuals are requested to rate their beliefs about, feelings toward, and/or behavioral intentions concerning the AO.

Single-item (basic) rating scales measure one's overall attitude toward an object, ranging from very favorable to very unfavorable.

Example: How do you like Pepsi Twist?

Very much	1	2	3	4	5	Not at all

Example: Do you oppose or favor the proposed legislation to crack down on Internet spam?
___ Favor
___ Oppose
___ Undecided

Most attitude scales assume attitude is a multidimensional construct and are therefore **multi-item (itemized) rating scales** consisting of a battery of items, each of which concerns a product attribute. Every item is arrayed along a continuum, with one end indicating an unfavorable attitude and the other end a favorable attitude. An individual's overall attitude score is simply the sum of the individual ratings.

The most typically used scales are **noncomparative (monadic) rating scales** that ask respondents to rate one AO in isolation, without comparison to other AOs. Alternatively, **comparative rating scales** that have respondents rate an AO by comparing it against a benchmark AO, such as an ideal, typical, favorite, or currently used brand. Comparative ratings indicate *preferences.* For example, respondents could be asked, "How does the taste of a Burger Buddy compare with other fast food hamburgers you have eaten?" followed by a scale anchored by "much better" at one end and "much worse" at the other end.

Noncomparative (Monadic) Rating Scales. Types of monadic attitude scales include the following.
➤ *1. Semantic differential scale.* A **semantic differential scale** is typically a seven-point rating scale. Bipolar adjectives (antonyms) anchor the poles (beginning and ending) of each scale item. Examples are sweet-sour, hot-cold, light-dark, and interesting-boring. (Note that monopolar adjectives such as sweet–not sweet aren't employed.)

Example: Please rate your new Kool Off air conditioning system on each of the following criteria:

Quiet	___	___	___	___	___	___	Noisy
Cools quickly	___	___	___	___	___	___	Cools slowly
Easy to operate	___	___	___	___	___	___	Difficult to operate

➤ *2. Numerical scale.* A **numerical scale** is similar to the semantic differential, except instead of using bipolar adjectives, it uses numbers to indicate scale positions that respondents rate an AO along regarding a series of adjectives.

Example: Please rate the new Sweet 'N Sour pork candy on each of the following criteria:

Tartness	+1	+2	+3	−1	−2	−3
Sweetness	+1	+2	+3	−1	−2	−3
Crunchiness	+1	+2	+3	−1	−2	−3

➤ *3. Likert scale.* A **Likert scale** is typically a five-point scale along which respondents indicate how strongly they either agree or disagree with a statement regarding their belief about or liking of a characteristic of an AO.

Example: Carr's Cars is an honest dealership from which to buy used automobiles.

Strongly agree	1	2	3	4	5	Strongly disagree

Example:

	Strongly agree	Moderately agree	Neither agree nor disagree	Moderately disagree	Strongly disagree
Above Board Corporation's products are of superior quality.	___	___	___	___	___
Above Board's products are overpriced.	___	___	___	___	___
Above Board is a trustworthy corporation.	___	___	___	___	___

➤ *4. Stapel scale.* A **Stapel scale** consists of a single adjective in the center of a rating scale. Scale values indicate how accurately the adjective describes the AO.

Example:

Sock 'Em Bop 'Em

+3
+2
+1
Exciting video game
−1
−2
−3

Comparative Rating Scales. The following are measures for comparing two or more alternatives:

➤ *1. Paired comparisons.* With **paired comparisons**, respondents are presented with pairs of AOs and asked to select the object preferred, either overall or in terms of a series of criteria. More than one pair of AOs can be evaluated so that all possible pairs are compared. Rank order preferences can be derived from these.

Example: Which of these two brands do you believe gives you the best deal? Which of the two brands has more attractive styling?

Such questions are given for each criterion. The process is repeated for all possible brand pairs.

➤ *2. Rank ordering.* Interviewees **rank order** AOs according to preference overall or else according to chosen criteria.

Example: Rank order these seven brands from the one giving you the best deal to the one giving you the poorest deal. Place a numeral 1 next to the brand that is the best deal, a 2 beside the brand that offers the second best deal, and so on, placing a 7 beside the brand giving you the poorest deal.

➤ *3. Constant sum scale.* For the **constant sum scale**, respondents divide a constant quantitative amount or sum (e.g., 10 points, 100 percentage points) among several AOs to indicate their relative preferences.

Example: Listed below are six brands of deodorant. Divide 100 points among them according to your preference for the brands.

Odorific	___	Spray 'N Go	___
Arm Pitts	___	SniffIt	___
Confident	___	Banish	___

All of the above are **closed-ended (fixed alternative) questions** to which respondents select from predetermined responses. Alternatively, researchers can use **open-ended (free answer) questions**, which allow interviewees to reply in their own words, usually administered in depth interviews and focus groups, although personal interviews are also used. These techniques allow more in-depth investigation of attitudes through follow-up and probing questions.

OBSERVATION AND EXPERIMENTATION

Besides questioning techniques, attitudes can also be measured using **scientific observation**, systematically recording people's behaviors. The thinking is that since behavior usually follows from attitude, the researcher can infer a person's attitude by observing behavior.

Researchers and managers learn customer attributes CB by waiting on customers, riding in repair trucks, milling around the mall, and watching shoppers interact with retail clerks. CB can also be observed in the context of a controlled laboratory experiment. For example, some food manufacturers set up "test kitchens" in which they invite people to cook, and toy manufacturers test out kids' reactions to new toys' "play value" by inviting kids into their play labs to try out the items. Here, the researchers watch the testers in rooms with one-way mirrors.

The overriding advantage of observational attitude research is that it is based on what people actually do, not say. We need not rely on questioning techniques' various response biases.

The major problem is that inferences on attitudes can be mistaken. For instance, if we witness that many people are not wearing seat belts, does this necessarily indicate that they have negative attitudes toward wearing them? Probably not, but they might believe they are such good drivers that the chance of their being involved in an accident is nil.

Another limit of observational techniques is that observers can be biased in recording what they see. And although attitude usually leads to a behavior having the same direction, sometimes behavior precedes attitude formation, that is, actions can occur in the absence of attitudes and so they do not reflect attitudes, (e.g., purchasing a new brand out of curiosity).

MEASURING THE ATTITUDE COMPONENTS

MEASURING THE COGNITIVE COMPONENT

Since the cognitive dimension is made up of descriptive beliefs, interviewees are asked for verbal statements regarding what criteria they use and their beliefs about an AO's performance or standing on these evaluative criteria, typically measured using rating scales to measure the beliefs. The overall pattern of their verbal statements and the summated score across all beliefs give an indication of respondents' overall attitude toward the AO. For Pepsi Max, respondents can be queried regarding how sweet they find it, how tasty it is, and how dark the color is.

MEASURING THE AFFECTIVE COMPONENT

Because the affective attitudinal dimension is composed of evaluative beliefs, it is ordinarily gauged by verbal measures asking respondents to evaluate the AO on the degree to which they like or dislike its overall performance using a single-item scale. Alternatively, or in addition, they can evaluate their liking of the AO's criteria using a multi-item scale. Consumers could be asked how they like Pepsi Max overall as well as the taste, the color, and so on.

Additionally, respondents can be requested to assign a weight to each product attribute, which is also an evaluative indicator since it tells how important the criterion is to them. Also, focus group and depth interview participants can be probed regarding their feelings for the AO.

Observational measures of physiological responses to stimuli can also be used to determine feelings. This technique is performed in a laboratory setting and provides biobehavioral measures of sympathetic nervous system reactions to stimuli such as ads and packages.

Such techniques include pupil dilation response (dilated pupils indicate emotional arousal), galvanic skin response (measures sweat gland activity that accompanies emotional excitement), and voice pitch analysis (determines changes in the relative frequency of the human voice that accompany emotional arousal). These measures are infrequently employed, however, because they require sophisticated equipment and skilled researchers. They often lack validity because in an artificial lab environment people are highly aware they are being monitored.

MEASURING THE CONATIVE COMPONENT

Since the connative component consists of both *behavioral intentions* and *actions* concerning an AO, separate measures are required if the researcher is interested in both of these aspects of connation.

To learn about behavioral intentions, survey respondents are queried directly regarding their marketplace intentions toward the AO. Such surveys employ **behavioral intentions scales** in which interviewees describe the probability that their beliefs and feelings will be acted upon, i.e., their purchase plans (propensities to purchase). Behavioral intentions scales relate to the attitude-toward-the-behavior model.

Example: What is the likelihood you will purchase Slurp the next time you buy a soft drink?
____ Definitely will buy
____ Probably will buy
____ Might buy
____ Probably will not buy
____ Definitely will not buy.

Example: How likely is it that you will purchase a new dishwasher during the next twelve months?
____ Very likely
____ Somewhat likely
____ Unlikely
____ Very unlikely

Closely related is the **behavioral differential scale**. This scale is similar to the semantic differential, except it measures behavioral intentions rather than beliefs or feelings.

Example: My teenage son or daughter

| Would buy | ___ | ___ | ___ | ___ | ___ | ___ | ___ | Would not buy |

Terrible Teen jeans.

Such conative scales provide additional information not gleaned from a cognitive or affective attitude scale because, although a person might be favorably predisposed toward an AO, he or she may not intend to act on that attitude. You might think a BMW Z3 Roadster is a cool car but you know there is a snowball's chance in Hades that you will be able to afford one anytime soon.

To learn about overt actions they already took regarding the AO, respondents are queried about their recent buyer behavior (since they are most likely to recall recent events). Examples include the last magazine read or restaurant most recently visited.

Example: The last brand of orange juice I drank was _____.

Also, observational measures of connation can be taken. An observational study reporting on the relative number and types of drivers and passengers who use seat belts could suggest attitudes toward seat belt usage.

Alternatively, experiments can be run whereby marketers test variations on elements of the marketing mix, such as packages, brand names, and sales presentations, to determine their influence on buying intentions and purchase behavior. For instance, in simulated test markets, consumers are given money and allowed to shop in a special store set up for the experiment, perhaps after exposure to advertising for some of the featured products. The products and brands that they purchase are presumably indicative of their attitudes toward the ads as well as the products.

Because each measurement method has its limitations, the safest approach is to use multiple measures of attitudes. If they agree, we can be more confident that we have an accurate read on attitudes.

THE ELABORATION LIKELIHOOD (ELM) MODEL

OVERVIEW OF THE ELABORATION LIKELIHOOD MODEL

The second key determinant for selecting among attitude models and strategies is the process whereby attitudes are likely to be formed. This process is described by Petty and Cacioppo's **elaboration likelihood model (ELM)** of attitude formation and change. The ELM considers the degree of **elaboration**, or how much effort consumers exert in learning about and forming attitudes for a given AO, that is, how deeply they process information on the AO.

The extent of consumers' elaboration is determined by the magnitude of their motivation, ability, and opportunity (MAO) to process information and make decisions:

- The *motivation* factor indicates the extent of consumer involvement.
- *Ability* suggests that buyers must have the skills to properly assess the information.
- *Opportunity* means consumers have access to the information.

The ELM suggests two distinctly different paths or routes to persuasion to mold attitudes: a central route and a peripheral route. When MOA is high, consumers use **central-route processing**, which involves a great deal of information acquisition, thinking, and decision making. Buyers undertake a deliberate, conscious, logical scrutiny of **strong arguments** which present the best or most convincing evidence regarding the AO's central merits or the significant issues embodied in evaluating an AO. The key is to offer compelling, relevant reasons for buying the brand. Examples of marketing communications encouraging central-route processing include detailed comparative advertisements, informative point-of-purchase brochures, and educational sales presentations.

Here, elaboration likelihood is high. The informational elements are elaborated on and combined into an overall attitude. The focus is on message content, that is, the substance of the message arguments; what is said. The result is the formation of strong central attitudes.

However, when MAO is low, consumer attitudes are based on a tangential or superficial examination of the information rather than an effortful analysis of its true merits. During this **peripheral-route processing**, the consumer expends limited effort, that is, there is little information search and low elaboration. This consumer uses **peripheral cues**, which are less relevant but easily processed stimuli associated with a message. Examples include background scenery, characteristics of people and music featured in advertising, attractive packaging, and brand name.

The fact that these stimuli are not relevant to a meaningful brand evaluation does not matter to the consumer. The focus is on creative execution or presentation technique—how the message is said—rather than the substance of the message. The result is the formation of a general, rather superficial impression of the AO, or weak peripheral attitudes.

REVIEW QUESTIONS

1. Where does attitude molding fit into the buyer decision process?
2. Describe how marketing objectives can be based on attitudes.
3. What types of AOs are marketers generally interested in influencing? Briefly explain each one.
4. Clarify how attitudes differ from, yet are related to, each of the following concepts: opinions, preferences, beliefs, and values.
5. Explain each of the following characteristics of attitudes: availability, accessibility, favorability (direction, valence), and strength (importance).
6. Name and describe the three attitude components, and describe the type of beliefs each is comprised of.
7. Explain the significance of inter-attitude consistency and of intra-attitude consistency for attitude molding strategies.
8. Describe how each of the major types of rating scales can be used to measure consumer attitudes. What is a major problem in using rating scales?

9. Which attitude measurement methods are most appropriate for measuring each of the three attitude components?
10. Describe the elaboration likelihood model of attitude molding. How does attitude molding differ during central-route versus peripheral-route processing?

IN-CLASS APPLICATIONS

1. Answer the following questions concerning the use of attitude molding strategies in each of the advertisements in Exhibits 15.4 through 15.7.
   a. Which of the four types of marketing objectives related to attitudes—forming, changing, adapting to, or reinforcing—does each ad appear to be trying to achieve? For those ads attempting to alter attitudes, does attitude change seem to be very feasible in light of product-market conditions?
   b. Describe which attitude component(s)—cognitive, affective, or conative—is (are) being appealed to in each ad in order to obtain a more favorable attitude toward the ad's brand. Do you believe that this approach will be effective?
   c. Describe how a different attitude component from what you described in part b, if any, could be appealed to for each product, using either advertising or another marketing communication tool. Which of the two approaches would be more effective and why?
   d. What is your attitude toward each advertisement? Do you think this would influence your attitude toward the advertised brand?
   e. Describe how any of these ads reflects cultural attitudes.
   f. Which "route" to persuasion does each ad seem to assume consumers use—the central route or peripheral route? Is this a good assumption for each advertised product?
2. Which attitude component(s) are being described in each of the following scenarios? Be as specific as possible. That is, for the cognitive and affective components, what types of beliefs are evident (e.g., descriptive beliefs about objective product attributes or affective subjective beliefs regarding emotional benefits)? For the conative dimension, is an appeal being made to behavioral intentions or overt behavior?
   → *Scenario A. Chris P. Crème's Donuts.* Chris P. Crème loves a good donut, but not just any old donut. It's got to be a fresh-made donut from a quick-serve restaurant, such as Dunkin' Donuts, Honey Dew Donuts, or, okay, yes, Krispy Kreme. He stops at one of these places every day for breakfast and lunch (but he has a sensible dinner).
   Store-bought donuts don't cut it, even if they are Krispy Kreme. No, they must be made fresh daily. "Mmmmmm. . . . donuts . . . ," Chris wistfully sighs in a manner reminiscent of Homer Simpson.
   → *Scenario B. Curt Does the Dew.* Curt likes Mountain Dew because he believes it's a hip soda popular with the young crowd, it's loaded with sugar and caffeine to give him a quick energy boost, and it runs fun TV commercials. So, Curt buys the Dew whenever possible when he's out and about with friends.
   → *Scenario C. FedEx Is One Honey of a Service.* Honey is one businesswoman who likes to move at warp speed. "He who hesitates is lost" is her motto. She dreads having to wait until the twelfth of never.
   Consequently, Honey uses Federal Express overnight services. She finds FedEx is very reliable and economical. And they are always willing to bend the rules a bit to fit her needs. Shipping packages via FedEx makes Honey feel safe and secure. Therefore, she recommends the company to all of her business associates.
   → *Scenario D. Ginger Snaps Cameras.* Ginger was out shopping at the Malta Mall for a camera for her upcoming vacation to Frostbite Falls, Minnesota. She decided to look at single-lens reflex cameras rather than automatics since they are more versatile and have better picture quality. Plus, she won't look like an amateur by snapping an automatic.
   She didn't find a camera at a price she could afford, so tomorrow Ginger plans to bop over to the Olive Grove Outlets to try snapping a few pix on the single-lens reflex cameras there.
   → *Scenario E. Order Orders O.J.* Marcie Order always buys Sun-Squished orange juice when grocery

EXHIBIT 15.4 L'Oréal Vive for Men Ad

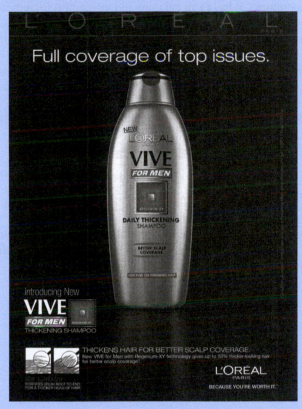

EXHIBIT 15.5 Lightlife Ad

EXHIBIT 15.6 Kellogg's Eggo Syrup Ad

You're sticky and we're sorry.

To our friends:

For years, you've had to eat your *Eggo®* waffles with syrup that can drip from the bottle onto your fingers.

But now we are putting an end to your suffering.

We're introducing *Eggo™* syrup, a great-tasting complement to America's favorite waffles.

And even better, it comes in a high-tech, no-drip bottle, so our syrup will wind up on your food, not your fingers.

Eggo™ syrup.
Better late than never.

William Wright
William Wright
Executive Vice President
Eggo Company

EXHIBIT 15.7 Mr. Clean AutoDry Carwash Ad

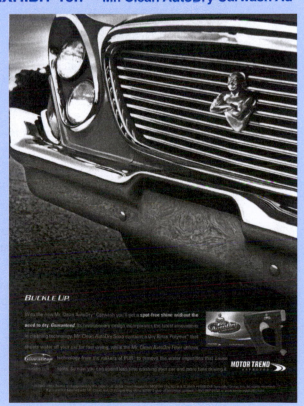

shopping for her family. She chooses this brand because it is higher in calories, giving her kids the energy they need (so they aren't couch potatoes); it has extra calcium and all-natural ingredients, making it nutritional; and it is very sweet, so her kids will drink it all. Personally, though, Marcie rarely drinks Sun-Squished or any other orange juice—she finds it too acidic for her sensitive stomach.

3. Identify the type of rating scale being used in each of the following questions. Formulate an alternative scaled attitude question for the same AO. For instance, if the question uses a semantic differential scale, try rewriting it as a numerical scale, Likert scale, or Stapel scale.

   a. For each factor listed below, please check the line that best describes Mrs. Beasley, your local Farma Sooticals salesperson.

   Knowledgeable ___ ___ ___ ___ ___ ___ ___ ___ Ignorant
   Experienced   ___ ___ ___ ___ ___ ___ ___ ___ Novice
   Sincere   ___ ___ ___ ___ ___ ___ ___ ___ Deceptive

   b. Below is a list of six characteristics of women's tennis sportswear. Please allocate 100 points among the characteristics to reflect the relative importance of each characteristic to you. The more points you assign to a characteristic, the more important it is.

Characteristic of tennis sportswear	Number of points
Comfortable to wear	___
Durable	___
Made by a well-known manufacturer	___
Made in America	___
Up-to-date styling	___
A good value for the money	___

   c. Select a number that most accurately describes the Second National Bank.

   + 4   + 3   + 2   + 1

   Competitive loan rates

   − 1   − 2   − 3   − 4

   d. Please rate the soap opera *As the Stomach Turns* on each of the following criteria:

Dramatic	+5	+4	+3	+2	+1	−1	−2	−3	−4	−5
Suspenseful	+5	+4	+3	+2	+1	−1	−2	−3	−4	−5
Boring	+5	+4	+3	+2	+1	−1	−2	−3	−4	−5

   e. For each of the following statements, please check the one response that best indicates to what extent you agree or disagree with that statement.

	Definitely agree	Generally agree	Slightly agree	Slightly disagree	Generally disagree	Definitely disagree
I buy many things with a credit card.	___	___	___	___	___	___
I wish I earned a lot more money.	___	___	___	___	___	___
You are what you own.	___	___	___	___	___	___

WRITTEN APPLICATIONS

1. Answer Question 1 in the In-Class Applications for three of the ads on p. 513. Be sure to select ads that allow you to analyze appeals to all three attitude dimensions.
2. Find three additional ads, each of which primarily appeals to a different attitude component, and repeat the analysis for Question 1 in the In-Class Applications.
3. Create a short questionnaire of about a half-dozen items to provide baseline measures of a target market's attitudes toward a particular AO. Such benchmark measures provide the springboard for the objective of changing, adapting to, or reinforcing those attitudes.

   Specifically, you must:

   a. Identify a target market. Briefly describe it demographically as well as either psychographically and/or behaviorally. (Hint: Since you'll be surveying members of this targeted group, you should select a segment easily accessible to you, such as students on your campus, or a segment thereof, or members of an organization you belong to.)

   b. Select an AO of interest to your target market (and, ideally, to you too!). It could be a product or service category (e.g., personal computers, cola drinks, airlines, perfume, fast food restaurants, automobiles, cosmetics, digital audio players, hotel/motel, etc.); company, retailer, e-tailer, or other type of organization; brand; media outlet; person (e.g., a celebrity, politician, or—gulp!—professor); place (e.g., country, state, city, or tourist destination); or issue (e.g., a political or social cause such as gun control or sexual abstinence before marriage).

      Also, identify one or more major "competitors" for your AO. For example, if it is a brand, specify rival brands, or if it is a cause, identify the other side of the issue (e.g., pro-choice vs. pro-life) or another cause people could instead support with their time and money.

   c. Develop a list of evaluative criteria that members of the target market use as the bases for their attitudes and decision making. You can do this by asking a few members of the market segment which features and benefits they use, using criteria from your own experience with the AO, and/or relying on available marketplace information from sources such as ads and packaging.

   d. Develop your questionnaire to learn about the target market's attitudes toward the AO as well as toward one or more "competitors." You should ask one question concerning each alternative's performance on each criterion. Include a variety of different noncomparative rating scales (semantic differential, Likert, etc.) as well as comparative rating scales (paired comparisons, rank ordering, and constant sum scales).

   e. Administer your questionnaire to a sample of about ten to twelve members of the target market. Tabulate and summarize the findings. What do these results suggest for setting attitude-based marketing objectives? If attitude change is among your goals, will it be feasible to achieve? Which components of consumer attitudes do your results suggest should be the focus of marketing objectives concerning attitudes? Should central-route or peripheral-route processing be the heart of attitude molding strategies?

EXERCISE 15.2. THE COGNITIVE DECISION-MAKING PERSPECTIVE

OBJECTIVES

1. To explain the various models and theories of cognitive attitude molding and to recognize their use in advertising and other marketing situations.
2. To recognize and analyze the strategies used by marketers to encourage consumers to generate support arguments and to not produce counterarguments, as well as to improve message credibility.
3. To recognize effective and ineffective use of various message structure characteristics: argument quality, order of presentation (serial position effects), message sidedness (one-sided versus two-sided messages), positive versus negative message framing, closed-ended versus open-ended (explicit) conclusion drawing, and use of distractions.

4. To practice distinguishing between credible and incredible communication sources that are credible and those that are not.
5. To become familiar with the concept of attitude toward the ad (A_{ad}).
6. To become familiar with several different types of multiattribute attitude models by applying them to your own CB, and determining marketing strategy implications from the results.
7. To recognize and evaluate advertisements using the various attitude-shaping strategies based on multiattribute attitude models.
8. To experience seeing applications of the functional theory of attitude change and critiquing them.
9. To discover how balance theory can be applied to shape attitudes.
10. To demonstrate the various ways the cognitive route can be used to mold attitudes, even under conditions of low-involvement peripheral-route processing, by working with simple beliefs.

BACKGROUND

This exercise concentrates on attitude-molding strategies grounded in the cognitive attitude dimension. Since they are based on forming beliefs and thinking, most of these approaches assume high-effort central-route processing. Together, these means for influencing attitudes are called the **decision-making perspective (DMP)**.

HIGH-EFFORT CENTRAL-ROUTE DECISION-MAKING PERSPECTIVE

Most cognitive approaches to persuasion assume reasoned, effortful decision making. There are four general models and theories for DMP cognitive attitude shaping: the cognitive response model, multiattribute models, functional theory, and balance theory.

THE COGNITIVE RESPONSE MODEL

Cognitive responses are the thoughtful reactions audience members have when exposed to persuasive marketing communications, from which they form descriptive beliefs (beliefs). Upon reading an advertisement in *TeenRager* magazine for new "miracle" Blotch Out acne medicine, a teenager could respond by thinking, "This is just what I need!" "It's too good to be true," "I wonder if any of my friends have tried this," "There's got to be a catch," or "I don't trust ads in this magazine." Each of these spur-of-the-moment responses will determine acceptance or rejection of the message (attitude toward the ad) as well as attitude toward the brand (Blotch Out). The **cognitive response model** provides a classification scheme for these thoughts as product/message thoughts, source-oriented thoughts, and ad-execution thoughts. The model offers suggestions for structuring the message by considering the impact of these beliefs on attitude toward the ad and brand attitude. Exhibit 15.8 summarizes this model.

Product/Message Thoughts: Support Arguments and Counterarguments. **Support arguments** and **counterarguments** concern cognitive responses aimed at the promoted product or the message itself. Support arguments are consumer thoughts agreeing with the message or confirming the product's worthiness, such as when the teen reading the Blotch Out ad responded, ""This is just what I need!" After reading an ad that claims, "GrimeOut stain remover gets rid of the toughest stains," a consumer might think, "That might solve my problem. I've got to buy GrimeOut."

Thoughts that conflict with or oppose the marketer's message are counterarguments. Counterarguing consumers express disbelief in or disapproval of a promotional claim. For instance, the teen's reactions, "It's too good to be true," and "There's got to be a catch," constitute counterarguments to the acne medicine ad. The U.S. Office of National Drug Control Policy's antidrug ad linking drugs to the war on terrorism caused skeptical college students to conclude that marijuana should be legalized rather than accepting the intended message that drugs are a bad thing.

A counterargument is formed when an audience member experiences **belief discrepancy**, believing that a marketing communication has little credibility, either because the claim itself seems to conflict with reality

EXHIBIT 15.8   **The Cognitive Response Model**

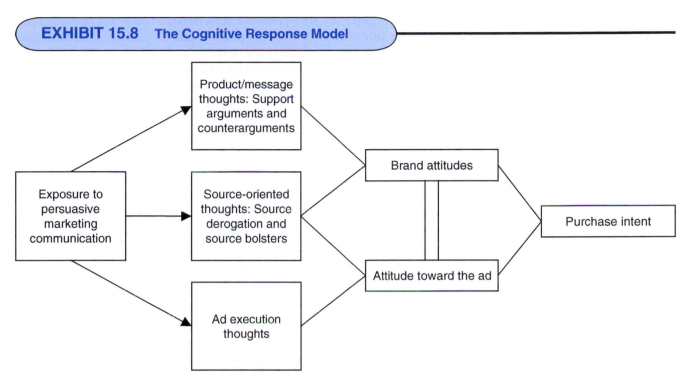

Source: This model is patterned after Figure 5–7 in George E. Belch and Michael A. Belch, *Advertising and Promotion,* 8th ed. (New York: McGraw-Hill Companies, 2009), p. 166.

or because the message conflicts with his or her own (especially central) beliefs. It is generally wiser for marketers to go with the flow and avoid going against the grain. It is easier to preach to the choir (current product and/or brand users) rather than attempting to convert lost souls (nonusers). An ad suggesting a newly discovered health benefit to prune juice would more likely persuade prune juice lovers than haters.

Message Structure Characteristics to Maximize Support Arguments and Minimize Counterarguments. The following **message structure characteristics**, or organization of the message elements, should be considered when attempting to minimize counterarguments and maximize support arguments and credibility.

➢ *Argument quality.* **Argument quality** concerns whether or not a communication employs *strong arguments*—compelling, relevant reasons for buying the brand. Strong arguments can be created through product demonstrations, testimonials of satisfied users, endorsements of third-party organizations, infomercials, and online advertising providing detailed, up-to-the-minute information. Message recipients are more prone to counterargue and disparage the message source when the message presents weak arguments. For example, suggesting that consumers patronize a firm because it has been "serving you for a half a dozen years!" is less compelling than explaining that the company has provided a century of excellence. Claiming that a pain reliever is better because it comes in a square pill instead of a round one is less convincing than saying it offers time-released dosage. A strong argument asserting that it works five times faster and offers 100 percent relief lasting three times longer should get sufferers down to the pharmacy pronto!

➢ *Serial position effects (order of presentation).* Exercise 14.1 explained that serial position effects (**order of presentation**) concerns whether the strongest arguments should be placed at the beginning, middle, or end of the marketing communication. Usually, there is either a **primacy effect**, that is, the first information presented is best remembered, or a **recency effect**, in which the last arguments are best recalled. Whether a primacy or recency effect will dominate depends on several other factors:

- If the target audience is initially opposed to the communicator's message, presenting strong points first reduces counterarguing. If weak arguments precede strong ones, there might be such a high level of counterarguing that the later stronger points would not be considered.

- Strong arguments should be placed early in the communication if the audience is disinterested since stronger arguments are inherently more interesting than weaker ones. Also, if weak assertions appear first, disinterested audience members are more likely to tune out the ad in disbelief before it is finished. For high-involvement consumers, however, attention-getters are not required.
- Where the message is long or detailed (e.g., salespeople with long presentations, infomercials, and long-copy ads), it is very important to use the strongest points both early and late in communications to take advantage of primacy and recency effects (see Exercise 14.1). For brief broadcast or outdoor ads, the issue of order of presentation is less critical. However, with a low-involvement audience, key elements (e.g., brand name and slogan) should occur early in the communiqué and then be repeated later (even several times) to bolster recall.

➤ *Message sidedness: one-sided versus two-sided messages.* Most marketing communications use **one-sided messages**, communications that only discuss the brand's merits without explaining its shortcomings or rivals' advantages because marketers fear that doing so will harm the brand. **Two-sided messages** present the brand's weaknesses as well as strengths, and/or they mention competitors' advantages. Such a balanced, relatively unbiased view bolsters the message's credibility. A classic example is Avis Rent-A-Car's 1960s ad campaign admitting, "Yes, we're only number two. But, we try harder." This created a believable and compelling strength for Avis. The market dominance of Hertz became a weakness, and underdog Avis was perceived as the "right choice."

One type of two-sided argument is the *mea culpa strategy* discussed in Exercise 14.2. Another kind is the **refutational appeal**, in which the communicator presents both sides of an issue and then refutes the opposing viewpoint. The purpose is to inoculate (immunize) recipients against a rival's countermessage or other opposing viewpoints. Salespeople do this when they raise and then refute potential customer concerns and objections. Refutational appeals are also used where the marketer faces strong competitive advertising, adverse publicity, or negative word-of-mouth communication.

Two-sided messages are most effective with highly knowledgeable or educated consumers who are probably aware of both sides anyway. For instance, pharmaceutical salespeople promoting to physicians should present a balanced perspective on the medications they are selling. Consumers with less education or information are less likely to see both sides, so negatives need not be addressed, although ethically they might be obligated to do so. One-sided messages are more effective for simple reinforcement of existing attitudes, since people look for confirmation of their opinions. For such individuals, a two-sided message might plant doubts in their mind about their positive beliefs, thereby creating dissonance.

➤ *Positive versus negative message framing.* **Message framing** entails whether one describes a condition in either positive terms ("The glass is half full") or using negative expressions ("The glass is half empty"). Low-fat milk is usually framed negatively as "1 percent fat" rather than positively as "99 percent fat free." However, beef is generally positively framed as "98 percent fat free" rather than negatively as "2 percent fat." This is because, generally, negative framing is superior, especially for health issues, and low-fat milk is bought primarily for its health qualities whereas beef is not.

➤ *Conclusion drawing.* Communications can be either **closed-ended (explicit) communications** that clearly draw conclusions for the audience or **open-ended (implicit) communications** that permit message recipients to come to their own conclusions. Usually, explicit conclusions are better understood and more persuasive.

On the other hand, letting people draw their own conclusions increases involvement, leading, in turn, to higher retention and hence stronger, more accessible attitudes. Some ambiguity in the message also lets them interpret benefits in a way that is most meaningful to them.

Whether or not to draw conclusions also depends on the following.

- *Education.* Highly educated people prefer to and are more capable of drawing their own conclusions, and they might feel pandered to if a conclusion is drawn for them. A clear conclusion should be given for less-educated people lest they might fail to draw their own conclusion or might draw an erroneous one.
- *Consumer involvement.* More involved consumers usually prefer to make up their own minds and resent efforts of marketers to do so for them.

- *Message complexity.* The more complex the topic, the more necessary it is to draw a conclusion for message recipients, regardless of their level of education or involvement.
- *Audience skepticism.* Skeptical audiences are more likely to be persuaded if they make up their own minds.
- *Privacy of issue.* People prefer to decide for themselves for more personal topics.
- *Direct vs. indirect response (action) objectives.* If a communication has a direct response (action) objective, such as an immediate purchase or inquiry for further information, it is more important for the communicator to come to an explicit conclusion. If there is an indirect action objective, such as building a positive image or increasing brand preference over a long time frame, an open-ended message can be used since consumers have time to develop their own conclusions.

➢ *Use of distractions.* Where people are opposed to the message and are consequently prone to counter-argue, it might be wise to include one or more **distractions**, attention-grabbing communication elements that are irrelevant to the message, such as humor, sexy presenters, catchy music, celebrities, or quirky situations and characters. Distractions can help slip the unwanted message below receivers' radar screens or otherwise soften them up. Pleasant distractions can increase the effectiveness of persuasive appeals by breaking through people's perceptual barriers, as illustrated by the salesperson who takes a client out to dinner. But beware: Too much distraction can drown out the message.

Source-Oriented Thoughts: Source Derogation and Source Bolsters. A second category of cognitive responses is targeted toward the source of the communication. The **communication source (source)** is anyone or any entity backing the message, including the message sponsor (company, organization, or brand), message presenter (e.g., "typical consumers," celebrities, and professional experts), and advertising media vehicle (e.g., TV show, corporate Web site).

Source derogation occurs when the message receiver attacks the message source, thereby rejecting the message. A *Teen* magazine reader might think, "I don't trust ads in this magazine." **Source bolsters** are favorable thoughts the message recipient has toward the communication source, leading to a higher probability of message acceptance.

Credibility is most important for a source's persuasiveness. Credible sources share several characteristics:

- *Trustworthiness.* The source is believed to be honest and ethical, with nothing to gain from manipulation. Examples include personal sources and third-party neutral (independent) sources, such as Consumers Union, government and scientific reports, and the American Dental Association, as well as professionals like doctors and scientists. To increase trustworthiness, advertisers use techniques such as straight-talking presenters, evidence from comparative tests, and hidden cameras to show consumers are not paid actors.
- *Expertise.* The source is perceived to have the requisite topic-relevant knowledge base to provide correct information. Examples include well-informed salespeople and certified professionals. However, marketing experts are often perceived as less trustworthy because they have a vested interest in product sales.
- *Status or prestige.* This is especially significant if the topic of persuasion relates to the source's role. A nuclear physicist would be credible discussing nuclear power but not necessarily nutrition, whereas a biologist would be persuasive explaining the latter but not the former. A sales manager might be more credible to customers than a salesperson.

Attractiveness also enhances source credibility and increases identification of message recipients with the message source. Attractive sources possess:

- *Similarity.* There is a perceived resemblance between the message source and receiver in terms of physical similarity (sex, dress, etc.) as well as attitudes and behavior. Salespeople should be similar to their prospects, advertising "typical consumers" should resemble targeted customers, and interviewers should be like respondents.
- *Likeability.* Likeability is affection for the source due to physical appearance, a pleasant personality,

and other positive personal traits. Sports celebrities such as Kurt Warner, Ken Griffey, Jr., and Shaquille O'Neal are selected as much for their likeability as for their athletic prowess.

- *Familiarity.* The source is recognized from prior exposure. This argues for long-running presenters and trade characters.
- *Confidence.* While not arrogant, effective presenters are self-assured.

A low-credibility source can become effective over time if a powerful message has been delivered. This is due to the **sleeper effect**, in which consumers forget the message source more rapidly than the message itself. Consequently the message's credibility increases with the passage of time as the low-credibility source and message become disassociated.

Ad Execution Thoughts: Attitude Toward the Ad. A third category of cognitive responses is **ad execution–related thoughts**, or reactions to ad execution or presentation, such as the ad's information, entertainment, and production values and voice tones. The receiver's thoughts about the ad constitute his or her attitude toward the ad (A_{ad}). If these thoughts are favorable (unfavorable), the consumer's attitude toward the advertised brand might also become positive (negative).

MULTIATTRIBUTE ATTITUDE MODELS

Descriptions of the Multiattribute Models. **Multiattribute attitude models** represent a consumer's attitude as determined by his or her beliefs about a brand's performance or rating on determinant criteria and assessment of either the weight (importance) or evaluation (goodness-badness) of those criteria. The following are all *weighted linear compensatory models*, which assume that a negative evaluation of an alternative on one attribute can be compensated for by a positive evaluation on another criterion.

➤ *The belief-importance (expectancy-value) model.* According to the **belief-importance (expectancy-value) model**, a consumer has a belief (subjective perception) about each alternative's performance or value (rating) on each evaluative criterion (e.g., "Walter's widgets are very energy efficient"). The buyer also decides the relative weight or importance of each attribute ("Energy efficiency is somewhat important").

Beliefs about values are measured using the rating scales discussed in Exercise 14.3. Attribute importance is typically measured either with rating scales anchored "very important" to "very unimportant" or by constant sum scales ("Divide 100 points among these five attributes according to their relative importance").

Multiplying a consumer's value or rating on each attribute by that attribute's importance weight and adding across all these cross-products determines an alternative's evaluation or attitude score. The formula (as we saw in Exercise 4.4) is as follows:

$$A_{jk} = \sum_{i=1}^{n} w_{ij} b_{ijk}$$

where i = attribute,
   j = brand,
   k = consumer,
   A_{jk} = a particular consumer's (k's) attitude score for brand j (A_B),
   w_{ik} = the importance weight assigned to attribute i by consumer k,
   b_{ijk} = consumer k's belief about the perfomance or value of brand j on attribute i,
   n = number of attributes considered.

As an example, Exhibit 15.9 is a *brand-attribute matrix* (decision matrix). It contains information on Millie's evoked set (brands evaluated) for three brands of athletic shoes. The matrix includes the criteria on which she evaluates athletic shoes (column 1), the importance weight Millie assigns to each alternative (column 2, using a 1-to-10 scale), and her belief about each brand's performance or value on each criterion (the remaining three columns, with each brand rated on a scale where 1 is "very poor performance" and 10 is "excellent value").

EXHIBIT 15.9	**Brand-Attribute Matrix for Athletic Shoes for Belief-Importance (Expectancy Value) Model**			

Criterion	Importance*	Sweathog**	Superjock	Powerman
Comfort	9	3	6	8
Durability	7	1	10	5
Shock absorbancy	6	4	5	3
Style	4	5	7	8
Price***	2	8	5	2

*Importance or weight of each criterion is scored on a rating scale where 1 = least important and 10 = most important.
**Brand ratings are scored on a rating scale where 1 = very poor performance/value and 10 = excellent performance/value.
***Price ratings assume that a lower price is preferred or valued more than a higher price.

To compute Millie's attitude score for the Sweathog brand, we multiply her evaluations of this brand on each attribute by each criterion's importance. Then, we sum up these cross-products as follows: $(9 \times 3) + (7 \times 1) + (6 \times 4) + (4 \times 5) + (2 \times 8) = 94$. Likewise, her evaluation of Superjock would be $(9 \times 6) + (7 \times 10) + (6 \times 5) + (4 \times 7) + (2 \times 5) = 192$. You should be able to compute that Millie's attitude score for Powerman is 161. Because Superjock received the highest summated score, it is the preferred brand. She least likes Sweathog.

These attitude scores have no meaning in an *absolute* sense. They are only used to get *relative* rankings to determine rank order of brand preferences. For instance, an attitude score of 80 is not twice as good as a score of 40. This is because the numbers on the rating scales only indicate relative positions. Hence, the number "6" on a scale is not necessarily twice as favorable as a "3."

If a consumer believes all attributes are equally important, she uses the **unweighted linear compensatory decision model (unweighted rule, simple additive rule, equal weight rule)**. The attitude score formula here is:

$$A_{jk} = \sum_{i=1}^{n} b_{ijk}$$

That is, we simply sum the consumer's brand ratings (beliefs or evaluations) on all evaluative criteria for a particular brand.

Thus, in the athletic shoe example, the brand ratings would be:

Sweathog = 3 + 1 + 4 + 5 + 8 = 21
Superjock = 6 + 10 + 5 + 7 + 5 = 33
Powerman = 8 + 5 +3+ 8 + 2 = 26

Although, in this example, the rank order preference for the three brands is the same regardless of whether weights are used, the unweighted simple additive rule and the weighted belief-importance model need not necessarily yield the same rank order preferences.

➤ *The finite ideal point (additive difference) belief-importance model.* The belief-importance model assumes that higher ratings on belief scales are preferable to lower ratings. In this **infinite ideal point (vector attribute, additive difference) attitude model**, a greater amount of an attribute is preferred to less.

On the other hand, the **finite ideal point (attribute adequacy, additive difference) attitude model**, which usually holds for experience products, assumes that people prefer a moderate amount of each attribute ("ideal point") rather than the most of each. For example, a pretzel usually tastes better with a little salt added, but too much salt will be unpleasing to the palate. A café latte that is somewhat sweet is tasty, but too much sugar can ruin it. At times, "less is more."

Each attribute has an ideal level somewhere between the end points of a rating scale. Consequently, data on the consumer's ideal level of each attribute must also be collected.

The difference between the ideal level and the perceived amount of each attribute in a brand is multiplied by the attribute's importance, and these products are summed according to the formula:

$$A_{jk} = \sum_{i=1}^{n} w_{ik} \left| b_{ijk} - I_{ik} \right|$$

where i = attribute,

    j = brand,

    k = consumer,

    A_{jk} = a particular consumer's (k's) attitude score for brand j (A_B),

    w_{ik} = the importance weight assigned to attribute i by consumer k,

    b_{ijk} = consumer k's belief about the level of attribute i in brand j,

    I_{ik} = consumer k's ideal level of attribute i,

$\left| b_{ijk} - I_{ik} \right|$ = the absolute value of the difference between consumer k's belief about the level of attribute i in brand j and her ideal level of attribute i,

    n = number of attributes considered.

Smaller AO scores indicate more favorable attitudes. In fact, the ideal brand would score a zero.

➤ *The Rosenberg (instrumentality-value) model.* Milton **Rosenberg's (instrumentality-value) model** is founded on the notion that an AO can be instrumental in helping people achieve various personal values or desired outcomes. Hence, a person's AO becomes more favorable the more that object is seen as helping to fulfill values such as security, saving money, and success.

Rosenberg's model is similar to the belief-importance model, except that the belief component measuring a brand's rating on an attribute is replaced with the brand's rated ability to help the buyer achieve a particular value.

The formula is:

$$A_{jk} = \sum_{i=1}^{n} I_{ik} V_{ijk}$$

where i = value,

    j = brand,

    k = consumer,

    A_{jk} = consumer k's attitude score for brand j (A_B),

    I_{ik} = the importance weight assigned to value i by consumer k,

    V_{ijk} = consumer k's belief about the instrumentality of brand j in obtaining value i,

    n = number of attributes considered.

For instance, using a rating scale, respondents could be asked to what degree buying a certain make and model of automobile will help to fulfill such values as family security, social respect, comfort, and an exciting life. Using a second rating scale, consumers would rate how important or desirable each value is. Otherwise, the computation of a consumer's attitude score is similar to the procedure used in the expectancy-value model.

➤ *The Fishbein model.* Martin **Fishbein's model** views an attitude as a function of a person's evaluation of or feelings about certain attributes (or consequences) as being either desirable or undesirable, and the individual's belief about whether an AO has those attributes (or consequences).

The Fishbein model used by consumer researchers is:

$$A_{jk} = \sum_{i=1}^{n} B_{ijk} E_{ik}$$

EXHIBIT 15.10	Brand-Attribute Matrix for Athletic Shoes for the Fishbein Model			
Criterion (consequences of attribute)	Evaluation of consequences of attribute*	Sweathog**	Superjock	Powerman
Feels comfortable	+9	3	6	8
Wears out quickly	−7	10	1	6
Absorbs shocks well	+6	4	5	3
Has attractive style	+4	5	7	8
Has a high price	−2	2	6	9

*Evaluation of the consequences of each attribute is scored on a +10 (very positive) to −10 (very negative) rating scale.
**Brand ratings are scored on a rating scale scoring a consumer's belief about a brand's delivery of the consequences, where 10 = the brand very much delivers the consequences and 1 = the brand does not at all deliver the consequences.

where i = attribute,

j = brand,

k = consumer,

A_{jk} = consumer k's attitude score for brand j (A_B),

B_{ijk} = consumer k's belief that brand j possesses attribute i (or has a certain consequence associated with attribute i),

E_{ik} = consumer k's evaluation of the desirability of attribute i (or the consequences affiliated with attribute i),

n = number of attributes considered.

Where Fishbein's model differs from Rosenberg's model and the expectancy-value model is that (except for the finite ideal point formulation) the latter two assume that more of an attribute is preferred to less, whereas Fishbein suggests that certain attributes or their consequences might be undesirable. Instead of rating the importance weights of attributes, Fishbein's ratings are evaluation weights of the degree of desirability of the attributes or of the consequences resulting from a brand having those attributes.

In Exhibit 15.10, the data from the athletic shoe example of Exhibit 15.9 have been modified so that the criteria (attributes) have been restated in terms of their consequences. Also shown are a consumer's evaluation of the goodness or badness of those consequences on a +10 (very positive) to −10 (very negative) scale and the consumer's ratings regarding perceptions of a brand's delivery of the various consequences on a 10 (very much delivers the consequences) to 1 (does not at all deliver the consequences) scale.

Notice that the importance ratings are the same as the evaluation of consequences ratings for positively stated consequences, whereas in the case of unfavorable evaluations, they are the same numbers, only negative. Also, note that the ratings remain the same as in Exhibit 15.9 if the consequences are stated in a positive way (e.g., comfort: feels comfortable) and are reversed where the outcomes are phrased in a negative way (e.g., durability: wears out quickly).

An outcome that one consumer views as positive another person could evaluate as negative. For instance, if a brand of mouthwash has a medicinal taste, Marcia Mellow might like this since she believes that a medicinal flavor suggests that the brand is effective in killing germs and fighting bad breath. However, Rita Book might view a medicinal taste as bad since she dislikes the flavor.

➤ *Fishbein's theory of reasoned action (TORA) (Fishbein's extended model of behavioral intention, behavioral intentions model).* A variation on the Fishbein attitude model is **Fishbein's theory of reasoned action (TORA)**, also known as **Fishbein's extended model of behavioral intention (behavioral intentions model)**. This is a paradigm explaining how, when, and why attitudes predict behavior. This model is an elaboration on, and hence an improvement of, the previous multiattribute models in two significant ways, which results in better predictions of behavioral intentions and behaviors than seen in previous models.

1. The model uses the principle of *attitude specificity*. The more specific the attitude is to the predicted behavior, the higher the probability that the attitude will correctly predict that conduct. That is, to accurately forecast actions, it is more critical to ascertain a person's attitude toward the behavior itself than

his or her attitude toward the object of the behavior (AO). In other words, TORA measures behavioral intentions rather than AO.

You might be convinced that a BMW is, indeed, "The ultimate driving machine" as the ads suggest. However, you could have a very negative attitude toward buying a BMW because you know it would break your bank account (and then some)! Nonetheless, you might have a very positive attitude toward taking a friend's BMW out for a spin.

2. The model takes into account not just a consumer's own attitude toward the behavior but also the attitudes of significant others, such as family and friends. This concern for social influences is captured by two variables: normative beliefs and motivation to comply with normative beliefs.

Normative beliefs (NB; social norms, subjective norms) are the individual's perceptions about significant others' desires or expectations regarding the individual acting a certain way toward an AO (perhaps in a given situation). NBs are perceived social pressure to conform to the behavioral norms (standards) of other important persons or social groups.

For example, a man might cringe at the idea of daily flossing his teeth but realizes that both his wife and dentist expect this of him. Or, a tightwad might prefer to spend her money on herself rather than donate to the Cause of the Month, but neighbors or coworkers might shame her into contributing. Hence, normative influence can cause someone to take positive action toward a negative AO.

The consumer's **motivation to comply with normative beliefs (MC)** is the willingness to go along with the perceived expectations of others. The person decides, for instance, "I do want to please my wife and dentist," or "I don't give a good golly what my neighbors and coworkers think—I'm hanging on to my wallet and not donating to the cause."

Combining NB and MC yield the consumer's **subjective norms (SN),** or the buyer's motivation to act in accordance with the perceived influence of significant others.

TORA says that, to predict a consumer's behavior regarding an AO, you must measure the person's behavioral intention, which, in turn, is determined by both the person's attitude toward the act regarding the AO (A_{Act}) and subjective norms (SN), each of which is then added together according to the TORA formula:

$$B \sim BI = W_1 A_{Act} + W_2 SN$$

where B = predicted behavior (e.g., brand purchase),
     BI = behavioral intention (e.g., intent to purchase a brand),
     $B \sim BI$ indicates that behavior is a function of intent to behave and is approximately predicted by
           it (disregarding situational influences),
     A_{Act} = attitude toward the act regarding the AO (e.g., attitude toward purchasing a brand),
     SN = subjective norms,
     W_1 = relative importance of A_{Act},
     W_2 = relative importance of SN,
         and where

$$A_{Act} = \sum_{i=1}^{n} B_i E_i$$

where B_i = beliefs about consequences of an act,
     E_i = evaluation of the consequences of an act,
     n = number of consequences,
         and where

$$SN = \sum_{i=1}^{n} NB_j \times MC_j$$

where NB_j = normative beliefs—belief that significant others (j) expect the consumer to act,
     MC_j = a consumer's motivation to comply with these beliefs regarding the expectations of significant
         others (j).

EXHIBIT 15.11   Elements in Fishbein's Theory of Reasoned Action (TORA)

| Beliefs about consequences of an act (B_i) | Evaluation of the consequences of an act (E_i) | Normative beliefs (NB) | Motivation to comply with normative beliefs (MC) |

B_i · E_i **influences** · **influences** NB · MC

Attitude toward the act (A_{Act})   **Subjective norms (SN)**

which in turn influences

Behavioral intention (BI)

which in turn influences

Behavior

Exhibit 15.11 summarizes the relationships among the components of the TORA model.

To learn about the likelihood of a consumer buying a package of Brand X English muffins, the elements of the TORA model could be captured as follows on two attributes:

Attitude Toward the Act of Buying (A_{Act})

Attribute 1:

BI   Brand X is light and airy inside and crisp and crunchy outside.

Very probable   ————————————————————   Very improbable

E_i   If a brand is light and airy inside and crisp and crunchy outside, how desirable is this?

Very desirable   ————————————————   Very undesirable

Attribute 2:

BI   Brand X has nooks and crannies to hold melted butter.

Very probable   ————————————————————   Very improbable

E_i   If a brand has nooks and crannies to hold melted butter, how desirable is this?

Very desirable   ————————————————   Very undesirable

SUBJECTIVE NORMS (SN)

Attribute 1:
NB My family cares about me serving English muffins that are light and airy inside and crisp and crunchy outside.

Very true ——————————————————————————— Very false

Attribute 2:
NB My family cares about me serving English muffins that have nooks and crannies.

Very true ——————————————————————————— Very false

MOTIVATION TO COMPLY (MC)

MC I care what my family thinks about my breakfasts.

Very true ——————————————————————————— Very false

Applications of Multiattribute Attitude Models for Attitude Shaping. The following attitude-molding strategies are based on the multiattribute attitude models. All of these strategies involve the cognitive component, whereby marketers use promotional or product modifications to frame or structure the decision-making process for buyers by getting them to think differently. Keep in mind that all of these strategies are easier to accomplish when trying to modify peripheral, not central, beliefs and attitudes.

➤ *1. Change a particular belief component (b_{ij}, V_{ij}, B_{ij}).* This is accomplished by altering consumer perceptions favorably about the performance or value of the marketer's brand *j* on attribute *i* (b_{ij}), beliefs regarding the instrumentality of brand *j* in obtaining value I (V_{ij}), or consumers' beliefs that brand *j* possesses attribute *i* or has certain associated consequences (B_{ij}). For instance, paper towel brands often tout their superior absorbency. Most marketing communications suggest that the brand is "better," "superior," "improved," and so on, on one or more important criteria. Product improvement can also alter beliefs.

Since an individual's beliefs tend to be mutually consistent, changing one brand belief might result in other brand beliefs shifting too. If consumers are convinced that a car is very safe, they might also deduce that it is solidly built and handles well in inclement weather.

Negative beliefs regarding the promoted brand's attributes can be corrected via product improvements or promotional messages that correct false beliefs. Hallmark developed an ad campaign convincing buyers that its cards are not expensive.

Another way to alter beliefs is to modify consumer beliefs regarding competitive brands' attributes so that they are less favorable. Comparative advertising that specifically names rival brands and shows how they are inferior regarding one or more criteria is a common approach.

➤ *2. Alter the importance weight consumers assign to an attribute (w_i, I_i) on which the brand excels, or their evaluation of the desirability of that attribute or of the desirability of consequences affiliated with it is very positive (E_i).* Changing the importance of a criterion was used when Michelin alerted the public to the significance of ruggedly built tires and their importance to safety. Heinz demonstrated that slow-pouring ketchup is desirable because this means that it is thick, not thin and runny.

Changing an attribute's importance or desirability can be a Herculean challenge if the personal values underlying weights or perceived desirability of an attribute or its consequences are founded on deep-seated social and cultural norms, such as status, comfort, conformity, and other embedded social values.

➤ *3. Introduce a new attribute associated with the alternative evaluation process (i) and convince consumers of its importance (w_i).* Then, persuade consumers that the brand performs well on that attribute (b_{ij}), its associated value (V_{ij}), or its affiliated consequences (B_{ij}).

This can be an existing brand attribute not previously promoted or considered by users. The dairy industry explained that yogurt has more potassium than a banana, Sure deodorant taught social worriers that a dry blouse does not necessarily mean deodorant users smell good, and Kellogg's educated the public on the cancer-prevention qualities of high-fiber breakfast cereals.

Another strategy is to physically add a new attribute to the brand. Over the years, gasoline brands have incorporated additives to help keep engines clean, toothpastes have included plaque fighters and whiteners, and packaged foods have been fortified with vitamins and minerals. Also, an undesirable characteristic can be deleted (unscented deodorant, calorie-and caffeine-free soda, and cigarettes with additives removed).

➢ *4. Change buyers' ideal brand (I$_i$).* For example, conservation organizations advocate buying brands that are environmentally friendly. Hybrid cars have helped move buyers away from their love affair with gas-guzzling SUVs.

➢ *5. Regarding the TORA model, communicate normative beliefs that endorse selecting a brand (NB) and the importance of complying with people who approve of the brand (MC).* This generally works best for socially conspicuous products where consumers decide to purchase a brand primarily for gaining social approval or avoiding social disapproval. Ads for such items often show their use in social settings with people praising the brand and buyers receiving social approbation.

➢ *6. Maintain existing beliefs.* Reminder advertising continuously links a brand and an attribute. For many years, Coke has reminded the public that it is the leading brand, Budweiser does not let us forget that they are the "King of beers," and BMW remains the "ultimate driving machine."

FUNCTIONAL THEORY OF ATTITUDE CHANGE

Psychologist Daniel Katz suggested that attitudes can serve four functions (i.e., satisfy four motives): knowledge, utility, value-expression, and ego-defense. This **functional theory of attitude change** suggests that marketers can modify attitudes by crafting marketing communications appealing to one or more of these four attitude functions.

We now discuss these four motives in order from those that consumers are most consciously aware of, that are easy for marketing researchers to measure, and that are less challenging to mold, to those that are more complex and subconscious, hard to measure, and difficult to transform.

The Utilitarian Attitude Function. The **utilitarian (instrumental, adjustment, adaptive) attitude function** relates to utilitarian needs and motives. People have favorable attitudes toward AOs that help secure rewards or avoid punishment. Adjustment is the inclination to develop attitudes that are most likely to result in rewards or in evading penalization. Utilitarian-based attitudes are held for products that satisfy pragmatic needs, such as having clean hands or working more efficiently. Functional attitudes are also held for items made to solve consumption-relevant problems such as preventing sickness or organizing information.

The marketing implication is to develop a product that shows superior performance in satisfying functional needs. Then, marketing communications should use a **utilitarian appeal** that demonstrates how the product fulfills functional needs. They should emphasize product features and the functional benefits they provide through techniques such as problem-solution advertising, comparative advertising, and sales promotions (e.g., coupons and samples) that encourage prospects to experience the product's superior performance.

The Knowledge Attitude Function. Attitudes held to satisfy the **knowledge attitude function** help consumers understand and adapt to a complex world and organize their beliefs about AOs. Such attitudes help people relate to the marketplace and simplify their decision making.

Keep it simple: Products should be easy to understand and operate, positioning must be unambiguous, and straightforward, and comprehensible information should be presented in marketing communications, owner's manuals, and other marketing materials.

The Value-Expressive Attitude Function. **Value-expressive attitudes** help us express our self-concept and live out our lifestyles and our central values. Such attitudes are tied to symbolic (value-expressive) needs. Value-expressive attitudes are most relevant for socially consumed or highly visible, relatively high-involvement products, such as cars, homes, and leisure pursuits. These suggest to others what we are really like. Going to the opera might imply that one has sophistication, class, and discriminating taste, while reading *The Economist* might suggest being learned and intelligent.

To influence value-expressive attitudes, marketers can use a **value-expressive appeal**, or a communication that crafts a brand image. One cosmetics brand might position itself as youthful while another comes across as suave and sophisticated. Promotional efforts can also show how buying the branded product helps fulfill cultural and personal values such as achievement, independence, wisdom, and freedom. However, the value-expressive attitude function deals with values that might be difficult to shape. The brand must be fit to the customer, not vice versa.

The Ego-Defensive Function. **Ego-defensive attitudes** are held to protect and defend one's self-concept and **self-ego** (i.e., one's sense of self-worth) from internal and external threats, anxieties, and insecurities. For example, apathetic or skeptical attitudes regarding the dangers of antisocial behaviors such as drinking and driving and doing drugs might reflect **ego defense**, in which one defends oneself against shame, anxiety, loss of self-esteem, conflict, or other unacceptable feelings or thoughts. Defense of the ego can be expressed through denial, projection, rationalization, and repression.

Examples: A man might deny that he is mechanically challenged because he believes "real men" know how to fix things. Prejudice against people of certain races, nationalities, or religions can be caused by one's own personal insecurities and feelings of inferiority, leading to projection of these onto others. At times, ego-defensive attitudes are rationalizations or justifications ("I'm not fat, just big-boned").

Attitudes toward products such as difficult-to-learn software and complex power tools might be negative if these things are seen as threats to one's competence, self-sufficiency, and other positive aspects of the self. Marketers of such products must design them to be "user-friendly" and promote them as such. When instant and frozen foods were launched during the 1950s, many homemakers were hesitant to accept them because they threatened women's self-images as hardworking, caring stewards of the home.

Conversely, products such as mouthwash and study guides might be held in high regard since they help prevent anxiety-producing situations. Sure brand deodorant is effectively positioned toward ego-defensive attitudes by promising social confidence. A brand promoted for "macho men" might appeal to insecure males.

Like value-expressive attitudes, ego-defensive attitudes are linked to symbolic needs, which are central to our lives, often subconsciously held, frequently idiosyncratic, and usually difficult to alter. Therefore, marketers should accept and adapt to existing ego-defensive attitudes rather than attempt to alter them. Instead of putting down drug users as not being cool, the antidrug marketer could try to persuade users that the risks just are not worth it.

Conclusion on Functional Theory. Any given attitude can perform multiple functions for a consumer. A buyer might like Sears Craftsman tools because they efficiently perform handy household tasks (utilitarian function); are clearly promoted as helping the do-it-yourself craftsman (knowledge function); assist with home improvements so as to create an attractive, comfortable abode (value-expressive function); and make being a handyman easier to achieve, even for those with two left thumbs (ego defensive function). Usually, one attitude function will predominate for a given product and market segment. Therefore, marketers should tap into the product-relevant functions and motives most important to the target market.

BALANCE THEORY

Fritz Heider's **balance theory** focuses on the relationship between beliefs and attitudes, suggesting that people seek balance between their thoughts (beliefs) and feelings (evaluations). This theory considers relationships among environmental elements a person might perceive as belonging together, describing these elements as composing attitude structure and occurring in groups of three, known as triads. Each triad contains: (1) a person (typically a consumer), (2) the individual's perceptions of an AO (brand, store, etc.), and (3) the consumer's perceptions of some other person or object that has a relationship with the AO (product endorser, advertising medium, etc.).

People desire relationships among these three elements to be balanced (harmonious). If they are unbalanced, the individual experiences a state of tension known as cognitive dissonance. People feeling

EXHIBIT 15.12   Illustration of Balance Theory

Unbalanced relationship

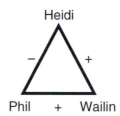

Restoring balance in the relationship

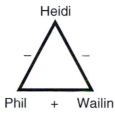 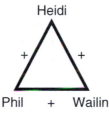 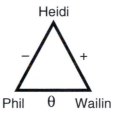

Note: The easy way to determine if a triad is balanced or unbalanced is to multiply the three signs, recalling that a positive times a positive is positive, a negative times a positive is negative, and a negative times a negative is positive. If the product of the three signs is positive, the relationship is balanced, and if this product is negative the relationship is unbalanced.

dissonance will alter their perceptions or evaluations in order to make relationships among the elements mutually consistent or balanced.

Two elements could be perceived to have either a unit relation, whereby one element is believed to belong to or be a part of the other, or a sentiment relation, where both elements are associated because one element has either a preference or a liking for the other element. For instance, a dating couple would have a positive sentiment relationship, and when married they would (hopefully) have a positive unit relation.

As an illustration, the first triangle in Exhibit 15.12 shows the relationships between Heidi, a consumer who initially likes Wailin brand guitars (indicated by a plus sign linking Heidi and Wailin but who despises the endorser for Wailin guitars, blues singer Phil N. Blue (shown by the negative sign connecting Heidi and Phil). There is a positive relationship between Phil and Wailin since Phil speaks highly of the guitar in their advertisements. This creates an unbalanced or incongruous relationship: Heidi does not like Phil, who endorses Wailin, yet she likes Wailin.

To restore balance among the relationships between these three elements of the triad, one of the three relationships must change (as shown in the next three triangles in Exhibit 15.12). The first possibility shown is for Heidi to decide that she likes neither Phil nor the guitars he is endorsing, that is, she changes her attitude toward Wailin guitars to be negative. A second scenario is to change her attitude toward Phil; maybe he is not such a bad guy after all. A third situation is for Heidi to disassociate Phil from Wailin guitars. She can decide that Phil really doesn't like Wailin after all; he is just endorsing it for the money, so there is no sentiment relationship (indicated by a "θ" in the illustration). In this third scenario, she maintains her original attitudes toward both Phil and Wailin guitars.

Generally, people are most prone to alter their weaker attitude. So, if Heidi does not have a very strong attitude toward Phil but has a more intense attitude toward Wailin, she will probably soften up her attitude toward Phil. However, if she feels very unfavorably about Phil but not very positively toward Wailin, she will likely sour on the guitar. Or, if both of these attitudes are strong, Heidi might change her perception about the reality or meaningfulness of the tie between Wailin and Phil.

As this example demonstrates, marketers use balance theory to affiliate their brand to some person or object (such as a spokescharacter or a logo) that people feel good about. The positive image of this person or object will presumably rub off onto the brand, that is, there is affect transferal. Conversely, marketers can associate a competitor's brand with something negative to induce negative evaluations of the rival's brand.

LOW-EFFORT PERIPHERAL-ROUTE DECISION-MAKING PERSPECTIVE

So far, we have assumed that beliefs are developed through a process of active information processing under conditions of moderate to high consumer involvement. However, where involvement is low, consumers might passively form **simple beliefs**, or perceptions that are relatively weak because buyers have not deeply processed the information underlying them. Marketers might find that simple beliefs are easier to change than beliefs formed via the central processing route.

Simple beliefs are founded on the basis of one or several peripheral cues. For instance, credible sources such as professional and celebrity experts can serve as peripheral cues for forming simple beliefs. Simple beliefs can also take the form of recognition of a marketing cue ("That's a familiar jingle," "I know whose logo that is"). Simple beliefs might also be acquired via **simple inferences**, in which consumers form beliefs based on straightforward associations. Line extensions get high trial rates because consumers figure that, if there is a quality flagship product (e.g., Cole Kutz lunch meats) from which the line extension derives (e.g., Cole Kutz cheese), the line extension is also of high quality.

Further, simple inferences can take the form of decision heuristics, such as "Buy the brand your neighbor uses" or "Purchase the same brand you bought last time." Simple inferences are sometimes formed based on surrogate indicators of product quality or performance, such as price, brand name, country of origin, and color. If Wetzels' pretzels come in a fancy-looking gold package, the belief might be, "Wetzel's is the high-priced, fancy pretzel."

Consumers might also observe that there are many message arguments supporting a product claim. Rather than processing all of these, they might use the **frequency heuristic**, which occurs when a belief is formed on the basis of the number of arguments made in its favor instead of on the nature of the arguments per se.

In all of these cases, however, after purchase and consumption, evaluation might occur and more complete attitudes might be formed based on experiential learning.

The marketing suggestion in such low-involvement learning situations is to keep the message simple and on target, repetitively hammering away at the selling appeal.

REVIEW QUESTIONS

1. Describe each of the four general models and theories for the decision-making perspective (DMP) on cognitive attitude shaping as well as some general marketing implications suggested by each.
2. Explain some of the ways marketers can encourage consumers to generate support arguments and to not produce counterarguments as well as try to enhance the credibility of their message.
3. Discuss under what kind of marketplace conditions each of the following marketing communications strategies would be most effective: placing the strongest arguments early in the message (i.e., assuming a primacy effect), using a two-sided message, employing negative message framing, drawing an explicit conclusion, and using distractions.
4. Explain the nature of the different types of communication sources. Describe why it is important to have a credible source, and cite the characteristics of credible communication sources.
5. Explain what determines a consumer's attitude toward the ad (A_{ad}) at the cognitive level.
6. Describe each of the following multiattribute attitude models: belief-importance (expectancy-value) model (including unweighted and finite ideal point models), Rosenberg's (instrumentality-value) model, Fishbein's model, and Fishbein's theory of reasoned action (Fishbein's extended model of behavioral intention, behavioral intentions model). Also, explain why multiattribute models are an improvement for understanding attitudes over simpler models of global attitude.
7. Explain each of the attitude-shaping strategies based on multiattribute attitude models.

8. Discuss the four functions of attitudes according to the functional theory of attitude change and how marketers can tap into each function.
9. Explain balance theory and how marketers can apply it.
10. How can marketers employ the cognitive route to attitude change under low-effort peripheral route processing?

IN-CLASS APPLICATIONS

1. Evaluate each of the ads in Exhibits 15.13 through 15.16 regarding as many message structure characteristics as you can find. Consider each ad's effectiveness in using argument quality; serial position effects (order of presentation); message sidedness (one-sided versus two-sided messages); positive versus negative message framing; closed-ended versus open-ended (explicit) conclusion drawing; and use of distractions.

2. Identify the communication source (or sources) in each of the following scenarios. Then, evaluate each source in terms of its credibility. Will this evaluation result in any kind of source derogation, source bolstering, or ad execution–related thoughts?

→ *Scenario A: Anna's Aquatic Antics.* Anna's Aqua World is a giant retail outlet, with corporate headquarters located in Marina Bay. With the slogan, "Proudly serving all your swimming and boating needs since 1901," Anna's carries everything and anything having to do with outdoor water sports, from swimwear and pool accessories to canoes and kayaks.

This emporium regularly schedules TV and radio commercials on the most popular local broadcast stations. The ads feature their beloved, cute and cuddly mascot, Sammy the Seal. Anna Pollagaro, CEO and daughter of the five-outlet chain's founder, makes regular appearances at each of the retailer's shops, doling out water wisdom to shoppers.

In the firm's annual "Twenty-five Grand in the Sand" contest, the winner of the treasure chest, buried somewhere on Boguski Bay, gets to keep the loot and dine at Larry's Lobster House with the beloved Anna.

→ *Scenario B: Wondering About Winky's.* Winky's Water Wonderland is Anna's Aqua World's major competitor. Winky's came on the scene in 2003, when Winky Wallace, founder and CEO, was released from prison after serving three years' time for corporate financial fraud at Humongous Conglomerate.

Winky's now has three outlets in the greater Marina Bay area, and they carry a more limited supply of water sports items than does Anna's. Winky's runs rather nasty late-night TV commercials on the Naughty Channel ("For sophisticated audiences"). The ads feature Winky with his infamous putdowns of Anna (e.g., "The old goat smells like a dead fish").

Winky's has been known to fail to honor their product and service guarantees. They also soak customers with exorbitant service charges. There have been several articles recently in *The Marina Bay Tattler* about the illegal gambling operations that Winky is alleged to be running out of one of his stores. He flat out denies any such dealings to media reporters, however.

→ *Scenario C: Pinky's Jewelry Isn't All Jewels.* Pinky's Jewelers is the Triboro Area's largest retail jeweler, with stores in several local malls. Pinky's absolutely will not be undersold—they buy in volume, hire homely looking, low-skilled high school kids to staff the stores to save on labor costs, and their outlets are bare bones, no-frills operations. All sales are final, with no returns.

Ads in the *Triboro Times* ("All the news that fits we print"), the area's most trusted local newspaper, feature pictures of gorgeous women and handsome men sporting the jewelry. Owner Pinky Finger appears in some ads wearing his trademark bow tie and loud plaid sports coat and striped pants, screaming "Come on down!" His slogan is, "We give you cheaper for less!"

Readers have reported that the ads are about as appealing as listening to fingernails scraping on a chalkboard. They also find that the quality of the jewelry often leaves something to be desired.

→ *Scenario D: Sandy's Saucy Super Subs.* Sandy's Submarine Sandwich Shops, "Home of the Super Sub," have arguably the best sub sandwiches in South Metro. They are the preferred late-night snack of Metro State College students. Not only do the subs have meat, cheese, and veggies piled high and deep, they also feature Sandy's Special Super Sauce, a concoction that adds extra zingy flavor. Plus, most of them are low in fat and carbohydrates.

EXHIBIT 15.13   Matrix Ad

EXHIBIT 15.14   Allegra Ad

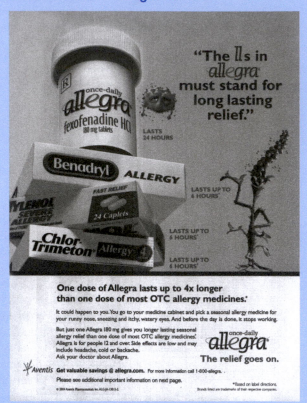

EXHIBIT 15.15   Kellogg's Hunny B's Ad

EXHIBIT 15.16   Partnership for a Drug-Free America Ad

Ads run in the local paper, *The Metro Reporter,* featuring Sam Ward, an actual consumer. Sam is a friendly, good-looking guy who allegedly lost 165 pounds by eating Sandy's sandwiches for breakfast, lunch, dinner, and evening snack for a year. The ads fail to mention, however, that he also ran ten miles a day and swam laps every morning to help him reach his weight loss goals, although word about this has leaked out.

Who is owner Sandy? Nobody really knows for sure, but rumor has it that it is Sandy Ribald, a jolly old soul who could devour a two-foot-long sub in under four minutes and founded the restaurant.

3. Analyze each of the ads you evaluated in Question 1 to determine which attitude-shaping strategy (or strategies) based on the multiattribute attitude model is being used: changing beliefs, altering importance weights, introducing new attributes, changing ideal levels, and maintaining belief levels. How effective do you think each ad is in shaping attitudes according to these strategies? Can you suggest any alternative cognitive attitude shaping strategies for any of the advertised brands?

4. Evaluate this same set of ads in terms of which theory or theories of functional attitude change each seems to be applying. How effective is each ad in applying the theory or theories?

WRITTEN APPLICATIONS

1. Find and discuss the effectiveness of advertisements demonstrating each of the following:
   a. Very strong arguments, considering both their quality and order of presentation.
   b. A two-sided message. If it is either a mea culpa strategy or refutational appeal, explain how so.
   c. A negatively framed message.
   d. Either a closed-ended (implicit) or an open-ended (explicit) conclusion.
   e. A distraction.
2. Select a product category that interests you (e.g., running shoes, MP3 players, video games, activewear, etc.). Your task is to use each of the following three multiattribute attitude models to compare three different brands for which, a priori, you have brand preferences (i.e., you can rank them first, second, and third in terms of your personal preference before applying the models to them): belief-importance (expectancy value) model (either weighted or unweighted, and either infinite ideal point or finite ideal point models), Rosenberg's (instrumentality-value) model, and Fishbein's model.

   You will need to determine four evaluative criteria and their relative importance to you, using a rating scale. You will also need to rate each brand on each criterion. If you use the finite ideal point model, you must additionally determine attribute ratings for your ideal brand. For Rosenberg's model, you will need to substitute valued states for attributes. For Fishbein's model, you must rate the desirability of each attribute (rather than importance). Describe how the three models compare in predicting your rank order brand preferences. Do you get different results with the different models? Do any of them correctly predict your rank-order preferences for the three brands? If not, why do you believe they don't?

   Assuming you are typical of your favorite brand's target market, suggest some marketing strategy implications from your findings. You might wish to think in terms of attitude-shaping strategies based on multiattribute models.
3. Answer Question 4 for in the In-Class Applications above for three of the ads. Then, find four different ads, each of which is an illustration of a different attitude function, and critique each ad's effectiveness.

EXERCISE 15.3. THE AFFECTIVE EXPERIENTIAL PERSPECTIVE AND THE CONATIVE BEHAVIORAL INFLUENCE PERSPECTIVE

OBJECTIVES

1. To explain the affective experiential perspective and the conative behavioral influence perspective for attitude formation and change under high- and low-effort information processing.
2. To identify and explain each of the theories and models of affective and conative attitude molding as

well as the kinds of products and situations for which each is relevant, their marketing applications, and the use of these models and theories in advertising and other marketing situations.

3. To understand the relevance of the attitude-toward-the-ad (A_{ad}) concept for both central route and peripheral route affective attitude molding.

4. To become familiar with attribution theory and self-perception theory, and to identify and "test" your own internal attributions and external attributions toward yourself, others, and objects.

5. To understand five models of hierarchy of communications effects, the type of conditions under which it is appropriate for marketers to tap into each hierarchy, and the tactics marketers use to move their targeted customers through each hierarchy.

Background

This concluding exercise examines attitude-shaping approaches based on the affective component (the experiential perspective) and the conative component (the behavioral influence perspective). These two perspectives are a mix of high-effort central-route processing and low-effort peripheral-route processing (see Exhibit 15.1). We conclude by describing five hierarchies of communications effects, each of which suggests a specific order in which marketers lead consumers through the cognitive, affective, and conative stages. The last two of these emphasize the primacy of the do (action) attitude component.

Appropriately, *Consumer Behavior in Action* concludes its journey with action!

The Affective Experiential Perspective

The **affective experiential perspective** is an outlook on attitude molding that tries to effect attitude change via consumers' feelings and emotions, employing strategies grounded in the affective dimension. Especially for hedonic products, consumers first evaluate a brand on an overall basis by relying on their feelings, emotions, and even fantasies, rather than on beliefs about brand-attribute performance. These beliefs are formed later, after purchase and use experience. Consequently, behavior influences subsequent experience-based attitudes.

When marketers use affective experiential strategies, consumers experience **affective responses**, or emotional reactions to marketing communications and anticipation of how the product will make them feel or how a brand will enhance their self-concepts. Affective responses also occur where the consumer has positive prior information on and experience with the product, such as when consumers are brand loyal. In such cases, consumers have holistic, positive brand attitudes.

As in the cognitive approach, under the affective experiential perspective a particular theory is applicable depending on whether consumers undertake high-effort central-route processing or low-effort peripheral-route processing.

Affective Change Under the High-Effort Central-Route Experiential Perspective

Under high-involvement circumstances, consumers experience **affective involvement**, strong emotional responses to a stimulus that lead to shaping of strong attitudes. In effect, buyers rely on their feelings, rather than on beliefs, as an information source. For example, a young couple buying their first house might happen upon an abode that they fall in love with before carefully inspecting it—it is their "dream house." Some high school seniors select a college based on "love at first sight."

We now examine two central-route affective approaches: emotional appeals and attitude toward the ad.

Emotional Appeals. **Emotional (affective) appeals** try to change the consumer's affect (i.e., to evoke an affective response) toward an AO via appeals such as fear, humor, sex, love, joy, and hope. Ads can present emotional situations so that consumers will vicariously experience these emotions via techniques such as transformational advertising, covert involvement advertising, and use of pleasurable peripheral cues including music, drama, and attractive presenters. Products ripe for emotional appeals include hedonic products, value-expressive products, and transformational products. The goal is to associate the brand with warm, emotional feelings. Ads for diamond rings feature loving, romantic couples; camera ads depict happy occasions such as weddings, birthday celebrations, and family reunions; soda ads show fun times and happy occasions; and greeting card ads display people emotionally connecting. In all cases, the hope is that audience members will connect to the brand.

Attitude Toward the Ad (A_{ad}). A_{ad} is concerned with whether or not an audience member likes a particular ad during a specific exposure occasion. If there is affect transfer, A_{ad} will influence the consumer's attitude toward an AO (e.g., brand) featured in the ad, such as the brand. When the affective response is favorable (unfavorable), the consumer's attitude toward the brand might also become favorable (unfavorable), and he or she will be more (less) likely to buy it.

Ads that create positive feelings (e.g., ads featuring exciting contests or nostalgic music), are interesting and intriguing, and feature techniques such as humor, upbeat music, interesting story lines, and celebrities can all create a positive A_{ad}.

AFFECTIVE CHANGE UNDER THE LOW-EFFORT PERIPHERAL-ROUTE DECISION-MAKING PERSPECTIVE

Most marketing communications that work on the affective plain are directed toward recipients engaged in low-involvement information processing. Such consumers lack the MOA to devote much effort to processing information. Here, attitudes are based on a few simple, relatively weak beliefs based on shallow information processing. Since the resulting attitudes are weak, they are relatively easy to change.

The four theories of attitude shaping that are relevant here all rely upon peripheral cues. There is much conceptual overlap among these theories, and so a given affective attitude alteration strategy can operate in accordance with several of these models simultaneously.

The Mere Exposure Effect. The **mere exposure effect** occurs when frequent exposure to a stimulus creates liking for it. For instance, we become attached to certain personal possessions, such as a favorite sweater, stuffed animal, or coffee mug, and are sometimes reluctant to junk them even after they have outlived their usefulness or have become old and worn out.

The mere exposure effect is most likely where elaboration likelihood is low. This suggests that brands bought due to inertia might eventually come to be preferred due to their familiarity. Recording artists hope their tunes get frequent airplay on radio, MTV, and YouTube so that the songs will "grow on" people.

Marketers should therefore work to get their low-involvement products in front of consumers regularly through strategies such as high-frequency advertising, intensive distribution, and peer-to-peer sharing on the Internet. There should be continuity in key ad elements such as slogans, jingles, and trade characters. However, care must be taken to avoid wearout by offering a variety of creative executions of the key ad elements.

Classical Conditioning: Attitudinal Conditioning. One type of classical conditioning is **attitudinal (emotional, affective) conditioning**, which occurs when learners attribute thoughts or feelings about the unconditioned stimulus to the conditioned stimulus upon repeated exposure to pairings of the stimuli.

For instance, through **affect transferal** the consumer's attitude toward an advertisement or emotional responses to that ad will transfer to the brand. Such ads use unconditioned affective stimuli such as a fun scenario, a celebrity, pleasant visuals, or enjoyable music that evoke unconditioned positive emotional reactions such as joy, excitement, relaxation, or sentimentality, feelings that then rub off onto the brand as a new conditioned response.

Attitude Toward the Ad (A_{ad}). As already noted, A_{ad} should be most influential on brand choices where consumers do not have solid reasons for selecting one alternative over another except for the fact that they like its advertising, as might occur in a low-involvement purchase situation.

According to the **dual-mediation hypothesis**, consumers can have a positive attitude toward the ad either because they have a favorable cognitive response (i.e., the ad provides them with useful information) or they have a positive affective response (i.e., they gain good feelings from or are interested in the ad).

In either case, A_{ad} is enhanced, leading to consumer acceptance of brand beliefs or claims, resulting in a more favorable brand attitude, or to affect transfer, in which positive feelings directly transfer to the brand (e.g., "I like the Squiddly Diddley character in Frank's frozen squid ads, so I like Frank's frozen squids").

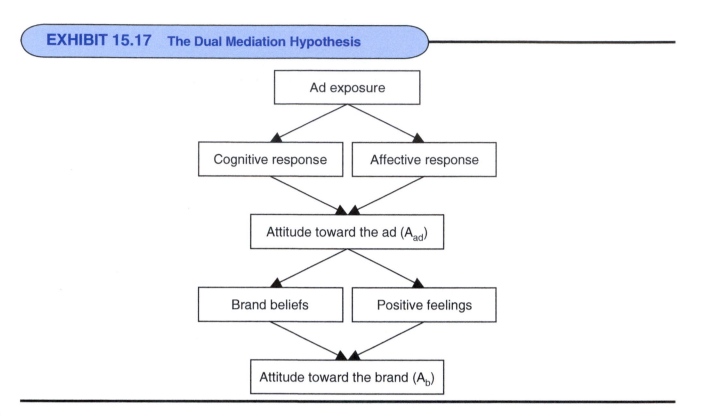

EXHIBIT 15.17   The Dual Mediation Hypothesis

Exhibit 15.17 outlines this hypothesis. Under low-effort peripheral-route processing, the affective response is at work, whereas under high-effort central-route processing, the cognitive response is operative.

Mood. The consumer's **mood** is a temporary feeling state that is usually not intense and is not tied to a specifiable behavior, event, or object. One's mood can create feelings like loneliness or anger upon exposure to a stimulus, thereby affecting attitude. That is why we are more favorable to new ideas when in a good mood. Most spouses realize that it is wise to approach their "better half" with a request or rebuke when their beloved is in a good frame of mind.

Consumers might like a brand better when either the commercials or the programming during which the ads appear put them in a good mood. Retailers can influence shoppers' moods through atmospherics (see Exercise 4.6).

THE CONATIVE BEHAVIORAL INFLUENCE PERSPECTIVE

The **conative behavioral influence perspective** seeks to first induce a change in CB, which will then lead to experience-based changes in buyers' knowledge and attitudes. Motion results in emotion. For instance, the OnStar security system is free for the first year after consumers purchase a new General Motors vehicle. Presumably buyers will have a good experience and then pay for the service (about 60 percent do so).

CONATIVE CHANGE UNDER THE HIGH-EFFORT CENTRAL-ROUTE BEHAVIORAL INFLUENCE PERSPECTIVE

There are three theories where behavioral modification occurs under relatively high-involvement conditions: instrumental conditioning, cognitive dissonance, and attribution theory.

Instrumental Conditioning. **Instrumental conditioning (operant conditioning, reinforcement theory)** learning theory suggests that reinforced behavior is more likely to be repeated because the learner's attitude has been strongly and favorably formed by a rewarding experience (Chapter 14). Such behavior-before-attitude learning occurs mostly in moderate- to high-involvement circumstances.

This suggests that marketers should induce targeted customers to purchase or consume the brand, especially for experience goods, and ensure that consumption will be a rewarding experience in order to gain more favorable attitudes. Incentives can provoke a purchase, notably sales promotions such as coupons and prepurchase sampling (e.g., "scratch n' sniff" scent strips for cologne, color strips for makeup, and calorie-free flavor strips for new toothpaste flavors), automobile test drives, and trial offers.

Cognitive Dissonance Theory. **Cognitive dissonance** is a psychologically uncomfortable state of tension caused by inconsistency among two or more attitude components (intra-attitude inconsistency). To achieve consistency, the consumer might shift her beliefs and attitudes to be consistent with her prior behavior, thereby reducing **postpurchase dissonance (buyer's remorse, regret)**. The probability of attitude change is directly proportional to the magnitude of dissonance.

Both the negative characteristics of selected alternatives and the positive attributes of rejected options induce dissonance. Therefore, buyers conduct postpurchase information search to confirm their decision, seeking out the marketer's promotional efforts that praise the brand while avoiding or counterarguing with dissonance-inducing competitive ads. They also seek reassurance and approval from others.

The marketer's task is to help lessen buyers' dissonance and thereby get more favorable postpurchase attitudes. This is accomplished primarily through dissonance-reducing communications (ads reassuring recent buyers, congratulatory phone calls, etc.) and follow-up service and complaint handling, suggestions for product care and maintenance, and relationship marketing programs.

Advertisers can also attempt to neutralize rivals' advertising that tries to create doubts in buyers' minds about the brands they bought by using strong arguments and two-sided messages to inoculate customers against competitive ads.

Attribution Theory. **Attribution** concerns the perception and crediting of the cause of an effect, that is, figuring out what caused an event to happen. According to Fritz Heider's **attribution theory**, people seek to understand reasons for observable environmental events. By attributing events to causes, people are able to understand the world around them.

Hence, consumers seek to determine attributions (causes—either credit or blame) for occurrences in the marketplace, often after the fact. One way they do this is by observing their own behavior and from that deducing what kind of attitude they have, especially for high-involvement purchases.

As was true of cognitive dissonance theory, attribution theory suggests that advertisers should provide consumers with positive reasons for selecting their brand after they have done so. Reinforcement advertising can assure customers that a brand's good performance is due to the brand and not some outside factor.

Self-Perception Theory. One type of attribution theory, Daryl Bem's **self-perception theory** says that when asked about attitudes of which they are uncertain, people sometimes reflect on their behavior and infer what their attitudes must be. Such individuals come up with judgments regarding whether the causes of their own behavior are of their own volition or due to external circumstances.

Accordingly, consumers can use either **internal attributions**, in which they assign credit or blame for an occurrence to themselves, or **external attributions**, in which an outcome is attributed to circumstances beyond their control. If they believe that they acted of their own free will, they deduce that their attitude must have been positive. However, if they believe their behavior was caused by outside circumstances, they are less likely to conclude that their attitude is favorable.

For instance, someone who volunteers at their child's school might do so thinking "I am helping out because I am a caring person." Alternatively, the volunteer might think, "I am assisting because Billy's teacher browbeat me into doing it." Each attribution results in a different attitude, and in this example each one concerns a different AO.

For example, after completing a home improvement do-it-yourself project, a person can admire the completed project and either think, "I'm really great at doing home improvement projects" (internal attribution), "The instructions the seller gave me were really helpful in getting the job done correctly" (external attribution), or "It looks wonderful—I lucked out" (external attribution).

From the seller's perspective, the first or second attributions are preferred. In the first attribution, the user's self-confidence is boosted and he or she might, consequently, purchase more do-it-yourself projects from the seller. In the second attribution, the user thinks more favorably of the marketer who provided excellent directions. The user will likely be a repeat customer. However, the third attribution could apply equally to a rival's brand.

This theory suggests that sales promotions might have the undesirable effect of causing consumers to ascribe purchase of the brand to the incentive rather than to their preference for the brand itself. The result is brand switching once the sales promotion terminates. Consequently, marketers can use advertising to provide nonprice-related reasons to repurchase so that consumers develop more favorable brand attitudes following purchase.

The principle of **defensive attribution** suggests that people tend to attribute their success to themselves (internal attribution) and their failures to others (external attribution). Consequently, our do-it-yourselfer will likely conclude that the project came out great due to his or her own skill. If it came out poorly blame would be placed on the marketer's instructions, the materials provided for the construction project, or other external causes.

Hence, a marketer should ensure that the product performs well for buyers. Marketing communications can also reassure buyers that good product performance is due to the product and its marketing and any possible problems are caused by nonmarketing factors (although the principle of defensive attribution suggests that care must be taken in ascribing blame to the customer).

➤ *Attributions toward others.* **Attributions toward others** concern why someone thinks other people (or groups or firms) do the things they do. For instance, if a salesperson recommends one brand of furniture over another, the buyer could attribute the seller's suggestion to a desire to earn a commission on it, to the salesperson having a friend who works for the furniture manufacturer, to the sales representative's personal preference, or to the seller's concern to ensure that the customer gets the best product. If the salesperson can convince the shopper that the seller has his or her best interests at heart, the customer is more likely to follow the seller's advice.

If a restaurant server is providing unusually slow service, the patron can chalk it up to the waitperson being lazy, incompetent, overworked, or just having a bad day. Alternatively, the customer can ascribe the poor service to factors outside the server's control, such as the kitchen crew being overworked or incompetent. Clearly, if the latter is true, it is in the waitperson's best self-interest to make the patron aware of this so that his or her tip does not suffer.

➤ *Attributions toward things.* **Attributions toward things** are formed when people try to figure out why products work or perform the way they do. If someone is having trouble getting software to download online, he or she could attribute the difficulty to the software provider or the program, to her Internet service provider, to the computer, or to personal technological ineptness (the latter being a self-perception). If the marketer knows of the buyer's difficulties but is not at fault, this should be made clear to the buyer. If the consumer is to blame, a software technician should diplomatically help out without making the customer feel foolish.

➤ *How consumers validate their attributions.* Harold Kelley suggested that someone's attribution is, in effect, a hypothesis. The observer then "tests" the hypothesis to ascertain its validity by gathering additional data in order to either confirm or disconfirm the initial hypothesis. In so doing, the individual uses four criteria:

- *Distinctiveness.* The person attributes an outcome to a cause if the outcome occurs when the cause is present and does not happen in the cause's absence.
- *Consistency over time.* Each time the alleged cause is present, the event occurs.
- *Consistency over modality.* The outcomes are consistent even though the situation in which the presumed cause is present varies.
- *Consensus.* Others perceive the cause-and-effect relationship the same way as the observer.

The more perfectly an individual's attributions fulfill these four criteria, the more confident he or she is that the attribution is, indeed, valid.

For example, suppose Otto's auto runs smoothly on Peter's Petroleum gasoline but the engine knocks on all other brands. Otto therefore attributes the superior performance of his car when filled with Otto's to the brand's high quality. His hypothesis is confirmed when he verifies that one or more of the following occur:

- *Distinctiveness.* The car runs smoothly on Peter's and only on Peter's.
- *Consistency over time.* Otto gets smooth operation each and every time he uses Peter's.
- *Consistency over modality.* Otto's car runs smoothly on Peter's no matter where or when he drives.
- *Consensus.* Everyone that Otto knows agrees that his or her car runs smoothest on this brand.

CONATIVE CHANGE UNDER THE LOW-EFFORT PERIPHERAL-ROUTE BEHAVIORAL INFLUENCE PERSPECTIVE

Passive learning does not require conscious attention or involvement on the learner's part (Chapter 14). In such low-involvement associative learning, the learner discovers that two events go together. Herbert Krugman's **passive learning theory** concerns the association of two stimuli. Krugman explained that in low-involvement situations, behavioral change tends to precede attitude change as follows:

- Consumers are exposed repeatedly to a brand's advertising in low-involvement media such as TV and radio.
- These ads create brand recognition and recall without altering attitudes. People might only remember the brand name (e.g., Hubba Bubba bubble gum) and some basic beliefs about the brand (Hubba Bubba is the best gum ever for blowing really huge bubbles).
- While in the supermarket, shoppers see the advertised brand (Hubba Bubba) on the store shelf. They then recall seeing an ad for it and remember one or more of these beliefs.
- Shoppers consequently buy the brand, not really knowing whether they like it or not.
- Upon trying it, they discover they enjoy the brand. Hence, their brand attitudes form after purchase and consumption behavior.

Marketers of such low-involvement items should encourage targeted customers to purchase or consume the brand, ensuring that consumption will be a rewarding experience. Trial can be induced via techniques such as high-frequency advertising to gain the requisite awareness for consumers to try the brand in a search for variety, memorable brand names (Hubba Bubba) and slogans ("Big bubbles—no troubles"), and eye-catching in-store displays.

FIVE HIERARCHIES OF COMMUNICATION EFFECTS

The **hierarchy of communication effects (HOCE)** is a series of states of thought and action through which people progress in response to marketing and nonmarketing communications. The HOCE concerns the order in which an individual's three attitude components are influenced by such communications. At least four hierarchies have been proposed in the CB literature: the standard learning (rational) hierarchy, the low-involvement hierarchy, the experiential hierarchy, and the dissonance attribution hierarchy. To these we add the passive learning hierarchy.

These hierarchies are summarized in Exhibit 15.18 in terms of the three attitude component–based perspectives and the degree of consumer elaboration. You might wish to compare this exhibit with Exhibit 15.1 at the start of this chapter, which shows the theories and models appropriate to each hierarchy.

STANDARD LEARNING (RATIONAL, PERSUASIVE) HIERARCHY: THINK-FEEL-DO

The "rational" five-stage buyer decision process model says that buyers put high effort into careful decision making by searching for and evaluating information on alternative brands (cognition) before feeling good about (affect) and then buying (behavior) a brand. Such buyers often engage in a think-feel-do process:

> **EXHIBIT 15.18   Five Hierarchies of Communications Effects**

	Decision-making perspective	Experiential perspective	Behavioral-influence perspective
High-effort central-route processing	Standard learning (rational) hierarchy: *Think-feel-do*	Experiential hierarchy: *Feel-do-think*	Dissonance-attribution hierarchy: *Do-feel-think*
Low-effort peripheral-route processing	Low-involvement hierarchy: *Think-do-feel*		Passive learning hierarchy: *Do-think-feel*

1. *Think.* Shoppers think by processing brand-attribute information, thereby forming brand beliefs.
2. *Feel.* They feel positive, negative, or neutral toward the brand based on their evaluation of data, thereby forming a brand attitude.
3. *Do.* Circumstances allowing, they do something (e.g., buy) if they feel sufficiently positive toward the brand.

This **standard learning (rational) hierarchy of communication effects** prevails where there is high involvement and perceived risk, as well as meaningful brand differences. This is the high-effort decision-making perspective. Wise advice here is to "Think before you act," "Look before you leap," and "Know what you are going to do before you do it." The multiattribute models and the cognitive response model apply here.

Advertising and promotion must move such shoppers sequentially through the cognitive, affective, and conative stages. Informative advertising copy appears in high-involvement print media. A sales pitch or discussion with informed personal sources such as friends and relatives might be required to move shoppers along through the hierarchy.

Low-Involvement Hierarchy: Think-Do-Feel

The low-effort, low-thought decision-making perspective is typified by the **low-involvement hierarchy**, with thinking occurring at minimal levels of processing. The procedure is *think-do-feel*, as follows:

1. *Think.* Consumers learn passively by being involuntarily exposed to simple information such as brand logos, slogans, and jingles, primarily in low-involvement broadcast media. This gains recognition and forms simple beliefs as a result of low levels of processing.
2. *Do.* There is in-store exposure to familiar reminder stimuli from the ads previously seen. Such cues, such as displays and packaging bearing the brand name, logos, and trade characters, trigger recognition and recall, prompting the consumer to purchase.
3. *Feel.* Postpurchase brand attitudes are formed on the basis of beliefs generated after the buyer consumes and evaluates the selected alternative.

Learning is of a passive or incidental nature in low-involvement media such as TV and radio. Ads are designed to gain recognition and form simple beliefs. This hierarchy occurs in low-involvement situations where brand differences are minor, often among mature products where consumers simply need reminders.

EXPERIENTIAL HIERARCHY: FEEL-DO-THINK

In the **experiential hierarchy**, consumers buy on the basis of emotional reactions to products and ads that contain emotional appeals or create favorable feelings through repetition (mere exposure), classical conditioning, or mood. After purchasing, there is experiential learning as buyers experience the product for themselves and think about its merits. Hence, the progression is *feel-do-think*.

This hierarchy holds for high- and low-involvement hedonic products satisfying experiential needs. How the purchase makes the consumer feel is important (rather than tangible attributes or functional benefits). In short, experiential consumers act on the basis of their emotional reactions to marketing communications and think about their product experience after consumption. Learning is primarily experiential. Hence, all of the experiential perspective attitude models apply here: emotional appeals, attitude toward the ad, mere exposure, classical conditioning, and mood.

DISSONANCE ATTRIBUTION HIERARCHY: DO-FEEL-THINK

In the dissonance-attribution hierarchy, the order of communication effects is *do-feel-think*. The process is as follows.

1. *Do.* A relatively uninformed purchase is made (e.g., "I bought the hair styling gel my hairdresser recommended").
2. *Feel.* Consequently, buyers feel dissonance regarding whether or not they chose correctly.
3. *Think.* This causes them to think about their purchase and figure out their attributions, or to what cause they attribute their behavior (e.g., "I bought the styling gel because I trust my hairdresser"). Such "doubting Thomases" might also seek out additional information to reinforce the wisdom of their decision, or if they realize it was not a prudent decision, to absolve themselves of responsibility (defensive attributions such as "It's difficult to say 'no' to a pushy hairdresser"). Clearly, this hierarchy is explained by both cognitive dissonance theory and attribution theory.

This process is likely to occur for high-involvement products with meaningful brand differences not easily discerned or understood by the buyer (e.g., professional service providers such as auto mechanics and lawyers). Hence, the purchaser seeks others' advice. This hierarchy also prevails for important decisions where consumers are forced to make a quick, uninformed choice (e.g., whether or not to undergo surgery). Either way, following purchase, buyers experience doubt. Consequently they form attributions, asking, "To what cause can I attribute my purchase behavior?"

For instance, the buyer of a KitchenAid dishwasher could conclude that she bought it because she really likes the brand or, alternatively, she purchased because the pushy sales rep snookered her into it. Either way, she must rationalize her decision. If she concludes that she likes the brand, she will seek out positive brand-attribute information supporting her attitude.

PASSIVE LEARNING HIERARCHY: DO-THINK-FEEL

In many low-involvement situations consumers merely (think, feel) "buy and try," (do) often with impulse purchases. On the basis of their usage experience, they form brand evaluations (think, feel). The low-effort **passive learning hierarchy** is *do-think-feel*. This can be explained in terms of passive learning theory.

REVIEW QUESTIONS

1. Explain how the affective experiential perspective and the conative behavioral influence perspective each differ from the cognitive decision-making perspective.
2. Describe the kinds of products for which the affective experiential perspective is most relevant as

well as each of the affective experiential perspective theories and models that apply for high-effort central-route processing as well as low-effort peripheral route processing.

3. Explain the types of advertisements that can positively affect attitude toward the ad (A_{ad}), explain the processing route relevant to each, and relate each to the dual-mediation hypothesis.

4. What are the marketing implications of each of the low-effort peripheral-route behavioral influence perspective affective models: mere exposure effect, classical conditioning, attitude toward the ad, and mood?

5. Describe the kinds of products and situations for which the conative behavioral influence perspective is most relevant as well as each of the theories and models that apply for both high-effort central-route processing and low-effort peripheral-route processing.

6. What are the marketing implications of each of the conative behavioral influence perspective models: operant conditioning, cognitive dissonance theory, attribution theory, and passive learning?

7. Explain the relationship between attribution theory and self-perception theory, as well as the nature and use of internal attributions and external attributions and how consumers "test" their hypotheses concerning their attributions toward self, others, and things.

8. Describe each of the five hierarchy of communications effects models, the type of route processing (high-effort central route vs. low-effort peripheral route) and attitude component perspective (decision-making, experiential, or cognitive) relevant to each hierarchy model, the types of products or situations for which each hierarchy is most relevant, and marketing implications for each hierarchy.

IN-CLASS APPLICATIONS

1. For each of the advertisements in Exhibits 15.19 through 15.23:
   a. Identify and explain the use of one or more theories and models for attitude molding.
   b. Demonstrate whether each theory or model is using an affective experiential approach or a conative behavioral influence approach to form and/or change consumer attitudes.
   c. Explain whether each theory or model assumes high-effort central-route or low-effort peripheral-route processing.
   d. Give your opinion regarding the appropriateness of the use of each theory or model given the nature of the product and situation.
   e. Explain which hierarchy of communications effects model each ad seems to be assuming, whether this is an appropriate model for each advertiser to use, at which point in the hierarchy the ad assumes targeted consumers are when they see the ad, and whether the ad will be effective in helping move readers through the hierarchy.

2. Discuss the use of attribution theory in each of the following scenarios. You should:
   a. Explain whether each person's attributions are toward self (self-perception theory), others, and/ or things. Describe the attributions. What other possible attributions could each person have made?
   b. If relevant (especially if self-perception is operative), explain whether the person uses an internal attribution or an external attribution and whether this is to be expected and why.
   c. Describe how the individual is testing or could test his or her attribution using as many of Harold Kelley's four criteria as are applicable.

→ *Scenario A. The Kids Are Alright.* Annie's three teenage children astonished her by throwing a surprise fiftieth birthday party for her. What amazed her was the fact that they had not been getting along with her and her husband, Buddy, ever since they each entered their "terrible teens."

   The children would regularly disobey and defy their parents' authority, whether it was by coming home late in the evening, not picking up their messes, or talking back. Once in a while they would even scream, "I hate you." What's more, the kids had consistently forgotten both parents' birthdays ever since they were tykes, including Buddy's fiftieth last year.

   Therefore, the party was a shock to Buddy as well. When Annie and Buddy returned home from the restaurant for which their kids had purchased a gift certificate, there waiting for them were fifty

EXHIBIT 15.19   Tylenol Ad

Taking a low-dose aspirin a day for your heart can be a smart thing to do.

Taking a pain reliever that won't interfere with it is even smarter.

More and more of you are taking a low-dose aspirin for your heart. Smart. But did you know that if you are also taking ibuprofen, you may not be getting the cardio protection you seek?

Clinical studies have shown that under certain circumstances, frequent use of ibuprofen can actually interfere with your aspirin therapy. It may be blocking your aspirin's ability to thin your blood.

If you are taking a low-dose aspirin a day for your heart, Tylenol may be a better choice. Unlike ibuprofen, Tylenol has not been shown to interfere with your aspirin heart therapy. That's why most doctors recommend Tylenol for people on aspirin therapy. Talk to your doctor about what's right for you.

TYLENOL®
A Better Choice.

For more information go to Tylenol.com or visit The American Heart Association at www.circulationaha.org.

McNeil ©McN-PPC Inc. 2004. Use as directed.

EXHIBIT 15.20   Freixenet Ad

EXHIBIT 15.21   Swanson Broth Ad

EXHIBIT 15.22   Cattlemen's Beef Board and National Cattlemen's Beef Association Ad

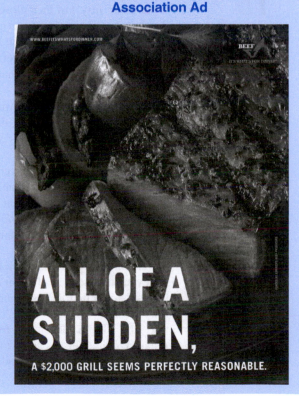

EXHIBIT 15.23   De Beer's "A Diamond Is Forever" Ad

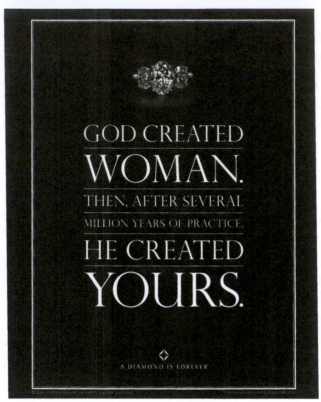

(count them: fifty!) of their closest, most personal friends and family members. The kids had even all chipped in to buy Annie earrings (albeit costume jewelry).

Everyone had a great time at the celebration. Many guests remarked about how thoughtful and kind the children were. However, afterward, Buddy and Annie, questioning their children's motives, had a chat in view of the fact that the moment the guests left, the young ones reverted to their usual rebellious behavior.

"I can't figure them out," Annie told Buddy. "Did they throw the birthday bash because they love me or is there something they want? Do they have an ulterior motive? This just wasn't like them at all. What's more, they were so courteous to us and the guests—they just didn't act like our kids."

"Well, even though they never say, 'I love you,' I think that deep down they do," replied Buddy. "They ordinarily act so despicably because teens' hormones rage uncontrollably."

"I don't know," answered Annie. "I think they're up to something."

→ *Scenario B. Block That Spam, Block That Spam.* Yule recently started receiving e-mail announcements for the new, free WipeClean spam and pop-up ad blocker. They came from a firm he had never heard of, Dr. Internet.

Every other offer he had previously received had been from companies whose names he recognized. However, because they all either charged a hefty one-time fee or smaller monthly payment, Yule had always ignored their offers, figuring that the darn pop-ups and spams were no worse than swatting pesky flies.

So why all of a sudden this free deal? Yule was suspicious. He thought there had to be a catch. Perhaps Dr. Internet was going to sell his name and Internet address to other firms. Maybe they were really hackers, and if he responded to an offer his computer would become infected with a virus or worm.

All of his friends say, "Buyer beware!" so Yule continues to tolerate the junk e-mail and pop-up ads.

→ *Scenario C. Val's Digital Frustration.* Val is having the darnedest time learning to operate her new Pixsher's digital video camera. There are so many buttons, so many features, and so many options. She has read through the owner's manual twice but swears it was meant to obfuscate, not enlighten. Virtually every time she tries to shoot a scene, something goes wrong. It doesn't matter whether she's indoors or outside, with friends or alone.

She wonders whether she's just technically challenged. Yet, she easily mastered her DVD player, camera phone, and digital music player. A good friend of hers who also purchased a Pixsher has also grumbled to her about its complexity.

For a minute-by-minute charge, the camera's manufacturer will offer online technical support. Val wonders if they aren't trying to make it so perplexing because they want to generate a revenue stream from online help.

→ *Scenario D. Doo-Gooders Does Shanda Wrong.* Shanda just turned down a high-powered position as a marketing officer with the Megamammoth Corp. at a six-figure income. Instead, she accepted a lower-income job as a marketing director with Doo-Gooders Charities. She figured that by doing so, she could "make a difference" in the world and "give back to society." After all, Shanda always thought of herself as a caring person, and many other people have remarked on how kind she is.

Following her first week (and measly paycheck!), she's having second thoughts. The hours were brutally long, her subordinates and boss were rude, and her clients were ungrateful. She's beginning to think that the Doo-Gooders interviewer just sweet-talked and suckered her into taking the position.

→ *Scenario E. Amber the Church Lady.* Amber is a regular churchgoer. Congregants at the Hellfire and Brimstone church are always impressed with her impromptu participation in the worship service. When people are invited to pray aloud, Amber always has a prayer of thanksgiving or one filled with all the right words and catch phrases—"Alleluia," "Praise the Lord," "Glory to God," and so on. She belts out the hymns so loud that people having Sunday brunch across the street at the Bagel Burgers Buffet can hear her.

Amber's favorite greeting is "God bless you brother" (or "sister"). She often lifts up "holy hands" as she sings, waving them wildly in the air. Amber has been known to dance in the sanctuary aisles on occasion. And throughout the sermon she mutters, "Jesus. Jesus."

However, a few church members wonder whether she isn't using Jesus' name as a curse word because, despite her pious behavior on Sunday morning, she lives like a veritable pagan the rest of the week. Not only does Amber never bother to help her terminally ill neighbor or even to visit her, she frequently goes out drinking till dawn, stumbling home in a stupor, and calling in "sick" the next morning to work.

The church elders are concerned about Amber's personal behavior, despite her religious fervor on Sunday. They think her holier-than-thou ways are all for show, to impress others and fool them into thinking she's a holy roller rather than a hypocrite.

3. Explain which hierarchy of communications effects model seems to be operative in each of the following scenarios. Describe how the buyer is moving through this hierarchy. What is the marketer doing to move consumers through the hierarchy? Can you suggest any other hierarchy that might be operative for this type of product? If so, explain how a marketer of the product could tap into that hierarchy.

→ *Scenario A. Brooke Breaks a Leg.* Brooke needed orthopedic surgery for a leg bone she broke while skiing far from home in Colorado. Not knowing anything about the local doctors, she inquired at the Rip Van Winkle Inn where she was staying. Both the desk clerk and hotel manager recommended Dr. Feelgood, who serviced all their ailing patrons. The clerk handed her a flier with the good doctor's handsome mug on it and his motto, "Pain, pain, go away. Never come again another day."

After finding out that her insurance plan would cover the surgery, Brooke went ahead with it. During the ensuing recovery, her leg continued to hurt. After the cast was removed, she was still extremely sore and creaky. Brooke began wondering whether she had made a big mistake.

Nevertheless, she didn't blame herself for not waiting until she got home to a familiar doctor. The bone break had needed attention, and the doctor had been highly recommended. Going online several weeks later to learn more about orthopedic surgery, she discovered that she should have gotten second opinions prior to surgery.

→ *Scenario B. Chuck Delights in Chicken.* Chuck was a late-night channel surfer. Typically arriving home from work around 9 P.M., he'd chow down and then break out the remote control, flipping from channel to channel until the wee hours.

Half asleep, Chuck would frequently come across a commercial for Chick'N Delite's chicken fries—"A bit less grease. Not quite as bad for you as chicken fingers or french fries." At least a dozen times a day he heard the brand name and slogan, and saw their silly advertising icon, Chip the Chicken.

When in the supermarket doing his weekly grocery shopping, Chuck was stopped by a marketing researcher who asked him about frozen foods. Chuck was stumped when she asked him to name a brand of chicken fries. Nonetheless, when passing by the frozen food aisle, he saw a section for Chick'N Delite's chicken fries, with packages featuring Chip the Chicken. He vaguely recalled the goofy chicken from TV commercials, squawking about less grease. So, being on a diet, he picked up a package.

That evening before his usual TV routine, Chuck heated up the fries and ate them along with his cheeseburger. "Not bad," he thought to himself. "I'll have to buy these again."

→ *Scenario C. Anita Lands a Job.* Anita Jobb was a college senior taking job interviews for an entry-level marketing position. She read through the relevant information at the university career services office and went online to gather and analyze more data on organizations that interested her.

Anita learned even more from the interviews she took with ten firms. Although she was still interested in five of these companies after interviewing, only two made her offers she couldn't refuse. After much thought, prayer, and discussions with her parents and a favorite professor, she accepted the position offered by the Aylward Corp.

And she lived happily ever after.

→ *Scenario D. Claire Rocks!* Claire loves alternative rock music. While listening to her favorite radio station, KRUM, she heard a commercial from the Soundcheck Music Center for the upcoming Benny and the Jets concert.

The ad featured a brief medley of some of the band's best-loved tunes with an overly enthusiastic announcer breathlessly encouraging listeners to visit TicketPurveyor.com to purchase tickets. Claire bought a pair and invited her boyfriend.

After sitting through almost three hours of hand-clapping, toe-tapping, foot-stomping music, Claire and her beau both agreed that this had been one awesome concert. On their way out of the concert hall, they each purchased a Benny and the Jets T-shirt and CD.

WRITTEN APPLICATIONS

1. Answer Question 1 in the In-Class Applications for three of the ads on pp. 543–44. Then find three more ads, each of which uses a different approach to attitude molding. Repeat the analysis for these ads.

2. Identify a situation in the marketplace where you had an attribution. Discuss the three issues in Question 2 in the In-Class Applications for this attribution situation. If you don't recall testing your attribution, describe how you could have done so. Are there any marketing implications here?

3. Answer Question 3 in the In-Class Applications. Then develop your own scenario and analyze it using the same questions.

4. Pretend you are the marketer of any product and brand you wish, real or imagined. Describe the theories and models for attitude molding that would be most relevant to you and why. Explain whether each theory or model would use a cognitive decision-making, an affective experiential, or a conative behavioral influence approach to mold consumer attitudes. Also, explain whether each theory or model assumes high-effort central-route or low-effort peripheral-route processing.

Design a marketing program to capitalize on these theories and move consumers through the appropriate hierarchy of communications effects model. Explain why you believe your program will be effective.

KEY CONCEPTS

ad execution–related thoughts

affect

affect transferal

affective attitude component

affective experiential perspective

affective involvement

affective responses

argument quality

attitude accessibility

attitude availability

attitude favorability (direction, valence)

attitude models

attitude molding

attitude object (AO)

attitude specificity

attitude strength (importance, intensity)

attitude structure

attitude toward the act (A_{act})

attitude toward the ad (A_{ad})

attitude-toward-the-behavior model

attitudes

attitude-toward-a-object model

attitudinal (emotional, affective) conditioning

attitudinal salience

attitudinal stability

attribution

attribution theory

attributions toward others

attributions toward things

balance theory

behavioral differential scale

behavioral intentions (behavioral tendencies, response tendencies)

behavioral intentions scales

belief

belief discrepancy

belief-importance (expectancy-value) model

brand attitude (A_b)

central attitudes

central beliefs

central-route processing

closed-ended (explicit) communications

closed-ended (fixed alternative) questions

cognitions

cognitive attitude component

cognitive dissonance

cognitive response model

cognitive responses

communication source (source)

comparative rating scales

conation

conative attitude component

conative behavioral influence perspective

constant sum scale

counterarguments

cultural attitudes

decision-making perspective (DMP)

defensive attribution

descriptive beliefs

dissonance-attribution hierarchy

distractions

dual-mediation hypothesis

ego defense

ego-defensive attitudes

elaboration

elaboration likelihood model (ELM)

emotional (affective) appeals

evaluative beliefs

experiential hierarchy

external attributions

finite ideal point (attribute adequacy, additive difference) attitude model

Fishbein's model

Fishbein's theory of reasoned action (TORA; Fishbein's extended model of behavioral intention, behavioral intentions model)

frequency heuristic

functional theory of attitude change

hierarchy of communication effects (HOCE)

infinite ideal point (vector attribute, additive difference) attitude model

instrumental conditioning (operant conditioning, reinforcement theory)

inter-attitude consistency

internal attributions

intra-attitude consistency

knowledge attitude function

Likert scale

low-involvement hierarchy

mere exposure effect

message framing

message structure characteristics

mood

motivation to comply with normative beliefs (MC)

multiattribute attitude models

multidimensional attitude

multi-item (itemized) rating scales

(continued)

KEY CONCEPTS *(continued)*

noncomparative (monadic) rating scales
normative beliefs (NB; social norms, subjective norms)
numerical scale
one-sided messages
open-ended (free answer) questions
open-ended (implicit) communications
opinion
paired comparisons
passive learning
passive learning hierarchy
passive learning theory
peripheral attitudes
peripheral beliefs
peripheral cues
peripheral-route processing
persuasion
postpurchase dissonance (buyer's remorse, regret)
preference
prescriptive (normative) beliefs
primacy effect
rank ordering
rating
recency effect
refutational appeal
Rosenberg's (instrumentality-value) model
scientific observation
self-ego
self-perception theory
semantic differential scale

serial position effects (order of presentation)
simple beliefs
simple inferences
single-item (basic) rating scales
sleeper effect
source bolsters
source derogation
standard learning (rational) hierarchy of communication effects
Stapel scale
strong arguments
strong (central) attitudes
subjective norms (SN)
support arguments
tricomponent (ABC—affect, behavior, cognition) attitude model
two-sided messages
unidimensional attitudes
unweighted linear compensatory decision model (unweighted rule, simple additive rule, equal weight rule)
utilitarian appeal
utilitarian (instrumental, adjustment, adaptive) attitude function
valence (direction)
value-expressive appeal
value-expressive attitudes
values
weak (peripheral) attitudes

SUMMARY

Attitudes develop during alternative evaluation. Buyers develop beliefs about and preferences for brands, forming the foundation for attitudes, which might again be altered during postpurchase behavior evaluation due to dissonance and changes in buyer satisfaction/dissatisfaction.

Effective attitude molding involves persuasion and is based on attitude models. You learned how to choose from among them based on: the attitude component to be molded and the degree of consumer elaboration—high-effort (central route) versus low-effort (peripheral route) information processing, as affected by the degree of consumer involvement and as reflected by how deep that information processing is.

Attitude molding is an important marketing objective, especially for marketing communications. Other marketing objectives besides forming and changing (i.e., molding) attitudes include adapting to and reinforcing existing attitudes.

Attitudes are held toward attitude objects (AOs). Marketers are concerned with attitude toward the object, brand attitude (A_b), attitude toward the ad (A_{ad}), attitude toward the behavior, and cultural attitude. Attitudes differ from but are related to each of the following concepts: opinions, preferences, beliefs (both central beliefs and peripheral beliefs), and values. Relative to attitudes and beliefs, values are more general, centrally held, widely accepted, and fewer in number.

There are several aspects of attitudes that determine the nature and degree of their behavioral influence:

- Attitude availability and attitude accessibility.
- Attitude favorability (direction, valence). There are unidimensional and multidimensional perspectives of attitude favorability.
- Attitude strength. There are strong attitudes and weak attitudes. Centrally held attitudes serve as anchoring points for other related peripheral attitudes. Attitudes formed by direct personal experience are stronger than those resulting from indirect personal experience. Attitudinal strength correlates with consumer involvement.
- Attitudinal stability. This correlates with attitude strength, and, therefore, involvement.
- Attitude salience. This varies across times and places.
- Attitude structure. The three attitudinal components are the cognitive, affective, and conative.

Models and strategies for attitude molding depend on two key dimensions: (1) which component of attitudes in the tricomponent (affect, behavior, cognition [ABC]) model should be the focus of persuasion and (2) the degree of consumer elaboration (see Exhibit 15.1).

Exercise 15.1 discussed the tricomponent (ABC) attitude model summarized in Exhibit 15.2. The first attitude component, cognitions, is organized as descriptive beliefs regarding physical product features and consumer benefits. The second attitude component, affect, entails evaluative beliefs. The third attitude component, connation, entails behavioral intentions as well as actions. Intention to buy is an intervening variable between attitudes and behavior.

Attitudes exhibit intra-attitude consistency due to the need for cognitive consistency. Otherwise, there is cognitive dissonance. Intra-attitude consistency exists along the dimensions of direction and strength. Regarding direction, thoughts, feelings, and behaviors toward a given AO tend to be in harmony. This suggests that if one attitude component is changed, the other two dimensions will tend to vary in the same direction. Hence, by altering one attitude component, a marketer can modify the entire package of attitude components. If brand beliefs are strong, the corresponding feelings will run deep and the buyer will likely buy the brand.

Attitudes also exhibit inter-attitude consistency since central attitudes serve as anchors for peripheral attitudes.

Knowledge of the three attitude dimensions can be used to measure the current state of consumer brand attitudes. From these baseline (benchmark) measures, the marketer can set attitude change objectives, devise and implement a marketing program to achieve the objectives, and conduct evaluative research to see whether or not the objectives were accomplished.

During marketing research, respondents are usually questioned regarding the cognitive and affective dimensions (descriptive and evaluative beliefs), and behavior is predicted from these dimensions. However, at times the conative component is measured, either through questions concerning behavioral intentions or by directly measuring behavior.

Exhibit 15.3 frames the stimulus-organism-response model (from Exhibit P4.1) in terms of attitude measurement. The stimulus is the AO, the hypothetical construct is the consumer's attitude, and the response is the measurement(s) of attitude component(s).

Questionnaires using rating scales present respondents with one or more items and request them to estimate the magnitude or favorability of traits along a numerically valued continuum or in one of a numerically ordered set of categories. Single-item rating scales assume attitude is a unidimensional concept. Most attitude scales assume attitude is a multidimensional construct and are therefore multi-item scales consisting of a battery of items. An individual's overall attitude score is the sum of the individual ratings, a summated attitude score.

There are noncomparative rating scales and comparative rating scales. Monadic scales include the semantic differential scale, numerical scale, Likert scale, and Stapel scale. Comparative rating scales include paired comparisons, rank ordering, and the constant sum scale.

All of these are closed-ended (fixed alternative) questions administered in large-scale survey research. Other small-sample interviews can get more in-depth information about people's attitudes using open-ended (free answer) questions during focus groups and depth interviews.

Scientific observation can also be used to learn about attitudes, such as observation of CB in the context of a controlled laboratory experiment. The overriding advantage of observational attitude research is that it lacks response bias. Problems with observational studies are that inferences on attitudes can be mistaken, observers can be biased in recording what they see, and behavior can occur without an attitude.

To learn about the cognitive dimension and its descriptive beliefs, participants in focus groups, depth interviews, and surveys (using rating scales) can be asked for verbal statements regarding their beliefs about the AO's performance or standing on the evaluative criteria.

Because the affective dimension is composed of evaluative beliefs, it is ordinarily gauged by verbal measures using rating scales asking survey respondents to evaluate the AO overall or else on its evaluative criteria. Also, focus group and depth interview participants can be probed regarding their feelings for the AO. Observational measures of physiological responses to stimuli can measure feelings.

Regarding the conative component, to learn about behavioral intentions, survey respondents are queried directly, typically using behavioral intentions scales and behavioral differential scales. These scales provide additional information not gleaned from other attitude scales because a person might have no intention to act on his or her attitude. To learn about overt actions toward the AO, respondents are queried about their CB, observational measures are taken, or experiments are run.

Exercise 15.1 also investigated the elaboration likelihood model of attitude molding. This concerns the consumer's extent of elaboration, which, in turn, is determined by the consumer's motivation (involvement), ability, and opportunity (MAO) to process information and make decisions. When MOA is high, elaboration likelihood is high, and consumers use central-route processing, scrutinizing strong arguments. The focus is on message content or what is said. Consequently, central attitudes are formed.

When MAO is low, consumer attitudes are based more on superficial information examination. During this peripheral-route processing, the consumer expends limited effort using peripheral cues. The focus is on creative execution—how the message is said—leading to formation of a general, superficial impression of the AO. The consequent peripheral attitudes are relatively weak.

Exercise 15.2 concentrated on attitude-molding strategies grounded in the cognitive attitude dimension, most of which assume high-effort central-route processing and take the decision-making perspective (DMP).

The cognitive response model provides a classification scheme for beliefs and offers suggestions for structuring the message taking into account cognitive responses. From these responses are formed descriptive beliefs. Exhibit 15.8 summarizes three broad categories of common cognitive reactions consumers can have to marketing communications: product/message thoughts, source-oriented thoughts, and ad-execution thoughts.

Concerning product/message thoughts, there are support arguments and counterarguments. The marketing communication counterargued against has little perceived credibility. Consumers are less likely to generate support arguments and are more prone to counterargue and derogate the source when there is belief discrepancy.

There are several message structure characteristics that should be taken into account to minimize counterarguments and maximize support arguments and credibility:

- *Argument quality.* Message recipients are more prone to counterargue and disparage the message source when the message presents weak arguments.
- *Serial position effects.* Usually there is either a primacy effect or a recency effect, depending on whether the target audience is opposed to the message (primacy effect), whether the recipients are disinterested (primacy), and whether the message is long or detailed, in which case strongest points should be made both early and late.
- *Message sidedness:* This concerns *one-sided versus two-sided messages.* Two-sided messages can bolster the message's credibility, especially in view of strongly held negative attitudes. One type of one-sided message is the mea culpa strategy. Another is the refutational appeal. Two-sided messages are most effective with highly knowledgeable or educated consumers, whereas one-sided messages are more effective for simple reinforcement of existing attitudes.
- *Positive versus negative message framing.* Generally, negative framing is superior.
- *Conclusion drawing:* This concerns *closed-ended versus open-ended communications.* Although usually explicit conclusions are better understood and more persuasive, letting people come to their own conclusions increases involvement, leading to higher retention and hence stronger, more accessible attitudes. Implicit conclusions are also more effective where the audience is educated, involved, and skeptical; the topic is not complex; the issue is private; and the message has an indirect action objective.

- *Distractions.* These can be effective where people are opposed to the message and are consequently prone to counterargument. However, too much distraction can drown out the message.

Regarding source-oriented thoughts, the communication source includes the message sponsor, message presenter, and the advertising medium. Source derogation results in less likelihood of message acceptance, whereas source bolsters lead to a higher probability of message acceptance.

Most important for a source to be persuasive is that it has credibility. Credible sources have trustworthiness, expertise, status or prestige, and attractiveness. Attractive sources possess similarity to audience members as well as likeability, familiarity, and confidence. A low-credibility source can become effective over time due to the sleeper effect as the source and message become disassociated.

Also important are ad execution–related thoughts, which constitute the receiver's attitude toward the ad (A_{ad}). If A_{ad} is favorable (unfavorable), the consumer's attitude toward the advertised product might also become favorable (unfavorable).

Multiattribute attitude models are based on a consumer's beliefs about brand-attribute ratings and assessment of either the weight (importance) or evaluation (goodness-badness) of each attribute. The multiattribute models discussed in this exercise are all weighted linear compensatory models.

In the belief-importance (expectancy-value) model, multiplying the consumer's value or rating on each attribute by that attribute's importance weight and adding across all these products determines an alternative's evaluation or attitude score. The formula is:

$$A_{jk} = \sum_{i=1}^{n} w_{ij} b_{ijk}$$

(See p. 520 for an explanation of the variables.) Exhibit 15.9 is a brand-attribute matrix. These attitude scores have no meaning in an absolute sense—they are only used to get relative rankings of brand preference.

If a consumer believes all attributes are equally important, she uses the unweighted linear compensatory decision model, the formula for which is:

$$A_{jk} = \sum_{i=1}^{n} b_{ijk}$$

That is, we simply sum the consumer's brand ratings on all evaluative criteria for a particular brand.

The belief-importance model is an infinite ideal point model. On the other had, the finite ideal point (additive difference) model, which usually holds for experience products, assumes that people prefer a moderate amount of each attribute ("ideal point").

In the finite ideal point model, the difference between the ideal and the perceived amount of each attribute in a brand is multiplied by the attribute's importance, and these products are summed according to the formula:

$$A_{jk} = \sum_{i=1}^{n} w_{ik} \left| b_{ijk} - I_{ik} \right|$$

(See p. 522 for an explanation of the variables.)

A second multiattribute model is Rosenberg's model, which says that an AO is instrumental in helping people achieve various values as evaluative criteria. The formula is:

$$A_{jk} = \sum_{i=1}^{n} I_{ik} V_{ijk}$$

(See p. 522 for an explanation of the variables.)

Fishbein's model views an attitude as a function of a person's evaluation of certain attributes (or consequences) as desirable or undesirable and the individual's belief about whether an AO has those attributes (or consequences). The Fishbein model formula is:

$$A_{jk} = \sum_{i=1}^{n} B_{ijk} E_{ik}$$

(See p. 522 for an explanation of the variables.) Instead of rating the importance weights of attributes, Fishbein's ratings are evaluation weights.

A variation on the Fishbein attitude model is Fishbein's theory of reasoned action (TORA), also known as Fishbein's extended model of behavioral intention (behavioral intentions model). This model better predicts behavioral intentions and behaviors than the previous multiattribute models because

1. It uses the principle of attitude specificity. To accurately forecast actions, it is more critical to ascertain a person's attitude toward the behavior (behavioral intentions) than his attitude toward the object of the behavior.
2. It takes into account not just a consumer's own attitude toward the behavior but also the attitudes of significant others. This concern for social influences is captured by two variables: (a) normative beliefs (NB) and (b) the consumer's motivation to comply with normative beliefs (MC). Combining NB and MC yield's the consumer's subjective norms (SN).

In the model, a behavioral intention is determined by both the person's attitude toward the act regarding the AO (A_{Act}) and her SN, each of which is multiplied by empirically derived weights indicating their relative importance. They are then added together according to the TORA formula:

$$B \sim BI = W_1 A_{Act} + W_2 SN$$

(See p. 524 for an explanation of the variables.) Exhibit 15.11 summarizes the relationships among the components of the TORA model.

Multiattribute attitude models are useful in suggesting specific attitude-shaping strategies based on the cognitive component, which can frame or structure buyers' decision-making processes. Marketers can:

- Change a particular belief component (b_{ij}, V_{ij}, B_{ij}).
- Alter the importance weight consumers assign to an attribute (w_i, I_i) on which the brand excels or their evaluation of the desirability of that attribute or of the consequences affiliated with it (E_i).
- Introduce a new attribute associated with the alternative evaluation process (b_{ij}) and convince consumers of its importance (w_i) and that the brand performs well on that attribute (b_{ij}), its associated value (V_{ij}), or its affiliated consequences (B_{ij}).
- Change buyers' ideal brand (I_i).
- Regarding the TORA model, communicate normative beliefs (NB) that endorse selecting a brand and the importance of complying with people who approve of the brand (MC).
- Maintain existing beliefs via reminder advertising that continuously links a brand and attribute.

The functional theory of attitude change suggests that marketers modify attitudes by crafting marketing communications appealing to consumers on the basis of one or more of four attitude functions:

1. *The utilitarian attitude function.* Adjustment is the inclination to develop attitudes that are most likely to result in rewards or in evading penalization. Utilitarian attitudes are held for utilitarian products. Here, marketers should develop a product with superior performance in satisfying functional needs and employ marketing communications using a utilitarian appeal.

2. *The knowledge attitude function.* Such attitudes help consumers in organizing their beliefs about AOs. The promotional suggestion is to keep it simple.

3. *The value-expressive attitude function.* Value-expressive attitudes help us express our self-concept and to live out our lifestyles and our central values. Value-expressive attitudes are tied to symbolic needs and are most relevant for socially consumed or highly visible, relatively high-involvement products. To influence such attitudes, marketers can use a value-expressive appeal or else show how buying the branded product helps fulfill cultural and personal values.

4. *The ego-defensive attitude function.* Such attitudes protect and defend one's self-concept and self-ego. Apathetic or skeptical attitudes regarding the dangers of anti-social behaviors might reflect ego defense. Such attitudes are usually difficult to alter. Instead, a marketer should accept and adapt to existing ego-defensive attitudes.

Balance theory describes environmental elements as composing attitude structure and occurring in triads, each containing: (1) a person (consumer), (2) the person's perceptions of an AO (brand), and (3) the consumer's perceptions of some other person or object that has a relationship with the AO (e.g., a product endorser or advertising medium). If these three elements are unbalanced, individuals experience cognitive dissonance, and they therefore alter their perceptions or evaluations to make relationships among the elements balanced.

Two of these three elements can have either (1) a unit relation, whereby one is perceived as belonging to or being a part of the other, or (2) a sentiment relation, where both elements are associated because one has either a preference or a liking for the other.

Exhibit 15.12 illustrates an initially unbalanced relationship and three ways that balance can be restored to the relationship. Generally, people are most prone to alter their weaker attitude in order to achieve balance. Marketers use balance theory to affiliate their brand with some person or object about which people feel good. Conversely, marketers can associate a competitor's brand with something negative.

Whereas all of these four cognitive theories assume high-effort central-route processing, under low-effort peripheral route processing, consumers passively form simple beliefs that are relatively easy to change. These beliefs are founded on one or several peripheral cues. They can take the form of simple recognition, simple inferences, decision heuristics, surrogate indicators, and the frequency heuristic. In such situations marketers should keep the message simple and on target.

Exercise 15.3 examined attitude-shaping approaches based on both the affective component (the experiential perspective) as well as the conative component (the behavioral influence perspective). These approaches are a mix of both high-effort central-route processing and low-effort peripheral-route processing.

According to the affective experiential perspective, for hedonic products, consumers first evaluate a brand by relying on their feelings, rather than based on beliefs about brand-attribute performance. These beliefs are formed after purchase and use experience. Consequently, behavior influences subsequent experience-based attitudes. Here, consumers experience affective responses.

When affective change occurs under high involvement circumstances, consumers experience affective involvement. The resulting information is general or holistic, not specific brand-attribute data. The associated consumer alternative evaluation strategy is affect referral.

There are two high-effort, central-route, affective approaches:

1. Emotional appeals work for hedonic products, value-expressive products, and transformational products. Advertising techniques here include transformational advertising, covert involvement advertising, and use of pleasurable peripheral cues. The goal is to associate the brand with warm, emotional feelings.

2. The attitude toward the ad (A_{ad}). This concept suggests that if someone's affective response toward an ad is favorable (unfavorable), the consumer's attitude toward the brand might also become favorable (unfavorable)—there is affect transfer.

There are four theories of affective attitude shaping operative under low-effort, peripheral-route processing:

1. *The mere exposure effect.* This suggests that marketers should get their low-involvement products in front of consumers often while avoiding causing message wearout.
2. *Classical conditioning, specifically, attitudinal conditioning.* Through this occurs affect transferal.
3. *The attitude toward the ad (A_{ad}) concept.* This is most relevant in low-involvement situations. The dual-mediation hypothesis suggests consumers have a positive attitude toward an ad either because: they have a favorable cognitive response or affective response. In either case, A_{ad} is enhanced. Exhibit 15.17 outlines this hypothesis. Under low-effort peripheral-route processing, the affective response is at work. Under high-effort central-route processing, the cognitive response is operative.
4. *Mood theory.* Consumers might like a brand better when they are put in a good mood by either the ads themselves or the surrounding programming or by retailers' atmospherics.

The conative behavioral influence perspective seeks to first induce a change in CB, which will then lead to experience-based changes in buyers' knowledge and attitudes. Under high-effort, central-route conditions, three theories are relevant to such behavioral modification:

1. *Operant (instrumental) conditioning (reinforcement theory) learning.* Here, marketers should induce customers to consume the brand and ensure that consumption will be a rewarding experience. Incentives to buy and pre-purchase sampling should be used to provoke a purchase.
2. *Cognitive dissonance theory.* At times consumers modify their attitudes to alleviate postpurchase doubts and confirm their actions. They do so via postpurchase information search using the marketer's promotions which can reduce dissonance, thereby getting more favorable postpurchase attitudes.
3. *Attribution theory.* Attribution theory suggests that under high-involvement conditions, buyers seek causes for events after the fact. Consequently, marketers can help their customers rationalize their purchases so that they feel better about them.

One attribution theory perspective, self-perception theory, suggests that if buyers believe that they made a free will choice, they will deduce that their attitude was positive. However, if they attribute their behavior to outside circumstances, they are less likely to conclude that their attitude is favorable.

Regarding their own behavior, consumers can use either internal attributions or external attributions. The principle of defensive attribution suggests that if a product does not work out well for buyers, they are likely to blame the marketer, not themselves. People also develop attributions toward others as well as attributions toward things.

Someone's attribution is a hypothesis needing validation through additional data, using four criteria: distinctiveness, consistency over time, consistency over modality, and consensus.

Under low-involvement conditions, passive learning theory suggests that consumers form attitudes after they purchase and evaluate, thereby gaining postpurchase information so as to form a judgment regarding whether or not they like the item. The marketing implications here are similar to those for operant conditioning: induce trial, and ensure that consumption will be a rewarding experience.

The hierarchy of communication effects (HOCE) concerns the order in which an individual's three attitude components are influenced as a consequence of exposure to marketing and nonmarketing communication sources. The following five hierarchies are summarized in Exhibit 15.18.

In the standard learning hierarchy, buyers engage in a think-feel-do process. First, they think by processing brand-attribute information. Second, by valuating this data, they develop feelings toward the brand. Last, they do something (i.e., buy) if they feel sufficiently positive toward the brand.

This hierarchy prevails in high involvement and high perceived risk situations as well where there are meaningful brand differences. Here, advertising and promotion must move the target audience sequentially through the cognitive, affective, and conative stages using long and informative advertising copy in high-involvement print media. This is the high-effort decision-making perspective.

In the low-effort decision-making perspective is the low-involvement hierarchy, think-do-feel, with thinking occurring at low levels of processing. Passive learning occurs in low-involvement media. Ads are designed to gain recognition and form simple beliefs.

Attitude change can also precede behavioral change in the experiential hierarchy: feel-do-think. Here, consumers react to products and ads containing emotional appeals or that create favorable feelings through repetition (mere exposure), classical conditioning, or mood. After purchasing, buyers experience the product for themselves and think about its merits.

The dissonance-attribution hierarchy is do-feel-think, and it can occur either for consumers lacking confidence or for high-involvement products with meaningful brand differences not easily discerned. Hence, buyers seek others' advice. This hierarchy is also relevant for those who must buy quickly. In either case their purchase is relatively uninformed—they take action first. Buyers therefore feel postpurchase doubt regarding whether or not they made a wise purchase. This causes them to think about their decision and figure out to what caused them to act (attribution). Such consumers might also seek out additional information to reinforce their decision.

In many low involvement situations consumers impulsively "buy and try." On the basis of their experience, they form brand evaluations. The passive learning hierarchy is do-think-feel.

REFERENCES

Bagozzi, Richard P., and Burnkrant, Robert E. (1979). "Attitude Organization and the Attitude-Behavior Relationship." *Journal of Personality and Social Psychology,* 37, 6, 913–929.

Belch, George E., and Belch, Michael A. (2009). *Advertising and Promotion,* 8th ed. New York: McGrath-Hill Companies.

Bem, Daryl J. (1967). "Self-Perception: An Alternative Interpretation of Cognitive Dissonance Phenomena." *Psychological Review,* 74, 183–200.

———. (1972). "Self-Perception Theory." In Leonard Berkowitz, ed. *Advances in Experimental Social Psychology.* New York: Academic Press, 1–62.

Bettman, James R., Capon, Noel, and Lutz, Richard J. (1975). "Multiattribute Measurement Models and Multiattribute Attitude Theory: A Test of Construct Validity." *Journal of Consumer Research,* 1, 4, 1–15.

Biethal, Gabriel, Stephens, Debra, and Curlo, Eleonara. (1992). "Attitude Toward the Ad and Brand Choice." *Journal of Advertising,* 21, 3, 19–36.

Bitner, Mary Jo, and Obermiller, Carl. (1985). "The Elaboration Likelihood Model: Limitations Extensions in Marketing." In Elizabeth C. Hirschman and Morris B. Holbrook, eds. *Advances in Consumer Research.* Provo, UT: Association for Consumer Research, 420–425.

Dasy, George S. (1973). "Theories of Attitude Structure and Change." In Scott Ward and Thomas S. Robertson, eds. *Consumer Behavior: Theoretical Sources.* Englewood Cliffs, NJ: Prentice-Hall, 303–353.

DeBono, Kenneth G., and Harnish, Richard J. (1988). "Source Expertise, Source Attractiveness, and the Processing of Persuasive Information: A Functional Approach." *Journal of Personality and Social Psychology,* 55, 541–546.

Fishbein, Leon. (1967). "Attitude and the Prediction of Behavior." In Martin Fishbein, ed. *Readings in Attitude Theory and Measurement.* New York: Wiley, 477–492.

Fishbein, Martin, and Ajzen, Icek. (1975). *Belief, Attitude, Intention, and Behavior.* Reading, MA: Addison-Wesley.

Golden, Linda L., and Alpert, Mark I. (1987). "Comparative Analysis of the Relative Effectiveness of One- and Two-Sided Communication for Contrasting Products." *Journal of Advertising,* 16, 18–25.

Grossman, Randi Priluck, and Till, Brian Dill. (1998). "The Persistence of Classically Conditioned Brand Attitudes." *Journal of Advertising,* 27, 1, 23–32.

Hannah, Darlene, and Sternthal, Brian. (1984). "Detecting and Explaining the Sleeper Effect." *Journal of Consumer Research,* 11, 2, 632–642.

Heider, Fritz. (1958). *The Psychology of Interpersonal Relations.* New York: Wiley.

Homer, Pamela Miles. (2006). "Relationships Among Ad-Induced Affect, Beliefs, and Attitudes." *Journal of Advertising,* 35, 1, 35–52.

Hovland, Carl I., and Weiss, W. (1952). "The Influence of Source Credibility on Communication Effectiveness." *Public Opinion Quarterly,* 15, 635–650.

Katz, Daniel. (1960). "The Functional Approach to the Study of Attitudes." *Public Opinion Quarterly,* 24 (Summer), 163–204.

Kelley, Harold H. (1973). "The Processes of Causal Attribution." *American Psychologist,* 28:107–128.

Krugman, Herman E. (1965). "The Impact of Television Advertising: Learning Without Involvement." *Public Opinion Quarterly,* 29, 3, 349–356.

Lutz, Richard J., and Bettman, James R. (1977). "Multiattribute Models in Marketing: A Bicentennial Review." In A. G. Woodside, J.N. Sheth, and P. D. Bennett, eds. *Consumer and Industrial Buying Behavior.* New York: North-Holland, 137–149.

Mackenzie, Scott B., Lutz, Richard J., and Belch, George E. (1986). "The Role of Attitude Toward the Ad as a Mediator of Advertising Effectiveness: A Test of Competing Explanations." *Journal of Marketing Research,* 23 (May), 130–143.

Mazis, Michael B., Ahtola, Olli T., and Klippel, R. Eugene. (1975). "A Comparison of Four Multi-Attribute Models in the Prediction of Consumer Attitudes." *Journal of Consumer Research,* 2, 1, 38–52.

McGuire, William J. (1969). "The Nature of Attitudes and Attitude Change." In Gardner Lindzey and Elliot Aronson, eds., *The Handbook of Social Psychology,* 3. Reading, MA: Addison-Wesley.

Mizerski, Richard W., Golden, Linda L., and Kernan, Jerome B. (1979). "The Attribution Process in Consumer Decision Making." *Journal of Consumer Research,* 6, 2, 123–140.

Palda, Kristian S. (1966). "The Hypothesis of a Hierarchy of Effects: A Partial Evaluation." *Journal of Marketing Research,* 3, 1, 13–24.

Petty, Richard E., Cacioppo, John T., and Schumann, David. (1983). "Central and Peripheral Routes to Advertising Effectiveness: The Moderating Role of Involvement." *Journal of Consumer Research,* 10, 2, 135–146.

Petty, R. E., Wegener, D. T., and Fabriger, L. R. (1997). "Attitudes and Attitude Change." *Annual Review of Psychology,* 48, 609–638.

Ray, Michael. (1973). "Marketing Communications and the Hierarchy-of-Effects." In P. Clarke, ed. *New Models for Mass Communication.* Beverly Hills, CA: Sage, 147–176.

Rescorla, R. A. (1988). "Pavlovian Conditioning of Attitudes: It's Not What You Think It Is." *American Psychologist,* 43, 151–160.

Rosenberg, Milton. (1956). "Cognitive Structure and Attitudinal Affect." *Journal of Abnormal and Social Psychology,* 53 (November), 376–382.

Ryan, Michael J., and Bonfield, Edward. (1975). "The Fishbein Extended Model and Consumer Behavior." *Journal of Consumer Research,* 2, 2, 118–136.

Sheppard, Blair H., Hartwick, Jon, and Warshaw, Paul R. (1988). "The Theory of Reasoned Action: A Meta-Analysis of Past Research with Recommendations for Modifications and Future Research." *Journal of Consumer Research,* 15, 3, 325–343.

Shimp, Terence A. (1981). "Attitude Toward the Brand as a Mediator of Consumer Brand Choice." *Journal of Advertising,* 10, 2, 9–15.

Stuart, Elnora W., Shimp, Terence A., and Engle, Randall W. (1987). "Classical Conditioning of Consumer Attitudes: Four Experiments in an Advertising Context." *Journal of Consumer Research,* 14, 3, 334–339.

Vakratsas, Demetrios, and Ambler, Tim. (1999). "How Advertising Works: What Do We Really Know?" *Journal of Marketing,* 63, 1, 26–43.

Wells, William D. (1985). "Attitudes and Behavior: Lessons from the Needham Life Style Study." *Journal of Advertising Research,* 25, 1, 40–44.

Wilkie, William L., and Pessemier, Edgar A. (1973). "Issues in Marketing's Use of Multi-Attribute Attitude Models." *Journal of Marketing Research,* 10, 4, 428–441.

Wilson, David T., Mathews, H. Lee, and Harvey, James W. (1975). "An Empirical Test of the Fishbein Behavioral Intention Model." *Journal of Consumer Research,* 1, 4, 39–48.

Zajonc, Robert B. (1968). "Attitudinal Effects of Mere Exposure." *Journal of Personality and Social Psychology,* 8, 1–29.

Absolute (lower, detection) threshold level. The minimum level of stimulus intensity that an individual can perceive.

Acceptance. When a person changes his or her beliefs and attitudes to be consistent with those of a reference group, i.e., he or she internalizes those ideas.

Accidental (incidental) search. Passive information acquisition via involuntary exposure. This yields data that is not necessarily of interest to the consumer. Such search occurs through passive viewing of ads. It contrasts with *deliberate search*.

Acculturation. Learning to function within the dominant culture while retaining one's original culture.

Achievement-inspired consumers. A VALS2 group; they are heavily influenced by the actions, approval, and opinions of others. These outer-directed consumers look for products and services that demonstrate their success to peers.

Achievers. A VALS2 type; they are achievement-oriented people with high resources.

Acquired (psychological, secondary psychogenic) needs. Desires people learn in response to their culture (reflecting its priorities) or environment (reflecting its demands). These needs are primarily psychological (psychogenic) in nature and are of secondary importance to more basic biological needs.

Activity (process) analysis. A *problem analysis* new product ideation technique that focuses on a particular activity or process. Consumer research is used to ascertain what problems consumers experience while performing the activity, how severe or important each problem is, and the frequency of occurrence of each problem.

Actual (real) self-image. How consumers view themselves or think they really are.

Ad execution–related thought. Reactions to ad execution or presentation, such as the ad's information, entertainment, and production values and voice tones.

Adaptation (sensory adaptation, habituation). The process of adjusting to or growing accustomed to a frequently occurring stimulus to the point where it is no longer noticed.

Adaptation level. The amount of stimulus intensity to which a person becomes accustomed. It serves as a reference point or standard of comparison for changes in the level of the stimulus.

Additions to existing product lines. These new products supplement or round out a current product line rather than replace it (as do new-and-improved products). They are variations on a firm's existing product, usually the *core (anchor, flagship) product*.

Adoption. The CB involved when potential users (individuals, families, or other social groups) decide whether or not to become committed to regularly using a new product. Adoption entails product purchase (high-priced durables) or a decision to regularly buy (nondurables).

Advertising. Any paid form of nonpersonal promotion by an identified sponsor making predominant use of the mass communication media.

Advertising appeal (selling premise, unique selling proposition [USP]). A basic advertising message that summarizes the brand's *positioning* in a statement explaining how a brand in a particular product category has a specific use that satisfies a target market's needs better than do competitive products and brands.

Advertising icons (product icons). People or animals that symbolize a brand.

Advertising retrieval cues. Visual or verbal stimuli uniquely associated with an ad and its brand that are also available when and where consumers make brand decisions.

Advocate channels. Biased marketer-controlled information sources.

Aesthetic needs. Desires for symmetry, order, and beauty.

Affect. Concerns, evaluations, feelings, emotions, and moods regarding either an AO or its performance on specific criteria.

Affect referral (affective choice, hedonic choice). A type of alternative evaluation strategy that entails *attitude-based choices*. It grounds decisions in global attitudes, holistic impressions, or emotions associated with a product or brand.

Affect transferal. A phenomenon whereby the advertiser connects the brand with good feelings, thereby forming emotional responses to the brand. The consumer's attitude toward an advertisement or emotional responses to that ad transfers to the brand featured in the ad.

Affective attitude component. The feeling, emotional, and mood attitude component.

Affective experiential perspective. A perspective on attitude molding that tries to effect attitude change via working on consumers' feelings and emotions, employing strategies grounded in the affective dimension.

Affective involvement. Emotional involvement related to hedonic or emotional motives. Here, consumers can be passionate about or experience intense feelings associated with value-expressive products that express their self-concepts. Affective involvement entails strong emotional responses to a stimulus, which can lead to shaping of strong attitudes.

Affective responses. Emotional reactions to marketing communications and to how buyers anticipate the product will make them feel or how a brand will enhance self-concept, stemming from overall memory and impressions from prior experiences.

Affinity marketing. Affiliating with a special interest group for which customers already feel loyalty.

After-market products. Goods and services, usually parts and accessories, associated with the upkeep or repair of a previously purchased product.

Age effects (life cycle effects). Age-related differences, including physical and psychological distinctions.

Aided (cued) recall. A memory-stimulating technique providing some memory-jogging stimuli during marketing research to measure consumer learning, providing the consumer with various amounts of *retrieval cues*.

AIOs. Activities, interests, and opinions, which are the variables measured in *psychographic* research.

Alpha moms. Educated, high-income, type A, tech-savvy, perfectionist women striving to achieve mommy excellence and be wonderful, can-do wives. These multitasking, kidcentric women are influential leaders and enthusiastically share their knowledge with other mothers.

Alternative evaluation. Second stage of the consumer decision-making process occurring simultaneously with external search. Here, the consumer decides which evaluative criteria will be used to compare alternatives and the relative importance (weights) of those criteria. She then compares the brands on the criteria to determine her most preferred one.

Altruism. The compassionate caring for one's fellow humans that leads to deemphasizing self interest and focusing on maximizing others' interests, usually at the expense of one's own concerns.

Analogy (analogical learning). An association technique in which a connection is established between things otherwise not affiliated. A type of *cognitive reasoning* whereby the consumer transfers knowledge from one domain to learn about another similar arena. He figures out how what he already knows can be applied to something he is not so sure about. An association technique that calls for *elaboration* rather than sheer repetition—establishing a connection between things otherwise not affiliated. Two analogy techniques are simile and metaphor.

Analytical attribute analysis. Examining product characteristics to generate new product ideas and design new as well as improved products.

Anglo. The mainstream culture in the United States, defined by the U.S. Census Bureau as "non-Hispanic whites."

Anticipatory aspiration group. An *aspiration group* that a person hopes and expects to join.

Approach-approach conflict. A motivational conflict scenario in which the choice is between two or more desirable alternatives (approach objects).

Approach-avoid conflict. A motivational conflict situation in which the goal object has aspects that are both positive (approach object) as well as negative (avoidance object).

Approach goal. The customer's desire to achieve the *approach object* because it either satisfies functional needs and wants or fulfills hedonic desires for pleasure.

Approach object. The ideal (desired) state consumers seek.

Argument quality. Whether or not a communication employs *strong arguments.*

Aspiration group. A nonmembership group with a positive attraction, causing people to want to join it.

Aspirational brand. A brand that will assist the customer in achieving the trappings of the next rung on the social ladder.

Assimilation. The process whereby ethnic group members learn and adapt to the values, language, and other cultural characteristics of the *host culture,* thereby replacing their native subcultural traits. Assimilation involves allowing one's native culture to be overridden by the dominant culture.

Association. Pairing stimuli to establish linkages between them. Such linkages are learned either through repetition (*associative learning*) or *elaboration* (*analogy*).

Associative (incidental) learning. Discovering that two events go together through a process of simple stimulus-response learning via repetition and association. The events might be two stimuli, as in *classical conditioning,* or a response and its consequences (rewards and punishments), as in *operant conditioning.*

Associative (semantic) network. A knowledge representation system comprised of concepts (ideas and memories) organized around a particular concept or event. The system consists of various nodes that are interconnected through links.

Atmospherics. The conscious designing of physical retail or service environment space (a servicescape) and its various dimensions to evoke certain mood and behavioral response effects in shoppers, creating a store atmosphere or retail environment to make the store an attractive place to shop.

Attention. The degree to which the consumer focuses on the incoming stimulus, thereby allocating information processing capacity to it so that the sensations enter the brain for processing.

Attitude. A favorable or unfavorable evaluation of an alternative based on the customer's beliefs about that option; positive or negative evaluations of marketplace phenomena; an overall evaluation of an attitude object that expresses a degree of favor or disfavor toward that object; a predisposition to think, feel, or behave in a positive or negative way toward an *attitude object.*

Attitude accessibility. Whether people can retrieve an available attitude from memory at any given moment.

Attitude availability. Whether consumers have an evaluation of an object in their *memory stores.*

Attitude favorability (direction, valence). The extent to which people like or dislike an attitude object.

Attitude models. Theories that portray the underlying dimensions of attitudes in order to help marketers mold those attitudinal dimensions.

Attitude molding. Attitude formation and change. This involves forming target customers' attitudes where none previously existed and/or changing their preexisting attitudes.

Attitude object (AO). The entity toward which the attitude is held. It can be abstract or concrete, individual or collective. The AO can be an object (person, group, place, or thing), issue, situation, activity, or behavior.

Attitude specificity. The principle saying that the more specific the attitude is to a predicted behavior, the higher the probability that the attitude will correctly predict conduct. That is, to accurately forecast actions, it is more critical to ascertain a person's attitude toward the behavior itself than attitude toward the attitude object.

Attitude strength (importance, intensity). The degree of influence an attitude has on someone's behavior.

Attitude structure. The components comprising an attitude, and their relationships to one another.

Attitude toward the ad (A_{ad}). Whether or not a message recipient likes a particular advertisement during a particular exposure occasion.

Attitude-based (affective, hedonic) choices. Decisions based not on specific brand-attribute comparisons but rather on general attitudes toward, summary impressions of, or feelings and emotions associated with the product.

Attitude-toward-the-behavior (attitude toward the act, A_{act}) model. A person's attitude concerning behavior with regard to an attitude object (e.g., purchasing a brand) rather than attitude toward the attitude object itself.

Attitude-toward-the-object model. This measures attitudes toward attitude objects. It is most commonly used by marketers to measure attitudes toward a product (or service) category or toward a specific brand.

Attitudinal (emotional) brand loyalty. An emotional attachment and brand preference.

Attitudinal (emotional, affective) conditioning. A form of classical conditioning, in which due to the constant stimulus-response pairing, learners attribute whatever feelings they have about the unconditioned stimulus to the conditioned stimulus.

Attitudinal salience. An attitude's relevance in a particular situation.

Attitudinal stability. The degree to which attitudes are not prone to waver, even in the face of attempts to change them.

Attribute extension (parameter analysis). This new product ideation method starts with a characteristic that has recently changed in the marketplace and then extends that change to see what (if any) benefits will accrue to consumers.

Attribute-based choices. Decisions comparing brands' performances on the determinant criteria.

Attribution. The perception and crediting of the cause of an effect, i.e., figuring out what caused an event to happen.

Attribution theory. This attitude change theory says people seek to understand observable events in their environment in terms of their reasons for being. By attributing events to causes, people are able to understand the world around them.

Attributions toward others. The way people decide why they think other people (or groups or firms) do the things they do.

Attributions toward things. The way that people decide why products work or perform the way they do.

Autobiographical memory. Episodic memory about a person and his or her past. It concerns an important, personal event that lasts for a long period of time and becomes part of someone's personal history. It includes prior experiences as well as the emotions and sensations affiliated with these experiences.

Autonomous (autonomic, autocratic, individualized) decisions. When either the husband or wife makes an individual decision, not both, during family decision making.

Avoidance goal. A consumer's objective to avoid an *avoidance object*.

Avoidance object. A consumer problem to be solved or a negative state of existence a consumer wishes to avoid, such as social disapproval, anxiety, or discomfort.

Avoid-avoid conflict. A motivational conflict situation in which buyers must choose between two or more undesirable alternatives (avoidance objects).

Awareness set (retrieval set). The brands in the product category of which consumers are aware during internal search.

Baby boom generation (baby boomers, boomers; 1946–1964). The largest bulge in population, boomers were born during the prosperous years following World War II, coming of age during the mass affluence of the 1960s and stagflation of the 1970s.

Baby boomerang (boomerangers, boomerang kids, back-to-the-bedroom kids, returning young adults, twixters). This emerging market of young adults, mostly in their twenties, either returns to or continues living with their parents.

Bachelor (young singles) phase. This family life cycle group consists of young (mostly 20s) single adults who have typically either graduated high school or college and are living on their own, establishing their independence, launching their careers, and enjoying recreational pursuits.

Backtranslation. Translating English to a foreign language by one person fluent in both languages, and then, having a second person conversant with both languages translate it back again to English.

Backward masking (backmasking, audio reversal). An undetected message is placed into an audio medium, such as a record, tape, CD, or DVD, by playing the message in reverse.

Balance theory. An attitude molding theory focusing on the relationship between beliefs and attitudes. It suggests that people seek balance between their thoughts (beliefs) and feelings (evaluations). This theory considers relationships among three elements that compose attitude structure, each containing a person, the person's perceptions of an attitude object, and the person's perceptions of some other person or object that has a relationship with the attitude object.

Behavioral brand loyalty. Repeat purchasing of a brand.

Behavioral differential scale. A marketing research scale similar to the *semantic differential scale*, except it measures behavioral intentions rather than beliefs or feelings.

Behavioral influence perspective (to attitude change). A general approach for attitude molding that employs strategies grounded in the conative dimension that seeks to first induce a change in CB, which will then lead to experience-based changes in buyers' knowledge and attitudes.

Behavioral influence techniques. Retail environmental stimuli and ecological design, such as merchandising and packaging that induce need recognition and modify buying behavior.

Behavioral intentions (behavioral tendencies, response tendencies). The likelihood that someone will undertake a specific behavior or act in a particular way regarding an attitude object, based on that person's knowledge and feelings.

Behavioral intentions scales. Scale items that ask interviewees about their subjective probabilities that their beliefs and feelings will be acted upon.

Behavioral (behaviorist, stimulus-response, associative, contiguity, connectionist, conditioning) learning school. Theories of learning that consider learning as a behavioral change caused by experiences with observable, external environmental influences (stimuli) that affect people's behaviors or outputs (responses). The emphasis is on how individuals learn by making simple stimulus-response associations. Observable reactions to external stimuli indicate that learning has occurred. The two behavioral learning theories are *classical conditioning* and *instrumental conditioning*.

Behavioral targeting (marketing, tracking). Matching Internet ads to interests indicated by recency and frequency of consumer behaviors, collected unobtrusively via cookies. Behavioral targeting uses collaborative filtering technology that recognizes when Web site visitors are seeking a particular product or service and then serves an ad relevant to their search at a later date on another Web page.

Behaviorism. The behavioral learning school. The focus is on how organisms respond to environmental stimuli rather than on their internal psychology.

Behavioristic (behavioral, usage) segmentation. Dividing the marketplace based on states of action. This includes a number of direct behavior measures, including end use, usage rate, usage experience, purchase or usage occasion, loyalty status, marketing factor sensitivity, innovativeness, opinion leadership, buyer readiness state, and benefits sought (benefit segmentation).

Belief discrepancy. When a message conflicts with consumers' existing beliefs, especially *central beliefs*.

Belief-importance (expectancy-value) model. A multiattribute attitude model suggesting a consumer has a belief (subjective perception) about each the alternative's performance or value (rating) on each criterion, plus the relative weight or importance of each attribute.

Beliefs. The consumer's perception about how each alternative in an evoked set for a particular product category performs on the important criteria. It is a subjective judgment linking an attitude object to a particular attribute of that object.

Believers. A VALS2 type; they are ideals-oriented people with moderate resources.

Benefit segmentation. A form of *behavioristic segmentation* that entails dividing the market based on benefits desired from a product because various groups of consumers seek different features and benefits for the same product.

Benefits. The psychological (subjective) satisfactions of buyers' needs and wants that are delivered by the product's objective features (physical characteristics). Benefits are what the features mean to consumers or what functions they perform. Benefits are the desired consequences of using the product or the buyer's consumption goals.

Between-group stratification. Ranking individuals or groups within society or a community as a whole, regarding prestige, respect, power, and influence, such as via social class and subculture.

Blended families (stepfamilies, reconstituted families, aggregate families, second chancers). Families consisting of a married couple, one or both of whom were previously married, and any children they produced as a couple, plus the offspring from the previous marriage of one or both parents, resulting in stepparents and stepsiblings.

Bottom-up (trickle-up, upward diffusion) model. When social change moves from the bottom rungs of the social ladder (or even from a counterculture) to mainstream society, perhaps even reaching the upper echelons.

Bounded rationality. The idea from economics that people are only as rational as their limited resources and other conditions will permit. Contrary to neoclassical decision theory, decision makers are not viewed as purely rational, optimizing individualistic outcomes. Rather, there are inherent limits on rational thought and decision making.

Boycott. Dissatisfied customers organizing to encourage people to abstain from purchasing the product.

Brand. A name, term, symbol, or design, or a combination of them that identifies the good or services of one seller or a group of sellers and distinguishes them from those of competitors.

Brand advocacy. A measure of *attitudinal brand loyalty* that entails plans to recommend or recommending the brand to others.

Brand ambassadors. *Buzz marketing* teams usually consisting of young adults planted in visible locations, like bars and city street corners, clad in outfits to promote and demonstrate products, and possibly land on the local TV news or in the newspapers.

Brand attitude (A_b). An overall evaluation of a brand on purchase criteria; consumers' learned tendencies to evaluate brands in a consistently favorable or unfavorable manner, as largely determined by consumers' evaluations of brands' performances on evaluative criteria.

Brand communities. Groups of consumers who feel a common bond or shared purpose associated with a consumer product.

Brand equity. The value consumers assign to a brand above and beyond its functional characteristics, including brand name awareness, perceived brand quality, brand associations, brand image, and brand loyalty.

Brand franchise extension (brand extension). When a new-to-the-company product is dubbed with an existing brand name.

Brand image (brand personality, brand character). A set of associations or mental impressions that reflects the brand's personality, i.e., what it would be like if it were a person.

Brand insight. A marketer's deep understanding of the brand.

Brand (customer) loyalty. Repeat buying of a particular brand due to a strong brand preference and emotional attachment; preferential attitudinal and behavioral responses toward *one or more brands* in a product category expressed by a decision-making unit over time.

Brand mark (logotype [logo]). An identifying graphic design, symbol, or brand name written in a distinctive typestyle.

Brand name. That part of a *brand* that can be vocalized, including letters, words, or numbers.

Brand (market) positioning. The final step in the process of choosing and serving markets by physically and/or psychologically differentiating the firm's offering for each target market from those of competitors pursuing the same or similar segments.

Brand ratings. Measures consumers' beliefs about how every brand performs on each attribute, as collected using *rating scales*.

Brand tradeoff analysis. A measure of brand loyalty based on how large a price differential between the customer's favored brand and second-preferred brand offered at a lower price would induce the consumer to switch to the second-preferred brand.

Brand-attribute information. Facts on various brands' performance on the important attributes.

Brand-attribute matrix (decision matrix). A chart showing brand ratings on *determinant attributes* for a product.

Brand-based evaluation strategy (choice by processing brands [CPB], processing by brands [PBB], brand-choice sequence). An alternative evaluation strategy used in *compensatory decision rules*, it is evaluating one brand at a time across all attributes (instead of comparing all brands across one criterion at a time).

Branding generalization (brand leveraging). Attempting to get buyers to generalize from the reputation of a marketer's brand and corporate names through employing *brand franchise extensions* and *product line extensions*.

Bundled pricing (price packaging). A group of related products is sold in a package where the total price of the component products is less than if each product were sold separately.

Business (business-to-business, B2C, organizational) customers. Those who buy on behalf of a business organization.

Buyer (family purchasing agent). The family member who buys the product during the purchase stage. Since deciding and buying often go hand in hand, the buyer is often the decider.

Buyer's market. A marketplace condition where supply outpaces demand.

Buying centers. Decision-making units within organizations. A network of people, including manufacturing engineers, purchasing specialists, and product managers.

Buying intention (purchase intention, intention to buy, behavioral intention, purchase plan, propensity to buy). A plan to buy the most favorable option: the one for which the consumer feels brand preference. An individual's subjective probability of acting on his or her beliefs and attitudes.

Buzz. As a verb, *buzz* involves seeding the media with news and information about a brand with the objective of creating favorable word-of-mouth. As a noun, buzz means an intense and interactive form of word-of-mouth referral that occurs both online and offline.

Buzz marketing. Efforts to gain awareness and trial of a new product by stimulating word-of-mouth communication about it.

Cachet (upgrading) by association. If one of two similar stimuli is perceived positively, so is the second cue.

Captive-product pricing. A pricing strategy whereby marketers break even in selling the main product (e.g., video game consoles sold at cost) or even take a loss (e.g., free cell phones or cable TV boxes), but they make a large profit margin on the captive product (e.g., video games, cell phone service) since the consumer feels required to purchase it.

Caste system. A *social stratification* system to stratify members of societies that are pre-industrial and very traditional. Under this system, status is ascribed or based on an individual's uncontrollable characteristics, formally defined and clearly identified using status markers, objectively assigned using clear criteria, and closed to social mobility.

Catch phrases. Words, phrases, or expressions that are so attention-grabbing and memorable that they become recognizable by their repeatable utterance, thereby becoming part of the cultural landscape.

Categorization. An *elaborative* process of labeling or identifying an object based on what a person already knows. A new stimulus is classified using familiar concepts or one's existing structure of meanings, known as a schema.

Census Bureau's Index of Socioeconomic Status. A three-factor social status index that is based on occupation, income, and education.

Central beliefs. Beliefs that are strongly held and lie at the core of a person's cognitive structure.

Central-route processing. In the elaboration likelihood model, this involves much effortful information acquisition, thinking, and decision making. Buyers undertake a deliberate, conscious, logical scrutiny of strong arguments.

Choice by processing attributes (CPA; processing by attributes [PBA], dimensional processing, attribute search sequence). A noncompensatory strategy that compares all brands across one criterion at a time.

Choice (shopping) process. All of the activities between formation of a purchase intention and buying the product.

Chunks. Units of memory, each storing a group of similar or related items that can easily be processed together to give it meaning.

Churn rate. Number or percentage of customers who defect in a given period of time.

Class average. Families having typical income levels for their social class.

Class system. A social stratification system to stratify members of most modern societies, using *social class* status. Under this system, status is achieved via one's contributions to society, informally defined without clear labels, subjectively assigned using criteria that are sometimes vague and open to dispute, and open to social mobility and interaction between members of different social classes.

Classical (respondent, Pavlovian) conditioning. A *behavioral learning* theory that considers behavior as learned through making a close connection between two stimuli. Stimulus-response linkages are learned through a process of repetition, contiguity (closeness in time and space), and association. Such conditioned learning is passive; it is unconscious, automatic, and involuntary. Classical conditioning is the process of using an existing stimulus-response relationship (association between an unconditioned stimulus and an unconditioned response) to create the learning of the same (or a very similar) response (a conditioned response to a different stimulus [a conditioned stimulus]).

Closed-ended (explicit) communications. Communications that clearly draw conclusions for the audience.

Closed-ended (fixed alternative) questions. Survey questions using predetermined responses from which respondents select.

Closure (mental completion) principle. A Gestalt psychology grouping principle that states that people tend to perceive incomplete patterns as being complete.

Club marketing programs. A way to encourage brand loyalty. Membership in some sort of semi-exclusive "club" is extended to regular customers.

Cluster analysis. A statistical technique for identifying groups of neighborhoods with households that are demographically similar.

Co-creation. When customers participate in creating their products.

Coercive power. A form of *social power* involving the capacity to punish undesirable behaviors by dispensing sanctions.

Cognition. A bit of knowledge, thoughts, or perceptions, i.e., peoples' mental activities associated with thinking, processing information, knowing, remembering, and communicating. In relation to attitudes, cognitions are called descriptive (existential) beliefs (or just beliefs)—the manner in which an attitude object is perceived. This entails bits of knowledge, ideas, and perceptions about an attitude object that are acquired through information acquisition.

Cognitive associative learning. A classical conditioning process entailing voluntary gaining of new knowledge about stimuli in the environment.

Cognitive attitude component. The knowledge or intellectual dimension of an attitude consisting of cognitions.

Cognitive components. Thoughts, values, ideas, and other intangibles in peoples' minds that influence and help define a society. A society's "collective consciousness."

Cognitive dissonance. Psychological discomfort caused when two *cognitions* are inconsistent or do not fit together. In attitude theory, cognitive dissonance is psychological discomfort caused by discrepancies among beliefs, feelings, and or actions.

Cognitive. Thoughtful involvement related to utilitarian needs. Consumers with high cognitive involvement wish to make a rational, informed decision and put lots of thought into it.

Cognitive learning. Purposeful and goal-directed learning by interpreting environmental information and creating new knowledge or meaning from it. Often cognitive learning entails discovering cause-and-effect relationships between associated environmental stimuli.

Cognitive learning school. Learning theories that center on how *cognitions* are actively engaged in the learning process. The focus is on actively thinking about acquired information, reasoning, and problem solving rather than doing.

Cognitive needs. Desires to know, to understand, to explore, for novelty, to achieve, and to find meaning. Such needs also include a desire to systematize, organize, and construct a value system.

Cognitive reasoning (reasoning). A *cognitive learning* school theory whose basic premise is that much human learning is the product of creative thinking and problem solving. The solution to a problem can come in a flash of brilliance, or it can come from education.

Cognitive reasoning process. Reasoned learning entails creative thinking to restructure and recombine existing and/or new information in order to form different associations and concepts, solve problems, and gain insights. During this active learning process consumers intuitively test hypotheses about products and adapt their beliefs in light of the data they acquire. This process consists of three steps: hypothesis generation, hypothesis testing, and hypothesis revision.

Cognitive response model. Provides a classification scheme for consumer thoughts following exposure to advertising communication as product/message thoughts, source-oriented thoughts, and ad execution thoughts, and offers suggestions for structuring the message by considering the impact of these beliefs on brand attitude and attitude toward the ad.

Cognitive responses. The thoughtful reactions audience members have when exposed to persuasive marketing communications, from which they form *descriptive beliefs*.

Cognitive school of psychology. Studies how the human mind works when processing information, especially regarding the formation of beliefs and attitudes. Suggests that the same stimulus can have different psychological meaning to different people.

Cognitive style. How consumers process information and make purchase decisions.

Cohabitating couples (domestic partnerships, POSSLQ). Unmarried couples living together. Persons of the opposite sex sharing living quarters (POSSLQ).

Cohesiveness. The degree to which social group participants are bonded through shared ideology.

Cohort analysis. A research method used to describe an aggregate of people (usually a birth cohort or marriage cohort), in terms of present as well as future values, attitudes, and lifestyles.

Cohort effects. Physical and psychological differences due to the year in which one was born and when he or she grew up, resulting in early generational shared experiences that form values and life skills.

Coleman-Rainwater social standing (social class) hierarchy. A social class hierarchy containing three general groupings with seven social classes as follows: Upper Americans (Upper-Upper, Lower-Upper, and Upper-Middle), Middle Americans (Middle Class and Working Class), and Lower Americans (Upper-Lower and Lower-Lower).

Collectivist cultures. Those cultures where people subordinate their personal goals to those of the group to which they owe allegiance, such as relatives, friends, and organizations. Decisions are made on the basis of group harmony and consensus.

Command system (socialism, collectivism, statism, centrally planned economies, command economies). When a government body arranges economic activities.

Commercially sponsored brand communities. Virtual communities that set up by companies as "relationship-building" Web sites.

Common knowledge. Educated beliefs shared by most members of society.

Communicability (observability). An innovation attribute concerning how readily visible the product and its benefits are to potential adopters, as well as how easy it is for users and marketers alike to explain the nature and relative advantages of the product to prospects.

Communication source (source). Anyone or any entity backing the message, including the message sponsor, presenter, and advertising medium.

Company loyal. Having favorable attitudinal and behavioral responses toward a company and its various offerings.

Comparative rating scales. Attitude rating scales that ask respondents to rate an attitude object by comparing it against a benchmark, such as an ideal, typical, favorite, or currently used brand.

Comparative reference group. A yardstick against which people compare their own attitudes and actions.

Comparison (comparative) advertising. Advertising claiming that the brand is superior to one or more explicitly named brands on one or more attributes.

Compatibility. An innovation attribute concerning the extent to which consumers believe that a new product is consistent with their current ways of thinking and behaving.

Compensatory decision rules (linear compensatory models). A category of decision models that uses brand-attribute information to compute for each brand in the product category one of two types of attitude scores: (1) a weighted score in the weighted linear compensatory model or (2) a summated score in the unweighted model.

Competitive advantage. An advantage over competitors gained by offering consumers greater value than rivals do.

Competitive insulation. The ability of a brand to exhibit resistance to the *conquest marketing* efforts of rivals attempting to win the brand's customers' favor via means such as price promotions and persuasive promotion.

Competitor myopia. Defining the competitive set too narrowly, thereby leaving the product vulnerable to new, unexpected indirect competition.

Complex decision making (CDM). A consumer purchasing decision situation in which high involvement is combined with *extended decision making*. The consumer thoroughly goes through the five-stage consumer decision process.

Complexity (converse is simplicity). An innovation attribute concerned with the innovation's perceived usability (ease of use).

Compliance. Conforming to a social group's expectations without accepting all its beliefs or behaviors.

Comprehension. As a verb, it is synonymous with interpretation and is how buyers organize and interpret information to derive meaning from or make sense of it (i.e., "getting it"). As a noun, it is the consumer's level of understanding and interpretation of a stimulus.

Comprehensive shopbots. A type of *shopping bot* that is comprehensive in coverage of many product categories.

Computerized Status Index (CSI). A *multi-item social class index* that combines education, occupation, area of residence, and income.

Conation. Behavioral intentions toward and actions taken concerning an attitude object.

Conative attitude component. The attitude component lying within the realm of the will (volition). It concerns people's behavioral intentions and overt behaviors.

Concentrated (niche) marketing. A *target market strategy* that involves dividing the market into groups and then focusing exclusively on one and only one, often narrowly defined, small, and underserved, segment, with one product and one marketing mix.

Concepts. Abstractions of, or generalized ideas about, reality—such as objects (brands, stores, endorsers, etc.) and their attributes. Concepts are analogous to the dictionary definition of a word and enable us to understand the meaning of things.

Conclusive research. Marketing research providing information that is useful in reaching conclusions or making decisions on alternative courses of action.

Conditioned response (CR). An unnatural, involuntary, reflexive reaction that is learned through the *classical conditioning* process.

Conditioned stimulus (CS). A secondary cue in the *classical conditioning* process that will lead to a conditioned response (CR).

Conditioning. A passively learned, low-involvement process of automatic responses or habits produced primarily by repetitious association of either two stimuli (classical conditioning) or of a stimulus and a response plus reinforcement of the responses (operant conditioning).

Confidence value. The consumer's self-perceived ability to use a product's attributes to correctly assess and thereby distinguish among brands.

Conformity. A change in group members' beliefs, attitudes, or actions as a reaction to real or perceived group pressure.

Conjunctive decision rule. A *noncompensatory* alternative evaluation strategy that considers all (or any, or the first) brands that surpass a cutoff—a minimum acceptable level or minimum standard of performance on *each* determinant criterion.

Conquest (acquisition) marketing. Efforts to attract competitors' customers.

Consonance. Psychological balance or consistency among *cognitions*, including knowledge of one's actions.

Conspicuous consumption. Consumption of consumer goods and leisure activities and display of social status to impress those around us.

Constant sum scale. A *rating scale* in which respondents are asked to divide a constant quantitative sum or amount among evaluative criteria of an attitude object to indicate their relative importance, or else among several attitude objects or else attitude object pairs to indicate relative preferences for them.

Consultative personal selling. A persuasive sales approach whereby salespeople are not merely order takers, but rather they probe deeply to find out what problems customers want to solve and then offer appropriate solutions.

Consumer behavior (CB). The thought processes and actions of those who purchase goods and services to satisfy their own or someone else's personal needs and wants or to solve personal marketplace problems.

Consumer brand franchise. A group of *brand loyal* customers.

Consumer buying power (state-of-wallet). How much a person can purchase, determined by three variables: (1) wealth, (2) income, and (3) access to credit, enabling borrowing against future earnings or wealth.

Consumer-complaining behavior (CCB). Courses of action a customer may take if s/he is dissatisfied. According to one commonly used classification scheme for CCB, these courses of action include: voice responses, private responses, publicity/third-party responses, or take no action.

Consumer decision. Selecting an alternative from among two or more choices.

Consumer decision-making process. The steps consumers go through in making decisions about choices among brands, products, stores, and other marketplace alternatives.

Consumer drawings (psychodrawings). A *projective technique* in which buyers are requested to express their perceptions of or feelings about a brand or its usage in pictorial format.

Consumer-driven brand communities. Social networking sites about brands created by consumers.

Consumer innovativeness. How receptive a person is to new products, services, practices, or experiences.

Consumer insight. A marketer's deep customer knowledge stemming from consumer research.

Consumer logistics. The speed and ease with which patrons are able to move into and through a store, including parking, entering, browsing, checkout, and exit.

Consumer materialism. The extent to which a consumer is attached to worldly possessions and regard products and possessions as central to their lives.

Consumer purchasing decision (decision-making) situations. The result of combining the degree of product *involvement* and the *level of decision making*, yielding six types of buying situations.

Consumer research. Marketing research that studies consumers to yield information about them of use to marketers.

Consumer satisfaction/dissatisfaction (CS/D). A postpurchase state in which a customer's desires and expectations are fulfilled (met or exceeded).

Consumer socialization. The process whereby children, teenagers, and young adults learn skills, knowledge, and attitudes to effectively function in the marketplace.

Consumer sovereignty. The notion that consumers can ultimately decide for themselves and cannot be manipulated by playing on their drives, creating moods, and otherwise controlling them.

Consumers. People who purchase and/or use products to satisfy their own or other people's personal needs and wants or to solve their personal marketplace problems. Ultimate end users (as opposed to business buyers or organizational consumers).

Consumption subcultures. Groups whose members share an avocational interest and hence a commitment to a particular product category, brand, or consumption activity.

Consumption-specific values. Values relevant to the marketplace; *evaluative criteria*.

Contactual groups. Membership reference groups about which an individual feels good.

Continuity principle (law of good continuation). A *Gestalt psychology* grouping principle that holds that people categorize stimuli into smooth, uninterrupted, continuous forms, rather than into discontinuous patterns.

Continuous innovations. Consumers view such new products as somewhat new since they require more behavior change than continuous innovations, although the degree of change in customer buying and product use is modest and usually makes buyers' lives easier.

Continuous (total) reinforcement. A reward schedule in which reinforcement is given each and every time the desired response is made.

Contrast principle. A Gestalt psychology context principle that suggests that a stimulus that stands out from or is different from its surroundings is more likely to be noticed.

Convenience goods. Products purchased frequently and with minimal shopping effort.

Conventions. Norms regarding proper conduct in everyday life or routine behavior.

Copycat products. Products that appear similar to one of their major (usually larger) competitors. They include imitative brands, value brands, and possible trade dress infringement in the forms of package knockoffs and counterfeit merchandise.

Core (anchor, flagship) product. A firm's mainstream product.

Corporate (organizational) cultures. An organization's clearly defined, informally shared values, assumptions, and ways of "doing business."

Corporate (trade, umbrella) name. The name under which a corporation conducts its business.

Corporate social responsibility (CSR). The obligation business assumes to optimize the positive effects and minimize the negative effects of its actions on society.

Cost reductions. New products whose primary benefit is that they are lower-priced than most (or all) competitors, due to lower manufacturing and/or marketing costs.

Counterarguing. Consumers who are fatigued, bored, or irritated (i.e., habituated) begin arguing against whatever a message is advocating because they experience attitude wearout, that is, their attitude toward the ad becomes negative, and so the learning curve turns downward.

Counterarguments. Thoughts that conflict with or oppose the marketer's message.

Counterfeit (knockoff) merchandise. An unauthorized *copycat product* claiming to be a well-known brand.

Covert involvement. The mental or emotional feelings that stimuli evoke.

Credence attributes. Features that are hidden or unknown, not easily discernible.

Credence goods. Products high in *credence attributes.*

Cross-elasticity of demand. How a change in the price of one alternative results in a change of sales in another option.

Cross-promote (cross-sell). When manufacturers simultaneously sell (promote) product sets (related items) in their line.

Crossover marketing (mainstreaming). Taking a product that was originally only marketed to a particular *subculture* and broadening its appeal to the macroculture (mainstream culture).

Cue association. A *classical conditioning* process that uses either unique marketing stimuli or else familiar environmental cues to identify and differentiate brands by linking the brand to the stimuli.

Cues (stimuli). Environmental signals (sights, sounds, smells, flavors, and tactile stimuli) received through our five senses.

Cultural activities. How people in a society generally spend time and money.

Cultural anthropologists. Social scientists who systematically investigate the various factors comprising society.

Cultural anthropology. The scientific study of the development of human cultures.

Cultural artifacts (material components). Physical, visible aspects of society. This includes privately owned consumer goods and public goods.

Cultural attitudes. Very general positive or negative evaluations in society regarding issues and practices such as the proper roles of men and women in society and if smoking in public is acceptable.

Cultural beliefs. A society's ideas about reality that might or might not be true.

Cultural components (cultural cues). The basic elements constituting a society's culture. The four broad categories of cultural cues are: *symbols*, *material artifacts*, cognitive components (knowledge and attitudes), and behaviors.

Cultural knowledge. A general awareness shared by society's citizens. It includes cultural values, cultural beliefs, language, and summary constructs like religion and politics.

Cultural norms. Informal societal rules or standards for appropriate or inappropriate behavior. These include *customs*, *conventions*, *etiquette*, and *rituals*.

Cultural truisms (folk wisdom). Pithy sayings that express commonly held beliefs, such as "Feed a cold, starve a fever" and "Brush your teeth after every meal."

Cultural values (core values, social values). Widely shared abstract ideals in a society about general goals and desirable means for achieving those goals. They are a culture's beliefs about what is and is not desirable regarding goals or ends (terminal values) and the means to achieve those objectives (instrumental values). Core values are general, abstract ideals, positive or negative, not tied to any specific object or situation.

Culture. The symbols, values, beliefs, and other cultural components, i.e., the total way of life, shared by members of a society (or, at a more micro level, of a social group).

Customer database. A list of all customers, along with their contact information (including address, phone number, and e-mail address), demographic and psychographic characteristics, and purchase transaction history.

Customer relationship management (CRM). Activities to encourage repeat patronage by offering reinforcement through incentives and rewards, including the capture, storage, and analysis of customer information that will help optimize those rewards.

Customer review sites. Web sites containing recommendations or warnings by other consumers.

Customs (traditions). *Norms* handed down over generations related to specific situations occurring infrequently.

Decay. A form of forgetting that occurs when memory or trace strength fades over time due to lack of refreshment via rehearsal, recirculation, or elaboration.

Deception. A form of impression management that entails deliberately creating perceptions that deviate from reality so as to mislead consumers acting reasonably.

Deceptive advertising. An ad that contains a material misrepresentation, omission, or other practice that can mislead a significant number of reasonable consumers to their detriment.

Decider. The family member or members who make the ultimate decisions on whether and what to purchase, as well as related choices such as where and when to buy during the choice stage.

Decision heuristics (choice heuristics, heuristics). Mental rules of thumb that generally focus on a single criterion to simplify consumer decision making, speed up the process, and help consumers cope with information overload.

Decision models (decision rules, alternative evaluation rules, decision strategies, information-processing strategies, choice rules). Shoppers' procedures to evaluate evoked set alternatives' performance on their choice criteria.

Decision-making perspective (DMP). A general approach for attitude molding that employs strategies based on forming beliefs and thinking grounded in the *cognitive* dimension. Most of these approaches assume high-effort *central-route processing*.

De-ethnicitization. Mainstreaming products originally marketed only to ethnic minorities.

Defense mechanisms. Unconscious, irrational strategies the Ego uses to reduce tension or maintain self-image.

Defensive attribution. Suggests that people tend to attribute their success to themselves (internal attribution) and their failures to others (external attribution).

Degree of search. How much consumers will search during an external search.

Deliberate search. Active information acquisition in either the form of prepurchase or ongoing search activity.

Delight. Positive disconfirmation of expectations and desires: A pleasant surprise ensues. The consumer gets more than expected and is therefore thrilled.

Demarketing (unselling, conversional marketing). Unselling products or behaviors associated with a *reference group* whom the marketer wishes to turn into a *disclaimant group*.

Demographic segmentation. Using demographic variables to describe a consumer's observable characteristics.

Demographics. States of being that describe the consumer's observable characteristics.

Demography. The science of describing a society's broad vital population characteristics.

Depression generation (silent generation, postwar cohort, bridge generation; 1930 to 1946**).** Living as youngsters during the Depression or World War II, they came of age during the 1950s or early 1960s, a period of economic growth and relative social tranquility.

Depth. Variety within a retailer's product category or department, which can be either shallow (little variety) or deep (much variety).

Depth interviews (in-depth interviews, one-on-ones, extended interviews). Unstructured (flexible and nondirective), probing, conversational thirty-minute-to-two-hour personal interviews based on the Freudian notion that through intensive, interactive conversation researchers can draw out people's inner thoughts and feelings by allowing them to talk freely.

Descriptive beliefs (beliefs). Perceptions about how an attitude object rates or performs on various product criteria. The total configuration of descriptive beliefs comprises a brand's *cognitive component*.

Desires. The consumer's needs and wants to be fulfilled or problems to be solved.

Determinant attributes. Criteria that are important and used to distinguish brands because not all alternatives are viewed by customers as performing equally.

Differential (difference) threshold (just noticeable difference, jnd). People's ability to sense changes in stimulus intensity. Specifically, this is either the minimum amount of change in the intensity of a stimulus that can barely be detected, or the difference between two similar stimuli that is barely noticeable by an individual or by the average person.

Differentiated marketing (multiple segmentation, multimarket strategy). A *target market strategy* that entails dividing the total market into two or more market segments and pursuing two or more of these groups with two or more marketing strategies (one strategy per segment).

Diffusion. The process whereby new product information spreads throughout and the new product is accepted within a social system.

Diffusion of innovations (DOI). The process whereby a new idea is communicated through certain channels over time among the members of a social system.

Dimensional analysis (attribute listing). This method of new product ideation begins with an exhaustive listing of all of the physical features (dimensions) of a product that developers think need improvement or modification. For each characteristic, the analyst asks either consumers or managers, "How can we change or improve this attribute to better deliver benefits?"

Direct analogies and symbolic analogies. *Projective techniques* in which consumers are asked to describe the brand as another object.

Direct marketing. Marketing by the manufacturer directly to the end user or buyer without use of any intermediaries.

Direct role model. *Role models* who have personal contact with their imitators.

Direction of search. Which information sources consumers use and the relative importance of each information source to them.

Disclaimant groups. Negative membership *reference groups* whose ideology the individual rejects.

Discontinuous innovations. New products perceived by customers to be radically new, causing buyers to significantly alter their behavior patterns, and also usually entailing extensive technological breakthroughs.

Disjunctive decision rule. A *noncompensatory* alternative evaluation strategy in which cutoffs are established, but there are minimum acceptable levels of performance for only two or three key criteria, and often at a very high performance level. Consideration is given to all (or any, or the first) brands that meet or exceed each of these key cutoffs, regardless of performance on the other less important criteria.

Disposer. The person who gets rid of the product by trashing, recycling, reselling, trading, or giving it away.

Dissatisfaction. Negative disconfirmation of expectations and desires. An unpleasant surprise occurs because the customer received less than what was expected and desired.

Dissociative groups (avoidance groups). Negative nonmembership reference groups whose values the individual rejects and with which the person wishes to avoid association.

Dissonance attribution hierarchy. A model of communication effects where the order is do-feel-think. This is the high-effort *behavioral influence perspective*.

Distractions. Attention-grabbing communication elements that are irrelevant to the message, such as humor, sexy presenters, catchy music, celebrities, or quirky situations and characters.

Doers (choleric). A Hippocratic personality type. Strengths: Take-charge, self-reliant leaders who like to make quick decisions, solve problems, and get immediate results. Weaknesses: These "movers and shakers" tend to be impatient, insensitive to others, inflexible, too risk-taking, and overly demanding of others. Typical positions include managers, producers, builders, and organizational leaders.

Dogmatism. Whether an individual is open-minded or closed-minded. Consumers low in dogmatism (open-minded) are more receptive to new ideas and experiences, prefer innovative products, and are innovators and early adopters who are *opinion leaders*.

Domain-specific values. Ideals which hold only for a particular set of activities, or values relevant only to a particular area of activity, such as family or religion.

Door-in-the-face compliance technique. A *multiple request shaping technique* that is a two-step process to get a desired response. Initially, the consumer is asked for a big favor that he or she is expected to refuse. Then, a second smaller request is posed, which the consumer will then more likely grant.

Drive. An internal tension state activated by unsatisfied needs and wants. An activated need, aroused energy state, or degree of internal tension that causes the consumer to attempt to reduce or eliminate the need. Drives include primary biological drives (needs), such as hunger, thirst, and sex, and secondary learned drives (wants), such as affiliation, self-esteem, power, and achievement.

Dual-income households (dual-career families). Families in which both spouses work outside the home, not just before kids arrive on the scene and after all children are back in school, but even while the children are very young.

Dual-mediation hypothesis. Consumers can have a positive attitude toward the ad either because they have a favorable cognitive response, i.e., the ad provides them with useful information, or they have a positive affective response, i.e., they gain good feelings from or are interested in the ad.

Dynamically continuous innovations. Consumers view such new products as somewhat new since they are more disruptive of their lives than *continuous innovations*, although the degree of change in customer buying and product use is modest.

Echoic memory. Very brief memory of things people hear, including words, jingles, and background music.

E-commerce. The direct sale of goods and services on the Internet.

Economic system. The means by which the economy is organized, setting the parameters for business decisions and consumer DM.

Economics. The social science concerned with the allocation of scarce resources (land, labor, and capital) to produce products satisfying consumers' unlimited needs and wants, given the society's institutional structures.

Economy. The institutional structure through which individuals in a society coordinate their diverse wants and desires.

Effort risk. The amount of effort that the consumer fears having to put into buying and using the product. It tends to be closely correlated with *time risk*.

Ego. That sector of Sigmund Freud's psychoanalytical mind representing the conscious mind under a person's control. It attempts to resolve the id-superego dispute by allowing the id's desires to be satisfied practically and sensibly in a manner socially acceptable to the superego.

Ego defense. Defending one's self through denial, *projection*, rationalization, and repression, to protect one's ego from shame, anxiety, conflict, loss of self-esteem, or other unacceptable feelings or thoughts.

Ego-defensive attitudes. A functional attitude theory that suggests that attitudes are held to protect and defend one's *self-concept* and *self-ego* from internal and external threats, anxieties, and insecurities.

Ego involvement. The importance of a product to a consumer's *self-concept*.

Ego risk. A perceived risk that entails potential loss of prestige, status, and respect due to purchasing and using a product.

Elaboration. The extent of effort consumers exert in learning about and forming an attitude for a given attitude object, i.e., how deeply they process information for meaning, such as by integrating new information with their existing knowledge and previous experiences.

Elaboration likelihood model (ELM). The ELM considers the degree of elaboration, or how much effort consumers exert in learning about and forming attitudes for a given AO, that is, how deeply they process information on the AO.

Elaborative activities. Entail relating or integrating new information with existing knowledge and prior experiences. They involve deep processing of the information, making connections between the stimulus and one's knowledge base to interpret and evaluate the stimulus.

Elaborative (meaning-level, semantic) processing. Storage of information in long-term memory by storing the information's meaning rather than the raw data.

Elimination-by-aspects rule (sequential elimination model). A *noncompensatory alternative evaluation strategy* that begins by ranking the criteria in order of perceived importance. The next step involves determining a cutoff for each criterion. Then, the customer compares brands on the most important criterion first, weeding out those alternatives that meet or exceed the cutoff. The remaining brands are then compared on the next-most important criterion to eliminate those that do not at least meet the consumer's cutoff on that characteristic. The process continues successively through the less important criteria, excluding brands from further consideration as they fail to meet each criterion's cutoff, until only one alternative remains, which is chosen.

Embeds. Hidden words and images, most of which appeal to subconscious drives such as sex and thanatos.

Emotional (affective) appeals. Marketing communication appeals that are directed toward the consumer's affect.

Emotions. Feelings that are not physically controllable, such as fun, excitement, and pride.

Empty Nest I (Postparental I, Childless I). In this family life cycle stage, an older married couple (mid-40s through mid-60s) no longer has children at home.

Empty Nest II (Postparental II, Childless II). In this family life cycle stage, the children of an older married couple (late 50s and older) have moved out and become financially independent.

Emulation. The process of imitating someone else's behavior because they are deemed superior in appearance, taste, knowledge, or experience.

Engagement. The amounts of time and effort consumers expend on an ad.

Episodic memory. A knowledge structure that entails remembering a particular sequence of events in which a person participated. Information is stored sequentially by episodes or events such as shopping trips, meal preparation, and packing for a vacation.

Esteem (ego, egotistic) needs. Needs for self-worth, self-confidence, and self respect. Esteem needs include inner-directed needs toward competency and self-confidence resulting from mastery of a task, and outer-directed needs—the attention and recognition that come from others, including respect, prestige, and status.

Ethical issues. Problems, situations, or opportunities that require a person or organization to choose among several courses of action (including no action) that must be evaluated as right or wrong.

Ethical values. Standards for acting morally and doing the right and proper thing. They are either good or helpful, or bad or harmful.

Ethics. The study of morality; a set of principles or rules of right and wrong designed to guide our thinking and behavior.

Ethnography. The study of living cultures through fieldwork and firsthand accounts.

Etiquette (decorum). *Cultural norms* entailing conventional ways of acting politely in social situations.

Euphemisms. The substitution of inoffensive, more pleasant-sounding, words for offensive, harsh, unpleasant, or embarrassing terms.

Evaluative beliefs. The goodness or badness of the attitude object overall as well as an evaluation of its performance on the attitude object's evaluative criteria. These subjective beliefs and emotional benefits entail feelings of like and dislike. The entire package of evaluative beliefs constitutes a brand's affective component.

Evaluative (choice, decision, buying, purchase) criteria (criteria). Those attributes or characteristics of alternatives consumers use to consider, compare, evaluate, and select one or more alternatives. These criteria include the product's physical *features* and consumer *benefits*.

Evaluative scale. An attribute importance *rating scale* which tells not only the magnitude but also the direction of the importance rating.

Evaluators. Family users and non-users in the postpurchase evaluation stage who assess the product's performance.

Evoked (consideration, choice, decision) set. A subset of the *awareness set*, this consists of the brands considered as possible solutions to the problem that the shopper will consider, compare, and evaluate.

Expectations. Prepurchase beliefs about the level of product performance on all important criteria.

Expected self-image. How consumers expect to see themselves at some identified future time, as they plan to move from their *actual self-image* to their *ideal self-image*.

Experience attributes. Attributes that are mostly intangible and subjectively evaluated. The best way to learn about how a brand performs on them is by personal experience with them, either through prepurchase sampling and demonstration or through postpurchase consumption and evaluation.

Experience goods. Products consisting mostly of *experience attributes*.

Experiencers. A VALS2 type; they are self-expression-oriented consumers with high resources.

Experiential (hedonic) benefits. These benefits answer the questions, "How does it feel to use the product?" and "What kind of experiences does the product provide?"

Experiential hierarchy. A model of communications effects in which consumers act on the basis of emotional reactions to products and ads that contain emotional appeals or that create favorable feelings through repetition (mere exposure), *classical conditioning*, or mood. After purchasing, buyers experience the product for themselves and think about its merits. Hence, the hierarchy is feel-do-think. This can be either high- or low-effort processing.

Experiential learning. Learning through personal experience, which usually involves using products.

Experiential marketing. Providing customers with experiences, not just products.

Experiential paradigm. A model of consumer behavior that recognizes that often consumers try not to solve practical problems but rather to pursue the more subjective, emotional, and symbolic aspects of consumption. The emphasis is on the experiential aspects of consumption, where feelings of enjoyment or pleasure are key outcomes.

Expert. A *social agent* having skill in or knowledge of the subject area through formal training, education, occupation, or experience. This agent has *expert power* based on the ability to provide an authoritative, objective evaluation.

Expert power. A form of *social power* based on the *social agent's* expertise.

Exploratory research. Preliminary research conducted in a marketing research project to: clarify and define the nature of a research problem or issue, develop and screen alternative solutions to the problem, and generate testable hypotheses.

Exposure. When a consumer confronts (or is confronted by) a stimulus so that one or more of the sensory organs are activated and information processing can begin. Exposure can be either random and involuntary or deliberate and voluntary.

Expressive roles. Family decision roles that are predominant for hedonic products and entail expressing the family's aesthetic, social, or emotional needs, with decisions on the likes of color, style, and design.

Extended decision making (EDM; extended problem solving, extensive DM, extensive problem solving, complex DM, midrange problem solving, considered purchases). A learning stage in which the consumer has little to no prior knowledge of and experience with the product class and alternative brands within that product category.

Extended family. A traditional family comprised of the nuclear family plus one or more additional blood relatives, such as grandparents, uncles and aunts, nephews and nieces, and parents-in-law, typically spanning three generations.

Extended self. The self, plus possessions and one's social network.

Extended warranties. Service contracts covering repairs, maintenance, or replacement for a specific time beyond the product's normal warranty period on product performance.

External attributions. Attributing an outcome to circumstances beyond one's control.

External (environmental) search. Motivated seeking of information from the marketing environment. External search is prepurchase search.

Extinction. The process whereby a previously established link between the stimulus and response is broken, reducing the likelihood that the response will be repeated.

Extrinsic cues (indirect indicators, non-product-related attributes). Product characteristics that are external to the physical product but are nonetheless closely associated with it, entailing elements of the marketing mix other than the physical product.

Extroverts. A Myers-Briggs Indicator Personality Inventory type; they are oriented toward people and their external environment and are highly communicative. With high energy, they are talkative, think out loud, enjoy being with people, are easily distracted, make decisions only after consulting others, and are aware of the environment, relying on it for stimulation and guidance.

Fads. Short-lived fashions that are taken up with great enthusiasm for a brief period of time, usually by relatively few people.

Family (umbrella) branding. Tagging a parent corporate (umbrella, trade) name or a brand name on a group of the firm's products.

Family (household) decision roles (consumption roles, purchase roles). Short-term roles taken in the family consumer decision process for a particular product.

Family household (family). Two or more people related by blood, marriage, or adoption who reside together.

Family life cycle (FLC; life stages, the household life cycle, the consumer life cycle). Describes the phases a family of procreation typically goes through in their process of formation, development, and ultimate dissolution.

Family of orientation (family of origin). The *nuclear family* into which one is born. It provides an orientation toward values, norms, political and religious beliefs, and other cultural characteristics.

Family of procreation. The family one establishes by marriage.

Family (lookalike, umbrella) packaging. Used in conjunction with *family branding*, it is the use of a package whose graphics resemble those on other products sold by an enterprise.

Fantasy solutions and **future scenarios.** *Projective techniques* in which consumers are presented with a consumer problem and asked to present their ideal solution or to otherwise imagine a fanciful situation, sometimes in the future.

Fashions. The adoption of a new style by a group of consumers for some time, typically several years to over a decade. They tend to be shorter-lived than *trends* but endure longer than do *fads*.

Fear (threat, problem-avoidance) appeal. Creating worry by suggesting problems or dire consequences that will arise or persist if the recommended course of action (e.g., brand purchase) is not taken.

Features. A product's physical attributes (characteristics) that provide *benefits*.

Feelers. A Myers-Briggs Indicator Personality Inventory type; they are personal and decide based on how their choice will affect people (especially their emotions and feelings), make decisions grounded on personal beliefs and personal and group values as well as personal attitudes and emotions, are warm and friendly, get their feelings hurt easily, are sensitive and diplomatic, try hard to please others, and are motivated by being appreciated.

Feminine cultures. In these societies, there are no rigid gender roles, and both sexes are concerned with quality of life, caring for others, and modesty.

Figure and ground (figure-ground) principle. A Gestalt psychology context principle that suggests that people interpret a stimulus in the context of its background. They tend to distinguish a prominent and well-defined stimulus in the foreground (the figure) from less prominent, indefinite stimuli in the background (the ground).

Financial (economic, monetary) risk. The likely loss of money associated with purchasing and using a product. It includes not only the product up-front sticker price (invoice cost or transaction price) but also costs of: acquisition, ownership and maintenance, and disposal.

Finite ideal point (attribute adequacy, additive difference) attitude model. A multiattribute attitude model (compensatory decision rule) that is appropriate for products for which a moderate amount of a characteristic is ideal.

Fishbein's model. This *multiattribute attitude model* views an attitude object as a function of: a person's evaluation of or feelings about certain attributes (or consequences) as being either desirable or undesirable, and the individual's belief about whether an attitude object has those attributes (or consequences).

Fishbein's theory of reasoned action (TORA; Fishbein's extended model of behavioral intention, behavioral intentions model). TORA measures behavioral intentions rather than their attitudes toward objects per se and takes into account not just a consumer's own attitude toward the behavior but also the attitudes of significant others. This concern for social influences is captured by two variables: normative beliefs (subjective norms) and motivation to comply with normative beliefs.

Fixed interval reinforcement. A reward schedule in which rewards are bestowed after a certain time interval elapses, even though several correct responses might have occurred during the time interval.

Fixed ratio reinforcement. A reward schedule in which rewards are given after a certain number of responses. The person is reinforced every "nth" time behavior occurs.

Fixed (systematic) reinforcement. A reward schedule in which reinforcement is only given some of the time the correct response occurs. Rewards are given regularly (not randomly) but only for some responses.

Flankers. Additions to an existing product line that carry a new brand name.

Flights. When heavy periods of advertising are followed by intervals of no advertising, such as during seasonal sales periods, special events, and sales promotions.

Focus group interview (group depth interview). A research technique that involves a moderator (interviewer) leading and focusing a discussion among six to twelve respondents. Participants are encouraged to talk freely about their feelings or thoughts regarding a particular topic, in effect probing one another.

Focus of orientation. A classification scheme for *values*, grouping them by personal, social, and material values.

Foot-in-the-door compliance technique. A *multiple request shaping technique* to get a desired response whereby a requester first gets the learner to agree to fulfill a small favor. Later, the learner is consequently more likely to carry out a larger demand (the desired response).

Forgetting. The loss of retention of previously learned material, due either to lack of repetition of the stimulus or message (decay) or because of *interference* from similar information.

Forgetting (decay) curve. A curve that demonstrates that forgetting is usually a logarithmic function of time elapsed since information was learned. Learning generally decays rapidly at first, and then the rate of decay slows.

Form (shape) perception. Gestalt perceptual principles dealing with how individual stimuli work together to create perceptions of one or more objects. They consist of *principles of grouping*, how people organize individual stimuli into groups or chunks of information, and *principles of context*, how the surrounding environment (context) helps determine individuals' perceptions of stimuli in that environment.

Formal groups. *Reference* groups having a formal, explicit organization, usually defined in writing, and possibly including a charter, regular meeting times, and officers or positions.

Formal legitimate power. A *social agent's* formal authority to set norms by virtue of position or role in the *social group*, providing the ability to demand *compliance*.

Framing. The way in which a decision problem is presented to the decision maker, such as by suggesting that certain criteria (those the brand best performs on) are most important.

Free market. A market in which the goods to be produced, their prices, and wages of workers producing the goods are not government controlled but are instead allowed to fluctuate according to the forces of supply and demand.

Frequency heuristic. When a simple belief is formed on the basis of the number of arguments made in its favor instead of on the nature of the arguments per se.

Full Nest I (Expanding I, Parenthood I). This family life cycle stage consists of young married couples (usually 30–40) with the youngest child under six.

Full Nest II (Expanding II, Parenthood II). Families in this family life cycle stage are comprised of young couples (usually under 45) with the youngest child six or over (school age) but still dependent.

Full Nest III (Contracting, Parenthood III). A life cycle stage when the older couple (late 30s through early 50s) still has one or more children at home, typically teens or very young adults.

Functional benefits. Benefits related to utilitarian (functional) needs and concerning the product's end uses or applications—the activity might yield desired *hedonic* benefits.

Functional theory of attitude change. This theory suggests that marketers modify attitudes by crafting marketing communications appealing to consumers on the basis of one or more of four attitude functions: *knowledge, utilitarian, value-expressive*, and *ego-defensive*.

Gap. The difference between consumers' ideal and actual states of affairs.

Gap analysis. Consumer research performed to identify a gap between consumers' ideal and actual states of affairs.

Gatekeeper. A family member who gathers and controls the flow of information to other family members and might also make a recommendation during the information search stage. In the *multistep flow of communication model*, someone who neither influences nor is influenced by others, but who merely passes along information they obtain from the media and personal sources to opinion leaders and opinion followers.

Gender (sex) roles. Behaviors considered appropriate for either males or females in society or within particular *social groups*.

Generalized opinion leaders. People who are "know-it-all," "Jack-of-all-trades" *opinion leaders*, not category-specific opinion leaders.

Generation (generational cohort, birth cohort, age subculture). A group of people born in the same era (typically seventeen to twenty-three years in duration) who have experienced a common social, political, historical, technological, and economic environment as well as similar significant, defining or formative life events.

Generation X (Gen X, baby bust, Busters, Xers, postboomers, shadow generation, MTV generation, Thirteeners, the Nike generation; 1965–1978). The Baby Bust was the first generation to largely grow up in either a dual-income household or else a single-parent home. They came of age during the prosperous 1980s and early 1990s.

Generation Y (Gen Y, Baby Boomlet, echo baby boom, Internet generation, Net generation, N-generation, Millennials, millennium generation, Generation Next; 1978–2000). Many members of this generation came of age during the birth of the Internet and grew up in an era of widespread computer literacy and unprecedented racial, ethnic, and socioeconomic diversity.

Generational marketing. A segmentation scheme that divides the marketplace on the basis of generational cohorts.

Generic goals. The general product category that consumers see as satisfying their desires.

Generic (primary) demand. *Generic goals*, i.e., demand for a general product category to satisfy people's desires.

Geodemographic data. Information that marries geographic location, demographic/socioeconomic statistics, and lifestyle information to describe micro-regions.

Geodemographic segmentation (geodemography). A *micromarketing* system that combines data on geography, demography (primarily age, degree of urbanity, and socioeconomic data such as education, occupation, income, and household type), lifestyle, and buyer behavior (notably consumption and media data).

Gestalt principles of perceptual organization. Perceptual principles concerning the process whereby people categorize and organize stimulus information into meaningful units to make sense of the stimuli.

Gestalt school of psychology. An early twentieth-century approach to studying perception suggesting that people acquire meaning from the totality of a group of stimuli rather than from any one individual stimulus. It concerns how humans arrange discrete stimuli or bits of information into holistic perceptions.

Global values. Values that are abstract and apply across many specific situations.

Goals (need fulfillment). The objects, activities, or conditions toward which motivated behavior is directed, i.e., goals are the desired state of affairs.

Grass roots (guerrilla) marketing tactics. Low-budget marketing efforts executed, often in unconventional ways, in local communities to deliver marketing messages to target audiences where they live, work, or play.

Grouping. A process whereby individuals are inclined to perceive stimuli as groups or chunks of information rather than as discrete bits of data, facilitating recognition and recall of those cues as a whole picture. Principles of grouping are similarity, proximity, continuity, closure, and simplicity.

Guarantee. A written promise about a product's integrity that ensures customer satisfaction; otherwise, money will be refunded.

Guilt. Violation of one's internal standards (values, norms, etc.) leading to lower self-esteem and/or remorse.

Guilt by association. If one of two similar cues is considered negatively, so is the second stimulus.

Habitual buying. Regularly and with little thought buying one (or more) brands in a given category.

Habituation. The process of adjusting to or growing accustomed to a frequently occurring stimulus to the point where it is no longer noticed, caused by fatigue, boredom, or even irritation.

Hard-sell advertising. Advertising that derives from high-pressure selling, using hard-hitting, hyperactive, and repetitive persuasion.

Hedonic (experiential, transformational) needs. Emotional, social, non-rational, subjective, abstract, symbolic, sensory, self-expressive, and aesthetic needs. The product creates feelings or experiences, providing an opportunity for indulgence rather than solving a pragmatic problem.

Hierarchy of communication effects (HOCE). A series of states of mind and action that people progress through in response to marketing and non-marketer communications. The HOCE concerns the order in which an individual's three attitude components are influenced by such communications.

Hierarchy of needs. Maslow organized human needs into a fixed sequential progression or hierarchy of needs. The hierarchy ranges from lower-level physiological needs to complex psychological motives.

High culture. Elite activities, such as museum-caliber art, opera, and ballet. It contrasts with *popular culture* because it requires more knowledge to understand, is less accessible, and is more exclusive in content, style, and appeal.

High-consideration products (considered purchases). Products typically bought under complex decision making. Most are shopping goods and search goods.

Hippocratic Temperament Survey. A standardized personality inventory that measures four personality traits: Choleric, Phlegmatic, Melancholy, and Sanguine. More descriptive, easier-to-remember labels are, respectively: Doers, Relaters, Thinkers, and Influencers.

Hispanics (Latinos). People having the Spanish language in common in either their primary language or the language of an ancestor, but who can be of various races and nationalities.

Hollingshead Index of Social Position (ISP). A two-item index that has been widely adopted to measure social class. Two variables are combined: occupation (weighted 7) and education (weighted 4).

Homophilous. Sharing similar demographic and socioeconomic characteristics and lifestyles. *Opinion* leaders and opinion receivers are homophilous, resulting in lateral (peer) influence (referent power).

Homophily. The "like-me" principle that says people mostly interact with and discuss issues with similar others with respect to sex, age, and socioeconomic status as well as beliefs, values, and the like.

Host culture. The culture immigrants have adopted.

Household (consumer unit, dwelling unit). Any occupied housing unit, regardless of the relationships among the people living there.

Humor appeals. Promotional appeals that rely on incongruity (deviation from expectations) and resolution of that incongruity, resulting in surprise.

Husband-dominant (patriarchal) decisions. When the husband largely controls the family decision, although the wife might have some input.

Hyperlinks (links). Electronic connections from one website to another website between documents that allow consumers to travel through cyberspace in a nonsequential manner.

Hypothesis generation. The first stage of the *cognitive reasoning process*, where the consumer formulates specific testable hypotheses or prior beliefs (assumptions about marketplace alternatives like products, brands, and stores).

Hypothesis revision. Stage three of the *cognitive reasoning process*, where after exposure to and evaluation of marketplace information, the consumer's prior beliefs (hypotheses) are either confirmed or revised if the information shows prior perceptions to be false.

Hypothesis testing. Stage two of the *cognitive reasoning process*, where the buyer gathers information relating to the hypothesis either through education or personal experience. He or she then evaluates the data to determine if the hypothesis is true or false.

Hypothetical constructs. Psychological variables that are not physical entities, but rather are unobservable, theoretical postulated states, conditions, or processes that are abstract constructs.

Iconic memory. Very brief recollection of things people see. Visual images can remain in our minds.

Id. That sector of Sigmund Freud's psychoanalytical mind consisting of primitive instincts and impulsive drives existing at birth. It encompasses basic physiological drives for which the id seeks immediate gratification.

Ideal (desired) self-image. How consumers would like to see themselves or would like to be.

Ideal social self-image. How consumers would like others to see them.

Ideals-inspired consumers. A VALS2 group; they are guided in their choices by abstract, idealized criteria, rather than by feelings, events, or desire for approval and opinions of others. They tend to be *inner-directed* consumers.

Identification. The process of attributing to one's self the characteristics of someone else or some other group. The social referent is perceived to be similar to the person to be influenced, resulting in a feeling of oneness with the social agent.

Image advertising. Retail advertising that helps to craft a *store image* via the people, places, and situations it includes.

Image congruence hypothesis. There should be a match between the *brand's image* and the consumers' *self-image*.

Imagery. Information stored in sensory form, representing an object in terms of its tangible sensory attributes: taste, feel, looks, sound, or smell.

Imitative (emulative) brands. "Me-too" alternatives that mimic successful brands.

Immoral. Wrong, bad, and improper decisions, behaviors, policies, and institutions.

Importance weights (weights). The relative importance of determinant attributes for a product, which can provide the data needed to identify benefit segments.

Important attributes. Criteria that are significant to the consumer.

Impression management (spin control). Selectively and positively reporting information to make one's self or firm look good; accentuating the positive and downplaying any negative.

Impulse (unplanned) purchase. A spontaneous buying situation where neither *problem recognition* nor a *buying intention* in a particular product category existed prior to entering a store or visiting a website. The brand bought differs from what the consumer originally planned (possibly including no planned purchase at all).

Incidental (accidental, passive, iconic rote, associative) learning. Low involvement learning that occurs by accident, without deliberate effort, when the consumer passively encounters unsought information, such as walking past and noticing in-store signs and displays or being exposed to TV commercials and billboards.

Income. A flow of money; the amount of money regularly coming into a household.

Incongruities. Portions of ad illustrations containing an inconsistency, i.e., two or more of its elements do not logically fit together.

Index measure (composite measure, composite variable, multi-item variable). A research measurement combining two or more variables to measure a single concept. Examples are *social class* and *family life* cycle, both of which combine two or more demographic and socioeconomic variables.

Indirect questions (disguised questions). Questions designed to conceal their true purpose that therefore are less threatening than asking a person potentially embarrassing direct questions.

Indirect reference groups. *Reference groups* or persons with whom a person lacks face-to-face contact.

Indirect (vicarious) role models. *Role models* lacking direct contact with the people who imitate or are influenced by them.

Individualism versus collectivism. The extent to which a *culture* focuses on individuals and their welfare rather than groups and their well being.

Individualistic cultures. *Cultures* where people are more concerned with personal goals, individual experiences, variety, pleasure, and freedom than they are with group welfare.

Individualized (one-to-one, segment-of-one, markets-of-one) marketing. Extreme segmentation, whereby marketers serve each individual consumer with a tailor-made marketing program.

Inept set. Alternatives in the *awareness* set the consumer views as unacceptable.

Inert set. Brands in the *awareness set* toward which the buyer is indifferent.

Inertia (repeat purchases, habitual buying). Regularly purchasing the same brand out of habit, convenience, or indifference.

Infinite ideal point attitude model (vector attribute model). The traditional *multiattribute attitude model* (compensatory decision rule) that specifies that consumers prefer an unlimited amount of each criterion.

Influencer. The person who provides other family members with information, advice, and persuasion during the *information search* and *alternative evaluation* stages.

Influencers (sanguine). A Hippocratic personality type. Strengths: Personable, helpful, enthusiastic, verbally articulate optimists. Weaknesses: Inclined to be impulsive, too talkative, overreaching, and over-committing. Typical occupations include actors, salespeople, and speakers.

Informal groups. *Reference groups* having implicit rather than explicit positions, roles, and goals. They are usually either socially based or founded on common interests rather than taking a formal organizational structure.

Informal legitimate power. An appeal to society's or the social group's *social values* and *norms* in an attempt to gain acceptance regarding what is proper.

Information. Data that reduces uncertainty, thereby lowering perceived risk, or that changes the buyer's beliefs.

Information input. Content of *sensory stimuli* adjusted so it is meaningful.

Information integration theory. The cognitive algebra consumers apply in using their brand-attribute knowledge to make marketplace decisions.

Information overload (sensory saturation). A consequence when people are bombarded by myriad stimuli assaulting their senses, due to limitations on people's ability to absorb and process all of these stimuli.

Information processing. The series of activities whereby *sensory stimuli* are perceived, transformed into information, and stored in a person's memory to be retrieved for later use. It includes *perception* plus the transformation and storage of that information in *memory* as part of the learning process.

Information-processing paradigm. A perspective of CB that views CB as largely objective and rational, oriented toward problem solving by acquiring and analyzing information to determine the best solution to the problem.

Information search. The second stage of the consumer decision process, during which the consumer seeks marketplace information.

Informational reference group influence. Where the consumer uses the attitudes and behaviors of *reference group* members to gain information and advice.

Initiator. The person who first suggests that the family has a need or want for a particular product, triggering the *problem recognition* stage.

Innate (physiological, primary, biogenic) needs. Needs that are biological and inborn. Sometimes termed needs, they include requirements for survival, such as food, water, sleep, air, shelter, clothing, and sex.

Inner-directed. People who are introverted and individualistic, self-sufficient, self-disciplined, and indifferent to group standards and opinions.

Innovation. A commercially successful new product. Also defined from a behavioral perspective as any product (good, service, or idea) perceived by the potential adopter to be new.

Innovation resistance. Preference for existing, familiar products and behaviors over less familiar ones.

Innovators. A VALS2 segment; they are achievement oriented with abundant resources.

Innovators (pioneers). The very first consumers (first 2.5 percent) to adopt a new product. Innovators are influential because of their early product experience and expertise.

In-store positioning. The section of the store in which a product is placed.

Instrumental conditioning (operant conditioning, reinforcement theory). This *behavioral learning* theory suggests that behavior is strengthened if followed by *reinforcement* (either positive or negative) or weakened if followed by *punishment*.

Instrumental performance. Outcomes of product purchase and usage related to *utilitarian*, *needs*.

Instrumental (functional, economic) roles. Family decision roles that relate to choosing functional products and to financial, performance, or other practical matters affecting the buying decision, such as when and how much to purchase, features and functions to consider, and budgeting.

Instrumental values. Ideal states of doing, means, or modes of conduct required to achieve terminal states of being. Examples: hard work, frugality, and helpfulness.

Integrated marketing communication (IMC). Using multiple promotional tools (advertising, sales promotion, publicity, packaging, etc.) that contain common elements, such as the same selling message, graphic design, and trade character.

Intellectual property. Any product of human intellect that is unique and not obvious, with some value in the marketplace. Intellectual property laws protect ideas, inventions, literary creations, unique names, business models, industrial processes, computer program code, and other intellectual works from appropriation by others.

Intentional (directed, purposive) learning. Prepurchase information search wherein highly involved consumers actively seek out and consciously process information in a goal-directed fashion.

Interactivity. Opportunities for e-shoppers to interact with a firm's personnel through e-mail, chat rooms, and blogs.

Inter-attitude consistency. A person's overall system of attitudes must remain in balance. Especially *peripheral attitudes* tend to be consistent with strong (central) attitudes.

Interference. When similar information subsequently or previously learned hinders recall or learning of new information.

Intergenerational influence. Early family influences in the marketplace that endure throughout one's lifetime.

Internal attributions. Assigning credit or blame for an occurrence to one's self. A consumer scans his or her *memory* to try to recall a satisfactory alternative solution to the problem.

Internal search. Following *problem recognition* and prior to *external search*, in this part of the information search stage in the consumer decision process, consumers scan their memories to try to recall a satisfactory alternative solution to the problem. That is, they try to recall whether, based on prior learning or personal product experience, they have enough information to make an intelligent purchase decision.

Internet. A worldwide means of exchanging information and communication via a computer network consisting of smaller, interconnected networks.

Interpersonal communication. The personal exchange of information between two or more individuals.

Interpersonal influence. When a consumer's attitude and/or behavior changes as a consequence of *interpersonal communication*.

Inter-role conflict. Mutually incompatible expectations among one's various roles, such as being expected to be in two different places at the same time and place or taking on too many tasks.

Intra-attitude consistency. The three internal attitude domains (cognitive, affective, and conative) tend to be interrelated, mutually influential, and mutually consistent.

Intraculturalism. The process of adopting characteristics of other cultures.

Intrarole conflict. When a given role places competing demands upon a person's time and energy.

Intrinsic cues (direct indicators, product-related attributes). Product characteristics that are part of the actual tangible product itself. They are inherent in the product's physical composition and are consumed, used up, worn out, or destroyed during the product's use.

Introverts. A Myers-Briggs Indicator Personality Inventory type; they are oriented internally toward the pursuit of concepts and ideas and are less communicative. Introverts tend to have quiet energy, talk less, think before they act, be comfortable spending time alone, have good concentration, and make decisions by internally processing information before asking others.

Intuiters. A Myers-Briggs Indicator Personality Inventory type; they rely more on their "sixth sense" or "gut feeling" when deciding, operate on hunches and possibilities, are creative, focus on ideas and the big picture, are theoretical, have roundabout thoughts, are imaginative, see possibilities, look for patterns and relationships, enjoy solving problems, dislike repetitive tasks, are future oriented, and are less patient with the decision-making process, although they are more tolerant of complicated situations.

Involvement. The extent to which the purchase decision has perceived personal importance and relevance for the buyer. Specifically, involvement is the degree of interest in and concern by the consumer in a particular situation for the purchase decision of a particular product (or the marketing communication for that product or any other object of involvement). It is an unobservable state of *motivation*, arousal, or interest in searching for and processing buying information on a product.

Irrationality (nonrationality). A failure to maximize utility or to shop wisely. This is not the same as acting emotionally.

Joint (syncratic) decisions. When both husband and wife make the decision together, especially where there exists high *perceived risk* and *high involvement.*

Judgers. A Myers-Briggs Indicator Personality Inventory type; they favor being organized and systematic, living in a planned and orderly way, making quick decisions, and being serious and formal. They are time-conscious, work first and play later, and prefer to finish projects, although they might experience trouble starting them.

Key informant. Someone who frequently engages in WOM communications within a social system.

Key informant method. A sociological method for identifying *opinion leaders* that asks them to identify opinion leaders for a particular product or situation through surveys.

Keyword search (contextual) advertising. A system through which ads get served up online to an individual viewer of a Web page based on the content the viewer is reading.

Keywords. Words that will trigger the advertiser's banner ad, known as a *keyword ad,* to appear whenever users select that keyword for an online search.

Kinesic communication. Nonverbal communication occurring through the movement of body parts such head nods, eye glances and winks, and movement of the hands, arms, legs, and torso.

Knowledge. Information stored in memory (knowledge content) and form for that information storage (knowledge structure).

Knowledge attitude function. This functional attitude theory suggests that attitudes help consumers in understanding and adapting to a complex world and in organizing their beliefs about attitude objects. Such attitudes help people better understand the marketplace and simplify their decision making.

Knowledge structures. Ways that information can be stored in long-term memory: semantic memory, episodic memory, and schematic memory.

Latent (subconscious, covert) problems (needs). Needs that are deep-seated, hidden below the surface, and must therefore be awakened and kindled by promotion. They are issues of which consumers are unaware, hidden below the surface of consciousness. Since they are unknown, consumers are unable to express them.

Learning. The procedure whereby *memory* and behavior are changed as a result of *perception* and conscious and unconscious *information processing.* A process in which behavioral tendencies are changed as a result of experience, provided they cannot be accounted for by instincts, maturation, temporary states of the organism, or reflex actions.

Learning curve. Displays how learning increases with repeated exposure to the same information, typically at a decreasing rate, i.e., there are usually diminishing returns to repetition. There are two different possible shapes for the learning curve.

Legal codes. A code of laws adopted by a state or nation enforcing *mores* via government sanctions for wrongdoing.

Legends. Stories about revered people who are a combination of myth and history. Examples: Elvis Presley, Babe Ruth, and Princess Dianna.

Legitimate power. A *social agent's* ability to establish social *norms* and then approve of people who follow the norms and disapprove of those who do not. Legitimate power can be both *formal* to gain compliance and *informal* to garner acceptance.

Level of decision making (consumer's learning stage, decision process continuum, consumer problem-solving approach). The degree of prior information and experience the consumer has with both the product category and some its brands. This is a continuum of decision-making complexity ranging from high to low.

Lexicographic decision rule. An alternative evaluation strategy in which the consumer first ranks the evaluative criteria in order of perceived importance. He or she then compares alternatives on the most important attribute and selects the one scoring highest, regardless of how it performs on the other criteria. If two or more brands tie their ratings on that most-critical criterion, the buyer then compares those tied brands on the second-most important characteristic, selecting the alternative performing best on that dimension. If there is again a tie, he or she proceeds to the third-highest-weighted attribute, comparing the remaining tied alternatives. If there continue to be ties, he or she proceeds through the remaining criteria in order of importance, until one of the remaining brands outperforms the others, selecting that one.

Libido (eros, sex). Life-seeking sexual drive.

Lifestage effects. Age-related distinctions arising from moving through important personal life events, such as getting a driver's license, going through parenthood, and confronting the uncertainties of retirement.

Lifestyle. The distinctive or characteristic modes of living of groups or individuals in society, including how they spend the valuable resources of time and money.

Lifetime value of a customer (LVC; lifetime customer value [LCV], lifetime value [LTV]). A calculation projecting a customer's financial worth over the entire history of that customer's relationship with a company. It is calculated by subtracting the acquisition costs plus ongoing costs of serving a customer from the revenue stream that results from building an enduring relationship with that consumer.

Light-bulb memories. Vivid recollections of significant historical events, such as the 9/11 attacks on the United States.

Likert scale. This is typically a five-point rating scale along which respondents indicate how strongly they either agree or disagree with a statement regarding their belief about or liking of a characteristic of an attitude object.

Limited decision making (LDM; limited problem solving). The consumer learning stage in which the consumer has some existing familiarity and perhaps experience with the product class and one or more of its brands and so needs to engage in a somewhat restricted information search, primarily on performance of some brands on the buying criteria.

Links. Connections through which *nodes* are joined to other nodes in an associative (semantic) network.

Locus of control. Whether an individual believes that events in that person's life are caused more by factors under his or her own control and actions (internal locus of control) or by uncontrollable conditions, i.e., other people or events (external locus of control).

Longitudinal research. Consumer research on attitudes and behavior of individual customers gathered over time.

Long-tail theory. As the Internet makes it easy and cheap to offer a vast array of content, consumers turn away from mass market hit products they sort of want, like best-selling books, chart-topping songs, and blockbuster movies, toward niche products they really desire, like obscure books, songs, and movies.

Long-term memory. A *memory store* containing unlimited, long-term storage of learned information.

Loss leaders. High-margin items sporting reduced prices to attract customers who, it is expected, will buy other merchandise at full price while in the store.

Lower-lower. Part of the lower Americans group. The poverty class or "bottom layer."

Lower-upper. Part of the upper Americans group. The newer social elite of first-generation earned wealth.

Low-involvement hierarchy. A model of communications effects for which the process is think-do-feel. However, due to low buyer involvement, the thinking typically occurs at low levels of processing. This is the *passive learning*, low-effort decision-making perspective.

Loyalty marketing (continuity programs, frequent buyer programs, frequency marketing). Encouraging repeat patronage by offering incentives and rewards such as accumulating points redeemable for prizes, instant discounts, and special privileges.

Ludicrous juxtaposition. Placing two objects side by side that normally are not found near one another.

Macroculture. The mainstream culture at large.

Macroeconomics. A major branch of economics that deals primarily with aggregates such as the total amount of products produced by society and the absolute levels of prices. It addresses issues such as level of growth of measures of national output like Gross National Product (GNP) and Gross Domestic Product (GDP), interest rates, unemployment, inflation, the availability of credit, and business cycles.

Macroenvironmental events. Happenings in society at large, such as changes in the sociocultural, technological, economic, natural, and political environments.

Maintainer. The person who keeps a durable good in tip-top shape by checking it regularly, getting it serviced, and taking it to be repaired or doing the repairs and servicing themselves.

Maintenance rehearsal (rehearsal). The silent, mental repetition of a piece of information in short-term memory. It is a form of inner speech, basically like silently talking to one's self.

Makers. A VALS2 type; they are self-expression-oriented individuals with moderate resources.

Manifest (expressed, overt) needs. Those psychological needs known and freely discussed by the respondent.

Market attractiveness. A gauge of how potentially profitable each segment will be, using measures such as whether the organization has the resources to serve each segment; each segment's size, growth rate, and buying power; costs of serving each segment; and size and nature of competitors serving the same segment and loyalty of consumers to those rivals.

Market beliefs. Assumptions about how product signals connote quality or performance.

Market damage. Harm done by dissatisfied customers, including exit or defection, and complaining, which can lead to negative word-of-mouth, legal action against the firm, negative publicity, and boycotts.

Market economy (laissez faire, capitalist, or free enterprise system). An economic system in which the means of production and distribution are privately or corporately owned and development is proportionate to the accumulation and reinvestment of profits gained in a free market. The government leaves its citizens alone regarding all economic activities (except for regulating illegal activities).

Market mavens. Consumers who have general marketplace information about many different types of products, places to shop, and brands to buy, rather than expertise on any particular product categories.

Market orientation. The firm's understanding of its customers and competitors.

Market segment profile. A description of a group of people emerging from the *market segmentation* process known as a market segment, using the selected segmentation variable(s).

Market segmentation. A managerial process that identifies groups of consumers who share similar or common needs and wants or problems to be solved as well as underlying *motivations* for marketplace behavior. It involves subdividing the marketplace into distinct and meaningful subsets of customers. Each group merits a separate marketing program to satisfy targeted consumers' particular needs and desires.

Market signals. Sometimes *surrogate indicators* are known as market signals because they signal, or indicate or suggest to the marketplace of consumers, something about the product that might not otherwise be known.

Marketer-controlled (commercial, advocate) sources. Information sources that originate with and are directed by the marketer.

Marketing. The business function that identifies and anticipates customers' needs and wants, creates products to satisfy those needs and wants, and then delivers the products through various techniques of pricing, distribution, and promotion. Marketing satisfies human needs and wants through the exchange of values between a buyer (customer) and a seller (marketer).

Marketing communication. Persuasive communication directed to people in the marketplace to encourage them to accept the marketer's product.

Marketing concept (marketing orientation). A marketing management philosophy that suggests that the ticket to business success is to identify what consumers want and need, and then to gear the entire marketing program to satisfying those needs and desires more effectively and efficiently than the competition.

Marketing intelligence. Information gathering to keep the marketer's eyes and ears open to the marketplace.

Marketing myopia. A narrow-sightedness or tunnel vision, leading to defining a company as a product producer or expert in a particular technology.

Marketing research. The formal, systematic, objective collection of information to solve a specific marketing problem.

Masculine cultures. These societies have clear distinctions between masculine values such as assertiveness, success, competition, and materialism, and feminine values like warm personal relationships, nurturance, equality, and preserving the environment.

Masculinity versus femininity. The extent to which sex roles are clearly defined in a culture.

Mass customization. Mass production of goods with differing individual specifications through the use of components that may be assembled in a number of different configurations. Producers can now achieve flexible, low-cost manufacturing without lengthy production runs of one product.

Massed advertising. When ads are bunched up in one or more short time periods during the entire ad campaign, often coinciding with peak buying periods.

Material values (environment-oriented values). This group of values prioritizes society's relationships with the various aspects of the broad environment: ecological (physical or natural environment), economic, and technical.

Mature market (seniors). Variously defined as people over 50, 55, or 60.

McClelland's trichotomy (trio) of social needs. A classification scheme of social motives that inform social dynamics between individuals, groups, and even entire nation-state societies: power, affiliation, and achievement.

Mea culpa strategy. A marketing strategy that involves admitting a marketing program shortcoming, apologizing for it, and assuring the audience that the problem has been recently rectified.

Means-end chain analysis. Is based on the idea that product features are the means for obtaining the ends, which are product *benefits* and personal values.

Mediating (contingency) variables. "It depends" factors of consumer behavior, viz. the consumer, product, and the purchase and consumption situation.

Membership groups. *Social groups* to which an individual belongs, i.e., has achieved formal or informal acceptance into the group.

Memories. Key elements from prior learning experiences.

Memory. The outcome of the learning process, providing a storehouse of information.

Memory stores. Processing areas in memory: *sensory memory, short-term memory, and long-term memory.*

Memory trace strength. The extent to which an association or link is strongly or weakly joined to a concept in memory.

Mental completion (closure). The human tendency to remember incomplete patterns better than those that are complete. We tend to perceive incomplete patterns as being complete, based on prior experiences.

Merchandising. The advertising, promotion, and organization of the sale of a particular brand within a store. Merchandising generally involves both in-store and outside-of-store promotional activities.

Mere exposure effect. Frequent exposure to a stimulus creates liking for that cue.

Message (theme, selling premise, selling appeal). The major point about the brand communicated to the target audience.

Message framing. Whether one describes a condition in either positive terms ("The glass is half full") or using negative expressions ("The glass is half empty").

Message structure characteristics. Organization of the message elements.

Message wearout (wearout, advertising wearout [in an advertising context]**).** A phenomenon in which the *learning curve*, after reaching the saturation point where the consumer has learned all he or she can or desires to learn, might actually start to turn downward as the consumer becomes satiated with too much repetition.

Message-response involvement (advertising involvement). The consumer's degree of interest in paying attention to and learning from (message-related involvement) and/or being entertained by (executional involvement) marketing communications.

Meta-engines (metasearch tool). A *search engine* that hunts multiple search engines simultaneously for words and phrases, combines results, removes duplicate entries, and presents a single listing.

Metaphor. A figure of speech using an implicit comparison suggesting two objects or experiences are alike, related, or identified with each other. It transfers a term or characteristic from the object it ordinarily designates to another object, saying, "A is to B as C is to D."

Microeconomics. A major branch of *economics* that has two perspectives: (1) Individual business decisions, known as the neoclassical (microeconomic) theory of the firm. (2) Individual consumer choices, called the neoclassical theory of consumption (consumer decision making).

Microenvironment (operating environment). Factors close to the company affecting its ability to effectively serve its customers, thereby causing buyers to either fulfill or not fulfill their original purchase intentions.

Micromarketing. Geographic targeting of a community down to the zip code and neighborhood levels.

Middle class. Part of the Middle American group. Average income white-collar workers; owners of small businesses; and highly paid, socially ambitious blue-collar workers.

Mixed economy. A blend of command and market economies, of socialism and capitalism. Economic decisions are primarily made freely as in a market economy, but there is more government intervention, such as through wage and price controls and import tariffs and quotas.

Mnemonics. Imposing a structure or organization upon material to be learned to give it meaning.

Mobile marketing (mobile commerce, m-commerce). Marketing and advertising over wireless networks so consumers can use their Internet-enabled smartphones, e-readers, portable entertainment players, and other wireless devices to get product/price and store information, find store locations, obtain coupons, and make purchases.

Modeling. The act of people copying the behavior of an idealized social lifestyle model in order to be like him or appear to be like him.

Moderator (interviewer). The person who leads a one-to-two hour discussion involving about six to twelve consumers in a *focus group interview*.

Monitor. The person who takes the task of keeping an eye on other family members' consumption during the postpurchase consumption stage.

Monochromic. A society's time orientation focused on doing one thing at a time (versus *polychromic*).

Mood. A temporary feeling state that is usually not intense, and is not tied to a specifiable behavior, event, or object.

Mood association. Advertisers attach a certain mood or feeling to their brands. Repeated association with particular stimuli such as music or celebrities evokes a conditioned or unconditioned response such as relaxation, recreation, and companionship.

Moral. Right, good, and proper decisions, behaviors, policies, and institutions.

Moral appeals. Advertising appeals to do the right thing based on social norms, such as vote or do volunteer work.

Moral norms (ethical norms). Standards of behavior that require, prohibit, or allow certain specific actions to avoid causing harm to others or to help people.

Moral reasoning (ethical reasoning). The rational reasoning process whereby people determine if human decisions, behaviors, institutions, or policies are in accordance with or in violation of moral standards.

Moral standards. Rules or guidelines by which we should live.

Mores. *Norms* with a strong moral overtone, usually entailing a taboo or forbidden behavior. Examples: incest and cannibalism.

Motivated behavior. Activities to satisfy a consumer's needs and wants.

Motivation. An activated internal need state leading to goal-directed behavior to satisfy that need.

Motivation (motivational) research. Consumer research based on Freud's notion of latent, subconscious motives and instincts that people are unable and/or unwilling to express, using probing and indirect questions to drill down deep into consumers' subconscious mind, to discover the motives or "real reasons" people buy that they are unable or unwilling to discuss. This research usually uses detailed analysis of the responses of a limited number of interviewees.

Motivation to comply with normative beliefs (MC). A component in the *Fishbein theory* of reasoned action representing a consumer's willingness to go along with the perceived expectations of others.

Motivational appeal. The nature of the driving force used to convey the advertiser's or salesperson's message. This message is the major point about the product communicated to the target audience.

Motivational conflict. Clashes concerning positively and/or negatively valenced objects.

Motivational direction. Unsatisfied motives direct people's actions toward a particular goal used to reduce the motivational tension and satisfy a desire.

Motivational process. This step-by-step process shows that *motivation* entails internal forces moving people from an actual or existing state of being toward a desired or ideal state. (See Figure 1 for Chapter 12 Introduction.)

Motivational strength. The degree to which a person is willing to expend energy to achieve a goal.

Motives. Relatively enduring, strong, and persistent internal stimuli which arouse and direct behavior toward certain goals. Internal drives that influence consumers to seek out, evaluate, and purchase goods and services.

Multiattribute attitude model. A representation of a consumer's attitude as determined by his or her beliefs about a brand's performance or rating on determinant criteria and assessment of either the weight (importance) or evaluation (goodness-badness) of that criterion. It is portrayed by the formula:

$$A_{jk} = \Sigma \; w_{ik} b_{ijk}$$

The consumer's overall attitude toward any given brand is a weighted sum of beliefs about the brand's performance on each of the characteristics. In this model, the higher the score, the more positive the attitude. (See also *weighted linear compensatory rule*, defined on p. 606.)

Multibrand loyalty (brand cluster loyalty). When a consumer is loyal to more than one brand in a category. Usually, this is for reasons of *variety seeking* while remaining loyal to the preferred brands.

Multicultural (ethnic, minority) marketing. Targeting groups whose members' share subcultural components based on a common racial, nationality, or language background.

Multiculturalism. The celebration of distinct ethnicities.

Multidimensional attitudes. A perspective on attitudes, taken by most surveys, that views the evaluation of an attitude object as occurring along several dimensions.

Multigenerational households. When grandparents and other relatives take up residence with the *nuclear family*.

Multi-item (itemized) rating scales. Attitude *rating scales* that assume attitude is a multidimensional construct and therefore consist of a battery of items, each arrayed along a continuum, with one end indicating an unfavorable predisposition and the other end a favorable attitude. An individual's overall attitude score is simply the sum of the individual ratings.

Multi-item (composite variable) social class index measures. Composite measures used to determine an individual's or household's *social class*, which recognize that social class is a multidimensional construct that is an amalgamation of several socioeconomic and demographic variables.

Multilevel marketing. A practice whereby a salesperson (distributor) earns extra commissions by persuading customers to also become distributors.

Multiple request techniques. Shaping techniques that entail gaining compliance with a "critical" request by first asking a person to fulfill a related favor. Multiple request methods include both *foot-in-the-door* and *door-in-the-face* techniques.

Multiple store theory. A theory suggesting there are three interrelated *memory stores*.

Multistep flow of communication model (multistage interaction model). This model of interpersonal communication flow suggests that not only do opinion leaders (OLs) get media information, but so do opinion followers. In fact, some information receivers receive marketplace information solely from the mass media rather than from OLs. Also, two-way flows of communication occur whereby OLs both influence and are influenced by opinion receivers.

Multitask (polychronic time use). To engage in two or more activities simultaneously in order to accomplish them all.

Myers-Briggs Type Indicator Personality Inventory. The most widely used psychological test in the world, it describes peoples' characteristic decision-making styles: Extroverts versus Introverts, Sensors versus Intuiters, Thinkers versus Feelers, and Judgers versus Perceivers.

Myths. Stories containing symbolic elements expressing a society's key values, ideals, emotions, and dreams. These often feature a clash between good and evil to serve as a moral guide. Examples: Superman and Santa Claus.

National brand. A well-known manufacturer's brand (not necessarily sold nationwide).

Navigational tools. Devices to help consumers efficiently navigate (find their way) through a website.

Need association. A *classical conditioning* process that repeatedly links a brand to a particular need or drive.

Need for cognition (NC). The extent to which a person craves or enjoys thinking, challenging information processing, and problem-solving activities.

Need recognition. A form of *problem recognition* in which the actual state declines.

Needs. States of felt deprivation of essential physiological requirements for optimal life conditions. Being mandatory, needs are satisfied by necessities (e.g., clothing, shelter, and rest).

Negative punishment. A form of *punishment* in which a wanted stimulus (reward) is removed as a result of undesirable behavior.

Negative reinforcement. A reward that induces a desired reaction by removing or else helping the learner avoid an adverse stimulus or unpleasant consequences following performance of that response.

Negativity bias. Bad news travels faster and farther than good news, and it has greater priority and influence in decision making than does positive communication.

Neoclassical microeconomic model of consumer decision making. Based on the theory of consumption, which says that consumer decisions are based on buyers' careful allocation of their scarce financial resources among various purchase alternatives so as to purchase a bundle of goods and services that maximize their utility. It suggests that buyers make careful, rational cost-benefit calculations using perfect information to determine the optimal combination of goods they can obtain, subject to their resource constraints.

Net promoter score. A measure of the relative number of advocates for versus complainers against a brand.

Neutral (independent) sources. Third-party information available to the general public, such as news editorials, consumer ratings, product-focused magazines, shopping magazines, government and scientific reports, J.D. Power satisfaction ratings, and personal blogs.

Neutral stimulus (NS). A cue that naturally would not produce any *response* on its own.

"New-and-improved" products (next-generation products). Modifications of existing products that result in replacing a previous version of the product (rather than supplementing an item, as with additions to existing product lines).

New product lines (new category entries). Such products are already established in the marketplace but are new to the firm launching them.

New-to-the-world products (new product categories). These new products either revolutionize existing product categories or define wholly new categories.

Newly married couples (Newlywed Game, Honeymooners). This family life cycle segment consists of young couples (generally under 35) without children.

Nodes. Beliefs or concepts in memory that are connected to other nodes through connections called *links*.

Nonbuying (nonfunctional) shopping motives. Needs unrelated to acquisition of one or more products but that are more *psychosocial* in nature.

Noncomparative (monadic) rating scales. Attitude *rating scales* that ask respondents to rate one attitude object in isolation, without comparison to other attitude objects.

Noncompensatory decision rules. A category of decision models that do not permit high performance on one attribute to compensate for a low rating on another criterion (no tradeoffs are allowed). Only the most important, not all, brand-attribute information is considered.

Nonfamily households. Dwelling units containing combinations of people other than families, such as cohabiting couples; others living together such as in a fraternity or sorority house or in a boarding house; same-sex homes; and persons living alone.

Non-marketer-controlled sources (noncommercial) sources. Information sources that stem from and are controlled by communicators other than marketers, such as friends, professionals, and the media.

Nonmembership groups. Social groups to which a person does not belong but might qualify to join.

Nonperformance (nonfunctional) attributes. Primarily extrinsic criteria irrelevant for judging a product's performance. They have low-to-no predictive value for understanding the difficult-to-discern product elements.

Nonpersonal sources. Information sources not involving other people, including mass media advertising, publicity, and *neutral sources.*

Nontraditional families. Families not consisting of a married couple with children. They fall outside the normative nuclear family but do contain people related by blood, marriage, or adoption. They include single-parent households, married couples without children, and *blended families.*

Nonverbal cues. Stimuli other than words.

Normative (prescriptive, evaluative). The *microeconomic theory* of the individual consumer explains the way the *rational* consumer should behave, based on deductive (inferential) reasoning, rather than being positive (descriptive), or founded on inductive (empirical) investigation.

Normative beliefs (NB; social norms). A component in the *Fishbein theory of reasoned action* representing an individual's perceptions about significant others' desires or expectations regarding the individual acting a certain way toward an attitude object (perhaps in a given situation). NBs are perceived social pressure to conform to the behavioral *norms* (standards) of other important persons or of a *social group.*

Nouveau riche. Literally means "new money, "or "new wealth," and refers to self-made people who are generally active in community affairs and public issues. They might be extremely wealthy, but since the money is still relatively new they have not yet been fully accepted by the community's upper crust.

Nuclear (conventional, normal, limited, typical) family. The most common family unit, consisting of two adults of opposite sexes, living in a socially approved sexual relationship with their own or adopted children.

Numerical scale. A rating scale that is similar to the semantic differential scale, except instead of using bipolar adjectives, it uses numbers to indicate scale positions that respondents rate an attitude object along regarding a series of adjectives.

Objective method. A sociological research method for identifying *opinion leaders* whereby a "controlled experiment" is run in which a new product (NP) or new product information is placed with selected persons. Then, the resulting chain of WOM communication is tracked by asking people if they received the information on and/or tried the NP and from where they received their product knowledge.

Objective methods. *Social class* research that collects data on various demographic and *socioeconomic status* variables such as occupation, education, and amount of income in order to identify people's social class.

Objective (actual, real) self. Who a person actually is. It can be objectively identified through a standardized personality test.

Obsolescence risk. The risk that the purchased product will quickly become outdated, being superseded by a new, advanced version. Hi-tech products and fashion and fad items are prone to this risk.

One-sided messages. Communications only discussing the brand's merits without explaining its shortcomings or rivals' strengths because marketers fear that doing so will harm the brand.

One-step flow of communication theory (top-down model, direct-flow model, hypodermic needle model). Another name for the top-down communication pattern entailing *top-down social change.* Mass media supposedly have a direct, immediate, and powerful effect on a mass audience.

Ongoing (exploratory) search. A regular search undertaken to gather a bank of information for potential future use or to experience fun or pleasure.

Open-ended (implicit) communications. Communications that permit recipients to come to their own conclusions.

Open-ended (free answer) questions. Survey questions allowing interviewees to reply in their own words, usually in depth interviews and focus groups, although personal interviews are also used.

Operant (instrumental) conditioning (reinforcement theory). A learning theory suggesting that responses are best learned if followed by *reinforcement* or weakened if followed by *punishment.* Through active, conscious, and voluntary trial and error learning, the learner discovers which stimuli are associated with the best rewards.

Opinion. Someone's verbal (spoken or written) expression of an attitude.

Opinion follower. The receiver of information and opinions from an *opinion leader.*

Opinion leaders (OLs, influentials, tastemakers, trendsetters, thought leaders, pioneer consumers, product enthusiasts). Influential individuals who are knowledgeable about products in a particular field and whose advice others take seriously.

Opinion leadership. The extent to which an individual directly (via verbal word of mouth) or indirectly (by being observed) changes others' attitudes and behaviors.

Opinion leadership overlap (quasi-generalized opinion leadership, polymorphic opinion leadership). Opinion leaders in one product class are often opinion leaders in one or more related categories.

Opinion receiver. An *opinion follower* who passively accepts information and advice from an opinion leader without having requested it.

Opinion seeker. When an *opinion follower* accepts information and advice when actively pursuing guidance from an opinion leader.

Opportunity cost. The next best use of the consumer's time after the current activity.

Opportunity recognition. A form of *problem recognition* in which the consumer's ideal state increases, and that person wants and expects more than previously.

Optimal decisions. Assumption underlying the traditional *microeconomic* perspective of consumer behavior is that consumers make choices so as to produce the very best results for themselves, given their resource (money, time, and energy) constraints.

Optimal stimulation level (OSL). People's preference for a simple, uncluttered and calm life as opposed to a novel, complex, and ever-changing existence. People have different optimal stimulation levels (OSLs)—desired levels of environmental arousal or excitement.

Outer-directed (other-directed). Consumers who are extroverted and conformists. Concerned with what others will think of them, they tend to give in to peer pressure and *reference group* influences and are thus less likely to be consumer innovators, preferring to wait until the innovators and early adopters are regular product users. They perceive high social risk in many products, are more social class/status conscious, and hence are into *conspicuous consumption*.

Overprivileged. Families with an income higher than the average in their *social class*.

Package downsizing (package shorting, weight out). Decreasing the amount and/or weight of package contents while holding price constant.

Package knockoffs (look-alike packaging). A potential form of *trade dress infringement* wherein aspects of a brand's unique packaging are imitated by another manufacturer.

Packaging. Entails the product's container or wrapper, plus inserts and labeling.

Paired comparisons. A rating scale that presents respondents with pairs of attitude objects and asks them to select the object preferred either overall or in terms of a series of criteria. More than one pair of attitude objects can be evaluated, so that all possible pairs are compared. From these, rank order preferences can be derived.

Paradigms. Models, perspectives, or worldviews providing fundamental assumptions regarding what we are studying and how to study it.

Pareto's Law (the heavy-half theory). Half of a brand's customers account for a disproportionately larger amount of a brand's overall sales volume. Frequently, 80 percent of the output results from 20 percent of the inputs.

Parody display. When the well-to-do deliberately mock status symbols by adopting items that originally skewed downscale, like ripped jeans, Jeeps, and tattoos.

Partial reinforcement. A reward schedule in which *reinforcement* is only given some of the time the correct response occurs.

Passive learning. Learning that does not require conscious attention or involvement on the learner's part. It is low-involvement (incidental) associative learning.

Passive learning hierarchy. A model of communication effects where the order is do-think-feel. In many low-involvement situations, consumers merely "buy and try." On the basis of their usage experience, they form brand evaluations. This is the low-effort *behavioral influence perspective*.

Passive learning theory. In low-involvement situations, behavioral change tends to precede attitude change. Consumers form attitudes after they purchase and evaluate, thereby gaining postpurchase information so as to form a judgment regarding whether or not they like the item.

Perceived risk. The extent of uncertainty the consumer believes (perceives) exists about possible negative consequences associated with the purchase and use of a product.

Perceivers. A Myers-Briggs Indicator Personality Inventory type, they like to live life flexibly and spontaneously, are open to new events, tend to wait for more information and procrastinate in decision-making, are playful and casual, are unaware of time, prefer to wait and see, play first then work later, and like to start projects.

Perception. The process whereby individuals receive, select, organize, and interpret *sensory stimuli* to produce a meaningful picture of their world. The interpretation of sensations to produce meaning.

Perceptual (informational) cues. Characteristics of stimulus objects, as consumers perceive them.

Perceptual defense. Individuals' tendency to ignore cues they find psychologically threatening or that contradict their beliefs or attitudes.

Perceptual predispositions. A person's needs and wants, interests, values, beliefs, and attitudes.

Perceptual (mental) set. What a person expects to perceive or is used to perceiving.

Perceptual vigilance. People are more likely to notice stimuli relevant to their needs and wants, interests, values, beliefs, and attitudes.

Performance (functional) attributes. Relevant traits for judging product performance. They have high *predictive value* and are mostly *intrinsic cues* since these directly affect product performance.

Performance (functional) risk. A perceived risk that involves the possibility that the product will not perform as expected, i.e., that it will not satisfy the functional needs that it is meant to fulfill.

Peripheral attitudes. Attitudes that are less important and weaker than *central attitudes*.

Peripheral beliefs. Beliefs that are less important than *central beliefs*, are not centrally held, and are anchored (tied) to central beliefs.

Peripheral cues. Less relevant, easily processed stimuli associated with a message. Examples include background scenery, characteristics of people and music featured in advertising; attractive packaging; and brand name.

Peripheral-route processing. In the *elaboration likelihood model*, this is where motivation, opportunity, and ability (MOA) are low, and so consumer attitudes are based more on a tangential or superficial examination of the information, rather than an effortful analysis of its true merits. The consumer expends limited effort, i.e., there is little information search and low *elaboration*.

Personal analogies. *Projective techniques* in which respondents are requested to imagine and describe themselves as the product.

Personal sources. Individuals with whom the consumer has direct, one-on-one contact, such as friends, family, colleagues, neighbors, and professionals.

Personal values (self-oriented values). Beliefs about ideal states of being. They are ideals most important to an individual, shaping how the person thinks and behaves in almost every situation. In the *focus-of-orientation values* system, personal values reflect the objectives and approaches to life that individual members of the culture find desirable.

Personality. Our relatively enduring, consistent, and distinguishing characteristic traits that differentiate us from others.

Personality inventory. An extensive list of statements with scales expressing likes or dislikes for certain objects, people, or situations, used to measure respondents' *personality traits*.

Personality traits. Characteristic behavior and thought patterns; any distinguishing, relatively enduring way that one person differs from another regarding the individual's typical responses to environmental stimuli.

Personification (anthropomorphism). A *projective technique* whereby consumers are asked to imagine that the brand comes to life as a person and are queried regarding what the brand is like in terms of its demographic characteristics, lifestyles, likes and dislikes, and so on.

Persuasion. An explicit attempt to influence people's beliefs, attitudes, and/or behaviors, i.e., to change their minds.

Phased decision strategy (multistage choice process). A two-step decision process. The first step entails quickly paring down a large number of alternatives to a more manageable number, using one of the quicker and easier *noncompensatory rules*. The second phase uses a *compensatory rule* to evaluate the remaining alternatives.

Philosophies of marketing management. How companies plan, implement, and control their marketing programs with their target markets in order to achieve their organizational and marketing objectives.

Physical positioning (physical product differentiation). Distinguishing the marketer's product from the competition via tangible product attributes (physical product characteristics) or by making it of better quality or higher performance.

Physical (safety) risk. Possible harm that can come from the product malfunctioning, thereby posing a physical hazard to the health and safety of users, others nearby the users, and possibly even the ecological environment.

Physical trace evidence. After a culture has dissipated, these *cultural artifacts* are sometimes left behind, which cultural anthropologists study via observational research.

Physiological (innate) needs. Basic biological requirements for living, including food, water, shelter, sleep, oxygen, relief from pain, waste elimination, a relatively constant body temperature, and sexual release.

Picture sorting. A *projective technique* in which respondents are given a deck of cards showing photos of different kinds of people who vary by gender, ethnicity, dress, etc. To enable researchers to learn about brand image, interviewees are asked to identify the brands in a particular product category that each person uses. Also, to reveal their own self-images, respondents are requested to identify pictures of people most like them.

Point of purchase (POP; point-of-sale advertising, in-store media). Includes banners, shelf signs, kiosks, ads on shopping carts, in-store broadcasts, and other ads found in retail outlets, including racks, shelves, or bins that hold the product. In conjunction with the package, they can clinch the sale.

Politics. The activities and affairs of government and politicians.

Polychromic. A society's time orientation toward multitasking.

Popular ("pop," mass) culture. The culture of mainstream appeal, such as movies, TV shows, popular books, music, fashion, sports, toys and games (including video games), and magazines. Without foundation in cultural tradition, it is mass-produced and standardized, shaped more by marketing surveys than by the spontaneous expression of a people's experience.

Positioning. Physically and/or psychologically differentiating the firm's offering for each target market from those of competitors pursuing the same or similar segments.

Positioning statement. A product description discussing a product's key points of distinction appealing to the targeted segment.

Positive (descriptive). A theory founded on inductive investigation (empirical; deriving general principles from specific facts or observations), as is done in *consumer research*.

Positive punishment. A form of punishment in which a negative stimulus (punishment) is administered for bad behavior.

Positive reinforcement. A form of reward that provokes the desired learned response by generating desired consequences following performance of the preferred behavior in response to a stimulus.

POSSLQ. Persons of the opposite sex sharing living quarters (unmarried couples living together).

Postpurchase dissonance (dissonance, buyer's remorse, regret). A consumer's post-choice doubt or anxiety over whether he or she selected the best alternative.

Postpurchase outcomes (postacquisition behaviors). Those aspects of CB that follow the purchase and acquisition of a product.

Postpurchase search. External search that sometimes occurs after purchase and use of the product for reasons such as reducing doubt and alleviating dissatisfaction.

Power distance. The degree to which members of a society are considered equal in terms of status, authority, and wealth, and there is acceptance of social inequality and hierarchical relationships, such as superiors versus subordinates.

Pre-Depression Generation (born before 1930). They grew up in tough times during the Depression and World War II and were deprived of material goods and a solid education, although they matured during the prosperous 1950s. This is the older end of today's mature market (seniors).

Predictive value. A perceptual cue's relevance or validity in predicting product performance.

Preference. Someone's attitude toward one attitude object in relation to another.

Preparer. The person who converts the product into a form consumable by family members during the postpurchase consumption stage.

Prepotency. Relative predominance of needs in Maslow's Hierarchy. A prepotent need has the greatest influence over people's actions, given where they are in the hierarchy of needs.

Prepurchase alternative evaluation. The third stage in the consumer decision-making process. It is the process of comparing various alternatives identified during information search in order to choose among them by comparing them on evaluative criteria.

Prepurchase search. Goal-oriented search following *problem recognition* driven by a desire to acquire a want-satisfying or problem-solving product.

Prescriptive normative beliefs. They prescribe what one will or should do, based upon the *cognitive* and affective dimensions. This behavioral component is usually an intention to buy.

Price-and-item advertising. Retail advertising whose message usually is "Here are the brands we are currently featuring at these spectacular prices." Other essential information can be included, such as hours of operation and location.

Primacy effect. The inclination to better recall information that occurs first or early in a sequence of information.

Primary (generic) demand. Understanding of and a felt need for the product category.

Primary (generic) demand advertising. Promotion that builds primary demand, being heavy with information, and often referring to another more detailed information source, such as a website or toll-free number.

Primary groups. These are contact groups characterized by small size and a highly shared ideology.

Primary motivation. In VALS2, that which determines what in particular about an individual or the world is the meaningful core governing that individual's activities.

Primary process thinking (fantasy). A self-induced shift in consciousness to compensate for lack of permissible external stimulation. The subconscious mind satisfies the id's longing for pleasure by fantasizing, i.e., enjoying thoughts about unrealized pleasures and forbidden fruits, thereby allowing day dreamers to gratify the id in an acceptable fashion.

Primary reinforcers. Rewards that satisfy primary motives.

Primary research. Information collected for the first time from original sources.

Principles of context. Perceptual principles concerning how the surrounding environment (context) helps determine individuals' perceptions of stimuli in that environment.

Principles of grouping. Gestalt perceptual principles concerning how people organize individual stimuli into groups or chunks of information.

Private (house, store, dealer) brand (own label). A wholesaler's or retailer's brand.

Private opinion leaders. *Opinion leaders* who have personal contact with people they influence.

Privately owned consumer goods. *Cultural artifacts* owned by individuals and households.

PRIZM. A geodemographic system developed by Claritas Corp. PRIZM (stands for Potential Rating Index by Zip Market) has identified 62 major types of neighborhoods or clusters, which can be grouped into 15 larger social groups based on degree of urbanization and socioeconomic status.

Proactive inhibition. A form of interference that happens when earlier information stored in long-term memory hinders learning later similar information because the latter is not processed.

Problem analysis (problem detection, needs analysis). An approach to finding and solving problems. The procedure is: determine an activity or product where consumers are believed to have unsatisfied needs or unsolved problems, use surveys or *focus groups* with target market consumers to gather a list of those needs and problems, and employ creative thinking to generate product ideas to solve one or more of the problems on the list.

Problem recognition (need arousal, need state). The first stage in the consumer decision process. It entails a significant gap between a consumer's actual or current state of affairs and the buyer's desired or ideal state of affairs caused by an unsolved problem or an unsatisfied need or want. Problem recognition is the result of a consumer's unsolved customer problem or a felt (unsatisfied) need or want.

Problem solving. The process whereby consumers taking thoughtful, reasoned action to find a solution to satisfy their needs, where the solution is purchase of a product.

Problem-based ideation (problem-solution route, problem find–problem solve approach). A new product ideation technique. The procedure is: (1) Discover unsolved consumer problems or unsatisfied needs and wants. Marketing research methodologies can be used to isolate the problems. Techniques include customer satisfaction surveys, *focus groups*, depth interviews, observation, complaint emails, and online community chatter; (2) Conceive, develop, test, and launch a new product that better solves the problem or satisfies the desires than anything else currently offered in the marketplace.

Problem-solution (problem-resolution) advertising. Advertising that raises a problem and dramatically shows how the product solves it.

Product analysis. A type of *problem analysis* that uncovers problems consumers associate with using a particular product, employing the same procedure as *activity analysis*.

Product class (category) positioning. Defining the boundaries of the product class, done either broadly or narrowly, suggesting other competitive product categories.

Product concept (product orientation). The marketing management philosophy alleging that consumers are interested in products that offer the most quality and performance and /or have unique features.

Product concept statement. A verbal description of the new product idea that describes its form (physical attributes), product functions (functional benefits), and delivered benefits (both hedonic and symbolic).

Product criteria. Attributes in a product, regardless of whether or not they matter to buyers. That is, they might or might not be *evaluative criteria* used to select among options.

Product differentiation. When items in a product line offered to consumers differ from each other and/or from rivals' offerings in one of the following three ways: being better than competitive brands, physically or tangibly; being superior to rivals psychologically or intangibly; and using product variety, offering multiple items in a product line differing from one another.

Product features (physical attributes, product specifications [specs]). These constitute the tangible product, the physical properties of a product. They also include intangible or abstract features.

Product generalization. A form of stimulus generalization occurring when consumers generalize from one product or brand to similar ones. It occurs because *copycat products* appear similar to one of their major (usually larger) competitors.

Product icons. Distinctive, enduring brand symbols holding significant nostalgia value or deep meaning for consumers, such as McDonald's Golden Arches, the Nike checkmark, and Ronald McDonald.

Product involvement. A consumer's inherent degree of interest in a particular product or brand, which is an enduring involvement.

Product line extension (line extension). The use of one of a firm's existing names on an addition to a product line. It is the most common means of adding variety to a product line.

Product missionaries. People who will spread the word about a product with evangelical zeal, converting unreached unbelievers into customers.

Product performance. The degree to which the product fulfills consumer desires and expectations, including *instrumental performance* and *symbolic performance*.

Product quality. Perceived quality entails giving buyers something for their money that meets their desires and fulfills their expectations, i.e., it satisfies its customers. Actual quality is competitive superiority or excellence on important evaluative criteria that can be objectively assessed.

Product semiotics. The study of the unique symbolic qualities of products and brands.

Product-specific goals. The branded products that consumers seek to fulfill their needs.

Product-specific values. *Evaluative criteria* buyers use for selecting among brands in a product category.

Production concept (production orientation). The organizational philosophy that says consumers are primarily interested in products that are readily affordable and easily available.

Products. Tangible goods, intangible services, ideas, or anything else that can satisfy customers' needs or desires.

Projection. A means by which people attribute their own thoughts and feelings (conscious and unconscious) to the external world.

Projective techniques. Consumer research techniques using indirect (disguised) questions.

Promotional mix. The specific combination of marketing communication techniques used in a marketing communication strategy.

Prototype. A member considered to be the best example of a product category.

Prototypical. Specific information that is exemplary or representative of a more general category.

Prototypical (master) brands. Brands that are viewed as the best examples of a product category. They have strong associations with the product class.

Proxemic communication. Nonverbal communication that occurs by varying the physical distance in face-to-face interactions.

Proximity (contiguity) principle. A Gestalt psychology *grouping* principle that suggests things that are in close proximity to one another are perceived as belonging together or as forming a gestalt.

Proxy factors (surrogate variables). Factors such as occupation, education, and income that serve as substitute (surrogate) indicators of social status.

Psychoanalytical theory of personality. Suggests that unconscious needs or drives (especially biological drives) underlie most human motivation, personality, and behavior.

Psychographics. Adds states of mind and consequent states of action to states of being. It includes internal and external personal factors like *personality* and *lifestyle*; *motivation*; and attitudes, interests, and opinions (*AIOs*).

Psychographics (lifestyle, values) research. The quantitative research method used for measuring consumer *lifestyles*. It captures buyers' *AIOs* (activities, interests, and opinions).

Psychological positioning (psychological product differentiation). Creating "induced" brand differences in buyers' minds via advertising and promotion.

Psychological risk. Perceived risk that entails uneasiness, mental anguish, and even fear that the product won't provide emotional or intellectual satisfaction.

Psychological value added (intangible value, perceptual value). Customers get extra utility from a product because of its psychological *positioning* and are therefore willing to pay more for it.

Psychology. The scientific study of the processes of thinking (states of mind) and behavior (states of action).

Psychophysics. The study of the how the physical environment is related to people's subjective (psychological) experience, i.e., the relationship between the nature and amount of a stimulus (cue) and the sensation that it produces.

Psychosocial (socio-psychological). Of a nature relating to or combining social and psychological factors, i.e., concerned with psychological development within and interaction with a social environment.

Public goods. *Cultural artifacts* owned and maintained by a governmental entity and available for everyone's use. Examples: highways, bridges, government buildings, museums, and parks.

Public opinion leader. An influential celebrity or person in the public limelight, various aspects of whose CB are reported by the media, thereby influencing the masses to follow suit.

Public relations (PR). The communications function that builds good relations and a good reputation with the organization's various *publics* by obtaining favorable publicity, building up a good "corporate image," and handling or heading off unfavorable rumors, stories, and events.

Publicity. Nonpaid, nonpersonal, newsworthy media exposure concerning a firm and its products.

Publics (stakeholders, constituencies). All individuals and groups that have an interest in the firm, can affect it by their behavior, and are affected by how the company conducts business. These include customers, stockholders, employees, suppliers and distributors, creditors, local communities, government regulatory agencies, and others.

Pulsing. When periods of high levels of advertising (pulses) are followed by intervals of little advertising.

Punishment. An environmental event that decreases the probability of an undesired response and is therefore avoided.

Purchase decision. The stage of the consumer decision-making process where a shopper makes a choice from among the considered alternatives.

Purchase pals. Opinion leaders (OLs) who accompany buyers on their shopping trips in order to provide information on and advice for their on-site purchase decisions.

Purchase situation. Consists of factors peculiar to a particular time, place, or location that affect the buyer's decision.

Purchase situation involvement (decision involvement). A consumer's extent of concern for and interest in the purchase process for a particular item, i.e., it is situational, short-term involvement.

Qualitative research. Collecting descriptions or narratives of events as contrasted with *quantitative research*.

Quantitative research. The systematic scientific investigation of quantitative properties and phenomena and their relationships, i.e., collecting data that take numerical form.

Rank ordering. A *rating scale* in which interviewees are asked to rank order attitude objects according to preference overall or else according to chosen criteria.

Rank-order importance scale. A *rating scale* allowing respondents to rank a list of product criteria in order of personal importance.

Rating. A measurement task presenting the respondent with one or more items—statements or questions regarding an attitude object's characteristics—and requesting an estimate of the magnitude or favorability of each trait along a numerically valued continuum or in one of a numerically ordered set of categories. Individuals are asked to rate their beliefs about, feelings toward, and/or behavioral intentions concerning an attitude object.

Rating scales. Questions that ask interviewees to estimate the magnitude of something on a continuum, such as the importance of an attribute or favorability of an attitude object.

Rational. One assumption that underlies the traditional *microeconomic* perspective of CB is that consumers make *optimal decisions*.

Rational (cognitive) appeals. Communication messages directed toward the message receiver's logic and self-interest, emphasizing hard facts, presenting reasoned arguments to buy, and focusing on informational needs.

Rationality. Reason, thought, logic, and physical control. Economic rationality means that decisions are made so as to produce the best possible or most preferred (optimal) results for the decision maker, given that person's resource constraints. Buyers make purchase decisions based on purposeful, thoughtful, self-interested economic calculations whereby each person wisely spends his or her limited income to get the most satisfaction for each dollar spent.

Recall. The ability to retrieve information from *memory*.

Recency effect. The tendency to better remember information that comes last or later in a series.

Recirculation. The process whereby information is remembered via a person being repeatedly exposed to that information without active rehearsal.

Recognition. A memory-stimulating technique in which a consumer remembers having previously encountered a visual stimulus shown to him, such as pictures of brand identity elements like logotypes, packages, brand names, trade characters, and advertisements.

Recovery process (customer winback). A procedure for counteracting bad customer experiences that develops reasonable strategies for rectifying complaints, thereby turning dissatisfaction into action, usually by making restitution.

Redundancy. To repeat information but in a different manner than previously presented, such as by providing similar information or *cues*, or by presenting the information through a different communication channel.

Reference group. A *social group* used as a reference point or frame of reference for shaping an individual's thinking and behavior.

Reference person (reference other, reference figure, or, if someone is a personally well-known individual, **significant other).** An influential individual used as a reference point or frame of reference for shaping someone's thinking and behavior.

Referent power. The ability to induce imitation of the referent's attitudes and behaviors through getting *social group* members to either identify with or emulate the *social agent*.

Referral communication. When one consumer recommends a particular good or service to another.

Referral systems (customer referrals, pyramiding, member-get-a-member programs, peer-to-peer marketing). Systems that recruit satisfied customers to encourage others to sign up, check out, or buy the product by offering those customers incentives such as product discounts or even cold cash.

Refutational appeal. The communicator presents both sides of the issue and then refutes the opposing viewpoint. The purpose is to inoculate (immunize) recipients against a rival's countermessage or other opposing viewpoints.

Regifting. Recycling new or used presents and passing them off as new gifts.

Reinforcement. The learner's reward resulting from a responding to a *cue*, leading to a reduction in a *drive's* strength. Reinforcement is an environmental event (stimulus, reinforcer) that increases the probability of generating a particular *response* in the future because it is sought by learners. Reinforcement takes the form of either *positive reinforcement* or *negative reinforcement*.

Reinforcement power (instrumental power). A social agent's ability to use instruments as rewards and punishments to affect attitudes and behavior.

Reinforcers. Reinforcements (rewards).

Relaters (phlegmatic). A Hippocratic personality type. Strengths: Loyal, agreeable, supportive team players who perform established work patterns and get along with virtually everybody. Weaknesses: They resist change, procrastinate, are overly lenient, and lack initiative. Typical careers include diplomats, accountants, teachers, and technicians.

Relationship (retention) marketing. All organizational activities whose goal is to develop long-term, value-laden relationships between brands and customers by marketers' efforts to continually fulfill buyers' unsatisfied desires.

Relative advantage. An *innovation* attribute concerning the degree to which consumers perceive the innovation as superior to existing products in satisfying their needs and solving their problems.

Relative income hypothesis. Suggests that although the *overprivileged* and *underprivileged* generally share the same patterns of thinking and behavior as other members of their social class, their purchasing patterns often differ due to their higher or lower incomes.

Relative occupational class income (ROCI). The relationship of a family's total income to the median income of other families in the same *social class*.

Reliability. The ability to obtain repeatable, consistent results when research studies are replicated.

Religion. Belief in and reverence for a supernatural power recognized as the creator and governor of the universe.

Reminder advertising. Advertising whose sole function is to keep in the target market's mind the brand name, slogan, important visuals such as the logo and package design, and other significant marketing stimuli.

Repeat purchase behavior (behavioral brand loyalty). Buying a brand repeatedly due to factors like indifference, convenience, low price, or unavailability of the preferred brand.

Repeated problem solving. A consumer purchasing decision situation where a consumer considers buying a different brand than previously, which can result in brand switching and *variety seeking*.

Repositioning (relaunching, restaging, remarketing). Staking out a new and different *brand position* due to marketplace dynamics.

Repressed needs (latent motives). Those desires pushed into the subconscious mind of which people are unaware.

Resources. A VALS2 dimension that is the full range of psychological, physical, demographic, and material means and capacities people have to draw upon.

Response. The third element of classical conditioning learning model, it is a consumer's reaction to the drive or stimulus in an effort to reduce the drive. The response can be either observable (overt) behavior or unobservable (covert) reactions.

Response bias. A survey respondent's conscious or unconscious misrepresentation of the truth.

Restitution (redress). During the recovery process, this is providing compensation for things gone wrong. It can be in the form of discounts, coupons, free gifts, even apologies.

Retail outlets. Commercial markets for goods or services that shoppers visit to purchase merchandise, i.e., retail stores (physical entities) and websites (virtual entities).

Retention. As a verb, the act of storing information in *short-term* and *long-term memory* at the conclusion of the *information processing* procedure so that it can be recalled. As a noun, the amount of previously learned material that is remembered.

Retrieval. The process whereby people recover (access or remember) information from long-term memory, i.e., the process of remembering.

Retrieval cues. Stimuli to aid remembering information stored in long-term memory.

Retro-acculturation. Developing a need to reconnect with one's ethnic roots and language.

Retroactive inhibition. A form of *interference that* occurs when later information interferes with recollection of information previously learned.

Reverse supply chain. A series of activities required to retrieve a used product from a customer and either dispose of or reuse it.

Reward power. The ability to gain compliance via administering rewards for desired actions.

Risk averse. Consumers who are more afraid of a loss than they are concerned with a gain of equal magnitude to the loss: Losses loom larger than gains.

Risk-reduction strategies (RRSs). Actions consumers take to handle and lessen *perceived risk*.

Risk relievers. Marketing strategies to lessen *perceived risk*.

Rites of passage. Ceremonies that observe people's change in social status, life situation, or other significant events. Examples: birthday parties, retirement dinners, and graduation ceremonies.

Ritual (ritual behavior). A series of expressive, symbolic behaviors that occur in a fixed sequence and are frequently repeated over time.

Ritual artifacts. Items used in conjunction with a ritual. Examples: a retirement gold watch, a white wedding gown.

Role acquisitions. When people take on important new roles in their lives as they mature and go through key life transition points when almost everything in their lives shift, causing them to change their behavior, including consumer behavior.

Role conflict. A situation where there are competing role expectations because one must take on two or more different and incompatible roles.

Role dominance. The extent to which husbands and wives influence the final decision relative to each other and additional family members.

Role load. The number of different roles people acquire in their various *social groups*.

Role model. A person whose attitudes and behaviors others imitate because they want to be like the model.

Role overload. A condition where consumers feel they have taken on more role demands than time or energy allows.

Role playing. A *projective technique* in which consumers act out the role of someone else in a particular situation.

Role set. All the various *social group* roles a person plays in life.

Role-related product clusters (consumption constellations). Groups of related products used to fulfill a particular role.

Rosenberg's (instrumentality-value) model. This *multi-attribute attitude model* is founded on the notion that an attitude object can be instrumental in helping people achieve various personal values. Hence, a person's attitude toward an object becomes more favorable the more that object is seen as helping to fulfill values. This model considers the realization of valued states (security, saving money, success, etc.) as evaluative criteria.

Routine decision making (RDM; routine problem solving, nominal DM, habitual DM, routinized response behavior, routine buying behavior, programmed decisions). The consumer learning stage in which the consumer has extensive information on and experience with both the product class and with one or (usually) many brands.

Safety (security) needs. Both physiological and psychological needs concerning establishing stability and consistency in one's life amidst a chaotic world. They include motives for physical safety, physical and psychological security, protection from the physical environment, and freedom from anxiety.

Sales promotion (promotions, promotional marketing). Short-term incentives to encourage immediate sale of a product.

Salience. The prominence of information; how well it stands out from other information surrounding it.

Salient attributes. Attributes that come readily to buyer's minds and are on the tip of their tongues if asked. They might not be important.

Sandwich generation. Those adults caring for their aging parents as well as their own children.

Satisfaction. Positive confirmation of expectations and desires: The buyer receives what is expected.

Satisfice. When a consumer settles for a satisfactory (rather than the optimal) brand as a satisfier of wants and needs.

Schedules of reinforcement. The regularity and timing of rewards.

Schema. Organized categories of *knowledge* (beliefs and feelings) held in memory that are structured around a focal concept and that determine how new stimuli will be processed; patterns of association among concepts and episodes that are brought to mind when a cue is activated.

Schematic memory. A *knowledge* structure in which both concepts and episodes acquire a depth of meaning by becoming associated with other concepts and episodes.

Scientific method. A systematic process for analyzing empirical evidence in an objective and accurate manner so as to confirm or disconfirm prior conceptions (hypotheses) in an ongoing, open-minded fashion.

Scientific observation. Systematically recording people's behaviors.

Script. An *episodic memory* for how an action sequence should occur.

Search attributes. Objective, tangible product attributes on which the consumer can get useful brand-attribute information prior to purchase through prepurchase search and alternative evaluation.

Search engines. Computer programs through which users can type in a name, word, or phrase, and the search engine will scour the Net to locate relevant information and website addresses.

Search goods. Products containing mostly *search attributes*.

Secondary data. Information gathered by someone else for another purpose.

Secondary (selective, brand) demand. A favorable attitude toward the marketer's brand.

Secondary (selective, brand) demand advertising. Promotion that emphasizes brand superiority in solving a consumer problem.

Secondary groups. Contact groups characterized by large size and a less strongly shared ideology.

Secondary reinforcers. Rewards that gratify secondary motives.

Secondary uses. New uses for a product.

Selective (secondary, brand) demand. A favorable attitude toward the marketer's branded product.

Selective perception (perceptual selection). People will consciously or subconsciously process only a fraction of the *sensory stimuli* to which they are exposed during each of the stages of the perceptual process.

Self-actualization. Self-initiated striving to become whatever people are able to become or whatever they are meant to be. Such needs relate to self-fulfillment and maximizing one's unique potential.

Self-actualization needs. Needs that relate to *self-actualization:* "What a man can be, he must be."

Self-designating method. A sociological research method for identifying *opinion leaders*. Respondents are asked a series of questions to determine whether they are more likely or less apt than their friends to be asked advice about some general product categories and whether friends and neighbors view them as a good information source for these products.

Self-ego. One's sense of self-worth.

Self-expression-inspired consumers. A VALS2 group; they are guided by a desire for social or physical activity, variety, and risk taking. They tend to be high sensation seekers and the "movers and shakers" who buy products to have an impact on the world around them.

Self-image (self-concept). One's conscious feelings and attitudes about himself or herself as a person, i.e., who a person believes he or she is at a given time. As such, self-image is subjective in nature and so might deviate somewhat from one's personality as objectively measured. The self-image answers the questions, "Who am I?" and "What am I like as a person?"

Self-interested. One assumption that underlies the traditional *microeconomic* perspective of CB that the basic buyer motivation is maximization of one's own utility (as long as it does not come at others' expense, which would be selfish).

Self-perception theory. An attitude change theory that says that when asked about their own attitudes of which they are uncertain, people sometimes reflect on their behavior and infer what their attitudes must be.

Seller's market. A marketplace condition where product demand exceeds product supply. There is lack of availability.

Selling concept (selling orientation). The marketing management philosophy that suggests that if people do not need a product, they can be persuaded to buy it via marketing communications.

Semantic differential scales. Measures consisting of a series of seven-point *rating scales* using bipolar (opposite) adjectives to anchor the beginning and end of each scale item (poles). Used to measure either level of *involvement* or consumer attitudes.

Semantic generalization. The process of establishing meaning for words that essentially have no meaning.

Semantic memory. A person's general knowledge and feelings about a concept, i.e., what the concept means to that individual, and is not tied to any particular object or event.

Semiotics (semiotic studies, semiology). The investigation of signs, i.e., something that has meaning, such as words, images, body language, etc., and *symbols*.

Sensation. The immediate and direct reception of sensory stimuli by the *sensory receptors*.

Sensors. A Myers-Briggs Indicator Personality Inventory type; they are prone to depend on their senses, to focus on the facts and concrete information, and to have a concern for specifics and details.

Sensory marketing (branding). Appealing to the five senses through the marketing program.

Sensory memory. A *memory store* that captures sensory stimuli that first enter the brain in a storage area known as a sensory store.

Sensory receptors (sensory organs). Human organs (eyes, ears, mouth, nose, and fingers and skin) that receive *sensory stimuli*.

Sensory stimuli (cues, sensory inputs). Sights, sounds, smells, tastes, and feelings.

Sensory store. A storage area known in sensory memory where sensory stimuli go when first entering the brain as information inputs. Here, information might register as no more than a fleeting sensation of size, shape, texture, or other stimuli.

Sensory systems (sensory functions). Senses of vision, hearing, smell, taste, and touch.

Sentence completion. A *projective technique* whereby interviewees complete a sentence with the first word or phrase that comes to mind.

Serial position effects (order of presentation). The influence of order of information presentation within a marketing communication on someone's ability to remember that information.

Service recovery. Responding when service goes wrong to turn potentially negative situations into positive ones.

Sex appeals. A selling appeal based on sexual imagery.

Shame appeal. This form of coercive power centers externally on other peoples' evaluation of one's behavior, leading to lower self-esteem and/or remorse.

Shaping. An *instrumental conditioning* technique that entails rewarding successive approximations of a complex desired behavior.

Share of category requirements. A measure of *brand loyalty* that measures a decision-making unit's proportion of purchases within a category devoted to particular brands.

Shelf positioning (shelving). The shelves on which a brand is located.

Shelf space. The number of shelf facings, i.e., rows displaying a product.

Shopper marketing. The orchestration of in-store marketing activities and the retail environment to turn browsers into buyers at point of sale.

Shopping bots (shopbots, buyer agents, virtual sales assistants, shopping search engines, comparison shopping sites, robot search engines). Specially designed Internet search engines used to locate and compare brand alternatives, telling users about brands with price information and/or providing product recommendations.

Shopping goods. Products for which consumers carefully comparatively evaluate alternatives during the shopping process.

Short-term memory (short-term store, working memory). A *memory store* that analyzes the *sensations* and information from *sensory memory* and assigns meaning to them based on prior *knowledge*.

Similarity principle. A Gestalt psychology *grouping* principle that says that things that are physically similar are perceived as belonging together or as forming a whole figure (gestalt).

Simile. An analogy technique that is a figure of speech using an explicit comparison in which two essentially unlike things are compared. Typically, simile uses a phrase including the words "like" or "as."

Simple beliefs. Perceptions that are relatively weak because consumers have not deeply processed the information underlying them. Consumers passively form these beliefs where *involvement* is low.

Simple inferences. When consumers form *simple beliefs* based on simple associations.

Simplicity principle (pragnänz). A Gestalt psychology *grouping* principle that suggests that individuals opt for relatively simple perceptions even when more complex perceptions can be derived. Every stimulus pattern is seen in such a way that the resulting structure is as simple as possible.

Single-item index. An objective method that estimates *social class* using a single proxy indicator.

Single-item (basic) rating scales. *Rating scales* that measure one's overall attitude toward an object, ranging from very favorable to very unfavorable. They assume attitude is a unidimensional concept.

Sleeper effect. Consumers forget the message source more rapidly than the message itself. Consequently, a message delivered by a source low in credibility can increase in credibility with the passage of time as the source and message become disassociated.

Social agents. Individuals, groups, or organizations that can affect an individual's thinking, attitudes, and behaviors.

Social aggregate. A bunch of people who have nothing in common except temporarily occupying the same time and place.

Social category. Aggregates of persons with a common status in a society demographically, socioeconomically, psychologically, and/or behaviorally, such as *subcultures* and *social classes*.

Social channels. Channels of communication consisting of friends, family members, neighbors, work associates, and acquaintances.

Social character. The degree to which an individual is *inner-directed* versus *outer-directed* (other-directed).

Social class. A means for ranking groups of people hierarchically in either an industrial or post-industrial society regarding social status.

Social desirability bias. A respondent's conscious or unconscious desire to appear proper, seem rational, gain prestige, or avoid embarrassment.

Social group. A set of individuals who regularly interact with one another to satisfy common needs or accomplish individual or mutual goals, and who share some significant commonality regarding *norms, values,* or beliefs.

Social group norms. Informal rules or standards regarding socially acceptable boundaries of proper behavior in a *social group*.

Social group role. Appropriate behavior for a particular person or position within a *social group*.

Social group socialization. The process of learning the values, norms, roles, and other characteristics of a social group in order to effectively function as a group member.

Social group status. The relative rankings of members of the *social group* regarding prestige, respect, power, and influence within the group.

Social group values. Widely shared values in a *social group*.

Social mobility. The ability to move up (upward mobility) and down (downward mobility) through the social hierarchy.

Social (love and belonging, affection, affiliation) needs. Needs oriented toward loving and being loved by others, affiliation, social recognition, and being accepted by people despite one's flaws.

Social networking sites. Online communities where literally thousands of people meet to form peer-to-peer social and business networks to help them accomplish goals around personal and career interests.

Social power. The degree to which the agent can influence others' thinking, attitudes, or behaviors.

Social psychologists. Social scientists who study *social psychology*.

Social psychology. The scientific inquiry into social behavior within *social groups* and among individuals, including the influence of group members on each other and the impact of the group on individual decisions, such as gaining conformity to the group's ideology.

Social referent. A *reference group* or *reference person*.

Social risk. A possible loss of face, prestige, and approval of significant others, such as friends and family, due to not buying and using a product or as a consequence of purchasing and using a socially unacceptable product.

Social sanctions. Penalties for violating norms, which can range from frowns, teasing, and ridicule to ostracism and imprisonment.

Social (behavioral) sciences. Scientific disciplines in which the actions and reactions of humans and animals are studied through observational and experimental methods.

Social (public, others, looking glass, apparent) self-image. How consumers believe others see them.

Social stratification. Ranking groups or individuals hierarchically within a *society* or *social group* with respect to social status, placing them into groups called strata.

Social system. One or more groups of individuals who interact fairly frequently, ranging from a local neighborhood to an entire *society*.

Social trends. Long-term, broad directions of change in a *society*.

Social values (other-oriented values). This set of values reflects a culture's view of what constitutes appropriate relationships between individuals and groups.

Socialization. The process whereby people learn the social roles and behaviors they need in order to effectively participate in society.

Socializing (societal) institutions (socialization agents). *Social groups* and organizations that teach people how to function in society.

Societal marketing concept. A marketing management philosophy that balances consumer interests and company requirements with societal well being. It mandates marketers to serve and satisfy customers more efficiently and effectively than competitors in a way that maintains or even enhances both the individual's and society's welfare, while maintaining the firm's profits.

Society. An aggregate group of people within a nation or group of nations who usually share a common language and heritage, i.e., a large cluster of people sharing a common *culture*.

Sociocultural (sociological) forces. Consists of influences on the consumer from the cultural and social environment. These range from the overall society and its culture to the effect of significant others such as family, friends, and colleagues.

Sociocultural influences. Societal and social influences ranging from the broad culture down to interpersonal relations.

Socioeconomic status (SES; social status). An individual's or group's position within a hierarchical social structure. SES is the relative ranking of members of each social class stratum (group) regarding factors like wealth, power, and prestige.

Socioeconomic status (SES) variables (stratification variables). Factors used to determine someone's social status, such as occupation, education, and amount of income.

Sociologists. Social scientists who study *sociology*.

Sociology. The social science that investigates social behavior and human groups within society. It studies the formation and functioning of social forces and institutions that affect both contemporary society (such as families, religious institutions, and workplaces) and peoples' personal lives (such as friendship cliques and juvenile gangs).

Sociometric method. A sociological research method for identifying *opinion leaders*, whereby members of a social system are asked to identify to whom they give advice and to whom they go for information and guidance about various products.

Solitary (Sole) Survivor I (dissolution). A *family life cycle* stage when one of the spouses has died and the other (usually the wife) continues or returns to work in order to live on earned income rather than savings and to remain socially active.

Solitary (Sole) Survivor II. A *family life cycle* stage in which one spouse lives on a relatively low retirement fixed income.

Source bolsters. Favorable thoughts the message recipient has toward the communication source, leading to a higher probability of message acceptance.

Source derogation. When the receiver of a marketing communication attacks the message source, thereby rejecting the message.

Sovereign. Consumers' ability to be in control of their decision making, personally responsible, and not controlled by outside forces.

Spaced (continuous, distributed) advertising. Ads are distributed fairly evenly throughout the campaign's duration, known as continuity in an advertising schedule.

Span of recall. The number of discrete items or bits of information someone can hold at one time in *short-term memory*.

Specialty goods. Items for which consumers have very strong brand preferences.

Spokescharacters. Animated "experts" serving as endorsers. They can be created characters or celebrity cartoon characters.

Spurious loyalty. Behavior which resembles *brand loyalty* but is not genuine loyalty caused by both true brand preference and regular buying. Rather, it is merely *repeat purchase behavior*.

Standard learning (rational) hierarchy of communication effects. A model of communications effects for which the process is think-feel-do. This prevails where there is high involvement and perceived risk, as well as meaningful brand differences. This is the high-effort decision-making perspective.

Stapel scale. A *rating scale* consisting of a single adjective in the center of a rating scale. Scale values indicate how accurately the adjective describes the attitude object.

Star perks (celebrity seeding, celebrity placements). Giving public *opinion leaders* various perquisites, ranging from special treatment, to product giveaways, to endorsements with lucrative incentives. The purpose is to have the famous folks seen using the product.

Status symbols. Visible, physical status-conveying representations of membership in, or aspiration to, a particular *social class* or status group. These serve as "badges" of achievement and distinction.

Stealth marketing. A form of *buzz marketing* whereby companies lure key customers with coveted items that are deliberately kept in short supply, such as hot news, cool gadgets, or free products.

Stereotyping. Attributing characteristics, attitudes, or behaviors to someone based on the social category (especially subculture) or social group to which the individual belongs.

Stimulus discrimination. From a learning perspective, when an organism learns to distinguish between similar but not identical stimuli.

Stimulus discrimination (sensory discrimination). From the perspective of *perception*, a person's ability to distinguish between slightly changing or similar stimuli.

Stimulus generalization. When an organism's response or reaction to a given stimulus is also evoked by a similar but nonidentical stimulus, i.e., when people respond in like fashion to similar stimuli.

Stimulus object. The physical object in the environment that is the source of the stimulus experienced through the five senses.

Stimulus-organism-response (S-O-R) model (input–process [throughput]–output model). A useful organizational framework for the study of psychological influences on CB. Illustrates how consumer behavior is studied within the context of psychology using its three elements: stimulus, organism, and response.

Store brands (private labels, dealer brands, in-house labels, own labels). Brands that are owned, sponsored, and controlled by the retailer.

Store image. The buyer's overall perception or impression of the store's personality and of the type of person who shops there.

Store loyal. Customers having favorable attitudinal and behavioral responses toward a store and its various offerings.

Storytelling. A *projective technique* in which consumers are requested to tell a story related to a setting or situation.

Strength of learning. How completely and rapidly learning occurs with repetition and how permanent the learning is.

Strivers. A VALS2 type; they are achievement-oriented consumers with moderate resources.

Strong arguments. Presentations of the best or most convincing evidence regarding the attitude object's central merits or the key issues embodied in evaluating an attitude object. The key is to offer compelling, relevant reasons for buying the brand. These are used to change attitudes where buyers are believed to employ *central route processing*.

Strong (central) attitudes. Attitudes that are highly accessible and strong, i.e., held with high confidence and commitment, and to which people are deeply committed, are able to easily access, and of which they are quite confident. Compared with *weak attitudes*, strong attitudes are more resistant to subsequent change because they are based on *central beliefs*.

Subaudible messages (subaudible communications, audio conditioning, threshold messaging, psychoacoustic persuasion). Accelerated (time-compressed) and/or garbled speech played at a low volume and masked under a "carrier," such as music or ocean waves, so that the message cannot be consciously heard.

Subconscious motives. Mostly social and psychological needs of a hedonic nature that consumers are either unable and/or unwilling to discuss, either because the needs are latent or because talking about and/or gratifying hedonic needs like vanity are socially unacceptable.

Subcultural identification. The degree to which ethnic group members retain their cultural identity, primarily through socializing institutions such as schools, churches, and neighborhoods.

Subcultural influences. The *values*, *norms*, *symbols*, and other unique *cultural components* of subcultures.

Subcultures (microcultures). Cultural subgroups within the macroculture who share some of their own unique cultural characteristics while retaining many of the significant cultural components from the society at large.

Subjective norms (SN). A component in the *Fishbein theory of reasoned action* representing the buyer's motivation to act in accordance with the perceived influence of significant others.

Subjective perception. How perception deviates from reality due to individual differences in the perceptual process.

Subjective social class. A special class with which consumers identify and perhaps to which they aspire but to which they do not belong.

Subliminal. Below the threshold of conscious perception (absolute threshold level), i.e., people cannot perceive a stimulus object at all.

Subliminal advertising (subliminal seduction). Advertising attempting to manipulate consumers by placing hidden images, words, or sounds in print, audio, or video advertising media that cannot be consciously perceived. The theory is that, although the stimulus is below the consumer's level of conscious awareness, the subconscious nonetheless processes the stimulus, leading to attitude change (e.g., brand preference), followed by behavioral change (e.g., a product purchase or a store visit).

Subliminal perception. A person's subconscious perception of *subliminal cues*.

Subliminal stimuli (subliminal messages). Cues that activate one or more sensory receptors but are below the threshold of perception (absolute threshold level).

Sub-subcultures. *Subcultures* within subcultures. Many subcultures can be sub-segmented into smaller, more homogenous groups, each with its own distinctive *cultural characteristics*.

Subvisual messages. Single-frame visual images or words, of milliseconds in duration, implanted into a film (and now also other electronic motion media). These messages are repeatedly flashed every few seconds, notably in motion pictures, television shows, videotapes, DVDs, video games, and on computer screens.

Suggestiveness. An advertisement that implies more than the written copy suggests. The message is not spelled out explicitly in words but rather is subtly implied via use of verbal language, body language, color, and other perceptual devices, often including sexual innuendo.

Superego. An element of the Freudian subconscious mind that is a person's conscience or internal representative of societal and parental *values* and *norms*.

Superstitions. Beliefs resulting from ignorance, fear of the unknown, or trust in magic or chance.

Support arguments. Consumer thoughts agreeing with the message or confirming the product's worthiness.

Surface-level processing (sensory processing). Storing information in *long-term memory* without analyzing it for meaning.

Surrogate buyers (shoppers, consumers). Professionals who are hired and paid to give information and recommendations, as well as to buy on behalf of their clients, such as wardrobe consultants, financial advisers, and interior decorators.

Surrogate (proxy) indicators (market signals). Readily observable product attributes that consumers use, often wrongly, to make probabilistic inferences on product characteristics unknown to them because they are not easily discerned.

Survey research. Asking direct (undisguised), straightforward questions in a highly structured (versus flexible) format, i.e., the same questions are asked of all respondents in a predetermined sequence.

Survivors. A VALS2 type; they are achievement-oriented folks with minimal resources.

Switching costs. The psychological, physical, and economic costs that buyers face in switching between technologies or products.

Symbolic (value-expressive, expressive) needs. *Hedonic needs* for self-expression that reflect a buyer's *self-concept*.

Symbolic performance. Outcomes of product purchase and usage related to *hedonic needs*.

Symbolic reference groups. Nonmembership *social groups* that an individual admires but does not expect to qualify to join.

Symbolism. The use of tangible representations of abstract concepts.

Symbols. Objects, characters, or other concrete representations of ideas, concepts, or other abstractions.

Tactile communication. Nonverbal communication that occurs via touching.

Target market. A group of current and prospective customers with common needs and wants.

Target market (market coverage) strategies. Plans for targeting a firm's marketing efforts to members of the marketplace.

Target marketing (market targeting). The act of evaluating, selecting, and serving the market segment(s) that the organization can accommodate most effectively and efficiently.

Teaser advertising. Involves planned secrecy for new products, new events, and other novelties, deliberately leaking bits of information over time in ads to keep people guessing and talking.

Technology. A body of knowledge, tools, and techniques derived from science and practical experience, which is used in the development, design, production, and application of products, processes, systems, and services.

Terminal values. Personal desirable end states of being (existence); how people would like to eventually experience their lives. Examples: mature love, true friendship, and wisdom.

Thanatos (death wish, death instinct). A primitive Freudian impulse for destruction, decay, death, misery, aggression, and self-hatred.

Theories. Propositions about various aspects of the world based on observation that allow marketers to describe, explain, predict and perhaps control certain phenomena.

Thinkers. A VALS2 type; they are ideal-oriented with high resources.

Thinkers. A Myers-Briggs Indicator Personality Inventory type; they are objective, make decisions based on facts and logic, have a high need for cognition (they enjoy and engage in thinking), and are cool and reserved, honest and direct, naturally critical, and motivated by achievement.

Thinkers (melancholy). A Hippocratic personality type. Strengths: Thorough, analytical, orderly, and conscientious planners and creators. Weaknesses: They can be indecisive, too detail-oriented, rigid, hesitant to try new things, and pessimistic.

Third-person (referent other) questioning. A *projective technique* whereby researchers ask respondents what another person (a friend, neighbor, colleague, etc.) or people in general think or do, rather than directly asking the interviewees about themselves.

Tie-in (captive) products. Related items, such as software, that must be used in conjunction with the main product, such as hardware.

Time capsule. A tool for preserving contemporary cultural artifacts for future generations to examine as *physical trade evidence* in order to learn more about a previous epoch.

Time orientation. The extent to which members of society are oriented more to either the past, present, or future.

Time risk. The perceived excessive time devoted to any stage in the consumer decision process.

Timesaving goods. Products designed to save consumers time and effort or allowing them to multitask.

Top-down social change (trickle-down influence, downward diffusion). Social change flowing from social system leaders to the masses, or from the upper to lower social strata in society.

Trade characters (advertising icons, product mascots). People or animals that symbolize a brand. Examples: The Pillsbury Dough Boy and the Jolly Green Giant.

Trade dress. A type of trademark encompassing the nonfunctional physical detail and design (color schemes, textures, sizes, designs, shapes, and placements of words, graphics, and decorations) of a product or its packaging. The general appearance or total image of a product.

Trade dress infringement. Unlawful copying of a marketer's *trade dress*.

Trade up. When people splurge on luxury goods that they find emotionally satisfying and that are symbolic of upward social mobility.

Trademark. Words, symbols, or devices, or any combination thereof, adopted and used by a manufacturer or merchant to identify a product's source and distinguish the product from those manufactured or sold by others.

Trait theory. Views *personality traits* as characteristic behavior and thought patterns, considering one's personality as comprised of a constellation of personality traits that describe that person's general response predispositions.

Transaction. A single exchange between a buyer and seller or one-time sale.

Transactional marketing. Emphasizes making the immediate sale and new customer acquisition via conquest (acquisition) marketing (efforts to attract competitors' customers) and enticing new product users (those who have never purchased the product category).

Transcendence needs. The very highest-level needs in Maslow's Needs Hierarchy to help others find self-fulfillment and realize their potential.

Trialability (divisibility). An innovation attribute concerning the extent to which the new product can be sampled or evaluated on a limited basis or small scale prior to adoption.

Tribal marketing. Pursuing like-minded consumers who spontaneously connect around a product or service (one type of consumption subculture).

Trickle across (lateral diffusion). Communication occurs horizontally within *social groups* (rather than vertically between individuals of unequal social status), typically between an opinion leader and an opinion follower.

Trickle-down diffusion. The original two-step flow of communication model, where marketers rely on mass media and public opinion leaders to spread product information.

Tricomponent (ABC—affect, behavior, cognition) attitude model. Attitudes toward attitude objects consist of three major dimensions or components: cognition, affect, and conation.

Truth effect. Exposure to repeated claims leads to increased belief in those claims.

Two-sided messages. Promotion that presents both the brand's weaknesses as well as strengths and possibly mentions competitors' strengths.

Two-step flow of communication theory. A theory of interpersonal influence suggesting that information flows, first, from the impersonal mass media to OLs, who have high media exposure. Second, opinion leaders operate as filters, interpreters, and transmitters of this information, which they pass on to the *opinion followers*.

Two-tier marketing. Targeting marketing efforts either up-market or down-market, not toward the middle market.

Unaided (free) recall. Remembering in the absence of *retrieval cues*.

Uncertainty avoidance. The degree to which a culture prefers structured to unstructured situations and is willing to tolerate ambiguity and unusual behavior.

Unconditioned response (UCR). A natural or instinctual reaction to an *unconditioned stimulus*.

Unconditioned stimulus (UCS). A primary cue or natural stimulus to which naturally occurs an *unconditioned response*.

Underprivileged. Families that are below their *social class* average income.

Undifferentiated marketing (mass marketing, market aggregation). A *target market strategy* that involves no market segmentation: The marketer pursues the entire or largest part of the market with one product and one marketing program.

Unidimensional. A view of attitudes that considers attitudes as a position on a continuum along one general dimension regarding an attitude object, ranging from very favorable to very unfavorable.

Universal cultural values. Values that are cherished across many different cultures due to underlying common human psychological needs.

Universal set. All brands in the product class.

Unsought goods. Products for which consumers have a dormant or latent need.

Unweighted linear compensatory decision model (unweighted rule, simple additive rule, equal weight rule). A linear compensatory decision model where the attributes are not weighted—i.e., all criteria are treated as equal in importance.

Upper-lower class. Part of the Lower Americans group. Some high school. Are working, not on welfare, although most are unskilled minimum-wage laborers.

Upper-middle class. Part of the Upper American group. The rest of college-graduate managers; intellectual elite; successful professionals, independent medium-size-businesspeople; and corporate managers. Income from profits and fees. College degrees, with many professional and graduate degrees.

Upper-upper class. Part of the Upper American group. The "capital S" society world of inherited wealth. Aristocratic names and socially prominent blue blood families. "Prep school" followed by Ivy League and masters' degrees.

Upward pull strategy. Positioning a brand as an *aspirational brand* that will assist the customer in achieving the trappings of the next rung on the social ladder.

Upward social mobility. Actions to achieve a higher social status, usually through educational or occupational achievement.

Upward stretch strategy (step-up extensions). Adding a classier or higher-end brand to a product line in hopes that its fine image will rub off on the entire product line.

Urban legend. A cultural belief passed along from person to person that is not true.

Urban marketing. Marketing efforts that reflect the trends and attitudes originating in cities, driven by young African-American and Hispanic consumers' choices in entertainment and fashion.

User (end user). The ultimate consumer of the product during the post-purchase consumption stage.

User-generated (created) content. Encouraging Web site visitors to create and pass along their own ads.

Utilitarian appeal. Discussing how the product fulfills functional needs by emphasizing product features and the functional benefits they provide.

Utilitarian (instrumental, adjustment, adaptive) attitude function. This *functional attitude theory* relates to *utilitarian needs* and motives. People have favorable attitudes toward those attitude objects that help us secure rewards or avoid punishment.

Utilitarian (functional, instrumental) needs. Practical, rational, objective, concrete, economic, and cognitive needs. The product performs a useful (utilitarian) function (functional), solves a specific consumption-related problem, or is instrumental in providing a material benefit.

Utilitarian (normative, instrumental) reference group influence. When an individual decides to conform to *social group* expectations and standards in order to gain rewards or to avoid punishment.

Utility. The satisfactions of needs or solutions of problems that the product provides.

Valence (direction). Goals and their underlying *motives* can be either positive or negative.

Validity. The degree to which research is correctly measuring the concept it should be measuring.

Value. When customers obtain the optimum combination of quantity and quality for their dollars. The optimum quantity plus quality per dollar spent.

Value brands. Low-priced brands similar to the market leaders but that charge less due to low-cost manufacturing or minimal marketing expenditures, notably advertising and packaging costs.

Value positioning. Differentiating a brand by suggesting it gives consumers more for their money.

Value proposition. An offer by a marketer that entails maximizing the ratio quantity + quality/price. Alternatively, value maximization means minimizing the difference between the customer's benefits and costs.

Value system. The relative weights of various values within a culture.

Value-expressive appeal. A communication crafting a *brand image*.

Value-expressive attitudes. The *functional attitude theory* suggests that such attitudes help us express our *self-concept*, and they also help us live out our lifestyles and our central values. Such attitudes are tied to symbolic (value-expressive) needs.

Value-expressive products. Products that provide social or aesthetic utility or have symbolic meaning regarding the user's *self-image*, suggesting to others something about whom they are as people (e.g., macho, intellectual, or thoroughly modern).

Value-expressive (comparative, identification) reference groups. Those *social groups* whose members' attitudes and behaviors are used as guides for others.

Values and Lifestyles 2 (VALS2™) System. The most popular standardized lifestyle research service, VALS2 is a psychographic tool that measures demographic, lifestyle, value, and attitude variables.

Variable interval reinforcement. A reward schedule in which the time that must pass before the learner is rewarded varies around an average. Since the learner is unaware of exactly when the reward will occur, that individual must consistently respond.

Variable ratio reinforcement. A reward schedule in which a certain percentage or number of a person's responses are rewarded, but the individual does not know what this reward ratio or number is. This causes learners to respond at very high and steady rates.

Variable (random) reinforcement. A reward schedule in which when and how often rewards are dispensed is purely by chance. There are two types of variable reinforcement: *variable interval* and *variable ratio reinforcement*.

Variety (novelty) seeking. A purchase decision situation characterized by a low-to-moderate involvement, moderate-to-high information search purchase decision situation. It entails searching for something new out of boredom or dissatisfaction, even though the consumer has been satisfied with past varieties and brands bought.

Verbal cues. Spoken or written words.

Verbalizers. Consumers who prefer print media.

Verbatims. Word-for-word consumer quotations from interviews.

Vicarious learning (modeling, observational learning, imitation, imitative behavior). *A cognitive* learning school theory that suggests that the outcomes of others' behaviors, not one's own actions, are scrutinized, and learners then modify their own responses correspondingly. That is, they imitate or model the other person's reinforced behavior.

Viral marketing. A marketing phenomenon that facilitates and encourages current and potential customers to pass along a marketing message or to tell others about the company's products and services, and in turn encourages those others to tell even more others. It usually entails creating an ad which is so informative or entertaining that consumers will want to pass it along to others, usually via e-mail, so that it spreads like the flu.

Virtual groups (virtual communities, online communities, cybercommunities, social media). Interactive media outlets containing user-generated content, in which consumers can comment or contribute to the medium's content or one another's comments, thereby building community.

Visual (mental) imagery. The imagery that is associated with visual, verbal, or aural material.

Visualizers. Consumers who opt for broadcast media.

Volitional control. When a decision is made of the consumer's free will.

Wants. The form that human needs take as determined by society and individual preferences. They are requirements for non-necessities (luxuries), i.e., products desirable but not mandatory.

Warner's Index of Status Characteristics (ISC). A social status index that combines and weights socioeconomic variables used to determine one's social class as follows (wights are in parentheses): occupation (4), source of income (3), house type (3), and dwelling area (2).

Warranty. A written promise about a product's integrity that spells out the manufacturer's responsibility for repairing or replacing defective parts. It spells out the terms of restitution—exactly what parts of the product are covered and the payout, plus the time period for coverage.

Weak (peripheral) attitudes. Attitudes that are founded on *peripheral beliefs*.

Wealth. Accumulated economic assets minus liabilities (debts), reflecting a lifetime's accumulation of income, investments, and inheritances.

Weber's law. States that the amount of change in a stimulus necessary to be noticed is related to the intensity of the original stimulus. The stronger the intensity of an initial stimulus, the greater a change in intensity that must occur for it to be noticed as different from the original stimulus.

Web (home, start, welcome) pages. The introductory page or opening screen of a website, making navigation simple and exciting.

Weighted linear compensatory rule (weighted additive rule). A weighted (consumers give attributes importance ratings or rankings) linear compensatory decision model. This is the traditional *multiattribute attitude model*.

Width. The number of different products a retailer carries. A store can offer either a wide assortment (many products) or a narrow selection (few products).

Wife-dominant (matriarchal) decisions. When the wife dominates the decision, perhaps with some input from her spouse.

Wikis. Websites where groups of users can collaboratively author content by adding, removing, or otherwise editing and changing available content.

Within-group stratification. The esteem, status, and power accorded an occupant of a certain position or role within a social group.

Word association. A projective technique in which the respondent is given a word or phrase and asked to respond with the first word or phrase that comes to mind.

Word-of-mouth (WOM) communication (interpersonal search, buzz). Unpaid and unsponsored transmission of personal messages between consumers, usually via reference persons and reference groups.

WOM marketing. Uses person-to-person consumer communication to raise awareness of an organization's offerings and generate sales.

Working class. Part of the Middle American group. Average pay, blue-collar workers. Includes skilled and semi-skilled employees in factories, construction, services (police, bartenders, deliverymen), and salespeople.

World Wide Web (WWW). The most popular component of the Internet and its main commercial constituent. The WWW is that portion of the Internet supporting a graphical interface retrieval system that organizes information into thousands of interconnected pages or documents called web pages (home pages, start pages, welcome pages).

INDEX

Italic page references indicate charts, graphs or illustrations.

Outer-directed needs, 380
Outer- (other-) directed people, 338
Outlet location choice, 145
Outlet type choice, 143
Overlearning, 447
Overprivileged social class, 216–217
Overt needs. *See* Manifest needs

P

Package downsizing/shorting, 413
Package knockoffs, 462–463
Packaging, brand differentiation and, 465
Packaging of brand, 329
Packaging, product, 147
Paired comparisons, 508
Paradigms, 4. *See also specific type*
Parameter analysis, 123
Pareto's Law, 37–38
Parody display, 298–299
Partial reinforcement, 466–468
Passive learning/hierarchy, 439, 539, *540,* 541
Patriarchal decisions, 266
Patrons, store, 145
Pavlov, Ivan, 23–24, 475–476
Pavlovian conditioning. *See* Classical conditioning
Payment methods, 148
Peer-to-peer marketing, 304
Perceived risks
  defining, 82–83
  involvement of consumer and, 82–85
  types of, 83–85
Perceivers, 336
Perception
  characteristics of, 388–391
  defining, 18–19, 388–389
  false, 395
  form/shape, 426
  process, 388, *389*
  selective, 390–394
  subjective, 390–391, 394–397
  subliminal, 405
  in toothpaste purchase, 19
Perception and information processing
  absolute threshold level and, 404–405
  characteristics of perception and, 388–391

Perception and information processing *(continued)*
  Gestalt psychology's principles and, 426–432
  marketing to selective, 391–402
  overview, 388, *389,* 391, 434–437
  stages, key, 388, 402–404, *403*
  subliminal advertising, 405–411
  surrogate indicators and, 416–425
  Weber's law and, 412–416
Perceptual cues, 388, 395–396, 417–418, *419*
Perceptual defense, 392
Perceptual predispositions, 392–393
Perceptual set, 429
Perceptual value, 44
Perceptual vigilance, 392
Performance attributes, 417
Performance, product, 151–152
Performance risk, 84
Peripheral attitudes, 500
Peripheral beliefs, 498
Peripheral cues, 511
Peripheral-route processing, 511
Personal analogies, 341
Personal selling, 12
Personal situational factors, 146
Personal sources, 115–116
Personal values, 120, 181–182, 185
Personality, 18, 317
Personality and lifestyle
  brand image and, building, 326–333
  Freudian theory, 317–326, *318*
  measuring
    Hippocratic Temperament Survey, 334, *335*
    Myers-Briggs Type Indicator Personality Inventory, 335–336
    overview, 333–334
    personality inventories, 334
  overview, 317, 358–359
  psychographics, 345–356, *349*
Personality inventories
  consumer research using, 336–337
  customized consumer personality research, 338
  defining, 334
  Hippocratic Temperament Survey, 334, *335*
  Myers-Briggs Type Indicator Personality Inventory, 335–336

Personality inventories *(continued)*
  problems using to predict consumer behavior, 337
  trait theory and, 334
Personality traits, 317
Personification, 341
Personnel, store, 145
Persuasion, 497
Phased decision strategy, 130
Philosophies of marketing management
  marketing concept and, *10,* 13–14
  overview, 7–8, *9, 10*
  product concept and, *10,* 11–12
  production concept and, 9–11, *10*
  selling concept and, *10,* 12–13
  societal marketing concept and, *10,* 14–15
Physical fear, 250, 369
Physical positioning/product differentiation, 44
Physical risk, 84
Physical trace of evidence, 179
Physiological needs, 364–365, 379
Picture sorting, 341
Pioneer consumers. *See* Opinion leaders (OLs)
Place in four P's, 33
Point-of-purchase (POP) displays, 147
Point-of-sale displays, 147
Politics, 174
Polychromic society, 183
Polychronic time use, 244
Popular (pop) culture, 179–180
Positioning, 39. *See also* Brand positioning
Positioning statement, 39
Positive behavioral approach, 61
Positive punishment, 468
Positive reinforcement, 465–466, *466*
Postacquisition behaviors. *See* Postpurchase behavior/outcomes stage of consumer decision making
Postboomers, 204
Postpurchase behavior/outcomes stage of consumer decision making
  customer relationships and, 149–150
  customer satisfaction/dissatisfaction and, 150–154
  defining, 69
  dissonance and, 154–156

Geoffrey P. Lantos is a Professor of Business Administration at Stonehill College in Massachusetts, where he has taught various undergraduate courses in marketing since 1986, including Consumer Behavior, Advertising Management, Marketing Research, New Product Management, and Marketing Principles, as well as a graduate Ethics and Accounting Profession course.

After earning his B.A. in business administration and economics from Gettysburg College, Dr. Lantos completed his M.B.A. at the University of Rochester and his Ph.D. at Lehigh University. He taught for one year at Eastern Michigan University and five years at Bentley College. He has also served as an instructor at a number of colleges in Pennsylvania and New Hampshire.

Dr. Lantos has published journal articles, professional manuals, conference papers, articles in books, case studies, book reviews, and instructional materials in the areas of consumer behavior, marketing education, marketing ethics, corporate social responsibility, advertising, and pricing.

He serves as book reviews editor at the *Journal of Consumer Marketing* and the *Journal of Product and Brand Management.* In addition, he is an editorial review board member and ad hoc reviewer for several marketing and business academic journals.